Customer Support Information

Plunkett's Real Estate & Construction Industry Almanac 2010

Please register your book immediately...

if you did not purchase it directly from Plunkett Research, Ltd. This will enable us to fulfill your replacement request if you have a damaged product, or your requests for assistance. Also it will enable us to notify you of future editions, so that you may purchase them from the source of your choice.

If you are an actual, original purchaser but did not receive a FREE CD-ROM version with your book...*

you may request it by returning this form.

____ YES, please register me as a purchaser of the book.
I did not buy it directly from Plunkett Research, Ltd.

____ YES, please send me a free CD-ROM version of the book.
I am an actual purchaser, but I did not receive one with my book. (Proof of purchase may be required.)

Customer Name ______________________________

Title ______________________________

Organization ______________________________

Address ______________________________

City ______________________ State ________ Zip ____________

Country (if other than USA) ______________________________

Phone ____________________ Fax ____________________

E-mail ______________________________

Mail or Fax to: **Plunkett Research, Ltd.**
Attn: FREE CD-ROM and/or Registration
P.O. Drawer 541737, Houston, TX 77254-1737 USA
713.932.0000 · Fax 713.932.7080 · www.plunkettresearch.com

* Purchasers of used books are not eligible to register. Use of CD-ROMs is subject to the terms of their end user license agreements.

PLUNKETT'S REAL ESTATE & CONSTRUCTION INDUSTRY ALMANAC 2010

The Only Comprehensive Guide to the Real Estate & Construction Industry

Jack W. Plunkett

Published by:
Plunkett Research, Ltd., Houston, Texas
www.plunkettresearch.com

PLUNKETT'S REAL ESTATE & CONSTRUCTION INDUSTRY ALMANAC 2010

Editor and Publisher:
Jack W. Plunkett

Executive Editor and Database Manager:
Martha Burgher Plunkett

Senior Editors and Researchers:
Brandon Brison
Michael Esterheld
Addie K. FryeWeaver
Christie Manck

Editors, Researchers and Assistants:
Kalonji Bobb
Elizabeth Braddock
Leslie Crow
Michelle Dotter
Lucinda Gaines
Leandra Hernandez
Abigail Meyer
Andrew Olsen
Jill Steinberg
Suzanne Zarosky

E-Commerce Managers:
Alejandra Avila
Emily Hurley
Geoffrey Trudeau

Information Technology Manager:
Wenping Guo

Cover Design:
Kim Paxson, Just Graphics
Junction, TX

Special Thanks to:
American Hotel & Lodging Association
National Association of Realtors
National Association of Home Builders
National Bureau of Statistics of China
Real Capital Analytics
U.S. Bureau of Economic Analysis
U.S. Bureau of Labor Statistics
U.S. Census Bureau
U.S. Federal Reserve

Plunkett Research, Ltd.
P. O. Drawer 541737, Houston, Texas 77254, USA
Phone: 713.932.0000 Fax: 713.932.7080 www.plunkettresearch.com

Published by:
Plunkett Research, Ltd.
P.O. Drawer 541737
Houston, Texas 77254-1737

Phone: 713.932.0000
Fax: 713.932.7080
Internet: www.plunkettresearch.com

ISBN13 # 978-1-59392-170-5

Disclaimer of liability for use and results of use:

The editors and publishers assume no responsibility for your own success in making an investment or business decision, in seeking or keeping any job, in succeeding at any firm or in obtaining any amount or type of benefits or wages. Your own results and the job stability or financial stability of any company depend on influences outside of our control. All risks are assumed by the reader. Investigate any potential employer or business relationship carefully and carefully verify past and present finances, present business conditions and the level of compensation and benefits currently paid. Each company's details are taken from sources deemed reliable; however, their accuracy is not guaranteed. The editors and publishers assume no liability, beyond the actual payment received from a reader, for any direct, indirect, incidental or consequential, special or exemplary damages, and they do not guarantee, warrant nor make any representation regarding the use of this material. Trademarks or tradenames are used without symbols and only in a descriptive sense, and this use is not authorized by, associated with or sponsored by the trademarks' owners. Ranks and ratings are presented as an introductory and general glance at corporations, based on our research and our knowledge of businesses and the industries in which they operate. The reader should use caution.

PLUNKETT'S
REAL ESTATE & CONSTRUCTION INDUSTRY
ALMANAC 2010

CONTENTS

Continued on the next page

Continued from previous page

A Short Real Estate & Construction Industry Glossary

10-K: An annual report filed by publicly held companies. It provides a comprehensive overview of the company's business and its finances. By law, it must contain specific information and follow a given form, the "Annual Report on Form 10-K." The U.S. Securities and Exchange Commission requires that it be filed within 90 days after fiscal year end. However, these reports are often filed late due to extenuating circumstances. Variations of a 10-K are often filed to indicate amendments and changes. Most publicly held companies also publish an "annual report" that is not on Form 10-K. These annual reports are more informal and are frequently used by a company to enhance its image with customers, investors and industry peers.

Abatement (Property Tax): A decrease in property taxes, due to a problem with the property or to an agreement by taxing authorities to delay taxing the property at full value.

Acceleration Clause: A clause in a contract of debt, such as a mortgage, which causes the entire amount to become due upon the borrower's default.

Accessibility: The degree to which customers can easily get into and out of a shopping center, store or office.

Acre: A measure of land equaling 43,560 square feet.

Adjustable-Rate Mortgage (ARM): A mortgage that changes interest rates periodically to match a specific index.

Adjusted Funds From Operations (AFFO): A measure of cash flow from operations, typically used to gauge REITs. AFFO is the result of subtracting from funds from operations (FFO) certain costs that otherwise would have been capitalized for depreciation, but are actually needed to maintain a property on a day-to-day basis, such as the replacement of carpeting, or leasing expenses such as remodeling allowances.

Air Rights: A sellable right to the air space above a property.

Alt-A: See "Alternative Documentation Mortgage (Alt-A)."

Alternative Documentation Mortgage (Alt-A): An alternative method of documenting a loan file, often referred to as "alt doc" or "Alt-A," that relies on unsubstantiated information provided by the borrower regarding personal income and assets, rather than positive proof such as income tax returns, W2 forms from employers, bank statements and investment account statements.

Amortization Schedule: A printed table showing the principal and interest payments and due dates of the payments owed on a mortgage or loan.

Amortization through Equal Monthly Payments: A repayment method in which the amount borrowed is repaid gradually through regular monthly payments of principal and interest. During the first few years, most of each payment is applied toward the interest owed. During the final years of the loan, payment amounts are applied almost exclusively to the remaining principal.

Anticompetitive Leasing Arrangement: A lease that limits the type and amount of competition a particular retailer faces within a trading area (e.g., a lease that will not allow two supermarkets in one shopping center).

Arbitration: A legal process wherein an impartial third party decides a dispute. This practice is used instead of a standard trial in court.

Assumable Mortgage (Assumable Loan): An existing mortgage that can be assumed by a future purchaser of a piece of real estate.

Atmosphere (Retail Stores): Architecture, layout, signs and displays, color, lighting, music and scents which together create an image of a store in the customer's mind.

Average Daily Rate (ADR): In hotels, room revenue divided by rooms sold.

Baby Boomer: Generally refers to people born in the U.S. and Western Europe from 1946 to 1964. In the U.S., the initial number of Baby Boomers totaled about 78 million. The term evolved to include the children of soldiers and war industry workers who were involved in World War II.

Back-End Ratio: See "Debt-to-Income Ratio (Mortgages)."

Balloon Loan: A loan in which a large payment for the remaining balance is due at the end of the loan.

Balloon Payment: The final principal payment due at the end of a balloon mortgage. Typically, lower monthly payments are provided for under a balloon mortgage, with a substantial final payment due later.

Basis Point: One 100th of 1%.

Below-Market Interest Rate (BMIR): An interest rate that is lower than rates generally charged on similar loans in the marketplace. In real estate, this is typically a subsidized interest rate provided by the Federal Government for low-income housing.

Biennial Payments: Loan payments that are due every other year.

Blanket Mortgage: A mortgage covering at least two pieces of real estate as security for the same mortgage.

Boiler Plate: A standard clause that appears in all similar contracts.

BPO: See "Business Process Outsourcing (BPO)."

BRAC: Base realignment and closure. The process whereby military bases are closed and repurposed into commercial, industrial or other real estate uses.

Branding: A marketing strategy that places a focus on the brand name of a product, service or firm in order to increase the brand's market share, increase sales, establish credibility, improve satisfaction, raise the profile of the firm and increase profits.

BRIC: An acronym representing Brazil, Russia, India and China. The economies of these four countries are seen as some of the fastest growing in the world. A 2003 report by investment bank Goldman Sachs is often credited for popularizing the term; the report suggested that by 2050, BRIC economies will likely outshine those countries which are currently the richest in the world.

B-to-B, or B2B: See "Business-to-Business."

B-to-C, or B2C: See "Business-to-Consumer."

Build-to-Suit: A building created by a landlord specifically for one tenant, designed to suit the tenant's particular needs.

Business Process Outsourcing (BPO): The process of hiring another company to handle business activities. BPO is one of the fastest-growing segments in the offshoring sector. Services include human resources management, billing and purchasing and call centers, as well as many types of customer service or marketing activities, depending on the industry involved. Also, see "Knowledge Process Outsourcing (KPO)."

Business-to-Business: An organization focused on selling products, services or data to commercial customers rather than individual consumers. Also known as B2B.

Business-to-Consumer: An organization focused on selling products, services or data to individual consumers rather than commercial customers. Also known as B2C.

Buy-down (Buydown): With a "temporary" buydown, a lender or homebuilder subsidizes a mortgage by lowering the interest rate during the first few years of the loan. While the payments are initially low, they increase when the subsidy expires. A "permanent" buydown, however, reduces the interest rate over the entire life of the loan.

Buying Power Index (BPI): An index indicating the percentage of total U.S. retail sales occurring in a specific geographic area. Used to forecast demand for new stores and to evaluate the performance of existing stores.

Call Option: 1) A contract giving the holder of an option the right to purchase (and obligating the writer of the option to sell) a specified number of shares of a stock at the given strike price. 2) The right of a lender to demand the outstanding balance of a loan at a given time.

Capital Expenditures: Expenditures to acquire or add to capital assets that will yield benefits over several years.

Capital Gain on Real Estate: The amount of increase in value of a property, other than a primary residence, that is taxable.

Capitalization Rate (Real Estate): A measure of a property's sale price, determined by dividing the annual net income of a property by the purchase price.

Captive Offshoring: Used to describe a company-owned offshore operation. For example, Microsoft owns and operates significant captive offshore research and development centers in China and elsewhere that are offshore from Microsoft's U.S. home base. Also see "Offshoring."

Cash Available for Distribution (CAD): A measure of a REIT's ability to generate cash and to distribute dividends. Also known as FAD (Funds Available for Distribution.)

Caveat Emptor: Latin for "buyer beware." In real estate it is generally incumbent upon the buyer to discover defects with the property unless those defects are known to the seller.

CDO: See "Collateralized Debt Obligation (CDO)."

Central Business District (CBD): The traditional downtown business area of a city or town.

Certificate of Eligibility: The document given to qualified veterans that entitles them to obtain VA-guaranteed loans for homes, businesses and mobile homes. Certificates of eligibility may be obtained by sending Form DD-214 (Separation Paper) to the local VA office with VA form 1880 (request for Certificate of Eligibility).

Certificate of Insurance: A document detailing the insurance coverage provided for a property, asset or business.

Certificate of Occupancy: A document issued by the local government stating that a property is ready for occupancy.

Chattel: An item not attached to the land or buildings in a purchase agreement unless otherwise specified.

CIS: See "Commonwealth of Independent States (CIS)."

Class A Building: The most visible, best-located, most prestigious buildings that rent to tenants at rates above typical buildings in the area.

Class B Building: Typical buildings within a given area, which rent to tenants seeking to pay average rates for the neighborhood. These buildings are well-maintained and well-located but are below the standards of Class A buildings.

Class C Building: Buildings that are maintained and located in a fashion that is satisfactory for tenants seeking to pay rents that are below average for the neighborhood. These buildings have a presence and level of finish that is well below those of Class A or B buildings.

Close-Out Store: A retailer offering low-priced merchandise obtained through liquidations.

Closing: The meeting between the buyer, seller and lender or their agents where the property or asset and funds legally change hands. Also called "settlement."

Closing Costs: Costs associated with the closing of a mortgage, including legal fees, taxes, mortgage application fees and other items.

CMO: See "Collateralized Mortgage Obligation (CMO)."

Collateralized Debt Obligation (CDO): A method of taking a pool of debts, such as mortgages, and selling pieces of that pool to multiple investors. CDOs can also be created for pools of bonds, loans, leases and other types of financial assets.

Collateralized Mortgage Obligation (CMO): A bond that is a debt instrument backed by a pool of underlying mortgages that pass through payments received to the holder of the CMO. A CMO is a popular way to trade large amounts of mortgages at once. The underlying pool may represent thousands of individual mortgages.

Combination Store: A store that combines grocery and drug products in the same building. See "Food/Drug Combo."

Commitment: 1) A promise by a lender to make a loan on specific terms or conditions to a borrower. 2) A promise by an investor to purchase mortgages from a lender with specific terms or conditions. 3) An agreement, often in writing, between a lender and a borrower to loan money at a future date subject to the completion of paperwork or compliance with stated conditions.

Common Area Maintenance (CAM) Assessments: Fees paid to a landlord or property owners association for the maintenance of common areas such as hallways, elevators, exterior lighting, sidewalks or recreational facilities.

Common Areas: Areas shared by tenants or property owners. For example, in a shopping center, the parking lots, sidewalks and hallways are common areas. In a housing development, recreational facilities, greenbelts and hike or bike trails may be common areas.

Commonwealth of Independent States (CIS): An organization consisting of 11 former members of the Soviet Union: Russia, Ukraine, Armenia, Moldova, Georgia, Belarus, Kazakhstan, Uzbekistan, Azerbaijan, Kyrgyzstan and Tajikistan. It was created in 1991. Turkmenistan recently left the Commonwealth as a permanent member, but remained as an associate member. The Commonwealth seeks to coordinate a variety of economic and social policies, including taxation, pricing, customs and economic regulation, as well as to promote the free movement of capital, goods, services and labor.

Community Center: A large shopping center that includes a discount store, specialty department store, super drugstore, home-improvement center and other convenience and shopping goods stores.

Compact Fluorescent Lamp (CFL): A type of light bulb that provides considerable energy savings over traditional incandescent light bulbs.

Condemnation: The claiming of private land by a government for public use or because of code violations. Also see "Eminent Domain."

Condominium: 1) In the travel industry, lodging similar to furnished, private apartments that are available to rent for days or weeks. 2) In real estate, a kind of property ownership in which the owner holds title to an individual unit in a multi-unit dwelling and shares ownership of common areas such as hallways or swimming pools.

Conforming Loan: See "Non-Conforming Loan."

Construction Loan: A short-term interim loan to pay for the construction a building or home. Such loans are usually designed to provide periodic disbursements to the builder as progress with construction is made.

Construction/Permanent Loan: A mortgage loan combining short-term financing of construction with long-term financing of the completed property.

Consumer Price Index (CPI): A measure of the average change in consumer prices over time in a fixed market basket of goods and services, such as food, clothing and housing. The CPI is calculated by the U.S. Federal Government and is considered to be one measure of inflation.

Consumerism: The activities of government, business and independent organizations designed to protect individuals from practices that infringe upon their rights as consumers.

Contract for Deed: A property transaction wherein the seller retains the title to the property until the buyer has paid a certain amount, usually the entire balance owned. This is generally a risky way for a buyer to enter into a purchase.

Convenience Center: A shopping center that typically includes such stores as a convenience store and a dry cleaner.

Convenience Stores: Stores between 3,000 and 8,000 square feet in size providing a limited assortment of merchandise at a convenient location and time (e.g., 7-Eleven). Many also sell gasoline.

Conventional Mortgage: A loan other than a government-financed loan (e.g., a loan that is not a VA mortgage).

Conventional Supermarket: A market that offers a complete line of groceries, meat and produce with a minimum of $2 million in annual revenue, at least 9% of which comes from GM/HBC. Stores typically carry approximately 15,000 items. Many stores offer bakery, deli, banking and other services.

Cooperative (Co-Op): In real estate, a type of multiple ownership in which members of the co-operative own shares in the corporation owning the property. Co-op owners typically have the right to occupy one unit in the co-op building. It is a distinctly different type of ownership from a condominium, wherein each unit's owner takes title to the condominium and then shares ownership of the common areas such as hallways.

Cost Plus Contract: A contract that sets the contractor's compensation as a percentage of the total cost of labor and materials.

Credit Risk: The risk assumed by the lender that the borrower may default on a loan or mortgage. The apparent credit risk is considered when setting an interest rate to be charged.

Customer Relationship Management (CRM): Refers to the automation, via sophisticated software, of business processes involving existing and prospective customers. CRM may cover aspects such as sales (contact management and contact history), marketing (campaign management and telemarketing) and customer service (call center history and field service history). Well known providers of CRM software include Salesforce, which delivers via a Software as a Service model (see "Software as a Service (Saas)"), Microsoft and Siebel, which as been acquired by Oracle.

Debt-to-Income Ratio (Mortgages): Also called the "back-end" ratio, this ratio, expressed as a percentage, is calculated by dividing a borrower's monthly payment obligations on long-term debt (including housing expense) by his or her gross monthly income.

Deed of Trust: In conjunction with a, this instrument is used in many western states to pledge the home or other real estate as security for a loan.

Deferred-Interest Mortgage: A mortgage that defers some of the interest to a later date.

Demographics: The breakdown of the population into statistical categories such as age, income, education and sex.

Department Stores: Very large stores carrying a wide variety and deep assortment while offering considerable customer services (e.g., Dillard's or Saks Fifth Avenue). Stores are organized into separate departments for displaying merchandise. However, the variety of departments has lessened in recent years, and these stores now tend to focus on apparel.

Depreciation: A method of amortizing the cost of an asset in equal dollar amounts over the useful life of an asset. For example, an item with a five-year life would be charged with a certain amount of its cost every year for five years.

Discount Broker: A broker or brokerage firm that executes buy and sell transactions at commission rates lower than a full-service broker or brokerage.

Discount Points (Mortgages): The amount paid either to maintain or to lower the interest rate charged on a mortgage. Each point is equal to 1% of the loan amount. (For example, two points on a $100,000 mortgage would equal $2,000.)

Discount Store: A general merchandise retailer offering a wide variety of merchandise, limited service and low prices (e.g., Target or Kmart).

Discount-Anchored Center: A shopping center that contains one or more discount stores plus smaller retail tenants.

Distributed Power Generation: A method of generating electricity at or near the site where it will be consumed, such as the use of small, local generators or fuel cells to power individual buildings, homes or neighborhoods. Distributed power is thought by many analysts to offer distinct advantages. For example, electricity generated in this manner is not reliant upon the grid for distribution to the end user.

Down Payment: The difference between the purchase price and that portion of the purchase price being financed.

DownREIT: A structure that enables an REIT to acquire properties in exchange for partnership units.

Earnest Money: Good faith money provided to the seller by the potential buyer to show that he or she is serious about purchasing a piece of real estate. This amount can be applied to the purchase at closing, but if the deal does not go through it may be forfeited, or in some cases returned, depending on the terms of the purchase contract.

Easement: A right of way giving persons other than the owner access to a property. A common use is to provide a driveway through one property owner's land for access to an adjacent property.

Echo Boomers: See "Generation Y."

E-Commerce: The use of online, Internet-based sales methods. The phrase is used to describe both business-to-consumer and business-to-business sales.

Eminent Domain: The right of a governmental unit to force an owner to sell his or her property for fair market value for public use. This is the legal basis for the condemnation of private property. For example, if a state needs property for the construction or widening of a highway, it may condemn the needed property under this feature of the law.

Encroachment: An intrusion onto a property. For example, if one property owner erects a fence along his property border and fails to properly stay inside of his property line, a portion of the fence lies on the adjacent property, forming an encroachment.

Encumbrance: Any claim on a title or property that might prevent the owner from passing good title at a sale.

End Caps: Display fixtures located at the end of an aisle. Also, in real estate, the end unit or corner unit in a shopping center.

Enterprise Resource Planning (ERP): An integrated information system that helps manage all aspects of a business, including accounting, ordering and human resources, typically across all locations of a major corporation or organization. ERP is considered to be a critical tool for management of large organizations. Suppliers of ERP tools include SAP and Oracle.

Equal Credit Opportunity Act (ECOA): A federal law that requires lenders to make credit equally available without discrimination based on race, religion, national origin, age, sex, marital status or receipt of income from public assistance programs.

Equity: 1) The net value of the common stockholders' interest in a company as listed on a company's balance sheet. 2) The difference between a company's assets and liabilities (it is possible for a company to have negative equity). 3) The difference between the value of a property and the amount owed on that property. 4) A share of stock.

Equity REIT: A REIT that owns real estate, as opposed to an REIT that specializes in making mortgage loans.

ERP: See "Enterprise Resource Planning (ERP)."

Escrow Account: A mortgage lender's method of accounting for escrow monies received from the borrower. See "Escrow(s)."

Escrow Waiver Fee: A fee paid by a home mortgage borrower who elects to pay insurance and property taxes directly, rather than paying them into an escrow account at the mortgage company. There is a one-time charge by the mortgage company of 0.25% to 0.375% of the loan amount.

Escrow(s): That portion of a borrower's monthly payments held by the lender or servicer to pay for taxes, hazard insurance, mortgage insurance and other items as they become due. Also known as impound(s).

EU: See "European Union (EU)."

EU Competence: The jurisdiction in which the EU can take legal action.

European Union (EU): A consolidation of European countries (member states) functioning as one body to facilitate trade. Previously known as the European Community (EC), the EU expanded to include much of Eastern Europe in 2004, raising the total number of member states to 25. In 2002, the EU launched a unified currency, the Euro. See europa.eu.int.

Expense Ratio: The comparison of the cost of operating a property, business or organization to its gross income.

Facilities Management: The management of a company's physical buildings and/or information systems on an outsourced basis.

Factory Outlet Stores: Off-price retail stores owned by manufacturers.

Fair Credit Reporting Act: A consumer protection law that regulates consumer credit report providers. For example, the act sets up procedures for correcting mistakes on an individual's credit record, provides certain restrictions on publishing credit reports and generally governs a consumer's rights.

Fair Market Value (FMV): A term used to indicate the value of a property on the open market.

Fannie Mae: See "Federal National Mortgage Association (FNMA)."

Farmers Home Administration (FmHA): A part of the U.S. Department of Agriculture that provides financing for farmers and residents of rural areas.

Federal Home Loan Bank Board (FHLBB): The agency of the federal government that supervises all federal savings and loan associations and federally insured state-chartered savings and loan associations. The FHLBB also operates the Federal Savings and Loan Insurance Corporation, which insures accounts at federal savings and loan associations and those state-chartered associations that apply and are accepted. In addition, the FHLBB directs the Federal Home Loan Bank System, which provides a flexible credit facility for member savings institutions to promote the availability of home financing. The FHL Banks also own the Federal Home Loan Mortgage Corporation, established in 1970 to promote secondary markets for mortgages.

Federal Home Loan Mortgage Corporation (FHLMC): A U.S. government-sponsored agency that purchases conventional mortgages from lending institutions, thus adding liquidity to the market. Also known as "Freddie Mac."

Federal Housing Administration (FHA): An agency of the U.S. Department of Housing and Urban Development (HUD). The FHA primarily insures housing loans.

Federal National Mortgage Association (FNMA): A major, government-sponsored investor that purchases mortgage loans from mortgage bankers. It is similar to FHLMC. Also known as "Fannie Mae."

Fee Simple: Absolute or sole ownership of a property.

FHA: See "Federal Housing Administration (FHA)."

FHLMC: See "Federal Home Loan Mortgage Corporation (FHLMC)."

First Mortgage: The mortgage that has legal precedence over other mortgage claims, usually, but not always, chronologically first in the history of the property. Also see "Second Mortgage."

Fixed-Rate Mortgage or Loan: A mortgage (or loan) that has an interest rate that does not change over the life of the loan.

FmHA: See "Farmers Home Administration (FmHA)."

FNMA: See "Federal National Mortgage Association (FNMA)."

Food/Drug Combo: A superstore and drug store that share checkout lanes. GM/HBC (General Merchandise/Health and Beauty Care) takes up at least one-third of retail space in the store, and accounts for 15% or more of revenue. Food/drug combos offer pharmacy services.

Forbearance (Mortgages): A temporary reprieve from paying a mortgage, usually granted because of some kind of hardship.

Foreclosure: The process whereby a borrower in default under a mortgage is deprived of his or her interest in a property, which is taken away by the lender via a legal procedure.

Franchising: A contractual agreement between a franchiser and a franchisee that allows the franchisee to operate a retail outlet or other type of business using a name and format developed and supported by the franchiser.

Freddie Mac: See "Federal Home Loan Mortgage Corporation (FHLMC)."

Free-Standing Retailer: A location for a retailer that is a building by itself, frequently on a pad site in front of a shopping center.

Front-End Ratio: See "Housing-Expenses-to-Income Ratio."

Full-Service Leasing: A program under which a vehicle or building is leased and the operation and maintenance are included in the lease fee.

GDP: See "Gross Domestic Product (GDP)."

General Merchandise, Apparel, Furniture and Other (GAFO): Usually used in reference to the retail sector, excluding automotive and food stores, and includes general merchandise, department, discount apparel, furniture and miscellaneous specialty stores.

Generation X: A loosely-defined and variously-used term that describes people born in the U.S. and Canada between approximately 1965 and 1980, but other time frames are recited. Generation X is often referred to as a group influential in defining tastes in consumer goods, entertainment and/or political and social matters.

Generation Y: Refers to people born between approximately 1980 and 2000, who number about 50 million in the U.S. They are also known as Echo Boomers, Millenials or the Millenial Generation. These are children of the Baby Boom generation who will be filling the work force as Baby Boomers retire.

Geological Information System (GIS): A computer software system which captures, stores, updates, manipulates, analyzes, and displays all forms of geographically referenced information.

Ginnie Mae: See "Government National Mortgage Association (GNMA)."

Globalization: The increased mobility of goods, services, labor, technology and capital throughout the world. Although globalization is not a new development, its pace has increased with the advent of new technologies, especially in the areas of telecommunications, finance and shipping.

GM/HBC: General Merchandise/Health and Beauty Care.

GNMA: See "Government National Mortgage Association (GNMA)."

Good Faith Estimate: A written estimate of closing costs that a lender must provide for the borrower within three days of submitting a new loan application.

Government National Mortgage Association (GNMA): A government-owned corporation within the U.S. Department of Housing and Urban Development (HUD) that specializes in the purchase of FHA and VA loans. Also known as "Ginnie Mae."

Graduated Payment Mortgage (GPM): A type of flexible-payment mortgage where the payments increase for a specified period of time and then level off. This type of mortgage has negative amortization built into it. For example, a homebuyer who believes that his or her income may increase a few years later may enter into a mortgage that has lower payments in the first five years but substantially higher monthly payments later in the loan.

Gross Domestic Product (GDP): The total value of a nation's output, income and expenditures produced with a nation's physical borders.

Gross Leasable Area (GLA): The total space that is leasable in a property. GLA may include common areas. Also see "Net Leasable Area (NLA)."

Gross National Product (GNP): A country's total output of goods and services from all forms of economic activity measured at market prices for one calendar year. It differs from Gross Domestic Product (GDP) in that GNP includes income from investments made in foreign nations.

Hard-Lines: Durable, non-apparel items, such as furniture, appliances and housewares.

Hectare (ha): A measurement of area equal to 10,000 square meters or 2.471 acres.

Historic District: A zoning classification for neighborhoods of historic value. This classification may limit what changes an owner can make to the property. For example, the colors of exterior paint or types of doors, windows and fences that may be used may be regulated.

Home Equity Loan: A fixed- or adjustable-rate loan obtained for a variety of purposes, secured by the equity in a home. Interest paid is usually tax-deductible. Often used for home improvement or the freeing of equity for investment. Home equity loans are tax-advantaged alternatives to consumer loans whose interest is not tax-deductible, such as auto or boat loans, credit card debt, medical debt and education loans.

Home Improvement Center: A category specialist combining the traditional hardware store and lumberyard (e.g., Home Depot).

Home Inspection: A thorough inspection by a professional that ensures that a property is mechanically and structurally sound. Home inspectors generally are licensed by the states in which they work.

Homeowners' Association: A nonprofit association that manages the common areas of a housing development or condominium project. In addition to owning and maintaining common areas, it may enforce deed restrictions and covenants.

Housing-Expenses-to-Income Ratio: Used in evaluating the income of a potential mortgage borrower. It is calculated by dividing the anticipated housing expense by the gross monthly income of the borrower. Also known as the "front-end" ratio.

HUD: The Department of Housing and Urban Development, a U.S. Government agency. HUD's mission is to increase homeownership, support community development and increase access to affordable housing free from discrimination.

HUD-I Settlement Statement: A form utilized at mortgage closing to itemize the costs associated with purchasing a home. Used universally by mandate of HUD (the U.S. Department of Housing and Urban Development).

Hybrid Mortgage: A type of mortgage that includes some compensation to the lender, such as a portion of income, in addition to the principal and interest on the loan.

Hybrid REIT: A REIT that combines the strategies of both an equity REIT and a mortgage REIT.

Hypermarket: A very large retail store that offers low prices and combines a discount store and a superstore food retailer in one warehouse-like building (e.g., a Wal-Mart Supercenter). These stores may be as large as 200,000 square feet.

Implied Equity Market Cap (REITs): The market value of all outstanding common stock of a company plus the value of all UPREIT partnership units as if they had been converted into stock.

Independent Retailer: A retailer that owns only one or a few retail stores and is not part of a large chain.

Indexed Lease: A rental agreement whereby the rent changes in accordance with a certain index, such as the consumer price index.

Infrastructure: 1) The equipment that comprises a system. 2) Public-use assets such as roads, bridges, sewers and other assets necessary for public accommodation and utilities. 3) The underlying base of a system or network.

Initial Public Offering (IPO): A company's first effort to sell its stock to investors (the public). Investors in an up-trending market eagerly seek stocks offered in many IPOs because the stocks of newly public companies that seem to have great promise may appreciate very rapidly in price, reaping great profits for those who were able to get the stock at the first offering. In the United States, IPOs are regulated by the SEC (U.S. Securities Exchange Commission) and by the state-level regulatory agencies of the states in which the IPO shares are offered.

Interim Loan: A loan that provides proceeds for the construction costs of a project. Often paid out in installments as the work progresses.

Interstate Sales Full Disclosure Act: A law that requires a residential development of 100 or more lots to file a disclosure statement with HUD.

Jumbo Loan: Also known as "non-conforming" loans, mortgage loans over the maximum "conforming" amount as set by FNMA are considered jumbo and are subject to different underwriting criteria. The benchmark loan amount is evaluated on a yearly basis by FNMA and adjusted accordingly. Interest rates on jumbo loans are generally 0.25% higher than their conforming counterparts. Also see "Non-Conforming Loan."

Knowledge Process Outsourcing (KPO): The use of outsourced and/or offshore workers to perform business tasks that require judgment and analysis. Examples include such professional tasks as patent research, legal research, architecture, design, engineering, market research, scientific research, accounting and tax return preparation. Also, see "Business Process Outsourcing (BPO)."

LAC: An acronym for Latin America and the Caribbean.

LDCs: See "Least Developed Countries (LDCs)."

Leased Department: A department in a retail store operated by an outside party. The outside party either pays fixed rent or a percentage of sales to the retailer for the space.

Least Developed Countries (LDCs): Nations determined by the U.N. Economic and Social Council to be the poorest and weakest members of the international community. There are currently 50 LDCs, of which 34 are in Africa, 15 are in Asia Pacific and the remaining one (Haiti) is in Latin America. The top 10 on the LDC list, in descending order from top to 10th, are Afghanistan, Angola, Bangladesh, Benin, Bhutan, Burkina Faso, Burundi, Cambodia, Cape Verde and the Central African Republic. Sixteen of the LDCs are also Landlocked Least Developed Countries (LLDCs) which present them with additional difficulties often due to the high cost of transporting trade goods. Eleven of the LDCs are Small Island Developing States (SIDS), which are often at risk of extreme weather phenomenon (hurricanes, typhoons, Tsunami); have fragile ecosystems; are often dependent on foreign energy sources; can have high disease rates for HIV/AIDS and malaria; and can have poor market access and trade terms.

Legal Description: A description of a property that fulfills legal requirements and properly identifies the property. A legal description is commonly used in conjunction with a boundary survey. Also see "Survey (Real Estate)."

Lifestyle Center: An open-air, highly landscaped configuration of approximately 50 stores. Generally located near upscale neighborhoods, lifestyle centers offer leasable retail area of 150,000 to 500,000 square feet (typically, at least 50,000 square feet are dedicated to upscale national specialty stores).

Limited-Assortment Store: A small, low-priced grocery store that provides limited service, few or no perishables and generally fewer than 2,000 items.

Loan Application Fee: A lender's fee, usually ranging from $75 to $300, which the buyer must pay when applying for a mortgage.

Loan Origination Fee: A fee charged by the lender for processing a mortgage or loan. The mortgage industry standard is 1% of the loan amount, but if the application is taken over the Internet, it is often reduced to 0.5% or even zero, depending on the lender.

Loan-to-Value Ratio (LTV): An underwriting ratio determined by dividing the sales price or appraised value into the loan amount, expressed as a percentage. For example, with a sales price of $100,000 and a mortgage loan of $80,000, the LTV ratio would be 80%. Loans with an LTV over 80% usually require private mortgage insurance. See "Private Mortgage Insurance (PMI)."

Lock (Lock In): A commitment that a borrower obtains from a lender assuring a particular interest rate for a limited time period, such as 30 days. A lock provides protection to the borrower should interest rates rise between the time the borrower applies for a loan, acquires loan approval and, subsequently, closes the purchase.

LOHAS: Lifestyles of Health and Sustainability. A marketing term that refers to consumers who choose to purchase and/or live with items that are natural, organic, less polluting, etc. Such consumers may also prefer products powered by alternative energy, such as hybrid cars.

Low-E: A coating for windows that can prevent warmth from escaping from the inside of a building during the winter, while preventing solar heat from entering the building during the summer. Significant savings in energy usage can result.

Market Segmentation: The division of a consumer market into specific groups of buyers based on demographic factors.

Market Value: An estimation of how much a property or asset would sell for on the open market.

Marketing: Includes all planning and management activities and expenses associated with the promotion of a product or service. Marketing can encompass advertising, customer surveys, public relations and many other disciplines. Marketing is distinct from selling, which is the process of sell-through to the end user.

Material Breach: The violation of a contract that causes invalidation or some other penalty.

Megapolitan: Massive corridors comprising several million residents across several cities. Examples include the IH35 Corridor anchored by Dallas and Ft. Worth, Texas, and the Atlantic Coast corridor anchored by Miami, Ft. Lauderdale and Boca Raton, Florida.

Mill: One 10th of a penny. Usually used in real estate taxation.

Millenials: See "Generation Y."

Mineral Interests: The rights of ownership to gas, oil or other minerals as they naturally occur at or below a tract of land. Also known as "mineral rights."

Mineral Rights: See "Mineral Interests."

MIP: See "Mortgage Insurance Premium (MIP)."

Mixed-Use Development: A development that has some combination of residential, office, retail and/or industrial space.

Mortgage Banker: An organization that specializes in underwriting mortgage loans. Mortgage bankers typically sell some or all of their loans to investors but may continue to own and/or service them. Also see "Mortgage Broker."

Mortgage Broker: An organization in the business of arranging funding for a borrower. In contrast to a mortgage banker, a broker does not actually loan the money. Brokers usually charge a fee or receive a commission for their services.

Mortgage Insurance Premium (MIP): Insurance purchased by the borrower to insure the lender against loss should he or she default. MIP is paid on government-insured loans (FHA or VA loans) regardless of the LTV (loan-to-value ratio). Should the borrower pay off a government-insured loan in advance of maturity, he or she may be entitled to a small refund of MIP. Also see "Private Mortgage Insurance (PMI)."

Mortgage REIT: A REIT that specializes in making mortgages rather than owning property outright.

Mortgage-Backed Security (MBS): A security that represents ownership of an undivided interest in a group of mortgages. Mortgage bankers often form MBSs in order to sell pools of their mortgages on the secondary market. Also see "Collateralized Debt Obligation (CDO)."

Municipal Utility District (MUD): A political unit, regulated by state authorities, that has been established to own and operate utilities within its boundaries. These utilities typically include water, sewer and/or drainage. MUDs may be inside or outside of city limits. MUDs generally are empowered to sell bonds in order to raise capital with which to install utility pipes and systems. Property owners within a MUD pay regular fees to the MUD for services.

National Flood Insurance Program (NFIP): A program offered by the Federal Emergency Management Association (FEMA) that provides flood insurance to individual property owners and tenants.

Negative Amortization: Amortization in which the payments made are insufficient to fund complete repayment of the loan at its termination. This usually occurs when the increase in the monthly payment on an adjustable-rate mortgage (ARM) is limited by a pre-set ceiling. The portion of the payment that should be paid is added to the remaining balance owed. The balance owed may increase rather than decrease at various times in the life of the loan.

Neighborhood Center: A shopping center that includes a supermarket, drugstore, home-improvement center or variety store. Neighborhood centers often include small stores, such as apparel, shoe, camera and other shopping goods stores.

Net Leasable Area (NLA): The square footage in a building or property that is leasable excluding common areas, common hallways, common baths, etc. Also, see "Gross Leasable Area (GLA)."

Net Lease: A lease that requires all maintenance expenses, such as heating, insurance and interior repair, to be paid for by the tenant.

New Urbanism: A relatively new term that refers to neighborhood developments that feature shorter blocks, more sidewalks and pedestrian ways, access to convenient mass transit, bicycle paths and conveniently placed open spaces. The intent is to promote walking and social interaction while decreasing automobile traffic. The concept may also include close proximity to stores and offices that may be reached by walking rather than driving.

Non-Conforming Loan: A loan that is not eligible to be purchased by Fannie Mae or Freddie Mac. These loan agencies have specific upper limits on how large a loan they will buy. These limits are adjusted on a regular basis. Also, several other factors regarding the loan must meet guidelines before they are considered to conform. Also see "Jumbo Loan."

Non-Store Retailing: A form of retailing that is not store-based. Non-store retailing can be conducted through vending machines, direct-selling, direct-marketing, party-based selling, catalogs, television programming, telemarketing and Internet-based selling.

OECD: See "Organisation for Economic Co-operation and Development (OECD)."

Office of Interstate Land Sales Registration: The HUD agency that is responsible for implementing the Interstate Sales Full Disclosure Act.

Off-Price Retailer: A retailer that offers an inconsistent assortment of brand-name, fashion-oriented soft goods at low prices.

Offshoring: The rapidly growing tendency among U.S., Japanese and Western European firms to send knowledge-based and manufacturing work overseas. The intent is to take advantage of lower wages and operating costs in such nations as China, India, Hungary and Russia. The choice of a nation for offshore work may be influenced by such factors as language and education of the local workforce, transportation systems or natural resources. For example, China and India are graduating high numbers of skilled engineers and scientists from their universities. Also, some nations are noted for large numbers of workers skilled in the English language, such as the Philippines and India. Also see "Captive Offshoring" and "Outsourcing."

Option ARM: An adjustable rate mortgage that lets the borrower decide how much to pay each month. The borrower may choose between the standard principal and interest amount, or simply pay the interest. Some plans allow the borrower to pay even less, adding the unpaid interest to the total amount due under the note.

Organisation for Economic Co-operation and Development (OECD): A group of 30 countries that are strongly committed to the market economy and democracy. Some of the OECD members include Japan, the U.S., Spain, Germany, Australia, Korea, the U.K., Canada and Mexico. Although not members, Chile, Estonia, Israel, Russia and Slovenia are invited to member talks; and Brazil, China, India, Indonesia and South Africa have enhanced engagement policies with the OECD. The Organisation provides statistics, as well as social and economic data; and researches social changes, including patterns in evolving fiscal policy, agriculture, technology, trade, the environment and other areas. It publishes over 250 titles annually; publishes a corporate magazine, the OECD Observer; has radio and TV studios; and has centers in Tokyo, Washington, D.C., Berlin and Mexico City that distributed the Organisation's work and organizes events.

Outsourcing: The hiring of an outside company to perform a task otherwise performed internally by the company, generally with the goal of lowering costs and/or streamlining work flow. Outsourcing contracts are generally several years in length. Companies that hire outsourced services providers often prefer to focus on their core strengths while sending more routine tasks outside for others to perform. Typical outsourced services include the running of human resources departments, telephone call centers and computer departments. When outsourcing is performed overseas, it may be referred to as offshoring. Also see "Offshoring."

Owner Financing: A mortgage transaction whereby the property seller provides some or all of the financing and takes back a mortgage loan at closing.

Pad Site: A location for a free-standing retail building that sits in front of a mall or shopping center.

Participating Mortgage: A mortgage in which the lender is entitled to a share of the income from the property.

Passive Solar: A system in which solar energy (heat from sunlight) alone is used for the transfer of thermal energy. Heat transfer devices that depend on energy other than solar are not used. A good example is a passive solar water heater on the roof of a building.

Pass-Through (Mortgages): See "Collateralized Mortgage Obligation (CMO)."

Percentage Lease: A lease in which rent payments are based on a store's sales.

Photovoltaic (PV) Cell: An electronic device consisting of layers of semiconductor materials fabricated to form a junction (adjacent layers of materials with different electronic characteristics) and electrical contacts, capable of converting incident light directly into electricity (direct current). Photovoltaic technology works by harnessing the movement of electrons between the layers of a solar cell when the sun strikes the material.

PITI: Principal, interest, taxes and insurance: the elements of a monthly mortgage payment.

Planned Unit Development (PUD): A housing subdivision that contains pre-planned community features, such as parks or adjacent office or retail districts. The common space is owned by a homeowners' association.

Power Shopping Center: A large, open-air shopping center with the majority of space leased to several well-known anchor retail tenants-typically specialty retailers operating large stores that specialize in one type of merchandise. Typical anchor tenants include OfficeMax, Linens 'n Things, Marshall's and Best Buy. Some of these tenants may be on pad sites. Convenient access and parking are emphasized. These centers usually sit on major intersections.

PPP: See "Purchasing Power Parity (PPP) or Point-to-Point Protocol (PPP)."

Prefabricated (Construction): A term for buildings erected onsite from factory-made components, or built entirely offsite and then set down on the property. A mobile home is prefabricated. However, a few manufacturers factory-build certain types of houses and buildings that are not considered in the same class as mobile homes.

Pre-Paid Expenses: At closing of a real estate purchase, monies necessary to create an escrow account. These typically include two month's worth of taxes, hazard insurance, private mortgage insurance and special assessments.

Pre-Paid Interest: The amount of interest paid to cover the period from the closing of a sale until the beginning of the first payment on the mortgage or loan.

Pre-Payment (Prepayment): The unscheduled payment of all or part of the outstanding principal of a loan or mortgage. Pre-payments are typically made, by the borrower, but may also result by foreclosures, condemnations or casualties, such as an insurance settlement resulting from a total loss by fire or flood.

Pre-Payment Penalty (Prepayment Penalty): A penalty found in a promissory note or mortgage, imposed by the lender if the principal of a loan is paid before it is due, thereby reducing the lender's stream of interest earned on the note.

Pre-Payment Privilege: The right to repay the principal of a loan before interest is due.

Pre-Payment Risk: The possibility that the mortgages underlying a mortgage-backed security are repaid faster or more slowly than expected.

Pre-Qualification (Mortgages): The process of determining how much money a prospective property buyer will be eligible to borrow before actually applying for a loan.

Private Mortgage Insurance (PMI): Insurance paid on those loans that are not government-insured when the loan to value ratio is greater than 80%. When you have accumulated 20% of your home's value as equity, your lender may waive PMI at your request. Note that such insurance does not constitute a form of life insurance that pays off the loan in case of death. Also see "Mortgage Insurance Premium (MIP)."

PUD: See "Planned Unit Development (PUD)."

Purchasing Power Parity (PPP): Currency conversion rates that attempt to reflect the actual purchasing power of a currency in its home market, as opposed to examining price levels and comparing an exchange rate. PPPs are always given in the national currency units per U.S. dollar.

R&D-Flex Building: Industrial-type buildings that are designed to satisfy tenants that require an above-average amount of office space as well as an above-average level of finish that presents a more office-like environment, such as more windows and better landscape. From 30% to 100% of the space in such buildings may be devoted to office or laboratory space, with the balance devoted to light assembly or warehouse space.

Radon: A radioactive gas that may cause health problems. Some state laws require that a property owner disclose any known radon gas conditions. Concerned buyers may include testing for radon in their property inspections.

Real Estate Investment Trust (REIT): Investments that work in a manner very similar to mutual funds in that money from several investors is pooled together to jointly own real estate and/or invest in mortgages. REITs are required to distribute almost all (90%) of their net income annually, directly to shareholders. Many REITs specialize in a specific kind of real estate, such as shopping centers or apartments. Investors generally buy shares in REITs with a two-fold purpose: 1) to earn current income and 2) for long-term capital gains on appreciation in the value of the real estate.

Real Estate Investment Trust Act of 1960: The federal law that established guidelines for establishing REITs.

Real Estate Settlement Procedures Act (RESPA): A federal law that allows consumers to review information on known or estimated settlement costs. A statement of estimated costs must be provided by the lender once after a mortgage application has been completed and once again prior to or at closing.

Refinancing: In mortgages, refinancing is the process of paying off an existing mortgage with a new mortgage, often to attain a certain interest rate or to obtain cash from the transaction by increasing the principal balance.

Regional Center: A shopping center or mall which includes up to three department stores plus shopping or specialty stores rather than convenience stores. Super-regionals are similar but have at least four department stores and at least 1 million square feet of retail space.

Regulation Z: A federal rule that requires a lender to disclose the terms of a loan to the borrower.

REIT Modernization Act of 1999: The federal law that enabled an REIT to own up to 100% of the stock of a taxable subsidiary that provides services to REIT tenants and other customers. The law also changed the minimum distribution requirement from 95% to 90% of a REIT's taxable income.

RESPA: See "Real Estate Settlement Procedures Act (RESPA)."

Retail Chain: A firm that consists of multiple retail units under common ownership and usually has some centralization of decision-making in defining and implementing its strategy.

Return on Investment (ROI): A measure of a company's profitability, expressed in percentage as net profit (after taxes) divided by total dollar investment.

Revenue Per Available Room (REVPAR): A hotel performance measure that divides revenue by the number of available rooms, as opposed to the number of occupied rooms.

Reverse Mortgage: Enables older homeowners (aged 62+) to convert part of the equity in their homes into tax-free income without having to sell the home, give up title, or take on a new monthly mortgage payment. The lender provides either a line of credit, steady monthly payments or one upfront payment to the borrower. In return, the lender receives a right to proceeds upon the eventual sale of the home, typically after the borrower's death. There are no monthly payments to be made by the borrower, and there are no income or health requirements. Sometimes called a reverse annuity mortgage or RAM.

Right of Rescission: The legal right to void or cancel a mortgage contract in such a way as to treat the contract as if it never existed. Right of rescission is not applicable to mortgages made to purchase a home, but may be applicable to other mortgages, such as cash-out refinances.

R-Value (R Value): A method of measuring the effectiveness of building materials such as insulation. Technically, it is the resistance that a material has to heat flow. The higher the R-Value, the better the insulation provided. It is the inverse of U-Value. See "U-Value."

Sales Per Square Foot of Selling Space: Net sales divided by square feet of selling space.

Same-Store Sales: Sales dollars generated only by those stores that have been open more than a year and have historical data to compare this year's sales to the same time-frame last year.

Savings and Loan (S&L, Thrift, Savings Association, Savings Bank): Depository institution historically engaged primarily in accepting consumer savings deposits and in originating and investing in securities and residential mortgage loans; now may offer checking-type deposits and make a wider range of loans. Federally-chartered and federally-insured savings and loans are supervised by the Federal Home Loan Bank Board (FHLBB).

Second Mortgage: A mortgage with collateralization rights that are secondary to a first mortgage. In the event that the borrower defaults, the second mortgage holder may be forced to pay off the first mortgage in order to protect the second mortgage's interests in the property. Second mortgages involve more risks to the mortgage holder and generally are written at higher interest rates. It is also possible to create third or fourth mortgages, etc.

Secondary Market: A market providing for securities to be bought or sold. This market is where the majority of trading occurs. The New York Stock Exchange, all other stock exchanges and the bond markets are secondary markets. In mortgages, large pools of mortgages are bought and sold by major investors in the secondary market.

Securitization: The process of financing a pool of similar assets (such as mortgages, automobile loans, corporate debt instruments or credit card debts) by issuing to investors interests in the funds generated by that pool. Such pools are generally in the range of $100 million or higher, and may represent the debts of dozens of companies or thousands of consumers. Securitization enables banks and other lenders to have ready markets into which they may sell loans that they generate.

Servicing (Mortgages): The steps and operations necessary to manage a mortgage or pool of mortgages, such as the collection of payments and the disbursement of escrowed funds for taxes and insurance. Servicing also includes following up on delinquent borrowers and foreclosure, if necessary. Servicing companies charge a fee to the investor that owns the loan.

Shared-Appreciation Mortgage: A loan that provides a share of the appreciation of the value of the property to the lender. Such loans are typically written at below-market interest rates.

Smart Buildings: Buildings or homes that have been designed with interconnected electronic and electrical systems which can be controlled by computers. Advantages include the ability to turn appliances and systems on or off remotely or on a set schedule, leading to greatly enhanced energy efficiency.

Soft Goods: Apparel and linens.

Software as a Service (SaaS): Refers to the practice of providing users with software applications that are hosted on remote servers and accessed via the Internet. Excellent examples include the CRM (Customer Relationship Management) software provided in SaaS format by Salesforce. An earlier technology that operated in a similar, but less sophisticated, manner was called ASP or Application Service Provider.

Specialty Department Store: A store with a department store format that focuses on apparel and soft home goods (e.g., Neiman Marcus).

Specialty Store: A store specializing in one category of merchandising, frequently fashion-related.

Straight-Lining (Real Estate): Required by GAAP (Generally Accepted Accounting Principles), straight-lining averages a tenant's rent payments over the life of a lease.

Strip Center: A small shopping center that includes several adjacent stores located along a major street or highway.

Subprime: A term used to describe mortgages offered to borrowers with less than perfect credit. Subprime rates are generally higher than typical interest rates.

Subsidiary, Wholly-Owned: A company that is wholly controlled by another company through stock ownership.

Super Warehouse: A large, high-volume warehouse store that offers expanded services similar to a superstore, such as a service deli and bakery. These stores typically focus largely on food and drug items, and offer reduced prices on merchandise.

Super-Regionals: See "Regional Center."

Superstore: A large specialty store, usually over 40,000 square feet. Many superstores focus on a particular field of merchandise. For example, BestBuy is a consumer electronics superstore.

Supply Chain: The complete set of suppliers of goods and services required for a company to operate its business. For example, a manufacturer's supply chain may include providers of raw materials, components, custom-made parts and packaging materials.

Survey (Real Estate): A technical drawing that shows the precise legal boundaries of a property. Also known as a boundary survey. Surveys are generally recognized only when they are drawn by licensed professionals known as registered surveyors. Also see "Legal Description."

Sustainable Development: Development that ensures that the use of resources and the environment today does not impair their availability to be used by future generations.

Sweat Equity: In mortgages, sweat equity created by a purchaser performing work on a property being purchased.

Three/Two (3/2) Option: An alternative mortgage plan that enables households whose earnings are no more than 100% of the median income in their regional area to make a 3% down payment with their own funds, coupled with a 2% gift from a relative or a 2% grant or unsecured loan from a nonprofit agency or state or local government program.

Time-share (Timeshare): A type of joint ownership in which a group of owners share a particular piece of property, agreeing to have use of the property only during set days each year. Typically, time-share properties are vacation properties in such areas as beach resorts or ski resorts. They typically are condominium properties in which each condominium is jointly owned by a large group of people. Each owner typically has access to one week's use per year and pays for a proportionate share of the property's upkeep, taxes and insurance as well as management fees.

Title Company: This is a generic term that generally refers to a company that provides services to buyers and sellers by facilitating the closing of a sale. While a title company charges various fees for services in connection with the closing, it makes most of its revenues from commissions received from the sale of title insurance. The title insurance itself is generally provided and guaranteed by a title insurance underwriter.

Title Examination Fee: A standard fee paid to a title company at closing of a real estate purchase. Also see "Title Search."

Title Insurance (Title Policy): Insurance to protect the lender (referred to as a "lender's policy" or "mortgage policy") or the buyer (an "owner's policy") against losses arising from disputes over ownership or unknown liens on a property.

Title Search: A check of property deed records to ensure that the seller is the legal owner of the property and that there are no unknown liens or other claims outstanding.

TND: Traditional Neighborhood Development. See "New Urbanism."

Traditional Neighborhood Development (TND): See "New Urbanism."

Truth-in-Lending Act: A federal law that requires lenders to fully disclose, in writing, the terms and conditions of a mortgage or loan, including the annual percentage rate and other charges.

Umbrella Partnership REIT (UPREIT): A real estate trust in which the partners of existing partnerships and a newly formed REIT become partners in a new entity called the operating partnership. The existing partners contribute property interests and the REIT contributes cash (typically proceeds from a public offering of stock).

Underwriter: The issuer of a publicly-held security, a loan or an insurance policy. Also see "Underwriting."

Underwriting: In lending, the reviewing of a loan file to determine the applicant's ability to meet the loan obligation. In insurance, underwriting is the process of reviewing the risk in a given insurance policy. In securities and investments, underwriting is the process of analyzing a bond or stock offering and then completing the necessary paperwork and regulatory filings necessary to offer the bond or stock for sale.

Universal Design: An approach to residential as well as commercial building design that attempts to accommodate as many people as possible, regardless of physical or mental limitations. For example, design elements may include wider doorways and stepless entries that are easy for the physically challenged to navigate.

Urban Development Action Grant (UDAG): A program under the department of Housing and Urban Development that lends money for redevelopment of urban commercial areas.

Urban Renewal: The process of the revitalization of urban areas, usually through redevelopment or older buildings or neighborhoods sponsored by a government or private organization.

Urban Sprawl: The growth of a city in a way that may be viewed by some as unsightly, crowded, unplanned or unproductive.

Urbanism: See “New Urbanism.”

U-Value (U Value): A measure of the amount of heat that is transferred into or out of a building. The lower the U-Value, the higher the insulating value of a window or other building material being rated. It is the reciprocal of an R-Value. See “R-Value.”

VA Mortgage: A mortgage that is guaranteed by the Veterans Administration, a Federal Government agency that provides benefits to U.S. veterans. VA mortgages tend to be made at below-market interest rates and may feature lower down payments or other benefits for the borrower.

Vacancy Rate: The percentage of units available to rent in a given area or building. For example, if 10 units are unrented in a 100-unit apartment building, then the vacancy rate is 10%.

Value Added Tax (VAT): A tax that imposes a levy on businesses at every stage of manufacturing based on the value it adds to a product. Each business in the supply chain pays its own VAT and is subsequently repaid by the next link down the chain; hence, a VAT is ultimately paid by the consumer, being the last link in the supply chain, making it comparable to a sales tax. Generally, VAT only applies to goods bought for consumption within a given country; export goods are exempt from VAT, and purchasers from other countries taking goods back home may apply for a VAT refund.

Variable-Maturity Mortgage: A long-term loan where the due date of the final payment may be changed when the amount of earlier payments has been altered.

Variable-Rate Mortgage: See “Adjustable-Rate Mortgage (ARM).”

Warehouse Store: A discount retailer offering merchandise in a no-frills environment. These stores often cut costs by reducing services and product variety.

Wholesale Club: A retail store that sells a limited assortment of general merchandise to customers who are members of the club. Memberships are generally fee-based, margins are small and there is little customer service provided to the members. Groceries are often sold in bulk sizes. The largest wholesale club chain is Sam's, owned by Wal-Mart. Costco is Sam's biggest competitor in the U.S.

World Trade Organization (WTO): One of the only globally active international organizations dealing with the trade rules between nations. Its goal is to assist the free flow of trade goods, ensuring a smooth, predictable supply of goods to help raise the quality of life of member citizens. Members form consensus decisions that are then ratified by their respective parliaments. The WTO’s conflict resolution process generally emphasizes interpreting existing commitments and agreements, and discovers how to ensure trade policies to conform to those agreements, with the ultimate aim of avoiding military or political conflict.

Wraparound Mortgage: A transaction whereby an old mortgage is included with a new loan. This is different from a second mortgage in that a second mortgage is legally subordinate to a first mortgage. The borrower makes payments on both loans to the holder of the wraparound.

WTO: See “World Trade Organization (WTO).”

ZigBee: May become the ultimate wireless control system for home and office lighting and entertainment systems. The ZigBee Alliance is an association of companies working together to enable reliable, cost-effective, low-power, wirelessly networked monitoring and control products based on an open global standard, 802.15.4 entertainment systems.

INTRODUCTION

PLUNKETT'S REAL ESTATE & CONSTRUCTION INDUSTRY ALMANAC, the seventh edition of our guide to the real estate and construction field, is designed as a general source for researchers of all types.

The data and areas of interest covered are intentionally broad, ranging from the various types of businesses involved in real estate and construction, to the online services and technologies that are changing the real estate and mortgage sectors, to an in-depth look at the major firms (which we call "THE REAL ESTATE AND CONSTRUCTION 400") within the many segments that make up the real estate and construction industry. Our definition of the types of businesses involved in real estate and construction is applied in a liberal sense. Accordingly, this book includes real estate brokerage, investment, development and management firms (both commercial and residential). It also covers companies involved in construction of all types, mortgages, hotels, shopping centers and apartments. In addition, this book covers companies that provide important services to the real estate industry, such as firms that write title insurance or operate industry databases and web sites.

This reference book is designed to be a general source for researchers. It is especially intended to assist with market research, strategic planning, employment searches, contact or prospect list creation (be sure to see the export capabilities of the accompanying CD-ROM that is available to book and eBook buyers) and financial research, and as a data resource for executives and students of all types.

PLUNKETT'S REAL ESTATE & CONSTRUCTION INDUSTRY ALMANAC takes a rounded approach for the general reader and presents a complete overview of the real estate and construction field (see "How To Use This Book").

THE REAL ESTATE AND CONSTRUCTION 400 is our unique grouping of the biggest, most successful corporations in all segments of the real estate and construction industry. Tens of thousands of pieces of information, gathered from a wide variety of sources, have been researched and are presented in a unique form that can be easily understood. This section includes thorough indexes to THE REAL ESTATE AND CONSTRUCTION 400, by geography, industry, sales, brand names, subsidiary names and many other topics. (See Chapter 4.)

Especially helpful is the way in which PLUNKETT'S REAL ESTATE & CONSTRUCTION INDUSTRY ALMANAC enables readers who have no business background to readily compare the financial records and growth plans of real estate and construction companies and major industry groups. You'll see the mid-term financial record of each firm, along with the impact of earnings, sales and strategic plans on each company's potential to fuel growth, to serve new markets and to provide investment and employment opportunities.

No other source provides this book's easy-to-understand comparisons of growth, expenditures, technologies, corporations and many other items of great importance to people of all types who may be studying this, one of the largest industry sectors in the world today.

By scanning the data groups and the unique indexes, you can find the best information to fit your personal research needs. The major companies in real estate and construction are profiled and then ranked using several different groups of specific criteria. Which firms are the biggest employers? Which companies earn the most profits? These things and much more are easy to find.

In addition to individual company profiles, a thorough analysis of trends in real estate and construction sectors is provided. These trends include the growth of discount residential brokerage firms, online real estate services and the changing nature of the mortgage industry. This book's job is to help you sort through easy-to-understand summaries of today's trends in a quick and effective manner.

Whatever your purpose for researching the real estate and construction field, you'll find this book to be a valuable guide. Nonetheless, as is true with all resources, this volume has limitations that the reader should be aware of:

- Financial data and other corporate information can change quickly. A book of this type can be no more current than the data that was available as of the time of editing. Consequently, the financial picture, management and ownership of the firm(s) you are studying may have changed since the date of this book. For example, this almanac includes the most up-to-date sales figures and profits available to the editors as of early 2010. That means that we have typically used corporate financial data as of late-2009.

- Corporate mergers, acquisitions and downsizing are occurring at a very rapid rate. Such events may have created significant change, subsequent to the publishing of this book, within a company you are studying.

- Some of the companies in THE REAL ESTATE AND CONSTRUCTION 400 are so large in scope, and in variety of business endeavors conducted within a parent organization, that we have been unable to completely list all subsidiaries, affiliations, divisions and activities within a firm's corporate structure.

- This volume is intended to be a general guide to a vast industry. That means that researchers should look to this book for an overview and, when conducting in-depth research, should contact the specific corporations or industry associations in question for the very latest changes and data. Where possible, we have listed contact names, toll-free telephone numbers and Internet site addresses for the companies, government agencies and industry associations involved so that the reader may get further details without unnecessary delay.

- Tables of industry data and statistics used in this book include the latest numbers available at the time of printing, generally through 2009. In a few cases, the only complete data available was for earlier years.

- We have used exhaustive efforts to locate and fairly present accurate and complete data. However, when using this book or any other source for business and industry information, the reader should use caution and diligence by conducting further research where it seems appropriate. We wish you success in your endeavors, and we trust that your experience with this book will be both satisfactory and productive.

Jack W. Plunkett
Houston, Texas
May 2010

HOW TO USE THIS BOOK

The two primary sections of this book are devoted first to the real estate and construction industry as a whole and then to the "Individual Data Listings" for THE REAL ESTATE 400. If time permits, you should begin your research in the front chapters of this book. Also, you will find lengthy indexes in Chapter 4 and in the back of the book.

THE REAL ESTATE AND CONSTRUCTION INDUSTRY

Glossary: A short list of real estate and construction industry terms.

Chapter 1: Major Trends Affecting the Real Estate and Construction Industry. This chapter presents an encapsulated view of the major trends that are creating rapid changes in the real estate and construction industry today.

Chapter 2: Real Estate and Construction Industry Statistics. This chapter presents in-depth statistics ranging from an industry overview to new and existing home sales, mortgage statistics, apartment vacancies and much more.

Chapter 3: Important Real Estate and Construction Industry Contacts – Addresses, Telephone Numbers and Internet Sites. This chapter covers contacts for important government agencies, industry organizations and trade groups. Included are numerous important Internet sites.

THE REAL ESTATE 400

Chapter 4: THE REAL ESTATE 400: Who They Are and How They Were Chosen. The companies compared in this book were carefully selected from the real estate and construction industry, largely in the United States. 112 of the firms are based outside the U.S. For a complete description, see THE REAL ESTATE 400 indexes in this chapter.

Individual Data Listings:

Look at one of the companies in THE REAL ESTATE 400's Individual Data Listings. You'll find the following information fields:

Company Name:

The company profiles are in alphabetical order by company name. If you don't find the company you are seeking, it may be a subsidiary or division of one of the firms covered in this book. Try looking it up in the Index by Subsidiaries, Brand Names and Selected Affiliations in the back of the book.

Ranks:

Industry Group Code: An NAIC code used to group companies within like segments. (See Chapter 4 for a list of codes.)

Ranks Within This Company's Industry Group: Ranks, within this firm's segment only, for annual sales and annual profits, with 1 being the highest rank.

Business Activities:

A grid arranged into six major industry categories and several sub-categories. A "Y" indicates that the firm operates within the sub-category. A complete Index by Industry is included in the beginning of Chapter 4.

Types of Business:

A listing of the primary types of business specialties conducted by the firm.

Brands/Divisions/Affiliations:

Major brand names, operating divisions or subsidiaries of the firm, as well as major corporate affiliations—such as another firm that owns a significant portion of the company's stock. A complete Index by Subsidiaries, Brand Names and Selected Affiliations is in the back of the book.

Contacts:

The names and titles up to 27 top officers of the company are listed, including human resources contacts.

Address:

The firm's full headquarters address, the headquarters telephone, plus toll-free and fax numbers where available. Also provided is the World Wide Web site address.

Financials:

Annual Sales (2009 or the latest fiscal year available to the editors, plus up to four previous years): These are stated in thousands of dollars (add three zeros if you want the full number). This figure represents consolidated worldwide sales from all operations. 2009 figures may be estimates.

Annual Profits (2009 or the latest fiscal year available to the editors, plus up to four previous years): These are stated in thousands of dollars (add three zeros if you want the full number). This figure represents consolidated, after-tax net profit from all operations. 2009 figures may be estimates.

Stock Ticker, International Exchange, Parent Company: When available, the unique stock market symbol used to identify this firm's common stock for trading and tracking purposes is indicated. Where appropriate, this field may contain "private" or "subsidiary" rather than a ticker symbol. If the firm is a publicly-held company headquartered outside of the U.S., its international ticker and exchange are given. If the firm is a subsidiary, its parent company is listed.

Total Number of Employees: The approximate total number of employees, worldwide, as of the end of 2009 (or the latest data available to the editors).

Apparent Salaries/Benefits:

(The following descriptions generally apply to U.S. employers only.) A "Y" in appropriate fields indicates "Yes."

Due to wide variations in the manner in which corporations report benefits to the U.S. Government's regulatory bodies, not all plans will have been uncovered or correctly evaluated during our effort to research this data. Also, the availability to employees of such plans will vary according to the qualifications that employees must meet to become eligible. For example, some benefit plans may be available only to salaried workers—others only to employees who work more than 1,000 hours yearly. Benefits that are available to employees of the main or parent company may not be available to employees of the subsidiaries. In addition, employers frequently alter the nature and terms of plans offered.

NOTE: Generally, employees covered by wealth-building benefit plans do not *fully* own ("vest in") funds contributed on their behalf by the employer until as many as five years of service with that employer have passed. All pension plans are voluntary—that is, employers are not obligated to offer pensions.

Pension Plan: The firm offers a pension plan to qualified employees. In this case, in order for a "Y" to appear, the editors believe that the employer offers a defined benefit or cash balance pension plan (see discussions below).The type and generosity of these plans vary widely from firm to firm. Caution: Some employers refer to plans as "pension" or "retirement" plans when they are actually 401(k) savings plans that require a contribution by the employee.

- Defined Benefit Pension Plans: Pension plans that do not require a contribution from the employee are infrequently offered. However, a few companies, particularly larger employers in high-profit-margin industries, offer defined benefit pension plans where the employee is guaranteed to receive a set pension benefit upon retirement. The amount of the benefit is determined by the years of service with the company and the employee's salary during the later years of employment. The longer a person works for the employer, the higher the retirement benefit. These defined benefit plans are funded entirely by the employer. The benefits, up to a reasonable limit, are guaranteed by the Federal Government's Pension Benefit Guaranty Corporation. These plans are not portable—if you leave the company, you cannot transfer your benefits into a different plan. Instead, upon retirement you will receive the benefits that vested during your service with the company. If your employer offers a pension plan, it must give you a summary plan description within 90 days of the date you join the plan. You can also request a summary annual report of the plan, and once every 12 months you may request an individual benefit statement accounting of your interest in the plan.

- Defined Contribution Plans: These are quite different. They do not guarantee a certain amount of pension benefit. Instead, they set out circumstances under which the employer will make a contribution to a plan on your behalf. The most common example is the 401(k) savings plan. Pension benefits are not guaranteed under these plans.
- Cash Balance Pension Plans: These plans were recently invented. These are hybrid plans—part defined benefit and part defined contribution. Many employers have converted their older defined benefit plans into cash balance plans. The employer makes deposits (or credits a given amount of money) on the employee's behalf, usually based on a percentage of pay. Employee accounts grow based on a predetermined interest benchmark, such as the interest rate on Treasury Bonds. There are some advantages to these plans, particularly for younger workers: a) The benefits, up to a reasonable limit, are guaranteed by the Pension Benefit Guaranty Corporation. b) Benefits are portable—they can be moved to another plan when the employee changes companies. c) Younger workers and those who spend a shorter number of years with an employer may receive higher benefits than they would under a traditional defined benefit plan.

ESOP Stock Plan (Employees' Stock Ownership Plan): This type of plan is in wide use. Typically, the plan borrows money from a bank and uses those funds to purchase a large block of the corporation's stock. The corporation makes contributions to the plan over a period of time, and the stock purchase loan is eventually paid off. The value of the plan grows significantly as long as the market price of the stock holds up. Qualified employees are allocated a share of the plan based on their length of service and their level of salary. Under federal regulations, participants in ESOPs are allowed to diversify their account holdings in set percentages that rise as the employee ages and gains years of service with the company. In this manner, not all of the employee's assets are tied up in the employer's stock.

Savings Plan, 401(k): Under this type of plan, employees make a tax-deferred deposit into an account. In the best plans, the company makes annual matching donations to the employees' accounts, typically in some proportion to deposits made by the employees themselves. A good plan will match one-half of employee deposits of up to 6% of wages. For example, an employee earning $30,000 yearly might deposit $1,800 (6%) into the plan. The company will match one-half of the employee's deposit, or $900. The plan grows on a tax-deferred basis, similar to an IRA. A very generous plan will match 100% of employee deposits. However, some plans do not call for the employer to make a matching deposit at all. Other plans call for a matching contribution to be made at the discretion of the firm's board of directors. Actual terms of these plans vary widely from firm to firm. Generally, these savings plans allow employees to deposit as much as 15% of salary into the plan on a tax-deferred basis. However, the portion that the company uses to calculate its matching deposit is generally limited to a maximum of 6%. Employees should take care to diversify the holdings in their 401(k) accounts, and most people should seek professional guidance or investment management for their accounts.

Stock Purchase Plan: Qualified employees may purchase the company's common stock at a price below its market value under a specific plan. Typically, the employee is limited to investing a small percentage of wages in this plan. The discount may range from 5 to 15%. Some of these plans allow for deposits to be made through regular monthly payroll deductions. However, new accounting rules for corporations, along with other factors, are leading many companies to curtail these plans—dropping the discount allowed, cutting the maximum yearly stock purchase or otherwise making the plans less generous or appealing.

Profit Sharing: Qualified employees are awarded an annual amount equal to some portion of a company's profits. In a very generous plan, the pool of money awarded to employees would be 15% of profits. Typically, this money is deposited into a long-term retirement account. Caution: Some employers refer to plans as "profit sharing" when they are actually 401(k) savings plans. True profit sharing plans are rarely offered.

Highest Executive Salary: The highest executive salary paid, typically a 2009 amount (or the latest year available to the editors) and typically paid to the Chief Executive Officer.

Highest Executive Bonus: The apparent bonus, if any, paid to the above person.

Second Highest Executive Salary: The next-highest executive salary paid, typically a 2009 amount (or the latest year available to the editors) and typically paid to the President or Chief Operating Officer.

Second Highest Executive Bonus: The apparent bonus, if any, paid to the above person.

Other Thoughts:

Apparent Women Officers or Directors: It is difficult to obtain this information on an exact basis, and employers generally do not disclose the data in a public way. However, we have indicated what our best efforts reveal to be the apparent number of women who either are in the posts of corporate officers or sit on the board of directors. There is a wide variance from company to company.

Hot Spot for Advancement for Women/Minorities: A "Y" in appropriate fields indicates "Yes." These are firms that appear either to have posted a substantial number of women and/or minorities to high posts or that appear to have a good record of going out of their way to recruit, train, promote and retain women or minorities. (See the Index of Hot Spots For Women and Minorities in the back of the book.) This information may change frequently and can be difficult to obtain and verify. Consequently, the reader should use caution and conduct further investigation where appropriate.

Growth Plans/ Special Features:

Listed here are observations regarding the firm's strategy, hiring plans, plans for growth and product development, along with general information regarding a company's business and prospects.

Locations:

A "Y" in the appropriate field indicates "Yes."

Primary locations outside of the headquarters, categorized by regions of the United States and by international locations. A complete index by locations is also in the front of this chapter.

Chapter 1

MAJOR TRENDS AFFECTING THE REAL ESTATE & CONSTRUCTION INDUSTRY

Major Trends Affecting the Real Estate and Construction Industry:

1) **Introduction to the Real Estate and Construction Industry**
2) **Subprime and Alt-A Mortgages/ Foreclosures Burn Overburdened Homeowners**
3) **Mortgage Originations Fall/Online Competition Changes the Industry**
4) **Home Sales Rebound Slightly**
5) **Real Estate Goes Online**
6) **Internet-Based Home Sales and Cheap Commissions Rock Residential Brokers**
7) **Homes and Commercial Buildings Go Green**
8) **Prefabricated Housing Causes a Stir**
9) **Baby Boomers Become a Strong Influence in the Housing Market/Universal Design Catches On**
10) **Commercial Construction Is Down as Vacancies Soar**
11) **Commercial Mortgage Defaults and Foreclosures Rise**
12) **Real Estate Markets in China and India Heat Up**
13) **Mixed-Use Developments Go Vertical**
14) **Shopping Center Tenants Face Slow Sales/Store Closings Force Landlords to Become Creative**
15) **Lifestyle Centers and Super-Regional Malls Falter/Mall Glut Anticipated**
16) **Malls Morph to Stay Afloat**
17) **Apartment House Vacancy Rates Stabilize**
18) **Hotel Operators Challenged/Pod Rooms Grow in Popularity**
19) **New Urbanism and Traditional Neighborhood Development are Retro Trends**
20) **Megapolitans Will Define America of the Future/Mega-Regions Defined Internationally**
21) **Destination Club Membership Growth Is Checked**
22) **Remodeling Rebounds/Home Sizes Shrink**

1) Introduction to the Real Estate and Construction Industry

Real estate, the residential sector in particular, has been making bleak headlines around the globe in 2008 and 2009. By early 2010, real estate had improved in some markets in the U.S., while real estate had enjoyed a significant boom in China, Canada and a few other select spots. Several important trends will shape the real estate industry of the near future.

Global Real Estate Trends to Watch for the Near- to Mid-Term

- A bottom will be reached eventually in virtually all markets. Business will pick up gradually. Assuming that the global recovery truly gets underway, home sales may rebound reasonably well by 2011 or 2012. However, many owners of homes and commercial properties will remain in a difficult position as their properties have a current value of less than what the owners paid, and many mortgage debts are at higher levels than what the underlying properties are worth.
- Many major development projects are downsized, delayed or cancelled.
- The commercial property investment sector remains slow. Vacancies remain high, particularly in retail shopping centers and many office markets.
- Commercial mortgage delinquencies and foreclosures will continue to be a big problem, and funding for speculative commercial projects remains extremely difficult to obtain. U.S. banks held $1.8 trillion in commercial property loans on their books as of early 2008, and write offs on those loans are projected to run as high as 12%, or more than $200 billion, by the end of 2010.
- On the corporate level, the trend will be towards consolidation of development and construction firms, particularly as stronger firms acquire weaker rivals. Cost control, debt reduction and risk management will be a core focus. Healthy development companies will acquire important tracts of land at bargain prices for future use. (In early 2009, Pulte agreed to acquire competitor Centex for $1.3 billion.)
- National government investments in transportation infrastructure such as highways, education facilities, government offices and health care facilities will offer opportunities to commercial construction firms. A large portion of national government "stimulus" construction spending will be funneled to state and local projects.

Source: Plunkett Research, Ltd.

During most of the 2001–2007 period, easy availability of development loans and mortgages, low interest rates, eager investors and unbridled optimism caused massive new developments of homes, shopping centers and office buildings to sprout on a global basis. The effect was widespread. For example, large portions of the national economies of Dubai, Ireland and Spain were driven by real estate speculation and investment. By 2009, however, Dubai had been forced to turn to neighboring nations for backup central bank funds. Ireland's real estate market spiraled downward. In Spain, where millions of workers had been added to construction and real estate positions in the previous decade, unemployment soared to more than 17% and remains stubbornly high.

Residential housing markets in America have been dismal. The hardest-hit sector may have been high rise condominiums, where new projects far exceeded potential demand by consumers. For February, 2009, the widely watched Case Shiller Index of home prices in the U.S. showed that prices in 20 of America's largest metropolitan areas had declined an average of 30.7% from their 2006 peak. Home prices in the Phoenix, Arizona area were down by 50.8%. In Miami, where tens of thousands of new high rise condominiums had broken ground in recent years, the drop was 45.1%. In Las Vegas, also home to vast numbers of new condominiums, the drop was 48.4% from peak prices.

For 2010, the National Association of Realtors estimates existing home sales in America will climb to 5.02 million from 4.69 million in 2009 and 4.91 million in 2008. These numbers remain down dramatically from 6.48 million existing homes sold in 2006. In total, the real estate and construction sectors, including the many professions and fields associated with them, make up one of the larger components of the global economy.

As of 2009, the U.S. Bureau of Labor estimates that 6.0 million Americans were employed in the construction industry, down from 7.2 million in 2008 and 7.6 million in 2007. The agency also estimates that 1.4 million Americans were employed in the real estate industry as of 2009, down from 1.5 million in 2008 and 1.5 million in 2007.

About $846.2 billion in new construction was put in place at a seasonally-adjusted annual rate as of February 2010, according to the U.S. Bureau of the Census. This was down from the 2006 yearly peak of $1.16 trillion.

There was $14.3 trillion in outstanding mortgage debt in America at year-end 2009, down from $14.6 trillion one year earlier, including $10.8 trillion in home mortgages (down from $11.0 trillion). However, many home mortgages remained in arrears as 2010 began, and mortgage owners will continue to suffer write downs to some degree.

Sales of newly-built, single-family homes plummeted to about 374,000 in 2009 from 485,000 in

2008 (according to the U.S. Bureau of the Census). These numbers are an immense reduction from the 1.05 million sold in 2006.

Clearly, homebuilders have been suffering. For example, Pulte Homes, Inc., one of the world's largest builders of new homes, saw its revenues soar from $8.8 billion in 2003 to $14.5 billion at its peak in 2005. In 2007-2008 the bottom fell out. Pulte's revenues dropped to $9.1 billion in 2007, with a net loss of $2.2 billion. Revenues dropped even further in 2008 to $6.1 billion, with a net loss recorded for the year of $1.4 billion. Now renamed PulteGroup after a merger with Centex, business remains dull. PulteGroup's 2009 revenues were only $3.9 billion and large losses continued.

On the opposite end of the spectrum, luxury home builder Toll Brothers saw sales rocket from $2.7 billion in 2003 to $6.1 billion at its peak in 2006. Buyers of these expensive homes (averaging about $688,000 during the boom) found it incredibly easy to get a mortgage, often a mortgage that they couldn't afford in the long run. For 2009, Toll Brothers' revenues were only $1.7 billion and the firm recorded a $755 million loss.

In the U.S., during 2009, only 433,600 single family homes were started, according to the Census Bureau (down from 622,000 in 2008). This is a stunning decrease form the 1.75 million new homes started in America in 2005 during the boom.

As of April 2010, the Mortgage Bankers Association forecast new single-family housing starts to total only 556,000 for 2010, growing to 790,000 in 2011 and 1,058,000 in 2012.

Many owners of retail centers and malls were hit hard by the recession. General Growth Properties, Inc., America's second largest mall operator, filed bankruptcy in early 2009. The company had been unable to refinance its massive mortgages as they came due. At $27.3 billion, this was the largest bankruptcy in U.S. real estate history.

Commercial construction spending was at record levels for several years. Private sector (non-governmental), non-residential construction put in place in the U.S. reached $357 billion in 2007 and $410 billion in 2008, according to figures compiled by the U.S. Census Bureau. Despite the slowing economy, strong growth was seen in construction in the hotel/motel sector, higher education, health care and office facilities. On a seasonally-adjusted annual basis, as of February 2010, the number had dropped to $302.7 billion.

In the U.S., commercial public sector (for government), non-residential construction totaled $287 billion in 2007 and $307 billion in 2008. On a seasonally-adjusted annual basis, as of February 2010, the number had dropped to $292.7 billion.

Over the long term, there will be continuing demand from the health care sector for new or remodeled properties as the percentage of Americans over age 65 continues to grow, increasing demand for medical care.

The median sales price for an existing home in the U.S. during 2006 was $221,900, according to the NAR, slipping to $219,000 in 2007 and $198,100 in 2008. The Mortgage Bankers Association estimates that the price was $172,800 in 2009 and would drop to $170,100 in 2010.

The median sales price for new homes in 2006 was $246,500, according to the NAR. The organization's figures showed that the number was nearly unchanged in 2007 at $247,200. The U.S. Bureau of the Census shows that number slipping to $230,600 in 2008. The Mortgage Bankers Association estimates the price at $214,200 during 2009, with $213,400 forecast for 2010.

2) Subprime and Alt-A Mortgages/ Foreclosures Burn Overburdened Homeowners

The American housing, lending and construction markets enjoyed booming times through early 2006. However, in 2007 and 2008 the picture turned black. Unfortunately, in many cases, the boom times were created by very aggressive lending to consumers who couldn't afford the mortgages that they signed. Now, the mortgage business and related sectors are paying the price. As of December 2008, an estimated 8.3 million U.S. homeowners (19.8% of American mortgage holders) owed more on their mortgages than their homes were actually worth, according to First American CoreLogic. RealtyTrac, Inc. reported that U.S. foreclosure filings rose 81% in 2008 over the previous year, and were up 225% from 2006. The trend continued in 2009 with filings increasing 21% from 2008. Overall in 2009, more than 3.9 million foreclosure filings were issued.

Homeowners aren't the only ones who are suffering. Non-payment on these mortgages and plummeting values of the houses that were used as collateral devastated the lenders and investors that hold the mortgages. Lenders have lost hundreds of billions of dollars, and the crashing values of mortgage securities touched off the global financial crisis.

There were many factors at work here, often related to an over-eager quest for profits. All parties are to blame. 1) Consumers wanted to cash in on what were once rising home prices. Many not only purchased and resold ("flipped") their own residences, but invested in additional condominiums and houses as well, hoping to flip them in short order for big profits. 2) Homebuilders had an unprecedented opportunity to sell to eager buyers, many of them first-time purchasers. Homebuilders found their inventories of land, as well as houses under construction, to be growing in value rapidly. They were able to raise prices consistently while their new homes sold quickly, often on a pre-construction basis. 3) The entire mortgage industry, from mortgage brokers to mortgage bankers to investment banks that packaged and traded pools of mortgages, had an unprecedented opportunity to earn extremely lucrative fees by generating new mortgages.

Profits were fast and furious during this boom. Once the bubble finally popped, and there was no longer a long line of buyers eager to snap up the offerings of flippers and homebuilders, the market crashed in a hurry. People who were the most recent investors often found that they were stuck with the homes and condos that they purchased, many of which they simply can't afford to hold.

How did this happen? Mortgage lending became so aggressive that virtually anyone could purchase a house, perhaps several of them at once, even if they had poor credit, modest incomes, high levels of existing debt and/or little money to use as a down payment. Exotic new types of mortgages, designed to make it easier and easier for buyers to borrow, proliferated, regardless of whether they made any economic or business sense. In total, exotic loans that were easier to qualify for, including interest-only mortgages and loans that required little or no documentation, accounted for 47% of the total mortgages written in the U.S. in 2006.

One of the biggest problems is the Alt-A or alternative documentation loan, sometimes sneeringly referred to as "liars' loans." A traditional mortgage requires the borrower to provide verifiable evidence of income and financial assets. The evidence might include copies of income tax returns, W2 forms, copies of bank and investment account statements, etc. Alt-A loans charge the borrower a slightly higher interest rate for the privilege of skipping the evidence. The borrower simply states his or her income and assets on the loan application while providing no actual evidence. Anything from a little lying to outright fraud was rampant.

A second large problem is the fact that buyers were able to purchase houses with either no money or very little money down, thanks to aggressive lending. This was particularly appealing to buyers who had few financial assets. They were empowered to go into debt for a house worth hundreds of thousands of dollars without a serious commitment in the form of a down payment. When home values decline, these buyers have little incentive to hang onto the houses. In fact, the borrowers find that they owe more than the actual value of these houses. Many of them have very little money on hand with which to ride out hard times. Even as late as 2007, there was no down payment on 29% of the mortgage loans originated, according to the U.S. Department of the Treasury.

Then there's the third problem, which has created huge repercussions throughout the financial world: subprime loans. These are mortgages provided to buyers who have low credit scores or are financially weak. Some lenders loved these loans because they could charge higher interest rates on them. There were plenty of eager home buyers on hand, but their incomes were low, or their credit scores were terrible, or both. Analysts at Barclays Capital estimate that there were about $1 trillion in subprime loans outstanding as of late 2008.

About 80% of subprime loans written in America in 2005-2006 were set up as adjustable interest rate mortgages (ARMs) that initially have low interest that soon balloon much higher. These are the loans that were creating immense problems for borrowers in 2008-2009 as rates reset. The "teaser" or introductory rate ARM and the Option-ARM emerged as popular vehicles for these situations. While they helped builders move houses and lenders move loans, they are time bombs waiting to explode in the faces of borrowers. In teaser rate loans, borrowers were given extremely low interest rates for the first year or two, sometimes as low as 1%. This made the initial monthly payments quite affordable, enabling the borrower to qualify under rules that state that a borrower's monthly payments cannot exceed a certain percentage of their monthly income.

Then there's the hybrid or "option" variation. In this case, the borrower is allowed to select from several payment choices each month. Borrowers even have the option of paying no principal for the month while paying only part of the interest due. This creates negative amortization of the loan. That is, the principal balance increases. After a set period, for example five years, borrowers have to start making full principal and interest payments on their now-larger loans. This means that their monthly payment is vastly larger than it was during the "option" payment period.

A large number of housing market support proposals and mortgage workout projects have poured forth from state and federal government, particularly in the wake of the federal seizure of Freddie Mac and Fannie Mae and the inauguration of a new administration in January 2009 under President Obama. Also, lenders in many cases are pressured, for various reasons and regulations, to offer loan workouts, reduce interest rates, delay foreclosures, and/or accept mortgage payoffs that are far below face value. As late as early 2010, these efforts had done little to stem the tide of foreclosures.

In March 2009, as a $75 billion part of the government's $787 billion economic stimulus package, a foreclosure-prevention plan was announced by the federal government. It was intended to provide loan workouts or refinancing in the following circumstances: primary homes only (not second or investment homes); the owners' present mortgage payment must be higher than 31% of their pretax monthly income; the existing mortgage must have been obtained prior to January 1, 2009; the owners must lack substantial financial assets that might be used to repay the mortgage; and other rules must be met. The loan modification plan, called the Home Affordable Modification Program (HAMP), expires at the end of 2012. Loan servicing firms will receive up to $3,500 per participating loan. The government will also match a portion of lenders' costs, while homeowners will benefit from as much as $5,000 each in funds to reduce their mortgage balance. Lenders would be required to lower interest rates to as little as 2% for the next five years in order to help borrowers meet their 31% mortgage payment ratios. Thereafter, interest rates would rise gradually. It remains to be seen whether this program will be effective to any great extent. Also, homeowners with little to no income, such as those who have lost their jobs, may not qualify. As of early 2010, more than 1.4 million borrowers in the U.S. had received modification offers, with approximately 1.2 million offers approved, resulting in modification trials. Of those in trials, 36% had received permanent modifications or were in the process of receiving modifications on a permanent basis.

A loan refinance segment of this plan ends in June 2010. The refinancing applies to people with mortgages held or issued by Fannie Mae or Freddie Mac. Modifications to HAMP were announced in early 2010. They include incentives for loan servicers to reduce principal for those owing more than 115% of the property's current value; relief for borrowers who have been making payments, in the form of shifting to loans that are reduced by 10% or more and are guaranteed by the FHA; a six-month payment assistance period for borrowers who lose their jobs; and, perhaps most importantly, federal funds of between 10 and 21 cents on the dollar to lenders holding second lien mortgages such as home-equity loans. Research company CreditSights estimates that Bank of America, Wells Fargo, JPMorgan Chase and Citigroup collectively hold $423 billion in home equity loans, with about $151 billion to borrowers deemed at risk.

3) Mortgage Originations Fall/Online Competition Changes the Industry

Despite the difficulties facing the mortgage market, online mortgage sites continue to offer financing to qualified borrowers. The Internet created a much more competitive landscape for home mortgages. Sites ranging from Ditech.com to LendingTree set low origination fees and make it simple to complete applications online, while the Internet itself makes it much simpler for consumers to compare interest rates and mortgage options. LendingTree claimed to have closed $207 billion in total transactions by early 2010. Ditech offers, in addition to low origination fees, the ability to apply for and process loans online and 24/7 availability of customer service staff. Bank of America, after acquiring the nation's largest mortgage broker, Countrywide, in 2008, offers low-fee home loans with online service. At Bank of America's user-friendly web site, prospective borrowers can apply online, view a breakdown of proposed fees, compare mortgage options and check the status of a loan in progress.

Mortgage competition online is really part of a much larger, global trend: fierce competition among financial services providers of all types. Firms throughout the consumer financial sector, from banks to insurance companies to stock brokerages, are fiercely battling to attract, retain and cross-market new services to consumers

Total home mortgage originations (which include loans for new purchases as well as refinancings) reached $3.81 trillion in America in 2003, during a low-interest-rate environment and a booming U.S. housing market. In 2006, originations were down to about $2.72 trillion. Experts at the Mortgage Bankers Association reported $2.10 trillion in home loans in 2009, but forecasted an abrupt drop in 2010 to $1.29 trillion due to falling home refinancing demand and a likely rise in mortgage rates.

Internet Research Tip: Online Mortgage Tools
For mortgage loan and loan provider advice, see
1) www.mtgprofessor.com, a site run by Jack M. Guttentag, Professor of Finance Emeritus at the Wharton School of the University of Pennsylvania.
2) www.myfico.com, a site operated by the credit analysis firm Fair Isaac Corp.
3) www.bankrate.com, a site that provides financial rate information.
4) www.hsh.com, a site run by financial publisher HSH Associates.

SPOTLIGHT: Reverse Mortgages

Reverse mortgages are U.S. federally-insured loans that allow older homeowners (age 62 and up) to take money out of their home equities without selling their homes. In this manner, they are enabled to continue to live in their homes, hopefully for the rest of their lives. Generally, no payment is due as long as the borrower remains in the house. These mortgages enable seniors to supplement retirement savings, which has been especially critical due to crushing losses on the stock market during the global economic crisis. In February 2009, Congress raised the maximum value that seniors can borrow against from \$417,000 to \$625,500; and capped mortgage origination fees at 2% on the first \$200,000 and 1% on any amount over that. Fees are not to exceed \$6,000.

4) Home Sales Rebound Slightly

According to the National Association of Realtors (NAR), sales of existing homes fell from 4.91 million units in 2008 to 4.69 million in 2009. However, the association projects sales of 5.02 million in 2010.

In response to crashing demand in recent years, home prices fell significantly. NAR reported a drop in median existing U.S. home prices to \$218,900 for 2007 (from the 2006 level of \$221,900), the first annual fall since the Great Depression. Prices fell further in 2008 to \$198,100, and to \$165,400 in 2009.

On a better note, for the first time since December 2006, the Standard & Poor's/Case-Shiller Home Price Index showed a slight increase of 0.6% in February 2010 compared to February 2009 in a study of 20 major American cities. Boston, Cleveland, Dallas, Denver, Los Angeles and San Francisco were among the cities showing positive growth in home prices, while Charlotte, Chicago, Detroit and most particularly Las Vegas showed declines for the period (Las Vegas was down 14.6%).

Homes in some stage of foreclosure or default have been increasing, up 21% in 2009 over 2008, to 3.9 million according to RealtyTrac, an online source for home foreclosures. Falling home values force some homeowners to put their homes on the market for asking prices that are lower than the value of their mortgages. These are typically homeowners who do not have the financial resources to keep their homes, due to rising adjustable mortgage payments or other factors. That is, they may be facing foreclosure. However, in a growing number of these cases, lenders are agreeing to accept a mortgage payoff that is less than face value. This is called a "short sale." Foreclosures can be terribly expensive to lenders. Also, values of nearby homes can drop as a ripple effect takes hold.

Nonetheless, many housing markets in the U.S. may have hit bottom and begun to achieve either growth or some sort of stability. The Mortgage Bankers Association (MBA) expects sales of existing homes to grow to 5.6 million in 2011, while it forecasts sales of new homes to grow to 528,000 that year. Positive factors supporting this trend in America include:

- Significantly lower new and existing home prices, including the fact that builders are cutting new home sizes and features in order to offer lower prices
- A growing number of individual investors snapping up homes at bargain rates
- Pent-up homebuyer demand in general
- A rebound in consumer wealth thanks to a large, recent boost in stock market values

(Significant, remaining negative factors include high unemployment rates and job insecurity in general.)

The U.S. government is helping further, on the low to mid end of the market, by encouraging FHA to make large quantities of mortgages with very small down payments. These loans come with strict income requirements. Buyers must submit proof of income and document employment history with two years of pay stubs and W-2 forms. Borrowers are typically limited to amounts that are about 31% of their income, or 43% when other debt is taken into account. In addition, down payments of at least 3.5% are required. The FHA's market share of home purchase financing was soaring in 2008; but so were its foreclosures, up a record 81%. (While the FHA programs may boost demand and borrowing, they also can lead to defaults by those buyers who fall behind financially and feel little regret at walking away from their very small home equities.)

In the past, real estate loans in the U.S. often stayed in the hands of federally insured lenders (such as savings associations and banks), but this changed dramatically when massive, securitized pools of mortgages became popular investments, snapped up by private investment funds, pension funds and other major accounts. Billions of dollars of these loans are held on the books of investment banks and commercial banks. By early 2007, more than one-half of all mortgages were owned in securitized pools. Sadly, this trend continued to balloon until the real estate speculation bubble burst, taking major mortgage holder and investment bank Bear Stearns down with it in early 2008. Managers of these mortgage pools are attempting to stem the tide of their losses, in some cases by agreeing to short sales. In other cases, managers are offering better terms, such as lower monthly payments, to homeowners in trouble.

Sales of newly-built, single-family homes plummeted to about 374,000 in 2009 from 485,000 in 2008 (according to the U.S. Bureau of the Census), These numbers are an immense reduction from the 1.05 million sold in 2006.

Clearly, homebuilders have been suffering. For example, Pulte Homes, Inc., one of the world's largest builders of new homes, saw its revenues soar from $8.8 billion in 2003 to $14.5 billion at its peak in 2005. In 2007-2008 the bottom fell out. Pulte's revenues dropped to $9.1 billion in 2007, with a net loss of $2.2 billion. Revenues dropped even further in 2008 to $6.1 billion, with a net loss recorded for the year of $1.4 billion. Now renamed PulteGroup after a merger with Centex, business remains dull. PulteGroup's 2009 revenues were only $3.9 billion and large losses continued.

On the opposite end of the spectrum, luxury home builder Toll Brothers saw sales rocket from $2.7 billion in 2003 to $6.1 billion at its peak in 2006. Buyers of these expensive homes (averaging about $688,000 during the boom) found it incredibly easy to get a mortgage, often a mortgage that they couldn't afford in the long run. For 2009, Toll Brothers' revenues were only $1.7 billion and the firm recorded a $755 million loss.

In the U.S., during 2009, only 433,600 single family homes were started, according to the Census Bureau (down from 622,000 in 2008). This is a stunning decrease form the 1.75 million new homes started in America in 2005 during the boom.

As of April 2010, the Mortgage Bankers Association forecast new single-family housing starts to total only 556,000 for 2010, growing to 790,000 in 2011 and 1,058,000 in 2012.

5) Real Estate Goes Online

According to a National Association of Realtors (NAR) survey, almost three out of four homebuyers go online to research the market before purchasing. Among the busiest sites are Realtor.com, Move.com, HomeGain.com, ZipRealty.com and Yahoo! Real Estate, along with the sites operated by RE/MAX and Coldwell Banker.

Sites such as HomeGain, ZipRealty and Move.com provide home listings as well as tools for calculating mortgages and researching schools in different neighborhoods. The sites make money by selling advertising, selling customer leads to real estate agents and placing home listings on their sites. Move.com, formerly Homestore, is among the most popular. It collaborates with the NAR to operate Realtor.com.

Home finance is also a hot Internet area. A large percent of homebuyers apply for mortgage pre-approval before deciding upon a house. Many of those buyers make their applications online. Sites such as LendingTree and E-Loan, Inc. make applying for a mortgage online simple and competitive, because they maintain relationships with a wide variety of lending institutions and can offer several options.

LendingTree, for example, sends each mortgage application to up to five different lenders. In return, the lenders offer competing interest rates, closing costs and terms. LendingTree earns an average of $500 at each loan's closing. The site also generates revenue through matching potential homebuyers with Realtors, taking a healthy fee from the Realtor.

Even eBay is having success selling real estate online. It's doing a significant volume of business auctioning houses, land, commercial property and time-share interests.

Zillow, www.zillow.com , is an extremely popular site launched in 2005. It provides online access to aerial home photos, and enables users to estimate home values based on a variety of factors, using a proprietary algorithm.

Internet Research Tip: Public Real Estate Data
For home value estimates, recent sales activity, tax information, title history and more, see:

Coldwell Banker's Home Value Estimation
www.coldwellbanker.com/real_estate/home_value_estimator

Property Shark	www.propertyshark.com
RealEstateABC	www.realestateabc.com
Zillow	www.zillow.com

Online listings are typically generated by Multiple Listing Services (MLS), which are run by groups of Realtors. The services feed information about homes for sale to brokers' web sites and national real estate sites, as well as sites representing a geographic area (most cities have real estate sites such as www.har.com which is operated by the Houston Association of Realtors in Houston, Texas). Most prospective buyers hope to see all available listings on these sites, as opposed to listings for a particular Realtor.

Savvy real estate agents are utilizing web sites such as YouTube and Facebook, blogs and text messages to reach younger, first time buyers. Some realty firms are hiring agents in their 20's to help reach this market.

6) Internet-Based Home Sales and Cheap Commissions Rock Residential Brokers

From around 2004 through 2007, residential real estate agents enjoyed a golden age. (In fact, making money by brokering real estate looked so easy that membership in the National Association of Realtors grew from about 750,000 in 2000 to more than 1,300,000 in 2007.) Residential real estate brokerage generated approximately $46.6 billion in commissions in 2008, down from $55 billion in 2007, (compared to $37.5 billion in 2000), according to ForSaleByOwner.com. Meanwhile, the amount of time or effort necessary to sell a house declined significantly in many markets before the real estate bubble burst, as eager buyers snapped up houses as soon as they came on the market. Many residential agents had been earning huge sums—sellers were paying ever-larger fees as home prices escalated. (The same scenario applied to mortgage brokers at the time—brisk home sales and rapid refinancing made this an extremely lucrative occupation before the real estate bust starting in 2007.)

However, the real estate broker as an intermediary is increasingly facing intense competition from Internet sites that connect buyers and sellers directly. A good analogy can be found in the travel agent industry, in which travel consumers have turned to the Internet for a vast portion of their purchases and information needs, and travel agents have been forced to downsize or become providers of new enhanced services and value-added packages.

The days of 6% commissions for real estate brokers are under pressure thanks to maverick real estate brokers such as Foxtons (www.foxtons.co.uk) and ZipRealty (www.ziprealty.com). Instead of the usual 6% commission, these upstart brokers' fees are as little as 3% and up to 5% of the selling price. They are able to cut costs by capitalizing on the power of the Internet to advertise homes for sale, listing homes with accompanying photographs and virtual tours, but not always including services such as conducting in-person showings and open houses or negotiating prices.

ZipRealty offers sellers a reduced commission structure that is about 5% of the sales price, compared to standard commissions of 6% elsewhere. At the same time, it attracts buyers with rebates of up to 20% of its commissions. For example, the seller of a $200,000 home might save $2,000 in commissions. When ZipRealty represents a buyer of a $200,000 home listed by another real estate firm, the buyer might receive a rebate of $1,200, assuming ZipRealty earns a co-brokerage commission of 3%. (ZipRealty's 3% commission would be $6,000 in this case, and the buyer would receive 20% of that amount, or $1,200.) Certain restrictions apply.

Competing against the extremely well-entrenched Realtors group is difficult at best. Discount brokerage Foxtons, which originated in the U.K., at one time charged sellers as little as 2% for listing their homes, provided the sellers did the showings and other tasks themselves. In 2000, Foxtons opened operations in the U.S., focused on the New York City area. In May 2007, before the current housing slump had gained much momentum in the U.K., Foxtons was acquired by a private equity firm for about $770 million. The acquisition excluded the U.S. operations. By September 2007, the U.S. unit filed for bankruptcy, despite the fact that it had listed about 4,400 homes for sale at the time. As of 2010, Foxtons continues to operate in London and Surrey in the U.K.

Another discount alternative for sellers is to pay a flat fee (usually around $500) to a discount broker to list their home in MLS. Sellers then do the showing and negotiating themselves.

Some online home-selling sites regularly mine MLS listings and then post those listings on their own sites. In order to have access to MLS data, a broker employed by the site must be a member of the local Realtors organization. Some online sites have been known to hire a member Realtor to feed MLS data to them. Disputes frequently break out between local boards of Realtors and such sites as to whether MLS data is proprietary.

Traditional brokers argue that in a declining home market, their services are more valuable. The National Association of Realtors (NAR) has spent millions on television and radio campaigns that highlight the benefits of using a Realtor and the difficulties homeowners face when selling on their own. Traditional brokers are also adding services to their portfolios. Full-service brokerage firm Real Living, Inc., for example, enhanced its web site (www.realliving.com) to enable sellers to see how many people have viewed their homes.

7) Homes and Commercial Buildings Go Green

In an increasingly growing trend, many homebuilders across the U.S. are constructing homes in accordance with the National Association of Home Builders' (NAHB) "green" specifications. These specifications require resource-efficient design, construction and operation, focusing on environmentally friendly materials. Today's much higher energy costs are spurring this trend. In addition, local building codes in many cities, such as Houston, are requiring that greater energy efficiency be incorporated in plans before a building permit can be issued.

There are several advantages to building along eco-sensitive lines. Lower operating costs are incurred because buildings built with highly energy-efficient components have superior insulation and require less heating and/or cooling. These practices include using oriented strand board instead of plywood; vinyl and fiber-cement sidings instead of wood products; and insulated foundations, windows and doors. Low-maintenance landscaping demands less water and weeding. Heating and cooling equipment with greater efficiency is being installed, as well as dishwashers, refrigerators and washing machines that use between 40% and 70% less energy than their 1970s counterparts. Wastewater heat recovery systems use hot wastewater to heat incoming water. Even toilets are more efficient than before. Current models use a mere 1.28 gallons of water per flush, as opposed to four gallons in the 70s.

The main disadvantage is that this kind of building is often more expensive than traditional construction methods. Added building costs often reach 10% to 15% and more per home; however, some homebuyers are willing to pay the increased price for future savings on utilities and maintenance. As energy prices increased over the last decade, builders became more amenable to constructing homes with energy-savings measures. In addition, some consumers are inclined to spend more when they feel they are buying environmentally friendly products, including homes. (Marketing analysts refer to this segment as "Lohas," a term that stands for "Lifestyles of Health and Sustainability." It refers to consumers who choose to purchase items that are natural, organic, less polluting and so forth. Such consumers may also prefer products powered by alternative energy, such as hybrid cars.)

The U.S. government and all 50 states offer tax incentives in varying amounts to builders using solar technology. A handful of "zero-energy homes" that produce as much electricity as they use are being built (see www.zeroenergy.com.) Examples include 20 duplex homes in Greenfield, Massachusetts built by nonprofit Rural Development, Inc. and a planned 30-unit apartment building in Berkeley, California by ZETA Communities, Inc. By installing photovoltaic panels to generate electricity and using improved insulation and energy-efficient appliances and lighting, the zero-energy goal is achieved, at least in sunny climates such as those in the American West and Southwest.

In the commercial sector, businesses may have several reasons to build greener, more energy-efficient buildings. To begin with, long-term operating costs will be lower, which will likely more than offset higher construction costs. Next, many companies see great public relations benefit in the ability to state that their new factory or headquarters building is environmentally friendly. Many office buildings, both public and private, are featuring alternative energy systems, ultra-high-efficiency heating and cooling, or high-efficiency lighting. In California, many public structures are incorporating solar power generation.

Even building maintenance is getting involved—building owners are finding that they can save huge amounts of money by scheduling janitorial service during the day, instead of the usual after-hours, after-dark schedule. In this manner, there is no need to leave lighting, heating or cooling running late at night for the cleaning crews.

An exemplary green office building is Bank of America Tower (formerly One Bryant Park), a 54-story skyscraper on the Avenue of the Americas in New York City. Completed in 2009, the $1.2-billion project is constructed largely of recycled and recyclable materials. Rainwater and wastewater is collected and reused, and a lighting and dimming system reduces electrical light levels when daylight is available. The building supplies about 70% of its own energy needs with an on-site natural gas burning power plant. It was the first skyscraper to rate platinum certification by adhering to the Leadership in Energy and Environmental Design (LEED) standards, set by the U.S. Green Building Council in 2000 (see www.usgbc.org).

The Pearl River Tower, a 71-story skyscraper set to open in the fall of 2010 in Guangzhou, China, may be the first major zero-energy building, or may at least come close. Designed by Chicago architecture firm SOM, the tower is planned to be 58% more energy efficient than traditional skyscrapers by using solar roof panels, novel wind turbines embedded in four openings spaced throughout the tower and walls with eight-inch air gaps that trap heat which then rises to power heat exchangers for use in cooling systems.

A growing number of buildings are being retrofitted to use energy more efficiently. One example is the initiative underway at Citigroup, Inc. The banking firm is turning off lobby escalators, incorporating more natural light and using recycled materials in dozens of its properties around the world. Citigroup says it can save as much as $1 per square foot a year by making its offices more efficient. Elsewhere, Google, Inc. installed a solar rooftop at its California headquarters as early as 2007, and retail chains such as Wal-Mart and Kohl's are installing solar panels on their California stores.

LEED standards have been adopted by companies such as Ford, Pfizer, Nestlé and Toyota, which have all built LEED-certified structures in the U.S. In addition, the standards have been adopted by 25 states and 48 cities for government-funded projects, including New York, Los Angeles and Chicago. Industry analysts estimate the value of government-financed construction projects at $200 billion per year. One of the world's largest green complexes is the new campus of King Abdullah University of Science and Technology (KAUST) in Saudi Arabia. The campus spans more than 118 million square feet of classrooms, laboratories and a coral reef ecosystem, and features more than 13,500 square feet of solar thermal panels and upwards of 54,300 square feet of photovoltaic arrays.

LEED is not without competition. Another green verification program called Green Globes is backed by the Green Building Initiative, a group led by a former timber company executive and funded by several timber and wood products firms. As of 2008, 14 states had adopted Green Globes guidelines instead of those supported by LEED for government-subsidized building projects. Green Globes is more wood friendly than LEED, which is not surprising considering the involvement of the timber industry. It promotes the use of wood and wood products in construction with fewer restrictions than LEED, which approves of wood if it comes from timber grown under sustainable forestry practices approved by the Forest Stewardship Council, an international accrediting group.

In a similar vein, the Environmental Protection Agency (EPA) established WaterSense, a voluntary public-private partnership program to promote water-efficient products and services; and EnergyStar, a program that promotes energy efficiency. WaterSense certifies low-flow toilets that use a mere 1.28 gallons per flush, creates standards for bathroom-sink faucets that flow at no more than 1.5 gallons per minute and offers a certification program for irrigation companies that use water-efficient practices. EnergyStar homes are at least 15% more efficient than homes built to the 2004 U.S. residential code.

Since 2005, retail giant Wal-Mart has been pursuing an aggressive policy to reduce energy use in its stores. The company is investing $500 million to reduce greenhouse gas emissions from its stores and distribution centers by 20% through 2012. The firm also pledged to increase the fuel efficiency of its trucking fleet by 25% by the year 2008, and up to 50% by 2015. Moreover, Wal-Mart opened two high-efficiency test stores in McKinney Texas and Aurora, Colorado in 2005, followed by the opening of a store in Kansas City, Missouri in January 2007 that meets the 20% energy reduction goal. The firm designed a new store concept that is at least 25% more energy-efficient than its current stores in 2008.

Green building materials suppliers are enjoying booming business, while traditional material sales have slumped. According to the U.S. Census Bureau, sales of lumber and construction materials fell 12% in December 2006 from the same month in 2005. Meanwhile, Honeywell International, Inc. saw sales of its energy-efficient "expanding" foam insulation rise by 20% and Carlisle Co.'s Ecostar roof shingles made of recycled rubber jumped 35%.

Dow Chemical has invested $100 million (plus a $10 million grant from the Department of Energy) in researching new plastic photovoltaic roof panels using thin-film solar cells. Prototypes of the product, called Powerhouse, were being tested in early 2010 with a goal of commercial release of the product by 2011. Dow has not published pricing, but observers estimate that Powerhouse (or products like it) would cost a homeowner about $10,000 after subsidies and tax rebates for approximately 1,000 square feet of roofing material. This compares to about $5,000 for traditional asphalt shingles. Dow projects the value of the solar shingles market could reach $5 billion by 2015.

Internet Research Tip: Green Buildings
For a look at government-sponsored projects in green commercial buildings, see:
1) Rebuilding America, www.energyfuturecoalition.org/What-Were-Doing/Energy-Efficiency/Rebuilding-America
2) U.S. Green Building Council, www.usgbc.org

In Europe, the EU has mandated that member states revisit building codes every five years and create standards of energy efficiency. Buildings are also required to submit an energy certificate that can be shown to prospective buyers and renters. Elsewhere, nations such as Japan that are focused on becoming much more energy-efficient are emphasizing the use of green methods in new construction.

8) Prefabricated Housing Causes a Stir

In this increasingly high-tech era, it's interesting to note that homebuilding is one of the last industries to remain focused on manufacturing by hand. For several decades, entrepreneurs have attempted to commercialize various kinds of prefabricated housing. For example, HUD (the U.S. Department of Housing and Urban Development) pushed a well-funded program in the late 1960s that sought to encourage lower-priced, high-quality housing through factory fabrication in materials that included steel as well as wood. Nonetheless, until recently, the market for prefabricated housing was tiny, and most homes are still constructed on-site by hand.

Enter "panelization," the practice of building and assembling elements such as foundations, walls and staircases off-site at a factory and then trucking them to a home site for assembly. Pulte Homes, Inc., one of the largest homebuilders in the U.S., is embracing the practice, as are many major builders across the nation. It is estimated that more than 10% of new homes constructed in the past decade have some panelized elements. The trend is not entirely new, as the Sears catalog sold home kits as early as 1908 (these now historic homes are considered highly desirable today). Post-World War II, William J. Levitt introduced modular housing to lukewarm response, which petered out once the housing boom subsided.

Today's panelization is more far-reaching than Levitt's practice, which merely assembled basic framing off-site. The quality of panelized flooring, walls and staircases has risen remarkably thanks to new techniques, and building these elements at a factory offers many advantages to working on-site. A foundation can be poured and cured indoors, thereby eliminating the need to wait for good weather at the home site. Substantial savings in construction time are a plus, and panelization also addresses the problem of the scarcity of skilled laborers in many areas. Homebuilders who have embraced at least some aspect of the prefab component trend include Pulte Homes, Toll Brothers, Inc. and Beazer Homes USA, Inc.

Spotlight: Resolution: 4 Architecture
Bucking a long-term, widely held distaste for prefabricated housing, a maverick firm called Resolution: 4 Architecture (www.re4a.com) is promoting manufactured, modular housing. Starting at around $200,000, modules can be manufactured in a factory and assembled into a completed house in one of several dozen designs.
The company won a competition sponsored by *Dwell*, a home design magazine, to design a house near Chapel Hill, North Carolina. In addition, the firm has designed a beach house in Ventura, California, a vacation home in East Hampton, New York and a 1,725-square-foot suburban home in Long Island, New York. Contemporary and hip in design, the homes generally appeal to young, cost-conscious homebuyers with cutting-edge tastes.

9) Baby Boomers Become a Strong Influence in the Housing Market/Universal Design Catches On

Americans aged 55 years or older are the fastest-growing segment of the population. 2006 marked the year that the first Baby Boomers turned 60. The term "Baby Boomer," generally referring to people born from 1946 to 1964, has evolved to include the children of soldiers and war industry workers who were involved in World War II. When those veterans and workers returned to civilian life, they started or added to families in large numbers. As a result, the Baby Boom generation is one of the largest demographic segments in the U.S. According to

MetLife, Baby Boomers make up about 27% of the U.S. population. As of early 2010, there were about 76 million surviving Baby Boomers. By 2011, millions will begin turning traditional retirement age (65), resulting in extremely rapid growth in the senior portion of the population.

The real estate industry is quickly evolving to meet the needs and tastes of the people in this rapidly growing population segment. Housing options that cater to aging homeowners include retirement communities (also referred to as "independent living"), continuing care (which provides a broad spectrum of living options from independent living to nursing homes), assisted living (which offers assistance in daily tasks such as shopping, cleaning, etc. but does not provide onsite medical care) and communities that provide medical care for specific conditions such as Alzheimer's disease.

Another trend in senior housing is cooperative or communal living, in which private dwellings are grouped around a communal area or "common house" which usually contains a living room, kitchen and dining area for group dinners. Some communities of this type also include housing for on-site medical caregivers. Watch for growth in all senior living real estate in the coming years as more Baby Boomers reach retirement age.

Spotlight: Universal Design

Universal design (UD) creates living spaces that are comfortably livable for the largest variety of people, including those who are older or dealing with physical challenges. As many homeowners age, they look for a house with elements such as wide, step-less doorways, sturdy hand rails, automatic faucets and stacked closets that can be converted to elevators. The Center for Universal Design promotes UD throughout the U.S. Located at North Carolina State University in Raleigh, North Carolina, the center conducts research and collaborates with builders and manufacturers. For more information, see www.design.ncsu.edu/cud.

10) Commercial Construction is Down as Vacancies Soar

The U.S. recession is hitting commercial real estate in the form of increased vacancy rates, lower property values and delinquent commercial mortgages. The office space vacancy rate in 2006, before the global recession, was 12.1%. 2010 saw vacancy rates rise to 17.2%, according to research firm Reis, Inc. Part of the reason for the rising vacancy rates is that many tenants either maintained or cut staff numbers in response to lower revenues. Also, consolidations of the business locations of tenants due to mergers, and a long list of major bankruptcies, particularly in retailing and financial services, put downward pressure on commercial property rentals. However, lease prices were firming as of the first quarter of 2010, indicating the beginning of a recovery.

Through 2005 and 2006, there was a tremendous construction market in such sectors as office buildings, hotels, hospitals, shopping centers and state and local government projects. These commercial projects remained a strong, positive influence on the construction market through much of 2007. However, by the end of 2007, demand slowed in some sectors, and it was vastly harder to obtain financial backing for speculative commercial projects.

Commercial construction spending had been at record levels. Private sector (non-governmental), non-residential construction put in place in the U.S. reached $298 billion in 2006, growing to $357 billion in 2007 and $410 billion in 2008, according to figures compiled by the U.S. Census Bureau. However, spending fell in 2009 to $367 billion.

In the U.S., commercial public sector (for government), non-residential construction was $249 billion in 2006, growing to $282 billion in 2007 and $299 billion in 2008. The $787 billion economic stimulus package passed by the federal government in early 2009 gave a big boost to spending on buildings and infrastructure for higher education, transportation (including highways), research laboratories and renewable energy. Total non-residential construction spending was $308 billion in 2009.

For the mid term, however, construction spending for certain sectors will remain slow, due to high unemployment, changes in consumer spending habits, difficulties in the banking and automobile industries, and a close scrutiny by corporations on their budgets for office and factory space. This slowdown will affect retail space, restaurant buildings, non-government office buildings, manufacturing/ warehouse space, automobile dealers, entertainment facilities and hotels/motels in particular.

11) Commercial Mortgage Defaults and Foreclosures Rise

Commercial mortgage delinquencies and foreclosures will rise over the short-term, and funding for speculative commercial projects remains extremely difficult to obtain. Write offs on those loans are running at extremely high rates. These loans cover both completed buildings and commercial projects under construction, many of which are now rusting away in uncompleted states. As of early 2010, commercial real estate debt totaled about $3.4 trillion (with banks holding $1.5 trillion and bondholders holding $708 billion), according to a recent panel of representatives from the Federal Reserve, U.S. Treasury Department and the Office of the Comptroller of the Currency (OCC). The same panel reported that from 2010 through 2014, about $1.4 trillion in commercial real estate loans will come due, with almost 50% of those loans worth more than the value of the properties concerned.

The delinquency rate on securitized loans backed by commercial properties such as office buildings, hotels and retail stores more than doubled from September 2008 to March 2009, reaching 1.8% according to Deutsche Bank AG.

There are two big issues here: The first is the fact that commercial property values, in many cases, are now far below the amount of the mortgages secured by them. During the 2003-2007 era of easy money and soaring property prices, many real estate investors overpaid dramatically for office buildings, hotels and shopping centers. Today, their investments are "underwater," and their equities are wiped out. The second issue that is devastating commercial properties, and therefore threatening the mortgages against them, is that rental incomes have fallen significantly. In some cases, tenants are unable to pay their rents or have taken bankruptcy. At the same time, vacancy rates are high, and it is very difficult to obtain tenants. When new leases are written, it is often at rental prices that are much lower than those of a few years ago. This situation will improve as the economic recovery takes hold, but it will remain a significant problem at least through 2010 and 2011.

In the U.S., an October 2009 guideline issued by federal bank regulators will allow banks to maintain property loans on their books as "performing," even though the market value of the underlying real estate has fallen to less than the mortgage amount. This is an attempt by regulators to encourage bankers to do "work outs," on such loans, rather than filing foreclosures. As of 2009, work outs were very common. Developers or property owners pay a bit of interest to the bank, if they can, and then promise to take all possible steps to improve the financial outlook of their properties. In many cases, lenders restructure these loans, trade some of their debt for equity, or agree to write-down the amount of the loan if the buildings' owners will inject new capital of their own into the project.

The most glaring example of troubled real estate financing may be giant mall owner General Growth Properties, which filed for bankruptcy protection in 2008 due to its inability to pay mortgages on hundreds of properties in a timely manner. However, there are myriad other examples, including the October 2009 bankruptcy of major commercial lender Capmark Financial Group and the September 2009 seizure of Chicago-based Corus Bank by the FDIC. Capmark Financial, based in Horsham, Pennsylvania, was one of the world's largest commercial lending companies, with $20.1 billion in assets. Corus Bank, based in Chicago, was one of the world's largest lenders to condominium developers. It had $7 billion in assets.

The problem is not limited to the United States. During the recent boom, commercial property prices skyrocketed and lending was very easy to obtain. As a result, commercial loans are in trouble to some extent in many markets worldwide. Newly developed shopping centers, office buildings and resorts have been particularly hard hit by the economic downturn. Morgan Stanley's real estate funds business, called Msref, is projected to lose as much as $5.4 billion on its commercial real estate investments, especially in properties outside the U.S. In Japan, for example, Msref's VI fund has $3.17 billion in equity with a projected return of only $320 million. In Europe, the fund has $3.14 billion in equity with a projected return of only $630 million.

12) Real Estate Markets in China and India Heat Up

After the global economic crisis wreaked havoc on the real estate markets in China and India in 2008 and early 2009, prices in major cities escalated almost exponentially from late 2009 and into 2010. For example, in Shanghai, analysts estimated that prices per square foot for luxury residential real estate rose 54% through September 2009 to $500 per square foot. In the month of November 2009 alone, prices for homes in 70 major Chinese cities jumped 5.7%, while housing starts across China skyrocketed 194%. Obviously, speculators are playing a major role in driving up these prices.

Leading up to the financial crisis, China had become the capital of offshored manufacturing. The Chinese government constructed a series of high-technology parks in addition to millions of square feet of new manufacturing space. Global manufacturing needs for everything from running shoes to hard drives are being met by millions of factory workers in China, who earn wages that are much lower than those paid in America and Europe, but are high enough to improve their former subsistence-level, agriculture-based lives significantly. A growing number of Chinese entrepreneurs and investors have become truly wealthy.

Companies like Microsoft hired large numbers of engineers for research and development in China, as did leading biopharmaceutical firms and a wide variety of other tech industry leaders. At the same time, the escalating number of commercial and leisure visitors to China created a boom in hotels, and the overall hot business climate fueled the need for millions of square feet in new office and shopping center space. China's economic growth remained very robust as of early 2010. However, it remains to be seen whether actual demand will catch up to very large recent growth in the square footage of newly-built offices, malls and residential condominiums.

Meanwhile, India suffered its own bust during the global economic crisis, but is enjoying a boom focused on low-income housing that began in 2009. India has become the global capital of business process outsourcing (BPO). While millions of Indians are enjoying a new life in the middle class as managers in call centers and as professionals in commercial complexes, lower income workers are leaving the remote villages and finding employment as drivers, factory staff and tailors. These workers earn enough to afford low income housing that commands between $4,500 and $10,000. Indian Consulting firm Monitor Group estimates that there are 23 million urban families in India earning annual incomes of between $1,300 and $3,000 per year. Two government owned banks, the National Bank for Agriculture and Rural Development and the National Housing Bank are backing mortgage companies to service higher-risk loans, provided that the buyer can put down a minimum of a quarter of the value of the home and that employers can verify income.

A growing number of builders are rushing to meet the demand. For example, Matheran Realty is building 15,000 flats in the town of Karjat, about 56 miles east of Mumbai, that start at about $4,500. Indian conglomerate Tata has a waiting list for 1,300 units in Boisar near Mumbai. According to a 2009 report from consulting giant McKinsey, 25 million additional homes are needed in urban areas in India.

13) Mixed Use Developments Go Vertical

Mixing office, retail, residential and entertainment space in one location is an idea on the rise, literally. For example, take the Time Warner Center in New York City. The 80-story, $1.7-billion building houses a 2.8-million-square-foot combination of condominiums, office space, a Mandarin Oriental hotel, CNN television studios, performance space, restaurants and retail space that includes a Whole Foods Market. It's a stupendous urban version of mixed-use developments that have cropped up in suburbs across the U.S. since the early 90s.

These spaces often outperform standard suburban real estate in office and retail lease rates, residential rents, retail sales, hotel room occupancy rates and property values, both on-site and in surrounding areas (according to a study by Charles Lockwood, a real estate historian and author). Many retailers in the Time Warner Center reported sales as high as 70% to 80% above their initial projections, before the current economic crisis. All this multi-use bounty comes at a price, however, since building these 24/7 communities costs more. Design is more complex because retail needs are often at odds with residential needs. Restaurants have different logistical requirements than office space. It's also difficult to find the right mix of high- and low-end retail tenants. Residents need groceries and dry cleaning far more often than luxury jewelry or clothing, making the right mix of tenants a top priority for developers. Nonetheless, in close-in urban areas or highly desirable waterfront or scenic locations, the extremely high cost of land often dictates dense, vertical mixed use development.

The vertical trend is expected to dominate built-out suburban cities with set boundaries over the mid-term and beyond. Michael Beyard at the Urban Land Institute projects that vertical, multi-use expansion of aging strip malls that are on prime land will promote significant reinvestment and tax base expansion.

Another twist to the vertical trend is to build "live, work, play" communities around sports arenas. Take the 75-acre Victory Park project in Dallas, Texas, for example (www.victorypark.com). Built around the American Airlines Center, home of the NBA Mavericks, Victory Park currently boasts the W Dallas Victory Hotel and Residences, and plans ultimately to offer an additional 850 apartments and condominiums. Developed by Hillwood and partly owned by Hicks Holding LLC, the multi-billion dollar project is expected to include large amounts of office, hotel, residential and retail space when complete.

A number of vertical developments are cropping up around light rail line terminals such as the new project in Carrollton, Texas near Dallas. The city approved, in 2009, a $38 million mixed-use development next to a commuter rail station that links Carrollton with Dallas. Commuters using rail are likely to look for housing, shopping and entertainment venues close to stations. Many communities are using funds from bonds and government subsidies to build new developments. Nonprofit Reconnecting America (which integrates transportation systems and the communities they serve) estimates that $250 billion in light-rail, street car and high-speed bus projects were in the planning stages in 2009, opening the door for nearby mixed use developments along the way. Examples of recent developments include the $1 billion revitalization of Union Station in Denver, Colorado and a $2.3 billion ($1.5 billion from private investors and $800 million in municipal, county, state and federal funds) redevelopment of central Columbus, Ohio.

14) Shopping Center Tenants Face Slow Sales/Store Closings Force Landlords to Become Creative

Many major chain store companies were cutting expansion plans for 2009 and beyond, as revenues per store are generally disappointing compared to the boom years that ended in 2007. Some chains that continue to expand are doing so with new formats that utilize less square footage and lower inventories. Store managers in malls found themselves facing light traffic and devastating losses in 2008 and into 2009. By early 2010, however, savvy retailers had learned to operate with lower overhead and lean inventories, while retail sales had finally begun to show positive growth that will help mall owners and retailers alike.

Retail industry analysts generally consider mall sales per square foot of $250 per year or less as an indicator of potential failure. As of mid-2009, Green Street Advisors, Inc. had 86 troubled malls in its list of 1,028 enclosed U.S. malls; and projected the number of malls in danger of failure would reach 120 by the end of 2010.

Macy's closed 11 stores across the U.S. in 2009. Worse still, a growing number of chains filed for bankruptcy over the past few years, including Sharper Image (high-end gifts), Domain, Inc. (furniture), Fortunoff (jewelry) Circuit City (electronics) and Linens 'n Things (housewares). More announcements of closings, retrenching and bankruptcy occurred throughout 2009, such as the June closing of Century Plaza Mall in Birmingham, Alabama. A leading trade group, the International Council of Shopping Centers (ICSC), reported that 4,763 stores announced closings in 2009. Apparel stores accounted for 26.4% of the closure announcements, jewelry stores 18.1%, home entertainment 17.6%, food and beverage 14.5% and home furnishings 6%.

According to Reis, Inc., occupied space in U.S. shopping centers and malls dropped a net 24.1 million square feel during all of 2009. The overall vacancy rate for malls and shopping centers in the top 77 U.S. markets in the first quarter of 2010 rose to 10.8%, up 0.2% from the previous quarter and 1.3% from the previous year.

The net effect of these store closings is hard on suppliers, employees and mall owners alike. Firms that own and operate malls and shopping centers are scrambling to find replacements for empty spaces. Meanwhile, landlords' rental income is falling. According to Reis, mall lease prices were $38.79 per square foot in the first quarter of 2010, 3% lower than a year earlier, while shopping center lease rates fell 3.4% to $16.62, compared to a year earlier.

Of particular difficulty for landlords is the task of finding tenants for empty "big boxes" and department store sites, for example when a department store abandons perhaps 200,000 square feet under one roof due to consolidation and store closings. Owners are having a tough time finding tenants for such large volumes of space. In some cases, cutting the boxes into smaller spaces is a viable option. Paradise Development Co., a Las Vegas owner and property developer, split a former large store into two 25,000 square foot spaces now leased by Copeland's Sporting Goods and Barnes & Noble. In a similar circumstance, the developer split a defunct Home Place store into a 30,000 square foot Bed, Bath & Beyond and a 20,000 square foot DSW Shoes discount store. Both projects cost a cool $2 million to renovate. Faced with tens of thousands of empty square feet in large spaces, many developers are biting the bullet and following suit.

Meanwhile, as some major chains have closed stores, mall operators are looking for new categories of niche tenants. For example, day spas or medical spas are becoming commonplace in malls, where clients can receive a botox shot or laser-based removal of unwanted hair. Mall owners are now more likely to consider incorporating nightclubs or additional food and drink venues in their empty spaces. In addition, rental agents are actively seeking unique locally-owned stores to expand into mall spaces when national chain store tenants vacate.

15) Lifestyle Centers and Super-Regional Malls Falter/Mall Glut Anticipated

Super-regional centers (that is, shopping centers or malls which include at least three department stores and at least 800,000 square feet of retail space) were favored in new construction up until 2008. New malls have been slightly smaller than those of the past, averaging 1,060,000 square feet between 2008 and 2009, compared to an average of 1,148,000 square feet from 1997 through 1999. Malls like these can cost more than $200 per square foot to build, making the new properties' investments in the range of $150 million to $250 million each.

Other types of shopping center properties, such as power centers and lifestyle centers, had been developing rapidly in recent years, in many cases robbing traffic from traditional malls. A "power center" is typically an open-air complex of category-dominant anchors such as category-killers, home improvement stores, discount stores and warehouse clubs. A "lifestyle center" is an open-air, highly landscaped configuration of approximately 50+ stores. Generally located near upscale neighborhoods, lifestyle centers offer leasable retail area of 150,000 to 500,000 square feet, with at least 50,000 square feet of space typically dedicated to upscale national specialty stores such as Williams-Sonoma.

There are also hybrid centers, and value oriented centers. Hybrids have some of the features of enclosed malls and lifestyle centers. That is, they have both open-air sections and enclosed sections. Value-oriented centers are built on formats that emphasize discounted prices. These include outlet malls. Many new value-oriented centers feature significant entertainment segments.

Fueled largely by investment money provided by pension funds, REITs and professional money managers, these newer shopping centers had been very popular, if not always profitable, investments. The global economic crisis is making developers painfully aware of recent over-development and putting the brakes on growing numbers of new projects. According to Property & Portfolio Research, Inc., developers built 1 billion square feet of retail space in the 54 largest markets in the U.S. from 2000 through 2008. This is 25% more that what was built during the same period in the 1990s. In 2007 alone, 37 lifestyle centers were built, totaling 12 million square feet. There are currently 38 square feet of retail space for every person in those 54 markets, up from 29 square feet in 1983.

The end result of the glut of mall space is a retail space shakeout. Property & Portfolio Research projected a decline in occupied retail space in major U.S. markets of 1.2 million square feet in 2008, the first decline since the 1990-1991 recession. As the financial crisis hit in late 2008, there were about 74 lifestyle centers under construction and more than 100 projects under planning or development. Expansion plans are being shelved and new projects are being postponed or cancelled altogether. Property & Portfolio Research forecasted that in 2009, mall and shopping center vacancies would reach 19.7% and rise to 20.2% in 2010.

At least one mall owner has gone from boom to bust. General Growth Properties, Inc., owner of some of the most admired retail centers in America, including Boston's Faneuil Hall, the Ala Moana Center in Honolulu, Fashion Show in Las Vegas and the South Street Seaport in Manhattan, filed bankruptcy in early 2009. The company had been unable to refinance its massive mortgages as they came due. These loans were the result of an acquisitions binge that drove General Growth to become America's second-largest mall owner. At $27.3 billion, this is the largest bankruptcy in U.S. real estate history. The filing will have at least some effect on a major European firm, Eurohypo AG, a business unit of Commerzbank AG that is owed $2.59 billion by General Growth. Eurohypo is administrator of the debts for a large group of creditors. As of mid-2009, Eurohypo was in the midst of a reorganization to curtail expansion plans and reduce its commercial real estate portfolio from approximately $115.4 billion in 2009 to about $87.6 billion by the end of 2011. In early 2010, Simon Property Group attempted to acquire General Growth with a $10 billion offer which was rejected. In April 2010, Simon Property altered its offer to a $2.5 billion investment for voting rights of about 20%. The end result remains to be seen.

Shopping mall performance in recent years was sharply delineated by economic scale. Low-end malls showed weak sales per square foot while high-end malls were the most successful. Malls catering to wealthier customers also cost more to build and operate, and are able to charge higher rental rates. For example, Taubman Centers, Inc., a luxury shopping center developer that owns 25 malls in 12 states, reported average sales per square foot of mall space of $550 in 2007, a figure much higher than typical malls, which often report average sales in the $350 range. 2008 sales per square foot increased 2.3% in the first nine months of the year. Although Taubman Center's financial performance continues to lag, sales per square foot for the first quarter of 2010 were up 10.8% from the first quarter of 2009.

Retailers who are successfully weathering the storm tend to be discount stores and outlets where low prices can still attract shoppers. Simon Property Group, which owns, develops and manages major shopping centers throughout the U.S. and Puerto Rico, reported that year-to-year growth in comparable sales per square foot was stronger at outlet centers than at traditional high-end malls as of early 2008. Overall, Simon Property regional mall comparable sales per square foot fell 11.2% for the 12 month period ending in September 2009 to $438, down from $493 per square foot for 2008 (rolling 12 month comparable sales per square foot for mall stores, less than 10,000 square feet in regional malls and all owned gross leasable area in premium outlets). However, sales per square foot improved for the 12 month period ending in the first quarter of 2010, reaching $467. Average rents per square foot reached $38.72, up from $37.51 for the first quarter in 2009. Simon also managed to open four new projects in the first quarter of 2010: a 600,000 square foot Phase II expansion of the Domain in Austin, Texas; the addition of a Target, Nordstrom and 138,000 square feet of small shops at South Shore Plaza in Boston, Massachusetts; a 300,000 square foot center anchored by Auchan in Naples, Italy (of which Simon has a 24% interest); and a 642,000 square foot shopping center also anchored by Auchan in Sicily, Italy (of which Simon has a similar 24% interest).

SPOTLIGHT: Mall of America

The largest mall in the U.S. is the Mall of America (www.mallofamerica.com), located in Bloomington, Minnesota. First opened in 1992, it contains 4.2 million square feet of gross building area (2.5 million leasable) and is visited by an average of 110,000 people daily (or 40 million people per year). Entertainment is everywhere in this mall: 14 movie screens, a comedy club, night clubs, a 1.2-million gallon walk-through aquarium, a seven-acre amusement park, the NASCAR Silicon Motor Speedway, LEGO building center, A.C.E.S. Flight Simulation and over 520 specialty shops. Total employment in the center ranges from 11,000 in normal times and up to 13,000 during holiday and summer seasons.

(Not everyone comes here just to shop: the Mall of America reports that more than 4,000 people have exchanged wedding vows in the Mall's "Chapel of Love" wedding chapel, and the mall's mall-walking list, the "Walksport Mall Stars!" has registered more than 4,000 people.)

With the addition of a 306,000-square-foot Ikea home furnishings store, the mall enters its newest phase of construction. Shoppers from far and wide visit Bloomington and stay several days specifically to shop this mammoth mall. International visitors are common. Overall, visitors from outside the mall's 150-mile radius hover at around 35%.

The Ikea store, while not directly connected to the original mall, is part of a 42-acre new Phase II development just north of the original site. Tentative plans for new tenants include several hotels, an office building, a spa and entertainment attractions, which may include a performing arts theater. In 2009, the Mayo Clinic signed a letter of intent to be part of the expansion. The Phase II mixed-use complex is zoned for up to 5.6 million square feet of new development.

16) Malls Morph to Stay Afloat

The days of the dull, old-fashioned enclosed mall are numbered. Anchor tenants such as major department stores are moving or going out of business, leaving mall owners with echoing empty spaces of painfully high square footage. An estimated one-third of the malls in the U.S. are obsolete or soon to become so. Malls are forced to adjust in order to stay in business.

One way to attract customers is to raise the roof—literally tear off the connecting roofs between stores to create an open-air environment. Parking garages are coming down as well so shoppers can park directly by the entrance of their favorite stores. Department store chains such as J.C. Penney and Macy's opened freestanding stores at mall sites. Typically built to have a single floor, the stand-alone locations have plenty of close-in parking, and offer shopping carts and centralized checkout stands for convenience.

For example, Bella Terra in Huntington Beach, California was an enclosed shopping mall built in 1966. Builder J.H. Snyder Company spent $170 million to tear off the roof and knock down walls, transforming the mall into an open-air lifestyle center with 74 shops and restaurants and a 4,000-seat, 20-screen cinema megaplex. The rebuilt center features Italian architecture and design accents.

Some operators of enclosed malls are scrambling to find alternative tenants to fill empty spaces. Wal-

Mart, for example, opened a two-story store in a mall in a suburb of New York City and a three-story location in a Los Angeles mall formerly occupied by a Macy's department store. The pluses for Wal-Mart in these locations are access to mall shoppers without having to acquire real estate that is scarce in congested areas, as well as favorable leases with mall owners who are anxious to fill large amounts of space. On the other hand, Wal-Mart faces increased security and logistics costs and the difficulty of having to switch from a single-floor sprawl to multi-story confusion.

Internet Research Tip: Shopping Centers
For up-to-the-minute facts and figures about shopping centers of all types, visit the International Council of Shopping Centers, www.icsc.org.

17) Apartment House Vacancy Rates Stabilize

Apartment developers, particularly in the high-end to luxury range, were facing softer rents and higher vacancy rates from 2003 through 2004. Renters by the millions turned into house buyers, lured by mortgage plans with low or no down payment and house payments that were suddenly lower than rental payments thanks to historically low interest rates. The tide turned, however, by the end of 2004 when interest rates began to rise and, more recently, homeowners with subprime mortgages in default began to be forced out of their homes. With the mortgage crisis of 2007-2008, apartment living became more popular than ever as some people lost their homes and others were reluctant or unable to buy.

In 2009, however, apartment owners saw vacancy rate rise along with unemployment rates. According to real estate research company Reis, Inc., the top 79 U.S. rental markets saw vacancy rates hit 8% in 2009. The rise occurred despite the fact that landlords reduced asking rents (which include concessions) by 3% overall in 2009. In the first quarter of 2010, vacancy rates remained flat at 8%, a sign of stabilization.

Landlords continue to offer enticements to sign or renew leases, including new carpet and paint, a free month's rent and gift cards from local retailers such as Starbucks. Rents throughout the U.S. fell during the economic recession by as much as 3% in 2009 according to Reis. Real estate investment services firm Marcus & Millichap forecast another 2% to 3% drop in rents through 2010. On a brighter note, major apartment complex owners and operators are reporting that renters are staying longer. The average stay in 2009 was 14 months, but in 2010, renters are leasing for 19 months.

Internet Research Tip: Apartments
Find out everything you ever wanted to know about apartments at the web site of the highly regarded National Apartment Association, www.naahq.org. Particularly useful are its archive of historical statistics and its commentary on the rental market.

18) Hotel Operators Challenged/Pod Rooms Grow in Popularity

With some signs of an economic recovery, the hotel industry was enjoying a rebound as of early 2010, but multiple challenges continued to face this business, particularly in terms of room prices and net profits. For example, for the first quarter of 2010, global hotel giant Marriott reported the arrival of increasing numbers of business travelers. Corporate room-nights booked at Marriott in North America for that quarter rose 16% over the same period of the previous year. A change to good news would be very welcome in this industry, particularly in light of the many foreclosures of major hotel and resort properties in recent months.

As the recession kept more and more travelers at home, hotels were starting to feel the pinch. According to Smith Travel Research, U.S. hotel occupancy levels were down about 5% for 2008 from 2007. Especially hard hit were destinations reached only by air such as Hawaii. Occupancy rates at hotels on the island of Maui fell from 85% in 2007 to 63% in 2008 according to research firm Hospitality Advisors. An even more dire projection came from PKF Consulting, an Atlanta, Georgia firm. It expected U.S. occupancy rates to drop to 58.3% for all of 2009 (a fall of 4.4% from 2008). This is lower even than the 59% reported by Smith Travel for 2002, the first full year following the 9/11 attacks.

PricewaterhouseCoopers forecast 2009 U.S. hotel revenue down 16.1% and remaining there for 2010. The firm expected occupancy rates would be 55.5% in 2009 and 56.1% in 2010.

PKF also predicted that U.S. revenue per available hotel room ("revpar") would drop by 4.3% in 2009 and hotel industry profits would drop by 7.9%. This is an excellent example of the devastating effect of the economic slowdown on business and leisure travel.

Marriott reported that its revpar was down 1.0% for the first quarter of 2010, compared to the first quarter of 2009 (on a company-operated, worldwide hotel basis, adjusted for the effects of inflation).

However, management at Marriott forecast that revpar at North American properties would increase by 3% to 6% for all of 2010, with even greater increases in the rest of their worldwide network. While revpar looks promising thanks to rising occupancy, room rates remain a challenge. In North America, Marriott's comparable company-operated revpar declined 1.9% in the first quarter of 2010. Revpar at the company's comparable company-operated North American full-service and luxury hotels (including Marriott Hotels & Resorts, The Ritz-Carlton and Renaissance Hotels) was down only 1.2%, but the firm faced a 7.8% decline in average daily rate.

The economic slowdown was particularly tough for a number of hotel companies that were in the midst of expansion. According to Lodging Econometrics, there were about 6,000 new hotels under construction in the U.S. as of mid-2008, totaling about 800,000 rooms. Still more projects that were on the drawing board were scrapped due to lack of financing. In 2009, 1,301 hotels with 146,929 rooms opened compared to 1,345 hotels with 154,667 rooms in 2008. Lodging Econometrics forecasted 717 hotels opening in 2010 with 82,620 rooms.

Many major hotel chains cut back on their growth plans over the past couple of years. Hyatt, for example, planned to open 80 hotels in 2008, but scaled back to 64. Likewise, several huge hotel developments planned for Las Vegas have been put on hold. The bright spots in hotel construction and expansion were in China. Hotel construction remains robust there. The long term need for additional rooms looks promising.

In early 2010, Marriott reported 95,000 rooms under construction, awaiting conversion or approved for development, at more than 600 properties. Meanwhile, Marriott's system already contained 3,457 properties and 603,000 rooms.

As hoteliers faced falling occupancy rates, many dropped prices significantly. Harrah's Las Vegas, for example, advertised rooms for as little as $60 per night during August 2009. Other hotels, however, are finding that lower rates are not attracting more hotel guests. After 9/11, many hotels lowered their rates but saw little increase in demand. People chose to stay at home more in 2001 and appeared to be doing so again in 2008 and 2009. Many hotels are attempting to create compelling package offerings at great prices in order to drive business. For example, room packages may include breakfast, spa credits, dinners in luxury on-site restaurants or other perks. Members of the loyalty reward programs of major hotel chains receive a continual stream of emails offering last minute discounts, resort travel packages or deep discounts on weekend rates. Hotels in Las Vegas are being particularly aggressive, and some owners are finding this strategy successful. The Wynn resort in Las Vegas opened its massive new ultra-luxury wing "Encore" in late 2008, just in time for the economic bust. The owners decided to use bargain pricing to drive up occupancy with good results. In their case, a relatively full hotel at lower rates was preferable to empty rooms.

Corporate and business travel destinations were especially hard hit. Major corporations cancelled or downsized meetings, while many firms instructed employees to curtail travel to visit clients and trips to conferences or conventions. The fall off in luxury retreats and meetings by hedge funds, investment banks and other financial industry companies was also a serious blow to the hotel and resort sector.

With travel budgets being tight, hotels are responding with new, cost effective room alternatives, especially in Europe and Japan. Busy travelers can now book tiny rooms or "pods" that typically measure about 100 square feet (some as small as 65 square feet) in size for the night or just a few hours to rest and freshen up. (In contrast, a more traditional motel is about 300 square feet, and luxury hotel rooms are 450 to 600 square feet.) Rooms generally have a small bed, flat screen TV and tiny bathrooms (some offered shared bathrooms), and windows, if there are any, may open onto a corridor instead of outside. Examples of hotels offering pods are Yotel at London's Heathrow Airport ($105 per night for a 117 square foot "premium cabin"), Pod Hotel in New York ($139 per night for 91.5 square feet) and EasyHotel in Zurich ($71 per night for 104 square feet).

The pod business model is similar to discount airlines in that only the basics are available and low prices are of supreme importance. Pod hotels do not generally offer perks such as fitness facilities, meeting rooms or lavish room service (some do not offer food of any kind). Yet, the services they do offer can be top of the line such as plasma TV screens and high-thread-count sheets. In addition to business travelers, the rooms attract vacationers looking for good deals in locations near major tourist attractions.

On the other end of the scale, a big trend in luxury hotels was the construction of adjacent condominiums. However, as the real estate bubble burst in 2008, owners of many of these properties saw their unit values plummet, and many developers ran into financial difficulty. Some of the residential units were selling for almost $2,000 per square foot before the crash. Of course, the condos make initial profits for the developers, when they are sold. Equally important, the condo owners pay hefty monthly common area fees to help defray the costs of luxurious lobbies, swimming pools, landscape and a high level of personal service. The economic crisis has weakened the luxury condominium market as it has in all other real estate sectors, so watch for project delays and price reductions for existing units through the mid-term.

19) New Urbanism and Traditional Neighborhood Developments are Retro Trends

New Urbanism, or traditional neighborhood development (TND) represent a strong trend among developers in many parts of America. TND is an attempt to create an old-fashioned aura in a newly built neighborhood. Typical elements include small lots, front porches and other features that encourage being outdoors, meeting your neighbors and walking or cycling (rather than driving) through the neighborhood. The architecture is frequently pre-1940s in style, and easy-to-walk-to retail spaces are often incorporated, sometimes in a town-center style. Also, live-work buildings are frequently placed in special parts of the neighborhood, encouraging entrepreneurs or professionals to work downstairs and live upstairs.

The most noted TND is a community in Florida called Seaside, www.seasidefl.com, which has been in place for more than a decade. Many other TNDs are attempting to emulate Seaside's success, which is based partly on its beachfront location, a tried-and-true draw for the retiree crowd and vacationers looking for something different from life back home.

TNDs are not necessarily instant successes, and they may not be suitable for development in many areas. To begin with, while many developers like the concept because municipal governments are likely to approve smaller lots in higher density arrangements, some elements of TNDs are more expensive to build, such as period streetlights, cobblestone streets or dense landscape. Also, the retail space offered in town-center sections of TNDs is often difficult to rent, resulting in costly high vacancy rates and unsightly empty storefronts. These high costs are especially problematic in the current economic crisis, and are causing new projects to be delayed or shelved altogether.

20) Megapolitans Will Define America of the Future/Mega-Regions Defined Internationally

The Metropolitan Institute (MI) at Virginia Tech University has done extensive research into what it calls "megapolitans;" that is, regional concentrations of population totaling 10 million people (now or by 2040) that comprise two or more contiguous metropolitan areas and feature other selected characteristics.

MI finds that 10 megapolitan areas exist within the U.S. today, comprising less than 20% of all land area in the lower 48 states, but holding almost 200 million people, about 66% of total U.S. population. By 2040, MI projects that these 10 areas will add 83 million additional residents and will attract more than 75% of all private real estate development investments from 2003 to 2040, or about $33 trillion.

MI lists the 10 megapolitans as 1) Cascadia in the Seattle/Portland area of the Pacific Northwest; 2) NorCal in Northern California; 3) Southland in Southern California; 4) Valley of the Sun in the Phoenix/Tucson area; 5) I-35 Corridor stretching from Dallas-Ft. Worth through central Oklahoma and parts of Kansas; 6) Gulf Coast comprising the coastal areas of Texas, Louisiana, Mississippi and Alabama; 7) Peninsula comprising all of Southern and Central Florida; 8) Piedmont in Central Georgia, the Carolinas, and nearby metro areas; 9) Northeast in the Northeast Corridor of the U.S.; and 10) Midwest in Chicago and the surrounding Midwestern metro areas.

Growth of these megapolitans can create unique new problems. For example, a migration of millions of people from suburban living in large homes to urban living on smaller lots could leave a surplus of as many as 22 million large-lot homes (built on at least one-sixth of an acre) in suburban areas by 2025 according to one estimate. Some analysts project that aging Baby Boomers will desire smaller, urban homes as they age, homes that are easier to care for and less expensive to operate than suburban houses on large lots.

The high gasoline prices of 2008 added fuel to the megapolitan fire. Dense population areas where people live and work close together foster the use of bicycles, public transportation and walking to get from place to place.

On the other hand, there is the possibility that urban living may not appeal to such a vast swath of the population. Advanced communication technologies centered on the Internet will continue to evolve quickly, making it ever more effective to work remotely while collaborating with associates, customers and suppliers who are far away. People will be able to use advances in communications to stay in touch with far-flung family and friends. This will encourage many people to live in communities with smaller populations that offer better recreation, cleaner air, lower crime, better weather and/or better public education than they would find in major cities. This could cause large numbers of knowledge workers to relocate to cities such as Boise, Idaho or the Spokane, Washington area. Communities that are even more rural, such as Taos, New Mexico; Grand Junction, Colorado or College Station, Texas could find an influx of knowledge workers who realize that they can live nearly anywhere that suits their unique individual tastes and budgets, as long as they have very fast Internet access and reasonable proximity to a major airport.

On a global scale, the Martin Prosperity Institute at the University of Toronto defines 40 mega-regions around the world that collectively power the global economy. While home to one-fifth of the world's population, these mega-regions produce two-thirds of global economic output and more than 85% of global innovation. Major mega-regions include Greater Tokyo (55 million people and $2.5 trillion in economic activity) and the 500-mile Boston-Washington corridor (54 million people and $2.2 trillion in output). Other regions of note include Chicago to Pittsburgh, Los Angeles to San Diego and the areas around global centers such as Amsterdam, London and Bangalore and Mumbai.

21) Destination Club Membership Growth Is Checked

In the same manner that corporations and wealthy individuals are enthusiastically participating in fractional bizjet ownership, wealthy travelers have bought into luxury fractional vacation home ownership. Participants, sometimes referred to as "members," purchase temporal ownership in a group of highly appealing properties. What makes this arrangement different from the standard time-share is the fact that members buy the right to use a variety of multi-million dollar houses (and sometimes yachts) in prime locations around the world, but do not actually own any property. In addition to posh accommodations, these programs offer stellar service. Concierges often handle everything from sports equipment rentals to stocking the refrigerator. The concept was a steady success until one of its originators, Tanner & Haley, filed for Chapter 11 bankruptcy in 2006, and the onset of the global recession soon thereafter.

Upfront deposits in such clubs typically range between $70,000 and $450,000, depending on the club and its levels of membership. Annual dues run between $7,000 and more than $50,000. Use of the homes in various destination clubs is usually flexible. Generally, members are limited to a 14-day stay in any property at any one time. Services may include assistance in chartering private jets to take members to their destinations for additional fees.

Most membership fees are from 80% to 100% refundable if the member decides to leave the program. On top of these up-front fees, however, are annual fees, which vary depending on the level of accommodations and the number of days.

So what happened to cause Tanner & Haley to file bankruptcy? Part of the problem was the firm's commitment to returning membership deposits, upon request, after tenure of at least 18 months. In addition to that potential capital drain, the company found itself having to lease luxury properties in addition to those it owned to meet client demand, further depleting the company's resources.

Tanner & Haley members found some solace in the 2007 purchase of the firm's real estate holdings by Ultimate Resort, a rival destination club firm based in Orlando, Florida. Thanks to the $100 million transaction, Tanner & Haley members were invited to join Ultimate without having to pay its initiation fee, which runs between $120,000 and $215,000 depending on the level of membership. Ultimate Resort further built up its portfolio with the 2008, $200 million merger with Private Escapes, another major destination club.

Other players in this business include Exclusive Resorts, which is 50%-owned by AOL's Steve Case, Solstice, The LUSSO Collection and Quintess. Each offers various packages and/or levels of service. Both Exclusive Resorts and the former Private Escapes issued letters to its members assuring them that their investments are safe and that their business models differ from that of Tanner & Haley.

Tanner & Haley's bankruptcy filing may be a serious blow to destination clubs in general if confidence in the overall concept is compromised. As of early 2009, there were fewer than 15 major destination club companies around the world. More consolidation may occur. The merging of two smaller clubs, Solstice and Parallel, for example, was completed in November 2006. Quintess also merged with Dream Catcher and Leading Residences of the World. In 2009, Quintess, Leading Residences of the

World and Dublin-based Oyster Circle formed a strategic alliance in which their members will be allowed to use properties in all three clubs.

One bright spot on the destination club horizon may be the formation of the Destination Club Association. Consisting of a small number of member clubs, the association is expected to operate as a governing body for the industry. It has established a list of best practices such as disclosure, financial responsibility and appropriate marketing and sales activity. Member clubs hope that prospective members will be assured of the safety of their investments and the quality of the clubs.

22) Remodeling Rebounds/Home Sizes Shrink

Home remodeling in the U.S. hit its peak in 2007 at $320 billion, according to the Joint Center for Housing Studies of Harvard University. By 2009, it had fallen to $246 billion. One result was declining profits at building center giants Home Depot and Lowe's. For example, at Home Depot net sales for the fiscal year ending February 3, 2008 were down by 2.1%, or $1.6 billion, to $77.3 billion, while net profits were off 23.7% to $4.4 billion. The fiscal year ending January 31, 2009 was significantly worse, with revenues decreasing to $71.2 billion and profits plummeting to $2.2 billion, a decrease of 48.6%.

However, there appears to be a faint glow on the remodeling horizon. Both the National Association of Home Builders (NAHB) and Harvard are forecasting a slow recovery beginning in the second quarter of 2010. Many homeowners are remodeling in order to increase energy efficiency, while others hope to capitalize on tax credits for new appliances and other energy saving improvements.

Important trends in remodeling:

- Consumers are in do-it-yourself mode to reduce costs. One interesting result is that the short-term rental of construction tools and equipment is soaring.
- Financing for remodeling via home equity loans is much harder to obtain.
- Projects are smaller and less expensive.
- There is a growing focus on green, energy-efficient remodeling projects.
- Federal and state government incentives, such as tax credits, will fuel investments in home solar projects, weather stripping, insulation and energy-efficient appliances and windows.
- As America's 76 million surviving Baby Boomers age, investments in remodeling for easier access for the aged will boom. Features such as wider doors for wheelchair access, firm handholds in bathrooms and better kitchen accessibility will be a focus. "Universal Design," a concept that focuses on ease of use by residents of limited physical ability, will grow.

Source: Plunkett Research, Ltd.

The size of the median new home in the U.S. grew steadily for several years, reaching 2,277 square feet in 2007, up from 1,940 in 1994. That trend was broken in 2008. Concerned about purchase price and energy expenses, American consumers are now looking for smaller homes. According to the U.S. Census Bureau, the median house started during the first quarter of 2009 was 2,065 square feet. In addition to smaller size overall, consumers are willing to accept fewer luxuries, such as only one fireplace instead of two, in order to save money. However, consumers are not willing to skimp on energy efficiency in their appliances, insulation and air conditioning systems. Energy efficiency is a high priority.

Chapter 2

REAL ESTATE & CONSTRUCTION INDUSTRY STATISTICS

CONTENTS:

Real Estate & Construction Industry Overview

	Quantity	Unit	Date	Source
Existing Home Sales, 2009, U.S.[1]	4.69	Million	2009	NAR
Existing Home Sales, 2010, U.S.[2]	5.02	Million	2010[2]	NAR
New Single Family Home Sales, U.S.	374	Thousand	2009	Census
New Single Family Homes For Sale, U.S., End of Period	232	Thousand	2009	Census
Single & Multi-family Home Housing Starts (Private), U.S.	554	Thousand	2009	Census
Median Sales Price of New Single-Family Houses Sold, U.S.	215,900	US$	2009	Census
Average Sales Price of New Single-Family Houses Sold, U.S.	270,400	US$	2009	Census
Median Existing Home Sales Price, 2009, U.S.	165,400	US$	2009	NAR
Median Existing Home Sales Price, 2010, U.S.	165,100	US$	2010[2]	NAR
Size of Median Newly Built Home, U.S.	2,065	Sq. Ft.	2009[3]	Census
Placements of New Manufactured Homes, U.S.	52,500	Units	2009	Census
Commercial Real Estate Sales Volume Worldwide: Last 6 Months	301.0	Bil. US$	Apr. 2010	RCA
U.S.	42.4	Bil. US$	Apr. 2010	RCA
U.K.	25.2	Bil. US$	Apr. 2010	RCA
Canada	4.4	Bil. US$	Apr. 2010	RCA
Value of U.S. Construction Put into Place	846.2	Bil. US$	2010[4]	Census
Private	553.5	Bil. US$	2010[4]	Census
Residential	250.8	Bil. US$	2010[4]	Census
Non-Residential	302.7	Bil. US$	2010[4]	Census
Public	292.7	Bil. US$	2010[4]	Census
State & Local	264.7	Bil. US$	2010[4]	Census
Federal	28.0	Bil. US$	2010[4]	Census
Foreign Direct Investment (Real Estate, Rental and Leasing)	52.0	Bil. US$	2008	BEA
Average 1-Year Adjustable Rate Mortgage	4.05	%	Apr. 2010	Freddie Mac
Average 15-Year Fixed-Rate Mortgage	4.39	%	Apr. 2010	Freddie Mac
Average 30-Year Fixed-Rate Mortgage	5.08	%	Apr. 2010	Freddie Mac
Total Outstanding Mortgage Debt, U.S.	14.3	Tril. US$	Q4 2009	Federal Reserve
Home Mortgage Debt, U.S.	10.8	Tril. US$	Q4 2009	Federal Reserve
Commercial Mortgage Debt, U.S.	2.5	Tril. US$	Q4 2009	Federal Reserve
Homeownership Rate (% of Households), U.S.	67.4	%	2009	Census
Residential Rental & Homeowner Vacancy Rate, End of Year, U.S.	10.6	%	2009	Census
Estimated Construction Industry Employment (NAICS 23), U.S.	6.0	Million	2009	BLS
Estimated Real Estate Industry Employment (NAICS 531), U.S.	1.4	Million	2009	BLS
Hotel Industry Revenue, U.S.	140.6	Bil. US$	2008	AH&LA
Gross Output Value, Current Construction Enterprises, China	1.1	Tril. US$	2009	NBSC
Total Investment in Construction, China	6.2	Tril. US$	2009	NBSC
Total Planned Investment in New Construction Projects, China	2.2	Tril. US$	2009	NBSC

[1] Existing home sales of single-family homes and condo/coops. [2] Estimate as of March 2010. [3] First three months of 2010. [4] Seasonally adjusted annual rate as of February 2010.

NAR = National Association of Realtors
RCA = Real Capital Analytics
BLS = U.S. Bureau of Labor Statistics
NBSC = National Bureau of Statistics of China
Census = U.S. Census Bureau
BEA = Bureau of Economic Analysis
AH&LA = American Hotel & Lodging Association

Plunkett's Real Estate & Construction Industry Almanac 2010

www.plunkettresearch.com

Value of U.S. Private Construction Put in Place: 2003-2009

(In Millions of US$)

Type of Construction	2003	2004	2005	2006	2007	2008	2009
Total Private Construction	675,370	771,378	868,543	912,169	861,615	766,170	619,277
Residential	446,035	532,900	611,899	613,731	493,246	350,078	251,364
New single family	310,575	377,557	433,510	415,997	305,184	185,776	106,288
New multi-family	35,116	39,944	47,297	52,803	48,959	44,158	29,264
Improvements	100,344	115,399	131,092	144,931	139,103	120,144	115,813
Nonresidential	229,335	238,478	256,644	298,438	368,369	416,092	367,913
Lodging	9,930	11,982	12,666	17,624	27,481	35,379	25,033
Office	30,579	32,879	37,276	45,680	53,815	57,084	40,286
General	27,380	28,679	32,962	41,085	48,945	51,939	36,265
Financial	3,174	4,186	4,285	4,542	4,785	4,819	3,806
Commercial	57,505	63,195	66,584	73,368	85,858	81,495	53,654
Automotive	5,039	5,235	5,614	5,528	6,281	5,387	4,608
Sales	2,099	2,443	2,834	2,285	2,571	2,279	1,658
Service/parts	1,866	1,978	1,805	2,184	2,356	1,846	1,979
Parking	1,074	814	975	1,059	1,354	1,262	971
Food/beverage	8,369	8,232	7,795	7,442	8,046	8,168	5,174
Food	4,234	3,590	3,128	2,752	2,779	3,149	2,132
Dining/drinking	3,321	3,937	4,078	3,780	3,957	4,071	2,386
Fast food	813	705	590	910	1,310	948	655
Multi-retail	15,400	18,828	22,750	29,218	34,751	32,227	20,782
General merchandise	5,341	6,416	6,740	5,699	7,572	4,522	4,532
Shopping center	6,867	9,256	12,462	18,417	22,197	22,958	12,919
Shopping mall	2,231	2,138	2,631	3,616	4,000	3,990	2,459
Other commercial	11,249	13,341	11,744	10,874	13,580	12,475	6,789
Drug store	1,790	1,427	1,315	1,238	1,500	1,940	1,991
Building supply store	2,268	2,521	2,416	2,594	3,507	2,649	1,284
Other stores	6,214	8,229	7,075	6,135	7,744	6,806	2,652
Warehouse	12,345	12,074	12,827	14,491	16,909	16,838	10,169
General commercial	11,004	10,830	11,468	13,493	15,641	15,661	9,165
Mini-storage	1,326	1,141	1,311	979	1,218	1,072	915
Farm	5,103	5,485	5,854	5,817	6,292	6,401	6,132
Health Care	24,217	26,272	28,495	32,016	35,588	39,101	36,760
Hospital	15,234	16,147	18,250	21,914	24,532	26,421	26,548
Medical building	6,068	7,615	8,031	7,165	7,981	8,995	7,032
Special care	2,915	2,510	2,213	2,937	3,074	3,684	3,180
Educational	13,424	12,701	12,788	13,839	16,691	18,585	16,619
Preschool	711	674	516	487	704	742	739
Primary/secondary	3,204	3,202	2,718	3,240	3,968	3,849	3,204
Higher education	7,259	6,496	6,946	7,611	9,424	11,568	10,696
Instructional	3,701	3,200	3,556	3,501	4,219	5,507	6,201
Dormitory	1,761	1,669	1,537	2,065	2,900	3,747	2,510
Sports/recreation	677	739	821	858	771	852	848
Other educational	1,785	1,998	2,294	2,090	2,167	2,014	1,655
Gallery/museum	1,371	1,335	1,745	1,697	1,939	1,722	1,368

(Continued on next page)

Value of U.S. Private Construction Put in Place: 2003-2009 (cont.)

(In Millions of US$)

Type of Construction	2003	2004	2005	2006	2007	2008	2009
Religious	8,559	8,153	7,715	7,740	7,522	7,097	6,287
House of worship	6,238	6,015	5,992	6,262	6,270	5,808	5,094
Other religious	2,322	2,138	1,723	1,478	1,252	1,289	1,194
Auxiliary building	1,296	1,258	1,251	1,219	1,099	1,096	1,060
Public Safety	185	289	408	419	595	650	463
Amusement & Recreation	7,781	8,432	7,507	9,326	10,193	10,316	7,718
Theme/amusement park	270	198	200	417	522	275	268
Sports	1,306	900	807	959	1,902	2,302	1,695
Fitness	1,262	1,141	1,425	2,028	1,945	2,058	1,772
Performance/meeting center	844	1,054	1,072	737	823	1,097	784
Social center	1,996	2,594	1,626	1,538	1,602	1,519	959
Movie theater/studio	855	1,218	1,248	1,309	1,159	572	333
Transportation	6,568	6,841	7,124	8,654	9,009	9,896	9,066
Air	1,012	869	748	719	732	745	503
Land	5,462	5,800	6,214	7,764	8,008	9,009	8,484
Railroad	4,851	5,392	5,816	7,313	7,423	8,367	8,019
Communication	14,456	15,468	18,846	22,187	27,488	25,496	20,229
Power	33,619	27,360	26,304	31,164	47,365	68,702	76,699
Electric	25,592	20,431	19,192	22,804	33,627	50,392	52,789
Gas	6,358	5,096	5,239	5,528	7,876	9,396	9,795
Oil	1,068	1,579	1,293	1,831	4,779	5,628	6,319
Sewage & Waste Disposal	278	331	240	305	408	548	458
Water Supply	393	405	326	477	516	696	345
Manufacturing	21,434	23,667	29,886	35,086	45,303	60,784	74,135
Food/beverage/tobacco	2,695	3,157	4,677	4,707	4,270	5,033	3,908
Textile/apparel/leather & allied	218	188	415	144	40	268	343
Wood	376	485	982	1,465	791	355	573
Paper	818	548	467	559	506	549	629
Print/publishing	630	654	777	727	265	295	204
Petroleum/coal	717	1,204	771	1,799	5,719	17,564	31,807
Chemical	5,368	5,507	6,588	9,235	14,958	13,719	12,887
Plastic/rubber	659	936	877	884	1,095	1,269	768
Nonmetallic mineral	865	896	1,163	2,603	3,848	3,343	2,547
Primary metal	436	312	836	1,441	1,757	3,846	5,786
Fabricated metal	662	595	699	562	1,050	1,913	1,948
Machinery	707	645	917	935	550	997	1,409
Computer/electronic/electrical	1,444	2,835	4,247	4,347	2,870	2,575	4,472
Transportation equipment	3,314	2,610	3,702	2,631	3,626	5,187	4,531
Furniture	278	217	96	122	180	40	(S)
Miscellaneous	2,248	2,878	2,674	2,928	3,781	3,831	2,324

Notes: Details may not add to totals since all types of construction are not shown separately. Total private construction includes the following categories of construction not shown: highway and street, and conservation and development.
S = Estimate does not meet publication standards.

Source: U.S. Census Bureau
Plunkett Research, Ltd.
www.plunkettresearch.com

Value of U.S. Public Construction Put in Place: 2003-2009

(In Millions of US$)

Type of Construction	2003	2004	2005	2006	2007	2008	2009
Total Public Construction[1]	**216,127**	**220,183**	**234,160**	**255,385**	**289,073**	**305,962**	**316,345**
Residential	5,216	5,508	5,608	6,083	7,222	7,330	8,093
Nonresidential	210,911	214,675	228,552	249,303	281,852	298,632	308,252
Office	8,839	9,525	8,487	8,507	11,445	13,222	14,919
Commercial	4,024	3,862	3,658	3,345	3,827	3,447	3,807
Health care	5,112	5,912	5,935	6,456	8,179	8,598	9,835
Educational	60,892	61,549	66,899	71,089	80,068	85,496	86,065
Public safety	6,976	6,730	6,906	7,350	9,606	12,286	13,727
Amusement & recreation	9,066	8,263	7,728	9,707	11,019	11,172	10,953
Transportation	18,142	18,219	17,928	19,310	22,868	24,057	26,206
Power	7,831	8,035	9,161	8,590	11,940	11,457	11,995
Highway and street	56,974	58,294	63,790	71,567	76,248	81,592	84,430
Sewage & waste disposal	16,304	17,598	19,627	22,881	24,464	24,596	24,392
Water supply	12,100	12,215	13,703	14,483	15,282	16,255	15,438
Conservation & development	3,694	3,869	4,322	5,047	5,155	5,350	5,767
Total State & Local Construction[1]	**198,214**	**201,841**	**216,860**	**237,831**	**268,494**	**282,122**	**288,542**
Residential	3,724	4,110	4,047	4,349	5,094	4,836	6,048
Nonresidential	194,490	197,731	212,813	233,482	263,399	277,286	282,493
Office	6,116	6,024	5,211	5,588	7,249	8,439	9,227
Commercial	2,207	1,979	1,882	1,567	1,777	1,817	2,293
Health care	4,005	5,025	5,059	5,615	7,028	7,065	7,110
Educational	59,340	59,741	65,750	69,790	78,376	83,759	83,846
Public safety	5,844	5,477	6,013	6,608	8,423	9,615	9,408
Amusement & recreation	8,354	7,794	7,340	9,444	10,670	10,826	10,553
Transportation	16,483	16,440	16,256	17,695	21,144	21,843	24,284
Power	6,785	7,044	8,320	7,766	11,449	10,623	10,908
Highway & street	56,251	57,351	63,157	71,032	75,455	80,835	83,682
Sewage & waste disposal	15,625	17,084	18,336	21,524	23,323	23,839	23,932
Water supply	11,711	11,977	13,483	14,299	15,029	15,835	15,128
Conservation & development	1,020	1,466	1,752	2,000	2,198	2,215	1,931
Total Federal Construction[2]	**17,913**	**18,342**	**17,300**	**17,555**	**20,580**	**23,840**	**27,803**
Residential	1,491	1,398	1,561	1,734	2,127	2,494	2,044
Nonresidential	16,422	16,944	15,739	15,821	18,452	21,346	25,759
Office	2,723	3,500	3,275	2,919	4,195	4,783	5,692
Commercial	1,817	1,882	1,776	1,778	2,049	1,629	1,513
Health care	1,107	887	877	842	1,150	1,533	2,724
Educational	1,552	1,808	1,149	1,299	1,691	1,737	2,220
Public safety	1,132	1,253	893	741	1,183	2,671	4,319
Amusement & recreation	712	469	388	263	349	345	400
Transportation	1,659	1,779	1,672	1,615	1,724	2,214	1,922
Power	1,045	990	842	824	491	834	1,086
Highway & street	723	943	633	536	792	757	749
Conservation & development	2,674	2,403	2,570	3,047	2,957	3,135	3,836

NA = Not applicable.

[1] Includes the following categories of construction not shown separately: lodging, religious, communication and manufacturing.

[2] Includes the following categories of federal construction not shown separately: lodging, religious, communication, sewage and waste disposal, water supply, and manufacturing.

Source: U.S. Census Bureau

Plunkett Research, Ltd.

www.plunkettresearch.com

Estimates of the Total Housing Inventory for the U.S.: 2008-2009

(In Thousands of Units)

Type of Housing	2008 Estimate	2009 Estimate	90-Percent Confidence Interval (+/-)*		2009 Percent of Total
			of 2009 Estimate	of Difference	
All housing units	129,019	130,159	(X)	(X)	100
Occupied	110,475	111,344	234	219	85.5
Owner occupied	74,931	75,014	563	480	57.6
Renter occupied	35,544	36,330	486	429	27.9
Vacant	18,543	18,815	299	270	14.5
Year-round vacant	13,816	14,143	310	279	10.9
For rent	4,021	4,393	141	145	3.4
For sale only	2,207	2,020	79	89	1.6
Rented or sold, awaiting occupancy	1,067	993	48	63	0.8
Held off market	6,522	6,737	222	201	5.2
For occasional use	2,053	2,068	127	116	1.6
Temporarily occupied by persons with usual residence elsewhere	1,160	1,187	96	88	0.9
For other reasons	3,310	3,482	161	144	2.7
Seasonal vacant	4,728	4,673	215	198	3.6

Estimates may not add to total due to rounding.

* A 90-percent confidence interval is a measure of an estimate's reliability. The larger the confidence interval is, in relation to the size of the estimate, the less reliable the estimate.

X = Not applicable. Because the number of housing units is set equal to an independent national measure, there is no sampling error, and hence no confidence interval.

Source: U.S. Census Bureau
Plunkett Research, Ltd.
www.plunkettresearch.com

Financial Assets and Liabilities of U.S. Real Estate Investment Trusts (REITs): 2005-2009

(In Billions of US$; Amounts Outstanding End of Period, Not Seasonally Adjusted)

Assets & Liabilities	2005	2006	2007	2008				2009			
				Q1	Q2	Q3	Q4	Q1	Q2	Q3	Q4
Total financial assets	**305.3**	**344.0**	**316.7**	**300.7**	**301.0**	**293.3**	**253.9**	**251.9**	**260.3**	**266.6**	**262.5**
Checkable deposits & currency	13.6	18.4	16.6	19.4	18.0	22.2	18.4	17.5	22.1	28.0	26.9
Credit market instruments	239.7	265.8	244.7	224.0	223.3	209.8	180.8	180.5	188.3	180.4	172.3
Agency- & GSE-backed securities	40.6	65.4	88.9	92.3	99.3	93.2	90.5	95.3	104.0	100.0	95.0
Corporate and foreign bonds	53.0	64.6	34.4	23.4	21.6	20.1	14.4	13.7	15.4	16.9	17.3
Mortgages	146.1	135.8	121.3	108.3	102.4	96.6	75.9	71.5	68.9	63.5	60.0
Home	127.4	103.7	79.2	65.9	60.3	55.1	36.7	33.7	32.8	31.5	30.3
Multi-family residential	1.9	5.0	5.2	5.2	5.0	4.4	3.9	3.7	3.3	2.0	1.9
Commercial	16.8	27.1	37.0	37.2	37.1	37.1	35.3	34.1	32.9	30.0	27.8
Miscellaneous assets	51.9	59.7	55.4	57.2	59.7	61.3	54.7	54.0	49.9	58.3	63.3
Total liabilities	**533.7**	**571.3**	**578.7**	**559.0**	**552.8**	**545.1**	**515.2**	**497.3**	**489.1**	**486.2**	**479.3**
Security repurchase agreements	83.5	97.9	91.7	89.9	91.6	89.6	80.5	83.2	85.5	93.2	94.3
Credit market instruments	395.5	411.0	421.2	403.8	397.5	389.9	372.6	364.0	352.5	347.8	340.7
Open market paper	0.0	0.0	0.0	0.0	0.0	0.0	0.0	0.0	0.0	0.0	0.0
Corporate bonds	216.7	230.6	231.3	207.7	206.8	194.8	176.2	168.3	161.0	159.6	156.3
Bank loans, nec	33.3	28.4	33.2	34.2	29.5	32.4	32.9	30.9	24.2	21.3	21.4
Mortgages	145.5	152.1	156.7	161.8	161.2	162.7	163.5	164.9	167.3	166.9	162.9
Miscellaneous liabilities	54.7	62.4	65.8	65.3	63.7	65.6	62.1	50.1	51.1	45.3	44.3
Memo:											
Securitized assets included above	107.3	110.0	92.1	72.2	66.7	59.4	50.4	46.6	43.9	40.6	38.8
Agency- & GSE-backed securities	0.0	0.0	0.0	0.0	0.0	0.0	0.0	0.0	0.0	0.0	0.0
Home mortgages	102.5	92.7	72.4	56.5	50.9	44.5	36.8	33.5	32.4	32.2	31.5
Multi-family residential mortgages	0.1	0.4	0.4	0.4	0.4	0.4	0.4	0.4	0.4	0.4	0.4
Commercial mortgages	4.7	17.0	19.3	15.3	15.4	14.5	13.2	12.7	11.2	8.1	6.9

GSE = Government sponsored enterprise. NEC = Not Elsewhere Classified.

Source: U.S. Federal Reserve
Plunkett Research, Ltd.
www.plunkettresearch.com

Assets & Liabilities, U.S. Agency- & Government Sponsored Enterprise (GSE)-Backed Securities by Holder: 2005-2009

(In Billions of US$; Amounts Outstanding End of Period, Not Seasonally Adjusted)

Assets & Liabilities	2005	2006	2007	2008				2009			
				Q1	Q2	Q3	Q4	Q1	Q2	Q3	Q4
Total liabilities	**6,158.0**	**6,488.6**	**7,396.9**	**7,563.0**	**7,885.1**	**8,067.7**	**8,166.1**	**8,182.7**	**8,143.6**	**8,123.4**	**8,112.7**
Budget agencies	23.8	23.5	23.1	23.5	23.5	23.1	23.3	22.5	22.3	23.2	23.5
Government-sponsored enterprises	2,592.2	2,627.8	2,910.2	2,938.1	3,102.1	3,152.7	3,181.9	3,118.3	2,948.1	2,800.5	2,706.2
Agency- & GSE-backed mortgage pools	3,541.9	3,837.3	4,463.5	4,601.4	4,759.5	4,891.9	4,960.8	5,041.8	5,173.3	5,299.7	5,383.0
Total assets	**6,158.0**	**6,488.6**	**7,396.9**	**7,563.0**	**7,885.1**	**8,067.7**	**8,166.1**	**8,182.7**	**8,143.6**	**8,123.4**	**8,112.7**
Household sector	488.2	402.6	682.2	641.6	659.0	829.1	701.1	486.1	190.1	185.0	35.0
Nonfinancial corporate business	18.8	16.4	12.8	8.6	9.1	8.0	9.1	5.8	10.8	10.6	12.2
State and local governments	401.6	439.9	454.6	451.0	447.2	440.3	434.2	425.9	412.8	403.7	392.2
Federal government	0.0	0.0	0.0	0.0	0.0	3.3	54.4	111.4	164.7	195.6	225.5
Rest of the world	1,012.9	1,262.3	1,582.4	1,606.1	1,631.1	1,535.7	1,445.2	1,386.2	1,379.8	1,331.2	1,315.1
Monetary authority	0.0	0.0	0.0	0.0	0.0	14.5	19.7	287.0	559.1	823.5	1,068.3
Commercial banking	1,089.6	1,135.6	1,022.3	1,016.2	1,095.7	1,080.0	1,169.4	1,175.4	1,221.3	1,185.8	1,276.8
U.S.-chartered commercial banks	992.7	1,040.3	928.9	923.2	985.7	991.3	1,068.7	1,085.4	1,136.8	1,106.5	1,200.0
Foreign banking offices in the U.S.	50.9	55.1	57.1	54.4	53.9	44.7	50.5	45.6	38.7	35.2	32.1
Bank holding companies	11.2	11.2	9.9	13.0	28.3	16.6	25.8	21.6	22.4	22.3	24.3
Banks in U.S.-affiliated areas	34.8	29.0	26.3	25.7	27.8	27.4	24.4	22.8	23.5	21.8	20.5
Savings institutions	192.3	177.0	177.4	173.0	176.6	169.9	173.8	175.9	187.6	197.4	201.6
Credit unions	86.4	72.5	68.4	73.5	80.8	82.4	82.9	91.9	100.7	105.2	105.5
Property-casualty insurance companies	117.9	122.0	125.8	123.0	120.5	117.0	114.3	106.8	101.7	98.2	94.5
Life insurance companies	368.5	377.4	382.9	381.4	379.1	373.6	366.2	350.5	334.7	319.6	310.1
Private pension funds	252.0	268.6	296.8	300.4	302.0	310.3	318.1	315.6	305.9	296.3	290.1
State and local government retirement funds	258.4	310.8	334.1	335.1	334.6	337.1	340.5	337.8	337.0	335.5	330.8
Federal government retirement funds	4.6	4.7	5.0	6.0	5.8	5.8	5.1	5.0	5.0	5.4	5.6
Money market mutual funds	160.1	131.4	235.9	388.9	424.9	518.4	756.2	776.3	733.2	635.2	543.0
Mutual funds	483.4	499.1	565.4	576.3	594.0	603.4	592.7	588.1	616.9	635.1	631.8
Government-sponsored enterprises	751.1	714.0	702.9	728.4	854.3	836.7	910.0	954.0	949.0	919.4	924.9
ABS Issuers	330.5	350.9	369.0	363.2	359.9	358.9	340.1	285.7	252.0	199.0	143.9
REITs	40.6	65.4	88.9	92.3	99.3	93.2	90.5	95.3	104.0	100.0	95.0
Brokers & dealers	101.0	138.0	290.2	298.1	311.2	350.0	242.6	222.0	177.2	141.6	110.9

Notes: Agency- and GSE-backed securities include: issues of federal budget agencies such as those for the TVA; issues of government sponsored enterprises such as FNMA and FHLB; and agency- and GSE-backed mortgage pool securities issued by GNMA, FNMA, FHLMC, and the Farmers Home Administration. Only the budget agency issues are considered officially to be part of the total debt of the federal government.

ABS = Asset-Backed Security. REIT = Real Estate Investment Trust.

Source: U.S. Federal Reserve

Plunkett Research, Ltd.

www.plunkettresearch.com

Commercial, Residential & Farm Mortgages by Holder, U.S.: 2005-2009

(In Billions of US$; Amounts Outstanding End of Period, Not Seasonally Adjusted)

Holder	2005	2006	2007	2008				2009			
				Q1	Q2	Q3	Q4	Q1	Q2	Q3	Q4
Total mortgages	**12,066.7**	**13,464.3**	**14,532.9**	**14,666.8**	**14,704.4**	**14,682.7**	**14,612.1**	**14,597.0**	**14,538.2**	**14,420.8**	**14,307.0**
Home	9,355.8	10,415.7	11,111.5	11,178.7	11,157.8	11,103.0	11,000.0	10,987.2	10,936.2	10,843.6	10,785.6
Multi-family residential	686.7	742.0	842.6	861.4	878.5	894.7	903.4	906.1	909.8	908.5	897.5
Commercial	1,919.5	2,198.5	2,466.1	2,509.7	2,546.7	2,559.3	2,578.6	2,571.6	2,557.9	2,532.3	2,485.5
Farm	104.8	108.0	112.7	117.0	121.3	125.7	130.1	132.2	134.2	136.3	138.5
Total liabilities	**12,066.7**	**13,464.3**	**14,532.9**	**14,666.8**	**14,704.4**	**14,682.7**	**14,612.1**	**14,597.0**	**14,538.2**	**14,420.8**	**14,307.0**
Household sector	9,035.0	10,039.5	10,724.6	10,797.2	10,794.1	10,757.4	10,678.3	10,675.3	10,636.7	10,562.3	10,504.6
Nonfinancial business	2,886.2	3,272.8	3,651.6	3,707.8	3,749.1	3,762.6	3,770.3	3,756.8	3,734.3	3,691.5	3,639.5
Corporate	773.8	875.9	945.8	960.0	973.9	973.5	983.4	978.3	973.3	960.0	949.9
Nonfarm noncorporate	2,007.5	2,288.9	2,593.1	2,630.8	2,653.9	2,663.4	2,656.8	2,646.4	2,626.7	2,595.2	2,551.2
Farm	104.8	108.0	112.7	117.0	121.3	125.7	130.1	132.2	134.2	136.3	138.5
Federal government	0.0	0.0	0.0	0.0	0.0	0.0	0.0	0.0	0.0	0.0	0.0
REITs	145.5	152.1	156.7	161.8	161.2	162.7	163.5	164.9	167.3	166.9	162.9
Total assets	**12,066.7**	**13,464.3**	**14,532.9**	**14,666.8**	**14,704.4**	**14,682.7**	**14,612.1**	**14,597.0**	**14,538.2**	**14,420.8**	**14,307.0**
Household sector	139.4	122.1	109.1	107.2	114.5	112.3	110.5	108.9	107.1	104.8	102.6
Nonfinancial corporate business	68.3	59.8	41.4	36.8	32.2	27.5	22.9	18.3	13.7	9.1	4.5
Nonfarm noncorporate business	36.2	34.6	42.1	43.2	43.9	44.5	44.6	44.1	43.4	42.5	41.7
State & local governments	151.9	166.4	176.9	176.3	175.9	174.5	171.3	167.6	165.1	163.1	161.5
Federal government	76.6	80.3	82.4	82.9	85.9	88.9	95.8	96.7	102.2	110.0	108.4
Commercial banking	2,958.0	3,403.1	3,644.4	3,684.5	3,660.7	3,853.4	3,841.4	3,853.3	3,897.6	3,795.4	3,819.0
Savings institutions*	1,152.7	1,076.8	1,094.0	1,112.4	1,116.1	884.1	860.6	849.8	752.2	725.8	633.3
Credit unions	219.7	249.7	281.5	290.0	301.0	309.0	314.7	316.3	319.0	317.7	316.7
Property-casualty insurance companies	2.7	3.5	4.8	4.9	5.0	4.7	5.0	5.0	5.0	4.8	4.6
Life insurance companies	285.5	303.8	326.2	330.9	336.4	340.9	342.4	338.6	335.0	332.4	330.1
Private pension funds	9.8	9.5	10.2	10.4	10.7	10.9	11.1	11.6	12.1	15.3	16.1
State & local government retirement funds	16.4	14.5	12.7	12.7	12.6	12.4	12.4	12.3	12.3	12.3	12.3
Government-sponsored enterprises*	588.8	607.2	643.1	659.0	671.6	669.0	701.4	719.1	704.8	701.4	696.7
Agency- & GSE-backed mortgage pools	3,541.9	3,837.3	4,463.5	4,601.4	4,759.5	4,891.9	4,960.8	5,041.8	5,173.3	5,299.7	5,383.0
ABS issuers	2,131.3	2,765.7	2,947.6	2,880.1	2,784.3	2,693.5	2,593.3	2,502.0	2,399.6	2,307.5	2,215.6
Finance companies	541.4	594.4	531.9	525.8	491.6	468.6	447.9	440.2	426.8	415.6	400.9
REITs	146.1	135.8	121.3	108.3	102.4	96.6	75.9	71.5	68.9	63.5	60.0

* FHLB loans to savings institutions are included in other loans and advances.

REIT = Real Estate Investment Trust. GSE = Government Sponsored Enterprise. ABS = Asset Backed Security.

Source: U.S. Federal Reserve
Plunkett Research, Ltd.
www.plunkettresearch.com

Commercial Mortgages by Holder, U.S.: 2005-2009

(In Billions of US$; Amounts Outstanding End of Period; Not Seasonally Adjusted)

Holder	2005	2006	2007	2008				2009			
				Q1	Q2	Q3	Q4	Q1	Q2	Q3	Q4
Total liabilities	**1,919.5**	**2,198.5**	**2,466.1**	**2,509.7**	**2,546.7**	**2,559.3**	**2,578.6**	**2,571.6**	**2,557.9**	**2,532.3**	**2,485.5**
Household sector	187.4	214.3	240.4	244.7	248.3	252.0	251.4	250.7	249.4	246.9	242.3
Nonfinancial corporate business	708.3	800.0	865.3	879.9	896.1	897.8	911.0	908.2	906.2	896.2	888.6
Nonfarm noncorporate business	903.1	1,057.3	1,226.5	1,247.3	1,265.1	1,271.3	1,277.8	1,273.5	1,262.2	1,249.6	1,216.8
REITs	120.7	127.0	134.0	137.9	137.2	138.2	138.4	139.2	140.1	139.7	137.8
Total assets	**1,919.5**	**2,198.5**	**2,466.1**	**2,509.7**	**2,546.7**	**2,559.3**	**2,578.6**	**2,571.6**	**2,557.9**	**2,532.3**	**2,485.5**
Household sector	14.9	17.0	19.1	19.4	19.7	19.8	20.0	19.9	19.8	19.6	19.2
Nonfinancial corporate business	26.3	23.0	15.8	14.2	12.4	10.6	8.8	7.1	5.3	3.5	1.7
Nonfarm noncorporate business	9.9	9.5	11.5	11.8	12.0	12.2	12.2	12.1	11.9	11.6	11.4
State & local governments	12.2	13.3	14.2	14.1	14.1	13.9	13.7	13.4	13.2	13.0	12.9
Federal government	45.2	48.9	51.0	51.6	53.8	56.6	61.4	62.5	65.4	69.0	67.8
Commercial banking	989.4	1,123.2	1,223.6	1,249.6	1,281.6	1,305.6	1,328.5	1,333.6	1,330.5	1,315.6	1,296.4
Savings institutions	100.0	112.4	121.5	132.0	133.7	126.4	128.1	128.2	128.8	126.9	123.9
Property-casualty insurance companies	2.7	3.5	4.8	4.9	5.0	4.7	5.0	5.0	5.0	4.8	4.6
Life insurance companies	224.3	235.4	252.2	256.6	261.8	266.0	267.1	264.1	261.3	259.3	257.5
Private pension funds	6.3	6.2	6.8	6.8	7.0	6.9	7.4	7.5	7.8	10.8	11.4
State & local government retirement funds	5.6	4.9	4.3	4.3	4.3	4.2	4.2	4.2	4.2	4.2	4.2
Agency- & GSE-backed mortgage pools	0.0	0.0	0.0	0.0	0.0	0.0	0.0	0.0	0.0	0.0	0.0
ABS issuers	420.1	523.0	650.5	644.9	639.1	628.7	620.3	613.8	606.6	598.9	582.3
Finance companies	46.0	51.1	54.0	62.3	65.2	66.7	66.6	66.2	65.2	65.1	64.5
REITs	16.8	27.1	37.0	37.2	37.1	37.1	35.3	34.1	32.9	30.0	27.8

REIT = Real Estate Investment Trust. GSE = Government Sponsored Enterprise. ABS = Asset Backed Security.

Source: U.S. Federal Reserve
Plunkett Research, Ltd.
www.plunkettresearch.com

Home Mortgages by Holder, U.S.: 2005-2009

(In Billions of US$; Amounts Outstanding End of Period; Not Seasonally Adjusted)

Holder	2005	2006	2007	2008				2009			
				Q1	Q2	Q3	Q4	Q1	Q2	Q3	Q4
Total liabilities	**9,355.8**	**10,415.7**	**11,111.5**	**11,178.7**	**11,157.8**	**11,103.0**	**11,000.0**	**10,987.2**	**10,936.2**	**10,843.6**	**10,785.6**
Household sector	8,847.7	9,825.2	10,484.2	10,552.5	10,545.8	10,505.4	10,426.9	10,424.6	10,387.3	10,315.5	10,262.3
Nonfinancial corporate business	31.1	39.4	42.2	41.5	38.8	36.3	32.7	30.0	26.8	23.3	20.3
Nonfarm noncorporate business	477.0	551.2	585.1	584.7	573.2	561.2	540.3	532.5	522.2	504.8	503.0
Total assets	**9,355.8**	**10,415.7**	**11,111.5**	**11,178.7**	**11,157.8**	**11,103.0**	**11,000.0**	**10,987.2**	**10,936.2**	**10,843.6**	**10,785.6**
Household sector	117.9	102.9	90.8	88.8	95.2	93.2	91.2	89.2	87.2	85.2	83.2
Nonfinancial corporate business	40.9	35.9	25.0	22.0	19.3	16.5	13.8	11.0	8.2	5.5	2.7
Nonfarm noncorporate business	13.3	12.7	15.4	15.8	16.0	16.3	16.3	16.1	15.9	15.5	15.3
State & local governments	77.5	84.9	90.2	89.9	89.7	89.2	87.5	85.6	84.4	83.3	82.4
Federal government	13.2	13.3	13.7	13.8	14.4	14.5	16.4	16.4	18.9	22.8	22.1
Commercial banking	1,792.1	2,082.1	2,210.5	2,218.4	2,157.7	2,286.0	2,249.0	2,253.4	2,300.0	2,211.7	2,260.8
Savings institutions	953.8	867.8	879.0	884.8	884.5	691.6	666.3	654.9	556.6	534.5	448.6
Credit unions	219.7	249.7	281.5	290.0	301.0	309.0	314.7	316.3	319.0	317.7	316.7
Life insurance companies	7.5	10.3	9.4	9.5	9.6	9.7	10.2	9.7	9.2	8.9	8.5
Private pension funds	1.4	1.3	1.2	1.3	1.3	1.4	1.3	1.7	1.8	1.9	2.0
State & local government retirement funds	5.9	5.2	4.6	4.6	4.5	4.5	4.5	4.4	4.4	4.4	4.4
Government-sponsored enterprises	453.9	457.6	447.9	450.8	451.2	434.9	456.9	470.6	452.2	444.4	438.5
Federally related mortgage pools	3,419.7	3,710.6	4,318.8	4,452.7	4,607.2	4,738.6	4,801.2	4,880.4	5,008.6	5,133.0	5,213.7
ABS issuers	1,621.9	2,139.5	2,171.7	2,112.5	2,025.3	1,947.4	1,858.6	1,775.3	1,680.9	1,598.3	1,525.2
Finance companies	489.8	538.1	472.7	458.0	420.5	395.2	375.4	368.4	356.1	345.1	331.3
REITs	127.4	103.7	79.2	65.9	60.3	55.1	36.7	33.7	32.8	31.5	30.3
Memo:											
Home equity loans included above[2]	914.8	1,066.1	1,129.8	1,126.7	1,126.5	1,115.9	1,113.5	1,095.9	1,074.2	1,051.1	1,032.4
Commercial banking	549.0	653.6	692.3	698.0	711.1	769.8	776.1	769.7	781.2	766.8	761.8
Savings institutions	151.6	137.6	180.5	180.5	180.3	119.7	119.5	116.0	90.0	87.9	80.0
Credit unions	75.9	86.9	94.1	94.5	95.3	97.2	98.7	97.0	96.1	95.0	94.4
ABS issuers	40.4	80.4	68.4	62.0	55.6	50.2	44.2	39.6	35.6	32.4	30.0
Finance companies	98.0	107.6	94.5	91.6	84.1	79.0	75.1	73.7	71.2	69.0	66.3

[1] Mortgages on 1-4 family properties.

[2] Loans made under home equity lines of credit and home equity loans secured by junior liens. Excludes home equity loans held by individuals.

REIT = Real Estate Investment Trust. ABS = Asset Backed Security.

Source: U.S. Federal Reserve
Plunkett Research, Ltd.
www.plunkettresearch.com

Farm Mortgages by Holder, U.S.: 2005-2009

(In Billions of US$; Amounts Outstanding End of Period; Not Seasonally Adjusted)

Holder	2005	2006	2007	2008				2009			
				Q1	Q2	Q3	Q4	Q1	Q2	Q3	Q4
Total liabilities	**104.8**	**108.0**	**112.7**	**117.0**	**121.3**	**125.7**	**130.1**	**132.2**	**134.2**	**136.3**	**138.5**
Total assets	**104.8**	**108.0**	**112.7**	**117.0**	**121.3**	**125.7**	**130.1**	**132.2**	**134.2**	**136.3**	**138.5**
Household sector	6.7	2.2	-0.8	-1.0	-0.4	-0.7	-0.6	-0.2	0.1	0.1	0.2
Nonfarm noncorporate business	0.7	0.7	0.8	0.9	0.9	0.9	0.9	0.9	0.9	0.9	0.8
State & local governments	1.5	1.7	1.8	1.8	1.8	1.7	1.7	1.7	1.7	1.6	1.6
Federal government	3.2	3.2	3.3	3.2	3.3	3.5	3.5	3.5	3.5	3.7	3.9
Commercial banking	37.9	40.1	41.9	43.6	45.3	47.1	48.8	49.6	50.3	51.1	51.9
Savings institutions	0.6	0.7	0.9	0.9	0.9	0.9	0.9	0.9	0.9	0.9	0.9
Life insurance companies	11.3	12.0	12.8	12.9	13.1	13.2	13.4	13.6	13.8	14.0	14.3
State & local government retirement funds	0.0	0.0	0.0	0.0	0.0	0.0	0.0	0.0	0.0	0.0	0.0
Government-sponsored enterprises	42.0	44.2	47.6	50.3	52.2	54.4	56.9	57.6	58.5	59.5	60.4
Agency & GSE-backed mortgage pools	0.8	3.2	4.5	4.5	4.3	4.7	4.7	4.6	4.6	4.5	4.5

GSE = Government Sponsored Enterprise.

Source: U.S. Federal Reserve
Plunkett Research, Ltd.
www.plunkettresearch.com

New Privately-Owned Housing Starts, U.S.: 1980-2009

(In Thousands)

Year	Single Unit	2-4 Units	5+ Units	Total
1980	852.2	109.5	330.5	1,292.2
1981	705.4	91.2	287.7	1,084.2
1982	662.6	80.1	319.6	1,062.2
1983	1,067.6	113.5	522.0	1,703.0
1984	1,084.2	121.4	543.9	1,749.5
1985	1,072.4	93.5	576.0	1,741.8
1986	1,179.4	84.0	542.0	1,805.4
1987	1,146.4	65.1	408.7	1,620.5
1988	1,081.3	58.7	348.0	1,488.1
1989	1,003.3	55.3	317.6	1,376.1
1990	894.8	37.6	260.4	1,192.7
1991	840.4	35.6	137.9	1,013.9
1992	1,029.9	30.9	139.0	1,199.7
1993	1,125.7	29.4	132.6	1,287.6
1994	1,198.4	35.2	223.5	1,457.0
1995	1,076.2	33.8	244.1	1,354.1
1996	1,160.9	45.3	270.8	1,476.8
1997	1,133.7	44.5	295.8	1,474.0
1998	1,271.4	42.6	302.9	1,616.9
1999	1,302.4	31.9	306.6	1,640.9
2000	1,230.9	38.7	299.1	1,568.7
2001	1,273.3	36.6	292.8	1,602.7
2002	1,358.6	38.5	307.9	1,704.9
2003	1,499.0	33.5	315.2	1,847.7
2004	1,610.5	42.3	303.0	1,955.8
2005	1,715.8	41.1	311.4	2,068.3
2006	1,465.4	42.7	292.8	1,800.9
2007	1,046.0	31.7	277.3	1,355.0
2008	622.0	17.5	266.0	905.5
2009	445.1	11.6	97.3	554.0

Note: Single-family estimates prior to 1999 include an upward adjustment of 3.3 percent made to account for structures started in permit-issuing areas without permit authorization.

Source: U.S. Census Bureau
Plunkett Research, Ltd.
www.plunkettresearch.com

Homeownership Rates by Region, U.S.: 1995-2009

(Percent of All Households)

Area	1995	2000	2003	2004	2005	2006	2007	2008	2009
United States	**64.7**	**67.4**	**68.3**	**69.0**	**68.9**	**68.8**	**68.1**	**67.8**	**67.4**
Inside Metropolitan Areas[1]	62.7	65.5	66.5	67.3	67.4	67.4	66.8	66.4	65.9
In Central Cities[1]	49.5	51.4	52.3	53.1	54.2	54.3	53.6	53.2	52.8
Not in Central Cities[1] (suburbs)	71.2	74.0	75.0	75.7	76.4	76.1	75.5	75.1	74.6
Outside Metropolitan Areas[1]	72.7	75.2	75.6	76.3	76.3	75.9	75.1	75.2	74.7
Northeast	62.0	63.4	64.4	65.0	65.2	65.2	65.0	64.6	64.0
Midwest	69.2	72.6	73.2	73.8	73.1	72.7	71.9	71.7	71.0
South	66.7	69.6	70.1	70.9	70.8	70.5	70.1	69.9	69.6
West	59.2	61.7	63.4	64.2	64.4	64.7	63.5	63.0	62.6

[1] Approximately every 10 years, metropolitan/nonmetropolitan area definitions are redefined by the Office of Management and Budget. Therefore metropolitan/nonmetropolitan data for 1986 to 1994, 1995 to 2004, and 2005 and later are not comparable to each other.

Source: U.S. Census Bureau
Plunkett Research, Ltd.
www.plunkettresearch.com

Homeownership Rates by Race & Ethnicity of Householder, U.S.: 2002-2009

(Percent of All Households)

	2002	2003	2004	2005	2006	2007	2008	2009
U.S. Total	**67.9**	**68.3**	**69.0**	**68.9**	**68.8**	**68.1**	**67.8**	**67.4**
White Alone, Total	71.7	72.1	72.8	72.7	72.6	72.0	71.7	71.4
Non-Hispanic White	74.7	75.4	76.0	75.8	75.8	75.2	75.0	74.8
Black, Total	47.4	48.1	49.1	48.2	47.9	47.2	47.4	46.2
All Other Races, Total*	54.5	56.0	58.6	59.2	59.9	59.2	58.5	57.8
American Indian or Alaskan Native	54.0	54.3	55.6	58.2	58.2	56.9	56.5	56.2
Asian or Native Hawaiian/Pacific Islander	54.6	56.3	59.8	60.1	60.8	60.0	59.5	59.3
Hispanic or Latino	47.0	46.7	48.1	49.5	49.7	49.7	49.1	48.4
Non-Hispanic	70.2	70.8	71.5	71.2	71.2	70.5	70.3	69.8

Notes: Beginning in 1996 to 2002, those answering 'other' for race were allocated to one of the 4 race categories-- White, Black, American Indian, Aleut, or Eskimo (one category), or Asian or Native Hawaiian.

* Asian, Native Hawaiian or other Pacific Islander, American Indian or Alaska Native (only one race reported) and Two or more races.

Source: U.S. Census Bureau

Plunkett Research, Ltd.

www.plunkettresearch.com

Homeownership Rates by Age of Householder, U.S.: Selected Years, 1985-2009

(In Percentage of Households)

Age Range	1985	1990	1995	2000	2008	2009
United States, Total	**63.9**	**63.9**	**64.7**	**67.4**	**67.8**	**67.4**
Less than 25years	17.2	15.7	15.9	21.7	23.6	23.3
25 to 29years	37.7	35.2	34.4	38.1	40.0	37.7
30 to 34 years	54.0	51.8	53.1	54.6	53.5	52.5
35 to 39 years	65.4	63.0	62.1	65.0	64.6	63.4
40 to 44 years	71.4	69.8	68.6	70.6	69.4	68.7
45 to 49 years	74.3	73.9	73.7	74.7	73.6	72.3
50 to 54 years	77.5	76.8	77.0	78.5	76.4	76.5
55 to 59years	79.2	78.8	78.8	80.4	79.4	78.6
60 to 64 years	79.9	79.8	80.3	80.3	80.9	80.6
65 to 69 years	79.5	80.0	81.0	83.0	81.6	82.0
70 to 74 years	76.8	78.4	80.9	82.6	81.7	81.9
75 years and over	69.8	72.3	74.6	77.7	78.6	78.9
Less than 35 years.	39.9	38.5	38.6	40.8	41.0	39.7
35 to 44 years	68.1	66.3	65.2	67.9	67.0	66.2
45 to 54 years	75.9	75.2	75.2	76.5	75.0	74.4
55 to 64 years	79.5	79.3	79.5	80.3	80.1	79.5
65 years and over	74.8	76.3	78.1	80.4	80.1	80.5

Source: U.S. Census Bureau
Plunkett Research, Ltd.
www.plunkettresearch.com

Median & Average Sales Price of New Single Family Homes by Region, U.S.: 1985-2009

(In US$)

Period	Median sales price					Average sales price				
	U.S.	Northeast	Midwest	South	West	U.S.	Northeast	Midwest	South	West
1985	84,300	103,300	80,300	75,000	92,600	100,800	121,900	95,400	88,900	111,800
1986	92,000	125,000	88,300	80,200	95,700	111,900	151,300	102,600	95,300	116,100
1987	104,500	140,000	95,000	88,000	111,000	127,200	170,900	115,500	106,600	134,600
1988	112,500	149,000	101,600	92,000	126,500	138,300	179,300	123,700	114,800	155,700
1989	120,000	159,600	108,800	96,400	139,000	148,800	188,600	130,600	123,100	173,900
1990	122,900	159,000	107,900	99,000	147,500	149,800	190,500	133,000	123,500	180,600
1991	120,000	155,900	110,000	100,000	141,100	147,200	188,800	134,500	123,000	176,400
1992	121,500	169,000	115,600	105,500	130,400	144,100	194,900	136,400	126,900	157,800
1993	126,500	162,600	125,000	115,000	135,000	147,700	183,600	143,100	133,600	161,900
1994	130,000	169,000	132,900	116,900	140,400	154,500	200,500	152,700	136,800	168,900
1995	133,900	180,000	134,000	124,500	141,000	158,700	216,600	157,200	142,000	169,800
1996	140,000	186,900	137,500	125,000	153,900	166,400	226,800	158,100	143,100	185,900
1997	146,000	190,000	149,900	129,600	160,000	176,200	234,100	173,000	151,400	198,200
1998	152,500	200,000	157,500	135,800	163,500	181,900	240,100	179,200	159,700	200,500
1999	161,000	210,500	164,000	145,900	173,700	195,600	247,900	186,800	173,000	221,700
2000	169,000	227,400	169,700	148,000	196,400	207,000	274,800	199,300	179,000	238,900
2001	175,200	246,400	172,600	155,400	213,600	213,200	294,300	201,300	185,700	250,000
2002	187,600	264,300	178,000	163,400	238,500	228,700	301,300	209,800	197,500	276,500
2003	195,000	264,500	184,300	168,100	260,900	246,300	315,700	218,200	208,900	306,800
2004	221,000	315,800	205,000	181,100	283,100	274,500	366,100	240,800	232,800	340,000
2005	240,900	343,800	216,900	197,300	332,600	297,000	397,000	249,800	249,200	388,700
2006	246,500	346,000	213,500	208,200	337,700	305,900	428,300	257,100	257,700	405,900
2007	247,900	320,200	208,600	217,700	330,900	313,600	437,700	256,800	269,800	403,700
2008	232,100	343,600	198,900	203,700	294,800	292,600	475,500	250,000	253,400	361,500
2009	215,900	297,400	189,700	193,300	264,800	270,400	409,600	224,600	241,000	322,300

Source: U.S. Census Bureau
Plunkett Research, Ltd.
www.plunkettresearch.com

New Single Family Homes Sold by Region, U.S.: 1985-2009

(Not Seasonally Adjusted; In Thousands.)

Period	U.S.	Northeast	Midwest	South	West
1985	688	112	82	323	171
1986	750	136	96	322	196
1987	671	117	97	271	186
1988	676	101	97	276	202
1989	650	86	102	260	202
1990	534	71	89	225	149
1991	509	57	93	215	144
1992	610	65	116	259	170
1993	666	60	123	295	188
1994	670	61	123	295	191
1995	667	55	125	300	187
1996	757	74	137	337	209
1997	804	78	140	363	223
1998	886	81	164	398	243
1999	880	76	168	395	242
2000	877	71	155	406	244
2001	908	66	164	439	239
2002	973	65	185	450	273
2003	1,086	79	189	511	307
2004	1,203	83	210	562	348
2005	1,283	81	205	638	358
2006	1,051	63	161	559	267
2007	776	65	118	411	181
2008	485	35	70	266	114
2009	374	31	54	202	87

Note: Components may not add to total because of rounding. Estimates prior to 1999 include an upward adjustment of 3.3 percent made to account for houses sold in permit-issuing areas that will never have a permit authorization.

Source: U.S. Census Bureau

Plunkett Research, Ltd.

www.plunkettresearch.com

New Single Family Homes Sold by Type of Financing, U.S.: 1988-2009

(In Thousands)

Period	Total Sold	Type of Financing				
		Conventional*	FHA Insured	VA Guaranteed	Rural Housing Service	Cash
1988	676	437	127	44	6	62
1989	650	416	118	44	14	58
1990	534	337	105	33	10	50
1991	509	329	92	36	9	43
1992	610	428	86	48	7	41
1993	666	476	92	55	6	37
1994	670	490	78	51	9	41
1995	667	490	79	50	9	39
1996	757	570	89	51	9	38
1997	804	616	90	47	6	46
1998	886	693	90	46	9	48
1999	880	689	106	37	6	41
2000	877	695	108	30	4	40
2001	908	726	106	35	2	39
2002	973	788	106	34	4	42
2003	1,086	911	94	36	4	41
2004	1,203	1,047	77	28	6	46
2005	1,283	1,151	51	28	1	52
2006	1,051	949	38	25	1	38
2007	776	695	28	24	2	30
2008	485	358	77	27	NA	23
2009	374	235	91	34	NA	15

* Includes houses reporting other types of financing. Beginning in 2005, also includes Rural Housing Service.

Note: Estimates prior to 1999 include an upward adjustment of 3.3 percent made to account for houses sold in permit-issuing areas that will never have a permit authorization.

Source: U.S. Census Bureau
Plunkett Research, Ltd.
www.plunkettresearch.com

New Single Family Homes for Sale at End of Period, by Region, U.S.: 1985-2009

(Not Seasonally Adjusted; In Thousands.)

Period	U.S.	Northeast	Midwest	South	West
1985	350	66	34	172	79
1986	361	88	32	153	87
1987	370	103	39	149	79
1988	371	112	43	133	82
1989	366	108	41	123	93
1990	321	77	42	105	97
1991	284	62	41	97	83
1992	267	48	41	104	74
1993	295	53	48	121	73
1994	340	55	63	140	82
1995	374	62	69	158	86
1996	326	38	67	146	74
1997	287	26	65	127	69
1998	300	28	63	142	68
1999	315	28	64	153	70
2000	301	28	65	146	62
2001	310	28	70	142	69
2002	344	36	77	161	70
2003	377	29	97	172	79
2004	431	30	111	200	91
2005	515	47	109	249	109
2006	537	54	97	267	119
2007	496	48	79	248	121
2008	352	37	57	175	83
2009	232	27	38	118	49

Note: Components may not add to total because of rounding. Estimates prior to 1999 include an upward adjustment of 3.3 percent made to account for houses for sale in permit-issuing areas that will never have a permit authorization.

Source: U.S. Census Bureau
Plunkett Research, Ltd.
www.plunkettresearch.com

Placements of New Manufactured Homes, U.S.: 1995-2009

(In Thousands)

Year	Total*	Single Units	Double-Wide
1995	319.4	163.0	152.1
1996	337.7	163.4	168.9
1997	336.3	144.0	186.2
1998	373.7	149.6	218.1
1999	338.3	122.5	213.0
2000	280.9	88.3	190.3
2001	196.2	53.3	139.3
2002	174.3	41.1	128.7
2003	139.8	29.4	106.0
2004	124.4	28.2	91.7
2005	122.9	28.7	89.4
2006	112.4	28.9	79.2
2007	94.8	28.6	63.1
2008	79.3	27.4	49.9
2009	52.5	19.3	32.1

* Includes manufactured homes with more than two sections.

Source: U.S. Census Bureau
Plunkett Research, Ltd.
www.plunkettresearch.com

Price Deflator (Fisher) Index of New One-Family Houses Under Construction, U.S.: 1970-February 2010

(2005 = 100)

Year	Annual		Monthly											
	Ann. Index	% Chg.	Jan	Feb	Mar	Apr	May	Jun	Jul	Aug	Sep	Oct	Nov	Dec
1970	15.4	2.7%	15.1	15.0	15.2	15.6	15.8	16.1	15.5	15.1	15.0	15.1	15.3	15.5
1971	16.3	5.6%	15.4	15.8	15.9	15.9	16.0	16.1	16.2	16.5	16.5	16.6	16.7	16.9
1972	17.5	7.3%	16.9	17.0	17.1	17.1	17.1	17.1	17.3	17.5	17.5	17.9	18.0	18.3
1973	19.1	9.5%	18.3	18.3	18.3	18.7	18.7	18.9	19.2	19.5	19.7	19.8	19.9	19.9
1974	21.1	10.1%	20.0	20.2	20.7	20.3	20.5	21.1	21.2	21.2	21.3	21.5	21.9	21.9
1975	22.9	8.8%	22.3	22.3	22.3	22.6	22.9	23.1	23.1	22.9	23.1	23.2	23.4	23.6
1976	24.4	6.4%	23.4	23.4	23.5	23.9	24.3	24.5	24.7	24.6	24.6	24.8	25.0	25.2
1977	27.0	10.6%	25.6	25.7	25.8	26.0	26.4	26.9	27.2	27.6	27.8	28.0	28.2	28.5
1978	30.6	13.5%	28.9	29.2	29.6	30.0	30.2	30.6	30.9	31.2	31.4	31.7	32.0	32.2
1979	34.3	12.1%	32.4	32.5	32.8	33.2	33.8	34.4	34.8	35.2	35.4	35.6	35.8	36.1
1980	37.9	10.3%	36.5	36.7	37.0	37.3	37.4	37.7	38.0	38.1	38.5	38.9	39.3	39.5
1981	40.5	7.0%	39.8	40.1	40.1	40.3	40.4	40.5	40.7	40.7	40.8	40.9	41.1	41.0
1982	41.7	3.0%	41.3	41.3	41.5	41.5	41.7	41.7	41.7	42.0	42.3	42.1	42.1	42.2
1983	42.9	2.7%	42.5	42.7	42.8	42.6	42.5	42.6	42.7	42.8	42.9	43.3	43.3	43.4
1984	44.5	3.9%	43.8	44.1	44.2	44.1	44.1	44.2	44.4	44.8	45.0	45.0	45.0	45.0
1985	45.4	1.9%	45.2	45.3	45.5	45.2	45.0	45.0	45.0	45.2	45.4	45.7	45.9	46.1
1986	47.4	4.5%	46.5	46.6	46.7	46.8	47.0	47.3	47.6	47.6	47.8	48.2	48.6	48.8
1987	49.6	4.6%	49.2	49.2	49.2	49.3	49.4	49.5	49.7	49.8	49.8	50.0	50.2	50.6
1988	51.6	4.0%	51.2	51.4	51.4	51.3	51.4	51.4	51.4	51.6	51.8	51.9	52.2	52.3
1989	53.7	4.0%	52.6	53.0	53.0	53.4	53.7	53.7	53.9	53.8	53.9	54.1	54.1	54.5
1990	55.4	3.2%	55.0	55.0	55.1	55.1	55.1	55.4	55.8	55.8	55.7	55.7	55.8	55.7
1991	55.9	0.8%	55.8	55.7	55.4	55.4	55.5	55.8	56.0	56.2	56.3	56.2	56.1	56.1
1992	57.0	2.0%	56.4	56.5	56.5	56.6	56.5	56.7	56.9	57.0	57.2	57.7	58.0	58.3
1993	59.8	4.9%	58.7	58.9	59.0	59.1	59.3	59.7	59.9	60.1	60.3	60.5	60.9	61.1
1994	62.5	4.4%	61.3	61.5	61.5	61.5	61.7	62.1	62.3	62.7	63.1	63.4	63.8	64.4
1995	65.2	4.4%	64.6	64.8	64.8	64.9	65.0	65.2	65.1	65.4	65.6	65.6	65.6	65.6
1996	66.4	1.9%	65.6	65.8	65.7	65.6	65.8	66.2	66.6	66.8	66.8	67.0	67.1	67.3
1997	68.4	2.9%	67.6	67.6	67.6	67.8	67.8	68.1	68.4	68.6	69.0	69.2	69.3	69.3
1998	70.2	2.6%	69.4	69.2	69.2	69.4	69.5	70.0	70.3	70.4	70.4	70.8	71.2	71.6
1999	73.3	4.5%	72.0	72.1	72.3	72.7	73.0	73.3	73.6	73.6	73.7	73.9	74.3	74.6
2000	76.7	4.6%	75.5	75.8	76.0	76.2	76.4	76.7	76.9	76.9	77.1	77.2	77.3	77.7
2001	80.2	4.6%	78.2	78.4	78.6	79.1	79.7	80.2	80.8	81.6	81.6	82.1	82.1	81.8
2002	82.1	2.4%	81.2	81.4	81.7	81.8	82.1	82.2	82.1	81.8	82.3	82.9	82.6	83.2
2003	86.1	4.9%	84.1	84.6	85.1	85.3	85.3	85.4	85.4	86.1	86.8	87.4	88.1	88.5
2004	93.0	8.0%	89.1	89.4	90.3	91.1	92.2	92.8	93.4	93.9	94.4	94.9	95.6	96.3
2005	100.0	7.5%	96.5	96.3	96.9	97.2	98.3	99.3	100.7	100.8	101.3	101.9	102.8	104.1
2006	106.2	6.2%	104.5	104.7	105.7	105.9	106.1	106.1	105.6	105.9	107.0	107.4	107.5	107.8
2007	107.2	0.9%	107.8	107.9	108.2	107.9	106.9	106.5	106.7	107.0	107.2	107.2	106.7	106.4
2008	104.1	-2.9%	105.8	105.5	105.2	104.8	105.2	104.0	104.1	103.4	102.6	102.2	102.2	102.6
2009	99.5	-4.4%	102.4	101.8	101.8	100.8	99.3	98.4	98.0	97.9	98.3	98.6	99.0	99.5
2010	--	--	99.8	99.5	--	--	--	--	--	--	--	--	--	--

Fisher Ideal Index (Price Deflator): This index helps answers the question, "What is the (unbiased) value of today's homes being constructed in constant dollars?" In doing this it attempts to eliminate two kinds of problems associated with two other indexes: the tendency to overstate inflation (Laspeyres); and the tendency to understate inflation (Paasche). The Fisher Ideal index is the geometric average of a Laspeyres and Paasche indexes for the same time period. The geometric average is calculated by multiplying the Laspeyres index by the Paasche index and then taking the square root of the result. The biases associated with each component index are minimized by calculating the geometric average.

Source: U.S. Census Bureau
Plunkett Research, Ltd.
www.plunkettresearch.com

Constant Quality (Laspeyres) Price Index of New One-Family Houses Under Construction, U.S.: 1970-February 2010

(2005 = 100)

Year	Annual		Monthly											
	Ann. Index	% Chg.	Jan	Feb	Mar	Apr	May	Jun	Jul	Aug	Sep	Oct	Nov	Dec
1970	15.9	2.7%	15.6	15.6	15.7	16.1	16.3	16.7	16.0	15.6	15.5	15.6	15.8	16.0
1971	16.8	5.6%	15.9	16.4	16.5	16.6	16.6	16.7	16.7	17.2	17.1	17.2	17.3	17.5
1972	18.0	6.9%	17.6	17.6	17.6	17.6	17.6	17.7	17.9	18.0	18.2	18.5	18.7	18.9
1973	19.8	9.9%	18.9	18.9	19.1	19.3	19.5	19.6	19.9	20.2	20.4	20.5	20.6	20.6
1974	21.8	10.1%	20.8	20.9	21.4	21.1	21.3	21.8	22.0	22.0	22.1	22.4	22.6	22.8
1975	23.7	8.8%	23.1	23.1	23.1	23.3	23.7	23.8	23.8	23.7	23.9	24.0	24.2	24.4
1976	25.2	6.4%	24.2	24.2	24.3	24.6	25.1	25.4	25.5	25.5	25.5	25.7	25.9	26.1
1977	28.2	12.0%	26.6	26.8	27.0	27.2	27.6	27.9	28.3	28.5	28.7	29.0	29.3	29.7
1978	31.7	12.4%	30.0	30.3	30.5	30.8	31.2	31.3	31.6	32.0	32.5	32.9	33.3	33.6
1979	35.7	12.8%	33.9	34.2	34.4	34.8	35.2	35.7	36.2	36.5	36.8	37.0	37.3	37.6
1980	39.8	11.3%	38.1	38.4	38.6	39.0	39.2	39.6	40.1	40.3	40.5	40.7	41.0	41.3
1981	42.6	7.1%	41.6	41.9	42.0	42.3	42.6	42.7	42.7	42.8	43.0	43.2	43.5	43.5
1982	43.4	1.9%	43.4	43.4	43.5	43.6	43.5	43.4	43.2	43.4	43.6	43.5	43.7	43.7
1983	44.7	2.8%	44.0	44.1	44.0	44.0	44.3	44.4	44.6	44.7	44.9	45.2	45.4	45.6
1984	46.7	4.6%	45.8	46.0	46.1	46.1	46.2	46.5	46.5	46.9	47.3	47.5	47.6	47.5
1985	47.9	2.5%	47.7	47.5	47.6	47.5	47.4	47.5	47.6	47.8	48.0	48.2	48.4	48.8
1986	50.4	5.2%	49.1	49.2	49.3	49.5	49.8	50.2	50.4	50.6	50.8	51.1	51.5	51.8
1987	52.7	4.6%	52.1	52.1	52.2	52.4	52.4	52.6	52.7	52.8	52.8	53.0	53.3	53.7
1988	54.5	3.5%	54.1	54.3	54.1	54.1	54.3	54.3	54.3	54.5	54.8	54.9	55.2	55.2
1989	56.4	3.4%	55.4	55.6	55.8	56.1	56.3	56.3	56.5	56.6	56.8	56.8	56.8	57.0
1990	58.0	2.9%	57.2	57.4	57.5	57.6	57.6	57.9	58.2	58.2	58.2	58.1	58.5	58.5
1991	58.2	0.2%	58.5	58.4	58.0	57.9	58.0	58.3	58.4	58.5	58.6	58.3	58.2	58.1
1992	58.9	1.2%	58.4	58.4	58.4	58.5	58.4	58.5	58.5	58.7	58.9	59.4	59.7	60.0
1993	61.8	4.9%	60.4	60.7	60.8	60.9	61.1	61.4	61.8	61.9	62.1	62.5	63.0	63.2
1994	64.6	4.6%	63.3	63.5	63.5	63.5	63.8	64.2	64.4	64.7	65.1	65.5	66.0	66.7
1995	67.3	4.3%	67.0	67.0	67.0	67.0	67.2	67.3	67.2	67.4	67.6	67.7	67.6	67.6
1996	68.6	1.9%	67.9	67.9	67.9	67.7	67.9	68.3	68.8	69.0	69.0	69.2	69.3	69.4
1997	70.6	2.9%	69.8	69.8	69.8	70.0	70.1	70.3	70.6	70.7	71.2	71.4	71.6	71.6
1998	72.5	2.6%	71.6	71.4	71.4	71.7	71.8	72.4	72.7	72.7	72.7	73.0	73.5	74.0
1999	72.7	0.3%	71.3	71.4	71.7	72.0	72.4	72.7	73.0	73.2	73.2	73.4	73.5	73.8
2000	75.9	4.4%	74.7	75.0	75.2	75.3	75.5	75.9	76.0	76.1	76.4	76.5	76.7	77.1
2001	79.7	5.0%	77.7	78.0	78.2	78.6	79.2	79.6	80.0	80.8	81.0	81.5	81.5	81.2
2002	81.7	2.5%	80.6	80.9	81.2	81.4	81.7	81.9	81.7	81.4	81.8	82.3	81.9	82.6
2003	85.9	5.1%	83.7	84.5	85.0	85.3	85.2	85.3	85.1	85.9	86.5	87.1	87.8	88.4
2004	93.1	8.4%	88.9	89.4	90.5	91.4	92.5	93.0	93.6	94.1	94.5	95.1	95.7	96.5
2005	100.0	7.4%	96.7	96.4	96.9	97.1	98.3	99.3	100.7	100.8	101.2	101.8	102.8	104.0
2006	106.0	6.0%	104.4	104.7	105.6	105.7	105.9	105.8	105.4	105.9	106.9	107.3	107.5	107.8
2007	107.0	0.9%	107.9	108.1	108.4	108.0	106.8	106.3	106.4	106.6	106.7	106.7	106.2	105.8
2008	103.3	-3.5%	105.1	104.9	104.5	103.8	104.1	103.0	103.3	102.7	101.8	101.4	101.6	102.0
2009	98.1	-5.0%	101.7	100.8	100.5	99.2	97.7	96.9	96.7	96.6	96.9	97.2	97.5	97.9
2010	--	--	98.3	98.2	--	--	--	--	--	--	--	--	--	--

Notes: Laspeyres Price Index (Constant Quality). This index answers the question, "How much is the sales price today for the same quality house as in the base year?" The base year we are now using is 1996; its index value is set to 100.0. Quality includes not only the physical size and amenities of the house, but also its geographic location. A hypothetical calculation is made in which the base year kind of house is held constant over time while its selling price is calculated in current dollars.

Source: U.S. Census Bureau

Plunkett Research, Ltd.

www.plunkettresearch.com

Constant Quality (Laspeyres) Price Index of New One-Family Houses Sold Including Value of Lot, U.S.: 1970-2009

(2005 = 100; Index Based on Kinds of Houses Sold in 2005)

Year	Quarterly					Annual			
	Annual	1Q	2Q	3Q	4Q	NE	MW	S	W
1970	14.9	14.7	15.2	14.8	15.0	13.4	17.9	18.2	10.2
1971	15.7	15.3	15.7	15.9	16.1	14.3	18.6	19.6	10.5
1972	16.8	16.4	16.5	16.8	17.4	15.4	19.8	20.8	11.1
1973	18.2	17.5	18.0	18.7	19.0	16.6	21.3	22.2	12.5
1974	19.9	19.4	19.8	20.3	20.8	18.1	23.1	24.0	14.1
1975	22.1	21.6	21.9	22.1	22.7	19.6	25.4	26.4	15.9
1976	24.0	23.1	23.8	24.5	24.9	20.4	27.7	28.2	17.6
1977	27.0	25.8	26.7	27.2	28.8	21.8	30.8	31.0	20.8
1978	30.9	29.2	30.4	31.7	32.7	24.2	35.2	34.8	24.7
1979	35.3	33.6	35.4	36.0	37.4	27.5	39.4	39.8	28.4
1980	38.9	38.1	38.7	39.6	39.9	30.2	41.2	44.4	31.9
1981	42.0	41.7	42.2	42.2	42.6	32.8	45.1	48.3	33.8
1982	43.0	43.6	43.4	43.0	42.6	34.0	46.4	49.8	34.3
1983	43.9	43.7	43.8	44.5	44.5	36.1	46.2	51.2	34.9
1984	45.7	44.9	45.8	46.3	46.8	39.2	49.0	52.8	36.2
1985	46.2	46.6	46.3	46.1	46.9	43.1	48.2	53.9	36.4
1986	48.0	47.2	48.4	49.1	48.7	49.5	51.0	55.5	37.3
1987	50.6	49.9	50.8	51.5	51.7	56.2	54.4	57.6	39.3
1988	52.5	52.4	52.6	53.2	53.1	57.6	56.8	58.8	41.4
1989	54.6	54.2	55.2	55.2	54.9	59.2	58.1	60.5	44.0
1990	55.7	56.1	55.5	56.3	55.7	58.0	58.6	60.6	46.2
1991	56.4	55.9	57.0	57.5	56.2	56.2	60.1	61.8	46.4
1992	57.2	56.6	56.6	56.7	58.2	60.5	61.2	62.4	46.7
1993	59.4	57.9	59.9	59.7	59.6	57.4	65.2	65.5	47.8
1994	62.9	62.5	62.9	63.1	63.4	62.1	69.4	68.1	51.9
1995	64.3	63.7	64.2	64.7	63.6	62.3	70.9	70.1	52.7
1996	66.0	65.9	65.7	67.1	65.6	63.2	72.5	71.2	55.3
1997	67.5	66.6	67.8	67.5	67.1	65.9	74.3	72.7	56.5
1998	69.2	68.8	68.2	69.4	70.1	66.1	76.0	74.4	58.4
1999	72.8	71.1	72.7	73.0	73.0	69.1	79.5	78.1	62.0
2000	75.6	74.3	74.5	75.8	76.2	73.0	83.5	80.7	64.4
2001	77.9	76.9	77.3	78.2	79.1	76.7	84.4	82.8	67.1
2002	81.4	80.9	81.3	80.6	83.8	80.2	86.1	86.3	71.5
2003	86.0	84.3	84.6	87.1	88.5	84.3	90.6	89.4	78.2
2004	92.8	91.3	91.8	94.8	95.1	91.6	96.7	94.4	88.2
2005	100.0	96.5	99.2	101.4	103.9	100.0	100.0	100.0	100.0
2006	104.8	104.1	105.7	104.8	103.8	102.6	102.9	105.4	105.2
2007	104.9	107.2	105.9	103.0	102.1	101.5	102.8	107.5	102.6
2008	99.5	98.8	102.2	100.2	95.7	100.8	98.9	103.7	92.7
2009	95.0	92.7	96.2	94.3	95.9	98.1	95.3	101.1	84.5

Notes: Laspeyres Price Index (Constant Quality). This index answers the question, "How much is the sales price today for the same quality house as in the base year?" The base year we are now using is 2005; its index value is set to 100.0. Quality includes not only the physical size and amenities of the house, but also its geographic location. A hypothetical calculation is made in which the base year kind of house is held constant over time while its selling price is calculated in current dollars.

Source: U.S. Census Bureau

Plunkett Research, Ltd.

www.plunkettresearch.com

Absorption Rates of U.S. Privately Financed, Nonsubsidized, Unfurnished Rental Apartments: 2003-3rd Quarter 2009

(Buildings with Five Units or More; Percents Computed Using Unrounded Data)

Quarter of Completion	Unfurnished Apartments Completed		Seasonally adjusted: rented within 3 months		Not seasonally adjusted; rented within:							
					3 months		6 months		9 months		12 months	
	Total	90% C.I. (+/-)*	%	90% C.I. (+/-)*	%	90% C.I. (+/-)*	%	90% C.I. (+/-)*	%	90% C.I. (+/-)*	%	90% C.I. (+/-)*
2009												
III[P]	43,500	4,290	52	1.8	52	1.8	NA	NA	NA	NA	NA	NA
II	48,300	4,010	48	2.0	51	2.1	69	1.9	NA	NA	NA	NA
I	28,400	2,770	52	2.4	51	2.4	74	2.9	83	1.9	NA	NA
2008												
IV	43,400	3,550	45	1.7	44	1.7	66	1.9	80	1.4	88	1.2
III	37,300	3,050	55	2.1	53	2.0	67	1.9	77	1.3	86	1.2
II	37,200	3,040	48	1.8	52	2.0	71	2.0	80	1.4	86	1.2
I	28,500	2,330	53	2.0	51	1.9	71	2.0	81	1.4	89	1.2
2007												
IV	24,000	1,960	57	2.2	57	2.2	76	2.1	89	1.5	94	1.3
III	26,100	2,140	55	2.1	53	2.0	71	2.0	82	1.4	90	1.3
II	26,500	2,170	53	2.0	59	2.2	76	2.1	85	1.5	90	1.3
I	28,200	6,370	53	5.6	51	5.4	75	4.8	89	2.4	93	1.6
2006												
IV	32,300	3,620	54	5.2	54	5.2	75	3.7	88	2.0	94	1.6
III	33,800	3,010	52	2.2	52	2.2	67	2.3	80	2.0	87	1.7
II	28,600	2,340	61	2.4	67	2.6	83	2.3	91	1.6	95	1.3
I	21,600	2,140	62	3.3	60	3.2	81	2.4	90	1.5	95	0.9
2005												
IV	25,600	2,370	63	2.9	59	2.7	81	2.0	90	1.6	95	1.2
III	30,500	5,340	63	5.7	64	5.8	82	2.8	91	1.7	96	0.9
II	30,800	4,900	65	3.6	71	3.9	88	2.0	93	1.2	97	0.7
I	26,100	3,350	61	3.8	59	3.7	84	2.9	93	1.9	96	1.2
2004												
IV	32,500	5,390	63	6.8	58	6.2	79	4.3	90	2.5	95	1.3
III	44,700	9,250	64	4.0	67	4.2	83	3.6	91	3.7	94	2.8
II	42,500	6,740	59	5.0	62	5.2	81	4.3	87	3.6	92	2.9
I	34,000	3,800	61	4.7	60	4.7	82	3.6	91	3.0	94	2.7
2003												
IV	38,800	6,360	63	4.3	58	3.9	78	4.1	88	3.6	92	3.8
III	42,500	6,060	56	4.3	59	4.5	74	4.6	84	4.2	91	3.6
II	47,600	5,820	61	4.3	65	4.6	85	2.5	91	2.0	96	1.0
I	37,600	4,620	62	4.9	60	5.1	79	3.9	87	3.8	94	2.3

P = Preliminary. NA = Not Available. Z = Fewer than 50 units or less than one-half of 1 percent.

* A 90-percent confidence interval is a measure of an estimate's variability. The larger the confidence interval in relation to the size of the estimate, the less reliable the estimate.

Source: U.S. Census Bureau

Plunkett Research, Ltd.

www.plunkettresearch.com

Absorption Rates of U.S. Condominium & Cooperative Apartments: 2003-3rd Quarter 2009

(Not Seasonally Adjusted; Privately Financed, Unsubsidized Condominium & Cooperative Apartments in Buildings with Five Units or More; Percents Computed Using Unrounded Data; Latest Year Available)

Quarter of Comp-letion	Total condo. & coop. apartments completed	90% C.I. (+/-)* (# of apts.)	% of all comp-letions	90% C.I. (+/-)* (%)	% ab-sorbed 3 mos.	90% C.I. (+/-)* (%)	% ab-sorbed 6 mos.	90% C.I. (+/-)* (%)	% ab-sorbed 9 mos.	90% C.I. (+/-)* (%)	% ab-sorbed 12 mos.	90% C.I. (+/-)* (%)
2009												
III[P]	9,600	1,340	13	1.6	45	1.4	NA	NA	NA	NA	NA	NA
II	9,600	1,650	13	1.9	36	1.9	49	2.4	NA	NA	NA	NA
I	12,400	1,010	23	2.1	42	2.9	57	2.0	65	1.0	NA	NA
2008												
IV	17,400	1,840	23	1.9	39	3.9	47	3.4	60	3.9	70	2.3
III	19,600	2,070	26	2.2	56	5.7	63	4.5	70	4.6	76	2.5
II	11,800	1,250	19	1.6	49	5.0	61	4.4	70	4.6	76	2.5
I	21,000	2,220	34	2.8	51	5.2	71	5.1	77	4.9	82	2.6
2007												
IV	22,100	2,330	35	2.9	56	5.7	68	4.9	75	4.9	79	2.6
III	26,900	2,840	37	3.1	63	6.4	72	5.2	80	5.2	87	2.8
II	20,900	2,210	37	3.1	64	6.5	74	5.3	79	5.2	83	2.7
I	21,100	4,100	35	6.7	60	6.4	72	4.0	77	4.2	82	3.4
2006												
IV	30,700	4,080	39	4.4	66	3.0	76	3.5	87	1.7	NA	NA
III	22,300	2,010	30	2.9	68	4.4	81	2.9	88	1.6	92	1.1
II	26,800	2,830	38	3.1	66	6.7	77	5.6	83	5.4	88	2.9
I	24,900	4,980	41	6.5	64	7.5	79	4.7	86	3.9	89	3.4
2005												
IV	23,100	4,300	35	4.9	71	5.9	81	5.0	87	4.5	91	4.5
III	19,300	3,750	28	6.0	79	6.3	86	5.3	89	5.2	93	5.1
II	26,200	6,230	36	6.9	79	10.6	88	7.9	91	7.4	93	6.0
I	13,200	2,650	26	5.9	75	8.6	90	4.1	94	3.4	96	2.9
2004												
IV	14,000	4,120	22	6.6	75	10.0	85	9.4	93	6.2	96	3.1
III	17,800	3,300	21	3.8	66	8.2	82	8.5	91	3.8	95	2.7
II	20,700	4,930	25	5.8	75	11.4	86	7.1	93	3.3	96	2.0
I	8,900	1,960	16	3.5	78	6.4	88	5.6	92	3.9	96	1.8
2003												
IV	9,300	2,200	16	4.1	76	6.5	87	4.3	93	2.0	95	1.5
III	9,800	2,470	14	3.8	75	4.7	84	3.5	90	2.8	96	1.7
II	10,900	4,330	15	8.4	76	6.7	87	4.1	90	4.4	96	3.9
I	11,100	3,370	18	5.4	69	2.1	78	2.5	86	1.8	94	3.1

P = Preliminary. NA = Not Available.

* A 90-percent confidence interval is a measure of an estimate's variability. The larger the confidence interval in relation to the size of the estimate, the less reliable the estimate.

Source: U.S. Census Bureau
Plunkett Research, Ltd.
www.plunkettresearch.com

Rental & Homeowner Vacancy Rates by Area, U.S.: 1995-2009

(Percentage of Rental Units; End of Year)

Area	1995	2000	2003	2004	2005	2006	2007	2008	2009
United States	**7.6**	**8.0**	**9.8**	**10.2**	**9.8**	**9.7**	**9.7**	**10.0**	**10.6**
Inside Metropolitan Areas	7.6	7.7	9.6	10.2	9.7	9.7	9.8	10.0	10.7
In Principal Cities[1]	8.4	8.2	10.0	10.8	10.0	10.0	10.0	10.2	11.1
Outside Principal Cities[1] (suburbs)	6.6	7.2	9.2	9.5	9.4	9.3	9.6	9.7	10.2
Outside Metropolitan Areas	7.9	9.5	10.6	10.2	10.5	10.0	9.3	10.4	10.4
Northeast	7.2	5.6	6.6	7.3	6.5	7.1	7.0	6.9	7.2
Midwest	7.2	8.8	10.8	12.2	12.6	12.4	11.5	10.8	10.7
South	8.3	10.5	12.5	12.6	11.8	11.6	12.3	13.0	13.6
West	7.5	5.8	7.7	7.5	7.3	6.8	6.7	7.5	9.0

[1] Approximately every 10 years, metropolitan/nonmetropolitan area definitions are redefined by the Office of Management and Budget. Therefore metropolitan/nonmetropolitan data prior to 1986, 1986 to 1994, 1995 to 2004, and 2005 and later are not comparable to each other.

Source: U.S. Census Bureau
Plunkett Research, Ltd.
www.plunkettresearch.com

U.S. Construction Industry Employment: 2004-2009

(In Thousands; Not Seasonally Adjusted)

NAICS Code	Industry Type	2004	2005	2006	2007	2008	2009
23	**Construction**	**6,976.0**	**7,336.0**	**7,691.0**	**7,630.0**	**7,162.0**	**6,037.0**
236	Construction of buildings	1,630.0	1,711.9	1,804.9	1,774.2	1,641.7	1,365.6
2361	Residential building	895.8	960.3	1,008.8	949.0	816.1	639.4
236115	New single-family general contractors	561.8	601.3	618.2	567.2	466.8	341.5
236116	New multifamily general contractors	28.2	31.1	32.8	30.9	29.2	25.3
236118	Residential remodelers	272.7	288.7	310.2	305.8	284.1	246.5
2362	Nonresidential building	734.2	751.5	796.1	825.2	825.6	726.2
23621	Industrial building	168.0	167.5	178.6	186.6	186.4	169.7
23622	Commercial building	566.2	584.0	617.5	638.7	639.2	556.5
237	**Heavy & civil engineering construction**	**907.4**	**951.2**	**985.1**	**1,005.4**	**964.5**	**846.9**
2371	Utility system construction	374.6	403.0	430.0	452.8	447.8	400.4
23711	Water & sewer system construction	188.9	199.6	209.8	209.1	192.7	164.3
23712	Oil & gas pipeline construction	68.7	70.5	84.3	99.6	109.1	107.1
23713	Power & communication system construction	117.1	132.9	135.9	144.0	146.1	129.0
2372	Land subdivision	85.8	91.8	95.7	93.2	79.6	62.0
2373	Highway, street & bridge construction	347.0	350.8	348.3	344.5	327.3	286.4
2379	Other heavy construction	100.0	105.7	111.2	115.0	109.8	98.1
238	**Specialty trade contractors**	**4,438.6**	**4,673.1**	**4,901.1**	**4,850.2**	**4,555.8**	**3,824.4**
238 pt.1	Residential specialty trade contractors	2,125.8	2,302.2	2,396.8	2,277.1	1,999.2	1,629.6
238 pt.2	Nonresidential specialty trade contractors	2,312.8	2,370.9	2,504.4	2,573.0	2,556.7	2,194.9
2381	Building foundation & exterior contractors	1,009.8	1,083.4	1,133.2	1,080.2	979.1	781.4
2381	Res. building foundation & ext. contractors	552.6	604.8	622.6	560.6	465.7	357.8
2381	Nonres. building foundation & ext. contractors	457.3	478.6	510.6	519.7	513.4	423.6
23811	Poured concrete structure contractors	212.8	230.6	250.4	241.0	220.5	171.2
23812	Steel and precast concrete contractors	82.7	87.9	97.4	101.6	101.2	76.8
23813	Framing contractors	154.3	174.6	164.1	134.3	98.1	65.7
23814	Masonry contractors	230.5	240.6	256.4	240.6	212.6	164.6
23815	Glass and glazing contractors	54.9	55.6	59.2	64.0	64.5	58.9
23816	Roofing contractors	189.4	203.3	204.5	197.7	191.4	168.9
23817	Siding contractors	44.1	46.1	48.8	47.1	40.9	33.0
23819	Other building exterior contractors	41.2	44.7	52.2	54.0	50.1	42.4
2382	Building equipment contractors	1,861.3	1,918.1	2,012.8	2,057.0	2,019.9	1,768.4
2382	Residential building equipment contractors	761.8	801.7	835.8	827.2	773.1	668.8
2382	Nonresidential building equipment contractors	1,099.4	1,116.4	1,177.0	1,229.8	1,246.8	1,099.6
23821	Electrical contractors	852.5	868.9	904.2	925.9	906.0	795.8
23822	Plumbing and HVAC contractors	899.1	936.1	987.4	1,003.3	982.0	850.7
23829	Other building equipment contractors	109.7	113.2	121.2	127.9	131.9	121.9
2383	Building finishing contractors	931.5	991.6	1,030.3	1,002.8	899.8	724.6
2383	Residential building finishing contractors	542.5	596.4	617.3	580.6	491.9	387.6
2383	Nonresidential building finishing contractors	388.9	395.3	413.1	422.2	407.9	337.0
23831	Drywall & insulation contractors	341.5	359.4	372.3	352.4	309.3	244.5
23832	Painting & wall covering contractors	224.5	240.0	245.2	241.4	220.6	178.8
23833	Flooring contractors	83.2	84.8	85.7	86.8	79.2	65.3
23834	Tile & terrazzo contractors	66.3	72.6	78.3	73.8	61.9	48.8
23835	Finish carpentry contractors	151.8	167.3	176.5	174.8	156.2	121.4
23839	Other building finishing contractors	64.1	67.5	72.4	73.6	72.8	65.9
2389	Other specialty trade contractors	636.1	680.0	724.9	710.2	657.0	550.1
2389	Other residential trade contractors	268.9	299.4	321.2	308.8	268.4	215.5
2389	Other nonresidential trade contractors	367.2	380.6	403.7	401.3	388.6	334.6
23891	Site preparation contractors	328.5	357.2	383.7	377.1	347.3	284.6
23899	All other specialty trade contractors	307.6	322.7	341.2	333.1	309.7	265.6

Source: U.S. Bureau of Labor Statistics
Plunkett Research, Ltd.
www.plunkettresearch.com

Miscellaneous Real Estate & Construction Industry Employment, U.S.: 2004-2009

(In Thousands; Not Seasonally Adjusted)

NAICS Code	Industry Type	2004	2005	2006	2007	2008	2009
Manufacturing							
321991	Manufactured & mobile homes	43.5	46.4	48.4	40.1	33.5	21.2
3271	Clay products & refractories	64.5	61.9	60.5	57.0	52.0	43.1
3273	Cement & concrete products	234.7	240.1	248.3	242.2	220.3	187.7
3323	Architectural & structural metals	388.9	397.9	411.6	417.2	405.9	348.3
33231	Plate work & fabricated structural products	166.0	170.9	179.8	186.1	188.8	161.1
332311	Prefabricated metal buildings & components	32.4	32.7	35.6	35.1	35.0	28.5
332312	Fabricated structural metal products	88.0	91.1	95.1	99.1	99.9	89.2
332313	Plate work	45.7	47.2	49.2	52.0	53.9	43.5
33232	Ornamental & architectural metal products	222.9	227.0	231.8	231.0	217.0	187.2
332321	Metal windows & doors	84.0	84.3	81.4	76.5	67.6	56.7
332322	Sheet metal work	101.0	103.4	108.7	112.4	107.7	94.2
332323	Ornamental & architectural metal work	37.9	39.3	41.8	42.1	41.8	36.2
33312	Construction machinery	63.1	71.4	77.7	78.9	82.3	67.4
Financial Activities							
522292	Real estate credit	341.0	349.0	351.4	292.2	225.8	196.9
52231	Mortgage & nonmortgage loan brokers	126.7	140.8	144.9	121.3	82.5	66.0
531	Real estate	1,418.7	1,460.8	1,499.0	1,500.4	1,485.0	1,416.7
5311	Lessors of real estate	603.4	603.4	602.4	599.3	596.2	574.3
53111	Lessors of residential buildings	377.6	374.8	371.8	365.5	365.4	350.5
53112	Lessors of nonresidential buildings	147.0	147.7	147.5	149.5	147.7	141.3
53113	Miniwarehouse & self-storage unit operators	36.8	38.7	42.0	43.6	43.7	43.1
53119	Lessors of other real estate property	42.0	42.2	41.2	40.7	39.4	39.4
5312	Offices of real estate agents & brokers	331.0	355.8	374.6	368.3	343.3	305.2
5313	Activities related to real estate	484.3	501.6	521.9	532.9	545.5	537.2
53131	Real estate property managers	408.0	421.8	438.0	451.9	468.8	467.2
531311	Residential property managers	289.0	300.2	310.6	321.8	334.1	336.7
531312	Nonresidential property managers	119.0	121.6	127.4	130.1	134.8	130.4
53132	Offices of real estate appraisers	42.2	41.9	41.8	41.4	37.9	35.1
53139	Other activities related to real estate	34.1	37.9	42.1	39.6	38.8	35.0
Professional & Business Services							
54131	Architectural services	184.6	193.1	205.1	214.1	213.1	179.0
54132	Landscape architectural services	42.3	42.1	45.1	43.7	41.5	33.6
54133,4	Engineering & drafting services	796.9	839.0	886.5	921.3	940.5	891.1
54135,6,7	Building inspection, surveying & mapping svcs.	91.4	95.5	101.9	102.6	94.6	78.1
Leisure & Hospitality							
7211,3	Traveler accommodations & other longer-term	1,737.4	1,765.4	1,778.0	1,812.4	1,815.0	1,704.6
72111	Hotels & motels, except casino hotels	1,426.6	1,443.9	1,458.6	1,493.9	1,501.1	1,412.4
72112	Casino hotels	275.4	286.3	283.6	281.8	275.6	255.8

Source: U.S. Bureau of Labor Statistics
Plunkett Research, Ltd.
www.plunkettresearch.com

Chapter 3

IMPORTANT REAL ESTATE & CONSTRUCTION INDUSTRY CONTACTS

Addresses, Telephone Numbers and Internet Web Sites

Contents:

I. Affordable Housing Associations

National Community Reinvestment Coalition (NCRC)
727 15th St. NW, Ste. 900
Washington, DC 20005 US
Phone: 202-628-8866
Fax: 202-628-9800
E-mail Address: *jvantol@ncrc.org*
Web Address: www.ncrc.org
The National Community Reinvestment Coalition (NCRC) is a national nonprofit 501(c)3 organization with 640 dues-paying chapters located in every state

in America. NCRC was founded in 1990 to unite efforts around the nation to increase the flow of private capital into traditionally underserved communities, with a focus on affordable mortgages and loans for housing and small businesses in low income neighborhoods.

II. Alternative Energy-General

Alliance to Save Energy (ASE)
1850 M St. NW, Ste. 600
Washington, DC 20036 US
Phone: 202-857-0666
Fax: 202-331-9588
E-mail Address: *info@ase.org*
Web Address: www.ase.org
The Alliance to Save Energy (ASE) promotes energy-efficiency worldwide to achieve a healthier economy, a cleaner environment and energy security.

American Council for an Energy-Efficient Economy (ACEEE)
529 14th St. NW, Ste. 600
Washington, DC 20045-1000 US
Phone: 202-507-4000
Fax: 202-429-2248
E-mail Address: *info@aceee.org*
Web Address: www.aceee.org
The American Council for an Energy-Efficient Economy (ACEEE) is a nonprofit organization dedicated to advancing energy-efficiency as a means of promoting both economic prosperity and environmental protection.

Center for Energy Efficiency and Renewable Technologies (CEERT)
1100 11th St., Ste. 311
Sacramento, CA 95814 US
Phone: 916-442-7785
Fax: 916-447-2940
Toll Free: 877-758-4462
E-mail Address: *info@ceert.org*
Web Address: www.ceert.org
The Center for Energy Efficiency and Renewable Technologies (CEERT) provides technical support to environmental advocates and clean technology developers.

III. Alternative Energy-Solar

American Solar Energy Society (ASES)
2400 Central Ave., Ste. A
Boulder, CO 80301 US
Phone: 303-443-3130
Fax: 303-443-3212
E-mail Address: *ases@ases.org*
Web Address: www.ases.org
The American Solar Energy Society (ASES) is committed to advancing the use of solar energy to benefit citizens and the global environment, promoting widespread solar energy use in the near future and long-term.

Solar Energy Industries Association (SEIA)
805 15th St. NW, Ste. 510
Washington, DC 20005 US
Phone: 202-682-0556
Fax: 202-682-7779
E-mail Address: *info@seia.org*
Web Address: www.seia.org
Solar Energy Industries Association (SEIA) operates a web site that provides news for the solar energy industry, links to related products and companies and solar energy statistics.

IV. Careers-First Time Jobs/New Grads

Black Collegian Online (The)
140 Carondelet St.
New Orleans, LA 70130 US
Phone: 504-523-0154
Web Address: www.black-collegian.com
The Black Collegian Online features listings for job and internship opportunities, as well as other tools for students of color; it is the web site of The Black Collegian Magazine, published by IMDiversity, Inc. The site includes a list of the top 100 minority corporate employers and an assessment of job opportunities.

Collegegrad.com, Inc.
234 E. College Ave., Ste. 200
State College, PA 16801 US
Phone: 262-375-6700
Toll Free: 1-800-991-4642
Web Address: www.collegegrad.com
Collegegrad.com, Inc. offers in-depth resources for college students and recent grads seeking entry-level jobs.

Job Web
Nat'l Association of Colleges & Employers (NACE)
62 Highland Ave.
Bethlehem, PA 18017-9085 US
Phone: 610-868-1421
Fax: 610-868-0208
Toll Free: 800-544-5272
E-mail Address: *editors@jobweb.com*
Web Address: www.jobweb.com
Job Web, owned and sponsored by National Association of Colleges and Employers (NACE), displays job openings and employer descriptions. The site also offers a database of career fairs, searchable by state or keyword, with contact information.

MBAjobs.net
Fax: 413-556-8849
E-mail Address: *contact@mbajobs.net*
Web Address: www.mbajobs.net
MBAjobs.net is a unique international service for MBA students and graduates, employers, recruiters and business schools. The MBAjobs.net service is provided by WebInfoCo.

MonsterTRAK
11845 W. Olympic Blvd., Ste. 500
Los Angeles, CA 90064 US
Toll Free: 800-999-8725
E-mail Address: *trakstudent@monster.com*
Web Address: www.college.monster.com
MonsterTRAK provides information about internships and entry-level jobs.

National Association of Colleges and Employers (NACE)
62 Highland Ave.
Bethlehem, PA 18017-9085 US
Phone: 610-868-1421
Fax: 610-868-0208
Toll Free: 800-544-5272
E-mail Address: *mcollins@naceweb.org*
Web Address: www.naceweb.org
The National Association of Colleges and Employers (NACE) is a premier U.S. organization representing college placement offices and corporate recruiters who focus on hiring new grads.

V. Careers-General Job Listings

Career Exposure, Inc.
805 SW Broadway, Ste. 2250
Portland, OR 97205 US
Phone: 503-221-7779
Fax: 503-221-7780
E-mail Address: *lisam@mackenzie-marketing.com*
Web Address: www.careerexposure.com
Career Exposure, Inc. is an online career center and job placement service, with resources for employers, recruiters and job seekers.

CareerBuilder, Inc.
200 N. LaSalle St., Ste. 1100
Chicago, IL 60601 US
Phone: 773-527-3600
Toll Free: 800-638-4212
Web Address: www.careerbuilder.com
CareerBuilder, Inc. focuses on the needs of companies and also provides a database of job openings. The site has 1.5 million jobs posted by 300,000 employers, and receives an average 23 million unique visitors monthly. The company also operates online career centers for 150 newspapers, 1,000 partners and other online portals such as America Online. Resumes are sent directly to the company, and applicants can set up a special e-mail account for job-seeking purposes. CareerBuilder is primarily a joint venture between three newspaper giants: The McClatchy Company (which recently acquired former partner Knight Ridder), Gannett Co., Inc. and Tribune Company. In 2007, Microsoft acquired a minority interest in CareerBuilder, allowing the site to ally itself with MSN.

CareerOneStop
Toll Free: 877-348-0502
E-mail Address: *info@careeronestop.org*
Web Address: www.careeronestop.org
CareerOneStop is operated by the employment commissions of various state agencies. It contains job listings in both the private sector and in government. CareerOneStop is sponsored by the U.S. Department of Labor. It includes a wide variety of useful career resources and workforce information.

HotJobs
45 W. 18th St., 6th Fl.
New York, NY 10011 US
Phone: 646-351-5300
Web Address: www.hotjobs.yahoo.com
HotJobs, designed for experienced professionals, employers and job seekers, is a Monster-owned site that provides company profiles, a resume posting service and a resume workshop. The site allows posters to block resumes from being viewed by certain companies and provides a notification service of new jobs.

JobCentral
DirectEmployers Association, Inc.
9002 N. Purdue Rd., Quad III, Ste. 100
Indianapolis, IN 46268 US
Phone: 317-874-9000
Fax: 317-874-9100
Toll Free: 866-268-6206
E-mail Address: *info@jobcentral.com*
Web Address: www.jobcentral.com
JobCentral, operated by the nonprofit DirectEmployers Association, Inc., links users directly to hundreds of thousands of job opportunities posted on the sites of participating employers, thus bypassing the usual job search sites. This saves employers money and allows job seekers to access many more job opportunities.

LaborMarketInfo
Employment Dev. Dept., Labor Market Info. Div.
800 Capitol Mall, MIC 83
Sacramento, CA 95814 US
Phone: 916-262-2162
Fax: 916-262-2352
Toll Free: 800-480-3287
Web Address: www.labormarketinfo.edd.ca.gov
LaborMarketInfo, formerly the California Cooperative Occupational Information System, is geared to providing job seekers and employers a wide range of resources, namely the ability to find, access and use labor market information and services. It provides demographical statistics for employment on both a local and regional level, as well as career searching tools for California residents. The web site is sponsored by California's Employment Development Office.

Recruiters Online Network
947 Essex Ln.
Medina, OH 44256 US
Phone: 888-364-4667
Fax: 888-237-8686
E-mail Address: *info@recruitersonline.com*
Web Address: www.recruitersonline.com
The Recruiters Online Network provides job postings from thousands of recruiters, Careers Online Magazine, a resume database, as well as other career resources.

True Careers, Inc.
Web Address: www.truecareers.com
True Careers, Inc. offers job listings and provides an array of career resources. The company also offers a search of over 2 million scholarships. It is partnered with CareerBuilder.com, which powers its career information and resume posting functions.

USAJOBS
U.S. Office of Personnel Management
1900 E St. NW
Washington, DC 20415 US
Phone: 202-606-1800
Web Address: usajobs.opm.gov
USAJOBS, a program of the U.S. Office of Personnel Management, is the official job site for the U.S. Federal Government. It provides a comprehensive list of U.S. government jobs, allowing users to search for employment by location; agency; type of work, using the Federal Government's numerical identification code, the General Schedule (GS) Series; or by senior executive positions. It also has a special veterans' employment section; an information center, offering resume and interview tips and other useful information such as hiring trends and a glossary of Federal terms; and allows users to create a profile and post a resume.

Wall Street Journal - CareerJournal
Wall Street Journal
200 Liberty St.
New York, NY 10281 US
Phone: 212-416-2000
Toll Free: 800-568-7625
E-mail Address: *onelinejournal@wsj.com*
Web Address: cj.careercast.com/careers/jobsearch
The Wall Street Journal's CareerJournal, an executive career site, features a job database with thousands of available positions; career news and employment related articles; and advice regarding resume writing, interviews, networking, office life and job hunting.

VI. Careers-Job Reference Tools

NewsVoyager
4401 Wilson Blvd., Ste. 900
Arlington, VA 22203-1867 US
Phone: 571-366-1000
Fax: 571-366-1195
E-mail Address: *sally.clarke@naa.org*
Web Address: www.newsvoyager.com
NewsVoyager, a service of the Newspaper Association of America (NAA), links individuals to local, national and international newspapers. Job seekers can search through thousands of classified sections.

Vault.com, Inc.
75 Varick St., 8th Fl.
New York, NY 10013 US
Phone: 212-366-4212
E-mail Address: *feedback@staff.vault.com*
Web Address: www.vault.com
Vault.com, Inc. is a comprehensive career web site for employers and employees, with job postings and valuable information on a wide variety of industries. Vault gears many of its features toward MBAs. The site has been recognized by Forbes and Fortune Magazines.

VII. Construction Industry Resources & Associations

American Concrete Institute (ACI)
38800 Country Club Dr.
Farmington Hills, MI 48331 US
Phone: 248-848-3700
Fax: 248-848-3701
E-mail Address: *BKStore@concrete.org*
Web Address: www.concrete.org
The American Concrete Institute (ACI) is a professional organization that provides information on the use of concrete for structures and facilities.

American Society of Professional Estimators (ASPE)
2525 Perimeter Place Dr., Ste. 103
Nashville, TN 37214 US
Phone: 615-316-9200
Fax: 615-316-9800
Toll Free: 888-378-6273
E-mail Address: *info@aspenational.com*
Web Address: www.aspenational.org
The American Society of Professional Estimators (ASPE) serves construction estimators by providing education, fellowships and opportunities for professional development.

American Subcontractors Association (ASA)
1004 Duke St.
Alexandria, VA 22314-3588 US
Phone: 703-684-3450
Fax: 703-836-3482
E-mail Address: *ASAoffice@asa-hq.com*
Web Address: www.asaonline.com
The American Subcontractors Association (ASA) is an association of professional construction contractors and suppliers.

Associated Builders and Contractors (ABC)
4250 N. Fairfax Dr., 9th Fl.
Arlington, VA 22203-1607 US
Phone: 703-812-2000
E-mail Address: *gotquestions@abc.org*
Web Address: www.abc.org
Associated Builders and Contractors (ABC) is a national trade association representing more than 23,000 merit shop contractors, subcontractors, material suppliers and related firms in 80 chapters across the United States.

Associated General Contractors of America (The, AGC)
2300 Wilson Blvd., Ste. 400
Arlington, VA 22201 US
Phone: 703-548-3118
Fax: 703-548-3119
Toll Free: 800-242-1767
Web Address: www.agc.org
The Associated General Contractors of America (AGC) is a membership organization dedicated to furthering the agenda of commercial construction contractors, improving job site safety, expanding the use of cutting edge technologies and techniques and strengthening the dialogue between contractors and owners.

Bookworkz-The Construction Industry Bookstore
P.O. Box 948
Valrico, FL 33595-0948 US
Phone: 813-662-6793
Fax: 888-533-5680
Toll Free: 800-997-2922
E-mail Address: *books@bookworkz.com*
Web Address: www.bookworkz.com
The Bookworkz web site offers users the opportunity to browse and purchase from thousands of construction, engineering and architectural titles.

Canadian Construction Association (CCA)
75 Albert St., Ste. 400
Ottawa, ON K1P 5E7 Canada
Phone: 613-236-9455
Fax: 613-236-9526
E-mail Address: *cca@cca-acc.com*
Web Address: www.cca-acc.com
The Canadian Construction Association (CCA), or, in French, the Association canadienne de la construction (ACC), is a Canadian organization devoted to setting standards for construction industry practices and labor issues nationwide.

Canadian Wood Council (The) (CWC)
99 Bank St., Ste. 400
Ottawa, ON K1P 6B9 Canada
Phone: 613-747-5544
Fax: 613-747-6264
Toll Free: 800-463-5091
E-mail Address: *info@cwc.ca*
Web Address: www.cwc.ca
The CWC is the Canadian national association of manufacturers of wood products that are used in construction.

Certified Aging in Place Specialist (CAPS)
National Association of Home Builders
1201 15th St. NW
Washington, DC 20005 US
Phone: 202-266-8200 x0
Fax: 202-266-8400
Toll Free: 800-368-5242
Web Address:
www.nahb.org/category.aspx?sectionID=686
The Certified Aging in Place Specialist (CAPS) designation program teaches the technical, business management and customer service skills necessary to make residential environments capable of housing people as they age. It is offered by the National Association of Home Builders (NAHB)

Construction Industry Institute (CII)
3925 W. Braker Ln.
Austin, TX 78759-5316 US
Phone: 512-232-3000
Fax: 512-499-8101
E-mail Address: *wcrew@mail.utexas.edu*
Web Address: www.construction-institute.org
The Construction Industry Institute (CII) is a consortium of leading owners, contractors and suppliers who work with academia to find better ways to plan and execute capital construction programs.

Contractors Group (The)
Diane Dennis Enterprises
555 NW Fairhaven Dr.
Oak Harbor, WA 98277 US
Fax: 866-480-7105
E-mail Address: *diane@TheContractorsGroup.com*
Web Address: www.thecontractorsgroup.com
The Contractors Group offers free editable construction forms, tutorials, forums and related links. It was founded, and is still run by Diane Dennis Enterprises.

McGraw-Hill Construction Sweets Network
The McGraw-Hill Companies
P.O. Box 182604
Columbus, OH 43272 US
Phone: 212-904-4376
Toll Free: 800-393-6343
E-mail Address: *kathy_malangone@mcgraw-hill.com*
Web Address: products.construction.com
The McGraw-Hill Construction Sweets Network on-line resource offers access to product and manufacturer information quickly and easily through a searchable database. Its design facilitates design specifications and document creation with downloadable, insertable product information. The service also offers access to the latest green products, trends, developments and innovations. The service is part of McGraw-Hill Construction, which is itself part of The McGraw-Hill Companies, Inc.

Metal Building Manufacturers Association (MBMA)
1300 Sumner Ave.
Cleveland, OH 44115-2851 US
Phone: 216-241-7333
Fax: 216-241-0105
E-mail Address: *mbma@mbma.com*
Web Address: www.mbma.com
The Metal Building Manufacturers Association (MBMA) promotes the design and construction of metal building and metal roofing systems in the low-rise, non-residential building and roofing marketplace.

National Asphalt Pavement Association (NAPA)
5100 Forbes Blvd.
Lanham, MD 20706 US
Phone: 301-731-4748
Fax: 301-731-4621
Toll Free: 888-468-6499
Web Address: www.hotmix.org
The National Asphalt Pavement Association is the only trade association that exclusively represents the interests of the hot-mix asphalt producer/contractor on the national level with Congress, government agencies, and other national trade and business organizations. NAPA supports an active research program designed to improve the quality of HMA pavements and paving techniques used in the construction of roads, streets, highways, parking lots, airports, and environmental and recreational facilities. The association provides technical, educational, and marketing materials and information

to its members; supplies product information to users and specifiers of paving materials; and conducts training courses. The association, which counts nearly 1,200 companies as its members, was founded in 1955.

National Association of Home Builders (NAHB)
1201 15th St. NW
Washington, DC 20005 US
Phone: 202-266-8200
Fax: 202-266-8400
Toll Free: 800-368-5242
E-mail Address: *cdouglas@nahb.com*
Web Address: www.nahb.org
The National Association of Home Builders (NAHB) exists to represent the building industry by serving its members and affiliated state and local builders associations.

National Association of Women in Construction (NAWIC)
327 S. Adams St.
Fort Worth, TX 76104 US
Phone: 817-877-5551
Fax: 817-877-0324
Toll Free: 800-552-3506
E-mail Address: *nawic@nawic.org*
Web Address: www.nawic.org
The National Association of Women in Construction (NAWIC) is an association to promote the advancement of women in the construction industry.

Precast/Prestressed Concrete Institute
209 W. Jackson Blvd., Ste. 500
Chicago, IL 60606 US
Phone: 312-786-0300
Fax: 312-786-0353
E-mail Address: *info@pci.org*
Web Address: www.pci.org
The Precast/Prestressed Concrete Institute (PCI) is an organization dedicated to the precast and prestressed concrete industry and includes a staff of technical and marketing specialists.

Public Works and Government Services Canada (PWGSC)
16A1, 102 Corporate Communications
Portage III
Gatineau, Quebec K1A 0S5 Canada
Fax: 819-956-9062
Toll Free: 800-622-6232
E-mail Address: *questions@pwgsc.gc.ca*
Web Address: www.pwgsc.gc.ca
Public Works and Government Services Canada (PWGSC) is a government agency that performs the following functions for all 106 Canadian federal departments: purchases goods and services; provides office accommodations for public servants; manages national heritage properties; oversees public construction; and offers information technology, telecommunications, translation, banking and auditing services to the government.

Singapore Contractors Association Ltd. (SCAL)
Construction House
Bukit Merah Ln. 2
159760 Singapore
Phone: 65-6278-9577
Fax: 65-6273-3977
E-mail Address: *enquiry@scal.com.sg*
Web Address: www.scal.com.sg
The Singapore Contractors Association (SCAL) has a membership of more than 2000 members under her wing, making it a representative of the construction industry in Singapore.

SmartMaket Report
Toll Free: 800-393-6343
Web Address: www.construction.com/SmartMarket
The SmartMarket Report series from McGraw-Hill Construction provides current, relevant intelligence about specific markets that offer significant opportunities for design and construction firms. The information is managed in the McGraw-Hill Construction statistical database, which has tracked the activity of over a million owners, designers, builders and supplier and the data of tens of millions of new, addition and renovation projects throughout the U.S. and Canada since 1967.

VIII. Construction Resources-Energy Efficient Buildings

EERE Rebuild America
1000 Independence Ave. SW
Mail Stop EE-1
Washington, DC 20585 US
Phone: 202-586-5463
Toll Free: 877-337-3463
Web Address: www.eere.energy.gov/buildings/program_areas/rebuild.html
The Building Technologies Program of the Office of Energy Efficiency and Renewable Energy (EERE), a division of the U.S. Department of Energy, operates Rebuild America, which is a network of hundreds of

community-based partnerships that are focused on increasing the number of energy-efficient buildings in the nation.

Efficient Windows Collaborative (EWC)
Nils Petermann, Alliance to Save Energy
1850 M St. NW, Ste. 600
Washington, DC 20036 US
Phone: 202-530-2254
Fax: 202-331-9588
E-mail Address: *ewc@ase.org*
Web Address: www.efficientwindows.org
The Efficient Windows Collaborative (EWC) web site provides unbiased information on the benefits of energy-efficient windows, descriptions of how they work and recommendations for their selection and use. The web site is sponsored by the U.S. Department of Energy's Windows and Glazings Program and the participation of industry members.

Green Building Initiative (GBI)
2104 SE Morrison
Portland, OR 97214 US
Fax: 503-961-8991
Toll Free: 877-424-4241
E-mail Address: *info@thegbi.org*
Web Address: www.thegbi.org
The Green Building Initiative (GBI) is a nonprofit network of building industry leaders committed to bringing green to mainstream residential and commercial construction. The GBI believes in building approaches that are environmentally progressive, but also practical and affordable for builders to implement.

GreenSource
2 Penn Plz.
New York, NY 10121-2298 US
Phone: 717-399-8900
Toll Free: 800-360-5549
E-mail Address: *greensourcemag@mcgraw-hill.com*
Web Address: www.greensource.construction.com
GreenSource is McGraw-Hill Construction's on-line directory of information on sustainable design, practice and products. It includes information from GreenSource, Architectural Record and Engineering News-Record magazines for architects, engineers, contractors and consumers. It also offers Internet-only exclusives.

Sustainable Buildings Industry Council (SBIC)
1112 16th St. NW, Ste. 240
Washington, DC 20036 US
Phone: 202-628-7400
Fax: 202-393-5043
E-mail Address: *sbic@sbicouncil.com*
Web Address: www.sbicouncil.org
The Sustainable Buildings Industry Council (SBIC) is an independent, nonprofit organization that concentrates on providing information on energy conservation in regards to building construction.

U.S. Green Building Council (USGBC)
1800 Massachusetts Ave. NW, Ste. 300
Washington, DC 20036 US
Phone: 202-742-3792
Fax: 202-828-5110
Toll Free: 800-795-1747
E-mail Address: *info@usgbc.org*
Web Address: www.usgbc.org
The United States Green Building Council (USGBC) is a coalition of building industry leaders working to promote environmentally responsible commercial and residential structures.

IX. Corporate Information Resources

bizjournals.com
120 W. Morehead St., Ste. 400
Charlotte, NC 28202 US
Web Address: www.bizjournals.com
Bizjournals.com is the online media division of American City Business Journals, the publisher of dozens of leading city business journals nationwide. It provides access to research into the latest news regarding companies small and large.

Business Wire
44 Montgomery St., 39th Fl.
San Francisco, CA 94104 US
Phone: 415-986-4422
Fax: 415-788-5335
Toll Free: 800-227-0845
Web Address: www.businesswire.com
Business Wire offers news releases, industry- and company-specific news, top headlines, conference calls, IPOs on the Internet, media services and access to tradeshownews.com and BW Connect On-line through its informative and continuously updated web site.

Edgar Online, Inc.
50 Washington St., 11th Fl.
Norwalk, CT 06854 US
Phone: 203-852-5666
Fax: 203-852-5667

Toll Free: 800-416-6651
Web Address: www.edgar-online.com
Edgar Online, Inc. is a gateway and search tool for viewing corporate documents, such as annual reports on Form 10-K, filed with the U.S. Securities and Exchange Commission.

PR Newswire Association LLC
810 7th Ave., 32nd Fl.
New York, NY 10019 US
Phone: 201-360-6700
Toll Free: 800-832-5522
E-mail Address: *information@prnewswire.com*
Web Address: www.prnewswire.com
PR Newswire Association LLC provides comprehensive communications services for public relations and investor relations professionals ranging from information distribution and market intelligence to the creation of online multimedia content and investor relations web sites. Users can also view recent corporate press releases. The Association is owned by United Business Media plc.

X. Design & Architectural Associations

American Institute of Architects (The) (AIA)
1735 New York Ave. NW
Washington, DC 20006-5292 US
Phone: 202-626-7300
Fax: 202-626-7547
Toll Free: 800-242-3837
E-mail Address: *infocentral@aia.org*
Web Address: www.aia.org
The American Institute of Architects (AIA) is a professional trade group for architects in the United States.

American Institute of Building Design (AIBD)
7059 Blair Rd. NW, Ste. 201
Washington, DC 20012 US
Fax: 202-249-2473
Toll Free: 800-366-2423
E-mail Address: *Info@AIBD.org*
Web Address: www.aibd.org
The American Institute of Building Design (AIBD) is a nonprofit professional organization dedicated to the development, recognition and enhancement of the profession of building design.

Center for Universal Design (The) (CUD)
College of Design, North Carolina State University
Campus Box 8613
Raleigh, NC 27695-8613 US
Phone: 919-515-3082
Fax: 919-515-8951
Toll Free: 800-647-6777
E-mail Address: *cud@ncsu.edu*
Web Address: www.design.ncsu.edu/cud/
The Center for Universal Design (CUD) is a national information, technical assistance and research center that evaluates, develops and promotes products and environments so that they can be used by all people, regardless of physical or mental limitations.

National Council of Architectural Registration Board (NCARB)
1801 K St. NW, Ste. 1100K
Washington, DC 20006-1310 US
Phone: 202-783-6500
Fax: 202-783-0290
E-mail Address: *customerservice@ncarb.org*
Web Address: www.ncarb.org
The National Council of Architectural Registration Board (NCARB) is a nonprofit federation of architectural licensing boards in the U.S. that provides state registration requirements, information on the Intern Development Program (IDP) and Architect Registration Examination (ARE) certification, continuing education and an architect database.

Royal Architectural Institute of Canada (RAIC)
330-55 Rue Murray St.
Ottawa, Ontario K1N 5M3 Canada
Phone: 613-241-3600
Fax: 613-241-5750
E-mail Address: *info@raic.org*
Web Address: www.raic.org
The Royal Architectural Institute of Canada (RAIC) is a voluntary national association representing professional architects, and faculty and graduates of accredited Canadian Schools of Architecture.

Royal Institute of British Architects (RIBA)
66 Portland Pl.
London, W1B 1AD UK
Phone: 44-20-7580-5533
Fax: 44-20-7255-1541
E-mail Address: *info@inst.riba.org*
Web Address: www.riba.org
The Royal Institute of British Architects (RIBA) is a professional association of architects in the United Kingdom, which also offers lectures, exhibitions and events, community architecture projects and community architecture schemes.

Singapore Institute of Architects (SIA)
79B Neil Rd.
088904 Singapore
Phone: 65-6226-2668
Fax: 65-6226-2663
E-mail Address: *info@sia.org.sg*
Web Address: www.sia.org.sg
The Singapore Institute of Architects (SIA) is the national organization representing architects in Singapore.

The Architectural Society of China (ASC)
No. 9 Sanlihe Rd.
Beijing, 100835 China
Phone: 86-10-88082224
Fax: 86-10-88082223
Web Address: www.chinaasc.org
The Architectural Society of China (ASC) represents professional architects in China.

XI. Economic Data & Research

Eurostat
Phone: 32-2-299-9696
Toll Free: 80-0-6789-1011
Web Address: www.epp.eurostat.ec.europa.eu
Eurostat is the European Union's service that publishes a wide variety of comprehensive statistics on European industries, populations, trade, agriculture, technology, environment and other matters.

Statistics Canada
150 Tunney's Pasture Driveway
Ottawa, ON K1A 0T6 Canada
Phone: 613-951-8116
Fax: 613-951-0581
Toll Free: 800-263-1136
Web Address: www.statcan.gc.ca
A complete portal to Canadian economic data and statistics.

STAT-USA/Internet
STAT-USA, HCHB, U.S. Dept. of Commerce
Rm. 4885
Washington, DC 20230 US
Phone: 202-482-1986
Fax: 202-482-2164
Toll Free: 800-782-8872
E-mail Address: *statmail@esa.doc.gov*
Web Address: www.stat-usa.gov
STAT-USA/Internet offers daily economic news, statistical releases and databases relating to export and trade, as well as the domestic economy. It is provided by STAT-USA, which is an agency in the Economics & Statistics Administration of the U.S. Department of Commerce. The site mainly consists of two main databases, the State of the Nation (SOTN), which focuses on the current state of the U.S. economy; and the Global Business Opportunities (GLOBUS) & the National Trade Data Bank (NTDB), which deals with U.S. export opportunities, global political/socio-economic conditions and other world economic issues.

XII. Economic Data-India

India Brand Equity Foundation (IBEF)
249-F Sector 18
Udyog Vihar Phase IV
Gurgaon, Haryana 122015 India
Phone: 91-124-4014060
Fax: 91-124-4013873
E-mail Address: *ceo@ibef.org*
Web Address: www.ibef.org
India Brand Equity Foundation (IBEF) is a public-private partnership between the Ministry of Commerce and Industry, Government of India, and the Confederation of Indian Industry. The Foundation's primary objective is to build positive economic perceptions of India globally. It aims to effectively present the India business perspective and leverage business partnerships in a globalizing market-place.

XIII. Engineering, Research & Scientific Associations

American National Standards Institute (ANSI)
1819 L St. NW, 6th Fl.
Washington, DC 20036 US
Phone: 202-293-8020
Fax: 202-293-9287
E-mail Address: *info@ansi.org*
Web Address: www.ansi.org
The American National Standards Institute (ANSI) is a private, nonprofit organization that administers and coordinates the U.S. voluntary standardization and conformity assessment system. Its mission is to enhance both the global competitiveness of U.S. business and the quality of life by promoting and facilitating voluntary consensus standards and conformity assessment systems and safeguarding their integrity.

American Society of Civil Engineers (ASCE)
1801 Alexander Bell Dr.
Reston, VA 20191-4400 US
Phone: 703-295-6300
Fax: 703-295-6222
Toll Free: 800-548-2723
Web Address: www.asce.org
The American Society of Civil Engineers (ASCE) is a leading professional organization serving civil engineers. It ensures safer buildings, water systems and other civil engineering works by developing technical codes and standards.

Association for Facilities Engineering (AFE)
12100 Sunset Hills Rd., Ste. 130
Reston, VA 20190 US
Phone: 703-234-4066
E-mail Address: *info@afe.org*
Web Address: www.afe.org
The Association for Facilities Engineering (AFE) provides education, certification, technical information and other relevant resources for plant and facility engineering, operations and maintenance professionals worldwide.

China Academy of Building Research (CABR)
30 Bei San Huan Dong Lu
Beijing, 100013 China
Phone: 010-84272233
Fax: 010-84281369
E-mail Address: *office@cabr.com.cn*
Web Address: www.cabr.cn
CABR is responsible for the development and management of the major engineering construction and product standards of China and is also the largest comprehensive research and development institute in the building industry in China. Some related institutes include Institute of Earthquake Engineering, Institute of Building Fire Research, Institute of Building Environment and Energy Efficiency (Building Physics), Institute of Foundation Engineering as well as many others.

Chinese Association of Earthquake Engineering (CAEE)
No. 29 Xuefu Rd. Harbin
Heilongjiang, 150080 China
Phone: 86-45186652663
Fax: 86-45186664755
Web Address: www.caee.org.cn
Chinese Association of Earthquake Engineering (CAEE) promotes the field of earthquake engineering and the research in seismic activity and earthquake sciences.

Civil Engineering Forum for Innovation (CEFI)
American Society of Civil Engineers
1801 Alexander Bell Dr.
Reston, VA 20191-4400 US
Phone: 703-295-6314
Fax: 703-295-6015
E-mail Address: *mdalton@asce.org*
Web Address: content.asce.org/cefi
The Civil Engineering Forum for Innovation (CEFI) is an independent nonprofit organization established by the American Society of Civil Engineers (ASCE) to strengthen the civil engineering profession and industry through technical innovation and public policy.

Earthquake Engineering Research Institute (EERI)
499 14th St., Ste. 320
Oakland, CA 94612-1934 US
Phone: 510-451-0905
Fax: 510-451-5411
E-mail Address: *eeri@eeri.org*
Web Address: www.eeri.org
The Earthquake Engineering Research Institute (EERI) is a national nonprofit technical organization of engineers, geoscientists, architects, planners, public officials and social scientists aimed at reducing earthquake risk by advancing the science and practice of earthquake engineering.

Illuminating Engineering Society of North America (IESNA)
120 Wall St., 17th Fl.
New York, NY 10005 US
Phone: 212-248-5000
Fax: 212-248-5017
E-mail Address: *iesna@iesna.org*
Web Address: www.iesna.org
A recognized authority on lighting in North America, the Illuminating Engineering Society of North America (IESNA) establishes scientific lighting recommendations. Members include engineers, architects, designers, educators, students, manufacturers and scientists.

Institute for Research in Construction (IRC)
National Research Council of Canada
1200 Montreal Rd., Bldg. M-24
Ottawa, ON K1A 0R6 Canada
Phone: 613-993-2607

Fax: 613-952-7673
E-mail Address: *irc.client-services@nrc-cnrc.gc.ca*
Web Address: irc.nrc-cnrc.gc.ca
The Institute for Research in Construction (IRC) provides research, building code development and materials evaluation services. The IRC is Canada's construction technology center and a division of the National Research Council.

Institute of Structural Engineers (IStructE)
11 Upper Belgrave St.
London, SW1X 8BH UK
Phone: 44-(0)20-7235-4535
Fax: 44-(0)20-7235-4294
Web Address: www.istructe.org.uk
The Institute of Structural Engineers (IStructE) is a professional organization, headquartered in the U.K., that sets and maintains standards for professional structural engineers.

National Academy of Building Inspection Engineers (NABIE)
P.O. Box 522158
Salt Lake City, UT 84152 US
Fax: 801-943-3689
Toll Free: 800-294-7729
E-mail Address: *director@nabie.org*
Web Address: www.nabie.org
The National Academy of Building Inspection Engineers (NABIE) is a chartered affinity group of the National Society of Professional Engineers. NABIE accepts only state-licensed engineers and architects as members in its building inspection association.

National Society of Professional Engineers (NSPE)
1420 King St.
Alexandria, VA 22314-2794 US
Phone: 703-684-2800
Fax: 703-836-4875
Toll Free: 888-285-6773
E-mail Address: *memserv@nspe.org*
Web Address: www.nspe.org
The National Society of Professional Engineers (NSPE) represents individual engineering professionals and licensed engineers across all disciplines. NSPE serves approximately 45,000 members and has more than 500 chapters.

World Federation of Engineering Organizations
Maison de l'UNESCO 1
rue Miollis
Paris, Cedex 15 F-75732 France
Phone: 33-1-45-68-48-46
Fax: 33-1-45-68-48-65
E-mail Address: *tl.fmoi@unesco.org*
Web Address: www.wfeo.org
World Federation of Engineering Organizations (WFEO) is an international non-governmental organization that represents major engineering professional societies in over 90 nations. It has several standing committees including engineering and the environment, technology, communications, capacity building, education, energy and women in engineering.

XIV. Environmental & Ecological Organizations

Global Footprint Network
312 Clay St., Ste. 300
Oakland, CA 94607-3510 US
Phone: 510-839-8879
Fax: 510-251-2410
E-mail Address: *info@footprintnetwork.org*
Web Address: www.footprintnetwork.org
Global Footprint Network publishes regional studies of human demands on the ecology which it calls an Ecological Footprint. The Footprint takes into consideration human use of land, water and other resources to fill needs for housing, agriculture, energy and more, along with nature's ability to fulfill those demands. The organization's analysis creates a scale by which one nation may compare its footprint against that of others.

XV. Financial Industry Resources

SNL Financial
1 SNL Plz., P.O. Box 2124
Charlottesville, VA 22902 US
Phone: 434-977-1600
Fax: 434-977-4466
Toll Free: 866-296-3743
E-mail Address: *support@snl.com*
Web Address: www.snl.com
SNL Financial provides industry-specific research and statistics in the banking, financial services, insurance, real estate and energy sectors.

XVI. Forest Products Associations

Canadian Lumbermen's Association (CLA)
30 Concourse Gate, Ste. 200
Ottawa, ON K2E 7V7 Canada
Phone: 613-233-6205

Fax: 613-233-1929
Web Address: www.canadianlumbermen.com
The CLA represents the interests of Canadian lumber manufacturers and various supporting industries as well.

XVII. Home Values Online

Trulia
208 Utah St., Ste. 310
San Francisco, CA 94103 US
E-mail Address: *customerservice@trulia.com*
Web Address: www.trulia.com
An excellent site for finding price trends for specific properties. The site includes many tools for buyers, sellers and real estate professionals. Trulia Voices, one of the largest real estate communities on the web, allows home buyers, sellers, agents and real estate enthusiasts to ask questions, receive advice and blog on topics such as the buying and selling process, foreclosures, refinancing and more.

Zillow
999 Third Ave., Ste. 4600
Seattle, WA 98104 US
Phone: 206-470-7167
E-mail Address: *press@zillow.com*
Web Address: www.zillow.com
Zillow is an extremely popular site launched in 2005. It provides online access to aerial home photos, and enables users to estimate home values based on a variety of factors, using a proprietary algorithm.

XVIII. Industry Research/Market Research

Forrester Research
400 Technology Sq.
Cambridge, MA 02139 US
Phone: 617-613-6000
Fax: 617-613-5200
Toll Free: 866-367-7378
Web Address: www.forrester.com
Forrester Research identifies and analyzes emerging trends in technology and their impact on business. Among the firm's specialties are the financial services, retail, health care, entertainment, automotive and information technology industries.

Marketresearch.com
11200 Rockville Pike, Ste. 504
Rockville, MD 20852 US
Phone: 240-747-3000
Fax: 240-747-3004
Toll Free: 800-298-5699
E-mail Address:
customerservice@marketresearch.com
Web Address: www.marketresearch.com
Marketresearch.com is a leading broker for professional market research and industry analysis. Users are able to search the company's database of research publications including data on global industries, companies, products and trends.

Plunkett Research, Ltd.
P.O. Drawer 541737
Houston, TX 77254-1737 US
Phone: 713-932-0000
Fax: 713-932-7080
E-mail Address:
customersupport@plunkettresearch.com
Web Address: www.plunkettresearch.com
Plunkett Research, Ltd. is a leading provider of market research, industry trends analysis and business statistics. Since 1985, it has served clients worldwide, including corporations, universities, libraries, consultants and government agencies. At the firm's web site, visitors can view product information and pricing and access a great deal of basic market information on industries such as financial services, infotech, e-commerce, health care and biotech.

STR Global
735 E. Main St.
Hendersonville, TN 37075 US
Phone: 615-824-8664
Fax: 615-824-3848
E-mail Address: *info@smithtravelresearch.com*
Web Address: www.strglobal.com
STR Global provides extensive market analysis to the U.S. lodging industry and provides benchmarking reports daily, weekly and monthly.

XIX. Long Term Care, Assisted Living Associations

Assisted Living Federation of America (ALFA)
1650 King St., Ste. 602
Alexandria, VA 22314-2747 US
Phone: 703-894-1805
Fax: 703-894-1831
E-mail Address: *info@alfa.org*
Web Address: www.alfa.org
The Assisted Living Federation of America (ALFA) represents for-profit and nonprofit providers of

assisted living, continuing care retirement communities, independent living and other forms of housing and services.

National Investment Center for the Seniors Housing & Care Industry (NIC)
1997 Annapolis Exchange Parkway, Ste. 110
Annapolis, MD 21401 US
Phone: 410-267-0504
Fax: 410-268-4620
Web Address: www.nic.org
NIC serves as a resource to lenders, investors, developers/operators, and others interested in meeting the housing and healthcare needs of America's seniors. NIC serves the entire industry as an objective purveyor of information: NIC's research and educational efforts are neither association-driven nor company-oriented. As an impartial observer and unbiased source, NIC has become the primary link between the financial markets and seniors housing developers/operators, connecting each side through relevant research and practical information.

XX. MBA Resources

MBA Depot
Phone: 512-499-8728
Web Address: www.mbadepot.com
MBA Depot is an online community for MBA professionals.

XXI. Mortgage Industry Associations

Council of Mortgage Lenders
Bush House, NW Wing, Aldwych
London, WC2B 4PJ UK
Phone: 44-845-373-6771
Fax: 44-845-373-6778
E-mail Address: *info@cml.org.uk*
Web Address: www.cml.org.uk
The Council of Mortgage Lenders is a trade organization whose members account for approximately 98% of U.K. mortgage lending industry.

Mortgage Bankers Association (MBA)
1331 L St. NW
Washington, DC 20005 US
Phone: 202-557-2700
Web Address: www.mbaa.org
The Mortgage Bankers Association (MBA) serves the real estate finance industry by representing its legislative and regulatory interests before Congress and federal agencies; providing educational programs, periodicals and publications; and supporting its business interests with research initiatives, products and services.

National Association of Professional Mortgage Women (NAPMW)
130 E. John Carpenter Fwy.
Irving, TX 75062 US
Fax: 469-524-5121
Toll Free: 800-827-3034
E-mail Address: *info@napmw.org*
Web Address: www.napmw.org
The National Association of Professional Mortgage Women (NAPMW) is an association for women in the banking and mortgage industry.

National Reverse Mortgage Lenders Association (NRMLA)
1400 16th St. NW, Ste. 420
Washington, DC 20036 US
Phone: 202-939-1760
Fax: 202-265-4435
E-mail Address: *dhicks@dworbell.com*
Web Address: www.nrmlaonline.org
The National Reverse Mortgage Lenders Association (NRMLA) was established in 1997 to provide consumer education, industry events and information, and public policy initiatives for the reverse mortgage industry.

XXII. Mortgage Industry Resources

1 Mortgage Loan Calculators
Web Address: www.1mortgageloancalculators.com
1 Mortgage Loan Calculators is a web site that allows users to determine their mortgage eligibility through various mortgage calculators and comparative data.

E-Loan
6230 Stoneridge Mall Rd.
Pleasanton, CA 94588 US
Phone: 925-847-6200
Fax: 925-847-0831
Toll Free: 888-533-5333
Web Address: www.eloan.com
E-Loan provides information on a large variety of loan types, debt consolidation, refinancing, home equity and mortgage management. Additionally, the companies website offers several loan calculators and free credit reports.

Fannie Mae
3900 Wisconsin Ave. NW
Washington, DC 20016-2892 US
Phone: 202-752-7000
Toll Free: 800-732-6643
E-mail Address: *headquarters@fanniemae.com*
Web Address: www.fanniemae.com
Fannie Mae is one of the world's largest non-bank financial services companies and one of the nation's largest sources of financing for home mortgages. It operates under special sanction by the U.S. Congress. It's purpose is to provide liquidity in the national mortgage market.

Federal Agricultural Mortgage Corporation
1133 21st St. NW, Ste. 600
Washington, DC 20036 US
Fax: 202-872-7713
Toll Free: 800-879-3276
Web Address: www.farmermac.com
Federal Agricultural Mortgage Corporation, known as Farmer Mac, is America's secondary market for agricultural real estate and rural housing mortgage loans. Congress created Farmer Mac in 1988 to improve the availability of mortgage credit to America's farmers, ranchers and rural homeowners, businesses and communities.

Federal Citizen Information Center (FCIC)
Dept. WWW
Pueblo, CO 81009 US
Fax: 719-948-9724
Toll Free: 888-878-3256
Web Address: www.pueblo.gsa.gov
The Federal Citizen Information Center (FCIC) offers information and resources for consumers on topics such as cars, children, education, housing, small businesses and more, as well as current consumer news.

Federal Home Loan Mortgage Corporation (Freddie Mac)
8200 Jones Branch Dr.
McLean, VA 22102-3110 US
Phone: 703-903-2000
E-mail Address: *corprel@freddiemac.com*
Web Address: www.freddiemac.com
The Federal Home Loan Mortgage Corporation (Freddie Mac) operates under special sanction by the U.S. Congress. Its purpose is to provide liquidity in the national mortgage market.

Government National Mortgage Association (Ginnie Mae)
451 7th St. SW, Rm. B-133
Washington, DC 20410-9000 US
Phone: 202-708-1535
Toll Free: 888-446-6434
E-mail Address: *ginniemae.helpdesk@lmco.com*
Web Address: www.ginniemae.gov
The Government National Mortgage Association (Ginnie Mae) is a Federal Government enterprise that provides mortgages to low-income families.

Homepath
Fannie Mae
3900 Wisconsin Ave. NW
Washington, DC 20016-2892 US
Phone: 202-752-7000
Toll Free: 800-732-6643
E-mail Address: *resource_center@fanniemae.com*
Web Address:
www.fanniemae.com/homebuyers/homepath
Homepath, powered by Fannie Mae, helps users find a home, get the most out of their current home, find lenders and other services that will assist in the purchase of a home and help customers avoid mortgage fraud.

LendingTree, LLC
11115 Rushmore Dr.
Charlotte, NC 28277 US
Toll Free: 800-555-8733
Web Address: www.lendingtree.com
LendingTree, LLC serves as an online loan center that connects borrowers to a nationwide network of lenders with exceptional speed and efficiency. LendingTree's simple online forms allow borrowers to provide required information in a matter of minutes. Additionally, the site's network of some of the most respected financial institutions in the United States allows for quick loan offers, often in less than 48 hours.

Mortgage 101
909 N. Sepulveda Blvd., 11th Fl.
El Segundo, CA 90245 US
Toll Free: 888-265-1110
Web Address: www.mortgage101.com
Mortgage 101 lets users find information on rates and local companies, as well as apply for financing. It also offers various calculators concerning refinancing, renting or buying and how much home can be afforded based on monthly mortgage

payments. Mortgage 101 is a division of Internet Brands, Inc.

Mortgage.com
Toll Free: 866-422-9432
Web Address: www.mortgage.com
Mortgage.com provides customers with rate quotes and with mortgages, home buying, refinancing and debt consolidation; it is powered by Citigroup, Inc.

Mortgage-calc.com
11760 US Hwy. 1, Ste. 500
North Palm Beach, FL 33408 US
Phone: 561-630-2400
Fax: 561-625-4540
E-mail Address: *webmaster@mortgage-calc.com*
Web Address: www.mortgage-calc.com
Mortgage-calc.com is a web site with a multitude of calculators for home mortgage, amortization, mortgage refinance, home equity loans and debt consolidation.

ReverseMortgage.org
E-mail Address: *dhicks@nrmlaonline.org*
Web Address: www.reversemortgage.org
ReverseMortgage.org is a web site that is maintained by the National Reverse Mortgage Lenders Association. ReverseMortgage.org offers excellent information to consumers who want to learn more about how reverse mortgages work.

XXIII. Real Estate Industry Associations

Affordable Housing Tax Credit Coalition
1900 K St. NW, Ste. 1200
Washington, DC 20006-1109 US
Phone: 202-419-2025
Fax: 202-828-3738
E-mail Address: *info@taxcreditcoalition.org*
Web Address: www.taxcreditcoalition.org
The Affordable Housing Tax Credit Coalition is a nonprofit organization of individuals and groups involved in providing affordable housing under the low-income housing tax credit program.

American Escrow Association (AEA)
211 N. Union St., Ste. 100
Alexandria, VA 22314 US
Phone: 703-519-1240
E-mail Address: *hq@a-e-a.org*
Web Address: www.a-e-a.org
The American Escrow Association (AEA) is a national trade association of settlement and escrow industry professionals.

American Institute of Inspectors
P.O. Box 248
Lower Lake, CA 95457 US
Fax: 707-277-7852
Toll Free: 800-877-4770
E-mail Address: *execdir@inspection.org*
Web Address: www.inspection.org
The American Institute of Inspectors is a nonprofit association for residential and commercial building inspectors across North America.

American Investors in Real Estate Online (AIREO)
1824 Sylvan Ave.
Dallas, TX 75208 US
Phone: 214-745-8900
Fax: 214-745-8922
Web Address: www.aireo.com
American Investors in Real Estate Online (AIREO) is a nonprofit organization of real estate investors and professionals dedicated to learning and sharing successful investment techniques.

American Property Tax Counsel (APTC)
77 W. Washington St., Ste. 900
Chicago, IL 60602 US
Toll Free: 877-829-2782
E-mail Address: *bulletin@aptcnet.com*
Web Address: www.aptcnet.com
The American Property Tax Counsel (APTC) is a professional association of property and tax attorneys.

American Society of Appraisers
555 Herndon Pkwy., Ste. 125
Herndon, VA 20170 US
Phone: 703-478-2228
Fax: 703-742-8471
E-mail Address: *asainfo@appraisers.org*
Web Address: www.appraisers.org
The American Society of Appraisers is an organization that provides education and accreditation for appraisers, plus an appraiser locator and electronic recruitment resource for employers and job seekers.

ApartmentAssociation.com
E-mail Address: *info@corp.admiralonline.com*
Web Address: www.apartmentassociation.com

ApartmentAssociation.com provides several online tools, including a directory of state and local apartment associations throughout the U.S.; a listing maker tool that can be added to member's websites; a credit check tool; and free PDA software.

Association of Foreign Investors in Real Estate (AFIRE)
1300 Pennsylvania Ave. NW
Ronald Reagan Bldg.
Washington, DC 20004 US
Phone: 202-312-1400
Fax: 202-312-1401
E-mail Address: *afireinfo@afire.org*
Web Address: www.afire.org
The Association of Foreign Investors in Real Estate (AFIRE) is the only not-for-profit association for the foreign real estate investment community, with more than 180 members representing 21 countries.

Building Owners and Managers Association (BOMA) International
1101 15th St. NW, Ste. 800
Washington, DC 20005 US
Phone: 202-408-2662
Fax: 202-326-6377
E-mail Address: *info@boma.org*
Web Address: www.boma.org
The Building Owners and Managers Association (BOMA) International is a premier network 92 local associations in the U.S. as well as 12 affiliates in 11 other countries, representing more than 16,500 commercial real estate professionals.

Certified Commercial Investment Member Institute (CCIM)
430 N. Michigan Ave., Ste. 800
Chicago, IL 60611-4092 US
Phone: 312-321-4460
Fax: 312-321-4530
Toll Free: 800-621-7027
E-mail Address: *info@ccim.com*
Web Address: www.ccim.com
The Certified Commercial Investment Member Institute (CCIM) is an organization that provides accreditation for certified commercial investment members.

Certified New Home Specialist
Dennis Walsh & Associates, Inc.
2222 Colony Plz.
Newport Beach, CA 92660 US
Phone: 949-706-3500
Toll Free: 800-428-1122
E-mail Address: *info@sellnewhomes.com*
Web Address: www.sellnewhomes.com
The Certified New Home Specialist web site offers certification as a New Home Specialist, an accreditation endorsed by GMAC, Coldwell Banker, ERA Real Estate and Prudential Real Estate. The web site is offered by Dennis Walsh & Associates, Inc.

China Commercial Real Estate Association
No. 3 Shijingshan Rd., Yuquan Mansion, Rm. 513
Beijing, 100049 China
Phone: 86-10-88255833
Fax: 86-10-88255149
E-mail Address: *ccreu@163.com*
Web Address: www.ccreu.com.cn
The China Commercial Real Estate Association (CCREA) primary members are commercial real estate development enterprises, retailers, chain store companies, commercial consultant companies, designing companies, funds companies, devices suppliers and professionals.

Commercial Real Estate Women Network (CREW Network)
1201 Wakarusa Dr., Ste. C3
Lawrence, KS 66049-3803 US
Phone: 785-832-1808
Fax: 785-832-1551
E-mail Address: *denisek@crewnetwork.org*
Web Address: www.crewnetwork.org
The Commercial Real Estate Women Network (CREW Network) is a national association of women in the commercial real estate industry.

Community Associations Institute (CAI)
225 Reinekers Ln., Ste. 300
Alexandria, VA 22314 US
Phone: 703-548-8600
Fax: 703-684-1581
Toll Free: 888-224-4321
Web Address: www.caionline.org
The Community Associations Institute (CAI) is an association of condominium, cooperative and homeowner associations.

Confederation of Real Estate Developer's Associations of India
105 Ansal Bhawan
16 Kasturba Gandhi Marg
New Delhi, 110 001 India
Phone: 91-11-4152 0549
Fax: 91-11-4152 0548

E-mail Address: *info@credai.org*
Web Address: www.cbec.gov.in
Confederation of Real Estate Developer's Associations of India (CREDAI) is the apex body of the organized real estate developers/builders across India.

Council of International Restaurant Real Estate Brokers (CIRB)
8350 N. Central Expwy., Ste. 1300
Dallas, TX 75206 US
Fax: 866-247-2329
Toll Free: 866-247-2123
E-mail Address: *cirbhq@cirb.net*
Web Address: www.cirb.net
The Council of International Restaurant Real Estate Brokers (CIRB) is the only international network of independent real estate brokers who specialize solely in restaurant and related real estate.

Council of Residential Specialists (CRS)
430 N. Michigan Ave., 3rd. Fl.
Chicago, IL 60611 US
Fax: 312-329-8882
Toll Free: 800-462-8841
Web Address: www.crs.com
The Council of Residential Specialists (CRS) is an association of realtors providing training for the Certified Residential Specialist designation.

Counselors of Real Estate (CRE)
430 N. Michigan Ave.
Chicago, Il 60611 US
Phone: 312-329-8427
E-mail Address: *pcoady@cre.org*
Web Address: www.cre.org
The Counselors of Real Estate (CRE) is an international group of high-profile professionals, including members of prominent real estate, financial, legal and accounting firms as well as leaders in government and academia, who provide objective advice on complex real property situations and land-related matters.

European Public Real Estate Association (EPRA)
Schiphol Blvd. 283
Schiphol Airport
1118 BH The Netherlands
Phone: 31-20-405-3830
Fax: 31-20-405-3840
E-mail Address: *info@epra.com*
Web Address: www.epra.com
The European Public Real Estate Association (EPRA) is a trade association of European real estate companies.

Foundation of Real Estate Appraisers (FREA)
4907 Morena Blvd., Ste. 1415
San Diego, CA 92117 US
Fax: 858-273-8206
Toll Free: 800-882-4410
E-mail Address: *info@frea.com*
Web Address: www.frea.com
The Foundation of Real Estate Appraisers (FREA) is an organization of appraisers, home inspectors and environmental site assessors offering errors and omissions insurance, continuing education and other benefits.

Hong Kong Institute of Surveyors (HKIS)
1 Connaught Pl.
8/F Jardine House, Ste. 801
Hong Kong, Hong Kong China
Phone: 852-2526-3679
Fax: 852-2868-4612
Web Address: www.hkis.org.hk
The Hong Kong Institute of Surveyors (HKIS) is the professional organization representing the surveying industry and surveying professionals in Hong Kong.

India Institute of Real Estate
Orchard Dr. Pai Marg, Nachiket Pk.
Baner,, Ste. 400
Pune, 411 045 India
Phone: 9890238936
E-mail Address: *support@iire.co.in*
Web Address: www.iire.co.in
The India Institute of Real Estate is a nonprofit organization supporting the real estate industry. The organization provides accreditation and certifications pertaining to the real estate practice in India.

Institute for Responsible Housing Preservation (IRHP)
401 9th St. NW, Ste. 900
Washington, DC 20004 US
Phone: 202-585-8739
Fax: 202-585-8080
E-mail Address: *info@HousingPreservation.org*
Web Address: www.housingpreservation.org
The Institute for Responsible Housing Preservation (IRHP) is a nonprofit association of owners and managers of Section 221(d)(3) and Section 236 projects participating in HUD preservation programs.

Institute of Housing Management (IHM)
2175 Sheppard Ave. E., Ste. 310
Toronto, ON M2J 1W8 Canada
Phone: 416-493-7382
Fax: 416-491-1670
Toll Free: 866-212-4377
E-mail Address: *ihm@taylorenterprises.com*
Web Address: www.ihm-canada.com
The Institute of Housing Management (IHM) is a Canadian organization of property management professionals.

Institute of Real Estate Management (IREM)
430 N. Michigan Ave.
Chicago, IL 60611 US
Fax: 800-338-4736
Toll Free: 800-837-0706
E-mail Address: *custserv@irem.org*
Web Address: www.irem.org
The Institute of Real Estate Management (IREM) seeks to educate real estate managers, certify their competence and professionalism, serve as an advocate on issues affecting the real estate management industry and enhance its members' professional competence so they can better identify and meet the needs of those who use their services.

International Association of Assessing Officers (IAAO)
314 West 10th St.
Kansas City, MO 64105-1616 US
Phone: 816-701-8100
Fax: 816-701-8149
Toll Free: 800-616-4226
E-mail Address: *daniels@iaao.org*
Web Address: www.iaao.org
The International Association of Assessing Officers (IAAO) is an association of professionals in the field of property assessment and taxation.

International Association of Certified Home Inspectors (InterNACHI)
1750 30th St.
Boulder, CO 80301 US
Phone: 303-502-6214
Fax: 650-429-2057
Toll Free: 877-346-3467
E-mail Address: *fastreply@nachi.org*
Web Address: www.nachi.org
The International Association of Certified Home Inspectors (InterNACHI) is a nonprofit organization designed to help home inspectors to achieve financial success and remain highly educated. The organizations web site provides free course material for home inspectors and online tools to help consumers find a qualified professional, mainly in the U.S. and Canada.

International Business Broker Association (IBBA)
401 N. Michigan Ave., Ste. 2200
Chicago, IL 60611-4267 US
Phone: 312-673-4097
Fax: 312-673-6599
Toll Free: 888-686-4222
E-mail Address: *admin@ibba.org*
Web Address: www.ibba.org
The International Business Broker Association (IBBA) is the largest international nonprofit association operating exclusively for the benefit of people and firms engaged in the various aspects of business brokerage and mergers and acquisitions.

International Facility Management Association (IFMA)
1 E. Greenway Plz., Ste. 1100
Houston, TX 77046-0194 US
Phone: 713-623-4362
Fax: 713-623-6124
E-mail Address: *ifma@ifma.org*
Web Address: www.ifma.org
The International Facility Management Association (IFMA) is a trade association of facilities managers. IFMA certifies facility managers, provides educational programs, conducts research, recognizes facility management degree and certificate programs and produces World Workplace, a facility management-related conference and exposition.

International Real Estate Institute (IREI)
1224 N. Nokomis NE
Alexandria, MN 56308 US
Phone: 320-763-4648
Fax: 320-763-9290
E-mail Address: *info@irei-assoc.org*
Web Address: irei-assoc.org
The International Real Estate Institute (IREI) is one of the largest international real estate associations in the world, with members in over more cities than any other organization.

International Society of Appraisers (ISA)
1131 SW 7th St., Ste. 105
Renton, WA 98057-1215 US
Phone: 206-241-0359
Fax: 206-241-0436
E-mail Address: *isa@isa-appraisers.org*

Web Address: www.isa-appraisers.org
The International Society of Appraisers (ISA) is a nonprofit association that provides education and organizational support to its members and serves the public by producing highly qualified and ethical appraisers who are recognized authorities in professional personal property appraising.

National Apartment Association (NAA)
4300 Wilson Blvd., Ste. 400
Arlington, VA 22203 US
Phone: 703-518-6141
Fax: 703-248-9440
E-mail Address: *webmaster@naahq.org*
Web Address: www.naahq.org
The National Apartment Association (NAA) is a national federation of state and local apartment associations designed to serve the interests of multifamily housing owners, managers, developers and suppliers.

National Association of Hispanic Real Estate Professionals (NAHREP)
1150 17th St. NW, Ste. 504
Washington, DC 20036 US
Fax: 202-955-1066
Toll Free: 800-964-5373
Web Address: www.nahrep.org
The National Association of Hispanic Real Estate Professionals (NAHREP) is an organization that serves real estate agents, brokers, loan officers, mortgage brokers, title officers, escrow officers, appraisers and insurance agents from diverse cultural backgrounds, as membership is not limited to professionals of Hispanic descent.

National Association of Home Inspectors (NAHI)
4248 Park Glen Rd.
Minneapolis, MN 55416 US
Phone: 952-928-4641
Fax: 952-929-1318
Toll Free: 800-448-3942
E-mail Address: *info@nahi.org*
Web Address: www.nahi.org
The National Association of Home Inspectors (NAHI) is a nonprofit association that exists to promote and develop the home inspection industry.

National Association of Housing and Redevelopment Officials (NAHRO)
630 Eye St. NW
Washington, DC 20001 US
Phone: 202-289-3500
Fax: 202-289-8181
Toll Free: 877-866-2476
E-mail Address: *nahro@nahro.org*
Web Address: www.nahro.org
The National Association of Housing and Redevelopment Officials (NAHRO) is an association of professionals in affordable housing and community redevelopment. Its members administer Hud programs such as Public Housing, Section 8, CDBG and HOME.

National Association of Independent Fee Appraisers (NAIFA)
401 N. Michigan Ave., Ste. 2200
Chicago, IL 60611 US
Phone: 312-321-6830
Fax: 312-673-6652
E-mail Address: *info@naifa.com*
Web Address: www.naifa.com
The National Association of Independent Fee Appraisers (NAIFA) offers education, professional designations, an online appraiser directory and other services for appraisers and the public.

National Association of Industrial and Office Properties (NAIOP)
2201 Cooperative Way, 3rd. Fl.
Herndon, VA 20171-3034 US
Phone: 703-904-7100
Fax: 703-904-7942
E-mail Address: *hamilton@naiop.org*
Web Address: www.naiop.org
The National Association of Industrial and Office Properties (NAIOP) is a trade association of commercial real estate professionals.

National Association of Mold Professionals (NAMP)
3250 Old Farm Ln., Ste. 1
Walled Lake, MI 48390 US
Phone: 248-669-5673
E-mail Address: *info@moldpro.org*
Web Address: www.moldpro.org
The National Association of Mold Professionals (NAMP) is a nonprofit organization that was established with the goal of developing and promoting the mold inspection and remediation industry.

National Association of Real Estate Brokers (NAREB)
9831 Greenbelt Rd., Ste. 309
Lanham, MD 20706 US

Phone: 301-552-9340
Fax: 301-552-9216
E-mail Address: *NAREB3@comcast.net*
Web Address: www.nareb.com
The National Association of Real Estate Brokers (NAREB) is a national trade organization dedicated to bringing together the nation's minority professionals in the real estate industry.

National Association of Real Estate Companies (NAREC)
216 W. Jackson Blvd., Ste. 625
Chicago, IL 60606 US
Phone: 312-263-1755
Fax: 312-750-1203
E-mail Address: *info@narec.org*
Web Address: www.narec.org
The National Association of Real Estate Companies (NAREC) is composed of representatives of publicly and privately owned real estate companies, significant subsidiaries of publicly owned companies and public accounting firms.

National Association of Real Estate Investment Trusts (NAREIT)
1875 I St. NW, Ste. 600
Washington, DC 20006 US
Phone: 202-739-9400
Fax: 202-739-9401
Toll Free: 800-362-7348
E-mail Address: *info@nareit.org*
Web Address: www.nareit.org
The National Association of Real Estate Investment Trusts (NAREIT) is the representative to governmental policymakers for U.S. Real Estate Investment Trusts (REITs) and publicly traded real estate companies worldwide.

National Association of Real Estate Property Managers (NARPM)
638 Independence Pkwy., Ste. 100
Chesapeake, VA 23320 US
Fax: 866-466-2776
Toll Free: 800-782-3452
E-mail Address: *info@narpm.org*
Web Address: www.narpm.org
National Association of Real Estate Property Managers (NARPM) is an association of real estate management professionals that specializes in single-family and small residential properties.

National Association of Real-Estate Inspection & Evaluation Services (NARIES)
P.O. Box 532
Edmonds, WA 98020 US
Phone: 206-778-1296
Toll Free: 800-583-5821
E-mail Address: *crmsnsky@verizon.net*
Web Address: www.naries.org
The National Association of Real-Estate Inspection & Evaluation Services (NARIES) is an association dedicated to the education of consumers hiring building and home inspectors, appraisers, real-estate professionals, architects, engineers and building officials.

National Association of Realtors (NAR)
430 N. Michigan Ave.
Chicago, IL 60611-4087 US
Phone: 202-383-1176
Toll Free: 800-874-6500
E-mail Address: *lsalvant@realtors.org*
Web Address: www.realtor.org
The National Association of Realtors (NAR) is composed of realtors involved in residential and commercial real estate as brokers, salespeople, property managers, appraisers and counselors and in other areas of the industry. NAR also sponsors Realtor.com, operated by Move, Inc.

National Council of Real Estate Investment Fiduciaries (NCREIF)
2 Prudential Plz., 180 N. Stetson Ave.
Chicago, IL 60601 US
Phone: 312-819-5890
Fax: 312-819-5891
E-mail Address: *dpoutasse@ncreif.org*
Web Address: www.ncreif.com
The National Council of Real Estate Investment Fiduciaries (NCREIF) is an association of institutional real estate professionals such as investment managers, plan sponsors, academicians, consultants, appraisers, CPAs and other service providers who have a significant involvement in pension fund real estate investments.

National Multi Housing Council (NMHC)
1850 M St. NW, Ste. 540
Washington, DC 20036-5803 US
Phone: 202-974-2300
Fax: 202-775-0112
E-mail Address: *info@nmhc.org*
Web Address: www.nmhc.org

The National Multi Housing Council (NMHC) is a trade association representing apartment owners, managers, developers, lenders and service providers.

Pension Real Estate Association (PREA)
100 Pearl St., 13th Fl.
Hartford, CT 06103 US
Phone: 860-692-6341
Fax: 860-692-6351
E-mail Address: *prea@prea.org*
Web Address: www.prea.org
The Pension Real Estate Association (PREA) is a nonprofit organization whose members are engaged in the investment of tax-exempt pension and endowment funds into real estate assets.

Property Management Association (PMA)
7900 Wisconsin Ave., Ste. 305
Bethesda, MD 20814 US
Phone: 301-657-9200
Fax: 301-907-9326
E-mail Address: *info@pma-dc.org*
Web Address: www.pma-dc.org
The Property Management Association (PMA) is a real estate management organization that promotes the knowledge and practical education of the industry through monthly meetings, seminars and publications.

Real Estate Developers' Association of Singapore (REDAS)
190 Clemenceau Ave.
07-01 Singapore Shopping Ctr.
Singapore
Phone: 65-6336-6655
Fax: 65-6337-2217
E-mail Address: *enquiry@redas.com*
Web Address: www.redas.com.sg
Real Estate Developers' Association of Singapore's (REDAS) website, Redas.com, is an information center as well as an electronic marketplace that offers a broad array of services and resources including but not limited to property search engines, market trends, policy updates, on-line purchases of products and services, business message exchange, and links to other trade associations, professional bodies, government agencies and statutory boards in Singapore and the region.

Real Estate Institute of Canada (REIC)
5407 Eglinton Ave. W., Ste. 208
Toronto, ON M9C 5K6 Canada
Phone: 416-695-9000
Fax: 416-695-7230
Toll Free: 800-542-7342
E-mail Address: *infocentral@reic.com*
Web Address: www.reic.ca
The Real Estate Institute of Canada (REIC) is an association of professionals dedicated to establishing, maintaining, promoting and advancing high standards of practice through education, certification and accreditation.

Realtors Land Institute (RLI)
430 N. Michigan Ave.
Chicago, IL 60611 US
Fax: 312-329-8633
Toll Free: 800-441-5263
E-mail Address: *rli@realtors.org*
Web Address: www.rliland.com
Realtors Land Institute (RLI) serves professionals specializing in land brokerage. The web site includes membership benefits, land listings and state chapters.

Research Institute for Housing America
Mortgage Bankers Association
1919 Pennsylvania Ave. NW
Washington, DC 20006 US
Phone: 202-557-2700
E-mail Address: *info@mortgagebankers.org*
Web Address: www.housingamerica.org
The Research Institute for Housing America of the Mortgage Bankers Association is a 501(c)(3) trust fund. Its chief purpose is to encourage and aid - through grants and sponsored research to distinguished scholars, educational institutions, research facilities, and government organizations - the pursuit of knowledge of mortgage markets and real estate finance. Excellent research papers on various housing issues are available on its web site.

Royal Institution of Chartered Surveyors
RICS Contact Ctr.
Surveyor Ct., Westwood Way
Coventry, CV4 8JE UK
Phone: 44-870-333-1600
Fax: 44-20-7-334-3811
E-mail Address: *contactrics@rics.org*
Web Address: www.rics.org
The Royal Institution of Chartered Surveyors (RICS) is a U.K.-based trade organization representing 140,000 members operating in 146 countries; it has offices around the globe, on every continent.

Society of Industrial and Office Realtors (SIOR)
1201 New York Ave. NW, Ste. 350

Washington, DC 20005-6126 US
Phone: 202-449-8200
Fax: 202-216-9325
E-mail Address: *admin@sior.com*
Web Address: www.sior.com
The Society of Industrial and Office Realtors (SIOR) provides support for industrial and office real estate specialists holding the SIOR designation.

Surveyors and Valuers Accreditation Association (SAVA)
SAVA, National Energy Ctr.
Davy Ave.
Milton Keynes, Surrey MK5 8NA UK
Phone: 44-1908-672787
Fax: 44-1908-662296
E-mail Address: *info@sava.org.uk*
Web Address: www.sava.org.uk
The Surveyors and Valuers Accreditation Association (SAVA) sets surveying standards for the Royal Institution of Chartered Surveyors.

TriState REALTORS Commercial Alliance
555 E. North Ln., Ste. 6125
Conshohocken, PA 19428-4425 US
Phone: 610-238-9950
Fax: 610-238-9959
E-mail Address: *tristate@tristaterca.com*
Web Address: www.tristaterca.com
The TriState REALTORS Commercial Alliance is an association of commercial real estate professionals in Pennsylvania, New Jersey and Delaware.

Women's Council of Realtors (WCR)
430 N. Michigan Ave.
Chicago, IL 60611 US
Toll Free: 800-245-8512
E-mail Address: *wcr@wcr.org*
Web Address: www.wcr.org
The Women's Council of Realtors (WCR) is a community of female real estate professionals.

XXIV. Real Estate Industry Resources

CoStar Group
2 Bethesda Metro Ctr., 10th Fl.
Bethesda, MD 20814-5388 US
Phone: 301-215-8300
Fax: 800-613-1301
Toll Free: 800-204-5960
E-mail Address: *info@costar.com*
Web Address: www.costar.com
CoStar Group operates a web site with extensive resources for brokers, owners and users of commercial real estate space. The group operates a listings database that allows users to analyze market trends, research property history and compare local rental rates for commercial real estate.

Marcus & Millichap Real Estate Investment Services, Inc.
16830 Ventura Blvd., Ste. 352
Encino, CA 91436 US
Phone: 818-907-0600
Fax: 818-501-8230
Web Address: www.marcusmillichap.com
Marcus & Millichap Real Estate Investment Services, Inc., a national investment real estate brokerage firm, offers in-depth reports on various commercial property and apartment sectors, by city and on a nationwide basis. Users can register to receive its e-mail reports.

Metropolitan Institute at Virginia Tech (MI)
1021 Prince St., Ste. 100
Alexandria, VA 22314 US
Phone: 703-706-8100
Fax: 703-518-8009
E-mail Address: *mivt@vt.edu*
Web Address: www.mi.vt.edu
The Metropolitan Institute at Virginia Tech (MI) conducts basic and applied research on national and international development patterns, focusing on key forces shaping metropolitan growth such as demographics, environment, technology, design, transportation, and governance. MI publishes several excellent white papers and reports yearly.

MSN Real Estate
Microsoft Corporation
1 Microsoft Way
Redmond, WA 98052-6399 US
Toll Free: 800-642-7676
Web Address: realestate.msn.com
MSN Real Estate features advice, links and services for buying and selling houses and managing and maintaining residential property.

Real Estate Library
200 SW Shining Mist
Depoe Bay, OR 97345 US
Phone: 541-765-3090
E-mail Address: *admin@relibrary.com*
Web Address: www.relibrary.com

The Real Estate Library contains resources such as mortgage loan assistance, online real estate courses for certification, real estate web design walkthroughs and other useful tools for buyers, sellers, home owners and real estate professionals.

REITNet
Web Address: www.reitnet.com
REITNet is a web site that offers a number of articles and glossaries for anyone researching or investing in real estate investment trusts (REITs). The REITNet.com domain is currently up for sale.

RentLaw.com
Phone: 732-539-2914
E-mail Address: *info@rentlaw.com*
Web Address: www.rentlaw.com
RentLaw.com provides landlords, tenants, investors, lawyers, agent associations and homeowners with extensive information regarding landlord-tenant laws and legal advice.

XXV. Remodeling Industry Associations

National Association of the Remodeling Industry (NARI)
780 Lee St., Ste. 200
Des Plaines, IL 60016 US
Phone: 847-298-9200
Fax: 847-298-9225
Toll Free: 800-298-6274
E-mail Address: *info@nari.org*
Web Address: www.nari.org
The National Association of the Remodeling Industry (NARI) provides certifications, education and support to professionals working in the remodeling industry, along with support to consumers.

National Kitchen & Bath Association (NKBA)
687 Willow Grove St.
Hackettstown, NJ 07840 US
Fax: 908-852-1695
Toll Free: 800-843-6522
E-mail Address: *feedback@nkba.org*
Web Address: www.nkba.org
The National Kitchen & Bath Association (NKBA) is a premier resource for kitchen and bath remodelers, designers, planners and consumers. It offers courses and certifications for professionals in design, installation and education. It is the owner of the Kitchen/Bath Industry Show & Conference each year and it sponsors annual design competitions.

XXVI. Science Parks

International Association of Science Parks (IASP)
29590 Campanillas
Malaga, Spain
Phone: 34 95 202 83 03
Fax: 34 95 202 04 64
E-mail Address: *iasp@iasp.ws*
Web Address: www.iasp.ws
The IASP is a worldwide network of science and technology parks. It enjoys Special Consultative status with the Economic and Social Council of the United Nations. Its 350 members represent science parks in 72 nations. It is also a founding member of the World Alliance for Innovation WAINOVA. World headquarters are in Spain, with an additional office in the Tsinghua University Science Park, Beijing, China.

XXVII. Shopping Center Directories

Chain Store Guide (CSG)
3922 Coconut Palm Dr.
Tampa, FL 33619 US
Fax: 813-627-6883
Toll Free: 800-778-9794
E-mail Address: *info@csgis.com*
Web Address: www.csgis.com
The Chain Store Guide (CSG) is a provider of comprehensive retail and foodservice intelligence. The CSG database contains over 200,000 retailers, foodservice operators, distributors and wholesalers in the U.S. and Canada.

National Research Bureau (NRB)
2 Bethesda Metro Ctr., 10th Fl.
Bethesda, MD 20814-5388 US
Phone: 301-215-8300
Fax: 800-613-1301
Toll Free: 800-204-5960
E-mail Address: *info@costar.com*
Web Address: www.nrbonline.com
CoStar Group, publishes The Shopping Center Information Products database, which contains approximately 41,000 U.S. shopping centers; Shopping Center Directory; the Shopping Center Directions Newsletter and Real Estate America.

The Directory of Major Malls, Inc.
20 N. Broadway
P.O. Box 837
Nyack, NY 10960 US

Phone: 845-348-7000
Fax: 845-348-7011
Toll Free: 800-898-6255
Web Address: www.directoryofmajormalls.com
The Directory of Major Malls, Inc. offers information on centers that have above 250,000 square feet of gross leaseable area (GLA). Information includes location, GLA, household income, area population and design of various centers.

Value Retail News
29399 US Hwy. 19 N, Ste. 370
Clearwater, FL 33761-2137 US
Phone: 727-781-7557
Fax: 727-781-9717
E-mail Address: *lhumphers@icsc.org*
Web Address: www.valueretailnews.com
Value Retail News, a division of the International Council of Shopping Centers, publishes several directories, including the Outlet Project Directory, a listing of factory outlet information; and the Value Retail Directory, which provides factory outlet tenant data.

XXVIII. Shopping Center Resources

ChainLinks Retail Advisors
2 Ravinia Dr., Ste. 1550
Atlanta, GA 30346 US
Phone: 678-336-8960
Fax: 678-336-8965
Toll Free: 800-394-3701
Web Address: www.chainlinks.com
ChainLinks is a major retail-only, full-service real estate broker in the United States and Canada.

CoreNet Global
260 Peachtree St. NW, Ste. 1500
Atlanta, GA 30303 US
Phone: 404-589-3200
Fax: 404-589-3201
Toll Free: 800-726-8111
E-mail Address: *sguree@corenetglobal.org*
Web Address: www2.corenetglobal.org
CoreNet Global is an organization for business leaders engaged in the strategic management of real estate for major corporations worldwide.

International Council of Shopping Centers (ICSC)
1221 Ave. of the Americas, 41st Fl.
New York, NY 10020-1099 US
Phone: 646-728-3800
Fax: 732 694 1800
E-mail Address: *icsc@icsc.org*
Web Address: www.icsc.org
The International Council of Shopping Centers (ICSC) is the global trade association of the shopping center industry, and includes shopping center owners, developers, managers, marketing specialists, investors, lenders and retailers. ICSC's 70,000 members reach to over 80 countries and the organization links with more than 25 national and regional shopping center councils throughout the world.

Retail Traffic Online
249 W. 17th St.
New York, NY 10011 US
Phone: 212-204-4200
Fax: 914-514-9050
E-mail Address: *david.bodamer@penton.com*
Web Address: www.retailtrafficmag.com
RetailTraffic Online serves as the web site for the Retail Traffic magazine. The site offers retail news, store expansion plans, financial news, research tools and much more.

XXIX. Spa Industry Associations

International Spa Association (ISPA)
2365 Harrodsburg Rd., Ste. A325
Lexington, KY 40504 US
Phone: 859-226-4326
Fax: 859-226-4445
Toll Free: 888-651-4772
E-mail Address: *ispa@ispastaff.com*
Web Address: www.experienceispa.com
The International Spa Association (ISPA) is recognized worldwide as one of the leading professional organizations and voices of the spa industry. It provides educational and networking opportunities, promotes the value of the spa experience and speaks as the authoritative voice to foster professionalism and growth. ISPA represents more than 3,000 health and wellness facilities and providers in 75 countries.

XXX. Telecommunications Industry Associations

FTTH Council (Fiber to the Home Council)
P. O. Box 21071
Spokane, WA 99201 US
Phone: 503-635-3114
E-mail Address: *info@ftthcouncil.org*

Web Address: www.ftthcouncil.org
The Fiber-to-the-Home (FTTH) Council is a nonprofit organization established in 2001 to educate the public on the opportunities and benefits of FTTH solutions. Its website is an excellent resource for statistics, general reference and trends in the delivery of fiber optic cable directly to the home and office.

XXXI. Trade Associations-General

BUSINESSEUROPE
168 Ave. de Cortenbergh
Brussels, 1000 Belgium
Phone: 32-0-2-237-65-11
Fax: 32-0-2-231-14-45
E-mail Address: *main@businesseurope.eu*
Web Address: www.businesseurope.eu
BUSINESSEUROPE is a major European trade federation that operates in a manner similar to a chamber of commerce. Its members are the central national business federations of the 34 countries throughout Europe from which they come. Companies cannot become direct members of BUSINESSEUROPE, though there is a support group which offers the opportunity for firms to encourage BUSINESSEUROPE objectives in various ways.

The Associated Chambers of Commerce and Industry of India (ASSOCHAM)
1 Community Ctr. Zamrudpur
Kailash Colony
New Delhi, 110 048 India
Phone: 46550555
Fax: 46536481
E-mail Address: *assocham@nic.in*
Web Address: www.assocham.org
The Associated Chambers of Commerce and Industry of India (ASSOCHAM) has a membership of more than 300 chambers and trade associations and serves members from all over India.

XXXII. Transportation Industry Associations

Reconnecting America
1707 L St. NW, Ste. 210
Washington, DC 20036 US
Phone: 202-429-6990
Fax: 202-315-3508
E-mail Address: *bsullivan@reconnectingamerica.org*
Web Address: www.reconnectingamerica.org
Reconnecting America is a nonprofit organization dedicated to integrating transportation systems and the communities they serve. It provides the Center for Transit-Oriented Development program to help spur investment in urban revitalization and a Transportation Networks program that works to link aviation, rail and intercity bus systems.

XXXIII. Travel-Local Transportation & Car Rental

American Public Transportation Association (APTA)
1666 K St. NW
Washington, DC 20006 US
Phone: 202-496-4800
Fax: 202-496-4321
Web Address: www.apta.com
APTA is a nonprofit international association of more than 1,500 member organizations including public transportation systems; planning, design, construction and finance firms; product and service providers; academic institutions; and state associations and departments of transportation. APTA members serve more than 90 percent of persons using public transportation in the United States and Canada.

XXXIV. U.S. Government Agencies

Bureau of Economic Analysis (BEA)
1441 L St. NW
Washington, DC 20230 US
Phone: 202-606-9900
E-mail Address: *customerservice@bea.gov*
Web Address: www.bea.gov
The Bureau of Economic Analysis (BEA), an agency of the U.S. Department of Commerce, is the nation's economic accountant, preparing estimates that illuminate key national, international and regional aspects of the U.S. economy.

Bureau of Labor Statistics (BLS)
2 Massachusetts Ave. NE
Washington, DC 20212-0001 US
Phone: 202-691-5200
Web Address: stats.bls.gov
The Bureau of Labor Statistics (BLS) is the principal fact-finding agency for the Federal Government in the field of labor economics and statistics. It is an independent national statistical agency that collects, processes, analyzes and disseminates statistical data to the American public, U.S. Congress, other federal agencies, state and local governments, business and

labor. The BLS also serves as a statistical resource to the Department of Labor.

Department of Housing and Urban Development (HUD)
451 7th St. SW
Washington, DC 20410 US
Phone: 202-708-1112
E-mail Address: *Helen.A.Savoye@hud.gov*
Web Address: www.hud.gov
The Department of Housing and Urban Development, commonly known as HUD, is a Federal Government agency involved in increasing homeownership, supporting community development and increasing access to affordable housing free from discrimination.

Energy Efficiency and Renewable Energy (EERE)
1000 Independence Ave. SW
Mail Stop EE-1
Washington, DC 20585 US
Phone: 202-586-4403
Toll Free: 877-337-3463
Web Address: www.eere.energy.gov
The Energy Efficiency and Renewable Energy (EERE), an office of the U.S. Department of Energy, provides information on bioenergy, geothermal, hydrogen, hydropower, tidal, hydropower, solar, wind and energy conservation methods. The Office also works with U.S. industries to advance the development of various alternative energy technologies.

Federal Housing Administration (FHA)
U.S. Dept of Housing & Urban Development
451 7th Street S.W.
Washington, DC 20410 US
Toll Free: 800-225-5342
Web Address: www.fha.gov
The Federal Housing Administration, generally known as FHA, is the largest government insurer of mortgages in the world, insuring over 35 million properties since its inception in 1934. A part of the United States Department of Housing and Urban Development (HUD), FHA provides mortgage insurance on single-family, multifamily, manufactured homes and hospital loans made by FHA-approved lenders throughout the United States and its territories.

National Institute of Standards and Technology (NIST)
100 Bureau Dr., Stop 1070
Gaithersburg, MD 20899-1070 US
Phone: 301-975-6478
E-mail Address: *inquiries@nist.gov*
Web Address: www.nist.gov
The National Institute of Standards and Technology (NIST) is an agency of the U.S. Department of Commerce's Technology Administration. It works with various industries to develop and apply technology, measurements and standards.

Office of Federal Housing Enterprise Oversight (OFHEO)
1700 G St. NW, 4th Fl.
Washington, DC 02552 US
Phone: 202-414-3800
Fax: 202-414-3823
E-mail Address: *fhfainfo@fhfa.gov*
Web Address: www.ofheo.gov
The Office of Federal Housing Enterprise Oversight (OFHEO) publishes a housing price index along with many other very useful statistics about America's housing and mortgage sectors.

U.S. Census Bureau
4600 Silver Hill Rd.
Washington, DC 20233-8800 US
Phone: 301-763-4636
Fax: 301-457-3670
Toll Free: 800-923-8282
E-mail Address: *pio@census.gov*
Web Address: www.census.gov
The U.S. Census Bureau is the official collector of data about the people and economy of the U.S. Founded in 1790, it provides official social, demographic and economic information.

U.S. Department of Commerce (DOC)
1401 Constitution Ave. NW
Washington, DC 20230 US
Phone: 202-482-2000
E-mail Address: *cgutierrez@doc.gov*
Web Address: www.commerce.gov
The U.S. Department of Commerce (DOC) regulates trade and provides valuable economic analysis of the economy.

U.S. Department of Labor (DOL)
Frances Perkins Bldg.
200 Constitution Ave. NW
Washington, DC 20210 US
Toll Free: 866-487-2365
Web Address: www.dol.gov

The U.S. Department of Labor (DOL) is the government agency responsible for labor regulations. This site provides tools to help citizens find out whether companies are complying with family and medical-leave requirements.

U.S. Securities and Exchange Commission (SEC)
100 F St. NE
Washington, DC 20549 US
Phone: 202-551-6000
Toll Free: 888-732-6585
E-mail Address: *publicinfo@sec.gov*
Web Address: www.sec.gov
The U.S. Securities and Exchange Commission (SEC) is a nonpartisan, quasi-judicial regulatory agency responsible for administering federal securities laws. These laws are designed to protect investors in securities markets and ensure that they have access to disclosure of all material information concerning publicly traded securities. Visitors to the web site can access the EDGAR database of corporate financial and business information.

Chapter 4

THE REAL ESTATE 400: WHO THEY ARE AND HOW THEY WERE CHOSEN

Includes Indexes by Company Name, Industry & Location, And a Complete Table of Sales, Profits and Ranks

The companies chosen to be listed in PLUNKETT'S REAL ESTATE & CONSTRUCTION INDUSTRY ALMANAC comprise a unique list. THE REAL ESTATE 400 (the actual count is 434 companies) were chosen specifically for their dominance in the many facets of the real estate and construction industry in which they operate. Complete information about each firm can be found in the "Individual Profiles," beginning at the end of this chapter. These profiles are in alphabetical order by company name.

THE REAL ESTATE 400 companies are from all parts of the United States, Asia, Canada, Europe and beyond. Essentially, THE REAL ESTATE 400 includes companies that are deeply involved in the services, trends and technologies that keep the entire industry forging ahead.

Simply stated, THE REAL ESTATE 400 contains the largest, most successful, fastest growing firms in real estate, construction and related industries in the world. To be included in our list, the firms had to meet the following criteria:

1) Generally, these are corporations based in the U.S., however, the headquarters of 112 firms are located in other nations.
2) Prominence, or a significant presence, in real estate, construction and supporting fields. (See the following Industry Codes section for a complete list of types of businesses that are covered).
3) The companies in THE REAL ESTATE 400 do not have to be exclusively in the real estate and construction field.
4) Financial data and vital statistics must have been available to the editors of this book, either directly from the company being written about or from outside sources deemed reliable and accurate by the editors. A small number of companies that we would like to have included are not listed because of a lack of sufficient, objective data.

INDEXES TO THE REAL ESTATE 400, AS FOUND IN THIS CHAPTER AND IN THE BACK OF THE BOOK:

INDUSTRY LIST, WITH CODES

This book refers to the following list of unique industry codes, based on the 2007 NAIC code system (NAIC is used by many analysts as a replacement for older SIC codes because NAIC is more specific to today's industry sectors, see www.census.gov/NAICS). Companies profiled in this book are given a primary NAIC code, reflecting the main line of business of each firm.

Automotive

Automotive Manufacturing

3363 Automobile Parts Manufacturing

Entertainment

Hotels & Accommodations

721110 Hotels/Resorts/Motels
721120 Casino Resorts

Financial Services

Banking, Credit & Finance

522220 Financing--Business
522291 Finance--Consumer
522310 Mortgages
522310E Mortgages, Online
522320 Payment & Transaction Processing Services

Stocks & Investments

523920 Investment Management/Mutual Funds/Pension Funds

Insurance

524126 Insurance--Property & Casualty, Specialty, Surety
524127 Insurance-Title (Real Estate)

Health Care

Nursing

623110 Long-Term Health Care & Assisted Living

InfoTech

Software

511210 Computer Software, Publisher
511210J Computer Software, Data Base & File Management

Internet

519130 Internet Publishing & Web Search Portals

Manufacturing

Manufactured Housing

321991 Housing (Mobile Homes), Manufactured

Paper Products/Forest Products

322 Forest Products/Paper, Manufacturing

Construction

326199 Building Products & Construction Materials in Plastic, Manufacturing

Nonmetallic Minerals/Rock/Aggregate

327 Nonmetallic Mineral, Rock & Aggregate Manufacturing

Fabricated Metals

332311 Prefabricated Metal Building & Component Manufacturing

Machinery & Manufacturing Equipment

333 Machinery, Manufacturing

Real Estate

Real Estate

525990 Real Estate Investment Trusts - Mortgage
531110 Real Estate Investment Trusts - Residential
531120 Real Estate Investment Trusts - Nonresidential

Retailing

Building Materials & Garden Supplies Stores

444110 Home Centers, Retail
444130 Building Materials/Hardware Stores

Services

Construction

23 Construction Services
2361 Construction, Residential
237 Construction, Heavy & Civil Engineering
238210 Electric Contractors

238220 Plumbing, Heating & Air Conditioning Contractors
2389 Construction--Other Special Trade Contractors

Real Estate

5311 Real Estate Operations & Development--General
531210 Real Estate Brokerage

Consulting & Professional Services

541310 Architectural Services
541330 Engineering Services

Personnel, Administrative & Support Services

561210 Facilities Support Services
561720 Janitorial Services

Travel Agencies

561599 Time Share Arrangements & Management

Transportation

Transportation-Manufacturing of Equipment

3366 Ship Manufacturing

Ships

483111 Shipping-Deep Sea

Truck

4885 Freight Forwarding & Support Services
532120 Trucks, Rental/Leasing

Wholesale Distribution-Other

Distribution-Durable Goods

4233 Lumber & Construction Materials, Wholesale Distribution

INDEX OF RANKINGS WITHIN INDUSTRY GROUPS

Company	Industry Code	2008 Sales (U.S. $ thousands)	Sales Rank	2008 Profits (U.S. $ thousands)	Profits Rank
Architectural Services					
SIEMENS BUILDING TECHNOLOGIES	541310				
Automobile Parts Manufacturing					
GEORG FISCHER LTD	3363	3,949,130	2	61,030	2
JOHNSON CONTROLS INC	3363	38,062,000	1	979,000	1
Building Materials/Hardware Stores					
84 LUMBER COMPANY	444130	2,100,000	1		
BUILDING MATERIALS HOLDING	444130	1,324,679	3	-214,809	3
FERGUSON ENTERPRISES INC	444130				
JEWETT CAMERON TRADING	444130	64,321	4	2,610	2
PACIFIC COAST BUILDING PRODUCTS	444130				
PLUM CREEK TIMBER CO INC	444130	1,614,000	2	233,000	1
STOCK BUILDING SUPPLY INC	444130				
TRUE HOME VALUE INC	444130				
Building Products & Construction Materials in Plastic, Manufacturing					
ROYAL GROUP INC	326199				
TRACO	326199				
Casino Resorts					
AMERISTAR CASINOS INC	721120	1,267,902	6	-130,672	3
BOYD GAMING CORP	721120	1,780,967	5	-223,005	5
HARRAH'S ENTERTAINMENT INC	721120	9,370,000	1	-5,197,200	8
KERZNER INTERNATIONAL LTD	721120				
LAS VEGAS SANDS CORP (THE VENETIAN)	721120	4,735,126	3	-163,558	4
MGM MIRAGE	721120	7,208,767	2	-855,286	7
RIO PROPERTIES INC	721120				
RIVIERA HOLDINGS CORP	721120	169,760	8	-11,862	2
SANDS REGENT	721120				
SOCIETE DES BAINS DE MER ET DU CERCLE	721120				
STATION CASINOS INC	721120				
STRATOSPHERE CORP	721120				
TRUMP ENTERTAINMENT RESORTS INC	721120	908,008	7	-232,203	6
WYNN RESORTS LIMITED	721120	2,987,324	4	210,479	1
Computer Software Publisher					
LENDER PROCESSING SERVICES INC	511210	1,837,590	1	230,888	1
Computer Software, Data Base & File Management					
REIS INC	511210J	47,621	1	-7,480	1
Construction Services					
CHINA COMMUNICATIONS CONSTRUCTION COMPANY LTD	23	22,008,100	1	881,490	1
SAMWHAN CORPORATION	23				
YIT CORPORATION	23	5,245,600	2	176,800	2
Construction, Heavy & Civil Engineering					
ACCIONA SA	237	17,094,300	10	626,280	6

Company	Industry Code	2008 Sales (U.S. $ thousands)	Sales Rank	2008 Profits (U.S. $ thousands)	Profits Rank
ACS ACTIVIDADES DE CONSTRUCCION Y SERVICIOS	237	20,786,400	6	2,412,200	1
AECOM TECHNOLOGY CORP	237	5,194,482	21	147,226	17
AECON GROUP INC	237	1,492,630	29	47,160	24
AMEC PLC	237	3,823,620	24	291,940	13
BALFOUR BEATTY PLC	237	12,658,800	11	396,460	11
BECHTEL GROUP INC	237	31,400,000	3		
BLACK & VEATCH HOLDING CO	237	3,200,000	25		
BOUYGUES SA	237	43,264,900	1	1,985,160	3
BURNS & MCDONNELL	237				
CAMP DRESSER & MCKEE INC	237				
CHICAGO BRIDGE & IRON COMPANY NV	237	5,944,981	18	-21,146	30
DAELIM INDUSTRIAL CO LTD	237	6,942,560	15	95,850	21
DESARROLLADORA HOMEX SAB DE CV	237	1,368,576	30	117,543	20
DOOSAN HEAVY INDUSTRY & CONSTRUCTION CO	237	8,943,400	13	217,500	16
EMPRESAS ICA SA DE CV	237	2,020,700	28	58,300	23
FLUOR CORP	237	22,325,900	5	748,903	5
FOMENTO DE CONSTRUCCIONES Y CONTRATAS SA (FCC)	237	18,563,200	9	446,330	8
GRANITE CONSTRUCTION INC	237	2,674,244	26	122,404	19
GRUPO ACS	237	19,320,500	7	1,769,040	4
GRUPO FERROVIAL SA	237	18,672,700	8	43,600	25
GS ENGINEERING & CONSTRUCTION CORP	237	4,971,500	22	266,300	14
HDR INC	237				
HOCHTIEF AG	237	25,783,870	4	419,100	10
HYUNDAI ENGINEERING & CONSTRUCTION COMPANY LTD	237	5,782,184	19	296,997	12
IMPREGILO SPA	237	3,991,960	23	226,220	15
JACOBS ENGINEERING GROUP	237	11,252,159	12	420,742	9
KUMHO INDUSTRIAL CO LTD	237	6,072,700	17	27,600	27
LAYNE CHRISTENSEN CO	237	868,274	31	37,256	26
LOUIS BERGER GROUP INC	237				
MATRIX SERVICE COMPANY	237	731,301	32	21,414	28
MEADOW VALLEY CORP	237				
MWH GLOBAL INC	237				
ODEBRECHT SA	237				
PARSONS BRINCKERHOFF INC	237	2,343,117	27	73,882	22
PCL CONSTRUCTION GROUP	237				
RAILWORKS CORP	237				
SEMBCORP INDUSTRIES LTD	237	6,548,910	16	482,170	7
SHAW GROUP INC	237	6,998,011	14	140,717	18
STERLING CONSTRUCTION CO	237	415,074	33	18,066	29
TDINDUSTRIES	237				
TUTOR PERINI CORPORATION	237	5,660,286	20	-75,140	31
VINCI	237	42,717,900	2	2,003,070	2
Construction, Residential					
AVATAR HOLDINGS INC	2361	110,366	20	-109,876	3

Company	Industry Code	2008 Sales (U.S. $ thousands)	Sales Rank	2008 Profits (U.S. $ thousands)	Profits Rank
BEAZER HOMES USA INC	2361	1,813,513	11	-951,912	13
BROOKFIELD HOMES CORP	2361	449,000	19	-116,000	5
CAPITAL PACIFIC HOLDINGS	2361				
CENTEX CORP	2361	8,275,562	2	-2,657,482	20
CYRELA BRAZIL REALTY SA EMPREEND PART	2361				
DOMINION HOMES INC	2361				
DR HORTON INC	2361	6,518,600	3	-2,633,600	19
HOVNANIAN ENTERPRISES INC	2361	3,308,111	7	-1,124,590	16
KB HOME	2361	3,033,936	9	-976,131	14
LENNAR CORPORATION	2361	4,575,417	5	-1,109,085	15
M/I HOMES INC	2361	607,659	15	-250,323	7
MDC HOLDINGS INC	2361	1,458,108	14	-380,545	10
MERITAGE HOMES CORP	2361	1,523,068	13	-291,935	8
NVR INC	2361	3,638,702	6	100,892	2
ORLEANS HOMEBUILDERS	2361	583,282	16	-143,413	6
PULTEGROUP INC	2361	6,112,038	4	-1,473,113	18
RYLAND GROUP INC	2361	1,976,000	10	-397,000	11
SEKISUI HOUSE LTD	2361	15,978,100	1	603,500	1
STANDARD PACIFIC CORP	2361	1,549,203	12	-1,233,615	17
TECHNICAL OLYMPIC USA INC	2361				
TOLL BROTHERS INC	2361	3,148,166	8	-297,810	9
WCI COMMUNITIES INC	2361	556,077	17	-936,796	12
WILLIAM LYON HOMES	2361	526,078	18	-111,638	4
Construction--Other Special Trade Contractors					
ACERGY SA	2389	2,522,400	1	307,200	1
ANTHONY & SYLVAN POOLS	2389				
INSITUFORM TECHNOLOGIES	2389	536,664	3	21,640	3
ORION MARINE GROUP INC	2389	261,802	4	14,475	4
SCHUFF INTERNATIONAL INC	2389	681,629	2	56,315	2
Electric Contractors					
EMCOR GROUP INC	238210	6,785,242	1	182,204	1
INTEGRATED ELECTRICAL SERVICES	238210	818,287	2	-187	2
Engineering Services					
AMEY PLC	541330				
ARCADIS NV	541330	2,277,630	5	83,350	6
CH2M HILL COMPANIES LTD	541330	5,589,900	4	32,056	7
CHIYODA CORPORATION	541330	6,035,600	3	96,410	5
ENGLOBAL CORP	541330	493,332	8	18,258	8
MCDERMOTT INTERNATIONAL	541330	6,572,423	2	429,302	1
SKIDMORE OWINGS & MERRILL	541330				
STV GROUP INC	541330	250,000	9		
TREVI-FINANZIARIA INDUSTRIALE SPA (TREVI GROUP)	541330	1,443,130	7	100,830	4
URS CORPORATION	541330	10,086,289	1	219,791	2
WS ATKINS PLC	541330	2,076,210	6	148,360	3
Facilities Support Services					
ABERTIS INFRAESTRUCTURAS	561210	4,883,650	1	820,360	1

Company	Industry Code	2008 Sales (U.S. $ thousands)	Sales Rank	2008 Profits (U.S. $ thousands)	Profits Rank
Financing--Business					
GENERAL ELECTRIC CO (GE)	522220	182,515,000	1	17,410,000	1
GMAC INC	522220	18,395,000	2	1,868,000	2
Financing--Consumer					
GE CAPITAL FINANCE	522291	67,008,000	1		
ORIGEN FINANCIAL INC	522291	0		-35,364	1
Freight Forwarding & Support Services					
ORIENT OVERSEAS (INTERNATIONAL) LTD	4885	6,545,140	1	275,529	1
Home Centers, Retail					
HOME DEPOT INC	444110	77,349,000	1	4,395,000	1
LOWE'S COMPANIES INC	444110	48,283,000	2	2,809,000	2
NATIONAL HOME CENTERS INC	444110				
Hotels/Resorts/Motels					
ACCOR NORTH AMERICA	721110				
ACCOR SA	721110	10,730,100	2	810,800	1
AMAN RESORTS	721110				
AMERICA'S BEST FRANCHISING	721110				
BANYON TREE HOTELS & RESORTS	721110				
BARCELO CRESTLINE CORP	721110				
BEST WESTERN INTERNATIONAL INC	721110	231,638	26	-1,657	21
CARLSON HOTELS WORLDWIDE	721110				
CHINA LODGING GROUP LTD	721110				
CHOICE HOTELS INTERNATIONAL INC	721110	641,680	17	100,211	8
CLUB MEDITERRANEE SA	721110	1,938,630	8	2,600	20
DAYS INN WORLDWIDE INC	721110				
DOYLE COLLECTION	721110				
FAIRMONT RAFFLES HOTELS INTERNATIONAL INC	721110				
FOUR SEASONS HOTELS	721110				
GAYLORD ENTERTAINMENT CO	721110	930,869	14	4,364	18
GOLDEN TULIP HOSPITALITY GROUP	721110				
GROUPE DU LOUVRE	721110				
GUOMAN HOTELS LIMITED	721110				
HILTON HOTELS CORP	721110	7,770,000	3		
HOME INNS & HOTELS MANAGEMENT INC	721110	257,922	25	14,838	16
HONGKONG AND SHANGHAI HOTELS LTD	721110	637,140	18	27,870	13
HOTEL PROPERTIES LTD	721110	78,960	30	5,160	17
HOWARD JOHNSON INTERNATIONAL INC	721110				
HVM LLC	721110				
HYATT HOTELS CORPORATION	721110	3,900,000	6		
INDIAN HOTEL COMPANY LTD	721110				
INTERCONTINENTAL HOTELS GROUP PLC	721110	1,854,000	9	302,000	4
INTERSTATE HOTELS AND RESORTS INC	721110	779,453	16	-18,023	24
INTOWN SUITES MANAGEMENT	721110				
JAMESON INN INC	721110				
JANUS HOTELS AND RESORTS	721110				
JOHN Q HAMMONS HOTELS	721110				

Company	Industry Code	2008 Sales (U.S. $ thousands)	Sales Rank	2008 Profits (U.S. $ thousands)	Profits Rank
JOIE DE VIVRE HOSPITALITY	721110				
KIMPTON HOTEL & RESTAURANT GROUP LLC	721110				
LODGIAN INC	721110	228,194	27	-11,984	23
LOEWS HOTELS HOLDING CORPORATION	721110				
LQ MANAGEMENT LLC	721110				
MANDARIN ORIENTAL INTERNATIONAL LTD	721110	530,000	20	66,200	10
MARCUS CORPORATION	721110	371,075	22	20,486	14
MARRIOTT INTERNATIONAL INC	721110	12,879,000	1	359,000	2
MERITUS HOTELS & RESORTS	721110				
MILLENNIUM & COPTHORNE HOTELS PLC	721110	1,158,530	12	116,860	7
MORGANS HOTEL GROUP CO	721110	314,467	23	-55,349	26
NH HOTELES SA	721110	1,997,070	7	34,930	12
OAKWOOD WORLDWIDE	721110				
OBEROI GROUP (EIH LTD)	721110	270,000	24	47,000	11
ORIENT-EXPRESS HOTELS LTD	721110	502,838	21	-26,551	25
QMH UK LTD	721110				
RAMADA WORLDWIDE INC	721110				
RED LION HOTELS CORP	721110	187,570	28	-1,704	22
RESORTQUEST INTERNATIONAL INC	721110				
REZIDOR SAS HOSPITALITY	721110				
RITZ-CARLTON HOTEL CO LLC	721110				
ROSEWOOD HOTELS & RESORTS LLC	721110				
SCANDIC HOTELS AB	721110	982,670	13	143,930	6
SHANGRI-LA ASIA LTD	721110	1,353,300	11	165,900	5
SHUN TAK HOLDINGS LIMITED	721110	561,240	19	14,860	15
SOL MELIA SA	721110	1,657,000	10	66,330	9
SONESTA INTERNATIONAL HOTELS CORP	721110	80,517	29	4,080	19
STARWOOD CAPITAL GROUP GLOBAL LLC	721110				
STARWOOD HOTELS & RESORTS WORLDWIDE INC	721110	5,754,000	4	329,000	3
STRATEGIC HOTELS AND RESORTS INC	721110	928,389	15	-317,291	27
SUNBURST HOSPITALITY CORP	721110				
SUPER 8 MOTELS INC	721110				
THARALDSON ENTERPRISES	721110				
TRT HOLDINGS	721110				
WYNDHAM WORLDWIDE	721110	4,281,000	5	-1,074,000	28
XANTERRA PARKS AND RESORTS	721110				
Housing (Mobile Homes), Manufactured					
CAVALIER HOMES INC	321991	164,405	4	3,349	2
CHAMPION ENTERPRISES INC	321991	1,033,193	1	-199,460	4
CLAYTON HOMES INC	321991				
DREW INDUSTRIES	321991	510,506	3	11,678	1
FAIRMONT HOMES INC	321991				
HORTON HOMES INC	321991				
MODTECH HOLDINGS INC	321991				

Company	Industry Code	2008 Sales (U.S. $ thousands)	Sales Rank	2008 Profits (U.S. $ thousands)	Profits Rank
PALM HARBOR HOMES INC	321991	555,096	2	-124,262	3
SOUTHERN ENERGY HOMES	321991				
Insurance--Property & Casualty, Specialty, Surety					
PMI GROUP INC	524126	907,787	2	-928,508	2
RADIAN GROUP INC	524126	1,808,036	1	-410,579	1
Insurance--Title (Real Estate)					
FIDELITY NATIONAL FINANCIAL	524127	4,251,200	2	-179,016	3
FIRST AMERICAN CORP	524127	6,213,758	1	-26,320	2
INVESTORS TITLE COMPANY	524127	71,123	5	-1,183	1
LANDAMERICA FINANCIAL GROUP INC	524127	2,876,000	3	-719,700	5
STEWART INFORMATION SERVICES CORP	524127	1,555,294	4	-247,455	4
Internet Publishing & Web Search Portals					
COSTAR GROUP INC	519130	212,428	2	24,623	1
MOVE INC	519130	242,069	1	-29,190	2
Investment Management/Mutual Funds/Pension Funds					
TRINITY LTD	523920				
Janitorial Services					
SERVICEMASTER COMPANY	561720	3,311,432	1	-126,399	1
Long-Term Health Care & Assisted Living					
ADVOCAT INC	623110	287,607	6	5,735	2
ATRIA SENIOR LIVING GROUP	623110				
BROOKDALE SENIOR LIVING	623110	1,928,054	2	-373,241	5
CAPITAL SENIOR LIVING CORP	623110	193,274	7	3,724	3
EMERITUS CORP	623110	772,443	5	-104,751	4
ERICKSON RETIREMENT COMMUNITIES	623110				
EXTENDICARE REAL ESTATE INVESTMENT TRUST	623110	1,686,690	3	11,350	1
MANOR CARE INC	623110	3,850,000	1		
SUNRISE SENIOR LIVING	623110	1,570,974	4	-439,179	6
Lumber & Construction Materials, Wholesale Distribution					
CEMEX INC	4233				
CEMEX SAB DE CV	4233	21,695,000	2	2,487,000	1
FIVE STAR PRODUCTS INC	4233				
LB FOSTER COMPANY	4233	512,592	3	27,746	3
WOLSELEY PLC	4233	24,071,500	1	437,820	2
Machinery, Manufacturing					
HYUNDAI ELEVATOR CO LTD	333				
Mortgages					
BANK OF AMERICA HOME LOANS	522310				
CAPMARK FINANCIAL GROUP	522310			-1,352,800	3
CITIMORTGAGE INC	522310				
FANNIE MAE	522310	17,436,000	1	-58,707,000	5
FEDERAL AGRICULTURAL MORTGAGE CORP (FARMER MAC)	522310	74,184	2	-154,080	2
FIRST MORTGAGE CORP	522310				
FIRSTCITY FINANCIAL CORP	522310	45,196	3	-46,675	1
FREDDIE MAC	522310	0		-50,119,000	4

Company	Industry Code	2008 Sales (U.S. $ thousands)	Sales Rank	2008 Profits (U.S. $ thousands)	Profits Rank
GE CAPITAL REAL ESTATE	522310				
MUNICIPAL MORTGAGE & EQUITY	522310				
Mortgages--Online					
DITECH.COM	522310E				
E-LOAN INC	522310E				
LENDINGTREE LLC	522310E				
Nonmetallic Mineral, Rock & Aggregate Manufacturing					
CRH PLC	327	27,220,600	1	1,644,680	1
Payment & Transaction Processing Services					
FIDELITY NATIONAL INFORMATION SERVICES INC	522320	3,427,700	1	214,800	1
Plumbing, Heating & Air Conditioning Contractors					
COMFORT SYSTEMS USA INC	238220	1,321,770	1	49,690	1
Prefabricated Metal Building & Component Manufacturing					
BUTLER MANUFACTURING CO	332311				
NCI BUILDING SYSTEMS INC	332311	1,764,159	1	78,881	1
SKYLINE CORPORATION	332311	301,765	2	-5,556	2
Real Estate Brokerage					
CB RICHARD ELLIS GROUP INC (CBRE)	531210	5,128,817	1	-1,012,066	3
CENTURY 21 REAL ESTATE	531210				
CHRISTIES GREAT ESTATES	531210				
COLDWELL BANKER REAL ESTATE CORP	531210				
COLLIERS INTERNATIONAL PROPERTY CONSULTANTS	531210	2,000,000	2		
CORE NETWORK	531210				
CUSHMAN & WAKEFIELD INC	531210				
GRUBB & ELLIS CO	531210	628,779	3	-330,870	2
HOMESERVICES OF AMERICA	531210				
NAI GLOBAL INC	531210				
NRT INCORPORATED	531210				
PRUDENTIAL REAL ESTATE AFFILIATES INC	531210				
RE/MAX INTERNATIONAL INC	531210				
ZIPREALTY INC	531210	107,450	4	-13,342	1
Real Estate Investment Trusts - Mortgage					
DYNEX CAPITAL INC	525990	29,653	2	15,121	2
MFA FINANCIAL INC	525990	519,788	1	45,797	1
Real Estate Investment Trusts - Nonresidential					
ALEXANDRIA REAL ESTATE EQUITIES INC	531120	451,637	39	120,097	23
AMLI RESIDENTIAL PROPERTIES TRUST	531120				
ANDERSON-TULLY LUMBER CO	531120				
ANNALY CAPITAL MANAGEMENT	531120	3,115,428	6	346,238	9
APARTMENT INVESTMENT AND MANAGEMENT CO	531120	1,243,170	14	627,002	3
ARC GROUP OF COMPANIES	531120				
ARDEN REALTY INC	531120				
BOSTON PROPERTIES INC	531120	1,488,400	10	125,232	22
BRANDYWINE REALTY TRUST	531120	589,421	30	38,525	37

Company	Industry Code	2008 Sales (U.S. $ thousands)	Sales Rank	2008 Profits (U.S. $ thousands)	Profits Rank
CAMDEN PROPERTY TRUST	531120	624,016	28	70,973	29
CAPITAL AUTOMOTIVE REIT	531120				
CBL & ASSOCIATES PROPERTIES INC	531120	1,138,218	16	57,434	33
CNL FINANCIAL GROUP INC	531120				
COLONY CAPITAL LLC	531120				
CORPORATE OFFICE PROPERTIES TRUST	531120	585,605	31	61,316	31
CRESCENT REAL ESTATE EQUITIES LP	531120				
DCT INDUSTRIAL TRUST INC	531120	248,542	50	9,486	49
DIVIDEND CAPITAL GROUP LLC	531120				
DUKE REALTY CORP	531120	1,292,183	12	110,408	24
EASTGROUP PROPERTIES INC	531120	168,575	58	34,142	41
ENTERTAINMENT PROPERTIES TRUST	531120	286,140	45	101,710	26
EQUITY OFFICE PROPERTIES TRUST	531120				
EQUITY ONE INC	531120	239,029	52	35,008	40
FEDERAL REALTY INVESTMENT TRUST	531120	520,188	34	129,246	21
FELCOR LODGING TRUST	531120	1,102,912	17	-120,487	58
FIRST INDUSTRIAL REALTY TRUST INC	531120	514,321	35	20,169	46
GENERAL GROWTH PROPERTIES INC	531120	3,361,525	4	4,719	52
GLENBOROUGH REALTY TRUST	531120				
GLIMCHER REALTY TRUST	531120	319,725	44	16,769	47
GRUBB & ELLIS REALTY INVESTORS LLC	531120				
HCP INC	531120	1,153,188	15	470,983	4
HEALTH CARE REIT INC	531120	526,406	33	283,425	10
HEALTHCARE REALTY TRUST	531120	213,931	54	41,760	36
HIGHWOODS PROPERTIES INC	531120	450,291	40	35,610	39
HOSPITALITY PROPERTIES TRUST	531120	1,252,674	13	133,995	19
HOST HOTELS & RESORTS LP	531120	5,139,000	2	414,000	6
HRPT PROPERTIES TRUST	531120	835,855	22	244,645	13
INLAND REAL ESTATE CORPORATION	531120	188,844	57	30,425	44
INNKEEPERS USA TRUST	531120				
ISTAR FINANCIAL INC	531120	1,354,254	11	-181,767	59
KILROY REALTY CORPORATION	531120	256,066	48	46,911	35
KIMCO REALTY CORP	531120	758,704	23	249,902	12
LASALLE HOTEL PROPERTIES	531120	683,377	26	33,127	42
LEXINGTON REALTY TRUST	531120	418,149	41	-3,468	53
LIBERTY PROPERTY TRUST	531120	731,352	24	180,106	16
LILLIBRIDGE HEALTHCARE REAL ESTATE TRUST	531120				
LINK REAL ESTATE INVESTMENT TRUST	531120	545,900	32	668,100	2
MACERICH COMPANY	531120	880,871	21	195,015	15
MACK-CALI REALTY CORP	531120	723,802	25	51,726	34
MISSION WEST PROPERTIES	531120	99,704	60	10,134	48
NATIONAL HEALTH INVESTORS	531120	58,005	63	57,510	32
NATIONWIDE HEALTH PROPERTIES	531120	368,319	42	268,138	11
NEW PLAN EXCEL REALTY TRUST INC	531120				
NEWCASTLE INVESTMENT	531120	468,867	37	-2,985,352	63
OMEGA HEALTHCARE INVESTORS	531120	193,762	56	78,137	27
PARKWAY PROPERTIES INC	531120	265,411	47	9,274	50

Company	Industry Code	2008 Sales (U.S. $ thousands)	Sales Rank	2008 Profits (U.S. $ thousands)	Profits Rank
PENNSYLVANIA REIT	531120	467,993	38	-16,355	55
PRIME GROUP REALTY TRUST	531120	64,840	62	-73,336	57
PRIME RETAIL INC	531120				
PROLOGIS	531120	5,565,983	1	-449,966	60
PS BUSINESS PARKS INC	531120	281,843	46	70,044	30
PUBLIC STORAGE INC	531120	1,723,593	9	935,176	1
REALTY INCOME CORP	531120	327,773	43	131,841	20
REGENCY CENTERS CORP	531120	495,895	36	136,188	18
RXR REALTY	531120				
SENIOR HOUSING PROPERTIES	531120	235,537	53	106,511	25
SIMON PROPERTY GROUP INC	531120	3,783,155	3	463,636	5
SL GREEN REALTY CORP	531120	1,079,422	18	360,935	8
SOVRAN SELF STORAGE INC	531120	200,193	55	37,399	38
SUN COMMUNITIES INC	531120	254,291	49	-34,448	56
SUNSTONE HOTEL INVESTORS	531120	881,494	20	71,238	28
SUPERTEL HOSPITALITY INC	531120	99,256	61	6,656	51
TANGER FACTORY OUTLET CENTERS	531120	245,391	51	25,786	45
TAUBMAN CENTERS INC	531120	671,498	27	-8,052	54
TRANSCONTINENTAL REALTY	531120	138,337	59	32,209	43
UNIBAIL-RODAMCO	531120	1,893,300	8	-1,484,300	61
VENTAS INC	531120	923,698	19	222,603	14
VORNADO REALTY TRUST	531120	2,692,686	7	411,445	7
WEINGARTEN REALTY INVESTORS	531120	592,748	29	154,595	17
WELLS REAL ESTATE FUNDS	531120				
WESTFIELD GROUP	531120	3,167,100	5	-1,581,600	62
Real Estate Investment Trusts - Residential					
ARCHSTONE TRUST	531110				
ASSOCIATED ESTATES REALTY CORPORATION	531110	130,642	18	34,627	9
AVALONBAY COMMUNITIES INC	531110	814,224	4	411,487	3
BOARDWALK REAL ESTATE INVESTMENT TRUST	531110	349,330	12	37,640	8
BRE PROPERTIES INC	531110	379,543	10	140,811	4
CAPREIT INC	531110				
CAPSTEAD MORTGAGE CORP	531110	400,489	9	125,923	5
COLONIAL PROPERTIES TRUST	531110	343,567	13	-55,429	17
COMMUNITY DEVELOPMENT TRUST	531110				
COUSINS PROPERTIES INC	531110	214,651	17	24,925	12
DEVELOPERS DIVERSIFIED REALTY CORP	531110	881,768	3	-93,095	18
EQUITY LIFESTYLE PROPERTIES INC	531110	419,349	7	18,303	13
EQUITY RESIDENTIAL	531110	1,975,669	1	436,413	2
ESSEX PROPERTY TRUST INC	531110	408,434	8	84,395	7
GABLES RESIDENTIAL TRUST	531110				
HOME PROPERTIES INC	531110	494,043	6	93,205	6
HOMETOWN AMERICA LLC	531110				
IMPAC MORTGAGE HOLDINGS	531110	1,476,972	2	-44,723	16
INLAND AMERICAN REAL ESTATE TRUST	531110				

Company	Industry Code	2008 Sales (U.S. $ thousands)	Sales Rank	2008 Profits (U.S. $ thousands)	Profits Rank
INVESTORS REAL ESTATE TRUST	531110	221,170	16	12,088	14
LIGHTSTONE GROUP LLC	531110				
MID-AMERICA APARTMENT COMMUNITIES INC	531110	370,011	11	30,249	10
POST PROPERTIES INC	531110	281,940	14	-8,370	15
SAWYER REALTY HOLDINGS	531110				
TRANSWESTERN INVESTMENT	531110				
UDR INC	531110	563,408	5	688,708	1
WASHINGTON REAL ESTATE INVESTMENT TRUST	531110	278,691	15	27,082	11
Real Estate Rental, Leasing, Development & Management					
ABM INDUSTRIES INC	5311	3,623,590	7	45,434	23
AMB PROPERTY CORPORATION	5311	693,842	24	-49,310	29
AMERICAN CAMPUS COMMUNITIES	5311	233,579	31	-13,055	27
AMERICAN REALTY INVESTORS	5311	177,367	33	26,634	26
BROOKFIELD ASSET MANAGEMENT INC	5311	12,909,000	2	649,000	11
CENTRO PROPERTIES GROUP	5311	491,360	27	-1,467,390	33
CHINA OVERSEAS LAND & INVESTMENT LIMITED	5311	2,437,530	12	654,440	10
CHINA STATE CONSTRUCTION ENGINEERING CORP	5311	29,564,000	1	401,630	14
CHINESE ESTATES HOLDINGS	5311	163,200	34	-187,880	30
CREST NICHOLSON PLC	5311				
DLF LIMITED	5311	3,155,320	8	1,678,670	3
EMAAR PROPERTIES PJSC	5311	4,360,000	5	1,519,000	4
EVERGRANDE REAL ESTATE GROUP	5311				
FIRSTSERVICE CORPORATION	5311	1,549,713	14	34,863	24
FOREST CITY ENTERPRISES	5311	1,286,470	18	52,425	22
GAFISA SA	5311	990,550	20	62,550	21
HANG LUNG GROUP LTD	5311	1,361,630	15	969,770	8
HANG LUNG PROPERTIES LTD	5311	1,300,600	17	661,010	9
HENDERSON LAND DEVELOPMENT COMPANY LTD	5311	1,754,000	13	2,011,400	2
HINES INTERESTS LP	5311				
HONGKONG LAND HOLDINGS	5311	1,022,300	19	-301,300	31
HUTCHISON WHAMPOA HOTEL & PROPERTIES LTD	5311				
HYPO REAL ESTATE HOLDING AG (HYPO BANK)	5311	309,400	28	594,100	13
HYSAN DEVELOPMENT CO LTD	5311	212,900	32	207,200	16
ICAHN ENTERPRISES LP	5311	5,027,000	3	-2,688,000	35
INDUSTRIAL DEVELOPMENTS INTERNATIONAL INC	5311				
JOHN LAING PLC	5311				
JONES LANG LASALLE INC	5311	2,697,586	11	84,883	18
LBA REALTY LLC	5311				
MAGUIRE PROPERTIES INC	5311	492,015	26	-323,338	32
MAX PROPERTY GROUP PLC	5311				
MRV ENGENHARIA E PARTICIPACOES SA	5311	634,050	25	131,870	17

Company	Industry Code	2008 Sales (U.S. $ thousands)	Sales Rank	2008 Profits (U.S. $ thousands)	Profits Rank
NEW WORLD DEVELOPMENT COMPANY LIMITED	5311	3,788,350	6	1,248,270	5
NEWHALL LAND & FARMING	5311				
PDG REALTY SA EMPREENDIMENTOS E PARTICIPACOES	5311				
REALOGY CORPORATION	5311	4,725,000	4	-1,912,000	34
RELATED GROUP	5311				
ROSSI RESIDENCIAL SA	5311	703,920	23	67,700	20
SAHA PATHANA INTER-HOLDING	5311	86,500	35	28,000	25
SHIMAO PROPERTY HOLDINGS	5311	1,356,270	16	598,280	12
SINO LAND COMPANY LIMITED	5311	812,600	22	1,003,700	7
ST JOE COMPANY	5311	258,158	29	-35,883	28
SUN HUNG KAI PROPERTIES	5311	3,154,710	9	2,956,560	1
TARRAGON CORPORATION	5311				
TRAMMELL CROW COMPANY	5311				
TRANSWESTERN COMMERCIAL SERVICES	5311				
TRIPLE FIVE GROUP	5311				
TRUMP ORGANIZATION	5311				
UNITECH LIMITED	5311	844,600	21	327,730	15
WATSON LAND COMPANY	5311				
WHARF (HOLDINGS) LIMITED	5311				
WHEELOCK AND COMPANY	5311	2,913,850	10	1,219,710	6
WP CAREY & CO LLC	5311	238,624	30	78,047	19
Ship Manufacturing					
HANJIN HEAVY INDUSTRIES CO	3366	3,068,630	1	56,810	1
Shipping-Deep Sea					
SWIRE PACIFIC LTD	483111	3,183,030	1	215,210	1
Steel & Metals, Fabricated Metals Components, Manufacturing					
BOISE CASCADE	322	2,977,498	1	-287,978	1
Time Share Arrangements & Management					
BLUEGREEN CORPORATION	561599	594,861	1	-516	1
DIAMOND RESORTS HOLDINGS	561599				
WORLDMARK BY WYNDHAM	561599				
WYNDHAM VACATION OWNERSHIP	561599				
Trucks, Rental/Leasing					
AMERCO	532120	2,049,174	1	67,784	1

ALPHABETICAL INDEX

DITECH.COM
DIVIDEND CAPITAL GROUP LLC
DLF LIMITED
DOMINION HOMES INC
DOOSAN HEAVY INDUSTRY & CONSTRUCTION CO
DOYLE COLLECTION (THE)
DR HORTON INC
DREW INDUSTRIES
DUKE REALTY CORP
DYNEX CAPITAL INC
EASTGROUP PROPERTIES INC
E-LOAN INC
EMAAR PROPERTIES PJSC
EMCOR GROUP INC
EMERITUS CORP
EMPRESAS ICA SA DE CV
ENGLOBAL CORP
ENTERTAINMENT PROPERTIES TRUST
EQUITY LIFESTYLE PROPERTIES INC
EQUITY OFFICE PROPERTIES TRUST
EQUITY ONE INC
EQUITY RESIDENTIAL
ERICKSON RETIREMENT COMMUNITIES
ESSEX PROPERTY TRUST INC
EVERGRANDE REAL ESTATE GROUP
EXTENDICARE REAL ESTATE INVESTMENT TRUST
FAIRMONT HOMES INC
FAIRMONT RAFFLES HOTELS INTERNATIONAL INC
FANNIE MAE
FEDERAL AGRICULTURAL MORTGAGE CORP (FARMER MAC)
FEDERAL REALTY INVESTMENT TRUST
FELCOR LODGING TRUST
FERGUSON ENTERPRISES INC
FIDELITY NATIONAL FINANCIAL INC
FIDELITY NATIONAL INFORMATION SERVICES INC
FIRST AMERICAN CORP
FIRST INDUSTRIAL REALTY TRUST INC
FIRST MORTGAGE CORP
FIRSTCITY FINANCIAL CORP
FIRSTSERVICE CORPORATION
FIVE STAR PRODUCTS INC
FLUOR CORP
FOMENTO DE CONSTRUCCIONES Y CONTRATAS SA (FCC)
FOREST CITY ENTERPRISES INC
FOUR SEASONS HOTELS
FREDDIE MAC
GABLES RESIDENTIAL TRUST
GAFISA SA
GAYLORD ENTERTAINMENT CO
GE CAPITAL FINANCE
GE CAPITAL REAL ESTATE
GENERAL ELECTRIC CO (GE)
GENERAL GROWTH PROPERTIES INC
GEORG FISCHER LTD
GLENBOROUGH REALTY TRUST
GLIMCHER REALTY TRUST
GMAC INC
GOLDEN TULIP HOSPITALITY GROUP
GRANITE CONSTRUCTION INC
GROUPE DU LOUVRE
GRUBB & ELLIS CO
GRUBB & ELLIS REALTY INVESTORS LLC
GRUPO ACS
GRUPO FERROVIAL SA
GS ENGINEERING & CONSTRUCTION CORP
GUOMAN HOTELS LIMITED
HANG LUNG GROUP LTD
HANG LUNG PROPERTIES LIMITED
HANJIN HEAVY INDUSTRIES CO LTD
HARRAH'S ENTERTAINMENT INC
HCP INC
HDR INC
HEALTH CARE REIT INC
HEALTHCARE REALTY TRUST INC
HENDERSON LAND DEVELOPMENT COMPANY LIMITED
HIGHWOODS PROPERTIES INC
HILTON HOTELS CORP
HINES INTERESTS LP
HOCHTIEF AG
HOME DEPOT INC
HOME INNS & HOTELS MANAGEMENT INC
HOME PROPERTIES INC
HOMESERVICES OF AMERICA INC
HOMETOWN AMERICA LLC
HONGKONG AND SHANGHAI HOTELS LTD
HONGKONG LAND HOLDINGS LTD
HORTON HOMES INC
HOSPITALITY PROPERTIES TRUST
HOST HOTELS & RESORTS LP
HOTEL PROPERTIES LTD
HOVNANIAN ENTERPRISES INC
HOWARD JOHNSON INTERNATIONAL INC
HRPT PROPERTIES TRUST
HUTCHISON WHAMPOA HOTEL & PROPERTIES LTD
HVM LLC
HYATT HOTELS CORPORATION
HYPO REAL ESTATE HOLDING AG (HYPO BANK)
HYSAN DEVELOPMENT CO LTD
HYUNDAI ELEVATOR CO LTD
HYUNDAI ENGINEERING & CONSTRUCTION COMPANY LTD
ICAHN ENTERPRISES LP
IMPAC MORTGAGE HOLDINGS INC
IMPREGILO SPA
INDIAN HOTEL COMPANY LIMITED (THE)
INDUSTRIAL DEVELOPMENTS INTERNATIONAL INC
INLAND AMERICAN REAL ESTATE TRUST INC

INLAND REAL ESTATE CORPORATION
INNKEEPERS USA TRUST
INSITUFORM TECHNOLOGIES
INTEGRATED ELECTRICAL SERVICES
INTERCONTINENTAL HOTELS GROUP PLC
INTERSTATE HOTELS AND RESORTS INC
INTOWN SUITES MANAGEMENT INC
INVESTORS REAL ESTATE TRUST
INVESTORS TITLE COMPANY
ISTAR FINANCIAL INC
JACOBS ENGINEERING GROUP INC
JAMESON INN INC
JANUS HOTELS AND RESORTS INC
JEWETT CAMERON TRADING CO LTD
JOHN LAING PLC
JOHN Q HAMMONS HOTELS LLC
JOHNSON CONTROLS INC
JOIE DE VIVRE HOSPITALITY
JONES LANG LASALLE INC
KB HOME
KERZNER INTERNATIONAL LIMITED
KILROY REALTY CORPORATION
KIMCO REALTY CORP
KIMPTON HOTEL & RESTAURANT GROUP LLC
KUMHO INDUSTRIAL CO LTD
LANDAMERICA FINANCIAL GROUP INC
LAS VEGAS SANDS CORP (THE VENETIAN)
LASALLE HOTEL PROPERTIES
LAYNE CHRISTENSEN COMPANY
LB FOSTER COMPANY
LBA REALTY LLC
LENDER PROCESSING SERVICES INC
LENDINGTREE LLC
LENNAR CORPORATION
LEXINGTON REALTY TRUST
LIBERTY PROPERTY TRUST
LIGHTSTONE GROUP LLC (THE)
LILLIBRIDGE HEALTHCARE REAL ESTATE TRUST
LINK REAL ESTATE INVESTMENT TRUST (THE)
LODGIAN INC
LOEWS HOTELS HOLDING CORPORATION
LOUIS BERGER GROUP INC (THE)
LOWE'S COMPANIES INC
LQ MANAGEMENT LLC
M/I HOMES INC
MACERICH COMPANY (THE)
MACK-CALI REALTY CORP
MAGUIRE PROPERTIES INC
MANDARIN ORIENTAL INTERNATIONAL LTD
MANOR CARE INC
MARCUS CORPORATION (THE)
MARRIOTT INTERNATIONAL INC
MATRIX SERVICE COMPANY
MAX PROPERTY GROUP PLC
MCDERMOTT INTERNATIONAL INC
MDC HOLDINGS INC
MEADOW VALLEY CORPORATION
MERITAGE HOMES CORP
MERITUS HOTELS & RESORTS INC
MFA FINANCIAL INC
MGM MIRAGE
MID-AMERICA APARTMENT COMMUNITIES INC
MILLENNIUM & COPTHORNE HOTELS PLC
MISSION WEST PROPERTIES
MODTECH HOLDINGS INC
MORGANS HOTEL GROUP CO
MOVE INC
MRV ENGENHARIA E PARTICIPACOES SA
MUNICIPAL MORTGAGE & EQUITY
MWH GLOBAL INC
NAI GLOBAL INC
NATIONAL HEALTH INVESTORS
NATIONAL HOME CENTERS INC
NATIONWIDE HEALTH PROPERTIES
NCI BUILDING SYSTEMS INC
NEW PLAN EXCEL REALTY TRUST INC
NEW WORLD DEVELOPMENT COMPANY LIMITED
NEWCASTLE INVESTMENT CORP
NEWHALL LAND & FARMING
NH HOTELES SA
NRT INCORPORATED
NVR INC
OAKWOOD WORLDWIDE
OBEROI GROUP (EIH LTD)
ODEBRECHT SA
OMEGA HEALTHCARE INVESTORS
ORIENT OVERSEAS (INTERNATIONAL) LTD
ORIENT-EXPRESS HOTELS LTD
ORIGEN FINANCIAL INC
ORION MARINE GROUP INC
ORLEANS HOMEBUILDERS
PACIFIC COAST BUILDING PRODUCTS
PALM HARBOR HOMES INC
PARKWAY PROPERTIES INC
PARSONS BRINCKERHOFF INC
PCL CONSTRUCTION GROUP INC
PDG REALTY SA EMPREENDIMENTOS E PARTICIPACOES
PENNSYLVANIA REIT
PLUM CREEK TIMBER CO INC
PMI GROUP INC (THE)
POST PROPERTIES INC
PRIME GROUP REALTY TRUST
PRIME RETAIL INC
PROLOGIS
PRUDENTIAL REAL ESTATE AFFILIATES INC
PS BUSINESS PARKS INC
PUBLIC STORAGE INC
PULTEGROUP INC
QMH UK LTD
RADIAN GROUP INC
RAILWORKS CORP
RAMADA WORLDWIDE INC
RE/MAX INTERNATIONAL INC
REALOGY CORPORATION
REALTY INCOME CORP

RED LION HOTELS CORPORATION
REGENCY CENTERS CORP
REIS INC
RELATED GROUP (THE)
RESORTQUEST INTERNATIONAL INC
REZIDOR HOTEL GROUP AB
RIO PROPERTIES INC
RITZ-CARLTON HOTEL COMPANY LLC (THE)
RIVIERA HOLDINGS CORP
ROSEWOOD HOTELS & RESORTS LLC
ROSSI RESIDENCIAL SA
ROYAL GROUP INC
RXR REALTY
RYLAND GROUP INC (THE)
SAHA PATHANA INTER-HOLDING PCL
SAMWHAN CORPORATION
SANDS REGENT
SAWYER REALTY HOLDINGS LLC
SCANDIC HOTELS AB
SCHUFF INTERNATIONAL INC
SEKISUI HOUSE LTD
SEMBCORP INDUSTRIES LTD
SENIOR HOUSING PROPERTIES
SERVICEMASTER COMPANY (THE)
SHANGRI-LA ASIA LTD
SHAW GROUP INC (THE)
SHIMAO PROPERTY HOLDINGS LTD
SHUN TAK HOLDINGS LIMITED
SIEMENS BUILDING TECHNOLOGIES
SIMON PROPERTY GROUP INC
SINO LAND COMPANY LIMITED
SKIDMORE OWINGS & MERRILL LLP
SKYLINE CORPORATION
SL GREEN REALTY CORP
SOCIETE DES BAINS DE MER ET DU CERCLE
SOL MELIA SA
SONESTA INTERNATIONAL HOTELS CORP
SOUTHERN ENERGY HOMES INC
SOVRAN SELF STORAGE INC
ST JOE COMPANY (THE)
STANDARD PACIFIC CORP
STARWOOD CAPITAL GROUP GLOBAL LLC
STARWOOD HOTELS & RESORTS WORLDWIDE INC
STATION CASINOS INC
STERLING CONSTRUCTION COMPANY
STEWART INFORMATION SERVICES CORP
STOCK BUILDING SUPPLY INC
STRATEGIC HOTELS AND RESORTS INC
STRATOSPHERE CORPORATION
STV GROUP INC
SUN COMMUNITIES INC
SUN HUNG KAI PROPERTIES
SUNBURST HOSPITALITY CORPORATION
SUNRISE SENIOR LIVING
SUNSTONE HOTEL INVESTORS INC
SUPER 8 MOTELS INC
SUPERTEL HOSPITALITY INC
SWIRE PACIFIC LTD
TANGER FACTORY OUTLET CENTERS
TARRAGON CORPORATION
TAUBMAN CENTERS INC
TDINDUSTRIES
TECHNICAL OLYMPIC USA INC
THARALDSON ENTERPRISES INC
TOLL BROTHERS INC
TRACO
TRAMMELL CROW COMPANY
TRANSCONTINENTAL REALTY
TRANSWESTERN COMMERCIAL SERVICES
TRANSWESTERN INVESTMENT CO LLC
TREVI-FINANZIARIA INDUSTRIALE SPA (TREVI GROUP)
TRINITY LTD
TRIPLE FIVE GROUP
TRT HOLDINGS
TRUE HOME VALUE INC
TRUMP ENTERTAINMENT RESORTS INC
TRUMP ORGANIZATION (THE)
TUTOR PERINI CORPORATION
UDR INC
UNIBAIL-RODAMCO
UNITECH LIMITED
URS CORPORATION
VENTAS INC
VINCI
VORNADO REALTY TRUST
WASHINGTON REAL ESTATE INVESTMENT TRUST
WATSON LAND COMPANY
WCI COMMUNITIES INC
WEINGARTEN REALTY INVESTORS
WELLS REAL ESTATE FUNDS INC
WESTFIELD GROUP (THE)
WHARF (HOLDINGS) LIMITED, THE
WHEELOCK AND COMPANY LIMITED
WILLIAM LYON HOMES
WOLSELEY PLC
WORLDMARK BY WYNDHAM INC
WP CAREY & CO LLC
WS ATKINS PLC
WYNDHAM VACATION OWNERSHIP
WYNDHAM WORLDWIDE
WYNN RESORTS LIMITED
XANTERRA PARKS AND RESORTS
YIT CORPORATION
ZIPREALTY INC

INDEX OF U.S. HEADQUARTERS LOCATION BY STATE

To help you locate members of the firms geographically, the city and state of the headquarters of each company are in the following index.

JANUS HOTELS AND RESORTS INC; Boca Raton
LENDER PROCESSING SERVICES INC; Jacksonville
LENNAR CORPORATION; Miami
REGENCY CENTERS CORP; Jacksonville
RELATED GROUP (THE); Miami
RESORTQUEST INTERNATIONAL INC; Fort Walton Beach
ST JOE COMPANY (THE); Jacksonville
TECHNICAL OLYMPIC USA INC; Hollywood
WCI COMMUNITIES INC; Bonita Springs
WYNDHAM VACATION OWNERSHIP; Orlando

GEORGIA
AMERICA'S BEST FRANCHISING INC; Atlanta
BEAZER HOMES USA INC; Atlanta
COUSINS PROPERTIES INC; Atlanta
GABLES RESIDENTIAL TRUST; Atlanta
HOME DEPOT INC; Atlanta
HORTON HOMES INC; Eatonton
INDUSTRIAL DEVELOPMENTS INTERNATIONAL INC; Atlanta
INTOWN SUITES MANAGEMENT INC; Atlanta
JAMESON INN INC; Smyrna
LODGIAN INC; Atlanta
POST PROPERTIES INC; Atlanta
WELLS REAL ESTATE FUNDS INC; Norcross

IDAHO
BOISE CASCADE; Boise
BUILDING MATERIALS HOLDING CORP; Boise

ILLINOIS
AMLI RESIDENTIAL PROPERTIES TRUST; Chicago
EQUITY LIFESTYLE PROPERTIES INC; Chicago
EQUITY OFFICE PROPERTIES TRUST; Chicago
EQUITY RESIDENTIAL; Chicago
FIRST INDUSTRIAL REALTY TRUST INC; Chicago
GENERAL GROWTH PROPERTIES INC; Chicago
HOMETOWN AMERICA LLC; Chicago
HYATT HOTELS CORPORATION; Chicago
INLAND AMERICAN REAL ESTATE TRUST INC; Oak Brook
INLAND REAL ESTATE CORPORATION; Oak Brook
JONES LANG LASALLE INC; Chicago
LILLIBRIDGE HEALTHCARE REAL ESTATE TRUST; Chicago
PRIME GROUP REALTY TRUST; Chicago
SKIDMORE OWINGS & MERRILL LLP; Chicago
STRATEGIC HOTELS AND RESORTS INC; Chicago
TRANSWESTERN INVESTMENT CO LLC; Chicago
VENTAS INC; Chicago

INDIANA
DUKE REALTY CORP; Indianapolis
FAIRMONT HOMES INC; Nappanee
SIMON PROPERTY GROUP INC; Indianapolis
SKYLINE CORPORATION; Elkhart

KANSAS
BLACK & VEATCH HOLDING COMPANY; Overland Park
LAYNE CHRISTENSEN COMPANY; Mission Woods

KENTUCKY
ATRIA SENIOR LIVING GROUP; Louisville
TRUE HOME VALUE INC; Louisville

LOUISIANA
SHAW GROUP INC (THE); Baton Rouge

MARYLAND
CAPREIT INC; Rockville
CHOICE HOTELS INTERNATIONAL INC; Silver Spring
CORPORATE OFFICE PROPERTIES TRUST; Columbia
COSTAR GROUP INC; Bethesda
ERICKSON RETIREMENT COMMUNITIES; Catonsville
FEDERAL REALTY INVESTMENT TRUST; Rockville
HOST HOTELS & RESORTS LP; Bethesda
LASALLE HOTEL PROPERTIES; Bethesda
MARRIOTT INTERNATIONAL INC; Bethesda
MUNICIPAL MORTGAGE & EQUITY; Baltimore
OMEGA HEALTHCARE INVESTORS; Hunt Valley
PRIME RETAIL INC; Baltimore
RITZ-CARLTON HOTEL COMPANY LLC (THE); Chevy Chase
SAWYER REALTY HOLDINGS LLC; College Park
SUNBURST HOSPITALITY CORPORATION; Silver Spring
WASHINGTON REAL ESTATE INVESTMENT TRUST; Rockville

MASSACHUSETTS
BOSTON PROPERTIES INC; Boston
CAMP DRESSER & MCKEE INC; Cambridge
COLLIERS INTERNATIONAL PROPERTY CONSULTANTS; Boston
HOSPITALITY PROPERTIES TRUST; Newton
HRPT PROPERTIES TRUST; Newton
SENIOR HOUSING PROPERTIES; Newton
SONESTA INTERNATIONAL HOTELS CORP; Boston

MICHIGAN
CHAMPION ENTERPRISES INC; Troy
GMAC INC; Detroit
ORIGEN FINANCIAL INC; Southfield
PULTEGROUP INC; Bloomfield Hills
SUN COMMUNITIES INC; Southfield
TAUBMAN CENTERS INC; Bloomfield Hills

MINNESOTA
CARLSON HOTELS WORLDWIDE; Minnetonka
HOMESERVICES OF AMERICA INC; Minneapolis

MISSISSIPPI
ANDERSON-TULLY LUMBER COMPANY; Vicksburg
EASTGROUP PROPERTIES INC; Jackson
PARKWAY PROPERTIES INC; Jackson

MISSOURI
BURNS & MCDONNELL; Kansas City
BUTLER MANUFACTURING CO; Kansas City
CITIMORTGAGE INC; O'Fallon
ENTERTAINMENT PROPERTIES TRUST; Kansas City
INSITUFORM TECHNOLOGIES; Chesterfield
JOHN Q HAMMONS HOTELS LLC; Springfield

NEBRASKA
HDR INC; Omaha
SUPERTEL HOSPITALITY INC; Norfolk

NEVADA
AMERCO; Reno
AMERISTAR CASINOS INC; Las Vegas
BOYD GAMING CORP; Las Vegas
DIAMOND RESORTS HOLDINGS LLC; Las Vegas
HARRAH'S ENTERTAINMENT INC; Las Vegas
LAS VEGAS SANDS CORP (THE VENETIAN); Las Vegas
MGM MIRAGE; Las Vegas
RIO PROPERTIES INC; Las Vegas
RIVIERA HOLDINGS CORP; Las Vegas
SANDS REGENT; Reno
STATION CASINOS INC; Las Vegas
STRATOSPHERE CORPORATION; Las Vegas
TRIPLE FIVE GROUP; Las Vegas
WYNN RESORTS LIMITED; Las Vegas

NEW JERSEY
ARC GROUP OF COMPANIES (THE); Clifton
CENTURY 21 REAL ESTATE CORP; Parsippany
COLDWELL BANKER REAL ESTATE CORP; Parsippany
DAYS INN WORLDWIDE INC; Parsippany
HOVNANIAN ENTERPRISES INC; Red Bank
HOWARD JOHNSON INTERNATIONAL INC; Parsippany
LOUIS BERGER GROUP INC (THE); Morristown
MACK-CALI REALTY CORP; Edison
NAI GLOBAL INC; Princeton
NRT INCORPORATED; Parsippany
RAMADA WORLDWIDE INC; Parsippany
REALOGY CORPORATION; Parsippany
SUPER 8 MOTELS INC; Parsippany
TRUMP ENTERTAINMENT RESORTS INC; Atlantic City
WYNDHAM WORLDWIDE; Parsippany

NEW MEXICO
CHRISTIES GREAT ESTATES; Santa Fe

NEW YORK
ABM INDUSTRIES INC; New York
ANNALY CAPITAL MANAGEMENT INC; New York
COMMUNITY DEVELOPMENT TRUST; New York
CUSHMAN & WAKEFIELD INC; New York
DREW INDUSTRIES; White Plains
HOME PROPERTIES INC; Rochester
ICAHN ENTERPRISES LP; New York
ISTAR FINANCIAL INC; New York
KIMCO REALTY CORP; New Hyde Park
LEXINGTON REALTY TRUST; New York
LIGHTSTONE GROUP LLC (THE); New York
LOEWS HOTELS HOLDING CORPORATION; New York
MFA FINANCIAL INC; New York
MORGANS HOTEL GROUP CO; New York
NEW PLAN EXCEL REALTY TRUST INC; New York
NEWCASTLE INVESTMENT CORP; New York
PARSONS BRINCKERHOFF INC; New York
RAILWORKS CORP; New York
REIS INC; New York
RXR REALTY; Uniondale
SL GREEN REALTY CORP; New York
SOVRAN SELF STORAGE INC; Williamsville
STARWOOD HOTELS & RESORTS WORLDWIDE INC; White Plains
TARRAGON CORPORATION; New York
TRUMP ORGANIZATION (THE); New York
VORNADO REALTY TRUST; New York
WP CAREY & CO LLC; New York

NORTH CAROLINA
HIGHWOODS PROPERTIES INC; Raleigh
INVESTORS TITLE COMPANY; Chapel Hill
LENDINGTREE LLC; Charlotte
LOWE'S COMPANIES INC; Mooresville
STOCK BUILDING SUPPLY INC; Raleigh
TANGER FACTORY OUTLET CENTERS; Greensboro

NORTH DAKOTA
INVESTORS REAL ESTATE TRUST; Minot
THARALDSON ENTERPRISES INC; Fargo

OHIO
ANTHONY & SYLVAN POOLS; Mayfield Village
ASSOCIATED ESTATES REALTY CORPORATION; Richmond Heights
DEVELOPERS DIVERSIFIED REALTY CORP; Beachwood
DOMINION HOMES INC; Dublin
FOREST CITY ENTERPRISES INC; Cleveland
GLIMCHER REALTY TRUST; Columbus
HEALTH CARE REIT INC; Toledo
M/I HOMES INC; Columbus
MANOR CARE INC; Toledo

OKLAHOMA
MATRIX SERVICE COMPANY; Tulsa

OREGON
JEWETT CAMERON TRADING CO LTD; North Plains

PENNSYLVANIA
84 LUMBER COMPANY; Eighty Four
BRANDYWINE REALTY TRUST; Radnor
CAPMARK FINANCIAL GROUP INC; Horsham
LB FOSTER COMPANY; Pittsburgh
LIBERTY PROPERTY TRUST; Malvern
ORLEANS HOMEBUILDERS; Bensalem
PENNSYLVANIA REIT; Philadelphia
RADIAN GROUP INC; Philadelphia
STV GROUP INC; Douglassville
TOLL BROTHERS INC; Horsham
TRACO; Cranberry Township

SOUTH CAROLINA
HVM LLC; Spartanburg

TENNESSEE
ADVOCAT INC; Brentwood
BROOKDALE SENIOR LIVING INC; Brentwood
CBL & ASSOCIATES PROPERTIES INC; Chattanooga
CLAYTON HOMES INC; Maryville
GAYLORD ENTERTAINMENT CO; Nashville
HEALTHCARE REALTY TRUST INC; Nashville
MID-AMERICA APARTMENT COMMUNITIES INC; Memphis
NATIONAL HEALTH INVESTORS; Murfreesboro
SERVICEMASTER COMPANY (THE); Memphis

TEXAS
ACCOR NORTH AMERICA; Carrollton
AMERICAN CAMPUS COMMUNITIES; Austin
AMERICAN REALTY INVESTORS INC; Dallas
CAMDEN PROPERTY TRUST; Houston
CAPITAL SENIOR LIVING CORP; Dallas
CAPSTEAD MORTGAGE CORPORATION; Dallas
CEMEX INC; Houston
CENTEX CORP; Dallas
COMFORT SYSTEMS USA INC; Houston
CORE NETWORK (THE); Dallas
CRESCENT REAL ESTATE EQUITIES LP; Fort Worth
DR HORTON INC; Fort Worth
ENGLOBAL CORP; Houston
FELCOR LODGING TRUST; Irving
FIRSTCITY FINANCIAL CORP; Waco
FLUOR CORP; Irving
HINES INTERESTS LP; Houston
INTEGRATED ELECTRICAL SERVICES; Houston
LQ MANAGEMENT LLC; Irving
MCDERMOTT INTERNATIONAL INC; Houston
NCI BUILDING SYSTEMS INC; Houston
ORION MARINE GROUP INC; Houston
PALM HARBOR HOMES INC; Addison
ROSEWOOD HOTELS & RESORTS LLC; Dallas
STERLING CONSTRUCTION COMPANY; Houston
STEWART INFORMATION SERVICES CORP; Houston
TDINDUSTRIES; Dallas
TRAMMELL CROW COMPANY; Dallas
TRANSCONTINENTAL REALTY; Dallas
TRANSWESTERN COMMERCIAL SERVICES; Houston
TRT HOLDINGS; Irving
WEINGARTEN REALTY INVESTORS; Houston

VIRGINIA
AVALONBAY COMMUNITIES INC; Alexandria
BARCELO CRESTLINE CORPORATION; Fairfax
BROOKFIELD HOMES CORP; Fairfax
CAPITAL AUTOMOTIVE REIT; McLean
DYNEX CAPITAL INC; Glen Allen
FERGUSON ENTERPRISES INC; Newport News
FREDDIE MAC; McLean
HILTON HOTELS CORP; McLean
INTERSTATE HOTELS AND RESORTS INC; Arlington
LANDAMERICA FINANCIAL GROUP INC; Glen Allen
NVR INC; Reston
SUNRISE SENIOR LIVING; McLean

WASHINGTON
EMERITUS CORP; Seattle
PLUM CREEK TIMBER CO INC; Seattle
RED LION HOTELS CORPORATION; Spokane
WORLDMARK BY WYNDHAM INC; Redmond

WISCONSIN
JOHNSON CONTROLS INC; Milwaukee
MARCUS CORPORATION (THE); Milwaukee

INDEX OF NON-U.S. HEADQUARTERS LOCATION BY COUNTRY

JAPAN
CHIYODA CORPORATION; Yokohama
SEKISUI HOUSE LTD; Osaka

KOREA
DAELIM INDUSTRIAL CO LTD; Seoul
DOOSAN HEAVY INDUSTRY & CONSTRUCTION CO; Changwon
GS ENGINEERING & CONSTRUCTION CORP; Seoul
HANJIN HEAVY INDUSTRIES CO LTD; Busan
HYUNDAI ELEVATOR CO LTD; Gyeonggi-do
HYUNDAI ENGINEERING & CONSTRUCTION COMPANY LTD; Seoul
KUMHO INDUSTRIAL CO LTD; Seoul
SAMWHAN CORPORATION; Seoul

MEXICO
CEMEX SAB DE CV; San Pedro Garza Garcia
DESARROLLADORA HOMEX SAB DE CV; Sinaloa
EMPRESAS ICA SA DE CV; Mexico City

MONACO
SOCIETE DES BAINS DE MER ET DU CERCLE; Monaco

SINGAPORE
AMAN RESORTS; Singapore
BANYON TREE HOTELS & RESORTS; Singapore
HOTEL PROPERTIES LTD; Singapore
MERITUS HOTELS & RESORTS INC; Singapore
SEMBCORP INDUSTRIES LTD; Singapore

SPAIN
ABERTIS INFRAESTRUCTURAS SA; Barcelona
ACCIONA SA; Alcobendas
ACS ACTIVIDADES DE CONSTRUCCION Y SERVICIOS SA; Madrid
FOMENTO DE CONSTRUCCIONES Y CONTRATAS SA (FCC); Madrid
GRUPO ACS; Madrid
GRUPO FERROVIAL SA; Madrid
NH HOTELES SA; Madrid
SOL MELIA SA; Palma de Mallorca

SWEDEN
SCANDIC HOTELS AB; Stockholm

SWITZERLAND
GEORG FISCHER LTD; Schaffhausen
SIEMENS BUILDING TECHNOLOGIES; Zug

THAILAND
SAHA PATHANA INTER-HOLDING PCL; Bangkok

THE NETHERLANDS
ARCADIS NV; Arnhem
CHICAGO BRIDGE & IRON COMPANY NV; The Hague
GOLDEN TULIP HOSPITALITY GROUP; Amersfoot

UNITED ARAB EMIRATES
EMAAR PROPERTIES PJSC; Dubai

UNITED KINGDOM
ACERGY SA; London
AMEC PLC; London
AMEY PLC; Oxford
BALFOUR BEATTY PLC; London
CREST NICHOLSON PLC; Chertsey
CRH PLC; Dublin
DOYLE COLLECTION (THE); Dublin
GUOMAN HOTELS LIMITED; Uxbridge
INTERCONTINENTAL HOTELS GROUP PLC; Denham
JOHN LAING PLC; London
MILLENNIUM & COPTHORNE HOTELS PLC; London
QMH UK LTD; Romford
WOLSELEY PLC; Theale
WS ATKINS PLC; Epsom

INDEX BY REGIONS OF THE U.S. WHERE THE FIRMS HAVE LOCATIONS

FIDELITY NATIONAL INFORMATION SERVICES INC
FIRST AMERICAN CORP
FIRST INDUSTRIAL REALTY TRUST INC
FIRST MORTGAGE CORP
FIRSTCITY FINANCIAL CORP
FIRSTSERVICE CORPORATION
FIVE STAR PRODUCTS INC
FLUOR CORP
FOREST CITY ENTERPRISES INC
FOUR SEASONS HOTELS
GABLES RESIDENTIAL TRUST
GE CAPITAL FINANCE
GE CAPITAL REAL ESTATE
GENERAL ELECTRIC CO (GE)
GENERAL GROWTH PROPERTIES INC
GEORG FISCHER LTD
GLENBOROUGH REALTY TRUST
GLIMCHER REALTY TRUST
GMAC INC
GRANITE CONSTRUCTION INC
GRUBB & ELLIS CO
GRUBB & ELLIS REALTY INVESTORS LLC
GUOMAN HOTELS LIMITED
HANJIN HEAVY INDUSTRIES CO LTD
HARRAH'S ENTERTAINMENT INC
HCP INC
HDR INC
HEALTH CARE REIT INC
HEALTHCARE REALTY TRUST INC
HILTON HOTELS CORP
HINES INTERESTS LP
HOCHTIEF AG
HOME DEPOT INC
HOMESERVICES OF AMERICA INC
HOMETOWN AMERICA LLC
HONGKONG AND SHANGHAI HOTELS LTD
HOSPITALITY PROPERTIES TRUST
HOST HOTELS & RESORTS LP
HOVNANIAN ENTERPRISES INC
HOWARD JOHNSON INTERNATIONAL INC
HRPT PROPERTIES TRUST
HVM LLC
HYATT HOTELS CORPORATION
HYUNDAI ELEVATOR CO LTD
ICAHN ENTERPRISES LP
IMPAC MORTGAGE HOLDINGS INC
INDIAN HOTEL COMPANY LIMITED (THE)
INDUSTRIAL DEVELOPMENTS INTERNATIONAL INC
INNKEEPERS USA TRUST
INSITUFORM TECHNOLOGIES
INTEGRATED ELECTRICAL SERVICES
INTERCONTINENTAL HOTELS GROUP PLC
INTERSTATE HOTELS AND RESORTS INC
INTOWN SUITES MANAGEMENT INC
INVESTORS REAL ESTATE TRUST
ISTAR FINANCIAL INC
JACOBS ENGINEERING GROUP INC
JEWETT CAMERON TRADING CO LTD
JOHN Q HAMMONS HOTELS LLC
JOHNSON CONTROLS INC
JOIE DE VIVRE HOSPITALITY
JONES LANG LASALLE INC
KB HOME
KILROY REALTY CORPORATION
KIMCO REALTY CORP
KIMPTON HOTEL & RESTAURANT GROUP LLC
LANDAMERICA FINANCIAL GROUP INC
LAS VEGAS SANDS CORP (THE VENETIAN)
LASALLE HOTEL PROPERTIES
LAYNE CHRISTENSEN COMPANY
LB FOSTER COMPANY
LBA REALTY LLC
LENDER PROCESSING SERVICES INC
LENDINGTREE LLC
LENNAR CORPORATION
LEXINGTON REALTY TRUST
LIGHTSTONE GROUP LLC (THE)
LODGIAN INC
LOEWS HOTELS HOLDING CORPORATION
LOUIS BERGER GROUP INC (THE)
LOWE'S COMPANIES INC
LQ MANAGEMENT LLC
MACERICH COMPANY (THE)
MAGUIRE PROPERTIES INC
MANDARIN ORIENTAL INTERNATIONAL LTD
MANOR CARE INC
MARCUS CORPORATION (THE)
MARRIOTT INTERNATIONAL INC
MATRIX SERVICE COMPANY
MCDERMOTT INTERNATIONAL INC
MDC HOLDINGS INC
MEADOW VALLEY CORPORATION
MERITAGE HOMES CORP
MGM MIRAGE
MILLENNIUM & COPTHORNE HOTELS PLC
MISSION WEST PROPERTIES
MODTECH HOLDINGS INC
MORGANS HOTEL GROUP CO
MOVE INC
MUNICIPAL MORTGAGE & EQUITY
MWH GLOBAL INC
NAI GLOBAL INC
NATIONAL HEALTH INVESTORS
NATIONWIDE HEALTH PROPERTIES
NCI BUILDING SYSTEMS INC
NEW PLAN EXCEL REALTY TRUST INC
NEWHALL LAND & FARMING
NRT INCORPORATED
OAKWOOD WORLDWIDE
OMEGA HEALTHCARE INVESTORS
ORIENT OVERSEAS (INTERNATIONAL) LTD
PACIFIC COAST BUILDING PRODUCTS
PALM HARBOR HOMES INC
PARSONS BRINCKERHOFF INC

PCL CONSTRUCTION GROUP INC
PLUM CREEK TIMBER CO INC
PMI GROUP INC (THE)
PRIME RETAIL INC
PROLOGIS
PRUDENTIAL REAL ESTATE AFFILIATES INC
PS BUSINESS PARKS INC
PUBLIC STORAGE INC
PULTEGROUP INC
RADIAN GROUP INC
RAILWORKS CORP
RAMADA WORLDWIDE INC
RE/MAX INTERNATIONAL INC
REALOGY CORPORATION
REALTY INCOME CORP
RED LION HOTELS CORPORATION
REGENCY CENTERS CORP
RELATED GROUP (THE)
RESORTQUEST INTERNATIONAL INC
RIO PROPERTIES INC
RITZ-CARLTON HOTEL COMPANY LLC (THE)
RIVIERA HOLDINGS CORP
ROSEWOOD HOTELS & RESORTS LLC
ROYAL GROUP INC
RYLAND GROUP INC (THE)
SAMWHAN CORPORATION
SANDS REGENT
SCHUFF INTERNATIONAL INC
SENIOR HOUSING PROPERTIES
SERVICEMASTER COMPANY (THE)
SHANGRI-LA ASIA LTD
SHAW GROUP INC (THE)
SIEMENS BUILDING TECHNOLOGIES
SIMON PROPERTY GROUP INC
SKIDMORE OWINGS & MERRILL LLP
SKYLINE CORPORATION
STANDARD PACIFIC CORP
STARWOOD CAPITAL GROUP GLOBAL LLC
STARWOOD HOTELS & RESORTS WORLDWIDE INC
STATION CASINOS INC
STERLING CONSTRUCTION COMPANY
STEWART INFORMATION SERVICES CORP
STOCK BUILDING SUPPLY INC
STRATEGIC HOTELS AND RESORTS INC
STRATOSPHERE CORPORATION
STV GROUP INC
SUN COMMUNITIES INC
SUNBURST HOSPITALITY CORPORATION
SUNRISE SENIOR LIVING
SUNSTONE HOTEL INVESTORS INC
SUPER 8 MOTELS INC
SUPERTEL HOSPITALITY INC
SWIRE PACIFIC LTD
TANGER FACTORY OUTLET CENTERS
TAUBMAN CENTERS INC
TECHNICAL OLYMPIC USA INC
THARALDSON ENTERPRISES INC
TOLL BROTHERS INC
TRAMMELL CROW COMPANY
TRANSCONTINENTAL REALTY
TRANSWESTERN COMMERCIAL SERVICES
TRANSWESTERN INVESTMENT CO LLC
TREVI-FINANZIARIA INDUSTRIALE SPA (TREVI GROUP)
TRIPLE FIVE GROUP
TRT HOLDINGS
TRUMP ORGANIZATION (THE)
TUTOR PERINI CORPORATION
UDR INC
URS CORPORATION
VENTAS INC
VINCI
VORNADO REALTY TRUST
WATSON LAND COMPANY
WEINGARTEN REALTY INVESTORS
WELLS REAL ESTATE FUNDS INC
WESTFIELD GROUP (THE)
WILLIAM LYON HOMES
WOLSELEY PLC
WORLDMARK BY WYNDHAM INC
WP CAREY & CO LLC
WS ATKINS PLC
WYNDHAM VACATION OWNERSHIP
WYNDHAM WORLDWIDE
WYNN RESORTS LIMITED
XANTERRA PARKS AND RESORTS
ZIPREALTY INC

SOUTHWEST
84 LUMBER COMPANY
ABERTIS INFRAESTRUCTURAS SA
ABM INDUSTRIES INC
ACCOR NORTH AMERICA
ACCOR SA
ACERGY SA
ADVOCAT INC
AECOM TECHNOLOGY CORPORATION
AMB PROPERTY CORPORATION
AMEC PLC
AMERCO
AMERICAN CAMPUS COMMUNITIES
AMERICAN REALTY INVESTORS INC
AMERICA'S BEST FRANCHISING INC
AMLI RESIDENTIAL PROPERTIES TRUST
ANTHONY & SYLVAN POOLS
APARTMENT INVESTMENT AND MANAGEMENT CO
ARC GROUP OF COMPANIES (THE)
ARCADIS NV
ARCHSTONE TRUST
ARDEN REALTY INC
ATRIA SENIOR LIVING GROUP
AVATAR HOLDINGS INC
BALFOUR BEATTY PLC
BANK OF AMERICA HOME LOANS

BARCELO CRESTLINE CORPORATION
BEAZER HOMES USA INC
BECHTEL GROUP INC
BEST WESTERN INTERNATIONAL INC
BLACK & VEATCH HOLDING COMPANY
BLUEGREEN CORPORATION
BOISE CASCADE
BRANDYWINE REALTY TRUST
BROOKDALE SENIOR LIVING INC
BROOKFIELD ASSET MANAGEMENT INC
BUILDING MATERIALS HOLDING CORP
BURNS & MCDONNELL
BUTLER MANUFACTURING CO
CAMDEN PROPERTY TRUST
CAMP DRESSER & MCKEE INC
CAPITAL AUTOMOTIVE REIT
CAPITAL PACIFIC HOLDINGS
CAPITAL SENIOR LIVING CORP
CAPMARK FINANCIAL GROUP INC
CAPREIT INC
CAPSTEAD MORTGAGE CORPORATION
CARLSON HOTELS WORLDWIDE
CAVALIER HOMES INC
CB RICHARD ELLIS GROUP INC (CBRE)
CBL & ASSOCIATES PROPERTIES INC
CEMEX INC
CEMEX SAB DE CV
CENTEX CORP
CENTRO PROPERTIES GROUP
CENTURY 21 REAL ESTATE CORP
CH2M HILL COMPANIES LTD
CHAMPION ENTERPRISES INC
CHICAGO BRIDGE & IRON COMPANY NV
CHIYODA CORPORATION
CHOICE HOTELS INTERNATIONAL INC
CHRISTIES GREAT ESTATES
CLAYTON HOMES INC
CNL FINANCIAL GROUP INC
COLDWELL BANKER REAL ESTATE CORP
COLLIERS INTERNATIONAL PROPERTY CONSULTANTS
COLONIAL PROPERTIES TRUST
COMFORT SYSTEMS USA INC
CORE NETWORK (THE)
CORPORATE OFFICE PROPERTIES TRUST
COSTAR GROUP INC
COUSINS PROPERTIES INC
CRESCENT REAL ESTATE EQUITIES LP
CRH PLC
CUSHMAN & WAKEFIELD INC
DAELIM INDUSTRIAL CO LTD
DAYS INN WORLDWIDE INC
DCT INDUSTRIAL TRUST INC
DEVELOPERS DIVERSIFIED REALTY CORP
DIAMOND RESORTS HOLDINGS LLC
DITECH.COM
DOOSAN HEAVY INDUSTRY & CONSTRUCTION CO
DR HORTON INC
DREW INDUSTRIES
DUKE REALTY CORP
EASTGROUP PROPERTIES INC
EMCOR GROUP INC
EMERITUS CORP
ENGLOBAL CORP
ENTERTAINMENT PROPERTIES TRUST
EQUITY LIFESTYLE PROPERTIES INC
EQUITY OFFICE PROPERTIES TRUST
EQUITY RESIDENTIAL
ERICKSON RETIREMENT COMMUNITIES
FAIRMONT RAFFLES HOTELS INTERNATIONAL INC
FEDERAL REALTY INVESTMENT TRUST
FELCOR LODGING TRUST
FERGUSON ENTERPRISES INC
FIDELITY NATIONAL FINANCIAL INC
FIDELITY NATIONAL INFORMATION SERVICES INC
FIRST AMERICAN CORP
FIRST INDUSTRIAL REALTY TRUST INC
FIRSTCITY FINANCIAL CORP
FIRSTSERVICE CORPORATION
FLUOR CORP
FOREST CITY ENTERPRISES INC
FOUR SEASONS HOTELS
GABLES RESIDENTIAL TRUST
GAYLORD ENTERTAINMENT CO
GE CAPITAL FINANCE
GE CAPITAL REAL ESTATE
GENERAL ELECTRIC CO (GE)
GENERAL GROWTH PROPERTIES INC
GLIMCHER REALTY TRUST
GMAC INC
GRANITE CONSTRUCTION INC
GRUBB & ELLIS CO
GRUBB & ELLIS REALTY INVESTORS LLC
GRUPO FERROVIAL SA
GUOMAN HOTELS LIMITED
HARRAH'S ENTERTAINMENT INC
HDR INC
HEALTH CARE REIT INC
HEALTHCARE REALTY TRUST INC
HILTON HOTELS CORP
HINES INTERESTS LP
HOCHTIEF AG
HOME DEPOT INC
HOMESERVICES OF AMERICA INC
HOMETOWN AMERICA LLC
HOSPITALITY PROPERTIES TRUST
HOST HOTELS & RESORTS LP
HOVNANIAN ENTERPRISES INC
HOWARD JOHNSON INTERNATIONAL INC
HRPT PROPERTIES TRUST
HVM LLC
HYATT HOTELS CORPORATION
ICAHN ENTERPRISES LP

IMPAC MORTGAGE HOLDINGS INC
INDUSTRIAL DEVELOPMENTS INTERNATIONAL INC
INLAND AMERICAN REAL ESTATE TRUST INC
INLAND REAL ESTATE CORPORATION
INNKEEPERS USA TRUST
INSITUFORM TECHNOLOGIES
INTEGRATED ELECTRICAL SERVICES
INTERCONTINENTAL HOTELS GROUP PLC
INTERSTATE HOTELS AND RESORTS INC
INTOWN SUITES MANAGEMENT INC
INVESTORS REAL ESTATE TRUST
ISTAR FINANCIAL INC
JACOBS ENGINEERING GROUP INC
JANUS HOTELS AND RESORTS INC
JOHN Q HAMMONS HOTELS LLC
JOHNSON CONTROLS INC
JONES LANG LASALLE INC
KB HOME
KIMCO REALTY CORP
KIMPTON HOTEL & RESTAURANT GROUP LLC
LANDAMERICA FINANCIAL GROUP INC
LASALLE HOTEL PROPERTIES
LAYNE CHRISTENSEN COMPANY
LB FOSTER COMPANY
LBA REALTY LLC
LENDER PROCESSING SERVICES INC
LENNAR CORPORATION
LEXINGTON REALTY TRUST
LIBERTY PROPERTY TRUST
LIGHTSTONE GROUP LLC (THE)
LILLIBRIDGE HEALTHCARE REAL ESTATE TRUST
LODGIAN INC
LOEWS HOTELS HOLDING CORPORATION
LOUIS BERGER GROUP INC (THE)
LOWE'S COMPANIES INC
LQ MANAGEMENT LLC
M/I HOMES INC
MACERICH COMPANY (THE)
MANOR CARE INC
MARCUS CORPORATION (THE)
MARRIOTT INTERNATIONAL INC
MATRIX SERVICE COMPANY
MCDERMOTT INTERNATIONAL INC
MDC HOLDINGS INC
MEADOW VALLEY CORPORATION
MERITAGE HOMES CORP
MID-AMERICA APARTMENT COMMUNITIES INC
MILLENNIUM & COPTHORNE HOTELS PLC
MOVE INC
MUNICIPAL MORTGAGE & EQUITY
MWH GLOBAL INC
NAI GLOBAL INC
NATIONAL HEALTH INVESTORS
NATIONWIDE HEALTH PROPERTIES
NCI BUILDING SYSTEMS INC
NEW PLAN EXCEL REALTY TRUST INC
NH HOTELES SA
NRT INCORPORATED
OAKWOOD WORLDWIDE
OMEGA HEALTHCARE INVESTORS
ORION MARINE GROUP INC
PALM HARBOR HOMES INC
PARKWAY PROPERTIES INC
PARSONS BRINCKERHOFF INC
PCL CONSTRUCTION GROUP INC
PLUM CREEK TIMBER CO INC
PMI GROUP INC (THE)
POST PROPERTIES INC
PRIME RETAIL INC
PROLOGIS
PRUDENTIAL REAL ESTATE AFFILIATES INC
PS BUSINESS PARKS INC
PUBLIC STORAGE INC
PULTEGROUP INC
RADIAN GROUP INC
RAILWORKS CORP
RAMADA WORLDWIDE INC
RE/MAX INTERNATIONAL INC
REALOGY CORPORATION
REALTY INCOME CORP
REGENCY CENTERS CORP
RESORTQUEST INTERNATIONAL INC
RITZ-CARLTON HOTEL COMPANY LLC (THE)
ROSEWOOD HOTELS & RESORTS LLC
ROYAL GROUP INC
RYLAND GROUP INC (THE)
SCHUFF INTERNATIONAL INC
SENIOR HOUSING PROPERTIES
SERVICEMASTER COMPANY (THE)
SHAW GROUP INC (THE)
SIEMENS BUILDING TECHNOLOGIES
SIMON PROPERTY GROUP INC
SKYLINE CORPORATION
SONESTA INTERNATIONAL HOTELS CORP
SOUTHERN ENERGY HOMES INC
SOVRAN SELF STORAGE INC
STANDARD PACIFIC CORP
STARWOOD HOTELS & RESORTS WORLDWIDE INC
STATION CASINOS INC
STERLING CONSTRUCTION COMPANY
STEWART INFORMATION SERVICES CORP
STOCK BUILDING SUPPLY INC
STRATEGIC HOTELS AND RESORTS INC
STV GROUP INC
SUN COMMUNITIES INC
SUNBURST HOSPITALITY CORPORATION
SUNRISE SENIOR LIVING
SUNSTONE HOTEL INVESTORS INC
SUPER 8 MOTELS INC
SWIRE PACIFIC LTD
TANGER FACTORY OUTLET CENTERS
TARRAGON CORPORATION
TAUBMAN CENTERS INC
TDINDUSTRIES

TECHNICAL OLYMPIC USA INC
THARALDSON ENTERPRISES INC
TOLL BROTHERS INC
TRAMMELL CROW COMPANY
TRANSCONTINENTAL REALTY
TRANSWESTERN COMMERCIAL SERVICES
TRANSWESTERN INVESTMENT CO LLC
TREVI-FINANZIARIA INDUSTRIALE SPA (TREVI GROUP)
TRIPLE FIVE GROUP
TRT HOLDINGS
TRUE HOME VALUE INC
UDR INC
URS CORPORATION
VENTAS INC
VINCI
VORNADO REALTY TRUST
WEINGARTEN REALTY INVESTORS
WELLS REAL ESTATE FUNDS INC
WILLIAM LYON HOMES
WOLSELEY PLC
WORLDMARK BY WYNDHAM INC
WP CAREY & CO LLC
WS ATKINS PLC
WYNDHAM VACATION OWNERSHIP
WYNDHAM WORLDWIDE
XANTERRA PARKS AND RESORTS
ZIPREALTY INC

MIDWEST
84 LUMBER COMPANY
ABM INDUSTRIES INC
ACCIONA SA
ACCOR NORTH AMERICA
ACCOR SA
ADVOCAT INC
AECOM TECHNOLOGY CORPORATION
AMB PROPERTY CORPORATION
AMEC PLC
AMERCO
AMERICAN CAMPUS COMMUNITIES
AMERICA'S BEST FRANCHISING INC
AMERISTAR CASINOS INC
AMLI RESIDENTIAL PROPERTIES TRUST
ANTHONY & SYLVAN POOLS
APARTMENT INVESTMENT AND MANAGEMENT CO
ARC GROUP OF COMPANIES (THE)
ARCADIS NV
ARDEN REALTY INC
ASSOCIATED ESTATES REALTY CORPORATION
ATRIA SENIOR LIVING GROUP
AVALONBAY COMMUNITIES INC
BANK OF AMERICA HOME LOANS
BARCELO CRESTLINE CORPORATION
BEAZER HOMES USA INC
BECHTEL GROUP INC
BEST WESTERN INTERNATIONAL INC
BLACK & VEATCH HOLDING COMPANY
BLUEGREEN CORPORATION
BOISE CASCADE
BOUYGUES SA
BOYD GAMING CORP
BROOKDALE SENIOR LIVING INC
BROOKFIELD ASSET MANAGEMENT INC
BUILDING MATERIALS HOLDING CORP
BURNS & MCDONNELL
BUTLER MANUFACTURING CO
CAMDEN PROPERTY TRUST
CAMP DRESSER & MCKEE INC
CAPITAL AUTOMOTIVE REIT
CAPITAL SENIOR LIVING CORP
CAPMARK FINANCIAL GROUP INC
CAPREIT INC
CARLSON HOTELS WORLDWIDE
CAVALIER HOMES INC
CB RICHARD ELLIS GROUP INC (CBRE)
CBL & ASSOCIATES PROPERTIES INC
CEMEX SAB DE CV
CENTEX CORP
CENTRO PROPERTIES GROUP
CENTURY 21 REAL ESTATE CORP
CH2M HILL COMPANIES LTD
CHAMPION ENTERPRISES INC
CHICAGO BRIDGE & IRON COMPANY NV
CHOICE HOTELS INTERNATIONAL INC
CHRISTIES GREAT ESTATES
CITIMORTGAGE INC
CLAYTON HOMES INC
CNL FINANCIAL GROUP INC
COLDWELL BANKER REAL ESTATE CORP
COLLIERS INTERNATIONAL PROPERTY CONSULTANTS
COMFORT SYSTEMS USA INC
CORE NETWORK (THE)
COSTAR GROUP INC
CRH PLC
CUSHMAN & WAKEFIELD INC
DAYS INN WORLDWIDE INC
DCT INDUSTRIAL TRUST INC
DEVELOPERS DIVERSIFIED REALTY CORP
DIAMOND RESORTS HOLDINGS LLC
DOMINION HOMES INC
DR HORTON INC
DREW INDUSTRIES
DUKE REALTY CORP
EMCOR GROUP INC
EMERITUS CORP
ENTERTAINMENT PROPERTIES TRUST
EQUITY LIFESTYLE PROPERTIES INC
EQUITY OFFICE PROPERTIES TRUST
EQUITY RESIDENTIAL
ERICKSON RETIREMENT COMMUNITIES
EXTENDICARE REAL ESTATE INVESTMENT TRUST
FAIRMONT HOMES INC

FAIRMONT RAFFLES HOTELS INTERNATIONAL INC
FEDERAL AGRICULTURAL MORTGAGE CORP (FARMER MAC)
FELCOR LODGING TRUST
FERGUSON ENTERPRISES INC
FIDELITY NATIONAL FINANCIAL INC
FIDELITY NATIONAL INFORMATION SERVICES INC
FIRST AMERICAN CORP
FIRST INDUSTRIAL REALTY TRUST INC
FIRSTSERVICE CORPORATION
FIVE STAR PRODUCTS INC
FLUOR CORP
FOREST CITY ENTERPRISES INC
FOUR SEASONS HOTELS
GE CAPITAL FINANCE
GE CAPITAL REAL ESTATE
GENERAL ELECTRIC CO (GE)
GENERAL GROWTH PROPERTIES INC
GLIMCHER REALTY TRUST
GMAC INC
GRANITE CONSTRUCTION INC
GRUBB & ELLIS CO
GRUBB & ELLIS REALTY INVESTORS LLC
GRUPO FERROVIAL SA
HARRAH'S ENTERTAINMENT INC
HDR INC
HEALTH CARE REIT INC
HEALTHCARE REALTY TRUST INC
HIGHWOODS PROPERTIES INC
HILTON HOTELS CORP
HINES INTERESTS LP
HOCHTIEF AG
HOME DEPOT INC
HOME PROPERTIES INC
HOMESERVICES OF AMERICA INC
HOMETOWN AMERICA LLC
HONGKONG AND SHANGHAI HOTELS LTD
HOSPITALITY PROPERTIES TRUST
HOST HOTELS & RESORTS LP
HOVNANIAN ENTERPRISES INC
HOWARD JOHNSON INTERNATIONAL INC
HRPT PROPERTIES TRUST
HVM LLC
HYATT HOTELS CORPORATION
ICAHN ENTERPRISES LP
IMPAC MORTGAGE HOLDINGS INC
INDUSTRIAL DEVELOPMENTS INTERNATIONAL INC
INLAND AMERICAN REAL ESTATE TRUST INC
INLAND REAL ESTATE CORPORATION
INNKEEPERS USA TRUST
INSITUFORM TECHNOLOGIES
INTEGRATED ELECTRICAL SERVICES
INTERCONTINENTAL HOTELS GROUP PLC
INTERSTATE HOTELS AND RESORTS INC
INTOWN SUITES MANAGEMENT INC
INVESTORS REAL ESTATE TRUST
INVESTORS TITLE COMPANY
ISTAR FINANCIAL INC
JACOBS ENGINEERING GROUP INC
JAMESON INN INC
JANUS HOTELS AND RESORTS INC
JOHN Q HAMMONS HOTELS LLC
JOHNSON CONTROLS INC
JONES LANG LASALLE INC
KB HOME
KIMCO REALTY CORP
KIMPTON HOTEL & RESTAURANT GROUP LLC
LANDAMERICA FINANCIAL GROUP INC
LASALLE HOTEL PROPERTIES
LAYNE CHRISTENSEN COMPANY
LB FOSTER COMPANY
LENDER PROCESSING SERVICES INC
LENNAR CORPORATION
LEXINGTON REALTY TRUST
LIBERTY PROPERTY TRUST
LIGHTSTONE GROUP LLC (THE)
LILLIBRIDGE HEALTHCARE REAL ESTATE TRUST
LODGIAN INC
LOUIS BERGER GROUP INC (THE)
LOWE'S COMPANIES INC
LQ MANAGEMENT LLC
M/I HOMES INC
MACERICH COMPANY (THE)
MANOR CARE INC
MARCUS CORPORATION (THE)
MARRIOTT INTERNATIONAL INC
MATRIX SERVICE COMPANY
MCDERMOTT INTERNATIONAL INC
MGM MIRAGE
MID-AMERICA APARTMENT COMMUNITIES INC
MILLENNIUM & COPTHORNE HOTELS PLC
MOVE INC
MUNICIPAL MORTGAGE & EQUITY
MWH GLOBAL INC
NAI GLOBAL INC
NATIONAL HEALTH INVESTORS
NATIONWIDE HEALTH PROPERTIES
NCI BUILDING SYSTEMS INC
NEW PLAN EXCEL REALTY TRUST INC
NRT INCORPORATED
NVR INC
OAKWOOD WORLDWIDE
OMEGA HEALTHCARE INVESTORS
ORIGEN FINANCIAL INC
ORLEANS HOMEBUILDERS
PALM HARBOR HOMES INC
PARKWAY PROPERTIES INC
PARSONS BRINCKERHOFF INC
PCL CONSTRUCTION GROUP INC
PENNSYLVANIA REIT
PLUM CREEK TIMBER CO INC
PMI GROUP INC (THE)
PRIME GROUP REALTY TRUST

PRIME RETAIL INC
PROLOGIS
PRUDENTIAL REAL ESTATE AFFILIATES INC
PUBLIC STORAGE INC
PULTEGROUP INC
RADIAN GROUP INC
RAILWORKS CORP
RAMADA WORLDWIDE INC
RE/MAX INTERNATIONAL INC
REALOGY CORPORATION
REALTY INCOME CORP
REGENCY CENTERS CORP
RITZ-CARLTON HOTEL COMPANY LLC (THE)
ROSEWOOD HOTELS & RESORTS LLC
ROYAL GROUP INC
RYLAND GROUP INC (THE)
SANDS REGENT
SCHUFF INTERNATIONAL INC
SENIOR HOUSING PROPERTIES
SERVICEMASTER COMPANY (THE)
SHAW GROUP INC (THE)
SIEMENS BUILDING TECHNOLOGIES
SIMON PROPERTY GROUP INC
SKIDMORE OWINGS & MERRILL LLP
SKYLINE CORPORATION
SOUTHERN ENERGY HOMES INC
SOVRAN SELF STORAGE INC
STARWOOD HOTELS & RESORTS WORLDWIDE INC
STEWART INFORMATION SERVICES CORP
STOCK BUILDING SUPPLY INC
STRATEGIC HOTELS AND RESORTS INC
STV GROUP INC
SUN COMMUNITIES INC
SUNBURST HOSPITALITY CORPORATION
SUNRISE SENIOR LIVING
SUNSTONE HOTEL INVESTORS INC
SUPER 8 MOTELS INC
SUPERTEL HOSPITALITY INC
SWIRE PACIFIC LTD
TANGER FACTORY OUTLET CENTERS
TAUBMAN CENTERS INC
THARALDSON ENTERPRISES INC
TOLL BROTHERS INC
TRAMMELL CROW COMPANY
TRANSCONTINENTAL REALTY
TRANSWESTERN COMMERCIAL SERVICES
TRANSWESTERN INVESTMENT CO LLC
TRIPLE FIVE GROUP
TRT HOLDINGS
TRUE HOME VALUE INC
TRUMP ORGANIZATION (THE)
URS CORPORATION
VENTAS INC
VINCI
VORNADO REALTY TRUST
WELLS REAL ESTATE FUNDS INC
WESTFIELD GROUP (THE)
WOLSELEY PLC
WORLDMARK BY WYNDHAM INC
WS ATKINS PLC
WYNDHAM VACATION OWNERSHIP
WYNDHAM WORLDWIDE
XANTERRA PARKS AND RESORTS
ZIPREALTY INC

SOUTHEAST
84 LUMBER COMPANY
ABERTIS INFRAESTRUCTURAS SA
ABM INDUSTRIES INC
ACCOR NORTH AMERICA
ACCOR SA
ADVOCAT INC
AECOM TECHNOLOGY CORPORATION
AMB PROPERTY CORPORATION
AMEC PLC
AMERCO
AMERICAN CAMPUS COMMUNITIES
AMERICA'S BEST FRANCHISING INC
AMERISTAR CASINOS INC
AMLI RESIDENTIAL PROPERTIES TRUST
ANDERSON-TULLY LUMBER COMPANY
ANTHONY & SYLVAN POOLS
APARTMENT INVESTMENT AND MANAGEMENT CO
ARC GROUP OF COMPANIES (THE)
ARCADIS NV
ARCHSTONE TRUST
ASSOCIATED ESTATES REALTY CORPORATION
ATRIA SENIOR LIVING GROUP
AVATAR HOLDINGS INC
BALFOUR BEATTY PLC
BANK OF AMERICA HOME LOANS
BARCELO CRESTLINE CORPORATION
BEAZER HOMES USA INC
BECHTEL GROUP INC
BEST WESTERN INTERNATIONAL INC
BLACK & VEATCH HOLDING COMPANY
BLUEGREEN CORPORATION
BOISE CASCADE
BOUYGUES SA
BOYD GAMING CORP
BROOKDALE SENIOR LIVING INC
BROOKFIELD ASSET MANAGEMENT INC
BUILDING MATERIALS HOLDING CORP
BURNS & MCDONNELL
BUTLER MANUFACTURING CO
CAMDEN PROPERTY TRUST
CAMP DRESSER & MCKEE INC
CAPITAL AUTOMOTIVE REIT
CAPITAL SENIOR LIVING CORP
CAPMARK FINANCIAL GROUP INC
CAPREIT INC
CARLSON HOTELS WORLDWIDE
CAVALIER HOMES INC
CB RICHARD ELLIS GROUP INC (CBRE)

CBL & ASSOCIATES PROPERTIES INC
CEMEX INC
CEMEX SAB DE CV
CENTEX CORP
CENTRO PROPERTIES GROUP
CENTURY 21 REAL ESTATE CORP
CH2M HILL COMPANIES LTD
CHAMPION ENTERPRISES INC
CHICAGO BRIDGE & IRON COMPANY NV
CHOICE HOTELS INTERNATIONAL INC
CHRISTIES GREAT ESTATES
CLAYTON HOMES INC
CLUB MEDITERRANEE SA
CNL FINANCIAL GROUP INC
COLDWELL BANKER REAL ESTATE CORP
COLLIERS INTERNATIONAL PROPERTY CONSULTANTS
COLONIAL PROPERTIES TRUST
COMFORT SYSTEMS USA INC
COMMUNITY DEVELOPMENT TRUST
CORE NETWORK (THE)
COSTAR GROUP INC
COUSINS PROPERTIES INC
CRESCENT REAL ESTATE EQUITIES LP
CRH PLC
CUSHMAN & WAKEFIELD INC
DAYS INN WORLDWIDE INC
DCT INDUSTRIAL TRUST INC
DEVELOPERS DIVERSIFIED REALTY CORP
DIAMOND RESORTS HOLDINGS LLC
DOOSAN HEAVY INDUSTRY & CONSTRUCTION CO
DR HORTON INC
DREW INDUSTRIES
DUKE REALTY CORP
EASTGROUP PROPERTIES INC
EMCOR GROUP INC
EMERITUS CORP
ENGLOBAL CORP
ENTERTAINMENT PROPERTIES TRUST
EQUITY LIFESTYLE PROPERTIES INC
EQUITY OFFICE PROPERTIES TRUST
EQUITY ONE INC
EQUITY RESIDENTIAL
ERICKSON RETIREMENT COMMUNITIES
FAIRMONT RAFFLES HOTELS INTERNATIONAL INC
FELCOR LODGING TRUST
FERGUSON ENTERPRISES INC
FIDELITY NATIONAL FINANCIAL INC
FIDELITY NATIONAL INFORMATION SERVICES INC
FIRST AMERICAN CORP
FIRST INDUSTRIAL REALTY TRUST INC
FIRSTSERVICE CORPORATION
FIVE STAR PRODUCTS INC
FLUOR CORP
FOMENTO DE CONSTRUCCIONES Y CONTRATAS SA (FCC)
FOUR SEASONS HOTELS
GABLES RESIDENTIAL TRUST
GAYLORD ENTERTAINMENT CO
GE CAPITAL FINANCE
GE CAPITAL REAL ESTATE
GENERAL ELECTRIC CO (GE)
GENERAL GROWTH PROPERTIES INC
GEORG FISCHER LTD
GLENBOROUGH REALTY TRUST
GLIMCHER REALTY TRUST
GMAC INC
GRANITE CONSTRUCTION INC
GRUBB & ELLIS CO
GRUBB & ELLIS REALTY INVESTORS LLC
HARRAH'S ENTERTAINMENT INC
HCP INC
HDR INC
HEALTH CARE REIT INC
HEALTHCARE REALTY TRUST INC
HIGHWOODS PROPERTIES INC
HILTON HOTELS CORP
HINES INTERESTS LP
HOCHTIEF AG
HOME DEPOT INC
HOME PROPERTIES INC
HOMESERVICES OF AMERICA INC
HOMETOWN AMERICA LLC
HORTON HOMES INC
HOSPITALITY PROPERTIES TRUST
HOST HOTELS & RESORTS LP
HOVNANIAN ENTERPRISES INC
HOWARD JOHNSON INTERNATIONAL INC
HRPT PROPERTIES TRUST
HVM LLC
HYATT HOTELS CORPORATION
ICAHN ENTERPRISES LP
IMPAC MORTGAGE HOLDINGS INC
INDUSTRIAL DEVELOPMENTS INTERNATIONAL INC
INLAND REAL ESTATE CORPORATION
INNKEEPERS USA TRUST
INSITUFORM TECHNOLOGIES
INTEGRATED ELECTRICAL SERVICES
INTERCONTINENTAL HOTELS GROUP PLC
INTERSTATE HOTELS AND RESORTS INC
INTOWN SUITES MANAGEMENT INC
ISTAR FINANCIAL INC
JACOBS ENGINEERING GROUP INC
JAMESON INN INC
JANUS HOTELS AND RESORTS INC
JOHN Q HAMMONS HOTELS LLC
JOHNSON CONTROLS INC
JONES LANG LASALLE INC
KB HOME
KIMCO REALTY CORP
KIMPTON HOTEL & RESTAURANT GROUP LLC

LANDAMERICA FINANCIAL GROUP INC
LAYNE CHRISTENSEN COMPANY
LB FOSTER COMPANY
LENDER PROCESSING SERVICES INC
LENNAR CORPORATION
LEXINGTON REALTY TRUST
LIBERTY PROPERTY TRUST
LIGHTSTONE GROUP LLC (THE)
LODGIAN INC
LOEWS HOTELS HOLDING CORPORATION
LOUIS BERGER GROUP INC (THE)
LOWE'S COMPANIES INC
LQ MANAGEMENT LLC
M/I HOMES INC
MACERICH COMPANY (THE)
MANDARIN ORIENTAL INTERNATIONAL LTD
MANOR CARE INC
MARRIOTT INTERNATIONAL INC
MCDERMOTT INTERNATIONAL INC
MDC HOLDINGS INC
MERITAGE HOMES CORP
MGM MIRAGE
MID-AMERICA APARTMENT COMMUNITIES INC
MILLENNIUM & COPTHORNE HOTELS PLC
MORGANS HOTEL GROUP CO
MUNICIPAL MORTGAGE & EQUITY
MWH GLOBAL INC
NAI GLOBAL INC
NATIONAL HEALTH INVESTORS
NATIONAL HOME CENTERS INC
NATIONWIDE HEALTH PROPERTIES
NCI BUILDING SYSTEMS INC
NEW PLAN EXCEL REALTY TRUST INC
NH HOTELES SA
NRT INCORPORATED
NVR INC
OAKWOOD WORLDWIDE
OMEGA HEALTHCARE INVESTORS
ORIENT OVERSEAS (INTERNATIONAL) LTD
ORION MARINE GROUP INC
ORLEANS HOMEBUILDERS
PALM HARBOR HOMES INC
PARKWAY PROPERTIES INC
PARSONS BRINCKERHOFF INC
PCL CONSTRUCTION GROUP INC
PENNSYLVANIA REIT
PLUM CREEK TIMBER CO INC
PMI GROUP INC (THE)
POST PROPERTIES INC
PRIME RETAIL INC
PROLOGIS
PRUDENTIAL REAL ESTATE AFFILIATES INC
PS BUSINESS PARKS INC
PUBLIC STORAGE INC
PULTEGROUP INC
RADIAN GROUP INC
RAILWORKS CORP
RAMADA WORLDWIDE INC
RE/MAX INTERNATIONAL INC
REALOGY CORPORATION
REALTY INCOME CORP
REGENCY CENTERS CORP
RELATED GROUP (THE)
RESORTQUEST INTERNATIONAL INC
RITZ-CARLTON HOTEL COMPANY LLC (THE)
ROSEWOOD HOTELS & RESORTS LLC
ROYAL GROUP INC
RYLAND GROUP INC (THE)
SCHUFF INTERNATIONAL INC
SENIOR HOUSING PROPERTIES
SERVICEMASTER COMPANY (THE)
SHAW GROUP INC (THE)
SIEMENS BUILDING TECHNOLOGIES
SIMON PROPERTY GROUP INC
SKYLINE CORPORATION
SONESTA INTERNATIONAL HOTELS CORP
SOUTHERN ENERGY HOMES INC
SOVRAN SELF STORAGE INC
ST JOE COMPANY (THE)
STANDARD PACIFIC CORP
STARWOOD CAPITAL GROUP GLOBAL LLC
STARWOOD HOTELS & RESORTS WORLDWIDE INC
STEWART INFORMATION SERVICES CORP
STOCK BUILDING SUPPLY INC
STRATEGIC HOTELS AND RESORTS INC
STV GROUP INC
SUN COMMUNITIES INC
SUNBURST HOSPITALITY CORPORATION
SUNRISE SENIOR LIVING
SUNSTONE HOTEL INVESTORS INC
SUPER 8 MOTELS INC
SUPERTEL HOSPITALITY INC
TANGER FACTORY OUTLET CENTERS
TARRAGON CORPORATION
TAUBMAN CENTERS INC
TECHNICAL OLYMPIC USA INC
THARALDSON ENTERPRISES INC
TOLL BROTHERS INC
TRAMMELL CROW COMPANY
TRANSCONTINENTAL REALTY
TRANSWESTERN COMMERCIAL SERVICES
TRANSWESTERN INVESTMENT CO LLC
TREVI-FINANZIARIA INDUSTRIALE SPA (TREVI GROUP)
TRIPLE FIVE GROUP
TRT HOLDINGS
TRUE HOME VALUE INC
TRUMP ORGANIZATION (THE)
TUTOR PERINI CORPORATION
UDR INC
URS CORPORATION
VENTAS INC
VINCI
VORNADO REALTY TRUST
WCI COMMUNITIES INC

WEINGARTEN REALTY INVESTORS
WELLS REAL ESTATE FUNDS INC
WESTFIELD GROUP (THE)
WOLSELEY PLC
WORLDMARK BY WYNDHAM INC
WS ATKINS PLC
WYNDHAM VACATION OWNERSHIP
WYNDHAM WORLDWIDE
ZIPREALTY INC

NORTHEAST
84 LUMBER COMPANY
ABM INDUSTRIES INC
ACCOR NORTH AMERICA
ACCOR SA
ACS ACTIVIDADES DE CONSTRUCCION Y SERVICIOS SA
ADVOCAT INC
AECOM TECHNOLOGY CORPORATION
ALEXANDRIA REAL ESTATE EQUITIES INC
AMB PROPERTY CORPORATION
AMEC PLC
AMERCO
AMERICAN CAMPUS COMMUNITIES
AMERICA'S BEST FRANCHISING INC
AMLI RESIDENTIAL PROPERTIES TRUST
ANNALY CAPITAL MANAGEMENT INC
ANTHONY & SYLVAN POOLS
APARTMENT INVESTMENT AND MANAGEMENT CO
ARC GROUP OF COMPANIES (THE)
ARCADIS NV
ARCHSTONE TRUST
ASSOCIATED ESTATES REALTY CORPORATION
ATRIA SENIOR LIVING GROUP
AVALONBAY COMMUNITIES INC
BANK OF AMERICA HOME LOANS
BARCELO CRESTLINE CORPORATION
BEAZER HOMES USA INC
BECHTEL GROUP INC
BEST WESTERN INTERNATIONAL INC
BLACK & VEATCH HOLDING COMPANY
BLUEGREEN CORPORATION
BOISE CASCADE
BOSTON PROPERTIES INC
BOUYGUES SA
BRANDYWINE REALTY TRUST
BROOKDALE SENIOR LIVING INC
BROOKFIELD ASSET MANAGEMENT INC
BROOKFIELD HOMES CORP
BUILDING MATERIALS HOLDING CORP
BURNS & MCDONNELL
BUTLER MANUFACTURING CO
CAMDEN PROPERTY TRUST
CAMP DRESSER & MCKEE INC
CAPITAL AUTOMOTIVE REIT
CAPITAL SENIOR LIVING CORP
CAPMARK FINANCIAL GROUP INC
CAPREIT INC
CARLSON HOTELS WORLDWIDE
CAVALIER HOMES INC
CB RICHARD ELLIS GROUP INC (CBRE)
CBL & ASSOCIATES PROPERTIES INC
CEMEX INC
CEMEX SAB DE CV
CENTEX CORP
CENTRO PROPERTIES GROUP
CENTURY 21 REAL ESTATE CORP
CH2M HILL COMPANIES LTD
CHAMPION ENTERPRISES INC
CHICAGO BRIDGE & IRON COMPANY NV
CHINA STATE CONSTRUCTION ENGINEERING CORP
CHOICE HOTELS INTERNATIONAL INC
CHRISTIES GREAT ESTATES
CLAYTON HOMES INC
CNL FINANCIAL GROUP INC
COLDWELL BANKER REAL ESTATE CORP
COLLIERS INTERNATIONAL PROPERTY CONSULTANTS
COLONIAL PROPERTIES TRUST
COLONY CAPITAL LLC
COMFORT SYSTEMS USA INC
COMMUNITY DEVELOPMENT TRUST
CORE NETWORK (THE)
CORPORATE OFFICE PROPERTIES TRUST
COSTAR GROUP INC
COUSINS PROPERTIES INC
CRH PLC
CUSHMAN & WAKEFIELD INC
DAYS INN WORLDWIDE INC
DCT INDUSTRIAL TRUST INC
DEVELOPERS DIVERSIFIED REALTY CORP
DIAMOND RESORTS HOLDINGS LLC
DOOSAN HEAVY INDUSTRY & CONSTRUCTION CO
DOYLE COLLECTION (THE)
DR HORTON INC
DREW INDUSTRIES
DUKE REALTY CORP
DYNEX CAPITAL INC
EASTGROUP PROPERTIES INC
EMCOR GROUP INC
EMERITUS CORP
ENTERTAINMENT PROPERTIES TRUST
EQUITY LIFESTYLE PROPERTIES INC
EQUITY OFFICE PROPERTIES TRUST
EQUITY ONE INC
EQUITY RESIDENTIAL
ERICKSON RETIREMENT COMMUNITIES
EXTENDICARE REAL ESTATE INVESTMENT TRUST
FAIRMONT RAFFLES HOTELS INTERNATIONAL INC
FANNIE MAE

FEDERAL AGRICULTURAL MORTGAGE CORP (FARMER MAC)
FEDERAL REALTY INVESTMENT TRUST
FELCOR LODGING TRUST
FERGUSON ENTERPRISES INC
FIDELITY NATIONAL FINANCIAL INC
FIDELITY NATIONAL INFORMATION SERVICES INC
FIRST AMERICAN CORP
FIRST INDUSTRIAL REALTY TRUST INC
FIRSTSERVICE CORPORATION
FIVE STAR PRODUCTS INC
FLUOR CORP
FOMENTO DE CONSTRUCCIONES Y CONTRATAS SA (FCC)
FOREST CITY ENTERPRISES INC
FOUR SEASONS HOTELS
FREDDIE MAC
GABLES RESIDENTIAL TRUST
GAYLORD ENTERTAINMENT CO
GE CAPITAL FINANCE
GE CAPITAL REAL ESTATE
GENERAL ELECTRIC CO (GE)
GENERAL GROWTH PROPERTIES INC
GLENBOROUGH REALTY TRUST
GLIMCHER REALTY TRUST
GMAC INC
GOLDEN TULIP HOSPITALITY GROUP
GRANITE CONSTRUCTION INC
GRUBB & ELLIS CO
HARRAH'S ENTERTAINMENT INC
HDR INC
HEALTH CARE REIT INC
HEALTHCARE REALTY TRUST INC
HIGHWOODS PROPERTIES INC
HILTON HOTELS CORP
HINES INTERESTS LP
HOCHTIEF AG
HOME DEPOT INC
HOME PROPERTIES INC
HOMESERVICES OF AMERICA INC
HOMETOWN AMERICA LLC
HONGKONG AND SHANGHAI HOTELS LTD
HORTON HOMES INC
HOSPITALITY PROPERTIES TRUST
HOST HOTELS & RESORTS LP
HOVNANIAN ENTERPRISES INC
HOWARD JOHNSON INTERNATIONAL INC
HRPT PROPERTIES TRUST
HVM LLC
HYATT HOTELS CORPORATION
HYPO REAL ESTATE HOLDING AG (HYPO BANK)
HYUNDAI ENGINEERING & CONSTRUCTION COMPANY LTD
ICAHN ENTERPRISES LP
IMPAC MORTGAGE HOLDINGS INC
INDIAN HOTEL COMPANY LIMITED (THE)
INDUSTRIAL DEVELOPMENTS INTERNATIONAL INC
INLAND AMERICAN REAL ESTATE TRUST INC
INNKEEPERS USA TRUST
INSITUFORM TECHNOLOGIES
INTEGRATED ELECTRICAL SERVICES
INTERCONTINENTAL HOTELS GROUP PLC
INTERSTATE HOTELS AND RESORTS INC
INTOWN SUITES MANAGEMENT INC
INVESTORS TITLE COMPANY
ISTAR FINANCIAL INC
JACOBS ENGINEERING GROUP INC
JAMESON INN INC
JANUS HOTELS AND RESORTS INC
JOHN Q HAMMONS HOTELS LLC
JOHNSON CONTROLS INC
JONES LANG LASALLE INC
KB HOME
KERZNER INTERNATIONAL LIMITED
KIMCO REALTY CORP
KIMPTON HOTEL & RESTAURANT GROUP LLC
LANDAMERICA FINANCIAL GROUP INC
LAS VEGAS SANDS CORP (THE VENETIAN)
LASALLE HOTEL PROPERTIES
LAYNE CHRISTENSEN COMPANY
LB FOSTER COMPANY
LENDER PROCESSING SERVICES INC
LENDINGTREE LLC
LENNAR CORPORATION
LEXINGTON REALTY TRUST
LIBERTY PROPERTY TRUST
LIGHTSTONE GROUP LLC (THE)
LODGIAN INC
LOEWS HOTELS HOLDING CORPORATION
LOUIS BERGER GROUP INC (THE)
LOWE'S COMPANIES INC
LQ MANAGEMENT LLC
M/I HOMES INC
MACERICH COMPANY (THE)
MACK-CALI REALTY CORP
MANDARIN ORIENTAL INTERNATIONAL LTD
MANOR CARE INC
MARRIOTT INTERNATIONAL INC
MATRIX SERVICE COMPANY
MCDERMOTT INTERNATIONAL INC
MDC HOLDINGS INC
MERITUS HOTELS & RESORTS INC
MFA FINANCIAL INC
MGM MIRAGE
MID-AMERICA APARTMENT COMMUNITIES INC
MILLENNIUM & COPTHORNE HOTELS PLC
MORGANS HOTEL GROUP CO
MOVE INC
MUNICIPAL MORTGAGE & EQUITY
MWH GLOBAL INC
NAI GLOBAL INC
NATIONAL HEALTH INVESTORS
NATIONWIDE HEALTH PROPERTIES

NCI BUILDING SYSTEMS INC
NEW PLAN EXCEL REALTY TRUST INC
NEWCASTLE INVESTMENT CORP
NH HOTELES SA
NRT INCORPORATED
NVR INC
OAKWOOD WORLDWIDE
OMEGA HEALTHCARE INVESTORS
ORIENT OVERSEAS (INTERNATIONAL) LTD
ORIENT-EXPRESS HOTELS LTD
ORION MARINE GROUP INC
ORLEANS HOMEBUILDERS
PALM HARBOR HOMES INC
PARKWAY PROPERTIES INC
PARSONS BRINCKERHOFF INC
PENNSYLVANIA REIT
PLUM CREEK TIMBER CO INC
PMI GROUP INC (THE)
POST PROPERTIES INC
PRIME RETAIL INC
PROLOGIS
PRUDENTIAL REAL ESTATE AFFILIATES INC
PS BUSINESS PARKS INC
PUBLIC STORAGE INC
PULTEGROUP INC
RADIAN GROUP INC
RAILWORKS CORP
RAMADA WORLDWIDE INC
RE/MAX INTERNATIONAL INC
REALOGY CORPORATION
REALTY INCOME CORP
REGENCY CENTERS CORP
REIS INC
RESORTQUEST INTERNATIONAL INC
RITZ-CARLTON HOTEL COMPANY LLC (THE)
ROSEWOOD HOTELS & RESORTS LLC
ROYAL GROUP INC
RXR REALTY
RYLAND GROUP INC (THE)
SAWYER REALTY HOLDINGS LLC
SENIOR HOUSING PROPERTIES
SERVICEMASTER COMPANY (THE)
SHANGRI-LA ASIA LTD
SHAW GROUP INC (THE)
SIEMENS BUILDING TECHNOLOGIES
SIMON PROPERTY GROUP INC
SKIDMORE OWINGS & MERRILL LLP
SKYLINE CORPORATION
SL GREEN REALTY CORP
SONESTA INTERNATIONAL HOTELS CORP
SOUTHERN ENERGY HOMES INC
SOVRAN SELF STORAGE INC
STANDARD PACIFIC CORP
STARWOOD CAPITAL GROUP GLOBAL LLC
STARWOOD HOTELS & RESORTS WORLDWIDE INC
STEWART INFORMATION SERVICES CORP
STOCK BUILDING SUPPLY INC
STRATEGIC HOTELS AND RESORTS INC
STV GROUP INC
SUN COMMUNITIES INC
SUNBURST HOSPITALITY CORPORATION
SUNRISE SENIOR LIVING
SUNSTONE HOTEL INVESTORS INC
SUPER 8 MOTELS INC
SUPERTEL HOSPITALITY INC
SWIRE PACIFIC LTD
TANGER FACTORY OUTLET CENTERS
TARRAGON CORPORATION
TAUBMAN CENTERS INC
TECHNICAL OLYMPIC USA INC
THARALDSON ENTERPRISES INC
TOLL BROTHERS INC
TRACO
TRAMMELL CROW COMPANY
TRANSCONTINENTAL REALTY
TRANSWESTERN COMMERCIAL SERVICES
TRANSWESTERN INVESTMENT CO LLC
TREVI-FINANZIARIA INDUSTRIALE SPA (TREVI GROUP)
TRIPLE FIVE GROUP
TRT HOLDINGS
TRUE HOME VALUE INC
TRUMP ENTERTAINMENT RESORTS INC
TRUMP ORGANIZATION (THE)
TUTOR PERINI CORPORATION
UDR INC
URS CORPORATION
VENTAS INC
VINCI
VORNADO REALTY TRUST
WASHINGTON REAL ESTATE INVESTMENT TRUST
WCI COMMUNITIES INC
WEINGARTEN REALTY INVESTORS
WELLS REAL ESTATE FUNDS INC
WESTFIELD GROUP (THE)
WOLSELEY PLC
WP CAREY & CO LLC
WS ATKINS PLC
WYNDHAM VACATION OWNERSHIP
WYNDHAM WORLDWIDE
ZIPREALTY INC

INDEX OF FIRMS WITH INTERNATIONAL OPERATIONS

GUOMAN HOTELS LIMITED
HANG LUNG GROUP LTD
HANG LUNG PROPERTIES LIMITED
HANJIN HEAVY INDUSTRIES CO LTD
HARRAH'S ENTERTAINMENT INC
HDR INC
HENDERSON LAND DEVELOPMENT COMPANY LIMITED
HILTON HOTELS CORP
HINES INTERESTS LP
HOCHTIEF AG
HOME DEPOT INC
HOME INNS & HOTELS MANAGEMENT INC
HONGKONG AND SHANGHAI HOTELS LTD
HONGKONG LAND HOLDINGS LTD
HOSPITALITY PROPERTIES TRUST
HOST HOTELS & RESORTS LP
HOTEL PROPERTIES LTD
HOWARD JOHNSON INTERNATIONAL INC
HUTCHISON WHAMPOA HOTEL & PROPERTIES LTD
HVM LLC
HYATT HOTELS CORPORATION
HYPO REAL ESTATE HOLDING AG (HYPO BANK)
HYSAN DEVELOPMENT CO LTD
HYUNDAI ELEVATOR CO LTD
HYUNDAI ENGINEERING & CONSTRUCTION COMPANY LTD
IMPREGILO SPA
INDIAN HOTEL COMPANY LIMITED (THE)
INSITUFORM TECHNOLOGIES
INTERCONTINENTAL HOTELS GROUP PLC
INTERSTATE HOTELS AND RESORTS INC
JACOBS ENGINEERING GROUP INC
JOHN LAING PLC
JOHNSON CONTROLS INC
JONES LANG LASALLE INC
KERZNER INTERNATIONAL LIMITED
KIMCO REALTY CORP
KIMPTON HOTEL & RESTAURANT GROUP LLC
KUMHO INDUSTRIAL CO LTD
LAS VEGAS SANDS CORP (THE VENETIAN)
LAYNE CHRISTENSEN COMPANY
LEXINGTON REALTY TRUST
LIBERTY PROPERTY TRUST
LINK REAL ESTATE INVESTMENT TRUST (THE)
LOEWS HOTELS HOLDING CORPORATION
LOUIS BERGER GROUP INC (THE)
LOWE'S COMPANIES INC
LQ MANAGEMENT LLC
MANDARIN ORIENTAL INTERNATIONAL LTD
MARRIOTT INTERNATIONAL INC
MATRIX SERVICE COMPANY
MAX PROPERTY GROUP PLC
MCDERMOTT INTERNATIONAL INC
MERITUS HOTELS & RESORTS INC
MGM MIRAGE
MILLENNIUM & COPTHORNE HOTELS PLC
MORGANS HOTEL GROUP CO
MOVE INC
MRV ENGENHARIA E PARTICIPACOES SA
MWH GLOBAL INC
NAI GLOBAL INC
NCI BUILDING SYSTEMS INC
NEW PLAN EXCEL REALTY TRUST INC
NEW WORLD DEVELOPMENT COMPANY LIMITED
NEWCASTLE INVESTMENT CORP
NH HOTELES SA
NRT INCORPORATED
OAKWOOD WORLDWIDE
OBEROI GROUP (EIH LTD)
ODEBRECHT SA
ORIENT OVERSEAS (INTERNATIONAL) LTD
ORIENT-EXPRESS HOTELS LTD
PACIFIC COAST BUILDING PRODUCTS
PARSONS BRINCKERHOFF INC
PCL CONSTRUCTION GROUP INC
PDG REALTY SA EMPREENDIMENTOS E PARTICIPACOES
PMI GROUP INC (THE)
PROLOGIS
PRUDENTIAL REAL ESTATE AFFILIATES INC
QMH UK LTD
RADIAN GROUP INC
RAILWORKS CORP
RAMADA WORLDWIDE INC
RE/MAX INTERNATIONAL INC
REALOGY CORPORATION
RED LION HOTELS CORPORATION
RESORTQUEST INTERNATIONAL INC
REZIDOR HOTEL GROUP AB
RITZ-CARLTON HOTEL COMPANY LLC (THE)
ROSEWOOD HOTELS & RESORTS LLC
ROSSI RESIDENCIAL SA
ROYAL GROUP INC
SAHA PATHANA INTER-HOLDING PCL
SAMWHAN CORPORATION
SCANDIC HOTELS AB
SEKISUI HOUSE LTD
SEMBCORP INDUSTRIES LTD
SENIOR HOUSING PROPERTIES
SERVICEMASTER COMPANY (THE)
SHANGRI-LA ASIA LTD
SHAW GROUP INC (THE)
SHIMAO PROPERTY HOLDINGS LTD
SHUN TAK HOLDINGS LIMITED
SIEMENS BUILDING TECHNOLOGIES
SIMON PROPERTY GROUP INC
SINO LAND COMPANY LIMITED
SKIDMORE OWINGS & MERRILL LLP
SOCIETE DES BAINS DE MER ET DU CERCLE
SOL MELIA SA
SONESTA INTERNATIONAL HOTELS CORP
STARWOOD CAPITAL GROUP GLOBAL LLC
STARWOOD HOTELS & RESORTS WORLDWIDE INC

STEWART INFORMATION SERVICES CORP
STRATEGIC HOTELS AND RESORTS INC
STV GROUP INC
SUN HUNG KAI PROPERTIES
SUNRISE SENIOR LIVING
SUPER 8 MOTELS INC
SWIRE PACIFIC LTD
TAUBMAN CENTERS INC
TRAMMELL CROW COMPANY
TRANSCONTINENTAL REALTY
TREVI-FINANZIARIA INDUSTRIALE SPA (TREVI GROUP)
TRINITY LTD
TRIPLE FIVE GROUP
TRT HOLDINGS
TRUMP ORGANIZATION (THE)
TUTOR PERINI CORPORATION
UNIBAIL-RODAMCO
UNITECH LIMITED
URS CORPORATION
VINCI
VORNADO REALTY TRUST
WESTFIELD GROUP (THE)
WHARF (HOLDINGS) LIMITED, THE
WHEELOCK AND COMPANY LIMITED
WOLSELEY PLC
WORLDMARK BY WYNDHAM INC
WP CAREY & CO LLC
WS ATKINS PLC
WYNDHAM VACATION OWNERSHIP
WYNDHAM WORLDWIDE
WYNN RESORTS LIMITED
YIT CORPORATION

Individual Profiles On Each Of THE REAL ESTATE 400

84 LUMBER COMPANY

www.84lumber.com

Industry Group Code: 444130 **Ranks within this company's industry group:** Sales: 1 Profits:

Properties:	Financial Services:	Construction/Development:		Investments:	Specialty Services:	Brokerage:
Apartments:	Mortgages:	Commercial Construction:		REIT:	Property Management:	Commercial Sales:
Malls/Shopping:	Title Insurance:	Residential Construction:			Online Services:	Residential Sales:
Offices:	Property Insurance:	Land Development:			Software/IT:	Specialty:
Hotels/Motels:		Support Services:	Y		Consulting:	
Industrial/Warehouses:		Design/Engineering:	Y			
Other:						

TYPES OF BUSINESS:

Hardware Stores
Building Materials
Construction Financing
Builder's Insurance
Travel Agency

BRANDS/DIVISIONS/AFFILIATES:

Affordable Collection
Oaks Collection
Builder Lending Program
Maggie's Management LLC
84 Travel
84 Components
84 Lumber Credit Card
84 Lumber Contractor Card

CONTACTS: *Note: Officers with more than one job title may be intentionally listed here more than once.*

Joseph A. Hardy III, CEO
Maggie H. Magerko, Pres.

Phone: 724-228-8820	**Fax:** 724-228-8058
Toll-Free:	
Address: 1019 Rte. 519, Eighty Four, PA 15330-2813 US	

GROWTH PLANS/SPECIAL FEATURES:

84 Lumber Company is one of the largest privately held suppliers of building materials, supplies and expertise to professional contractors, remodelers and individuals in the U.S. The company operates 319 locations nationwide, including six component manufacturing facilities. 84 Lumber has store locations in 37 states, which offer lumber, plywood, insulation, trim, molding, flooring, siding, drywall, trusses, roofing, skylights, engineered lumber, hardware, doors and windows. In addition to its retail store operations, 84 Lumber offers a variety of good and services. 84 Components is the company's manufacturing division, which builds metal plate connected roof and floor trusses and wall panels. 84 Travel is a full-service accredited travel agency offering no-fee service to professional contractors and to the general public. Along with builder's risk, general liability, workers compensation, commercial auto and personal insurance provided by Maggie's Management, LLC, the company provides financing for professional builders through its Builder Lending Program with Liberty Savings Bank. The 84 Lumber Credit Card and the 84 Lumber Contractor Card are available to general customers and contractors respectively. The firm offers installed services that include framing, roofing, insulation, windows, doors, trip and siding. 84 Lumber also sells entire home packages such as the Affordable Collection, which contains plans for easy-to-build homes from 500 square feet up to 2,576 square feet; and the Oaks Collection, which includes more elaborate designs in sizes up to nearly 5,000 square feet. In addition, 84 Lumber has an affiliation with Nelson Design Group, an online provider of over 900 house plans.

The company offers its employees medical and dental; a 401(K) plan; a profit sharing plan; disability and life insurance; and training and development programs.

FINANCIALS: **Sales and profits are in thousands of dollars—add 000 to get the full amount. 2009 Note: Financial information for 2009 was not available for all companies at press time.**

2009 Sales: $	2009 Profits: $	**U.S. Stock Ticker: Private**
2008 Sales: $2,100,000	2008 Profits: $	**Int'l Ticker:** Int'l Exchange:
2007 Sales: $3,100,000	2007 Profits: $	Employees: 4,500
2006 Sales: $3,920,000	2006 Profits: $	Fiscal Year Ends: 12/31
2005 Sales: $	2005 Profits: $	Parent Company:

SALARIES/BENEFITS:

Pension Plan:	ESOP Stock Plan:	Profit Sharing: Y	Top Exec. Salary: $	Bonus: $
Savings Plan: Y	Stock Purch. Plan:		Second Exec. Salary: $	Bonus: $

OTHER THOUGHTS:

Apparent Women Officers or Directors: 2
Hot Spot for Advancement for Women/Minorities: Y

LOCATIONS: ("Y" = Yes)

West:	Southwest:	Midwest:	Southeast:	Northeast:	International:
Y	Y	Y	Y	Y	

ABERTIS INFRAESTRUCTURAS SA

www.abertis.com

Industry Group Code: 561210 **Ranks within this company's industry group:** Sales: 1 Profits: 1

Properties:		Financial Services:		Construction/Development:		Investments:		Specialty Services:		Brokerage:	
Apartments:		Mortgages:		Commercial Construction:		REIT:		Property Management:	Y	Commercial Sales:	
Malls/Shopping:		Title Insurance:		Residential Construction:				Online Services:		Residential Sales:	
Offices:		Property Insurance:		Land Development:				Software/IT:		Specialty:	
Hotels/Motels:				Support Services:				Consulting:			
Industrial/Warehouses:				Design/Engineering:							
Other:	Y										

TYPES OF BUSINESS:

Transport & Communications
Logistics Services
TV & Radio Broadcasting
Airport Operations
Parking Facilities Management
Motorway Construction & Management
Warehouses
Heavy Construction

BRANDS/DIVISIONS/AFFILIATES:

Saba
Tradia
Retevision
Abertis Logistica
Abertis Telecom
Desarrollo de Concesiones Aeroportuarias SA

CONTACTS:

Note: Officers with more than one job title may be intentionally listed here more than once.

Salvador Alemany Mas, CEO
Jose Aljaro Navarro, CFO
Joan Rafel Herrero, Dir.-Personnel & Organization
Marta Casas, Dir.-Legal Svcs.
David Diaz Almazan, Dir.-Corp. Dev.
Antoni Brunet Mauri, Dir.-Corp. Comm.
Luis Subira Laborda, Dir.-Corp. Finance
Juan A. M. Padros, Company Sec.
Sergi Loughney Castells, Dir.-Institutional Rel.
Tobias Martinez Gimeno, Managing Dir.-Abertis Telecom
Manel Cruces Socasau, Managing Dir.-Toll Roads South America
Isidre Faine Casas, Chmn.
Jordi Graells Ferrandez, Managing Dir.-Toll Roads North America & Int'l

Phone: 34-932-305-000 **Fax:** 34-932-305-001
Toll-Free:
Address: 12-20 Parc Logistic Ave., Barcelona, 08040 Spain

GROWTH PLANS/SPECIAL FEATURES:

Abertis Infraestructuras S.A., a private transport and communications infrastructure management company based in Barcelona, is a leading Spain-based operator of motorways and car parks. The company, which is active in 17 countries in Europe, North America and South America, also offers logistics parks, telecommunications infrastructure and airport operation services. Abertis is the head of a number of business units made up of over 60 directly-managed or associate companies. The firm's motorways division, representing approximately 76% of revenues, directly manages a network of 2,063 miles of motorways, including 59% of all toll routes in Spain. Abertis manages an additional 3,355 miles of motorways through interests in Italy, the U.K., Argentina, Chile and Portugal. The company's car park division is headed by Saba and manages facilities in over 70 municipalities in Spain, Italy, Portugal, Chile, Morocco and Andorra. The company's logistics activities, headed by Abertis Logistica, consist of warehouses and offices in Spain and abroad. Industrial facilities under the firm's management total approximately 8.6 million square feet and currently house the operations of more than 300 companies. Abertis Telecom, the company's telecommunications division, consists of two companies, Tradia and Retevision. Tradia's activities include provision of radio and TV signal broadcasting services and the renting of space for telecommunications operators. Retevision, which provides national coverage with its analog and digital network, focuses on audiovisual signal transportation and broadcasting. In the field of airport operations, the company operates directly in 16 airports in six countries, including the U.S., as well as providing airport-related consulting services. Recently, the firm completed its acquisition of Desarrollo de Concesiones Aeroportuarias, S.A., with stakes in 15 airports in Mexico, Jamaica, Chile and Columbia. In 2009, Abertis announced that it would install a satellite-based toll system for heavy vehicles on a 1,240-mile road network in Slovakia.

FINANCIALS:

Sales and profits are in thousands of dollars—add 000 to get the full amount. 2009 Note: Financial information for 2009 was not available for all companies at press time.

2009 Sales: $5,252,880	2009 Profits: $889,560
2008 Sales: $4,883,650	2008 Profits: $820,360
2007 Sales: $4,805,330	2007 Profits: $905,310
2006 Sales: $4,880,810	2006 Profits: $775,660
2005 Sales: $2,257,200	2005 Profits: $609,800

U.S. Stock Ticker: ABE
Int'l Ticker: ABE Int'l Exchange: Madrid-MCE
Employees: 11,894
Fiscal Year Ends: 12/31
Parent Company:

SALARIES/BENEFITS:

Pension Plan:	ESOP Stock Plan:	Profit Sharing:	Top Exec. Salary: $	Bonus: $
Savings Plan:	Stock Purch. Plan:		Second Exec. Salary: $	Bonus: $

OTHER THOUGHTS:

Apparent Women Officers or Directors: 2
Hot Spot for Advancement for Women/Minorities:

LOCATIONS: ("Y" = Yes)

West:	Southwest:	Midwest:	Southeast:	Northeast:	International:
	Y		Y		Y

ABM INDUSTRIES INC

www.abm.com

Industry Group Code: 5311 **Ranks within this company's industry group:** Sales: 7 Profits: 23

Properties:		Financial Services:		Construction/Development:		Investments:		Specialty Services:		Brokerage:	
Apartments:		Mortgages:		Commercial Construction:		REIT:		Property Management:	Y	Commercial Sales:	
Malls/Shopping:		Title Insurance:		Residential Construction:				Online Services:		Residential Sales:	
Offices:		Property Insurance:		Land Development:				Software/IT:		Specialty:	
Hotels/Motels:				Support Services:	Y			Consulting:			
Industrial/Warehouses:				Design/Engineering:							
Other:											

TYPES OF BUSINESS:

Janitorial Services
Parking Facilities
Maintenance Personnel
Security Services
Lighting Services
Billing & Accounting Services
Supplier Management
Call Center Services

BRANDS/DIVISIONS/AFFILIATES:

ABM Janitorial Services
American Building Maintenance
ABM Security Services
Security Services of America
Silverhawk Security Specialists
Elite Protection Services
ABM Engineering Services
Amtech Lighting Services

CONTACTS: *Note: Officers with more than one job title may be intentionally listed here more than once.*

Henrik C. Slipsager, CEO
Henrik C. Slipsager, Pres.
James Lusk, CFO/Exec. VP
Gary R. Wallace, Chief Mktg. Officer
Erin M. Andre, Sr. VP-Human Resources
Sarah Hlavinka McConnell, General Counsel/Sr. VP/Corp. Sec.
Gary R. Wallace, Sr. VP-Bus. Dev.
Tony Mitchell, VP-Corp. Comm.
David L. Farwell, Sr. VP-Investor Rel.
James P. McClure, Exec. VP/Pres., ABM Janitorial Svcs.
Steven M. Zaccagnini, Exec. VP/Pres., ABM Facility Svcs.
David L. Farwell, Sr. VP/Chief of Staff
Chris Hansen, Pres., Ampco System Parking
Maryellen C. Herringer, Chmn.

Phone: 212-297-0200	**Fax:** 415-733-7333
Toll-Free:	
Address: 551 5th Ave., Ste. 300, New York, NY 10176 US	

GROWTH PLANS/SPECIAL FEATURES:

ABM Industries, Inc. is one of the country's largest facility services providers. Founded in California in 1909 as a one-man window cleaning business, today the firm provides janitorial, parking, engineering, security, and mechanical services to commercial, industrial, institutional and retail facilities throughout the U.S. and Canada. ABM operates through a number of subsidiaries, which are grouped into four segments: janitorial, parking, security and engineering. The company's janitorial services companies include ABM Janitorial Services and American Building Maintenance. Services provided include floor cleaning and finishing; window washing; furniture polishing; and carpet cleaning and dusting. Through its subsidiaries the company provides parking and transportation services in 35 states. These include three types of parking services, managed, leased and allowance locations; it also provides shuttle services to 14 nationwide airports. ABM's security services subsidiaries include ABM Security Services, SSA Security, Security Services of America, Silverhawk Security Specialists and Elite Protection Services. Security services offered by these subsidiaries include security officers; investigative services; electronic monitoring of fire, life safety systems and access control devices; and security consulting. ABM Engineering Services is the company's primary engineering subsidiary, offering on-site engineers to operate and maintain mechanical, electrical and plumbing systems at such facilities as high-rise office buildings, schools, computer centers, shopping malls, manufacturing facilities, museums and universities. The engineering segment also provides facility services through ABM Facility Services, which provides streamlined, centralized control and coordination of multiple facility service needs. In addition, this segment also provides an energy management service, which helps clients identify and amend drains on energy efficiency. The company also provides landscaping and golf services through its subsidiary OneSource.

ABM offers its employees a tuition reimbursement program, credit union membership, an employee assistance program and medical, dental, vision, life, AD&D and disability insurance.

FINANCIALS: **Sales and profits are in thousands of dollars—add 000 to get the full amount. 2009 Note: Financial information for 2009 was not available for all companies at press time.**

2009 Sales: $3,481,823	2009 Profits: $54,293	**U.S. Stock Ticker: ABM**
2008 Sales: $3,623,590	2008 Profits: $45,434	**Int'l Ticker:** Int'l Exchange:
2007 Sales: $2,706,105	2007 Profits: $52,440	Employees: 91,000
2006 Sales: $2,579,351	2006 Profits: $93,205	Fiscal Year Ends: 10/31
2005 Sales: $2,587,761	2005 Profits: $57,941	Parent Company:

SALARIES/BENEFITS:

Pension Plan:	ESOP Stock Plan:	Profit Sharing:	Top Exec. Salary: $765,000	Bonus: $1,040,000
Savings Plan: Y	Stock Purch. Plan:		Second Exec. Salary: $550,000	Bonus: $449,708

OTHER THOUGHTS:

Apparent Women Officers or Directors: 4
Hot Spot for Advancement for Women/Minorities: Y

LOCATIONS: ("Y" = Yes)

West:	Southwest:	Midwest:	Southeast:	Northeast:	International:
Y	Y	Y	Y	Y	Y

ACCIONA SA

www.acciona.es

Industry Group Code: 237 **Ranks within this company's industry group:** Sales: 16 Profits: 6

Properties:		Financial Services:		Construction/Development:		Investments:		Specialty Services:		Brokerage:	
Apartments:		Mortgages:		Commercial Construction:	Y	REIT:		Property Management:		Commercial Sales:	
Malls/Shopping:		Title Insurance:		Residential Construction:				Online Services:		Residential Sales:	
Offices:		Property Insurance:		Land Development:				Software/IT:		Specialty:	
Hotels/Motels:				Support Services:	Y			Consulting:			
Industrial/Warehouses:				Design/Engineering:							
Other:											

TYPES OF BUSINESS:

Heavy Construction
Infrastructure Services
Road Concessions
Logistics Services
Airport Services
Passenger Ferries
Urban & Environmental Services
Alternative Energy Installation

BRANDS/DIVISIONS/AFFILIATES:

Acciona Infraestructuras SA
Acciona Agua
Acciona Facility Services
Acciona Environmental Services
Acciona Urban Services
Acciona Logistics
Acciona Airport Services
Acciona TrasMediterranea

CONTACTS: *Note: Officers with more than one job title may be intentionally listed here more than once.*

Juan Ignacio Entrecanales Franco, CEO/Vice Chmn.
Valentin Montoya Moya, CFO
Juan Ramon Silva Ferrada, Chief Mktg. Officer
Jorge Vega-Penichet Lopez, General Counsel/Corp. Sec.
Juan Muro-Lara, Head-Corp. Dev.
Pio Cabanillas, Chief Comm. Officer
Juan Muro-Lara, Head-Investor Rel.
Juan Gallardo, Controller
Carmen Becerril, Pres., Energy Div.
Pedro Martinez, Pres., Infrastructure Div.
Luis Castilla, Pres., Water Div.
Isabel Antunez, Head-Real Estate
Jose M. E. Domecq, Chmn.
Frank Gelardin, Head-Int'l
Antonio Gravalos, Head-Logistics & Transport Svcs.

Phone: 34-91-663-28-50 **Fax:** 34-91-663-28-51
Toll-Free:
Address: Ave. De Europa, 18, Parque Empresarial La Moreleja, Alcobendas, 28108 Spain

GROWTH PLANS/SPECIAL FEATURES:

Acciona SA develops and manages infrastructure and related projects in Spain and internationally. The company has six primary divisions: Infrastructure; Real Estate; Energy; Water; Environmental & Urban Services; and Logistics & Transport Services. The infrastructure division includes Acciona Infrastructure SA, a leading construction and civil engineering group formed in 1850. The firm builds roads, bridges, railways, dams, canals, sewer systems, hospitals, seaports and airports, industrial facilities and municipal buildings. The real estate division is involved in property management, car park operations, apartments, shopping centers, office buildings and general real estate development, with a strong focus in Latin American markets such as Mexico and Brazil, where the division currently maintains more than half of its investments. The energy division is focused on the development of renewable energy facilities, primarily through the installation of wind farms and solar arrays. Roughly three-fourths of the energy division's business has been outside Spain in recent years. The water division is involved in the engineering, construction and management of drinking water plants, sewage treatment plants and reverse-osmosis desalination plants. Subsidiary Acciona Agua has built some 400 water treatment plans and 70 desalination plants in 20 countries. The environmental and urban services division offers street cleaning, municipal solid waste collection, park design and maintenance and facility management services through subsidiaries Acciona Facility Services, Acciona Environmental Services and Acciona Urban Services. The logistics and transport services division encompasses subsidiaries such as Acciona Logistics; Acciona Rail Services; Acciona Airport Services; and Acciona TrasMediterranea, a passenger ferry and cargo shipping firm. Some key markets worldwide include Canada, the U.S., Mexico, Chile, Brazil, Poland, Spain, the U.A.E., India and Australia. Overall, the firm is active in over 30 countries across Europe, North and South America, Africa, the Middle East and Asia.

FINANCIALS: **Sales and profits are in thousands of dollars—add 000 to get the full amount. 2009 Note: Financial information for 2009 was not available for all companies at press time.**

2009 Sales: $10,374,100 | 2009 Profits: $1,720,540
2008 Sales: $17,094,300 | 2008 Profits: $626,280
2007 Sales: $10,734,400 | 2007 Profits: $1,282,240
2006 Sales: $7,418,400 | 2006 Profits: $452,500
2005 Sales: $5,838,200 | 2005 Profits: $389,800

U.S. Stock Ticker: ACXIF.PK
Int'l Ticker: ANA Int'l Exchange: Madrid-MCE
Employees:
Fiscal Year Ends: 12/31
Parent Company:

SALARIES/BENEFITS:

Pension Plan: | ESOP Stock Plan: | Profit Sharing: | Top Exec. Salary: $ | Bonus: $
Savings Plan: | Stock Purch. Plan: | | Second Exec. Salary: $ | Bonus: $

OTHER THOUGHTS:

Apparent Women Officers or Directors: 2
Hot Spot for Advancement for Women/Minorities:

LOCATIONS: ("Y" = Yes)

West:	Southwest:	Midwest:	Southeast:	Northeast:	International:
Y		Y			Y

ACCOR NORTH AMERICA

www.accor-na.com

Industry Group Code: 721110 **Ranks within this company's industry group:** Sales: Profits:

Properties:		Financial Services:	Construction/Development:	Investments:	Specialty Services:	Brokerage:
Apartments:		Mortgages:	Commercial Construction:	REIT:	Property Management:	Commercial Sales:
Malls/Shopping:		Title Insurance:	Residential Construction:		Online Services:	Residential Sales:
Offices:		Property Insurance:	Land Development:		Software/IT:	Specialty:
Hotels/Motels:	Y		Support Services:		Consulting:	
Industrial/Warehouses:			Design/Engineering:			
Other:						

TYPES OF BUSINESS:

Hotels

BRANDS/DIVISIONS/AFFILIATES:

Accor SA
Accor Economy Lodging
Motel 6
Studio 6
Red Roof Inn
Novotel
Ibis
Sofitel

CONTACTS:

Note: Officers with more than one job title may be intentionally listed here more than once.

Yann Caillere, CEO-Sofitel Worldwide
Didier Obeuf, Sr. VP-Oper., Canada

Phone: 972-360-9000 **Fax:** 972-716-6590
Toll-Free:
Address: 4001 International Parkway, Carrollton, TX 75007 US

GROWTH PLANS/SPECIAL FEATURES:

Accor North America, a subsidiary of French hotel and human resources conglomerate Accor SA, operates more than 1,052 hotels with 107,104 rooms across the U.S., Canada and Mexico. The firm's North American hotel chains include Sofitel, which is a French luxury brand that incorporates the local culture into its décor. It offers visitors first-rate accommodations with upscale restaurants, complete business facilities, fitness centers, fine art and antiques. The Novotel Chain is another of the company's more upscale offerings that consists of a relaxed modern decor that makes it accessible to both business and leisure travelers. Novotel properties offer rooms with sitting/working areas, mid-scale restaurants and pools and golf course privileges, with locations in the U.S. and Canada. The company's Accor Economy Lodging properties brand names include Motel 6, which offers visitors only the essentials at one of the lowest prices for a national chain. Studio 6 hotels offer extended stay lodging at fiscally convenient prices, with locations in the central business districts of major metropolitan areas. Ibis is the company's international economy hotel that has seven locations in Mexico. It offers visitors 24/7 hotel services, an en-suite bedroom and on-site food and beverage locations. Accor incorporates a green policy into all of its chains that consists of water saving shower heads, Energy Star program participation, recycled paper and soy ink for its directories, energy efficient fluorescent lighting and the use of green Ecolab products for laundry and cleaning.

FINANCIALS:

Sales and profits are in thousands of dollars—add 000 to get the full amount. 2009 Note: Financial information for 2009 was not available for all companies at press time.

2009 Sales: $	2009 Profits: $
2008 Sales: $	2008 Profits: $
2007 Sales: $	2007 Profits: $
2006 Sales: $	2006 Profits: $
2005 Sales: $1,534,900	2005 Profits: $

U.S. Stock Ticker: Subsidiary
Int'l Ticker: Int'l Exchange:
Employees:
Fiscal Year Ends: 12/31
Parent Company: ACCOR SA

SALARIES/BENEFITS:

Pension Plan:	ESOP Stock Plan:	Profit Sharing:	Top Exec. Salary: $	Bonus: $
Savings Plan:	Stock Purch. Plan:		Second Exec. Salary: $	Bonus: $

OTHER THOUGHTS:

Apparent Women Officers or Directors: 6
Hot Spot for Advancement for Women/Minorities: Y

LOCATIONS: ("Y" = Yes)

West:	Southwest:	Midwest:	Southeast:	Northeast:	International:
Y	Y	Y	Y	Y	Y

ACCOR SA

www.accor.com

Industry Group Code: 721110 **Ranks within this company's industry group:** Sales: 2 Profits: 1

Properties:		Financial Services:		Construction/Development:		Investments:		Specialty Services:		Brokerage:	
Apartments:		Mortgages:		Commercial Construction:		REIT:		Property Management:	Y	Commercial Sales:	
Malls/Shopping:		Title Insurance:		Residential Construction:				Online Services:		Residential Sales:	
Offices:		Property Insurance:		Land Development:				Software/IT:		Specialty:	
Hotels/Motels:	Y			Support Services:				Consulting:			
Industrial/Warehouses:				Design/Engineering:							
Other:											

TYPES OF BUSINESS:

Hotels
Vacation Services
Cruises
Internal Corporate Services

BRANDS/DIVISIONS/AFFILIATES:

Accor North America
Etap
Formula 1
Novotel
Sofitel
Ticket Restaurant
Ticket Childcare Vouchers
Pullman

CONTACTS:

Note: Officers with more than one job title may be intentionally listed here more than once.

Gilles Pelisson, CEO
Jacques Stern, CFO
Jean-Luc Chretien, Exec. VP-Mktg. & Dist.
Patrick Ollivier, Exec. VP-Human Resources
Pascal Quint, Corp. Sec.
Jacques Stern, Sr. Exec. VP-Finance
Michael Issenberg, COO-Asia Pacific
Michael Flaxman, COO-Americas
Jacques Stern, Sr. Exec. VP-Svcs.
Gilles Pelisson, Chmn.
Yann Caillere, COO-EMEA

Phone: 33-0169-36-8080	**Fax:** 33-0169-36-7900
Toll-Free:	
Address: 2 rue de la Mare-Neuve, Evry Cedex, 91021 France	

GROWTH PLANS/SPECIAL FEATURES:

Accor SA is a European company operating through two divisions: Hotels and Services. Hotel operations accounted for 74% of 2009 revenue, Services accounted for 13% and other businesses accounted for 13% of revenue. The company derives its profits primarily from France, which alone accounts for 37%; with 38% coming from the rest of Europe, 9% from North America, 8% from Latin America and 8% from the rest of the world. Accor has 4,111 hotels in 90 countries worldwide. The hotels vary in price scale from budget, which includes brands Motel6, Studio6, Etap, hotelF1 and Formule 1; economy, which includes All Seasons and Ibis; upscale and midscale, which includes Mercure, Novotel, Adagio, Suite Hotel, Gallery M, and Pullman; and luxury, which include Sofitel. Accor's Services is divided into three families of products: employee and public benefits; rewards and motivation; and expense management. Accor Services are used by 32 million people in 40 countries. Its flagship brand, Ticket, is a line of prepaid charge cards. Its employee and public benefits offerings include Ticket Restaurant, allowing employees to have lunch outside of their workplace; Ticket Alimentacion, whereby employees use food vouchers to pay for groceries in neighborhood stores; Ticket Service, a prepaid voucher for food and essential service purchases; Ticket CESU, which gives employees low-cost access to housekeeping, childcare and other services. Reward and motivation services include Accentiv, a group that designs, executes and manages customer loyalty programs, employee rewards and incentives for distribution networks; Ticket Kadeos, a gift card brand; and Ticket Compliments, a gift card and voucher service for employees and public social welfare programs. Expense management products are comprised of Ticket Car, a leading Latin American corporate gasoline payment card for company cars; and Ticket Clean Way, a corporate dry cleaning service.

FINANCIALS:

Sales and profits are in thousands of dollars—add 000 to get the full amount. 2009 Note: Financial information for 2009 was not available for all companies at press time.

2009 Sales: $9,351,450	2009 Profits: $-373,260	**U.S. Stock Ticker:**
2008 Sales: $10,730,100	2008 Profits: $810,800	**Int'l Ticker: AC** Int'l Exchange: Paris-Euronext
2007 Sales: $11,951,184	2007 Profits: $1,299,596	Employees:
2006 Sales: $11,194,761	2006 Profits: $737,291	Fiscal Year Ends: 12/31
2005 Sales: $	2005 Profits: $	Parent Company:

SALARIES/BENEFITS:

Pension Plan:	ESOP Stock Plan:	Profit Sharing:	Top Exec. Salary: $	Bonus: $
Savings Plan:	Stock Purch. Plan:		Second Exec. Salary: $	Bonus: $

OTHER THOUGHTS:

Apparent Women Officers or Directors: 2
Hot Spot for Advancement for Women/Minorities: Y

LOCATIONS: ("Y" = Yes)

West:	Southwest:	Midwest:	Southeast:	Northeast:	International:
Y	Y	Y	Y	Y	Y

ACERGY SA

www.acergy-group.com

Industry Group Code: 2389 **Ranks within this company's industry group:** Sales: 1 Profits: 1

Properties:		Financial Services:		Construction/Development:		Investments:		Specialty Services:		Brokerage:	
Apartments:		Mortgages:		Commercial Construction:		REIT:		Property Management:		Commercial Sales:	
Malls/Shopping:		Title Insurance:		Residential Construction:				Online Services:		Residential Sales:	
Offices:		Property Insurance:		Land Development:				Software/IT:		Specialty:	
Hotels/Motels:				Support Services:	Y			Consulting:			
Industrial/Warehouses:				Design/Engineering:	Y						
Other:											

TYPES OF BUSINESS:

Offshore Platform Construction
Pipeline Construction
Offshore Support Services
Design Services
Oil Field Services

BRANDS/DIVISIONS/AFFILIATES:

NKT Flexibles
Seaway Heavy Lifting
Sapura-Acergy
Sonamet
Stanislav Yudin
Acergy M.S. Limited

CONTACTS:

Note: Officers with more than one job title may be intentionally listed here more than once.

Jean Cahuzac, CEO
Bruno Chabas, COO
Simon Crowe, CFO
Mark Preece, Corp. VP-Mktg. & Bus. Dev.
Keith Tipson, Corp. VP-Human Resources
Allen Leatt, CTO
Allen Leatt, Corp. VP-Eng.
Johan Rasmussen, General Counsel/Corp. VP
Jean-Luc Laloe, Corp. VP-Corp. Dev.
Andy Culwell, Corp. VP-Health, Safety, Environment & Quality
Tony Duncan, Regional VP-North America & Mexico
Olivier Carre, Regional VP-Africa & Mediterranean
Oyvind Mikaelsen, Regional VP-Northern Europe & Canada
Mark Woolveridge, Chmn.
Jeff Champion, Regional VP-Asia & Middle East

Phone: 44--8210-5500	**Fax:** 44-8210-5501
Toll-Free:	
Address: 200 Hammersmith Rd., London, W6 7DL UK	

GROWTH PLANS/SPECIAL FEATURES:

Acergy S.A., formerly Stolt Offshore S.A., is a U.K.-based company that offers contract seabed-to-surface engineering and construction for the offshore oil and gas industry throughout the world. The company provides products and services to companies looking to produce oil in an offshore location, from flowline and pipeline construction to subsea wells and fixed or floating platforms. Acergy manages its marine assets through a global asset organization based in Aberdeen, U.K. and operates through five geographical regions, with 53% of operating revenue in Africa and the Mediterranean. The majority of the firm's activities fall into the areas of engineering, procurement, installation, and commissioning (EPIC) project delivery. Within the restraints of these activities, the company can be further branched into several additional types including deepwater operations; inspection, maintenance and repair; conventional field development; and truckline expertise. The deepwater division provides design, installation and commissioning of subsea infrastructure, umbilical, riser and flowline systems. Inspection, maintenance and repair services includes both diver and remotely operated vehicle inspection as well as maintenance and repair services that keep oil and gas fields producing at a desired level. The conventional field development division focuses on hydrocarbon extraction and field development problems. The truckline expertise segment operates one of the world's largest semi-submersible pipelay barges, the Acergy Piper.

FINANCIALS:

Sales and profits are in thousands of dollars—add 000 to get the full amount. 2009 Note: Financial information for 2009 was not available for all companies at press time.

2009 Sales: $2,208,800	2009 Profits: $265,700	**U.S. Stock Ticker: ACGY**
2008 Sales: $2,522,400	2008 Profits: $307,200	**Int'l Ticker: ACY** Int'l Exchange: Oslo-OBX
2007 Sales: $2,406,300	2007 Profits: $134,500	Employees: 6,385
2006 Sales: $2,124,200	2006 Profits: $236,700	Fiscal Year Ends: 11/30
2005 Sales: $1,483,300	2005 Profits: $139,500	Parent Company:

SALARIES/BENEFITS:

Pension Plan:	ESOP Stock Plan:	Profit Sharing:	Top Exec. Salary: $2,100,000	Bonus: $
Savings Plan:	Stock Purch. Plan:		Second Exec. Salary: $111,499	Bonus: $

OTHER THOUGHTS:

Apparent Women Officers or Directors:
Hot Spot for Advancement for Women/Minorities:

LOCATIONS: ("Y" = Yes)

West:	Southwest:	Midwest:	Southeast:	Northeast:	International:
	Y				Y

ACS ACTIVIDADES DE CONSTRUCCION Y SERVICIOS SA

www.grupoacs.com

Industry Group Code: 237 **Ranks within this company's industry group:** Sales: 6 Profits: 1

Properties:		Financial Services:		Construction/Development:		Investments:		Specialty Services:		Brokerage:	
Apartments:		Mortgages:		Commercial Construction:		REIT:		Property Management:		Commercial Sales:	
Malls/Shopping:		Title Insurance:		Residential Construction:				Online Services:		Residential Sales:	
Offices:		Property Insurance:		Land Development:				Software/IT:		Specialty:	
Hotels/Motels:				Support Services:	Y			Consulting:			
Industrial/Warehouses:				Design/Engineering:							
Other:											

TYPES OF BUSINESS:

Construction Services

BRANDS/DIVISIONS/AFFILIATES:

Dragados S.A.
Vias Y Construcciones S.A.
Drace Medio Ambiente
Iridium Concesiones de Infraestructuras, S.A.
Dragados S.P.L.
Cobra Gestion de Infraestructuras, S.A.
Abertis
John Picone

CONTACTS:

Note: Officers with more than one job title may be intentionally listed here more than once.

Florentino Perez Rodriguez, CEO
Jose Luis del Valle Perez, Sec. Gen.
Eugenio Llorente Gomez, CEO-Industrial Services
Marcelino Fernandez Verdes, CEO-Construction, Services & Concessions
Antonio Garcia Ferrer, Exec. Vice Chmn.
Angel Garcia Altozano, Corp. Gen. Mgr.
Florentino Perez Rodriguez, Exec. Chmn.

Phone: 34-91-3439200	**Fax:** 34-91-3439456
Toll-Free:	
Address: Avenida Pio XII 102, Madrid, 28036 Spain	

GROWTH PLANS/SPECIAL FEATURES:

ACS Actividades de Construccion Y Servicios is a Spanish-based construction group. The company and its subsidiaries are primarily involved in five areas: Construction (civil works, residential and non-residential building); concessions; environmental and facility management; industrial services; and strategic investments. The group's primary construction subsidiaries include Dragados S.A., a general-purpose contracting; Vias Y Construcciones S.A. railway construction; Drace Medio Ambiente water and waste treatment plant specialists; Flota Proyectos Singulars maritime and port specialists; Seis modular and pre-fabricated construction; Dravo S.A. dredging and beach reconstruction specialists; Geocisa foundation and land engineering; Dycvensa civil works in Venezuela; Dycasa roadway construction in Argentina; Chiavone civil works in the U.S.; Cogesa real-estate; Pol-Aqua civil works in Poland; Pulice roads and highways; and John Picone tunnels and infrastructure in the U.S. The firm has been involved in several major civil works and building projects, many of which are in Spain. The concessions division, through Iridium Concesiones de Infraestructuras, S.A., is involved in project identification, financing, and all activities related. The environmental segment, which includes Urbaser S.A.; Dragados S.P.L.; and Cleve S.A., works to deal with waste handling and transportation management. The industrial services segment, through Cobra Gestion de Infraestructuras, S.A. and Dragados Industrial, builds, operates and maintains industrial and energy infrastructure. The strategic investments division, which consists of Abertis, Iberdrola, Hochtief, invests in infrastructure and energy sectors. The company is active in about 44 countries worldwide.

FINANCIALS:

Sales and profits are in thousands of dollars—add 000 to get the full amount. 2009 Note: Financial information for 2009 was not available for all companies at press time.

2009 Sales: $21,045,400	2009 Profits: $2,607,980
2008 Sales: $20,786,400	2008 Profits: $2,412,200
2007 Sales: $20,917,300	2007 Profits: $2,072,890
2006 Sales: $	2006 Profits: $
2005 Sales: $	2005 Profits: $

U.S. Stock Ticker:
Int'l Ticker: ACS Int'l Exchange: Madrid
Employees:
Fiscal Year Ends: 12/31
Parent Company:

SALARIES/BENEFITS:

Pension Plan:	ESOP Stock Plan:	Profit Sharing:	Top Exec. Salary: $	Bonus: $
Savings Plan:	Stock Purch. Plan:		Second Exec. Salary: $	Bonus: $

OTHER THOUGHTS:

Apparent Women Officers or Directors:
Hot Spot for Advancement for Women/Minorities:

LOCATIONS: ("Y" = Yes)

West:	Southwest:	Midwest:	Southeast:	Northeast:	International:
				Y	Y

ADVOCAT INC

www.irinfo.com/avc

Industry Group Code: 623110 **Ranks within this company's industry group:** Sales: 6 Profits: 2

Properties:		Financial Services:		Construction/Development:		Investments:		Specialty Services:		Brokerage:	
Apartments:		Mortgages:		Commercial Construction:		REIT:		Property Management:		Commercial Sales:	
Malls/Shopping:		Title Insurance:		Residential Construction:				Online Services:		Residential Sales:	
Offices:		Property Insurance:		Land Development:				Software/IT:		Specialty:	
Hotels/Motels:				Support Services:				Consulting:			
Industrial/Warehouses:				Design/Engineering:							
Other:	Y										

TYPES OF BUSINESS:

Nursing Homes
Assisted Living Facilities

BRANDS/DIVISIONS/AFFILIATES:

CONTACTS:

Note: Officers with more than one job title may be intentionally listed here more than once.

William R. Council, III, CEO
Kelly J. Gill, COO/Exec. VP
William R. Council, III, Pres.
L. Glynn Riddle, CFO
David White, VP-Bus. Dev.
Raymond L. Tyler, Sr. VP-Nursing Home Oper.
Wallace E. Olson, Chmn.

Phone: 615-771-7575	**Fax:** 615-771-7409
Toll-Free:	
Address: 1621 Galleria Blvd., Brentwood, TN 37027 US	

GROWTH PLANS/SPECIAL FEATURES:

Advocat, Inc. provides long-term care services to nursing home patients and residents of assisted living facilities in eight states, primarily in the Southeast. The company's total operations are composed of 50 nursing homes containing approximately 5,773 licensed nursing beds and 66 assisted living facilities units. Facilities are located in the states of Alabama, Arkansas, Florida, Kentucky, Ohio, Tennessee, Texas and West Virginia. The company's leased and managed homes provide a range of health care services to its residents. In addition to the nursing and social services usually provided in long-term care facilities, Advocat offers a variety of rehabilitative, nutritional, respiratory and other specialized ancillary services. The firm's nursing centers provide skilled nursing health care services, including room and board; nutrition services; recreational therapy; social services; and housekeeping and laundry services. In addition, nursing centers dispense medications prescribed by the patients' physicians, and a plan of care is developed by professional nursing staff for each resident as well as providing for the delivery of ancillary medical services. These specialty services include rehabilitation therapy services, such as audiology, speech, occupational and physical therapies, which are provided through licensed therapists and registered nurses, and the provision of medical supplies, nutritional support, infusion therapies, and related clinical services. The majority of these services are provided using internal resources and clinicians. In January 2010, the company finished its expansion and renovation of its 13th facility. Advocat plans to continue renovations on its remaining facilities throughout 2010.

FINANCIALS:

Sales and profits are in thousands of dollars—add 000 to get the full amount. 2009 Note: Financial information for 2009 was not available for all companies at press time.

2009 Sales: $302,031	2009 Profits: $2,601	**U.S. Stock Ticker: AVCA**
2008 Sales: $287,607	2008 Profits: $5,735	**Int'l Ticker:** Int'l Exchange:
2007 Sales: $243,907	2007 Profits: $9,387	Employees: 5,800
2006 Sales: $214,653	2006 Profits: $22,395	Fiscal Year Ends: 12/31
2005 Sales: $203,653	2005 Profits: $25,302	Parent Company:

SALARIES/BENEFITS:

Pension Plan:	ESOP Stock Plan:	Profit Sharing:	Top Exec. Salary: $442,000	Bonus: $53,000
Savings Plan: Y	Stock Purch. Plan:		Second Exec. Salary: $308,000	Bonus: $20,000

OTHER THOUGHTS:

Apparent Women Officers or Directors:
Hot Spot for Advancement for Women/Minorities:

LOCATIONS: ("Y" = Yes)

West:	Southwest:	Midwest:	Southeast:	Northeast:	International:
	Y	Y	Y	Y	

AECOM TECHNOLOGY CORPORATION

www.aecom.com

Industry Group Code: 237 **Ranks within this company's industry group:** Sales: 21 Profits: 17

Properties:		Financial Services:		Construction/Development:		Investments:		Specialty Services:		Brokerage:	
Apartments:		Mortgages:		Commercial Construction:		REIT:		Property Management:		Commercial Sales:	
Malls/Shopping:		Title Insurance:		Residential Construction:				Online Services:		Residential Sales:	
Offices:		Property Insurance:		Land Development:	Y			Software/IT:		Specialty:	
Hotels/Motels:				Support Services:				Consulting:			
Industrial/Warehouses:				Design/Engineering:	Y						
Other:											

TYPES OF BUSINESS:

Engineering & Design Services
Transportation Projects
Environmental Projects
Power & Mining Support
Consulting
Economic Development Consulting

BRANDS/DIVISIONS/AFFILIATES:

AGS
CTE
DMJM Aviation
Faber Maunsell
Tecsult, Inc
Boyle Engineering
Totten Sims Hubicki Associates
Earth Tech Inc

CONTACTS: *Note: Officers with more than one job title may be intentionally listed here more than once.*

John M. Dionisio, CEO
James R. Royer, COO/Exec. VP
John M. Dionisio, Pres.
Michael S. Burke, CFO/Sr. VP
Ian R. MacLeod, Sr. VP-Human Resources
Raul Cruz, CIO/Sr. VP
James T. Walsh, CTO/Sr. VP
Stephanie Hunter, Chief Admin. Officer
Eric Chen, General Counsel
Robert L. Costello, Exec. VP-Global Oper.
Glenn R. Robson, Chief Strategy Officer/Sr. VP
Paul J. Gennaro, Jr., Chief Comm. Officer
Paul J. Gennaro, Jr., Sr. VP-Investor Rel.
Eric Chen, Sr. VP-Finance
John L. Kinley, CEO-Canada
Glenn R. Robson, Chief Strategy Officer/Sr. VP-Finance
Frederick W. Werner, CEO-U.S.
Jane Chmielinski, CEO-Corp. Dev.
Richard G. Newman, Chmn.
Anthony C. K. Shum, CEO-Hong Kong, China & Asia

Phone: 213-593-8000	**Fax:** 213-593-8730
Toll-Free:	
Address: 555 S. Flower St., Ste. 3700, Los Angeles, CA 90071-2300 US	

GROWTH PLANS/SPECIAL FEATURES:

AECOM Technology Corporation is a global engineering and design company engaged in facility, transportation, environment and specialty engineering projects for corporate, institutional and government clients. Certain specialized services are available in mining, power, international development, and operations and maintenance. The firm's facility design and construction projects encompass land development assignments and a wide variety of building projects. Transportation services include feasibility studies, planning, design, engineering, construction management and asset management for transit and rail, highway, bridge, port, harbor and airport projects. AECOM offers water resource, wastewater, wet weather, hazardous waste management and other environmental engineering services. The power sector offers design, construction management and commissioning services. The company operates largely through a network of subsidiaries, including AGS, AECOM's government services arm; CTE, an infrastructure engineering firm (with a wastewater treatment plant in Antarctica); DMJM Aviation, the firm's flagship aviation design and construction management company; Faber Maunsell, a European engineering consultancy firm; Metcalf & Eddy, an environmental engineering group; UMA, a Canadian division; Hayes, Seay, Mattern & Mattern, Inc., an architectural and engineering firm; and PADCO, a firm that promotes sustainable economic development in more than 100 countries. AECOM Austin, another subsidiary, is devoted to serving engineering and development clients in a variety of sectors, including pharmaceutical, industrial and aviation companies. In January 2010, the company's joint venture, Tishman Construction Corp, was contracted by the U.S. Dept. of Homeland Security to begin construction of its new headquarters. Also in January 2010, another of the company's joint ventures, Greenman-Pedersen and Parsons Brinckerhoff, was contracted to widen the New Jersey Turnpike, by the New Jersey Turnpike Authority.

The company offers its employees medical, dental and life insurance; a stock purchase program with company match; a 401(k) and Roth IRA; and a merit based scholarship program for the children of employees.

FINANCIALS: **Sales and profits are in thousands of dollars—add 000 to get the full amount. 2009 Note: Financial information for 2009 was not available for all companies at press time.**

2009 Sales: $6,119,465	2009 Profits: $189,696	**U.S. Stock Ticker: ACM**
2008 Sales: $5,194,482	2008 Profits: $147,226	**Int'l Ticker:** Int'l Exchange:
2007 Sales: $4,237,270	2007 Profits: $100,297	Employees: 43,200
2006 Sales: $3,421,492	2006 Profits: $53,686	Fiscal Year Ends: 9/30
2005 Sales: $2,395,340	2005 Profits: $53,814	Parent Company:

SALARIES/BENEFITS:

Pension Plan: Y	ESOP Stock Plan:	Profit Sharing:	Top Exec. Salary: $1,056,245	Bonus: $2,500,000
Savings Plan: Y	Stock Purch. Plan: Y		Second Exec. Salary: $1,016,613	Bonus: $1,800,000

OTHER THOUGHTS:

Apparent Women Officers or Directors: 2
Hot Spot for Advancement for Women/Minorities: Y

LOCATIONS: ("Y" = Yes)

West:	Southwest:	Midwest:	Southeast:	Northeast:	International:
Y	Y	Y	Y	Y	Y

AECON GROUP INC

www.aecon.com

Industry Group Code: 237 **Ranks within this company's industry group:** Sales: 29 Profits: 24

Properties:		Financial Services:		Construction/Development:		Investments:		Specialty Services:		Brokerage:	
Apartments:		Mortgages:		Commercial Construction:	Y	REIT:		Property Management:		Commercial Sales:	
Malls/Shopping:		Title Insurance:		Residential Construction:				Online Services:		Residential Sales:	
Offices:		Property Insurance:		Land Development:				Software/IT:		Specialty:	
Hotels/Motels:				Support Services:	Y			Consulting:			
Industrial/Warehouses:				Design/Engineering:	Y						
Other:											

TYPES OF BUSINESS:

Construction
Infrastructure Development
Utility Systems
Steam Power Generation
Renovation

BRANDS/DIVISIONS/AFFILIATES:

Aecon Concessions
Aecon Buildings
Aecon Civil & Utilities
Lockerbie & Hole, Inc.
Aecon Atlantic
Group Aecon Quebec Ltee.
Innovative Steam Technologies, Inc.
South Rock, Ltd.

CONTACTS:

Note: Officers with more than one job title may be intentionally listed here more than once.

John M. Beck, CEO
Scott C. Balfour, Pres.
David Smales, CFO/Exec. VP
Mitch Patten, VP-Human Resources
Andy DeHaan, VP-IT
L. Brian Swartz, Sr. VP-Legal & Commercial Svcs.
Mitch Patten, Sr. VP-Corp. Affairs
Gerard A. Kelly, Sr. VP-Finance
Terrance L. McKibbon, CEO-Aecon Infrastructure
Paul P. Koenderman, Exec. VP/CEO-Aecon Industrial Group
Mike Archambault, VP-Safety & Loss Control
Frank Ross, Pres., Aecon Buildings
John M. Beck, Chmn.

Phone: 416-293-7004 **Fax:** 416-754-8736
Toll-Free: 877-232-2677
Address: 20 Carlson Ct., Ste. 800, Toronto, ON M9W 7K6 Canada

GROWTH PLANS/SPECIAL FEATURES:

Aecon Group, Inc., formerly Aecon Enterprises, is one of Canada's largest construction and infrastructure development companies. The firm operates in four principal segments: Buildings, Infrastructure, Industrial and Concessions. The Buildings segment provides construction and construction management, retrofit and renovation, design build, general contracting and green construction services for commercial office buildings, institutional and educational facilities, retail facilities, multi-unit residential properties, industrial buildings and high technology, health care, environment, hospitality, government and aviation buildings. The Infrastructure segment, through its various business units, provides all aspects of the construction of both public and private infrastructure, including roads, highways, bridges, airport facilities, dams, tunnels, marine facilities, transit systems and power projects. This segment also offers design, project management and construction management services; and utility infrastructure services for gas projects, hydro distribution networks, telecommunication networks, water mains and sewers. The Industrial segment encompasses all of Aecon's industrial construction and manufacturing activities, including platform construction and assembly, as well as installation and maintenance for specialized industrial systems and equipment. Activities within the Concessions segment include the development, financing and operation of infrastructure projects by way of build-operate-transfer and other public-private partnership contract structures. The company operates through eight subsidiaries: Aecon Atlantic; Aecon Buildings; Aecon Civil and Utilities; Aecon Concessions; Aecon Constructors; Aecon Industrial; Innovative Steam Technologies, Inc.; and Group Aecon Quebec Ltee., a Quebec-based construction company with expertise primarily in civil buildings and industrial construction. In January 2009, Aecon Group acquired South Rock, Ltd., an infrastructure construction business. In April 2009, the firm acquired Lockerbie & Hole, Inc., a mechanical construction contractor.

Aecon Group offers its employees medical, dental, life insurance and disability plans; a retirement savings plan and pension plan; an employee stock purchase program; group home and auto insurance; and an employee assistance program.

FINANCIALS:

Sales and profits are in thousands of dollars—add 000 to get the full amount. 2009 Note: Financial information for 2009 was not available for all companies at press time.

2009 Sales: $2,196,360	2009 Profits: $43,130
2008 Sales: $1,492,630	2008 Profits: $47,160
2007 Sales: $1,187,260	2007 Profits: $38,410
2006 Sales: $1,091,000	2006 Profits: $11,300
2005 Sales: $972,000	2005 Profits: $- 954

U.S. Stock Ticker:
Int'l Ticker: ARE Int'l Exchange: Toronto-TSX
Employees:
Fiscal Year Ends: 12/31
Parent Company:

SALARIES/BENEFITS:

Pension Plan: Y	ESOP Stock Plan:	Profit Sharing:	Top Exec. Salary: $489,770	Bonus: $946,894
Savings Plan: Y	Stock Purch. Plan: Y		Second Exec. Salary: $431,781	Bonus: $834,782

OTHER THOUGHTS:

Apparent Women Officers or Directors:
Hot Spot for Advancement for Women/Minorities:

LOCATIONS: ("Y" = Yes)

West:	Southwest:	Midwest:	Southeast:	Northeast:	International:
Y					Y

ALEXANDRIA REAL ESTATE EQUITIES INC

www.labspace.com

Industry Group Code: 531120 **Ranks within this company's industry group:** Sales: 39 Profits: 23

Properties:		Financial Services:		Construction/Development:		Investments:		Specialty Services:		Brokerage:	
Apartments:		Mortgages:		Commercial Construction:		REIT:	Y	Property Management:	Y	Commercial Sales:	
Malls/Shopping:		Title Insurance:		Residential Construction:				Online Services:		Residential Sales:	
Offices:	Y	Property Insurance:		Land Development:				Software/IT:		Specialty:	
Hotels/Motels:				Support Services:				Consulting:			
Industrial/Warehouses:				Design/Engineering:							
Other:	Y										

TYPES OF BUSINESS:

Real Estate Investment Trust
Scientific Properties
Office & Laboratory Space
Property Development

BRANDS/DIVISIONS/AFFILIATES:

CONTACTS:

Note: Officers with more than one job title may be intentionally listed here more than once.

Joel S. Marcus, CEO
Joel S. Marcus, Pres.
Dean A. Shigenaga, CFO
Joel S. Marcus, Chmn.

Phone: 626-578-0777 **Fax:** 626-578-0896
Toll-Free:
Address: 385 E. Colorado Blvd., Ste. 299, Pasadena, CA 91101 US

GROWTH PLANS/SPECIAL FEATURES:

Alexandria Real Estate Equities, Inc. is a real estate investment trust (REIT) that owns, acquires, operates, manages, expands and redevelops scientific properties containing a mixture of office and laboratory space. The firm focuses its activities principally in the life science markets of California (in the San Diego and San Francisco Bay areas); Seattle; suburban Washington, D.C. (both in Maryland and Virginia); eastern Massachusetts; New Jersey; New York City; suburban Philadelphia; and the Southeast, as well as certain parts of Canada. Alexandria's portfolio currently consists of 156 properties, 152 in ten states in the U.S. and 4 in Canada, comprising approximately 12.7 million rentable square feet of office/laboratory space. The company's portfolio also includes roughly 980,000 rentable square feet undergoing ground-up development and an imbedded pipeline for future ground-up development, approximating 11.1 million developable square feet. The company's goal is to acquire high-quality life science facilities that it can then expand or to redevelop existing office, warehouse or vacant space into genetic laboratory space. The firm's properties are leased principally to tenants in a broad spectrum of sectors within the life science industry, such as institutional (universities and independent not-for-profit institutions), pharmaceutical, biopharmaceutical, medical device, life science product, service and translational entities, as well as government agencies. Some of its tenants include ZymoGenetics; GlaxoSmithKline; the Massachusetts Institute of Technology; Theravance; Genentech; Quest Diagnostics Incorporated; Johnson & Johnson; and the U.S. government. In July 2009, the company announced that it signed Eli Lilly and Company, a biopharmaceutical company, as the anchor tenant at the Alexandria Center for Science and Technology. Lilly leased approximately 91,000 rentable square feet and 9,000 rentable square feet of core services space. This space will become the new research headquarters for ImClone Systems to be New York City's life science collaboration and research epicenter.

FINANCIALS:

Sales and profits are in thousands of dollars—add 000 to get the full amount. 2009 Note: Financial information for 2009 was not available for all companies at press time.

2009 Sales: $480,140	2009 Profits: $141,648	**U.S. Stock Ticker: ARE**
2008 Sales: $451,637	2008 Profits: $120,097	**Int'l Ticker:** Int'l Exchange:
2007 Sales: $388,339	2007 Profits: $89,980	Employees: 142
2006 Sales: $302,061	2006 Profits: $73,416	Fiscal Year Ends: 12/31
2005 Sales: $238,138	2005 Profits: $63,433	Parent Company:

SALARIES/BENEFITS:

Pension Plan:	ESOP Stock Plan:	Profit Sharing:	Top Exec. Salary: $750,000	Bonus: $1,375,000
Savings Plan:	Stock Purch. Plan:		Second Exec. Salary: $535,000	Bonus: $267,500

OTHER THOUGHTS:

Apparent Women Officers or Directors:
Hot Spot for Advancement for Women/Minorities:

LOCATIONS: ("Y" = Yes)

West:	Southwest:	Midwest:	Southeast:	Northeast:	International:
Y				Y	Y

AMAN RESORTS

www.amanresorts.com

Industry Group Code: 721110 **Ranks within this company's industry group:** Sales: Profits:

Properties:		Financial Services:	Construction/Development:	Investments:	Specialty Services:		Brokerage:
Apartments:		Mortgages:	Commercial Construction:	REIT:	Property Management:	Y	Commercial Sales:
Malls/Shopping:		Title Insurance:	Residential Construction:		Online Services:		Residential Sales:
Offices:		Property Insurance:	Land Development:		Software/IT:		Specialty:
Hotels/Motels:	Y		Support Services:		Consulting:		
Industrial/Warehouses:			Design/Engineering:				
Other:							

TYPES OF BUSINESS:

Hotels & Resorts

BRANDS/DIVISIONS/AFFILIATES:

DLF Limited
Aman-i-Khas
Amandari
Amankora
Amansara
Le Melezin
Amangani
Aman at Summer Palace

CONTACTS:

Note: Officers with more than one job title may be intentionally listed here more than once.

K. P. Singh, Exec. Chmn.-DLF Limited
T. C. Goyal, Managing Dir.-DLF Limited

Phone: 65-6883-2555	**Fax:** 65-6883-0555
Toll-Free: 800-477-9780	
Address: 1 Orchard Spring Ln., #05-01 Tourism Ct., Singapore, 247729 Singapore	

GROWTH PLANS/SPECIAL FEATURES:

Aman Resorts (also known as Amanresorts), majority-owned by DLF Limited, owns and operates luxury resorts. The company name derives from the Sanskrit word aman, meaning peace. Since opening its first location, the Amanpuri (meaning place of peace) in Phuket, Thailand, in 1988, the firm has expanded to operating 24 resorts in 15 countries, mostly in and around Southeast Asia. These resorts are small, ranging from 10 luxurious, air-conditioned tents at the Aman-i-Khas, located near a wildlife sanctuary in Ranthambhore, India, to the 70 pavilions and villas in Amanpuri. In total, the firm offers more than 800 private rooms, suites, villas, tents, bungalows and pavilions, with a mean size of 40 rooms per resort. Besides those listed above, its other resorts include Amandari, Amankila, Amanusa, Amanwana and Amanjiwo, all located in Indonesia. Amankora is spread across five towns in Bhutan; Amansara is in Cambodia; and Amanpulo is in the Philippines. Hotel Bora Bora in French Polynesia is currently closed for renovations. Amanbagh and Aman New Delhi comprise its other Indian locations. Amangalla and Amanwella are in Sri Lanka. Amanjena is in Morocco. Le Melezin is in Courcheval, France while Amangani is in Wyoming, near the Grand Tetons and Yellowstone. Amanyara is located in Turks and Caicos, in the Caribbean. Amangiri, a small 34 suite resort was opened in Southern Utah in 2009. The firm also recently opened an Aman Spa in The Connaught Hotel in Mayfair, London. The company sources the decor for its resorts locally, in order to reflect the natural surroundings and local cultures. In early 2010, the Amanfayun resort, featuring a spa, tea house and restaurants, modeled after an ancient Chinese village, was opened in China near Hangzhou. In February 2010, the company's parent, DLF Limited began looking for a buyer for Aman Resorts.

FINANCIALS:

Sales and profits are in thousands of dollars—add 000 to get the full amount. 2009 Note: Financial information for 2009 was not available for all companies at press time.

2009 Sales: $	2009 Profits: $	**U.S. Stock Ticker: Subsidiary**
2008 Sales: $	2008 Profits: $	**Int'l Ticker:** Int'l Exchange:
2007 Sales: $	2007 Profits: $	Employees:
2006 Sales: $	2006 Profits: $	Fiscal Year Ends:
2005 Sales: $	2005 Profits: $	Parent Company: DLF LIMITED

SALARIES/BENEFITS:

Pension Plan:	ESOP Stock Plan:	Profit Sharing:	Top Exec. Salary: $	Bonus: $
Savings Plan:	Stock Purch. Plan:		Second Exec. Salary: $	Bonus: $

OTHER THOUGHTS:

Apparent Women Officers or Directors:
Hot Spot for Advancement for Women/Minorities:

LOCATIONS: ("Y" = Yes)

West:	Southwest:	Midwest:	Southeast:	Northeast:	International:
Y					Y

AMB PROPERTY CORPORATION

www.amb.com

Industry Group Code: 5311 **Ranks within this company's industry group:** Sales: 24 Profits: 29

Properties:		Financial Services:		Construction/Development:		Investments:		Specialty Services:		Brokerage:	
Apartments:		Mortgages:		Commercial Construction:		REIT:	Y	Property Management:	Y	Commercial Sales:	
Malls/Shopping:		Title Insurance:		Residential Construction:				Online Services:		Residential Sales:	
Offices:		Property Insurance:		Land Development:				Software/IT:		Specialty:	
Hotels/Motels:				Support Services:				Consulting:			
Industrial/Warehouses:	Y			Design/Engineering:							
Other:											

TYPES OF BUSINESS:

Real Estate Operations- Industrial
Port Facilities
Distribution Centers

BRANDS/DIVISIONS/AFFILIATES:

AMB Capital Partners LLC
AMB Property LP

CONTACTS:

Note: Officers with more than one job title may be intentionally listed here more than once.

Hamid R. Moghadam, CEO
Thomas S. Olinger, CFO
Tamra D. Browne, General Counsel/Sr. VP/Sec.
Tracy A. Ward, VP-Corp. Comm.
Tracy A. Ward, VP-Investor Rel.
Eugene F. Reilly, Pres., The Americas
Guy F. Jaquier, Pres., AMB Capital Partners, LLC
Hamid R. Moghadam, Chmn.
Guy F. Jaquier, Pres., Europe & Asia

Phone: 415-394-9000	**Fax:** 415-394-9001
Toll-Free:	
Address: Pier 1, Bay 1, San Francisco, CA 94111 US	

GROWTH PLANS/SPECIAL FEATURES:

AMB Property Corporation is a global owner, developer and operator of industrial real estate focused on major hub and gateway distribution markets, such as shipping port facilities, throughout North America, Europe and Asia. The company's portfolio of owned and managed properties and renovation and development projects spans 155.1 million square feet in 47 markets within 14 countries. Through its primary operating subsidiary company AMB Property, L.P., AMB invests in high-throughput distribution centers that have a variety of characteristics allowing for the rapid transport of goods from point-to-point, include numerous dock doors, shallower building depths, fewer columns, large truck courts and more space for trailer parking. These facilities function best when located in convenient proximity to transportation infrastructure such as major airports and seaports. The firm's AMB Capital Partners, LLC subsidiary co-invests with private capital sources instead of shareholder investments. In November 2009, the company launched the AMB Industrial Business Indicator (AMB IBI), a diffusion index that combines information from customers with economic variables to study business activity in the industrial real estate market.

Employees are offered medical, dental and vision insurance; flexible spending accounts; life insurance; disability coverage; a 401(k) plan; a bonus program; wellness programs; education reimbursement; a stock option plan; and an employee assistance program.

FINANCIALS:

Sales and profits are in thousands of dollars—add 000 to get the full amount. 2009 Note: Financial information for 2009 was not available for all companies at press time.

2009 Sales: $633,842	2009 Profits: $-43,001	**U.S. Stock Ticker: AMB**
2008 Sales: $693,842	2008 Profits: $-49,310	**Int'l Ticker:** Int'l Exchange:
2007 Sales: $650,886	2007 Profits: $314,260	Employees:
2006 Sales: $712,391	2006 Profits: $224,072	Fiscal Year Ends: 12/31
2005 Sales: $660,875	2005 Profits: $257,807	Parent Company:

SALARIES/BENEFITS:

Pension Plan:	ESOP Stock Plan:	Profit Sharing:	Top Exec. Salary: $657,750	Bonus: $570,000
Savings Plan: Y	Stock Purch. Plan:		Second Exec. Salary: $440,500	Bonus: $400,000

OTHER THOUGHTS:

Apparent Women Officers or Directors: 1
Hot Spot for Advancement for Women/Minorities:

LOCATIONS: ("Y" = Yes)

West:	Southwest:	Midwest:	Southeast:	Northeast:	International:
Y	Y	Y	Y	Y	Y

AMEC PLC

www.amec.com

Industry Group Code: 237 **Ranks within this company's industry group:** Sales: 24 Profits: 13

Properties:		Financial Services:		Construction/Development:		Investments:		Specialty Services:		Brokerage:	
Apartments:		Mortgages:		Commercial Construction:		REIT:		Property Management:		Commercial Sales:	
Malls/Shopping:		Title Insurance:		Residential Construction:				Online Services:		Residential Sales:	
Offices:		Property Insurance:		Land Development:				Software/IT:		Specialty:	
Hotels/Motels:				Support Services:	Y			Consulting:			
Industrial/Warehouses:				Design/Engineering:	Y						
Other:											

TYPES OF BUSINESS:

Architectural & Engineering Services
Commercial & Heavy Construction
Environmental Services
Nuclear Power Services
Renewable Energy Services
Support & Maintenance Services
Consulting
Mining

BRANDS/DIVISIONS/AFFILIATES:

GRD Limited
Currie & Brown
Entec Holdings Ltd

CONTACTS:

Note: Officers with more than one job title may be intentionally listed here more than once.

Samir Brikho, CEO
Neil Bruce, COO
Ian McHoul, CFO
Keith Bradford, Dir.-Human Resources
Michael Blacker, General Counsel
Francois-Philippe Champagne, Dir.-Strategic Dev.
Sue Scholes, Dir.-Comm.
Sue Scholes, Dir.-Investor Rel.
Roger Jinks, Pres., Earth & Environmental Div.
Jock Green-Armytage, Chmn.

Phone: 44-20-7539-5800	**Fax:** 44-20-7539-5900
Toll-Free:	
Address: 76 - 78 Old St., London, EC1V 9RU UK	

GROWTH PLANS/SPECIAL FEATURES:

AMEC plc, headquartered in London, is a global engineering and construction management firm with operations in more than 40 countries worldwide. Its operations are divided into four segments: Natural Resources; Power & Process ; Earth & Environmental; and Investments and other. The Natural Resources segment focuses on the oil and gas, oil sands and mining industries. Services include design, delivery, commissioning and decommissioning of oil and gas facilities, surface mining and oil sands engineering services, as well as minerals and metals mining consultancy, design and project management. The Power & Process segment is concerned with power transmission and distribution, nuclear power, renewables, bio-process energy and conventional power delivery. The company's nuclear service areas include new build, the licensing, regulatory and project support; reactor support, life time extension and asset performance improvement; clean up, specialist decommissioning and waste management services; and nuclear defense, engineering and technical services. The power and utilities sector includes engineering; project management; risk and reputation management; environmental impact assessments and sustainable solutions, for the Americas and Europe; and a Power Training School. The Earth & Environmental segment is organized into federal government, mining, oil and gas, transportation and water units. Environmental services include consultancy and engineering, as well as specialty services such as environmental assessment, materials testing, specialty water services and clean-up. In November 2009, AMEC completed the acquisition of Australian engineering firm GRD Limited. In January 2010, the company acquired Australian cost and commercial management consulting firm Currie & Brown for approximately $33.9 million. In March 2010, AMEC acquired Entec Holdings Ltd., an environmental and engineering consultancy based in the U.K. for approximately $94 million.

FINANCIALS:

Sales and profits are in thousands of dollars—add 000 to get the full amount. 2009 Note: Financial information for 2009 was not available for all companies at press time.

2009 Sales: $3,865,270	2009 Profits: $261,380	**U.S. Stock Ticker:**
2008 Sales: $3,823,620	2008 Profits: $291,940	**Int'l Ticker: AMEC** Int'l Exchange: London-LSE
2007 Sales: $3,456,570	2007 Profits: $505,240	Employees: 21,000
2006 Sales: $3,112,410	2006 Profits: $321,569	Fiscal Year Ends: 12/31
2005 Sales: $8,564,860	2005 Profits: $145,910	Parent Company:

SALARIES/BENEFITS:

Pension Plan:	ESOP Stock Plan:	Profit Sharing:	Top Exec. Salary: $	Bonus: $
Savings Plan:	Stock Purch. Plan:		Second Exec. Salary: $	Bonus: $

OTHER THOUGHTS:

Apparent Women Officers or Directors: 3
Hot Spot for Advancement for Women/Minorities: Y

LOCATIONS: ("Y" = Yes)

West:	Southwest:	Midwest:	Southeast:	Northeast:	International:
Y	Y	Y	Y	Y	Y

AMERCO

www.amerco.com

Industry Group Code: 532120 **Ranks within this company's industry group:** Sales: 1 Profits: 1

Properties:		Financial Services:		Construction/Development:		Investments:		Specialty Services:		Brokerage:	
Apartments:		Mortgages:		Commercial Construction:		REIT:		Property Management:		Commercial Sales:	Y
Malls/Shopping:	Y	Title Insurance:		Residential Construction:				Online Services:		Residential Sales:	
Offices:	Y	Property Insurance:	Y	Land Development:				Software/IT:		Specialty:	
Hotels/Motels:				Support Services:				Consulting:			
Industrial/Warehouses:	Y			Design/Engineering:							
Other:	Y										

TYPES OF BUSINESS:

Truck Rental & Leasing Services
Moving & Storage Services & Supplies
Property & Casualty Insurance
Life Insurance
Annuities
Self-Storage Properties

BRANDS/DIVISIONS/AFFILIATES:

U-Haul International, Inc.
Republic Western Insurance Company
Oxford Life Insurance Company
AMERCO Real Estate Company
Safemove
Safetow
Safestor

CONTACTS:

Note: Officers with more than one job title may be intentionally listed here more than once.

Edward J. Shoen, Pres.
Laurence J. De Respino, General Counsel
Jennifer Flachman, Dir.-Investor Rel.
Jason A. Berg, Principal Acct. Officer
Mark A. Haydukovich, Treas.
Edward J. Shoen, CEO-U-Haul
Carlos Vizcarra, Pres., AMERCO Real Estate Co.
Richard M. Amoroso, Pres., Republic Western Insurance Co.
Edward J. Shoen, Chmn.

Phone: 775-688-6300	**Fax:** 775-688-6338
Toll-Free:	
Address: 1325 Airmotive Way, Ste. 100, Reno, NV 89502 US	

GROWTH PLANS/SPECIAL FEATURES:

AMERCO is a holding company that operates U-Haul International, Inc.'s moving and storage operations; AMERCO Real Estate Company; Republic Western Insurance Company; and Oxford Life Insurance Company. Accordingly, the firm has three reportable business segments: moving and storage; property and casualty insurance; and life insurance. The moving and storage segment consists of U-Haul, with its rental equipment fleet of trucks, trailers and tow dollies being offered by approximately 14,500 independent dealers. It also provides furniture pads, utility dollies and hand trucks; sells a wide selection of other moving supplies; and offers protection packages for moving and storage. U-Haul owns more than 100,000 trucks, 78,500 trailers and 31,100 towing devices. The firm's Emove.com and Uhaul.com online reservation portals are significant drivers of U-Haul's rental transaction volume. The company also offers moving and storage protection packages such as Safemove and Safetow, providing moving and towing customers a damage waiver; cargo protection; and medical and life coverage. Additionally, Safestor protects storage customers from loss on their goods in storage. AMERCO Real Estate Company markets commercial properties available for sale or lease. The property and casualty insurance business consists of Republic Western Insurance Company's business activities, which includes coverage for U-Haul customers, independent dealers, fleet owners and employees of AMERCO. The life insurance operating segment consists of Oxford Life Insurance Company, which offers annuities, credit life and disability, critical illness insurance, single premium whole life, group life and disability coverage as well as Medicare supplement insurance. Oxford also administers self-insured group health and dental plans for AMERCO.

Employees are offered medical, dental and vision insurance; life and AD&D insurance; disability coverage; a 401(k) plan; and an employee stock ownership plan.

FINANCIALS:

Sales and profits are in thousands of dollars—add 000 to get the full amount. 2009 Note: Financial information for 2009 was not available for all companies at press time.

2009 Sales: $1,992,266	2009 Profits: $13,410	**U.S. Stock Ticker: UHAL**
2008 Sales: $2,049,174	2008 Profits: $67,784	**Int'l Ticker:** Int'l Exchange:
2007 Sales: $2,069,298	2007 Profits: $90,553	Employees: 17,700
2006 Sales: $2,087,525	2006 Profits: $121,154	Fiscal Year Ends: 3/31
2005 Sales: $2,008,100	2005 Profits: $89,400	Parent Company:

SALARIES/BENEFITS:

Pension Plan:	ESOP Stock Plan: Y	Profit Sharing:	Top Exec. Salary: $675,004	Bonus: $
Savings Plan: Y	Stock Purch. Plan:		Second Exec. Salary: $623,077	Bonus: $

OTHER THOUGHTS:

Apparent Women Officers or Directors:
Hot Spot for Advancement for Women/Minorities:

LOCATIONS: ("Y" = Yes)

West:	Southwest:	Midwest:	Southeast:	Northeast:	International:
Y	Y	Y	Y	Y	Y

AMERICAN CAMPUS COMMUNITIES

www.studenthousing.com

Industry Group Code: 5311 **Ranks within this company's industry group:** Sales: 31 Profits: 27

Properties:		Financial Services:		Construction/Development:		Investments:		Specialty Services:		Brokerage:	
Apartments:	Y	Mortgages:		Commercial Construction:		REIT:		Property Management:	Y	Commercial Sales:	
Malls/Shopping:		Title Insurance:		Residential Construction:	Y			Online Services:		Residential Sales:	
Offices:		Property Insurance:		Land Development:				Software/IT:		Specialty:	
Hotels/Motels:				Support Services:	Y			Consulting:			
Industrial/Warehouses:				Design/Engineering:							
Other:	Y										

TYPES OF BUSINESS:

Student Housing Development

BRANDS/DIVISIONS/AFFILIATES:

American Campus Communities Operating Partnership
GMH Communities Trust
American Campus Equity

CONTACTS:

Note: Officers with more than one job title may be intentionally listed here more than once.

William C. Bayless, Jr., CEO
Greg A. Dowell, COO/Sr. VP
William C. Bayless, Jr., Pres.
Jonathan A. Graf, CFO/Exec. VP
Brian B. Nickel, CIO/Sr. VP
Jonathan A. Graf, Treas.
James C. Hopke Jr., Exec. VP-Project Mgmt. & Construction
James E. Wilhelm III, Exec. VP-Public & Private Transactions
Clint Braun, Sr. VP-Construction Mgmt.
Steve Crawford, Sr. VP-Mgmt. Svcs.
R.D. Burck, Chmn.

Phone: 512-732-1000	**Fax:** 517-732-2450
Toll-Free:	
Address: 805 Las Cimas Pkwy., Ste. 400, Austin, TX 78746 US	

GROWTH PLANS/SPECIAL FEATURES:

American Campus Communities, Inc. (ACC) is a real estate investment trust with expertise in the acquisition, design, financing, development, construction management, leasing and management of student housing properties. The company, operating primarily via subsidiary American Campus Communities Operating Partnership LP, is one of the largest owners, managers and developers of student housing properties in the U.S. in terms of beds owned, developed, and under management. ACC's property portfolio consists of 85 student housing properties with approximately 52,100 beds and approximately 17,000 apartment units, including 30 properties containing approximately 22,800 beds and approximately 7,300 units through subsidiary GMH Communities. The company operates in four segments that include wholly-owned properties, on-campus participating properties, development services and property management services. The wholly-owned property segment consists of all properties in proximity to college campus; these include 79 wholly-owned complexes. The on-campus participation segment consists of facilities leased from universities that are managed by the company. The development services segment provides consulting services, through the company's subsidiaries, to colleges and universities for all stages of property construction. The property management segment is conducted primarily through subsidiaries for college or university clients and includes all aspect of facility maintenance and administration. ACC provides property management services to 31 properties. The company also owns a minority interest in two joint ventures with American Campus Equity that include 21 student housing properties. ACC's communities contain modern housing units and are supported by a resident assistant system and other student-oriented programming, with many offering resort-style amenities.

FINANCIALS:

Sales and profits are in thousands of dollars—add 000 to get the full amount. 2009 Note: Financial information for 2009 was not available for all companies at press time.

2009 Sales: $309,590	2009 Profits: $-12,840	**U.S. Stock Ticker: ACC**
2008 Sales: $233,579	2008 Profits: $-13,055	**Int'l Ticker:** Int'l Exchange:
2007 Sales: $147,135	2007 Profits: $-1,686	Employees: 2,183
2006 Sales: $118,953	2006 Profits: $1,662	Fiscal Year Ends: 12/31
2005 Sales: $	2005 Profits: $	Parent Company:

SALARIES/BENEFITS:

Pension Plan:	ESOP Stock Plan:	Profit Sharing:	Top Exec. Salary: $352,000	Bonus: $496,232
Savings Plan:	Stock Purch. Plan:		Second Exec. Salary: $312,125	Bonus: $300,000

OTHER THOUGHTS:

Apparent Women Officers or Directors:
Hot Spot for Advancement for Women/Minorities:

LOCATIONS: ("Y" = Yes)

West:	Southwest:	Midwest:	Southeast:	Northeast:	International:
Y	Y	Y	Y	Y	

AMERICAN REALTY INVESTORS INC

www.amrealtytrust.com

Industry Group Code: 5311 **Ranks within this company's industry group:** Sales: 33 Profits: 26

Properties:		Financial Services:		Construction/Development:		Investments:		Specialty Services:		Brokerage:	
Apartments:	Y	Mortgages:		Commercial Construction:		REIT:	Y	Property Management:	Y	Commercial Sales:	
Malls/Shopping:		Title Insurance:		Residential Construction:				Online Services:		Residential Sales:	
Offices:	Y	Property Insurance:		Land Development:				Software/IT:		Specialty:	
Hotels/Motels:	Y			Support Services:				Consulting:			
Industrial/Warehouses:				Design/Engineering:							
Other:	Y										

TYPES OF BUSINESS:

Real Estate Development & Management
Real Estate Investments
Apartments
Land
Commercial/Office buildings
Hotels

BRANDS/DIVISIONS/AFFILIATES:

Transcontinental Realty Investors
Mercer Crossing
HarmInvest GmbH Berlin

CONTACTS:

Note: Officers with more than one job title may be intentionally listed here more than once.

Daniel J. Moos, COO
Daniel J. Moos, Pres.
Gene S. Bertcher, CFO/Exec. VP
Louis J. Corna, General Counsel/Exec. VP-Tax/Corp. Sec.
Gene S. Bertcher, Chief Acct. Officer/Exec. VP
Alfred Crozier, Exec. VP-Residential Construction
Ted P. Stokely, Chmn.

Phone: 469-522-4200	**Fax:** 469-522-4299
Toll-Free: 800.400.6407	
Address: 1800 Valley View Ln., Ste. 300, Dallas, TX 75234 US	

GROWTH PLANS/SPECIAL FEATURES:

American Realty Investors (ARI), Inc. owns, develops and manages property throughout the U.S. The company holds investments in apartments, commercial/office buildings, hotels, parcels of land and other equity ownership interests. ARI generates revenue through its income producing properties, third party development strategies and land acquisitions in high growth suburban markets. The firm's property portfolio consists of 5.7 million square feet of rentable commercial properties that include 21 office buildings, six industrial facilities, four retail properties and 344,975 square feet of trade show and exhibit hall. Other properties include five hotels four of which are located in California and one in Colorado with a combined total of 808 rooms. ARI owns 61 residential apartment communities with a total of 11,942 units; the company has several units currently under construction including a 224 unit complex in Garland, Texas and a 240 unit complex in Gautier, Mississippi. The company develops residential complexes through third party agreements, in which it contributes land and in some cases cash support. ARI also buys large tracts of underdeveloped or partially developed land in areas that are or will be likely growth communities; these tracts of land are located primarily in suburban communities. The company uses the purchased land for its own developments or sells it for a profit to other developers. Current development projects of this nature include a joint venture with HarmInvest GmbH Berlin to develop a decommissioned navel base into a family resort in Schleswig-Holstein, Germany. ARI, through its subsidiary, Transcontinental Realty Investors, Inc.(TRI) and its affiliates invest in under-valued properties; TRI currently holds 7,688 acres for development, with a total of nine projects under construction. One of its current projects includes Mercer Crossing, a mixed-use development in Dallas, Texas.

FINANCIALS:

Sales and profits are in thousands of dollars—add 000 to get the full amount. 2009 Note: Financial information for 2009 was not available for all companies at press time.

2009 Sales: $183,657	2009 Profits: $-82,659	**U.S. Stock Ticker: ARL**
2008 Sales: $177,367	2008 Profits: $26,634	**Int'l Ticker:** Int'l Exchange:
2007 Sales: $164,622	2007 Profits: $26,562	Employees:
2006 Sales: $142,138	2006 Profits: $13,066	Fiscal Year Ends: 12/31
2005 Sales: $123,147	2005 Profits: $47,417	Parent Company:

SALARIES/BENEFITS:

Pension Plan:	ESOP Stock Plan:	Profit Sharing:	Top Exec. Salary: $	Bonus: $
Savings Plan:	Stock Purch. Plan:		Second Exec. Salary: $	Bonus: $

OTHER THOUGHTS:

Apparent Women Officers or Directors: 1
Hot Spot for Advancement for Women/Minorities:

LOCATIONS: ("Y" = Yes)

West:	Southwest:	Midwest:	Southeast:	Northeast:	International:
Y	Y				

AMERICA'S BEST FRANCHISING INC

www.abestfranchise.com

Industry Group Code: 721110 **Ranks within this company's industry group:** Sales: Profits:

Properties:		Financial Services:		Construction/Development:		Investments:		Specialty Services:		Brokerage:	
Apartments:		Mortgages:		Commercial Construction:		REIT:		Property Management:	Y	Commercial Sales:	
Malls/Shopping:		Title Insurance:		Residential Construction:				Online Services:	Y	Residential Sales:	
Offices:		Property Insurance:		Land Development:				Software/IT:		Specialty:	
Hotels/Motels:	Y			Support Services:				Consulting:			
Industrial/Warehouses:				Design/Engineering:							
Other:											

TYPES OF BUSINESS:

Hotels
Hospitality Services
Hotel Franchising
Hotel Management
Back Office Services

BRANDS/DIVISIONS/AFFILIATES:

Buckhead America Corporation
America's Best Inns & Suites
Country Hearth Inn
EverGreen Rooms
Lodge Keeper Group (The)
KI Group, Inc.
America's Best Hotels Services, Inc.
3 Palms Hotels & Resorts

CONTACTS:

Note: Officers with more than one job title may be intentionally listed here more than once.

Douglas C. Collins, CEO
Douglas C. Collins, Pres.
Jason Yarbrough, VP-Franchise Sales
Ed Selby, Dir.-IT
Lori Whatley, VP-Franchise Admin.
Chris Elbers, VP-Franchise Oper.
Jason Yarbrough, VP-Dev.
David Van Matre, Corp. Controller
Douglas C. Collins, Chmn.

Phone: 770-393-2662	**Fax:** 770-393-2480
Toll-Free: 800-432-7992	
Address: 50 Glenlake Pkwy., Ste. 350, Atlanta, GA 30328 US	

GROWTH PLANS/SPECIAL FEATURES:

America's Best Franchising, Inc. is a holding and franchising company for mid-priced hotels, hotel loan portfolios and other hospitality-related assets. The company franchises consist of America's Best Inns & Suites, which is geared toward the business traveler; Country Hearth Inns & Suites, which strives to combine the intimate atmosphere of a bed-and-breakfast with all the conveniences of a contemporary hotel. Other Hotels include the Vagabond Inn, which offers California ranch style accommodations and the Vagabond Inn Executive, which offers the same California ranch style accommodations with extra services geared towards business travelers, such as high speed internet and free incoming fax documents. Budgetel Inns & Suites is marketed towards leisure travelers that include seniors, families, tour groups, with most locations offering free parking and liberal pet policies. The company's more upscale offering is the 3 Palms Hotels & Resorts that has six locations located in proximity to major family oriented attractions, and offers a condo-hotel style brand. The 3 Palms amenities include guest spa packages, pillow top mattresses, guest laundry, golf packages, shuttle and valet service. Each of the hotel chains possesses different special services, such as the EverGreen Room accommodations, which offers rooms designed to support allergen- and irritant-free air, water and mattresses. America's Best and Country Hearth lines offers visitors the EcoRooms opinion, which offers energy efficient, water efficient, waste-reducing and biodegradable products; this is similar to the Green Suites Certification offered by the 3 Palms. The company has an approximate total of 225 hotels under its various brands that are located throughout the U.S. Additionally, the firm formed America's Best Hotel Services, Inc., a company intended to provide hospitality and back office services to independent hotels, other franchisors and emerging brands. The offered services include web site design, Central Reservation Services, Internet marketing, training, quality assurance programs and environmental programs.

FINANCIALS:

Sales and profits are in thousands of dollars—add 000 to get the full amount. 2009 Note: Financial information for 2009 was not available for all companies at press time.

2009 Sales: $	2009 Profits: $	**U.S. Stock Ticker: Private**
2008 Sales: $	2008 Profits: $	**Int'l Ticker:** Int'l Exchange:
2007 Sales: $	2007 Profits: $	Employees:
2006 Sales: $	2006 Profits: $	Fiscal Year Ends: 12/31
2005 Sales: $	2005 Profits: $	Parent Company:

SALARIES/BENEFITS:

Pension Plan:	ESOP Stock Plan:	Profit Sharing:	Top Exec. Salary: $	Bonus: $
Savings Plan:	Stock Purch. Plan:		Second Exec. Salary: $	Bonus: $

OTHER THOUGHTS:

Apparent Women Officers or Directors: 1
Hot Spot for Advancement for Women/Minorities: Y

LOCATIONS: ("Y" = Yes)

West:	Southwest:	Midwest:	Southeast:	Northeast:	International:
Y	Y	Y	Y	Y	Y

AMERISTAR CASINOS INC

www.ameristarcasinos.com

Industry Group Code: 721120 **Ranks within this company's industry group:** Sales: 6 Profits: 3

Properties:		Financial Services:		Construction/Development:		Investments:		Specialty Services:		Brokerage:	
Apartments:		Mortgages:		Commercial Construction:		REIT:		Property Management:	Y	Commercial Sales:	
Malls/Shopping:		Title Insurance:		Residential Construction:				Online Services:		Residential Sales:	
Offices:		Property Insurance:		Land Development:				Software/IT:		Specialty:	
Hotels/Motels:	Y			Support Services:				Consulting:			
Industrial/Warehouses:				Design/Engineering:							
Other:	Y										

TYPES OF BUSINESS:

Casino Resorts
Casino Management

BRANDS/DIVISIONS/AFFILIATES:

Cactus Pete's Resort Casino
Ameristar Kansas City
Ameristar St. Charles
Ameristar Council Bluffs
Ameristar Vicksburg
Horseshu Hotel & Casino
Ameristar Black Hawk
Resorts East Chicago

CONTACTS:

Note: Officers with more than one job title may be intentionally listed here more than once.

Gordon R. Kanofsky, CEO/Vice Chmn.
Larry A. Hodges, COO
Larry A. Hodges, Pres.
Thomas M. Steinbauer, CFO/Sr. VP-Finance/Treas./Sec.
Peter C. Walsh, Chief Admin. Officer
Peter C. Walsh, General Counsel/Sr. VP
Troy Stremming, Sr. VP-Gov't Rel. & Public Affairs
Heather Rollo, Chief Acct. Officer
George Stadler, Sr. VP/Gen. Mgr.-Ameristar Casino Vicksburg
Reginald (Reggie) Fullwood, Sr. VP/Gen. Mgr.-Ameristar Casino Black Hawk
Sean Barnard, Sr. VP/Gen. Mgr.-Ameristar Casino Kansas City
Roxann M. Kinkade, Dir.-External Comm.
Ray H. Neilsen, Chmn.

Phone: 702-567-7000 **Fax:** 702-369-8860
Toll-Free:
Address: 3773 Howard Hughes Pkwy., Ste. 490S, Las Vegas, NV 89169 US

GROWTH PLANS/SPECIAL FEATURES:

Ameristar Casinos, Inc. (ASCA), founded in 1954, is a gaming and entertainment company that develops, owns and operates casino facilities. Its subsidiaries include Ameristar St. Charles and Ameristar Kansas City in Missouri; Ameristar Council Bluffs in southwestern Iowa; Ameristar Vicksburg in Mississippi; Ameristar Black Hawk in Denver, Colorado; Resorts East Chicago; and Cactus Pete's Resort Casino and Horseshu Hotel and Casino, both near the Idaho boarder in Jackpot, Nevada. The casinos typically offer slot machines, including video poker and keno; and a variety of table games, including blackjack, craps, roulette, baccarat and numerous live poker variations such as Texas Hold 'Em and Pai Gow. In addition, some locations offer sports book wagering. Ameristar is a leader in the casino industry in the implementation of cashless slot technology and new-generation multi-coin (nickel and penny denomination) slot machines. The casinos also offer a variety of casual dining and upscale restaurants; sports bars; and private clubs for Star Awards members. Ameristar St. Charles offers two ballrooms for its guests, five meeting rooms and an executive board room. Ameristar Kansas City features an 18-screen movie theater, a 4,280 square foot arcade and an activity center named Kids Quest. Ameristar Vicksburg is a permanently docked riverboat casino located on the Mississippi River, while Ameristar Council Bluffs offers a cruising riverboat casino that travels down the Missouri River, as well as landside amenities such as the Ameristar Hotel and Main Street Pavilion. Cactus Pete's features an outdoor amphitheater, arcades, an 18-hole golf course and tennis courts. Resorts East Chicago is a 56,000 square foot property that features a 550-seat ballroom and a nearly 2,000 space parking garage.

Employees are offered medical, dental and vision insurance; a 401(k) plan; life insurance, additional voluntary life insurance and supplemental life insurance for spouses and children; disability insurance; flexible spending accounts; an employee assistance program; and tuition reimbursement.

FINANCIALS:

Sales and profits are in thousands of dollars—add 000 to get the full amount. 2009 Note: Financial information for 2009 was not available for all companies at press time.

2009 Sales: $1,215,445	2009 Profits: $-4,667
2008 Sales: $1,267,902	2008 Profits: $-130,672
2007 Sales: $1,080,523	2007 Profits: $69,433
2006 Sales: $1,000,298	2006 Profits: $59,565
2005 Sales: $961,358	2005 Profits: $66,285

U.S. Stock Ticker: ASCA
Int'l Ticker: Int'l Exchange:
Employees: 7,600
Fiscal Year Ends: 12/31
Parent Company:

SALARIES/BENEFITS:

Pension Plan:	ESOP Stock Plan:	Profit Sharing:	Top Exec. Salary: $674,134	Bonus: $426,997
Savings Plan: Y	Stock Purch. Plan:		Second Exec. Salary: $483,173	Bonus: $228,624

OTHER THOUGHTS:

Apparent Women Officers or Directors: 3
Hot Spot for Advancement for Women/Minorities: Y

LOCATIONS: ("Y" = Yes)

West:	Southwest:	Midwest:	Southeast:	Northeast:	International:
Y		Y	Y		

AMEY PLC

www.amey.co.uk

Industry Group Code: 541330 **Ranks within this company's industry group:** Sales: Profits:

Properties:		Financial Services:		Construction/Development:		Investments:		Specialty Services:		Brokerage:	
Apartments:		Mortgages:		Commercial Construction:		REIT:		Property Management:	Y	Commercial Sales:	
Malls/Shopping:		Title Insurance:		Residential Construction:				Online Services:		Residential Sales:	
Offices:		Property Insurance:		Land Development:				Software/IT:		Specialty:	
Hotels/Motels:				Support Services:	Y			Consulting:	Y		
Industrial/Warehouses:				Design/Engineering:	Y						
Other:											

TYPES OF BUSINESS:

Engineering Services
Facilities Management
Design Services
Consulting Services
Asset Management
Infrastructure Services
Highway Design Services
IT Services

BRANDS/DIVISIONS/AFFILIATES:

Grupo Ferrovial SA

CONTACTS:

Note: Officers with more than one job title may be intentionally listed here more than once.

Mel Ewell, CEO
Chris Webster, COO
Andrew Nelson, Group Dir.-Finance
Valerie Hughes-D'Aeth, Dir.-Human Resources
Wayne Robertson, Head-Legal
Andy Ractliffe, Dir.-Acct.
Keith Cottrell, Managing Dir.-Amey Ventures
Keith Sexton, Dir.-Health, Safety, Environment & Quality
Chris Fenton, Managing Dir.-Tube Svcs.
Richard Shackell, Bus. Mgr.-Signaling
Richard Mottram, Chmn.

Phone: 44-18-6571-3100 **Fax:** 44-18-6571-3357
Toll-Free:
Address: The Sherard Bldg., Edmund Halley Rd., Oxford, OX4 4DQ UK

GROWTH PLANS/SPECIAL FEATURES:

Amey plc, a subsidiary of the Spanish Grupo Ferrovial, provides business and infrastructure support services through more than 200 locations across the U.K. and Ireland. The company identifies its services as belonging to the following four areas: transport systems; school and youth support; community development; and public services. In the transport systems division, Amey offers design and advisory services, such as feasibility studies, technical surveys and environmental assessments; ensures the delivery and renewal of road and rail infrastructure; provides management services; and designs, provides and manages transport information solutions across the road and rail networks. Amey holds a 30-year contract to upgrade and maintain London's Jubilee, Northern and Piccadilly tube lines. The properties administered in this area include 100 stations, over 200 miles of track and 255 subway trains. With regard to school and youth support, Amey designs and builds schools/colleges, manages school facilities, implements new technology in school management solutions and provides education improvement consultation services. In the vein of community development, the company designs and manages public spaces, consults with local and government organizations to improve community services and works to maximize community resources through community centers. The firm's public services division includes financing services, managing estates, business support services and transportation solutions. In November 2009, Amey opened a new international design office in Birmingham, U.K.

The firm offers its employees life, dental, travel and personal accident insurance; parental leave; paid time off; and a pension plan.

FINANCIALS:

Sales and profits are in thousands of dollars—add 000 to get the full amount. 2009 Note: Financial information for 2009 was not available for all companies at press time.

2009 Sales: $	2009 Profits: $	**U.S. Stock Ticker: Subsidiary**
2008 Sales: $	2008 Profits: $	**Int'l Ticker:** Int'l Exchange:
2007 Sales: $	2007 Profits: $	Employees:
2006 Sales: $2,613,130	2006 Profits: $127,413	Fiscal Year Ends: 12/31
2005 Sales: $2,122,990	2005 Profits: $91,985	Parent Company: GRUPO FERROVIAL SA

SALARIES/BENEFITS:

Pension Plan: Y	ESOP Stock Plan:	Profit Sharing:	Top Exec. Salary: $	Bonus: $
Savings Plan:	Stock Purch. Plan:		Second Exec. Salary: $	Bonus: $

OTHER THOUGHTS:

Apparent Women Officers or Directors: 1
Hot Spot for Advancement for Women/Minorities:

LOCATIONS: ("Y" = Yes)

West:	Southwest:	Midwest:	Southeast:	Northeast:	International:
					Y

AMLI RESIDENTIAL PROPERTIES TRUST

www.amli.com

Industry Group Code: 531120 **Ranks within this company's industry group:** Sales: Profits:

Properties:		Financial Services:		Construction/Development:		Investments:		Specialty Services:		Brokerage:	
Apartments:	Y	Mortgages:		Commercial Construction:		REIT:	Y	Property Management:	Y	Commercial Sales:	
Malls/Shopping:		Title Insurance:		Residential Construction:	Y			Online Services:		Residential Sales:	
Offices:		Property Insurance:		Land Development:				Software/IT:		Specialty:	
Hotels/Motels:				Support Services:				Consulting:			
Industrial/Warehouses:				Design/Engineering:							
Other:											

TYPES OF BUSINESS:

Real Estate Investment Trust
Apartment Communities
Construction & Landscape Services
Management & Leasing Services
Investment Services

BRANDS/DIVISIONS/AFFILIATES:

AMLI Management Company
AMLI Institutional Advisors
AMLI Residential Construction
AMLI Residential Properties, LP
Morgan Stanley Real Estate
FAMLI
AMLI Nest Egg

CONTACTS:

Note: Officers with more than one job title may be intentionally listed here more than once.

Gregory T. Mutz, CEO
Allan J. Sweet, Pres.
Robert J. Chapman, CFO/Exec. VP
Leslie Silverman, Sr. VP-Human Resources
Stephen C. Ross, Exec. VP-Dev.
Rosita A. Lina, Controller/VP
Philip N. Tague, Exec. VP
Steve F. Hallsey, Pres./CEO-AMLI Mgmt. Co.
Mark T. Evans, Pres., AMLI Residential Construction
Taylor Bowen, Exec. VP-Dev., Texas
Gregory T. Mutz, Chmn.

Phone: 312-283-4700	**Fax:** 312-283-4720
Toll-Free:	
Address: 200 W. Monroe St., Ste. 2200, Chicago, IL 60606 US	

GROWTH PLANS/SPECIAL FEATURES:

AMLI Residential Properties Trust, a subsidiary of Morgan Stanley Real Estate, is a self-administered and self-managed real estate investment trust engaged in the development, acquisition and management of luxury apartment communities. The company manages 66 apartment communities in Atlanta, Georgia; Austin, Texas; Chicago, Illinois; Dallas, Texas; Denver, Colorado; West Palm Beach, Florida; Houston, Texas; Kansas City, Kansas; Kansas City, Missouri; Seattle, Washington; Morristown, New Jersey; Sherman Oaks, California; and Rancho Cucamonga, California. Overall, AMLI manages 61 apartment communities, comprised of approximately 22,000 units and about 2,000 additional apartment complexes that are in lease-up or under development. The company also provides property management, institutional advisory and construction management services through its subsidiary companies, AMLI Management Company; AMLI Institutional Advisors, Inc.; and AMLI Residential Construction, LLC. AMLI's growth strategies employ a combination of brand and market promotions, acquisition, development and co-investments with institutional investors in new apartment communities. The company offers its tenants the AMLI Nest Egg program, an equity credit plan that allows 20% of base apartment rent to be applied as non-monetary credit towards the purchase price of a new home from KB Home, Ryland Homes or Belgravia Realty Group. AMLI also created the FAMLI volunteer program as a means of connecting AMLI residents and employees with local non-profit organizations.

AMLI offers its employees a benefits package that includes health and dependent care flexible spending accounts; a 401(k) plan; bonus programs; adoption assistance; medical, dental and vision coverage; life insurance; tuition assistance; and housing discounts.

FINANCIALS:

Sales and profits are in thousands of dollars—add 000 to get the full amount. 2009 Note: Financial information for 2009 was not available for all companies at press time.

2009 Sales: $	2009 Profits: $	**U.S. Stock Ticker: Subsidiary**
2008 Sales: $	2008 Profits: $	**Int'l Ticker:** Int'l Exchange:
2007 Sales: $	2007 Profits: $	Employees:
2006 Sales: $	2006 Profits: $	Fiscal Year Ends: 12/31
2005 Sales: $	2005 Profits: $	Parent Company: MORGAN STANLEY

SALARIES/BENEFITS:

Pension Plan:	ESOP Stock Plan:	Profit Sharing:	Top Exec. Salary: $	Bonus: $
Savings Plan: Y	Stock Purch. Plan:		Second Exec. Salary: $	Bonus: $

OTHER THOUGHTS:

Apparent Women Officers or Directors: 2
Hot Spot for Advancement for Women/Minorities: Y

LOCATIONS: ("Y" = Yes)

West:	Southwest:	Midwest:	Southeast:	Northeast:	International:
Y	Y	Y	Y	Y	

ANDERSON-TULLY LUMBER COMPANY

www.andersontully.com

Industry Group Code: 531120 **Ranks within this company's industry group:** Sales: Profits:

Properties:		Financial Services:		Construction/Development:		Investments:		Specialty Services:		Brokerage:	
Apartments:		Mortgages:		Commercial Construction:		REIT:	Y	Property Management:		Commercial Sales:	
Malls/Shopping:		Title Insurance:		Residential Construction:				Online Services:		Residential Sales:	
Offices:		Property Insurance:		Land Development:	Y			Software/IT:		Specialty:	
Hotels/Motels:				Support Services:	Y			Consulting:			
Industrial/Warehouses:				Design/Engineering:							
Other:	Y										

TYPES OF BUSINESS:

Real Estate Investment Trust
Timber Tract Operations
Hardwood Products
Hardwood Flooring

BRANDS/DIVISIONS/AFFILIATES:

Anderson Tully Lumber Company
Anderson Tully Veneers
Anderson Tully Engineered Wood/Capella
ForestMark
Patton Tully Transportation, LLC

CONTACTS:

Note: Officers with more than one job title may be intentionally listed here more than once.

E. J. (Buddy) Irby, Jr., VP-Sales
Mike Myrick, Mgr.-Human Resources
Tom Evans, Industrial Engineer
Roy James, VP-Mfg.
Ellis Screws, Mgr.-Oper. Support
Kimberly Opiela, Mgr.-Acct.
Richard Wilkerson, Exec. VP
Norman Davis, Exec. VP-Land Acquisition & Sales
Mike Gross, Computer Operations
Tony Davidson, Specialist-Applications

Phone: 601-629-3283	**Fax:** 601-629-3284
Toll-Free:	
Address: 1725 N. Washington St., P.O. Box 38, Vicksburg, MS 39181 US	

GROWTH PLANS/SPECIAL FEATURES:

Anderson-Tully Lumber Company (ATCO) is a REIT (Real Estate Investment Trust) focusing entirely on timberland investments. ATCO is one of the few REITs that manage timberlands, and one of the only ones to focus on hardwood timberlands. Originally a crate manufacturing company, the company moved into the timberland ownership business in 1889 to provide itself with sustainable operations, eventually shifting its focus away from crates and boxes to exclusively operating its timberlands. Today, it owns approximately 300,000 acres of hardwood timber tracts along the Mississippi River in Mississippi, Louisiana and Arkansas. The firm was one of the first major Southeastern timber companies certified by the Forest Stewardship Council, an organization devoted to the promotion of responsible forestry. ATCO operates its own sawmills, lumber inspectors, holding facilities and transport networks. Customers may choose between a variety of hardwoods, including cottonwood, hackberry, pecan, poplar, red oak, sweetgum, sycamore, white ash, white oak and willow. Its operating companies include Anderson-Tully Worldwide, the firm's sales and marketing arm; Anderson-Tully China, with offices in Shanghai and Guangzhou; Anderson-Tully de Mexico, based in Mexico City; Anderson-Tully Vietnam, based in Ho Chi Minh City; and Anderson-Tully Lumber Company. Patton Tully Transportation, a sister company, provides shipping for the firm's products along the Mississippi, Ohio, Tombigbee, Black, Tennessee, Cumberland, Yazoo, Arkansas, Red, White and Missouri river systems. Additionally, ATCO created a network of producers called the International Hardwood Resource, designed to insure the smooth flow of hardwood to its customers. The Resource currently has seven members, besides ATCO subsidiaries, including six U.S. firms and one based in Italy. The firm is owned by the Heartwood Forestland Fund V, an affiliate of The Forestland Group LLC.

FINANCIALS:

Sales and profits are in thousands of dollars—add 000 to get the full amount. 2009 Note: Financial information for 2009 was not available for all companies at press time.

2009 Sales: $	2009 Profits: $	**U.S. Stock Ticker: Subsidiary**
2008 Sales: $	2008 Profits: $	**Int'l Ticker:** Int'l Exchange:
2007 Sales: $	2007 Profits: $	Employees:
2006 Sales: $	2006 Profits: $	Fiscal Year Ends: 12/31
2005 Sales: $	2005 Profits: $	Parent Company: FORESTLAND GROUP LLC (THE)

SALARIES/BENEFITS:

Pension Plan:	ESOP Stock Plan:	Profit Sharing:	Top Exec. Salary: $	Bonus: $
Savings Plan:	Stock Purch. Plan:		Second Exec. Salary: $	Bonus: $

OTHER THOUGHTS:

Apparent Women Officers or Directors: 9
Hot Spot for Advancement for Women/Minorities: Y

LOCATIONS: ("Y" = Yes)

West:	Southwest:	Midwest:	Southeast:	Northeast:	International:
			Y		Y

ANNALY CAPITAL MANAGEMENT INC

www.annaly.com

Industry Group Code: 531120 **Ranks within this company's industry group:** Sales: 6 Profits: 9

Properties:		Financial Services:		Construction/Development:		Investments:		Specialty Services:		Brokerage:	
Apartments:		Mortgages:	Y	Commercial Construction:		REIT:	Y	Property Management:		Commercial Sales:	
Malls/Shopping:		Title Insurance:		Residential Construction:				Online Services:		Residential Sales:	
Offices:		Property Insurance:		Land Development:				Software/IT:		Specialty:	
Hotels/Motels:				Support Services:				Consulting:			
Industrial/Warehouses:				Design/Engineering:							
Other:											

TYPES OF BUSINESS:

Real Estate Investment Trust
Mortgage-Backed Securities

BRANDS/DIVISIONS/AFFILIATES:

Annaly Mortgage Management, Inc.
Fixed Income Discount Advisory Company
Sentry Select FIDAC U.S. Mortgage Trust
Ranger Capital Corp
Merganser Capital Management Inc.
RCap Securities, Inc.

CONTACTS:

Note: Officers with more than one job title may be intentionally listed here more than once.

Michael A. J. Farrell, CEO
Wellington J. Denahan-Norris, COO
Michael A. J. Farrell, Pres.
Kathryn F. Fagan, CFO
R. Nicholas Singh, General Counsel/Sec./Exec. VP
Kathryn F. Fagen, Treas.
Wellington J. Denahan-Norris, Chief Investment Officer/Vice Chmn.
Ronald D. Kazel, Managing Dir.
James P. Fortescue, Managing Dir./Head-Liabilities
Kristopher R. Konrad, Managing Dir./Co-Head-Portfolio Mgmt.
Michael A. J. Farrell, Chmn.

Phone: 212-696-0100 **Fax:** 212-696-9809
Toll-Free: 888-826-6259
Address: 1211 Ave. of the Americas, Ste. 2902, New York, NY 10036 US

GROWTH PLANS/SPECIAL FEATURES:

Annaly Capital Management, Inc., formerly Annaly Mortgage Management, Inc., is a self-managed, self-administered real estate investment trust (REIT) that focuses entirely on owning and managing a portfolio of mortgage-backed securities. The company has three wholly-owned subsidiaries: Fixed Income Discount Advisory Company (FIDAC); Merganser Capital Management, Inc.; and RCap Securities, Inc (RCap). FIDAC and Merganser manage multiple investment vehicles and separate accounts. RCap operates as a broker dealer. The firm owns and manages a portfolio of investment securities including collateralized mortgage obligations (CMOs), mortgage pass-through certificates and agency callable debentures. All of Annaly's assets are securities issued by Fannie Mae, Ginnie Mae or Freddie Mac, carrying an AAA rating or better from Standard & Poor's, with a mix of adjustable, floating and fixed rates. Approximately 74% of the company's investment securities are fixed-rate CMOs, 21% are adjustable-rate, while 5% are CMO floaters. The firm also uses moderate leverage, or debt, to increase returns by borrowing money at a low interest rate and then investing it in high-interest mortgages. All of Annaly's assets are easily priced and traded in the mortgage-backed securities market. The company has some of the lowest operating costs of any company in the business (an average of 0.15% of assets managed). Since Annaly has elected to be taxed as a REIT, it must pay out at least 90% of its earnings to its shareholders in order to avoid taxation at the corporate level.

FINANCIALS:

Sales and profits are in thousands of dollars—add 000 to get the full amount. 2009 Note: Financial information for 2009 was not available for all companies at press time.

2009 Sales: $2,922,602	2009 Profits: $1,961,471	**U.S. Stock Ticker: NLY**
2008 Sales: $3,115,428	2008 Profits: $346,238	**Int'l Ticker:** Int'l Exchange:
2007 Sales: $2,355,447	2007 Profits: $414,384	Employees: 87
2006 Sales: $1,221,882	2006 Profits: $93,816	Fiscal Year Ends: 12/31
2005 Sales: $740,671	2005 Profits: $-9,247	Parent Company:

SALARIES/BENEFITS:

Pension Plan:	ESOP Stock Plan:	Profit Sharing:	Top Exec. Salary: $2,430,000	Bonus: $17,722,781
Savings Plan:	Stock Purch. Plan:		Second Exec. Salary: $972,000	Bonus: $7,089,113

OTHER THOUGHTS:

Apparent Women Officers or Directors: 2
Hot Spot for Advancement for Women/Minorities: Y

LOCATIONS: ("Y" = Yes)

West:	Southwest:	Midwest:	Southeast:	Northeast:	International:
				Y	

ANTHONY & SYLVAN POOLS

www.anthonysylvan.com

Industry Group Code: 2389 **Ranks within this company's industry group:** Sales: Profits:

Properties:		Financial Services:		Construction/Development:		Investments:		Specialty Services:		Brokerage:	
Apartments:		Mortgages:		Commercial Construction:		REIT:		Property Management:		Commercial Sales:	
Malls/Shopping:		Title Insurance:		Residential Construction:	Y			Online Services:		Residential Sales:	
Offices:		Property Insurance:		Land Development:				Software/IT:		Specialty:	
Hotels/Motels:				Support Services:				Consulting:			
Industrial/Warehouses:				Design/Engineering:							
Other:											

TYPES OF BUSINESS:

Special Trade Contractors-Pools
Residential Swimming Pools & Spas
Pool-Related Products & Services

BRANDS/DIVISIONS/AFFILIATES:

CONTACTS:

Note: Officers with more than one job title may be intentionally listed here more than once.

Stuart D. Neidus, CEO
Richard Mills, COO
Howard P. Wertman, Pres.
William J. Evanson, CFO/Exec. VP
Ken F. Sloan, VP-Human Resources
Stuart D. Neidus, Chmn.

Phone: 440-720-3301	**Fax:** 440-720-3303
Toll-Free: 877-729-7946	
Address: 6690 Beta Dr., Ste. 300, Mayfield Village, OH 44143 US	

GROWTH PLANS/SPECIAL FEATURES:

Anthony & Sylvan Pool Corporation (ASP) is among the largest U.S. installers of custom-designed, in-ground concrete residential swimming pools and spas. Its operations span a network of approximately 35 company-owned sales offices serving nine major metropolitan markets in 11 states. In addition to designing and offering residential swimming pools, the company provides pool renovation services in select markets; operates retail stores that sell spa- and pool-related products such as chemicals, replacement parts, toys, accessories and equipment; and operates service centers that offer post-installation services such as weekly maintenance, as well as parts, equipment and accessories. ASP also offers eco-friendly swimming pools with filtration systems that are more energy efficient and do not require chlorine. Historically, its sales have been seasonally strongest in the second and third quarters, the peak period for pool installation and use, and weakest in the first and fourth quarters, corresponding with the colder seasons of the year. ASP sells its products primarily to residential homeowners and homebuilders. The company also offers its customers financing options.

The firm offers employee benefits that include health care insurance; dental coverage; company-paid life insurance; discounted prescription drugs; short and long-term disability insurance; 401(k) with company match; and career development training.

FINANCIALS:

Sales and profits are in thousands of dollars—add 000 to get the full amount. 2009 Note: Financial information for 2009 was not available for all companies at press time.

2009 Sales: $	2009 Profits: $	**U.S. Stock Ticker: Private**
2008 Sales: $	2008 Profits: $	**Int'l Ticker:** Int'l Exchange:
2007 Sales: $	2007 Profits: $	Employees:
2006 Sales: $	2006 Profits: $	Fiscal Year Ends: 12/31
2005 Sales: $250,000	2005 Profits: $	Parent Company:

SALARIES/BENEFITS:

Pension Plan:	ESOP Stock Plan:	Profit Sharing:	Top Exec. Salary: $	Bonus: $
Savings Plan: Y	Stock Purch. Plan:		Second Exec. Salary: $	Bonus: $

OTHER THOUGHTS:

Apparent Women Officers or Directors:
Hot Spot for Advancement for Women/Minorities:

LOCATIONS: ("Y" = Yes)

West:	Southwest:	Midwest:	Southeast:	Northeast:	International:
Y	Y	Y	Y	Y	

APARTMENT INVESTMENT AND MANAGEMENT CO www.aimco.com

Industry Group Code: 531120 **Ranks within this company's industry group:** Sales: 14 Profits: 3

Properties:		Financial Services:		Construction/Development:		Investments:		Specialty Services:		Brokerage:	
Apartments:	Y	Mortgages:		Commercial Construction:		REIT:	Y	Property Management:	Y	Commercial Sales:	
Malls/Shopping:		Title Insurance:		Residential Construction:				Online Services:		Residential Sales:	
Offices:		Property Insurance:		Land Development:				Software/IT:		Specialty:	
Hotels/Motels:				Support Services:				Consulting:			
Industrial/Warehouses:				Design/Engineering:							
Other:											

TYPES OF BUSINESS:

Real Estate Investment Trust
Apartment Communities
Property Management Services

BRANDS/DIVISIONS/AFFILIATES:

AIMCO
AIMCO-GP, Inc.
AIMCO-LP, Inc.
AIMCO Properties, L.P.

CONTACTS:

Note: Officers with more than one job title may be intentionally listed here more than once.

Terry Considine, CEO
Timothy J. Beaudin, COO
Timothy J. Beaudin, Pres.
Ernest M. Freedman, CFO/Exec. VP
Miles Cortez, Chief Admin. Officer/Exec. VP
Lisa R. Cohn, General Counsel/Exec. VP/Sec.
Anthony R. D'Alto, Exec. VP-Property Oper.
Elizabeth Coalson, VP-Investor Rel.
Patti K. Fielding, Treas./Exec. VP-Securities & Debt
Robert Y. Walker IV, Exec. VP/CFO-Property Oper.
Terry Considine, Chmn.

Phone: 303-757-8101 **Fax:** 303-759-3226
Toll-Free: 888-789-8600
Address: 4582 S. Ulster St. Pkwy., Ste. 1100, Denver, CO 80237 US

GROWTH PLANS/SPECIAL FEATURES:

Apartment Investment and Management Co. (AIMCO) is a self-administered and self-managed real estate investment trust (REIT) engaged in the acquisition, ownership, management and redevelopment of apartment properties that holds a nationwide portfolio of apartment communities. AIMCO owns and operates around 870 properties that include approximately 135,654 units, and serves around 500,000 annually. The company operates in two segments: real estate, which focuses on the owning and operating of apartments; and investment management, which provides portfolio and asset management. The firm's portfolio is divided into two business components: conventional and affordable. Conventional operations consist of market-rate apartments in which rent is paid by the resident. Affordable operations consist of mostly apartments in which rent is subsidized or paid by a government agency. These operations are almost completely conducted through the AIMCO Operating Partnership that consists of subsidiaries AIMCO-GP, Inc., and AIMCO-LP, Inc., which, together, hold a majority interest in AIMCO Properties, L.P. The company's properties are located in 44 states, Washington, D.C. and Puerto Rico.

Employees are offered medical, dental and vision insurance; life insurance; disability coverage; a 401(k) plan' an employee assistance program; flexible spending accounts; fitness club discounts; professional certification reimbursement; a tuition aid program; an apartment discount; and discounted legal services.

FINANCIALS:

Sales and profits are in thousands of dollars—add 000 to get the full amount. 2009 Note: Financial information for 2009 was not available for all companies at press time.

2009 Sales: $1,195,763	2009 Profits: $-44,800
2008 Sales: $1,243,170	2008 Profits: $627,002
2007 Sales: $1,174,457	2007 Profits: $125,506
2006 Sales: $1,274,163	2006 Profits: $176,787
2005 Sales: $1,408,464	2005 Profits: $70,982

U.S. Stock Ticker: AIV
Int'l Ticker: Int'l Exchange:
Employees: 3,500
Fiscal Year Ends: 12/31
Parent Company:

SALARIES/BENEFITS:

Pension Plan: ESOP Stock Plan: Profit Sharing: Top Exec. Salary: $600,000 Bonus: $710,535
Savings Plan: Y Stock Purch. Plan: Second Exec. Salary: $534,722 Bonus: $

OTHER THOUGHTS:

Apparent Women Officers or Directors: 3
Hot Spot for Advancement for Women/Minorities: Y

LOCATIONS: ("Y" = Yes)

West:	Southwest:	Midwest:	Southeast:	Northeast:	International:
Y	Y	Y	Y	Y	Y

ARC GROUP OF COMPANIES (THE)

www.arcproperties.com

Industry Group Code: 531120 **Ranks within this company's industry group:** Sales: Profits:

Properties:		Financial Services:		Construction/Development:		Investments:		Specialty Services:		Brokerage:	
Apartments:	Y	Mortgages:		Commercial Construction:		REIT:	Y	Property Management:	Y	Commercial Sales:	
Malls/Shopping:	Y	Title Insurance:		Residential Construction:				Online Services:		Residential Sales:	
Offices:	Y	Property Insurance:		Land Development:				Software/IT:		Specialty:	
Hotels/Motels:				Support Services:				Consulting:			
Industrial/Warehouses:				Design/Engineering:							
Other:											

TYPES OF BUSINESS:

Real Estate Investment Trust
Credit Lease Properties

BRANDS/DIVISIONS/AFFILIATES:

ARC International Fund
ARC Corporate Realty Trust
ARC Properties, Inc.

CONTACTS:

Note: Officers with more than one job title may be intentionally listed here more than once.

Robert J. Ambrosi, CEO
Marc Perel, COO
Marc Perel, Pres.
Bruce Nelson, CFO
Michael R. Ambrosi, Mktg. & Leasing
Michael R. Ambrosi, Administrator-IT & Bus. Tech.
Gary S. Baumann, General Counsel
Gil Revera, VP-Bus. Dev.
Catherine Buck, Acct.
Steven L. Maloy, Sr. VP-Investments
Joseph Morena, Exec. VP
Claudia L. Gibson, VP-Capital Markets
Neil Doornheim, Sr. Mgr.-Property
Robert J. Ambrosi, Chmn.

Phone: 973-249-1000	**Fax:** 973-249-1001
Toll-Free:	
Address: 1401 Broad St., Clifton, NJ 07013 US	

GROWTH PLANS/SPECIAL FEATURES:

The ARC Group of Companies consists of three operating companies: ARC International Fund; ARC Property Trust (the firm's publicly listed REIT); and ARC Properties, Inc., a development and management wing. Together the companies specialize in the acquisition and development of credit lease properties throughout the U.S., with special emphasis on metropolitan areas east of the Mississippi. Credit lease properties are general retail, office or industrial buildings leased long-term to credit-worthy clients, who in turn pay the majority or entirety of operating expenses and insurance. Major retail tenants include Home Depot, Lowe's, Staples, Walgreen's and Bed, Bath & Beyond. The company seeks undeveloped land from 1-100 acres in size, generally along the Eastern seaboard from New York City to Washington, D.C. and in Miami. Its preferences are less narrow concerning the location of its developed properties, but it tends to focus on the metropolitan areas of Miami, Florida; Boston, Massachusetts; Washington, D.C.; Philadelphia, Pennsylvania; Chicago, Illinois; and Charlotte, North Carolina. These tend to range anywhere from $1 million to $50 million. Additionally, ARC has leased residential properties near greater New York, Philadelphia and Baltimore. In January 2010, following the liquidation of the group's former REIT, Arc Corporate Realty Trust, Arc Properties, Inc. established ARC Property Trust.

FINANCIALS:

Sales and profits are in thousands of dollars—add 000 to get the full amount. 2009 Note: Financial information for 2009 was not available for all companies at press time.

2009 Sales: $	2009 Profits: $	**U.S. Stock Ticker: Private**
2008 Sales: $	2008 Profits: $	**Int'l Ticker:** Int'l Exchange:
2007 Sales: $	2007 Profits: $	Employees:
2006 Sales: $	2006 Profits: $	Fiscal Year Ends: 12/31
2005 Sales: $	2005 Profits: $	Parent Company:

SALARIES/BENEFITS:

Pension Plan:	ESOP Stock Plan:	Profit Sharing:	Top Exec. Salary: $	Bonus: $
Savings Plan:	Stock Purch. Plan:		Second Exec. Salary: $	Bonus: $

OTHER THOUGHTS:

Apparent Women Officers or Directors: 7
Hot Spot for Advancement for Women/Minorities: Y

LOCATIONS: ("Y" = Yes)

West:	Southwest:	Midwest:	Southeast:	Northeast:	International:
	Y	Y	Y	Y	

ARCADIS NV

www.arcadis-global.com

Industry Group Code: 541330 **Ranks within this company's industry group:** Sales: 5 Profits: 6

Properties:		Financial Services:		Construction/Development:		Investments:		Specialty Services:		Brokerage:	
Apartments:		Mortgages:		Commercial Construction:	Y	REIT:		Property Management:	Y	Commercial Sales:	
Malls/Shopping:		Title Insurance:		Residential Construction:	Y			Online Services:		Residential Sales:	
Offices:		Property Insurance:		Land Development:	Y			Software/IT:		Specialty:	
Hotels/Motels:				Support Services:	Y			Consulting:			
Industrial/Warehouses:				Design/Engineering:	Y						
Other:											

TYPES OF BUSINESS:

Engineering Services
Consulting Services
Project Management
Environmental Services
Infrastructure Construction Management
Power Generation Facilities
Industrial & Residential Development

BRANDS/DIVISIONS/AFFILIATES:

ARCADIS Geraghty & Miller Inc
HOMOLA Projectmanagement AG
Bessent, Hammack & Ruckman Inc
Logos Engenharia
Eurolatina
Arcadis Euroconsult
Bohemiaplan
Plan & Projectpartners

CONTACTS:

Note: Officers with more than one job title may be intentionally listed here more than once.

Harrie L. J. Noy, Exec. Chmn.
Renier Vree, CFO
Tom W. Haak, Dir.-Human Resources
Anja M. Van Bergen-van Kruijsbergen, General Counsel/Corp. Sec.
Joost Slloten, Investor Rel. Officer
Craig E. Eisen, Dir.-Mergers & Acquisitions
C. Michiel Jaski, Member-Exec. Board
Friedrich M.T. Schneider, Member-Exec. Board
Rijnhard W. F. van Tets, Chmn.
Steven B. Blake, CEO-Arcadis U.S.

Phone: 31-26-377-8911	**Fax:** 31-26-351-5235
Toll-Free:	
Address: Nieuwe Stationsstraat 10, Arnhem, 6800 LE The Netherlands	

GROWTH PLANS/SPECIAL FEATURES:

Arcadis N.V., based in the Netherlands, is an international provider of consulting, engineering and project management services for infrastructure, environment and facilities. The company develops, designs, implements, maintains and operates projects for private and public sector clients through three activity divisions: Infrastructure, which accounts for 41% of Arcadis' business; Environment, which accounts for 36%; and Buildings, which accounts for 23%. The infrastructure division consults, designs and manages the construction of infrastructure projects, including railroads, highways, airports, harbors, waterways, dikes and retention ponds. The company also develops utilities for rail signaling, safety, communications and energy supply; constructs bridges and tunnels; and develops small power plants, wind farms and hydroelectric facilities. In addition, the infrastructure division designs and develops new industrial parks and residential areas and oversees the redevelopment of old sites. The environment division provides consulting on environmental policy for companies and governments; conducts environmental impact assessments; and supports environmental management and environmentally conscious engineering practices. The division provides soil and groundwater contamination testing and develops cost-effective solutions for the remediation of contaminated soil and water. Lastly, the buildings division develops and maintains buildings, including offices, stores, commercial properties, schools, museums, prisons, stadiums and railway stations. To carry out the activities of these divisions, Arcadis works from its strong home market positions in Europe, the U.S. and South America, with approximately 200 locations in 100 countries. The firm is also seeking to expand into new markets, with select offices in the Middle East, Japan and China. Recently, the company acquired SET, an Italian firm specializing in environmental consulting.

Arcadis offers its U.S. employees benefits including medical, dental and vision coverage; flexible spending accounts; an employee assistance program; a 401(k) plan; a discount stock purchase plan; and life and AD&D insurance.

FINANCIALS:

Sales and profits are in thousands of dollars—add 000 to get the full amount. 2009 Note: Financial information for 2009 was not available for all companies at press time.

2009 Sales: $2,426,260	2009 Profits: $98,910	**U.S. Stock Ticker: ARCAY**
2008 Sales: $2,277,630	2008 Profits: $83,350	**Int'l Ticker: ARCAD** Int'l Exchange: Amsterdam-Euronext
2007 Sales: $2,235,000	2007 Profits: $81,260	Employees: 15,000
2006 Sales: $1,825,000	2006 Profits: $66,460	Fiscal Year Ends: 12/31
2005 Sales: $873,000	2005 Profits: $41,200	Parent Company:

SALARIES/BENEFITS:

Pension Plan:	ESOP Stock Plan:	Profit Sharing:	Top Exec. Salary: $	Bonus: $
Savings Plan: Y	Stock Purch. Plan: Y		Second Exec. Salary: $	Bonus: $

OTHER THOUGHTS:

Apparent Women Officers or Directors:
Hot Spot for Advancement for Women/Minorities:

LOCATIONS: ("Y" = Yes)

West:	Southwest:	Midwest:	Southeast:	Northeast:	International:
Y	Y	Y	Y	Y	Y

ARCHSTONE TRUST

www.archstoneapartments.com

Industry Group Code: 531110 **Ranks within this company's industry group:** Sales: Profits:

Properties:		Financial Services:		Construction/Development:		Investments:		Specialty Services:		Brokerage:	
Apartments:	Y	Mortgages:		Commercial Construction:		REIT:	Y	Property Management:	Y	Commercial Sales:	
Malls/Shopping:		Title Insurance:		Residential Construction:				Online Services:		Residential Sales:	
Offices:		Property Insurance:		Land Development:	Y			Software/IT:		Specialty:	
Hotels/Motels:				Support Services:				Consulting:	Y		
Industrial/Warehouses:				Design/Engineering:							
Other:											

TYPES OF BUSINESS:

Real Estate Investment Trust
Apartments
Land Development
Garden Communities

BRANDS/DIVISIONS/AFFILIATES:

Archstone Communities
Archstone B.V.
Archstone Real Estate Advisory Services

CONTACTS:

Note: Officers with more than one job title may be intentionally listed here more than once.

R. Scot Sellers, CEO
Charles E. Mueller, COO
Daniel E. Amedro, Chief Mktg. Officer
Daniel E. Amedro, CIO
Al Neely, Chief Dev. Officer
R. Scot Sellers, Chmn.
Dana K. Hamilton, Managing Dir.-Archstone B.V./Pres.-European Oper.

Phone: 303-708-5959 **Fax:** 303-708-5999
Toll-Free: 877-272-4786
Address: 9200 E. Panorama Cir., Ste. 400, Englewood, CO 80112 US

GROWTH PLANS/SPECIAL FEATURES:

Archstone Trust (formerly Archstone-Smith Trust) is a real estate investment trust (REIT) focused on acquiring, developing and managing apartment properties. The company administers a portfolio concentrated in desirable neighborhoods in the Washington, D.C. metro area, Southern California, the San Francisco Bay area, the New York City metropolitan area, Boston, Southeast Florida, Chicago, Atlanta, Houston, Seattle and other major cities. The firm manages garden-style apartment complexes and high-rise apartments. All of the market areas in which the company owns property are characterized by three traits: high income levels; limited land available for housing development and a strong, diversified economic base. The firm also offers advisory services to lenders and investors through Archstone Real Estate Advisory Services including asset strategy services such as market analysis and valuations; development services consisting of entitlement and pre-construction services such as permits, estimates, design management and value engineering; construction management including bidding, contracting, cost/schedule control, reporting, risk management and construction completion; and asset management services consisting of marketing/leasing, property maintenance, asset repositioning, disposition analysis/execution and performance monitoring. Archstone foreign subsidiary, Archstone B.V. develops and manages apartment properties in Europe. In July 2009, the company opened an apartment community in Boston that prohibits smoking within the development.

The firm offers its employees health, disability, life, and AD&D insurance; housing discounts at the firm's apartment communities; paid holidays, vacation and sick time; flexible spending accounts, transportation benefits; an employee assistance program; tuition reimbursement; and discount programs on various services.

FINANCIALS:

Sales and profits are in thousands of dollars—add 000 to get the full amount. 2009 Note: Financial information for 2009 was not available for all companies at press time.

2009 Sales: $	2009 Profits: $	**U.S. Stock Ticker: Private**
2008 Sales: $	2008 Profits: $	**Int'l Ticker:** Int'l Exchange:
2007 Sales: $	2007 Profits: $	Employees:
2006 Sales: $1,133,586	2006 Profits: $727,434	Fiscal Year Ends: 12/31
2005 Sales: $833,633	2005 Profits: $616,172	Parent Company:

SALARIES/BENEFITS:

Pension Plan:	ESOP Stock Plan:	Profit Sharing:	Top Exec. Salary: $	Bonus: $
Savings Plan: Y	Stock Purch. Plan:		Second Exec. Salary: $	Bonus: $

OTHER THOUGHTS:

Apparent Women Officers or Directors: 1
Hot Spot for Advancement for Women/Minorities:

LOCATIONS: ("Y" = Yes)

West:	Southwest:	Midwest:	Southeast:	Northeast:	International:
Y	Y		Y	Y	Y

ARDEN REALTY INC

www.ardenrealty.com

Industry Group Code: 531120 **Ranks within this company's industry group:** Sales: Profits:

Properties:		Financial Services:		Construction/Development:		Investments:		Specialty Services:		Brokerage:	
Apartments:		Mortgages:		Commercial Construction:	Y	REIT:	Y	Property Management:	Y	Commercial Sales:	
Malls/Shopping:		Title Insurance:		Residential Construction:				Online Services:	Y	Residential Sales:	
Offices:	Y	Property Insurance:		Land Development:	Y			Software/IT:		Specialty:	
Hotels/Motels:				Support Services:	Y			Consulting:			
Industrial/Warehouses:				Design/Engineering:	Y						
Other:											

TYPES OF BUSINESS:

Real Estate Investment Trust
Office Properties
Property & Asset Management
Property Development
Construction
Consulting-Energy Efficiency

BRANDS/DIVISIONS/AFFILIATES:

GE Real Estate
Arden At Your Service
Concierge At Large, Inc.

GROWTH PLANS/SPECIAL FEATURES:

Arden Realty, Inc., a subsidiary of GE Real Estate, is a fully-integrated real estate investment trust (REIT) that leases, manages, constructs, develops and acquires commercial properties throughout the West Coast. GE Real Estate acquired Arden in 2006 for $4.8 billion as its West Coast growth platform. The company owns and manages 230 buildings (102 Office buildings and 128 industrial properties) covering 28 million square feet in Southern California, Northern California, Seattle, Portland, Phoenix, Chicago and Utah. The firm's Arden at Your Service program is a free online concierge service for its tenants offered in partnership with Concierge At Large, Inc., a provider of luxury and corporate concierge services. Arden additionally surveys its tenants twice a year and provides special discounts, events and energy solutions. The company's portfolio includes a number of EPA Energy Star labeled buildings as a result of its portfolio-wide energy conservation program.

CONTACTS: *Note: Officers with more than one job title may be intentionally listed here more than once.*

Joaquin de Monet, CEO
Joaquin de Monet, Pres.
David Stippich, CFO
Brooke Lauter, First VP-Mktg.
Noel Clark, CIO/First VP
Scott Lyle, Sr. VP-Oper.
Brooke Lauter, First VP-Corp. Comm.
Iris Almaraz, First VP-Acct.
Lee Halford, Managing Dir.-Industrial
Gary Hansel, VP-Portfolio Oper.
Eric Hasserjian, First VP-Northern Region
Paul King, First VP-Southern Region

Phone: 310-966-2600 **Fax:** 310-966-2699
Toll-Free:
Address: 11601 Wilshire Blvd., Ste. 400, Los Angeles, CA 90025 US

FINANCIALS: **Sales and profits are in thousands of dollars—add 000 to get the full amount. 2009 Note: Financial information for 2009 was not available for all companies at press time.**

2009 Sales: $ | 2009 Profits: $
2008 Sales: $ | 2008 Profits: $
2007 Sales: $ | 2007 Profits: $
2006 Sales: $ | 2006 Profits: $
2005 Sales: $441,903 | 2005 Profits: $65,499

U.S. Stock Ticker: Subsidiary
Int'l Ticker: Int'l Exchange:
Employees:
Fiscal Year Ends: 12/31
Parent Company: GE REAL ESTATE

SALARIES/BENEFITS:

Pension Plan: ESOP Stock Plan: Profit Sharing: Top Exec. Salary: $ Bonus: $
Savings Plan: Stock Purch. Plan: Second Exec. Salary: $ Bonus: $

OTHER THOUGHTS:

Apparent Women Officers or Directors: 2
Hot Spot for Advancement for Women/Minorities: Y

LOCATIONS: ("Y" = Yes)

West:	Southwest:	Midwest:	Southeast:	Northeast:	International:
Y	Y	Y			

ASSOCIATED ESTATES REALTY CORPORATION

www.associatedestates.com

Industry Group Code: 531110 **Ranks within this company's industry group:** Sales: 18 Profits: 9

Properties:		Financial Services:		Construction/Development:		Investments:		Specialty Services:		Brokerage:	
Apartments:	Y	Mortgages:		Commercial Construction:	Y	REIT:	Y	Property Management:	Y	Commercial Sales:	
Malls/Shopping:		Title Insurance:		Residential Construction:	Y			Online Services:		Residential Sales:	
Offices:		Property Insurance:		Land Development:				Software/IT:		Specialty:	
Hotels/Motels:				Support Services:				Consulting:			
Industrial/Warehouses:				Design/Engineering:							
Other:											

TYPES OF BUSINESS:

Real Estate Investment Trust
Apartment Communities
Multifamily
Construction Services

BRANDS/DIVISIONS/AFFILIATES:

CONTACTS:

Note: Officers with more than one job title may be intentionally listed here more than once.

Jeffrey I. Friedman, CEO
Jeffrey I. Friedman, Pres.
Lou Fatica, CFO/VP
Patrick Duffy, VP-Strategic Mktg.
Daniel E. Gold, VP-Human Resources
Martin A. Fishman, General Counsel/VP/Corp. Sec.
John T. Shannon, Sr. VP-Oper.
Lou Fatica, Treas.
Beth L. Stoll, VP-Oper.
Miria C. Rabideau, VP-Oper.
Michelle B. Creger, VP/Associate General Counsel
Jason A. Friedman, VP-Construction & Dev.
Jeffrey I. Friedman, Chmn.

Phone: 216-261-5000	**Fax:** 216-289-9600
Toll-Free: 800-440-2372	
Address: 1 AEC Pkwy., Richmond Heights, OH 44143-1467 US	

GROWTH PLANS/SPECIAL FEATURES:

Associated Estates Realty Corporation (AEC) is an equity real estate investment trust (REIT) engaged in property acquisition, advisory, development, construction, management, disposition, operation and ownership activities. The firm focuses on high barrier-to-entry markets in the Midwest, Mid-Atlantic and Southeastern U.S. The company also owns two taxable REIT subsidiaries that provide management and other services to AEC and third party owners. AEC's property portfolio includes 48 owned apartment communities containing 12,108 units in seven states; one apartment community that the firm manages for a third party owner, consisting of 258 units; and a 186-unit apartment community and a commercial property containing approximately 145,000 square feet that the company manages. Multifamily properties account for about 98% of the firm's total revenue. In addition, the company offers a number of construction and development services for commercial construction, including design and rehabilitation services for offices, warehouses, public and government-assisted projects; residential construction services for single family property design, development and rehabilitation; commercial and residential construction site development services; and tax credit preparation services. In January 2009, AEC completed the sale of a 96-unit property located in northeast Ohio. In July 2009, the firm completed the sale of a 468-unit apartment community in Pittsburgh, Pennsylvania.

AEC offers its employees health, dental, life and vision insurance, long-term disability coverage, tuition and educational reimbursement, medical and dependent care flexible spending accounts, a 401(k) plan, employee discounts and rent discounts for employees residing in AEC-owned apartment communities.

FINANCIALS:

Sales and profits are in thousands of dollars—add 000 to get the full amount. 2009 Note: Financial information for 2009 was not available for all companies at press time.

2009 Sales: $130,419	2009 Profits: $6,263	**U.S. Stock Ticker: AEC**
2008 Sales: $130,642	2008 Profits: $34,627	**Int'l Ticker:** Int'l Exchange:
2007 Sales: $126,980	2007 Profits: $10,165	Employees: 360
2006 Sales: $119,364	2006 Profits: $27,021	Fiscal Year Ends: 12/31
2005 Sales: $129,382	2005 Profits: $36,206	Parent Company:

SALARIES/BENEFITS:

Pension Plan:	ESOP Stock Plan:	Profit Sharing:	Top Exec. Salary: $487,479	Bonus: $690,758
Savings Plan: Y	Stock Purch. Plan:		Second Exec. Salary: $290,000	Bonus: $203,580

OTHER THOUGHTS:

Apparent Women Officers or Directors: 3
Hot Spot for Advancement for Women/Minorities: Y

LOCATIONS: ("Y" = Yes)

West:	Southwest:	Midwest:	Southeast:	Northeast:	International:
Y		Y	Y	Y	

ATRIA SENIOR LIVING GROUP

www.arvi.com

Industry Group Code: 623110 **Ranks within this company's industry group:** Sales: Profits:

Properties:		Financial Services:		Construction/Development:		Investments:		Specialty Services:		Brokerage:	
Apartments:		Mortgages:		Commercial Construction:		REIT:		Property Management:	Y	Commercial Sales:	
Malls/Shopping:		Title Insurance:		Residential Construction:				Online Services:		Residential Sales:	
Offices:		Property Insurance:		Land Development:				Software/IT:		Specialty:	
Hotels/Motels:				Support Services:				Consulting:			
Industrial/Warehouses:				Design/Engineering:							
Other:	Y										

TYPES OF BUSINESS:

Long-Term Health Care
Assisted Living Centers
Alzheimer Care

BRANDS/DIVISIONS/AFFILIATES:

Engage Life Program
Life Guidance Program
Independent Living Program
Assisted Living Program

CONTACTS:

Note: Officers with more than one job title may be intentionally listed here more than once.

John A. Moore, CEO
Julie Harding, COO
Mark Jesse, CFO
Doug Owens, CIO
Bryan Hudson, General Counsel/Sr. VP/Sec.

Phone: 502-779-4700 **Fax:** 502-779-4701
Toll-Free: 888-287-4201
Address: 401 S. 4th Ave., Ste. 1900, Louisville, KY 40202 US

GROWTH PLANS/SPECIAL FEATURES:

Atria Senior Living Group is one of the nation's largest operators of facilities providing assisted living services for the country's burgeoning senior population. The company currently operates more than 120 communities across 26 states, which provide housing and support services for over 13,000 seniors. Each program that Atria offers is tailored to the individual, with residents free to bring their own furnishings and even pets. Atria provides seniors with the following programs: The Independent Living program, which is a retirement lifestyle that frees seniors from the worries of home maintenance, encourages them to engage in activities and hobbies and allows them to choose their own degree of privacy or sociability; the Assisted Living program, which is available to help seniors with daily activities such as bathing, eating, dressing and medication management; the Life Guidance program, which is available at some communities to provide a separate and secure environment for seniors with Alzheimer's disease and other forms of memory impairment; and respite stay programs, which are tailored for seniors on a temporary basis for seasonal stays, hospital recovery or trial-period stays. Also, Atria's Engage Life program strives to provide residents with other interesting and meaningful activities, such as book clubs, exercise classes, gardening, arts and crafts, bingo and card games which are coordinated by Engage Life Directors that spend individual time with each resident to help them plan activities according to their interests.

FINANCIALS:

Sales and profits are in thousands of dollars—add 000 to get the full amount. 2009 Note: Financial information for 2009 was not available for all companies at press time.

2009 Sales: $ | 2009 Profits: $
2008 Sales: $ | 2008 Profits: $
2007 Sales: $ | 2007 Profits: $
2006 Sales: $ | 2006 Profits: $
2005 Sales: $ | 2005 Profits: $

U.S. Stock Ticker: Private
Int'l Ticker: Int'l Exchange:
Employees:
Fiscal Year Ends: 12/31
Parent Company:

SALARIES/BENEFITS:

Pension Plan: ESOP Stock Plan: Profit Sharing: Top Exec. Salary: $ Bonus: $
Savings Plan: Stock Purch. Plan: Second Exec. Salary: $ Bonus: $

OTHER THOUGHTS:

Apparent Women Officers or Directors:
Hot Spot for Advancement for Women/Minorities:

LOCATIONS: ("Y" = Yes)

West:	Southwest:	Midwest:	Southeast:	Northeast:	International:
Y	Y	Y	Y	Y	

AVALONBAY COMMUNITIES INC

www.avalonbay.com

Industry Group Code: 531110 **Ranks within this company's industry group:** Sales: 4 Profits: 3

Properties:		Financial Services:		Construction/Development:		Investments:		Specialty Services:		Brokerage:	
Apartments:	Y	Mortgages:		Commercial Construction:		REIT:	Y	Property Management:	Y	Commercial Sales:	
Malls/Shopping:		Title Insurance:		Residential Construction:	Y			Online Services:		Residential Sales:	
Offices:		Property Insurance:		Land Development:				Software/IT:		Specialty:	
Hotels/Motels:				Support Services:				Consulting:			
Industrial/Warehouses:				Design/Engineering:							
Other:	Y										

TYPES OF BUSINESS:

Real Estate Investment Trust
Apartment Complexes
Residential Construction

BRANDS/DIVISIONS/AFFILIATES:

CONTACTS:

Note: Officers with more than one job title may be intentionally listed here more than once.

Bryce Blair, CEO
Timothy J. Naughton, Pres.
Thomas J. Sargeant, CFO
Kevin Thompson, VP-Mktg.
Suzanne Jakstavich, VP-Human Resources
Tsippora Dingott, VP-Info. Svcs.
Mike Nootens, VP-Eng. & Maintenance
Edward M. Schulman, General Counsel/Sr. VP/Corp. Sec.
Leo S. Horey, Exec. VP-Oper.
Jonathan B. Cox, Sr. VP-Dev.
Joanne M. Lockridge, Sr. VP-Finance/Asst. Treas./Asst. Sec.
David W. Bellman, Sr. VP-Construction
Kevin P. O'Shea, Sr. VP-Investment Mgmt.
Lyn C. Lansdale, Sr. VP-Strategic Bus. Svcs.
Keri A. Shea, VP-Finance/Treas.
Bryce Blair, Chmn.

Phone: 703-329-6300 **Fax:** 703-329-1459
Toll-Free:
Address: 2900 Eisenhower Ave., Ste. 300, Alexandria, VA 22314 US

GROWTH PLANS/SPECIAL FEATURES:

AvalonBay Communities, Inc. is a real estate investment trust (REIT) engaged in the development, redevelopment, acquisition, ownership and operation of multifamily communities in high barrier-to-entry markets in the U.S. The firm's investments are divided into three segments: Established Communities; Other Stabilized Communities; and Development/Redevelopment Communities. Established Communities are generally operating communities that were owned and had stabilized occupancy and operating expenses as of the beginning of the prior year. Other Stabilized Communities are generally all other operating communities that have stabilized occupancy and operating expenses during the current year, but that had not achieved stabilization as of the beginning of the prior year. Development/ Redevelopment Communities consist of communities that are under construction, communities where substantial redevelopment is in progress or is planned to begin during the current year and communities under lease-up. The company's markets are located in the New England, New York/New Jersey metro, Midwest, Pacific Northwest and the Northern and Southern California regions of the U.S. The company owns or operates 164 apartment communities containing over 47,631 apartment units in 10 states and Washington, D.C. AvalonBay also holds development rights for 28 additional communities. Current properties are primarily garden-style apartment communities consisting of two- and three-story buildings in landscaped settings, as well as high-rise and mid-rise apartment communities. AvalonBay's primary markets are Boston, Massachusetts; Chicago, Illinois; San Jose and Los Angeles, California; Shelton, Connecticut; Virginia Beach, Virginia; Seattle, Washington; and the New York City and Washington, D.C. areas.

Employees are offered medical, dental, and vision insurance; disability benefits; accidental death and dismemberment (AD&D) insurance; flexible spending accounts; a health care account; a dependent care account; an employee assistance program; an employee stock purchase plan; relocation assistance; a 401(k) plan; professional development opportunities through AvalonBay University and tuition reimbursement; and a housing discount for employees who live at an AvalonBay community.

FINANCIALS:

Sales and profits are in thousands of dollars—add 000 to get the full amount. 2009 Note: Financial information for 2009 was not available for all companies at press time.

2009 Sales: $851,582	2009 Profits: $155,647
2008 Sales: $814,224	2008 Profits: $411,487
2007 Sales: $727,786	2007 Profits: $358,160
2006 Sales: $677,641	2006 Profits: $266,546
2005 Sales: $655,211	2005 Profits: $310,468

U.S. Stock Ticker: AVB
Int'l Ticker: Int'l Exchange:
Employees: 1,877
Fiscal Year Ends: 12/31
Parent Company:

SALARIES/BENEFITS:

Pension Plan:	ESOP Stock Plan: Y	Profit Sharing:	Top Exec. Salary: $855,036	Bonus: $965,389
Savings Plan: Y	Stock Purch. Plan:		Second Exec. Salary: $778,847	Bonus: $693,758

OTHER THOUGHTS:

Apparent Women Officers or Directors: 11
Hot Spot for Advancement for Women/Minorities: Y

LOCATIONS: ("Y" = Yes)

West:	Southwest:	Midwest:	Southeast:	Northeast:	International:
Y		Y		Y	

AVATAR HOLDINGS INC

www.avatarhomes.com

Industry Group Code: 2361 **Ranks within this company's industry group:** Sales: 20 Profits: 3

Properties:		Financial Services:		Construction/Development:		Investments:		Specialty Services:		Brokerage:	
Apartments:	Y	Mortgages:		Commercial Construction:	Y	REIT:		Property Management:	Y	Commercial Sales:	
Malls/Shopping:	Y	Title Insurance:	Y	Residential Construction:	Y			Online Services:		Residential Sales:	
Offices:	Y	Property Insurance:		Land Development:	Y			Software/IT:		Specialty:	
Hotels/Motels:				Support Services:	Y			Consulting:			
Industrial/Warehouses:				Design/Engineering:							
Other:	Y										

TYPES OF BUSINESS:

Property Development
Retirement Communities
Residential Properties
Commercial Properties
Home Building
Property Management
Utility Operations
Title Insurance Agency

BRANDS/DIVISIONS/AFFILIATES:

Avatar Properties, Inc.
Solivita
Poinciana
Villages of Rio Rico
Prominent Title Insurance Agency Inc

CONTACTS:

Note: Officers with more than one job title may be intentionally listed here more than once.

Gerald D. Kelfer, CEO
Michael Levy, COO/Exec. VP
Gerald D. Kelfer, Pres./Vice Chmn.
Randy L. Kotler, CFO/Exec. VP
Patricia Kimball Fletcher, General Counsel/Exec. VP
Randy L. Kotler, Treas.
Michael F. Levy, Exec. VP/COO-Avatar Properties, Inc.
Jonathan Fels, Pres., Avatar Properties, Inc.
Juanita I. Kerrigan, VP/Corp. Sec.
Joshua Lionel Nash, Chmn.

Phone: 305-442-7000 **Fax:** 305-443-3844
Toll-Free:
Address: 201 Alhambra Cir., Coral Gables, FL 33134 US

GROWTH PLANS/SPECIAL FEATURES:

Avatar Holdings, Inc. is a diverse real estate company engaged primarily in the development of lifestyle communities, including active adult and primary residential communities in Florida and Arizona. It handles development through subsidiary Avatar Properties, Inc. Avatar has ventured into areas other than development, including property management, home building, commercial/industrial properties and various activities in Florida and Arizona. For example, the company operates a small shopping center in Rio Rico, Arizona; a 38-story high-rise condominium joint venture in Hollywood, Florida; and a title insurance agency. Avatar's chief retirement community, Solivita, is located within its master-planned community of Poinciana in central Florida and encompasses approximately 126,000 square feet of recreation and service facilities, including a fitness center, a golf clubhouse, restaurants, arts and crafts room, a newsstand and meeting and theater facilities. The property also features two 18-hole golf courses and other sporting and games facilities, including a softball field and five tennis courts. The community was designed to accommodate in excess of 4,000 homes. The Poinciana community is large enough to require 14 primary and secondary schools, its own business and shopping district and a planned hospital. Overall, Avatar owns over 17,000 acres of developed, partially developed or developable residential, commercial and industrial property. Within Florida and Arizona, Avatar also owns more than 15,000 acres of preserves, wetlands, open space and other areas that are not developable, but which the company considers potentially valuable for preservation or conservation purposes. In September 2009, the company acquired 87 completed and partially completed homes, 267 developed lots, 364 partially developed lots and approximately 400 undeveloped master planned lots in a residential community located at Seasons at Tradition in St. Lucie County, Florida. In December 2009, the company acquired 86 developed lots located at Estancias del Corazon in Pima County, Arizona.

FINANCIALS:

Sales and profits are in thousands of dollars—add 000 to get the full amount. 2009 Note: Financial information for 2009 was not available for all companies at press time.

2009 Sales: $73,501	2009 Profits: $-28,983
2008 Sales: $110,366	2008 Profits: $-109,876
2007 Sales: $291,832	2007 Profits: $20,997
2006 Sales: $835,079	2006 Profits: $174,726
2005 Sales: $516,848	2005 Profits: $63,127

U.S. Stock Ticker: AVTR
Int'l Ticker: Int'l Exchange:
Employees: 233
Fiscal Year Ends: 12/31
Parent Company:

SALARIES/BENEFITS:

Pension Plan:	ESOP Stock Plan:	Profit Sharing:	Top Exec. Salary: $500,000	Bonus: $500,000
Savings Plan: Y	Stock Purch. Plan:		Second Exec. Salary: $500,000	Bonus: $400,000

OTHER THOUGHTS:

Apparent Women Officers or Directors: 3
Hot Spot for Advancement for Women/Minorities: Y

LOCATIONS: ("Y" = Yes)

West:	Southwest:	Midwest:	Southeast:	Northeast:	International:
	Y		Y		

BALFOUR BEATTY PLC

www.balfourbeatty.com

Industry Group Code: 237 **Ranks within this company's industry group:** Sales: 11 Profits: 11

Properties:		Financial Services:		Construction/Development:		Investments:		Specialty Services:		Brokerage:	
Apartments:		Mortgages:		Commercial Construction:	Y	REIT:		Property Management:		Commercial Sales:	
Malls/Shopping:		Title Insurance:		Residential Construction:				Online Services:		Residential Sales:	
Offices:		Property Insurance:		Land Development:				Software/IT:		Specialty:	
Hotels/Motels:				Support Services:	Y			Consulting:			
Industrial/Warehouses:				Design/Engineering:							
Other:											

TYPES OF BUSINESS:

Heavy Construction
Engineering Services
Railway Services
Property Management
Utility & Roadway Infrastructure Management

BRANDS/DIVISIONS/AFFILIATES:

Heery International
Parsons Brinckerhoff Inc
Balfour Beatty Rail, Inc.
Balfour Beatty Capital Projects
Dean & Dyball
Blackpool International Airport
Colledge Trundle and Hall Limited
Schreck-Mieves

CONTACTS: *Note: Officers with more than one job title may be intentionally listed here more than once.*

Ian Tyler, CEO
Andrew McNaughton, COO
Paul Raby, Dir.-Human Resources
Brian Osborne, Managing Dir.-Civil & Ground Eng.
Chris Vaughan, General Counsel/Corp. Sec.
Peter Zinkin, Dir.-Planning & Dev.
Duncan Magrath, Dir.-Finance
Anthony Rabin, Deputy CEO
Manfred Leger, Managing Dir.-Railroad Bus.
Brian Osborne, Managing Dir.-Utilities, Road & Facilities Mgmt.
Mike Peasland, Managing Dir.-UK Building Construction & Building
Steve Marshall, Chmn.

Phone: 44-20-7216-6800	**Fax:** 44-20-7216-6950
Toll-Free:	
Address: 130 Wilton Rd., London, SW1V 1LQ UK	

GROWTH PLANS/SPECIAL FEATURES:

Balfour Beatty plc provides engineering, construction and financial services for rail, road, power and building projects worldwide. It is one of the largest fixed rail infrastructure contracting companies in the world. Balfour divides its business into four categories: professional services, construction services, support services and infrastructure investments. The professional services division provides program and project management, architectural services, project design, technical services, planning and consultancy. Construction services include building design; construction management; refurbishment and fit-out; and mechanical and electrical services. The firm has an established presence in the U.K. and U.S., through its subsidiaries, and is expanding its business in South Africa and the Middle East. Balfour Beatty provides ongoing operation and maintenance of assets after construction and offers business services outsourcing through its support services division. The division encompasses the company's utilities, facilities management, rail renewals and highway management activities. It conducts business mainly through long-term contracts, ranging from 5-30 years. The infrastructure investments segment is a leader in the public private partnership (PPP) contracts in the U.K. with 31 concessions, primarily in the education, health and roads/street lighting sectors. Balfour Beatty also has a portfolio of long-term military accommodation PPP concessions in the U.S. In October 2009, the company completed its acquisition of Parsons Brinckerhoff, Inc., a leader in professional services, bringing in Parson's 100 offices and 12,500 employees. In December 2009, the firm completed its acquisition of SpawMaxwell Company, a leading Texas-based interior construction contractor.

FINANCIALS: **Sales and profits are in thousands of dollars—add 000 to get the full amount. 2009 Note: Financial information for 2009 was not available for all companies at press time.**

2009 Sales: $13,771,300	2009 Profits: $327,600	**U.S. Stock Ticker:**
2008 Sales: $12,658,800	2008 Profits: $396,460	**Int'l Ticker: BBY** Int'l Exchange: London-LSE
2007 Sales: $9,494,480	2007 Profits: $230,530	Employees: 41,000
2006 Sales: $8,936,980	2006 Profits: $497,270	Fiscal Year Ends: 12/31
2005 Sales: $7,642,340	2005 Profits: $587,570	Parent Company:

SALARIES/BENEFITS:

Pension Plan:	ESOP Stock Plan:	Profit Sharing:	Top Exec. Salary: $	Bonus: $
Savings Plan:	Stock Purch. Plan:		Second Exec. Salary: $	Bonus: $

OTHER THOUGHTS:

Apparent Women Officers or Directors:
Hot Spot for Advancement for Women/Minorities:

LOCATIONS: ("Y" = Yes)

West:	Southwest:	Midwest:	Southeast:	Northeast:	International:
	Y		Y		Y

BANK OF AMERICA HOME LOANS

www.countrywide.com

Industry Group Code: 522310 **Ranks within this company's industry group:** Sales: Profits:

Properties:		Financial Services:		Construction/Development:		Investments:		Specialty Services:		Brokerage:	
Apartments:		Mortgages:	Y	Commercial Construction:		REIT:		Property Management:		Commercial Sales:	
Malls/Shopping:		Title Insurance:		Residential Construction:				Online Services:	Y	Residential Sales:	
Offices:		Property Insurance:		Land Development:				Software/IT:		Specialty:	
Hotels/Motels:				Support Services:				Consulting:			
Industrial/Warehouses:				Design/Engineering:							
Other:											

TYPES OF BUSINESS:

Mortgage Banking
Banking
Insurance

BRANDS/DIVISIONS/AFFILIATES:

Bank of America Corp
Countrywide Financial Corp

CONTACTS:

Note: Officers with more than one job title may be intentionally listed here more than once.

Barbara Desoer, Pres., Bank of America Mortgage, Home Equity & Insurance Svcs.
Anne D. McCallion, CFO

Phone: 818-225-3000 **Fax:**
Toll-Free: 800-283-8875
Address: 4500 Park Granada, Calabasas, CA 91302 US

GROWTH PLANS/SPECIAL FEATURES:

Bank of America Home Loans (BOAHL), formerly Countrywide Financial Corp, a wholly-owned subsidiary of Bank of America, is engaged in mortgage lending and other real estate finance-related businesses, including mortgage banking; banking and mortgage warehouse lending; securities; and insurance underwriting. The company operates in three segments: home loans, banking and insurance. Home loan products include home loans, refinancing, home equity lines of credit, construction loans and reverse mortgages. Through the banking division, BOAHL takes deposits and invests in mortgage loans and home equity lines of credit, sourced primarily through its mortgage banking operation as well as through purchases from non-affiliates. The segment also offers short-term secured financing to mortgage lenders. Banking products include certificates of deposit, money market accounts, savings accounts and credit cards. The insurance division offers property, casualty, life and disability insurance as an underwriter and as an insurance agency. Insurance products include homeowners/condo, auto, home warranty, renters, life, commercial and other products. Countrywide was a major influence in the creation of subprime mortgages. After massive losses suffered in 2007, the firm agreed to be acquired by Bank of America. In July 2008, Bank of America completed the acquisition of the company for approximately $4 billion. Following the acquisition, the firm ceased offering subprime mortgages and certain other non-traditional mortgages.

FINANCIALS:

Sales and profits are in thousands of dollars—add 000 to get the full amount. 2009 Note: Financial information for 2009 was not available for all companies at press time.

2009 Sales: $
2008 Sales: $
2007 Sales: $6,061,437
2006 Sales: $11,417,128
2005 Sales: $10,016,708

2009 Profits: $
2008 Profits: $
2007 Profits: $-703,538
2006 Profits: $2,674,846
2005 Profits: $2,528,090

U.S. Stock Ticker: Subsidiary
Int'l Ticker: Int'l Exchange:
Employees:
Fiscal Year Ends: 12/31
Parent Company: BANK OF AMERICA CORP

SALARIES/BENEFITS:

Pension Plan: ESOP Stock Plan: Profit Sharing: Top Exec. Salary: $ Bonus: $
Savings Plan: Y Stock Purch. Plan: Second Exec. Salary: $ Bonus: $

OTHER THOUGHTS:

Apparent Women Officers or Directors: 1
Hot Spot for Advancement for Women/Minorities:

LOCATIONS: ("Y" = Yes)

West:	Southwest:	Midwest:	Southeast:	Northeast:	International:
Y	Y	Y	Y	Y	Y

BANYAN TREE HOTELS & RESORTS

www.banyantree.com

Industry Group Code: 721110 **Ranks within this company's industry group:** Sales: Profits:

Properties:		Financial Services:		Construction/Development:		Investments:		Specialty Services:		Brokerage:	
Apartments:		Mortgages:		Commercial Construction:		REIT:		Property Management:		Commercial Sales:	Y
Malls/Shopping:	Y	Title Insurance:		Residential Construction:				Online Services:		Residential Sales:	
Offices:		Property Insurance:		Land Development:				Software/IT:		Specialty:	
Hotels/Motels:	Y			Support Services:				Consulting:			
Industrial/Warehouses:				Design/Engineering:	Y						
Other:	Y										

TYPES OF BUSINESS:

Hotels & Resorts
Spas

BRANDS/DIVISIONS/AFFILIATES:

Laguna Resorts & Hotels Public Company Limited
Architrave Design & Project Services Pte Ltd
Banyan Tree Hotels
Angsana Hotels

CONTACTS: *Note: Officers with more than one job title may be intentionally listed here more than once.*

Ariel P. Vera, Group Managing Dir.
Eddy See Hock Lye, CFO
Arthur Kiong Kim Hock, Managing Dir.-Sales & Mktg.
Foong Pohmun, VP-People Dev.
Michael Lee, CIO
Bernold Olaf Schroeder, Managing Dir.-Hotel Oper.
Paul Chong, VP-Bus. Dev.
Hokan Limin, VP-Hotel Finance
Chiang See Ngoh Claire, Managing Dir.-Retail Oper.
Ho KwonCjan, Managing Dir.-Design Oper.
Tee Hwee Liang, Sr. VP-China Desk
Sachiko Shiina, VP-Japan
Ho KwonPing, Exec. Chmn.

Phone: 65-6849-5888	**Fax:** 65-6462-2463
Toll-Free: 800-591-0439	
Address: 211 Upper Bukit Timah Rd., Singapore, 588182 Singapore	

GROWTH PLANS/SPECIAL FEATURES:

Banyan Tree Hotels & Resorts is a Singapore-based hospitality company that develops, manages, operates and invests in resorts, hotels, spas and property. The company's portfolio includes more than 27 hotels and resorts, 67 spas, 71 retail galleries and two golf clubs across 23 countries, and the Banyan Tree and Angsana brand names. Banyan Tree's operations are split into seven segments: Hotel investments; hotel management; hotel residences; spa operations; property sales; design services; and gallery operations. The majority of the firm's 2009 revenue, about 60%, came from investments in luxury hotels that are managed by third-party operators. Banyan Tree's hotel management segment, which manages properties owned by other companies, accounted for about 8% of revenues. The hotel residences segment accounted for roughly 7% of revenues, and includes Banyan Tree Residences properties sold in Asia and Mexico. About 9% of revenue came from the spa operations segment, which manages spas located within Banyan Tree's properties and other hotels. The property sales segment, which is mostly conducted through the firm's Laguna Resorts & Hotels subsidiary, made up 8% of the company's 2009 revenues. Banyan Tree's in-house design division, Architrave, conducts designing services as well as operates the firm's golf properties, and accounted for 7% of the company's revenue. Finally, the gallery operations branch offers works of art and other retail sales, and accounted for 2% of 2009 revenue. The majority of Banyan Tree's properties and operations are located in the Asia Pacific region and Mexico, with destinations in Bahrain, China, Indonesia, Korea, Maldives, Seychelles, Thailand and the United Arab Emirates. In 2010, the firm plans to open hotels or spas in Mexico, China, South Korea, Thailand, India, Portugal and Kenya. In October 2009, the company announced a joint venture with Jiuzhaigou HonYee Investment Company Limited to develop a hotel in Jiuzhaigou, China.

FINANCIALS: **Sales and profits are in thousands of dollars—add 000 to get the full amount. 2009 Note: Financial information for 2009 was not available for all companies at press time.**

2009 Sales: $	2009 Profits: $	**U.S. Stock Ticker:**
2008 Sales: $	2008 Profits: $	**Int'l Ticker:** Int'l Exchange:
2007 Sales: $	2007 Profits: $	Employees:
2006 Sales: $	2006 Profits: $	Fiscal Year Ends: 12/31
2005 Sales: $	2005 Profits: $	Parent Company:

SALARIES/BENEFITS:

Pension Plan:	ESOP Stock Plan:	Profit Sharing:	Top Exec. Salary: $	Bonus: $
Savings Plan:	Stock Purch. Plan:		Second Exec. Salary: $	Bonus: $

OTHER THOUGHTS:

Apparent Women Officers or Directors:
Hot Spot for Advancement for Women/Minorities:

LOCATIONS: ("Y" = Yes)

West:	Southwest:	Midwest:	Southeast:	Northeast:	International:
					Y

BARCELO CRESTLINE CORPORATION

www.barcelocrestline.com

Industry Group Code: 721110 **Ranks within this company's industry group:** Sales: Profits:

Properties:		Financial Services:		Construction/Development:		Investments:		Specialty Services:		Brokerage:	
Apartments:		Mortgages:		Commercial Construction:		REIT:		Property Management:	Y	Commercial Sales:	
Malls/Shopping:		Title Insurance:		Residential Construction:				Online Services:		Residential Sales:	
Offices:		Property Insurance:		Land Development:				Software/IT:		Specialty:	
Hotels/Motels:	Y			Support Services:				Consulting:			
Industrial/Warehouses:				Design/Engineering:							
Other:											

TYPES OF BUSINESS:

Hotels

BRANDS/DIVISIONS/AFFILIATES:

Barcelo Corporacion Empresarial SA
Crestline Hotels & Resorts, Inc.

CONTACTS:

Note: Officers with more than one job title may be intentionally listed here more than once.

James Carroll, COO
Ed Hoganson, Sr. VP-Finance
Deanne Johnson-Anderson, VP-Human Resources
Jerry Galindo, VP-IT
Elizabeth Lieberman, General Counsel/Exec. VP
Bruce Nelker, Sr. VP-Oper.
Ed Hoganson, Sr. VP-Dev.
Keith F. Hansen, VP-Hotel Acct. & Finance
Shaun Kirby, Sr. VP-Oper.
Al Wiles, Sr. VP-Oper.
Joy Jolin, Regional VP-Oper.
Terri Ryan, Regional VP-Oper.

Phone: 571-529-6000	**Fax:** 571-529-6050
Toll-Free:	
Address: 3950 University Dr., Fairfax, VA 22030 US	

GROWTH PLANS/SPECIAL FEATURES:

Barcelo Crestline Corporation is a leading independent hospitality management company. It is a privately-owned subsidiary of Barcelo Corporacion Empresarial S.A. (based in Palma de Mallorca, Spain). Through its operating company, wholly-owned subsidiary Crestline Hotels & Resorts, Inc. (Crestline), the company manages properties including 65 hotels, resorts and conference and convention centers with nearly 13,500 rooms in 13 states and Washington, D.C. Crestline operates 14 independent hotels, with the remainder falling under brands such as Hilton, Hilton Garden Inn, Homewood Suites, Sheraton, Renaissance, Crowne Plaza, Four Points, Residence Inn, Marriott and Courtyard by Marriott. Crestline typically seeks to acquire 250-750 room hotels in the U.S., Caribbean or Mexico. It generally acquires boutique or premium branded limited-service hotels; or first class, full service hotels located in either suburban or urban markets. In December 2009, the firm opened the 410- room Renaissance Palm Springs Hotel, formerly the Wyndham Palm Springs, in Palm Springs California.

The firm offers its employees medical, vision and dental insurance; life and disability insurance; a 401(k) plan; and hotel discounts.

FINANCIALS:

Sales and profits are in thousands of dollars—add 000 to get the full amount. 2009 Note: Financial information for 2009 was not available for all companies at press time.

2009 Sales: $
2008 Sales: $
2007 Sales: $88,100
2006 Sales: $
2005 Sales: $

2009 Profits: $
2008 Profits: $
2007 Profits: $
2006 Profits: $
2005 Profits: $

U.S. Stock Ticker: Subsidiary
Int'l Ticker: Int'l Exchange:
Employees:
Fiscal Year Ends: 12/31
Parent Company: BARCELO CORPORATION EMPRESARIAL SA

SALARIES/BENEFITS:

Pension Plan: ESOP Stock Plan: Profit Sharing: Top Exec. Salary: $ Bonus: $
Savings Plan: Y Stock Purch. Plan: Second Exec. Salary: $ Bonus: $

OTHER THOUGHTS:

Apparent Women Officers or Directors: 6
Hot Spot for Advancement for Women/Minorities: Y

LOCATIONS: ("Y" = Yes)

West:	Southwest:	Midwest:	Southeast:	Northeast:	International:
Y	Y	Y	Y	Y	

BEAZER HOMES USA INC

www.beazer.com

Industry Group Code: 2361 **Ranks within this company's industry group:** Sales: 11 Profits: 13

Properties:		Financial Services:		Construction/Development:		Investments:		Specialty Services:		Brokerage:	
Apartments:		Mortgages:	Y	Commercial Construction:		REIT:		Property Management:		Commercial Sales:	
Malls/Shopping:		Title Insurance:		Residential Construction:	Y			Online Services:		Residential Sales:	Y
Offices:		Property Insurance:		Land Development:				Software/IT:		Specialty:	
Hotels/Motels:				Support Services:				Consulting:			
Industrial/Warehouses:				Design/Engineering:							
Other:											

TYPES OF BUSINESS:

Homebuilding
Home Design

BRANDS/DIVISIONS/AFFILIATES:

Beazer Mortgage Corporation
ZC Sterling

CONTACTS:

Note: Officers with more than one job title may be intentionally listed here more than once.

Ian J. McCarthy, CEO
Michael H. Furlow, COO/Exec. VP
Ian J. McCarthy, Pres.
Allan P. Merrill, CFO/Exec. VP
Kathi James, Chief Mktg. Officer/Sr. VP
Fred Fratto, Sr. VP-Human Resources
Cindy B. Tierney, CIO/Sr. VP
Kenneth Khoury, General Counsel/Exec. VP
Robert Salomon, Chief Acct. Officer/Sr. VP
Peggy J. Caldwell, Deputy General Counsel/Sr. VP
Brian C. Beazer, Chmn.

Phone: 770-829-3700	**Fax:** 770-481-2808
Toll-Free:	
Address: 1000 Abernathy Rd., Ste. 1200, Atlanta, GA 30328 US	

GROWTH PLANS/SPECIAL FEATURES:

Beazer Homes USA, Inc., a top national homebuilder, designs, sells and builds single-family and multi-family homes with markets in Arizona, California, Nevada, New Mexico, Texas, Maryland/Delaware, New Jersey/Pennsylvania, Virginia, North Carolina, Indiana, Tennessee, Florida, Georgia and South Carolina. The company provides its services through three homebuilding segments and one financial services segment. Beazer's homes are designed primarily for first-time buyers and are designed at various price points to appeal to a wide demographic. They are also generally offered for sale in advance of their construction. Most homes are built from standardized plans, which help facilitate a greater profit margin through faster construction times and standard materials. The company does offer some measure of customization in the form of flooring, cabinetry, countertop and wall covering options. The average sales price of a Beazer home was about $230,900 during 2009. Beazer's business strategy involves geographically diverse project development to minimize losses caused by local economic downturns and a localized management scheme based upon local market knowledge and expertise. Part of this business strategy is the company's eSmart initiative. The eSmart homes are engineered to be energy-efficient and less expensive. The company also seeks to make energy saving, water conservation and improved air quality standard components in all homes. The company's home warranties are issued, administered and insured by independent third parties. The company is a national sponsor of HomeAid America, a nonprofit national program that provides housing for the temporarily homeless.

FINANCIALS:

Sales and profits are in thousands of dollars—add 000 to get the full amount. 2009 Note: Financial information for 2009 was not available for all companies at press time.

2009 Sales: $1,005,212	2009 Profits: $-189,383	**U.S. Stock Ticker: BZH**
2008 Sales: $1,813,513	2008 Profits: $-951,912	**Int'l Ticker:** Int'l Exchange:
2007 Sales: $3,036,988	2007 Profits: $-411,000	Employees: 901
2006 Sales: $5,321,702	2006 Profits: $388,761	Fiscal Year Ends: 9/30
2005 Sales: $4,995,353	2005 Profits: $262,524	Parent Company:

SALARIES/BENEFITS:

Pension Plan:	ESOP Stock Plan:	Profit Sharing:	Top Exec. Salary: $1,200,000	Bonus: $
Savings Plan:	Stock Purch. Plan:		Second Exec. Salary: $760,272	Bonus: $

OTHER THOUGHTS:

Apparent Women Officers or Directors: 7
Hot Spot for Advancement for Women/Minorities: Y

LOCATIONS: ("Y" = Yes)

West:	Southwest:	Midwest:	Southeast:	Northeast:	International:
Y	Y	Y	Y	Y	

BECHTEL GROUP INC

www.bechtel.com

Industry Group Code: 237 **Ranks within this company's industry group:** Sales: 3 Profits:

Properties:		Financial Services:		Construction/Development:		Investments:		Specialty Services:		Brokerage:	
Apartments:		Mortgages:		Commercial Construction:	Y	REIT:		Property Management:		Commercial Sales:	
Malls/Shopping:		Title Insurance:		Residential Construction:				Online Services:		Residential Sales:	
Offices:		Property Insurance:		Land Development:	Y			Software/IT:		Specialty:	
Hotels/Motels:				Support Services:	Y			Consulting:			
Industrial/Warehouses:				Design/Engineering:	Y						
Other:											

TYPES OF BUSINESS:

Engineering, Construction & Project Management Services
Civic Engineering
Outsourcing
Financial Services
Atomic Propulsion Systems Engineering
Airport Construction
Electric Power Plant Construction
Nuclear Power Plant Construction

BRANDS/DIVISIONS/AFFILIATES:

CONTACTS:

Note: Officers with more than one job title may be intentionally listed here more than once.

Riley P. Bechtel, CEO
Bill Dudley, COO
Bill Dudley, Pres.
Peter Dawson, CFO
John MacDonald, Dir.-Human Resources
Geir Ramleth, Dir.-Info. Systems
Geir Ramleth, Dir.-Tech.
Michael Bailey, General Counsel
Jim Jackson, Pres., Oil, Gas & Chemicals
Mike Adams, Pres., Civil
Scott Ogilvie, Pres., Bechtel Systems & Infrastructure, Inc.
Andy Greig, Pres., Mining & Metals
Riley P. Bechtel, Chmn.
David Hammerle, Mgr.-Contracts & Procurement

Phone: 415-768-1234	**Fax:** 415-768-9038
Toll-Free:	
Address: 50 Beale St., San Francisco, CA 94105-1895 US	

GROWTH PLANS/SPECIAL FEATURES:

Bechtel Group, Inc., founded in 1906 by Warren A. Bechtel, is one of the world's largest engineering companies. The privately-owned firm offers engineering, construction and project management services, with a broad project portfolio including road and rail systems, airports and seaports, nuclear power plants, petrochemical facilities, mines, defense and aerospace facilities, environmental cleanup projects, telecommunication networks, pipelines and oil fields development. The firm has participated in such notable endeavors as the construction of the Hoover Dam, the creation of the Bay Area Rapid Transit system in San Francisco, the massive James Bay Hydroelectric Project in Quebec and the quelling of oil field fires in Kuwait following the Persian Gulf War. Bechtel also constructed the Trans-Alaska Oil Pipeline, covering 800 miles between the Prudhoe Bay oil field and Valdez. Bechtel has also been contracted to develop the New Doha International Airport in Qatar, Iraq. An 11-year, multi-billion-dollar project, the new airport will be designed to accommodate six Airbus A380-800's, the largest passenger aircraft in the world. In December 2009, Bechtel formed a strategic alliance with Calera Corporation to jointly build facilities using carbon capture technology that reduces emissions.

FINANCIALS:

Sales and profits are in thousands of dollars—add 000 to get the full amount. 2009 Note: Financial information for 2009 was not available for all companies at press time.

2009 Sales: $30,800,000	2009 Profits: $	**U.S. Stock Ticker: Private**
2008 Sales: $31,400,000	2008 Profits: $	**Int'l Ticker:** Int'l Exchange:
2007 Sales: $27,000,000	2007 Profits: $	Employees: 44,000
2006 Sales: $20,500,000	2006 Profits: $	Fiscal Year Ends: 12/31
2005 Sales: $18,600,000	2005 Profits: $	Parent Company:

SALARIES/BENEFITS:

Pension Plan:	ESOP Stock Plan:	Profit Sharing:	Top Exec. Salary: $	Bonus: $
Savings Plan:	Stock Purch. Plan:		Second Exec. Salary: $	Bonus: $

OTHER THOUGHTS:

Apparent Women Officers or Directors: 4
Hot Spot for Advancement for Women/Minorities: Y

LOCATIONS: ("Y" = Yes)

West:	Southwest:	Midwest:	Southeast:	Northeast:	International:
Y	Y	Y	Y	Y	Y

BEST WESTERN INTERNATIONAL INC

www.bestwestern.com

Industry Group Code: 721110 **Ranks within this company's industry group:** Sales: 26 Profits: 21

Properties:		Financial Services:		Construction/Development:		Investments:		Specialty Services:		Brokerage:	
Apartments:		Mortgages:		Commercial Construction:		REIT:		Property Management:		Commercial Sales:	
Malls/Shopping:		Title Insurance:		Residential Construction:				Online Services:		Residential Sales:	
Offices:		Property Insurance:		Land Development:				Software/IT:		Specialty:	
Hotels/Motels:	Y			Support Services:				Consulting:			
Industrial/Warehouses:				Design/Engineering:							
Other:											

TYPES OF BUSINESS:

Hotels

BRANDS/DIVISIONS/AFFILIATES:

Gold Crown Club International
Travel Card

CONTACTS:

Note: Officers with more than one job title may be intentionally listed here more than once.

David T. Kong, CEO
David T. Kong, Pres.
Mark Straszynski, CFO
Dorothy Dowling, Sr. VP-Mktg. & Sales
Barbara Bras, VP-Human Resources
Scott Gibson, CIO/Sr. VP-Dist.
Larry Cuculic, General Counsel/VP
David Velasquez, VP-Info. Systems Oper.
Mark Williams, VP-North American Dev.
Julie Montmaneix, Treas./Sec.
Glenn De Souza, VP-Int'l Oper. Asia
Renee Ryan, VP-Mktg.
Ron Pohl, Sr. VP-Brand Mgmt. & Member Svcs.
Beth Campbell, Chmn.
Suzi Y. MacDonald, VP-Int'l Oper.
Rich Bennett, VP-Supply & Design

Phone: 602-957-4200	**Fax:** 602-957-5641
Toll-Free:	
Address: 6201 N. 24th Pkwy., Phoenix, AZ 85016 US	

GROWTH PLANS/SPECIAL FEATURES:

Best Western International, Inc. is one of the largest lodging companies in the world, providing more than 308,237 rooms in 80 countries and territories worldwide, with over 4,000 independently owned and operated hotels. Its unique organizational structure allows individual hotels to maintain local control and autonomy while reaping the benefits of a large international lodging firm, such as a global reservations system. The company, which is organized as a nonprofit association of member hotels, continues to grow as it establishes new hotels in the U.S. and across the world. Its international expansion includes hotels in Europe, South America and other regions of the world, with the newest additions in Suriname and Malaysia. In addition, Best Western has a partnership with MasterCard that provides cardholders with special offers and benefits, as well as its own benefits program, Best Western Rewards. Some other customer benefit programs such as Speed Rewards, for race fans, and Ride Rewards for Harley-Davidson owners, offer discounted room rates, free room upgrades, meal certificates and other promotional offerings. Regular amenities include breakfast services, data port connections, free local calls and a variety of other services that are already offered in many locations and are currently being extended to other facilities. In the past few years, Best Western has begun to offer the Travel Card, a gift card that can be filled with U.S. or Canadian dollars, euros, or British pounds. Additionally, all Best Western hotels in the U.S., Canada and the Caribbean offer free high-speed Internet access to guests. In November 2009, Best Western Germany announced plans to open 200 new hotels in Germany in 2010.

FINANCIALS:

Sales and profits are in thousands of dollars—add 000 to get the full amount. 2009 Note: Financial information for 2009 was not available for all companies at press time.

2009 Sales: $	2009 Profits: $	**U.S. Stock Ticker: Nonprofit**
2008 Sales: $231,638	2008 Profits: $-1,657	**Int'l Ticker:** Int'l Exchange:
2007 Sales: $220,911	2007 Profits: $-2,983	Employees:
2006 Sales: $205,539	2006 Profits: $4,052	Fiscal Year Ends: 11/30
2005 Sales: $198,842	2005 Profits: $-2,125	Parent Company:

SALARIES/BENEFITS:

Pension Plan:	ESOP Stock Plan:	Profit Sharing:	Top Exec. Salary: $	Bonus: $
Savings Plan: Y	Stock Purch. Plan:		Second Exec. Salary: $	Bonus: $

OTHER THOUGHTS:

Apparent Women Officers or Directors: 7
Hot Spot for Advancement for Women/Minorities: Y

LOCATIONS: ("Y" = Yes)

West:	Southwest:	Midwest:	Southeast:	Northeast:	International:
Y	Y	Y	Y	Y	Y

BLACK & VEATCH HOLDING COMPANY

www.bv.com

Industry Group Code: 237 **Ranks within this company's industry group:** Sales: 25 Profits:

Properties:	Financial Services:	Construction/Development:		Investments:	Specialty Services:	Brokerage:
Apartments:	Mortgages:	Commercial Construction:	Y	REIT:	Property Management:	Commercial Sales:
Malls/Shopping:	Title Insurance:	Residential Construction:			Online Services:	Residential Sales:
Offices:	Property Insurance:	Land Development:			Software/IT:	Specialty:
Hotels/Motels:		Support Services:			Consulting:	
Industrial/Warehouses:		Design/Engineering:	Y			
Other:						

TYPES OF BUSINESS:

Construction, Heavy & Civil Engineering
Infrastructure & Energy Services
Environmental & Hydrologic Engineering
Consulting Services
IT Services
Power Plant Engineering and Construction
LNG and Gas Processing Plant Engineering

BRANDS/DIVISIONS/AFFILIATES:

BV Solutions Group, Inc.
Fortegra
B&V China
B&V Corporation
B&V Construction, Inc.
B&V Europe
BV Solutions Group, Inc.
B&V International Co.

CONTACTS: *Note: Officers with more than one job title may be intentionally listed here more than once.*

Leonard C. Rodman, CEO
Leonard C. Rodman, Pres.
Karen L. Daniel, CFO
John G. Voeller, CTO
Howard G. Withey, Chief Admin. Officer
Daniel W. McCarthy, Pres./CEO-B&V Water
Leonard C. Rodman, Chmn.

Phone: 913-458-2000	**Fax:** 913-458-2934
Toll-Free:	
Address: 11401 Lamar Ave., Overland Park, KS 66211 US	

GROWTH PLANS/SPECIAL FEATURES:

Black & Veatch Holding Company (B&V) is a leading engineering, consulting and construction company specializing in infrastructure development for the energy, water and telecommunications, federal, management consulting and environmental markets. The company is employee-owned and operates over 100 offices worldwide. B&V provides its clients with conceptual and preliminary engineering services, engineering design, procurement, construction, financial management, asset management, information technology, environmental, security design and consulting, and management consulting services. The firm's energy market services include energy engineering and construction services for cogeneration, coal, nuclear and renewable energy sources; energy services, such as asset optimization, strategic market analysis, asset valuation and asset addition; gas, oil and chemical construction and consulting services for natural gas processing, sulfur recovery, LNG, petroleum refining, petrochemicals and cogeneration; and power delivery services for substations, overhead transmission, underground transmission, power system studies and distributed generation. B&V's water sector provides a broad range of water and environmental study, consulting, design, design-build and construction management services to utilities, agencies and industrial clients in the Americas, Europe and Asia Pacific. It develops water treatment facilities, distribution systems for potable water and wastewater collection systems and provides water reclamation and reuse consulting services. The company's information market services include telecommunications services, A&E services, integrated networks, federal and state government networks, as well as offerings through BV Solutions Group, Inc., a wholly-owned IT service provider subsidiary. In January 2010, the company was contracted by Thames Water to modify the Mogden Sewage Treatment Works in London. Also in January 2010, the company was contracted to redesign the Davyhulme Wastewater Treatment Works, which is one of the largest in the U.K. In March 2010, the company acquired Enspiria Solutions, which provides smart grid solutions.

The company offers employees private medical insurance; income protection; an employee assistance program; a pension program; and life insurance.

FINANCIALS: **Sales and profits are in thousands of dollars—add 000 to get the full amount. 2009 Note: Financial information for 2009 was not available for all companies at press time.**

2009 Sales: $	2009 Profits: $	**U.S. Stock Ticker: Private**
2008 Sales: $3,200,000	2008 Profits: $	**Int'l Ticker:** Int'l Exchange:
2007 Sales: $3,200,000	2007 Profits: $	Employees: 9,600
2006 Sales: $1,800,000	2006 Profits: $	Fiscal Year Ends: 12/31
2005 Sales: $1,600,000	2005 Profits: $	Parent Company:

SALARIES/BENEFITS:

Pension Plan:	ESOP Stock Plan:	Profit Sharing:	Top Exec. Salary: $	Bonus: $
Savings Plan:	Stock Purch. Plan:		Second Exec. Salary: $	Bonus: $

OTHER THOUGHTS:

Apparent Women Officers or Directors: 2
Hot Spot for Advancement for Women/Minorities: Y

LOCATIONS: ("Y" = Yes)

West:	Southwest:	Midwest:	Southeast:	Northeast:	International:
Y	Y	Y	Y	Y	Y

BLUEGREEN CORPORATION

www.bluegreencorp.com

Industry Group Code: 561599 **Ranks within this company's industry group:** Sales: 1 Profits: 1

Properties:		Financial Services:		Construction/Development:		Investments:		Specialty Services:		Brokerage:	
Apartments:		Mortgages:		Commercial Construction:		REIT:		Property Management:	Y	Commercial Sales:	
Malls/Shopping:		Title Insurance:		Residential Construction:				Online Services:		Residential Sales:	Y
Offices:		Property Insurance:		Land Development:	Y			Software/IT:		Specialty:	
Hotels/Motels:	Y			Support Services:				Consulting:			
Industrial/Warehouses:				Design/Engineering:							
Other:	Y										

TYPES OF BUSINESS:

Timeshare Resorts
Time shares
Residential Properties
Property Development & Subdivisions
Resort Management Services

BRANDS/DIVISIONS/AFFILIATES:

Bluegreen Resorts
Bluegreen Vacation Club
Bluegreen Communities
Cibola Vista Resort and Spa

CONTACTS:

Note: Officers with more than one job title may be intentionally listed here more than once.

John M. Maloney, Jr., CEO
John M. Maloney, Jr., Pres.
Anthony M. Puleo, CFO/Sr. VP/Treas.
Susan J. Saturday, Chief Human Resources Officer/Sr. VP
Allan J. Herz, Sr. VP-Mortgage Oper./Assistant Treas.
Stephen Wilke, Contact-Media
Raymond S. Lopez, Chief Acct. Officer/VP
Daniel C. Koscher, Sr. VP/CEO & Pres., Bluegreen Communities
David A. Bidgood, Pres., Field Sales & Mktg.-Bluegreen Resorts
David L. Pontius, Sr. VP/Pres., Bluegreen Management Svcs.
Alan B. Levan, Chmn.

Phone: 561-912-8000	**Fax:** 561-912-8100
Toll-Free:	
Address: 4960 Conference Way N., Ste. 100, Boca Raton, FL 33431 US	

GROWTH PLANS/SPECIAL FEATURES:

Bluegreen Corporation markets and develops both residential and vacation homes. It is known for its registered slogan, Colorful Places to Live and Play. The firm is organized into two segments: Bluegreen Resorts and Bluegreen Communities. Bluegreen Resorts markets, sells and manages real estate-based vacation ownership interests in resorts generally located in popular high-volume vacation destinations. This division also provides sales, marketing, mortgage servicing, construction management, title and resort management services to third-party resort developers and owners. Bluegreen currently markets timeshare interests for over 45 U.S. resorts. Customers are eligible to enter the Bluegreen Vacation Club, a customer rewards system similar to a frequent flyer program. U.S. resort locations include Myrtle Beach, South Carolina; numerous locations in Florida, including Orlando, Panama City Beach and Surfside; Las Vegas, Nevada; New Orleans, Louisiana; and locations in Aruba, the Bahamas and Hawaii. Bluegreen Communities, Bluegreen's residential land and golf business, acquires, develops and subdivides property and markets residential land homesites. These homesites are generally sold directly to retail customers seeking to build a home, in some cases on properties featuring a golf course. This division's strategy is to locate its properties near major metropolitan centers but outside the perimeter of intense subdivision development, and in popular retirement areas. The division has sold homesites in planned residential and golf communities in 32 states, with projects located in Texas, North Carolina, Virginia, Tennessee and Georgia. Bluegreen Resorts accounts for about 92% of the company's sales of real estate, with Bluegreen Communities comprising the remaining 8%. In July 2009, Bluegreen announced an agreement to provide timeshare services and resort management operations for four resorts in Virginia, Massachusetts, New Hampshire and the Bahamas. In September 2009, the firm agreed to provide similar services for the Cibola Vista Resort and Spa in Arizona.

FINANCIALS:

Sales and profits are in thousands of dollars—add 000 to get the full amount. 2009 Note: Financial information for 2009 was not available for all companies at press time.

2009 Sales: $365,961	2009 Profits: $-3,572	**U.S. Stock Ticker: BXG**
2008 Sales: $594,861	2008 Profits: $- 516	**Int'l Ticker:** Int'l Exchange:
2007 Sales: $683,917	2007 Profits: $31,926	Employees: 3,651
2006 Sales: $673,373	2006 Profits: $29,817	Fiscal Year Ends: 12/31
2005 Sales: $684,156	2005 Profits: $46,551	Parent Company:

SALARIES/BENEFITS:

Pension Plan:	ESOP Stock Plan:	Profit Sharing:	Top Exec. Salary: $600,000	Bonus: $
Savings Plan:	Stock Purch. Plan:		Second Exec. Salary: $500,000	Bonus: $653,277

OTHER THOUGHTS:

Apparent Women Officers or Directors: 1
Hot Spot for Advancement for Women/Minorities: Y

LOCATIONS: ("Y" = Yes)

West:	Southwest:	Midwest:	Southeast:	Northeast:	International:
Y	Y	Y	Y	Y	

BOARDWALK REAL ESTATE INVESTMENT TRUST

www.boardwalkreit.com

Industry Group Code: 531110 **Ranks within this company's industry group:** Sales: 12 Profits: 8

Properties:		Financial Services:		Construction/Development:		Investments:		Specialty Services:		Brokerage:	
Apartments:	Y	Mortgages:		Commercial Construction:		REIT:	Y	Property Management:	Y	Commercial Sales:	
Malls/Shopping:		Title Insurance:		Residential Construction:				Online Services:		Residential Sales:	
Offices:		Property Insurance:		Land Development:				Software/IT:		Specialty:	
Hotels/Motels:				Support Services:				Consulting:			
Industrial/Warehouses:				Design/Engineering:							
Other:											

TYPES OF BUSINESS:

Real Estate Investment Trust
Apartment Development & Management

BRANDS/DIVISIONS/AFFILIATES:

Boardwalk Equities Inc

CONTACTS:

Note: Officers with more than one job title may be intentionally listed here more than once.

Sam Kolias, CEO
Roberto Geremia, Pres.
William Wong, CFO/Sr. VP
Helen Mix, VP-Human Resources
Michael Guyette, CIO
Dean Burns, VP-Legal Affairs
Michael Guyette, VP-Oper., Southern Alberta & BC
William Chidley, Sr. VP-Corp. Dev.
David McIlveen, Contact-Media Rel.
Zoe Geddes-Soltess, Contact-Investor Rel.
Van Kolias, Sr. VP-Quality Control
Jonathan Brimmell, VP-Oper., Ontario & Quebec
Kelly Mahajan, VP-Customer Service & Process Design
Jean Denis, VP-Quebec Acquisitions
Sam Kolias, Chmn.
Ian Dingle, VP-Purchasing & Contracts

Phone: 403-531-9255	**Fax:** 403-531-9565
Toll-Free:	
Address: 1501 1st St. SW, Ste. 200, Calgary, AB T2R 0W1 Canada	

GROWTH PLANS/SPECIAL FEATURES:

Boardwalk Real Estate Investment Trust, formerly Boardwalk Equities, Inc., is Canada's largest owner and operator of multi-family rental communities. The company currently owns and operates more than 260 properties with more than 36,000 units, totaling approximately 31 million rentable square feet. Boardwalk's portfolio includes properties in the provinces of Alberta, British Columbia, Saskatchewan, Ontario and Quebec, with approximately 55% of its rentable portfolio and nearly 62% of its net operating income concentrated in Alberta. The firm is not involved in construction and only looks to purchase existing structures within its acquisition program, especially high-rise buildings with more than 100 suites, townhomes and certain other property types to ensure a diversified portfolio. The company targets well-located properties that it believes have been poorly managed, creating a higher-than-average vacancy rate. Boardwalk's strength is in its operating, leasing and financing capabilities and its ability to enhance the long-term value of a property. The firm attempts to acquire properties at a substantial discount to replacement cost. It then restores the apartment buildings and focuses on adding high-tech amenities, such as fiber-optic cable. Boardwalk sometimes sells its properties after renovation, either entirely to other companies or as individual condos to residents. During 2009, the firm disposed of four properties, one each in Calgary, Quebec, Levis and Surrey.

FINANCIALS:

Sales and profits are in thousands of dollars—add 000 to get the full amount. 2009 Note: Financial information for 2009 was not available for all companies at press time.

2009 Sales: $	2009 Profits: $	**U.S. Stock Ticker:**
2008 Sales: $349,330	2008 Profits: $37,640	**Int'l Ticker: BEI** Int'l Exchange: Toronto-TSX
2007 Sales: $309,000	2007 Profits: $-48,880	Employees:
2006 Sales: $316,200	2006 Profits: $25,100	Fiscal Year Ends: 12/31
2005 Sales: $258,174	2005 Profits: $4,365	Parent Company:

SALARIES/BENEFITS:

Pension Plan:	ESOP Stock Plan:	Profit Sharing:	Top Exec. Salary: $	Bonus: $
Savings Plan:	Stock Purch. Plan:		Second Exec. Salary: $	Bonus: $

OTHER THOUGHTS:

Apparent Women Officers or Directors: 5
Hot Spot for Advancement for Women/Minorities: Y

LOCATIONS: ("Y" = Yes)

West:	Southwest:	Midwest:	Southeast:	Northeast:	International:
					Y

BOISE CASCADE

www.bc.com

Industry Group Code: 322 **Ranks within this company's industry group:** Sales: 1 Profits: 1

Properties:		Financial Services:		Construction/Development:		Investments:		Specialty Services:		Brokerage:	
Apartments:		Mortgages:		Commercial Construction:		REIT:		Property Management:		Commercial Sales:	
Malls/Shopping:		Title Insurance:		Residential Construction:				Online Services:		Residential Sales:	
Offices:		Property Insurance:		Land Development:				Software/IT:		Specialty:	
Hotels/Motels:				Support Services:	Y			Consulting:			
Industrial/Warehouses:				Design/Engineering:							
Other:											

TYPES OF BUSINESS:

Lumber Products, Manufacturing
Engineered Wood Products
Wholesale Building Materials Distribution
Packaging & Newsprint
Cottonwood Fiber Farming

BRANDS/DIVISIONS/AFFILIATES:

Kettle Falls Lumber
Elgin Studs
Florien Plywood
St. Jacques, NB

CONTACTS:

Note: Officers with more than one job title may be intentionally listed here more than once.

Thomas Carlile, CEO
Wayne Rancourt, CFO/Sr. VP/Treas.
John Sahlberg, VP-Human Resources
Dave Gadda, General Counsel/Sec./VP
Kelly Hibbs, Dir.-Strategic Planning
John Sahlberg, VP-Comm.
Bernadette Madarieta, Controller/VP-Tax
Nick Stokes, VP/Mgr.-Oper.-Building Materials Div.
Thomas Lovlien, Pres., Wood Prod.
Thomas Corrick, VP-Boise Wood Prod.
Duane McDougall, Chmn.
Stanley Bell, Pres., Building Materials Dist.

Phone: 208-384-6161	**Fax:** 208-384-7189
Toll-Free:	
Address: 1111 W. Jefferson St., Ste. 300, Boise, ID 83702-5389 US	

GROWTH PLANS/SPECIAL FEATURES:

Boise Cascade Corp. is a major wholesale distributor of wood products and building materials. The firm controls significant amounts of timberland in the United States. Boise Cascade produces structural panels, lumber and particleboard, as well as engineered wood products consisting of laminated veneer lumber, wood I-joists and laminated beams. These products are used primarily in housing, industrial construction and a variety of manufactured products. The company operates its wood products division in Louisiana, Oregon, Washington, Idaho and Canada. Operating names include Kettle Falls Lumber; Elgin Studs; Kinzua Lumber; Florien Plywood; and St. Jacques, NB. Boise Cascade's materials distribution division maintains distribution centers throughout the U.S. The firm holds many environmental sustainability certificates, including compliance with Forest Stewardship Council, Programme for Endorsement of Forest Certification and Sustainable Forestry Initiative. The company is controlled by private equity investors Madison Dearborn Partners. During 2009, the firm closed its lumber manufacturing facility in La Grande, Oregon; its veneer operations in St. Helens, Oregon; and its plywood manufacturing facility in White City, Oregon. In May 2009, Boise Cascade acquired Total Structural Systems (TSS), formerly Wood Structures, Inc.

The firm offers its employees health, medical, prescription drug, dental and vision coverage; flexible spending accounts; 16-31 days paid-time off; life, AD&D and long term disability insurance; a 401(k) plan with a 4% employer match; and an employee assistance program.

FINANCIALS:

Sales and profits are in thousands of dollars—add 000 to get the full amount. 2009 Note: Financial information for 2009 was not available for all companies at press time.

2009 Sales: $1,973,250
2008 Sales: $2,977,498
2007 Sales: $5,413,456
2006 Sales: $5,779,865
2005 Sales: $

2009 Profits: $-19,057
2008 Profits: $-287,978
2007 Profits: $127,697
2006 Profits: $71,571
2005 Profits: $

U.S. Stock Ticker: Private
Int'l Ticker: Int'l Exchange:
Employees: 4,600
Fiscal Year Ends: 12/31
Parent Company:

SALARIES/BENEFITS:

Pension Plan: ESOP Stock Plan: Profit Sharing: Top Exec. Salary: $ Bonus: $
Savings Plan: Y Stock Purch. Plan: Second Exec. Salary: $ Bonus: $

OTHER THOUGHTS:

Apparent Women Officers or Directors: 2
Hot Spot for Advancement for Women/Minorities: Y

LOCATIONS: ("Y" = Yes)

West:	Southwest:	Midwest:	Southeast:	Northeast:	International:
Y	Y	Y	Y	Y	Y

BOSTON PROPERTIES INC

www.bostonproperties.com

Industry Group Code: 531120 **Ranks within this company's industry group:** Sales: 10 Profits: 22

Properties:		Financial Services:		Construction/Development:		Investments:		Specialty Services:		Brokerage:	
Apartments:		Mortgages:		Commercial Construction:		REIT:	Y	Property Management:		Commercial Sales:	
Malls/Shopping:		Title Insurance:		Residential Construction:				Online Services:		Residential Sales:	
Offices:	Y	Property Insurance:		Land Development:				Software/IT:		Specialty:	
Hotels/Motels:	Y			Support Services:				Consulting:			
Industrial/Warehouses:	Y			Design/Engineering:							
Other:											

TYPES OF BUSINESS:

Real Estate Investment Trust
Offices
Hotel
Industrial Space

BRANDS/DIVISIONS/AFFILIATES:

Boston Properties Office Value-Added Fund LP
Times Square Tower
Embarcadero Center
Prudential Center
Prudential Tower
Metropolitan Square
General Motors Building

CONTACTS:

Note: Officers with more than one job title may be intentionally listed here more than once.

Mortimer B. Zuckerman, CEO
E. Mitchell Norville, COO/Exec. VP
Douglas T. Linde, Pres.
Michael E. LaBelle, CFO/Sr. VP
Raymond A. Ritchey, Dir.-Dev. & Acquisitions/Exec. VP
Arista Joyner, Mgr.-Investor Rel.
Michael E. LaBelle, Treas.
Bryan J. Koop, Sr. VP/Mgr.-Boston Office
Robert E. Selsam, Sr. VP/Mgr.-New York Office
Robert E. Pester, Sr. VP/Mgr.-San Francisco Office
Mitchell S. Landis, Sr. VP/Mgr.-Princeton Office
Mortimer B. Zuckerman, Chmn.

Phone: 617-236-3300 **Fax:** 617-536-5087
Toll-Free:
Address: The Prudential Ctr., 800 Boylston St., Ste. 1900, Boston, MA 02199-8103 US

GROWTH PLANS/SPECIAL FEATURES:

Boston Properties, Inc. is a fully integrated, self-administered and self-managed real estate investment trust (REIT) and one of the largest owners and developers of office properties in the U.S. The trust develops, redevelops, acquires, manages, operates and owns a diverse portfolio of Class A offices. It holds properties in the U.S., with holdings concentrated in five core markets: Boston, Massachusetts; Washington, D.C.; midtown Manhattan; San Francisco, California; and Princeton, New Jersey. The company's subsidiary, Boston Properties Limited Partnership, conducts the vast majority of its business. Boston Properties owns or has interests in 146 properties, including 140 office properties, one hotel, three retail properties and two residential properties (under construction). The sum of this property is 37.7 million net rentable square feet and 12.8 million square feet of structured parking. In addition, the trust owns or controls approximately 509.3 acres of undeveloped land. The company has a minority interest in the Boston Properties Office Value-Added Fund, L.P., which acquires deficient properties and remodels/refurbishes them for resale. Examples of the company's properties are Prudential Tower and Prudential Center in Boston; Times Square Tower and General Motors Building (60% owned) in New York; Metropolitan Square in Washington, D.C.; One, Two, Three and Four Embarcadero Center in San Francisco; and 17 office buildings in Carnegie Center in Princeton.

The company offers employees health, dental, life, business travel accident and disability insurance; an employee assistance program; a 401(k); a stock purchase plan; paid time off; legal referral services; tuition reimbursement; commuter benefits; and a scholarship program.

FINANCIALS:

Sales and profits are in thousands of dollars—add 000 to get the full amount. 2009 Note: Financial information for 2009 was not available for all companies at press time.

2009 Sales: $1,522,249	2009 Profits: $274,499	**U.S. Stock Ticker: BXP**
2008 Sales: $1,488,400	2008 Profits: $125,232	**Int'l Ticker:** Int'l Exchange:
2007 Sales: $1,482,289	2007 Profits: $1,324,690	Employees: 700
2006 Sales: $1,417,627	2006 Profits: $873,635	Fiscal Year Ends: 12/31
2005 Sales: $1,382,866	2005 Profits: $438,292	Parent Company:

SALARIES/BENEFITS:

Pension Plan:	ESOP Stock Plan:	Profit Sharing:	Top Exec. Salary: $986,538	Bonus: $2,000,000
Savings Plan: Y	Stock Purch. Plan: Y		Second Exec. Salary: $986,538	Bonus: $1,800,000

OTHER THOUGHTS:

Apparent Women Officers or Directors: 3
Hot Spot for Advancement for Women/Minorities: Y

LOCATIONS: ("Y" = Yes)

West:	Southwest:	Midwest:	Southeast:	Northeast:	International:
Y				Y	

BOUYGUES SA

www.bouygues.fr

Industry Group Code: 237 **Ranks within this company's industry group:** Sales: 1 Profits: 3

Properties:		Financial Services:		Construction/Development:		Investments:		Specialty Services:		Brokerage:	
Apartments:		Mortgages:		Commercial Construction:	Y	REIT:		Property Management:		Commercial Sales:	
Malls/Shopping:		Title Insurance:		Residential Construction:				Online Services:		Residential Sales:	
Offices:		Property Insurance:		Land Development:				Software/IT:	Y	Specialty:	
Hotels/Motels:				Support Services:	Y			Consulting:			
Industrial/Warehouses:	Y			Design/Engineering:	Y						
Other:											

TYPES OF BUSINESS:

Construction & Telecommunications
Construction
Road Building
Property Development
Precasting
Cellular Phone Service
Media Operation
Research & Development

BRANDS/DIVISIONS/AFFILIATES:

Bouygues Construction
Bouygues Immobilier
Bouygues Telecom
Bouygues e-Lab
Colas
TF1
Finagestion

CONTACTS:

Note: Officers with more than one job title may be intentionally listed here more than once.

Martin Bouygues, CEO
Philippe Marien, CFO
Jean-Claude Tostivin, Sr. VP-Human Resources
Alain Pouyat, Exec. VP-Info. Systems
Alain Pouyat, Exec. VP-New Tech.
Jean-Claude Tostivin, Sr. VP-Admin.
Jean-Francois Guillemin, Corp. Sec.
Pierre Auberger, Dir.-Corp. Comm.
Valarie Agathon, Dir.-Investor Rel.
Olivier Bouygues, Deputy CEO
Yves Gabriel, CEO-Bouygues Construction
Nonce Paolini, CEO-TF1
Francois Bertiere, CEO-Bouygues Immobilier
Martin Bouygues, Chmn.

Phone: 33-1-44-20-10-00	**Fax:** 33-1-44-20-12-42
Toll-Free:	
Address: 32 Ave. Hoche, Paris, 75008 France	

GROWTH PLANS/SPECIAL FEATURES:

Buoygues SA, based in Paris, France, was founded in 1952 as a construction and industrial works company. Operating through its subsidiaries, the firm now primarily serves two distinct areas: construction and telecoms/media. Company subsidiaries working within the construction sector include Bouygues Construction, dedicated to electrical contracting and civil works; Bouygues Immobilier, committed to property development; and Colas, dedicated to building roads. Subsidiaries serving the telecoms/media branch include TF1 and Buoygues Telecom. The firm also maintains the Bouygues e-Lab, a research and development city which supports all areas of the company with innovations in their particular fields and in the digital technologies sector. Recent research projects include acoustics, vibration and energy performance for the Construction sector; strategic marketing and the development of new products for the Immobilier sector; various asphalts and mixing processes for the Colas sector; television capabilities on mobile phones as well as high-definition TV for the TF1 sector; and mobile videos, broadband innovations and contactless applications for the Telecom sector. The firm maintains operations in Europe, Central and South America, North America, Asia, the Middle East and Africa. In November 2009, Bouygues SA sold 35.7% of its interest in Finagestion, a holding company that owns water management operations in Senegal and Ivory Coast, reducing its stake in the company to 35%.

FINANCIALS:

Sales and profits are in thousands of dollars—add 000 to get the full amount. 2009 Note: Financial information for 2009 was not available for all companies at press time.

2009 Sales: $41,783,500	2009 Profits: $1,757,800	**U.S. Stock Ticker:**
2008 Sales: $43,264,900	2008 Profits: $1,985,160	**Int'l Ticker: EN** Int'l Exchange: Paris-Euronext
2007 Sales: $39,131,900	2007 Profits: $1,819,840	Employees:
2006 Sales: $36,022,600	2006 Profits: $2,157,970	Fiscal Year Ends: 12/31
2005 Sales: $32,714,700	2005 Profits: $1,415,920	Parent Company:

SALARIES/BENEFITS:

Pension Plan:	ESOP Stock Plan:	Profit Sharing:	Top Exec. Salary: $	Bonus: $
Savings Plan:	Stock Purch. Plan:		Second Exec. Salary: $	Bonus: $

OTHER THOUGHTS:

Apparent Women Officers or Directors: 2
Hot Spot for Advancement for Women/Minorities:

LOCATIONS: ("Y" = Yes)

West:	Southwest:	Midwest:	Southeast:	Northeast:	International:
Y		Y	Y	Y	Y

BOYD GAMING CORP

www.boydgaming.com

Industry Group Code: 721120 **Ranks within this company's industry group:** Sales: 5 Profits: 5

Properties:		Financial Services:		Construction/Development:		Investments:		Specialty Services:		Brokerage:	
Apartments:		Mortgages:		Commercial Construction:		REIT:		Property Management:	Y	Commercial Sales:	
Malls/Shopping:		Title Insurance:		Residential Construction:				Online Services:		Residential Sales:	
Offices:		Property Insurance:		Land Development:				Software/IT:		Specialty:	
Hotels/Motels:	Y			Support Services:				Consulting:			
Industrial/Warehouses:				Design/Engineering:							
Other:	Y										

TYPES OF BUSINESS:

Casinos & Hotels
Casino Management

BRANDS/DIVISIONS/AFFILIATES:

California Hotel & Casino
Borgata Hotel, Casino, & Spa
Blue Chip Hotel and Casino
Delta Downs Racetrack & Casino
Gold Coast Hotel and Casino
Water Club (The)
Club Coast
B Connected

CONTACTS: *Note: Officers with more than one job title may be intentionally listed here more than once.*

Keith E. Smith, CEO
Paul J. Chakmak, COO/Exec. VP
Keith E. Smith, Pres.
John Hirsberg, CFO/Sr. VP/Treas.
Tom Balance, Sr. VP-Prod. Design & Construction
William J. Noonan, Sr. VP-Admin.
Brian A. Larson, General Counsel/Sec./Exec. VP
Christopher R. Gibase, Sr. VP-Oper., Midwest & South
Robert L. Boughner, Chief Bus. Dev. Officer/Exec. VP
Jeff Santoro, Controller/Sr. VP
Marianne Boyd Johnson, Vice Chmn./Exec. VP
William R. Boyd, VP
Stephan S. Thompson, Sr. VP-Oper., Nevada
William S. Boyd, Exec. Chmn.

Phone: 702-792-7200 **Fax:** 702-792-7313
Toll-Free:
Address: 3883 Howard Hughes Pkwy., 9th Fl., Las Vegas, NV 89169 US

GROWTH PLANS/SPECIAL FEATURES:

Boyd Gaming Corp. is a multi-jurisdictional gaming company and one of the country's leading casino operators. It currently owns and operates 15 casinos totaling 812,500 square feet, and housing 21,400 slot machines, 425 table games and 7,550 hotel rooms. Its Las Vegas, Nevada properties include The Orleans Hotel and Casino; Sam's Town Hotel & Gambling Hall; Gold Coast Hotel and Casino; Eldorado Casino; Jokers Wild Casino; California Hotel and Casino; Main Street Station Hotel, Casino and Brewery; Suncoast Hotel and Casino; and Fremont Hotel & Casino. Its properties in other states include a Sam's Town Hotel and Gambling Hall, in Tunica, Mississippi; the Delta Downs Racetrack and Casino, the Sam's Town Hotel and Casino Shreveport (formerly Shreveport Hotel and Casino) and the Treasure Chest Casino, in Louisiana; the Par-a-Dice Hotel and Casino in East Peoria, Illinois; Borgata Hotel, Casino and Spa in Atlantic City, New Jersey (jointly owned with MGM Mirage); and the Blue Chip Hotel and Casino in Michigan City, Indiana. In addition to these properties, the firm owns and operates a jai-alai facility in Dania Beach, Florida; a travel agency; an insurance agency specializing in travel-related insurance; and 85 contiguous acres of land on the Las Vegas Strip. The company maintains a loyalty program which allows customers to use Club Coast or B Connected cards to earn and redeem points at any Boyd gaming property in Nevada, Illinois, Indiana, Louisiana and Mississippi. Boyd has one delayed property in development, the Echelon, which is a multi-billion dollar facility on the Las Vegas Strip. In 2009, gaming operations alone accounted for 75% of the company's revenue, with food and beverage sales being the only other significant source of income at 13%.

Employees are offered medical, dental and vision coverage; a 401(k) plan; short-term disability coverage; and life insurance.

FINANCIALS: **Sales and profits are in thousands of dollars—add 000 to get the full amount. 2009 Note: Financial information for 2009 was not available for all companies at press time.**

2009 Sales: $1,640,986	2009 Profits: $156,193	**U.S. Stock Ticker: BYD**
2008 Sales: $1,780,967	2008 Profits: $-223,005	**Int'l Ticker:** Int'l Exchange:
2007 Sales: $1,997,119	2007 Profits: $303,035	Employees: 15,400
2006 Sales: $2,192,634	2006 Profits: $116,778	Fiscal Year Ends: 12/31
2005 Sales: $2,161,085	2005 Profits: $144,610	Parent Company:

SALARIES/BENEFITS:

Pension Plan:	ESOP Stock Plan:	Profit Sharing:	Top Exec. Salary: $1,100,000	Bonus: $770,000
Savings Plan: Y	Stock Purch. Plan:		Second Exec. Salary: $1,100,000	Bonus: $577,500

OTHER THOUGHTS:

Apparent Women Officers or Directors: 2
Hot Spot for Advancement for Women/Minorities: Y

LOCATIONS: ("Y" = Yes)

West:	Southwest:	Midwest:	Southeast:	Northeast:	International:
Y		Y	Y		

BRANDYWINE REALTY TRUST

www.brandywinerealty.com

Industry Group Code: 531120 **Ranks within this company's industry group:** Sales: 30 Profits: 37

Properties:		Financial Services:		Construction/Development:		Investments:		Specialty Services:		Brokerage:	
Apartments:		Mortgages:		Commercial Construction:		REIT:	Y	Property Management:	Y	Commercial Sales:	
Malls/Shopping:		Title Insurance:		Residential Construction:				Online Services:		Residential Sales:	
Offices:	Y	Property Insurance:		Land Development:	Y			Software/IT:		Specialty:	
Hotels/Motels:				Support Services:				Consulting:	Y		
Industrial/Warehouses:	Y			Design/Engineering:							
Other:											

TYPES OF BUSINESS:

Real Estate Investment Trust
Office & Industrial Properties
Property Management Services
Development Support Services
Consulting

BRANDS/DIVISIONS/AFFILIATES:

Brandywine Operating Partnership, LP
Brandywine Development Services
e-tenants.com
Prentiss Properties

CONTACTS: *Note: Officers with more than one job title may be intentionally listed here more than once.*

Gerard H. Sweeney, CEO
Gerard H. Sweeney, Pres.
Howard M. Sipzner, CFO/Exec. VP
Beth R. Glassman, VP-Human Resources
Robert J. Juliano, CIO/VP
Brad A. Molotsky, General Counsel/Sr. VP/Corp. Sec.
George D. Johnstone, Sr. VP-Oper.
Gabe Mainardi, VP-Acct./Treas.
H. Jeffrey DeVuono, Exec. VP/Sr. Managing Dir.-Pennsylvania Region
George D. Sowa, Exec. VP/Sr. Managing Dir.-NJ & DE Region
William D. Redd, Sr. VP/Sr. Managing Dir.-Richmond & Austin Region
Anthony S. Rimikis, Sr. VP-Urban Development
Walter D'Alessio, Chmn.

Phone: 610-325-5600 **Fax:** 610-325-5622
Toll-Free:
Address: 555 East Lancaster Ave., Ste. 100, Radnor, PA 19087 US

GROWTH PLANS/SPECIAL FEATURES:

Brandywine Realty Trust is a real estate investment trust (REIT) that acquires, develops, redevelops, manages and leases office and industrial properties across the U.S. The firm owns 22 industrial facilities, 212 office properties, three mixed-use properties and 23.3 million square feet available for rent (single property). Brandywine also has two properties under development and three properties under redevelopment, containing a total of 1.9 million net rentable square feet. The company has several divions, including Asset and Property Management; Development/Construction; Investment Services; Marketing and Leasing Services; Property Management; and Tenant Services. The asset and property management programs include acquisition and disposition, capital allocation and deployment, and project management. The development/construction program's capabilities include development, site selection, land purchase, renovation and construction management. The investment services program has a variety of transactions in core markets and works with opportunities such as existing office buildings, developable land and redevelopment properties. The marketing and leasing services program works with tenants to provide office space and other alternatives. As part of the company's Tenant Services division, Brandywine launched e-tenants.com, designed to streamline delivery of service and amenities to its tenants online. In April 2010, the company announced that it signed over 1 million square feet in new and renewed leases. Some of the tenants include Ametek, GSI Commerce Solutions and PPD Development.

Employees are offered medical, dental, prescription drug and vision insurance; short- and long-term disability coverage; a 401(k) plan with company match; reimbursement accounts for health, dependent care and public transportation; an employee stock purchase plan; military leave with pay for training or reserve duty; tuition reimbursement; scholarships for employees' children; and business casual environment in the corporate and property management offices.

FINANCIALS: **Sales and profits are in thousands of dollars—add 000 to get the full amount. 2009 Note: Financial information for 2009 was not available for all companies at press time.**

2009 Sales: $582,219	2009 Profits: $8,089	**U.S. Stock Ticker: BDN**
2008 Sales: $589,421	2008 Profits: $38,525	**Int'l Ticker:** Int'l Exchange:
2007 Sales: $604,811	2007 Profits: $55,335	Employees: 402
2006 Sales: $568,883	2006 Profits: $9,814	Fiscal Year Ends: 12/31
2005 Sales: $364,435	2005 Profits: $42,766	Parent Company:

SALARIES/BENEFITS:

Pension Plan:	ESOP Stock Plan:	Profit Sharing:	Top Exec. Salary: $600,000	Bonus: $1,050,000
Savings Plan: Y	Stock Purch. Plan:		Second Exec. Salary: $402,069	Bonus: $392,700

OTHER THOUGHTS:

Apparent Women Officers or Directors: 5
Hot Spot for Advancement for Women/Minorities: Y

LOCATIONS: ("Y" = Yes)

West:	Southwest:	Midwest:	Southeast:	Northeast:	International:
Y	Y			Y	

BRE PROPERTIES INC

www.breproperties.com

Industry Group Code: 531110 **Ranks within this company's industry group:** Sales: 10 Profits: 4

Properties:		Financial Services:		Construction/Development:		Investments:		Specialty Services:		Brokerage:	
Apartments:	Y	Mortgages:		Commercial Construction:		REIT:	Y	Property Management:		Commercial Sales:	
Malls/Shopping:		Title Insurance:		Residential Construction:				Online Services:		Residential Sales:	
Offices:		Property Insurance:		Land Development:				Software/IT:		Specialty:	
Hotels/Motels:				Support Services:				Consulting:			
Industrial/Warehouses:				Design/Engineering:							
Other:											

TYPES OF BUSINESS:

Real Estate Investment Trust
Apartment Communities

BRANDS/DIVISIONS/AFFILIATES:

H.O.M.E. Plan

CONTACTS:

Note: Officers with more than one job title may be intentionally listed here more than once.

Constance B. Moore, CEO
Edward F. Lange, Jr., COO/Exec. VP
Constance B. Moore, Pres.
John A. Schissel, CFO/Exec. VP
Todd E. Katler, Sr. VP-Mktg. & Sales
Kerry Fanwick, General Counsel/Exec. VP
Stephanie Andre, Treas./VP
Stephen C. Dominiak, Chief Investment Officer/Exec. VP
Irving F. Lyons III, Chmn.

Phone: 415-445-6530	**Fax:** 415-445-6505
Toll-Free:	
Address: 525 Market St., 4th Fl., San Francisco, CA 94105 US	

GROWTH PLANS/SPECIAL FEATURES:

BRE Properties, Inc. is a real estate investment trust (REIT) that develops, acquires and manages multifamily apartment communities. BRE operates communities in six targeted metropolitan markets of the western U.S., including 73 wholly- or majority-owned stabilized multifamily communities, including 21,245 apartment units, in California, Washington and Arizona; 13 stabilized multifamily communities owned through joint venture agreements comprised of 4,080 apartment units; and six apartment communities in various stages of construction. The company's strategy for acquiring new property involves targeting high-quality communities in high-demand, supply-constrained, attractive locations, especially coastal California. Furthermore, its communities are generally built after 1980, include 100 or more units and are located near business, transportation, employment and recreation centers. BRE's H.O.M.E. Plan offers renters the option of putting a portion of monthly rent toward the purchase of a home. In 2009, the company sold two communities totaling 752 units. Also in 2009, the firm completed construction of three development communities: Taylor 28, with 197 units in Seattle, Washington; 5600 Wilshire, with 284 units in Los Angeles, California; and Park Viridian with 320 units in Anaheim, California.

Employees are offered medical and dental insurance; life insurance; flexible spending accounts; disability coverage; a 401(k) plan; a scholarship program for employees' children and grandchildren; and tuition reimbursement.

FINANCIALS:

Sales and profits are in thousands of dollars—add 000 to get the full amount. 2009 Note: Financial information for 2009 was not available for all companies at press time.

2009 Sales: $	2009 Profits: $	**U.S. Stock Ticker: BRE**
2008 Sales: $379,543	2008 Profits: $140,811	**Int'l Ticker:** Int'l Exchange:
2007 Sales: $362,561	2007 Profits: $128,081	Employees: 793
2006 Sales: $364,586	2006 Profits: $102,195	Fiscal Year Ends: 12/31
2005 Sales: $298,133	2005 Profits: $80,948	Parent Company:

SALARIES/BENEFITS:

Pension Plan:	ESOP Stock Plan:	Profit Sharing:	Top Exec. Salary: $475,000	Bonus: $567,373
Savings Plan: Y	Stock Purch. Plan:		Second Exec. Salary: $416,000	Bonus: $409,731

OTHER THOUGHTS:

Apparent Women Officers or Directors: 4
Hot Spot for Advancement for Women/Minorities: Y

LOCATIONS: ("Y" = Yes)

West:	Southwest:	Midwest:	Southeast:	Northeast:	International:
Y					

BROOKDALE SENIOR LIVING INC

www.brookdaleliving.com

Industry Group Code: 623110 **Ranks within this company's industry group:** Sales: 2 Profits: 5

Properties:		Financial Services:		Construction/Development:		Investments:		Specialty Services:		Brokerage:	
Apartments:		Mortgages:		Commercial Construction:		REIT:		Property Management:		Commercial Sales:	
Malls/Shopping:		Title Insurance:		Residential Construction:				Online Services:		Residential Sales:	
Offices:		Property Insurance:		Land Development:				Software/IT:		Specialty:	
Hotels/Motels:				Support Services:				Consulting:			
Industrial/Warehouses:				Design/Engineering:							
Other:	Y										

TYPES OF BUSINESS:

Long-Term Health Care & Assisted Living
Retirement Communities
Assisted Living Communities
Continued Care Retirement Communities (CCRCs)
Managed Facilities

BRANDS/DIVISIONS/AFFILIATES:

Innovative Senior Care
Optimum Life
Freedom Pointe Rehabilitation & Healthcare Center

CONTACTS: *Note: Officers with more than one job title may be intentionally listed here more than once.*

Bill E. Sheriff, CEO
John P. Rijos, COO
John P. Rijos, Co-Pres.
Mark W. Ohlendorf, CFO/Co-Pres.
Bryan D. Richardson, Chief Admin. Officer/Exec. VP
T. Andrew Smith, General Counsel/Sec./Exec. VP
Gregory B. Richard, Exec. VP-Field Oper.
H. Todd Kaestner, Exec. VP-Dev.
Ross Roadman, Contact-Investor Rel.
George T. Hicks, Exec. VP-Finance
Kristin A. Ferge, Exec. VP/Treas.
Wesley R. Edens, Chmn.

Phone: 615-221-2250	**Fax:** 615-221-2289
Toll-Free: 866-785-9025	
Address: 111 Westwood Place, Ste. 200, Brentwood, TN 37027 US	

GROWTH PLANS/SPECIAL FEATURES:

Brookdale Senior Living, Inc. (BSL) is one of the largest senior living facility operators in the U.S. It operates 564 owned, leased or managed senior living facilities in 35 states that can serve approximately 53,000 residents. BSL operates four segments, representing different types of facilities. It has 80 retirement centers with 14,867 beds, 430 assisted living communities with 22,954 beds, 36 continuing care retirement communities (CCRCs) with 12,017 beds and it provides management services for 19 third-party facilities with 3,788 beds. At the end of 2009, these facilities were 88.9% occupied. The facilities strive to offer residents a home-like setting and typically feature assistance with daily living, multiple forms of therapy and various home health services. For example, many locations offer the Innovative Senior Care program, which focuses on rehabilitation, fitness and educational offerings in addition to home health services. Additionally, its Optimum Life program is a nationwide wellness initiative that offers a holistic approach to health, life and aging. BSL offers a full spectrum of care options, including independent living, personalized assisted living, Alzheimer's and dementia care, rehabilitation and skilled nursing. The company maintains its own culinary arts institute, which offers a training ground for chefs and dining staff. Leased communities generated the largest share (59.7%) of 2009 revenues, followed by owned communities (40%) and managed communities (0.3%). BSL generated 83% of its 2009 revenue from private pay customers, with the remainder generated by Medicare, Medicaid and other various third-party payor programs. In September 2009, the company opened the Freedom Pointe Rehabilitation & Healthcare Center, a nursing and rehabilitation center at its facility in The Villages, Florida.

Employees are offered medical, dental and vision insurance; flexible spending accounts; disability coverage; an employee assistance plan; access to onsite clinics that offer free healthcare services; adoption benefits; legal insurance; and tuition reimbursement.

FINANCIALS: **Sales and profits are in thousands of dollars—add 000 to get the full amount. 2009 Note: Financial information for 2009 was not available for all companies at press time.**

2009 Sales: $2,023,068	2009 Profits: $-66,255	**U.S. Stock Ticker: BKD**
2008 Sales: $1,928,054	2008 Profits: $-373,241	**Int'l Ticker:** Int'l Exchange:
2007 Sales: $1,839,296	2007 Profits: $-161,979	Employees: 36,800
2006 Sales: $1,309,913	2006 Profits: $-108,087	Fiscal Year Ends: 12/31
2005 Sales: $790,577	2005 Profits: $-50,986	Parent Company:

SALARIES/BENEFITS:

Pension Plan:	ESOP Stock Plan:	Profit Sharing:	Top Exec. Salary: $446,442	Bonus: $100,500
Savings Plan: Y	Stock Purch. Plan: Y		Second Exec. Salary: $233,654	Bonus: $114,000

OTHER THOUGHTS:

Apparent Women Officers or Directors: 2
Hot Spot for Advancement for Women/Minorities: Y

LOCATIONS: ("Y" = Yes)

West:	Southwest:	Midwest:	Southeast:	Northeast:	International:
Y	Y	Y	Y	Y	

BROOKFIELD ASSET MANAGEMENT INC

www.brookfield.com

Industry Group Code: 5311 **Ranks within this company's industry group:** Sales: 2 Profits: 11

Properties:		Financial Services:		Construction/Development:		Investments:		Specialty Services:		Brokerage:	
Apartments:		Mortgages:		Commercial Construction:		REIT:		Property Management:		Commercial Sales:	Y
Malls/Shopping:	Y	Title Insurance:		Residential Construction:				Online Services:		Residential Sales:	Y
Offices:	Y	Property Insurance:		Land Development:				Software/IT:		Specialty:	
Hotels/Motels:	Y			Support Services:	Y			Consulting:			
Industrial/Warehouses:				Design/Engineering:							
Other:	Y										

TYPES OF BUSINESS:

Real Estate Operations
Asset Management
Hydroelectric Generation & Transmission
Paper Production
Agriculture
Financial Services
Timber Development
Wind Power Development

BRANDS/DIVISIONS/AFFILIATES:

Longview Fibre Company
Norbord, Inc.
Brookfield Renewable Power Fund
Brookfield Incorporacoes SA
Brookfield Homes Corporation
Brookfield Renewable Power Inc

CONTACTS:

Note: Officers with more than one job title may be intentionally listed here more than once.

J. Bruce Flatt, CEO
Brian D. Lawson, CFO
Lori Pearson, Sr. VP-Human Resources
Joseph S. Freedman, General Counsel
Richard Clark, Sr. Managing Partner-Property Oper.
Jeff Blidner, Sr. Managing Partner-Strategic Planning
Katherine Vyse, Sr. VP-Comm.
Katherine Vyse, Sr. VP-Investor Rel.
Sachin G. Shah, Sr. VP-Finance
Richard Legault, CEO/Pres., Brookfield Power
Marcel R. Coutu, Chmn.
Denis Couture, Sr. VP-Int'l Affairs

Phone: 416-363-9491 **Fax:** 416-365-9642
Toll-Free:
Address: Brookfield Pl., 181 Bay St., Ste. 300, Toronto, ON M5J 2T3 Canada

GROWTH PLANS/SPECIAL FEATURES:

Brookfield Asset Management, Inc. is a Canadian holding company that owns and manages assets in the areas of real estate and power generation. The company's assets, totaling approximately $90 billion, includes commercial properties, 162 conventional hydroelectric power generating facilities(with 3,129 gigawatts of capacity), one wind farm and two thermal plants. These properties are located in Canada, North America and South America. Brookfield's subsidiaries include Norbord, a paper production firm; Brookfield Renewable Power, Inc., which operates over 160 hydroelectric power facilities with a combined production capacity of roughly 4,000 megawatts; Brookfield Homes Corporation, which deals in residential real estate; Brookfield Properties Corporation, a commercial real estate management agency; Brookfield Renewable Power Fund, which owns assets that produce electricity exclusively from environmentally friendly hydroelectric resources; Brookfield Incorporacoes SA, a high-end and luxury residential real estate company based in Brazil; and Longview Fibre Company, which owns and manages Oregon and Washington timberlands for the purpose of commercial logging. Longview Fibre Company also owns and operates a pulp and paper mill and seven converting plants for production of craft paper, paperboard, and finished products such as corrugated containers. Brookfield manages office properties and development sites located in eight core markets: New York, Los Angeles, Houston, San Diego, Washington, D.C., Toronto, Ottowa and Calgary. The firm also owns retail and hotel properties in the U.K. and Brazil. In March 2009, Brookfield Asset Management agreed to acquire all remaining interest in MediSolution Ltd., of which it previously owned a controlling interest. In mid 2009, Brookfield Renewable Power agreed to sell its Ontario electric distribution business to FortisOntario Inc., and the remainder of its Canadian renewable power generation business to Great Lakes Hydro Income Fund.

FINANCIALS:

Sales and profits are in thousands of dollars—add 000 to get the full amount. 2009 Note: Financial information for 2009 was not available for all companies at press time.

2009 Sales: $12,082,000
2008 Sales: $12,909,000
2007 Sales: $9,343,000
2006 Sales: $6,897,000
2005 Sales: $5,220,000

2009 Profits: $454,000
2008 Profits: $649,000
2007 Profits: $787,000
2006 Profits: $1,170,000
2005 Profits: $1,662,000

U.S. Stock Ticker: BAM
Int'l Ticker: BAM Int'l Exchange: Toronto-TSX
Employees:
Fiscal Year Ends: 12/31
Parent Company:

SALARIES/BENEFITS:

Pension Plan: ESOP Stock Plan: Profit Sharing: Top Exec. Salary: $374,445 Bonus: $
Savings Plan: Stock Purch. Plan: Second Exec. Salary: $374,445 Bonus: $

OTHER THOUGHTS:

Apparent Women Officers or Directors: 2
Hot Spot for Advancement for Women/Minorities: Y

LOCATIONS: ("Y" = Yes)

West:	Southwest:	Midwest:	Southeast:	Northeast:	International:
Y	Y	Y	Y	Y	Y

BROOKFIELD HOMES CORP

www.brookfieldhomes.com

Industry Group Code: 2361 **Ranks within this company's industry group:** Sales: 19 Profits: 5

Properties:		Financial Services:		Construction/Development:		Investments:		Specialty Services:		Brokerage:	
Apartments:		Mortgages:		Commercial Construction:		REIT:		Property Management:		Commercial Sales:	
Malls/Shopping:		Title Insurance:		Residential Construction:	Y			Online Services:		Residential Sales:	
Offices:		Property Insurance:		Land Development:	Y			Software/IT:		Specialty:	
Hotels/Motels:				Support Services:				Consulting:			
Industrial/Warehouses:				Design/Engineering:							
Other:											

TYPES OF BUSINESS:

Construction, Residential
Land Development

BRANDS/DIVISIONS/AFFILIATES:

Brookfield Homes San Diego, Inc.
Brookfield Washington, Inc.
Brookfield Homes Southland, Inc.
Brookfield Homes Bay Area, Inc.
Brookfield Blue
Brookfield Homes Hawaii

CONTACTS: *Note: Officers with more than one job title may be intentionally listed here more than once.*

Ian G. Cockwell, CEO
Ian G. Cockwell, Pres.
Craig J. Laurie, CFO/Exec. VP
Shane D. Pearson, General Counsel/VP
Linda T. Northwood, Dir.-Investor Rel.
Jessica Caldwell, Controller/VP
William B. Seith, Exec. VP-Risk Mgmt.
Stephen P. Doyle, Pres., Brookfield San Diego Holdings LLC
John J. Ryan, Pres., Brookfield Bay Area Holdings LLC
Robert Hubbell, Pres., Brookfield Washington LLC
Robert L. Stelzl, Chmn.

Phone: 703-270-1700	**Fax:** 703-270-1401
Toll-Free:	
Address: 8500 Executive Park Ave., Ste. 300, Fairfax, VA 22031 US	

GROWTH PLANS/SPECIAL FEATURES:

Brookfield Homes Corp. is a residential homebuilder and land developer. The company builds homes and develops land in master-planned communities and infill locations in five markets: the San Francisco Bay Area; Sacramento; Southland/Los Angeles; San Diego/Riverside; and the Washington D.C. area. It develops land for its own communities and sells lots to other homebuilders. In its communities, the company designs, constructs and markets single-family and multi-family homes primarily to move-up and luxury homebuyers. In each of its markets, the firm operates through local business units that are involved in all phases of the planning and building of master-planned communities and infill developments. These phases include sourcing and evaluating land acquisitions; site planning; obtaining entitlements; developing the land; product design; constructing, marketing and selling homes; and homebuyer customer services. The firm owns over 13,000 lots and controls another 11,000 through land options. The company's work begins with the purchase of raw or semi-developed land. It then involves itself with gaining governmental permission in regards to infrastructure development, such as new roads, water and power lines. Upon approval, single-family homes or planned communities of homes with recreational amenities are constructed. In 2009, the company closed a total of 703 homes and sold 469 lots to other homebuilders.

FINANCIALS: **Sales and profits are in thousands of dollars—add 000 to get the full amount. 2009 Note: Financial information for 2009 was not available for all companies at press time.**

2009 Sales: $376,000	2009 Profits: $-33,000	**U.S. Stock Ticker: BHS**
2008 Sales: $449,000	2008 Profits: $-116,000	**Int'l Ticker:** Int'l Exchange:
2007 Sales: $583,000	2007 Profits: $16,000	Employees: 291
2006 Sales: $872,000	2006 Profits: $148,000	Fiscal Year Ends: 12/31
2005 Sales: $1,231,052	2005 Profits: $218,740	Parent Company:

SALARIES/BENEFITS:

Pension Plan:	ESOP Stock Plan:	Profit Sharing:	Top Exec. Salary: $350,000	Bonus: $140,000
Savings Plan:	Stock Purch. Plan:		Second Exec. Salary: $210,000	Bonus: $40,000

OTHER THOUGHTS:

Apparent Women Officers or Directors: 2
Hot Spot for Advancement for Women/Minorities: Y

LOCATIONS: ("Y" = Yes)

West:	Southwest:	Midwest:	Southeast:	Northeast:	International:
Y				Y	

BUILDING MATERIALS HOLDING CORP

www.bmhc.com

Industry Group Code: 444130 **Ranks within this company's industry group:** Sales: 3 Profits: 3

Properties:		Financial Services:		Construction/Development:		Investments:		Specialty Services:		Brokerage:	
Apartments:		Mortgages:		Commercial Construction:		REIT:		Property Management:		Commercial Sales:	
Malls/Shopping:		Title Insurance:		Residential Construction:				Online Services:		Residential Sales:	
Offices:		Property Insurance:		Land Development:				Software/IT:		Specialty:	
Hotels/Motels:				Support Services:	Y			Consulting:			
Industrial/Warehouses:				Design/Engineering:	Y						
Other:											

TYPES OF BUSINESS:

Building Materials & Hardware Stores, Retail
Building & Construction Services

BRANDS/DIVISIONS/AFFILIATES:

BMC West Corporation
SelectBuild Construction
BBP Companies
Campbell Companies
Leaman Building Materials
Riggs Plumbing LLC

CONTACTS: *Note: Officers with more than one job title may be intentionally listed here more than once.*

Robert E. Mellor, CEO
Stanley M. Wilson, COO
Stanley M. Wilson, Pres.
William M. Smartt, CFO/Sr. VP
Steven H. Pearson, Sr. VP-Human Resources
Paul S. Street, Chief Admin. Officer
Paul S. Street, General Counsel/Corp. Sec./Sr. VP
Michael D. Mahre, Sr. VP-Corp. Dev.
Mark R. Kailer, VP/Treas.
Hank L. Finchett, VP-Infrastructure Svcs.
Terrill F. Rust, VP-Application Svcs.
John D. Fa, VP-Real Estate
Eric R. Beem, Controller
Robert E. Mellor, Chmn.

Phone: 208-331-4300	**Fax:** 208-331-4366
Toll-Free:	
Address: 720 Park Blvd., Ste. 200, Boise, ID 83712 US	

GROWTH PLANS/SPECIAL FEATURES:

Building Materials Holding Corporation (BMHC), through wholly-owned subsidiaries BMC West Corporation and SelectBuild Construction, is a leading provider of building materials and services to residential, commercial and industrial contractors as well as professional repair and remodeling contractors and builders. BMC West operates building materials centers primarily in the western U.S. The division's principal products include lumber, panel products, engineered wood products, roofing materials, pre-hung doors and millwork, roof and floor trusses, pre-assembled windows, cabinets, hardware, paint and tools. In addition, BMC West provides value-added services such as pre-cutting lumber and pre-assembling windows to meet customer specifications. The company targets primarily professional contractors and builders engaged in residential construction and, to a lesser extent, light commercial and industrial construction. The firm's other subsidiary, SelectBuild Construction, provides construction services to high-volume production homebuilders. Services include framing, concrete, plumbing, other construction trades, managing labor and construction schedules as well as sourcing materials. BMHC's primary growth plans consist of expansion through acquisitions, focusing on those that complement existing operations in growing building markets, and those that provide entry into fast-growing, attractive new markets. In June 2009, BMHC began a restructuring plan that was initiated under Chapter 11 proceedings. The company will continue to conduct its ordinary business during the reorganization process. As part of the reorganization process, BMHC will close all of its facilities in Nevada; will consolidate its Portland operations with its Vancouver, Washington facility; will consolidate its California facilities; and additional consolidations will take place in Texas, Arizona and Colorado.

The company offers its employees a 401(k) plan; profit sharing and stock ownership; and medical, dental and health.

FINANCIALS:

Sales and profits are in thousands of dollars—add 000 to get the full amount. 2009 Note: Financial information for 2009 was not available for all companies at press time.

2009 Sales: $	2009 Profits: $	**U.S. Stock Ticker: BLGM**
2008 Sales: $1,324,679	2008 Profits: $-214,809	**Int'l Ticker:** Int'l Exchange:
2007 Sales: $2,179,073	2007 Profits: $-312,713	Employees: 8,200
2006 Sales: $2,951,162	2006 Profits: $102,074	Fiscal Year Ends: 12/31
2005 Sales: $2,878,408	2005 Profits: $129,507	Parent Company:

SALARIES/BENEFITS:

Pension Plan:	ESOP Stock Plan: Y	Profit Sharing: Y	Top Exec. Salary: $	Bonus: $833,690
Savings Plan: Y	Stock Purch. Plan:		Second Exec. Salary: $	Bonus: $

OTHER THOUGHTS:

Apparent Women Officers or Directors: 1
Hot Spot for Advancement for Women/Minorities:

LOCATIONS: ("Y" = Yes)

West:	Southwest:	Midwest:	Southeast:	Northeast:	International:
Y	Y	Y	Y	Y	

BURNS & MCDONNELL

www.burnsmcd.com

Industry Group Code: 237 **Ranks within this company's industry group:** Sales: Profits:

Properties:		Financial Services:		Construction/Development:		Investments:		Specialty Services:		Brokerage:	
Apartments:		Mortgages:		Commercial Construction:	Y	REIT:		Property Management:		Commercial Sales:	
Malls/Shopping:		Title Insurance:		Residential Construction:				Online Services:		Residential Sales:	
Offices:		Property Insurance:		Land Development:				Software/IT:		Specialty:	
Hotels/Motels:				Support Services:				Consulting:			
Industrial/Warehouses:				Design/Engineering:	Y						
Other:											

TYPES OF BUSINESS:

Engineering
Construction
Consulting
Environmental Consulting
Architecture & Design
Energy Transmission

BRANDS/DIVISIONS/AFFILIATES:

CONTACTS:

Note: Officers with more than one job title may be intentionally listed here more than once.

Greg Graves, CEO
Greg Graves, Pres.
Joe Brooks, Dir.-Corp. Mktg.
Kathleen Huttmann, Mgr.-Bus. Dev.
Roger Dick, Mgr.-Mktg. Comm.
Mark Taylor, VP/Treas.
Michael S. DeBacker, Dir.-Transportation Practice
Stephen A. Brown, Dir.-Global Security Svcs.
John Mitchell, Dir.-Wastewater Practice
John Lionberger, VP
Greg Graves, Chmn.

Phone: 816-333-9400	**Fax:** 816-822-3412
Toll-Free:	
Address: 9400 Ward Pkwy., Kansas City, MO 64114 US	

GROWTH PLANS/SPECIAL FEATURES:

Burns & McDonnell provides engineering, architectural, construction, environmental and consulting services across the U.S. and worldwide. The company divides its businesses into 10 global practice units and an operations division. The Aviation and Facilities unit designs and constructs airport terminals; military facilities; aerospace manufacturing facilities; runways and airfield infrastructure; and aviation support facilities. The Business and Technology Services unit provides business consulting services such as project development, analysis and forecasting; energy services; and information technology services. The Construction/Design-Build unit provides post-construction services to companies in the power, process, aviation, infrastructure and commercial industries. The Energy unit is focused on sustainability in construction and renovation, with projects ranging from the construction of baseload coal-fired power generation plants and high-voltage transmission networks to comprehensive energy system overhauls. The Environmental unit's services include hazardous waste remediation, solid waste management and emergency response. The Environmental Studies and Permitting unit offers permitting, ecology, studies and land management services. The Healthcare and Research Facilities unit constructs hospitals, laboratories and research facilities, and offers additional planning, management and landscape architecture services. The Infrastructure unit is focused on water and transportation projects, providing collection system construction, wastewater services and watershed management. The Process and Industrial unit designs manufacturing plants, refineries, warehouses and assembly facilities. The Transmission and Distribution unit includes the construction of transportation infrastructure and electrical energy transmission services. Burns & McDonnell's customers include companies in a wide variety of industries, including the energy, environmental, government and defense, healthcare, manufacturing, telecommunications and water and wastewater markets.

Employees of the firm are offered health and life insurance; short and long-term disability; flexible spending accounts; personal time off; eight paid holidays; educational seminars; fitness center; and tuition assistance. The company is 100% employee-owned through its employee stock ownership plan.

FINANCIALS:

Sales and profits are in thousands of dollars—add 000 to get the full amount. 2009 Note: Financial information for 2009 was not available for all companies at press time.

2009 Sales: $	2009 Profits: $	**U.S. Stock Ticker: Private**
2008 Sales: $	2008 Profits: $	**Int'l Ticker:** Int'l Exchange:
2007 Sales: $	2007 Profits: $	Employees: 2,850
2006 Sales: $	2006 Profits: $	Fiscal Year Ends: 12/31
2005 Sales: $	2005 Profits: $	Parent Company:

SALARIES/BENEFITS:

Pension Plan:	ESOP Stock Plan: Y	Profit Sharing:	Top Exec. Salary: $	Bonus: $
Savings Plan: Y	Stock Purch. Plan:		Second Exec. Salary: $	Bonus: $

OTHER THOUGHTS:

Apparent Women Officers or Directors: 3
Hot Spot for Advancement for Women/Minorities: Y

LOCATIONS: ("Y" = Yes)

West:	Southwest:	Midwest:	Southeast:	Northeast:	International:
Y	Y	Y	Y	Y	

BUTLER MANUFACTURING CO

www.butlermfg.com

Industry Group Code: 332311 **Ranks within this company's industry group:** Sales: Profits:

Properties:		Financial Services:		Construction/Development:		Investments:		Specialty Services:		Brokerage:	
Apartments:		Mortgages:		Commercial Construction:	Y	REIT:		Property Management:		Commercial Sales:	
Malls/Shopping:		Title Insurance:		Residential Construction:				Online Services:		Residential Sales:	
Offices:		Property Insurance:		Land Development:				Software/IT:		Specialty:	
Hotels/Motels:				Support Services:	Y			Consulting:			
Industrial/Warehouses:				Design/Engineering:	Y						
Other:											

TYPES OF BUSINESS:

Construction Materials
Prefabricated Metal Building & Component Manufacturing
Pre-Engineered Building Systems & Components
Architectural Aluminum Systems & Components
Construction & Real Estate Services

BRANDS/DIVISIONS/AFFILIATES:

BlueScope Steel, Ltd.
Vistawall Group
Butler Heavy Construction
Butler Buildings North America

CONTACTS:

Note: Officers with more than one job title may be intentionally listed here more than once.

Ted Wolfe, Pres.
Tom Gilligan, VP-Mktg. & Sales
Kim Moyer, Mgr.-Human Resources
Kostas Kariotis, Mgr.-Oper.
Patrick Finan, Pres., Butler Buildings North America
Ron Miller, VP-Mktg.

Phone: 816-968-3000 **Fax:** 816-968-3279
Toll-Free:
Address: 1540 Genessee St., Kansas City, MO 64102 US

GROWTH PLANS/SPECIAL FEATURES:

Butler Manufacturing Co., a subsidiary of BlueScope Steel Limited, markets, designs and manufactures steel building systems for nonresidential buildings. It also executes construction and real estate operations. The firm manufactures five main types of product: structural systems, consisting of support systems (trusses, joists and anything else that keeps a building standing up); wall systems, which come in a variety of textures but are generally utilitarian in design; roofs; Vistawall architectural products, covering a variety of different components, such as doors, windows, skylights and store fronts, among many other things; and environmental designs, mainly with a focus on reduced energy consumption. Butler's largest division designs, manufactures, markets and sells steel building systems. This division's products are mostly custom-designed and engineered one- to eight-story steel buildings for use as offices, manufacturing facilities, warehouses, schools, shopping centers, agricultural buildings and other applications. Butler's specialized construction services segment consists of BlueScope Construction, a construction company specializing in large, multiple-site projects and Butler Heavy Structures,a supplier of pre-engineered building shell materials, offering design, delivery, installation and complete turnkey construction services. The company offers specialized government construction services through Butler GSA, which has experience in military base construction, Air Force hangars, Coast Guard marine storage and maintenance facilities and more. Additionally the Butler Research Center simulates worst case scenario weather conditions designed to test Butler products and ensure their durability. The company has subsidiaries and joint-ventures located throughout the U.S., China, Europe, Japan, Saudi Arabia and Latin America. Current projects include a 16,000 square foot infant and daycare facility at Fort Riley, Kansas, for military families returning from a 10-year station in Germany.

FINANCIALS:

Sales and profits are in thousands of dollars—add 000 to get the full amount. 2009 Note: Financial information for 2009 was not available for all companies at press time.

2009 Sales: $	2009 Profits: $	**U.S. Stock Ticker: Subsidiary**
2008 Sales: $	2008 Profits: $	**Int'l Ticker:** Int'l Exchange:
2007 Sales: $	2007 Profits: $	Employees:
2006 Sales: $	2006 Profits: $	Fiscal Year Ends: 6/30
2005 Sales: $	2005 Profits: $	Parent Company: BLUESCOPE STEEL LIMITED

SALARIES/BENEFITS:

Pension Plan:	ESOP Stock Plan:	Profit Sharing:	Top Exec. Salary: $	Bonus: $
Savings Plan:	Stock Purch. Plan:		Second Exec. Salary: $	Bonus: $

OTHER THOUGHTS:

Apparent Women Officers or Directors: 1
Hot Spot for Advancement for Women/Minorities:

LOCATIONS: ("Y" = Yes)

West:	Southwest:	Midwest:	Southeast:	Northeast:	International:
Y	Y	Y	Y	Y	Y

CAMDEN PROPERTY TRUST

www.camdenliving.com

Industry Group Code: 531120 **Ranks within this company's industry group:** Sales: 28 Profits: 29

Properties:		Financial Services:		Construction/Development:		Investments:		Specialty Services:		Brokerage:	
Apartments:	Y	Mortgages:		Commercial Construction:		REIT:	Y	Property Management:		Commercial Sales:	
Malls/Shopping:		Title Insurance:		Residential Construction:	Y			Online Services:		Residential Sales:	
Offices:		Property Insurance:		Land Development:				Software/IT:		Specialty:	
Hotels/Motels:				Support Services:	Y			Consulting:	Y		
Industrial/Warehouses:				Design/Engineering:							
Other:											

TYPES OF BUSINESS:

Real Estate Investment Trust
Apartment Communities
Construction Services
Consulting Services

BRANDS/DIVISIONS/AFFILIATES:

Onex Real Estate Partners
Camden Plaza
Camden Main & Jamboree

CONTACTS:

Note: Officers with more than one job title may be intentionally listed here more than once.

Richard J. Campo, CEO
H. Malcolm Stewart, COO
D. Keith Oden, Pres.
Dennis M. Steen, CFO/Sr. VP-Finance
John Selindh, VP-Mktg.
Cynthia B. Scharringhausen, Sr. VP-Human Resources
Jimmy Whorton, VP-IT
Robert Fisher, General Counsel/VP/Sec.
Kim Callahan, VP-Investor Rel.
Michael P. Gallagher, Chief Acct. Officer/VP
Ross Wehman, VP-Tax
Sarah Barletta, VP-Employee Benefits
Kip Zacharias, VP-Bus. Svcs.
Stephen R. Hefner, Sr. VP-Construction
Richard J. Campo, Chmn.

Phone: 713-354-2500	**Fax:** 713-354-2700
Toll-Free: 800-922-6336	
Address: 3 Greenway Plz., Ste. 1300, Houston, TX 77046 US	

GROWTH PLANS/SPECIAL FEATURES:

Camden Property Trust is one of the largest real estate investment trusts (REIT) in the U.S, specializing in several disciplines within the residential real estate industry. The company acquires, develops, manages, disposes and redevelops apartment home communities and offers consulting, building and construction services for third-party clients. Camden currently owns interests in and operates 183 communities consisting of approximately 63,286 apartment homes geographically dispersed in 13 states through the Sunbelt and Midwestern markets. The company has pursued an aggressive growth strategy over the past decade, with more than a $1 billion in construction since 1996. Camden maintains a diversified portfolio of residential properties ranging from upscale urban residences to middle-class housing in established suburban neighborhoods. Camden has two joint ventures with Onex Real Estate Partners valued at a total of $150 million: Camden Main & Jamboree in Irvine California, which features 290 luxury apartments; and Camden Plaza, which is a 271-unit facility in Houston, Texas. The company currently has two properties under development, and after completion, the firm's portfolio is expected to increase to 63,658 homes in 185 properties. In March 2010, the company launched web sites specifically designed for mobile phone users, which allow people to view floor plans, search for and reserve apartments.

Employees are offered medical, dental and vision insurance; flexible spending accounts; life insurance; disability coverage; adoption benefits; a 401(k) plan; an employee stock purchase plan; apartment discounts; education assistance; scholarship funds for children of employees; and an employee assistance program.

FINANCIALS:

Sales and profits are in thousands of dollars—add 000 to get the full amount. 2009 Note: Financial information for 2009 was not available for all companies at press time.

2009 Sales: $623,926	2009 Profits: $-50,800	**U.S. Stock Ticker: CPT**
2008 Sales: $624,016	2008 Profits: $70,973	**Int'l Ticker:** Int'l Exchange:
2007 Sales: $588,319	2007 Profits: $148,457	Employees: 1,750
2006 Sales: $561,029	2006 Profits: $232,846	Fiscal Year Ends: 12/31
2005 Sales: $504,061	2005 Profits: $199,086	Parent Company:

SALARIES/BENEFITS:

Pension Plan:	ESOP Stock Plan:	Profit Sharing:	Top Exec. Salary: $447,700	Bonus: $403,750
Savings Plan: Y	Stock Purch. Plan: Y		Second Exec. Salary: $447,700	Bonus: $403,750

OTHER THOUGHTS:

Apparent Women Officers or Directors: 12
Hot Spot for Advancement for Women/Minorities: Y

LOCATIONS: ("Y" = Yes)

West:	Southwest:	Midwest:	Southeast:	Northeast:	International:
Y	Y	Y	Y	Y	

CAMP DRESSER & MCKEE INC

www.cdm.com

Industry Group Code: 237 **Ranks within this company's industry group:** Sales: Profits:

Properties:		Financial Services:		Construction/Development:		Investments:		Specialty Services:		Brokerage:	
Apartments:		Mortgages:		Commercial Construction:	Y	REIT:		Property Management:		Commercial Sales:	
Malls/Shopping:		Title Insurance:		Residential Construction:				Online Services:		Residential Sales:	
Offices:		Property Insurance:		Land Development:				Software/IT:		Specialty:	
Hotels/Motels:				Support Services:				Consulting:			
Industrial/Warehouses:				Design/Engineering:	Y						
Other:											

TYPES OF BUSINESS:

Engineering & Construction
Water Management
Environmental Services
Design Services
Information Management & Technology
Consulting
Facilities Design
Geotechnical Services

BRANDS/DIVISIONS/AFFILIATES:

CDM
CDM International Inc
CDM Constructors Inc
CDM Federal Programs Corporation
CDM Consult GmbH

CONTACTS:

Note: Officers with more than one job title may be intentionally listed here more than once.

Richard D. Fox, CEO
John D. Manning, COO
John D. Manning, Pres.
Paul R. Brown, Chief Mktg. Officer
William S. Howard, CTO/Exec. VP
Paul G. Camell, Chief Admin. Officer
Paul R. Brown, Exec. VP-Global Market Dev.
John L. Roberts, Exec. VP
Paul G. Camell, Exec. VP-Mergers & Acquisitions
Timothy B. Wall, Pres., Federal Svcs. Group
Stephen J. Hickox, Group Pres., Public Svcs., N. Amer.E.&Latin Amer.
Richard D. Fox, Chmn.
Alex H. Makled, Group Pres., Client Svcs., EU, Middle East, Africa

Phone: 617-452-6000 **Fax:** 617-452-8000
Toll-Free:
Address: 1 Cambridge Pl., 50 Hampshire St., Cambridge, MA 02139 US

GROWTH PLANS/SPECIAL FEATURES:

Camp Dresser & McKee, Inc. (CDM) provides services in engineering, consulting, construction and operations. The company has five operating units: client services - Europe, Middle East and Africa; federal services; industrial services; public services - North America east & Latin America; and public services - North America west/central & Asia. Supporting these units are the consulting services; engineering services; construction services; and the operations services. Consulting services include architecture; asset, energy and program management; environmental management systems; information management and technology; management consulting; security; and sustainable development. Engineering services include 3D design; automation and instrumentation; and civil, electrical, geotechnical, mechanical, process and structural engineering. Construction services include constructability and value engineering reviews; cost estimating; design-build and alternative delivery methods; engineering services during construction; general contracting; procurement; and project controls. Operations services include contract management; contract operations; operations and maintenance; and operations optimization. CDM's work has involved solid waste and wastewater purification facilities; municipal data management systems; airports, dams, harbors and bridges; a wildlife refuge; major universities; municipal railways; and sports facilities. The firm has a number of subsidiaries including CDM International, Inc., offering CDM's full range of services in Europe, Latin America, the Middle East and Asia; CDM Constructors, Inc., providing design, construction, remediation, general contracting and equipment fabrication services worldwide; and CDM Federal Programs Corporation, offering environmental management services for the EPA, Department of Energy, Department of Defense and other U.S. government agencies. Additionally, CDM owns a majority interest in geotechnical and environmental consulting and design firm, CDM Consult GmbH, in Germany.

Employees of CDM receive medical, dental and vision plans; life insurance; spouse and domestic partner benefits; a commuter program; flexible spending accounts; an employee assistance program; and tuition assistance.

FINANCIALS:

Sales and profits are in thousands of dollars—add 000 to get the full amount. 2009 Note: Financial information for 2009 was not available for all companies at press time.

2009 Sales: $ | 2009 Profits: $
2008 Sales: $ | 2008 Profits: $
2007 Sales: $ | 2007 Profits: $
2006 Sales: $ | 2006 Profits: $
2005 Sales: $ | 2005 Profits: $

U.S. Stock Ticker: Private
Int'l Ticker: Int'l Exchange:
Employees: 4,500
Fiscal Year Ends: 12/31
Parent Company:

SALARIES/BENEFITS:

Pension Plan: | ESOP Stock Plan: | Profit Sharing: Y | Top Exec. Salary: $ | Bonus: $
Savings Plan: Y | Stock Purch. Plan: | | Second Exec. Salary: $ | Bonus: $

OTHER THOUGHTS:

Apparent Women Officers or Directors:
Hot Spot for Advancement for Women/Minorities:

LOCATIONS: ("Y" = Yes)

West:	Southwest:	Midwest:	Southeast:	Northeast:	International:
Y	Y	Y	Y	Y	Y

CAPITAL AUTOMOTIVE REIT

www.capitalautomotive.com

Industry Group Code: 531120 **Ranks within this company's industry group:** Sales: Profits:

Properties:		Financial Services:		Construction/Development:		Investments:		Specialty Services:		Brokerage:	
Apartments:		Mortgages:		Commercial Construction:		REIT:	Y	Property Management:		Commercial Sales:	
Malls/Shopping:		Title Insurance:		Residential Construction:				Online Services:		Residential Sales:	
Offices:		Property Insurance:		Land Development:				Software/IT:		Specialty:	
Hotels/Motels:				Support Services:				Consulting:			
Industrial/Warehouses:				Design/Engineering:							
Other:	Y										

TYPES OF BUSINESS:

Real Estate Investment Trust
Automotive Retail Real Estate

BRANDS/DIVISIONS/AFFILIATES:

DRA Investors, LLC
Sonic Automotive, Inc.

CONTACTS:

Note: Officers with more than one job title may be intentionally listed here more than once.

Thomas D. Eckert, CEO
Jay M. Ferriero, COO/Exec. VP
Thomas D. Eckert, Pres.
David S. Kay, CFO/Sr. VP
John M. Weaver, General Counsel/Exec. VP/Corp. Sec.
P. James Kahler, Treas./VP
Joseph P. Connolly, VP-Western Region Acquisitions
Daniel E. Garces, VP/Sr. Portfolio Mgr.-Midwest Acquisitions
John J. Pohanka, Chmn.
Willie Beck, VP-Eastern U.S. & Canadian Acquisitions

Phone: 703-288-3075	**Fax:** 703-288-3375
Toll-Free: 877-422-7288	
Address: 8270 Greensboro Dr., Ste. 950, McLean, VA 22102 US	

GROWTH PLANS/SPECIAL FEATURES:

Capital Automotive REIT (CARS), a private real estate investment trust owned by DRA Advisors LLC, is a finance company focused on automotive retail real estate, with almost $3.8 billion invested in more than 550 automotive properties. The company's properties are located in 37 states and Canada, and make up more than 17.5 million square feet of retail building space on over 3,000 acres of land. Capital's tenants operate franchises representing 46 brands of motor vehicles. Capital's strategy is to acquire real estate throughout the U.S. and then make improvements so that operators of multi-site, multi-franchised automotive dealerships and related businesses can use the piece of property. The company engages in a sale-leaseback transaction with automotive dealers, in which the dealers sell their real estate to the firm and then lease it back. This allows the dealers to tap into 100% of their real estate equity while maintaining long-term control of their property. The initial lease term is generally 15-20 years with options for renewal. Capital seeks to invest in properties used by high-quality, well-managed dealer groups that have demonstrated a consistent growth and strong operating results in top metropolitan markets. A typical investment begins at $10 million but the firm will consider an investment as small as $5 million. The firm can also purchase properties with operating partnership units, which are exchangeable for common stock. This allows dealers to defer large portions of their tax liability from selling their properties for cash.

DRA offers employees medical, dental and vision; a prescription drug plan; 401(k) savings and matching plan; flexible spending account; commuter subsidy; an employee assistance program; short and long term disability; life insurance; a discount program; and gym memberships.

FINANCIALS:

Sales and profits are in thousands of dollars—add 000 to get the full amount. 2009 Note: Financial information for 2009 was not available for all companies at press time.

2009 Sales: $	2009 Profits: $	**U.S. Stock Ticker: Private**
2008 Sales: $	2008 Profits: $	**Int'l Ticker:** Int'l Exchange:
2007 Sales: $	2007 Profits: $	Employees:
2006 Sales: $	2006 Profits: $	Fiscal Year Ends: 12/31
2005 Sales: $	2005 Profits: $	Parent Company: DRA ADVISORS LLC

SALARIES/BENEFITS:

Pension Plan:	ESOP Stock Plan:	Profit Sharing:	Top Exec. Salary: $	Bonus: $
Savings Plan: Y	Stock Purch. Plan:		Second Exec. Salary: $	Bonus: $

OTHER THOUGHTS:

Apparent Women Officers or Directors:
Hot Spot for Advancement for Women/Minorities:

LOCATIONS: ("Y" = Yes)

West:	Southwest:	Midwest:	Southeast:	Northeast:	International:
Y	Y	Y	Y	Y	

CAPITAL PACIFIC HOLDINGS

www.capitalpacifichomes.com

Industry Group Code: 2361 **Ranks within this company's industry group:** Sales: Profits:

Properties:		Financial Services:		Construction/Development:		Investments:		Specialty Services:		Brokerage:	
Apartments:		Mortgages:	Y	Commercial Construction:		REIT:		Property Management:		Commercial Sales:	
Malls/Shopping:		Title Insurance:		Residential Construction:	Y			Online Services:		Residential Sales:	
Offices:		Property Insurance:		Land Development:	Y			Software/IT:		Specialty:	
Hotels/Motels:				Support Services:				Consulting:			
Industrial/Warehouses:				Design/Engineering:							
Other:											

TYPES OF BUSINESS:

Homebuilding
Land Development
Mortgage Brokerage
Commercial Properties Management

BRANDS/DIVISIONS/AFFILIATES:

Capital Pacific Homes
Capital Pacific Holdings, LLC
Capital Pacific Home Loans, LP
Makar Properties

CONTACTS:

Note: Officers with more than one job title may be intentionally listed here more than once.

Hadi Makarechian, CEO
Hadi Makarechian, Pres.
Matthew C. Kern, CFO
Sherry S. Irani, Treas.
Hadi Makarechian, Chmn.

Phone: 949-622-8400	**Fax:** 949-622-8404
Toll-Free:	
Address: 4100 MacArthur Blvd., Ste. 120, Newport Beach, CA 92660 US	

GROWTH PLANS/SPECIAL FEATURES:

Capital Pacific Holdings, Inc. (CPHI) is a diversified real estate development company. The Newport Beach, California-based firm has two main segments: homebuilding and mixed-use land development. CPHI develops communities of new homes for buyers (under Capital Pacific Homes) with varying lifestyles and budgets throughout Arizona, California, Colorado and Texas. The company builds entry-level, move-up, and semi-custom homes, as well as commercial properties. CPHI's operations are divided into five divisions: Residential, commercial, mixed-use land development, joint ventures and managed projects. The residential division has constructed homes for more than 23,000 customers and closes as many as 1,470 homes and lots annually; homes built by the firm range from $180,000 to $1 million. The residential division also builds, decorates, furnishes and landscapes model homes for its company developments and maintains on-site sales offices. Acting as a general contractor, CPHI subcontracts its construction operations to smaller firms. The commercial properties division operates under the Makar Properties subsidiary, which manages a variety of commercial properties, including the St. Regis Hotel in Monarch Beach, California. The mixed-use land development division is also managed by Makar. The joint ventures division acts in tandem with partners that provide capital and specific expertise needed by the company in order to increase access to financing and quality sites. Lastly, the managed projects division develops new home communities for third party owners.

FINANCIALS:

Sales and profits are in thousands of dollars—add 000 to get the full amount. 2009 Note: Financial information for 2009 was not available for all companies at press time.

2009 Sales: $	2009 Profits: $	**U.S. Stock Ticker: Private**
2008 Sales: $	2008 Profits: $	**Int'l Ticker:** Int'l Exchange:
2007 Sales: $	2007 Profits: $	Employees:
2006 Sales: $	2006 Profits: $	Fiscal Year Ends: 2/28
2005 Sales: $	2005 Profits: $	Parent Company:

SALARIES/BENEFITS:

Pension Plan:	ESOP Stock Plan:	Profit Sharing:	Top Exec. Salary: $	Bonus: $
Savings Plan:	Stock Purch. Plan:		Second Exec. Salary: $	Bonus: $

OTHER THOUGHTS:

Apparent Women Officers or Directors: 1
Hot Spot for Advancement for Women/Minorities:

LOCATIONS: ("Y" = Yes)

West:	Southwest:	Midwest:	Southeast:	Northeast:	International:
Y	Y				

CAPITAL SENIOR LIVING CORP

www.capitalsenior.com

Industry Group Code: 623110 **Ranks within this company's industry group:** Sales: 7 Profits: 3

Properties:		Financial Services:		Construction/Development:		Investments:		Specialty Services:		Brokerage:	
Apartments:		Mortgages:		Commercial Construction:		REIT:		Property Management:		Commercial Sales:	
Malls/Shopping:		Title Insurance:		Residential Construction:				Online Services:		Residential Sales:	
Offices:		Property Insurance:		Land Development:				Software/IT:		Specialty:	
Hotels/Motels:				Support Services:				Consulting:			
Industrial/Warehouses:				Design/Engineering:							
Other:	Y										

TYPES OF BUSINESS:

Long-Term Health Care
Nursing Homes
Assisted Living Services
Home Care Services

BRANDS/DIVISIONS/AFFILIATES:

CONTACTS:

Note: Officers with more than one job title may be intentionally listed here more than once.

Lawrence A. Cohen, CEO
Keith N. Johannessen, COO
Keith N. Johannessen, Pres.
Ralph A. Beattie, CFO/Exec. VP
Rob Goodpaster, VP-Nat'l Mktg.
David R. Brickman, General Counsel/VP/Sec.
David Beathard, VP-Oper.
Glen Campbell, VP-Dev.
Gloria Holland, VP-Finance
Robert Hollister, Property Controller

Phone: 972-770-5600	**Fax:** 972-770-5666
Toll-Free:	
Address: 14160 Dallas Pkwy., Ste. 300, Dallas, TX 75254 US	

GROWTH PLANS/SPECIAL FEATURES:

Capital Senior Living Corporation (CSL) is one of the nation's largest operators and developers of residential communities for seniors. The firm operates 66 communities: one managed for a third party; 25 which are leased; and 40 in which it maintains at least partial ownership. CSL offers its senior living services in 23 states. Its combined facilities can support approximately 10,000 residents. Approximately 94% of the company's revenue is generated through private pay parties at these communities. The firm provides senior living services to the elderly, including independent living, assisted living, skilled nursing and home care services. Many of CSL's communities offer a continuum of care to meet its residents' needs as they change over time. This continuum of care, which integrates independent living, assisted living and home care through independent home care agencies or the company's home care agency, sustains residents' autonomy and independence based on their physical and mental abilities. Each Capital community features social and recreational programs, maid service, restaurant-quality meals and complimentary laundry rooms.

Employees are offered medical and dental insurance; life insurance; and a 401(k) plan.

FINANCIALS:

Sales and profits are in thousands of dollars—add 000 to get the full amount. 2009 Note: Financial information for 2009 was not available for all companies at press time.

2009 Sales: $191,991	2009 Profits: $2,759	**U.S. Stock Ticker: CSU**
2008 Sales: $193,274	2008 Profits: $3,724	**Int'l Ticker:** Int'l Exchange:
2007 Sales: $189,052	2007 Profits: $4,360	Employees: 3,676
2006 Sales: $159,070	2006 Profits: $-2,600	Fiscal Year Ends: 12/31
2005 Sales: $126,404	2005 Profits: $-5,354	Parent Company:

SALARIES/BENEFITS:

Pension Plan:	ESOP Stock Plan:	Profit Sharing:	Top Exec. Salary: $422,173	Bonus: $189,053
Savings Plan: Y	Stock Purch. Plan:		Second Exec. Salary: $351,811	Bonus: $118,742

OTHER THOUGHTS:

Apparent Women Officers or Directors: 2
Hot Spot for Advancement for Women/Minorities:

LOCATIONS: ("Y" = Yes)

West:	Southwest:	Midwest:	Southeast:	Northeast:	International:
Y	Y	Y	Y	Y	

CAPMARK FINANCIAL GROUP INC

www.capmark.com

Industry Group Code: 522310 **Ranks within this company's industry group:** Sales: Profits: 3

Properties:		Financial Services:		Construction/Development:		Investments:		Specialty Services:		Brokerage:	
Apartments:		Mortgages:	Y	Commercial Construction:		REIT:		Property Management:		Commercial Sales:	
Malls/Shopping:		Title Insurance:		Residential Construction:				Online Services:		Residential Sales:	
Offices:		Property Insurance:		Land Development:				Software/IT:		Specialty:	
Hotels/Motels:				Support Services:				Consulting:	Y		
Industrial/Warehouses:				Design/Engineering:							
Other:											

TYPES OF BUSINESS:

Commercial Real Estate & Construction Lending
Loan Services
Investments
Investment Research

BRANDS/DIVISIONS/AFFILIATES:

Capmark Investments LP

CONTACTS:

Note: Officers with more than one job title may be intentionally listed here more than once.

Jay N. Levine, CEO
Jay N. Levine, Pres.
Frederick Arnold, CFO/Exec. VP
Linda A. Pickles, Exec. VP-Human Resources
Linda A. Pickles, Chief Admin. Officer/Exec. VP
Thomas L. Fairfield, General Counsel/Exec. VP
Paul W. Kopsky, Jr., Controller/Chief Acct. Officer/Exec. VP
Michael I. Lipson, Exec. VP/Pres., Capmark Finance, Inc.
William Gallagher, Chief Risk Officer/Exec. VP
Dennis D. Dammerman, Chmn.

Phone: 215-328-4622	**Fax:**
Toll-Free: 888-848-2276	
Address: 116 Welsh Rd., Horsham, PA 19044 US	

GROWTH PLANS/SPECIAL FEATURES:

Capmark Financial Group, Inc., is a real estate finance company. The firm has three core businesses: lending and mortgage banking; investments and funds management; and services. The lending and mortgage banking unit originated $10.5 billion in primarily commercial loans worldwide in 2008. The investments unit, comprising subsidiary Capmark Investments LP, offers investors private funds and separate accounts in equity real estate and higher-yield mortgage plans. Capmark Investments has approximately $9 billion in investments under management and supervision. The services unit offers clients the ability to outsource commercial loan servicing needs for managing and resolving real estate asset portfolios. Services customers include government agencies, investment banks, CMBS (commercial mortgage backed securities) trusts and public retirement funds. In total, the firm's servicing portfolio includes approximately 49,000 loans, equaling an outstanding principal balance of over $362 billion. Capmark has operations in the U.S., Japan, India, China and the U.K. In early 2008, the company's subsidiaries sold significant interests in 34 European loans to GE Real Estate. Capmark filed for bankruptcy protection in October 2009 as a result of a steep decline in commercial property values underlying its mortgages and a very high default rate by its borrowers..

Capmark offers its employees health benefits, a 401(k) plan, ongoing training and educational opportunities including tuition assistance.

FINANCIALS:

Sales and profits are in thousands of dollars—add 000 to get the full amount. 2009 Note: Financial information for 2009 was not available for all companies at press time.

2009 Sales: $	2009 Profits: $	**U.S. Stock Ticker: Private**
2008 Sales: $	2008 Profits: $-1,352,800	**Int'l Ticker:** Int'l Exchange:
2007 Sales: $1,212,100	2007 Profits: $280,300	Employees:
2006 Sales: $	2006 Profits: $	Fiscal Year Ends: 12/31
2005 Sales: $	2005 Profits: $	Parent Company:

SALARIES/BENEFITS:

Pension Plan:	ESOP Stock Plan:	Profit Sharing:	Top Exec. Salary: $1,549,039	Bonus: $
Savings Plan: Y	Stock Purch. Plan:		Second Exec. Salary: $500,000	Bonus: $

OTHER THOUGHTS:

Apparent Women Officers or Directors: 1
Hot Spot for Advancement for Women/Minorities:

LOCATIONS: ("Y" = Yes)

West:	Southwest:	Midwest:	Southeast:	Northeast:	International:
Y	Y	Y	Y	Y	Y

CAPREIT INC

www.capreit.com

Industry Group Code: 531110 **Ranks within this company's industry group:** Sales: Profits:

Properties:		Financial Services:		Construction/Development:		Investments:		Specialty Services:		Brokerage:	
Apartments:	Y	Mortgages:		Commercial Construction:		REIT:	Y	Property Management:	Y	Commercial Sales:	
Malls/Shopping:		Title Insurance:		Residential Construction:				Online Services:		Residential Sales:	
Offices:		Property Insurance:		Land Development:				Software/IT:		Specialty:	
Hotels/Motels:				Support Services:				Consulting:			
Industrial/Warehouses:				Design/Engineering:							
Other:											

TYPES OF BUSINESS:

Real Estate Investment Trust
Apartments
Property Management

BRANDS/DIVISIONS/AFFILIATES:

CONTACTS:

Note: Officers with more than one job title may be intentionally listed here more than once.

Dick Kadish, Pres.
Bruce Esposito, CFO
Sandra Becker, Sr. VP

Phone: 301-231-8700 **Fax:** 301-468-8391
Toll-Free:
Address: 11200 Rockville Pk., Ste. 100, Rockville, MD 20852 US

GROWTH PLANS/SPECIAL FEATURES:

CAPREIT Inc. is a real estate investment trust (REIT) and property manager. Its focus is on the acquisition of multi-family residential properties. Since its founding in 1993, CAPREIT has owned or operated over 200 rental and condominium apartment homes consisting of over 30,000 units and housing over 100,000 families. The company's current holdings include apartment units spread over a broad market area of 19 states. CAPREIT also manages a portfolio of properties for third parties. Most of its properties are spread over the Northeast and Southeast, with additional properties in the Midwest and in California. In acquiring properties, the firm stresses both a viable knowledge of the local market and establishing consistent relationships with its brokers, many of whom have made the company a preferred customer. It targets markets that have both high economic growth characteristics and identifiable barriers to entry. CAPREIT specializes in financing its acquisitions with tax-exempt multifamily housing revenue bonds and, to date, has acquired over $1.5 billion. Its acquisitions team works directly with municipal and state issuing authorities, bond trustees and monitoring agents in closing these financing transactions. CAPREIT has a team of over 400 real estate professionals that handles day-to-day on-site management of its multifamily communities.

FINANCIALS:

Sales and profits are in thousands of dollars—add 000 to get the full amount. 2009 Note: Financial information for 2009 was not available for all companies at press time.

2009 Sales: $ 2009 Profits: $
2008 Sales: $ 2008 Profits: $
2007 Sales: $ 2007 Profits: $
2006 Sales: $ 2006 Profits: $
2005 Sales: $ 2005 Profits: $

U.S. Stock Ticker: Private
Int'l Ticker: Int'l Exchange:
Employees:
Fiscal Year Ends: 12/31
Parent Company:

SALARIES/BENEFITS:

Pension Plan: ESOP Stock Plan: Profit Sharing: Top Exec. Salary: $ Bonus: $
Savings Plan: Stock Purch. Plan: Second Exec. Salary: $ Bonus: $

OTHER THOUGHTS:

Apparent Women Officers or Directors: 1
Hot Spot for Advancement for Women/Minorities:

LOCATIONS: ("Y" = Yes)

West:	Southwest:	Midwest:	Southeast:	Northeast:	International:
Y	Y	Y	Y	Y	

CAPSTEAD MORTGAGE CORPORATION

www.capstead.com

Industry Group Code: 531110 **Ranks within this company's industry group:** Sales: 9 Profits: 5

Properties:		Financial Services:		Construction/Development:		Investments:		Specialty Services:		Brokerage:	
Apartments:		Mortgages:	Y	Commercial Construction:		REIT:	Y	Property Management:		Commercial Sales:	
Malls/Shopping:		Title Insurance:		Residential Construction:				Online Services:		Residential Sales:	
Offices:		Property Insurance:		Land Development:				Software/IT:		Specialty:	
Hotels/Motels:				Support Services:				Consulting:			
Industrial/Warehouses:				Design/Engineering:							
Other:											

TYPES OF BUSINESS:

Real Estate Investment Trust
Mortgage-Backed Securities
Commercial Real Estate

BRANDS/DIVISIONS/AFFILIATES:

CONTACTS:

Note: Officers with more than one job title may be intentionally listed here more than once.

Andrew F. Jacobs, CEO
Andrew F. Jacobs, Pres.
Phillip A. Reinsch, CFO/Exec. VP
Kelly L. Sargent, Contact-Investor Rel.
Robert R. Spears, Jr., Exec. VP-Residential Mortgage Investments
Michael W. Brown, Sr. VP-Asset & Liability Mgmt.
Jack E. Biegler, Chmn.

Phone: 214-874-2323	**Fax:** 214-874-2398
Toll-Free: 800-358-2323	
Address: 8401 N. Central Expressway, Ste. 800, Dallas, TX 75225 US	

GROWTH PLANS/SPECIAL FEATURES:

Capstead Mortgage Corporation, headquartered in Dallas, Texas, operates as a real estate investment trust earning income from investing in real estate-related assets on a leveraged basis and from other investment strategies. For the most part, these investments are limited to single-family residential adjustable-rate mortgage securities issued by such government agencies and government-sponsored entities as Fannie Mae, Freddie Mac and Ginnie Mae. The firm also invests in credit-sensitive commercial mortgage assets. Capstead tends to focus on ARM securities that reset annually or semi-annually and are particularly liquid. Up until 1998, Capstead provided mortgage servicing, but this portfolio was dispensed to GMAC Mortgage Corporation. In recent years, the company acquired an additional 25% of its commercial real estate loan joint venture with Redtail Capital Partners L.P. Capstead previously held a 75% interest; the takeover price was $4 million.

The firm offers its employees benefits such as basic life and AD&D insurance, as well as a 401(k) plan.

FINANCIALS:

Sales and profits are in thousands of dollars—add 000 to get the full amount. 2009 Note: Financial information for 2009 was not available for all companies at press time.

2009 Sales: $314,595	2009 Profits: $129,263	**U.S. Stock Ticker: CMO**
2008 Sales: $400,489	2008 Profits: $125,923	**Int'l Ticker:** Int'l Exchange:
2007 Sales: $311,643	2007 Profits: $24,713	Employees: 16
2006 Sales: $243,272	2006 Profits: $3,843	Fiscal Year Ends: 12/31
2005 Sales: $24,396	2005 Profits: $57,192	Parent Company:

SALARIES/BENEFITS:

Pension Plan:	ESOP Stock Plan:	Profit Sharing:	Top Exec. Salary: $908,000	Bonus: $1,450,000
Savings Plan: Y	Stock Purch. Plan:		Second Exec. Salary: $695,500	Bonus: $1,150,000

OTHER THOUGHTS:

Apparent Women Officers or Directors: 1
Hot Spot for Advancement for Women/Minorities:

LOCATIONS: ("Y" = Yes)

West:	Southwest:	Midwest:	Southeast:	Northeast:	International:
	Y				

CARLSON HOTELS WORLDWIDE

www.carlsonhotels.com

Industry Group Code: 721110 **Ranks within this company's industry group:** Sales: Profits:

Properties:		Financial Services:		Construction/Development:		Investments:		Specialty Services:		Brokerage:	
Apartments:		Mortgages:		Commercial Construction:		REIT:		Property Management:	Y	Commercial Sales:	
Malls/Shopping:		Title Insurance:		Residential Construction:				Online Services:		Residential Sales:	
Offices:		Property Insurance:		Land Development:				Software/IT:		Specialty:	
Hotels/Motels:	Y			Support Services:				Consulting:			
Industrial/Warehouses:				Design/Engineering:							
Other:											

TYPES OF BUSINESS:

Hotels & Resorts

BRANDS/DIVISIONS/AFFILIATES:

Regent Hotels & Resorts
Radisson Hotels & Resorts
Park Plaza Hotels & Resorts
Country Inns & Suites By Carlson
Park Inn Hotels
Carlson Companies Inc

CONTACTS: *Note: Officers with more than one job title may be intentionally listed here more than once.*

Hubert Joly, CEO
Hubert Joly, Pres.
Gordon McKinnon, Chief Branding Officer/Exec. VP
Robert Kleinschmidt, Chief Dev. Officer, Carlson Hotels, The Americas
Joan Cronson, Sr. Dir.-Public Rel.
Thorsten Kirschke, Exec. VP/COO-Carlson Hotels, The Americas
Steve Mogck, Exec. VP/COO-Country Inns & Suites, The Americas
Fredrik Korallus, Exec. VP-Global Revenue Generation
Steve Mogck, COO-Country Inns & Suites By Carlson - Americas

Phone: 763-212-4000	**Fax:**
Toll-Free:	
Address: 701 Carlson Pkwy., Minnetonka, MN 55305 US	

GROWTH PLANS/SPECIAL FEATURES:

Carlson Hotels Worldwide, a subsidiary of Carlson Companies, Inc., is a world-leading hotel franchisor. The firm includes more than 1,060 locations in 77 countries. Specific brands include Regent Hotels & Resorts; Radisson Hotels & Resorts; Park Plaza Hotels & Resorts; Park Inn; Country Inns & Suites by Carlson; and Park Inn Hotels. The Regent brand offers luxury accommodations at seven locations with nine more scheduled to open between 2010 and 2012. These new locations include Abu Dhabi, Doha, Bangkok, Phuket, Puerto Rico, Maldives, Kuala Lumpur, Bali and Dubrovnik. The company's Radisson chain owns full-service hotels at 422 locations throughout North America, Latin America, Asia Pacific, Europe, the Middle East and Africa. Radisson Hotels offer pre-arrival online check-in; Sleep Number beds by Select Comfort; a fitness center; and free high-speed Internet access. The Park Inn is the company's economy brand with approximately 100 hotels in operation worldwide. The firm's 36 Park Plaza Hotels are generally 150 rooms or larger and include restaurants, meeting rooms, catering, suites and recreational facilities. Country Inns & Suites By Carlson is a mid-tier lodging chain with more than 485 locations in the Americas, Europe and India and 80 more under development. Specialty services include an in-hotel Read It and Return Lending Library, in which guests can borrow a book and return it on their next stay. In addition to hotels, the firm's parent company, Carlson Companies, owns subsidiaries in the travel, restaurant, cruise and marketing industries. During 2009, the company added a total of 92 hotels to its portfolio. In April 2010, Carlson Hotels announced renovations on a new Radisson Hotel and Spa in Martinique, beginning in June 2010, are scheduled to be completed by late 2011.

FINANCIALS: **Sales and profits are in thousands of dollars—add 000 to get the full amount. 2009 Note: Financial information for 2009 was not available for all companies at press time.**

2009 Sales: $	2009 Profits: $	**U.S. Stock Ticker: Subsidiary**
2008 Sales: $	2008 Profits: $	**Int'l Ticker:** Int'l Exchange:
2007 Sales: $	2007 Profits: $	Employees:
2006 Sales: $	2006 Profits: $	Fiscal Year Ends: 12/31
2005 Sales: $6,000,000	2005 Profits: $	Parent Company: CARLSON COMPANIES INC

SALARIES/BENEFITS:

Pension Plan:	ESOP Stock Plan:	Profit Sharing:	Top Exec. Salary: $	Bonus: $
Savings Plan:	Stock Purch. Plan:		Second Exec. Salary: $	Bonus: $

OTHER THOUGHTS:

Apparent Women Officers or Directors: 1
Hot Spot for Advancement for Women/Minorities: Y

LOCATIONS: ("Y" = Yes)

West:	Southwest:	Midwest:	Southeast:	Northeast:	International:
Y	Y	Y	Y	Y	Y

CAVALIER HOMES INC

www.cavalierhomebuilders.com

Industry Group Code: 321991 **Ranks within this company's industry group:** Sales: 4 Profits: 2

Properties:		Financial Services:		Construction/Development:		Investments:		Specialty Services:		Brokerage:	
Apartments:		Mortgages:	Y	Commercial Construction:		REIT:		Property Management:		Commercial Sales:	
Malls/Shopping:		Title Insurance:		Residential Construction:	Y			Online Services:		Residential Sales:	Y
Offices:		Property Insurance:	Y	Land Development:				Software/IT:		Specialty:	
Hotels/Motels:				Support Services:				Consulting:			
Industrial/Warehouses:				Design/Engineering:							
Other:											

TYPES OF BUSINESS:

Manufactured Housing
Financial Services & Insurance

BRANDS/DIVISIONS/AFFILIATES:

CIS Financial Services Inc
Southern Energy Homes Inc
Clayton Homes Inc
Berkshire Hathaway Inc

CONTACTS:

Note: Officers with more than one job title may be intentionally listed here more than once.

Keith O. Holdbrooks, CEO-Southern Energy Homes
James L. Stariha, CFO-Southern Energy Homes

Phone: 256-747-1575	**Fax:** 256-747-3044
Toll-Free: 866-896-2737	
Address: 47 Wilson Blvd., Addison, AL 35540 US	

GROWTH PLANS/SPECIAL FEATURES:

Cavalier Homes, Inc. designs, manufactures and sells a wide range of mobile homes. The company primarily serves markets in the South Central and South Atlantic regions of the U.S. and sells its homes through a network of independent dealers as well as exclusive dealers. Cavalier offers approximately 250 different models of manufactured homes including modular homes, with a variety of decors that are marketed under multiple brand names. It operates four manufacturing facilities that oversee the entire operation of manufactured home production. This includes producing laminated wallboards, attaching home frames to wheeled axles and overseeing sub-assemblies were various components are attached. It takes between two and six days to complete each home, depending on the size and selected options. Its brands and affiliates include Cavalier Home Builders Addison; Buccaneer Homes; Cavalier Home Builders Nashville; and Mansion Homes. The company now operates as a wholly-owned subsidiary of Southern Energy Homes, Inc., which is itself a subsidiary of Clayton Homes, Inc., a Berkshire Hathaway portfolio company.

FINANCIALS:

Sales and profits are in thousands of dollars—add 000 to get the full amount. 2009 Note: Financial information for 2009 was not available for all companies at press time.

2009 Sales: $	2009 Profits: $	**U.S. Stock Ticker: Subsidiary**
2008 Sales: $164,405	2008 Profits: $3,349	**Int'l Ticker:** Int'l Exchange:
2007 Sales: $206,884	2007 Profits: $-8,519	Employees: 1,012
2006 Sales: $224,602	2006 Profits: $ 172	Fiscal Year Ends: 12/31
2005 Sales: $272,032	2005 Profits: $10,915	Parent Company: SOUTHERN ENERGY HOMES INC

SALARIES/BENEFITS:

Pension Plan:	ESOP Stock Plan:	Profit Sharing:	Top Exec. Salary: $	Bonus: $
Savings Plan:	Stock Purch. Plan:		Second Exec. Salary: $	Bonus: $

OTHER THOUGHTS:

Apparent Women Officers or Directors:
Hot Spot for Advancement for Women/Minorities:

LOCATIONS: ("Y" = Yes)

West:	Southwest:	Midwest:	Southeast:	Northeast:	International:
	Y	Y	Y	Y	

CB RICHARD ELLIS GROUP INC (CBRE)

www.cbre.com

Industry Group Code: 531210 **Ranks within this company's industry group:** Sales: 1 Profits: 3

Properties:		Financial Services:		Construction/Development:		Investments:		Specialty Services:		Brokerage:	
Apartments:		Mortgages:	Y	Commercial Construction:		REIT:		Property Management:		Commercial Sales:	
Malls/Shopping:		Title Insurance:		Residential Construction:				Online Services:		Residential Sales:	
Offices:		Property Insurance:		Land Development:				Software/IT:		Specialty:	
Hotels/Motels:				Support Services:				Consulting:			
Industrial/Warehouses:				Design/Engineering:							
Other:											

TYPES OF BUSINESS:

Real Estate Brokerage
Real Estate Management Services
Mortgage Banking
Investment Management
Consulting Services
Real Estate Investment Trust

BRANDS/DIVISIONS/AFFILIATES:

Trammel Crow
CB Richard Ellis Investors, LLC

CONTACTS: *Note: Officers with more than one job title may be intentionally listed here more than once.*

Brett White, CEO
Bob Sulentic, Pres.
Gil Borok, CFO
Chris Kirk, Dir.-Human Resources
Laurence Midler, General Counsel/Exec. VP
Jim Groch, Global Strategy Officer/Chief Investment Officer
Robert W. McGrath, Sr. Dir.-Media
Arlin E. Gaffner, Chief Acct. Officer
Ray Torto, Global Chief Economist
Mike J. Lafitte, Pres., Americas
Calvin W. Frese, Jr., Pres., Global Svcs.
Brian F. Stoffers, Pres., Capital Markets
Richard C. Blum, Chmn.
Michael J. Strong, CEO/Pres., EMEA

Phone: 310-405-8900	**Fax:**
Toll-Free:	
Address: 11150 Santa Monica Blvd., Ste. 1600, Los Angeles, CA 90025 US	

GROWTH PLANS/SPECIAL FEATURES:

CB Richard Ellis Group, Inc. is one of the world's largest commercial real estate services companies, with more than 300 offices in more than 52 countries. It offers a full range of services to occupiers, owners, lenders and investors in office, retail, industrial, multi-family and other commercial real estate assets. The firm's core services include commercial property and corporate facilities management; tenant representation; property/agency leasing; property sales; valuation; real estate investment management; commercial mortgage origination and servicing; capital markets (equity and debt); development services; and proprietary research. The firm operates its three regional segments through many indirect wholly-owned subsidiaries. The Americas segment accounts for 62.3% of the company's revenue. The Europe, Middle East and Africa, segment has offices in 33 countries, with its largest operations located in the U.K., France, Spain, the Netherlands and Germany. This segment accounts for 19.6% of the firm's revenue. The third, and final, segment is the firm's Asia Pacific segment, which operates in 12 countries. The Asia Pacific division accounts for 12.6% of revenue. The firm's principal operations in Asia are located in China, Hong Kong, India, Japan, Singapore, South Korea and Taiwan. In addition, the company has agreements with affiliated offices in the Philippines, Thailand, Indonesia and Vietnam that generate royalty fees and support cross-referral arrangements. The firm's global investment management business, handled by subsidiary CB Richard Ellis Investors, L.L.C., accounts for 3.4% of revenue and its development services, provided by subsidiary Trammel Crow Company, account for 2.1%. In March 2010, the company launched a solar energy services company, CBRE Solar, which will provide a range of solar energy services covering solar power purchase agreements, roof leases, project development/management and advisory services as well as investment opportunities in solar power projects.

The company offers its employees medical, dental and vision insurance; 401(k); flexible spending accounts; an employee assistance program and paid vacation and holidays.

FINANCIALS: **Sales and profits are in thousands of dollars—add 000 to get the full amount. 2009 Note: Financial information for 2009 was not available for all companies at press time.**

2009 Sales: $4,165,820	2009 Profits: $33,341	**U.S. Stock Ticker: CBG**
2008 Sales: $5,128,817	2008 Profits: $-1,012,066	**Int'l Ticker:** Int'l Exchange:
2007 Sales: $6,034,249	2007 Profits: $390,505	Employees: 29,000
2006 Sales: $4,032,027	2006 Profits: $318,571	Fiscal Year Ends: 12/31
2005 Sales: $3,194,026	2005 Profits: $217,341	Parent Company:

SALARIES/BENEFITS:

Pension Plan:	ESOP Stock Plan:	Profit Sharing:	Top Exec. Salary: $781,346	Bonus: $843,200
Savings Plan: Y	Stock Purch. Plan:		Second Exec. Salary: $562,038	Bonus: $447,300

OTHER THOUGHTS:

Apparent Women Officers or Directors: 2
Hot Spot for Advancement for Women/Minorities: Y

LOCATIONS: ("Y" = Yes)

West:	Southwest:	Midwest:	Southeast:	Northeast:	International:
Y	Y	Y	Y	Y	Y

CBL & ASSOCIATES PROPERTIES INC

www.cblproperties.com

Industry Group Code: 531120 **Ranks within this company's industry group:** Sales: 16 Profits: 33

Properties:		Financial Services:		Construction/Development:		Investments:		Specialty Services:		Brokerage:	
Apartments:		Mortgages:		Commercial Construction:		REIT:	Y	Property Management:	Y	Commercial Sales:	
Malls/Shopping:	Y	Title Insurance:		Residential Construction:				Online Services:		Residential Sales:	
Offices:		Property Insurance:		Land Development:				Software/IT:		Specialty:	
Hotels/Motels:				Support Services:				Consulting:			
Industrial/Warehouses:				Design/Engineering:							
Other:											

TYPES OF BUSINESS:

Malls & Shopping Centers
Retail Property Management
Retail Property Development
Real Estate Investment Trust

BRANDS/DIVISIONS/AFFILIATES:

CBL Holdings I, Inc.
CBL Holdings II, Inc.
CBL & Associates Management, Inc.

CONTACTS:

Note: Officers with more than one job title may be intentionally listed here more than once.

Stephen D. Lebovitz, CEO
Augustus N. Stephas, COO/Exec. VP
Stephen D. Lebovitz, Pres.
John N. Foy, CFO/Treas./Sec.
Barb J. Faucette, VP-Mall Mktg.
Maggie Carrington, VP-Human Resources
Steve Newton, VP-IT
Michael I. Lebovitz, Exec. VP-Admin.
Victoria Berghel, General Counsel/Sr. VP
Michael I. Lebovitz, Exec. VP-Dev.
Katie Reinsmidt, VP-Corp. Rel.
Katie Reinsmidt, VP-Investor Rel.
Farzana K. Mitchell, Exec. VP-Finance
John N. Foy, Vice Chmn.
Ben S. Landress, Exec. VP-Mgmt.
Howard B. Grody, Sr. VP-Leasing
Andrew F. Cobb, VP/Dir.-Acct.
Charles B. Lebovitz, Chmn.

Phone: 423-855-0001	**Fax:** 423-490-8390
Toll-Free: 800-333-7310	
Address: 2030 Hamilton Place Blvd., Ste. 500, Chattanooga, TN 37421-6000 US	

GROWTH PLANS/SPECIAL FEATURES:

CBL & Associates Properties, Inc. is a self-managed, self-administered real estate investment trust (REIT) engaged in the ownership, development, acquisition, leasing, management and operation of regional shopping malls, open-air centers, community centers and office properties. The firm's properties are located principally in the Southeastern and Midwestern U.S., with its top markets in St. Louis, Missouri; Nashville, Tennessee; Kansas City, Kansas; Madison, Wisconsin; and Chattanooga, Tennessee. CBL owns, holds interests in or manages 84 regional malls/open-air centers, 34 associated centers, 13 community centers, one mixed-use center and 19 office buildings. The properties are located in 27 states. The firm also has mortgages on 13 properties. The company conducts substantially all of its business through two REIT subsidiaries, CBL Holdings I, Inc. and CBL Holdings II, Inc. Additionally, the company conducts its property management operations through subsidiary CBL & Associates Management, Inc. This subsidiary operates property management at all but three of CBL's properties, Governor's Square and Governor's Plaza in Clarksville, Tennessee, and Kentucky Oaks Mall, in Paducah, Kentucky, which are owned as joint ventures and operated by third parties. CBL's key tenants include The Limited, Footlocker, Gap, Luxottica, Abercrombie & Fitch, Signet, American Eagle Outfitters, J.C. Penny, Zales and The Finish Line. The firm's on-site property management functions include leasing, management, data processing, rent collection, budgeting and promotions.

FINANCIALS:

Sales and profits are in thousands of dollars—add 000 to get the full amount. 2009 Note: Financial information for 2009 was not available for all companies at press time.

2009 Sales: $1,089,489	2009 Profits: $-7,065	**U.S. Stock Ticker: CBL**
2008 Sales: $1,138,218	2008 Profits: $57,434	**Int'l Ticker:** Int'l Exchange:
2007 Sales: $1,039,944	2007 Profits: $147,608	Employees: 969
2006 Sales: $995,502	2006 Profits: $17,501	Fiscal Year Ends: 12/31
2005 Sales: $900,419	2005 Profits: $162,475	Parent Company:

SALARIES/BENEFITS:

Pension Plan:	ESOP Stock Plan:	Profit Sharing:	Top Exec. Salary: $596,836	Bonus: $337,500
Savings Plan: Y	Stock Purch. Plan: Y		Second Exec. Salary: $532,906	Bonus: $337,500

OTHER THOUGHTS:

Apparent Women Officers or Directors: 7
Hot Spot for Advancement for Women/Minorities: Y

LOCATIONS: ("Y" = Yes)

West:	Southwest:	Midwest:	Southeast:	Northeast:	International:
Y	Y	Y	Y	Y	

CEMEX INC

www.cemexusa.com

Industry Group Code: 4233 **Ranks within this company's industry group:** Sales: Profits:

Properties:		Financial Services:		Construction/Development:		Investments:		Specialty Services:		Brokerage:	
Apartments:		Mortgages:		Commercial Construction:		REIT:		Property Management:		Commercial Sales:	
Malls/Shopping:		Title Insurance:		Residential Construction:				Online Services:		Residential Sales:	
Offices:		Property Insurance:		Land Development:	Y			Software/IT:		Specialty:	
Hotels/Motels:				Support Services:	Y			Consulting:			
Industrial/Warehouses:	Y			Design/Engineering:							
Other:	Y										

TYPES OF BUSINESS:

Cement Materials & Production
Cement Materials & Production
Ready-Mix Cement

BRANDS/DIVISIONS/AFFILIATES:

CEMEX SAB de CV

CONTACTS:

Note: Officers with more than one job title may be intentionally listed here more than once.

Gilberto Perez, Pres.
Andy Miller, Exec. VP-Human Resources
Adolfo Garza, Exec. VP-Technical Svcs.
Leslie White, General Counsel/Exec. VP
Luis Oropeza, Exec. VP-Cement Oper.
Jesus Gonzalez, Exec. VP-Planning
Jennifer Borgen, Dir.-External Comm.
Frank Craddock, Exec. VP-Commercial
Ira Fialkow, Exec. VP-Shared Service Organization
Karl Watson Jr., Pres., Eastern Region
Steven Wise, Pres., Western Region
Juan Carlos Herrera, Exec. VP-Logistics

Phone: 713-650-6200	**Fax:** 713-653-6815
Toll-Free:	
Address: 840 Gessner Rd., Ste. 1400, Houston, TX 77024 US	

GROWTH PLANS/SPECIAL FEATURES:

CEMEX Inc., a subsidiary of Mexico-based CEMEX, S.A. de C.V., is among the largest cement and ready-mix companies in the U.S. Headquartered in Houston, Texas, the firm also has operations in California, Colorado and throughout the Northeast and Southeast. The firm's network includes 14 cement plants, over 50 distribution channels, 100 aggregate quarries and 370 ready-mix concrete plants. CEMEX divides its operations into the following four categories: Cement, aggregates, ready mix and related products. Cement products, which vary by region in terms of availability, include portland cement, masonry cement, oil well cement, low-alkali cement, plastic cement and moderate heat cement. Aggregate products include sand, gravel and crushed stone, all of which are used in concrete products as well as in landscaping settings. The firm's ready-mix concrete, which consists of cement, water and aggregates, is a cost-effective and versatile building material used in almost all types of construction. The related products unit manufactures concrete block, architectural products (such as architectural block, concrete brick and pavers), asphalt, building materials (such as mortar and lime), pipe and landscaping materials.

FINANCIALS:

Sales and profits are in thousands of dollars—add 000 to get the full amount. 2009 Note: Financial information for 2009 was not available for all companies at press time.

2009 Sales: $	2009 Profits: $	**U.S. Stock Ticker: Subsidiary**
2008 Sales: $	2008 Profits: $	**Int'l Ticker:** Int'l Exchange:
2007 Sales: $	2007 Profits: $	Employees:
2006 Sales: $	2006 Profits: $	Fiscal Year Ends: 12/31
2005 Sales: $	2005 Profits: $	Parent Company: CEMEX SAB DE CV

SALARIES/BENEFITS:

Pension Plan:	ESOP Stock Plan:	Profit Sharing:	Top Exec. Salary: $	Bonus: $
Savings Plan:	Stock Purch. Plan:		Second Exec. Salary: $	Bonus: $

OTHER THOUGHTS:

Apparent Women Officers or Directors: 1
Hot Spot for Advancement for Women/Minorities:

LOCATIONS: ("Y" = Yes)

West:	Southwest:	Midwest:	Southeast:	Northeast:	International:
Y	Y		Y	Y	

CEMEX SAB DE CV

www.cemex.com

Industry Group Code: 4233 **Ranks within this company's industry group:** Sales: 2 Profits: 1

Properties:		Financial Services:		Construction/Development:		Investments:		Specialty Services:		Brokerage:	
Apartments:		Mortgages:		Commercial Construction:		REIT:		Property Management:		Commercial Sales:	
Malls/Shopping:		Title Insurance:		Residential Construction:				Online Services:		Residential Sales:	
Offices:		Property Insurance:		Land Development:				Software/IT:		Specialty:	
Hotels/Motels:				Support Services:	Y			Consulting:			
Industrial/Warehouses:				Design/Engineering:							
Other:											

TYPES OF BUSINESS:

Cement & Concrete Production
Construction Materials Production

BRANDS/DIVISIONS/AFFILIATES:

CEMEX Deutschland AG
CEMEX Mexico
CEMEX Corp.
CEMEX Inc
CEMEX France Gestion SAS
CEMEX Southeast, LLC
Empresas Tolteca de Mexico
Ready Mix USA, LLC

CONTACTS: *Note: Officers with more than one job title may be intentionally listed here more than once.*

Lorenzo H. Zambrano, CEO
Rodrigo Trevino, CFO
Victor M. Romo, Exec. VP-Admin.
Fernando A. Gonzalez, Exec. VP-Planning
Fernando A. Gonzalez, Exec. VP-Finance
Francisco Garza, Pres., Americas
Lorenzo H. Zambrano, Chmn.
Juan Romero, Pres., EMEA & Asia Region

Phone: 52-81-8888-8888 **Fax:** 52-81-8888-4417
Toll-Free:
Address: Av. Ricardo Margain Zozaya 325, San Pedro Garza Garcia, 66265 Mexico

GROWTH PLANS/SPECIAL FEATURES:

Cemex S.A.B. de C.V. (formerly CEMEX, S.A. de C.V.), founded in Mexico in 1906, is a holding company that produces, distributes, markets and sells cement, ready-mix concrete, aggregates, clinker and other construction materials through its operating subsidiaries. The company has operations in over 50 countries across five continents, with annual production levels of around 107 tons of cement. Cemex wholly owns 63 cement plants; over 2,000 ready-mix concrete facilities; and has a minority participation in 12 cement plants. The firm also operates 391 aggregate quarries, 223 land-distribution centers and 72 marine terminals. The firm's operations in Mexico are run by subsidiaries CEMEX Mexico and Empresas Tolteca de Mexico. In the U.S., the company owns holding company CEMEX Corp., which manages companies such as CEMEX Southeast, LLC and Ready Mix USA, LLC through CEMEX, Inc. The company operates through a number of subsidiaries throughout Europe: CEMEX France Gestion SAS; CEMEX UK; CEMEX Espana S.A.; CEMEX Deutchland AG in Germany; with additional operations in Poland, Croatia, the Czech Republic, Denmark, Ireland, Italy, Finland, Norway and Sweden. In South and Central America, the company operates facilities in Venezuela, Colombia, Argentina, Costa Rica, the Dominican Republic, Panama, Nicaragua, Puerto Rico and Jamaica. CEMEX also has operations in Egypt, the U.A.E., Israel, the Philippines, Singapore, Thailand, Malaysia and Taiwan. In October 2009, the company completed the sale of its Australian operations to Holcim Group for approximately $1.7 billion.

FINANCIALS: **Sales and profits are in thousands of dollars—add 000 to get the full amount. 2009 Note: Financial information for 2009 was not available for all companies at press time.**

2009 Sales: $16,220,500	2009 Profits: $115,544	**U.S. Stock Ticker: CX**
2008 Sales: $21,695,000	2008 Profits: $2,487,000	**Int'l Ticker:** Int'l Exchange:
2007 Sales: $21,673,000	2007 Profits: $2,971,000	Employees: 47,624
2006 Sales: $21,376,700	2006 Profits: $2,785,500	Fiscal Year Ends: 12/31
2005 Sales: $15,131,937	2005 Profits: $2,056,695	Parent Company:

SALARIES/BENEFITS:

Pension Plan:	ESOP Stock Plan:	Profit Sharing:	Top Exec. Salary: $	Bonus: $
Savings Plan:	Stock Purch. Plan:		Second Exec. Salary: $	Bonus: $

OTHER THOUGHTS:

Apparent Women Officers or Directors:
Hot Spot for Advancement for Women/Minorities:

LOCATIONS: ("Y" = Yes)

West:	Southwest:	Midwest:	Southeast:	Northeast:	International:
Y	Y	Y	Y	Y	Y

CENTEX CORP

www.centex.com

Industry Group Code: 2361 **Ranks within this company's industry group:** Sales: 2 Profits: 20

Properties:		Financial Services:		Construction/Development:		Investments:		Specialty Services:		Brokerage:	
Apartments:		Mortgages:	Y	Commercial Construction:		REIT:		Property Management:		Commercial Sales:	
Malls/Shopping:		Title Insurance:	Y	Residential Construction:	Y			Online Services:		Residential Sales:	Y
Offices:		Property Insurance:	Y	Land Development:	Y			Software/IT:		Specialty:	
Hotels/Motels:				Support Services:	Y			Consulting:			
Industrial/Warehouses:				Design/Engineering:	Y						
Other:											

TYPES OF BUSINESS:

Residential Construction
Mortgages
Real Estate Development
Commercial Construction
Construction Supply Services

BRANDS/DIVISIONS/AFFILIATES:

Centex Homes
Pulte Homes Inc
PulteGroup Inc

CONTACTS:

Note: Officers with more than one job title may be intentionally listed here more than once.

Timothy R. Eller, CEO
Cathy R. Smith, CFO/Exec. VP
Joe Bosch, Sr. VP-Human Resources
Michael S. Albright, Sr. VP-Admin.
Mark D. Kemp, Controller
Timothy R. Eller, Chmn.

Phone: 214-981-5000 **Fax:** 214-981-6859
Toll-Free:
Address: 2728 N. Harwood, Dallas, TX 75201 US

GROWTH PLANS/SPECIAL FEATURES:

Centex Corp., a subsidiary of PulteGroup, Inc. (formerly Pulte Homes, Inc.) focuses principally on residential construction and related activities, including mortgage financing. The firm's home building operations involve the purchase and development of land or lots and the construction and sale of detached and attached single-family homes, including resort and second home properties and lots, and land or lots. Centex's financial services include mortgage lending, conducted through Pulte Motrgage LLC; title insurance, handled by Commerce Title and Closing Services, LLC; and insurance with Westwood Insurance Agency, offering homeowners, auto, life and commercial insurance. In partnership with HomeTeam Pest Defense, Centex installs pest control systems in its homes as they are being built including Taexx, built-in pest control systems and Tubes Under the Slab termite control systems. All new Centex homes include energy saving features such as radiant-barrier roof decking, enhanced insulation, low-emissivity windows and Energy Star appliances. In August 2009, Centex was acquired by competitor, Pulte Homes, Inc. for approximately $1.4 billion.

The company offers its employees medical, dental and vision insurance; life and AD&D insurance; short- and long-term disability insurance; a 401(k) plan; a college savings plan; tuition reimbursement; and an employee assistance program.

FINANCIALS:

Sales and profits are in thousands of dollars—add 000 to get the full amount. 2009 Note: Financial information for 2009 was not available for all companies at press time.

2009 Sales: $	2009 Profits: $	**U.S. Stock Ticker: Subsidiary**
2008 Sales: $8,275,562	2008 Profits: $-2,657,482	**Int'l Ticker:** Int'l Exchange:
2007 Sales: $11,887,601	2007 Profits: $268,366	Employees: 6,530
2006 Sales: $12,742,666	2006 Profits: $1,289,313	Fiscal Year Ends: 3/31
2005 Sales: $9,934,282	2005 Profits: $1,011,364	Parent Company: PULTEGROUP INC

SALARIES/BENEFITS:

Pension Plan:	ESOP Stock Plan:	Profit Sharing:	Top Exec. Salary: $920,000	Bonus: $216,459
Savings Plan: Y	Stock Purch. Plan:		Second Exec. Salary: $542,375	Bonus: $492,188

OTHER THOUGHTS:

Apparent Women Officers or Directors: 1
Hot Spot for Advancement for Women/Minorities: Y

LOCATIONS: ("Y" = Yes)

West:	Southwest:	Midwest:	Southeast:	Northeast:	International:
Y	Y	Y	Y	Y	Y

CENTRO PROPERTIES GROUP

www.centro.com.au

Industry Group Code: 5311 **Ranks within this company's industry group:** Sales: 27 Profits: 33

Properties:		Financial Services:		Construction/Development:		Investments:		Specialty Services:		Brokerage:	
Apartments:		Mortgages:		Commercial Construction:		REIT:	Y	Property Management:	Y	Commercial Sales:	
Malls/Shopping:	Y	Title Insurance:		Residential Construction:				Online Services:		Residential Sales:	
Offices:	Y	Property Insurance:		Land Development:	Y			Software/IT:		Specialty:	
Hotels/Motels:				Support Services:				Consulting:			
Industrial/Warehouses:				Design/Engineering:	Y						
Other:											

TYPES OF BUSINESS:

Real Estate Development-Shopping Centers
Property Ownership
Leasing
Funds Management

BRANDS/DIVISIONS/AFFILIATES:

Centro US
Centro Retail Trust
Centro MCS Manager Limited

CONTACTS:

Note: Officers with more than one job title may be intentionally listed here more than once.

Robert Tsenin, CEO
Chris Nunn, CFO
Dimitri Kiriacoulacos, General Counsel
Paul Belcher, Gen. Mgr.-Finance
Michael Benett, Gen. Mgr.-Institutional Funds
Gerard Condon, Gen. Mgr.-Syndicate Funds
Paul Cooper, Chmn.

Phone: 61-3-8847-0000	**Fax:** 61-3-9886-1234
Toll-Free:	
Address: 235 Springvale Rd., 3rd Fl., Glen Waverly, VIC 3150 Australia	

GROWTH PLANS/SPECIAL FEATURES:

Centro Properties Group (Centro), based in Australia, is a retail property ownership firm concerned with property investment, property management, property development and funds management. The firm has offices in Australia, New Zealand and the U.S. In Australia and New Zealand, Centro maintains regional and neighborhood shopping centers in metropolitan and non-metropolitan markets. In the U.S., the firm manages neighborhood as well as mall and large retail shopping centers primarily based in suburban areas. Centro's shopping centers are primarily concerned with non-discretionary retail spending, focusing on fresh food, supermarkets and other everyday needs. Centro Retail Trust is a CER, or an Australian Real Estate Investment Trust (REIT), managed by Centro Subsidiary Centro MCS Manager Limited, which connects investors to Australian and US shopping center investments. Subsidiary Centro US is responsible for carrying out asset management; property management and development; and leasing activities with U.S. properties. Centro US has a portfolio of approximately 600 properties in 39 states; properties include various malls and shopping centers. Centro Properties Group currently has $22.6 billion in properties under management. The group is a major provider of retail space to Wesfarmers and Woolworths in Australia and TJX and Kroger in the U.S.

FINANCIALS:

Sales and profits are in thousands of dollars—add 000 to get the full amount. 2009 Note: Financial information for 2009 was not available for all companies at press time.

2009 Sales: $1,850,360	2009 Profits: $-3,284,920	**U.S. Stock Ticker:**
2008 Sales: $491,360	2008 Profits: $-1,467,390	**Int'l Ticker: CNP** Int'l Exchange: Sydney-ASX
2007 Sales: $261,490	2007 Profits: $336,150	Employees:
2006 Sales: $677,800	2006 Profits: $611,100	Fiscal Year Ends: 6/30
2005 Sales: $444,100	2005 Profits: $712,400	Parent Company:

SALARIES/BENEFITS:

Pension Plan:	ESOP Stock Plan:	Profit Sharing:	Top Exec. Salary: $	Bonus: $
Savings Plan:	Stock Purch. Plan:		Second Exec. Salary: $	Bonus: $

OTHER THOUGHTS:

Apparent Women Officers or Directors: 2
Hot Spot for Advancement for Women/Minorities:

LOCATIONS: ("Y" = Yes)

West:	Southwest:	Midwest:	Southeast:	Northeast:	International:
Y	Y	Y	Y	Y	Y

CENTURY 21 REAL ESTATE CORP

www.century21.com

Industry Group Code: 531210 **Ranks within this company's industry group:** Sales: Profits:

Properties:		Financial Services:		Construction/Development:		Investments:		Specialty Services:		Brokerage:	
Apartments:		Mortgages:	Y	Commercial Construction:		REIT:		Property Management:		Commercial Sales:	Y
Malls/Shopping:		Title Insurance:		Residential Construction:				Online Services:	Y	Residential Sales:	Y
Offices:		Property Insurance:		Land Development:				Software/IT:		Specialty:	Y
Hotels/Motels:				Support Services:	Y			Consulting:			
Industrial/Warehouses:				Design/Engineering:							
Other:											

TYPES OF BUSINESS:

Real Estate Brokerage
Commercial Brokerage
Residential & Specialty Brokerage
Mortgage Services
Construction Support Services
Relocation Services

BRANDS/DIVISIONS/AFFILIATES:

Realogy Corporation
Century 21 Mortgage
Century 21 Commercial
Century 21 Fine Homes and Estates

CONTACTS:

Note: Officers with more than one job title may be intentionally listed here more than once.

Richard W. Davidson, CEO
Richard W. Davidson, Pres.
Beverly Thorne, Chief Mktg. Offficer
Matt Gentile, Contact-Public Rel.
James Ramsay, VP-Franchise Sales

Phone: 877-221-2765 **Fax:**
Toll-Free: 866-732-6139
Address: 1 Campus Dr., Parsippany, NJ 07054 US

GROWTH PLANS/SPECIAL FEATURES:

Century 21 Real Estate Corp., a subsidiary of Realogy Corp., is the franchiser of one of the world's largest residential real estate sales organizations. It has more than 7,700 independently owned and operated franchised broker offices in 68 countries. The firm helps clients find, buy, sell and finance their residential property or new home, as well as find, buy, sell and sometimes lease commercial property and vacation properties. It also provides relocation services for individuals, businesses and members of the military. Century 21's web site gives the public access to its vast database of listed homes, as well as allowing clients to list their homes on said database. The company has offices in every state, providing customers with brokers familiar with their area and current market conditions. Century 21 Mortgage offers mortgage services to its clients in person, over the phone or online. Other subsidiaries include Century 21 Commercial, helping clients invest in or sell commercial real estate and Century 21 Fine Homes and Estates, for those looking for higher-priced luxury homes. Its magazine, At Home with Century 21, provides information on remodeling, gardening, cooking and personal finance. In recent years, the firm has expanded into Albania, India and the Czech Republic. In June, Century 21 signed a master franchise agreement to open offices in Thailand and in August 2009 the company announced the opening of its first franchise in Bermuda.

Employees receive training in marketing, sales, business planning and development.

FINANCIALS:

Sales and profits are in thousands of dollars—add 000 to get the full amount. 2009 Note: Financial information for 2009 was not available for all companies at press time.

2009 Sales: $	2009 Profits: $	**U.S. Stock Ticker: Subsidiary**
2008 Sales: $	2008 Profits: $	**Int'l Ticker:** Int'l Exchange:
2007 Sales: $41,300	2007 Profits: $	Employees:
2006 Sales: $	2006 Profits: $	Fiscal Year Ends: 12/31
2005 Sales: $	2005 Profits: $	Parent Company: REALOGY CORPORATION

SALARIES/BENEFITS:

Pension Plan:	ESOP Stock Plan:	Profit Sharing:	Top Exec. Salary: $	Bonus: $
Savings Plan:	Stock Purch. Plan:		Second Exec. Salary: $	Bonus: $

OTHER THOUGHTS:

Apparent Women Officers or Directors: 1
Hot Spot for Advancement for Women/Minorities:

LOCATIONS: ("Y" = Yes)

West:	Southwest:	Midwest:	Southeast:	Northeast:	International:
Y	Y	Y	Y	Y	Y

CH2M HILL COMPANIES LTD

www.ch2m.com

Industry Group Code: 541330 **Ranks within this company's industry group:** Sales: 4 Profits: 7

Properties:		Financial Services:		Construction/Development:		Investments:		Specialty Services:		Brokerage:	
Apartments:		Mortgages:		Commercial Construction:	Y	REIT:		Property Management:	Y	Commercial Sales:	
Malls/Shopping:		Title Insurance:		Residential Construction:				Online Services:		Residential Sales:	
Offices:		Property Insurance:		Land Development:				Software/IT:		Specialty:	
Hotels/Motels:				Support Services:	Y			Consulting:	Y		
Industrial/Warehouses:				Design/Engineering:	Y						
Other:											

TYPES OF BUSINESS:

Engineering Services-Consultation
Environmental Engineering & Consulting
Nuclear Management Services
Water & Electrical Utility Services
Decommissioning & Decontamination
Facilities Design & Construction
Project Financing & Procurement
Nanotechnology Research

BRANDS/DIVISIONS/AFFILIATES:

Operations Management International
CH2M HILL Canada, Ltd.
Lockwood Greene
Industrial Design and Construction
CH2M-IDC China
Wade & Assoicates, Inc.
Goldston Engineering, Inc.
VECO

CONTACTS:

Note: Officers with more than one job title may be intentionally listed here more than once.

Lee A. McIntire, CEO
Catherine Santee, CFO
Bob Allen, Chief Human Resources Officer/Sr. VP
Catherine Santee, VP-Finance
Margaret McLean, Chief Legal Officer
William T. Dehn, VP-Special Projects
Nancy R. Tuor, VP-Sustainability
Michael E. McKelvy, Sr. VP- Gov't, Environment & Nuclear Div.
Lee A. McIntire, Chmn.
Thomas G. Searle, Pres., CH2M HILL Int'l

Phone: 303-771-0900	**Fax:** 720-286-9250
Toll-Free: 888-242-6445	
Address: 9191 S. Jamaica St., Englewood, CO 80112 US	

GROWTH PLANS/SPECIAL FEATURES:

CH2M HILL Companies, Ltd. is an employee-owned firm that offers engineering, consulting, design, construction, procurement, operations, maintenance and program and project management services to clients in the public and private sectors. CH2M HILL conducts business in several countries worldwide. The company's environmental services division offers its clients ecological and natural resource damage assessments, environmental consulting for remediation projects and treatment systems for properties that have been contaminated by toxic or radioactive waste. The nuclear services segment manages the decontamination and demolition of weapons production facilities and designs nuclear waste treatment and handling facilities. CH2M HILL's Operations Management International subsidiary provides water, wastewater and electrical utility services to private and public clients. CH2M HILL Canada, Ltd. is the Canadian division of the company. CH2M HILL Lockwood Greene is a major engineering and construction firm focused on national and multinational industrial and power clients worldwide. CH2M HILL Industrial Design and Construction, Inc. (IDC) is a high-technology facilities design, construction, maintenance and operations company serving process-intensive technology clients. IDC also has interests in nanotechnology research and manufacturing. CH2M-IDC China provides full-service solution to manufacturing companies that are building or have plants in China. In September 2009, firm sold its Enterprise Management Solutions business' IT solutions operations to CRITIGEN. In November 2009,

In 2009, CH2M HILL was ranked 84 on FORTUNE Magazine's 12th annual list of the100 Best Companies to Work For.

FINANCIALS:

Sales and profits are in thousands of dollars—add 000 to get the full amount. 2009 Note: Financial information for 2009 was not available for all companies at press time.

2009 Sales: $5,499,318	2009 Profits: $103,742	**U.S. Stock Ticker: Private**
2008 Sales: $5,589,900	2008 Profits: $32,056	**Int'l Ticker:** Int'l Exchange:
2007 Sales: $4,376,200	2007 Profits: $65,999	Employees: 23,500
2006 Sales: $4,000,000	2006 Profits: $	Fiscal Year Ends: 12/31
2005 Sales: $3,152,200	2005 Profits: $81,600	Parent Company:

SALARIES/BENEFITS:

Pension Plan:	ESOP Stock Plan:	Profit Sharing:	Top Exec. Salary: $	Bonus: $
Savings Plan:	Stock Purch. Plan:		Second Exec. Salary: $	Bonus: $

OTHER THOUGHTS:

Apparent Women Officers or Directors: 4
Hot Spot for Advancement for Women/Minorities: Y

LOCATIONS: ("Y" = Yes)

West:	Southwest:	Midwest:	Southeast:	Northeast:	International:
Y	Y	Y	Y	Y	Y

CHAMPION ENTERPRISES INC

www.championhomes.com

Industry Group Code: 321991 **Ranks within this company's industry group:** Sales: 1 Profits: 4

Properties:		Financial Services:		Construction/Development:		Investments:		Specialty Services:		Brokerage:	
Apartments:		Mortgages:		Commercial Construction:		REIT:		Property Management:		Commercial Sales:	
Malls/Shopping:		Title Insurance:		Residential Construction:	Y			Online Services:		Residential Sales:	
Offices:		Property Insurance:		Land Development:				Software/IT:		Specialty:	
Hotels/Motels:				Support Services:				Consulting:			
Industrial/Warehouses:				Design/Engineering:							
Other:											

TYPES OF BUSINESS:

Manufactured Housing
Housing Retailing
Steel-Frame Building

BRANDS/DIVISIONS/AFFILIATES:

Champion Enterprises Inc
Champion Home Centers
GO House
Genesis Homes
Building Systems Limited
Moduline Industries
SRI Homes

CONTACTS:

Note: Officers with more than one job title may be intentionally listed here more than once.

William C. Griffiths, CEO
William C. Griffiths, Pres.
Kevin Flaherty, VP-Mktg.
Roger K. Scholten, General Counsel/Sr. VP/Sec.

Phone: 248-614-8200	**Fax:** 248-273-4279
Toll-Free:	
Address: 755 W. Big Beaver, Ste. 1000, Troy, MI 48084 US	

GROWTH PLANS/SPECIAL FEATURES:

Champion Enterprises, Inc. is the holding company for a family of companies that manufacture and retail manufactured and modular housing. Founded in 1953, the company has sold over 1.7 million factory-built homes since its inception. The Champion family of companies is one of the largest housing manufacturers and retailers in the U.S., manufacturing approximately 11,000 homes annually through 27 manufacturing facilities in North America and the U.K. The company sells homes largely through its 15 company-owned retail home centers in California. The Champion family of homebuilders includes Carolina Building Solutions, Commander, Dutch, Fortune, Highland, Homes of Merit, New Era, New Image, North American, Redman, Silvercrest, Summit Crest and Titan. Most of the homes built are multi-section, ranch-style units, but one and two-story homes, colonial-style homes, Cape Cod style homes and multi-family units are also offered. Homes generally range in size from 600 to 3,000 square feet and typically include 2-4 bedrooms, a living room or family room, dining room, kitchen and two full bathrooms. Additional floor plan options include vaulted ceilings, entertainment centers, spa-style bathrooms, fireplaces, custom cabinetry and various floor covering options. In Canada, Champion produces and sells factory-built homes through two divisions: Moduline Industries, operating in western Canada; and SRI Homes, operating in western and central Canada. Additionally, Champion produces pre-engineered and steel-framed modular buildings in the U.K through Caledonian Building Systems Limited. In January 2010, the firm launched the GO House, an environmentally conscious modular home marketed under the Genesis Homes brand. In March 2010, the company's domestic and international operations were acquired by Champion Enterprises Holdings LLC.

FINANCIALS:

Sales and profits are in thousands of dollars—add 000 to get the full amount. 2009 Note: Financial information for 2009 was not available for all companies at press time.

2009 Sales: $	2009 Profits: $	**U.S. Stock Ticker: CJHBQ**
2008 Sales: $1,033,193	2008 Profits: $-199,460	**Int'l Ticker:** Int'l Exchange:
2007 Sales: $1,273,465	2007 Profits: $7,192	Employees: 4,100
2006 Sales: $1,364,648	2006 Profits: $138,308	Fiscal Year Ends: 12/31
2005 Sales: $1,272,590	2005 Profits: $37,805	Parent Company:

SALARIES/BENEFITS:

Pension Plan:	ESOP Stock Plan:	Profit Sharing:	Top Exec. Salary: $	Bonus: $
Savings Plan:	Stock Purch. Plan:		Second Exec. Salary: $	Bonus: $

OTHER THOUGHTS:

Apparent Women Officers or Directors:
Hot Spot for Advancement for Women/Minorities:

LOCATIONS: ("Y" = Yes)

West:	Southwest:	Midwest:	Southeast:	Northeast:	International:
Y	Y	Y	Y	Y	Y

CHICAGO BRIDGE & IRON COMPANY NV

www.cbiepc.com

Industry Group Code: 237 **Ranks within this company's industry group:** Sales: 18 Profits: 30

Properties:		Financial Services:		Construction/Development:		Investments:		Specialty Services:		Brokerage:	
Apartments:		Mortgages:		Commercial Construction:		REIT:		Property Management:		Commercial Sales:	
Malls/Shopping:		Title Insurance:		Residential Construction:				Online Services:		Residential Sales:	
Offices:		Property Insurance:		Land Development:				Software/IT:		Specialty:	
Hotels/Motels:				Support Services:	Y			Consulting:			
Industrial/Warehouses:				Design/Engineering:	Y						
Other:											

TYPES OF BUSINESS:

Heavy Construction & Civil Engineering
Specialty Engineering & Procurement Services
Liquid & Gas Storage Facilities
Maintenance & Support Services

BRANDS/DIVISIONS/AFFILIATES:

John Brown Hydrocarbons Ltd.
CB&I Howe-Baker
CB&I TPA
CB&I Matrix
ABB Lummus Global, Inc.
ABB Oil & Gas Europe B.V.

CONTACTS:

Note: Officers with more than one job title may be intentionally listed here more than once.

Phillip K. Asheman, CEO
Lasse Petterson, COO
Phillip K. Asheman, Pres.
Ronald A. Ballschmiede, CFO/Exec. VP
David P. Bordages, VP-Human Resources
David P. Bordages, VP-Admin.
David A. Delman, General Counsel/Chief Legal Officer/VP
John W. Redmon, Exec. VP-Oper.
Mark Coscio, VP-Corp. Planning
Ronald E. Blum, Pres., Steele Plate Structures
Daniel M. McCarthy, Pres., CB&I Lummus Technology
David A. Delman, Sec.
Luciano Reyes, Treas./VP
Jerry H. Ballengee, Chmn.
Ronald E. Blum, Exec. VP-Global Bus. Dev.

Phone: 31-70-373-2722 **Fax:**
Toll-Free:
Address: Oostduinlaan 75, Hoofddorp, The Hague, 2596JJ The Netherlands

GROWTH PLANS/SPECIAL FEATURES:

Chicago Bridge & Iron Company N.V. (CB&I), a global engineering, procurement and construction (EPC) company, provides specialty construction for liquid and gas storage facilities. Company operations include over 80 offices, warehouses and other facilities on six continents. CB&I offers conceptual design, engineering, procurement, fabrication, field construction, mechanical installation and commissioning, serving customers in the oil and gas; petrochemical and chemical; power; water and wastewater; and metals and mining industries. Projects include hydrocarbon processing plants, liquid natural gas (LNG) terminals and peak shaving plants, offshore structures, pipelines, bulk liquid terminals and water storage and treatment facilities. The company provides complete service, from the initial design and engineering through procurement and construction and maintenance. The company also offers a range of complementary products and services including low temperature or cryogenic tanks and systems, primarily used by petroleum, chemical, petrochemical, natural gas and power generation companies to store, transport and handle liquefied gases and specialty structures including iron and aluminum processing facilities and hydroelectric structures. CB&I operates through several subsidiaries including CB&I Howe-Baker, which provides oil and gas engineering services and CBI TPA, which provides engineering and services for sulfur reduction and removal projects. In October 2009, CB&I finalized a $100 million contract with Petroterminal de Panama SA, which is located in Panama City, Panama. CB&I will execute the Phase II expansion of Trans Panama pipeline. In addition, the firm has received a contract from Royal Dutch Shell plc, worth approximately $60 million, for procurement and construction of a diesel hydrotreater at the Pernis Refinery in Rotterdam.

The firm offers its U.S. employees medical, dental and vision plans; employee and dependent life insurance options; a 401(k) plan; profit sharing; a stock purchase program; and an educational assistance plan.

FINANCIALS:

Sales and profits are in thousands of dollars—add 000 to get the full amount. 2009 Note: Financial information for 2009 was not available for all companies at press time.

2009 Sales: $4,556,503	2009 Profits: $174,289
2008 Sales: $5,944,981	2008 Profits: $-21,146
2007 Sales: $4,363,492	2007 Profits: $165,640
2006 Sales: $3,125,307	2006 Profits: $116,968
2005 Sales: $2,257,517	2005 Profits: $15,977

U.S. Stock Ticker: CBI
Int'l Ticker: BDZ Int'l Exchange: Frankfurt-Euronext
Employees: 15,755
Fiscal Year Ends: 12/31
Parent Company:

SALARIES/BENEFITS:

Pension Plan:	ESOP Stock Plan:	Profit Sharing: Y	Top Exec. Salary: $955,000	Bonus: $286,249
Savings Plan: Y	Stock Purch. Plan: Y		Second Exec. Salary: $720,000	Bonus: $467,109

OTHER THOUGHTS:

Apparent Women Officers or Directors:
Hot Spot for Advancement for Women/Minorities:

LOCATIONS: ("Y" = Yes)

West:	Southwest:	Midwest:	Southeast:	Northeast:	International:
Y	Y	Y	Y	Y	Y

CHINA COMMUNICATIONS CONSTRUCTION COMPANY LTD

www.ccccltd.com.cn

Industry Group Code: 23 **Ranks within this company's industry group:** Sales: 1 Profits: 1

Properties:		Financial Services:		Construction/Development:		Investments:		Specialty Services:		Brokerage:	
Apartments:		Mortgages:		Commercial Construction:	Y	REIT:		Property Management:		Commercial Sales:	
Malls/Shopping:		Title Insurance:		Residential Construction:				Online Services:		Residential Sales:	
Offices:		Property Insurance:		Land Development:				Software/IT:		Specialty:	
Hotels/Motels:				Support Services:	Y			Consulting:			
Industrial/Warehouses:				Design/Engineering:	Y						
Other:	Y										

TYPES OF BUSINESS:

Transport Infrastructure, Construction & Design
Port Construction
Dredging
Container Cranes

BRANDS/DIVISIONS/AFFILIATES:

CONTACTS:

Note: Officers with more than one job title may be intentionally listed here more than once.

Fengchao Meng, Exec. Dir.
Fengchao Meng, Pres./Vice Chmn.
Junyuan Fu, CFO
Wensheng Liu, Sec./Chief Economist
Yun Chen, VP
Yusheng Chen, VP
Jinlong Hou, VP
Liqiang Yang, VP/Head-Trade Union
Jichang Zhou, Chmn.

Phone: 86-10-8201-6655	**Fax:** 86-10-8201-6500
Toll-Free:	
Address: 85 Deshengmenwai St., Xicheng District, Beijing, 100088 China	

GROWTH PLANS/SPECIAL FEATURES:

China Communications Construction Company Ltd. (CCCC) is one of China's largest port construction and design companies, as well as one of the world's largest container crane manufacturers. The firm's principal activities include the design and construction of transportation infrastructure, dredging and heavy machinery manufacturing. CCCC's operations are separated into five business units: infrastructure construction, infrastructure design, dredging, heavy machinery manufacturing and others. The infrastructure construction business, operating through 16 direct subsidiaries, offers construction and transportation services for ports, roads, bridges and tunnel works. It currently has the only three top-tier qualification certificates granted by the Ministry of Construction for port construction work in China. The infrastructure design business, comprised of 10 subsidiaries, offers a range of design services including consulting and planning; feasibility studies; design services; engineering consulting; engineering surveys and technical studies; project management and supervision; construction; and more. The dredging business, one of the largest in the world, made up of three subsidiaries, is involved in major dredging and reclamation operations along the China coast and internationally. The port machinery manufacturing business, operating through two major subsidiaries, mainly supplies container cranes, and bulk material handling machinery. The other businesses, comprised of four subsidiaries, have completed projects in a variety of fields, including railway, road, bridge, machinery manufacturing, logistics services and the trading of construction materials and equipment.

FINANCIALS:

Sales and profits are in thousands of dollars—add 000 to get the full amount. 2009 Note: Financial information for 2009 was not available for all companies at press time.

2009 Sales: $33,195,800	2009 Profits: $1,053,280	**U.S. Stock Ticker: HSI**
2008 Sales: $22,008,100	2008 Profits: $881,490	**Int'l Ticker:** Int'l Exchange:
2007 Sales: $16,788,200	2007 Profits: $467,490	Employees: 87,022
2006 Sales: $16,386,300	2006 Profits: $456,300	Fiscal Year Ends: 12/31
2005 Sales: $11,876,700	2005 Profits: $313,090	Parent Company:

SALARIES/BENEFITS:

Pension Plan:	ESOP Stock Plan:	Profit Sharing:	Top Exec. Salary: $	Bonus: $
Savings Plan:	Stock Purch. Plan:		Second Exec. Salary: $	Bonus: $

OTHER THOUGHTS:

Apparent Women Officers or Directors:
Hot Spot for Advancement for Women/Minorities:

LOCATIONS: ("Y" = Yes)

West:	Southwest:	Midwest:	Southeast:	Northeast:	International:
					Y

CHINA LODGING GROUP LTD

www.htinns.com

Industry Group Code: 721110 **Ranks within this company's industry group:** Sales: Profits:

Properties:		Financial Services:	Construction/Development:	Investments:	Specialty Services:	Brokerage:
Apartments:		Mortgages:	Commercial Construction:	REIT:	Property Management:	Commercial Sales:
Malls/Shopping:		Title Insurance:	Residential Construction:		Online Services:	Residential Sales:
Offices:		Property Insurance:	Land Development:		Software/IT:	Specialty:
Hotels/Motels:	Y		Support Services:		Consulting:	
Industrial/Warehouses:			Design/Engineering:			
Other:						

TYPES OF BUSINESS:

Hotels & Resorts

BRANDS/DIVISIONS/AFFILIATES:

HanTing Express Hotels
HanTing Seasons Hotels
HanTing Hi Inn

CONTACTS:

Note: Officers with more than one job title may be intentionally listed here more than once.

Tuo (Matthew) Zhang, CEO
Min (Jenny) Zhang, CFO
Haijun Wang, Exec. VP
Qi Ji, Exec. Chmn.

Phone: 86-21-51539477 **Fax:**
Toll-Free:
Address: 5th Fl., Bl. 57, #461 Hongcao Rd., Xuhui District, Shanghai, 200233 China

GROWTH PLANS/SPECIAL FEATURES:

China Lodging Group, Limited is a China-based holding group for hotels. The firm conducts operations through HanTing Inn & Hotels, a leading chain of economy hotels. The company's properties include about 236 hotels across 39 cities, mostly in western China. China Lodging employs both a lease-and-operate model, which is used to directly operate hotels in prime locations, and a franchise-and-manage model, which is used to expand network coverage. The firm has three primary brands: HanTing Express Hotels; HanTing Seasons Hotels; and HanTing Hi Inn. The flagship HanTing Express Hotels is targeted towards value-conscious travelers and workers. The premium HanTing Seasons Hotel is geared primarily towards corporate managers and owners of small- to mid-level business. The HanTing Hi Inn serves budget customers. The company hopes to harness rapidly growing levels of leisure travel and disposable income in China to help fuel its growth. In March 2010, the company became listed on the NASDAQ stock index.

FINANCIALS:

Sales and profits are in thousands of dollars—add 000 to get the full amount. 2009 Note: Financial information for 2009 was not available for all companies at press time.

2009 Sales: $	2009 Profits: $	**U.S. Stock Ticker: HTHT**
2008 Sales: $	2008 Profits: $	**Int'l Ticker:** Int'l Exchange:
2007 Sales: $	2007 Profits: $	Employees:
2006 Sales: $	2006 Profits: $	Fiscal Year Ends: 12/31
2005 Sales: $	2005 Profits: $	Parent Company:

SALARIES/BENEFITS:

Pension Plan:	ESOP Stock Plan:	Profit Sharing:	Top Exec. Salary: $	Bonus: $
Savings Plan:	Stock Purch. Plan:		Second Exec. Salary: $	Bonus: $

OTHER THOUGHTS:

Apparent Women Officers or Directors: 1
Hot Spot for Advancement for Women/Minorities:

LOCATIONS: ("Y" = Yes)

West:	Southwest:	Midwest:	Southeast:	Northeast:	International:
					Y

CHINA OVERSEAS LAND & INVESTMENT LIMITED www.coli.com.hk

Industry Group Code: 5311 **Ranks within this company's industry group:** Sales: 12 Profits: 10

Properties:		Financial Services:		Construction/Development:		Investments:		Specialty Services:		Brokerage:	
Apartments:	Y	Mortgages:		Commercial Construction:	Y	REIT:		Property Management:	Y	Commercial Sales:	
Malls/Shopping:		Title Insurance:		Residential Construction:	Y			Online Services:		Residential Sales:	
Offices:		Property Insurance:		Land Development:	Y			Software/IT:		Specialty:	
Hotels/Motels:	Y			Support Services:	Y			Consulting:			
Industrial/Warehouses:				Design/Engineering:	Y						
Other:	Y										

TYPES OF BUSINESS:

Real Estate Holdings & Development
Property Management Services
Construction Design Services

BRANDS/DIVISIONS/AFFILIATES:

China State Construction Engineering Corporation
China Overseas Property Management
Hua Yi Designing Consultants Ltd.

CONTACTS: *Note: Officers with more than one job title may be intentionally listed here more than once.*

Jian Min Hao, CEO/Vice Chmn.
Wu Jianbin, CFO/Exec. Dir.
Da Ping Dong, Exec. Dir.-Human Resources
Da Ping Dong, Exec. Dir.-Admin.
Doris Chung, Contact-Media
Michael Jiang, Dir.-Investor Rel.
Yun Wing Nip, Exec. Dir.-Finance & Treasury
Xiao Xiao, Vice Chmn./Exec. Dir.
Bin Chen, Exec. Dir.
Yafei Ge, VP/Gen. Mgr.-China Overseas Property Group Co Ltd
Yan Jian Guo, Gen. Mgr.-COB Development (Shanghai) Co Ltd
Qing Ping Kong, Chmn.

Phone: 852-2823-7888	**Fax:** 852-2865-5939
Toll-Free:	
Address: 3 Pacific Place, 1 Queen's Rd. East, 10th Fl., Hong Kong, China	

GROWTH PLANS/SPECIAL FEATURES:

China Overseas Land & Investment Limited (COLI) is a Hong Kong-based real estate investment holding firm and a publicly listed subsidiary of government-owned China State Construction Engineering Corporation. The firm operates in three segments: property development, property investment and other related businesses. The property development business, the company's largest business segment, engaged in the development and sale of property, completed 29 projects in 2009, 70% of which were sold. The property investment business holds approximately 329 million square feet of land, 2 million square feet of investment properties and about 13 million square feet of property under development. The firm's portfolio includes properties in 22 Chinese cities and regions, including Beijing, Shanghai, Guangzhou, Shenzhen, Chengdu, Changchun, Nanjing, Xian, Zhongshan, Foshan, Zhuhai, Suzhou, Ningbo, Chongqing, Hangzhou, Qingdao, Dalian, Shenyang, Tianjin, Jinan, Hong Kong and Macau. Some of the major properties held by the company include luxury apartment communities such as Mt. Riviera, a 1,071 unit housing and high-rise apartment complex in Hangzhou; Blossom Riverine, a 766,670 square-foot residential development in Foshan; Olympic City Phase One, a 1.2 million square-foot multi-storey apartment complex in Shenzhen; The Arch, a 293,800 square-foot luxury high-rise apartment and hotel property in Nanjing; International Community, a 4.8 million square-foot residential development in Xi'an; the Orchid Garden, a 1 million square-foot residential garden-style community in Chengdu; and One South Lake, a 293,400 square-foot upscale apartment complex in Changchun. The firm is also engaged in several related business areas, including property management, provided by subsidiary China Overseas Property Management; construction design services, offered through subsidiary Hua Yi; and several long-term investments in infrastructure and provincial facilities projects.

FINANCIALS: **Sales and profits are in thousands of dollars—add 000 to get the full amount. 2009 Note: Financial information for 2009 was not available for all companies at press time.**

2009 Sales: $4,807,250	2009 Profits: $962,040
2008 Sales: $2,437,530	2008 Profits: $654,440
2007 Sales: $2,145,970	2007 Profits: $544,110
2006 Sales: $	2006 Profits: $
2005 Sales: $	2005 Profits: $

U.S. Stock Ticker: Subsidiary
Int'l Ticker: 0688 Int'l Exchange: Hong Kong-HKE
Employees:
Fiscal Year Ends: 12/31
Parent Company: CHINA STATE CONSTRUCTION ENGINEERING CORP

SALARIES/BENEFITS:

Pension Plan:	ESOP Stock Plan:	Profit Sharing:	Top Exec. Salary: $	Bonus: $
Savings Plan:	Stock Purch. Plan:		Second Exec. Salary: $	Bonus: $

OTHER THOUGHTS:

Apparent Women Officers or Directors: 1
Hot Spot for Advancement for Women/Minorities:

LOCATIONS: ("Y" = Yes)

West:	Southwest:	Midwest:	Southeast:	Northeast:	International:
					Y

CHINA STATE CONSTRUCTION ENGINEERING CORP

www.cscec.com.cn

Industry Group Code: 5311 **Ranks within this company's industry group:** Sales: 1 Profits: 14

Properties:		Financial Services:		Construction/Development:		Investments:		Specialty Services:		Brokerage:	
Apartments:		Mortgages:		Commercial Construction:	Y	REIT:		Property Management:		Commercial Sales:	
Malls/Shopping:		Title Insurance:		Residential Construction:				Online Services:		Residential Sales:	
Offices:		Property Insurance:		Land Development:	Y			Software/IT:		Specialty:	
Hotels/Motels:				Support Services:				Consulting:			
Industrial/Warehouses:				Design/Engineering:							
Other:											

TYPES OF BUSINESS:

Construction & Real Estate Development
Contract Engineering
Property Development

BRANDS/DIVISIONS/AFFILIATES:

China State Construction International Co
China Construction Development Co. Ltd.
China Construction Decoration Engineering Co.
CSCEC Property Management Co.
CSC& EC (PTY) Ltd.
China Construction Namibia Co. Ltd.
China Construction American Co.

CONTACTS:

Note: Officers with more than one job title may be intentionally listed here more than once.

Sun Wenjie, Pres.
Guo Tao, VP
Yi Jun, VP
Guo Aihua, VP

Phone:	**Fax:**
Toll-Free: 086-010-8808-2888	
Address: 15 Sanlihe Rd. Haidan Dist., Beijing, 100037 China	

GROWTH PLANS/SPECIAL FEATURES:

China State Construction Engineering Corporation (CSCEC), founded in 1982, is primarily engaged in real estate, construction and contract engineering. The company also conducts design and planning; property development; machinery leasing; project supervision; property management; and trading activities. The firm has worked on office buildings, public facilities, airports, hotels, educational institutions, sports facilities, residential complexes, hospitals and military buildings. Its technologies are used for many applications such as constructing high-rises; installing large industrial works; complex deep pit support and dewatering activities; concrete manufacturing; project management; and general contracting of international projects. Specific projects include the Hada Express Way, Wuhan Railway Station, Shaanxi LanShang Expressway, the Tianjin Cihan Ferris Wheel, the Beijing Subway Line 4, Hongheyan Nuclear Station, China World Trade Center. The company has various domestic affiliated companies such as China State Construction International Co; China Construction Development Co. Ltd.; China Construction Decoration Engineering Co.; and CSCEC Property Management Co. The firm also has various international affiliated companies such as China Construction (South Pacific) Development Co. Pte. Ltd. in Singapore; CSC& EC (PTY) Ltd. in Botswana; China Construction Namibia Co. Ltd. in Namibia; and China Construction American Co. in Jersey City, New Jersey, with additional branches in Algeria, Barbados; Seychelles; Thailand; the Philippines; United Arab Emirates (U.A.E.), Japan, Korea, Ireland, Russia and the Middle East.

FINANCIALS:

Sales and profits are in thousands of dollars—add 000 to get the full amount. 2009 Note: Financial information for 2009 was not available for all companies at press time.

2009 Sales: $	2009 Profits: $	**U.S. Stock Ticker:**
2008 Sales: $29,564,000	2008 Profits: $401,630	**Int'l Ticker: 601668** Int'l Exchange:
2007 Sales: $24,620,900	2007 Profits: $719,290	Employees:
2006 Sales: $	2006 Profits: $	Fiscal Year Ends: 12/31
2005 Sales: $	2005 Profits: $	Parent Company:

SALARIES/BENEFITS:

Pension Plan:	ESOP Stock Plan:	Profit Sharing:	Top Exec. Salary: $	Bonus: $
Savings Plan:	Stock Purch. Plan:		Second Exec. Salary: $	Bonus: $

OTHER THOUGHTS:

Apparent Women Officers or Directors:
Hot Spot for Advancement for Women/Minorities:

LOCATIONS: ("Y" = Yes)

West:	Southwest:	Midwest:	Southeast:	Northeast:	International:
				Y	Y

CHINESE ESTATES HOLDINGS LTD

www.chineseestates.com

Industry Group Code: 5311 **Ranks within this company's industry group:** Sales: 34 Profits: 30

Properties:		Financial Services:		Construction/Development:		Investments:		Specialty Services:		Brokerage:	
Apartments:	Y	Mortgages:		Commercial Construction:	Y	REIT:		Property Management:		Commercial Sales:	
Malls/Shopping:	Y	Title Insurance:		Residential Construction:	Y			Online Services:		Residential Sales:	
Offices:	Y	Property Insurance:		Land Development:	Y			Software/IT:		Specialty:	
Hotels/Motels:	Y			Support Services:				Consulting:			
Industrial/Warehouses:	Y			Design/Engineering:							
Other:	Y										

TYPES OF BUSINESS:

Real Estate Holdings & Development
Commercial Property Development
Residential Property Development

BRANDS/DIVISIONS/AFFILIATES:

Chi Cheung Investment Company, Ltd.
Power Jade Limited
G-Prop (Holdings) Limited

CONTACTS:

Note: Officers with more than one job title may be intentionally listed here more than once.

Luen-hung (Joseph) Lau, CEO
Mun-yi Cheung, Sr. Mgr.-Legal
Matthew Veng-va Cheong, Gen. Mgr.-Oper.
Alison Yeung, Dir.-Corp. Comm.
Kwong-wai Lam, Controller/Company Sec.
Chi-ming (Alec) Kong, Head-Mainland China Bus.
Ming-yan (Hazel) Lai, Sr. Mgr.-Contracts, Project Dev.
Mun-chie (Teresa) Poon, Sr. Mgr.-Project Dev. Dept.
Yik-hei (Kenneth) Ng, Sr. Mgr.-Project Dev. Dept.
Luen-hung (Joseph) Lau, Chmn.

Phone: 852-2866-6999	**Fax:** 852-2866-2822
Toll-Free:	
Address: 38 Gloucester Rd., 26th Fl., Wanchai, Hong Kong, China	

GROWTH PLANS/SPECIAL FEATURES:

Chinese Estates Holdings Limited is a Hong Kong-based property development firm. Its core business is focused on investments in properties for rent and the development of properties for sale. Over the course of its 20 year history, the company's primary work has been in Hong Kong, though it has been expanding its activities in Mainland China in recent years. The firm's property portfolio is comprised of approximately 1 million square feet of retail property and approximately 1.2 million square feet of office property, mostly situated in commercial areas of Hong Kong such as Causeway Bay, Tsim Sha Tsui and Wanchai. The company's Hong Kong rental properties include nine shopping centers, four industrial sites and three commercial properties, including the MassMutual Tower, where the firm has its headquarters. Hong Kong properties currently for sale include 13 residential complexes, primarily consisting of high-rise apartments and condominiums. On the Chinese mainland, Chinese Estates owns commercial buildings in Beijing and Shanghai; a five-star hotel in Beijing; and part of a shopping arcade located in Shenzhen. The firm specializes in developing mid to high-end residential and commercial properties, and it currently has a land bank totaling approximately 30 million square feet in various parts of Hong Kong, Macau and Mainland China. The company's long-term strategy involves leveraging this sizeable land bank to provide itself with the flexibility necessary to respond to local real estate cycles over time. Chinese Estates has several partially-owned subsidiaries also engaged in property investment and development: Chi Cheung Investment Company, Ltd., in which the firm holds a 61.96% share; Power Jade Limited, in which the company holds 50%; and G-Prop (Holdings) Limited, in which Chinese Estates hold a 41.93% share. In addition to its Hong Kong headquarters, the company maintains offices in Beijing, Chengdu, Shanghai and Shenzhen.

FINANCIALS:

Sales and profits are in thousands of dollars—add 000 to get the full amount. 2009 Note: Financial information for 2009 was not available for all companies at press time.

2009 Sales: $292,890	2009 Profits: $1,114,000	**U.S. Stock Ticker:**
2008 Sales: $163,200	2008 Profits: $-187,880	**Int'l Ticker: 0127** Int'l Exchange: Hong Kong-HKE
2007 Sales: $577,770	2007 Profits: $1,075,120	Employees:
2006 Sales: $	2006 Profits: $	Fiscal Year Ends: 12/31
2005 Sales: $	2005 Profits: $	Parent Company:

SALARIES/BENEFITS:

Pension Plan:	ESOP Stock Plan:	Profit Sharing:	Top Exec. Salary: $	Bonus: $
Savings Plan:	Stock Purch. Plan:		Second Exec. Salary: $	Bonus: $

OTHER THOUGHTS:

Apparent Women Officers or Directors: 5
Hot Spot for Advancement for Women/Minorities: Y

LOCATIONS: ("Y" = Yes)

West:	Southwest:	Midwest:	Southeast:	Northeast:	International:
					Y

CHIYODA CORPORATION

www.chiyoda-corp.com

Industry Group Code: 541330 **Ranks within this company's industry group:** Sales: 3 Profits: 5

Properties:		Financial Services:		Construction/Development:		Investments:		Specialty Services:		Brokerage:	
Apartments:		Mortgages:		Commercial Construction:		REIT:		Property Management:		Commercial Sales:	
Malls/Shopping:		Title Insurance:		Residential Construction:				Online Services:	Y	Residential Sales:	
Offices:		Property Insurance:		Land Development:				Software/IT:		Specialty:	
Hotels/Motels:				Support Services:				Consulting:	Y		
Industrial/Warehouses:				Design/Engineering:	Y						
Other:											

TYPES OF BUSINESS:

Engineering & Construction Services
Plant Lifecycle Engineering
Computer-Aided Engineering
Risk Management
Pollution Prevention Systems
Industrial Equipment-Online Procurement
Mining

BRANDS/DIVISIONS/AFFILIATES:

Chiyoda Advanced Solutions Corporation
EREKA
Biofiner
CTG Engineering Method
CT-121 FGD Process
Chiyoda International Corporation

CONTACTS:

Note: Officers with more than one job title may be intentionally listed here more than once.

Takashi Kubota, CEO
Takashi Kubota, Pres.
Kimura Katsutoshi, CFO
Sumio Nakashima, Dir.-Tech.
Sumio Nakashima, Dir.-Eng.
Satoru Yokoi, Dir.-Bus. Dev.
Toshiyuki Ohnuma, Dir.-Finance
Manabu Mitani, Dir.-Project Logistics & Construction
Tsuyoshi Kakizaki, Gen. Mgr.-SQE Office
Eisaku Yamashita, Dir.-Domestic Project Oper.
Madoka Koda, Mgr.-Saudi Arabia/Dir.-Oil & Chemical Project
Atsuo Minamoto, Dir.-Logistics

Phone: 81-45-521-1231 **Fax:** 81-45-503-0200
Toll-Free:
Address: 12-1, Tsurumichuo, 2-Chome, Tsurumi-ku, Yokohama, 230-8601 Japan

GROWTH PLANS/SPECIAL FEATURES:

Chiyoda Corporation is a Japanese engineering firm that operates in the hydrocarbon and chemical industries. Many of the firm's activities involve facilities that prevent disasters, improve the environment and control pollution. Chiyoda provides comprehensive engineering services that range from feasibility studies of design to maintenance, engineering, procurement, construction and start-up assistance. The firm's EREKA process provides a process of producing clean fuel from heavy residual materials. The first Eureka unit was installed in Japan over 20 years ago and is still in operation. Chiyoda has also developed many environmental preservation and pollution prevention systems, such as Biofiner, the CTG Engineering Method and the CT-121 FGD Process. Through Chiyoda Advanced Solutions Corporation, the firm provides technological support for engineering projects, including computer-aided engineering analysis and plant lifecycle engineering and risk management. The firm's U.S. activities are overseen by Chiyoda International Corporation, headquartered in Houston, Texas. The company has offices in countries throughout the world, including Indonesia, the U.K., the U.S., the Philippines, Australia, China, Brazil, Malaysia, Saudi Arabia, Singapore, Thailand, Qatar, India and Indonesia. The company has 17 consolidated subsidiaries and three associated companies.

FINANCIALS:

Sales and profits are in thousands of dollars—add 000 to get the full amount. 2009 Note: Financial information for 2009 was not available for all companies at press time.

2009 Sales: $4,963,910	2009 Profits: $72,250	**U.S. Stock Ticker:**
2008 Sales: $6,035,600	2008 Profits: $96,410	**Int'l Ticker: 6366** Int'l Exchange: Tokyo-TSE
2007 Sales: $4,800,500	2007 Profits: $233,000	Employees:
2006 Sales: $3,869,700	2006 Profits: $192,100	Fiscal Year Ends: 3/31
2005 Sales: $2,649,800	2005 Profits: $127,300	Parent Company:

SALARIES/BENEFITS:

Pension Plan:	ESOP Stock Plan:	Profit Sharing:	Top Exec. Salary: $	Bonus: $
Savings Plan:	Stock Purch. Plan:		Second Exec. Salary: $	Bonus: $

OTHER THOUGHTS:

Apparent Women Officers or Directors:
Hot Spot for Advancement for Women/Minorities:

LOCATIONS: ("Y" = Yes)

West:	Southwest:	Midwest:	Southeast:	Northeast:	International:
	Y				Y

CHOICE HOTELS INTERNATIONAL INC

www.choicehotels.com

Industry Group Code: 721110 **Ranks within this company's industry group:** Sales: 17 Profits: 8

Properties:		Financial Services:		Construction/Development:		Investments:		Specialty Services:		Brokerage:	
Apartments:		Mortgages:		Commercial Construction:		REIT:		Property Management:		Commercial Sales:	
Malls/Shopping:		Title Insurance:		Residential Construction:				Online Services:		Residential Sales:	
Offices:		Property Insurance:		Land Development:				Software/IT:		Specialty:	
Hotels/Motels:	Y			Support Services:				Consulting:			
Industrial/Warehouses:				Design/Engineering:							
Other:											

TYPES OF BUSINESS:

Hotels
Motels
Suites
Franchising

BRANDS/DIVISIONS/AFFILIATES:

Econo Lodge
MainStay Suites
Rodeway Inn
Quality Inn
Clarion Hotels
Comfort Inn
Sleep Inn
Comfort Suites

CONTACTS: *Note: Officers with more than one job title may be intentionally listed here more than once.*

Stephen P. Joyce, CEO
Stephen P. Joyce, Pres.
David White, CFO
Bruce N. Haase, Exec. VP-Mktg.
Patrick Cimerola, Sr. VP-Human Resources
Patrick Pacious, Sr. VP-IT
Patrick Cimerola, Sr. VP-Admin.
Bruce Haase, Exec. VP-Global Brand Oper.
Patrick Pacious, Sr. VP-Corp. Strategy
Mary Beth Knight, Sr. VP-e-commerce
Anne Madison, Sr. VP-Corp. Comm.
Scott Oaksmith, Controller
William Carlson, Sr. VP-Performance Analytics & Loyalty
David Pepper, Sr. VP-Global Dev.
Bret Limage, Assistant General Counsel/Asst. Sec.
Ron Parisotto, Assistant General Counsel/Asst. Sec.
Stewart W. Bainum, Jr., Chmn.

Phone: 301-592-5000 **Fax:** 301-592-6157
Toll-Free:
Address: 10750 Columbia Pike, Silver Spring, MD 20901 US

GROWTH PLANS/SPECIAL FEATURES:

Choice Hotels International, Inc. is one of the world's largest franchisers of hotel properties. It has 6,021 hotels open and 843 hotels under development in 49 states, Washington D.C. and over 40 foreign countries and territories around the globe. More than 1,165 of these hotels are international. The firm's 11 proprietary brand names include Comfort Inn, Comfort Suites, Quality, Clarion, Sleep Inn, Econo Lodge, Rodeway Inn, MainStay Suites, Suburban Extended Stay Hotel, Cambria Suites and the Ascend Collection. Choice Hotel's business is based on franchise revenues that consist of initial fees and ongoing royalty fees. The company also collects marketing and reservation fees to support centralized activities. The Econo Lodge and Rodeway Inn brands compete in the limited-service economy market; the Comfort Inn, Comfort Suites and Sleep Inn brands compete in the limited-service midscale without food and beverage market; the MainStay brand and the Extended Stay Hotel brand compete in the extended stay market; and the Clarion and Quality brands compete primarily in the full-service midscale with food and beverage market. The firm's largest brand is Comfort, which provides mid-scale rooms without food and beverage service, targeted primarily to business and leisure travelers. To support its hotel operations, Choice Hotels maintains call centers, proprietary web sites and global distribution systems to help deliver customers to franchisees through multiple channels. Through these channels, customers can check hotel rates and locations as well as make reservations and apply for the company loyalty program. In February 2010, the company announced the opening of six newly added properties in Poland.

Employees are offered a 401(k) plan; an employee stock purchase plan; medical, dental, vision and prescription coverage; life insurance; accidental death and dismemberment coverage; flexible spending accounts; disability coverage; long term care coverage; an employee assistance program; paid leave; tuition reimbursement; adoption assistance; legal services; hotel discounts; employee banking; pet insurance; and vendor/retail discounts.

FINANCIALS: **Sales and profits are in thousands of dollars—add 000 to get the full amount. 2009 Note: Financial information for 2009 was not available for all companies at press time.**

2009 Sales: $564,178	2009 Profits: $98,250	**U.S. Stock Ticker: CHH**
2008 Sales: $641,680	2008 Profits: $100,211	**Int'l Ticker:** Int'l Exchange:
2007 Sales: $615,494	2007 Profits: $111,301	Employees: 1,560
2006 Sales: $539,903	2006 Profits: $112,787	Fiscal Year Ends: 12/31
2005 Sales: $472,098	2005 Profits: $87,565	Parent Company:

SALARIES/BENEFITS:

Pension Plan:	ESOP Stock Plan:	Profit Sharing:	Top Exec. Salary: $775,000	Bonus: $775,000
Savings Plan: Y	Stock Purch. Plan: Y		Second Exec. Salary: $360,000	Bonus: $199,980

OTHER THOUGHTS:

Apparent Women Officers or Directors: 3
Hot Spot for Advancement for Women/Minorities: Y

LOCATIONS: ("Y" = Yes)

West:	Southwest:	Midwest:	Southeast:	Northeast:	International:
Y	Y	Y	Y	Y	Y

CHRISTIES GREAT ESTATES

www.christiesgreatestates.com

Industry Group Code: 531210 **Ranks within this company's industry group:** Sales: Profits:

Properties:		Financial Services:		Construction/Development:		Investments:		Specialty Services:		Brokerage:	
Apartments:	Y	Mortgages:		Commercial Construction:		REIT:		Property Management:		Commercial Sales:	
Malls/Shopping:		Title Insurance:		Residential Construction:				Online Services:		Residential Sales:	Y
Offices:		Property Insurance:		Land Development:				Software/IT:		Specialty:	Y
Hotels/Motels:				Support Services:				Consulting:			
Industrial/Warehouses:				Design/Engineering:							
Other:											

TYPES OF BUSINESS:

Real Estate Brokerage
Luxury Home Sales

BRANDS/DIVISIONS/AFFILIATES:

Christie's International plc
Christie's Auction House
Great Estates, Inc.
Christie's Great Estates Magazine

CONTACTS:

Note: Officers with more than one job title may be intentionally listed here more than once.

Kay Coughlin, CEO
Kay Coughlin, Pres.
David Wilson, Dir.-Advertising Sales
Gregg Antonsen, Sr. VP-Bus. Dev.
Joachim Wrang-Widen, Dir.-Real Estate, Europe
Kathleen Coumou, VP-Eastern Region
Richard M. Moeser, VP-Southeast Region

Phone: 505-983-8733	**Fax:** 505-982-0348
Toll-Free:	
Address: 125 Lincoln Ave., Ste. 300, Santa Fe, NM 87501 US	

GROWTH PLANS/SPECIAL FEATURES:

Christie's Great Estates, a wholly-owned subsidiary of Christie's International plc, was formed when Christie's Auction House acquired Great Estates, Inc. It is the largest international network of real estate companies that are dedicated to the marketing and selling of high-end properties. The network boasts over 800 real estate offices and approximately 35,000 sales associates in over 40 countries. The company brings buyers and sellers of luxury real estate together throughout the world. Through an exclusive system of advertising, marketing and listing tools, Christie's Great Estates provides access to a worldwide audience. Properties are showcased in Christie's Great Estates magazine, which is published four times a year; in custom-designed property brochures distributed worldwide; on the Christie's Great Estates Web site; and in Christie's Magazine and other highly regarded international publications. The Great Estates magazine is also available worldwide in all of the firm's offices; at newsstands and bookstores in affluent communities; and many luxury hotels and inns. Christie's clients include some of the highest-salaried executives and heads of major international corporations, celebrities, sports figures and other high-net-worth individuals.

FINANCIALS:

Sales and profits are in thousands of dollars—add 000 to get the full amount. 2009 Note: Financial information for 2009 was not available for all companies at press time.

2009 Sales: $	2009 Profits: $	**U.S. Stock Ticker: Subsidiary**
2008 Sales: $	2008 Profits: $	**Int'l Ticker:** Int'l Exchange:
2007 Sales: $	2007 Profits: $	Employees:
2006 Sales: $	2006 Profits: $	Fiscal Year Ends: 12/31
2005 Sales: $	2005 Profits: $	Parent Company: CHRISTIES INTERNATIONAL PLC

SALARIES/BENEFITS:

Pension Plan:	ESOP Stock Plan:	Profit Sharing:	Top Exec. Salary: $	Bonus: $
Savings Plan:	Stock Purch. Plan:		Second Exec. Salary: $	Bonus: $

OTHER THOUGHTS:

Apparent Women Officers or Directors: 2
Hot Spot for Advancement for Women/Minorities: Y

LOCATIONS: ("Y" = Yes)

West:	Southwest:	Midwest:	Southeast:	Northeast:	International:
Y	Y	Y	Y	Y	Y

CITIMORTGAGE INC

www.citimortgage.com

Industry Group Code: 522310 **Ranks within this company's industry group:** Sales: Profits:

Properties:		Financial Services:		Construction/Development:		Investments:		Specialty Services:		Brokerage:	
Apartments:		Mortgages:	Y	Commercial Construction:		REIT:		Property Management:		Commercial Sales:	
Malls/Shopping:		Title Insurance:		Residential Construction:				Online Services:		Residential Sales:	
Offices:		Property Insurance:		Land Development:				Software/IT:		Specialty:	
Hotels/Motels:				Support Services:				Consulting:			
Industrial/Warehouses:				Design/Engineering:							
Other:											

TYPES OF BUSINESS:

Mortgages
Refinancing
Home Equity Loans

BRANDS/DIVISIONS/AFFILIATES:

Citigroup Inc
Smith Barney
ABN AMRO Mortgage Group

CONTACTS:

Note: Officers with more than one job title may be intentionally listed here more than once.

Sanjiv Das, CEO
Sanjiv Das, Pres.
Paul Ince, CFO

Phone: 636-261-2484	**Fax:** 636-261-2387
Toll-Free: 800-667-8424	
Address: 1000 Technology Dr., O'Fallon, MO 63368-2240 US	

GROWTH PLANS/SPECIAL FEATURES:

CitiMortgage, Inc., the mortgage lending unit of Citigroup, Inc., is one of the nation's leading residential mortgage originators, with over 100 retail branch locations throughout the country. The company offers products to help first-time homebuyers, as well as those interested in building a new home, refinancing or salvaging the equity built up in an existing home through its retail, telesales and corporate loan origination channels. CitiMortgage allows customers to apply online, by phone or in person at various locations throughout the country. Its web site provides various tools that help customers choose the right mortgage product, determine how much they can realistically expect to receive, what their rate will be and compare home equity versus refinancing and renting versus buying. In addition, it provides mortgage assistance to relocating employees of many Fortune 500 companies. The firm receives customer referrals from Citigroup and its subsidiaries, which have over 200 million customers. CitiMortgage allows the customers of its sister subsidiary, Smith Barney, a global private wealth management and equity research unit, to use its accounts as collateral for down payments. Citigroup incurred heavy losses in 2008, partially due to a rise in delinquent mortgage payments and foreclosures. As a result of a rising number of defaults, Citimortgage reduced its brokers to 1,000. Between October and March 2009, Citigroup received $45 billion in government bailout funds.

CitiMortgage offers its employees benefits including tuition reimbursement, formal training packages, mortgage assistance, discount banking services, stock ownership programs, LifeWorks family support, 2-4 weeks of paid vacation and 10 paid holidays per year.

FINANCIALS:

Sales and profits are in thousands of dollars—add 000 to get the full amount. 2009 Note: Financial information for 2009 was not available for all companies at press time.

2009 Sales: $	2009 Profits: $	**U.S. Stock Ticker: Subsidiary**
2008 Sales: $	2008 Profits: $	**Int'l Ticker:** Int'l Exchange:
2007 Sales: $	2007 Profits: $	Employees:
2006 Sales: $	2006 Profits: $	Fiscal Year Ends: 12/31
2005 Sales: $	2005 Profits: $	Parent Company: CITIGROUP INC

SALARIES/BENEFITS:

Pension Plan:	ESOP Stock Plan:	Profit Sharing:	Top Exec. Salary: $	Bonus: $
Savings Plan: Y	Stock Purch. Plan: Y		Second Exec. Salary: $	Bonus: $

OTHER THOUGHTS:

Apparent Women Officers or Directors:
Hot Spot for Advancement for Women/Minorities:

LOCATIONS: ("Y" = Yes)

West:	Southwest:	Midwest:	Southeast:	Northeast:	International:
		Y			

CLAYTON HOMES INC

www.claytonhomes.com

Industry Group Code: 321991 **Ranks within this company's industry group:** Sales: Profits:

Properties:		Financial Services:		Construction/Development:		Investments:		Specialty Services:		Brokerage:	
Apartments:		Mortgages:	Y	Commercial Construction:		REIT:		Property Management:		Commercial Sales:	
Malls/Shopping:		Title Insurance:		Residential Construction:	Y			Online Services:		Residential Sales:	Y
Offices:		Property Insurance:	Y	Land Development:				Software/IT:		Specialty:	
Hotels/Motels:				Support Services:				Consulting:			
Industrial/Warehouses:				Design/Engineering:							
Other:											

TYPES OF BUSINESS:

Construction Services
Manufactured Housing
Insurance & Financing

BRANDS/DIVISIONS/AFFILIATES:

Vanderbilt Mortgage & Finance, Inc.
Berkshire Hathaway Inc
Schult
Clayton
Crest Homes
Marlette
SE Homes
I-House

CONTACTS: *Note: Officers with more than one job title may be intentionally listed here more than once.*

Kevin T. Clayton, CEO
Kevin T. Clayton, Pres.
John J. Kalec, CFO/Exec. VP

Phone: 865-380-3000	**Fax:** 865-380-3742
Toll-Free: 800-822-0633	
Address: 500 Alcoa Trail, Maryville, TN 37804 US	

GROWTH PLANS/SPECIAL FEATURES:

Clayton Homes, Inc., a subsidiary of Berkshire Hathaway, Inc., produces, sells, finances and insures modular and manufactured homes, in addition to commercial and educational relocatable buildings. The company's 36 manufacturing plants in 12 states produce homes that are marketed in 48 states through 1,500 independent retailers and approximately 385 company-owned sales centers. Its homes are designed and built through 35 facilities. Clayton's factory-built manufactured homes are completely finished dwellings that are constructed under federal code in factories and then transported by trucks to its targeted location. The homes are designed to be permanent, owner-occupied residential sites with attached utilities. Clayton manufactures a variety of single- and multi-sectional homes from 500 to 2,000 square feet and larger under brand names such as Clayton, Schult, Crest Homes, Marlette, Karsten, Norris, Golden West, Giles and SEhomes. Standard features offered in Clayton Homes include central heating, flooring systems and wall and floor treatments. Customers can choose predesigned homes or custom-design a home by size, number of bedrooms and other features. Through Clayton's financial subsidiary, Vanderbilt Mortgage and Finance, Inc. (VMF), the firm offers financing to manufactured home customers, as well as customers purchasing homes from certain third parties. VMF's financing products include manufactured home loans, Federal Housing Authority (FHA) loans, Land Home financing and more. Clayton and its subsidiaries provide financing to 325,000 customers and insurance to 160,000 customers. Additionally, Clayton acts as a reinsurance agent for physical damage, family protection and homebuyer protection insurance and other policies issued by insurance companies in connection with the firm's homes. In 2009, the firm introduced its newest home design, the I-House, a more environmentally friendly plan with a sleek design that offers several energy-saving features.

Clayton offers its employees a 401(k) plan; medical, dental vision and life insurance; training programs; and tuition and fitness reimbursement.

FINANCIALS: **Sales and profits are in thousands of dollars—add 000 to get the full amount. 2009 Note: Financial information for 2009 was not available for all companies at press time.**

2009 Sales: $	2009 Profits: $	**U.S. Stock Ticker: Subsidiary**
2008 Sales: $	2008 Profits: $	**Int'l Ticker:** Int'l Exchange:
2007 Sales: $	2007 Profits: $	Employees:
2006 Sales: $	2006 Profits: $	Fiscal Year Ends: 6/30
2005 Sales: $	2005 Profits: $	Parent Company: BERKSHIRE HATHAWAY INC

SALARIES/BENEFITS:

Pension Plan:	ESOP Stock Plan:	Profit Sharing:	Top Exec. Salary: $	Bonus: $
Savings Plan: Y	Stock Purch. Plan:		Second Exec. Salary: $	Bonus: $

OTHER THOUGHTS:

Apparent Women Officers or Directors:
Hot Spot for Advancement for Women/Minorities:

LOCATIONS: ("Y" = Yes)

West:	Southwest:	Midwest:	Southeast:	Northeast:	International:
Y	Y	Y	Y	Y	

CLUB MEDITERRANEE SA

www.clubmed.com

Industry Group Code: 721110 **Ranks within this company's industry group:** Sales: 8 Profits: 20

Properties:		Financial Services:		Construction/Development:		Investments:		Specialty Services:		Brokerage:	
Apartments:		Mortgages:		Commercial Construction:		REIT:		Property Management:		Commercial Sales:	
Malls/Shopping:		Title Insurance:		Residential Construction:				Online Services:		Residential Sales:	
Offices:		Property Insurance:		Land Development:				Software/IT:		Specialty:	
Hotels/Motels:	Y			Support Services:				Consulting:			
Industrial/Warehouses:				Design/Engineering:							
Other:	Y										

TYPES OF BUSINESS:

Resort Hotels
Tour Marketing/Packaging
Cruise Ships
Seminars, Conventions & Event Planning
Gyms
Licensed Apparel Products

BRANDS/DIVISIONS/AFFILIATES:

Club Med
Club Med Decouverte

CONTACTS:

Note: Officers with more than one job title may be intentionally listed here more than once.

Henri G. d'Estaing, CEO
Michel Wolfovski, CFO/Exec. VP
Caroline Puechoultres, VP-Strategic Mktg. & Quality
Olivier Sastre, Sr. VP-Human Resources
Caroline Puechoultres, VP-Dev.
Thierry Orsoni, VP-Comm.
Anne Bouferguene, Managing Dir.-Jet Tours
Patrick Calvet, VP-Villages, Europe & Africa
Caroline Puechoultres, VP-Asia-Pacific
Sylvain Rabuel, VP-Sales & Mktg. New Markets-Europe & Africa
Henri G. d'Estaing, Chmn.
Janyck Daudet, CEO/Pres., Latin America

Phone: 33-1-53-35-35-53	**Fax:** 33-1-53-35-36-16
Toll-Free:	
Address: 11 Rue de Cambrai, Paris, 75019 France	

GROWTH PLANS/SPECIAL FEATURES:

Club Mediterranee S.A. (Club Med) is an international operator of resort hotels and tours, operating in over 40 countries worldwide. Club Med is known for being the originator of all-inclusive vacations, which means that every meal, drink, activity and amenity is included in the price of the vacation. The core business of the company is the operation of vacation villages, resorts organized like small towns. These villages and villas include streets with shops and houses and feature a large number of luxury accommodations in hand-picked locations. The company operates approximately 80 properties, concentrated in equatorial locations, including the Caribbean, Southeast Asia and the Mediterranean. It also operates two ski resorts. The company sells licensed products such as sportswear and children's clothing. In addition, Club Med offers Club Med Decouverte, a tour guide service that takes small groups to places such as Phuket, Cancun Yucatan as well as weekend getaways to Venice, Istanbul and other well-known cities. The company organizes corporate events, weddings and other events at its villages and other venues. In recent years, the company has divested its jet tours, Club Met World and Club Med Gym operations as well as its resort in Bora Bora. In February 2010, the company signed an agreement with Melco China Resorts Holding Limited to open its first Chinese resort village, the Sun Mountain Yabuli Resort, which is scheduled to open in November 2010. Under the agreement, Club Med will operate and market the village and MCR will handle all ski activities.

FINANCIALS:

Sales and profits are in thousands of dollars—add 000 to get the full amount. 2009 Note: Financial information for 2009 was not available for all companies at press time.

2009 Sales: $1,801,630	2009 Profits: $-77,750	**U.S. Stock Ticker: CU**
2008 Sales: $1,938,630	2008 Profits: $2,600	**Int'l Ticker: CU** Int'l Exchange: Paris-Euronext
2007 Sales: $1,829,630	2007 Profits: $-10,380	Employees:
2006 Sales: $2,468,100	2006 Profits: $7,400	Fiscal Year Ends: 10/31
2005 Sales: $2,337,300	2005 Profits: $13,200	Parent Company:

SALARIES/BENEFITS:

Pension Plan:	ESOP Stock Plan:	Profit Sharing:	Top Exec. Salary: $	Bonus: $
Savings Plan:	Stock Purch. Plan:		Second Exec. Salary: $	Bonus: $

OTHER THOUGHTS:

Apparent Women Officers or Directors: 3
Hot Spot for Advancement for Women/Minorities: Y

LOCATIONS: ("Y" = Yes)

West:	Southwest:	Midwest:	Southeast:	Northeast:	International:
Y			Y		Y

CNL FINANCIAL GROUP INC

www.cnl.com

Industry Group Code: 531120 **Ranks within this company's industry group:** Sales: Profits:

Properties:		Financial Services:		Construction/Development:		Investments:		Specialty Services:		Brokerage:	
Apartments:		Mortgages:		Commercial Construction:	Y	REIT:	Y	Property Management:	Y	Commercial Sales:	
Malls/Shopping:	Y	Title Insurance:		Residential Construction:				Online Services:		Residential Sales:	
Offices:	Y	Property Insurance:		Land Development:	Y			Software/IT:		Specialty:	
Hotels/Motels:				Support Services:				Consulting:	Y		
Industrial/Warehouses:	Y			Design/Engineering:							
Other:	Y										

TYPES OF BUSINESS:

Real Estate Investment Trust
Banking Services
Commercial Financing
Investment Advisory Services
Real Estate Development & Management
Health Care & Assisted Living Properties
Industrial Properties
Retail, Hotel & Entertainment Properties

BRANDS/DIVISIONS/AFFILIATES:

CNL Fund Management Company
CNL Income Company, LLC
CNL Lifestyle Properties
CNL Commercial Real Estate
CNL Private Equity Corp.
CNL Real Estate Advisors
CNL Real Estate & Development Corp.
CNL Fund Advisors Company

CONTACTS: *Note: Officers with more than one job title may be intentionally listed here more than once.*

James M. Seneff, Jr., CEO
Timothy J. Seneff, Pres.
Tracy G. Schmidt, CFO
Lisa A. Schultz, Chief Human Capital Officer
Joel Schwalbe, CIO
Timothy J. Manor, General Counsel
Carolyn B. Gosselin, Chief Comm. Officer
Tammy Tipton, Chief Acct. Officer/Sr. VP
Robert A. Bourne, Vice Chmn.
R. Byron Carlock, Jr., CEO/Pres., CNL Lifestyle Company LLC
Timothy Edmond, Pres., CNL Real Estate & Dev.
Paul Ellis, Pres., CNL Commercial Real Estate
James M. Seneff, Jr., Chmn.

Phone: 407-650-1000 **Fax:** 407-650-1011
Toll-Free: 800-522-3863
Address: 450 S. Orange Ave., CNL Ctr. at City Commons, Orlando, FL 32801-3336 US

GROWTH PLANS/SPECIAL FEATURES:

CNL Financial Group is the flagship company for a group of real estate investment trusts (REITs) and financial services and advisory companies. CNL Fund Management Company collaborates with prominent investment managers in the real estate industry to create and manage real estate investment products. CNL Income Company, LLC is an advisor to CNL Lifestyle Properties (formerly CNL Income Properties), an REIT primarily investing in lifestyle properties in the U.S. and Canada. CNL Private Equity Corp. invests in business and real estate opportunities and manages a select portfolio of CNL's private offerings and investments. CNL Real Estate Advisors acquires, develops and manages real estate investments across a wide variety of sectors. CNL Real Estate & Development Corp. is a comprehensive development group specializing in master-planned communities, corporate offices, urban infill and other mixed-use projects throughout the Southeast U.S. CNL Commercial Real Estate provides real estate services including brokerage; property and facilities management; project management; commercial development and investment; and corporate services. CNL Securities Corp. sources capital for CNL and its joint venture partners. CNL Fund Advisors Company provides mutual funds to global real estate securities. CNL Private Equity Corp., is a non REIT strategy that manages investments in both real estate and business opportunities. Other CNL related companies are CNL Bank, which provides financial services; CNL Macquire Global Growth Advisors, provides management and administrative services to CNL Macquarie Global Growth Trust, Inc.; and lastly CNL Macquire Global Growth Trust Inc., a private real estate investment trust company. In March 2010, CNL Lifestyle Properties, Inc. acquired four California marinas for $55 million from Almar Management, Inc.

Employees of the firm receive educational assistance, a 529 college savings account, an adoption assistance program, flexible spending accounts and medical, prescription, dental, vision, disability and life insurance.

FINANCIALS: **Sales and profits are in thousands of dollars—add 000 to get the full amount. 2009 Note: Financial information for 2009 was not available for all companies at press time.**

2009 Sales: $	2009 Profits: $	**U.S. Stock Ticker: Private**
2008 Sales: $	2008 Profits: $	**Int'l Ticker:** Int'l Exchange:
2007 Sales: $77,400	2007 Profits: $	Employees:
2006 Sales: $	2006 Profits: $	Fiscal Year Ends: 12/31
2005 Sales: $	2005 Profits: $	Parent Company:

SALARIES/BENEFITS:

Pension Plan:	ESOP Stock Plan:	Profit Sharing:	Top Exec. Salary: $	Bonus: $
Savings Plan: Y	Stock Purch. Plan:		Second Exec. Salary: $	Bonus: $

OTHER THOUGHTS:

Apparent Women Officers or Directors: 4
Hot Spot for Advancement for Women/Minorities: Y

LOCATIONS: ("Y" = Yes)

West:	Southwest:	Midwest:	Southeast:	Northeast:	International:
Y	Y	Y	Y	Y	

COLDWELL BANKER REAL ESTATE CORP www.coldwellbanker.com

Industry Group Code: 531210 **Ranks within this company's industry group:** Sales: Profits:

Properties:		Financial Services:		Construction/Development:		Investments:		Specialty Services:		Brokerage:	
Apartments:		Mortgages:	Y	Commercial Construction:		REIT:		Property Management:		Commercial Sales:	Y
Malls/Shopping:		Title Insurance:		Residential Construction:				Online Services:	Y	Residential Sales:	Y
Offices:		Property Insurance:		Land Development:				Software/IT:		Specialty:	Y
Hotels/Motels:				Support Services:				Consulting:			
Industrial/Warehouses:				Design/Engineering:							
Other:											

TYPES OF BUSINESS:

Real Estate Brokerage
Residential & Resort Brokerage
Commercial Brokerage
Mortgage Services
Online Information & Lending

BRANDS/DIVISIONS/AFFILIATES:

Realogy
Coldwell Banker Preview International
Coldwell Banker Concierge
Coldwell Banker Mortgage
Coldwell Banker Commercial
Coldwell Banker Integrity
Coldwell Banker Select Professionals
CBU.com

CONTACTS:

Note: Officers with more than one job title may be intentionally listed here more than once.

Jim Gillespie, CEO
Jim Gillespie, Pres.
Michael Fischer, Sr. VP-Mktg.
Greg Sexton, VP-Oper.
David Siroty, Dir.-Public Rel.
Steve Bright, Sr. VP/Regional Dir.-Western Region
Nelson Bennett, Sr. VP/Regional Dir.-Northern Region
Frank Lindsey, Sr. VP/Regional Dir.-Southern Region
John Geha, Pres., Coldwell Banker Canada

Phone: 973-407-2000	**Fax:** 973-496-7217
Toll-Free: 877-373-3829	
Address: 1 Campus Dr., Parsippany, NJ 07054 US	

GROWTH PLANS/SPECIAL FEATURES:

Coldwell Banker Real Estate Corporation, a subsidiary of Realogy Corporation, offers a full array of commercial and residential real estate services including buying, selling, leasing, lending, refinancing and a variety of support services. The Coldwell Banker website provides resources for buyers and sellers of homes such as local real estate office information, agent locators, general information for first time buyers/sellers and a property locator. The website's Personal Retriever feature allows customers to keep track of properties they are interested in by creating a personal online account to which they can save home and real estate agent information as well as receive alerts when new properties are listed that meet their search criteria. The firm's Concierge Service Program, provides customers with information on local service providers specializing in everything from car and truck rental to home maintenance. Coldwell's sales associates act as local market experts and can help clients with everything from selling, buying and financing to moving into a new home. Coldwell Banker Mortgage is a leading telephone- and web-based lender in the U.S. Coldwell Banker International markets and sells luxury homes in the Americas, Europe, Africa, the Middle East, Asia and Australia. The firm has over 3,300 franchised residential and commercial real estate offices in 49 countries. Each office is independently owned and operated, except for offices owned and operated by NRT, Inc. Coldwell provides its brokers and sales associates with exclusive access to its Internet portal, CBNet, which has the most up-to-date information on all of the company's products and services, its listings, selling and prospecting and networking tools. Coldwell also provides CBU.com, an education site with a wide variety of classes and continuing education programs that can be taken in person, by phone or via the Internet.

FINANCIALS:

Sales and profits are in thousands of dollars—add 000 to get the full amount. 2009 Note: Financial information for 2009 was not available for all companies at press time.

2009 Sales: $	2009 Profits: $	**U.S. Stock Ticker: Subsidiary**
2008 Sales: $	2008 Profits: $	**Int'l Ticker:** Int'l Exchange:
2007 Sales: $	2007 Profits: $	Employees:
2006 Sales: $	2006 Profits: $	Fiscal Year Ends: 12/31
2005 Sales: $	2005 Profits: $	Parent Company: REALOGY CORPORATION

SALARIES/BENEFITS:

Pension Plan:	ESOP Stock Plan:	Profit Sharing:	Top Exec. Salary: $	Bonus: $
Savings Plan:	Stock Purch. Plan:		Second Exec. Salary: $	Bonus: $

OTHER THOUGHTS:

Apparent Women Officers or Directors:
Hot Spot for Advancement for Women/Minorities:

LOCATIONS: ("Y" = Yes)

West:	Southwest:	Midwest:	Southeast:	Northeast:	International:
Y	Y	Y	Y	Y	Y

COLLIERS INTERNATIONAL PROPERTY CONSULTANTS

www.colliers.com

Industry Group Code: 531210 **Ranks within this company's industry group:** Sales: 2 Profits:

Properties:		Financial Services:		Construction/Development:		Investments:		Specialty Services:		Brokerage:	
Apartments:		Mortgages:		Commercial Construction:		REIT:		Property Management:	Y	Commercial Sales:	Y
Malls/Shopping:		Title Insurance:		Residential Construction:				Online Services:		Residential Sales:	Y
Offices:		Property Insurance:		Land Development:	Y			Software/IT:		Specialty:	Y
Hotels/Motels:				Support Services:				Consulting:	Y		
Industrial/Warehouses:				Design/Engineering:							
Other:	Y										

TYPES OF BUSINESS:

Property Representation & Agency
Facilities Management
Commercial Sales
Consulting Services
Valuation & Advisory Services
Portfolio Management
Development & Project Management
Debt, Mezzanine & Equity Capital Financing

BRANDS/DIVISIONS/AFFILIATES:

Colliers Legal Resources Group
Colliers Investment Services Group
Colliers MultiModal Services Group
Colliers Facility Management Group

CONTACTS:

Note: Officers with more than one job title may be intentionally listed here more than once.

Doug Frye, CEO
Peter Humphries, COO
Doug Frye, Global Pres.
Peter Humphries, CFO
Kristen Okerman, VP-Global Mktg.
Mindy Geisser, VP-Global Human Resources
Ross Moore, Exec. VP-Research
Veresh Sita, CIO
Amyn Bhayani, Int'l Corp. Sec.
Carolyn Sidor, Exec. VP-Oper.
Amyn Bhayani, VP-Corp. Dev.
Chris McLernon, CEO-Latin American Region & EMEA
Dylan Taylor, CEO-Colliers USA
Annya Hawkins, Exec. VP-EMEA
David Kahnweiler, CEO/Chmn.-Colliers Bennett & Kahnweiler, Inc.
Doug Frye, Chmn.
Achim Degen, CEO-Germany

Phone: 617-722-0221	**Fax:** 617-722-0224
Toll-Free:	
Address: 50 Milk St., Fl. 20, Boston, MA 02109 US	

GROWTH PLANS/SPECIAL FEATURES:

Colliers International Property Consultants, Inc. (CIPC) is one of the world's largest commercial real estate organizations, with 294 offices in 61 countries. It is a partnership of more than 40 independently owned firms. The company's services include property representation and agency; tenant representation; portfolio management; mergers and acquisitions; facilities management; multi-family property advisement; development and project management; valuation and advisory services; and consulting. CIPC provides its services to a wide range of clients and industries through 11 practice groups. The Logistics, Healthcare, Not For Profit, Telecommunications and Hotel groups serve clients in their respective industries. The Colliers Legal Resources Group provides specialized services to law firms, while the Colliers Investment Services Group serves institutional and private investors. The Life Sciences group caters to research centers and pharmaceutical and biotechnology companies, while the Colliers MultiModal Services Group provides services to the global shipping and transportation industry. The Advanced Technology Real Estate group helps clients buy and sell advanced technology buildings. The Structured Finance group arranges more than $2 billion in debt, mezzanine and equity capital annually on behalf of clients. The Colliers Facility Management Group manages over 670 million square feet of client facilities. The Colliers Automotive Real Estate Services Group (Cars) offers commercial real estate to the automotive industry. The Call Center Service Group offers call center services to the real estate industry. Colliers Investment Service Group provides market research, data on emerging capital sources and sales transaction information. Colliers Land Advisory Group represents both buyer and sellers in land acquisitions and dispositions. Recently, four key subsidiaries; Colliers Turley Martin Tucker; Colliers Pinkard; Cassidy & Pinkard Colliers; and Colliers ABR; combined to form one holding company within its corporate solutions group. In January 2010, property management firm FirstService acquired Colliers International. In April 2010, the company acquired a majority ownership in commercial real estate firm Colliers Bennett & Kahnweiler.

FINANCIALS:

Sales and profits are in thousands of dollars—add 000 to get the full amount. 2009 Note: Financial information for 2009 was not available for all companies at press time.

2009 Sales: $	2009 Profits: $	**U.S. Stock Ticker: Subsidiary**
2008 Sales: $2,000,000	2008 Profits: $	**Int'l Ticker:** Int'l Exchange:
2007 Sales: $	2007 Profits: $	Employees: 11,000
2006 Sales: $	2006 Profits: $	Fiscal Year Ends: 12/31
2005 Sales: $	2005 Profits: $	Parent Company: FIRSTSERVICE CORPORATION

SALARIES/BENEFITS:

Pension Plan:	ESOP Stock Plan:	Profit Sharing:	Top Exec. Salary: $	Bonus: $
Savings Plan:	Stock Purch. Plan:		Second Exec. Salary: $	Bonus: $

OTHER THOUGHTS:

Apparent Women Officers or Directors: 4
Hot Spot for Advancement for Women/Minorities: Y

LOCATIONS: ("Y" = Yes)

West:	Southwest:	Midwest:	Southeast:	Northeast:	International:
Y	Y	Y	Y	Y	Y

COLONIAL PROPERTIES TRUST

www.colonialprop.com

Industry Group Code: 531110 **Ranks within this company's industry group:** Sales: 13 Profits: 17

Properties:		Financial Services:		Construction/Development:		Investments:		Specialty Services:		Brokerage:	
Apartments:	Y	Mortgages:		Commercial Construction:		REIT:	Y	Property Management:	Y	Commercial Sales:	
Malls/Shopping:	Y	Title Insurance:		Residential Construction:				Online Services:		Residential Sales:	
Offices:	Y	Property Insurance:		Land Development:				Software/IT:		Specialty:	
Hotels/Motels:				Support Services:				Consulting:			
Industrial/Warehouses:				Design/Engineering:							
Other:											

TYPES OF BUSINESS:

Real Estate Investment Trust
Multi-Family Apartments
Office Properties
Retail Properties
Property Management

BRANDS/DIVISIONS/AFFILIATES:

Colonial Realty, LP
Colonial Properties Services, Inc.
Cornerstone Realty Income Trust, Inc.
Colonnade Properties, LLC

CONTACTS:

Note: Officers with more than one job title may be intentionally listed here more than once.

Thomas Lowder, CEO
Paul F. Earle, COO
C. Reynolds Thompson, III, Pres.
C. Reynolds Thompson, III, CFO
John P. Rigrish, Chief Admin. Officer
John P. Rigrish, Corp. Sec.
Jerry A. Brewer, Exec. VP-Finance
Bradley P. Sandidge, Exec. VP-Acct.
Ed Wright, Exec. VP-Dev. & Construction
Bo Jackson, Exec. VP-Commercial Properties
Thomas Lowder, Chmn.

Phone: 205-250-8700 **Fax:** 205-250-8890
Toll-Free: 800-645-3917
Address: 2101 6th Ave. N., Ste. 750, Birmingham, AL 35203 US

GROWTH PLANS/SPECIAL FEATURES:

Colonial Properties Trust is a self-administered equity real estate investment trust (REIT) that owns, develops and operates multi-family, office, retail and mixed-use properties in Alabama, Arizona, Florida, Georgia, Nevada, North Carolina, South Carolina, Tennessee, Texas, and Virginia. Colonial owns and operates a diversified portfolio of 156 wholly- and partially-owned properties. At the end of 2009, the company owned or maintained a partial ownership in 111 multifamily apartment communities containing a total of 33,520 apartment units and 45 commercial properties containing 12.8 million square feet. The company holds an 89.1% interest in Colonial Realty, LP. Through this partnership, Colonial conducts management services for its properties as well as other business. Moreover, through Colonial Properties Services, Inc., the company provides management services for properties owned by third parties. Colonial also creates additional value by managing commercial assets, primarily through joint venture investments, and pursuing development opportunities. In November 2009, Colonial disposed of its 15% ownership interest in the DRA/CRA office joint venture with DRA Advisors LLC. As part of this transaction, the company acquired full ownership of the Three Ravinia, one of the joint venture's properties. In December 2009, the company exited two joint ventures, one with OZRE Retail LLC and one with the Mansell Group. Also in December 2009, Colonial sold the Colonial Promenade Winter Haven, one of its wholly-owned retail assets located in Orlando, Florida, for $20.7 million.

Employees are offered medical, dental and vision insurance; a 401(k) plan; a stock purchase plan; flexible spending accounts; life and AD&D insurance; short- and long-term disability coverage; an employee assistance program; education assistance; adoption assistance; and access to onsite fitness facilities.

FINANCIALS:

Sales and profits are in thousands of dollars—add 000 to get the full amount. 2009 Note: Financial information for 2009 was not available for all companies at press time.

2009 Sales: $340,352	2009 Profits: $- 509	**U.S. Stock Ticker: CLP**
2008 Sales: $343,567	2008 Profits: $-55,429	**Int'l Ticker:** Int'l Exchange:
2007 Sales: $421,571	2007 Profits: $342,102	Employees: 1,037
2006 Sales: $466,037	2006 Profits: $203,480	Fiscal Year Ends: 12/31
2005 Sales: $542,240	2005 Profits: $219,641	Parent Company:

SALARIES/BENEFITS:

Pension Plan:	ESOP Stock Plan:	Profit Sharing:	Top Exec. Salary: $405,000	Bonus: $150,000
Savings Plan: Y	Stock Purch. Plan: Y		Second Exec. Salary: $350,000	Bonus: $

OTHER THOUGHTS:

Apparent Women Officers or Directors:
Hot Spot for Advancement for Women/Minorities:

LOCATIONS: ("Y" = Yes)

West:	Southwest:	Midwest:	Southeast:	Northeast:	International:
Y	Y		Y	Y	

COLONY CAPITAL LLC

www.colonyinc.com

Industry Group Code: 531120 **Ranks within this company's industry group:** Sales: Profits:

Properties:		Financial Services:		Construction/Development:		Investments:		Specialty Services:		Brokerage:	
Apartments:		Mortgages:		Commercial Construction:		REIT:	Y	Property Management:		Commercial Sales:	
Malls/Shopping:		Title Insurance:		Residential Construction:				Online Services:		Residential Sales:	
Offices:		Property Insurance:		Land Development:				Software/IT:		Specialty:	
Hotels/Motels:	Y			Support Services:				Consulting:			
Industrial/Warehouses:				Design/Engineering:							
Other:	Y										

TYPES OF BUSINESS:

Real Estate Investment Trust
Private Equity

BRANDS/DIVISIONS/AFFILIATES:

Colony Reality Partners LP
Colony Investment Management LLC
La Tour
Brownfields
Carrefour SA
Challenger Financial Services
Station Casinos Inc
Meadowlands Xanadu

CONTACTS:

Note: Officers with more than one job title may be intentionally listed here more than once.

Thomas J. Barrack Jr., CEO
Richard B. Saltzman, Pres.
Mark M. Hedstrom, CFO
Jonathan Grunzweig, CIO
Ronald M. Sanders, General Counsel/Principal
Duyen Tran, VP-Oper. & Finance
Toshio Masui, Dir.-New Bus. Dev. Japan
Brent Elkins, Contact-Investor Rel.
Richard S. Welch, Sr. VP-Finance
Ed C. Daily, VP-Risk Mgmt. & Asset Mgmt.
Naji E. Boutros, Dir.-Middle East & North Africa
Henry G. Brauer, Sr. Managing Dir.-Colony Realty Partners LLC
Justin Chang, Principal
Thomas J. Barrack Jr., Chmn.
Sebastien Bazin, CEO-Colony Capital SAS/Managing Dir.-Europe

Phone: 310-282-8820	**Fax:** 310-282-8808
Toll-Free:	
Address: 2450 Broadway, Santa Monica, CA 90404 US	

GROWTH PLANS/SPECIAL FEATURES:

Colony Capital, LLC is a private international investment firm focusing primarily on real estate related assets and operating companies with a strategic dependence on such assets. The firm has invested over $39 billion in over 8,500 assets since 1991. The company's current fund, its eighth, has stakes in Station Casinos, a Las Vegas locals gaming business and Native American gaming management company; Meadowlands Xanadu, a retail development of a 2.2 million-square-foot sports, leisure, shopping and entertainment location in New Jersey; Ambassy Court, a 484,000-square-foot apartment building in Beijing; Brownfields, a platform specializing in the purchase, de-pollution and resale of contaminated industrial sites in Europe; La Tour, consisting of two private hospitals in Geneva, Switzerland; Challenger Financial Services Group, an Australian financial services company with $62.6 billion assets in management, administration and advice; Accor SA, a French Hotel Group with 4,000 hotels and 500,000 rooms; and 9.1% public shares of Carrefour SA, a food retailer with 12,000 locations in 29 countries. The company has two subsidiaries Colony Reality Partners L.P., real estate investment company that acquires and manages commercial real estate properties and Colony Investment Management LLC, manages investments for its clients. The firm operates through offices in Los Angeles, New York, Boston, Hawaii, Paris, Rome, London, Madrid, Beirut, Hong Kong, Beijing, Tokyo, Seoul and Taipei. In April 2010, as a co-owner with the Station executives Frank and Lorenzo Fertitta, the company formed a new entity called "PropCo" and would manage and have an ownership stake in five of Station's properties: Red Rock Resort, Sunset Station, Boulder Station, Palace Station and the Wild Wild West in Nevada.

FINANCIALS:

Sales and profits are in thousands of dollars—add 000 to get the full amount. 2009 Note: Financial information for 2009 was not available for all companies at press time.

2009 Sales: $	2009 Profits: $	**U.S. Stock Ticker: Private**
2008 Sales: $	2008 Profits: $	**Int'l Ticker:** Int'l Exchange:
2007 Sales: $475,100	2007 Profits: $	Employees:
2006 Sales: $	2006 Profits: $	Fiscal Year Ends:
2005 Sales: $	2005 Profits: $	Parent Company:

SALARIES/BENEFITS:

Pension Plan:	ESOP Stock Plan:	Profit Sharing:	Top Exec. Salary: $	Bonus: $
Savings Plan:	Stock Purch. Plan:		Second Exec. Salary: $	Bonus: $

OTHER THOUGHTS:

Apparent Women Officers or Directors: 5
Hot Spot for Advancement for Women/Minorities: Y

LOCATIONS: ("Y" = Yes)

West:	Southwest:	Midwest:	Southeast:	Northeast:	International:
Y				Y	Y

COMFORT SYSTEMS USA INC

www.comfortsystemsusa.com

Industry Group Code: 238220 **Ranks within this company's industry group:** Sales: 1 Profits: 1

Properties:		Financial Services:		Construction/Development:		Investments:		Specialty Services:		Brokerage:	
Apartments:		Mortgages:		Commercial Construction:		REIT:		Property Management:		Commercial Sales:	
Malls/Shopping:		Title Insurance:		Residential Construction:				Online Services:		Residential Sales:	
Offices:		Property Insurance:		Land Development:				Software/IT:		Specialty:	
Hotels/Motels:				Support Services:	Y			Consulting:			
Industrial/Warehouses:				Design/Engineering:	Y						
Other:											

TYPES OF BUSINESS:

Plumbing, Heating & Air Conditioning Contractors
Industrial & Commercial HVAC Systems & Services
Facility Automation Services

BRANDS/DIVISIONS/AFFILIATES:

Acorn Industrial, Inc.

CONTACTS:

Note: Officers with more than one job title may be intentionally listed here more than once.

William F. Murdy, CEO
Brian Lane, COO
William George, CFO
Trent McKenna, General Counsel/VP
Kimberlee Cotter, Sr. VP-Service Oper.
Julie Shaeff, Chief Acct. Officer/Sr. VP
Melissa Frazier, VP-Audit & Controls
W. Brewster Earle, Sr. VP-Energy Svcs.
Thomas N. Tanner, Sr. VP-Region 1
Dean Tillison, Sr. VP-Region 2
William F. Murdy, Chmn.

Phone: 713-803-9600	**Fax:** 713-830-9696
Toll-Free: 800-723-8431	
Address: 675 Bering, Ste. 400, Houston, TX 77057 US	

GROWTH PLANS/SPECIAL FEATURES:

Comfort Systems USA, Inc. is a national heating, ventilation and air conditioning (HVAC) and building automation services company with more than 80 locations in 72 cities nationwide. It provides installation, maintenance, repair and replacement services for a large and growing base of national, multi-location clients in both commercial and industrial markets. The company's technical experts design, install and fine-tune HVAC systems for downtown high-rises, hospitals, universities, national hotels, factories and industrial plants. Comfort offers two types of service: Installation services, accounting for 52% of revenues; and maintenance, repair and replacement services, accounting for 48% of revenues. Installation services involve the design, engineering, integration, installation and start-up of HVAC, building automation controls and related systems. The company provides design-and-build services, in which Comfort determines the needed capacity and energy efficiency of the HVAC system that best suits the proposed facility and then estimates the amount of time, labor, materials and equipment needed to build the specified system; and plan-and-spec services, in which it participates in a bid process to provide labor, equipment, materials and installation based on plans and engineering specifications provided by a customer, general contractor or consulting engineer, for office buildings, retail centers, apartment complexes, manufacturing plants, health care, education and government facilities and other commercial, industrial, and institutional facilities. Additionally, the firm installs process cooling systems and building automation controls and monitoring systems. The maintenance, repair and replacement services include the maintenance, repair, replacement, reconfiguration and monitoring of HVAC systems and industrial process piping. Maintenance and repair services are provided either in response to service calls or under a service agreement. In January 2010, the company acquired construction firm, Acorn Industrial, Inc. and mechanical services company, Dillingham & Smith Mechanical and Sheet Metal Contractors, LLC.

FINANCIALS:

Sales and profits are in thousands of dollars—add 000 to get the full amount. 2009 Note: Financial information for 2009 was not available for all companies at press time.

2009 Sales: $1,128,907	2009 Profits: $34,182	**U.S. Stock Ticker: FIX**
2008 Sales: $1,321,770	2008 Profits: $49,690	**Int'l Ticker:** Int'l Exchange:
2007 Sales: $1,101,579	2007 Profits: $32,466	Employees: 5,623
2006 Sales: $1,056,525	2006 Profits: $28,724	Fiscal Year Ends: 12/31
2005 Sales: $892,549	2005 Profits: $-6,226	Parent Company:

SALARIES/BENEFITS:

Pension Plan:	ESOP Stock Plan:	Profit Sharing:	Top Exec. Salary: $	Bonus: $
Savings Plan:	Stock Purch. Plan:		Second Exec. Salary: $	Bonus: $

OTHER THOUGHTS:

Apparent Women Officers or Directors: 3
Hot Spot for Advancement for Women/Minorities: Y

LOCATIONS: ("Y" = Yes)

West:	Southwest:	Midwest:	Southeast:	Northeast:	International:
Y	Y	Y	Y	Y	

COMMUNITY DEVELOPMENT TRUST

www.cdt.biz

Industry Group Code: 531110 **Ranks within this company's industry group:** Sales: Profits:

Properties:		Financial Services:		Construction/Development:		Investments:		Specialty Services:		Brokerage:	
Apartments:	Y	Mortgages:	Y	Commercial Construction:		REIT:	Y	Property Management:		Commercial Sales:	
Malls/Shopping:	Y	Title Insurance:		Residential Construction:				Online Services:		Residential Sales:	
Offices:	Y	Property Insurance:		Land Development:				Software/IT:		Specialty:	
Hotels/Motels:				Support Services:				Consulting:			
Industrial/Warehouses:				Design/Engineering:							
Other:											

TYPES OF BUSINESS:

Real Estate Investment Trust
Equity & Mortgage Investments
Apartments
Offices
Retail Properties

BRANDS/DIVISIONS/AFFILIATES:

Local Initiative Support Corporation

CONTACTS:

Note: Officers with more than one job title may be intentionally listed here more than once.

Joseph F. Reilly, CEO
John J. Divers, COO
Joseph F. Reilly, Pres.
John J. Divers, CFO
Susan Robbins, General Counsel/Corp. Sec.
John J. Divers, Treas.
Brian Gallagher, Sr. VP-Debt
Warren Horvath, Chief Investment Officer
Shelly Cleary, VP-Debt
Joan B. Berkowitz, Sr. VP-Asset Mgmt.
Peter J. Weidhorn, Chmn.

Phone: 212-271-5080 **Fax:** 212-271-5079
Toll-Free:
Address: 1350 Broadway, Ste. 700, New York, NY 10018-7702 US

GROWTH PLANS/SPECIAL FEATURES:

Community Development Trust (CDT) is a real estate investment trust (REIT) entirely devoted to investment in the community development market through both an equity program and a debt program. In the past ten years, the company has committed $724 million in debt and equity capital to affordable housing properties across the country. Through CDT's debt and equity programs, the firm invests long-term debt capital by purchasing smaller, fixed-rate multifamily mortgages from community lenders and equity capital in cash or by providing a tax advantaged transition for existing properties to a new set of owners committed to long-term affordability. All of CDT's investments must satisfy Community Reinvestment Act requirements. The company currently has investments in 28,000 housing units in 39 states across the country representing a broad mix of types ranging from scattered-site developments to in-fill urban family apartments and redeveloped high rises. The firm's average investment per transaction is approximately $5 million. Major investors in CDT include Allstate Insurance; Bank of America; California Bank and Trust; Citibank Community Development; Deutsche Bank; Fannie Mae; HSBC Bank USA; JPMorgan Chase Community Development Group; Key Community Development; Local Initiatives Support Corporation; MetLife; Merrill Lynch Community Development Company LLC; NCB Capital Impact; Prudential Financial; The Reinvestment Fund; Wachovia Corporation; Washington Mutual Bank; and Wells Fargo.

FINANCIALS:

Sales and profits are in thousands of dollars—add 000 to get the full amount. 2009 Note: Financial information for 2009 was not available for all companies at press time.

2009 Sales: $ 2009 Profits: $
2008 Sales: $ 2008 Profits: $
2007 Sales: $ 2007 Profits: $
2006 Sales: $ 2006 Profits: $
2005 Sales: $ 2005 Profits: $

U.S. Stock Ticker: Private
Int'l Ticker: Int'l Exchange:
Employees:
Fiscal Year Ends: 12/31
Parent Company:

SALARIES/BENEFITS:

Pension Plan: ESOP Stock Plan: Profit Sharing: Top Exec. Salary: $ Bonus: $
Savings Plan: Stock Purch. Plan: Second Exec. Salary: $ Bonus: $

OTHER THOUGHTS:

Apparent Women Officers or Directors: 9
Hot Spot for Advancement for Women/Minorities: Y

LOCATIONS: ("Y" = Yes)

West:	Southwest:	Midwest:	Southeast:	Northeast:	International:
Y			Y	Y	

CORE NETWORK (THE)

www.corenetwork.org

Industry Group Code: 531210 **Ranks within this company's industry group:** Sales: Profits:

Properties:		Financial Services:		Construction/Development:		Investments:		Specialty Services:		Brokerage:	
Apartments:		Mortgages:		Commercial Construction:		REIT:		Property Management:	Y	Commercial Sales:	Y
Malls/Shopping:		Title Insurance:		Residential Construction:				Online Services:	Y	Residential Sales:	
Offices:		Property Insurance:		Land Development:				Software/IT:		Specialty:	Y
Hotels/Motels:				Support Services:				Consulting:	Y		
Industrial/Warehouses:				Design/Engineering:							
Other:											

TYPES OF BUSINESS:

Office & Industrial Consulting
Retail Planning
Real Estate Development
Financial Services & Mortgages
Property Management
Real Estate Brokerage

BRANDS/DIVISIONS/AFFILIATES:

Project Tracking System

CONTACTS:

Note: Officers with more than one job title may be intentionally listed here more than once.

Perry Morita, Exec. Dir.
Michael B. Divaris, Chmn.

Phone: 972-980-3994	**Fax:** 972-980-3993
Toll-Free:	
Address: 15150 Preston Rd., Ste. 300, Dallas, TX 75248 US	

GROWTH PLANS/SPECIAL FEATURES:

The CORE Network is a consortium of approximately 28 mid-sized commercial real estate companies providing services to office and retail businesses. Through its member firms Core offers clients a variety of services including tenant representation, in which a specialist assists clients in negotiating leases, moving into a new facility and defining goals for surplus property and space requirements. The leasing and management service offers clients basic property management, as well as providing an evaluation of occupancy alternatives. The investment advisory services offer investors consultation in advantageous portfolio acquisitions through the firm's knowledge of local real estate opportunities. In addition, it offers finance and investment banking services to large corporate and institutional clients that consists of financing, transaction assistance, providing capital and negotiation tactics. The facility management services helps reduce cost and facilitate tenant services; construction management provides budgeting, general contracting, project and scheduling management; and development management services provides assistance to those clients wanting to occupy a property or for corporate clients entering into a joint venture. CORE's portfolio management offers tracking and administrative services to clients with numerous real estate acquisitions. The network's strategic planning and general advisory services incorporate long term consulting and analytical methods for financial growth. Additionally, CORE offers fundamental research, analysis and planning through specialized department within each member firm. The company employs the expertise of industry-specific account teams and specialists from various member firms in the network, allowing companies to provide better service collectively. Most clients of network members are major property holders with at least 100 leased or owned properties. CORE supports client projects through the Project Tracking System, which allows network members to access an index of project progress online.

FINANCIALS:

Sales and profits are in thousands of dollars—add 000 to get the full amount. 2009 Note: Financial information for 2009 was not available for all companies at press time.

2009 Sales: $	2009 Profits: $	**U.S. Stock Ticker: Private**
2008 Sales: $	2008 Profits: $	**Int'l Ticker:** Int'l Exchange:
2007 Sales: $	2007 Profits: $	Employees:
2006 Sales: $	2006 Profits: $	Fiscal Year Ends:
2005 Sales: $	2005 Profits: $	Parent Company:

SALARIES/BENEFITS:

Pension Plan:	ESOP Stock Plan:	Profit Sharing:	Top Exec. Salary: $	Bonus: $
Savings Plan:	Stock Purch. Plan:		Second Exec. Salary: $	Bonus: $

OTHER THOUGHTS:

Apparent Women Officers or Directors: 1
Hot Spot for Advancement for Women/Minorities:

LOCATIONS: ("Y" = Yes)

West:	Southwest:	Midwest:	Southeast:	Northeast:	International:
Y	Y	Y	Y	Y	

CORPORATE OFFICE PROPERTIES TRUST

www.copt.com

Industry Group Code: 531120 **Ranks within this company's industry group:** Sales: 31 Profits: 31

Properties:		Financial Services:		Construction/Development:		Investments:		Specialty Services:		Brokerage:	
Apartments:		Mortgages:		Commercial Construction:	Y	REIT:	Y	Property Management:	Y	Commercial Sales:	
Malls/Shopping:		Title Insurance:		Residential Construction:				Online Services:		Residential Sales:	
Offices:	Y	Property Insurance:		Land Development:	Y			Software/IT:		Specialty:	
Hotels/Motels:				Support Services:	Y			Consulting:			
Industrial/Warehouses:				Design/Engineering:	Y						
Other:											

TYPES OF BUSINESS:

Real Estate Investment Trust
Commercial Development & Construction Services
Office Properties
Property Management
HVAC Services
Lease, Audit & Consulting Services

BRANDS/DIVISIONS/AFFILIATES:

Corporate Office Properties, LP
COPT Development & Construction Services, LLC
COPT Property Management Services, LLC
COPT Environmental Systems, LLC

CONTACTS:
Note: Officers with more than one job title may be intentionally listed here more than once.

Randall M. Griffin, CEO
Roger A. Waesche, Jr., COO/Exec. VP
Randall M. Griffin, Pres.
Stephen E. Riffee, CFO/Exec. VP
Holly G. Edington, Sr. VP-Human Resources
Stephen B. Kutzer, CIO
Karen M. Singer, General Counsel/Sr. VP/Corp. Sec.
Frank W. Ziegler, Sr. VP-New Bus. & Dev., Gov't Svcs.
Michelle Layne, Contact-Media
Michelle Layne, Contact-Investor Rel.
Mary Ellen Fowler, Treas./Sr. VP
Clay W. Hamlin, III, Vice Chmn.
Wayne Lingafelter, Pres., COPT Dev. & Construction Svcs. LLC
Charles J. Fiala, Jr., Sr. VP-Gov't Svcs.
Carl M. Nelson, Sr. VP-Dev. & Construction
Jay H. Shidler, Chmn.

Phone: 443-285-5400 **Fax:** 443-285-7650
Toll-Free:
Address: 6711 Columbia Gateway Dr., Ste. 300, Columbia, MD 21046 US

GROWTH PLANS/SPECIAL FEATURES:

Corporate Office Properties Trust (COPT) is a fully integrated and self-managed real estate investment trust (REIT) focused on strategic customer relationships and specialized tenant requirements in the U.S. government, defense information technology and data sectors. The company wholly-owns 249 office properties in Maryland, Virginia, Colorado, Texas, Pennsylvania and New Jersey, containing 19.1 million rentable square feet that were 90.7% occupied at the beginning of 2010. COPT also wholly-owns 17 office properties under construction or development and land parcels totaling 1,521 acres. In addition, the company has partial ownership interests, primarily through joint ventures, in 20 operational properties, totaling approximately 1.1 million square feet; one property under redevelopment; and land parcels totaling 297 acres. Subsidiary COPT Development & Construction Services, LLC (CDCS) provides development and construction services to government and private sector clients. CDCS specializes in suburban office buildings and handles all aspects of real estate development including project planning, design and construction. Subsidiary COPT Property Management Services, LLC manages most of firm's properties and provide corporate facilities management for third parties. Subsidiary COPT Environmental Systems, LLC provides heating and air conditioning installation, maintenance, repair and control services. COPT's largest tenant is the U.S. Government, representing approximately 18.6% of 2009 rental revenues. Over the course of 2009, the company acquired a 474,000-square foot office tower in Baltimore, Maryland for approximately $123.2 million, as well as two other office properties totaling 223,000 square feet that were acquired for $50.5 million. In March 2010, the firm announced a joint venture with Jim Wilson & Associates, LLC to develop a 468-acre property in Huntsville, Alabama.

The company offers its employees a benefits package that includes a 401(k) plan with company match; a college savings plan; an adoption assistance program; life and disability insurance; flexible spending accounts for health and dependent care; and medical, dental and vision coverage.

FINANCIALS:
Sales and profits are in thousands of dollars—add 000 to get the full amount. 2009 Note: Financial information for 2009 was not available for all companies at press time.

2009 Sales: $767,519	2009 Profits: $61,299
2008 Sales: $585,605	2008 Profits: $61,316
2007 Sales: $404,466	2007 Profits: $35,942
2006 Sales: $351,528	2006 Profits: $49,227
2005 Sales: $316,043	2005 Profits: $39,031

U.S. Stock Ticker: OFC
Int'l Ticker: Int'l Exchange:
Employees: 382
Fiscal Year Ends: 12/31
Parent Company:

SALARIES/BENEFITS:

Pension Plan:	ESOP Stock Plan:	Profit Sharing:	Top Exec. Salary: $625,000	Bonus: $1,558,500
Savings Plan: Y	Stock Purch. Plan:		Second Exec. Salary: $475,000	Bonus: $720,000

OTHER THOUGHTS:

Apparent Women Officers or Directors: 8
Hot Spot for Advancement for Women/Minorities: Y

LOCATIONS: ("Y" = Yes)

West:	Southwest:	Midwest:	Southeast:	Northeast:	International:
Y	Y			Y	

COSTAR GROUP INC

www.costar.com

Industry Group Code: 519130 **Ranks within this company's industry group:** Sales: 2 Profits: 1

Properties:		Financial Services:		Construction/Development:		Investments:		Specialty Services:		Brokerage:	
Apartments:		Mortgages:		Commercial Construction:		REIT:		Property Management:		Commercial Sales:	Y
Malls/Shopping:		Title Insurance:		Residential Construction:				Online Services:	Y	Residential Sales:	
Offices:		Property Insurance:		Land Development:				Software/IT:		Specialty:	
Hotels/Motels:				Support Services:				Consulting:			
Industrial/Warehouses:				Design/Engineering:							
Other:											

TYPES OF BUSINESS:

Online Commercial Real Estate Information
Data Hosting Services
Advertising Services

BRANDS/DIVISIONS/AFFILIATES:

CoStar Property Professional
CoStar Tenant
CoStar COMPS Professional
FOCUS
CoStar UK Ltd.
Resolve Technology, Inc.
Property Portfolio Research, Inc.

CONTACTS:

Note: Officers with more than one job title may be intentionally listed here more than once.

Andrew C. Florance, CEO
Andrew C. Florance, Pres.
Brian Radecki, CFO
John Stanfill, Sr. VP-Sales & Customer Svc.
Jennifer Kitchen, Sr. VP-Research
Frank Simuro, CIO
Jonathan Coleman, General Counsel/Corp. Sec.
Jim Black, VP-Electronic Media
Dan Kimball, VP-Mktg.
Michael R. Klein, Chmn.
Paul Marples, Managing Dir.-CoStar UK Ltd.

Phone: 301-215-8300 **Fax:** 301-718-2444
Toll-Free: 800-204-5960
Address: 2 Bethesda Metro Ctr., 10th Fl., Bethesda, MD 20814 US

GROWTH PLANS/SPECIAL FEATURES:

CoStar Group, Inc. is a leading national provider of commercial real estate sales information. The company offers customers online access to a comprehensive, verified database of commercial real estate information in 81 U.S. markets, as well as in London, other U.K. markets and France. CoStar has a highly developed data collection system that includes sales prices, income and expenses, capitalization rates, loan data, property photographs, buyers, sellers, brokers and other key details. The firm provides commercial real estate professionals with critical knowledge that enables them to complete transactions by offering the most up-to-date, consolidated and standardized information on U.S. commercial real estate. CoStar's subscription-based information services consist primarily of CoStar Property Professional, the firm's flagship services which provides a comprehensive inventory of office, industrial, retail, multifamily properties and land in markets throughout the U.S., including for-lease and for-sales listings, historical data, building photographs, maps and floor plans; CoStar Tenant, a an online business-to-business prospecting and analytical tool providing commercial real estate professionals with commercial U.S. tenant information; CoStar COMPS Professional, a provider of comprehensive coverage of comparable sales information in the U.S. commercial real estate industry; and FOCUS (offered by CoStar U.K Limited, the firm's U.K. subsidiary), a digital online service offering information on the U.K. real estate market. These services generate over 90% of the company's total revenues. The company's database, which it has spent more than 21 years building, contains information on approximately 59 billion square feet of U.S. commercial real estate, and over 7 billion square feet of leasable space. A diverse portfolio of customers consists of asset managers, mortgage lenders, investors, security analysts and property managers. In 2009, the company acquired Resolve Technology, Inc. a portfolio management software and business intelligence provider and Property Portfolio Research, Inc., a real estate and market analyzer.

FINANCIALS:

Sales and profits are in thousands of dollars—add 000 to get the full amount. 2009 Note: Financial information for 2009 was not available for all companies at press time.

2009 Sales: $209,659	2009 Profits: $18,693	**U.S. Stock Ticker: CSGP**
2008 Sales: $212,428	2008 Profits: $24,623	**Int'l Ticker:** Int'l Exchange:
2007 Sales: $192,805	2007 Profits: $15,951	Employees: 1,438
2006 Sales: $158,889	2006 Profits: $12,410	Fiscal Year Ends: 12/31
2005 Sales: $134,338	2005 Profits: $6,457	Parent Company:

SALARIES/BENEFITS:

Pension Plan:	ESOP Stock Plan:	Profit Sharing:	Top Exec. Salary: $456,154	Bonus: $
Savings Plan: Y	Stock Purch. Plan:		Second Exec. Salary: $268,383	Bonus: $40,517

OTHER THOUGHTS:

Apparent Women Officers or Directors: 1
Hot Spot for Advancement for Women/Minorities:

LOCATIONS: ("Y" = Yes)

West:	Southwest:	Midwest:	Southeast:	Northeast:	International:
Y	Y	Y	Y	Y	Y

COUSINS PROPERTIES INC

www.cousinsproperties.com

Industry Group Code: 531110 **Ranks within this company's industry group:** Sales: 17 Profits: 12

Properties:		Financial Services:		Construction/Development:		Investments:		Specialty Services:		Brokerage:	
Apartments:		Mortgages:		Commercial Construction:		REIT:	Y	Property Management:	Y	Commercial Sales:	
Malls/Shopping:	Y	Title Insurance:		Residential Construction:	Y			Online Services:		Residential Sales:	Y
Offices:	Y	Property Insurance:		Land Development:	Y			Software/IT:		Specialty:	
Hotels/Motels:				Support Services:				Consulting:			
Industrial/Warehouses:				Design/Engineering:							
Other:	Y										

TYPES OF BUSINESS:

Real Estate Investment Trust
Residential Communities
Office Properties
Retail Properties
Property Management
Land Development
Open Air Malls
Industrial

BRANDS/DIVISIONS/AFFILIATES:

Avenue (The)
Cousins Properties Services, LP
Georgian (The)

CONTACTS:

Note: Officers with more than one job title may be intentionally listed here more than once.

Larry L. Gellerstedt, III, CEO
Larry L. Gellerstedt, III, Pres.
James A. Fleming, CFO/Exec. VP
Robert M. Jackson, General Counsel/Sr. VP/Corp. Sec.
John D. Harris, Jr, Chief Acct. Officer/Sr. VP
Craig B. Jones, Chief Investment Officer/Exec. VP
Steve Yenser, Chief Leasing & Asset Management Officer
R. Dary Stone, Vice Chmn.
S. Taylor Glover, Chmn.

Phone: 404-407-1000	**Fax:** 770-857-2360
Toll-Free:	
Address: 191 Peachtree St., Ste. 3600, Atlanta, GA 30303 US	

GROWTH PLANS/SPECIAL FEATURES:

Cousins Properties, Inc., a real estate investment trust (REIT) located in Atlanta, Georgia, owns, develops and manages its own real estate portfolio. The new structure contains three functional groups through which all company activities are conducted: Development; Leasing and Asset Management; and Investment and Corporate. The Development Group is responsible for identifying new development projects among all product types and managing all phases of the development and construction process through project stabilization or sale. This process includes not only construction management, but also leasing and tenant coordination for first generation office and retail space. It also includes marketing, selling and move-in coordination for multi-family projects. In addition, this group is responsible for all residential lot and tract development from project identification to lot and tract sales to end users. The Leasing and Asset Management Group is responsible for the activities of all operating properties. These activities include property management, leasing and asset management of each property. This division controls 22 operating office properties equaling 6.9 million square feet, 14 operating retail centers equaling 4.7 million square feet and three operating industrial properties equaling 2 million square feet. The Investment and Corporate groups comprises the firm's investment and corporate functions, including regulatory compliance and reporting, treasury and finance. The firm's subsidiary, Cousins Properties Services LP, focuses on development leasing. The company's portfolio includes The Avenue, a shopping center concept consisting of major retailers, local merchants and specialty restaurants with eight locations; and The Georgian, a neighborhood in South Paulding, Georgia consist of 1110 acres with 1400 homesites and an 18-hole golf course.

FINANCIALS:

Sales and profits are in thousands of dollars—add 000 to get the full amount. 2009 Note: Financial information for 2009 was not available for all companies at press time.

2009 Sales: $224,882	2009 Profits: $29,547	**U.S. Stock Ticker: CUZ**
2008 Sales: $214,651	2008 Profits: $24,925	**Int'l Ticker:** Int'l Exchange:
2007 Sales: $165,357	2007 Profits: $34,578	Employees: 387
2006 Sales: $162,288	2006 Profits: $217,441	Fiscal Year Ends: 12/31
2005 Sales: $147,480	2005 Profits: $49,741	Parent Company:

SALARIES/BENEFITS:

Pension Plan:	ESOP Stock Plan:	Profit Sharing:	Top Exec. Salary: $432,565	Bonus: $
Savings Plan: Y	Stock Purch. Plan:		Second Exec. Salary: $350,000	Bonus: $

OTHER THOUGHTS:

Apparent Women Officers or Directors: 1
Hot Spot for Advancement for Women/Minorities:

LOCATIONS: ("Y" = Yes)

West:	Southwest:	Midwest:	Southeast:	Northeast:	International:
Y	Y		Y	Y	

CRESCENT REAL ESTATE EQUITIES LP

www.crescent.com

Industry Group Code: 531120 **Ranks within this company's industry group:** Sales: Profits:

Properties:		Financial Services:		Construction/Development:		Investments:		Specialty Services:		Brokerage:	
Apartments:	Y	Mortgages:	Y	Commercial Construction:		REIT:	Y	Property Management:	Y	Commercial Sales:	
Malls/Shopping:		Title Insurance:		Residential Construction:	Y			Online Services:		Residential Sales:	
Offices:	Y	Property Insurance:		Land Development:	Y			Software/IT:		Specialty:	
Hotels/Motels:	Y			Support Services:				Consulting:			
Industrial/Warehouses:	Y			Design/Engineering:							
Other:											

TYPES OF BUSINESS:

Real Estate Investment Trust
Property Management
Land Development
Leasing
Offices
Hotels & Resorts
Residential Properties
Temperature-Controlled Logistics Facilities

BRANDS/DIVISIONS/AFFILIATES:

Barclays Capital
Goff Capital, Inc
Crescent Resort Development
Desert Mountain Development
Canyon Ranch
Fairmont Sonoma Mission Inn & Spa
Kelsey-Seybold Clinic
Crescent Real Estate Equities, Ltd

CONTACTS: *Note: Officers with more than one job title may be intentionally listed here more than once.*

Jason Anderson, COO
Suzanne M. Stevens, CFO
Peggy Haynes, VP-Human Resources
C. Robert Baird, General Counsel/Sr. VP
Joseph Pitchford, Sr. VP-Dev.
Jason Phinney, Controller/Sr. VP
Joe D. Dobbs, Sr. VP-Property Mgmt.
Anthony B. Clark, VP-Leasing
Randall C. Kostroske, VP-Risk Mgmt.

Phone: 817-321-2100	**Fax:** 817-321-2000
Toll-Free:	
Address: 777 Main St., Ste. 2100, Fort Worth, TX 76102 US	

GROWTH PLANS/SPECIAL FEATURES:

Crescent Real Estate Equities Limited Partnership, registered as a real estate investment trust (REIT), conducts property management, leasing and development activities through its operating partnership, Crescent Real Estate Equities, Ltd. The company owns and operates 36 premier office buildings with 17.6 million square feet of rentable space. The company's properties are concentrated in Dallas, Texas; Houston, Texas; Denver, Colorado; Miami, Florida; and Las Vegas, Nevada. The firm also holds three resort/spa properties in its portfolio including the Canyon Ranch in Tucson, Arizona; the Canyon Ranch in Lenox, Massachusetts; and the Fairmont Sonoma Mission Inn & Spa in Sonoma, California. Crescent also maintains interests in two high-end residential development corporations that include the Desert Mountain Development in Arizona and the Crescent Resort Development in both Colorado and California. The company is jointly owned by Barclays Capital & Goff Capital, Inc. In April 2010, the company opened a Kelsey-Seybold Clinic in Houston, Texas, marking the company's first venture into medical services development.

The company offers its employees medial, dental and vision; a 401(k) plan; an employee assistance plan; AD&D insurance; short and long term disability; paid parking; an adoption assistance program; a flexible spending account; and a scholarship program for children of employees.

FINANCIALS: **Sales and profits are in thousands of dollars—add 000 to get the full amount. 2009 Note: Financial information for 2009 was not available for all companies at press time.**

2009 Sales: $	2009 Profits: $	**U.S. Stock Ticker: Subsidiary**
2008 Sales: $	2008 Profits: $	**Int'l Ticker:** Int'l Exchange:
2007 Sales: $	2007 Profits: $	Employees:
2006 Sales: $928,696	2006 Profits: $33,433	Fiscal Year Ends: 12/31
2005 Sales: $1,018,100	2005 Profits: $101,585	Parent Company: BARCLAYS CAPITAL

SALARIES/BENEFITS:

Pension Plan:	ESOP Stock Plan:	Profit Sharing:	Top Exec. Salary: $	Bonus: $
Savings Plan: Y	Stock Purch. Plan:		Second Exec. Salary: $	Bonus: $

OTHER THOUGHTS:

Apparent Women Officers or Directors: 5
Hot Spot for Advancement for Women/Minorities: Y

LOCATIONS: ("Y" = Yes)

West:	Southwest:	Midwest:	Southeast:	Northeast:	International:
Y	Y		Y		

CREST NICHOLSON PLC

www.crestnicholson.com

Industry Group Code: 5311 **Ranks within this company's industry group:** Sales: Profits:

Properties:		Financial Services:		Construction/Development:		Investments:		Specialty Services:		Brokerage:	
Apartments:		Mortgages:		Commercial Construction:		REIT:		Property Management:		Commercial Sales:	
Malls/Shopping:		Title Insurance:		Residential Construction:	Y			Online Services:		Residential Sales:	
Offices:		Property Insurance:		Land Development:	Y			Software/IT:		Specialty:	
Hotels/Motels:				Support Services:				Consulting:			
Industrial/Warehouses:				Design/Engineering:							
Other:											

TYPES OF BUSINESS:

Real Estate Development
Environmental Communities
Mixed-Use Developments

BRANDS/DIVISIONS/AFFILIATES:

Castle Bidco Ltd
HBOS plc
West Coast Capital
Building Research Establishment
EcoHomes
Hardy's Gate
Rosebery Heights

CONTACTS:

Note: Officers with more than one job title may be intentionally listed here more than once.

Stephen Stone, CEO
Peter Darby, Dir.-Finance
Pippa Bugby, Dir.-Sales & Mktg.
Adrian Willet, Dir.-Dev.
Paul Callcutt, Exec. Dir.-Land
Chris Tinker, Chmn.-Regeneration
Alen Goldman, Chmn.

Phone: 01-93-258-0555 **Fax:** 08-70-336-3990
Toll-Free:
Address: Crest House, Pyrcroft Rd., Chertsey, Surrey KT16 9GN UK

GROWTH PLANS/SPECIAL FEATURES:

Crest Nicholson plc is a British real estate developer focusing on the construction of environmentally sound master-planned communities and mixed-use developments. The firm is a subsidiary of Castle Bidco Ltd. is a joint venture between HBOS plc and West Coast Capital. The company's master planned communities feature distinctive residential areas and a good deal of open space, as well as amenities such as schools, shops and sports facilities. The company also focuses on building communities that do not rely on the use of a car, featuring designated cycling routes and integrated bus service that link outlying residential areas to the town center. Crest Nicholson actively supports the Building Research Establishment's EcoHomes rating scheme, which accesses the environmental performance of buildings in the areas of energy, transport, pollution, materials, water, land use, ecology, health and well being. In April 2010, the company was given final approval to begin it Penarth Heights redevelopment project that will include 377 new houses. Also in April 2010, the company announced several new developments including Hardy's Gate in Dartford, which will consist of cottage and detached homes and Rosebery Heights in Epsom will consists of approximately 72 townhomes and apartments.

FINANCIALS:

Sales and profits are in thousands of dollars—add 000 to get the full amount. 2009 Note: Financial information for 2009 was not available for all companies at press time.

2009 Sales: $
2008 Sales: $
2007 Sales: $
2006 Sales: $1,365,090
2005 Sales: $1,381,050

2009 Profits: $
2008 Profits: $
2007 Profits: $
2006 Profits: $196,060
2005 Profits: $195,465

U.S. Stock Ticker: Subsidiary
Int'l Ticker: Int'l Exchange:
Employees:
Fiscal Year Ends: 10/31
Parent Company: CASTLE BIDCO LTD

SALARIES/BENEFITS:

Pension Plan: ESOP Stock Plan: Profit Sharing: Top Exec. Salary: $ Bonus: $
Savings Plan: Stock Purch. Plan: Second Exec. Salary: $ Bonus: $

OTHER THOUGHTS:

Apparent Women Officers or Directors: 1
Hot Spot for Advancement for Women/Minorities:

LOCATIONS: ("Y" = Yes)

West:	Southwest:	Midwest:	Southeast:	Northeast:	International:
					Y

CRH PLC

www.crh.com

Industry Group Code: 327 **Ranks within this company's industry group:** Sales: 1 Profits: 1

Properties:		Financial Services:		Construction/Development:		Investments:		Specialty Services:		Brokerage:	
Apartments:		Mortgages:		Commercial Construction:		REIT:		Property Management:		Commercial Sales:	
Malls/Shopping:		Title Insurance:		Residential Construction:				Online Services:		Residential Sales:	
Offices:		Property Insurance:		Land Development:				Software/IT:		Specialty:	
Hotels/Motels:				Support Services:	Y			Consulting:			
Industrial/Warehouses:				Design/Engineering:							
Other:											

TYPES OF BUSINESS:

Building Materials
Aggregates
Asphalt
Cement & Concrete Products
Distribution
Glass Fabrications
Security Gates & Fencing
Insulation Products

BRANDS/DIVISIONS/AFFILIATES:

Oldcastle, Inc.
Ancon Building Products
My Home Industries Limited, India
Tyco International Ltd.

CONTACTS: *Note: Officers with more than one job title may be intentionally listed here more than once.*

M. Lee, CEO
A. Manifold, COO
G. Culpepper, Dir.-Finance
Jack Golden, Dir.-Human Resources
Angela Malone, Corp. Sec.
Albert Manifold, Dir.-Dev.
Elmear O'Flynn, Head-Investor Rel.
Maeve Carton, Group Treas.
Mark Towe, CEO-Old Castle, Inc.
Liam Hughes, Dir.-Bus. Support
Kieran McGowan, Chmn.
Erik Bax, Managing Dir.-European Prod. & Dist.

Phone: 353-1-404-1000	**Fax:** 353-1-404-1007
Toll-Free:	
Address: Belgard Castle, Clondalkin, Dublin, Ireland L2 22 UK	

GROWTH PLANS/SPECIAL FEATURES:

CRH plc is a building materials company focusing on three core businesses: primary materials, value-added building products and specialty building materials distribution. With operations in 35 countries, CRH is divided into four regionally focused business segments: European materials; European products and distribution; Americas materials; and Americas products and distribution. The European materials division, which operates in 15 countries, produces primary materials and value-added manufactured products, including cement, aggregates, ready-mixed concrete and pre-cast concrete products. The Europe products and distribution segment is comprised of four groups: concrete products, which manufactures products for architectural and structural use; clay products, which manufactures bricks and blocks; building products, which manufactures construction accessories, insulation, fences, security products, awnings and roller shutters; and distribution, comprised of 331 professional builders merchants locations in Austria, France, Germany, the Netherlands and Switzerland, and 206 DIY (do-it-yourself) stores in the Benelux, Germany and Portugal. The Americas materials segment produces aggregates, asphalt and ready-mixed concrete throughout the U.S. The Americas products and distribution segment, which is run by Oldcastle, Inc., has operations throughout the U.S. and Canada, with five product groups: architectural products, precast, glass, MMI (management and maintenance inspection) and distribution. The segment additionally produces clay tile products in Argentina and operates glass fabrication businesses in Argentina and Chile. The company owns stakes in several companies including My Home Industries Ltd; Jilin Yatai Group's cement operations; Ancon Building Products; and Tyco International Ltd.

FINANCIALS: Sales and profits are in thousands of dollars—add 000 to get the full amount. 2009 Note: Financial information for 2009 was not available for all companies at press time.

2009 Sales: $23,288,500	2009 Profits: $801,620	**U.S. Stock Ticker: CRH**
2008 Sales: $27,220,600	2008 Profits: $1,644,680	**Int'l Ticker:** Int'l Exchange:
2007 Sales: $27,357,400	2007 Profits: $1,874,040	Employees:
2006 Sales: $25,450,820	2006 Profits: $2,176,520	Fiscal Year Ends: 12/31
2005 Sales: $17,100,700	2005 Profits: $1,181,000	Parent Company:

SALARIES/BENEFITS:

Pension Plan:	ESOP Stock Plan:	Profit Sharing:	Top Exec. Salary: $	Bonus: $
Savings Plan:	Stock Purch. Plan:		Second Exec. Salary: $	Bonus: $

OTHER THOUGHTS:

Apparent Women Officers or Directors: 2
Hot Spot for Advancement for Women/Minorities:

LOCATIONS: ("Y" = Yes)

West:	Southwest:	Midwest:	Southeast:	Northeast:	International:
Y	Y	Y	Y	Y	Y

CUSHMAN & WAKEFIELD INC

www.cushmanwakefield.com

Industry Group Code: 531210 **Ranks within this company's industry group:** Sales: Profits:

Properties:		Financial Services:		Construction/Development:		Investments:		Specialty Services:		Brokerage:	
Apartments:		Mortgages:		Commercial Construction:		REIT:		Property Management:	Y	Commercial Sales:	Y
Malls/Shopping:		Title Insurance:		Residential Construction:				Online Services:	Y	Residential Sales:	
Offices:		Property Insurance:		Land Development:				Software/IT:		Specialty:	
Hotels/Motels:				Support Services:				Consulting:			
Industrial/Warehouses:				Design/Engineering:							
Other:											

TYPES OF BUSINESS:

Real Estate Brokerage
Property Management
Real Estate Documentation Web Site
Advisory Services
Research Services

BRANDS/DIVISIONS/AFFILIATES:

IFIL Group
Rockefeller Group (The)
CW-ONE SharePlace
Alston Nock
Sonnenblick Goldman
Cushman & Wakefield Residential
Cushman & Wakefield Hotels
RH International

CONTACTS:

Note: Officers with more than one job title may be intentionally listed here more than once.

Glenn Rufrano, CEO
John C. Santora, COO
Glenn Rufrano, Pres.
Robert P. Rozek, CFO/Exec. VP
Tony Marano, CEO-Americas
John C. Cushman III, Chmn.
Paul Bacon, CEO-Europe

Phone: 212-841-7500	**Fax:** 212-841-7767
Toll-Free:	
Address: 51 W. 52nd St., New York, NY 10019-6178 US	

GROWTH PLANS/SPECIAL FEATURES:

Cushman & Wakefield, Inc. (C&W), founded in 1917, is a global commercial real estate brokerage and services company with nearly 231 offices in 58 countries. The company's brokerage services include industrial brokerage services, landlord representation, lease advisory, offices, retail services, supply chain and tenant representation. Additional services offered by C&W include capital markets, comprised of agency executions, advisory services and investment management; client solutions, comprised of corporate and investor services; global consulting, comprised of business and real estate consulting; practice groups, comprised of hospitality, law and pharmaceutical; and research. C&W provides its services on both a regional and worldwide basis to major corporations, pension funds, REITs, developers, entrepreneurs, government entities, financial institutions and small- and mid-size companies. C&W manages approximately 5,500 properties with a total of nearly 300 million square feet. It actively advises, implements and manages properties on behalf of landlords, tenants and investors through every stage of the real estate process. The company's CW-ONE SharePlace proprietary system is a highly secure, web-based site that allows all portfolio documentation to be posted, reviewed and modified for the benefit of C&W's clients and team members. Recent acquisitions of the company include Laing+Simmons Commercial, Inc; Cushman & Wakefield Residential; and Cushman & Wakefield Hotels. In April 2010, CRH announce the formation of two partnerships that include Ecological LLC, which will help assist clients in complying with sustainability mandates and a one with Saffronart, a leading Indian auction house, which will offer clients access to online real estate auctions.

FINANCIALS:

Sales and profits are in thousands of dollars—add 000 to get the full amount. 2009 Note: Financial information for 2009 was not available for all companies at press time.

2009 Sales: $	2009 Profits: $	**U.S. Stock Ticker: Subsidiary**
2008 Sales: $	2008 Profits: $	**Int'l Ticker:** Int'l Exchange:
2007 Sales: $	2007 Profits: $	Employees:
2006 Sales: $	2006 Profits: $	Fiscal Year Ends: 12/31
2005 Sales: $1,200,000	2005 Profits: $	Parent Company: IFIL GROUP

SALARIES/BENEFITS:

Pension Plan:	ESOP Stock Plan:	Profit Sharing:	Top Exec. Salary: $	Bonus: $
Savings Plan:	Stock Purch. Plan:		Second Exec. Salary: $	Bonus: $

OTHER THOUGHTS:

Apparent Women Officers or Directors:
Hot Spot for Advancement for Women/Minorities:

LOCATIONS: ("Y" = Yes)

West:	Southwest:	Midwest:	Southeast:	Northeast:	International:
Y	Y	Y	Y	Y	Y

CYRELA BRAZIL REALTY SA EMPREEND PART

www.brazilrealty.com.br

Industry Group Code: 2361 **Ranks within this company's industry group:** Sales: Profits:

Properties:		Financial Services:		Construction/Development:		Investments:		Specialty Services:		Brokerage:	
Apartments:		Mortgages:		Commercial Construction:		REIT:		Property Management:		Commercial Sales:	
Malls/Shopping:		Title Insurance:		Residential Construction:	Y			Online Services:		Residential Sales:	
Offices:		Property Insurance:		Land Development:				Software/IT:		Specialty:	
Hotels/Motels:				Support Services:				Consulting:			
Industrial/Warehouses:				Design/Engineering:							
Other:											

TYPES OF BUSINESS:

Residential Construction

BRANDS/DIVISIONS/AFFILIATES:

SKR
LIDER
Irsa Cyrela
Cury Construtora e Incorporadora
Plano & Plano Construcoes e Participacoes
MAC Construtora e Incorporadora
Lucio Engenharia

CONTACTS:

Note: Officers with more than one job title may be intentionally listed here more than once.

Elie Horn, CEO
Luis Largman, CFO
Saulo de Tarso Alves de Lara, Planning Officer
Luis Largman, Investor Rel. Officer
Saulo de Tarso Alves de Lara, Financial Control Officer
Rogerio J. Zylbersztajn, VP
Ubirajara Spessotto de Camargo de Freitas, Gen. Exec. Officer
Cassio Mantelmacher, Real Estate Dev. Officer
Elie Horn, Chmn.

Phone: 55-11-4502-3000	**Fax:** 55-11-4502-3140
Toll-Free:	
Address: 1455 Presidente Juscelino Kubitscheck Ave., 3rd Fl, Sao Paulo, SP 04543-011 Brazil	

GROWTH PLANS/SPECIAL FEATURES:

Cyrela Brazil Realty S.A. Empreendimentos e Participacoes is one of Brazil's largest developers of residential properties. In its 50 years of operation, the firm has built 17,000 units totaling over 53.8 million square feet for 37,000 customers. The company operates in 17 states and 55 cities in Brazil; Cyrela Brazil also operates in Argentina. Middle class housing accounts for approximately 29% of the firm's sales; economic housing, 23%; luxury real estate, 23%; mid-high housing, 22%; and super economic housing, 3%. Cyrela Brazil also offers residential construction through seven joint ventures: MAC Construtora e Incorporadora and Lucio Engenharia, which both build middle and mid-high housing; Irsa Cyrela, which builds all economic levels of housing in Buenos Aires; SKR, a mid-high and luxury home builder in Sao Paulo; Cury Construtora e Incorporadora and Plano & Plano Construcoes e Participacoes, both of which build economic and super-economic housing; and LIDER, which builds all economic levels of housing in Minas Gerais and Distrito Federal, Brazil. The company owns 50% of each of these joint ventures with the exception of Plano & Plano (79% owned). The majority of Cyrela Brazil's sales are derived from Sao Paulo (46%) and Rio de Janeiro (16%).

FINANCIALS:

Sales and profits are in thousands of dollars—add 000 to get the full amount. 2009 Note: Financial information for 2009 was not available for all companies at press time.

2009 Sales: $	2009 Profits: $	**U.S. Stock Ticker:**
2008 Sales: $	2008 Profits: $	**Int'l Ticker: CYRE3** Int'l Exchange: Sao Paulo-SAO
2007 Sales: $	2007 Profits: $	Employees:
2006 Sales: $	2006 Profits: $	Fiscal Year Ends: 12/31
2005 Sales: $	2005 Profits: $	Parent Company:

SALARIES/BENEFITS:

Pension Plan:	ESOP Stock Plan:	Profit Sharing:	Top Exec. Salary: $	Bonus: $
Savings Plan:	Stock Purch. Plan:		Second Exec. Salary: $	Bonus: $

OTHER THOUGHTS:

Apparent Women Officers or Directors:
Hot Spot for Advancement for Women/Minorities:

LOCATIONS: ("Y" = Yes)

West:	Southwest:	Midwest:	Southeast:	Northeast:	International:
					Y

DAELIM INDUSTRIAL CO LTD

www.daelim.co.kr

Industry Group Code: 237 **Ranks within this company's industry group:** Sales: 15 Profits: 21

Properties:		Financial Services:		Construction/Development:		Investments:		Specialty Services:		Brokerage:	
Apartments:		Mortgages:		Commercial Construction:	Y	REIT:		Property Management:		Commercial Sales:	
Malls/Shopping:		Title Insurance:		Residential Construction:	Y			Online Services:		Residential Sales:	
Offices:		Property Insurance:		Land Development:	Y			Software/IT:		Specialty:	
Hotels/Motels:				Support Services:				Consulting:			
Industrial/Warehouses:				Design/Engineering:	Y						
Other:											

TYPES OF BUSINESS:

Construction
Petrochemicals Distribution

BRANDS/DIVISIONS/AFFILIATES:

CONTACTS:

Note: Officers with more than one job title may be intentionally listed here more than once.

Yong Koo Lee, CEO
Jong In Kim, Pres./CEO-Eng. & Construction Div.
Jong Kook Park, Sr. VP-Finance
Joo Hee Han, Pres./CEO-Petrochemical Div.
Jong Kook Park, Sr. VP
Yong Koo Lee, Chmn.

Phone: 82-2-2011-7114 **Fax:** 82-2-2011-8000
Toll-Free:
Address: 146-12 Susong-Dong, Jongno-Gu, Seoul, 110-732 Korea

GROWTH PLANS/SPECIAL FEATURES:

Daelim Industrial Co., Ltd. is a construction and engineering firm operating in four primary divisions: building, housing, civil works and plants. The building division is engaged in the construction of offices; cultural and assembly facilities; commercial buildings, such as markets and department stores; educational facilities, such as university buildings; medical and sports facilities, such as the King Abdul Aziz University Hospital; and others, such as the Seoul Court House Complex and the U.S. Embassy in Bangladesh. Some of the division's projects include constructing the main stadium for the 1988 Seoul Olympics, the Sejong Performing Arts Center and the main campus of the Arabian Gulf University in Bahrain. The housing division has three main activities: constructing apartments and stores; redevelopment and reconstruction, primarily in residential areas of Korea; and remodeling, primarily of commercial and cultural facilities, such as Meyongdong Cathedral, the Daelim Contemporary Art Museum and the main building of the Bank of Korea. The civil works division has three broad categories of projects. The first combines expressways, airports, airfields and bridges. The second encompasses railroads, subways and tunnels. The third is engaged in the construction of dams; irrigation infrastructure; and harbors and marine facilities. Some of the division's projects include constructing the King Fahad International Airport in Saudi Arabia, the Ayer Rajah Expressway in Singapore, the Hwacheon Dam and the Dintulu Deepwater Port in Malaysia. Finally, the firm's plants division constructs chemical plants, such as oil refineries and petrochemical processing facilities, including plants in India, the Middle East, Africa, the U.S., Southeast Asia and Korea; and power plants, which Daelim has constructed both in Korea and abroad.

FINANCIALS:

Sales and profits are in thousands of dollars—add 000 to get the full amount. 2009 Note: Financial information for 2009 was not available for all companies at press time.

2009 Sales: $6,873,200
2008 Sales: $6,942,560
2007 Sales: $3,641,270
2006 Sales: $3,412,040
2005 Sales: $6,138,686

2009 Profits: $309,460
2008 Profits: $95,850
2007 Profits: $339,070
2006 Profits: $188,700
2005 Profits: $355,780

U.S. Stock Ticker:
Int'l Ticker: 000210 Int'l Exchange: Seoul-KRX
Employees:
Fiscal Year Ends: 12/31
Parent Company:

SALARIES/BENEFITS:

Pension Plan: ESOP Stock Plan: Profit Sharing: Top Exec. Salary: $ Bonus: $
Savings Plan: Stock Purch. Plan: Second Exec. Salary: $ Bonus: $

OTHER THOUGHTS:

Apparent Women Officers or Directors:
Hot Spot for Advancement for Women/Minorities:

LOCATIONS: ("Y" = Yes)

West:	Southwest:	Midwest:	Southeast:	Northeast:	International:
	Y				Y

DAYS INN WORLDWIDE INC

www.daysinn.com

Industry Group Code: 721110 **Ranks within this company's industry group:** Sales: Profits:

Properties:		Financial Services:		Construction/Development:		Investments:		Specialty Services:		Brokerage:	
Apartments:		Mortgages:		Commercial Construction:		REIT:		Property Management:		Commercial Sales:	
Malls/Shopping:		Title Insurance:		Residential Construction:				Online Services:	Y	Residential Sales:	
Offices:		Property Insurance:		Land Development:				Software/IT:		Specialty:	
Hotels/Motels:	Y			Support Services:				Consulting:			
Industrial/Warehouses:				Design/Engineering:							
Other:											

TYPES OF BUSINESS:

Motels

BRANDS/DIVISIONS/AFFILIATES:

Wyndham Worldwide
Days Hotel
Days Inn & Suites
Days Inn Business Place
TripRewards Card

CONTACTS: *Note: Officers with more than one job title may be intentionally listed here more than once.*

Clyde Guinn, Pres.

Phone: 973-428-9700	**Fax:** 973-496-7658
Toll-Free: 800-329-7466	
Address: 1 Sylvan Way, Parsippany, NJ 07054 US	

GROWTH PLANS/SPECIAL FEATURES:

Days Inn Worldwide, Inc., a subsidiary of Wyndham Worldwide, operates one of the world's largest franchised hotel networks. Its operations span over 1,858 low-cost hotels with a total of 149,633 rooms that are located throughout the U.S. and around the world. These worldwide locations include Argentina, Canada, China, Egypt, Hungary, India, Jordan, Mexico, the Philippines, South Africa, the U.K. and Uruguay, with openings planned in Japan, Morocco and Korea. Every night, over 200,000 guests sleep in Days Inns. The franchised hotels come in four varieties: Days Inn, a standard roadside motel; Days Hotel, a slightly larger property, usually in an urban center or near an airport, that features restaurants, lounges and meeting and banquet rooms in addition to guest rooms; Days Inn & Suites, similar to Days Inn but providing larger rooms, often for guests who plan to stay for relatively long periods of time; and Days Inn Business Place, inns offering specialized services catering to the needs of business travelers. Some universal amenities that the chain offers its guests include hairdryers, alarm clocks and complimentary copies of USA Today. The firm inspects and rates its properties three times per year. At the company's web site customers can make reservations online and access special promotions and other information. Additionally, Wyndham's hotel group offers a best-available-rate guarantee, providing its online customers with the lowest rates available for all its hotel brands, including Days Inn. It also offers the Wyndham Rewards Card, which allows customers to earn points at any of Wyndham's hotel chains, a total of more than 6,000 hotels. The program offers over 250 point-redemption options, and is one of the world's largest hotel loyalty programs based on the number of participation hotels. The Mobile Days application allows guest to connect to the nearest Days Inn location using a mobile phone browser.

FINANCIALS: **Sales and profits are in thousands of dollars—add 000 to get the full amount. 2009 Note: Financial information for 2009 was not available for all companies at press time.**

2009 Sales: $	2009 Profits: $	**U.S. Stock Ticker: Subsidiary**
2008 Sales: $	2008 Profits: $	**Int'l Ticker:** Int'l Exchange:
2007 Sales: $	2007 Profits: $	Employees:
2006 Sales: $	2006 Profits: $	Fiscal Year Ends: 12/31
2005 Sales: $	2005 Profits: $	Parent Company: WYNDHAM WORLDWIDE

SALARIES/BENEFITS:

Pension Plan:	ESOP Stock Plan:	Profit Sharing:	Top Exec. Salary: $	Bonus: $
Savings Plan:	Stock Purch. Plan:		Second Exec. Salary: $	Bonus: $

OTHER THOUGHTS:

Apparent Women Officers or Directors:
Hot Spot for Advancement for Women/Minorities:

LOCATIONS: ("Y" = Yes)

West:	Southwest:	Midwest:	Southeast:	Northeast:	International:
Y	Y	Y	Y	Y	Y

DCT INDUSTRIAL TRUST INC

www.dctindustrial.com

Industry Group Code: 531120 **Ranks within this company's industry group:** Sales: 50 Profits: 49

Properties:		Financial Services:		Construction/Development:		Investments:		Specialty Services:		Brokerage:	
Apartments:		Mortgages:		Commercial Construction:		REIT:	Y	Property Management:	Y	Commercial Sales:	
Malls/Shopping:		Title Insurance:		Residential Construction:				Online Services:		Residential Sales:	
Offices:		Property Insurance:		Land Development:				Software/IT:		Specialty:	
Hotels/Motels:				Support Services:				Consulting:			
Industrial/Warehouses:	Y			Design/Engineering:							
Other:											

TYPES OF BUSINESS:

Industrial Property Leasing
REIT
Property Management Services

BRANDS/DIVISIONS/AFFILIATES:

DCT Fund I LLC
Phelan Development Company

CONTACTS:
Note: Officers with more than one job title may be intentionally listed here more than once.

Philip L. Hawkins, CEO
Stuart B. Brown, CFO
Stephen K. Schutte, General Counsel/Corp. Sec./Sr. VP
Matthew T. Murphy, Sr. VP-Finance/Treas.
Michael J. Ruen, Managing Dir.-East Region
Daryl H. Mechem, Managing Dir.-West Region
Teresa L. Corral, Sr. VP-Fund Mgmt. & Dispositions
Bonnie B. Micus, Sr. VP/National Dir.-Property Mgmt.
Thomas G. Wattles, Chmn.

Phone: 303-597-2400 **Fax:** 303-228-2201
Toll-Free:
Address: 518 17th St., Ste. 800, Denver, CO 80202 US

GROWTH PLANS/SPECIAL FEATURES:

DCT Industrial Trust, formerly Dividend Capital Trust Inc., is a real estate investment trust (REIT) specializing in the ownership, acquisition, development and management of bulk distribution and light industrial properties in the U.S. and Mexico. The company owns, manages, or has under development 450 real estate buildings totaling over 75.4 million square feet leased to more than 800 corporate customers. DCT seeks to acquire properties that have convenient access to major transportation arteries; proximity to densely populated markets; and quality design standards that allow for easy reconfiguration of space. The firm concentrates its acquisitions into 25 key markets: Atlanta, Georgia; Nashville and Memphis, Tennessee; Baltimore, Maryland/Washington, D.C.; Orlando, Florida; Central Pennsylvania; New Jersey; Miami, Florida; Cincinnati and Columbus, Ohio; Indianapolis, Indiana; Chicago, Illinois; Charlotte, North Carolina; Louisville, Kentucky; Dallas, Houston and San Antonio, Texas; Minneapolis, Minnesota; Kansas City, Missouri; Northern California; Southern California; Phoenix, Arizona; Seattle, Washington; Denver, Colorado; and Mexico. DCT also manages and owns interests in properties through its institutional capital management program. During 2009, the company acquired three development properties comprised of 0.4 million square feet located in Monterrey, Mexico, and two parcels of land comprised of 12.3 acres. Additionally, the company sold three operating properties comprised of approximately 0.9 million square feet and two land parcels comprised of 43 acres. In March 2009, DCT sold 53 acres of land at Southern California Logistics Airport to Dr Pepper Snapple Group, Inc. In March 2010, the firm acquired the Phelan Development Company, as well as a Class A bulk distribution property in Sayreville, New Jersey. Additionally, DCT opened two regional offices in Orlando, Florida, and Houston, Texas.

The company offers its employees medical and dental insurance; life and AD&D insurance; long-term disability insurance; and a 401(k) plan.

FINANCIALS:
Sales and profits are in thousands of dollars—add 000 to get the full amount. 2009 Note: Financial information for 2009 was not available for all companies at press time.

2009 Sales: $244,006	2009 Profits: $-18,585	**U.S. Stock Ticker: DCT**
2008 Sales: $248,542	2008 Profits: $9,486	**Int'l Ticker:** Int'l Exchange:
2007 Sales: $245,816	2007 Profits: $40,112	Employees: 87
2006 Sales: $209,851	2006 Profits: $-158,043	Fiscal Year Ends: 12/31
2005 Sales: $117,220	2005 Profits: $-11,960	Parent Company:

SALARIES/BENEFITS:

Pension Plan:	ESOP Stock Plan:	Profit Sharing:	Top Exec. Salary: $600,000	Bonus: $480,000
Savings Plan: Y	Stock Purch. Plan:		Second Exec. Salary: $265,000	Bonus: $180,000

OTHER THOUGHTS:

Apparent Women Officers or Directors: 2
Hot Spot for Advancement for Women/Minorities:

LOCATIONS: ("Y" = Yes)

West:	Southwest:	Midwest:	Southeast:	Northeast:	International:
Y	Y	Y	Y	Y	Y

DESARROLLADORA HOMEX SAB DE CV

www.homex.com.mx

Industry Group Code: 237 **Ranks within this company's industry group:** Sales: 30 Profits: 20

Properties:		Financial Services:		Construction/Development:		Investments:		Specialty Services:		Brokerage:	
Apartments:		Mortgages:		Commercial Construction:		REIT:		Property Management:		Commercial Sales:	
Malls/Shopping:		Title Insurance:		Residential Construction:	Y			Online Services:		Residential Sales:	
Offices:		Property Insurance:		Land Development:				Software/IT:		Specialty:	
Hotels/Motels:				Support Services:				Consulting:			
Industrial/Warehouses:				Design/Engineering:							
Other:											

TYPES OF BUSINESS:

Home Building
Construction

BRANDS/DIVISIONS/AFFILIATES:

Homex
Homex India Private Limited

CONTACTS:

Note: Officers with more than one job title may be intentionally listed here more than once.

Gerardo de Nicolas Gutierrez, CEO
Carlos J. Monctezuma, CFO
Daniel Leal Diaz-Conti, Dir.-Sales & Mktg.
Monica Lafaire Cruz, VP-Human Resources & Social Responsibility
Ramon Lafarga Batiz, Chief Admin. Officer
Carlos J. Monctezuma, Dir.-Strategic Planning
Lorena Andrade, Dir.-Public Rel.
Vania Fueyo, Dir.-Investor Rel.
Ramon Lafarga Batiz, Chief Acct. Officer
Ruben Izabal Gonzalez, VP-Construction
Alberto Menchaca Valenzuela, VP-Affordable Entry Division
Julian de Nicolas Gutierrez, VP-Middle Income Division
Eustaquio Tomas De Nicolas Gutierrez, Chmn.
Alberto Urquiza Quiroz, VP-Int'l Div.

Phone: 52-667-758-5800 **Fax:**

Toll-Free: 800-224-6639

Address: Boulevard Alfonso Zaragoza M. 2204 Norte, Sinaloa, 80200 Mexico

GROWTH PLANS/SPECIAL FEATURES:

Desarrolladora Homex SAB de CV (Homex) is a homebuilding and construction company based in Culiacan, Mexico. The firm focuses primarily on building entry-level and middle-income housing throughout Mexico. Homex has operations in 34 cities in 21 states, including Culiacan, Mexico City, Puebla, Guadalajara, Acapulco, Nuevo Laredo, Juarez, Tijuana, Tuxtla, Coahuila, Queretaro, Cancun, Cuernavaca, Veracruz and Puerto Vallarta. Most of the firm's largest entry-level housing developments are located in Guadalajara, Monterrey, Tijuana, Puebla, and Nuevo Laredo. Entry-level developments range in size from 500 to 20,000 homes, which typically include one to three bedrooms and one bathroom and are sold at an average price of $20,038. Sales of entry-level housing account for approximately 91.2% of the company's revenues. Its mid-level developments range in size from 400 to 2,000 homes, which include two to three bedrooms and two bathrooms and averages $59,316 in price. It sold 57,955 units in 2009, a slight increase from 2008, when it sold a total of 57,498 homes. It derives roughly 35% of its revenue from the Mexico City Metropolitan Area, its largest market and 8% from Guadalajara. The firm's newly established vacation homes division, HXMTD Las Villas de Mexico, builds resort-style communities, featuring pools, fitness centers and golf courses, which are targeted at foreigners. In December 2009, Homex announced the sale of the first 15 homes in its first Brazilian entry-level development project, Jardin das Paineiras, in Sao Jose dos Campos, Brazil. In March 2010, the company's Indian subsidiary, Homex India Private Limited established a joint venture company with Puravankara Projects Limited to develop affordable entry-level housing in and around Chennai, in South India.

FINANCIALS:

Sales and profits are in thousands of dollars—add 000 to get the full amount. 2009 Note: Financial information for 2009 was not available for all companies at press time.

2009 Sales: $	2009 Profits: $	**U.S. Stock Ticker: HXM**
2008 Sales: $1,368,576	2008 Profits: $117,543	**Int'l Ticker:** Int'l Exchange:
2007 Sales: $1,622,300	2007 Profits: $223,300	Employees:
2006 Sales: $1,344,000	2006 Profits: $139,100	Fiscal Year Ends: 12/31
2005 Sales: $793,900	2005 Profits: $113,100	Parent Company:

SALARIES/BENEFITS:

Pension Plan:	ESOP Stock Plan:	Profit Sharing:	Top Exec. Salary: $	Bonus: $
Savings Plan:	Stock Purch. Plan:		Second Exec. Salary: $	Bonus: $

OTHER THOUGHTS:

Apparent Women Officers or Directors: 2
Hot Spot for Advancement for Women/Minorities:

LOCATIONS: ("Y" = Yes)

West:	Southwest:	Midwest:	Southeast:	Northeast:	International:
					Y

DEVELOPERS DIVERSIFIED REALTY CORP

www.ddrc.com

Industry Group Code: 531110 **Ranks within this company's industry group:** Sales: 3 Profits: 18

Properties:		Financial Services:		Construction/Development:		Investments:		Specialty Services:		Brokerage:	
Apartments:		Mortgages:		Commercial Construction:	Y	REIT:	Y	Property Management:	Y	Commercial Sales:	
Malls/Shopping:	Y	Title Insurance:		Residential Construction:				Online Services:		Residential Sales:	
Offices:	Y	Property Insurance:		Land Development:	Y			Software/IT:		Specialty:	
Hotels/Motels:				Support Services:				Consulting:			
Industrial/Warehouses:				Design/Engineering:							
Other:											

TYPES OF BUSINESS:

Real Estate Investment Trust
Shopping Centers
Business Centers
Property Management
Commercial Construction & Land Development

BRANDS/DIVISIONS/AFFILIATES:

CONTACTS:

Note: Officers with more than one job title may be intentionally listed here more than once.

Daniel B. Hurwitz, CEO
Daniel B. Hurwitz, Pres.
David J. Oakes, Interim CFO/Sr. Exec. VP
Nan Zieleniec, Sr. VP-Human Resources
Kevin Moss, Sr. VP-IT
David E. Weiss, General Counsel/Sr. VP
Marc Feldman, Sr. VP-New Bus. Dev.
Christa A. Vesy, Chief Acct. Officer/Sr. VP
John S. Kokinchak, Sr. Exec. VP-Property Mgmt.
Joan U. Allgood, Exec. VP-Corp. Transactions & Governance
Robin R. Walker-Gibbons, Exec. VP-Leasing
Paul Freddo, Sr. VP-Leasing & Dev.
Scott A. Wolstein, Chmn.
Richard E. Brown, Exec. VP-Int'l

Phone: 216-755-5500 **Fax:** 216-755-1500
Toll-Free: 877-225-5337
Address: 3300 Enterprise Pkwy., Beachwood, OH 44122 US

GROWTH PLANS/SPECIAL FEATURES:

Developers Diversified Realty Corp. (DDR) is a self-administered and self-managed real estate investment trust (REIT). The company is in the business of acquiring, developing, owning, leasing and managing shopping centers and business centers. The firm currently owns and manages approximately 665 shopping centers and six business centers (over 148 million square feet) in 44 states, Puerto Rico and Brazil. The company has 274 shopping centers that are owned through joint ventures. DDR also owns nearly 2,000 acres of undeveloped land. The company focuses on earning rent payments in properties already owned; and the acquisition, development, redevelopment, renovation and expansion of income-producing real estate properties (primarily shopping centers). DDR's primary interest is in open-air shopping centers and lifestyle centers between 250,000 and 1 million square feet in size. The firm prefers properties with strong national tenant anchor stores such as Wal-Mart, Circuit City, PetSmart and Lowe's Home Improvement. In early 2009, DDR partnered with SunEdison, a provider of solar energy, to bring solar systems to DDR's Colorado, California, New Jersey and Puerto Rico shopping centers; SunEdison has the option to extend service to hundreds of DDR's North American locations. In 2009, the company sold 30 million common shares, as well as entitlement warrants for 10 million additional shares, to Alexander Otto and other members of the Otto family. As a result of this deal, the Otto family is DDR's biggest individual shareholder.

FINANCIALS:

Sales and profits are in thousands of dollars—add 000 to get the full amount. 2009 Note: Financial information for 2009 was not available for all companies at press time.

2009 Sales: $819,307 | 2009 Profits: $-317,107
2008 Sales: $881,768 | 2008 Profits: $-93,095
2007 Sales: $885,025 | 2007 Profits: $186,237
2006 Sales: $773,351 | 2006 Profits: $253,264
2005 Sales: $678,109 | 2005 Profits: $282,643

U.S. Stock Ticker: DDR
Int'l Ticker: Int'l Exchange:
Employees: 722
Fiscal Year Ends: 12/31
Parent Company:

SALARIES/BENEFITS:

Pension Plan: ESOP Stock Plan: Profit Sharing:
Savings Plan: Stock Purch. Plan:

Top Exec. Salary: $875,000 Bonus: $4,963,522
Second Exec. Salary: $616,000 Bonus: $3,146,240

OTHER THOUGHTS:

Apparent Women Officers or Directors: 4
Hot Spot for Advancement for Women/Minorities: Y

LOCATIONS: ("Y" = Yes)

West:	Southwest:	Midwest:	Southeast:	Northeast:	International:
Y	Y	Y	Y	Y	Y

DIAMOND RESORTS HOLDINGS LLC

www.diamondresorts.com

Industry Group Code: 561599 **Ranks within this company's industry group:** Sales: Profits:

Properties:		Financial Services:		Construction/Development:		Investments:		Specialty Services:		Brokerage:	
Apartments:		Mortgages:		Commercial Construction:		REIT:		Property Management:		Commercial Sales:	
Malls/Shopping:		Title Insurance:		Residential Construction:				Online Services:	Y	Residential Sales:	
Offices:		Property Insurance:		Land Development:				Software/IT:		Specialty:	
Hotels/Motels:	Y			Support Services:				Consulting:			
Industrial/Warehouses:				Design/Engineering:							
Other:											

TYPES OF BUSINESS:

Time-Share Resorts

BRANDS/DIVISIONS/AFFILIATES:

Diamond Resorts International
THE Club
Sunterra Corporation
Owner Advisory Board

CONTACTS:

Note: Officers with more than one job title may be intentionally listed here more than once.

Stephen J. Cloobeck, CEO
Simon Crawford-Welch, COO
Simon Crawford-Welch, Pres.
David Palmer, CFO
Brian P. Garavuso, CIO/Exec. VP
Stephen J. Cloobeck, Chmn.

Phone: 702-804-8600	**Fax:** 702-304-7066
Toll-Free:	
Address: 10600 W. Charleston Blvd., Las Vegas, NV 89135 US	

GROWTH PLANS/SPECIAL FEATURES:

Diamond Resorts Holdings, LLC, which does business as Diamond Resorts International (DRI), is a vacation ownership firm, offering over 150 affiliated and branded resorts and over 23,000 beds in 21 countries. DRI operates THE Club, a points-based vacation system with over 380,000 member-owners. Points, which are renewed annually, may be spent as currency on resort vacations, cruises, airline tickets and other travel purchases. Members may search for a resort by an activity or interest they wish to pursue, browsing through categories such as History & Heritage; Outdoor; Ski & Snow; Spa; Beaches; Family Resorts; and Golf Resorts. Alternatively, resorts may be located by geographical area; the firm currently has resorts in the U.S., the Caribbean, Mexico and Canada, and nine countries in Europe: Austria, France, Germany, Italy, Malta, Norway, Portugal, Spain and the U.K. Amenities vary by resort, buy may include a full bath, kitchen, dishwasher, washer/dryer, satellite TV, fireplace, deck, pool, sauna, spa, beauty salon, fitness center, movie rentals, broadband Internet, childcare/babysitting, 24-hour reception and safe deposit boxes. Besides resort reservations, DRI directly offers flight, cruise and car rental reservations (provided by various third-parties such as British Airways, Hertz and Royal Caribbean) on its DiamondResorts.com site, as well as offering hotel reservations through its Travel.ian.com site. Recently, Diamond Resorts acquired Sunterra Corporation, an operator of 97 timeshare resorts, for $700 million, including the assumption of $375 million in debt. The company has created the Owner Advisory Board, which consists of a group of member-owners from the U.S. and Europe. It will assist DRI corporate leaders plan new projects, programs and products.

FINANCIALS:

Sales and profits are in thousands of dollars—add 000 to get the full amount. 2009 Note: Financial information for 2009 was not available for all companies at press time.

2009 Sales: $	2009 Profits: $	**U.S. Stock Ticker: Private**
2008 Sales: $	2008 Profits: $	**Int'l Ticker:** Int'l Exchange:
2007 Sales: $	2007 Profits: $	Employees:
2006 Sales: $	2006 Profits: $	Fiscal Year Ends: 9/30
2005 Sales: $423,930	2005 Profits: $-34,734	Parent Company:

SALARIES/BENEFITS:

Pension Plan:	ESOP Stock Plan:	Profit Sharing:	Top Exec. Salary: $	Bonus: $
Savings Plan:	Stock Purch. Plan:		Second Exec. Salary: $	Bonus: $

OTHER THOUGHTS:

Apparent Women Officers or Directors:
Hot Spot for Advancement for Women/Minorities: Y

LOCATIONS: ("Y" = Yes)

West:	Southwest:	Midwest:	Southeast:	Northeast:	International:
Y	Y	Y	Y	Y	Y

DITECH.COM

www.ditech.com

Industry Group Code: 522310E **Ranks within this company's industry group:** Sales: Profits:

Properties:		Financial Services:		Construction/Development:		Investments:		Specialty Services:		Brokerage:	
Apartments:		Mortgages:	Y	Commercial Construction:		REIT:		Property Management:		Commercial Sales:	
Malls/Shopping:		Title Insurance:		Residential Construction:				Online Services:		Residential Sales:	
Offices:		Property Insurance:		Land Development:				Software/IT:		Specialty:	
Hotels/Motels:				Support Services:				Consulting:			
Industrial/Warehouses:				Design/Engineering:							
Other:											

TYPES OF BUSINESS:

Mortgage Origination
Direct Lending
Online Services

BRANDS/DIVISIONS/AFFILIATES:

GMAC Mortgage Corporation
ditechatwork.com
Real Life Plan

CONTACTS:

Note: Officers with more than one job title may be intentionally listed here more than once.

Richard D. Powers, Gen. Mgr./Sr. VP
Phil Armstrong, VP-Mktg.

Phone: 714-800-5800 **Fax:** 714-800-5801
Toll-Free: 800-803-7656
Address: 3200 Park Ctr. Dr., Ste. 150, Costa Mesa, CA 92626 US

GROWTH PLANS/SPECIAL FEATURES:

Ditech.com, a business unit of GMAC Mortgage Corporation, is a leader in the direct lending industry. As a direct lender, customers are offered mortgages without the intermediary of a broker. The company offers a variety of products, including first mortgages, fixed-rate second mortgages, variable equity lines of credit and no-closing-cost-option equity seconds. Its online capabilities allow customers to communicate with loan agents from home, work or on the road and provide 24-hour-a-day access to information, loan calculator tools and customer service. Customers are asked to take part in a five-step process which involves determining the customer's purchasing power; the customer's goals and situation; and choosing a loan appropriate to the home they wish to purchase. The firm has found that its flat-fee program, which opened in 1995, is a popular solution for customers wary of hidden fees when refinancing. Within the first 18 months of launching the program, ditech.com had signed up over 30,000 customers for the $395 flat-fee program. The firm's ditechatwork.com is designed to be a financing program used by employers as an employee benefit resource, entitling employees to discounts on mortgage rates integrated in their benefits packages. The firm offers Real Life Plan, a service which combines a mortgage or refinance with a home equity line of credit, and the Ditech Equity Rewards MasterCard, to help pay down the loan principal with use.

FINANCIALS:

Sales and profits are in thousands of dollars—add 000 to get the full amount. 2009 Note: Financial information for 2009 was not available for all companies at press time.

2009 Sales: $ — 2009 Profits: $
2008 Sales: $ — 2008 Profits: $
2007 Sales: $ — 2007 Profits: $
2006 Sales: $ — 2006 Profits: $
2005 Sales: $ — 2005 Profits: $

U.S. Stock Ticker: Subsidiary
Int'l Ticker: Int'l Exchange:
Employees:
Fiscal Year Ends: 12/31
Parent Company: GMAC INC

SALARIES/BENEFITS:

Pension Plan: ESOP Stock Plan: Profit Sharing: Top Exec. Salary: $ Bonus: $
Savings Plan: Stock Purch. Plan: Second Exec. Salary: $ Bonus: $

OTHER THOUGHTS:

Apparent Women Officers or Directors: 1
Hot Spot for Advancement for Women/Minorities:

LOCATIONS: ("Y" = Yes)

West:	Southwest:	Midwest:	Southeast:	Northeast:	International:
Y	Y				

DIVIDEND CAPITAL GROUP LLC

www.dividendcapital.com

Industry Group Code: 531120 **Ranks within this company's industry group:** Sales: Profits:

Properties:		Financial Services:		Construction/Development:		Investments:		Specialty Services:		Brokerage:	
Apartments:		Mortgages:		Commercial Construction:		REIT:	Y	Property Management:		Commercial Sales:	
Malls/Shopping:		Title Insurance:		Residential Construction:				Online Services:		Residential Sales:	
Offices:		Property Insurance:		Land Development:				Software/IT:		Specialty:	
Hotels/Motels:				Support Services:				Consulting:			
Industrial/Warehouses:	Y			Design/Engineering:							
Other:											

TYPES OF BUSINESS:

Real Estate Investment
REIT Holding
Mutual Funds
Investment Advisory Services

BRANDS/DIVISIONS/AFFILIATES:

DCT Industrial Trust, Inc.
Dividend Capital Total Realty Trust
Dividend Capital Investments
DCA Total Return Fund
DCW Total Return Fund
Industrial Income Trust
Dividend Capital Securities

CONTACTS:

Note: Officers with more than one job title may be intentionally listed here more than once.

Thomas G. Wattles, Managing Principal
Eric Paul, Contact-Media
John Kendall, Regional Dir.-Central California
Guy Arnold, Pres., Dividend Capital Total Realty Trust
Glenn R. Mueller, Real Estate Investment Strategist
Evan H. Zucker, Managing Principal

Phone: 303-228-2200 **Fax:** 303-228-0128
Toll-Free: 866-324-7348
Address: 518 17th St., Fl. 17, Denver, CO 80202 US

GROWTH PLANS/SPECIAL FEATURES:

Dividend Capital Group LLC (DCG) is a real estate investment holding company for DCT Industrial Trust, Inc. (DCT); Dividend Capital Total Realty Trust (TRT); Dividend Capital Investments (DCI); and Industrial Income Trust (IIT). DCT is a public REIT that owns, operates and develops primarily bulk distribution warehouses and light industrial properties in the U.S. and Mexico. DCT invests in industrial properties through active leasing and management, which allows the company to more easily control operating expenses and maintain its properties; and an ongoing strategy of recycling capital by disposing of underperforming assets. TRT is a private REIT with a diverse portfolio of 76 properties in 26 markets, offering a sampling of multiple real estate sectors. DCI is the registered investment advisor for DCA Total Return Fund (formerly Dividend Capital Realty Income Allocation Fund), a closed-end management investment company that invests in the financial, healthcare, materials, energy, information technology, industrial, consumer staples, telecommunications services and real estate sectors; and DCW Total Return Fund (formerly Dividend Capital Global Realty Exposure Fund), a non-closed-end management investment company investing in similar segments, with at least 30% of its net assets invested in real estate. IIT is a private REIT with investments in industrial and distribution properties, which it leases to corporate customers. IIT invests in industrial properties principally because of industrial real estate's typically lower rent volatility; the generally lower operating costs; and larger diversity of tenants, which reduces risk of cash flow instability. Securities for DCG are offered through Dividend Capital Securities LLC. Recently, DCG acquired properties in Austin and Houston, Texas; Princeton, New Jersey; and Washington, D.C.

DCG offers its employees medical, dental and vision coverage; life, AD&D and short- and long-term disability insurance; parking and transportation plans; a health savings account; and a 401(k) plan.

FINANCIALS:

Sales and profits are in thousands of dollars—add 000 to get the full amount. 2009 Note: Financial information for 2009 was not available for all companies at press time.

2009 Sales: $	2009 Profits: $	**U.S. Stock Ticker: Private**
2008 Sales: $	2008 Profits: $	**Int'l Ticker:** Int'l Exchange:
2007 Sales: $	2007 Profits: $	Employees:
2006 Sales: $	2006 Profits: $	Fiscal Year Ends: 12/31
2005 Sales: $	2005 Profits: $	Parent Company:

SALARIES/BENEFITS:

Pension Plan:	ESOP Stock Plan:	Profit Sharing:	Top Exec. Salary: $	Bonus: $
Savings Plan: Y	Stock Purch. Plan:		Second Exec. Salary: $	Bonus: $

OTHER THOUGHTS:

Apparent Women Officers or Directors:
Hot Spot for Advancement for Women/Minorities:

LOCATIONS: ("Y" = Yes)

West:	Southwest:	Midwest:	Southeast:	Northeast:	International:
Y					

DLF LIMITED

www.dlf.in

Industry Group Code: 5311 **Ranks within this company's industry group:** Sales: 8 Profits: 3

Properties:		Financial Services:		Construction/Development:		Investments:		Specialty Services:		Brokerage:	
Apartments:		Mortgages:		Commercial Construction:	Y	REIT:		Property Management:	Y	Commercial Sales:	
Malls/Shopping:	Y	Title Insurance:		Residential Construction:	Y			Online Services:		Residential Sales:	
Offices:	Y	Property Insurance:		Land Development:				Software/IT:		Specialty:	
Hotels/Motels:	Y			Support Services:				Consulting:			
Industrial/Warehouses:				Design/Engineering:							
Other:											

TYPES OF BUSINESS:

Real Estate Development
Commercial Real Estate Management & Leasing
Hotels
Luxury Resorts
Airport Infrastructure

BRANDS/DIVISIONS/AFFILIATES:

DLF Hotels
Aman Resorts

CONTACTS:

Note: Officers with more than one job title may be intentionally listed here more than once.

T.C. Goyal, Managing Dir.
Ashkok Tyagi, CFO
Kameshwar Swarup, Sr. Exec. Dir.-Legal
Sanjey Roy, Contact-Corp. Comm.
Subhash C. Setia, Corp. Sec./Compliance Officer
Rajiv Singh, Vice Chmn.
Pia Singh, Dir.-Retail Segment
K.P. Singh, Chmn.

Phone: 91-11-4210-2030	**Fax:**
Toll-Free:	
Address: DLF Centre Sansad Marg, New Delhi, 110001 India	

GROWTH PLANS/SPECIAL FEATURES:

DLF Limited is an India-based real estate development and construction company. The firm has over 238 million square feet (msf) of completed development, with another 423 msf of planned projects, in 30 cities across India. DLF is primarily engaged in the development of residential, commercial and retail properties. It is divided into two business units: development and annuity. The development unit develops mid-income, luxury and super luxury residential communities. Products offered include condominiums, duplexes, row houses and apartments as well as commercial facilities. The annuity business is engaged in the rental of office and retail properties. Through subsidiaries Aman resorts and DLF Hotels the firm participates in the hospitality business, developing and managing hotels internationally. The firm's business model allows it to earn revenues from both development activities and the leasing of completed properties. The company hopes to continue to grow its business through projects in India's special economic zones (SEZs), which are specially- legislated areas designed to encourage foreign investment and exports from the country. The company has approximately 243 subsidiaries, including DLF Commercial Complexes Limited, which is responsible for the development and construction of the firm's commercial structures across India. In 2009, the firm delayed construction of some luxury properties and lowered prices on some homes in the affordable category, to as little as $30,000, in reaction to the global financial slowdown. In February 2010, DLF began construction on its largest township project outside of Guragon, the Panchkula Valley project, which will include over 1200 apartments, a community center, nursery, schools, shopping centers, offices, a hospital and a rain water collection system.

FINANCIALS:

Sales and profits are in thousands of dollars—add 000 to get the full amount. 2009 Note: Financial information for 2009 was not available for all companies at press time.

2009 Sales: $2,241,520	2009 Profits: $960,220	**U.S. Stock Ticker:**
2008 Sales: $3,155,320	2008 Profits: $1,678,670	**Int'l Ticker: 532868** Int'l Exchange: Bombay-BSE
2007 Sales: $1,085,870	2007 Profits: $415,510	Employees: 2,882
2006 Sales: $	2006 Profits: $	Fiscal Year Ends: 3/31
2005 Sales: $	2005 Profits: $	Parent Company:

SALARIES/BENEFITS:

Pension Plan:	ESOP Stock Plan:	Profit Sharing:	Top Exec. Salary: $	Bonus: $
Savings Plan:	Stock Purch. Plan:		Second Exec. Salary: $	Bonus: $

OTHER THOUGHTS:

Apparent Women Officers or Directors: 1
Hot Spot for Advancement for Women/Minorities:

LOCATIONS: ("Y" = Yes)

West:	Southwest:	Midwest:	Southeast:	Northeast:	International:
					Y

DOMINION HOMES INC

www.dominionhomes.com

Industry Group Code: 2361 **Ranks within this company's industry group:** Sales: Profits:

Properties:		Financial Services:		Construction/Development:		Investments:		Specialty Services:		Brokerage:	
Apartments:		Mortgages:	Y	Commercial Construction:		REIT:		Property Management:		Commercial Sales:	
Malls/Shopping:		Title Insurance:		Residential Construction:	Y			Online Services:		Residential Sales:	Y
Offices:		Property Insurance:		Land Development:	Y			Software/IT:		Specialty:	
Hotels/Motels:				Support Services:				Consulting:			
Industrial/Warehouses:				Design/Engineering:							
Other:											

TYPES OF BUSINESS:

Residential Construction
Financial Services
Residential Sales

BRANDS/DIVISIONS/AFFILIATES:

Founders Collection
Metropolitan Collection
Celebration Collection
Grand Reserve Collection
Tradition Collection
Angelo Gordon & Co LP
Silver Point Capital LP
BRC Properties Inc

CONTACTS: *Note: Officers with more than one job title may be intentionally listed here more than once.*

William G. Cornely, COO
William G. Cornely, CFO
William G. Cornely, Exec. VP-Finance
Douglas G. Borror, Chmn.

Phone: 614-356-5000	**Fax:** 614-356-6010
Toll-Free:	
Address: 4900 Tuttle Crossing Blvd., Dublin, OH 43016 US	

GROWTH PLANS/SPECIAL FEATURES:

Dominion Homes, Inc. is a leading builder of high-quality homes in central Ohio, as well as in Louisville and Lexington, Kentucky. Dominion targets entry-level and move-up home buyers, offering a variety of homes differentiated by price, size, standard features and available options. These homes range in price from approximately $100,000 to over $300,000 and in size from approximately 1,000 to 3,500 square feet. The company currently offers five distinct series of homes: the Founders Collection, a neo-traditional housing concept targeting entry-level home buyers; the Metropolitan Collection, targeting the young, single home buyer; the Celebration Collection, targeting entry-level and first-time move-up home buyers; the Tradition Collection with styles ranging from contemporary to traditional designs, targeting move-up home buyers; and the Grand Reserve Collection, which targets active adults who want luxury patio homes built in private communities with convenient amenities like pools and clubhouses. In recent years, Dominion became a private company upon being acquired by a buyout group comprised of Angelo Gordon & Co., L.P.; Silver Point Capital L.P.; and BRC Properties, Inc.

Dominion offers its employees benefits including life, accidental death, medical, dental and vision insurance; flexible spending accounts; a 401(k); training/development programs; tuition assistance; and home purchase discounts.

FINANCIALS: **Sales and profits are in thousands of dollars—add 000 to get the full amount. 2009 Note: Financial information for 2009 was not available for all companies at press time.**

2009 Sales: $	2009 Profits: $	**U.S. Stock Ticker: Private**
2008 Sales: $	2008 Profits: $	**Int'l Ticker:** Int'l Exchange:
2007 Sales: $147,991	2007 Profits: $-82,159	Employees:
2006 Sales: $256,760	2006 Profits: $-34,009	Fiscal Year Ends: 12/31
2005 Sales: $415,700	2005 Profits: $5,326	Parent Company:

SALARIES/BENEFITS:

Pension Plan:	ESOP Stock Plan:	Profit Sharing:	Top Exec. Salary: $	Bonus: $
Savings Plan: Y	Stock Purch. Plan:		Second Exec. Salary: $	Bonus: $

OTHER THOUGHTS:

Apparent Women Officers or Directors: 2
Hot Spot for Advancement for Women/Minorities:

LOCATIONS: ("Y" = Yes)

West:	Southwest:	Midwest:	Southeast:	Northeast:	International:
		Y			

DOOSAN HEAVY INDUSTRY & CONSTRUCTION CO

www.doosanheavy.com

Industry Group Code: 237 **Ranks within this company's industry group:** Sales: 13 Profits: 16

Properties:		Financial Services:		Construction/Development:		Investments:		Specialty Services:		Brokerage:	
Apartments:		Mortgages:		Commercial Construction:	Y	REIT:		Property Management:		Commercial Sales:	
Malls/Shopping:		Title Insurance:		Residential Construction:	Y			Online Services:		Residential Sales:	
Offices:		Property Insurance:		Land Development:	Y			Software/IT:		Specialty:	
Hotels/Motels:				Support Services:	Y			Consulting:			
Industrial/Warehouses:				Design/Engineering:	Y						
Other:											

TYPES OF BUSINESS:

Construction
Power Plant Construction
Desalination Plant Construction
Civil Works Projects
Architecture Works Projects
Casting & Forging

BRANDS/DIVISIONS/AFFILIATES:

Doosan Power Systems
Skoda Power
Doosan Babcock Energy
DPS Europe
DPS Americas

CONTACTS: *Note: Officers with more than one job title may be intentionally listed here more than once.*

Geewon Park, CEO
Geewon Park, Pres.
Jong Il Choi, CFO/Exec. VP
C. John Yoon, Exec. VP-Corp. R&D Institute
C. John Yoon, CTO/Exec. VP
Kim Ha-Bang, Sr. VP-Nuclear Power Plant Mktg.
Lee Dong-kyu, VP-HRSG Bus. Unit
Chung Yong-Gyun, VP-Material Handling Equipment Bus. Unit
Kim Sung-Soo, Sr. VP-Power Plant Svcs. Bus. Unit
Yong-Sung Park, Chmn.
Hyun sang Ahn, VP-Water Bus. Group, Middle East

Phone: 82-55-278-6114	**Fax:** 82-55-264-5551
Toll-Free:	
Address: 555 Guigok-dong, Gyeongsangnam-do, Changwon, 641-792 Korea	

GROWTH PLANS/SPECIAL FEATURES:

Doosan Heavy Industry and Construction Co., established in 1962, has built over 300 thermal, hydro, nuclear and combined cycle power plants, and is currently building more than 60 plants in Korea, China, India, the U.S. and other countries. It is also developing wind power systems, fuel cells and other environmentally friendly energy sources. Doosan built the Shuaibah Desalination Plant Phase 3 in Saudi Arabia, one of the world's largest desalination facilities, with a daily capacity of 880,000 tons. The company also built one of the world's first hybrid desalination plants, located in Fujairah, in the United Arab Emirates. The plant combines two desalination technologies: Multi-Stage Flash (MSF), which desalinates through a repeated cycle of evaporation and condensation; and Reverse Osmosis (RO), which forces the water across a filtering membrane. The firm is one of the few with proprietary technologies in all three areas of desalination: MSF, RO and MED (Multi-Effect Distillation, where the heat from boiling one chamber, or effect, is used to heat another effect and so on, in a series). In addition to constructing plants, Doosan supplies forging and casting products, and constructs highways, ports, airports, high-speed railroads, tunnels, subways, apartments and power transmission lines. Its casting and forging products include rotor shafts and turbine casings for nuclear and thermal power plants; shells for reactors and steam generators in nuclear power plants; crank shafts, rudder horns and propeller shafts for ships; components for steel mills such as mill housing and rolls; die steel, used in the manufacture of plastic products; and tool steel, used to manufacture machine tools. In February 2010, the firm established Doosan Power Systems, a holding company, to manage its U.S. and European companies, including Doosan Babcock (U.K.); Skoda Power (Czech Republic); DPS Europe; and DPS Americas.

FINANCIALS: **Sales and profits are in thousands of dollars—add 000 to get the full amount. 2009 Note: Financial information for 2009 was not available for all companies at press time.**

2009 Sales: $	2009 Profits: $	**U.S. Stock Ticker:**
2008 Sales: $8,943,400	2008 Profits: $217,500	**Int'l Ticker: 034020** Int'l Exchange: Seoul-KRX
2007 Sales: $7,651,000	2007 Profits: $48,300	Employees:
2006 Sales: $5,907,300	2006 Profits: $112,000	Fiscal Year Ends: 12/31
2005 Sales: $327,698	2005 Profits: $142,394	Parent Company:

SALARIES/BENEFITS:

Pension Plan:	ESOP Stock Plan:	Profit Sharing:	Top Exec. Salary: $	Bonus: $
Savings Plan:	Stock Purch. Plan:		Second Exec. Salary: $	Bonus: $

OTHER THOUGHTS:

Apparent Women Officers or Directors:
Hot Spot for Advancement for Women/Minorities:

LOCATIONS: ("Y" = Yes)

West:	Southwest:	Midwest:	Southeast:	Northeast:	International:
	Y		Y	Y	Y

DOYLE COLLECTION (THE)

www.doylecollection.com

Industry Group Code: 721110 **Ranks within this company's industry group:** Sales: Profits:

Properties:		Financial Services:		Construction/Development:		Investments:		Specialty Services:		Brokerage:	
Apartments:		Mortgages:		Commercial Construction:		REIT:		Property Management:	Y	Commercial Sales:	
Malls/Shopping:		Title Insurance:		Residential Construction:				Online Services:		Residential Sales:	
Offices:		Property Insurance:		Land Development:				Software/IT:		Specialty:	
Hotels/Motels:	Y			Support Services:				Consulting:			
Industrial/Warehouses:				Design/Engineering:							
Other:											

TYPES OF BUSINESS:

Hotels
Hotel Management

BRANDS/DIVISIONS/AFFILIATES:

Jurys Doyle Hotel Group
Westbury Hotel (The)
Croke Park Hotel (The)
River Lee Hotel (The)
Normandy Hotel (The)
Courtyard by Marriott Northwest
Back Bay Hotel (The)
Marylebone Hotel (The)

CONTACTS:

Note: Officers with more than one job title may be intentionally listed here more than once.

Bill Walshe, CEO
Patrick King, CFO
Seamus Daly, Corp. Sec.
Bernadette C. Gallagher, Chmn.

Phone: 353-1-607-0070	**Fax:** 353-1-667-2370
Toll-Free:	
Address: 146 Pembroke Rd., Ballsbridge, Dublin, Ireland 4 UK	

GROWTH PLANS/SPECIAL FEATURES:

The Doyle Collection (TDC), formerly known as Jurys Doyle Hotel Group plc, is an international hotel operator headquartered in Dublin, Ireland. It has properties in Ireland, the U.K. and the U.S. Currently, the company offers business and leisure travelers a portfolio of 11 luxury hotels in six cities with a combined total of 2,300 rooms. The firm's Irish properties are located in Dublin and Cork; its U.K. properties are located in London and Bristol; and its U.S. properties are located in Boston, Massachusetts and Washington, D.C. Hotels are generally located centrally in their respective cities, giving corporate clients easy access to local business and financial districts. Additionally, the firm's hotels offer corporate hospitality, conference, event and meeting suites to accommodate meetings and events of various sizes. Several of the group's hotels have professional wedding planners on staff to help coordinate wedding and reception activities. The company's individual properties include the Westbury Hotel and the Croke Park Hotel, in Dublin; The River Lee Hotel, in Cork; the Marylebone Hotel, the Great Russell Hotel and the Kensington Hotel, in London; the Bristol Hotel, in Bristol; the Normandy Hotel, the Dupont Hotel and the Courtyard by Marriott Northwest, in Washington, D.C.; and the Back Bay Hotel, in Boston. In March 2010, the Jurys Cork Hotel was renamed the River Lee Hotel.

The Doyle Collection offers its employees a benefits package that includes a pension plan; medical coverage; discounts on accommodation and food; death-in-service benefits; and educational assistance.

FINANCIALS:

Sales and profits are in thousands of dollars—add 000 to get the full amount. 2009 Note: Financial information for 2009 was not available for all companies at press time.

2009 Sales: $	2009 Profits: $	**U.S. Stock Ticker: Private**
2008 Sales: $	2008 Profits: $	**Int'l Ticker:** Int'l Exchange:
2007 Sales: $	2007 Profits: $	Employees:
2006 Sales: $	2006 Profits: $	Fiscal Year Ends: 12/31
2005 Sales: $	2005 Profits: $	Parent Company:

SALARIES/BENEFITS:

Pension Plan: Y	ESOP Stock Plan:	Profit Sharing:	Top Exec. Salary: $	Bonus: $
Savings Plan:	Stock Purch. Plan:		Second Exec. Salary: $	Bonus: $

OTHER THOUGHTS:

Apparent Women Officers or Directors: 1
Hot Spot for Advancement for Women/Minorities: Y

LOCATIONS: ("Y" = Yes)

West:	Southwest:	Midwest:	Southeast:	Northeast:	International:
				Y	Y

DR HORTON INC

www.drhorton.com

Industry Group Code: 2361 **Ranks within this company's industry group:** Sales: 3 Profits: 19

Properties:		Financial Services:		Construction/Development:		Investments:		Specialty Services:		Brokerage:	
Apartments:		Mortgages:	Y	Commercial Construction:		REIT:		Property Management:		Commercial Sales:	
Malls/Shopping:		Title Insurance:	Y	Residential Construction:	Y			Online Services:		Residential Sales:	
Offices:		Property Insurance:		Land Development:				Software/IT:		Specialty:	
Hotels/Motels:				Support Services:				Consulting:			
Industrial/Warehouses:				Design/Engineering:							
Other:											

TYPES OF BUSINESS:

Construction, Residential
Mortgages
Title Insurance

BRANDS/DIVISIONS/AFFILIATES:

DHI Mortgage

CONTACTS:

Note: Officers with more than one job title may be intentionally listed here more than once.

Donald J. Tomnitz, CEO
Donald J. Tomnitz, Pres./Vice Chmn.
Bill W. Wheat, CFO/Exec. VP
Ted I. Harbour, Chief Legal Officer
Jessica Hansen, Dir.-Investor Rel.
Stacey H. Dwyer, Treas./Exec. VP
Randy Present, Pres., Financial Svcs.
Chris Chambers, Pres., West Region
Rick Horton, Pres., South Region
George Seagraves, Pres., North Region
Donald R. Horton, Chmn.

Phone: 817-390-8200	**Fax:** 817-436-6717
Toll-Free:	
Address: 301 Commerce St., Ste. 500, Fort Worth, TX 76102 US	

GROWTH PLANS/SPECIAL FEATURES:

D. R. Horton is a leading national builder of single-family homes with a diversified set of holdings, and operating divisions in 27 states and 75 metropolitan markets. The firm generally builds homes between 1,000 to 4,000 square feet, ranging in price from $90,000 to $700,000, with construction often completed in four to six months. In fiscal 2009, the company closed approximately 16,703 homes, with an average closing sales price approximating $213,400. The company is divided into six regional homebuilding segments and one financial services segment. The homebuilding segments are East, operating in eight states; Midwest, four states; Southeast, three states; South Central, four states; Southwest, two states; and West, seven states. Approximately 81% of D.R. Horton's 2009 home sale revenues came from detached home building. The building services section constructs residences, tailored to the particular community where they are being built, including single-family residential homes, townhouses, condominiums, duplexes and triplexes. Subcontractors under the supervision of D. R. Horton do substantially all of the actual building. The financial services segment of the company provides mortgage financing and title insurance through its wholly-owned subsidiary, DHI Mortgage. Though the company has been affected by shifting conditions in U.S. housing demand, D. R. Horton foresees a strong long-term recovery, due namely to population growth and household formation. The home builder's business strategy going forward from 2009 is to strengthen its financials by reducing inventories of homes and land, and controlling and reducing construction and overhead costs.

FINANCIALS:

Sales and profits are in thousands of dollars—add 000 to get the full amount. 2009 Note: Financial information for 2009 was not available for all companies at press time.

2009 Sales: $3,603,900	2009 Profits: $-545,300	**U.S. Stock Ticker: DHI**
2008 Sales: $6,518,600	2008 Profits: $-2,633,600	**Int'l Ticker:** Int'l Exchange:
2007 Sales: $11,088,800	2007 Profits: $-712,500	Employees: 2,926
2006 Sales: $14,760,500	2006 Profits: $1,233,300	Fiscal Year Ends: 9/30
2005 Sales: $13,628,600	2005 Profits: $1,470,500	Parent Company:

SALARIES/BENEFITS:

Pension Plan:	ESOP Stock Plan:	Profit Sharing:	Top Exec. Salary: $400,000	Bonus: $2,340,014
Savings Plan: Y	Stock Purch. Plan:		Second Exec. Salary: $300,000	Bonus: $2,340,014

OTHER THOUGHTS:

Apparent Women Officers or Directors: 1
Hot Spot for Advancement for Women/Minorities:

LOCATIONS: ("Y" = Yes)

West:	Southwest:	Midwest:	Southeast:	Northeast:	International:
Y	Y	Y	Y	Y	

DREW INDUSTRIES

www.drewindustries.com

Industry Group Code: 321991 **Ranks within this company's industry group:** Sales: 3 Profits: 1

Properties:		Financial Services:		Construction/Development:		Investments:		Specialty Services:		Brokerage:	
Apartments:		Mortgages:		Commercial Construction:		REIT:		Property Management:		Commercial Sales:	
Malls/Shopping:		Title Insurance:		Residential Construction:	Y			Online Services:		Residential Sales:	
Offices:		Property Insurance:		Land Development:				Software/IT:		Specialty:	
Hotels/Motels:				Support Services:	Y			Consulting:			
Industrial/Warehouses:				Design/Engineering:							
Other:											

TYPES OF BUSINESS:

Recreational Vehicle Components
Manufactured Housing Components
Modular Housing & Office Unit Products
Chassis & Chassis Parts

BRANDS/DIVISIONS/AFFILIATES:

Kinro Inc
Lippert Components Inc
Seating Technology Inc

CONTACTS:

Note: Officers with more than one job title may be intentionally listed here more than once.

Fredric M. Zinn, CEO
Fredric M. Zinn, Pres.
Joseph S. Giordano, III, CFO
Harvey F. Milman, Chief Legal Officer/VP/Corp. Sec.
Christopher L. Smith, Controller
Jason Lippert, Pres./CEO-Kinro, Inc.
Scott T. Mereness, Exec. VP/COO-Kinro, Inc.
Leigh J. Abrams, Chmn.

Phone: 914-428-9098 **Fax:** 914-428-4581
Toll-Free:
Address: 200 Mamaroneck Ave., White Plains, NY 10601 US

GROWTH PLANS/SPECIAL FEATURES:

Drew Industries, Inc., operating through its wholly-owned subsidiaries Kinro, Inc. and Lippert Components, Inc., supplies a broad array of components for recreational vehicles (RVs) and manufactured homes (MH). Kinro manufactures and markets components primarily for RVs and manufactured homes, including windows, doors and screens, and thermoformed bath and kitchen products. Lippert manufactures and markets components primarily for RVs and manufactured homes, including steel chassis; steel chassis parts; slide-out mechanisms and related power units; electric stabilizer jacks; leveling devices; bed lifts; suspension systems; axles; and steps. Lippert also manufactures specialty trailers for hauling equipment, boats, personal watercraft and snowmobiles, as well as axles for specialty trailers. With 24 manufacturing facilities located in 12 states, Drew is an important supplier to nearly all of the leading producers of RVs and manufactured homes. The company's two subsidiaries each operate in two segments: the recreational vehicle and leisure product segment (the RV Segment) and the manufactured housing products segment (the MH Segment), with the RV segment accounting for approximately 79% of net sales and the MH segment accounting for approximately 21%. Certain products manufactured by the subsidiaries are also used in modular homes and office units. In March 2010, Drew announced that Lippert Components, Inc. completed the acquisition of some intellectual property and other assets from Schwintek, Inc. The acquisition includes products such as an aluminum cylinder for use in leveling devices, a new tent camper device and a wall slide-out mechanism. Patents for these products are still pending. Also in March 2010, the company announced that Lippert Components received the patent-pending design for Level Up, a six-point leveling system for fifth-wheel RVs. In April 2010, the firm announced plans to create a manufacturing plant for Kinro, Inc. in Chester, South Carolina.

FINANCIALS:

Sales and profits are in thousands of dollars—add 000 to get the full amount. 2009 Note: Financial information for 2009 was not available for all companies at press time.

2009 Sales: $397,839	2009 Profits: $-24,053
2008 Sales: $510,506	2008 Profits: $11,678
2007 Sales: $668,625	2007 Profits: $39,767
2006 Sales: $729,232	2006 Profits: $31,023
2005 Sales: $669,147	2005 Profits: $33,602

U.S. Stock Ticker: DW
Int'l Ticker: Int'l Exchange:
Employees: 3,054
Fiscal Year Ends: 12/31
Parent Company:

SALARIES/BENEFITS:

Pension Plan:	ESOP Stock Plan:	Profit Sharing:	Top Exec. Salary: $700,000	Bonus: $244,569
Savings Plan: Y	Stock Purch. Plan:		Second Exec. Salary: $450,000	Bonus: $34,680

OTHER THOUGHTS:

Apparent Women Officers or Directors:
Hot Spot for Advancement for Women/Minorities:

LOCATIONS: ("Y" = Yes)

West:	Southwest:	Midwest:	Southeast:	Northeast:	International:
Y	Y	Y	Y	Y	Y

DUKE REALTY CORP

www.dukerealty.com

Industry Group Code: 531120 **Ranks within this company's industry group:** Sales: 12 Profits: 24

Properties:		Financial Services:		Construction/Development:		Investments:		Specialty Services:		Brokerage:	
Apartments:		Mortgages:		Commercial Construction:	Y	REIT:	Y	Property Management:		Commercial Sales:	
Malls/Shopping:	Y	Title Insurance:		Residential Construction:				Online Services:		Residential Sales:	
Offices:	Y	Property Insurance:		Land Development:	Y			Software/IT:		Specialty:	
Hotels/Motels:				Support Services:				Consulting:			
Industrial/Warehouses:	Y			Design/Engineering:	Y						
Other:											

TYPES OF BUSINESS:

Real Estate Investment Trust
Real Estate Development
Commercial Real Estate
Construction & Design Services
Commercial Construction
Warehouses

BRANDS/DIVISIONS/AFFILIATES:

Duke Realty LP
Duke Realty Services LP
Duke Construction LP

CONTACTS: *Note: Officers with more than one job title may be intentionally listed here more than once.*

Dennis D. Oklak, CEO
Christie Kelly, CFO/Exec. VP
Howard L. Feinsand, General Counsel/Exec. VP/Corp. Sec.
Steve R. Kennedy, VP-Construction
James B. Connor, Exec. VP-Midwest
Jeffrey D. Turner, Exec. VP-South & West Regions
Sam O'Briant, Exec. VP-Southeast & East Regions
Dennis D. Oklak, Chmn.

Phone: 317-808-6000 **Fax:** 317-808-6770
Toll-Free: 800-875-3366
Address: 600 E. 96th St., Ste. 100, Indianapolis, IN 46240 US

GROWTH PLANS/SPECIAL FEATURES:

Duke Realty Corp. is a self-administered and self-managed real estate investment trust (REIT) providing in-house leasing, management, development and construction services. The company's diversified portfolio of 762 office, industrial, healthcare and retail rental properties, including 211 jointly controlled in-service properties with more than 43.2 million square feet, encompasses approximately136 million rentable square feet, leased by a diverse and stable base of approximately 3,500 tenants whose businesses include manufacturing, retailing, wholesale trade, distribution, healthcare and professional services. The firm's portfolio includes 427 industrial properties, consisting primarily of bulk warehouses, totaling approximately 95.5 million square feet. Properties also include service center properties also known as flex buildings or light industrial properties. Office properties owned by the firm include 298 office buildings totaling approximately 35.4 million square feet, primarily in suburban locations. Duke also owns interests in 37 healthcare and retail buildings totaling more than 4.6 million square feet. It also owns or controls more than 7,000 acres of land ready for development. The company conducts rental operations through subsidiary Duke Realty, LP. It conducts service operations through Duke Realty Services, LP, in which the company is the sole general partner. The company also operates Duke Construction, LP, which offers office, industrial, medical and retail building and design services in the Midwestern, Southeastern and Southwestern U.S.

Employees are offered medical, dental and vision insurance; health savings accounts; flexible spending accounts; an employee assistance program; a 401(k) plan; an employee stock purchase plan; life and AD&D insurance; disability coverage; adoption assistance; a scholarship program; an employer assisted housing program; and an associate referral bonus program.

FINANCIALS: **Sales and profits are in thousands of dollars—add 000 to get the full amount. 2009 Note: Financial information for 2009 was not available for all companies at press time.**

2009 Sales: $1,344,089
2008 Sales: $1,292,183
2007 Sales: $1,122,095
2006 Sales: $805,296
2005 Sales: $713,552

2009 Profits: $-271,490
2008 Profits: $110,408
2007 Profits: $291,059
2006 Profits: $204,147
2005 Profits: $309,183

U.S. Stock Ticker: DRE
Int'l Ticker: Int'l Exchange:
Employees: 1,000
Fiscal Year Ends: 12/31
Parent Company:

SALARIES/BENEFITS:

Pension Plan: ESOP Stock Plan: Profit Sharing: Top Exec. Salary: $ Bonus: $
Savings Plan: Y Stock Purch. Plan: Y Second Exec. Salary: $ Bonus: $

OTHER THOUGHTS:

Apparent Women Officers or Directors: 3
Hot Spot for Advancement for Women/Minorities: Y

LOCATIONS: ("Y" = Yes)

West:	Southwest:	Midwest:	Southeast:	Northeast:	International:
	Y	Y	Y	Y	

DYNEX CAPITAL INC

www.dynexcapital.com

Industry Group Code: 525990 **Ranks within this company's industry group:** Sales: 2 Profits: 2

Properties:		Financial Services:		Construction/Development:		Investments:		Specialty Services:		Brokerage:	
Apartments:		Mortgages:	Y	Commercial Construction:		REIT:		Property Management:		Commercial Sales:	
Malls/Shopping:		Title Insurance:		Residential Construction:				Online Services:		Residential Sales:	
Offices:		Property Insurance:		Land Development:				Software/IT:		Specialty:	
Hotels/Motels:				Support Services:				Consulting:			
Industrial/Warehouses:				Design/Engineering:							
Other:											

TYPES OF BUSINESS:

Mortgage REIT
Real Estate Investment Trust
Collateralized Bonds

BRANDS/DIVISIONS/AFFILIATES:

CONTACTS:

Note: Officers with more than one job title may be intentionally listed here more than once.

Thomas B. Akin, CEO
Stephen J. Benedetti, COO/Exec. VP
Stephen J. Benedetti, CFO/Exec. VP
John L. Goodhue, VP-Info. Systems
Stephen J. Benedetti, Corp. Sec.
Alison G. Griffin, VP-Investor Rel.
Jeffrey Childress, Controller
Robert M. Nilson, Jr., VP-Risk Mgmt.
Wayne E. Brockwell, VP-Portfolio
Stephen J. Benedetti, Treas.
Byron L Boston, Chief Investment Officer
Thomas B. Akin, Chmn.

Phone: 804-217-5800	**Fax:** 804-217-5860
Toll-Free:	
Address: 4991 Lake Brook Dr., Ste. 100, Glen Allen, VA 23060-6740 US	

GROWTH PLANS/SPECIAL FEATURES:

Dynex Capital, Inc., organized as a real estate investment trust (REIT), is a financial services company that invests in loans and securities consisting primarily of single-family residential and commercial mortgage loans. These loans and securities are financed through a combination of non-recourse securitization financing, repurchase agreements and equity. Its investment policy allocates the firm's capital amongst short-term, highly liquid investments, investment grade fixed income investments, subordinate and credit, as well as strategic investments in equity and equity-like securities of other companies, including other REIT companies. In addition, the firm owns some non-investment grade investments. Its ownership of non-investment grade securities is usually in the form of the first-loss or subordinate classes of securitization trusts, most of which the company sponsors. Its primary source of income is net interest income, which is the excess of the interest income earned on its investments over the cost of financing these investments. The firm holds approximately $172 million in securitized commercial mortgage loans and approximately $71.9 million in single-family mortgage loans.

FINANCIALS:

Sales and profits are in thousands of dollars—add 000 to get the full amount. 2009 Note: Financial information for 2009 was not available for all companies at press time.

2009 Sales: $	2009 Profits: $	**U.S. Stock Ticker: DX**
2008 Sales: $29,653	2008 Profits: $15,121	**Int'l Ticker:** Int'l Exchange:
2007 Sales: $30,778	2007 Profits: $8,899	Employees: 13
2006 Sales: $50,449	2006 Profits: $4,909	Fiscal Year Ends: 12/31
2005 Sales: $74,395	2005 Profits: $9,585	Parent Company:

SALARIES/BENEFITS:

Pension Plan:	ESOP Stock Plan:	Profit Sharing:	Top Exec. Salary: $277,429	Bonus: $14,135
Savings Plan: Y	Stock Purch. Plan:		Second Exec. Salary: $239,864	Bonus: $

OTHER THOUGHTS:

Apparent Women Officers or Directors:
Hot Spot for Advancement for Women/Minorities:

LOCATIONS: ("Y" = Yes)

West:	Southwest:	Midwest:	Southeast:	Northeast:	International:
				Y	

EASTGROUP PROPERTIES INC

www.eastgroup.net

Industry Group Code: 531120 **Ranks within this company's industry group:** Sales: 58 Profits: 41

Properties:		Financial Services:		Construction/Development:		Investments:		Specialty Services:		Brokerage:	
Apartments:		Mortgages:		Commercial Construction:		REIT:	Y	Property Management:	Y	Commercial Sales:	
Malls/Shopping:		Title Insurance:		Residential Construction:				Online Services:		Residential Sales:	
Offices:		Property Insurance:		Land Development:				Software/IT:		Specialty:	
Hotels/Motels:				Support Services:				Consulting:			
Industrial/Warehouses:	Y			Design/Engineering:							
Other:											

TYPES OF BUSINESS:

Real Estate Investment Trust
Industrial Properties
Property Management

BRANDS/DIVISIONS/AFFILIATES:

Fairgrounds Business Park
Nations Ford Business Park
Centennial Park Distribution Center
Ocean View Corporate Center

CONTACTS:

Note: Officers with more than one job title may be intentionally listed here more than once.

David H. Hoster, II, CEO
David H. Hoster, II, Pres.
N. Keith McKey, CFO/Exec. VP/Treas.
Brian Laird, VP-IT
N. Keith McKey, Corp. Sec.
Bruce Corkern, Chief Acct. Officer/Controller/Sr. VP
William D. Petsas, Sr. VP/Head-Arizona Western Regional Office
John F. Coleman, Sr. VP-Florida Regional Office
Brent W. Wood, Sr. VP/Head-Texas Regional Office
Jann W. Puckett, VP/Asset Mgr.
Leland R. Speed, Chmn.

Phone: 601-354-3555 **Fax:** 601-352-1441
Toll-Free:
Address: 190 E. Capital St., Ste. 400, Jackson, MS 39201-2195 US

GROWTH PLANS/SPECIAL FEATURES:

EastGroup Properties, Inc. is an equity real estate investment trust (REIT) focused on the acquisition, operation and development of industrial properties in major Sunbelt markets throughout the U.S., with an emphasis in the states of Florida, Texas, Arizona and California. The company focuses on acquiring distribution facilities in the 5,000 to 50,000 square foot range, generally clustered near major transportation features in supply constrained markets. Over 99% of EastGroup's revenue is generated from renting real estate. The company's portfolio is comprised of 238 industrial properties and one office building, and includes 5.1 million square feet of properties under development. EastGroup has developed approximately 33% of its total portfolio, including real estate properties and development properties in lease-up and under construction. EastGroup's focus is the ownership of business distribution space (78% of its portfolio), with the remainder in bulk distribution space (17% of its portfolio) and business service space (5% of its portfolio). Business distribution space properties are typically multi-tenant buildings with a building depth of 200 feet or less, clear height of 20-24 feet, office finish of 10% to 25% and truck courts with a depth of 100-120 feet. In addition to direct property acquisitions and developments, the company seeks to expand its portfolio through the acquisition of other public and private real estate companies and REITs. EastGroup owns Fairgrounds Business Park, comprised of four distribution buildings in San Antonio; Nations Ford Business Park, comprised of four buildings in Charlotte; and Centennial Park Distribution Center, in Denver. In 2009, the company purchased two multi-tenant business distribution complexes with a total of five buildings and 35.9 acres of developable land for a combined cost of $22.7 million. In 2010, the company acquired two business distribution buildings for approximately $5.3 million; and a three building complex in San Diego called the Ocean View Corporate Center for $17 million.

FINANCIALS:

Sales and profits are in thousands of dollars—add 000 to get the full amount. 2009 Note: Financial information for 2009 was not available for all companies at press time.

2009 Sales: $	2009 Profits: $	**U.S. Stock Ticker: EGP**
2008 Sales: $168,575	2008 Profits: $34,142	**Int'l Ticker:** Int'l Exchange:
2007 Sales: $150,730	2007 Profits: $29,734	Employees: 69
2006 Sales: $133,145	2006 Profits: $29,234	Fiscal Year Ends: 12/31
2005 Sales: $121,014	2005 Profits: $22,191	Parent Company:

SALARIES/BENEFITS:

Pension Plan:	ESOP Stock Plan:	Profit Sharing:	Top Exec. Salary: $525,000	Bonus: $583,800
Savings Plan: Y	Stock Purch. Plan:		Second Exec. Salary: $317,200	Bonus: $330,681

OTHER THOUGHTS:

Apparent Women Officers or Directors: 3
Hot Spot for Advancement for Women/Minorities: Y

LOCATIONS: ("Y" = Yes)

West:	Southwest:	Midwest:	Southeast:	Northeast:	International:
Y	Y		Y	Y	

E-LOAN INC

www.eloan.com

Industry Group Code: 522310E **Ranks within this company's industry group:** Sales: Profits:

Properties:		Financial Services:		Construction/Development:		Investments:		Specialty Services:		Brokerage:	
Apartments:		Mortgages:	Y	Commercial Construction:		REIT:		Property Management:		Commercial Sales:	
Malls/Shopping:		Title Insurance:		Residential Construction:				Online Services:	Y	Residential Sales:	
Offices:		Property Insurance:		Land Development:				Software/IT:		Specialty:	
Hotels/Motels:				Support Services:				Consulting:			
Industrial/Warehouses:				Design/Engineering:							
Other:											

TYPES OF BUSINESS:

Online Mortgage Broker
Debt Consolidation
Small Business Loans
Credit Cards
Education Loans

BRANDS/DIVISIONS/AFFILIATES:

Popular Inc

CONTACTS:

Note: Officers with more than one job title may be intentionally listed here more than once.

Mark E. Lefanowicz, Pres.
Alberto J. Paracchini, CFO/Exec. VP
Imran Khan, Chief Mktg. Officer
Jay Shah, CIO
Scott McKinlay, Sr. VP-Corp. Dev.
Harold (Pete) Bonnikson, Sr. VP-First Mortgage
Rick Folgmann, Sr. VP-Home Equity
Tess Koleczek, Chief Privacy Officer
Jim Gallagher, VP-Bus. Dev.
Christian A. Larsen, Chmn.

Phone: 925-847-6200	**Fax:** 925-847-0831
Toll-Free: 888-533-5333	
Address: 6230 Stoneridge Mall Rd., Pleasanton, CA 94588 US	

GROWTH PLANS/SPECIAL FEATURES:

E-LOAN, Inc., a wholly-owned subsidiary of Banco Popular North America (a subsidiary of Popular Inc.), is an online provider and direct-to-consumer lender of a full range of mortgages; credit cards; and home equity, auto, education and personal loans. The E-LOAN web site offers a variety of services for borrowers, including comparisons of loans from the nation's leading lenders; tools for managing debt; credit reports and scores; exclusive 24-hour loan status access; automatic notification regarding new products that meet specific customer needs; and a variety of other services. E-LOAN originates loans through its web site and by telephone; funds the loans using warehouse and other lines of credit; and then sells closed loans. The gain on the sale of these loans is the company's primary source of income. The firm showcases a low-cost guarantee, assuring customers that its combination of low rate, points and lender or broker fees is the lowest-cost loan available. Products offered by E-LOAN include fixed-rate mortgage products, including 30 year and 15 year terms; adjustable rate mortgage products, including 10, seven, five and three year terms; stated income mortgage products, for individuals who are self-employed or write off a large portion of their income; and home equity lines of credit, home equity loans and installment vehicle loans. Lending partners for the company include First Street, Option One Mortgage Corporation (a subsidiary of H&R Block), Irwin Home Equity and HSBC Auto Finance. In 2008, E-LOAN announced that it will offer federally insured Federal Housing Administration (FHA) loans to assist consumers facing a tight credit market.

FINANCIALS:

Sales and profits are in thousands of dollars—add 000 to get the full amount. 2009 Note: Financial information for 2009 was not available for all companies at press time.

2009 Sales: $	2009 Profits: $	**U.S. Stock Ticker: Subsidiary**
2008 Sales: $	2008 Profits: $	**Int'l Ticker:** Int'l Exchange:
2007 Sales: $147,000	2007 Profits: $	Employees:
2006 Sales: $	2006 Profits: $	Fiscal Year Ends: 12/31
2005 Sales: $	2005 Profits: $	Parent Company: POPULAR INC

SALARIES/BENEFITS:

Pension Plan:	ESOP Stock Plan:	Profit Sharing:	Top Exec. Salary: $	Bonus: $
Savings Plan:	Stock Purch. Plan:		Second Exec. Salary: $	Bonus: $

OTHER THOUGHTS:

Apparent Women Officers or Directors: 1
Hot Spot for Advancement for Women/Minorities:

LOCATIONS: ("Y" = Yes)

West:	Southwest:	Midwest:	Southeast:	Northeast:	International:
Y					

EMAAR PROPERTIES PJSC

www.emaar.com

Industry Group Code: 5311 **Ranks within this company's industry group:** Sales: 5 Profits: 4

Properties:		Financial Services:		Construction/Development:		Investments:		Specialty Services:		Brokerage:	
Apartments:	Y	Mortgages:		Commercial Construction:	Y	REIT:		Property Management:	Y	Commercial Sales:	
Malls/Shopping:	Y	Title Insurance:		Residential Construction:	Y			Online Services:		Residential Sales:	
Offices:	Y	Property Insurance:		Land Development:	Y			Software/IT:		Specialty:	
Hotels/Motels:	Y			Support Services:				Consulting:			
Industrial/Warehouses:				Design/Engineering:							
Other:	Y										

TYPES OF BUSINESS:

Real Estate Development
Retail Construction
Residential Construction
Education & Health Care Construction

BRANDS/DIVISIONS/AFFILIATES:

Burj Dubai
Emaar Malls Group LLC
Emaar Hotels and Resorts LLC
Emaar Hospitality Group LLC
Bali Tourism Development Corp.
Emaar Misr
SEGA Corp
Emaar International

CONTACTS: *Note: Officers with more than one job title may be intentionally listed here more than once.*

Vinod Kumar Gomber, CEO
Amit Jain, CFO
Kenneth Foong, CIO
Ayman Hamdy, Exec. Dir.-Legal/Company Sec.
Low Ping, Exec. Dir.-Finance & Risk
Nasser Rafi, CEO-Emaar Malls Group LLC
Marc-Francois Dardenne, CEO-Emaar Hospitality Group LLC
Arif Amiri, CEO-Amaar Retail LLC
Robert Booth, CEO-North America
H.E. Mohamed Bin Ali Alabbar, Chmn.
Sergio Casari, CEO-Emaar Int'l

Phone: 971-4-367-3333 **Fax:** 971-4-367-3000
Toll-Free:
Address: Emaar Business Park, Bldg. 3, P.O. Box 9440, Dubai, UAE

GROWTH PLANS/SPECIAL FEATURES:

Emaar Properties PJSC is a Dubai-based real estate developer whose projects are primarily located in Dubai, though the group encompasses more than 60 active companies with operations spanning the Middle East, North Africa, Pan-Asia, Europe and North America. Emaar Properties PJSC's operating divisions include Emaar United Arab Emirates, principally active in Dubai; Emaar International, with focus on partnerships in the Middle East, North Africa and India; Emaar Malls Group LLC; Emaar Education, which manages over 100 educational institutions through a subsidiary; Emaar Healthcare Group, which plans to develop and manage hospitals and health clinics in the Middle East, North Africa and southeastern Asia; Emaar Hotels and Resorts LLC, a joint venture with Giorgio Armani SPA; and Emaar Hospitality Group LLC, which manages the company's hospitality and leisure projects. The company's most ambitious project to-date is the Downtown Burj Dubai or Burj Khalifa in Dubai, the world's tallest tower. Other projects include the Dubai Mall, which will be one of the world's largest shopping malls; and the Old Town, a residence community designed to reflect traditional Arabian architecture including the Old Town Island, Emaar Square, the Residences and Burj Dubai Boulevard and featuring a manmade lake and fountain, as well as parks and gardens. In March 2009, the company sold its education business in Dubai, including two schools, six nurseries and a vocational training institute, to Innoventure Educational Investments LLC. In April 2010, the Armani Hotel Dubai, the world's first Armani hotel, located in the Burj Khalifa, opened for business.

FINANCIALS: **Sales and profits are in thousands of dollars—add 000 to get the full amount. 2009 Note: Financial information for 2009 was not available for all companies at press time.**

2009 Sales: $2,290,040	2009 Profits: $89,090	**U.S. Stock Ticker:**
2008 Sales: $4,360,000	2008 Profits: $1,519,000	**Int'l Ticker: EMAAR** Int'l Exchange: Abu Dhabi-ADSM
2007 Sales: $4,865,000	2007 Profits: $1,790,000	Employees:
2006 Sales: $3,813,000	2006 Profits: $1,730,000	Fiscal Year Ends: 12/31
2005 Sales: $2,276,000	2005 Profits: $1,288,000	Parent Company:

SALARIES/BENEFITS:

Pension Plan:	ESOP Stock Plan:	Profit Sharing:	Top Exec. Salary: $	Bonus: $
Savings Plan:	Stock Purch. Plan:		Second Exec. Salary: $	Bonus: $

OTHER THOUGHTS:

Apparent Women Officers or Directors: 1
Hot Spot for Advancement for Women/Minorities:

LOCATIONS: ("Y" = Yes)

West:	Southwest:	Midwest:	Southeast:	Northeast:	International:
Y					Y

EMCOR GROUP INC

www.emcorgroup.com

Industry Group Code: 238210 **Ranks within this company's industry group:** Sales: 1 Profits: 1

Properties:		Financial Services:		Construction/Development:		Investments:		Specialty Services:		Brokerage:	
Apartments:		Mortgages:		Commercial Construction:		REIT:		Property Management:	Y	Commercial Sales:	
Malls/Shopping:		Title Insurance:		Residential Construction:				Online Services:		Residential Sales:	
Offices:		Property Insurance:		Land Development:				Software/IT:		Specialty:	
Hotels/Motels:				Support Services:	Y			Consulting:	Y		
Industrial/Warehouses:				Design/Engineering:	Y						
Other:											

TYPES OF BUSINESS:

Electric Contractors
Mechanical Construction
Technical Consulting Services
Facilities Management

BRANDS/DIVISIONS/AFFILIATES:

Ohmstede Ltd
Redman Equipment & Manufacturing Co
MOR PPM Inc
Building Technology Engineers Inc
Central Mechanical Construction Co Inc
Comstock Canada Ltd
Design Air Ltd
F&G Mechanical Corp

CONTACTS:

Note: Officers with more than one job title may be intentionally listed here more than once.

Frank T. MacInnis, CEO
Anthony J. Guzzi, COO
Anthony J. Guzzi, Pres.
Mark A. Pompa, CFO/Exec. VP
Mava K. Heffler, VP-Mktg.
Joseph A. Puglisi, CIO/VP
Sheldon I. Cammaker, General Counsel/Exec. VP/Corp. Sec.
Mava K. Heffler, VP-Comm.
William E. Feher, VP-Finance & Compliance
R. Kevin Matz, Exec. VP-Shared Svcs.
Joseph A. Serino, Treas.
Rex C. Thrasher, VP-Risk Mgmt.
David Copley, VP-Safety & Quality Mgmt.
Frank T. MacInnis, Chmn.
Geoff Birkbeck, CEO-Comstock Canada

Phone: 203-849-7800 **Fax:** 203-849-7900
Toll-Free: 866-890-7794
Address: 301 Merritt Seven, Norwalk, CT 06851 US

GROWTH PLANS/SPECIAL FEATURES:

EMCOR Group, Inc. is a global leader in mechanical and electrical construction, energy infrastructure and facilities services. The company offers its services through approximately 75 subsidiaries and 170 offices located throughout the U.S. (which accounted for approximately 85% of 2009 revenues), as well as in Canada and the U.K. In the Middle East, the firm carries on business through a joint venture. Services provided to its customers include the design, integration, installation, start-up, operation and maintenance of systems for generation and distribution of electrical power; lighting systems; low-voltage systems, such as fire alarm, security, communications and process control systems; voice and data communication systems; heating, ventilation, air conditioning, refrigeration and clean-room process ventilation systems; plumbing, process and high-purity piping systems; water and wastewater treatment systems; and central plant heating and cooling systems. In addition to its construction services, EMCOR offers facilities services, such as site-based operations and maintenance, mobile maintenance and service, facilities management, installation and support for building systems, technical consulting and diagnostic services, small modification and retrofit projects and program development and management for energy systems. Most of the firm's business is done with corporations, municipalities and other government agencies, owner/developers and tenants of buildings. Additional services are provided to a range of general and specialty contractors, with EMCOR operating as a subcontractor.

Employees are offered medical, dental and vision coverage; flexible spending accounts; life insurance; disability coverage; a 401(k) plan; and an employee assistance program.

FINANCIALS:

Sales and profits are in thousands of dollars—add 000 to get the full amount. 2009 Note: Financial information for 2009 was not available for all companies at press time.

2009 Sales: $5,547,942	2009 Profits: $160,756	**U.S. Stock Ticker: EME**
2008 Sales: $6,785,242	2008 Profits: $182,204	**Int'l Ticker:** Int'l Exchange:
2007 Sales: $5,927,152	2007 Profits: $126,808	Employees: 25,000
2006 Sales: $4,901,783	2006 Profits: $86,634	Fiscal Year Ends: 12/31
2005 Sales: $4,592,990	2005 Profits: $60,042	Parent Company:

SALARIES/BENEFITS:

Pension Plan:	ESOP Stock Plan:	Profit Sharing:	Top Exec. Salary: $950,000	Bonus: $4,055,000
Savings Plan: Y	Stock Purch. Plan:		Second Exec. Salary: $650,000	Bonus: $2,240,000

OTHER THOUGHTS:

Apparent Women Officers or Directors: 1
Hot Spot for Advancement for Women/Minorities: Y

LOCATIONS: ("Y" = Yes)

West:	Southwest:	Midwest:	Southeast:	Northeast:	International:
Y	Y	Y	Y	Y	Y

EMERITUS CORP

www.emeritus.com

Industry Group Code: 623110 **Ranks within this company's industry group:** Sales: 5 Profits: 4

Properties:		Financial Services:		Construction/Development:		Investments:		Specialty Services:		Brokerage:	
Apartments:		Mortgages:		Commercial Construction:		REIT:		Property Management:		Commercial Sales:	
Malls/Shopping:		Title Insurance:		Residential Construction:				Online Services:		Residential Sales:	
Offices:		Property Insurance:		Land Development:				Software/IT:		Specialty:	
Hotels/Motels:				Support Services:				Consulting:			
Industrial/Warehouses:				Design/Engineering:							
Other:	Y										

TYPES OF BUSINESS:

Long-Term Health Care
Assisted Living Communities

BRANDS/DIVISIONS/AFFILIATES:

Arbor Place at Silverlake

CONTACTS:

Note: Officers with more than one job title may be intentionally listed here more than once.

Daniel R. Baty, Co-CEO
Chris Hyatt, COO/Exec. VP
Granger Cobb, Pres./Co-CEO
Robert C. Bateman, CFO/Exec. VP-Finance
Jayne Sallerson, Exec. VP-Mktg. & Sales
Melanie Werdel, Exec. VP-Admin.
Raymond R. Brandstrom, Corp. Sec.
Eric Mendelsohn, Sr. VP-Corp. Dev.
Jayne Sallerson, Exec. VP-Comm.
Jim L. Hanson, Sr. VP-Financial Svcs./Controller
Budgie Amparo, Exec. VP-Quality & Risk Mgmt.
Martin D. Roffe, Sr. VP-Financial Planning
John Cincotta, Sr. VP-Sales
Leo Watterson, VP-Corp. Acct.
Daniel R. Baty, Chmn.

Phone: 206-298-2909	**Fax:** 206-301-4500
Toll-Free: 800-429-4828	
Address: 3131 Elliott Ave., Ste. 500, Seattle, WA 98121 US	

GROWTH PLANS/SPECIAL FEATURES:

Emeritus Corp. operates assisted living residential communities in the U.S. These communities cater to senior citizens who need help with daily living, but do not require the intensive care provided in skilled nursing facilities. It operates or has an interest in 308 communities, consisting of 27,100 residential rooms or suites with a capacity for 32,300 residents. The firm's communities are located in 36 states and include 167 owned communities, 105 leased communities and 36 managed communities. Emeritus holds joint venture interests in 24 managed communities. Assisted living generally provides housing and 24-hour personal support services. Seniors reside in a private or semi-private residential unit for a monthly fee based on each resident's individual service needs. Emeritus's specialty is Alzheimer's disease and dementia-related care, for which the company has developed a program that links memory training, familiar environments and personalized care services. Accessing the market for Alzheimer's care is one of the firm's key business strategies. In its other assisted living programs, Emeritus business strategy calls for customer service that addresses both physical and social health. The firm's target customers are middle to upper-middle income seniors, 75 and older, living in smaller cities (50,000 to 150,000 persons). Emeritus attempts to generate growth through increases in residential occupancy rates and revenue per occupied unit, as well as through investments in IT infrastructure and through the selective acquisition of assisted living communities. In recent years, the company has sought to increase the number of communities it owns and decrease the number it merely manages. In January 2010, Emeritus entered into a joint venture agreement with Columbia Pacific Advisors and Blackstone Real Estate Advisors VI, L.P. to acquire 134 senior living communities from Sunwest Management.

Employees are offered health care benefits; a 401(k) plan; a stock purchase plan; tuition assistance; and sick, vacation and holiday pay.

FINANCIALS:

Sales and profits are in thousands of dollars—add 000 to get the full amount. 2009 Note: Financial information for 2009 was not available for all companies at press time.

2009 Sales: $898,732	2009 Profits: $-53,875	**U.S. Stock Ticker: ESC**
2008 Sales: $772,443	2008 Profits: $-104,751	**Int'l Ticker:** Int'l Exchange:
2007 Sales: $538,874	2007 Profits: $-48,741	Employees: 17,409
2006 Sales: $411,375	2006 Profits: $-14,618	Fiscal Year Ends: 12/31
2005 Sales: $387,732	2005 Profits: $11,703	Parent Company:

SALARIES/BENEFITS:

Pension Plan:	ESOP Stock Plan:	Profit Sharing:	Top Exec. Salary: $641,533	Bonus: $242,850
Savings Plan: Y	Stock Purch. Plan: Y		Second Exec. Salary: $636,952	Bonus: $243,500

OTHER THOUGHTS:

Apparent Women Officers or Directors: 2
Hot Spot for Advancement for Women/Minorities: Y

LOCATIONS: ("Y" = Yes)

West:	Southwest:	Midwest:	Southeast:	Northeast:	International:
Y	Y	Y	Y	Y	

EMPRESAS ICA SA DE CV

www.ica.com.mx

Industry Group Code: 237 **Ranks within this company's industry group:** Sales: 28 Profits: 23

Properties:		Financial Services:		Construction/Development:		Investments:		Specialty Services:		Brokerage:	
Apartments:		Mortgages:		Commercial Construction:	Y	REIT:		Property Management:		Commercial Sales:	
Malls/Shopping:		Title Insurance:		Residential Construction:	Y			Online Services:		Residential Sales:	
Offices:		Property Insurance:		Land Development:	Y			Software/IT:		Specialty:	
Hotels/Motels:				Support Services:				Consulting:			
Industrial/Warehouses:				Design/Engineering:	Y						
Other:											

TYPES OF BUSINESS:

Heavy Construction
Civic Construction
Industrial Construction
Transportation Infrastructure Management
Residential Construction
Design & Engineering Services
Airport Operations

BRANDS/DIVISIONS/AFFILIATES:

CasaFlex
FRAMEX
Consorcio del Mayab S.A. de. C.V.
Kronsa
ICA Fluor Daniel
ICA Reichmann
ICA CPC Argentina
Construcciones Y Trituraciones, S.A. de C.V.

CONTACTS: *Note: Officers with more than one job title may be intentionally listed here more than once.*

Jose Luis Guerrero, CEO
Bernardo Quintana Isaac, Pres.
Alonso Quintana Kawage, CFO
Alonso Quintana Kawage, Exec. VP-Finance
Juan Carlos Santos, Dir. Gen.-ICA Fluor
Luis Z. Rocha, VP-Housing
Bernardo Quintana Isaac, Chmn.

Phone: 52-55-5272-9991	**Fax:** 52-55-52771428
Toll-Free:	
Address: Mineria No. 145, Edificio Central, Mexico City, 11800 Mexico	

GROWTH PLANS/SPECIAL FEATURES:

Empresas ICA S.A. de C.V. (ICA) is one of Mexico's largest engineering, procurement and construction companies. Its operates three divisions: construction (divided into the civil construction and industrial construction segments), infrastructure and housing. The company's civil construction segment builds highways, dams, airports, bridges, tunnels, subways and port facilities primarily in Mexico, with occasional projects in Latin America, the Caribbean, Asia and the U.S. The industrial construction division, through majority owned subsidiary ICA Fluor, builds industrial factories such as refineries, petrochemical plants, cement factories, automotive factories and electrical generation plants. ICA's construction divisions accounted for nearly 79% of the firm's revenues. The infrastructure segment mainly operates airports in Mexico through subsidiary OMA, as well as operating three highway concessions. The housing segment has built over 40,000 homes across Mexico. The firm has entered partnerships with leading companies around the world to develop and carry out new projects. Some of its current permanent partnerships include ICA Fluor (with Fluor Corporation), a construction partnership in the U.S.; Radio (with Solentanche Bachy), specializing in foundations and geotechnical work in Portugal, Spain and Central America; and Los Portales (with Grupo Raffo), developing real estate in Peru. In September 2009, the firm acquired Construcciones Y Trituraciones, S.A. de C.V. for $23.7 million.

FINANCIALS: **Sales and profits are in thousands of dollars—add 000 to get the full amount. 2009 Note: Financial information for 2009 was not available for all companies at press time.**

2009 Sales: $2,441,780	2009 Profits: $-3,240	**U.S. Stock Ticker: ICA**
2008 Sales: $2,020,700	2008 Profits: $58,300	**Int'l Ticker: ICA** Int'l Exchange: Mexico City-BMV
2007 Sales: $2,060,000	2007 Profits: $-72,000	Employees:
2006 Sales: $1,982,000	2006 Profits: $92,000	Fiscal Year Ends: 12/31
2005 Sales: $1,730,800	2005 Profits: $47,200	Parent Company:

SALARIES/BENEFITS:

Pension Plan:	ESOP Stock Plan:	Profit Sharing:	Top Exec. Salary: $	Bonus: $
Savings Plan:	Stock Purch. Plan:		Second Exec. Salary: $	Bonus: $

OTHER THOUGHTS:

Apparent Women Officers or Directors:
Hot Spot for Advancement for Women/Minorities:

LOCATIONS: ("Y" = Yes)

West:	Southwest:	Midwest:	Southeast:	Northeast:	International:
					Y

ENGLOBAL CORP

www.englobal.com

Industry Group Code: 541330 **Ranks within this company's industry group:** Sales: 8 Profits: 8

Properties:		Financial Services:		Construction/Development:		Investments:		Specialty Services:		Brokerage:	
Apartments:		Mortgages:		Commercial Construction:		REIT:		Property Management:		Commercial Sales:	
Malls/Shopping:		Title Insurance:		Residential Construction:				Online Services:		Residential Sales:	
Offices:		Property Insurance:		Land Development:				Software/IT:	Y	Specialty:	
Hotels/Motels:				Support Services:				Consulting:	Y		
Industrial/Warehouses:				Design/Engineering:	Y						
Other:											

TYPES OF BUSINESS:

Engineering Services
Petrochemicals Industry Support Services
Control & Instrumentation Systems
Consulting & Inspection Services
Project Management

BRANDS/DIVISIONS/AFFILIATES:

ENGlobal Power Group

CONTACTS:

Note: Officers with more than one job title may be intentionally listed here more than once.

William A. Coskey, CEO
William A. Coskey, Pres.
Robert W. Raiford, CFO
Robert J. Church, Corp. Mgr.-Human Resources
Alex Schroeder, Mgr.-Corp. IT
Natalie S. Hairston, Corp. Sec./Chief Governance Officer
Michael M. Patton, Sr. VP-Bus. Dev.
Natalie S. Hairston, VP-Investor Rel.
Robert W. Raiford, Treas.
R. David Kelley, Sr. VP-Corp. Svcs.
Don A. Johnson, Mgr.-Health, Safety & Environmental
H. Paul Cohen, VP-Legal Affairs & Contracts
David W. Smith, Pres., ENGlobal Engineering, Inc.
William A. Coskey, Chmn.

Phone: 281-878-1000 **Fax:** 281-878-1010
Toll-Free: 800-411-6040
Address: 654 N. Sam Houston Pkwy E., Ste. 400, Houston, TX 77060-5914 US

GROWTH PLANS/SPECIAL FEATURES:

ENGlobal Corp. is an international provider of engineering services and systems to the petroleum refining, petrochemical, pipeline, production and processing industries. The firm operates in four segments: Engineering, Construction, Automation and Land. The engineering segment provides consulting services including feasibility studies, engineering, design, procurement and construction management. The segment provides these services to the upstream, midstream and downstream energy industries and branches of the U.S. military, and in some instances it delivers its services via in-plant personnel assigned throughout the U.S. and internationally. The construction segment provides construction management personnel and services in the areas of inspection, mechanical integrity, vendor and turnaround surveillance, field support, construction, quality assurance and plant asset management. Its customers include pipeline, refining, utility, chemical, petroleum, petrochemical, oil and gas, and power industries throughout the U.S. Construction segment personnel are typically assigned to client facilities throughout the U.S. The automation segment provides services related to the design, fabrication, and implementation of process distributed control and analyzer systems, advanced automation and information technology projects. This segment's customers include members of the domestic and foreign energy related industries. Automation segment personnel assist in on-site commissioning, start-up and training for the company's specialized systems. The land segment provides land management, right-of-way, environmental compliance and governmental regulatory compliance services primarily to the pipeline, utility and telecom companies and other owner/operators of infrastructure facilities throughout the U.S. and Canada. In August 2009, the firm acquired PCI Management and Consulting Company, which was rebranded as ENGlobal Power Group.

Employees are offered medical, dental and vision insurance; life insurance; flexible spending accounts; disability coverage; a 401(k) plan; educational reimbursement; and employee referral bonuses.

FINANCIALS:

Sales and profits are in thousands of dollars—add 000 to get the full amount. 2009 Note: Financial information for 2009 was not available for all companies at press time.

2009 Sales: $343,462	2009 Profits: $1,233	**U.S. Stock Ticker: ENG**
2008 Sales: $493,332	2008 Profits: $18,258	**Int'l Ticker:** Int'l Exchange:
2007 Sales: $363,227	2007 Profits: $12,464	Employees: 2,000
2006 Sales: $303,090	2006 Profits: $-3,486	Fiscal Year Ends: 12/31
2005 Sales: $233,585	2005 Profits: $4,782	Parent Company:

SALARIES/BENEFITS:

Pension Plan:	ESOP Stock Plan:	Profit Sharing:	Top Exec. Salary: $260,000	Bonus: $116,250
Savings Plan: Y	Stock Purch. Plan:		Second Exec. Salary: $245,000	Bonus: $65,000

OTHER THOUGHTS:

Apparent Women Officers or Directors: 2
Hot Spot for Advancement for Women/Minorities: Y

LOCATIONS: ("Y" = Yes)

West:	Southwest:	Midwest:	Southeast:	Northeast:	International:
Y	Y		Y		Y

ENTERTAINMENT PROPERTIES TRUST

www.eprkc.com

Industry Group Code: 531120 **Ranks within this company's industry group:** Sales: 45 Profits: 26

Properties:		Financial Services:		Construction/Development:		Investments:		Specialty Services:		Brokerage:	
Apartments:		Mortgages:		Commercial Construction:		REIT:	Y	Property Management:		Commercial Sales:	
Malls/Shopping:	Y	Title Insurance:		Residential Construction:				Online Services:		Residential Sales:	
Offices:		Property Insurance:		Land Development:				Software/IT:		Specialty:	
Hotels/Motels:				Support Services:				Consulting:			
Industrial/Warehouses:				Design/Engineering:							
Other:	Y										

TYPES OF BUSINESS:

REIT-Entertainment Properties
Megaplex Movie Theaters
Entertainment Retail Centers
Ski Resorts
Vineyards & Wineries

BRANDS/DIVISIONS/AFFILIATES:

EPR Canada, Inc.

CONTACTS:

Note: Officers with more than one job title may be intentionally listed here more than once.

David M. Brain, CEO
Gregory K. Silvers, COO/VP
David M. Brain, Pres.
Mark A. Peterson, CFO/VP
Gregory K. Silvers, General Counsel/VP
Jonathan Weis, Dir.-Corp. Comm.
Michael Hirons, VP-Finance
Morgan G. (Jerry) Earnest, II, Chief Investment Officer
Robert J. Druten, Chmn.

Phone: 816-472-1700	**Fax:** 816-472-5794
Toll-Free: 888-377-7348	
Address: 30 W. Pershing Rd., Ste. 201, Kansas City, MO 64108 US	

GROWTH PLANS/SPECIAL FEATURES:

Entertainment Properties Trust (EPR) is a self-administered REIT (Real Estate Investment Trust) with approximately 95 multiplex movie theaters, nine entertainment retail centers (ERCs) and other specialty properties. EPR's collection of properties totals 11.9 million square feet, including 7.8 million square feet of multiplex theatre properties and 4.1 million square feet of retail centers, restaurant and other miscellaneous properties. Its multiplex theatres usually have at least 10 screens with elevated, stadium-style seating and amenities such as digital cinema, which allow greater enhancement to audio and visual experiences for theatre patrons. EPR operates multiplexes in 33 U.S. states and Ontario, Canada, and leases to theatre operators such as American Multi-Cinema, Inc. (AMC), which leases 43% of the firm's properties; Muvico Entertainment, LLC; Regal Entertainment Group; Rave Cinemas, LLC; AmStar Cinemas, LLC; Southern Theatres; and Kerasotes Theatres. The firm's ERCs are located in Colorado, New York, California and Ontario, Canada. Land parcels are often leased to restaurant and retail operators adjacent to its theater properties. Tenants of EPR's restaurant properties include Texas Roadhouse, Cherrydale Shops, Stir Crazy, Mad River Mountain, Johnny Carino's, On The Border and Wing Factory, among others. Some of its specialty properties include 10 wineries and eight vineyards located in California and Washington; a metropolitan ski area in Bellefontaine, Ohio; and 22 public charter schools in eight states and Washington, D.C. In December 2009, the company completed its $121 million acquisition of 15 theatres located in Connecticut, Massachusetts, New Jersey, Virginia, Kentucky, Ohio, Michigan and Iowa; collectively, the acquisition adds roughly 52,730 seats and 230 screens to EPR's portfolio, including 59 screens equipped for digital projection and three IMAX screens. In March 2010, the firm acquired a 330,000-square foot entertainment retail property in downtown Toronto, Ontario for approximately $120 million.

FINANCIALS:

Sales and profits are in thousands of dollars—add 000 to get the full amount. 2009 Note: Financial information for 2009 was not available for all companies at press time.

2009 Sales: $270,811	2009 Profits: $-22,199	**U.S. Stock Ticker: EPR**
2008 Sales: $286,140	2008 Profits: $101,710	**Int'l Ticker:** Int'l Exchange:
2007 Sales: $235,615	2007 Profits: $81,251	Employees: 22
2006 Sales: $195,860	2006 Profits: $70,432	Fiscal Year Ends: 12/31
2005 Sales: $144,950	2005 Profits: $57,707	Parent Company:

SALARIES/BENEFITS:

Pension Plan:	ESOP Stock Plan:	Profit Sharing:	Top Exec. Salary: $530,250	Bonus: $400,000
Savings Plan:	Stock Purch. Plan:		Second Exec. Salary: $383,250	Bonus: $287,500

OTHER THOUGHTS:

Apparent Women Officers or Directors:
Hot Spot for Advancement for Women/Minorities:

LOCATIONS: ("Y" = Yes)

West:	Southwest:	Midwest:	Southeast:	Northeast:	International:
Y	Y	Y	Y	Y	Y

EQUITY LIFESTYLE PROPERTIES INC

www.equitylifestyles.com

Industry Group Code: 531110 **Ranks within this company's industry group:** Sales: 7 Profits: 13

Properties:		Financial Services:		Construction/Development:		Investments:		Specialty Services:		Brokerage:	
Apartments:		Mortgages:		Commercial Construction:		REIT:	Y	Property Management:		Commercial Sales:	
Malls/Shopping:		Title Insurance:		Residential Construction:				Online Services:		Residential Sales:	
Offices:		Property Insurance:		Land Development:				Software/IT:		Specialty:	
Hotels/Motels:				Support Services:				Consulting:			
Industrial/Warehouses:				Design/Engineering:							
Other:	Y										

TYPES OF BUSINESS:

Real Estate Investment Trust
Manufactured Home & RV Communities

BRANDS/DIVISIONS/AFFILIATES:

MHC Operating Limited Partnership

CONTACTS:

Note: Officers with more than one job title may be intentionally listed here more than once.

Thomas P. Heneghan, CEO
Joe B. McAdams, Pres.
Michael B. Berman, CFO/Exec. VP
Marguerite Nader, Exec. VP-Sales & Mktg.
Ellen Kelleher, Corp. Sec./Exec. VP
Roger A. Maynard, Exec. VP-Asset Management
Ellen Kelleher, Exec. VP-Property Management
Samuel Zell, Chmn.

Phone: 312-279-1400	**Fax:** 312-279-1710
Toll-Free:	
Address: 2 N. Riverside Plz., Ste. 800, Chicago, IL 60606 US	

GROWTH PLANS/SPECIAL FEATURES:

Equity Lifestyle Properties, Inc. (ELS) is an integrated real estate investment trust (REIT) that owns and operates communities of developed residential sites as well as recreational vehicle (RV) resorts. The company primarily operates through an operating partnership, MHC Trust. The firm owns or has an interest in 304 properties in 27 U.S. states and the Canadian province of British Columbia, consisting of about 110,575 residential sites. The heaviest concentrations of these properties are located in Florida, California and Arizona, with 86 properties, 48 properties and 35 properties, respectively. Additional U.S. sites are located in Texas, Pennsylvania, Washington, Colorado, Oregon, North Carolina, Delaware, New York, Nevada, Virginia, Wisconsin, Indiana, Maine, Illinois, Massachusetts, New Jersey, Michigan, South Carolina, New Hampshire, Ohio, Tennessee, Utah, Alabama and Kentucky. These communities are designed and improved for the placement of detached, single-family manufactured homes and RVs that are produced off-site, then installed and set on residential sites within the community. The owner of each home leases the site on which it is located, while the firm handles property infrastructure issues, such as water, sewage and power. Sites typically contain centralized entrances, paved streets, curbs, gutters, parkways, clubhouses for social activities and recreation, swimming pools, shuffleboard courts, tennis courts, laundry facilities and cable television service, among other amenities. Each community is designed to attract, and is marketed to, retirees, empty-nesters, families or first-time homeowners. The company focuses on owning properties in or near large metropolitan markets, as well as popular retirement and vacation destinations.

ELS offers its employees medical coverage, life and disability insurance, a 401(k) plan and a bonus program, among other benefits.

FINANCIALS:

Sales and profits are in thousands of dollars—add 000 to get the full amount. 2009 Note: Financial information for 2009 was not available for all companies at press time.

2009 Sales: $479,295	2009 Profits: $34,005	**U.S. Stock Ticker: ELS**
2008 Sales: $419,349	2008 Profits: $18,303	**Int'l Ticker:** Int'l Exchange:
2007 Sales: $376,154	2007 Profits: $32,102	Employees: 3,200
2006 Sales: $346,383	2006 Profits: $16,632	Fiscal Year Ends: 12/31
2005 Sales: $315,018	2005 Profits: $-2,333	Parent Company:

SALARIES/BENEFITS:

Pension Plan:	ESOP Stock Plan:	Profit Sharing:	Top Exec. Salary: $382,454	Bonus: $573,681
Savings Plan: Y	Stock Purch. Plan:		Second Exec. Salary: $311,428	Bonus: $370,210

OTHER THOUGHTS:

Apparent Women Officers or Directors: 3
Hot Spot for Advancement for Women/Minorities: Y

LOCATIONS: ("Y" = Yes)

West:	Southwest:	Midwest:	Southeast:	Northeast:	International:
Y	Y	Y	Y	Y	Y

EQUITY OFFICE PROPERTIES TRUST

www.equityoffice.com

Industry Group Code: 531120 **Ranks within this company's industry group:** Sales: Profits:

Properties:		Financial Services:		Construction/Development:		Investments:		Specialty Services:		Brokerage:	
Apartments:		Mortgages:		Commercial Construction:		REIT:	Y	Property Management:	Y	Commercial Sales:	
Malls/Shopping:		Title Insurance:		Residential Construction:				Online Services:		Residential Sales:	
Offices:	Y	Property Insurance:		Land Development:				Software/IT:		Specialty:	
Hotels/Motels:				Support Services:				Consulting:			
Industrial/Warehouses:				Design/Engineering:							
Other:											

TYPES OF BUSINESS:

Real Estate Investment Trust
Office Properties
Property Management

BRANDS/DIVISIONS/AFFILIATES:

Beacon Properties, Inc.
Cornerstone Properties, Inc.
Spieker Properties, Inc.
Blackstone Group (The)
CarrAmerica Properties
Trizec Properties, Inc.
EOP Operating Limited Partnership

CONTACTS:

Note: Officers with more than one job title may be intentionally listed here more than once.

Christopher Peatross, CEO
Kurt Heister, COO
Christopher Peatross, Pres.
Laura Klimenko, VP-Human Resources
Brian Campbell, Chief Acct. Officer/VP
Tom Bakke, Market Managing Dir.-Boston
Adam Goldenberg, Market Managing Dir.-New York
Joe Moe, Market Managing Dir.-Northern California
Frank Campbell, Market Managing Dir.-Southern California

Phone: 312-466-3300	**Fax:**
Toll-Free:	
Address: 2 N. Riverside Plz., Chicago, IL 60606 US	

GROWTH PLANS/SPECIAL FEATURES:

Equity Office Properties Trust (EOP), operating through its various affiliates and subsidiaries, is one of the largest real estate investment trusts (REITs) in the U.S. At last count, the company owned over 300 properties, most of which are Class A office buildings, in Denver, Colorado; Los Angeles, San Diego and Northern California; Seattle, Washington; Austin and Dallas Texas; Minneapolis, Minnesota; New Orleans, Louisiana; Atlanta, Georgia; Boston, Massachusetts; Columbus, Ohio; Miami, Florida; and New York City. EOP provides a wide range of office options for local, regional and national customers. The firm has a history of strategic acquisitions that have enabled it to quadruple in size since its 1997 initial public offering. These acquisitions, totaling more than $17 billion in value, include mergers with Beacon Properties, Inc.; Cornerstone Properties, Inc.; and Spieker Properties, Inc. The Blackstone Group owns the firm. Subsidiary, Equity Office Properties was merged with EOP Operating Limited Partnership and affiliates of Blackstone Real Estate Partners, including CarrAmerica Properties and Trizec Properties. Since the acquisition, Blackstone has sold $14.6 billion worth of EOP buildings.

Employees of the firm are offered a benefits package that includes a 401(k) savings program with company match, health and dependent care flexible spending accounts, insurance benefits for domestic partners, adoption assistance, flexible work arrangements, educational assistance, an employee assistance program and a commuter program.

FINANCIALS:

Sales and profits are in thousands of dollars—add 000 to get the full amount. 2009 Note: Financial information for 2009 was not available for all companies at press time.

2009 Sales: $	2009 Profits: $	**U.S. Stock Ticker: Private**
2008 Sales: $	2008 Profits: $	**Int'l Ticker:** Int'l Exchange:
2007 Sales: $	2007 Profits: $	Employees:
2006 Sales: $	2006 Profits: $	Fiscal Year Ends: 12/31
2005 Sales: $3,000,589	2005 Profits: $42,939	Parent Company: BLACKSTONE GROUP LP (THE)

SALARIES/BENEFITS:

Pension Plan:	ESOP Stock Plan:	Profit Sharing:	Top Exec. Salary: $	Bonus: $
Savings Plan: Y	Stock Purch. Plan:		Second Exec. Salary: $	Bonus: $

OTHER THOUGHTS:

Apparent Women Officers or Directors: 1
Hot Spot for Advancement for Women/Minorities: Y

LOCATIONS: ("Y" = Yes)

West:	Southwest:	Midwest:	Southeast:	Northeast:	International:
Y	Y	Y	Y	Y	

EQUITY ONE INC

www.equityone.net

Industry Group Code: 531120 **Ranks within this company's industry group:** Sales: 52 Profits: 40

Properties:		Financial Services:		Construction/Development:		Investments:		Specialty Services:		Brokerage:	
Apartments:		Mortgages:		Commercial Construction:		REIT:	Y	Property Management:	Y	Commercial Sales:	
Malls/Shopping:	Y	Title Insurance:		Residential Construction:				Online Services:		Residential Sales:	
Offices:		Property Insurance:		Land Development:				Software/IT:		Specialty:	
Hotels/Motels:				Support Services:				Consulting:			
Industrial/Warehouses:				Design/Engineering:							
Other:											

TYPES OF BUSINESS:

Real Estate Investment Trust
Property Management
Shopping Centers

BRANDS/DIVISIONS/AFFILIATES:

Global Retail Investors LLC
DIM Vastgoed NV

CONTACTS:

Note: Officers with more than one job title may be intentionally listed here more than once.

Jeffrey S. Olson, CEO
Thomas Caputo, Pres.
Gregory R. Andrews, CFO/Exec. VP
Mark Langer, Chief Admin. Officer
Arthur L. Gallagher, General Counsel/Exec. VP
Michael J. Berfield, VP-Dev.
Deborah Cheek, Chief Acct. Officer
Lauren Holden, VP-Portfolio Mgmt.
Chaim Katzman, Chmn.

Phone: 305-947-1664	**Fax:** 305-947-1734
Toll-Free:	
Address: 1600 NE Miami Gardens Dr., North Miami Beach, FL 33179 US	

GROWTH PLANS/SPECIAL FEATURES:

Equity One, Inc. is a Florida-based real estate investment trust (REIT) that acquires, renovates, develops and manages neighborhood shopping centers anchored by national and regional supermarket chains and other necessity-oriented retailers, such as drug stores or discount retail stores. Its 19 million-square-foot portfolio consists of 182 properties primarily located in Alabama, Connecticut, Florida, Georgia, Louisiana, Massachusetts, Mississippi, New York, North Carolina, South Carolina and Virginia. These properties include 168 shopping centers, three development/redevelopment properties, six non-retail properties and five parcels of land. The firm owns a 10% interest in GRI-EQY I, LLC, a joint venture with Global Retail Investors LLC, which owns ten neighborhood shopping centers. It also owns a 20% interest in G&I VI Investment South Florida Portfolio, LLC, an affiliate of DRA Advisors LLC, which owns one office building and two neighborhood shopping centers. The company seeks to maximize the value of its existing shopping centers by leasing and re-leasing properties at higher rental rates and acquiring new commercial properties for rent. The company has leased to supermarkets, such as Albertsons, Food Lion, H.E.B., Kash N' Karry and Publix Super Markets (the leading Equity One tenant with 52 leases), as well as national retailers such as Bed Bath & Beyond, Office Depot, Best Buy, Blockbuster, CVS Pharmacy, Eckerd, Home Depot, Kmart, Lowe's, Walgreens and Wal-Mart. In November 2009, the company acquired a 22-acre property on Long Island, New York. In April 2010, the firm acquired two shopping centers: Veranda Shoppes in Plantation, Florida, and Copps Hill Plaza in Ridgefield, Connecticut.

The company offers its employees benefits that include medical and dental insurance; flexible spending accounts; short- and long-term disability insurance; a 401(k) plan; an employee stock purchase plan; and a tuition assistance program.

FINANCIALS:

Sales and profits are in thousands of dollars—add 000 to get the full amount. 2009 Note: Financial information for 2009 was not available for all companies at press time.

2009 Sales: $237,449	2009 Profits: $35,008	**U.S. Stock Ticker: EQY**
2008 Sales: $239,029	2008 Profits: $35,008	**Int'l Ticker:** Int'l Exchange:
2007 Sales: $246,109	2007 Profits: $69,385	Employees: 160
2006 Sales: $224,937	2006 Profits: $176,955	Fiscal Year Ends: 12/31
2005 Sales: $201,781	2005 Profits: $92,741	Parent Company:

SALARIES/BENEFITS:

Pension Plan:	ESOP Stock Plan:	Profit Sharing:	Top Exec. Salary: $605,475	Bonus: $1,014,000
Savings Plan: Y	Stock Purch. Plan:		Second Exec. Salary: $540,000	Bonus: $150,000

OTHER THOUGHTS:

Apparent Women Officers or Directors: 4
Hot Spot for Advancement for Women/Minorities: Y

LOCATIONS: ("Y" = Yes)

West:	Southwest:	Midwest:	Southeast:	Northeast:	International:
Y			Y	Y	

EQUITY RESIDENTIAL

www.equityresidential.com

Industry Group Code: 531110 **Ranks within this company's industry group:** Sales: 1 Profits: 2

Properties:		Financial Services:		Construction/Development:		Investments:		Specialty Services:		Brokerage:	
Apartments:	Y	Mortgages:		Commercial Construction:		REIT:	Y	Property Management:	Y	Commercial Sales:	
Malls/Shopping:		Title Insurance:		Residential Construction:				Online Services:		Residential Sales:	
Offices:		Property Insurance:		Land Development:				Software/IT:		Specialty:	
Hotels/Motels:				Support Services:				Consulting:			
Industrial/Warehouses:				Design/Engineering:							
Other:											

TYPES OF BUSINESS:

Real Estate Investment Trust
Apartment Communities
Property Management

BRANDS/DIVISIONS/AFFILIATES:

425 Mass

CONTACTS:

Note: Officers with more than one job title may be intentionally listed here more than once.

David J. Neithercut, CEO
David J. Neithercut, Pres.
Mark J. Parrell, CFO/Exec. VP
John Powers, Exec. VP-Human Resources
Bruce C. Strohm, General Counsel/Exec. VP
David S. Santee, Exec. VP-Oper.
Mark N. Tennison, Exec. VP-Dev.
Alan W. George, Chief Investment Officer/Exec. VP
Frederick C. Tuomi, Pres., Property Mgmt.
Yasmina Duwe, Sr. VP/Sec.
Samuel Zell, Chmn.

Phone: 312-474-1300	**Fax:**
Toll-Free:	
Address: 2 N. Riverside Plz., Chicago, IL 60606 US	

GROWTH PLANS/SPECIAL FEATURES:

Equity Residential is a real estate investment trust (REIT) engaged in the acquisition, development and management of apartment properties across the U.S. The firm conducts all operations through operating partnership ERP Operating Limited Partnership, of which it owns 95.2%. One of the leading publicly traded owners and operators of multiple-family properties in the U.S., the firm owns all or a portion of 494 properties throughout 23 states and Washington, D.C., totaling around 136,886 units. Its properties are highly diversified with respect to design and geography, ranging from high-rise to garden styles. Specially designed corporate and military housing plans are available. Corporate housing benefits include fully furnished units, free local calling, basic cable, short-term leases and direct billing options. Military housing provides similar benefits in addition to government credit card acceptance and military discounts. The firm's corporate housing and condominium conversion businesses are handled through subsidiaries. In 2010, the company acquired luxury apartment, 425 Mass, in Washington, D.C. for $167 million; as well as three high-rise apartment towers in Manhattan for a combined total of $475 million.

Employees are offered medical, dental and vision coverage; life and AD&D insurance; travel accident insurance; disability insurance; flexible spending accounts; a 401(k) plan; an employee stock purchase plan; profit sharing; discounts on apartment rent; home and auto insurance discounts; and credit card union membership.

FINANCIALS:

Sales and profits are in thousands of dollars—add 000 to get the full amount. 2009 Note: Financial information for 2009 was not available for all companies at press time.

2009 Sales: $1,943,711	2009 Profits: $382,029	**U.S. Stock Ticker: EQR**
2008 Sales: $1,975,669	2008 Profits: $436,413	**Int'l Ticker:** Int'l Exchange:
2007 Sales: $1,824,046	2007 Profits: $1,047,356	Employees: 4,100
2006 Sales: $1,702,541	2006 Profits: $1,072,844	Fiscal Year Ends: 12/31
2005 Sales: $1,495,510	2005 Profits: $861,793	Parent Company:

SALARIES/BENEFITS:

Pension Plan:	ESOP Stock Plan:	Profit Sharing: Y	Top Exec. Salary: $625,000	Bonus: $719,063
Savings Plan: Y	Stock Purch. Plan: Y		Second Exec. Salary: $425,000	Bonus: $346,587

OTHER THOUGHTS:

Apparent Women Officers or Directors: 2
Hot Spot for Advancement for Women/Minorities:

LOCATIONS: ("Y" = Yes)

West:	Southwest:	Midwest:	Southeast:	Northeast:	International:
Y	Y	Y	Y	Y	

ERICKSON RETIREMENT COMMUNITIES

www.ericksonliving.com

Industry Group Code: 623110 **Ranks within this company's industry group:** Sales: Profits:

Properties:		Financial Services:		Construction/Development:		Investments:		Specialty Services:		Brokerage:	
Apartments:	Y	Mortgages:		Commercial Construction:		REIT:		Property Management:		Commercial Sales:	
Malls/Shopping:		Title Insurance:		Residential Construction:				Online Services:		Residential Sales:	
Offices:		Property Insurance:		Land Development:				Software/IT:		Specialty:	
Hotels/Motels:				Support Services:				Consulting:			
Industrial/Warehouses:				Design/Engineering:							
Other:	Y										

TYPES OF BUSINESS:

Retirement Communities
Supplemental Health Insurance

BRANDS/DIVISIONS/AFFILIATES:

Erickson Advantage

CONTACTS:

Note: Officers with more than one job title may be intentionally listed here more than once.

Rick Grindrod, CEO
Mark R. Erickson, COO
Jeffrey A. Jacobson, CFO
Tom Neubauer, Exec. VP-Sales
Diane Flanders, VP-Benefits & Compensation
Matthew J. Narrett, Chief Medical Officer/Exec. VP
Gerald F. Doherty, General Counsel/Exec. VP
Debra B. Doyle, Exec. VP-Health & Oper.
Scott Gensler, Sr. VP-Planning
Thomas L. Brod, Exec. VP-Finance
Scott Gensler, Sr. VP-Mktg. Oper.
Gary D. Hibbs, Regional Exec. Dir.-Northeast
Kerry Jones, Sr. VP-Oper.
William F. Walker, Sr. VP-Acquisitions
John C. Erickson, Chmn.

Phone: 410-242-2880	**Fax:** 410-737-8854
Toll-Free:	
Address: 701 Maiden Choice Lane, Catonsville, MD 21228 US	

GROWTH PLANS/SPECIAL FEATURES:

Erickson Retirement Communities is a real estate firm focused on the development and operation of retirement communities for men and women ages 62 and up. The firm's portfolio consists of 19 properties spread throughout Colorado, Illinois, Kansas, Maryland, Massachusetts, Michigan, New Jersey, Pennsylvania, Texas, and Virginia, which altogether house more than 22,000 senior citizens. The firm's communities feature apartment homes with a variety of floor plans, primarily in one- or two-bedroom options. Each apartment home is designed to promote an independent lifestyle and all Erickson communities provide residents with services including transportation, grounds maintenance, and housekeeping. Erickson's retirement communities feature amenities including restaurants, stores and a Fitness Center with full-time trainers. Additionally, each community features a medical center staffed by geriatricians who practice exclusively in Erickson communities. Residents pay an all-inclusive monthly service fee, which covers all rent and maintenance service costs. In addition to its retirement communities, Erickson provides the Erickson Advantage supplemental health insurance plan and the Erickson Health health and wellness maintenance system, which focuses on fitness and preventative wellness programs. In 2009, Erickson's latest community, Renaissance Gardens, commenced operations in Lincolnshire, Illinois.

FINANCIALS:

Sales and profits are in thousands of dollars—add 000 to get the full amount. 2009 Note: Financial information for 2009 was not available for all companies at press time.

2009 Sales: $	2009 Profits: $	**U.S. Stock Ticker: Private**
2008 Sales: $	2008 Profits: $	**Int'l Ticker:** Int'l Exchange:
2007 Sales: $	2007 Profits: $	Employees:
2006 Sales: $	2006 Profits: $	Fiscal Year Ends:
2005 Sales: $	2005 Profits: $	Parent Company:

SALARIES/BENEFITS:

Pension Plan:	ESOP Stock Plan:	Profit Sharing:	Top Exec. Salary: $	Bonus: $
Savings Plan:	Stock Purch. Plan:		Second Exec. Salary: $	Bonus: $

OTHER THOUGHTS:

Apparent Women Officers or Directors: 9
Hot Spot for Advancement for Women/Minorities: Y

LOCATIONS: ("Y" = Yes)

West:	Southwest:	Midwest:	Southeast:	Northeast:	International:
Y	Y	Y	Y	Y	

ESSEX PROPERTY TRUST INC

www.essexpropertytrust.com

Industry Group Code: 531110 **Ranks within this company's industry group:** Sales: 8 Profits: 7

Properties:		Financial Services:		Construction/Development:		Investments:		Specialty Services:		Brokerage:	
Apartments:	Y	Mortgages:		Commercial Construction:		REIT:	Y	Property Management:	Y	Commercial Sales:	
Malls/Shopping:		Title Insurance:		Residential Construction:				Online Services:		Residential Sales:	
Offices:	Y	Property Insurance:		Land Development:				Software/IT:		Specialty:	
Hotels/Motels:				Support Services:				Consulting:			
Industrial/Warehouses:				Design/Engineering:							
Other:											

TYPES OF BUSINESS:

Real Estate Investment Trust
Apartments
Residential Brokerage
Property Management

BRANDS/DIVISIONS/AFFILIATES:

Essex Portfolio, L.P.

CONTACTS:

Note: Officers with more than one job title may be intentionally listed here more than once.

Keith R. Guericke, CEO
Michael J. Schall, COO/Sr. Exec. VP
Keith R. Guericke, Pres.
Michael T. Dance, CFO/Exec. VP
Darcey Forbes, Dir.-Mktg.
Suzanne M. Golden, VP-Human Resources
Jamie Williams, VP-IT
Jordan E. Ritter, General Counsel/Sr. VP
John D. Eudy, Exec. VP-Dev.
Bryan G. Hunt, Chief Acct. Officer/VP
Craig K. Zimmerman, Exec. VP-Acquisitions
John F. Burkart, Sr. VP/Fund Mgr.-Essex Apartment Value Fund
Mark J. Mikl, Sr. VP-Asset Management
Maura Lederer, VP-Regional Dev. Mgr.
George M. Marcus, Chmn.

Phone: 650-494-3700	**Fax:** 650-494-8743
Toll-Free:	
Address: 925 E. Meadow Dr., Palo Alto, CA 94303 US	

GROWTH PLANS/SPECIAL FEATURES:

Essex Property Trust, Inc. (EPT) is a self-administered and self-managed real estate investment trust (REIT) that acquires, develops, redevelops and manages multifamily residential properties in West Coast communities. The firm owns all of its interest in properties either directly or through Essex Portfolio, L.P., in which EPT owns about 92% general partnership interest and is the sole general partner. The company's holdings encompass 133 apartment communities, aggregating approximately 27,248 units; five office buildings, totaling roughly 215,840 square feet; and four active development projects, with 581 units in various stages of completion. Most of the firm's holdings are concentrated in coastal markets in Southern California, the San Francisco Bay area and the Seattle, Washington metropolitan area. EPT's investment strategy has various components, including monitoring of current markets as well as the evaluation of new markets in search of areas with relatively high rental growth potential. The company utilizes a research model that examines property liquidity, demand for housing, enhanced demand for rentals and demand based on quality of life factors in order to evaluate potential acquisitions. EPT's development program allows the company to acquire land outright or form a joint venture with a developer. Acquisitions can also be structured as all-cash or through the assumption of a loan. The company typically targets properties with over 100 units with a total value greater than $10 million. Over the course of 2009, the firm sold five apartment complexes, for a total of $38 million. In December 2009, EPT purchased a 75-unit apartment community in Encino, California for approximately $16 million. In January 2010, the company acquired a 115-unit condominium development project in Irvine, California for $27 million.

FINANCIALS:

Sales and profits are in thousands of dollars—add 000 to get the full amount. 2009 Note: Financial information for 2009 was not available for all companies at press time.

2009 Sales: $411,389	2009 Profits: $53,739	**U.S. Stock Ticker: ESS**
2008 Sales: $408,434	2008 Profits: $84,395	**Int'l Ticker:** Int'l Exchange:
2007 Sales: $374,749	2007 Profits: $203,061	Employees: 938
2006 Sales: $334,102	2006 Profits: $62,748	Fiscal Year Ends: 12/31
2005 Sales: $314,186	2005 Profits: $79,716	Parent Company:

SALARIES/BENEFITS:

Pension Plan:	ESOP Stock Plan:	Profit Sharing:	Top Exec. Salary: $350,000	Bonus: $400,000
Savings Plan: Y	Stock Purch. Plan:		Second Exec. Salary: $300,000	Bonus: $300,000

OTHER THOUGHTS:

Apparent Women Officers or Directors: 8
Hot Spot for Advancement for Women/Minorities: Y

LOCATIONS: ("Y" = Yes)

West:	Southwest:	Midwest:	Southeast:	Northeast:	International:
Y					

EVERGRANDE REAL ESTATE GROUP

www.evergrande.com

Industry Group Code: 5311 **Ranks within this company's industry group:** Sales: Profits:

Properties:		Financial Services:		Construction/Development:		Investments:		Specialty Services:		Brokerage:	
Apartments:	Y	Mortgages:		Commercial Construction:	Y	REIT:		Property Management:	Y	Commercial Sales:	
Malls/Shopping:		Title Insurance:		Residential Construction:	Y			Online Services:		Residential Sales:	
Offices:	Y	Property Insurance:		Land Development:	Y			Software/IT:		Specialty:	
Hotels/Motels:	Y			Support Services:	Y			Consulting:			
Industrial/Warehouses:				Design/Engineering:	Y						
Other:											

TYPES OF BUSINESS:

Real Estate Development
Architectural Engineering Services
Architectural Design Services
Property Management Services

BRANDS/DIVISIONS/AFFILIATES:

Evergrande Real Estate Development Co., Ltd.
Evergrande Architectural Engineering Company
Evergrande Architectural Design Institute
Evergrande Property Management Company
Splendor Property Group Co., Ltd.

CONTACTS: *Note: Officers with more than one job title may be intentionally listed here more than once.*

Xia Haijun, CEO
Tse Wai Wah, CFO
He Miaoling, VP-Mktg.
Li Gang, Exec. VP
Xu Xiangwu, VP
Xu Wen, VP
Lai Lixin, VP

Phone: 86-20-3830-2222 **Fax:** 86-20-3830-2233
Toll-Free:
Address: Talent Building, 45 Tianhe Rd., 23rd Fl., Guangzhou City, 510075 China

GROWTH PLANS/SPECIAL FEATURES:

Evergrande Real Estate Group is one of the largest real estate developers in China. The firm is primarily engaged in the planning, design, development and construction of real estate, and also offers various property management activities. Evergrande's portfolio of real estate comprises 57 properties throughout China. Major projects, comprising high-end residential, hotel and commercial properties, include the Evergrande Palace, Evergrande Metropolis, Evergrande City, Evergrande Oasis and Evergrande Splendor. The firm operates in 25 major Chinese including Guangzhou, Tianjin, Chongqing, Shenyang, Wuhan, Chengdu, Nanjing, Xi'an, Changsha, Taiyuan, Kunming, and Hefei. Evergrande's subsidiaries include Evergrande Real Estate Development Co., Ltd., which is a real estate development company that develops roughly 74.2 million square feet per year. Evergrande Architectural Engineering Company is an architectural engineering company that focuses primarily on residential buildings. Evergrande Architectural Design Institute offers architectural design services for residential buildings. Evergrande Property Management Company, operating via Splendor Property Group Co., Ltd., manages a variety of properties throughout China, including multi-storey residential buildings, high-rise residential buildings, independent villas and commercial properties.

FINANCIALS: **Sales and profits are in thousands of dollars—add 000 to get the full amount. 2009 Note: Financial information for 2009 was not available for all companies at press time.**

2009 Sales: $	2009 Profits: $	**U.S. Stock Ticker:**
2008 Sales: $	2008 Profits: $	**Int'l Ticker: 3333** Int'l Exchange: Hong Kong-HKEX
2007 Sales: $	2007 Profits: $	Employees:
2006 Sales: $	2006 Profits: $	Fiscal Year Ends:
2005 Sales: $	2005 Profits: $	Parent Company:

SALARIES/BENEFITS:

Pension Plan:	ESOP Stock Plan:	Profit Sharing:	Top Exec. Salary: $	Bonus: $
Savings Plan:	Stock Purch. Plan:		Second Exec. Salary: $	Bonus: $

OTHER THOUGHTS:

Apparent Women Officers or Directors: 1
Hot Spot for Advancement for Women/Minorities:

LOCATIONS: ("Y" = Yes)

West:	Southwest:	Midwest:	Southeast:	Northeast:	International:
					Y

EXTENDICARE REAL ESTATE INVESTMENT TRUST

www.extendicare.com

Industry Group Code: 623110 **Ranks within this company's industry group:** Sales: 3 Profits: 1

Properties:		Financial Services:		Construction/Development:		Investments:		Specialty Services:		Brokerage:	
Apartments:		Mortgages:		Commercial Construction:		REIT:		Property Management:		Commercial Sales:	
Malls/Shopping:		Title Insurance:		Residential Construction:				Online Services:		Residential Sales:	
Offices:		Property Insurance:		Land Development:				Software/IT:		Specialty:	
Hotels/Motels:				Support Services:				Consulting:			
Industrial/Warehouses:				Design/Engineering:							
Other:	Y										

TYPES OF BUSINESS:

Long-Term Care
Assisted Living Facilities
Sub-Acute Care
Rehabilitative Services

BRANDS/DIVISIONS/AFFILIATES:

Extendicare Health Services, Inc.
Extendicare REIT
Extendicare Canada, Inc.
ProStep
ParaMed

CONTACTS:

Note: Officers with more than one job title may be intentionally listed here more than once.

Timothy L. Lukenda, CEO
Timothy L. Lukenda, Pres.
Douglas J. Harris, CFO/Sr. VP
Jillian E. Fountain, Corp. Sec.
Elaine E. Everson, Controller/VP
Mel Rhinelander, Vice Chmn.
Paul Tuttle, Pres., Canadian Oper.
Cristina McKey, VP-Eastern Oper., Extendicare Canada
Wayne McKendrick, VP-Western Oper., Extendicare Canada
Mel Rhinelander, Chmn.

Phone: 905-470-4000	**Fax:** 905-470-5588
Toll-Free:	
Address: 3000 Steeles Ave. E., Ste. 700, Markham, ON L3R 9W2 Canada	

GROWTH PLANS/SPECIAL FEATURES:

Extendicare Real Estate Investment Trust, formerly Extendicare, Inc., is a Canadian real estate investment trust (REIT) operating long-term care facilities and related services. Through its subsidiaries it operates roughly 266 (185 in the U.S.) long-term care and assisted living facilities across North America, with a total capacity of 30,000 residents. Through its operations in the U.S., Extendicare offers nursing care, assisted living and related medical specialty services, while home health care services are provided in Canada. All of these facilities are operated through two operating subsidiaries: Extendicare Health Services, Inc. (EHSI), based in the U.S., and Extendicare Canada, Inc., based in Canada. EHSI offers, in addition to standard nursing and assistance, specialty care services such as sub-acute care and rehabilitative therapy services through ProStep, the company's progressive step rehabilitation service. Virtual Care Provider, Inc., also operating in the U.S., provides information technology services to small long-term care providers. In Canada, Extendicare offers ParaMed, which provides home health care services to subscribers. In addition to these subsidiaries and products, the firm offers management and consulting services and group supply purchasing services for third-party customers.

Extendicare offers its employees and their children educational assistance programs, as well as scholarship programs for those pursuing health care professions.

FINANCIALS:

Sales and profits are in thousands of dollars—add 000 to get the full amount. 2009 Note: Financial information for 2009 was not available for all companies at press time.

2009 Sales: $2,166,230	2009 Profits: $77,720	**U.S. Stock Ticker:**
2008 Sales: $1,686,690	2008 Profits: $11,350	**Int'l Ticker: EXE** Int'l Exchange: Toronto-TSX
2007 Sales: $1,441,150	2007 Profits: $57,500	Employees: 38,000
2006 Sales: $1,664,300	2006 Profits: $-34,300	Fiscal Year Ends: 12/31
2005 Sales: $1,698,634	2005 Profits: $81,930	Parent Company:

SALARIES/BENEFITS:

Pension Plan:	ESOP Stock Plan:	Profit Sharing:	Top Exec. Salary: $544,685	Bonus: $370,453
Savings Plan:	Stock Purch. Plan:		Second Exec. Salary: $276,727	Bonus: $54,315

OTHER THOUGHTS:

Apparent Women Officers or Directors: 5
Hot Spot for Advancement for Women/Minorities: Y

LOCATIONS: ("Y" = Yes)

West:	Southwest:	Midwest:	Southeast:	Northeast:	International:
Y		Y		Y	Y

FAIRMONT HOMES INC

www.fairmonthomes.com

Industry Group Code: 321991 **Ranks within this company's industry group:** Sales: Profits:

Properties:		Financial Services:		Construction/Development:		Investments:		Specialty Services:		Brokerage:	
Apartments:		Mortgages:		Commercial Construction:		REIT:		Property Management:		Commercial Sales:	
Malls/Shopping:		Title Insurance:		Residential Construction:	Y			Online Services:		Residential Sales:	
Offices:		Property Insurance:		Land Development:				Software/IT:		Specialty:	
Hotels/Motels:				Support Services:				Consulting:			
Industrial/Warehouses:				Design/Engineering:							
Other:											

TYPES OF BUSINESS:

Manufactured Housing
Recreational Vehicles

BRANDS/DIVISIONS/AFFILIATES:

Owens Corning
Moen
Georgia-Pacific Corp
Whirpool Appliances
Gulf Stream Coach Inc
Supernova
Touring Cruiser
Canyon Trail

CONTACTS: *Note: Officers with more than one job title may be intentionally listed here more than once.*

James F. Shea, CEO
Edward Ludwick, Pres.
Rick Jones, Dir.-Human Resources
Judy Stapleton, Mgr.-Safety
Tim Rock, Dir.-Quality
James F. Shea, Chmn.
Bob Hasse, Dir.-Purchasing

Phone: 574-773-7941	**Fax:** 574-773-2185
Toll-Free:	
Address: 502 S. Oakland Ave., Nappanee, IN 46550 US	

GROWTH PLANS/SPECIAL FEATURES:

Fairmont Homes, Inc., a family owned and operated business, makes manufactured housing, including single- and multi-section homes with up to 2,330 square feet. It offers several floor plans that feature 2-5 bedrooms, 1-3 bathrooms and extra features such as a study, retreat room, library, utility room, family room, great room, porch, basement, den, breakfast nook, dining room, living room, sunroom, morning room, sitting room and park trailer. The company also offers luxury features such as Amish-crafted cabinetry and custom designed kitchens. Fairmont has retailers located in 21 states throughout the Midwestern and Northeastern U.S. The firm's suppliers include Owens Corning, Moen, Georgia-Pacific, Whirlpool Appliances, Trane Furnaces, Style Crest Siding, Honeywell Thermostats, Congoleum Flooring and Shaw Carpets. In addition to manufactured housing, Fairmont's Gulf Stream Coach subsidiary manufactures a full line of recreational vehicles, offering 26 brands and more than 100 models. Gulf Stream brands include the luxury brands, Scenic Cruiser, Independence, Sun Voyager, Constellation, Canyon Trail, Caribbean, Conquest, Yellowstone, Sedona, Supernova, Touring Cruiser and Montaj.

Employees of the company receive medical and dental coverage; an on-site country club with a swimming pool and golf course; a 401(k) plan; life insurance; cancer insurance; wellness benefits; and prescription plan.

FINANCIALS: **Sales and profits are in thousands of dollars—add 000 to get the full amount. 2009 Note: Financial information for 2009 was not available for all companies at press time.**

2009 Sales: $	2009 Profits: $	**U.S. Stock Ticker: Private**
2008 Sales: $	2008 Profits: $	**Int'l Ticker:** Int'l Exchange:
2007 Sales: $	2007 Profits: $	Employees:
2006 Sales: $	2006 Profits: $	Fiscal Year Ends: 12/31
2005 Sales: $	2005 Profits: $	Parent Company:

SALARIES/BENEFITS:

Pension Plan:	ESOP Stock Plan:	Profit Sharing:	Top Exec. Salary: $	Bonus: $
Savings Plan: Y	Stock Purch. Plan:		Second Exec. Salary: $	Bonus: $

OTHER THOUGHTS:

Apparent Women Officers or Directors: 1
Hot Spot for Advancement for Women/Minorities:

LOCATIONS: ("Y" = Yes)

West:	Southwest:	Midwest:	Southeast:	Northeast:	International:
		Y			

FAIRMONT RAFFLES HOTELS INTERNATIONAL INC

www.fairmont.com

Industry Group Code: 721110 **Ranks within this company's industry group:** Sales: Profits:

Properties:		Financial Services:		Construction/Development:		Investments:		Specialty Services:		Brokerage:	
Apartments:		Mortgages:		Commercial Construction:		REIT:		Property Management:	Y	Commercial Sales:	
Malls/Shopping:		Title Insurance:		Residential Construction:				Online Services:	Y	Residential Sales:	
Offices:		Property Insurance:		Land Development:				Software/IT:		Specialty:	
Hotels/Motels:	Y			Support Services:				Consulting:			
Industrial/Warehouses:				Design/Engineering:							
Other:	Y										

TYPES OF BUSINESS:

Hotels, Luxury
Spa Services
Real Estate Holdings

BRANDS/DIVISIONS/AFFILIATES:

Fairmont Hotels & Resorts
Farimont Gold
Raffles Hotels & Resorts
Fairmont Golf
Fairmont Residences
Fairmont San Francisco

CONTACTS:

Note: Officers with more than one job title may be intentionally listed here more than once.

William R. Fatt, CEO
Chris J. Cahill, COO
Thomas Storey, Pres.
Beatriz Fuentes, Sr. Mgr.-Sales & Mktg.
Beatriz Fuentes, Sr. Mgr.-Public Rel.

Phone: 416-874-2600 **Fax:** 416-874-2601
Toll-Free: 800-257-7544
Address: 100 Wellington St. W., Canadian Pacific Tower, Toronto, ON M5K 1B7 Canada

GROWTH PLANS/SPECIAL FEATURES:

Fairmont Raffles Hotels International, created in mid-2006 by the combination of Fairmont Hotels and Raffles Hotels, is one of the world's largest luxury hotel firms. It operates approximately 100 hotels worldwide under the Raffles, Fairmont and Swissotel brand names. Owners of the firm include Kingdom Holding Company and Colony Capital. The firm offers many services to its business travel clients such as high-speed Internet access; a 24 hour technology help desk; work centers with photocopying services, secretarial services, a private lounge and boardroom; printers for in-room use; a 24 hour fax service; and express checkout. The Fairmont offers various types of resort accommodations including spa resorts, golf resorts, ski resorts, Fairmont Gold and Fairmont Residences. Fairmont Spas feature Willow Stream spa facilities in many of its hotels. Fairmont Golf properties are located in cities around the world such as Acapulco, Mexico; St. Andrews, Scotland; Zimbali, South Africa; and Southhampton, Bermuda. Fairmont Ski designations include the Fairmont Chateau Whistler, Fairmont Vail, Fairmont Tremblant and many others. Fairmont Gold is an exclusive, private floor of the hotel with its own private check-in and check-out desk. Fairmont Gold offers a private lounge; a healthy continental breakfast; afternoon canapes and honor bar; complimentary newspapers; computer access in lounge; in-room high-speed Internet access; and a selection of DVD's , CD's, books and games. Fairmont Residences are located worldwide in locations such as Dubai, U.A.E.; Zimbali, South Africa; and Vancouver, Canada. These properties are designed to be utilized as primary dwelling or as getaway retreats. Additional residences located in Cairo, Egypt; Angulla, British West Indies and Colorado, U.S. are scheduled to open during 2010. Raffles Hotels includes the signature Raffles Hotel, built in 1887 in Singapore.

FINANCIALS:

Sales and profits are in thousands of dollars—add 000 to get the full amount. 2009 Note: Financial information for 2009 was not available for all companies at press time.

2009 Sales: $	2009 Profits: $	**U.S. Stock Ticker: Private**
2008 Sales: $	2008 Profits: $	**Int'l Ticker:** Int'l Exchange:
2007 Sales: $	2007 Profits: $	Employees:
2006 Sales: $	2006 Profits: $	Fiscal Year Ends: 12/31
2005 Sales: $857,500	2005 Profits: $167,500	Parent Company:

SALARIES/BENEFITS:

Pension Plan:	ESOP Stock Plan:	Profit Sharing:	Top Exec. Salary: $	Bonus: $
Savings Plan:	Stock Purch. Plan:		Second Exec. Salary: $	Bonus: $

OTHER THOUGHTS:

Apparent Women Officers or Directors: 1
Hot Spot for Advancement for Women/Minorities:

LOCATIONS: ("Y" = Yes)

West:	Southwest:	Midwest:	Southeast:	Northeast:	International:
Y	Y	Y	Y	Y	Y

FANNIE MAE

www.fanniemae.com

Industry Group Code: 522310 **Ranks within this company's industry group:** Sales: 1 Profits: 5

Properties:		Financial Services:		Construction/Development:		Investments:		Specialty Services:		Brokerage:	
Apartments:		Mortgages:	Y	Commercial Construction:		REIT:		Property Management:		Commercial Sales:	
Malls/Shopping:		Title Insurance:		Residential Construction:				Online Services:		Residential Sales:	
Offices:		Property Insurance:		Land Development:				Software/IT:	Y	Specialty:	
Hotels/Motels:				Support Services:				Consulting:			
Industrial/Warehouses:				Design/Engineering:							
Other:											

TYPES OF BUSINESS:

Mortgages, Secondary Market
Mortgage-Related Securities
Financial Software

BRANDS/DIVISIONS/AFFILIATES:

Federal National Mortgage Association

CONTACTS:

Note: Officers with more than one job title may be intentionally listed here more than once.

Michael J. Williams, CEO
Michael J. Williams, Pres.
David M. Johnson, CFO/Exec. VP
Rahul Merchant, CIO/Exec. VP
Edward G. Watson, Exec. VP-Tech
Timothy J. Mayopoulos, General Counsel/Exec. VP/Corp. Sec.
Edward G. Watson, Exec. VP-Oper.
Michael A. Shaw, Chief Credit Officer/Exec. VP
David Benson, Exec. VP-Capital Markets
Linda Knight, Exec. VP-Securities
Kenneth J. Phelan, Exec. VP-Single Family Mortgage Bus.
Phillip Laskawy, Chmn.

Phone: 202-752-7000	**Fax:**
Toll-Free: 800-732-6643	
Address: 3900 Wisconsin Ave. NW, Washington, DC 20016 US	

GROWTH PLANS/SPECIAL FEATURES:

Fannie Mae is a government-sponsored enterprise chartered by the U.S. Congress under the name Federal National Mortgage Association. The firm's activities include providing funds to mortgage lenders through purchase of mortgage assets. The firm then issues and guarantees mortgage-related securities that facilitate the flow of additional funds into the mortgage market. Fannie Mae does not offer mortgages directly to homebuyers. The firm operates exclusively in the secondary mortgage market securities from primary market institutions. These include commercial banks, savings and loan associations, mortgage companies and securities dealers. The company operates in three segments: single-family credit guaranty, housing and community development and capital markets. The single-family credit guaranty segment works with lender customers to securitize single-family mortgage loans into Fannie Mae mortgage-backed securities (MBS) and to facilitate the purchase of single-family mortgage loans. The housing and community development segment works with lender customers to securitize multifamily mortgage loans into Fannie Mae MBS and to facilitate the purchase of multifamily mortgage loans. The capital markets segment manages the firm's investment activity in mortgage loans and mortgage-related securities. This segment is also responsible for managing the company's assets, liabilities and its liquidity and capital positions. In September 2008, after suffering devastating losses in it mortgage portfolio, Fannie Mae was placed in conservatorship by the U.S. federal government, which has taken effective control of the company. Over the near term, its focus will be on less aggressive lending, attempting to facilitate stability in the housing market and workouts of existing mortgages. In September 2009, Fannie Mae added an automated software program for processing mortgage applications called the eMason Clarifire Application for Home Affordability Program Workout (HAMP).

The company offers its employees medical and dental insurance; life insurance; and education assistance.

FINANCIALS:

Sales and profits are in thousands of dollars—add 000 to get the full amount. 2009 Note: Financial information for 2009 was not available for all companies at press time.

2009 Sales: $22,494,000	2009 Profits: $-72,022,000	**U.S. Stock Ticker: FNM**
2008 Sales: $17,436,000	2008 Profits: $-58,707,000	**Int'l Ticker:** Int'l Exchange:
2007 Sales: $11,206,000	2007 Profits: $-2,050,000	Employees: 6,000
2006 Sales: $12,012,000	2006 Profits: $4,059,000	Fiscal Year Ends: 12/31
2005 Sales: $50,149,000	2005 Profits: $6,347,000	Parent Company:

SALARIES/BENEFITS:

Pension Plan: Y	ESOP Stock Plan: Y	Profit Sharing:	Top Exec. Salary: $951,923	Bonus: $
Savings Plan: Y	Stock Purch. Plan: Y		Second Exec. Salary: $788,000	Bonus: $

OTHER THOUGHTS:

Apparent Women Officers or Directors: 1
Hot Spot for Advancement for Women/Minorities:

LOCATIONS: ("Y" = Yes)

West:	Southwest:	Midwest:	Southeast:	Northeast:	International:
				Y	

FEDERAL AGRICULTURAL MORTGAGE CORP (FARMER MAC)

www.farmermac.com

Industry Group Code: 522310 **Ranks within this company's industry group:** Sales: 2 Profits: 2

Properties:		Financial Services:		Construction/Development:		Investments:		Specialty Services:		Brokerage:	
Apartments:		Mortgages:	Y	Commercial Construction:		REIT:		Property Management:		Commercial Sales:	
Malls/Shopping:		Title Insurance:		Residential Construction:				Online Services:		Residential Sales:	
Offices:		Property Insurance:		Land Development:				Software/IT:		Specialty:	
Hotels/Motels:				Support Services:				Consulting:			
Industrial/Warehouses:				Design/Engineering:							
Other:											

TYPES OF BUSINESS:

Mortgages
Agricultural Real Estate Loans
Rural Housing Mortgage Loans

BRANDS/DIVISIONS/AFFILIATES:

Farmer Mac I
Farmer Mac II
Rural Utilities

CONTACTS:

Note: Officers with more than one job title may be intentionally listed here more than once.

Michael A. Gerber, CEO
Tom D. Stenson, COO
Michael A. Gerber, Pres.
Nancy E. Corsiglia, CFO
Jerome G. Oslick, General Counsel/Corp. Sec./VP
Mary K. Waters, VP-Corp. Rel.
Nancy E. Corsiglia, Exec. VP-Finance/Treas.
Paul N. Peiffer, VP-Agricultural Credit
Timothy L. Buzby, Controller/VP/Acting Treas.
Tom D. Stenson, Exec. VP-Agricultural Finance
Lowell L. Junkins, Acting Chmn.

Phone: 202-872-7700	**Fax:** 202-872-7713
Toll-Free: 800-879-3276	
Address: 1133 21st St. NW, Ste. 600, Washington, DC 20036 US	

GROWTH PLANS/SPECIAL FEATURES:

Federal Agricultural Mortgage Corporation, known as Farmer Mac, is a secondary market for agricultural real estate and rural housing mortgage loans. Congress created the company in 1987 to improve the availability of mortgage credit to America's farmers, ranchers and rural homeowners, businesses and communities. Farmer Mac does this through providing liquidity and lending capacity to agricultural mortgage lenders by purchasing newly originated and pre-existing mortgage loans directly from lenders; guaranteeing securities backed by eligible mortgage loans, referred to as Farmer Mac I Guaranteed Securities; exchanging newly issued Farmer Mac I Guaranteed Securities for newly originated and seasoned eligible mortgage loans that back those securities in so-called swap transactions; and issuing long-term standby purchase commitments for both newly originated and seasoned mortgage loans. The firm does this through two programs: Farmer Mac I and Farmer Mac II. Under Farmer Mac I, Farmer Mac purchases eligible mortgage loans, securitizes purchased loans and guarantees the timely payment of principal and interest on the securities backed by the loans. Under Farmer Mac II, the company purchases the guaranteed portions of loans guaranteed by the United States Department of Agriculture (USDA) and guarantees securities backed by those USDA-guaranteed portions purchased by Farmer Mac. Although created by Congress, Farmer Mac is a publicly traded corporation owned by its stockholders. Farmer Mac's primary sources of revenue are the fees it receives from outstanding Farmer Mac Guaranteed Securities and its purchase commitments and net interest income from Farmer Mac Guaranteed Securities.

FINANCIALS:

Sales and profits are in thousands of dollars—add 000 to get the full amount. 2009 Note: Financial information for 2009 was not available for all companies at press time.

2009 Sales: $83,055	2009 Profits: $82,298	**U.S. Stock Ticker: AGM**
2008 Sales: $74,184	2008 Profits: $-154,080	**Int'l Ticker:** Int'l Exchange:
2007 Sales: $44,668	2007 Profits: $4,421	Employees:
2006 Sales: $40,686	2006 Profits: $29,773	Fiscal Year Ends: 12/31
2005 Sales: $92,500	2005 Profits: $47,000	Parent Company:

SALARIES/BENEFITS:

Pension Plan:	ESOP Stock Plan:	Profit Sharing:	Top Exec. Salary: $573,776	Bonus: $84,177
Savings Plan:	Stock Purch. Plan:		Second Exec. Salary: $368,082	Bonus: $72,089

OTHER THOUGHTS:

Apparent Women Officers or Directors: 2
Hot Spot for Advancement for Women/Minorities: Y

LOCATIONS: ("Y" = Yes)

West:	Southwest:	Midwest:	Southeast:	Northeast:	International:
		Y		Y	

FEDERAL REALTY INVESTMENT TRUST

www.federalrealty.com

Industry Group Code: 531120 **Ranks within this company's industry group:** Sales: 34 Profits: 21

Properties:		Financial Services:		Construction/Development:		Investments:		Specialty Services:		Brokerage:	
Apartments:		Mortgages:		Commercial Construction:		REIT:	Y	Property Management:		Commercial Sales:	
Malls/Shopping:	Y	Title Insurance:		Residential Construction:				Online Services:		Residential Sales:	
Offices:	Y	Property Insurance:		Land Development:				Software/IT:		Specialty:	
Hotels/Motels:				Support Services:				Consulting:			
Industrial/Warehouses:				Design/Engineering:							
Other:											

TYPES OF BUSINESS:

Real Estate Investment Trust
Retail Properties
Real Estate Development & Redevelopment

BRANDS/DIVISIONS/AFFILIATES:

CONTACTS:

Note: Officers with more than one job title may be intentionally listed here more than once.

Donald C. Wood, CEO
Dawn Becker, COO/Exec. VP
Donald C. Wood, Pres.
Andrew Blocher, CFO/Treas./Sr. VP
Lisa Denson, VP-IT & Special Projects
Debbie Colson, Sr. VP-Legal Oper.
Don Briggs, Sr. VP-Dev.
Janelle Stevenson, Corp. Comm.
Phillip Mays, Chief Acct. Officer/VP
Wendy Seher, VP-Leasing
Chris Weilminster, Sr. VP-Leasing
Jeff Berkes, Chief Investment Officer/Exec. VP
Joseph S. Vassalluzzo, Chmn.

Phone: 301-998-8100	**Fax:** 301-998-3700
Toll-Free: 800-658-8980	
Address: 1626 E. Jefferson St., Rockville, MD 20852-4041 US	

GROWTH PLANS/SPECIAL FEATURES:

Federal Realty Investment Trust is an equity real estate investment trust (REIT) engaged in the ownership, management, development and redevelopment of retail and mixed-use properties. Federal Realty's portfolio encompasses approximately 84 community and neighborhood shopping centers and mixed-used properties in 13 states and Washington, D.C., comprising a total of 18.2 million square feet. The company also holds a 30% share in a joint venture that owns seven properties totaling approximately 1 million square feet. The company focuses on the acquisition of commercial properties that have expansion, redevelopment and remerchandising potential. The company particularly targets affluent and densely populated communities throughout the Northeast, Mid-Atlantic and California. Federal Realty's operating portfolio is 95% leased to national, regional, and local retailers. Its leasing clients include Urban Outfitters Banana Republic, Borders Books, Safeway, Toys 'R' Us, TJ Maxx, Giant Food, Rite Aid and Barnes & Noble, among many others.

Employees are offered medical and dental insurance; a vision discount program; a 401(k) plan; tuition reimbursement; disability coverage; flexible spending accounts; life insurance; AD&D insurance; an incentive bonus program; and housing discounts.

FINANCIALS:

Sales and profits are in thousands of dollars—add 000 to get the full amount. 2009 Note: Financial information for 2009 was not available for all companies at press time.

2009 Sales: $531,019	2009 Profits: $97,763	**U.S. Stock Ticker: FRT**
2008 Sales: $520,188	2008 Profits: $129,246	**Int'l Ticker:** Int'l Exchange:
2007 Sales: $482,788	2007 Profits: $195,095	Employees: 376
2006 Sales: $426,816	2006 Profits: $118,712	Fiscal Year Ends: 12/31
2005 Sales: $390,808	2005 Profits: $114,612	Parent Company:

SALARIES/BENEFITS:

Pension Plan:	ESOP Stock Plan:	Profit Sharing:	Top Exec. Salary: $650,000	Bonus: $487,500
Savings Plan: Y	Stock Purch. Plan:		Second Exec. Salary: $350,000	Bonus: $150,000

OTHER THOUGHTS:

Apparent Women Officers or Directors: 8
Hot Spot for Advancement for Women/Minorities: Y

LOCATIONS: ("Y" = Yes)

West:	Southwest:	Midwest:	Southeast:	Northeast:	International:
Y	Y			Y	

FELCOR LODGING TRUST

www.felcor.com

Industry Group Code: 531120 **Ranks within this company's industry group:** Sales: 17 Profits: 58

Properties:		Financial Services:		Construction/Development:		Investments:		Specialty Services:		Brokerage:	
Apartments:		Mortgages:		Commercial Construction:		REIT:	Y	Property Management:		Commercial Sales:	
Malls/Shopping:		Title Insurance:		Residential Construction:				Online Services:		Residential Sales:	
Offices:		Property Insurance:		Land Development:				Software/IT:		Specialty:	
Hotels/Motels:	Y			Support Services:				Consulting:			
Industrial/Warehouses:				Design/Engineering:							
Other:											

TYPES OF BUSINESS:

Real Estate Investment Trust
Hotel Ownership

BRANDS/DIVISIONS/AFFILIATES:

FelCor Lodging Limited Partnership

CONTACTS:

Note: Officers with more than one job title may be intentionally listed here more than once.

Richard A. Smith, CEO
Richard A. Smith, Pres.
Andrew J. Welch, CFO/Exec. VP
Jack C. Marraccini, Sr. VP-Eng.
Jonathan H. Yellen, General Counsel/Exec. VP/Corp. Sec.
Stephen A. Schafer, VP-Strategic Planning
Stephen A. Schafer, VP-Investor Rel.
Lester C. Johnson, Chief Acct. Officer/Sr. VP
Michael A. DeNicola, Chief Investment Officer/Exec. VP
Troy A. Pentecost, Exec. VP/Dir.-Asset Management
Robert P. Carl, Sr. VP/Dir.-Design & Construction
Eric U. Nylen, Sr. VP-Dev.
Thomas J. Corcoran, Jr., Chmn.

Phone: 972-444-4900 **Fax:** 972-444-4949
Toll-Free:
Address: 545 E. John Carpenter Freeway., Ste. 1300, Irving, TX 75062 US

GROWTH PLANS/SPECIAL FEATURES:

FelCor Lodging Trust, Inc. (FelCor) is a hotel real estate investment trust (REIT) that, through its 99% partnership interest in FelCor Lodging LP, holds ownership interests in 85 hotels in 23 states and the city of Toronto in Canada, with a total of approximately 24,000 rooms and suites. The company is among the largest U.S. owners of upper-upscale, all-suite style hotel properties. Of the 85 hotels in which FelCor holds an ownership interest, it owns a 100% interest in 64 hotels, a 90% or greater interest in entities owning four hotels, an 81% interest in an entity owning one hotel, a 60% interest in an entity owning one hotel and a 50% interest in entities owning 15 hotels. Its hotel brands include Embassy Suites Hotels (representing approximately 60% of FelCor 2009 earnings), Holiday Inn (18%), Sheraton and Westin (9%), Doubletree (7%), Renaissance and Marriot (3%), and Hilton (3%). FelCor's properties are located in major markets including San Francisco, southern Florida, Atlanta, Los Angeles, Orlando, Dallas, San Antonio, San Diego, northern New Jersey, Boston, Minneapolis and Philadelphia. In 2009, roughly 97% of revenues were derived from U.S. properties, with the remaining 3% derived from the properties in the Toronto area in Canada. The firm has alliances with the four brand owners that manage most of FelCor's hotels: Hilton Hotels Corporation, whose brands include Embassy Suites Hotels, Hilton and Doubletree; InterContinental Hotels Group, owner of the Holiday Inn brand; Starwood Hotels & Resorts, whose brands include Sheraton and Westin; and Marriott International, Inc., which owns the Marriott and Renaissance hotel brands. During 2009 the company generally limited its redevelopment spending, but ongoing renovations and redevelopment of the San Francisco Marriott Union Square were completed in June 2009.

FINANCIALS:

Sales and profits are in thousands of dollars—add 000 to get the full amount. 2009 Note: Financial information for 2009 was not available for all companies at press time.

2009 Sales: $908,701	2009 Profits: $-109,091
2008 Sales: $1,102,912	2008 Profits: $-120,487
2007 Sales: $993,834	2007 Profits: $89,824
2006 Sales: $991,038	2006 Profits: $51,045
2005 Sales: $914,655	2005 Profits: $-251,615

U.S. Stock Ticker: FCH
Int'l Ticker: Int'l Exchange:
Employees: 68
Fiscal Year Ends: 12/31
Parent Company:

SALARIES/BENEFITS:

Pension Plan: ESOP Stock Plan: Profit Sharing: Top Exec. Salary: $600,000 Bonus: $1,776,184
Savings Plan: Y Stock Purch. Plan: Second Exec. Salary: $321,360 Bonus: $694,828

OTHER THOUGHTS:

Apparent Women Officers or Directors: 10
Hot Spot for Advancement for Women/Minorities:

LOCATIONS: ("Y" = Yes)

West:	Southwest:	Midwest:	Southeast:	Northeast:	International:
Y	Y	Y	Y	Y	Y

FERGUSON ENTERPRISES INC

www.ferguson.com

Industry Group Code: 444130 **Ranks within this company's industry group:** Sales: Profits:

Properties:		Financial Services:		Construction/Development:		Investments:		Specialty Services:		Brokerage:	
Apartments:		Mortgages:		Commercial Construction:		REIT:		Property Management:		Commercial Sales:	
Malls/Shopping:		Title Insurance:		Residential Construction:				Online Services:		Residential Sales:	
Offices:		Property Insurance:		Land Development:				Software/IT:		Specialty:	
Hotels/Motels:				Support Services:	Y			Consulting:			
Industrial/Warehouses:				Design/Engineering:							
Other:											

TYPES OF BUSINESS:

Plumbing Supplies, Retail
Wholesale Distribution
Construction Supplies, Retail
Waterworks Supplies
HVAC Equipment, Retail
PVF Supplies, Retail

BRANDS/DIVISIONS/AFFILIATES:

Wolseley plc
Endries International Inc.
Mastercraft Cabinets Inc.
Ferguson Xpress

CONTACTS: *Note: Officers with more than one job title may be intentionally listed here more than once.*

Frank W. Roach, CEO
Kevin Murphy, COO
Frank W. Roach, Pres.
Shawn Washington, Mgr.-Oper.
Bill Stevens, Mgr.-Bus. Dev., Ferguson Integration Svcs.
Stacy Hackworth, Gen. Mgr.-Frostproof Dist. Center
Frank W. Roach, CEO-Wolseley North America

Phone: 757-874-7795	**Fax:** 757-989-2501
Toll-Free:	
Address: 12500 Jefferson Ave., Newport News, VA 23602 US	

GROWTH PLANS/SPECIAL FEATURES:

Ferguson Enterprises, Inc. is one of the largest wholesale distributors of plumbing supplies in the U.S. The company has been a subsidiary of Wolseley plc, one of largest distributors of plumbing and heating products in the world, since 1982. Ferguson has approximately 1,350 retail locations in all 50 U.S. states, Washington, D.C., Puerto Rico, the Caribbean and Mexico. Additionally, the firm operates Ferguson Xpress stores, largely self-service locations that market plumbing and light commercial products to contractors. In general, Ferguson's customers include homeowners, builders, contractors, engineers and other trade professionals. Ferguson operates in seven business groups: residential; heating and cooling equipment (HVAC); industrial; commercial and mechanical; waterworks; government; and integrated. The company's product offerings include plumbing supplies; pipes, valves and fittings; HVAC; waterworks; lighting; appliances; tools and safety equipment; gas fireplaces; and fire protection products. An internal delivery service moves products from distribution hubs to Ferguson branches, satellites and customers. The firm has recently opened showrooms in Indiana, Tennessee, Florida, California, Texas, Minnesota, Colorado, Michigan and Virginia. Through other divisions, the company is also involved in nuclear power provision; fire protection supply; valve assembly and testing; and geosynthetic product supply to the mining industry. In February 2008, Ferguson acquired Mastercraft Cabinets, Inc. In November 2008, the company announced the opening of the 545,000-square foot distribution center in Frostproof, Florida. This center will support all its branches in Florida, Georgia, Puerto Rico and South Carolina.

Employees of Ferguson are offered medical, dental and vision coverage; a 401(k) plan; short and long term disability; life insurance; flexible spending accounts; educational assistance; on-site employee training courses; and a performance awards program.

FINANCIALS: **Sales and profits are in thousands of dollars—add 000 to get the full amount. 2009 Note: Financial information for 2009 was not available for all companies at press time.**

2009 Sales: $	2009 Profits: $	**U.S. Stock Ticker: Subsidiary**
2008 Sales: $	2008 Profits: $	**Int'l Ticker:** Int'l Exchange:
2007 Sales: $9,650,000	2007 Profits: $	Employees:
2006 Sales: $9,650,000	2006 Profits: $	Fiscal Year Ends: 7/31
2005 Sales: $5,000,000	2005 Profits: $	Parent Company: WOLSELEY PLC

SALARIES/BENEFITS:

Pension Plan:	ESOP Stock Plan:	Profit Sharing:	Top Exec. Salary: $	Bonus: $
Savings Plan: Y	Stock Purch. Plan:		Second Exec. Salary: $	Bonus: $

OTHER THOUGHTS:

Apparent Women Officers or Directors: 1
Hot Spot for Advancement for Women/Minorities:

LOCATIONS: ("Y" = Yes)

West:	Southwest:	Midwest:	Southeast:	Northeast:	International:
Y	Y	Y	Y	Y	Y

FIDELITY NATIONAL FINANCIAL INC

www.fnf.com

Industry Group Code: 524127 **Ranks within this company's industry group:** Sales: 2 Profits: 3

Properties:		Financial Services:		Construction/Development:		Investments:		Specialty Services:		Brokerage:	
Apartments:		Mortgages:		Commercial Construction:		REIT:		Property Management:		Commercial Sales:	
Malls/Shopping:		Title Insurance:	Y	Residential Construction:				Online Services:		Residential Sales:	
Offices:		Property Insurance:		Land Development:				Software/IT:		Specialty:	
Hotels/Motels:				Support Services:				Consulting:			
Industrial/Warehouses:				Design/Engineering:							
Other:											

TYPES OF BUSINESS:

Title Insurance
Escrow Services
Collection & Trust Activities
Electronic Data Interchange Software
Payment Processing
Equipment Lease Services
Insurance Claims Management

BRANDS/DIVISIONS/AFFILIATES:

Fidelity National Title Group, Inc.
Lawyers Title Insurance Corporation
Ceridian Corporation
Sedgwick CMS
Fidelity National title de Mexico SA de CV
Commonwealth Land Title Insurance Company
United Capital Title Insurance Company

CONTACTS: *Note: Officers with more than one job title may be intentionally listed here more than once.*

Alan L. Stinson, CEO
Raymond R. Quirk, Pres.
Anthony J. Park, CFO
Peter T. Sadowski, Chief Legal Officer/Exec. VP
Brent Bickett, Exec. VP-Finance
Raymond R. Quirk, CEO-Fidelity National Title Group
Michael L. Gravelle, Corp. Sec
Daniel Kennedy Murphy, Sr. VP/Treas.
William P. Foley, II, Chmn.

Phone: 904-854-8100	**Fax:** 904-357-1007
Toll-Free: 888-934-3354	
Address: 601 Riverside Ave., Jacksonville, FL 32204 US	

GROWTH PLANS/SPECIAL FEATURES:

Fidelity National Financial, Inc. (FNF) is a holding company that provides outsourced products and services to a variety of industries. FNF operates in three segments: Fidelity National Title Group, Inc. (FNT); Specialty Insurance; and Corporate and Other. Fidelity National Title Group, Inc., a majority-owned, publicly traded company, is responsible for the title operations of FNF. Through FNT, the company is one of the nation's largest title insurance companies. Through its Specialty Insurance segment, FNF is a leading provider of specialty insurance products, including flood insurance, homeowners insurance and home warranty insurance. The company's Corporate and Other segment includes certain other unallocated corporate overhead expenses, other smaller operations and the firm's interests in Ceridian Corporation and Sedgwick CMS Holdings. Ceridian Corporation, the firm's minority-owned subsidiary, provides information services to the transportation, human resources and retail industries; Sedgwick CMS Holdings, another minority-owned subsidiary, offers outsourced claims management services to large corporate and public sector clients. In July 2008, the company opened Fidelity National title de Mexico S.A. de C.V., a title insurance operation in Mexico with its principle office in Mexico City. In August 2008, FNF acquired Mercury Companies, Inc.'s Colorado title insurance operations, which includes United Title; Security Title; First American Heritage Title; and Title America. In December 2008, the company acquired three of the subsidiaries of LandAmerica Financial Group, Inc.: Lawyers Title Insurance Corporation, Commonwealth Land Title Insurance Company and United Capital Title Insurance Company. In May 2009, the firm agreed to acquire LoanCare Servicing Center, Inc., a national loan subservicing services provider.

FINANCIALS: **Sales and profits are in thousands of dollars—add 000 to get the full amount. 2009 Note: Financial information for 2009 was not available for all companies at press time.**

2009 Sales: $5,828,400	2009 Profits: $222,300	**U.S. Stock Ticker: FNF**
2008 Sales: $4,251,200	2008 Profits: $-179,016	**Int'l Ticker:** Int'l Exchange:
2007 Sales: $5,465,600	2007 Profits: $129,769	Employees: 17,200
2006 Sales: $9,434,399	2006 Profits: $437,761	Fiscal Year Ends: 12/31
2005 Sales: $9,654,580	2005 Profits: $964,106	Parent Company:

SALARIES/BENEFITS:

Pension Plan: Y	ESOP Stock Plan:	Profit Sharing:	Top Exec. Salary: $709,167	Bonus: $
Savings Plan: Y	Stock Purch. Plan: Y		Second Exec. Salary: $536,667	Bonus: $

OTHER THOUGHTS:

Apparent Women Officers or Directors:
Hot Spot for Advancement for Women/Minorities:

LOCATIONS: ("Y" = Yes)

West:	Southwest:	Midwest:	Southeast:	Northeast:	International:
Y	Y	Y	Y	Y	Y

FIDELITY NATIONAL INFORMATION SERVICES INC

www.fisglobal.com

Industry Group Code: 522320 **Ranks within this company's industry group:** Sales: 1 Profits: 1

Properties:		Financial Services:		Construction/Development:		Investments:		Specialty Services:		Brokerage:	
Apartments:		Mortgages:		Commercial Construction:		REIT:		Property Management:		Commercial Sales:	
Malls/Shopping:		Title Insurance:		Residential Construction:				Online Services:		Residential Sales:	
Offices:		Property Insurance:		Land Development:				Software/IT:	Y	Specialty:	
Hotels/Motels:				Support Services:				Consulting:			
Industrial/Warehouses:				Design/Engineering:							
Other:											

TYPES OF BUSINESS:

Payment & Transaction Processing Services
IT Consulting
Outsourcing Services
Due Diligence Services
Mortgage Loan Processing

BRANDS/DIVISIONS/AFFILIATES:

Metavante Technologies Inc

CONTACTS:

Note: Officers with more than one job title may be intentionally listed here more than once.

Frank R. Martire, CEO
Gary A. Norcross, COO/Exec. VP
Frank R. Martire, Pres.
Michael D. Hayford, CFO/Exec. VP
Marcia Danzeisen, Sr. VP-Global Mktg.
Michael P. Oates, Chief Human Resources Officer/Exec. VP
Brian Hurdis, Exec. VP-Tech. Svcs.
Michael Gravelle, Chief Legal Officer/Exec. VP/Corp. Sec.
James Susoreny, Exec. VP-Bus. Dev.
Marcia Danzeisen, Sr. VP-Global Comm.
Mary K. Waggoner, Sr. VP-Investor Rel.
George Scanlon, Exec. VP-Finance
Brent Bickett, Exec. VP-Corp. Finance
Frank Sanchez, Exec. VP-Strategic Solutions
Frank D'Angelo, Exec. VP-Payment Solutions
Anthony Jabbour, Exec. VP-Financial Solutions
William P. Foley, II, Chmn.
Mark Davey, Exec. VP-Int'l

Phone: 904-854-5000	**Fax:** 904-357-1105
Toll-Free: 888-323-0310	
Address: 601 Riverside Ave., Jacksonville, FL 32204 US	

GROWTH PLANS/SPECIAL FEATURES:

Fidelity National Information Services, Inc. (FIS) offers banking/payments technology solutions, processing services and information-based services. The firm provides core financial institution processing; card issuer and transaction processing services; and outsourcing services to financial institutions and retailers worldwide. The company has processing and technology relationships with 40 of the top 50 global banks, including nine of the top 10. Headquartered in Jacksonville, Florida, FIS maintains a global presence, serving more than 14,000 financial institutions through 210 offices worldwide. The company operates in four segments: Financial Solutions, Payment Solutions, International Solutions and Corporate/Other. The Financial Solutions Group offers core processing software applications designed to run critical banking processes; channel, decision and risk management solutions; syndicated loan applications; and global commercial services. The Payment Solutions division offers settlement and card management solutions for financial institution card issuers; check and transaction ticket data capture; healthcare payments solutions; and card issuer services, enabling financial institutions and others to issue VISA and MasterCard branded credit and debit cards, private label cards, and other electronic payment cards for use by both consumer and business accounts. FIS' International Solutions segment provides the firm's services in over 100 countries. The Corporate/Other division includes corporate overhead costs that are not allocated to operating segments. In July 2009, FIS agreed to sell the assets of Certegy Australia, Ltd. to Flexigroup Limited for roughly $30 million. In October 2009, the firm acquired Metavante Technologies, Inc., a Milwaukee-based transaction processing firm with 5,900 employees. Also in October 2009, the company agreed to sell its ClearPar automated syndicated loan trade settlement operations to financial information services firm Markit.

FINANCIALS:

Sales and profits are in thousands of dollars—add 000 to get the full amount. 2009 Note: Financial information for 2009 was not available for all companies at press time.

2009 Sales: $3,769,500	2009 Profits: $105,900	**U.S. Stock Ticker: FIS**
2008 Sales: $3,427,700	2008 Profits: $214,800	**Int'l Ticker:** Int'l Exchange:
2007 Sales: $2,892,900	2007 Profits: $561,222	Employees: 3,100
2006 Sales: $2,416,500	2006 Profits: $259,087	Fiscal Year Ends: 12/31
2005 Sales: $2,688,218	2005 Profits: $130,319	Parent Company:

SALARIES/BENEFITS:

Pension Plan:	ESOP Stock Plan:	Profit Sharing:	Top Exec. Salary: $886,250	Bonus: $2,481,500
Savings Plan: Y	Stock Purch. Plan:		Second Exec. Salary: $627,500	Bonus: $3,067,500

OTHER THOUGHTS:

Apparent Women Officers or Directors: 2
Hot Spot for Advancement for Women/Minorities:

LOCATIONS: ("Y" = Yes)

West:	Southwest:	Midwest:	Southeast:	Northeast:	International:
Y	Y	Y	Y	Y	Y

FIRST AMERICAN CORP

www.firstam.com

Industry Group Code: 524127 **Ranks within this company's industry group:** Sales: 1 Profits: 2

Properties:		Financial Services:		Construction/Development:		Investments:		Specialty Services:		Brokerage:	
Apartments:		Mortgages:		Commercial Construction:		REIT:		Property Management:		Commercial Sales:	
Malls/Shopping:		Title Insurance:	Y	Residential Construction:				Online Services:		Residential Sales:	
Offices:		Property Insurance:		Land Development:				Software/IT:		Specialty:	
Hotels/Motels:				Support Services:				Consulting:			
Industrial/Warehouses:				Design/Engineering:							
Other:											

TYPES OF BUSINESS:

Title Insurance
Real Estate Services
Escrow Services
Screening Services
Credit Reporting
Property & Casualty Insurance
Trust Services
Internet Services

BRANDS/DIVISIONS/AFFILIATES:

First Advantage Corporation
First Title plc
First American CoreLogic
BasePoint Analytics LLC

CONTACTS:

Note: Officers with more than one job title may be intentionally listed here more than once.

Parker S. Kennedy, CEO
Dennis J. Gilmore, COO
Anthony Piszel, CFO/Treas.
William J. Sherakas, VP/Dir.-Nat'l Mktg. & Sales
Frank V. McMahon, Exec. VP/CEO-Info. Solutions Group
Evan H. Jafa, CTO
Kenneth D. DeGiorgio, General Counsel/Sr. VP/Interim Sec.
Jo Etta Bandy, Sr. VP-Corp. Comm.
Mark Seaton, Dir.-Investor Rel.
Max O. Valdes, Chief Acct. Officer/Sr. VP
Dennis J. Gilmore, Exec. VP/CEO-Financial Svcs. Group
George Livermore, Pres., Data & Analytic Solutions
Anand K. Nallathambi, CEO-First Advantage Corp./Pres., Bus. Solutions
Barry M. Sando, Pres., Info. & Outsourcing Solutions
Parker S. Kennedy, Chmn.
Jodee L. Barnett, VP-National Procurement

Phone: 714-250-3000	**Fax:**
Toll-Free: 800-854-3643	
Address: 1 First American Way, Santa Ana, CA 92707 US	

GROWTH PLANS/SPECIAL FEATURES:

First American Corp. provides business information and related products and services. The company conducts its operations through two major units: the financial services group and the information solutions group. The financial services group includes the title insurance and services segment, which issues residential and commercial title insurance policies and provides escrow services, investment advisory services and trust services; and the specialty insurance segment, which issues property and casualty insurance policies and provides home warranties. The firm's information technology group encompasses the information and outsourcing solutions segment, which provides tax monitoring, flood zone certification, default management services and asset management services; the data and analytic solutions segment, offering database management and appraisal services; and the risk mitigation and business solutions segment, comprised of First Advantage Corporation (FAC). FAC operates in six business groups: lender services, data services, dealer services, employer services, multifamily services and investigation and litigation support services. The lender services group provides consumer credit reporting solutions for mortgage and home equity companies. The data services group offers motor vehicle records, transportation industry credit reporting, criminal records reselling and lead generation services. The dealer services group offers consumer credit reports and lead development services to auto dealers and lenders. FAC's employer services group provides employment screening, occupation health and human resource management. The multifamily service group offers resident screening services, property management software and renters' insurance services. The investigative and litigation support services segment offers computer forensics, electronic discovery and data recovery services. In January 2008, First American announced plans to spin off its financial services and information solutions companies. In March 2009, subsidiary First Title plc entered the Russian title insurance market. In June 2009, First American CoreLogic, another subsidiary, acquired BasePoint Analytics LLC, a risk management services provider. Also in June, First American agreed to acquire FAC stock.

FINANCIALS:

Sales and profits are in thousands of dollars—add 000 to get the full amount. 2009 Note: Financial information for 2009 was not available for all companies at press time.

2009 Sales: $5,972,777	2009 Profits: $199,651	**U.S. Stock Ticker: FAF**
2008 Sales: $6,213,758	2008 Profits: $-26,320	**Int'l Ticker:** Int'l Exchange:
2007 Sales: $8,222,383	2007 Profits: $-3,119	Employees: 30,922
2006 Sales: $8,533,597	2006 Profits: $287,676	Fiscal Year Ends: 12/31
2005 Sales: $8,104,751	2005 Profits: $480,380	Parent Company:

SALARIES/BENEFITS:

Pension Plan:	ESOP Stock Plan:	Profit Sharing:	Top Exec. Salary: $750,000	Bonus: $
Savings Plan:	Stock Purch. Plan:		Second Exec. Salary: $698,629	Bonus: $800,000

OTHER THOUGHTS:

Apparent Women Officers or Directors: 10
Hot Spot for Advancement for Women/Minorities: Y

LOCATIONS: ("Y" = Yes)

West:	Southwest:	Midwest:	Southeast:	Northeast:	International:
Y	Y	Y	Y	Y	Y

FIRST INDUSTRIAL REALTY TRUST INC

www.firstindustrial.com

Industry Group Code: 531120 **Ranks within this company's industry group:** Sales: 35 Profits: 46

Properties:		Financial Services:		Construction/Development:		Investments:		Specialty Services:		Brokerage:	
Apartments:		Mortgages:		Commercial Construction:	Y	REIT:	Y	Property Management:	Y	Commercial Sales:	
Malls/Shopping:		Title Insurance:		Residential Construction:				Online Services:		Residential Sales:	
Offices:		Property Insurance:		Land Development:				Software/IT:		Specialty:	
Hotels/Motels:				Support Services:				Consulting:			
Industrial/Warehouses:	Y			Design/Engineering:							
Other:											

TYPES OF BUSINESS:

Real Estate Investment Trust-Industrial Properties
Development Services
Warehouses

BRANDS/DIVISIONS/AFFILIATES:

GROWTH PLANS/SPECIAL FEATURES:

First Industrial Realty Trust, Inc. owns, manages, acquires, sells, develops and redevelops industrial real estate in the U.S. Organized as a real estate investment trust (REIT), First Industrial owns and operates approximately 783 in-service industrial properties located in 28 states and containing approximately 69 million square feet of gross leasable areas. These properties fall into five primary sub-groups: light industrial (of which the firm's portfolio contains approximately 369 properties), R&D flex (131 properties), bulk warehouse (174 properties), regional warehouse (89 properties) and manufacturing (20 properties). Most of its properties are located in business parks, with easy access to highways, rail lines or airports. The tenants that occupy them do business in the manufacturing, retail, wholesale trade, distribution and professional service industries. First Industrial's properties and land parcels are held through partnerships, corporations and limited liability companies controlled directly or indirectly by the firm, including a number of joint ventures. During 2009, the company sold 15 industrial properties and several parcels of land.

Employees are offered medical, dental and vision insurance; retirement planning; employee stock programs; and life insurance.

CONTACTS: *Note: Officers with more than one job title may be intentionally listed here more than once.*

Bruce W. Duncan, CEO
Bruce W. Duncan, Pres.
Scott Musil, Acting CFO
Christopher Schneider, CIO
John Clayton, VP-Legal
Christopher Schneider, Sr. VP-Oper.
Michael Damone, Dir.-Strategic Planning
Johannson Yap, Chief Investment Officer
Donald Stoffle, Exec. Dir.-Dispositions
Robert Walter, Sr. VP-Capital Markets
David Harker, Exec. VP-Central
W. Ed Tyler, Chmn.

Phone: 312-344-4300 **Fax:** 312-922-6320
Toll-Free:
Address: 311 S. Wacker Dr., Ste. 3900, Chicago, IL 60606 US

FINANCIALS: **Sales and profits are in thousands of dollars—add 000 to get the full amount. 2009 Note: Financial information for 2009 was not available for all companies at press time.**

2009 Sales: $411,958	2009 Profits: $-13,783	**U.S. Stock Ticker: FR**
2008 Sales: $514,321	2008 Profits: $20,169	**Int'l Ticker:** Int'l Exchange:
2007 Sales: $369,874	2007 Profits: $130,368	Employees: 229
2006 Sales: $300,183	2006 Profits: $112,082	Fiscal Year Ends: 12/31
2005 Sales: $287,663	2005 Profits: $87,104	Parent Company:

SALARIES/BENEFITS:

Pension Plan:	ESOP Stock Plan:	Profit Sharing:	Top Exec. Salary: $1,065,274	Bonus: $
Savings Plan:	Stock Purch. Plan: Y		Second Exec. Salary: $501,134	Bonus: $

OTHER THOUGHTS:

Apparent Women Officers or Directors:
Hot Spot for Advancement for Women/Minorities:

LOCATIONS: ("Y" = Yes)

West:	Southwest:	Midwest:	Southeast:	Northeast:	International:
Y	Y	Y	Y	Y	Y

FIRST MORTGAGE CORP

www.firstmortgage.com

Industry Group Code: 522310 **Ranks within this company's industry group:** Sales: Profits:

Properties:		Financial Services:		Construction/Development:		Investments:		Specialty Services:		Brokerage:	
Apartments:		Mortgages:	Y	Commercial Construction:		REIT:		Property Management:		Commercial Sales:	
Malls/Shopping:		Title Insurance:		Residential Construction:				Online Services:		Residential Sales:	
Offices:		Property Insurance:		Land Development:				Software/IT:		Specialty:	
Hotels/Motels:				Support Services:				Consulting:			
Industrial/Warehouses:				Design/Engineering:							
Other:											

TYPES OF BUSINESS:

Mortgages
Loan Origination
Loan Purchasing

BRANDS/DIVISIONS/AFFILIATES:

CONTACTS:
Note: Officers with more than one job title may be intentionally listed here more than once.

Clement Ziroli, CEO
Bruce G. Norman, COO
Bruce G. Norman, Pres.
Pac W. Dong, CFO/Exec. VP
Tammy Russ, VP-Human Resources
Robyn S. Fredericks, Corp. Sec./Sr. VP
Pac W. Dong, Controller/Exec. VP
Ronald T. Vargas, Sr. VP
Scott Lehrer, Sr. VP
Clement Ziroli, Chmn.

Phone: 909-595-1996	**Fax:** 909-598-7351
Toll-Free: 800-395-4778	
Address: 3230 Fallow Field Dr., Diamond Bar, CA 91765 US	

GROWTH PLANS/SPECIAL FEATURES:

First Mortgage Corporation (FMC) is a mortgage banking firm. The company originates, purchases, warehouses, sells and services mortgage loans for owner-occupied residences, principally in California. FMC provides seven different loan programs. Its conventional loans are mortgages that are not insured or guaranteed by any governmental agency, and thus may be eligible for purchase on the secondary mortgage market. These loans are available with either fixed or adjustable interest rates and have individualized repayment terms. FHA loans are originated by FMC and insured by the Federal Housing Administration. These loans have either fixed or adjustable interest rates, with 30-year repayment terms. The Department of Housing and Urban Development (HUD) determines the designated maximum loan amount. Jumbo or non-conforming loans are those that exceed the maximum amount allowed for conventional loans and may be up to $1 million. These are either a fixed or adjustable rate mortgages, with parameters varying depending on the down payment and actual loan amount so terms are individualized. FMC is an approved lender to offer California's Housing Finance Agency Homeownership Loan Program; it offers California State Teachers Retirement System loan programs; and it is approved lender of the California Public Employees Retirement System. These California programs allow certain public officials, teachers, judges and state legislators and homebuyers to benefit from low or no down payments, reduced fees and closing cost assistance. In addition to these, the company provides VA loans and three California-specific programs. The VA loans, guaranteed by the Veteran's Association, are for those who have served or are currently in the U.S. armed forces that meet eligibility requirements. They do not require a down payment. The firm originates mortgage loans through three primary sources: referrals from real estate brokers and builders; direct marketing; and consumers interested in refinancing.

FINANCIALS:
Sales and profits are in thousands of dollars—add 000 to get the full amount. 2009 Note: Financial information for 2009 was not available for all companies at press time.

2009 Sales: $	2009 Profits: $	**U.S. Stock Ticker: Private**
2008 Sales: $	2008 Profits: $	**Int'l Ticker:** Int'l Exchange:
2007 Sales: $	2007 Profits: $	Employees:
2006 Sales: $	2006 Profits: $	Fiscal Year Ends: 3/31
2005 Sales: $	2005 Profits: $	Parent Company:

SALARIES/BENEFITS:

Pension Plan:	ESOP Stock Plan:	Profit Sharing:	Top Exec. Salary: $	Bonus: $
Savings Plan:	Stock Purch. Plan:		Second Exec. Salary: $	Bonus: $

OTHER THOUGHTS:

Apparent Women Officers or Directors: 2
Hot Spot for Advancement for Women/Minorities: Y

LOCATIONS: ("Y" = Yes)

West:	Southwest:	Midwest:	Southeast:	Northeast:	International:
Y					

FIRSTCITY FINANCIAL CORP

www.fcfc.com

Industry Group Code: 522310 **Ranks within this company's industry group:** Sales: 3 Profits: 1

Properties:		Financial Services:		Construction/Development:		Investments:		Specialty Services:		Brokerage:	
Apartments:		Mortgages:	Y	Commercial Construction:		REIT:		Property Management:		Commercial Sales:	
Malls/Shopping:		Title Insurance:		Residential Construction:				Online Services:		Residential Sales:	
Offices:		Property Insurance:		Land Development:				Software/IT:		Specialty:	
Hotels/Motels:				Support Services:				Consulting:			
Industrial/Warehouses:				Design/Engineering:							
Other:											

TYPES OF BUSINESS:

Mortgages
Portfolio Acquisitions
Flexible Capital Structuring Arrangements

BRANDS/DIVISIONS/AFFILIATES:

CONTACTS:

Note: Officers with more than one job title may be intentionally listed here more than once.

James T. Sartain, CEO
Jim W. Moore, COO/Exec. VP
James T. Sartain, Pres.
J. Bryan Baker, CFO/Sr. VP
Jim W. Moore, Treas.
James C. Holmes, Sr. VP
Terry R. DeWitt, Sr. VP
Joe S. Greak, Sr. VP/Dir.-Tax
C. Ivan Wilson, Vice Chmn.
Richard E. Bean, Chmn.

Phone: 254-761-2800	**Fax:** 254-751-7648
Toll-Free: 800-247-4274	
Address: 6400 Imperial Dr., Waco, TX 76712 US	

GROWTH PLANS/SPECIAL FEATURES:

FirstCity Financial Corporation is a diversified financial services company. The firm has offices throughout the U.S. and a presence in France, Mexico, Japan and South America. The company operates in two segments: portfolio asset acquisition/resolution and special situations platform. FirstCity Financial purchases and resolves portfolios of performing and non-performing commercial/consumer loans, as well as other assets generally acquired at a discount. Assets are acquired either in the form of pools or single assets, and are only purchased after an extensive evaluation has been completed. This evaluation includes an examination of the local economic and market trends; and an analysis of a given asset's projected cash flow and sources of repayment. Sellers of portfolio assets have included financial institutions, insurance companies and government agencies such as the Small Business Association (SBA). FirstCity Financial's special situation platform segment provides investment capital to privately-held middle-market companies through flexible capital structuring arrangements. These capital investments are primarily senior and junior financing arrangements; other investments include common equity warrants, distressed debt transactions, direct equity investments and leveraged buyouts. FirstCity's other services include debt purchases; due diligence underwriting; loan servicing and management; and debt obligation negotiation and resolution.

FINANCIALS:

Sales and profits are in thousands of dollars—add 000 to get the full amount. 2009 Note: Financial information for 2009 was not available for all companies at press time.

2009 Sales: $79,787	2009 Profits: $18,744	**U.S. Stock Ticker: FCFC**
2008 Sales: $45,196	2008 Profits: $-46,675	**Int'l Ticker:** Int'l Exchange:
2007 Sales: $43,656	2007 Profits: $2,185	Employees: 365
2006 Sales: $28,387	2006 Profits: $9,802	Fiscal Year Ends: 12/31
2005 Sales: $24,093	2005 Profits: $8,231	Parent Company:

SALARIES/BENEFITS:

Pension Plan:	ESOP Stock Plan:	Profit Sharing: Y	Top Exec. Salary: $500,000	Bonus: $
Savings Plan: Y	Stock Purch. Plan: Y		Second Exec. Salary: $315,000	Bonus: $

OTHER THOUGHTS:

Apparent Women Officers or Directors:
Hot Spot for Advancement for Women/Minorities:

LOCATIONS: ("Y" = Yes)

West:	Southwest:	Midwest:	Southeast:	Northeast:	International:
Y	Y				Y

FIRSTSERVICE CORPORATION

www.firstservice.com

Industry Group Code: 5311 **Ranks within this company's industry group:** Sales: 14 Profits: 24

Properties:		Financial Services:		Construction/Development:		Investments:		Specialty Services:		Brokerage:	
Apartments:		Mortgages:		Commercial Construction:		REIT:		Property Management:	Y	Commercial Sales:	
Malls/Shopping:		Title Insurance:		Residential Construction:				Online Services:		Residential Sales:	
Offices:		Property Insurance:		Land Development:				Software/IT:	Y	Specialty:	
Hotels/Motels:				Support Services:	Y			Consulting:	Y		
Industrial/Warehouses:				Design/Engineering:	Y						
Other:											

TYPES OF BUSINESS:

Real Estate Services
Residential Property Management
Security Services
Maintenance Services
Outsourcing Services
IT & Logistics Support
Security Systems Design

BRANDS/DIVISIONS/AFFILIATES:

Colliers International Property Consultants
PGP Property Valuation
PKF Hotel & Hospitality Consulting
Pillar to Post
MHPM Project Managers
Floorcoverings International
Field Asset Services
CertaPro Painters

CONTACTS: *Note: Officers with more than one job title may be intentionally listed here more than once.*

Jay S. Hennick, CEO
D. Scott Patterson, COO
D. Scott Patterson, Pres.
John B. Friedrichsen, CFO/Sr. VP
Douglas G. Cooke, Corp. Sec.
Roman Kocur, Sr. VP-Corp. Dev. & Strategy
Christian Mayer, VP-Finance
Elias Mulamoottil, VP-Corp. Dev. & Strategy
Neil D. Chander, VP-Tax
Douglas G. Cooke, Corp. Controller/VP
Peter F. Cohen, Chmn.

Phone: 416-960-9500	**Fax:** 416-960-5333
Toll-Free:	
Address: FirstService Bldg., 1140 Bay St., Ste. 4000, Toronto, ON M5S 2B4 Canada	

GROWTH PLANS/SPECIAL FEATURES:

FirstService Corporation is a diversified provider of services to residential and commercial tenants worldwide. The company has three main operating segments: residential property management, property services and commercial real estate services. The residential property management segment oversees residential communities in 18 states provide sales and leasing brokerage; valuation and advisory services; standard property management (leasing, maintenance, etc.) and specialty management (such as pools), mostly to private residential communities. In total, the residential property management unit oversees roughly 3,700 U.S. residential communities containing over 1 million housing units. The property services segment offers property reservation services through Field Asset Services; owns and operates seven franchise systems, including Paul Davis Restoration, CertaPro Painters, Pillar to Post and Floorcoverings International; and branchising services (the reacquisition of profitable franchises). The commercial real estate services segment, which operates primarily through its subsidiary Colliers International Property Consultants, offers full service commercial real estate services through over 480 offices in 61 countries. Other brands in this segment include PGP Property Valuation, PKF Hotel & Hospitality Consulting and MHPM Project Managers. In October 2009, FirstService acquired 29.99% ownership of U.K.-based real estate consultancy firm Colliers CRE plc. In January 2010, Colliers International Property Consultants and FirstService Real Estate Advisors agreed to combine under the Colliers International name. In April 2010, Colliers International acquired a controlling stake in commercial real estate services company Colliers Bennett & Kahnweiler.

FINANCIALS: **Sales and profits are in thousands of dollars—add 000 to get the full amount. 2009 Note: Financial information for 2009 was not available for all companies at press time.**

2009 Sales: $1,703,222	2009 Profits: $-7,279	**U.S. Stock Ticker: FSRV**
2008 Sales: $1,549,713	2008 Profits: $34,863	**Int'l Ticker: FSV** Int'l Exchange: Toronto-TSX
2007 Sales: $1,152,821	2007 Profits: $34,863	Employees: 18,000
2006 Sales: $918,668	2006 Profits: $69,497	Fiscal Year Ends: 12/31
2005 Sales: $812,300	2005 Profits: $23,200	Parent Company:

SALARIES/BENEFITS:

Pension Plan:	ESOP Stock Plan:	Profit Sharing:	Top Exec. Salary: $1,155,300	Bonus: $3,347,300
Savings Plan:	Stock Purch. Plan:		Second Exec. Salary: $469,200	Bonus: $

OTHER THOUGHTS:

Apparent Women Officers or Directors:
Hot Spot for Advancement for Women/Minorities:

LOCATIONS: ("Y" = Yes)

West:	Southwest:	Midwest:	Southeast:	Northeast:	International:
Y	Y	Y	Y	Y	Y

FIVE STAR PRODUCTS INC

www.fivestarproducts.com

Industry Group Code: 4233 **Ranks within this company's industry group:** Sales: Profits:

Properties:		Financial Services:		Construction/Development:		Investments:		Specialty Services:		Brokerage:	
Apartments:		Mortgages:		Commercial Construction:		REIT:		Property Management:		Commercial Sales:	
Malls/Shopping:		Title Insurance:		Residential Construction:				Online Services:		Residential Sales:	
Offices:		Property Insurance:		Land Development:				Software/IT:	Y	Specialty:	
Hotels/Motels:				Support Services:	Y			Consulting:			
Industrial/Warehouses:				Design/Engineering:	Y						
Other:											

TYPES OF BUSINESS:

Hardware
Decorating & Finishing Products
Hardware Distribution
Painting Supplies
Technical Services

BRANDS/DIVISIONS/AFFILIATES:

National Patent Development Corporation
Five Star Special Grout 400
Five Star Fast Set Cement
Five Star Fluid Epoxy
Five Star High Temperature Grout
Five Star Group, Inc.
Novolac
Design-A-Spec

CONTACTS:

Note: Officers with more than one job title may be intentionally listed here more than once.

David Babcock, CEO
David Babcock, Pres.
Terry Stysly, VP-Sales
Chris Piekos, Mgr.-Technical Svcs.
Steven P. Fenelli, VP-Prod. Dev.
Steven P. Fenelli, VP-Mfg.
Bobby Carlson, Mgr.-Southeast Region
Rick Dufresne, Mgr.-Northeast Region
Walt Cooper, Mgr.-Central Region
Simon Ross, Mgr.-Int'l Sales

Phone: 203-336-7900	**Fax:** 203-336-7930
Toll-Free:	
Address: 750 Commerce Dr., Fairfield, CT 06825 US	

GROWTH PLANS/SPECIAL FEATURES:

Five Star Products, Inc. is engaged in the wholesale distribution of home decorating, hardware and finishing products. It is a wholly-owned subsidiary of National Patent Development Corporation. Five Star serves over 3,000 retail dealers in the Northeast and Mid Atlantic states, making it one of the largest independent distributors in the Northeastern U.S. The firm and its subsidiary, Five Star Group, Inc., operate two warehouse facilities located in Newington, Connecticut and East Hanover, New Jersey. The company has 100 patents worldwide and offers a variety of high performance cement and epoxy based construction solutions for the industrial, infrastructure and marine markets. Specific products produced by Five Star include concrete restoration, advanced vibration dampening products, waterproofing coatings, adhesives and machinery foundation systems. The firm is also a major distributor of paint sundry items, interior and exterior stains, brushes, rollers, caulking compounds and hardware products. Five Star additionally offers products from manufacturers such as Valspar/Cabot Stain; William Zinsser; DAP; General Electric Corporation; Newell/Irwin; USG; Stanley Tools; Minwax; and 3M Company. The company offers its own line of patented products, which include Five Star Special Grout 400, Five Star Fluid Epoxy and Five Star Fast Set Cement. It distributes its products to lumberyards, do-it-yourself centers, hardware stores and paint stores throughout the world. Five Star has also developed elastomeric grout, which absorbs vibration in the train and trolley industries; a line of Novolac products for coatings, structural concrete and grout; and a new computer program, Design-A-Spec, which assists engineers in selecting the proper products for applications, giving specifications for general conditions, materials, preparation, application, finishing and curing.

FINANCIALS:

Sales and profits are in thousands of dollars—add 000 to get the full amount. 2009 Note: Financial information for 2009 was not available for all companies at press time.

2009 Sales: $	2009 Profits: $	**U.S. Stock Ticker: Subsidiary**
2008 Sales: $	2008 Profits: $	**Int'l Ticker:** Int'l Exchange:
2007 Sales: $123,713	2007 Profits: $1,199	Employees:
2006 Sales: $108,088	2006 Profits: $ 285	Fiscal Year Ends: 12/31
2005 Sales: $106,451	2005 Profits: $- 287	Parent Company: NATIONAL PATENT DEVELOPMENT CORP

SALARIES/BENEFITS:

Pension Plan:	ESOP Stock Plan:	Profit Sharing:	Top Exec. Salary: $	Bonus: $
Savings Plan:	Stock Purch. Plan:		Second Exec. Salary: $	Bonus: $

OTHER THOUGHTS:

Apparent Women Officers or Directors: 1
Hot Spot for Advancement for Women/Minorities:

LOCATIONS: ("Y" = Yes)

West:	Southwest:	Midwest:	Southeast:	Northeast:	International:
Y		Y	Y	Y	Y

FLUOR CORP

www.fluor.com

Industry Group Code: 237 **Ranks within this company's industry group:** Sales: 5 Profits: 5

Properties:		Financial Services:		Construction/Development:		Investments:		Specialty Services:		Brokerage:	
Apartments:		Mortgages:		Commercial Construction:		REIT:		Property Management:	Y	Commercial Sales:	
Malls/Shopping:		Title Insurance:		Residential Construction:				Online Services:		Residential Sales:	
Offices:		Property Insurance:		Land Development:				Software/IT:		Specialty:	
Hotels/Motels:				Support Services:				Consulting:	Y		
Industrial/Warehouses:				Design/Engineering:	Y						
Other:											

TYPES OF BUSINESS:

Construction, Heavy & Civil Engineering
Power Plant Construction and Management
Facilities Management
Procurement Services
Consulting Services
Project Management
Asset Management
Staffing Services

BRANDS/DIVISIONS/AFFILIATES:

Fluor Constructors International, Inc.
Fluor Canada

CONTACTS:
Note: Officers with more than one job title may be intentionally listed here more than once.

Alan L. Boeckmann, CEO
David T. Seaton, COO
D. Michael Steuert, CFO/Sr. VP
Glenn Gilkey, Sr. VP-Human Resources
Ray F. Barnard, CIO/VP
Glenn Gilkey, Sr. VP-Admin.
Carlos M. Hernandez, Chief Legal Officer/Corp. Sec.
David E. Constable, Group Pres., Oper.
John L. Hopkins, Group Exec.-Bus. Dev.
Lee Tashjian, VP-Corp. Affairs
Kenneth H. Lockwood, VP-Investor Rel.
Kenneth H. Lockwood, VP-Corp. Finance
Wendy Hallgren, VP-Corp. Compliance
David Marventano, Sr. VP-Gov't Rel.
Joanna M. Oliva, Treas./VP
Richard P. Carter, Pres., Fluor Constructors International, Inc.
Alan L. Boeckmann, Chmn.
Kirk D. Grimes, Pres., Global Svcs.

Phone: 469-398-7000	**Fax:** 469-398-7255
Toll-Free:	
Address: 6700 Las Colinas Blvd., Irving, TX 75039 US	

GROWTH PLANS/SPECIAL FEATURES:

Fluor Corp. is a global provider of engineering, procurement, construction and maintenance services, with offices in over 25 countries spanning across six continents. As well as being a primary service provider to the U.S. federal government, Fluor serves a diverse set of industries including oil and gas; chemical and petrochemicals; transportation; mining and metals; power; life sciences; and manufacturing. Fluor operates in five business segments: oil and gas; industrial and infrastructure; government; global services; and power. The oil and gas segment offers design, engineering, procurement, construction and project management services to energy-related industries. The industrial and infrastructure segment provides design, engineering and construction services to the transportation, mining, life sciences, telecommunications, manufacturing, microelectronics and healthcare sectors. The government segment provides project management services, including environmental restoration, engineering, construction, site operations and maintenance, to the U.S. government, particularly to the Department of Energy, the Department of Homeland Security and the Department of Defense. The global services segment provides operations, maintenance and construction services, as well as industrial fleet outsourcing, plant turnaround services, temporary staffing, procurement services and construction-related support. The power segment provides such services as engineering, procurement, construction, program management, start-up, commissioning and maintenance to the gas fueled, solid fueled, renewable and nuclear marketplaces. Fluor Constructors International, Inc., which operates separately from the rest of the businesses, provides unionized management and construction services in the U.S. and Canada, both independently.

Employees are offered medical, dental and vision insurance; life insurance; disability coverage; a retirement plan; a 401(k) savings plan; an employee assistance program; a tax savings account; and education assistance; automobile and home insurance; and legal services.

FINANCIALS:
Sales and profits are in thousands of dollars—add 000 to get the full amount. 2009 Note: Financial information for 2009 was not available for all companies at press time.

2009 Sales: $21,990,300	2009 Profits: $732,875	**U.S. Stock Ticker: FLR**
2008 Sales: $22,325,900	2008 Profits: $748,903	**Int'l Ticker:** Int'l Exchange:
2007 Sales: $16,691,000	2007 Profits: $527,961	Employees: 36,152
2006 Sales: $14,078,500	2006 Profits: $263,500	Fiscal Year Ends: 12/31
2005 Sales: $13,161,100	2005 Profits: $227,300	Parent Company:

SALARIES/BENEFITS:

Pension Plan: Y	ESOP Stock Plan:	Profit Sharing:	Top Exec. Salary: $1,232,270	Bonus: $6,873,200
Savings Plan: Y	Stock Purch. Plan:		Second Exec. Salary: $781,871	Bonus: $2,563,000

OTHER THOUGHTS:

Apparent Women Officers or Directors: 3
Hot Spot for Advancement for Women/Minorities: Y

LOCATIONS: ("Y" = Yes)

West:	Southwest:	Midwest:	Southeast:	Northeast:	International:
Y	Y	Y	Y	Y	Y

FOMENTO DE CONSTRUCCIONES Y CONTRATAS SA (FCC)

www.fcc.es

Industry Group Code: 237 **Ranks within this company's industry group:** Sales: 9 Profits: 8

Properties:		Financial Services:		Construction/Development:		Investments:		Specialty Services:		Brokerage:	
Apartments:		Mortgages:		Commercial Construction:	Y	REIT:		Property Management:		Commercial Sales:	
Malls/Shopping:		Title Insurance:		Residential Construction:				Online Services:		Residential Sales:	
Offices:		Property Insurance:		Land Development:	Y			Software/IT:		Specialty:	
Hotels/Motels:				Support Services:				Consulting:			
Industrial/Warehouses:				Design/Engineering:							
Other:											

TYPES OF BUSINESS:

Heavy Construction
Airport Operations
Urban Sanitation
Commuter Bus & Rail Lines
Logistics Services
Real Estate Development
Cement Manufacturing
Engineering Services

BRANDS/DIVISIONS/AFFILIATES:

Cementos Portland Valderrivas
FCC Medio Ambiente, S.A.
FCC Versia, S.A.
Aqualia, S.A.
Torre Picasso
Realia Business, S.A.
Global Via Infrastructures SA (GlobalVia)

CONTACTS: *Note: Officers with more than one job title may be intentionally listed here more than once.*

Baldomero Falcones Jaquotot, Exec. Dir.
Antonio Perez Colmenero, Corp. Mgr.-Human & Other Resources
Jose Luis Vasco Hernando, Mgr.-Admin.
Felipe Bernabe Garcia Perez, General Sec.
Victor Pastor Fernandez, Gen. Mgr.-Finance
Dieter Kiefer, Chmn.-Cementos Portland Valderrivas, Spain
Jose Mayor Oreja, Chmn.-FCC Construccion, S.A.
Jose Luis de la Torre Sanchez, Chmn.-FCC Servicios
Antonio Gomez Ciria, Gen. Mgr.-Internal Audit
Baldomero Falcones Jaquotot, Chmn.
Jose Liebana Alcantarilla, Mgr.-Int'l Corp. Dev.

Phone: 34-91-359-54-00	**Fax:** 34-91-359-49-23
Toll-Free:	
Address: Federico Salmon 13, Madrid, 28016 Spain	

GROWTH PLANS/SPECIAL FEATURES:

Fomento de Construcciones Y Contratas S.A. (FCC) is parent company to one of Spain's leading construction and service groups. It divides its business between construction, which generates 55.2% of the firm's revenues; cement production, 10.2%; other services, 32.3%; and Real Estate, 3.1%. The firm's construction business consists of civil engineering, non-residential building and residential building. Construction projects have included oil and gas pipelines; highways; airports; and railways. The firm's cement business, with operations in the U.S. as well in Argentina, Uruguay, Canada, the U.K. and Tunisia, is conducted by Cementos Portland Valderrivas, a leading Spanish cement firm with control over 15 cement factories. FCC's services are conducted by its Environmental Services division, which generated 25.9% of FCC's total net revenue Versia (a part of Environmental Services), and Torre Picasso. The firm's environmental services are conducted by FCC itself, FCC Medio Ambiente, S.A.; FCC Versia, S.A.; and Aqualia, S.A. Services include sewer system maintenance; street cleaning; collecting, treating and eliminating solid urban waste; park and garden maintenance; full-service water management; and treating and eliminating industrial waste. Versia's services include logistics; parking; passenger transportation; urban furniture; handling; conservation and systems; and technical vehicle inspections. Torre Picasso provides real estate services, as does Realia Business, S.A., in which FCC owns a 30% interest. Realia is involved in real estate development, rental and other services. In January 2009, the company acquired 14 wind farms in Spain from Australian firm, Babcock & Brown Wind Partners.

FINANCIALS: **Sales and profits are in thousands of dollars—add 000 to get the full amount. 2009 Note: Financial information for 2009 was not available for all companies at press time.**

2009 Sales: $17,496,500	2009 Profits: $414,637	**U.S. Stock Ticker: FCC**
2008 Sales: $18,563,200	2008 Profits: $446,330	**Int'l Ticker: FCC** Int'l Exchange: Madrid-MCE
2007 Sales: $17,777,800	2007 Profits: $977,430	Employees:
2006 Sales: $13,747,300	2006 Profits: $776,500	Fiscal Year Ends: 12/31
2005 Sales: $9,640,270	2005 Profits: $572,430	Parent Company:

SALARIES/BENEFITS:

Pension Plan:	ESOP Stock Plan:	Profit Sharing:	Top Exec. Salary: $	Bonus: $
Savings Plan:	Stock Purch. Plan:		Second Exec. Salary: $	Bonus: $

OTHER THOUGHTS:

Apparent Women Officers or Directors:
Hot Spot for Advancement for Women/Minorities:

LOCATIONS: ("Y" = Yes)

West:	Southwest:	Midwest:	Southeast:	Northeast:	International:
			Y	Y	Y

FOREST CITY ENTERPRISES INC

www.fceinc.com

Industry Group Code: 5311 **Ranks within this company's industry group:** Sales: 18 Profits: 22

Properties:		Financial Services:		Construction/Development:		Investments:		Specialty Services:		Brokerage:	
Apartments:	Y	Mortgages:		Commercial Construction:		REIT:		Property Management:	Y	Commercial Sales:	
Malls/Shopping:	Y	Title Insurance:		Residential Construction:				Online Services:		Residential Sales:	
Offices:	Y	Property Insurance:		Land Development:	Y			Software/IT:		Specialty:	
Hotels/Motels:	Y			Support Services:				Consulting:			
Industrial/Warehouses:	Y			Design/Engineering:							
Other:											

TYPES OF BUSINESS:

Real Estate Development & Management
Office Buildings
Apartments
Retail Centers
Hotels
Land Development
Industrial Development
Military Housing

BRANDS/DIVISIONS/AFFILIATES:

Mesa del Sol
New Jersey Nets

CONTACTS:

Note: Officers with more than one job title may be intentionally listed here more than once.

Charles A. Ratner, CEO
David J. LaRue, COO/Exec. VP
Charles A. Ratner, Pres.
Robert G. O'Brien, CFO/Exec. VP
Nancy W. McCann, Sr. VP-Mktg. & Public Rel.
Andy Passen, Exec. VP-Human Resources
Charles L. Rau, CTO/VP
Linda M. Kane, Chief Admin. Officer/Sr. VP
Geralyn M. Presti, General Counsel/Sr. VP
Nancy W. McCann, Sr. VP-Public Rel.
Linda M. Kane, Chief Acct. Officer
David J. LaRue, Pres./COO-Commercial Group
Robert F. Monchein, Pres., Land Group
Ronald A. Ratner, Exec. VP/Pres./CEO-Residential Group
Bruce C. Ratner, Exec. VP/CEO- Forest City Ratner Co.
Albert B. Ratner, Co-Chmn.

Phone: 216-621-6060 **Fax:** 216-263-4808
Toll-Free:
Address: 1100 Terminal Tower, 50 Public Sq., Cleveland, OH 44113 US

GROWTH PLANS/SPECIAL FEATURES:

Forest City Enterprises, Inc., a $10.9 billion real estate company, primarily owns, develops, acquires and manages premier commercial and residential real estate throughout the U.S. Its portfolio consists of hotels, office buildings, apartment communities and retail centers. It operates through three strategic business units (SBUs). The Commercial Group, its largest SBU, has 96 completed projects, including 44 retail centers with 12.8 million square feet of gross leasable area; five hotels with 1,823 rooms; 47 office buildings with 13.1 million square feet; and mixed-use facilities, such as the 12,900 acre Mesa del Sol urban community in Albuquerque, New Mexico. The Residential Group deals with apartments, adaptive re-use developments, federally assisted housing, senior housing, mixed-use facilities, military housing and new condos and town homes. It has more than 31,891 units in 116 properties across 20 states and Washington, D.C.; and almost 1,260 syndicated senior subsidized housing in eight properties. The Land Development Group acquires and sells raw land and developed lots to commercial, residential and industrial customers; and develops raw land into master-planned communities, mixed-use projects and other residential developments. It currently owns over 10,497 acres of undeveloped land. Forest leases retail space, with its largest retail tenants consisting of Bass Pro Shops, Inc.; AMC Entertainment, Inc.; Regal Entertainment Group; and The Gap. It also leases office space, with its largest tenants consisting of the City of New York; Millennium Pharmaceuticals, Inc.; and the U.S. Government. Forest also reports its 21% ownership interest in the New Jersey Nets NBA franchise as a segment. Ownership in the Nets is the first step in a development called Atlantic Yards, which will include a new entertainment arena complex and adjacent urban developments combining housing, offices, shops and public open space.

Employees are offered medical, dental, vision and life insurance; disability coverage; tuition reimbursement and flexible spending accounts.

FINANCIALS:

Sales and profits are in thousands of dollars—add 000 to get the full amount. 2009 Note: Financial information for 2009 was not available for all companies at press time.

2009 Sales: $1,290,390	2009 Profits: $-112,200
2008 Sales: $1,286,470	2008 Profits: $52,425
2007 Sales: $1,116,639	2007 Profits: $177,251
2006 Sales: $1,085,857	2006 Profits: $83,519
2005 Sales: $887,362	2005 Profits: $85,206

U.S. Stock Ticker: FCE.A
Int'l Ticker: Int'l Exchange:
Employees: 3,237
Fiscal Year Ends: 1/31
Parent Company:

SALARIES/BENEFITS:

Pension Plan:	ESOP Stock Plan:	Profit Sharing:	Top Exec. Salary: $	Bonus: $
Savings Plan: Y	Stock Purch. Plan:		Second Exec. Salary: $	Bonus: $

OTHER THOUGHTS:

Apparent Women Officers or Directors: 10
Hot Spot for Advancement for Women/Minorities: Y

LOCATIONS: ("Y" = Yes)

West:	Southwest:	Midwest:	Southeast:	Northeast:	International:
Y	Y	Y		Y	

FOUR SEASONS HOTELS

www.fourseasons.com

Industry Group Code: 721110 **Ranks within this company's industry group:** Sales: Profits:

Properties:		Financial Services:		Construction/Development:		Investments:		Specialty Services:		Brokerage:	
Apartments:	Y	Mortgages:		Commercial Construction:		REIT:		Property Management:	Y	Commercial Sales:	
Malls/Shopping:		Title Insurance:		Residential Construction:				Online Services:		Residential Sales:	
Offices:		Property Insurance:		Land Development:				Software/IT:		Specialty:	
Hotels/Motels:	Y			Support Services:				Consulting:			
Industrial/Warehouses:				Design/Engineering:							
Other:	Y										

TYPES OF BUSINESS:

Hotels, Luxury
Luxury Condominiums
Conference Centers
Resort Time Shares

BRANDS/DIVISIONS/AFFILIATES:

Regent Hotels
Four Seasons Hotels
Four Seasons Private Residences

CONTACTS: *Note: Officers with more than one job title may be intentionally listed here more than once.*

Isadore Sharp, CEO
Kathleen Taylor, COO
Kathleen Taylor, Pres.
John Davison, CFO
Susan Helstab, Exec. VP-Mktg.
Nick Mutton, Exec. VP-Human Resources
Nick Mutton, Exec. VP-Admin.
Jim FitzGibbon, Exec. VP/Pres., Worldwide Hotel Oper.
Scott Woroch, Exec. VP-Worldwide Dev.
Nicola Blazier, Dir.-Corp. Public Rel.
John Davison, Exec. VP-Residential
Isadore Sharp, Chmn.
Antoine Corinthios, Pres., EMEA

Phone: 416-449-1750	**Fax:** 416-441-4374
Toll-Free:	
Address: 1165 Leslie St., Toronto, ON M3C 2K8 Canada	

GROWTH PLANS/SPECIAL FEATURES:

Four Seasons Hotels, Inc. is a leading operator of luxury hotels and resorts. Headquartered in Toronto, the company manages 83 properties in 35 countries, mostly operated under the Four Seasons and Regent brands, owning roughly half of them. The firm offers its guests amenities such as monogrammed terry-cloth bathrobes, concierge service, in-room fax machines, overnight sandal and golf shoe repair and even in-room exercise equipment installation, if the guest should request it. The No Luggage Required program provides a variety of crucial loan-items to customers who have lost their belongings. Many hotels provide experienced meeting and conference personnel to help guests plan business events such as award galas and multimedia presentations. Moreover, the firm offers a number of branded vacation ownership properties and private residences in Jackson Hole, Wyoming; Scottsdale, Arizona; San Francisco, California; Miami, Florida; and Houston, Texas, with new properties under development in Toronto, Canada. New locations where Four Seasons Hotels have opened include the Maldives; northern Thailand; Damascus, Syria; Geneva, Switzerland; Palo Alto, California; Beirut, Lebanon and Lana'i, Hawaii. In January 2010, the firm opened a hotel in Beirut, Lebanon.

In 2010, for the 13th consecutive year, the Four Seasons was listed on Fortune magazine's list of the 100 Best Companies to Work For.

FINANCIALS: **Sales and profits are in thousands of dollars—add 000 to get the full amount. 2009 Note: Financial information for 2009 was not available for all companies at press time.**

2009 Sales: $	2009 Profits: $	**U.S. Stock Ticker: Private**
2008 Sales: $	2008 Profits: $	**Int'l Ticker:** Int'l Exchange:
2007 Sales: $	2007 Profits: $	Employees:
2006 Sales: $253,425	2006 Profits: $50,287	Fiscal Year Ends: 12/31
2005 Sales: $248,338	2005 Profits: $-28,223	Parent Company:

SALARIES/BENEFITS:

Pension Plan:	ESOP Stock Plan:	Profit Sharing:	Top Exec. Salary: $	Bonus: $
Savings Plan:	Stock Purch. Plan:		Second Exec. Salary: $	Bonus: $

OTHER THOUGHTS:

Apparent Women Officers or Directors: 3
Hot Spot for Advancement for Women/Minorities: Y

LOCATIONS: ("Y" = Yes)

West:	Southwest:	Midwest:	Southeast:	Northeast:	International:
Y	Y	Y	Y	Y	Y

FREDDIE MAC

www.freddiemac.com

Industry Group Code: 522310 **Ranks within this company's industry group:** Sales: Profits: 4

Properties:		Financial Services:		Construction/Development:		Investments:		Specialty Services:		Brokerage:	
Apartments:		Mortgages:	Y	Commercial Construction:		REIT:		Property Management:		Commercial Sales:	
Malls/Shopping:		Title Insurance:		Residential Construction:				Online Services:		Residential Sales:	
Offices:		Property Insurance:		Land Development:				Software/IT:		Specialty:	
Hotels/Motels:				Support Services:				Consulting:			
Industrial/Warehouses:				Design/Engineering:							
Other:											

TYPES OF BUSINESS:

Mortgage Purchasing
Credit Services

BRANDS/DIVISIONS/AFFILIATES:

Federal Home Loan Mortgage Corp.

CONTACTS:

Note: Officers with more than one job title may be intentionally listed here more than once.

Charles E. Haldeman, Jr., CEO
Bruce M. Witherell, COO
Ross J. Kari, CFO
Paul G. George, Exec. VP-Human Resources
Mike Perlman, Exec. VP-Tech.
Robert E. Bostrom, General Counsel/Exec. VP
Mike Perlman, Exec. VP-Oper.
Ralph F. Boyd, Jr., Exec. VP-Comm. Rel.
Michael C. May, Sr. VP-Multifamily Sourcing
Hollis McLoughlin, Sr. VP-External Rel.
Paul E. Mullings, Sr. VP-Single Family Sourcing
Anurag Saksena, Chief Enterprise Risk Officer/Sr. VP
John A. Koskinen, Chmn.

Phone: 703-903-2000	**Fax:**
Toll-Free: 800-424-5401	
Address: 8200 Jones Branch Dr., McLean, VA 22102 US	

GROWTH PLANS/SPECIAL FEATURES:

Freddie Mac, officially known as Federal Home Loan Mortgage Corporation, is a public corporation chartered by the U.S. Congress to create a continuous flow of funds to mortgage lenders in support of home ownership and rental housing. The company purchases residential mortgages from lenders then packages them into securities, which are sold to investors worldwide. The firm also lends money directly to homebuyers. The firm purchases 30-year, 20-year, 15-year and 10-year fixed-rate single-family mortgages, adjustable-rate mortgages (ARMs) and balloon/reset mortgages. Freddie Mac's mortgage securitization business receives the mortgage payments from the original lender or loan servicer, deducts a timeliness guarantee fee and other fees, passing the remainder on to the holder or holders of the mortgage-backed securities. The company implements regular public risk-based capital stress tests, initiates public interest-rate risk sensitivity analyses, discloses credit risk sensitivity analyses and obtains annual ratings from statistical rating organizations. In September 2008, after suffering devastating losses in it mortgage portfolio, Freddie Mac was placed in conservatorship by the U.S. federal government, which has taken effective control of the company. Over the near term, its focus will be on less aggressive lending, attempting to facilitate stability in the housing market and workouts of existing mortgages. Initially, the U. S. Treasury committed to provide up to $100 billion under the senior preferred stock purchase agreement. In February 2009, the Treasury increased its commitment to $200 billion. The program to buy mortgage-related securities issued by Freddie Mac is set to expire at the end of 2009.

The company provides employee benefits include health insurance, a 401(k) plan, a stock purchase and pension plan.

FINANCIALS:

Sales and profits are in thousands of dollars—add 000 to get the full amount. 2009 Note: Financial information for 2009 was not available for all companies at press time.

2009 Sales: $	2009 Profits: $-21,553,000	**U.S. Stock Ticker: FRE**
2008 Sales: $	2008 Profits: $-50,119,000	**Int'l Ticker:** Int'l Exchange:
2007 Sales: $1,009,000	2007 Profits: $-3,094,000	Employees: 4,927
2006 Sales: $42,264,000	2006 Profits: $2,327,000	Fiscal Year Ends: 12/31
2005 Sales: $36,327,000	2005 Profits: $	Parent Company:

SALARIES/BENEFITS:

Pension Plan: Y	ESOP Stock Plan:	Profit Sharing:	Top Exec. Salary: $	Bonus: $
Savings Plan: Y	Stock Purch. Plan: Y		Second Exec. Salary: $	Bonus: $

OTHER THOUGHTS:

Apparent Women Officers or Directors: 2
Hot Spot for Advancement for Women/Minorities: Y

LOCATIONS: ("Y" = Yes)

West:	Southwest:	Midwest:	Southeast:	Northeast:	International:
				Y	

GABLES RESIDENTIAL TRUST

www.gables.com

Industry Group Code: 531110 **Ranks within this company's industry group:** Sales: Profits:

Properties:		Financial Services:		Construction/Development:		Investments:		Specialty Services:		Brokerage:	
Apartments:	Y	Mortgages:	Y	Commercial Construction:		REIT:	Y	Property Management:	Y	Commercial Sales:	
Malls/Shopping:		Title Insurance:		Residential Construction:				Online Services:		Residential Sales:	
Offices:		Property Insurance:		Land Development:				Software/IT:		Specialty:	
Hotels/Motels:				Support Services:				Consulting:	Y		
Industrial/Warehouses:				Design/Engineering:							
Other:											

TYPES OF BUSINESS:

Real Estate Investment Trust
Apartment Communities

BRANDS/DIVISIONS/AFFILIATES:

Gables Realty, LP
Gables Advantage Home Mortgage Program
Gables Corporate Accommodations
Express Luxury
ING Clarion
Lehman Brothers

CONTACTS:

Note: Officers with more than one job title may be intentionally listed here more than once.

David Fitch, CEO
Susan Ansel, COO/Exec. VP
David D. Fitch, Pres.
Dawn Severt, CFO/Exec. VP
Philip Altschuler, VP-Human Resources
Robert D. Lamb, VP-IT
Cristina Sullivan, Sr. VP-Property Oper.
David Reece, Sr. VP-Finance & Capital Markets
Dennis E. Rainosek, Sr. VP-Portfolio Mgmt.
Darin Botelho, VP-Retail Oper.
Joseph Wilber, Sr. VP-Investments, East
Douglas Chesnut, Sr. VP-Investments, West
Chris D. Wheeler, Chmn.

Phone: 404-923-5500	**Fax:**
Toll-Free:	
Address: 3399 Peachtree Road N.E., Ste. 600, Atlanta, GA 30326 US	

GROWTH PLANS/SPECIAL FEATURES:

Gables Residential Trust, owned by a closed-end fund managed by a joint venture between ING Clarion and Lehman Brothers, is a real estate investment trust (REIT) engaged in the business of multi-family apartment community management, development, construction, disposition and acquisition. The company owns upscale apartment communities primarily in Atlanta, Georgia; South Florida; Houston, Austin and Dallas, Texas; Tampa, Florida; San Diego/Inland Empire, California; and Washington, D.C. Gables manages over 38,000 apartment homes in over 120 communities; owns 57 communities with over 14,500 apartment homes; and is in the process of developing an additional 20 communities. As a real estate investment trust (REIT), substantially all of the company's business is conducted through Gables Realty, LP. Management solutions offered by Gables includes NOI and performance improvement; leasing and marketing strategy; customized accounting and reporting; development; construction and renovation; and asset preservation planning. Gables offers its tenants Gables Great Awards, a program which provides carpet cleaning and home-improvements such as paint, patio/balcony detailing and vinyl replacement. Additional services provided by the firm are property management and consulting and development services. In addition to residential apartments, the company also offers Gables Corporate Accommodations, a temporary housing provider for business travel, insurance claims and entertainment industry projects. Express Luxury packages for corporate accommodations include a studio, 1-, 2- or 3-bedroom apartment with utensils, cookware, dishes, utilities, a washer and dryer and maid service.

The company offers employees medical, dental and vision coverage; flexible spending plans; a rental housing allowance; a 401(k) plan; an employee assistance plan; a bonus program; short- and long-term disability insurance; and continuing career development with Gables University.

FINANCIALS:

Sales and profits are in thousands of dollars—add 000 to get the full amount. 2009 Note: Financial information for 2009 was not available for all companies at press time.

2009 Sales: $	2009 Profits: $	**U.S. Stock Ticker: Private**
2008 Sales: $	2008 Profits: $	**Int'l Ticker:** Int'l Exchange:
2007 Sales: $	2007 Profits: $	Employees:
2006 Sales: $	2006 Profits: $	Fiscal Year Ends: 12/31
2005 Sales: $	2005 Profits: $	Parent Company:

SALARIES/BENEFITS:

Pension Plan:	ESOP Stock Plan:	Profit Sharing:	Top Exec. Salary: $	Bonus: $
Savings Plan: Y	Stock Purch. Plan:		Second Exec. Salary: $	Bonus: $

OTHER THOUGHTS:

Apparent Women Officers or Directors: 15
Hot Spot for Advancement for Women/Minorities: Y

LOCATIONS: ("Y" = Yes)

West:	Southwest:	Midwest:	Southeast:	Northeast:	International:
Y	Y		Y	Y	

GAFISA SA

www.gafisa.com.br

Industry Group Code: 5311 **Ranks within this company's industry group:** Sales: 20 Profits: 21

Properties:		Financial Services:		Construction/Development:		Investments:		Specialty Services:		Brokerage:	
Apartments:		Mortgages:		Commercial Construction:	Y	REIT:		Property Management:	Y	Commercial Sales:	Y
Malls/Shopping:		Title Insurance:		Residential Construction:	Y			Online Services:		Residential Sales:	Y
Offices:	Y	Property Insurance:		Land Development:	Y			Software/IT:		Specialty:	
Hotels/Motels:				Support Services:				Consulting:			
Industrial/Warehouses:				Design/Engineering:							
Other:	Y										

TYPES OF BUSINESS:

Construction & Real Estate Services
Construction Services
Real Estate Services
Residential Communities
Commercial Buildings
Third Party Construction Services

BRANDS/DIVISIONS/AFFILIATES:

Gafisa Vendas
Alphaville Urbanismo S.A.
Cipesa Engenharia S.A.
Construtora Tenda S.A.

CONTACTS:

Note: Officers with more than one job title may be intentionally listed here more than once.

Wilson Amaral de Oliveira, CEO
Alceu Duilio Calciolari, CFO
Mario Rocha Neto, Exec. Officer-Oper.
Odair Garcia Senra, Dir.-Dev.
Alceu Duilio Calciolari, Investor Rel. Officer
Antonio Carlos Ferreira Rosa, Exec. Officer-New Markets
Gary R. Garrabrant, Chmn.

Phone: 55-11-3025-9000 **Fax:** 55-11-3025-9348
Toll-Free:
Address: Ave. Nacoes Unidas, 8501 19th Fl., Sao Paulo, 05425-070 Brazil

GROWTH PLANS/SPECIAL FEATURES:

Gafisa S.A., based in Sao Paulo, Brazil, is a provider of construction and real estate services. Since its founding, Gafisa has completed and sold more than 970 developments and constructed over 36 million square feet of residential space. The firm focuses primarily on residential markets, and over half of its construction revenues annually derive from middle and upper-income residential developments. The company's real estate services are likewise geared toward middle and upper-income customers. However, Gafisa also sells residential units, land subdivisions, commercial buildings, construction services and entry-level housing units, in large part through its brokerage subsidiary Gafisa Vendas. Gafisa provides construction services to third parties across Brazil, primarily to developers of residential and commercial projects who do not construct their own designs. The company has a presence in roughly 94 Brazilian municipalities, including Sao Paulo, Rio de Janeiro, Salvador, Fortaleza, Natal, Curitiba, Belo Horizonte, Manaus, Porto Alegre and Belem, across 18 states. More than half of new projects are typically located in the populous states of Sao Paulo and Rio de Janeiro. The firm owns 60% of subsidiary Alphaville Urbanismo S.A., a residential community developer focused on premium metropolitan markets; a 70% stake in Cipesa Engenharia S.A., a homebuilding company in the state of Alagoas; and a 60% share of Construtora Tenda S.A., a developer of low-income residential projects. In March 2009 Gafisa exited Bairro Novo, a joint venture partnership with Odebrecht Empreendimentos Imobiliarios Ltda which had been focused on the development, construction and management of low-income residential projects. In November 2009, Bank of America Corporation acquired an approximate 5% stake in Gafisa.

FINANCIALS:

Sales and profits are in thousands of dollars—add 000 to get the full amount. 2009 Note: Financial information for 2009 was not available for all companies at press time.

2009 Sales: $1,720,150	2009 Profits: $121,510	**U.S. Stock Ticker: GFA**
2008 Sales: $990,550	2008 Profits: $62,550	**Int'l Ticker:** Int'l Exchange:
2007 Sales: $682,430	2007 Profits: $52,130	Employees:
2006 Sales: $411,600	2006 Profits: $28,600	Fiscal Year Ends: 12/31
2005 Sales: $192,000	2005 Profits: $13,200	Parent Company:

SALARIES/BENEFITS:

Pension Plan:	ESOP Stock Plan:	Profit Sharing:	Top Exec. Salary: $	Bonus: $
Savings Plan:	Stock Purch. Plan:		Second Exec. Salary: $	Bonus: $

OTHER THOUGHTS:

Apparent Women Officers or Directors:
Hot Spot for Advancement for Women/Minorities:

LOCATIONS: ("Y" = Yes)

West:	Southwest:	Midwest:	Southeast:	Northeast:	International:
					Y

GAYLORD ENTERTAINMENT CO

www.gaylordentertainment.com

Industry Group Code: 721110 **Ranks within this company's industry group:** Sales: 14 Profits: 18

Properties:		Financial Services:		Construction/Development:		Investments:		Specialty Services:		Brokerage:	
Apartments:		Mortgages:		Commercial Construction:		REIT:		Property Management:		Commercial Sales:	
Malls/Shopping:		Title Insurance:		Residential Construction:				Online Services:		Residential Sales:	
Offices:		Property Insurance:		Land Development:				Software/IT:		Specialty:	
Hotels/Motels:	Y			Support Services:				Consulting:			
Industrial/Warehouses:				Design/Engineering:							
Other:											

TYPES OF BUSINESS:

Hotels & Convention Centers
Vacation Property Management
Live Entertainment Venues
Online Vacation Rental Booking
Radio Station Operation
Golf Courses
Theme Parks

BRANDS/DIVISIONS/AFFILIATES:

Gaylord Opryland Resort & Convention Center
Gaylord Palms Resort & Convention Center
Gaylord Texan Resort & Convention Center
Gaylord National Resort & Convention Center
Grand Ole Opry
General Jackson Showboat
Gaylord Springs Golf Links
Ryman Auditorium

CONTACTS: *Note: Officers with more than one job title may be intentionally listed here more than once.*

Colin V. Reed, CEO
David C. Kloeppel, COO
David C. Kloeppel, Pres.
Mark Fioravanti, CFO/Sr. VP
Rich Maradik, Chief Mktg. Officer/Sr. VP
Gara Pryor, Sr. VP-Human Resources
Bennett D. Westbrook, Sr. VP-Dev. & Design & Construction
Carter R. Todd, General Counsel/Exec. VP/Corp. Sec.
Brian Abrahamson, VP-Corp. Comm.
Stephen G. Buchanan, Sr. VP-Media & Entertainment
Phil Coffey, Sr. VP/Gen. Mgr.-Gaylord National Resort
Kemp Gallineau, Chief Sales Officer/Sr. VP
Mike Mason, Sr. VP-Sales
Colin V. Reed, Chmn.

Phone: 615-316-6000	**Fax:** 615-316-6555
Toll-Free:	
Address: 1 Gaylord Dr., Nashville, TN 37214 US	

GROWTH PLANS/SPECIAL FEATURES:

Gaylord Entertainment Company is a hospitality company focused on the large group meetings and conventions sector of the lodging market. The firm's hospitality business includes its Gaylord branded hotels, consisting of the Gaylord Opryland Resort & Convention Center in Nashville, Tennessee; the Gaylord Palms Resort & Convention Center near Orlando, Florida; the Gaylord Texan Resort & Convention Center near Dallas, Texas; and the Gaylord National Resort & Convention Center near Washington, D.C. It also owns and operates the Radisson Hotel at Opryland in Nashville. The company's hotels incorporate lodging; meeting, convention and exhibition space; food and beverage options; and retail and spa facilities. Gaylord also owns and operates several attractions in Nashville, including the Grand Ole Opry, a live country music variety show and one of the longest-running radio shows in the U.S. The firm's hospitality operations generated approximately 93% of its 2009 revenues, while its Opry and Attractions division, which includes its Nashville attractions and assets related to the Grand Ole Opry, generated 7%. The firm's Opry and Attractions group operates country radio station WSM-AM radio; the General Jackson Showboat; the Gaylord Springs Golf Links, a championship golf course; and live music venues such as the Grand Ole Opry, the Ryman Auditorium and the Wildhorse Saloon. These attractions are located on the firm's Opry Complex property in Nashville, Tennessee.

Gaylord offers its employees medical, dental, vision, prescription, life and AD&D insurance; short- and long-term disability; medical and dependent care reimbursement accounts; a 401(k) savings plan; an employee stock purchase plan; an adoption assistance program; discounts at the hotel and with local merchants; and free laundered uniforms and a meal allowance for employees who work at the hotels.

FINANCIALS: **Sales and profits are in thousands of dollars—add 000 to get the full amount. 2009 Note: Financial information for 2009 was not available for all companies at press time.**

2009 Sales: $879,121	2009 Profits: $- 23	**U.S. Stock Ticker: GET**
2008 Sales: $930,869	2008 Profits: $4,364	**Int'l Ticker:** Int'l Exchange:
2007 Sales: $747,723	2007 Profits: $111,911	Employees: 1,365
2006 Sales: $722,272	2006 Profits: $-79,435	Fiscal Year Ends: 12/31
2005 Sales: $644,536	2005 Profits: $-33,950	Parent Company:

SALARIES/BENEFITS:

Pension Plan:	ESOP Stock Plan:	Profit Sharing:	Top Exec. Salary: $897,960	Bonus: $400,000
Savings Plan: Y	Stock Purch. Plan: Y		Second Exec. Salary: $564,423	Bonus: $200,000

OTHER THOUGHTS:

Apparent Women Officers or Directors: 2
Hot Spot for Advancement for Women/Minorities:

LOCATIONS: ("Y" = Yes)

West:	Southwest:	Midwest:	Southeast:	Northeast:	International:
	Y		Y	Y	

GE CAPITAL FINANCE

www.gecapital.com

Industry Group Code: 522291 **Ranks within this company's industry group:** Sales: 1 Profits:

Properties:		Financial Services:		Construction/Development:		Investments:		Specialty Services:		Brokerage:	
Apartments:		Mortgages:	Y	Commercial Construction:		REIT:		Property Management:		Commercial Sales:	
Malls/Shopping:		Title Insurance:		Residential Construction:				Online Services:		Residential Sales:	
Offices:		Property Insurance:		Land Development:				Software/IT:		Specialty:	
Hotels/Motels:				Support Services:				Consulting:			
Industrial/Warehouses:				Design/Engineering:							
Other:											

TYPES OF BUSINESS:

Financial Products & Services
Consumer Financial Products & Services
Real Estate
Commercial Financial Products & Services

BRANDS/DIVISIONS/AFFILIATES:

General Electric

CONTACTS:

Note: Officers with more than one job title may be intentionally listed here more than once.

Michael A. Neal, CEO
William H. Cary, COO
Jeffrey S. Bornstein, CFO
Jack Ryan, Sr. VP-Human Resources
Keith Morgan, General Counsel/Sr. VP
Mark W. Begor, Pres./CEO-Retail Finance & Restructuring Oper.
Russell Wilkerson, Managing Dir.-Comm. & Public Affairs
Kathy Cassidy, Treas./Sr. VP
Alex Urquhart, Pres./CEO-GE Energy Financial Svcs.
James Colica, Sr. VP-Global Risk Mgmt.
Ronald R. Pressman, Pres./CEO-GE Capital Real Estate
Michael A. Neal, Chmn.
Richard A. Laxer, Pres./CEO-GE Capital EMEA

Phone: 203-373-2211	**Fax:** 203-373-3131
Toll-Free:	
Address: 3135 Easton Turnpike, Fairfield, CT 06828-0001 US	

GROWTH PLANS/SPECIAL FEATURES:

GE Capital Finance, a division of General Electric Co. (GE), manages all of the GE's lending and financial services units, as well as its real estate activities. GE Capital offers a broad range of financial products and services worldwide. Services include commercial loans, operating leases, fleet management, financial programs, home loans, credit cards, personal loans and other financial services. It divides its operations into Commercial Lending and Leasing (CLL); Consumer Finance; Energy Financial Services; Capital Aviation Services (GECAS); and Real Estate. CLL offers loans, leases and other financial services to customers including manufacturers, distributors and end-users for a variety of equipment and major capital assets such as industrial-related facilities and equipment; vehicles; corporate aircraft; and equipment used in many industries, including the construction, manufacturing, transportation, telecommunications and healthcare industries. GE Consumer Finance provides financial services such as credit cards; personal loans; bank cards; auto loans and leases; mortgages; debt consolidation; home equity loans; deposit and other savings products; and small and medium enterprise lending through GE Money. GE Energy Financial Services offers structured equity, debt, leasing, partnership financing, project finance and broad-based commercial finance to the global energy and water industries. GECAS is involved in commercial aircraft leasing and finance. The unit's airport financing unit makes debt and equity investments primarily in mid-sized regional airports. Real Estate offers equity capital for acquisition or development, as well as mortgages for new acquisitions or re-capitalizations of commercial real estate worldwide. Other businesses operating under the GE Capital banner include GE Healthcare Financial Services; GE Media, Communications & Entertainment; GE Capital Fleet Services; GE Money Bank and GECAS Engine Services. It also owns a controlling interest in Regency Energy Partners LP. In December 2009, Bank BPH, a Polish Bank, and GE Money Bank of Poland merged.

FINANCIALS:

Sales and profits are in thousands of dollars—add 000 to get the full amount. 2009 Note: Financial information for 2009 was not available for all companies at press time.

2009 Sales: $	2009 Profits: $	**U.S. Stock Ticker: Subsidiary**
2008 Sales: $67,008,000	2008 Profits: $	**Int'l Ticker:** Int'l Exchange:
2007 Sales: $66,301,000	2007 Profits: $	Employees: 80,500
2006 Sales: $56,378,000	2006 Profits: $	Fiscal Year Ends: 12/31
2005 Sales: $49,071,000	2005 Profits: $	Parent Company: GENERAL ELECTRIC CO (GE)

SALARIES/BENEFITS:

Pension Plan:	ESOP Stock Plan:	Profit Sharing:	Top Exec. Salary: $	Bonus: $
Savings Plan:	Stock Purch. Plan:		Second Exec. Salary: $	Bonus: $

OTHER THOUGHTS:

Apparent Women Officers or Directors:
Hot Spot for Advancement for Women/Minorities:

LOCATIONS: ("Y" = Yes)

West:	Southwest:	Midwest:	Southeast:	Northeast:	International:
Y	Y	Y	Y	Y	Y

GE CAPITAL REAL ESTATE

www.gerealestate.com

Industry Group Code: 522310 **Ranks within this company's industry group:** Sales: Profits:

Properties:		Financial Services:		Construction/Development:		Investments:		Specialty Services:		Brokerage:	
Apartments:	Y	Mortgages:	Y	Commercial Construction:		REIT:	Y	Property Management:		Commercial Sales:	
Malls/Shopping:	Y	Title Insurance:		Residential Construction:				Online Services:		Residential Sales:	
Offices:	Y	Property Insurance:		Land Development:				Software/IT:		Specialty:	
Hotels/Motels:				Support Services:				Consulting:			
Industrial/Warehouses:	Y			Design/Engineering:							
Other:	Y										

TYPES OF BUSINESS:

Commercial Real Estate Operations
Commercial Real Estate Mortgages & Finance
Asset Management
Joint Ventures
Capital Market Securitization
Restructuring & Acquisition Capital
Niche Equity Investments

BRANDS/DIVISIONS/AFFILIATES:

Arden Realty, Inc.
Merrill Lynch Capital Real Estate

CONTACTS: *Note: Officers with more than one job title may be intentionally listed here more than once.*

Ron Pressman, CEO
Ron Pressman, Pres.
Stewart Koenigsberg, CFO
Bernard Garrigues, Sr. VP-Global Human Resources
Hank Zupnick, CIO
Eileen Brumback, General Counsel/Sr. VP
Kathleen Carey, Sr. VP-eBusiness & Quality
Joseph Parsons, Pres./CEO-Global Investment Mgmt. Div.
Jonathan Kern, Global Chief Investment Officer
Bruce Nelson, CEO/Pres., Bus. Property
Francois Trausch, Head-Asia/Pacific
Mark Hutchinson, Pres., GE Real Estate Int'l
Tony Kinnel, Sr. VP-Sourcing

Phone: 203-750-2900 **Fax:**
Toll-Free: 888-433-4778
Address: 901 Main Ave., Norwalk, CT 06581 US

GROWTH PLANS/SPECIAL FEATURES:

GE Capital Real Estate, a subsidiary of General Electric Co. (GE) operating under the GE Capital division, is one of the leading global resources for commercial real estate mortgages and investment capital, with approximately $84 billion in total assets and 43 offices in 31 countries. It provides a range of financing, equity and real estate services, including mortgage financing; restructuring and acquisition capital; niche equity investments/joint ventures; capital market securitization and placements; and asset management services. GE Capital Real Estate operates in four divisions: Global Investment Management; Global Asset Management; North America; and International. The Global Investment Management segment creates real estate investment funds for institutional investors, and controls all fundraising and investor relations activities for GE Capital Real Estate. The Global Asset Management division manages the firm's real estate holdings. It is responsible for creating business plans for each investment as well as managing tenant improvements with the goal of retaining tenants and maximizing property value. The North America division provides and purchases commercial real estate debt in the U.S., Canada and Mexico. The International division controls the group's real estate activities in the U.K., France, Germany, Scandinavia, Spain, Italy, Australia, Japan and Korea, among others. The company has roughly 11,400 properties owned or financed around the world.

FINANCIALS: **Sales and profits are in thousands of dollars—add 000 to get the full amount. 2009 Note: Financial information for 2009 was not available for all companies at press time.**

2009 Sales: $ 2009 Profits: $
2008 Sales: $ 2008 Profits: $
2007 Sales: $ 2007 Profits: $
2006 Sales: $ 2006 Profits: $
2005 Sales: $ 2005 Profits: $

U.S. Stock Ticker: Subsidiary
Int'l Ticker: Int'l Exchange:
Employees:
Fiscal Year Ends: 12/31
Parent Company: GENERAL ELECTRIC CO (GE)

SALARIES/BENEFITS:

Pension Plan: ESOP Stock Plan: Profit Sharing: Top Exec. Salary: $ Bonus: $
Savings Plan: Y Stock Purch. Plan: Second Exec. Salary: $ Bonus: $

OTHER THOUGHTS:

Apparent Women Officers or Directors: 2
Hot Spot for Advancement for Women/Minorities: Y

LOCATIONS: ("Y" = Yes)

West:	Southwest:	Midwest:	Southeast:	Northeast:	International:
Y	Y	Y	Y	Y	Y

GENERAL ELECTRIC CO (GE)

www.ge.com

Industry Group Code: 522220 **Ranks within this company's industry group:** Sales: 1 Profits: 1

Properties:		Financial Services:		Construction/Development:		Investments:		Specialty Services:		Brokerage:	
Apartments:		Mortgages:		Commercial Construction:		REIT:		Property Management:		Commercial Sales:	
Malls/Shopping:		Title Insurance:		Residential Construction:				Online Services:		Residential Sales:	
Offices:		Property Insurance:		Land Development:				Software/IT:		Specialty:	
Hotels/Motels:				Support Services:	Y			Consulting:			
Industrial/Warehouses:				Design/Engineering:							
Other:											

TYPES OF BUSINESS:

Business Leasing & Finance
Energy Systems & Consulting
Financial Services
Industrial & Electrical Equipment & Consumer Products
Television & Film Production & Distribution
Real Estate Investments & Finance
Medical Equipment
Transportation, Aircraft Engines, Rail Systems & Truck Fleet Management

BRANDS/DIVISIONS/AFFILIATES:

GE Energy Infrastructure
GE Technology Infrastructure
GE Capital Finance
NBC Universal
GE Money
GE Aviation
GE Healthcare
GE Global Research

CONTACTS: *Note: Officers with more than one job title may be intentionally listed here more than once.*

Jeffrey R. Immelt, CEO
Keith S. Sherin, CFO
Beth Comstock, Chief Mktg. Officer/Sr. VP
John Lynch, Sr. VP-Corp. Human Resources
Mark M. Little, Sr. VP/Dir.-Global Research
Brackett B. Denniston, III, General Counsel/Sr. VP
Wayne Hewett, VP-Oper.
Pamela Daley, Sr. VP-Corp. Bus. Dev.
Trevor Schauenberg, VP-Corp. Investor Comm.
Kathryn A. Cassidy, Treas./Sr. VP
John Krenicki, Jr., CEO/Pres., GE Energy Infrastructure
Michael A. Neal, CEO-GE Capital
John G. Rice, CEO/Pres., GE Technology Infrastructure
Susan P. Peters, Chief Learning Officer/VP-Exec. Dev.
Jeffrey R. Immelt, Chmn.
Ferdinando Beccalli-Falco, CEO/Pres., Int'l

Phone: 203-373-2211	**Fax:** 203-373-3131
Toll-Free:	
Address: 3135 Easton Turnpike, Fairfield, CT 06828-0001 US	

GROWTH PLANS/SPECIAL FEATURES:

General Electric Co. (GE) is one of the largest technology, media, and financial services corporations in the world. The company's products, which range from aircraft engines, power generation, water processing, and security technology to medical imaging, business financing, media content and industrial products, are designed and manufactured by GE's five operating divisions: Energy Infrastructure, Technology Infrastructure, NBC Universal, Capital Finance, and Consumer & Industrial. The Energy Infrastructure division serves power generation, industrial, government and other customers worldwide with products and services related to energy production, distribution and management. The Technology Infrastructure division comprises the firm's aviation, enterprise solutions, healthcare technology and transportation technology operations. NBC Universal, 80%-owned by GE with the remaining 20% owned by Vivendi S.A., consolidates GE's media operations, and is engaged in the production and distribution of film and television programming; the operation of cable/satellite television networks around the world; the broadcast of network television; and investment and programming activities in digital media and the Internet. The Capital Finance division manages all of the firm's lending and financial services units, as well as its real estate activities. GE's Consumer & Industrial division manufactures, sells and services major home appliances including refrigerators, freezers, and residential water systems. In December 2009, GE agreed to purchase Vivendi Universal Entertainment's 20% stake in NBC Universal and subsequently sell a 51% stake in NBC Universal to Comcast Corp. Once the transaction is complete, GE and Comcast will create a joint venture to consolidate NBC Universal's operations with Comcast's cable networks. The new joint venture will retain the NBC Universal name. In March 2010, GE announced plans to expand its wind turbine manufacturing, engineering and service facilities in Norway, Sweden, Germany and the U.K.

FINANCIALS: **Sales and profits are in thousands of dollars—add 000 to get the full amount. 2009 Note: Financial information for 2009 was not available for all companies at press time.**

2009 Sales: $156,783,000	2009 Profits: $11,025,000	**U.S. Stock Ticker: GE**
2008 Sales: $182,515,000	2008 Profits: $17,410,000	**Int'l Ticker:** Int'l Exchange:
2007 Sales: $172,488,000	2007 Profits: $22,208,000	Employees: 304,000
2006 Sales: $151,568,000	2006 Profits: $20,742,000	Fiscal Year Ends: 12/31
2005 Sales: $136,580,000	2005 Profits: $16,720,000	Parent Company:

SALARIES/BENEFITS:

Pension Plan:	ESOP Stock Plan:	Profit Sharing:	Top Exec. Salary: $3,300,000	Bonus: $
Savings Plan: Y	Stock Purch. Plan:		Second Exec. Salary: $1,750,000	Bonus: $2,900,000

OTHER THOUGHTS:

Apparent Women Officers or Directors: 11
Hot Spot for Advancement for Women/Minorities: Y

LOCATIONS: ("Y" = Yes)

West:	Southwest:	Midwest:	Southeast:	Northeast:	International:
Y	Y	Y	Y	Y	Y

GENERAL GROWTH PROPERTIES INC

www.ggp.com

Industry Group Code: 531120 **Ranks within this company's industry group:** Sales: 4 Profits: 52

Properties:		Financial Services:		Construction/Development:		Investments:		Specialty Services:		Brokerage:	
Apartments:		Mortgages:		Commercial Construction:		REIT:	Y	Property Management:	Y	Commercial Sales:	
Malls/Shopping:	Y	Title Insurance:		Residential Construction:				Online Services:		Residential Sales:	
Offices:	Y	Property Insurance:		Land Development:				Software/IT:		Specialty:	
Hotels/Motels:				Support Services:				Consulting:			
Industrial/Warehouses:	Y			Design/Engineering:							
Other:	Y										

TYPES OF BUSINESS:

Real Estate Investment Trust
Property Management
Shopping Malls
Office & Industrial Properties
Planned Community Developments

BRANDS/DIVISIONS/AFFILIATES:

GGP Limited Partnership

CONTACTS:

Note: Officers with more than one job title may be intentionally listed here more than once.

Adam Metz, CEO
Thomas Nolan, COO
Thomas Nolan, Pres.
Ed Hoyt, Interim CFO/Sr. VP
Wally Brewster, Sr. VP-Mktg.
Ronald L. Gern, General Counsel/Sr. VP/Sec.
Wally Brewster, Sr. VP-Comm.
Robert A. Michaels, Vice Chmn.
Sharon Polonia, Exec. VP-Asset Mgmt.
Joel Bayer, Chief Investment Officer
John Bucksbaum, Chmn.

Phone: 312-960-5000	**Fax:**
Toll-Free:	
Address: 110 N. Wacker Dr., Chicago, IL 60606 US	

GROWTH PLANS/SPECIAL FEATURES:

General Growth Properties, Inc. (GGP) is a real estate investment trust (REIT) with ownership interest in or management responsibility for over 200 regional shopping malls in 43 U.S. states, as well as ownership in master planned communities and commercial office buildings. Operated by GGP Limited Partnership, the company is primarily engaged in the operation, development and management of retail and other rental property, primarily shopping centers but also including festival market places, urban mixed-use centers and strip/community centers; and the development and sale of land, primarily in large-scale, long-term community development projects in and around Columbia, Maryland; Summerlin, Nevada; and Houston, Texas and its one residential condominium project located in Boston, Massachusetts. The company operates approximately 7 million square feet of office and industrial space, primarily components of large-scale mixed-use properties (which include retail, parking and other uses) but also including free-standing office or industrial properties in office parks in the Baltimore/Washington, D.C. and Las Vegas markets. It maintains around 200 million square feet of retail space with 24,000 stores all over the U.S. The company also holds ownership interests in joint ventures in Brazil, Turkey and Costa Rica. In recent years, the company has been focused less on acquisitions and more on development activities, including ground-up development and redevelopment and expansion of already built properties. The firm has been heavily in debt. Difficulty in obtaining refinancing when needed drove it to bankruptcy in April 2009, in what was the largest real bankruptcy in U.S. history. A large number of its prime properties may be sold in order to pay off creditors.

Employees are offered medical, dental and vision insurance; life insurance; disability coverage; same sex domestic partner coverage; a 401(k) savings plan; flexible spending accounts; an employee assistance program; credit union membership; and various employee discounts.

FINANCIALS:

Sales and profits are in thousands of dollars—add 000 to get the full amount. 2009 Note: Financial information for 2009 was not available for all companies at press time.

2009 Sales: $3,135,814	2009 Profits: $-1,284,689	**U.S. Stock Ticker: GGP**
2008 Sales: $3,361,525	2008 Profits: $4,719	**Int'l Ticker:** Int'l Exchange:
2007 Sales: $3,261,801	2007 Profits: $273,642	Employees: 3,200
2006 Sales: $3,256,283	2006 Profits: $59,273	Fiscal Year Ends: 12/31
2005 Sales: $3,072,704	2005 Profits: $75,553	Parent Company:

SALARIES/BENEFITS:

Pension Plan:	ESOP Stock Plan:	Profit Sharing:	Top Exec. Salary: $1,200,000	Bonus: $125,000
Savings Plan: Y	Stock Purch. Plan:		Second Exec. Salary: $1,059,425	Bonus: $

OTHER THOUGHTS:

Apparent Women Officers or Directors: 3
Hot Spot for Advancement for Women/Minorities: Y

LOCATIONS: ("Y" = Yes)

West:	Southwest:	Midwest:	Southeast:	Northeast:	International:
Y	Y	Y	Y	Y	Y

GEORG FISCHER LTD

www.georgfischer.com

Industry Group Code: 3363 **Ranks within this company's industry group:** Sales: 2 Profits: 2

Properties:		Financial Services:		Construction/Development:		Investments:		Specialty Services:		Brokerage:	
Apartments:		Mortgages:		Commercial Construction:		REIT:		Property Management:		Commercial Sales:	
Malls/Shopping:		Title Insurance:		Residential Construction:				Online Services:		Residential Sales:	
Offices:		Property Insurance:		Land Development:				Software/IT:		Specialty:	
Hotels/Motels:				Support Services:				Consulting:			
Industrial/Warehouses:				Design/Engineering:	Y						
Other:											

TYPES OF BUSINESS:

Automotive Components
Iron Casting
Manufacturing Technology
Machine Tools
Piping Systems
Design
Control systems

BRANDS/DIVISIONS/AFFILIATES:

Agie Charmilles Group
Actspark
Engemaq
Mikron
Step-Tec
Central Plastics
JRG Gunzenhauser AG

CONTACTS:

Note: Officers with more than one job title may be intentionally listed here more than once.

Yves Serra, CEO
Yves Serra, Pres.
Stephan Wittmann, Dir.-Human Resources
Roland Groebil, Sec.
Yves Serra, Corp. Dev.
Bettina Schmidt, Head-Comm.
Daniel Boesiger, Head-Investor Rel.
Roland Abt, Dir.-Finance & Controlling
Josef Edbauer, Dir.-GF Automotive
Pietro Lori, Dir.-GF Piping Systems
Michael Hauser, Dir.-GF AgieCharmilles
Barbara Senn, Head-Corp. Compliance
Martin Huber, Chmn.

Phone: 41-52-631-1111 **Fax:** 41-52-631-2837
Toll-Free:
Address: Amsler-Laffon-Strasse 9, Schaffhausen, CH-8201 Switzerland

GROWTH PLANS/SPECIAL FEATURES:

Georg Fischer Ltd. is a design and manufacturing firm with 150 subsidiaries operating through three divisions: automotive, piping systems and machine tools. The automotive division designs and manufactures cast components and systems for auto chassis, powertrains and bodies. The firm performs large-scale iron casting, sand and die-casting and pressure die casting of iron and light metals. In addition, the firm sells automotive products such as mounting plates, mounting kits and the TRILEX Wheel System. The piping systems division supplies plastic and metal piping systems for industrial applications, gas and water utilities and construction projects. Products include industrial piping systems; piping system control and regulation products; distribution systems for gas and water; drinking water installation systems; and machines and tools for jointing plastic and metal piping systems. The division has a sales presence in over 100 countries to ensure round-the-clock customer support. The machine tools segment, also known as AgieCharmilles Group, designs and manufactures precision machinery for tool and mold making. The firm's wire-cut and die sinking electric discharge machines (EDM) and high-speed milling (HSM) technologies create forms down to the micro and nano ranges. Molds are produced for the mass production of consumer goods such as phone handsets, as well as for complex, customized precision components. The segment produces products under a number of brand names, including Agie, Charmilles, Actspark, Engemaq, Mikron, Step-Tec, System 3R and Intech EDM. The firm's subsidiaries Central Plastics and JRG Gunzenhauser AG, is a supplier of piping systems to gas and water utilities. In November 2009, Georg Fischer opens a new pipe-manufacturing factory in Ratnagiri, India.

FINANCIALS:

Sales and profits are in thousands of dollars—add 000 to get the full amount. 2009 Note: Financial information for 2009 was not available for all companies at press time.

2009 Sales: $2,735,600	2009 Profits: $-230,860	**U.S. Stock Ticker:**
2008 Sales: $3,949,130	2008 Profits: $61,030	**Int'l Ticker: FI-N** Int'l Exchange: Zurich-SWX
2007 Sales: $3,977,430	2007 Profits: $216,690	Employees: 12,481
2006 Sales: $4,007,500	2006 Profits: $226,700	Fiscal Year Ends: 12/31
2005 Sales: $3,655,100	2005 Profits: $153,500	Parent Company:

SALARIES/BENEFITS:

Pension Plan:	ESOP Stock Plan:	Profit Sharing:	Top Exec. Salary: $	Bonus: $
Savings Plan:	Stock Purch. Plan:		Second Exec. Salary: $	Bonus: $

OTHER THOUGHTS:

Apparent Women Officers or Directors: 3
Hot Spot for Advancement for Women/Minorities: Y

LOCATIONS: ("Y" = Yes)

West:	Southwest:	Midwest:	Southeast:	Northeast:	International:
Y			Y		Y

GLENBOROUGH REALTY TRUST

www.glenborough.com

Industry Group Code: 531120 **Ranks within this company's industry group:** Sales: Profits:

Properties:		Financial Services:		Construction/Development:		Investments:		Specialty Services:		Brokerage:	
Apartments:		Mortgages:		Commercial Construction:		REIT:		Property Management:	Y	Commercial Sales:	
Malls/Shopping:		Title Insurance:		Residential Construction:				Online Services:		Residential Sales:	
Offices:	Y	Property Insurance:		Land Development:				Software/IT:		Specialty:	
Hotels/Motels:				Support Services:	Y			Consulting:			
Industrial/Warehouses:	Y			Design/Engineering:							
Other:											

TYPES OF BUSINESS:

Real Estate Investment Trust
Office Properties
Property Management
Property Development

BRANDS/DIVISIONS/AFFILIATES:

Morgan Stanley

CONTACTS:

Note: Officers with more than one job title may be intentionally listed here more than once.

Andrew Batinovich, CEO
Michael A. Steele, COO/Exec. VP
Andrew Batinovich, Pres.
Brian S. Peay, CFO/Exec. VP
Carlos Santmaria, Dir.-Eng. & Portfolio Mgmt.
G. Lee Burns, General Counsel/Sec./Sr. VP
Sandra L. Boyle, Exec. VP-Dev.
Terri Garnick, Sr. VP-Acct.
Sandra L. Boyle, Exec. VP-Project Mgmt.
Michael Williams, VP-Property Mgmt,, Eastern Region
Edward Edmistion, VP-Property Mgmt., Western Region
Alan Shapiro, VP-Acquisitions

Phone: 650-343-9300	**Fax:** 650-343-7438
Toll-Free:	
Address: 400 S. El Camino Real, San Mateo, CA 94402-1708 US	

GROWTH PLANS/SPECIAL FEATURES:

Glenborough, LLC is a firm focused on acquiring, managing, leasing and developing high-quality office properties. The company holds a portfolio of 45 properties, primarily high-quality, multi-tenant office properties, with some industrial and multi-use buildings. Of these, two properties are under development. The company's portfolio encompasses approximately 4 million square feet in seven core markets: Southern California; Denver, Colorado; Washington, D.C.; San Francisco, California; Tampa, Florida; Las Vegas, Nevada; and New Jersey. In addition, the firm participates in several alliances to develop property both for its portfolio and for sale to third parties. The company performs all property management, leasing, construction supervision, accounting, finance, acquisition and disposition activities for its portfolio of properties. Glenborough has projects under development constituting over 44,000 square feet of office space and 160,000 square feet of retail space. It also performs all portfolio management activities, including on-site property management, lease negotiations and construction supervision of tenant improvements, property renovations and capital expenditures. The firm is owned by Morgan Stanley Real Estate. The firm recently completed development of its Foundry Square I, Lima Ridge Professional Center, Three Parkside and Vanderbilt Plaza properties.

FINANCIALS:

Sales and profits are in thousands of dollars—add 000 to get the full amount. 2009 Note: Financial information for 2009 was not available for all companies at press time.

2009 Sales: $	2009 Profits: $	**U.S. Stock Ticker: Subsidiary**
2008 Sales: $	2008 Profits: $	**Int'l Ticker:** Int'l Exchange:
2007 Sales: $	2007 Profits: $	Employees:
2006 Sales: $	2006 Profits: $	Fiscal Year Ends: 12/31
2005 Sales: $162,870	2005 Profits: $ 520	Parent Company: MORGAN STANLEY

SALARIES/BENEFITS:

Pension Plan:	ESOP Stock Plan:	Profit Sharing:	Top Exec. Salary: $	Bonus: $
Savings Plan:	Stock Purch. Plan:		Second Exec. Salary: $	Bonus: $

OTHER THOUGHTS:

Apparent Women Officers or Directors: 3
Hot Spot for Advancement for Women/Minorities: Y

LOCATIONS: ("Y" = Yes)

West:	Southwest:	Midwest:	Southeast:	Northeast:	International:
Y			Y	Y	

GLIMCHER REALTY TRUST

www.glimcher.com

Industry Group Code: 531120 **Ranks within this company's industry group:** Sales: 44 Profits: 47

Properties:		Financial Services:		Construction/Development:		Investments:		Specialty Services:		Brokerage:	
Apartments:		Mortgages:		Commercial Construction:		REIT:	Y	Property Management:		Commercial Sales:	
Malls/Shopping:	Y	Title Insurance:		Residential Construction:				Online Services:		Residential Sales:	
Offices:		Property Insurance:		Land Development:				Software/IT:		Specialty:	
Hotels/Motels:				Support Services:				Consulting:			
Industrial/Warehouses:				Design/Engineering:							
Other:											

TYPES OF BUSINESS:

Real Estate Investment Trust
Malls & Shopping Centers

BRANDS/DIVISIONS/AFFILIATES:

CONTACTS:

Note: Officers with more than one job title may be intentionally listed here more than once.

Michael P. Glimcher, CEO
Marshall A. Loeb, COO
Marshall A. Loeb, Pres.
Mark E. Yale, CFO/Exec. VP/Treas.
Grace E. Schmitt, VP-Human Resources
Cheryl Southworth, VP-Info. Svcs.
Kim A. Rieck, General Counsel/Corp. Sec./Sr. VP
Melissa Indest, VP-Finance & Acct.
George A. Schmidt, Chief Investment Officer/Exec. VP
Thomas J. Drought, Jr., Sr. VP/Dir.-Leasing
Kenneth D. Cannon, Sr. VP-Dev.
Carrie Dworek, VP-Leasing
Michael P. Glimcher, Chmn.

Phone: 614-621-9000 **Fax:** 614-621-9321
Toll-Free:
Address: 180 E. Broad St., Columbus, OH 43215 US

GROWTH PLANS/SPECIAL FEATURES:

Glimcher Realty Trust is a fully integrated, self-administered and self-managed real estate investment trust (REIT) that owns, leases, acquires, develops and operates a portfolio of retail properties consisting of enclosed regional and super-regional malls and community shopping centers (including single-tenant retail properties) located in 13 states. The company's portfolio consists of 21 malls containing an aggregate of 19.1 million square feet of gross leasable area (GLA) and four community centers containing 779,000 square feet of GLA. During 2009, the occupancy rate for the firm's properties was 93.3% of GLA. Glimcher's malls are anchored by multiple department stores, such as Dillard's, Herberger's, JCPenney, Kohl's, Macy's, Nordstrom, Saks and Sears. Mall stores include national retailers such as Abercrombie & Fitch, American Eagle Outfitters, Banana Republic, Barnes & Noble, Footlocker, Gap, Hallmark, The Limited, New York & Company, Pacific Sunwear, Radio Shack and Victoria's Secret. Malls also generally include at least one theme restaurant, a food court and movie theaters or other entertainment. The firm's community centers are designed to attract local and regional area customers and are typically anchored by a combination of discount department stores, supermarkets and/or drug stores, including retailers such as Target and supermarkets such as Kroger. Tenants typically offer day-to-day necessities and value-oriented merchandise. The company has recently sold off many of its non-mall properties in an effort to develop a more focused portfolio. In June 2009, the firm partnered with Columbus-based technology company eProximiti to launch a mobile marketing platform nationwide. In March 2010, Glimcher closed on a $320 million joint venture with The Blackstone Group for the acquisition of two regional malls, which are located in Oregon and Florida. Glimcher will retain 40% of the joint venture, whereas Blackstone will retain 60%.

FINANCIALS:

Sales and profits are in thousands of dollars—add 000 to get the full amount. 2009 Note: Financial information for 2009 was not available for all companies at press time.

2009 Sales: $308,425	2009 Profits: $4,581	**U.S. Stock Ticker: GRT**
2008 Sales: $319,725	2008 Profits: $16,769	**Int'l Ticker:** Int'l Exchange:
2007 Sales: $302,900	2007 Profits: $39,992	Employees: 1,038
2006 Sales: $292,551	2006 Profits: $-77,165	Fiscal Year Ends: 12/31
2005 Sales: $287,918	2005 Profits: $20,850	Parent Company:

SALARIES/BENEFITS:

Pension Plan:	ESOP Stock Plan:	Profit Sharing:	Top Exec. Salary: $575,000	Bonus: $322,575
Savings Plan: Y	Stock Purch. Plan:		Second Exec. Salary: $425,000	Bonus: $153,000

OTHER THOUGHTS:

Apparent Women Officers or Directors: 4
Hot Spot for Advancement for Women/Minorities: Y

LOCATIONS: ("Y" = Yes)

West:	Southwest:	Midwest:	Southeast:	Northeast:	International:
Y	Y	Y	Y	Y	

GMAC INC

www.gmacfs.com

Industry Group Code: 522220 **Ranks within this company's industry group:** Sales: 2 Profits: 2

Properties:		Financial Services:		Construction/Development:		Investments:		Specialty Services:		Brokerage:	
Apartments:		Mortgages:	Y	Commercial Construction:		REIT:		Property Management:		Commercial Sales:	
Malls/Shopping:		Title Insurance:		Residential Construction:				Online Services:		Residential Sales:	
Offices:		Property Insurance:	Y	Land Development:				Software/IT:		Specialty:	
Hotels/Motels:				Support Services:				Consulting:			
Industrial/Warehouses:				Design/Engineering:							
Other:											

TYPES OF BUSINESS:

Automobile Financing
Leasing Services
Insurance
Mortgage Banking
Bank Holding Company
Commercial Credit
Commercial Mortgages
Residential Mortgages

BRANDS/DIVISIONS/AFFILIATES:

GMAC Mortgage
Cerberus Capital Management LP
Residential Capital LLC (ResCap)
Ally Bank
GMAC-CIS
General Motors Acceptance Corporation
Chrysler Financial Services LLC

CONTACTS: *Note: Officers with more than one job title may be intentionally listed here more than once.*

Michael A. Carpenter, CEO
Cliff Skelton, COO
William F. Muir, Pres.
James G. Mackey, Interim CFO
Sanjay Gupta, Chief Mktg. Officer
Anthony S. (Tony) Marino, Chief Human Resources Officer
Cliff Skelton, CTO
William B. Solomon, Jr., General Counsel
Gina Proia, Chief Comm. Officer
Jeffrey Brown, Treas.
Samuel Ramsey, Chief Risk Officer
William (Bill) Hall, Jr., Pres./CEO-GMAC Commercial Finance
Thomas Marano, CEO-GMAC Mortgage
Mark H. Weintraub, Gen. Auditor
Lenard B. Tessler, Chmn.

Phone: 313-556-5000	**Fax:**
Toll-Free:	
Address: 200 Renaissance Ctr., Detroit, MI 48265-2000 US	

GROWTH PLANS/SPECIAL FEATURES:

GMAC, Inc., formerly doing business as GMAC Financial Services, is a global financial services company providing automotive finance, real estate finance, insurance and commercial finance in roughly 40 countries. GMAC operates in four primary business lines: global automotive finance; mortgage, through wholly-owned subsidiary Residential Capital LLC (ResCap); insurance; and other. The automotive finance segment offers wholesale and retail automotive financing services primarily to GM dealers and their customers. Through ResCap, the company originates, purchases, sells and securitizes residential mortgage loans, primarily in the U.S.; provides collateralized lines of credit; and provides specialty financing and equity capital to residential land developers and homebuilders. GMAC's insurance offerings include automobile service contracts, personal automobile insurance coverages, selected commercial insurance coverages and other consumer products. The company's other solutions include commercial finance services, such as asset-based lending, structured finance, factoring, health capital and resort finance; equity investments; and other corporate offerings. Ally Bank is an online bank offering money market savings accounts and fixed-rate certificates. The U.S. Treasury department owns roughly 56.3% of GMAC; Cerberus Capital Management, L.P., a private equity firm, owns 14.9%; General Motors Trust owns 9.9%; and GM owns 6.7%. The remainder is owned by third party investors. In early 2009, the U.S. federal government injected $7 billion into GMAC in efforts to keep the firm afloat. Another $7.5 billion was allocated to GMAC in May 2009. In April 2009, GMAC Financial Services replaced Chrysler Financial Services LLC as the primary retail and commercial lender for Chrysler dealers. In May 2009, the company re-branded its GMAC Bank division as Ally Bank. Following GM's bankruptcy filing in June 2009, the company announced that it would not be seeking bankruptcy protection. In March 2010, the firm sold its U.S. consumer property and casualty insurance business to American Capital Acquisition Corporation. In April 2010, ResCap agreed to sell its European mortgage assets and businesses.

FINANCIALS: **Sales and profits are in thousands of dollars—add 000 to get the full amount. 2009 Note: Financial information for 2009 was not available for all companies at press time.**

2009 Sales: $	2009 Profits: $	**U.S. Stock Ticker: Private**
2008 Sales: $18,395,000	2008 Profits: $1,868,000	**Int'l Ticker:** Int'l Exchange:
2007 Sales: $21,187,000	2007 Profits: $-2,332,000	Employees: 22,700
2006 Sales: $23,103,000	2006 Profits: $2,125,000	Fiscal Year Ends: 12/31
2005 Sales: $21,312,000	2005 Profits: $2,282,000	Parent Company:

SALARIES/BENEFITS:

Pension Plan:	ESOP Stock Plan:	Profit Sharing:	Top Exec. Salary: $	Bonus: $
Savings Plan:	Stock Purch. Plan:		Second Exec. Salary: $	Bonus: $

OTHER THOUGHTS:

Apparent Women Officers or Directors: 3
Hot Spot for Advancement for Women/Minorities: Y

LOCATIONS: ("Y" = Yes)

West:	Southwest:	Midwest:	Southeast:	Northeast:	International:
Y	Y	Y	Y	Y	Y

GOLDEN TULIP HOSPITALITY GROUP

www.goldentulip.com

Industry Group Code: 721110 **Ranks within this company's industry group:** Sales: Profits:

Properties:		Financial Services:		Construction/Development:		Investments:		Specialty Services:		Brokerage:	
Apartments:		Mortgages:		Commercial Construction:		REIT:		Property Management:	Y	Commercial Sales:	
Malls/Shopping:		Title Insurance:		Residential Construction:				Online Services:		Residential Sales:	
Offices:		Property Insurance:		Land Development:				Software/IT:		Specialty:	
Hotels/Motels:	Y			Support Services:				Consulting:			
Industrial/Warehouses:				Design/Engineering:							
Other:											

TYPES OF BUSINESS:

Hotels & Resorts

BRANDS/DIVISIONS/AFFILIATES:

Golden Tulip Hotels
Tulip Inns
Royal Tulip
BRANCHE Restaurant, Bar & Lounge
Golden Tulip Resort
Tulip Residences

CONTACTS:

Note: Officers with more than one job title may be intentionally listed here more than once.

Pierre-Frederic Roulot, Pres.
Haike Blaauw, Sr. VP-Franchise Oper.

Phone: 31-33-25-44-800 **Fax:** 31-33-25-44-815
Toll-Free: 800-448-8355
Address: Arnhemseweg 2 P.O. Box 448, Amersfoot, 3800 AK The Netherlands

GROWTH PLANS/SPECIAL FEATURES:

Golden Tulip Hospitality Group is a Swiss hospitality company with over 230 branded and hotels featuring more than 27,000 rooms in more than 40 countries. Since the company's acquisition in 2009 by Starwood Capital Group, owner of Louvre Hotels, Golden Tulip has expanded its network of hotels to include 1072 hotels with the addition of Louvre Hotels brands, Kyriad, Kyriad Prestige, Campanile and Premiere Classe. The company's original brands include Royal Tulip, reserved for five-star hotels located in prime areas near city centers and business districts; Golden Tulip Hotels, which are four-star hotels situated in key locations near city centers, airports, conference venues and business districts; and Tulip Inns, which are three-star budget hotels with fewer amenities than company's other brands. Golden Tulip also owns and operates the Branche Restaurant, Bar & Lounge chain; George & Co. casual dining restaurants; and The State Room, exclusively in Royal Tulip Hotels. These facilities are generally located in or near a Golden Tulip hotel. In addition to its facilities, the company offers several services to business customers including group rates and the Golden Tulip Central Meeting Line, a reservation and planning service for businesses or large groups. The Ambassador Club is the company's frequent stay program through which guests have access to special events and discounts. Golden Tulip franchises and manages hotels in Europe, the Middle East and Africa, the Asia-Pacific Region and the Americas. In June 2008, the company added a new brand concept, Tulip Residences, which provides travelers with extended-stay studios and one-bedroom suites. The accommodations are four-star rated and offer amenities such as high-definition televisions, free Wi-Fi connection, en suite bathrooms and a fully equipped kitchen facility. In July 2009, Golden Tulip was acquired by Starwood Capital Group Global, L.P., owner of Louvre Hotels SAS.

FINANCIALS:

Sales and profits are in thousands of dollars—add 000 to get the full amount. 2009 Note: Financial information for 2009 was not available for all companies at press time.

2009 Sales: $ | 2009 Profits: $
2008 Sales: $ | 2008 Profits: $
2007 Sales: $ | 2007 Profits: $
2006 Sales: $ | 2006 Profits: $
2005 Sales: $ | 2005 Profits: $

U.S. Stock Ticker: Private
Int'l Ticker: Int'l Exchange:
Employees:
Fiscal Year Ends:
Parent Company: STARWOOD CAPITAL GROUP GLOBAL LLC

SALARIES/BENEFITS:

Pension Plan: ESOP Stock Plan: Profit Sharing: Top Exec. Salary: $ Bonus: $
Savings Plan: Stock Purch. Plan: Second Exec. Salary: $ Bonus: $

OTHER THOUGHTS:

Apparent Women Officers or Directors: 1
Hot Spot for Advancement for Women/Minorities:

LOCATIONS: ("Y" = Yes)

West:	Southwest:	Midwest:	Southeast:	Northeast:	International:
				Y	Y

GRANITE CONSTRUCTION INC

www.graniteconstruction.com

Industry Group Code: 237 **Ranks within this company's industry group:** Sales: 26 Profits: 19

Properties:		Financial Services:		Construction/Development:		Investments:		Specialty Services:		Brokerage:	
Apartments:		Mortgages:		Commercial Construction:	Y	REIT:		Property Management:		Commercial Sales:	
Malls/Shopping:		Title Insurance:		Residential Construction:				Online Services:		Residential Sales:	
Offices:		Property Insurance:		Land Development:				Software/IT:		Specialty:	
Hotels/Motels:				Support Services:				Consulting:			
Industrial/Warehouses:				Design/Engineering:							
Other:											

TYPES OF BUSINESS:

Construction, Heavy & Civil Engineering
Infrastructure Projects
Site Preparation Services
Construction Materials Processing
Heavy Construction Equipment

BRANDS/DIVISIONS/AFFILIATES:

Granite Construction Northeast Inc
Granite Northwest Inc
Granite Land Company
Granite Construction Supply
Intermountain Slurry Seal Inc

CONTACTS:

Note: Officers with more than one job title may be intentionally listed here more than once.

William G. Dorey, CEO
James H. Roberts, COO/Exec. VP
William G. Dorey, Pres.
LeAnne M. Stewart, CFO/Sr. VP
Margaret B. Wynn, VP-Human Resources
Michael Flutch, General Counsel/VP/Sec.
Kent H. Marshall, VP-Bus. Dev.
Laurel J. Krzeminski, Controller/VP
Michael F. Donnino, Sr. VP/Group Mgr.
Thomas S. Case, Sr. VP/Group Mgr.
Randy J. Kremer, VP/Mgr.-Construction Materials
Jigisha Desai, VP/Treas.
William H. Powell, Chmn.

Phone: 831-724-1011	**Fax:** 831-722-9657
Toll-Free:	
Address: 585 W. Beach St., Watsonville, CA 95076 US	

GROWTH PLANS/SPECIAL FEATURES:

Granite Construction, Inc. is one of the largest heavy civil construction contractors in the U.S. The firm operates nationwide, serving both public and private sector clients. Within the public sector, the company primarily concentrates on infrastructure projects, including the construction of roads, highways, bridges, dams, tunnels, canals, mass transit facilities and airports. Within the private sector, it performs site preparation services for commercial/industrial buildings, residential buildings and other facilities. Granite owns and leases substantial aggregate reserves and owns 158 construction materials processing plants. In addition, the company has one of the largest contractor-owned heavy construction equipment fleets in the U.S., with over 7,000 units. Granite Construction operates in four segments: Construction, Large Project Construction, Construction Materials and Real Estate. The Construction division operates out of 14 branch offices that serve local markets, as well as major infrastructure projects in the western region of the U.S. Each of its branch locations is aligned under one of three operating groups: Northwest, Northern California and Southwest. The Large Project Construction segment focuses on the firm's larger projects, such as mass transit facilities, highways, dams, bridges and airports. It operates out of three regional offices in Lewisville, Texas; Tampa, Florida; and Tarrytown, New York. The Construction Materials division (Granite Construction Supply) produces concrete, gravel, ready-mix asphalt, sand, and other products. Granite Construction's Real Estate segment, formerly Granite Land Company, purchases, develops, operates, sells and invests in real estate. Its current portfolio includes residential, retail and office site development projects held for rental income or for sale to home and commercial property developers. Granite Construction's subsidiaries and affiliates include Granite Construction Northeast, Inc.; Granite Northwest, Inc.; and Intermountain Slurry Seal, Inc.

Employee benefits include life, AD&D, medical, dental and vision coverage; a 401(k); stock purchase plan; flexible spending accounts; education reimbursement; and domestic partner benefits.

FINANCIALS:

Sales and profits are in thousands of dollars—add 000 to get the full amount. 2009 Note: Financial information for 2009 was not available for all companies at press time.

2009 Sales: $1,963,479	2009 Profits: $100,201	**U.S. Stock Ticker: GVA**
2008 Sales: $2,674,244	2008 Profits: $122,404	**Int'l Ticker:** Int'l Exchange:
2007 Sales: $2,737,914	2007 Profits: $112,065	Employees: 3,600
2006 Sales: $2,969,604	2006 Profits: $80,509	Fiscal Year Ends: 12/31
2005 Sales: $2,641,352	2005 Profits: $83,150	Parent Company:

SALARIES/BENEFITS:

Pension Plan:	ESOP Stock Plan:	Profit Sharing:	Top Exec. Salary: $500,000	Bonus: $503,606
Savings Plan: Y	Stock Purch. Plan: Y		Second Exec. Salary: $400,000	Bonus: $279,590

OTHER THOUGHTS:

Apparent Women Officers or Directors: 4
Hot Spot for Advancement for Women/Minorities: Y

LOCATIONS: ("Y" = Yes)

West:	Southwest:	Midwest:	Southeast:	Northeast:	International:
Y	Y	Y	Y	Y	

GROUPE DU LOUVRE

www.groupedulouvre.com

Industry Group Code: 721110 **Ranks within this company's industry group:** Sales: Profits:

Properties:		Financial Services:		Construction/Development:		Investments:		Specialty Services:		Brokerage:	
Apartments:		Mortgages:		Commercial Construction:		REIT:		Property Management:	Y	Commercial Sales:	
Malls/Shopping:		Title Insurance:		Residential Construction:				Online Services:		Residential Sales:	
Offices:		Property Insurance:		Land Development:				Software/IT:		Specialty:	
Hotels/Motels:	Y			Support Services:				Consulting:			
Industrial/Warehouses:				Design/Engineering:							
Other:	Y										

TYPES OF BUSINESS:

Hotels
Luxury Goods
Perfume House

BRANDS/DIVISIONS/AFFILIATES:

Starwood Capital Group
Crillon
Concorde
Kyriad Prestige
Campanile
Premiere Classe
Annick Goutal
Baccarat

CONTACTS:

Note: Officers with more than one job title may be intentionally listed here more than once.

Jeffrey Dishner, Managing Dir.
Pascal Malbequi, General Counsel
Franck Hebrard, VP-Finance
Brigitte Taitttinger, Pres., Annick Goutal
Bernard Granier, COO-Concorde Hotels & Resorts
Pierre Frederic Roulot, Pres., Louvre Hotels
Herve Martin, Pres., Baccarat
Barry Sternlicht, Chmn.

Phone: 33-1-42-91-4500 **Fax:**
Toll-Free:
Address: Village 5, 50 Place de l'Ellipse, Paris, 92081 France

GROWTH PLANS/SPECIAL FEATURES:

Groupe du Louvre (Louvre) is a French hotel and luxury goods company. It is owned by an affiliate of Starwood Capital Group. The company operates in four segments: luxury hotel, budget hotel, crystal manufacturer and perfume house. The luxury hotel division encompasses the Crillon and Concorde hotels and resorts. The segment gathers more than 30 prestigious hotels in locations such as Amsterdam, Barcelona, Cannes, London, Nice, Paris, Prague and Tokyo. The budget hotel division is comprised of more than 800 hotels with a capacity of roughly 52,000 rooms in nine European countries under four brands: Kyriad Prestige, Kyriad, Campanile and Premiere Classe. The crystal manufacturer division operates through subsidiary Societe du Louvre, which is the majority shareholder of Baccarat, one of the most prestigious crystal manufacturers in the world. Products, which include jewelry, accessories and wristwatches, are sold through a network of 47 owned stores and points of sales worldwide. The perfume house division operates through Annick Goutal, a unique luxury perfume house created in 1980 that distributes products in a selective way in more than 20 countries. Annick Goutal offers more than 25 fragrances composed mainly of natural elements, as well as a skin care line with active rose serum. The perfumery has 11 boutiques and 1,000 prestigious points of sale such as Saks Avenue, Isetan, Bergdorf Goodman, Harrods and Harvey Nichols.

FINANCIALS:

Sales and profits are in thousands of dollars—add 000 to get the full amount. 2009 Note: Financial information for 2009 was not available for all companies at press time.

2009 Sales: $ | 2009 Profits: $
2008 Sales: $ | 2008 Profits: $
2007 Sales: $ | 2007 Profits: $
2006 Sales: $ | 2006 Profits: $
2005 Sales: $ | 2005 Profits: $

U.S. Stock Ticker: Subsidiary
Int'l Ticker: Int'l Exchange:
Employees:
Fiscal Year Ends: 12/31
Parent Company: STARWOOD CAPITAL GROUP GLOBAL LLC

SALARIES/BENEFITS:

Pension Plan: ESOP Stock Plan: Profit Sharing: Top Exec. Salary: $ Bonus: $
Savings Plan: Stock Purch. Plan: Second Exec. Salary: $ Bonus: $

OTHER THOUGHTS:

Apparent Women Officers or Directors: 1
Hot Spot for Advancement for Women/Minorities: Y

LOCATIONS: ("Y" = Yes)

West:	Southwest:	Midwest:	Southeast:	Northeast:	International:
					Y

GRUBB & ELLIS CO

www.grubb-ellis.com

Industry Group Code: 531210 **Ranks within this company's industry group:** Sales: 3 Profits: 2

Properties:		Financial Services:		Construction/Development:		Investments:		Specialty Services:		Brokerage:	
Apartments:		Mortgages:		Commercial Construction:		REIT:	Y	Property Management:	Y	Commercial Sales:	Y
Malls/Shopping:		Title Insurance:		Residential Construction:				Online Services:		Residential Sales:	
Offices:		Property Insurance:		Land Development:				Software/IT:		Specialty:	
Hotels/Motels:				Support Services:				Consulting:	Y		
Industrial/Warehouses:				Design/Engineering:	Y						
Other:											

TYPES OF BUSINESS:

Real Estate Brokerage & Leasing
Property Management
Engineering Services
Strategic Planning
Market Research
Retail Services
Valuation Services
Consulting Services

BRANDS/DIVISIONS/AFFILIATES:

Grubb & Ellis Securities Inc
Grubb & Ellis Healthcare REIT II Inc
Grubb & Ellis Alesco Global Advisors LLC
Center for Neurosurgery and Spine
Lacombe Medical Office Building
Grubb & Ellis Realty Investors LLC
Grubb & Ellis Apartment REIT Inc
Energy & Infrastructure Advisors LLC

CONTACTS:

Note: Officers with more than one job title may be intentionally listed here more than once.

Thomas P. D'Arcy, CEO
Jack Van Berkel, COO/Exec. VP/Pres., Real Estate Svcs.
Thomas P. D'Arcy, Pres.
Richard W. Pehlke, CFO/Exec. VP
Andrea R. Biller, General Counsel/Exec. VP/Corp. Sec.
Jeffrey T. Hanson, Exec. VP/Pres., Grubb & Ellis Equity Advisors
Jay P. Leupp, Pres., Grubb & Ellis Alesco Global Advisors
Kevin K. Hull, CEO/Pres., Grubb & Ellis Securities
Stanley J. Olander, Jr., Pres., Grubb & Ellis Apartment REIT
C. Michael Kojaian, Chmn.

Phone: 714-667-8252	**Fax:** 312-207-1822
Toll-Free: 800-877-9066	
Address: 1551 N. Tustin Ave., Ste. 300, Santa Ana, CA 92705 US	

GROWTH PLANS/SPECIAL FEATURES:

Grubb & Ellis Co. (G&E) is a leading commercial real estate services and investment management company operating through 126 owned and affiliate offices worldwide. The firm provides property owners, corporate occupants and program investors with transactions, management, consulting and investment advisory services. G&E operates through three segments: Investment Management, Transaction Services and Management Services. Its Investment Management segment provides acquisition, financing and disposition services with respect to its programs; asset management services related to its programs; and dealer-manager services by its securities broker-dealer, which facilitates capital raising transactions for its tenant in common (TIC), REIT and other investment programs. Investment management products are distributed through G&E's subsidiary Grubb & Ellis Securities, Inc. The firm's Transaction Services segment comprises its real estate brokerage operations, which are conducted through over 1,800 brokers. G&E's Management Services segment includes property, corporate facilities and project management; client accounting; business services; and engineering services for unrelated third parties and the properties owned by the programs it sponsors. G&E recently started a family of U.S. and global open and closed end mutual funds that focus on real estate securities and manage private investment funds exclusively for qualified investors through its 51% ownership in Grubb & Ellis Alesco Global Advisors, LLC. In June 2009, the firm sold Danbury Corporate Center to The Matrix Realty Group Inc. for $72.4 million; and formed Energy & Infrastructure Advisors LLC, a joint venture with the Meridian Companies. In early 2010, the company's Grubb & Ellis Healthcare REIT II, Inc. fund acquired the Center for Neurosurgery and Spine in Minnesota, Lacombe Medical Office Building in Louisiana and Parkway Medical Center in Ohio. In March 2010, another fund, Grubb & Ellis Apartment REIT, Inc., acquired Bella Ruscello Luxury Apartment Homes in Texas. Also in March 2010, G&E opened a new office in San Diego, California.

FINANCIALS:

Sales and profits are in thousands of dollars—add 000 to get the full amount. 2009 Note: Financial information for 2009 was not available for all companies at press time.

2009 Sales: $535,645	2009 Profits: $-78,838	**U.S. Stock Ticker: GBE**
2008 Sales: $628,779	2008 Profits: $-330,870	**Int'l Ticker:** Int'l Exchange:
2007 Sales: $229,657	2007 Profits: $21,072	Employees: 5,000
2006 Sales: $108,543	2006 Profits: $19,971	Fiscal Year Ends: 12/31
2005 Sales: $92,859	2005 Profits: $18,124	Parent Company:

SALARIES/BENEFITS:

Pension Plan:	ESOP Stock Plan:	Profit Sharing:	Top Exec. Salary: $401,889	Bonus: $
Savings Plan: Y	Stock Purch. Plan:		Second Exec. Salary: $400,000	Bonus: $

OTHER THOUGHTS:

Apparent Women Officers or Directors: 1
Hot Spot for Advancement for Women/Minorities: Y

LOCATIONS: ("Y" = Yes)

West:	Southwest:	Midwest:	Southeast:	Northeast:	International:
Y	Y	Y	Y	Y	Y

GRUBB & ELLIS REALTY INVESTORS LLC equityadvisors.grubb-ellis.com

Industry Group Code: 531120 **Ranks within this company's industry group:** Sales: Profits:

Properties:		Financial Services:		Construction/Development:		Investments:		Specialty Services:		Brokerage:	
Apartments:		Mortgages:		Commercial Construction:		REIT:	Y	Property Management:	Y	Commercial Sales:	
Malls/Shopping:		Title Insurance:		Residential Construction:				Online Services:		Residential Sales:	
Offices:		Property Insurance:		Land Development:				Software/IT:		Specialty:	Y
Hotels/Motels:				Support Services:				Consulting:	Y		
Industrial/Warehouses:				Design/Engineering:							
Other:											

TYPES OF BUSINESS:

Real Estate Investment Trust
Commercial Properties
Advising & Redevelopment Services

BRANDS/DIVISIONS/AFFILIATES:

Grubb & Ellis Co
Grubb & Ellis Equity Advisors

CONTACTS:

Note: Officers with more than one job title may be intentionally listed here more than once.

Michael Rispoli, CFO
Mathieu Streiff, Sr. VP-Investment Oper.
Michael Rispoli, Sr. VP-Strategic Planning
Julia McCartney, Contact-Media
Michael Rispoli, Sr. VP-Investor Rel.
Jeffery T. Hanson, Chief Investment Officer
Kent Peters, Exec. VP-Asset Mgmt.
Talle Voorhies, Exec. VP-Investor Svcs.
Christine Teagle, Sr. VP-Asset Mgmt.

Phone: 714-667-8252	**Fax:** 714-667-6860
Toll-Free: 877-888-7348	
Address: 1551 N. Tustin Ave., Ste. 300, Santa Ana, CA 92705 US	

GROWTH PLANS/SPECIAL FEATURES:

Grubb & Ellis Realty Investors, LLC (GERI) is the asset management and real estate investment subsidiary of Grubb & Ellis Company. GERI and its affiliates manage more than $6.9 billion in assets in 32 states on behalf of roughly 4,500 investors. The company specializes in tenant-in-common (TIC) investment strategies for investors structuring like-kind or tax-deferred exchanges under Section 1031 of the Tax Code, which allows a property owner to sell a property, buy another and defer the sale-generated taxable income. GERI currently has more than 150 TIC programs comprised of nearly 23 million square feet and has completed 59 TIC programs. In addition to TIC programs, the firm has experience in non-traded public real estate investment trusts (REITs); multi-member limited liability companies (LLCs); and other institutional investments. GERI offers high net worth investors specialized, comprehensive programs through Grubb & Ellis Private Client Management. In January 2010, Grubb & Ellis Equity Advisors LLC, another subsidiary of Grubb & Ellis Company, purchased all of the rights, title and interests in Grubb & Ellis Apartment REIT advisor, LLC and Grubb & Ellis Apartment Management, LLC from Grubb & Ellis Realty Investors, LLC. Grubb & Ellis Equity Advisors LLC is the real estate investment and asset management subsidiary of Grubb & Ellis Company.

FINANCIALS:

Sales and profits are in thousands of dollars—add 000 to get the full amount. 2009 Note: Financial information for 2009 was not available for all companies at press time.

2009 Sales: $	2009 Profits: $	**U.S. Stock Ticker: Subsidiary**
2008 Sales: $	2008 Profits: $	**Int'l Ticker:** Int'l Exchange:
2007 Sales: $	2007 Profits: $	Employees:
2006 Sales: $	2006 Profits: $	Fiscal Year Ends: 12/31
2005 Sales: $	2005 Profits: $	Parent Company: GRUBB & ELLIS CO

SALARIES/BENEFITS:

Pension Plan:	ESOP Stock Plan:	Profit Sharing:	Top Exec. Salary: $	Bonus: $
Savings Plan:	Stock Purch. Plan:		Second Exec. Salary: $	Bonus: $

OTHER THOUGHTS:

Apparent Women Officers or Directors: 3
Hot Spot for Advancement for Women/Minorities: Y

LOCATIONS: ("Y" = Yes)

West:	Southwest:	Midwest:	Southeast:	Northeast:	International:
Y	Y	Y	Y		

GRUPO ACS

www.grupoacs.com

Industry Group Code: 237 **Ranks within this company's industry group:** Sales: 7 Profits: 4

Properties:		Financial Services:		Construction/Development:		Investments:		Specialty Services:		Brokerage:	
Apartments:		Mortgages:		Commercial Construction:	Y	REIT:		Property Management:		Commercial Sales:	
Malls/Shopping:		Title Insurance:		Residential Construction:				Online Services:	Y	Residential Sales:	
Offices:		Property Insurance:		Land Development:				Software/IT:		Specialty:	
Hotels/Motels:				Support Services:	Y			Consulting:	Y		
Industrial/Warehouses:				Design/Engineering:	Y						
Other:											

TYPES OF BUSINESS:

Heavy Construction
Engineering Services
Civic Construction & Infrastructure
Industrial Services
Facility Maintenance
Passenger Transportation
Transportation Concessions

BRANDS/DIVISIONS/AFFILIATES:

Grupo Dragados, S.A.
Vias
Drace
Geocisa
Tecsa Empresa
Constructora S.A.
FPS
John Picone

CONTACTS:

Note: Officers with more than one job title may be intentionally listed here more than once.

Florentino P. Rodriguez, CEO
Angel G. Altozano, Corp. Gen. Mgr.
Jose L. V. Perez, Sec.
Antonio G. Ferrer, Exec. Vice Chmn.
Marcelino F. Verdes, CEO-Construction
Jose Maria Aguirre Fernandez, Gen. Mgr.-Tecsa
Alejandro C. Botteghelz, CEO-Seis
Florentino P. Rodriguez, Chmn.

Phone: 34-91-343-92-00	**Fax:** 34-91-343-94-56
Toll-Free:	
Address: Avda. Pio XII, No. 102, Madrid, 28036 Spain	

GROWTH PLANS/SPECIAL FEATURES:

Grupo ACS is a leading Spanish construction and engineering firm that services a wide variety of sectors, including transportation infrastructure, real estate, offshore activities, energy, hydraulics, environment, industrial equipment, concessions and maintenance. The company performs operates through many subsidiaries, the most significant being Grupo Dragados, S.A., the Spanish construction giant. Other ACS companies include Vias Y Construcciones S.A., Drace Medio Ambiente, Geocisa, Tecsa Empresa Constructora S.A., FPS, Schiavone, Seis and John Picone. The firm has operations in 43 countries. ACS operates primarily in four major areas: construction; concessions; environmental & logistical services; and industrial services. The construction business, builds a variety of civil works projects, as well as commercial and residential structures. The concessions segment is managed by Iridium, which promotes concessions and private-public partnership contracts for infrastructural projects such as toll ways and public facilities services. The environmental and logistical services segment specializes in waste management and recycling and treatment. This segment also manages port activities such as the handling of bulk materials, general cargo and perishables. The industrial services division largely serves the energy and communications sectors through its applied design, installation and maintenance of the industrial infrastructure.

FINANCIALS:

Sales and profits are in thousands of dollars—add 000 to get the full amount. 2009 Note: Financial information for 2009 was not available for all companies at press time.

2009 Sales: $20,818,700	2009 Profits: $2,642,050	**U.S. Stock Ticker:**
2008 Sales: $19,320,500	2008 Profits: $1,769,040	**Int'l Ticker: ACS** Int'l Exchange: Barcelona-BME
2007 Sales: $16,713,900	2007 Profits: $3,505,000	Employees: 141,002
2006 Sales: $19,016,796	2006 Profits: $1,721,450	Fiscal Year Ends: 12/31
2005 Sales: $16,376,220	2005 Profits: $855,723	Parent Company:

SALARIES/BENEFITS:

Pension Plan:	ESOP Stock Plan:	Profit Sharing:	Top Exec. Salary: $	Bonus: $
Savings Plan:	Stock Purch. Plan:		Second Exec. Salary: $	Bonus: $

OTHER THOUGHTS:

Apparent Women Officers or Directors: 1
Hot Spot for Advancement for Women/Minorities:

LOCATIONS: ("Y" = Yes)

West:	Southwest:	Midwest:	Southeast:	Northeast:	International:
					Y

GRUPO FERROVIAL SA

www.ferrovial.com

Industry Group Code: 237 **Ranks within this company's industry group:** Sales: 8 Profits: 25

Properties:		Financial Services:		Construction/Development:		Investments:		Specialty Services:		Brokerage:	
Apartments:		Mortgages:		Commercial Construction:	Y	REIT:		Property Management:	Y	Commercial Sales:	
Malls/Shopping:		Title Insurance:		Residential Construction:				Online Services:		Residential Sales:	
Offices:		Property Insurance:		Land Development:	Y			Software/IT:		Specialty:	
Hotels/Motels:				Support Services:				Consulting:			
Industrial/Warehouses:				Design/Engineering:							
Other:	Y										

TYPES OF BUSINESS:

Airport Management
Construction
Infrastructure Services
Toll Roads
Civil Engineering

BRANDS/DIVISIONS/AFFILIATES:

Swissport International Ltd
Webber
BAA PLC
Cespa
Cadagua
Budimex
Amey PLC
Cintra

CONTACTS: *Note: Officers with more than one job title may be intentionally listed here more than once.*

Inigo Meiras Amusco, CEO
Ernesto Lopez Mozo, CFO
Jaime Aguirre de Carcer Y Moreno, Dir.-Human Resources
Federico Florez Gutierrez, CIO
Santiago Ortiz Vaamonde, General Sec.
Alejandro De la Joya Ruiz, CEO-Ferrovial Agroman
Alvaro Echaniz Urcelay, CEO-Real Estate Div.
Nicolas Villen Jiminez, CEO-Ferrovial Aeropuertos
Enrique Diaz-Rato Revuelta, CEO-Cintra
Rafael del Pino, Chmn.

Phone: 34-91-586-25-00	**Fax:** 34-91-586-26-77
Toll-Free:	
Address: Principe de Vergara, 135, Madrid, 28002 Spain	

GROWTH PLANS/SPECIAL FEATURES:

Grupo Ferrovial S.A. is a leading infrastructure and industrial group with operations in 49 countries worldwide. The company's investments target four business areas: airports; toll roads and car parks; services; and construction. Ferrovial's airports segment is one of the leading private airport operators in the world, with nine airports handling 152 million passengers annually. It serves 434 airlines that fly to approximately 1,000 destinations worldwide. The largest company in the airport division, BAA, owns and manages six airports in the U.K.: Heathrow, Stansted, Southampton, Glasgow, Edinburgh and Aberdeen. The firm's other two airports are the Cerro Moreno Airport in Chile and the Naples Airport. Cintra is the firm's toll road and car parks division. It manages 1,765 miles of toll road in Spain, North America, Portugal, Ireland, Greece and Chile and 296,146 parking spaces in Spain, Andorra and the U.K. The company's services segment consists of Amey, a British infrastructure maintenance subsidiary; Cespa, a municipal and waste-water treatment subsidiary; Swissport, an airport handling services company; and various other infrastructure and maintenance companies, chiefly in Spain and Portugal. Construction, the firm's original business, covers all aspects of civil engineering and building, including roads, railways, hydraulic works, maritime works, hydroelectric and industrial works. This division includes several subsidiaries: Cadagua, a water and waste treatment plant engineering and construction company; Ferrovial Agroman, the group's flagship construction company, engaged in civil engineering; Budimex, one of Poland's largest construction companies; and Webber, a construction group in Texas. In October 2009, BAA sold London Gatwick airport to Global Infrastructure Partners for $2.47 billion. In December 2009, the firm completed its acquisition and integration of Cintra Concesiones de Infrastructura de Transporte S.A., which it has renamed Ferrovial, S.A.

FINANCIALS: **Sales and profits are in thousands of dollars—add 000 to get the full amount. 2009 Note: Financial information for 2009 was not available for all companies at press time.**

2009 Sales: $	2009 Profits: $	**U.S. Stock Ticker: GRFRF.PK**
2008 Sales: $18,672,700	2008 Profits: $43,600	**Int'l Ticker: FER** Int'l Exchange: Madrid-MCE
2007 Sales: $21,360,000	2007 Profits: $1,070,000	Employees:
2006 Sales: $17,033,300	2006 Profits: $1,965,970	Fiscal Year Ends: 12/31
2005 Sales: $11,470,500	2005 Profits: $530,580	Parent Company:

SALARIES/BENEFITS:

Pension Plan:	ESOP Stock Plan:	Profit Sharing:	Top Exec. Salary: $	Bonus: $
Savings Plan:	Stock Purch. Plan:		Second Exec. Salary: $	Bonus: $

OTHER THOUGHTS:

Apparent Women Officers or Directors:
Hot Spot for Advancement for Women/Minorities:

LOCATIONS: ("Y" = Yes)

West:	Southwest:	Midwest:	Southeast:	Northeast:	International:
	Y	Y			Y

GS ENGINEERING & CONSTRUCTION CORP

www.gsconst.co.kr

Industry Group Code: 237 **Ranks within this company's industry group:** Sales: 22 Profits: 14

Properties:		Financial Services:		Construction/Development:		Investments:		Specialty Services:		Brokerage:	
Apartments:		Mortgages:		Commercial Construction:	Y	REIT:		Property Management:		Commercial Sales:	
Malls/Shopping:		Title Insurance:		Residential Construction:				Online Services:		Residential Sales:	
Offices:		Property Insurance:		Land Development:	Y			Software/IT:		Specialty:	
Hotels/Motels:				Support Services:				Consulting:			
Industrial/Warehouses:				Design/Engineering:	Y						
Other:											

TYPES OF BUSINESS:

Construction

BRANDS/DIVISIONS/AFFILIATES:

Xi
Eclat

CONTACTS:

Note: Officers with more than one job title may be intentionally listed here more than once.

Myung-Soo Huh, CEO
Myung-Soo Huh, Pres.
Si-Min Kim, CFO/Exec. VP
Jong-Gyu Kim, Sr. VP-Human Resources
Young-Nam Lee, CTO/Sr. Exec. VP
Hwi-Sung Lee, Sr. Exec. VP-Civil Eng.
Yong-Deug Ha, Chief Legal Officer
Chang-Deuk Do, Sr. VP-Strategic Planning
Yong-Deug Ha, Sr. Exec. VP-Public Rel.
Geon-Soo Jang, Sr. Exec. VP-Architecture
Chan-Ho Lee, Sr. Exec. VP-Housing
Jung-Jae Huh, Sr. Exec. VP-Power & Environment
Hwi-Sung Lee, Sr. Exec. VP-Domestic Bus.
Chang-Soo Huh, Chmn.
Kee-Ju Jang, Exec. VP-Procurement & Project Monitoring

Phone: 82-2-2005-1114	**Fax:**
Toll-Free:	
Address: GS Yeokjeon Twr., 537 Namdaemun-ro 5-ga, Joong-gu, Seoul, Korea	

GROWTH PLANS/SPECIAL FEATURES:

GS Engineering and Construction Corporation (GS E&C), established in 1969, has six main construction divisions: Civil Engineering, Plant, Environment, Architecture, Housing and Power. The civil engineering division focuses on roads, bridges and railroads; underground spaces; and harbors and dredging. Projects of note include the 4.54 mile West Sea Grand Bridge, the Hopo Subway Yard in Busan and an LPG (Liquefied Petroleum Gas) offloading terminal in Incheon. The plant division constructs oil refineries and gas processing plants; petrochemical plants; and power plants and other energy related facilities, such as pipelines and storage facilities. Some of its major projects include the Azerpetrochim refinery in Azerbaijan, the $700 million QP Refinery Expansion in Qatar, a VCM/PVC (Vinyl Chloride Monomer is used to make Polyvinyl Chloride) plant in Saudi Arabia, and the coal-fired Power Plant No. 5 and 6 in Taean. The environment division handles water and wastewater treatment facilities, as well as waste treatment and recycling facilities. Some of its projects include the China Sanghae Songjiang sewage treatment facilities and the Incheon Namdong-gu food waste recycling center. The architecture division constructs intelligent buildings; research, educational and medical health care facilities; and cultural and sports facilities. Major projects include the COEX Convention Center, the Buddhist Hospital for Dongkook University and the main stadium for Iman University in Saudi Arabia. GS E&C's housing division constructs residential complexes under the Xi brand and studio apartments under the Eclat brand. One of its major accomplishments was being selected as the contractor for the Korea National Housing Corp. project. The Power segment focuses on the construction of combined cycle power plant and thermal fired power plants; co-generation plants and district heating; and nuclear power plants. This division is currently constructing Nuclear Power Plant No.1 & 2 in the southeastern part of Korea.

FINANCIALS:

Sales and profits are in thousands of dollars—add 000 to get the full amount. 2009 Note: Financial information for 2009 was not available for all companies at press time.

2009 Sales: $6,822,640	2009 Profits: $339,260	**U.S. Stock Ticker:**
2008 Sales: $4,971,500	2008 Profits: $266,300	**Int'l Ticker: 006360** Int'l Exchange: Seoul-KRX
2007 Sales: $4,431,100	2007 Profits: $294,850	Employees:
2006 Sales: $4,234,760	2006 Profits: $285,220	Fiscal Year Ends: 12/31
2005 Sales: $6,255,637	2005 Profits: $285,291	Parent Company:

SALARIES/BENEFITS:

Pension Plan:	ESOP Stock Plan:	Profit Sharing:	Top Exec. Salary: $	Bonus: $
Savings Plan:	Stock Purch. Plan:		Second Exec. Salary: $	Bonus: $

OTHER THOUGHTS:

Apparent Women Officers or Directors:
Hot Spot for Advancement for Women/Minorities:

LOCATIONS: ("Y" = Yes)

West:	Southwest:	Midwest:	Southeast:	Northeast:	International:
					Y

GUOMAN HOTELS LIMITED

www.thistlehotels.com

Industry Group Code: 721110 **Ranks within this company's industry group:** Sales: Profits:

Properties:		Financial Services:		Construction/Development:		Investments:		Specialty Services:		Brokerage:	
Apartments:		Mortgages:		Commercial Construction:		REIT:		Property Management:	Y	Commercial Sales:	
Malls/Shopping:		Title Insurance:		Residential Construction:				Online Services:		Residential Sales:	
Offices:		Property Insurance:		Land Development:				Software/IT:		Specialty:	
Hotels/Motels:	Y			Support Services:				Consulting:			
Industrial/Warehouses:				Design/Engineering:							
Other:											

TYPES OF BUSINESS:

Hotels
Hotel Management

BRANDS/DIVISIONS/AFFILIATES:

Thistle Hotels plc
GuocoLeisure Limited
BIL International Limited
Thistle Marble Arch
Charing Cross
Otium Health and Leisure Club
Just Gym
Roomexpress

CONTACTS:
Note: Officers with more than one job title may be intentionally listed here more than once.

Timothy J. Scoble, CEO
Timothy J. Scoble, COO
Jeff Karlson, VP-Global Sales
Heiko Figge, Managing Dir.-Hotel Oper., UK
Ahmed Al Makkawy, Mgr.-Int'l Sales, New Markets-Middle East
Sandro Volpato, Dir.-Sales, Middle East
Mauricio Gonzalez, Gen. Sales Agent-Mexico
Tan Sri Quek Leng Chan, Chmn.
Sanjay Nijhawan, COO-Int'l

Phone: 44-20-7138-0000	**Fax:** 44-20-7138-0001
Toll-Free:	
Address: Bath Rd., Uxbridge, UB8 9FH UK	

GROWTH PLANS/SPECIAL FEATURES:

Guoman Hotels Limited, formerly Thistle Hotels plc, owns and operates a chain of 39 hotels throughout the U.K. and Malaysia, primarily under the Guoman and Thistle brands. The company is owned by GuocoLeisure Limited (formerly BIL International Limited). Guoman features 16 hotels in London alone. These hotels include the Thistle Marble Arch, overlooking Oxford Street; the Charing Cross Hotel, near Trafalgar Square; and the Tower Hotel, with views of the Tower of London and Tower Bridge. All of Guoman's properties are located near financial centers, tourist attractions and shopping districts. The company has locations in most business centers and resort areas of the U.K., including Birmingham, Bristol, Edinburgh, Glasgow, Liverpool, Manchester and Newcastle. Hotel amenities include computer and modem hookups, conference rooms, Roomexpress (its delivery room service), lounges and coffee shops. In addition, Guoman properties feature a portfolio of restaurant brands, including CoMotion, a fusion of a New York deli and Italian café, and Gengis, a mixture of Asian and Mediterranean food. Many sites feature Otium Health and Leisure Clubs that have swimming pools, whirlpools and fitness centers; others have Just Gym workout facilities; while some include full-service spas.

FINANCIALS:
Sales and profits are in thousands of dollars—add 000 to get the full amount. 2009 Note: Financial information for 2009 was not available for all companies at press time.

2009 Sales: $	2009 Profits: $	**U.S. Stock Ticker: Subsidiary**
2008 Sales: $	2008 Profits: $	**Int'l Ticker:** Int'l Exchange:
2007 Sales: $	2007 Profits: $	Employees:
2006 Sales: $	2006 Profits: $	Fiscal Year Ends: 12/31
2005 Sales: $302,400	2005 Profits: $94,500	Parent Company: GUOCOLEISURE LTD

SALARIES/BENEFITS:

Pension Plan:	ESOP Stock Plan:	Profit Sharing:	Top Exec. Salary: $	Bonus: $
Savings Plan:	Stock Purch. Plan:		Second Exec. Salary: $	Bonus: $

OTHER THOUGHTS:

Apparent Women Officers or Directors: 1
Hot Spot for Advancement for Women/Minorities: Y

LOCATIONS: ("Y" = Yes)

West:	Southwest:	Midwest:	Southeast:	Northeast:	International:
Y	Y				Y

HANG LUNG GROUP LTD

www.hanglunggroup.com

Industry Group Code: 5311 **Ranks within this company's industry group:** Sales: 15 Profits: 8

Properties:		Financial Services:		Construction/Development:		Investments:		Specialty Services:		Brokerage:	
Apartments:	Y	Mortgages:		Commercial Construction:		REIT:		Property Management:	Y	Commercial Sales:	
Malls/Shopping:	Y	Title Insurance:		Residential Construction:				Online Services:		Residential Sales:	
Offices:	Y	Property Insurance:		Land Development:	Y			Software/IT:		Specialty:	
Hotels/Motels:	Y			Support Services:				Consulting:			
Industrial/Warehouses:				Design/Engineering:							
Other:											

TYPES OF BUSINESS:

Real Estate Holdings & Development
Carpark Management
Hotel Management
Dry Cleaning

BRANDS/DIVISIONS/AFFILIATES:

Hang Lung Properties Limited
Hang Lung-Hakuyosha Dry Cleaning
AP City Limited
AP Success Limited
AP Win Limited
Bonna Estates Company Limited

CONTACTS: *Note: Officers with more than one job title may be intentionally listed here more than once.*

Nelson Wai Leung Yuen, Managing Dir.
Velencia Lee, Corp. Sec.
William Pak Yau Ko, Exec. Dir.-Property Dev. & Project Mgmt.
Terry Szeyuen Ng, Executive Dir.
Shang Shing Yin, Vice-Chmn.
Ronnie Chichung Chan, Chmn.

Phone: 852-2879-0111	**Fax:** 852-2868-6086
Toll-Free:	
Address: 4 Des Voeux Rd., 28th Fl., Hong Kong, China	

GROWTH PLANS/SPECIAL FEATURES:

The Hang Lung Group LTD, through its subsidiary, Hang Lung Properties Limited, develops property in Hong Kong and China for both sale and lease. The company's Hong Kong portfolio, accounting for approximately 59% of revenue, consists of residential, office and commercial properties. Its China portfolio, accounting for nearly 41% of revenue, includes two large scale developments in Shanghai: The Grand Gateway, a commercial, office and residential structure; and Plaza 66, a commercial and office complex. The firm is currently expanding in other large cities such as Tianjin, Shenyang, Wuxi and Jinan, where it is developing a variety of mixed use commercial, office and residential buildings. The Hang Lung Group also manages shopping centers, office buildings, apartments and car parks and the Wesley Hotel in Hong Kong. The Group derives the majority of its revenue from Hang Lung Properties Limited. The company owns a 50% stake in Hang Lung-Hakuyosha Dry Cleaning, a joint-venture. The company's subsidiaries include AP City Limited, AP Properties Limited, AP Success Limited, AP Win Limited and Bonna Estates Company Limited.

FINANCIALS: **Sales and profits are in thousands of dollars—add 000 to get the full amount. 2009 Note: Financial information for 2009 was not available for all companies at press time.**

2009 Sales: $649,410	2009 Profits: $339,790	**U.S. Stock Ticker: HNLGF**
2008 Sales: $1,361,630	2008 Profits: $969,770	**Int'l Ticker: 0010** Int'l Exchange: Hong Kong-HKE
2007 Sales: $616,490	2007 Profits: $617,530	Employees: 2,116
2006 Sales: $552,750	2006 Profits: $365,540	Fiscal Year Ends: 6/30
2005 Sales: $	2005 Profits: $	Parent Company:

SALARIES/BENEFITS:

Pension Plan:	ESOP Stock Plan:	Profit Sharing:	Top Exec. Salary: $	Bonus: $
Savings Plan:	Stock Purch. Plan:		Second Exec. Salary: $	Bonus: $

OTHER THOUGHTS:

Apparent Women Officers or Directors: 2
Hot Spot for Advancement for Women/Minorities:

LOCATIONS: ("Y" = Yes)

West:	Southwest:	Midwest:	Southeast:	Northeast:	International:
					Y

HANG LUNG PROPERTIES LIMITED

www.hanglung.com

Industry Group Code: 5311 **Ranks within this company's industry group:** Sales: 17 Profits: 9

Properties:		Financial Services:		Construction/Development:		Investments:		Specialty Services:		Brokerage:	
Apartments:	Y	Mortgages:		Commercial Construction:		REIT:		Property Management:		Commercial Sales:	
Malls/Shopping:	Y	Title Insurance:		Residential Construction:				Online Services:		Residential Sales:	
Offices:	Y	Property Insurance:		Land Development:	Y			Software/IT:		Specialty:	
Hotels/Motels:	Y			Support Services:				Consulting:			
Industrial/Warehouses:				Design/Engineering:							
Other:											

TYPES OF BUSINESS:

Real Estate Holdings & Development
Leasing

BRANDS/DIVISIONS/AFFILIATES:

Harbourside
Summit (The)
Grand Gateway (The)
Wesley (The)
Hang Lung Group Ltd
AP City Limited
AP Properties Limited
AP Success Limited

CONTACTS:

Note: Officers with more than one job title may be intentionally listed here more than once.

Nelson W. L. Yuen, Managing Dir.
Eric Wing Hong Szeto, Sr. Mgr.-Mktg.
Walter King Yee Wong, Sr. Mgr.-IT
Yun Zhang, Sr. Mgr.-Legal
May Lam K., Sr. Mgr.-Corp. Comm.
Andrew Chee Man Lee, Sr. Mgr.-Finance
Mina Pou Lam Lai, Sr. Mgr.-Leasing & Mgmt.
Shiu Wo Lam, Sr. Mgr.-Project. Dev.
Velencia Lee, Corp. Sec.
Desmond Chun Cheong Lai, Sr. Mgr.-Internal Audit
Ronnie C. Chan, Chmn.

Phone: 852-2879-0111	**Fax:** 852-2868-6086
Toll-Free:	
Address: 4 Des Voeux Rd., 28th Fl., Hong Kong, China	

GROWTH PLANS/SPECIAL FEATURES:

Hang Lung Properties Limited is a property investment holding company for the retail, commercial, office, residential and industrial sectors. As a publicly listed subsidiary of Hang Lung Group Ltd., the firm operates in both Hong Kong and mainland China. In Hong Kong, Hang Lung has developed shopping malls, and mixed use commercial and residential complexes concentrated along the MTR Line, the city's mass transit system. The company also develops luxury residential properties such as The Summit and its latest, Harbourside, which consists of three blocks of 80 story residences. Its mainland China developments include Plaza 66, a five story shopping mall and office building, and The Grand Gateway, a complex consisting of retail, office and residential facilities, in Shanghai. Development projects are also underway in the mainland Chinese cities of Tianjin, Shenyang, Wuxi, Jinan and Dalian. In addition, Hang Sung is involved with leasing. Its commercial leasing portfolio in Hong Kong includes properties in strategic locations along busy shopping centers in the city, such as Causeway Bay and Mongkok. Its office properties are located along mass transit railway lines and other transportation networks. The Summit, with 60 stories is one of the company's luxury leasing residences. It also leases its Plaza 66 and Grand Gateway properties in Shanghai, China and is pre-leasing space in its Palace 66 mall under construction in Shenyang. The firm operates car parks located in densely populated areas and manages The Wesley Hotel in Hong Kong, with 250 rooms and targeted toward both commercial and business travelers.

FINANCIALS:

Sales and profits are in thousands of dollars—add 000 to get the full amount. 2009 Note: Financial information for 2009 was not available for all companies at press time.

2009 Sales: $539,870	2009 Profits: $531,490	**U.S. Stock Ticker: HLPPY**
2008 Sales: $1,300,600	2008 Profits: $661,010	**Int'l Ticker: 0101** Int'l Exchange: Hong Kong-HKE
2007 Sales: $566,300	2007 Profits: $264,250	Employees: 1,955
2006 Sales: $	2006 Profits: $	Fiscal Year Ends: 6/30
2005 Sales: $	2005 Profits: $	Parent Company: HANG LUNG GROUP LTD

SALARIES/BENEFITS:

Pension Plan:	ESOP Stock Plan:	Profit Sharing:	Top Exec. Salary: $	Bonus: $
Savings Plan:	Stock Purch. Plan:		Second Exec. Salary: $	Bonus: $

OTHER THOUGHTS:

Apparent Women Officers or Directors: 7
Hot Spot for Advancement for Women/Minorities: Y

LOCATIONS: ("Y" = Yes)

West:	Southwest:	Midwest:	Southeast:	Northeast:	International:
					Y

HANJIN HEAVY INDUSTRIES CO LTD

www.hanjinsc.com

Industry Group Code: 3366 **Ranks within this company's industry group:** Sales: 1 Profits: 1

Properties:		Financial Services:		Construction/Development:		Investments:		Specialty Services:		Brokerage:	
Apartments:		Mortgages:		Commercial Construction:	Y	REIT:		Property Management:		Commercial Sales:	
Malls/Shopping:		Title Insurance:		Residential Construction:	Y			Online Services:		Residential Sales:	
Offices:		Property Insurance:		Land Development:	Y			Software/IT:		Specialty:	
Hotels/Motels:				Support Services:	Y			Consulting:			
Industrial/Warehouses:				Design/Engineering:	Y						
Other:											

TYPES OF BUSINESS:

Construction & Manufacturing
Shipbuilding

BRANDS/DIVISIONS/AFFILIATES:

HHIC Shipping Limited

CONTACTS:

Note: Officers with more than one job title may be intentionally listed here more than once.

Su Sin Lee, Co-CEO
Cho Nam Ho, Co-CEO
Song Hwa Yeong, Co-CEO
Nam Ho Cho, Chmn.

Phone: 82-51-410-3114	**Fax:** 82-51-410-8465
Toll-Free:	
Address: 29, 5-Ga, Bongnae-dong, Youngdo-gu, Busan, 606-796 Korea	

GROWTH PLANS/SPECIAL FEATURES:

Hanjin Heavy Industries and Construction Co., Ltd. (HHIC), established in 1937, has two main divisions: Shipbuilding and Construction. Hanjin's oldest division, shipbuilding, manufactures container carriers; LNG and LPG (Liquefied Natural Gas and Liquefied Petroleum Gas) carriers; chemical tankers; oil and petroleum product carriers; bulk, cement and woodchip carriers; ro-ro (roll-on/roll-off, which handle wheeled cargo) and reefer (or refrigerated) vessels; and special purpose vessels such as cable layers, icebreakers, dredgers, oceanographic vessels and semi-submersible drilling rigs. It also manufactures less standard ships, such as military patrol boats, amphibious transport ships, assault hovercraft and salvage ships. The construction division's architectural operations encompass commercial buildings, mainly large office complexes; hospitals and hotels; schools and campuses; apartment complexes and housing; airport terminals; cultural and sports facilities; and military facilities. The division's infrastructure projects encompass bridges, tunnels and roadways; subways and railroads; airfield runways; harbors, marine works and landscaping; dams and irrigation; and water and sewage systems. Electricity projects include signal lights for airport runways, power lines and electrified railway tracks. The construction division's plants and facilities segment constructs power generation, energy, waste treatment and industrial plants, as well as steel structures and material handling equipment, such as bridges, cranes and sorting systems for cargo terminals. The firm's shipbuilding R&D efforts include structural analysis, such as collision analysis; hydrodynamic performance, such as hull form development and propeller performance research; vibration and noise analysis; and automated ship manufacturing systems, including laser sensing technology and multi-axis welding robotics research.

FINANCIALS:

Sales and profits are in thousands of dollars—add 000 to get the full amount. 2009 Note: Financial information for 2009 was not available for all companies at press time.

2009 Sales: $	2009 Profits: $	**U.S. Stock Ticker:**
2008 Sales: $3,068,630	2008 Profits: $56,810	**Int'l Ticker: 003480** Int'l Exchange: Seoul-KRX
2007 Sales: $1,071,120	2007 Profits: $21,060	Employees:
2006 Sales: $1,924,560	2006 Profits: $72,490	Fiscal Year Ends: 12/31
2005 Sales: $2,172,300	2005 Profits: $	Parent Company:

SALARIES/BENEFITS:

Pension Plan:	ESOP Stock Plan:	Profit Sharing:	Top Exec. Salary: $	Bonus: $
Savings Plan:	Stock Purch. Plan:		Second Exec. Salary: $	Bonus: $

OTHER THOUGHTS:

Apparent Women Officers or Directors:
Hot Spot for Advancement for Women/Minorities:

LOCATIONS: ("Y" = Yes)

West:	Southwest:	Midwest:	Southeast:	Northeast:	International:
Y					Y

HARRAH'S ENTERTAINMENT INC

www.harrahs.com

Industry Group Code: 721120 **Ranks within this company's industry group:** Sales: 1 Profits: 8

Properties:		Financial Services:		Construction/Development:		Investments:		Specialty Services:		Brokerage:	
Apartments:		Mortgages:		Commercial Construction:		REIT:		Property Management:	Y	Commercial Sales:	
Malls/Shopping:		Title Insurance:		Residential Construction:				Online Services:		Residential Sales:	
Offices:		Property Insurance:		Land Development:				Software/IT:		Specialty:	
Hotels/Motels:	Y			Support Services:				Consulting:			
Industrial/Warehouses:				Design/Engineering:							
Other:	Y										

TYPES OF BUSINESS:

Casino Hotels
Dockside & Riverboat Casinos
Racing Venues
Casino Management
Golf Facility

BRANDS/DIVISIONS/AFFILIATES:

Harrah's Operating Company Inc
Flamingo
Caesars Entertainment Inc
Horseshoe
Total Rewards
Hamlet Holdings LLC
TPG Capital LP
Apollo Management LP

CONTACTS:

Note: Officers with more than one job title may be intentionally listed here more than once.

Gary Loveman, CEO
Gary W. Loveman, Pres.
Jonathan S. Halkyard, CFO/Sr. VP/Treas.
David Norton, Chief Mktg. Officer/Sr. VP
Mary Thomas, Sr. VP-Human Resources
Katrina Lane, CTO/Sr. VP
Tim Donovan, General Counsel/Sr. VP
Peter Murphy, Pres., Bus. & Strategy
Jan Jones, Sr. VP-Comm. & Gov't Rel.
Tom M. Jenkin, Pres., Western Div.
John Payne, Pres., Central Div.
Don Marrandino, Pres., Eastern Div.
John Baker, Sr. VP-Enterprise Effectiveness
Gary Loveman, Chmn.

Phone: 702-407-6000	**Fax:** 702-407-6037
Toll-Free: 800-318-0047	
Address: 1 Caesars Palace Dr., Las Vegas, NV 89109 US	

GROWTH PLANS/SPECIAL FEATURES:

Harrah's Entertainment, Inc., owned by Hamlet Holdings LLC, an affiliate of TPG Capital, LP and Apollo Management, L.P., is one of the largest gaming companies in the world. The firm owns or manages approximately 40 casinos throughout the world. Harrah's also earns fees from managing three casinos for Indian tribes: Harrah's Phoenix Ak-Chin, located near Phoenix, Arizona; Harrah's Rincon Casino and Resort, near San Diego, California; and Harrah's Cherokee Casino and Hotel, in Cherokee, North Carolina. These contracts expire in 2011. Additional brands operated and/or owned by Harrah's, Caesars; Horseshoe; Bally's; Flamingo; Grand Biloxi; Harveys; Imperial Palace; Paris; Rio; and Showboat. The firm offers casino entertainment facilities primarily under the Harrah's, Caesars and Horseshoe brands in the U.S., including land-based casinos; riverboat or dockside casinos; casino clubs; and three racing venues. Besides casinos, the firm's properties generally include hotel and convention space; restaurants; and non-gaming entertainment facilities. Harrah's properties total approximately 3 million square feet of gaming space and 38,000 hotel rooms. For returning customers in the U.S., the firm offers the Total Rewards card plan, allowing holders to earn reward credits for prizes such as vacations, event tickets and cars; Total Rewards currently has over 40 million members. The company owns and operates the World Series of Poker tournament and brand.

Employees of Harrah's receive medical, dental and vision plans; educational assistance; a health and wellness programs.

FINANCIALS:

Sales and profits are in thousands of dollars—add 000 to get the full amount. 2009 Note: Financial information for 2009 was not available for all companies at press time.

2009 Sales: $8,907,400	2009 Profits: $846,400	**U.S. Stock Ticker: Private**
2008 Sales: $9,370,000	2008 Profits: $-5,197,200	**Int'l Ticker:** Int'l Exchange:
2007 Sales: $10,825,200	2007 Profits: $619,400	Employees: 80,000
2006 Sales: $9,673,900	2006 Profits: $535,800	Fiscal Year Ends: 12/31
2005 Sales: $7,010,000	2005 Profits: $236,400	Parent Company: HAMLET HOLDINGS LLC

SALARIES/BENEFITS:

Pension Plan:	ESOP Stock Plan:	Profit Sharing:	Top Exec. Salary: $	Bonus: $
Savings Plan: Y	Stock Purch. Plan:		Second Exec. Salary: $	Bonus: $

OTHER THOUGHTS:

Apparent Women Officers or Directors: 2
Hot Spot for Advancement for Women/Minorities: Y

LOCATIONS: ("Y" = Yes)

West:	Southwest:	Midwest:	Southeast:	Northeast:	International:
Y	Y	Y	Y	Y	Y

HCP INC

www.hcpi.com

Industry Group Code: 531120 **Ranks within this company's industry group:** Sales: 15 Profits: 4

Properties:		Financial Services:		Construction/Development:		Investments:		Specialty Services:		Brokerage:	
Apartments:		Mortgages:		Commercial Construction:		REIT:	Y	Property Management:		Commercial Sales:	
Malls/Shopping:		Title Insurance:		Residential Construction:				Online Services:		Residential Sales:	
Offices:		Property Insurance:		Land Development:				Software/IT:		Specialty:	
Hotels/Motels:				Support Services:				Consulting:			
Industrial/Warehouses:				Design/Engineering:							
Other:	Y										

TYPES OF BUSINESS:

Real Estate Investment Trust
Health Care Properties

BRANDS/DIVISIONS/AFFILIATES:

Health Care Property Investors
Investment Management Program

CONTACTS:

Note: Officers with more than one job title may be intentionally listed here more than once.

James F. (Jay) Flaherty, III, CEO
Thomas M. Herzog, CFO/Exec. VP
Alberto Gonzalez-Pita, General Counsel/Exec. VP
Paul F. Gallagher, Chief Investment Officer/Exec. VP
Thomas M. Klaritch, Exec. VP-Medical Office Properties
Susan M. Tate, Exec VP-Asset Mgmt. & Senior Housing
Timothy M. Schoen, Exec. VP-Life Science & Investment Mgmt.
James F. (Jay) Flaherty, III, Chmn.

Phone: 562-733-5100 **Fax:** 562-733-5200
Toll-Free: 888-604-1990
Address: 3760 Kilroy Airport Way, Ste. 300, Long Beach, CA 90806 US

GROWTH PLANS/SPECIAL FEATURES:

HCP, Inc., formerly Health Care Property Investors, invests primarily in real estate serving the healthcare industry in the U.S. Headquartered in Long Beach, California, the firm has additional offices in Nashville and San Francisco. HCP's portfolio of investments is comprised of 256 senior housing facilities, 98 life science facilities, 251 medical offices, 22 hospitals and 48 skilled nursing facilities. Included in its portfolio are joint venture investments through its Investment Management Program in 25 senior housing facilities, four life science facilities, 67 medical offices and four hospitals. Senior housing facilities, which generate approximately 30% of its revenue, include independent living facilities, assisted living facilities and continuing care retirement communities. HCP's life science properties, which generate approximately 22% of its revenue, are primarily configured in business park formats and contain laboratory and office space primarily for scientific research institutions, government agencies and biotechnology and pharmaceutical companies. Its medical office facilities, which generate approximately 27% of its revenue, typically contain physicians' offices and examination rooms, and may also include pharmacies, hospital ancillary service space and outpatient services such as diagnostic centers, rehabilitation clinics and day-surgery operating rooms. All of the company's hospitals, which include acute care hospitals, long-term acute care hospitals, specialty hospitals and rehabilitation hospitals, are leased to single tenants under net lease structures. The firm's hospital properties generate approximately 11% of its revenue. HCP's skilled nursing facilities, which generate approximately 10% of its revenue, offer restorative, rehabilitative and custodial nursing care for people not requiring the more extensive and sophisticated treatment available at hospitals. In June 2009, HCP announced plans to transition 15 Sunrise Senior Living, Inc. housing communities to new operators.

FINANCIALS:

Sales and profits are in thousands of dollars—add 000 to get the full amount. 2009 Note: Financial information for 2009 was not available for all companies at press time.

2009 Sales: $1,157,030 2009 Profits: $146,151
2008 Sales: $1,153,188 2008 Profits: $470,983
2007 Sales: $953,743 2007 Profits: $614,115
2006 Sales: $464,247 2006 Profits: $396,417
2005 Sales: $364,735 2005 Profits: $151,927

U.S. Stock Ticker: HCP
Int'l Ticker: Int'l Exchange:
Employees: 142
Fiscal Year Ends: 12/31
Parent Company:

SALARIES/BENEFITS:

Pension Plan: ESOP Stock Plan: Profit Sharing: Top Exec. Salary: $600,000 Bonus: $1,462,500
Savings Plan: Y Stock Purch. Plan: Second Exec. Salary: $350,000 Bonus: $650,000

OTHER THOUGHTS:

Apparent Women Officers or Directors: 3
Hot Spot for Advancement for Women/Minorities: Y

LOCATIONS: ("Y" = Yes)

West:	Southwest:	Midwest:	Southeast:	Northeast:	International:
Y			Y		

HDR INC

www.hdrinc.com

Industry Group Code: 237 **Ranks within this company's industry group:** Sales: Profits:

Properties:		Financial Services:		Construction/Development:		Investments:		Specialty Services:		Brokerage:	
Apartments:		Mortgages:		Commercial Construction:		REIT:		Property Management:		Commercial Sales:	
Malls/Shopping:		Title Insurance:		Residential Construction:				Online Services:		Residential Sales:	
Offices:		Property Insurance:		Land Development:				Software/IT:		Specialty:	
Hotels/Motels:				Support Services:				Consulting:			
Industrial/Warehouses:				Design/Engineering:	Y						
Other:											

TYPES OF BUSINESS:

Engineering Services
Architectural Services
Consulting Services

BRANDS/DIVISIONS/AFFILIATES:

iTrans
e2M
TransDec
RailDec
GradeDec
RAP
AirLib
Interactive Value Assessment (IVA)

CONTACTS: *Note: Officers with more than one job title may be intentionally listed here more than once.*

Richard R. Bell, CEO
Terrence C. Cox, CFO
Jackie Fox, Contact-Media
Pierre Vilain, VP-Finance & Economics
George A. Little, Vice Chmn./Pres., HDR Eng., Inc.
Merle S. Bachman, Pres., HDR Architecture
Richard R. Bell, Chmn.

Phone: 402-399-1000 **Fax:** 402-399-1238
Toll-Free: 800-366-4411
Address: 8404 Indian Hills Dr., Omaha, NE 68114-4049 US

GROWTH PLANS/SPECIAL FEATURES:

HDR, Inc. is an architectural, engineering and consulting firm that specializes in managing complex projects and solving engineering and architectural challenges for its clients. The company has more than 165 locations globally, including operations in all 50 states and within 60 countries worldwide. The employee-owned firm offers design-build services and program management for a variety of markets, including community architecture; hospitals and other health care projects; science and technology construction; transportation; power; justice; and wastewater and water resources. HDR's economic tools include StratBENCOST, an investment analysis tool for state and local transportation agencies engaged in multi-year strategic planning and budgeting for highways; TransDec, a cost-benefit analysis tool for both large and small urban areas and projects; RailDec, a decision support tool for state and local transportation agencies engaged in strategic planning and budgeting for rail and rail-related intermodal projects; GradeDec, a highway-rail grade crossing investment analysis tool; RAP, a suite of risk analysis tools; AirLib, a model for investigating the costs and benefits associated with liberalizing international air travel agreements; Interactive Value Assessment (IVA), a tool for conducting real-time business case evaluations; and Sustainability Business Case Tool (SBC), a tool for assessing the costs and benefits related to sustainable design. Repeat clients account for roughly 80% of the company's business. Subsidiaries of the firm include, E.T. Archer Corporation, Claunch & Miller, Inc., and Doherty & Associates. In January 2009, the firm acquired Devine Tarbell & Associates, Inc., an architectural, engineering and consulting firm. In June 2009, the company acquired e2M, an engineering and environmental management firm. In July 2009, HDR acquired iTrans, a Canadian consulting firm.

Employees are offered medical, dental and vision coverage; tuition assistance; a 401(k) plan; a flexible spending accounts; life insurance; short and long term disability; part-time employee benefits (for employees who work a minimum of 30 hours per week).

FINANCIALS: **Sales and profits are in thousands of dollars—add 000 to get the full amount. 2009 Note: Financial information for 2009 was not available for all companies at press time.**

2009 Sales: $ | 2009 Profits: $
2008 Sales: $ | 2008 Profits: $
2007 Sales: $ | 2007 Profits: $
2006 Sales: $ | 2006 Profits: $
2005 Sales: $ | 2005 Profits: $

U.S. Stock Ticker: Private
Int'l Ticker: Int'l Exchange:
Employees:
Fiscal Year Ends: 12/31
Parent Company:

SALARIES/BENEFITS:

Pension Plan: | ESOP Stock Plan: Y | Profit Sharing: | Top Exec. Salary: $ | Bonus: $
Savings Plan: Y | Stock Purch. Plan: | | Second Exec. Salary: $ | Bonus: $

OTHER THOUGHTS:

Apparent Women Officers or Directors: 1
Hot Spot for Advancement for Women/Minorities: Y

LOCATIONS: ("Y" = Yes)

West:	Southwest:	Midwest:	Southeast:	Northeast:	International:
Y	Y	Y	Y	Y	Y

HEALTH CARE REIT INC

www.hcreit.com

Industry Group Code: 531120 **Ranks within this company's industry group:** Sales: 33 Profits: 10

Properties:		Financial Services:		Construction/Development:		Investments:		Specialty Services:		Brokerage:	
Apartments:		Mortgages:		Commercial Construction:		REIT:	Y	Property Management:	Y	Commercial Sales:	
Malls/Shopping:		Title Insurance:		Residential Construction:				Online Services:		Residential Sales:	
Offices:	Y	Property Insurance:		Land Development:	Y			Software/IT:		Specialty:	
Hotels/Motels:				Support Services:	Y			Consulting:			
Industrial/Warehouses:				Design/Engineering:							
Other:	Y										

TYPES OF BUSINESS:

Real Estate Investment Trust
Health Care Properties

BRANDS/DIVISIONS/AFFILIATES:

Paramount Real Estate Services Inc
HCN Development Services Group Inc
Windrose Southside Properties Ltd
Lake Mead Medical Investors LP
Med Properties Asset Group LLC
Windrose Medical Properties Management LLC
HCRI Eden Holdings Inc

CONTACTS:

Note: Officers with more than one job title may be intentionally listed here more than once.

George L. Chapman, CEO
George L. Chapman, Pres.
Scott A. Estes, CFO/Exec. VP
Charles J. Herman, Jr., CIO/Exec. VP
Erin C. Ibele, Sr. VP-Admin./Corp. Sec.
Jeffrey H. Miller, General Counsel/Exec. VP
Jeffrey H. Miller, Exec. VP-Oper.
Michael A. Crabtree, Treas./VP
Daniel R. Loftus, Sr. VP
Frederick L. Farrar, Exec. VP
Fred S. Klipsch, Vice Chmn.
John T. Thomas, Exec. VP-Medical Facilities
George L. Chapman, Chmn.

Phone: 419-247-2800 **Fax:** 419-247-2826
Toll-Free:
Address: 1 SeaGate, Ste. 1500, Toledo, OH 43603 US

GROWTH PLANS/SPECIAL FEATURES:

Health Care REIT, Inc. (HC) is a self-administered, equity real estate investment trust (REIT) that invests in continuing care retirement communities; hospitals; medical office buildings; and skilled nursing, assisted living and specialty health care facilities. The company's holdings include 633 properties across 39 states, leased to about 50 health care operating companies. Of these properties, 186 are assisted living facilities, which combine housing, personalized supportive services and health care; 225 are skilled nursing facilities, which provide inpatient skilled nursing, rehabilitative, restorative and transitional medical services; 31 are specialty care facilities, including acute care hospitals and long-term care hospitals; 128 are medical office buildings; and 63 are continuing care retirement facilities. Properties are further diversified by geographical dispersion and the variety of operators to which they are leased. Major operators include Emeritus Corporation; Merrill Gardens LLC; Life Care Centers of America, Inc.; Senior Living Communities LLC; Signature Healthcare LLC; and Brookdale Senior Living, Inc. Through HCN Development Services Group, Inc. (HCN), a subsidiary, HC also has capabilities in property development; facility planning; medical equipment planning and implementation services; and leasing and property management services. HCN primarily develops specialty medical properties for its parent, although it also provides some services to third parties. In September 2008, HC announced that it would acquire a 90% share in 29 senior housing properties managed by Sunrise Senior Living, Inc., for approximately $643.5 million. Sunrise Senior Living will continue to hold a 10% interest in the properties, which are located primarily in the New York, Los Angeles and Chicago metropolitan areas. In October 2008, the company completed the sale of 29 communities to Emeritus Corporation for approximately $300 million. The properties had previously been under long-term leases to Emeritus.

FINANCIALS:

Sales and profits are in thousands of dollars—add 000 to get the full amount. 2009 Note: Financial information for 2009 was not available for all companies at press time.

2009 Sales: $568,973	2009 Profits: $192,927	**U.S. Stock Ticker: HCN**
2008 Sales: $526,406	2008 Profits: $283,425	**Int'l Ticker:** Int'l Exchange:
2007 Sales: $429,486	2007 Profits: $138,593	Employees: 217
2006 Sales: $288,242	2006 Profits: $89,975	Fiscal Year Ends: 12/31
2005 Sales: $264,622	2005 Profits: $84,286	Parent Company:

SALARIES/BENEFITS:

Pension Plan:	ESOP Stock Plan:	Profit Sharing:	Top Exec. Salary: $	Bonus: $
Savings Plan: Y	Stock Purch. Plan:		Second Exec. Salary: $	Bonus: $

OTHER THOUGHTS:

Apparent Women Officers or Directors: 2
Hot Spot for Advancement for Women/Minorities:

LOCATIONS: ("Y" = Yes)

West:	Southwest:	Midwest:	Southeast:	Northeast:	International:
Y	Y	Y	Y	Y	

HEALTHCARE REALTY TRUST INC

www.healthcarerealty.com

Industry Group Code: 531120 **Ranks within this company's industry group:** Sales: 54 Profits: 36

Properties:		Financial Services:		Construction/Development:		Investments:		Specialty Services:		Brokerage:	
Apartments:		Mortgages:	Y	Commercial Construction:	Y	REIT:	Y	Property Management:	Y	Commercial Sales:	
Malls/Shopping:		Title Insurance:		Residential Construction:				Online Services:		Residential Sales:	
Offices:	Y	Property Insurance:		Land Development:				Software/IT:		Specialty:	
Hotels/Motels:				Support Services:				Consulting:			
Industrial/Warehouses:				Design/Engineering:							
Other:	Y										

TYPES OF BUSINESS:

Real Estate Investment Trust
Health Care Properties
Medical Facility Construction
Property Management
Mortgages

BRANDS/DIVISIONS/AFFILIATES:

Healthcare Realty Services, Inc.
HR Assets LLC

CONTACTS: *Note: Officers with more than one job title may be intentionally listed here more than once.*

David R. Emery, CEO
B. Douglas Whitman, II, COO/Exec. VP
Scott W. Holmes, CFO/Exec. VP
Revell Michael, Dir-Mktg./Associate VP
Rebecca T. Oberlander, Associate VP-Human Resources
William R. Davis, Associate VP-IT
John M. Bryant, Jr., General Counsel/Exec. VP
Gilbert T. Irvin, VP-Oper.
Frederick M. Langreck, Treas./Sr. VP
Todd Meredith, Sr. VP-Real Estate Investments
Julie A. Wilson, Sr. VP/Dir.-Asset Mgmt.
Christine Acosta, Associate VP/Dir.-Real Estate, Western Region
Leigh Ann Stach, VP-Financial Reporting
David R. Emery, Chmn.

Phone: 615-269-8175	**Fax:** 615-269-8461
Toll-Free:	
Address: 3310 West End Ave., 4th Fl., Ste. 700, Nashville, TN 37203 US	

GROWTH PLANS/SPECIAL FEATURES:

Healthcare Realty Trust, Inc. (HRT) is a self-managed and self-administered real estate investment trust (REIT) that owns, acquires, manages and develops real estate properties in the health care industry. HRT has investments of approximately $2.3 billion in mortgage investments and 204 real estate properties in 28 states with approximately 12.3 million square feet. The company also provides property management services for 140 healthcare-related properties nationwide, totaling approximately 9.3 million square feet.

Unlike the majority of real estate firms, HRT funds all acquisitions and developments from internal capital instead of third-party lenders or equity partners, which allows the firm to expedite investments and accept shorter operating leases. The company's portfolio consists of six major facility types, including medical offices; ambulatory care and surgery; physician clinics; specialty outpatient; specialty inpatient; and other specialty healthcare fields. HRT has also constructed over two dozen medical real estate facilities valued at more than $500 million in an effort to improve acute care facilities, technology and services for healthcare providers. Although HRT invests in properties nationwide, the majority of its investments are concentrated in the Southern and Western U.S. The company's most prominent client is HealthSouth Corporation, which accounted for 11% of HRT's 2009 revenue. During 2009, the company acquired $106.4 million in real estate assets. Four of the properties, which total $43.9 million, were acquired by a joint venture in which HRT has an 80% controlling interest. Also during 2009, the company disposed of seven real estate properties. In 2010, the company disposed of five properties in Virginia.

FINANCIALS: **Sales and profits are in thousands of dollars—add 000 to get the full amount. 2009 Note: Financial information for 2009 was not available for all companies at press time.**

2009 Sales: $253,304	2009 Profits: $51,148	**U.S. Stock Ticker: HR**
2008 Sales: $213,931	2008 Profits: $41,760	**Int'l Ticker:** Int'l Exchange:
2007 Sales: $197,081	2007 Profits: $60,062	Employees: 229
2006 Sales: $198,219	2006 Profits: $39,719	Fiscal Year Ends: 12/31
2005 Sales: $206,745	2005 Profits: $52,668	Parent Company:

SALARIES/BENEFITS:

Pension Plan:	ESOP Stock Plan:	Profit Sharing:	Top Exec. Salary: $959,711	Bonus: $
Savings Plan: Y	Stock Purch. Plan: Y		Second Exec. Salary: $411,521	Bonus: $

OTHER THOUGHTS:

Apparent Women Officers or Directors: 12
Hot Spot for Advancement for Women/Minorities: Y

LOCATIONS: ("Y" = Yes)

West:	Southwest:	Midwest:	Southeast:	Northeast:	International:
Y	Y	Y	Y	Y	

HENDERSON LAND DEVELOPMENT COMPANY LIMITED

www.hld.com

Industry Group Code: 5311 **Ranks within this company's industry group:** Sales: 13 Profits: 2

Properties:		Financial Services:		Construction/Development:		Investments:		Specialty Services:		Brokerage:	
Apartments:	Y	Mortgages:		Commercial Construction:	Y	REIT:		Property Management:	Y	Commercial Sales:	
Malls/Shopping:	Y	Title Insurance:		Residential Construction:	Y			Online Services:		Residential Sales:	
Offices:	Y	Property Insurance:		Land Development:	Y			Software/IT:		Specialty:	
Hotels/Motels:	Y			Support Services:				Consulting:			
Industrial/Warehouses:				Design/Engineering:							
Other:											

TYPES OF BUSINESS:

Real Estate Holdings & Development
Property Management
Construction
Hotel Operation

BRANDS/DIVISIONS/AFFILIATES:

Hong Kong Ferry (Holdings) Company Limited
Henderson Investment Limited
Hong Kong & China Gas Company Limited (The)
Miramar Hotel & Investment Company, Limited
Towngas China
Citistore

CONTACTS:
Note: Officers with more than one job title may be intentionally listed here more than once.

Tat Man Lam, Gen. Mgr-Sales
Cheung Yuen Liu, Corp. Sec.
Wing Kee Wong, Gen. Mgr.-Accounts
David Francis Dumigan, Gen. Mgr.-Project Mgmt. Unit
Ho Ming Wong, Gen. Mgr.-Property Dev.
Kam Leung Leung, Gen. Mgr-Property Planning
Wing Hoo Wong, Gen. Mgr-Construction
Shau Kee Lee, Chmn.

Phone: 852-2908-8888 **Fax:** 852-2908-8838
Toll-Free:
Address: International Finance Centre, 8 Finance St., Fl. 2, Hong Kong, China

GROWTH PLANS/SPECIAL FEATURES:

Henderson Land Development Company Limited is an investment holding firm that focuses on property development and investment; property management; construction; and hotel operation in Hong Kong and China. The total land bank of the company and its subsidiaries in Hong Kong equals approximately 19 million square feet of total attributable floor space. It also holds 32.4 million square feet of agricultural land. The firm develops property in both urban and suburban areas in Hong Kong. Its investment portfolio in Hong Kong is around 10 million square feet. Henderson's landmark investment project in the city is the International Finance Centre, which consists of retail shopping centers and office buildings, which account for 80% of the company's investment properties. Henderson also participates in hotel development, having established the Mira Hong Kong, Four Seasons Hotel Hong Kong and Newton Hotel Hong Kong. In addition, the company holds a place in the department store market, under the trade name, Citistore, which targets young and fashion forward clientele. The firm's total land bank in China is approximately 130.4 million square feet in developable gross floor area. Henderson has participated in the development and investment of the Henderson Centre in Beijing, Office Tower II of The Grand Gateway in Shanghai, the Shanghai Skycity and the Heng Bao Garden in Guangzhou. The company's subsidiaries include Hong Kong Ferry (Holdings) Company Limited, which focuses on property development and investment; Henderson Investment Limited, which is involved in infrastructure; The Hong Kong and China Gas Company Limited, which produces and distributes gas in Hong Kong and China; Miramar Hotel and Investment Company, Limited, which is involved in hotel operation and the travel business; and Towngas China, a distributor of liquefied petroleum and natural gas in China.

FINANCIALS:
Sales and profits are in thousands of dollars—add 000 to get the full amount. 2009 Note: Financial information for 2009 was not available for all companies at press time.

2009 Sales: $1,341,060
2008 Sales: $1,754,000
2007 Sales: $1,086,300
2006 Sales: $880,500
2005 Sales: $

2009 Profits: $1,693,750
2008 Profits: $2,011,400
2007 Profits: $1,276,300
2006 Profits: $1,761,300
2005 Profits: $

U.S. Stock Ticker:
Int'l Ticker: 0012 Int'l Exchange: Hong Kong-HKE
Employees: 7,700
Fiscal Year Ends: 12/31
Parent Company:

SALARIES/BENEFITS:

Pension Plan: ESOP Stock Plan: Profit Sharing: Top Exec. Salary: $ Bonus: $
Savings Plan: Stock Purch. Plan: Second Exec. Salary: $ Bonus: $

OTHER THOUGHTS:

Apparent Women Officers or Directors: 3
Hot Spot for Advancement for Women/Minorities: Y

LOCATIONS: ("Y" = Yes)

West:	Southwest:	Midwest:	Southeast:	Northeast:	International:
					Y

HIGHWOODS PROPERTIES INC

www.highwoods.com

Industry Group Code: 531120 **Ranks within this company's industry group:** Sales: 40 Profits: 39

Properties:		Financial Services:		Construction/Development:		Investments:		Specialty Services:		Brokerage:	
Apartments:	Y	Mortgages:		Commercial Construction:	Y	REIT:	Y	Property Management:	Y	Commercial Sales:	
Malls/Shopping:		Title Insurance:		Residential Construction:	Y			Online Services:		Residential Sales:	
Offices:	Y	Property Insurance:		Land Development:	Y			Software/IT:	Y	Specialty:	
Hotels/Motels:				Support Services:	Y			Consulting:			
Industrial/Warehouses:	Y			Design/Engineering:							
Other:											

TYPES OF BUSINESS:

Real Estate Investment Trust
Real Estate Development
Property Management & Leasing
Office, Retail & Industrial Properties
Apartments
Construction Services
Asset Management
Corporate Hosting

BRANDS/DIVISIONS/AFFILIATES:

Highwoods Realty Limited Partnership
ServiceLink

CONTACTS:

Note: Officers with more than one job title may be intentionally listed here more than once.

Edward J. Fritsch, CEO
Michael E. Harris, COO/Exec. VP
Edward J. Fritsch, Pres.
Terry L. Stevens, CFO/Sr. VP
Peter T. Jardine, VP-Mktg.
Art H. McCann, CIO
Jeffrey D. Miller, General Counsel/Corp. Sec./VP
Kevin E. Penn, VP-Strategy
Tabitha N. Zane, VP-Corp. Comm.
Tabitha N. Zane, VP-Investor Rel.
Daniel L. Clemmens, Chief Acct. Officer/VP
S. Hugh Esleek, Treas.
Carman J. Liuzzo, VP-Investments
Michael D. Starchville, VP-Asset Mgmt.
O. Temple Sloan, Jr., Chmn.

Phone: 919-872-4924	**Fax:** 919-876-2448
Toll-Free: 866-449-6637	
Address: 3100 Smoketree Ct., Ste. 600, Raleigh, NC 27604 US	

GROWTH PLANS/SPECIAL FEATURES:

Highwoods Properties, Inc. is a self-administered real estate investment trust engaged in the acquisition, development and operation of rental real estate properties, including office, industrial, retail and residential properties. Highwoods conducts nearly all of its activities through the Highwoods Realty Limited Partnership, in which it is the sole general partner. The firm's property holdings consist of 378 wholly-owned, in-service office, industrial and retail properties; an interest in approximately 70 in-service office and industrial properties and 418 rental residential units; 581 acres of wholly-owned undeveloped land; and 44 for-sale residential condominiums. The company's properties and development land are located in Florida, Georgia, Iowa, Mississippi, Missouri, North Carolina, South Carolina, Tennessee and Virginia. Highwoods also provides services including asset management, tenant services and corporate hosting. Highwoods' tenant services include ServiceLink, its customer service system enabling telephone or online system access, wireless service technician notification and online real-time service request tracking. In May 2009, the firm sold its non-core assets in Kansas City for $62.1 million. In November 2009, the company acquired a 220,000 square foot, 10 story office building in Tampa, Florida. Also in November 2009, the company sold 39,700 square feet of retail space in Winston-Salem, North Carolina, as well as 1.9 acres of land.

Employees are offered medical, dental and vision insurance; life insurance; flexible reimbursement accounts; disability coverage; a 401(k) savings plan; an employee stock purchase plan; educational assistance; credit union membership; an interest free computer purchase program; and discounted auto and homeowner's insurance.

FINANCIALS:

Sales and profits are in thousands of dollars—add 000 to get the full amount. 2009 Note: Financial information for 2009 was not available for all companies at press time.

2009 Sales: $454,026	2009 Profits: $61,694	**U.S. Stock Ticker: HIW**
2008 Sales: $450,291	2008 Profits: $35,610	**Int'l Ticker:** Int'l Exchange:
2007 Sales: $418,409	2007 Profits: $97,095	Employees: 407
2006 Sales: $401,304	2006 Profits: $53,744	Fiscal Year Ends: 12/31
2005 Sales: $387,929	2005 Profits: $62,458	Parent Company:

SALARIES/BENEFITS:

Pension Plan:	ESOP Stock Plan:	Profit Sharing:	Top Exec. Salary: $540,750	Bonus: $1,054,461
Savings Plan: Y	Stock Purch. Plan: Y		Second Exec. Salary: $360,500	Bonus: $513,712

OTHER THOUGHTS:

Apparent Women Officers or Directors: 3
Hot Spot for Advancement for Women/Minorities: Y

LOCATIONS: ("Y" = Yes)

West:	Southwest:	Midwest:	Southeast:	Northeast:	International:
		Y	Y	Y	

HILTON HOTELS CORP

www.hiltonworldwide.com

Industry Group Code: 721110 **Ranks within this company's industry group:** Sales: 3 Profits:

Properties:		Financial Services:		Construction/Development:		Investments:		Specialty Services:		Brokerage:	
Apartments:		Mortgages:		Commercial Construction:		REIT:		Property Management:	Y	Commercial Sales:	
Malls/Shopping:		Title Insurance:		Residential Construction:				Online Services:	Y	Residential Sales:	
Offices:		Property Insurance:		Land Development:				Software/IT:		Specialty:	
Hotels/Motels:	Y			Support Services:				Consulting:			
Industrial/Warehouses:				Design/Engineering:							
Other:	Y										

TYPES OF BUSINESS:

Hotels & Resorts
Timeshare Properties
Conference Centers
Franchising
Management Services
Online Reservations

BRANDS/DIVISIONS/AFFILIATES:

Blackstone Group LP
Hilton Group plc
Hampton Inn
Conrad Hotels and Resorts
Waldorf Astoria Collection
Embassy Suites
Hilton Garden Vacations Company LLC
Hhonors

CONTACTS:

Note: Officers with more than one job title may be intentionally listed here more than once.

Christopher Nassetta, CEO
Christopher J. Nassetta, Pres.
Tom Kennedy, CFO/Exec. VP
Matthew W. Schuyler, Chief Human Resources Officer/Exec. VP
Rich Lucas, General Counsel/Exec. VP
Ian R. Carter, Pres., Global Oper.
Kevin Jacobs, Sr. VP-Corp. Strategy
Ellen Gonda, Sr. VP-Global Corp. Comm.
Kevin Jacobs, Treas.
Paul Brown, Pres., Global Brands & Commercial Svcs.
Mark Wang, Pres., Hilton Grand Vacations Co., LLC
Matt Richardson, Head-Architecture/Design/Construction/Real Estate

Phone: 703-883-1000	**Fax:**
Toll-Free: 800-445-8667	
Address: 7930 Jones Branch Dr. Ste. 1100, McLean, VA 22102 US	

GROWTH PLANS/SPECIAL FEATURES:

Hilton Hotels Corp. (HHC), founded in 1919, owns, manages and develops hotels, resorts and timeshare properties; and franchises lodging properties. HHC consists of 10 hotel brands and more than 3,500 hotels in 81 countries around the world. Its hotel brands include Hilton, Hilton Garden Inn, Doubletree, Embassy Suites, Homewood Suites, Home2 Suites, Hampton Inn, Conrad Hotels and Resorts and The Waldorf Astoria Collection. HHC owns the worldwide rights to develop and market Hilton and Conrad brands. Although the majority of the company's hotels are located within the U.S., the company also operates luxury lodgings in locations such as Thailand, Ireland, Singapore, Uruguay, Indonesia and Egypt. Hilton Worldwide Resorts offers 54 self-contained resorts in the Middle East, Asia Pacific, Europe, the Americas, the Indian Ocean and the Caribbean. Through Hilton Garden Vacations Company, LLC, the firm also owns and manages approximately 48 vacation timeshare properties with three more under development. HHonors, the firm's loyalty enrollment program for returning customers, has over 25 million members and includes partner benefits with JetBlue Airlines. The firm is investing in technologies such as check-in kiosks to facilitate an easier and faster check-in process for its customers in partnership with IBM. HHC, in separate deals with three real estate groups, is developing over 55 properties in Russia, the U.K. and Central America, all planned to be completed by 2012. Over the next decade, the firm plans to open 300 new hotels in Asia, including properties in India and China. In February 2010, Hilton concluded an agreement for the management of a Hilton hotel in Riyadh, Saudi Arabia scheduled to open in 2013. In March 2010, Hilton signed a management agreement for a new Hilton branded hotel scheduled to open in Egypt, along the Nile River in July 2010.

FINANCIALS:

Sales and profits are in thousands of dollars—add 000 to get the full amount. 2009 Note: Financial information for 2009 was not available for all companies at press time.

2009 Sales: $	2009 Profits: $	**U.S. Stock Ticker: Private**
2008 Sales: $7,770,000	2008 Profits: $	**Int'l Ticker:** Int'l Exchange:
2007 Sales: $8,090,000	2007 Profits: $121,000	Employees: 130,000
2006 Sales: $7,438,000	2006 Profits: $572,000	Fiscal Year Ends: 12/31
2005 Sales: $3,218,000	2005 Profits: $460,000	Parent Company: BLACKSTONE GROUP LP (THE)

SALARIES/BENEFITS:

Pension Plan:	ESOP Stock Plan:	Profit Sharing:	Top Exec. Salary: $	Bonus: $
Savings Plan: Y	Stock Purch. Plan:		Second Exec. Salary: $	Bonus: $

OTHER THOUGHTS:

Apparent Women Officers or Directors: 1
Hot Spot for Advancement for Women/Minorities: Y

LOCATIONS: ("Y" = Yes)

West:	Southwest:	Midwest:	Southeast:	Northeast:	International:
Y	Y	Y	Y	Y	Y

HINES INTERESTS LP

www.hines.com

Industry Group Code: 5311 **Ranks within this company's industry group:** Sales: Profits:

Properties:		Financial Services:		Construction/Development:		Investments:		Specialty Services:		Brokerage:	
Apartments:	Y	Mortgages:		Commercial Construction:	Y	REIT:		Property Management:	Y	Commercial Sales:	
Malls/Shopping:		Title Insurance:		Residential Construction:				Online Services:		Residential Sales:	
Offices:	Y	Property Insurance:		Land Development:	Y			Software/IT:		Specialty:	
Hotels/Motels:	Y			Support Services:	Y			Consulting:			
Industrial/Warehouses:	Y			Design/Engineering:	Y						
Other:	Y										

TYPES OF BUSINESS:

Real Estate Development
Property Management
Property Development
Engineering Services
Office Buildings
Industrial Properties
Hotels
Residential Properties

BRANDS/DIVISIONS/AFFILIATES:

Two MacArthus Ridge

CONTACTS:

Note: Officers with more than one job title may be intentionally listed here more than once.

Charles N. Hazen, CEO
Jeffrey C. Hines, Pres.
C. Hastings Johnson, CFO/Exec. VP
Stephanie Fore, Sr. VP-Human Resources
Jesse Carrillo, CIO
Clayton Ulrich, Sr. VP-Eng. Svcs.
David LeVrier, Chief Admin. Officer/Sr. VP
Ilene Allen, VP-Corp. Oper. Svcs.
George C. Lancaster, Sr. VP-Corp. Comm.
Kay P. Forbes, Sr. VP-Corp. Finance
Charles M. Baughn, Exec. VP/CEO-Capital Markets
Jerrold P. Lea, Sr. VP-Conceptual Construction
Tom Owens, Chief Risk Officer/Exec. VP
James C. Buie, Jr., Exec. VP/CEO-West Region
Gerald D. Hines, Chmn.

Phone: 713-621-8000 **Fax:** 713-966-2636
Toll-Free:
Address: 2800 Post Oak Blvd., Williams Tower, Houston, TX 77056-6118 US

GROWTH PLANS/SPECIAL FEATURES:

Hines Interests, LP is a private commercial real estate development firm handling many aspects of development, including site selection, acquisition, zoning, design, construction management, financing and property management. The company has offices in 68 U.S. cities and 17 other countries in Europe, South America and North America and controls assets valued at approximately $22.9 billion. Hines' portfolio of projects completed, underway, acquired and managed for third parties includes more than 1,100 properties representing more than 249 million square feet of office, mixed-use, industrial, hotel, medical, sports facilities and residential properties, as well as large, master-planned communities and land developments. The firm specializes in integrated design projects, working with potential tenants and other clients in order to develop the most valuable and most beautiful buildings and rentable spaces possible. Hines' services include investment management; development; asset and property management; acquisition and disposition; and marketing and leasing. Throughout its history, the company has worked on such notable properties as Penzoil Place in Houston, Texas; the J.P. Morgan Chase Tower, in Houston; the EDF Tower in Paris, France; the Comerica Tower at Detroit Center; and the Torre Del Angel and Del Bosque in Mexico. Hines has worked in partnership with many of the most notable architects in the world, including Frank Gehry, I.M. Pei and Philip Johnson. Recently, Hines acquired properties in Dallas and Houston, Texas; Phoenix, Arizona; Minneapolis, Minnesota; Kansas City, Missouri; Chicago, Illinois; Los Angeles, California; Frankfurt, Germany; and Denver, Colorado. In April 2010, the firm began construction on the Arboretum, a 12-story 315-unit residential building located in Lodz, Poland.

Hines offers its employees a 401(k) plan with matching funds; adoption benefits; benefits advocacy services; credit union membership; dependent and health care reimbursement accounts; an educational reimbursement program; an employee assistance program; employee referral bonuses; and wellness benefits.

FINANCIALS:

Sales and profits are in thousands of dollars—add 000 to get the full amount. 2009 Note: Financial information for 2009 was not available for all companies at press time.

2009 Sales: $	2009 Profits: $	**U.S. Stock Ticker: Private**
2008 Sales: $	2008 Profits: $	**Int'l Ticker:** Int'l Exchange:
2007 Sales: $	2007 Profits: $	Employees:
2006 Sales: $	2006 Profits: $	Fiscal Year Ends: 12/31
2005 Sales: $	2005 Profits: $	Parent Company:

SALARIES/BENEFITS:

Pension Plan:	ESOP Stock Plan:	Profit Sharing:	Top Exec. Salary: $	Bonus: $
Savings Plan: Y	Stock Purch. Plan:		Second Exec. Salary: $	Bonus: $

OTHER THOUGHTS:

Apparent Women Officers or Directors: 3
Hot Spot for Advancement for Women/Minorities: Y

LOCATIONS: ("Y" = Yes)

West:	Southwest:	Midwest:	Southeast:	Northeast:	International:
Y	Y	Y	Y	Y	Y

HOCHTIEF AG

www.hochtief.de

Industry Group Code: 237 **Ranks within this company's industry group:** Sales: 4 Profits: 10

Properties:		Financial Services:		Construction/Development:		Investments:		Specialty Services:		Brokerage:	
Apartments:		Mortgages:		Commercial Construction:	Y	REIT:		Property Management:		Commercial Sales:	
Malls/Shopping:		Title Insurance:		Residential Construction:				Online Services:		Residential Sales:	
Offices:		Property Insurance:		Land Development:				Software/IT:		Specialty:	
Hotels/Motels:				Support Services:				Consulting:			
Industrial/Warehouses:				Design/Engineering:							
Other:											

TYPES OF BUSINESS:

Heavy Construction
Airport Management & Consulting Services
Infrastructure Development
Geothermal Plant Construction
Green Building Engineering Services

BRANDS/DIVISIONS/AFFILIATES:

Turner Construction Company
HOCHTIEF do Brasil
HOCHTIEF Construction A.G.
HOCHTIEF Facility Management GmbH
HOCHTIEF Property Management
HOCHTIEF Projektentwicklung
HOCHTIEF PPP Solutions
HOCHTIEF AirPort

CONTACTS: *Note: Officers with more than one job title may be intentionally listed here more than once.*

Herbert Lutkestratkotter, CEO
Burkhard Lohr, CFO
Albrecht Ehlers, Dir.-Svcs. & Labor Rel.
Herbert Lutkestratkotter, Dir.-Corp. Dev.
Herbert Lutkestratkotter, Dir.-Corp. Comm.
Burkhard Lohr, Dir.-Controlling, Auditing & Tax
Martin Rohr, Dir.-Real Estate
Martin Kohlhaussen, Chmn.
Peter Noe, Dir.-Asia Pacific
Martin Rohr, Dir.-Global Procurement

Phone: 49-201-824-0	**Fax:** 49-201-824-2777
Toll-Free:	
Address: Opernplatz 2, Essen, 45128 Germany	

GROWTH PLANS/SPECIAL FEATURES:

HOCHTIEF AG is a construction services provider that designs, builds, finances and operates facilities worldwide. The company operates through six divisions: HOCHTIEF Americas; HOCHTIEF Europe; HOCHTIEF Asia Pacific; HOCHTIEF Concessions; HOCHTIEF Real Estate; and HOCHTIEF Services. The Americas division includes the activities of subsidiaries in the U.S. and Brazil, including Turner Construction Company, a leading U.S. general construction contractor and green building engineering firm, and HOCHTIEF do Brasil, providing construction and facilities management services. The Europe division's leading company, HOCHTIEF Construction A.G., provides civil and structural engineering, as well as building construction services. The core of the Asia-Pacific division is Leighton Holdings, Ltd., which operates the Australian subsidiaries Leighton Contractors Pty., Leighton Properties Pty., John Holland Group Pty., Thiess Pty.; and Leighton Asia (Northern), Ltd. and Leighton Asia (Southern), Ltd., in Hong Kong. The concessions division covers business areas such as airports, roads, municipal infrastructure and public-private partnership (PPP) projects, including the operations of subsidiaries HOCHTIEF AirPort and HOCHTIEF PPP Solutions. The company's concessions portfolio contains approximately six airports, seven roads, 89 schools, several municipal buildings; a military base and two geothermal energy projects. The real estate division develops, markets and manages a range of property types through such subsidiaries as HOCHTIEF Projektentwicklung, an inner-city property developer; HOCHTIEF Property Management, which manages real estate for various investors; and joint venture subsidiary Aurelis Real Estate GmbH & Co. KG, which redevelops urban retail sites in Germany. The services division includes subsidiaries HOCHTIEF Facility Management GmbH and HOCHTIEF Energy Management, which works with clients to improve the energy efficiency of both public and private buildings. In addition to these primary divisions, subsidiary HOCHTIEF Insurance Broking & Risk Management Solutions handles insurance services for the company's units, while HOCHTIEF ViCon offers virtual design and construction services to HOCHTIEF units and outside clients.

FINANCIALS: **Sales and profits are in thousands of dollars—add 000 to get the full amount. 2009 Note: Financial information for 2009 was not available for all companies at press time.**

2009 Sales: $24,519,300	2009 Profits: $263,470	**U.S. Stock Ticker: HOCFF.PK**
2008 Sales: $25,783,870	2008 Profits: $419,100	**Int'l Ticker: HOT** Int'l Exchange: Frankfurt-Euronext
2007 Sales: $22,205,420	2007 Profits: $165,870	Employees:
2006 Sales: $21,065,480	2006 Profits: $273,520	Fiscal Year Ends: 12/31
2005 Sales: $18,545,954	2005 Profits: $212,208	Parent Company:

SALARIES/BENEFITS:

Pension Plan:	ESOP Stock Plan:	Profit Sharing:	Top Exec. Salary: $	Bonus: $
Savings Plan:	Stock Purch. Plan:		Second Exec. Salary: $	Bonus: $

OTHER THOUGHTS:

Apparent Women Officers or Directors:
Hot Spot for Advancement for Women/Minorities:

LOCATIONS: ("Y" = Yes)

West:	Southwest:	Midwest:	Southeast:	Northeast:	International:
Y	Y	Y	Y	Y	Y

HOME DEPOT INC

www.homedepot.com

Industry Group Code: 444110 **Ranks within this company's industry group:** Sales: 1 Profits: 1

Properties:		Financial Services:		Construction/Development:		Investments:		Specialty Services:		Brokerage:	
Apartments:		Mortgages:		Commercial Construction:		REIT:		Property Management:		Commercial Sales:	
Malls/Shopping:	Y	Title Insurance:		Residential Construction:				Online Services:	Y	Residential Sales:	
Offices:		Property Insurance:		Land Development:				Software/IT:		Specialty:	
Hotels/Motels:				Support Services:	Y			Consulting:			
Industrial/Warehouses:				Design/Engineering:							
Other:											

TYPES OF BUSINESS:

Home Centers, Retail
Home Improvement Products
Building Materials
Lawn & Garden Products
Online & Catalog Sales
Tool & Truck Rental
Installation & Design Services

BRANDS/DIVISIONS/AFFILIATES:

THD Design Center
EXPO Design Centers
Yardbirds

CONTACTS: *Note: Officers with more than one job title may be intentionally listed here more than once.*

Francis S. Blake, CEO
Carol B. Tome, CFO
Frank Bifulco, Sr. VP/Chief Mktg. Officer
Timothy M. Crow, Exec. VP-Human Resources
Cara Kinzey, Sr. VP-IT
Craig A. Menear, Exec. VP-Merch.
Jack A. VanWoerkom, General Counsel/Exec. VP/Corp. Sec.
Mark Powers, Sr. VP-Oper.
Carol B. Tome, Exec. VP-Corp. Svcs.
Brad Shaw, Sr. VP-Corp Comm. & External Affairs
Dianne Dayhoff, Sr. VP-Investor Rel.
Ted Decker, Sr. VP-Retail Finance
Kelly Barrett, Sr. VP-Enterprise Program Mgmt.
Ricardo E. Saldivar, Pres., The Home Depot Mexico
Anne-Marie Campbell, Pres., Southern Div.
Marvin R. Ellison, Exec. VP-U.S. Stores
Francis S. Blake, Chmn.
Annette M. Verschuren, Pres., The Home Depot Canada & Asia
Mark Holifield, Sr. VP-Supply Chain

Phone: 770-433-8211 **Fax:** 770-384-2356
Toll-Free: 800-553-3199
Address: 2455 Paces Ferry Rd., Atlanta, GA 30339 US

GROWTH PLANS/SPECIAL FEATURES:

Home Depot, Inc. is one of the world's largest home improvement retailers. The company operates 2,233 Home Depot stores throughout the U.S., Canada, China, Puerto Rico, the Virgin Islands and Mexico. A typical store encompasses 105,000 square feet of enclosed space with a 24,000 square foot outdoor garden center; these locations usually stock between 35,000 and 45,000 items. These stores sell an assortment of building materials, plumbing materials, electrical materials, kitchen products, hardware, seasonal items, paint, flooring and wall coverings. Home Depot markets its products primarily to three types of customers: professional customers, such as remodelers, contractors, repairmen and small business owners; do-it-for-me shoppers, who are homeowners that personally purchase Home Depot products but hire third party individuals for installation and/or project completion; and do-it-yourself customers, who are homeowners that both shop for and personally install and/or utilize the firm's materials. In early 2009, the firm announced plans to close its five Yardbirds stores, two THD Design Center stores and 34 full-service interior design and home furnishing EXPO Design Centers. The nationwide real estate slowdown of 2007-2009 hurt Home Depot's business. In mid 2008, the firm canceled plans for about 50 new store openings, and announced that it was closing 15 underperforming stores. In 2009, sales per square foot of store space were averaging $300. Home Depot is focusing on improvements to existing stores rather than expansion.

The company offers its employees medical, dental, vision, life, AD&D and disability insurance; a 401(k) plan; a stock purchase plan; adoption, education and relocation assistance; flexible spending accounts; a legal services plan; auto and homeowners insurance; and veterinary coverage.

FINANCIALS: **Sales and profits are in thousands of dollars—add 000 to get the full amount. 2009 Note: Financial information for 2009 was not available for all companies at press time.**

2009 Sales: $71,288,000 — 2009 Profits: $2,260,000
2008 Sales: $77,349,000 — 2008 Profits: $4,395,000
2007 Sales: $79,022,000 — 2007 Profits: $5,761,000
2006 Sales: $77,019,000 — 2006 Profits: $5,838,000
2005 Sales: $73,094,000 — 2005 Profits: $5,001,000

U.S. Stock Ticker: HD
Int'l Ticker: Int'l Exchange:
Employees: 322,000
Fiscal Year Ends: 1/31
Parent Company:

SALARIES/BENEFITS:

Pension Plan:	ESOP Stock Plan:	Profit Sharing:	Top Exec. Salary: $1,013,461	Bonus: $
Savings Plan: Y	Stock Purch. Plan: Y		Second Exec. Salary: $901,923	Bonus: $666,346

OTHER THOUGHTS:

Apparent Women Officers or Directors: 6
Hot Spot for Advancement for Women/Minorities: Y

LOCATIONS: ("Y" = Yes)

West:	Southwest:	Midwest:	Southeast:	Northeast:	International:
Y	Y	Y	Y	Y	Y

Note: Financial information, benefits and other data can change quickly and may vary from those stated here.

HOME INNS & HOTELS MANAGEMENT INC

www.homeinns.com

Industry Group Code: 721110 **Ranks within this company's industry group:** Sales: 25 Profits: 16

Properties:		Financial Services:		Construction/Development:		Investments:		Specialty Services:		Brokerage:	
Apartments:		Mortgages:		Commercial Construction:		REIT:		Property Management:		Commercial Sales:	
Malls/Shopping:		Title Insurance:		Residential Construction:				Online Services:		Residential Sales:	
Offices:		Property Insurance:		Land Development:				Software/IT:		Specialty:	
Hotels/Motels:	Y			Support Services:				Consulting:			
Industrial/Warehouses:				Design/Engineering:							
Other:											

TYPES OF BUSINESS:

Economy Hotels

BRANDS/DIVISIONS/AFFILIATES:

Ctrip.com International, Ltd.

CONTACTS:

Note: Officers with more than one job title may be intentionally listed here more than once.

David Sun, CEO
Jason Zong, COO
May Wu, CFO
May Wu, Chief Strategy Officer
Ethan Ruan, Mgr.-Investor Rel.
Nanpeng Shen, Co-Chmn.
Yunxin Mei, Co-Chmn.

Phone: 86-21-3401-9898	**Fax:** 86-21-6483-5660
Toll-Free:	
Address: Number 124, Caobao Rd., Shanghai, 200235 China	

GROWTH PLANS/SPECIAL FEATURES:

Home Inns & Hotels Management, Inc. (Home Inns) is an economy hotel chain in China. The company develops and operates economy hotels across China under its Home Inns brand. Home Inns leases real estate properties on which it develops; operates hotels; franchises its brand to hotel owners; and manages these hotel properties. For the leased and operated hotels, the company is responsible for hotel development and customization to conform to the standards of Home Inns, as well as repairs, maintenance and operating expenses. For the franchised and managed hotels, Home Inns is responsible for managing the hotel, while the franchisee is responsible for cost of development and customization. The company's hotel chain consists of 390 leased-and-operated hotels in operation, with an additional 6 leased-and-operated hotels under development; and 226 franchised-and-managed hotels in operation and an additional 63 franchised-and-managed hotels under development. The firm's properties cover 108 cities in China. Beijing and Shanghai are the cities with the most hotels, with 70 and 62 Home Inns hotels in operation, respectively. A typical Home Inns hotel has 80-160 guest rooms. Each hotel has a standardized design, appearance, decor, color scheme, lighting scheme and set of guest amenities in each room, including free in-room broadband Internet access, a work space, air conditioning and a supply of cold and hot drinking water. Home Inns hotels are strategically located to provide guests with convenient access to major business districts, ground transportation hubs, major highways, shopping centers, industrial development zones, colleges and universities, and large residential neighborhoods. In May 2009, Home Inns announced the sale of $50 million in equity to Ctrip.com International, Ltd., increasing Ctrip's ownership in the company to approximately 18%.

FINANCIALS:

Sales and profits are in thousands of dollars—add 000 to get the full amount. 2009 Note: Financial information for 2009 was not available for all companies at press time.

2009 Sales: $	2009 Profits: $	**U.S. Stock Ticker: HMIN**
2008 Sales: $257,922	2008 Profits: $14,838	**Int'l Ticker:** Int'l Exchange:
2007 Sales: $130,098	2007 Profits: $4,902	Employees: 12,686
2006 Sales: $71,055	2006 Profits: $6,009	Fiscal Year Ends: 12/31
2005 Sales: $	2005 Profits: $	Parent Company:

SALARIES/BENEFITS:

Pension Plan:	ESOP Stock Plan: Y	Profit Sharing:	Top Exec. Salary: $	Bonus: $
Savings Plan:	Stock Purch. Plan:		Second Exec. Salary: $	Bonus: $

OTHER THOUGHTS:

Apparent Women Officers or Directors: 1
Hot Spot for Advancement for Women/Minorities: Y

LOCATIONS: ("Y" = Yes)

West:	Southwest:	Midwest:	Southeast:	Northeast:	International:
					Y

HOME PROPERTIES INC

www.homeproperties.com

Industry Group Code: 531110 **Ranks within this company's industry group:** Sales: 6 Profits: 6

Properties:		Financial Services:		Construction/Development:		Investments:		Specialty Services:		Brokerage:	
Apartments:	Y	Mortgages:		Commercial Construction:		REIT:	Y	Property Management:	Y	Commercial Sales:	
Malls/Shopping:		Title Insurance:		Residential Construction:				Online Services:		Residential Sales:	
Offices:		Property Insurance:		Land Development:				Software/IT:		Specialty:	
Hotels/Motels:				Support Services:				Consulting:			
Industrial/Warehouses:				Design/Engineering:							
Other:											

TYPES OF BUSINESS:

Real Estate Investment Trust
Apartment Communities
Property Management

BRANDS/DIVISIONS/AFFILIATES:

Home Properties LP
Home Properties Resident Services Inc

CONTACTS:

Note: Officers with more than one job title may be intentionally listed here more than once.

Edward J. Pettinella, CEO
Edward J. Pettinella, Pres.
David P. Gardner, CFO/Exec. VP
Lisa M. Critchley, Sr. VP-Human Resources
Ann M. McCormick, General Counsel/Exec. VP/Corp. Sec.
Bernard J. Quinn, Sr. VP-Property Mgmt. Oper.
Donald R. Hague, Sr. VP-Dev.
Robert J. Luken, Chief Acct. Officer/Treas./Sr. VP
Scott A. Doyle, Sr. VP-Strategic Property Mgmt.
John E. Smith, Sr. VP/Chief Investment Officer
Norman P. Leenhouts, Co-Chmn.
Nelson B. Leenhouts, Co-Chmn.

Phone: 585-546-4900 **Fax:** 585-546-5433
Toll-Free: 866-243-6256
Address: 850 Clinton Sq., Rochester, NY 14604 US

GROWTH PLANS/SPECIAL FEATURES:

Home Properties, Inc. specializes in the acquisition, development, rehabilitation, ownership and operation of apartment complexes. The company is a self-administered and self-managed real estate investment trust (REIT). Home Properties operates in Washington, D.C., and the following states: Florida; Illinois; Maine; Massachusetts; Virginia; Pennsylvania; Maryland; New Jersey; and New York. The firm conducts its business through Home Properties, L.P., in which it owns about 74.7% interest; and its management subsidiary Home Properties Resident Services, Inc. Home Properties operates 107 complexes totaling approximately 36,947 apartment units. The company typically manages and owns apartment communities with 150 or more units, which are 20-40 years old and located in suburban markets with substantial barriers to new development. Other characteristics the firm uses to evaluate markets include acquisition opportunities below replacement costs, a mature housing stock, high average single-family home prices and stable or moderate job growth. The suburban areas the trust has targeted for growth are the suburbs of New York City, Baltimore, Boston, Philadelphia, and Washington, D.C. Home Properties' business strategy involves aggressively managing and improving communities to achieve increased net operating income, as well as maintaining a conservative capital structure with efficient access to the capital markets. In April 2010, the firm acquired Westminster Apartments and Middlebrooke Apartments, which consist of a combined 318 units.

The company offers its employees life, medical and dental insurance; a 401(k) plan; paid time off; an employee stock purchase program; apartment rental discounts; and flexible spending accounts.

FINANCIALS:

Sales and profits are in thousands of dollars—add 000 to get the full amount. 2009 Note: Financial information for 2009 was not available for all companies at press time.

2009 Sales: $503,609	2009 Profits: $47,078	**U.S. Stock Ticker: HME**
2008 Sales: $494,043	2008 Profits: $93,205	**Int'l Ticker:** Int'l Exchange:
2007 Sales: $472,973	2007 Profits: $82,509	Employees: 1,100
2006 Sales: $424,061	2006 Profits: $110,485	Fiscal Year Ends: 12/31
2005 Sales: $387,362	2005 Profits: $81,512	Parent Company:

SALARIES/BENEFITS:

Pension Plan:	ESOP Stock Plan:	Profit Sharing:	Top Exec. Salary: $550,000	Bonus: $346,071
Savings Plan: Y	Stock Purch. Plan: Y		Second Exec. Salary: $334,970	Bonus: $145,913

OTHER THOUGHTS:

Apparent Women Officers or Directors: 3
Hot Spot for Advancement for Women/Minorities: Y

LOCATIONS: ("Y" = Yes)

West:	Southwest:	Midwest:	Southeast:	Northeast:	International:
		Y	Y	Y	

HOMESERVICES OF AMERICA INC

www.homeservices.com

Industry Group Code: 531210 **Ranks within this company's industry group:** Sales: Profits:

Properties:		Financial Services:		Construction/Development:		Investments:		Specialty Services:		Brokerage:	
Apartments:		Mortgages:		Commercial Construction:		REIT:		Property Management:		Commercial Sales:	Y
Malls/Shopping:		Title Insurance:		Residential Construction:				Online Services:		Residential Sales:	Y
Offices:		Property Insurance:		Land Development:				Software/IT:		Specialty:	
Hotels/Motels:				Support Services:				Consulting:			
Industrial/Warehouses:				Design/Engineering:							
Other:											

TYPES OF BUSINESS:

Real Estate Brokerage
Settlement Services
Title Services
Mortgage Services

BRANDS/DIVISIONS/AFFILIATES:

Woods Bros. Realty
Rector-Hayden Realtors
HomeServices of Kentucky, Inc.
Prudential Carolinas Realty
Long Realty Companies
CBSHOME Real Estate
HomeServices of Nebraska
Huff Realty

CONTACTS: *Note: Officers with more than one job title may be intentionally listed here more than once.*

Ronald J. Peltier, CEO
Robert R. Moline, COO
Robert R. Moline, Pres.
Cynthia L. Sattler, CFO/Sr. VP
Clifford Faddis Jr., Sr. VP-Human Resources
Patty Czepowski, VP-IT
Cynthia L. Sattler, Chief Admin. Officer
Mike Warmka, Chief Acct. Officer/Sr. VP
Mary Lee Blaylock, Pres., HomeServices of America Relocation LLC
Melissa J. Buscho, Pres., HomeServices Insurance, Inc.
Jerry D. Reece, CEO-Reece & Nichols
Greg Mason, Managing Dir.-Title Services
Ronald J. Peltier, Chmn.

Phone:	**Fax:** 612-336-5590
Toll-Free: 888-485-0018	
Address: 333 S. 7th St., 27th Fl., Minneapolis, MN 55402 US	

GROWTH PLANS/SPECIAL FEATURES:

HomeServices of America, Inc., a subsidiary of MidAmerican Energy Holdings Co. (which is owned by Berkshire Hathaway, Inc.), is a real estate brokerage firm and provider of brokerage-owned settlement services. The firm is comprised of 20 real-estate brands and operates through several offices and more than 17,000 sales associates in 19 states. Though HomeServices maintains operations all over the U.S., 10 of its 20 brands are located in the Midwest. Midwest brands include Edina Realty Home Services; CBSHOME Real Estate; Home Real Estate; Prudential First Realty; Rector-Hayden Realtors; Woods Bros. Realty; Iowa Realty; Semonin Realtors; Champion Realty; and Huff Realty. Brands in the Northeast and Southeast include Prudential Carolinas Realty; Harry Norman Realtors; Prudential York Simpson Underwood Realty; Esslinger-Wooten-Maxwell Realtors; and RealtySouth. In the Western portion of the U.S., brands include Prudential California Realty and Long Realty Company. Of the aforementioned brands, Edina Realty Home Services in one of the largest. Started by a housewife in Edina, Minnesota in 1955, the firm is now one of the nation's largest real estate companies, currently overseeing the following companies: Edina Realty; Edina Realty Title; Edina Realty Mortgage; and Edina Realty Relocation. In September 2009, the company acquired Koenig & Strey GMAC Real Estate, a residential real estate brokerage firm, from Brookfield Residential Property Services. In April 2010, the firm acquired Schiller Real Estate, an Illinois-based residential real estate firm.

FINANCIALS: **Sales and profits are in thousands of dollars—add 000 to get the full amount. 2009 Note: Financial information for 2009 was not available for all companies at press time.**

2009 Sales: $
2008 Sales: $
2007 Sales: $
2006 Sales: $
2005 Sales: $

2009 Profits: $
2008 Profits: $
2007 Profits: $
2006 Profits: $
2005 Profits: $

U.S. Stock Ticker: Subsidiary
Int'l Ticker: Int'l Exchange:
Employees:
Fiscal Year Ends: 12/31
Parent Company: MIDAMERICAN ENERGY HOLDINGS CO

SALARIES/BENEFITS:

Pension Plan:	ESOP Stock Plan:	Profit Sharing:	Top Exec. Salary: $	Bonus: $
Savings Plan:	Stock Purch. Plan:		Second Exec. Salary: $	Bonus: $

OTHER THOUGHTS:

Apparent Women Officers or Directors: 4
Hot Spot for Advancement for Women/Minorities: Y

LOCATIONS: ("Y" = Yes)

West:	Southwest:	Midwest:	Southeast:	Northeast:	International:
Y	Y	Y	Y	Y	

HOMETOWN AMERICA LLC

www.hometownamerica.com

Industry Group Code: 531110 **Ranks within this company's industry group:** Sales: Profits:

Properties:		Financial Services:		Construction/Development:		Investments:		Specialty Services:		Brokerage:	
Apartments:		Mortgages:		Commercial Construction:		REIT:		Property Management:	Y	Commercial Sales:	
Malls/Shopping:		Title Insurance:		Residential Construction:				Online Services:		Residential Sales:	Y
Offices:		Property Insurance:		Land Development:				Software/IT:		Specialty:	
Hotels/Motels:				Support Services:				Consulting:			
Industrial/Warehouses:				Design/Engineering:							
Other:	Y										

TYPES OF BUSINESS:

Manufactured Home Communities
RV Parks
Property Management
Brokerage Services

BRANDS/DIVISIONS/AFFILIATES:

Hometown America Family Communities
Hometown America
Providence Age-qualified Communities
Providence
Hometown America Foundation

CONTACTS:

Note: Officers with more than one job title may be intentionally listed here more than once.

Gregory O'Berry, Pres.

Phone: 312-604-7500	**Fax:** 312-604-7501
Toll-Free: 888.735.4310	
Address: 150 N. Wacker Dr., Ste. 2800, Chicago, IL 60606-1610 US	

GROWTH PLANS/SPECIAL FEATURES:

Hometown America, LLC develops, acquires and manages manufactured housing communities and age-qualified communities. Hometown currently owns roughly 130 communities with over 48,000 home sites in 20 states. The company operates through two divisions: The Hometown America Family Communities division and the Providence Age-qualified Communities division. The Providence communities are targeted toward active seniors. All of the firm's communities are provided with on-site management and new home and resale brokerage services. The Hometown America Foundation provides funding to nonprofit organizations that addresses the needs of the homelessness. Many of Hometown's communities feature recreational facilities such as swimming pools, clubhouses, golf courses and basketball courts. Nearly half of Hometown's properties are located in Florida and Michigan.

Employees of the company are offered an employee assistance program; comprehensive medical, dental, vision, life and short and long-term disability insurance; bonus opportunities; paid vacation; sick and holiday pay; and dependent care flexible spending accounts.

FINANCIALS:

Sales and profits are in thousands of dollars—add 000 to get the full amount. 2009 Note: Financial information for 2009 was not available for all companies at press time.

2009 Sales: $	2009 Profits: $	**U.S. Stock Ticker: Private**
2008 Sales: $	2008 Profits: $	**Int'l Ticker:** Int'l Exchange:
2007 Sales: $	2007 Profits: $	Employees:
2006 Sales: $	2006 Profits: $	Fiscal Year Ends: 12/31
2005 Sales: $	2005 Profits: $	Parent Company:

SALARIES/BENEFITS:

Pension Plan:	ESOP Stock Plan:	Profit Sharing:	Top Exec. Salary: $	Bonus: $
Savings Plan: Y	Stock Purch. Plan:		Second Exec. Salary: $	Bonus: $

OTHER THOUGHTS:

Apparent Women Officers or Directors:
Hot Spot for Advancement for Women/Minorities:

LOCATIONS: ("Y" = Yes)

West:	Southwest:	Midwest:	Southeast:	Northeast:	International:
Y	Y	Y	Y	Y	

HONGKONG AND SHANGHAI HOTELS LTD

www.hshgroup.com

Industry Group Code: 721110 **Ranks within this company's industry group:** Sales: 18 Profits: 13

Properties:		Financial Services:		Construction/Development:		Investments:		Specialty Services:		Brokerage:	
Apartments:	Y	Mortgages:		Commercial Construction:	Y	REIT:		Property Management:	Y	Commercial Sales:	
Malls/Shopping:	Y	Title Insurance:		Residential Construction:				Online Services:		Residential Sales:	
Offices:	Y	Property Insurance:		Land Development:				Software/IT:		Specialty:	
Hotels/Motels:	Y			Support Services:				Consulting:			
Industrial/Warehouses:				Design/Engineering:	Y						
Other:	Y										

TYPES OF BUSINESS:

Hotels
Commercial Properties
Resorts & Luxury Clubs
Apartments
Golf Courses
Property Management
Laundry Services
Park Attractions & Tramways

BRANDS/DIVISIONS/AFFILIATES:

Peninsula Group (The)
Landmark (The)
Peninsula Merchandising, Ltd.
Peak Tramways
Phataraprasit Group (The)
Quail Lodge Resort & Golf Club
Peninsula Clubs and Consultancy Services, Ltd.
Tai Pan Laundry

CONTACTS: *Note: Officers with more than one job title may be intentionally listed here more than once.*

Clement K. M. Kwok, CEO
Peter C. Borer, COO
Neil J. Galloway, CFO
Jean Forrest, Gen. Mgr.-Mktg.
Sindy Tsui, Gen. Mgr.-Human Resources
Ingvar Herland, Gen. Mgr-R&D
Shane Izaks, Gen. Mgr.-IT
Ingvar Herland, Gen. Mgr.-Tech.
Christobelle Liao, Corp. Counsel/Sec.
David Batchelor, Gen. Mgr.-Oper.
John H. Miller, Gen. Mgr.-Design & Planning
Offer Nissenbaum, Managing Dir.-Peninsula Beverly Hills
Jonathan Crook, Gen. Mgr.-Peninsula Manila
Rainy Chan, Area VP-Hong Kong & Bangkok
Nicolas Beliard, Gen. Mgr.-Peninsula Bangkok
Michael D. Kadoorie, Chmn.
Maria Razumich-Zec, Regional VP-USA East Coast, Chicago & New York

Phone: 852-2840-7788 **Fax:** 852-2810-4306
Toll-Free:
Address: St. George's Bldg., 2 Ice House St., 8th Fl., Hong Kong, China

GROWTH PLANS/SPECIAL FEATURES:

Hongkong and Shanghai Hotels, Ltd. (HSH) owns and operates luxury hotels, resorts and other commercial properties. The Peninsula Group is HSH's hotel management division. The firm's Peninsula hotels are located in Hong Kong, Beijing, Chicago, New York, Bangkok, Manila, Beverly Hills, Tokyo and Shanghai. HSH also owns the Repulse Bay, a self-contained residential, retail and commercial complex. The firm's Landmark property in Ho Chi Minh City features 65 fully furnished apartments on the upper floors, a restaurant, a bar, a rooftop swimming pool with a poolside bar, deck, gymnasium, sauna and squash court and office space on the lower levels. HSH also owns the Peninsula Office Tower, part of the extension of the Peninsula Hong Kong. The Office Tower includes nine floors of high-end office space with office units ranging from 6,200 to 11,200 square feet. Another office property owned by HSH is the St. John's Building in Hong Kong, with 21 floors of office space. The company's subsidiary Peninsula Clubs and Consultancy Services, Ltd., manages high-end clubs such as The Hong Kong Club, The Hong Kong Bankers Club and Butterfield's. The Thai Country Club, a 72-hole golf course in Thailand is 75% owned by HSH. The firm's other operations include Peak Tramways (one of the oldest operating funicular railways in the world) operating out of Hong Kong, Peninsula Merchandising, Ltd. (a subsidiary that owns and operates boutiques selling Peninsula-brand products) and Tai Pan Laundry (a commercial laundry service for major hotels, clubs and restaurants, as well as a valet service). The company's latest project, The Peninsula Paris is scheduled to open in 2012.

FINANCIALS: **Sales and profits are in thousands of dollars—add 000 to get the full amount. 2009 Note: Financial information for 2009 was not available for all companies at press time.**

2009 Sales: $543,330 — 2009 Profits: $296,010
2008 Sales: $637,140 — 2008 Profits: $27,870
2007 Sales: $590,500 — 2007 Profits: $446,800
2006 Sales: $483,200 — 2006 Profits: $272,200
2005 Sales: $420,400 — 2005 Profits: $140,400

U.S. Stock Ticker:
Int'l Ticker: 0045 Int'l Exchange: Hong Kong-HKEX
Employees:
Fiscal Year Ends: 12/31
Parent Company:

SALARIES/BENEFITS:

Pension Plan: ESOP Stock Plan: Profit Sharing: Top Exec. Salary: $ Bonus: $
Savings Plan: Stock Purch. Plan: Second Exec. Salary: $ Bonus: $

OTHER THOUGHTS:

Apparent Women Officers or Directors: 7
Hot Spot for Advancement for Women/Minorities: Y

LOCATIONS: ("Y" = Yes)

West:	Southwest:	Midwest:	Southeast:	Northeast:	International:
Y		Y		Y	Y

HONGKONG LAND HOLDINGS LTD

www.hkland.com

Industry Group Code: 5311 **Ranks within this company's industry group:** Sales: 19 Profits: 31

Properties:		Financial Services:		Construction/Development:		Investments:		Specialty Services:		Brokerage:	
Apartments:	Y	Mortgages:		Commercial Construction:		REIT:		Property Management:	Y	Commercial Sales:	
Malls/Shopping:	Y	Title Insurance:		Residential Construction:				Online Services:		Residential Sales:	
Offices:	Y	Property Insurance:		Land Development:	Y			Software/IT:		Specialty:	
Hotels/Motels:				Support Services:	Y			Consulting:			
Industrial/Warehouses:				Design/Engineering:							
Other:	Y										

TYPES OF BUSINESS:

Property Investment, Management & Development
Office Properties
Homes & Apartments
Highway Development
Water Company Development

BRANDS/DIVISIONS/AFFILIATES:

Alexandra House
Jardine House
CityLink Mall
Gaysorn
Central Park
Marina Bay Suites
MCL Land
Jardine Matheson Group

CONTACTS:

Note: Officers with more than one job title may be intentionally listed here more than once.

Y. K. Pang, CEO
A. J. L. Nightingale, Managing Dir.
John R. Witt, CFO
Catherine Chau, Head-Human Resources
Angie Fung, Head-Administrative & Secretarial Svcs.
Cissy Leung, Head-Legal Svcs.
Angela Yeung, Head-Comm.
Geoffrey M. Brown, Dir.-Finance
James Robinson, Exec. Dir.-Projects
Raymond Chow, Exec. Dir.-Commercial Property
Robert Wong, Exec. Dir.-Residential Property
Mark Whitehead, Exec. Dir.-Property Mgmt.
Simon Keswick, Chmn.

Phone: 852-2842-8428 **Fax:** 852-2845-9226
Toll-Free:
Address: 8th Fl., 1 Exchange Square Central, Hong Kong, China

GROWTH PLANS/SPECIAL FEATURES:

Hongkong Land Holdings Ltd., founded in 1889, is a property investment, management and development group with a portfolio encompassing approximately 5 million square feet of commercial and residential property in Hong Kong. The firm operates in two main sectors: Commercial and Residential. The Commercial sector owns several prime office and retail locations in Hong Kong's Central Business District, as well as other high-end retail properties and prime office locations in South East Asia. Its commercial Hong Kong properties include Alexandra House; Chater House; One & Two Exchange Square; Three Exchange Square; Jardine House; The Hong Kong Club Building; The Landmark; Edinburgh Tower; Gloucester Tower; York House; Prince's Building; and Tradeport Hong Kong. Its other commercial properties include One Raffles Link, CityLink Mall, One Raffles Quay and Marina Bay Financial Centre, in Singapore; Gaysorn, in Thailand; Central Building and 63 Ly Thai To, in Vietnam; One Central, in Macau; and Jakarta Land, in Indonesia. The Residential sector focuses on luxury and high-end properties in Hong Kong and Southeast Asia. Its Hong Kong residential properties consist of 15 Tai Hang Road and The Sail at Victoria. Its other Asian properties include Central Park and Maple Place at Beijing Riviera, in Beijing; Bamboo Grove, in Chongqing; One Central Residences, in Macau; Marina Bay Suites and Marina Bay Residences, in Singapore; and North Pine and Roxas Triangle Tower, in the Philippines. The firm's assets in Hong Kong represent approximately 66% of its portfolio. The company also holds a 77% ownership interest in Singapore-based residential property developer MCL Land. Asian-based trading group Jardine Matheson owns a 49% stake in Hongkong Land.

FINANCIALS:

Sales and profits are in thousands of dollars—add 000 to get the full amount. 2009 Note: Financial information for 2009 was not available for all companies at press time.

2009 Sales: $1,322,600	2009 Profits: $1,641,100	**U.S. Stock Ticker: HNGKY.PK**
2008 Sales: $1,022,300	2008 Profits: $-301,300	**Int'l Ticker: H78** Int'l Exchange: Singapore-SIN
2007 Sales: $933,200	2007 Profits: $3,037,700	Employees: 1,104
2006 Sales: $556,900	2006 Profits: $358,400	Fiscal Year Ends: 12/31
2005 Sales: $368,000	2005 Profits: $272,000	Parent Company:

SALARIES/BENEFITS:

Pension Plan:	ESOP Stock Plan:	Profit Sharing:	Top Exec. Salary: $	Bonus: $
Savings Plan:	Stock Purch. Plan:		Second Exec. Salary: $	Bonus: $

OTHER THOUGHTS:

Apparent Women Officers or Directors: 4
Hot Spot for Advancement for Women/Minorities: Y

LOCATIONS: ("Y" = Yes)

West:	Southwest:	Midwest:	Southeast:	Northeast:	International:
					Y

HORTON HOMES INC

www.hortonhomes.com

Industry Group Code: 321991 **Ranks within this company's industry group:** Sales: Profits:

Properties:		Financial Services:		Construction/Development:		Investments:		Specialty Services:		Brokerage:	
Apartments:		Mortgages:		Commercial Construction:		REIT:		Property Management:		Commercial Sales:	
Malls/Shopping:		Title Insurance:		Residential Construction:	Y			Online Services:		Residential Sales:	
Offices:		Property Insurance:		Land Development:				Software/IT:		Specialty:	
Hotels/Motels:				Support Services:				Consulting:			
Industrial/Warehouses:				Design/Engineering:							
Other:											

TYPES OF BUSINESS:

Manufactured & Modular Homes

BRANDS/DIVISIONS/AFFILIATES:

Horton Industries
Dynasty Homes
Modular Builder's Series

CONTACTS: *Note: Officers with more than one job title may be intentionally listed here more than once.*

Nevils D. Horton, Jr., CEO
Nevils D. Horton, Jr., Pres.
Steve M. Sinclair, CFO/VP
Rus W. Hicks, VP-Sales
Nevils D. Horton, Jr., Chmn.

Phone: 706-485-8506	**Fax:** 706-485-4446
Toll-Free: 800-657-4000	
Address: 101 Industrial Blvd., Eatonton, GA 31024 US	

GROWTH PLANS/SPECIAL FEATURES:

Horton Homes, Inc., a subsidiary of Horton Industries, is a leading manufacturer of houses and modular homes for sale in the southeastern U.S. Its sister subsidiary, Dynasty Homes, also makes manufactured houses. Horton produces approximately 100 floors a week at its 100-acre facility in Georgia. Manufactured homes are homes made or manufactured in a factory and designed to be transported to a site. They can be large or small, and while they are constructed in the same manner as mobile homes, manufactured homes are permanently attached to the site using conventional on-site construction, as opposed to mobile homes, which can be moved from one location to another. The company sells its houses through more than 90 retail centers in seven states, where buyers can choose from more than 80 floor plans, including 14-feet, 16-feet, 24-feet, 27-feet, 32-feet and 41-feet wide. The firm's homes feature brand-name appliances, a 30- or 50-gallon water heater and moisture-protected deck flooring, as well as the option of various amenities, such as bay windows, vaulted ceilings, walk-in closets and skylights. The firm's modular division, the Modular Builder's Series, builds modular homes (offering five floor plans) for the commercial modular industry. These modular buildings are mainly used for construction offices, classrooms, church assembly buildings, retail offices and golf proshops, and are marketed throughout 11 Southeastern states.

FINANCIALS: **Sales and profits are in thousands of dollars—add 000 to get the full amount. 2009 Note: Financial information for 2009 was not available for all companies at press time.**

2009 Sales: $	2009 Profits: $	**U.S. Stock Ticker: Subsidiary**
2008 Sales: $	2008 Profits: $	**Int'l Ticker:** Int'l Exchange:
2007 Sales: $	2007 Profits: $	Employees:
2006 Sales: $	2006 Profits: $	Fiscal Year Ends: 8/31
2005 Sales: $	2005 Profits: $	Parent Company: HORTON INDUSTRIES INC

SALARIES/BENEFITS:

Pension Plan:	ESOP Stock Plan:	Profit Sharing:	Top Exec. Salary: $	Bonus: $
Savings Plan:	Stock Purch. Plan:		Second Exec. Salary: $	Bonus: $

OTHER THOUGHTS:

Apparent Women Officers or Directors:
Hot Spot for Advancement for Women/Minorities:

LOCATIONS: ("Y" = Yes)

West:	Southwest:	Midwest:	Southeast:	Northeast:	International:
			Y	Y	

HOSPITALITY PROPERTIES TRUST

www.hptreit.com

Industry Group Code: 531120 **Ranks within this company's industry group:** Sales: 13 Profits: 19

Properties:		Financial Services:		Construction/Development:		Investments:		Specialty Services:		Brokerage:	
Apartments:		Mortgages:		Commercial Construction:		REIT:	Y	Property Management:		Commercial Sales:	
Malls/Shopping:		Title Insurance:		Residential Construction:				Online Services:		Residential Sales:	
Offices:		Property Insurance:		Land Development:				Software/IT:		Specialty:	
Hotels/Motels:	Y			Support Services:				Consulting:			
Industrial/Warehouses:				Design/Engineering:							
Other:	Y										

TYPES OF BUSINESS:

Real Estate Investment Trust
Hotels
Travel Centers

BRANDS/DIVISIONS/AFFILIATES:

Reit Management & Research LLC
TravelCenters of America LLC

CONTACTS:

Note: Officers with more than one job title may be intentionally listed here more than once.

John G. Murray, COO
John G. Murray, Pres.
Mark L. Kleifges, CFO
Jennifer B. Clark, Sec.
Mark L. Kleifges, Treas.
Ethan S. Bornstein, Sr. VP-Asset Mgmt.
Thomas O'Brien, Pres./CEO-TravelCenters of America LLC

Phone: 617-964-8389	**Fax:** 617-969-5730
Toll-Free:	
Address: 400 Centre St., Newton, MA 02458 US	

GROWTH PLANS/SPECIAL FEATURES:

Hospitality Properties Trust (HPT) is a real estate investment trust. The company owns 289 hotels with 42,880 rooms or suites, as well as 185 travel centers, located in 44 U.S. states, Puerto Rico and Canada. HPT hotel properties are currently operated under the following brands: Courtyard by Marriott, Candlewood Suites, Staybridge Suites, Residence Inn by Marriott, Crowne Plaza Hotels & Resorts, Hyatt Place, InterContinental Hotels & Resorts, Marriott Hotels and Resorts, Radisson Hotels & Resorts, TownePlace Suites by Marriott, Country Inns & Suites by Carlson, Holiday Inn Hotels & Resorts, SpringHill Suites by Marriott, and Park Plaza Hotels & Resorts. The company's 185 travel centers include 145 operated under the TravelCenters of America (TA) brand names and 40 operated under the Petro Stopping Centers brand name. All of HPT's management agreements or leases share eight points: first, managers are required to pay a fixed minimum rent; second, operators must pay percentage returns on gross hotel revenues exceeding a certain threshold; third, all agreements are long-term (15 years or more); fourth, each hotel is a part of a combination of hotels and is subject to cross-default obligations with respect to all other hotels in the same combination; fifth, each combination of hotels is geographically diverse; sixth, contract renewals may only be pursued for a combination of hotels, not for each hotel individually; seventh, the firm's agreements require the deposit of 5% to 6% of gross hotel revenues into escrows to fund periodic renovations; finally, each management agreement or lease includes security terms to ensure payments to HPT. Generally, the firm prefers to purchase multiple properties in a single transaction, rather than individual properties.

FINANCIALS:

Sales and profits are in thousands of dollars—add 000 to get the full amount. 2009 Note: Financial information for 2009 was not available for all companies at press time.

2009 Sales: $1,037,247	2009 Profits: $193,341	**U.S. Stock Ticker: HPT**
2008 Sales: $1,252,674	2008 Profits: $133,995	**Int'l Ticker:** Int'l Exchange:
2007 Sales: $1,285,479	2007 Profits: $330,968	Employees: 600
2006 Sales: $1,022,946	2006 Profits: $169,039	Fiscal Year Ends: 12/31
2005 Sales: $818,013	2005 Profits: $129,903	Parent Company:

SALARIES/BENEFITS:

Pension Plan:	ESOP Stock Plan:	Profit Sharing:	Top Exec. Salary: $92,565	Bonus: $
Savings Plan:	Stock Purch. Plan:		Second Exec. Salary: $89,880	Bonus: $

OTHER THOUGHTS:

Apparent Women Officers or Directors: 1
Hot Spot for Advancement for Women/Minorities:

LOCATIONS: ("Y" = Yes)

West:	Southwest:	Midwest:	Southeast:	Northeast:	International:
Y	Y	Y	Y	Y	Y

HOST HOTELS & RESORTS LP

www.hosthotels.com

Industry Group Code: 531120 **Ranks within this company's industry group:** Sales: 2 Profits: 6

Properties:		Financial Services:		Construction/Development:		Investments:		Specialty Services:		Brokerage:	
Apartments:		Mortgages:		Commercial Construction:		REIT:	Y	Property Management:		Commercial Sales:	
Malls/Shopping:		Title Insurance:		Residential Construction:				Online Services:		Residential Sales:	
Offices:		Property Insurance:		Land Development:				Software/IT:		Specialty:	
Hotels/Motels:	Y			Support Services:				Consulting:			
Industrial/Warehouses:				Design/Engineering:							
Other:											

TYPES OF BUSINESS:

Real Estate Investment Trust
Hotels

BRANDS/DIVISIONS/AFFILIATES:

Marriott
Ritz-Carlton
Four Seasons
Hilton/Embassy Suites
Hyatt
Westin
Sheraton
Starwood Hotels & Resorts Worldwide, Inc.

CONTACTS:

Note: Officers with more than one job title may be intentionally listed here more than once.

W. Edward Walter, CEO
W. Edward Walter, Pres.
Larry K. Harvey, CFO/Exec. VP/Treas.
Joanne G. Hamilton, Exec. VP-Human Resources
James F. Risoleo, CIO/Exec. VP
Elizabeth A. Abdoo, General Counsel/Sec./Exec. VP
Brian G. Macnamara, Sr. VP-Corp. Controller
Minaz Abji, Exec. VP-Asset Mgmt.
Gregory J. Larson, Exec. VP-Corp. Strategy & Fund Mgmt.
James F. Risoleo, Chief Investment Officer/Exec. VP
Richard E. Marriott, Chmn.

Phone: 240-744-1000	Fax:
Toll-Free:	
Address: 6903 Rockledge Dr., Ste. 1500, Bethesda, MD 20817-1109 US	

GROWTH PLANS/SPECIAL FEATURES:

Host Hotels & Resorts, L.P. (HST), formerly Host Marriott Corporation, is a leading hotel real estate investment trust (REIT) formed through the recent merger of Host Marriott with Starwood Hotels and Resorts. The firm conducts the entirety of its business through an umbrella partnership structure with Host Hotels & Resorts, Inc. as its sole general partner. Host Hotels & Resorts, Inc. holds 98% of HST's outstanding partnership interests. HST itself is self-managed and self-administered, with 121 upper upscale and luxury full-service hotels consisting of 64,511 rooms in the U.S., U.K., Spain, Poland, Mexico, Chile and Canada to name a few. HST operates 66 Marriott's; seven Sheraton's; 11 Westin's; nine Ritz-Carlton's; six Hyatt's; two W Hotel's; one Fairmont; two Four Seasons; two Hilton/Embassy Suites; one Swissotel; and three other hotels. All hotel locations are generally confined in the business districts of major cities, airports areas, resorts and convention destinations. HST properties typically include meeting and banquet facilities; a variety of restaurants and lounges; swimming pools; exercise facilities and/or spas; gift shops; and parking facilities. The company operates through several segments, including brand names such as the Marriott, Ritz-Carlton, Four Seasons, Hilton/Embassy Suites, Hyatt, Delta, Westin and Sheraton. The company is always actively seeking acquisitions and focusing its resources on upgrading and expanding existing hotels. In September 2009, the firm sold its remaining 3.6% limited partnership interest in CBM Joint Venture Limited Partnership.

HST offers its employees medical, dental, prescription, vision and hearing coverage; free on-site fitness centers; associate assistance programs (AAP) to provide help for issues on health; long- and short-term disability and life insurance; a 401(k) plan; company paid parking; hotel discounts; health and dependent care spending accounts; long term care coverage; employee stock purchase plan; and tuition assistance.

FINANCIALS:

Sales and profits are in thousands of dollars—add 000 to get the full amount. 2009 Note: Financial information for 2009 was not available for all companies at press time.

2009 Sales: $4,158,000	2009 Profits: $-258,000	**U.S. Stock Ticker: HST**
2008 Sales: $5,139,000	2008 Profits: $414,000	**Int'l Ticker:** Int'l Exchange:
2007 Sales: $5,249,000	2007 Profits: $734,000	Employees: 186
2006 Sales: $4,802,000	2006 Profits: $738,000	Fiscal Year Ends: 12/31
2005 Sales: $3,694,000	2005 Profits: $166,000	Parent Company:

SALARIES/BENEFITS:

Pension Plan:	ESOP Stock Plan:	Profit Sharing:	Top Exec. Salary: $704,589	Bonus: $673,154
Savings Plan: Y	Stock Purch. Plan: Y		Second Exec. Salary: $500,000	Bonus: $350,769

OTHER THOUGHTS:

Apparent Women Officers or Directors: 3
Hot Spot for Advancement for Women/Minorities: Y

LOCATIONS: ("Y" = Yes)

West:	Southwest:	Midwest:	Southeast:	Northeast:	International:
Y	Y	Y	Y	Y	Y

HOTEL PROPERTIES LTD

www.hotelprop.com

Industry Group Code: 721110 **Ranks within this company's industry group:** Sales: 30 Profits: 17

Properties:		Financial Services:		Construction/Development:		Investments:		Specialty Services:		Brokerage:	
Apartments:	Y	Mortgages:		Commercial Construction:		REIT:		Property Management:		Commercial Sales:	
Malls/Shopping:	Y	Title Insurance:		Residential Construction:				Online Services:		Residential Sales:	
Offices:		Property Insurance:		Land Development:				Software/IT:		Specialty:	
Hotels/Motels:	Y			Support Services:				Consulting:			
Industrial/Warehouses:				Design/Engineering:							
Other:	Y										

TYPES OF BUSINESS:

Hotels
Condominiums
Restaurants
Retail Properties & Operations
Food Distribution

BRANDS/DIVISIONS/AFFILIATES:

Four Seasons Resort
Hard Rock Hotel
Rihiveli Beach Resort
Concorde Hotel
Lakehouse (The)
Le Meriden
Hard Rock Cafe
HPL Hotels & Resorts Pte Ltd

CONTACTS:

Note: Officers with more than one job title may be intentionally listed here more than once.

Ong Beng Seng, Managing Dir.
Chuang Sheue Ling, Corp. Sec.
Buong Lik Lau, Head-Hotel Div.
Tien Lock Lim, Exec. Dir.
Joseph Grimberg, Chmn.

Phone: 65-734-5250 **Fax:** 65-732-0347
Toll-Free:
Address: 50 Cuscaden Rd., 08-01 HPL House, Singapore, 249724 Singapore

GROWTH PLANS/SPECIAL FEATURES:

Hotel Properties Ltd. (HPL) is a diversified hotel holding company headquartered in Singapore that invests in premium commercial and residential properties in Asia and the Pacific, including hotels, condominiums, shopping centers, restaurants, a food distribution chain and retail operations. It owns or has interests in 19 hotels in Singapore, Malaysia, Thailand, Indonesia, Bhutan, Vanuatu and the Maldives. These include three Four Seasons properties and a Hard Rock Hotel in Indonesia; two Four Seasons Resorts, one Holiday Inn Resort and the Rihiveli Beach Resort in the Maldives; two Concorde Hotels, a Casa Del Mar, a Hard Rock Hotel and The Lakehouse Cameron Highlands in Malaysia; a Four Seasons Hotel, a Hilton and a Concorde Hotel in Singapore; a Hard Rock Hotel and a Metropolitan in Thailand; and the Palms Resort and Casino in Vanuatu. The company owns three shopping centers and five residential areas in Singapore, as well as a residential property in Thailand. In its Lifestyle division, the company owns Hard Rock Cafes in China, Hong Kong, Indonesia, Malaysia, Philippines, Singapore, and Thailand. In addition, it owns a Planet Hollywood restaurant in Malaysia and Haagen-Dazs ice cream stores in Malaysia and Singapore. In May 2009, the firm's wholly-owned subsidiary, NYC 55 Corp., established two new subsidiaries, Concorde Hotel Management Inc. and Concorde Hotel New York Inc. In June 2009, the company acquired 100% of the shares of HRH merchandise Singapore Ltd., a company specializing in souvenirs, gifts, apparel and accessories, and a 50% interest in HRH Merchandise Sdn Bhd, based in Malaysia.

FINANCIALS:

Sales and profits are in thousands of dollars—add 000 to get the full amount. 2009 Note: Financial information for 2009 was not available for all companies at press time.

2009 Sales: $323,320	2009 Profits: $25,680
2008 Sales: $78,960	2008 Profits: $5,160
2007 Sales: $59,120	2007 Profits: $20,940
2006 Sales: $263,000	2006 Profits: $73,200
2005 Sales: $225,100	2005 Profits: $28,400

U.S. Stock Ticker:
Int'l Ticker: H15 Int'l Exchange: Singapore-SIN
Employees:
Fiscal Year Ends: 12/31
Parent Company:

SALARIES/BENEFITS:

Pension Plan:	ESOP Stock Plan:	Profit Sharing:	Top Exec. Salary: $	Bonus: $
Savings Plan:	Stock Purch. Plan:		Second Exec. Salary: $	Bonus: $

OTHER THOUGHTS:

Apparent Women Officers or Directors:
Hot Spot for Advancement for Women/Minorities:

LOCATIONS: ("Y" = Yes)

West:	Southwest:	Midwest:	Southeast:	Northeast:	International:
					Y

HOVNANIAN ENTERPRISES INC

www.khov.com

Industry Group Code: 2361 **Ranks within this company's industry group:** Sales: 7 Profits: 16

Properties:		Financial Services:		Construction/Development:		Investments:		Specialty Services:		Brokerage:	
Apartments:		Mortgages:		Commercial Construction:	Y	REIT:		Property Management:		Commercial Sales:	
Malls/Shopping:		Title Insurance:		Residential Construction:	Y			Online Services:		Residential Sales:	
Offices:		Property Insurance:		Land Development:				Software/IT:		Specialty:	
Hotels/Motels:				Support Services:				Consulting:			
Industrial/Warehouses:				Design/Engineering:	Y						
Other:											

TYPES OF BUSINESS:

Home Building
Mortgages
Title Insurance
Residential Communities
Commercial Construction

BRANDS/DIVISIONS/AFFILIATES:

K. Hovnanian American Mortgage, LLC

CONTACTS:

Note: Officers with more than one job title may be intentionally listed here more than once.

Ara K. Hovnanian, CEO
Thomas J. Pellerito, COO
Ara K. Hovnanian, Pres.
J. Larry Sorsby, CFO/Exec. VP
Robyn T. Mingle, Sr. VP-Human Resources
Peter S. Reinhart, General Counsel/Sr. VP
Paul W. Buchanan, Sr. VP/Chief Acct. Officer
Ara K. Hovnanian, Chmn.

Phone: 732-747-7800	**Fax:** 732-747-7159
Toll-Free:	
Address: 110 W. Front St., Red Bank, NJ 07701 US	

GROWTH PLANS/SPECIAL FEATURES:

Hovnanian Enterprises, Inc. designs, constructs, markets and sells single-family detached homes, attached townhomes and condominiums, mid-rise and high-rise condominiums, urban infill and active adult homes in planned residential communities. The firm organizes its operations into two divisions: homebuilding and financial services. Homebuilding operations are conducted in six segments: Northeast, Mid-Atlantic, Midwest, Southeast, Southwest and West. Hovnanian's financial services operations provide mortgage loans and title services. With more than 285,000 total homes sold since its inception in 1959, including 5,659 homes delivered in 2008, the firm is one of the largest homebuilders in the U.S. Hovnanian markets its homes primarily to first-time buyers, first-time and second-time move-up buyers, luxury buyers, active adult buyers and empty nesters. Base home prices range from $36,000 to $1,800,000 in the Northeast; from $155,000 to $1,262,000 in the Mid-Atlantic; from $80,000 to $499,000 in the Midwest; from $95,000 to $600,000 in the Southeast; from $81,000 to $1,034,000 in the Southwest; and from $102,000 to $706,000 in the West, with an average sales price of $283,900 in 2009. Its homes are available in 179 communities in 39 markets in 18 states, and are generally located in suburban areas easily accessible through public and personal transportation. Development activities include site planning and engineering; obtaining environmental and other regulatory approvals; constructing roads, sewer, water and drainage facilities; and recreational facilities and other amenities for residential developments. In November 2009, Hovnanian entered into a joint venture agreement with GoldenTree InSite Partners to acquire a portfolio of homebuilding projects.

Employees are offered medical, dental and vision insurance; an employee assistance program; flexible spending accounts; life insurance; short- and long-term disability; a 401(k) plan; an annual 401(k) profit sharing plan; a 529 collegebound savings plan; tuition assistance; US government bonds; a home purchase discount; entertainment discounts; and discounted home, auto, boater's and renter's insurance.

FINANCIALS:

Sales and profits are in thousands of dollars—add 000 to get the full amount. 2009 Note: Financial information for 2009 was not available for all companies at press time.

2009 Sales: $1,596,290	2009 Profits: $-716,712	**U.S. Stock Ticker: HOV**
2008 Sales: $3,308,111	2008 Profits: $-1,124,590	**Int'l Ticker:** Int'l Exchange:
2007 Sales: $4,798,921	2007 Profits: $-627,119	Employees: 1,750
2006 Sales: $6,148,235	2006 Profits: $149,533	Fiscal Year Ends: 10/31
2005 Sales: $5,348,417	2005 Profits: $471,847	Parent Company:

SALARIES/BENEFITS:

Pension Plan:	ESOP Stock Plan:	Profit Sharing: Y	Top Exec. Salary: $1,092,606	Bonus: $699,500
Savings Plan: Y	Stock Purch. Plan:		Second Exec. Salary: $1,058,911	Bonus: $444,700

OTHER THOUGHTS:

Apparent Women Officers or Directors: 1
Hot Spot for Advancement for Women/Minorities:

LOCATIONS: ("Y" = Yes)

West:	Southwest:	Midwest:	Southeast:	Northeast:	International:
Y	Y	Y	Y	Y	

HOWARD JOHNSON INTERNATIONAL INC

www.hojo.com

Industry Group Code: 721110 **Ranks within this company's industry group:** Sales: Profits:

Properties:		Financial Services:		Construction/Development:		Investments:		Specialty Services:		Brokerage:	
Apartments:		Mortgages:		Commercial Construction:		REIT:		Property Management:		Commercial Sales:	
Malls/Shopping:		Title Insurance:		Residential Construction:				Online Services:		Residential Sales:	
Offices:		Property Insurance:		Land Development:				Software/IT:		Specialty:	
Hotels/Motels:	Y			Support Services:				Consulting:			
Industrial/Warehouses:				Design/Engineering:							
Other:											

TYPES OF BUSINESS:

Hotels
Restaurants
Vacation Specials
Travel Packages

BRANDS/DIVISIONS/AFFILIATES:

Wyndham Worldwide
Hotel Package Deals
TripFinder Vacation Packages
Guaranteed Best Rate
Wyndham Rewards
Rise & Dine

CONTACTS:

Note: Officers with more than one job title may be intentionally listed here more than once.

Ken Greene, Pres.
Rui Barros, Pres, Brand-Howard Johnson Int'l/Travelodge Hotels

Phone: 973-428-9700	**Fax:** 973-496-7658
Toll-Free: 800-544-9881	
Address: 22 Sylvan Way, Parsippany, NJ 07054 US	

GROWTH PLANS/SPECIAL FEATURES:

Howard Johnson International, Inc., a subsidiary of Wyndham Worldwide, owns and franchises mid-priced hotels. Its portfolio currently includes approximately 470 hotels located in the U.S., China, Mexico and other international regions. The firm's Hotel Package Deals feature several destinations for a given week, offering various packages viewable on the firm's web site. These packaged specials often include discounted hotel fees and location-specific promotions. TripFinder Vacation Packages offer a travel package program through which costumers can rent cars or purchase airlines in addition to securing hotel reservations. Howard Johnson additionally features the Guaranteed Best Rate program, which guarantees customers a 10% lower price than any competitor. Howard Johnson participates in the Wyndham Rewards, which is a free program that offers customers redeemable points or airline miles for staying at any one of Wyndham's hotel locations. Howard Johnson's hotels feature a variety of amenities. Customers can search for a hotel on the firm's web site using any or all of these amenities as search criteria. Amenities include an airport shuttle, business center, free high-speed Internet, free Rise & Dine breakfast, gym/fitness center, meeting/banquet facilities, pet friendly, pool and restaurant.

FINANCIALS:

Sales and profits are in thousands of dollars—add 000 to get the full amount. 2009 Note: Financial information for 2009 was not available for all companies at press time.

2009 Sales: $	2009 Profits: $	**U.S. Stock Ticker: Subsidiary**
2008 Sales: $	2008 Profits: $	**Int'l Ticker:** Int'l Exchange:
2007 Sales: $	2007 Profits: $	Employees:
2006 Sales: $	2006 Profits: $	Fiscal Year Ends: 12/31
2005 Sales: $	2005 Profits: $	Parent Company: WYNDHAM WORLDWIDE

SALARIES/BENEFITS:

Pension Plan:	ESOP Stock Plan:	Profit Sharing:	Top Exec. Salary: $	Bonus: $
Savings Plan:	Stock Purch. Plan:		Second Exec. Salary: $	Bonus: $

OTHER THOUGHTS:

Apparent Women Officers or Directors:
Hot Spot for Advancement for Women/Minorities:

LOCATIONS: ("Y" = Yes)

West:	Southwest:	Midwest:	Southeast:	Northeast:	International:
Y	Y	Y	Y	Y	Y

HRPT PROPERTIES TRUST

www.hrpreit.com

Industry Group Code: 531120 **Ranks within this company's industry group:** Sales: 22 Profits: 13

Properties:		Financial Services:		Construction/Development:		Investments:		Specialty Services:		Brokerage:	
Apartments:		Mortgages:		Commercial Construction:		REIT:	Y	Property Management:		Commercial Sales:	
Malls/Shopping:		Title Insurance:		Residential Construction:				Online Services:		Residential Sales:	
Offices:	Y	Property Insurance:		Land Development:				Software/IT:		Specialty:	
Hotels/Motels:				Support Services:				Consulting:			
Industrial/Warehouses:	Y			Design/Engineering:							
Other:											

TYPES OF BUSINESS:

Real Estate Investment Trust
Office Buildings

BRANDS/DIVISIONS/AFFILIATES:

Reit Management & Research LLC

CONTACTS:

Note: Officers with more than one job title may be intentionally listed here more than once.

David M. Lepore, COO/Sr. VP
John A. Mannix, Pres.
John C. Popeo, CFO
Jennifer B. Clark, Sec.
Tim Bonang, VP-Investor Rel.
John C. Popeo, Treas.
William J. Sheehan, Dir.-Internal Audit & Compliance
John A. Mannix, Chief Investment Officer

Phone: 617-332-3990	**Fax:** 617-332-2261
Toll-Free:	
Address: 400 Centre St., Newton, MA 02458 US	

GROWTH PLANS/SPECIAL FEATURES:

HRPT Properties Trust, which is managed by Reit Management & Research LLC, is a real estate investment trust (REIT) that owns and operates office and industrial buildings and leases industrial land. The company owns 518 properties: 332 office properties with a total of approximately 35.3 million square feet; and 186 industrial properties with 31.5 million square feet of space. HRPT's income is derived primarily from rent on these properties. The properties are located in central business districts and suburban areas in four major market regions: Metro Philadelphia, Pennsylvania; Metro Washington, D.C.; Metro Boston, Massachusetts; and Oahu, Hawaii. HRPT operates in a total of 34 states, with 17.9 million square feet of the land area of the firm's industrial properties concentrated in Oahu, Hawaii. In evaluating potential investments and asset sales, HRPT considers historic and projected rents received and operating expenses; the growth, tax and regulatory environment of the market; the quality, experience and credit worthiness of the property's tenants; the occupancy, demand for and pricing of similar properties in nearby markets; the construction quality, physical condition and design of the property; and the geographic area and type of property. HRPT's tenants include U.S. government agencies, GlaxoSmithKline plc; Expedia, Inc.; Wells Fargo Bank; and The Bank of New York Mellon Financial Corporation.

FINANCIALS:

Sales and profits are in thousands of dollars—add 000 to get the full amount. 2009 Note: Financial information for 2009 was not available for all companies at press time.

2009 Sales: $849,722	2009 Profits: $164,674	**U.S. Stock Ticker: HRP**
2008 Sales: $835,855	2008 Profits: $244,645	**Int'l Ticker:** Int'l Exchange:
2007 Sales: $783,266	2007 Profits: $124,255	Employees: 600
2006 Sales: $744,008	2006 Profits: $250,580	Fiscal Year Ends: 12/31
2005 Sales: $708,841	2005 Profits: $164,984	Parent Company:

SALARIES/BENEFITS:

Pension Plan:	ESOP Stock Plan:	Profit Sharing:	Top Exec. Salary: $	Bonus: $
Savings Plan:	Stock Purch. Plan:		Second Exec. Salary: $	Bonus: $

OTHER THOUGHTS:

Apparent Women Officers or Directors: 1
Hot Spot for Advancement for Women/Minorities:

LOCATIONS: ("Y" = Yes)

West:	Southwest:	Midwest:	Southeast:	Northeast:	International:
Y	Y	Y	Y	Y	

HUTCHISON WHAMPOA HOTEL & PROPERTIES LTD

www.hwpg.com/en/res/index.asp

Industry Group Code: 5311 **Ranks within this company's industry group:** Sales: Profits:

Properties:		Financial Services:		Construction/Development:		Investments:		Specialty Services:		Brokerage:	
Apartments:	Y	Mortgages:		Commercial Construction:		REIT:		Property Management:	Y	Commercial Sales:	
Malls/Shopping:	Y	Title Insurance:		Residential Construction:				Online Services:	Y	Residential Sales:	
Offices:	Y	Property Insurance:		Land Development:				Software/IT:		Specialty:	
Hotels/Motels:	Y			Support Services:	Y			Consulting:			
Industrial/Warehouses:	Y			Design/Engineering:	Y						
Other:	Y										

TYPES OF BUSINESS:

Real Estate Operations & Development
Hotels
Office & Industrial Properties
Residential Properties
Marine Docks & Repair Yards

BRANDS/DIVISIONS/AFFILIATES:

Hutchison Whampoa Limited
Property & Hotels Group
Hongkong & Whampoa Dock Company Limited
Hutchison Properties Limited
Cavendish International Holdings Limited
Hutchison Premium Services
Pacific Property Net
Harbour Plaza Hotels & Resorts

CONTACTS: *Note: Officers with more than one job title may be intentionally listed here more than once.*

Phone: 852-2128-7500	**Fax:** 852-2128-7888
Toll-Free:	
Address: 3/F, 1 Harbourfront, 18 Tak Fung St., Hunghom, Hong Kong, China	

GROWTH PLANS/SPECIAL FEATURES:

Hutchison Whampoa Properties Ltd. (Hutchison) is the property development and investment subsidiary of Hutchison Whampoa Limited (HWL). Hutchison was established by HWL to hold the property interests of Hongkong & Whampoa Dock Company Limited (HWD), Hutchison Properties Limited (HPL) and Cavendish International Holdings Limited (CIHL). The company operates within HWL's Property & Hotels Group, which was established through the merger of HWD and HPL in 1980. HWL's other Property & Hotels Group subsidiary is joint-venture Harbour Plaza Hotels & Resorts. Hutchison's properties are organized by type into six categories: residential, office, industrial, commercial, hotel and golf. The company has numerous residential properties in such locations as Hong Kong, London, Singapore, the Bahamas, Beijing and Shanghai. Hutchinson has office properties in seven different locations throughout China. The firm's five industrial properties are all located in Hong Kong. Its commercial properties are located in London and 12 locations throughout China. The company's hotels are located in the Bahamas and Hong Kong, Chongqing and Kunming, China. Hutchison has one golf property located Dongguan, China. The firm's services include property management, project management, marketing and e-business. Property management services offered by Hutchison include the deployment of security guards, caretakers and maintenance workers. The company's project management team is comprised of architects, engineers and quantity surveyors who supervise and coordinate the design and construction of its developments through external consultants and contractors. Hutchison's in-house marketing team is responsible for the leasing and sale of its properties, and provides property-related services to other HWL subsidiaries, including tenancy negotiations, valuations, feasibility studies and general real estate guidance. The company's e-business operations comprise subsidiaries Hutchison Premium Services and Pacific Property Net, both of which operate real estate web sites.

FINANCIALS: **Sales and profits are in thousands of dollars—add 000 to get the full amount. 2009 Note: Financial information for 2009 was not available for all companies at press time.**

2009 Sales: $	2009 Profits: $	**U.S. Stock Ticker: Subsidiary**
2008 Sales: $	2008 Profits: $	**Int'l Ticker:** Int'l Exchange:
2007 Sales: $	2007 Profits: $	Employees:
2006 Sales: $	2006 Profits: $	Fiscal Year Ends: 12/31
2005 Sales: $	2005 Profits: $	Parent Company: HUTCHISON WHAMPOA LIMITED

SALARIES/BENEFITS:

Pension Plan:	ESOP Stock Plan:	Profit Sharing:	Top Exec. Salary: $	Bonus: $
Savings Plan:	Stock Purch. Plan:		Second Exec. Salary: $	Bonus: $

OTHER THOUGHTS:

Apparent Women Officers or Directors:
Hot Spot for Advancement for Women/Minorities:

LOCATIONS: ("Y" = Yes)

West:	Southwest:	Midwest:	Southeast:	Northeast:	International:
					Y

HVM LLC

www.extendedstayhotels.com

Industry Group Code: 721110 **Ranks within this company's industry group:** Sales: Profits:

Properties:		Financial Services:		Construction/Development:		Investments:		Specialty Services:		Brokerage:	
Apartments:		Mortgages:		Commercial Construction:		REIT:		Property Management:		Commercial Sales:	
Malls/Shopping:		Title Insurance:		Residential Construction:				Online Services:		Residential Sales:	
Offices:		Property Insurance:		Land Development:				Software/IT:		Specialty:	
Hotels/Motels:	Y			Support Services:				Consulting:			
Industrial/Warehouses:				Design/Engineering:							
Other:											

TYPES OF BUSINESS:

Hotels, Extended Stay
Hotels

BRANDS/DIVISIONS/AFFILIATES:

Lightstone Group (The)
Homestead Studio Suites
Extended Stay Hotels
Extended Stay Deluxe
Studio PLUS
Crossland
Extended Stay America
Lowest Internet Price Guarantee

CONTACTS:

Note: Officers with more than one job title may be intentionally listed here more than once.

Gary A. DeLapp, CEO
Gary A. DeLapp, Pres.
Stephen T. Woolridge, Sr. Exec. VP-Oper.
Joseph Rodgers, Exec. VP-Acct.

Phone: 864-573-1600	**Fax:** 864-573-1695
Toll-Free: 800-804-3724	
Address: 100 Dunbar St., Spartanburg, SC 29306 US	

GROWTH PLANS/SPECIAL FEATURES:

HVM, LLC, formerly Homestead Village Management, LLC, is the operator of the Extended Stay Hotels network, which has nearly 700 extended-stay properties in Canada and most of the major metro areas in the U.S. The firm is a subsidiary of the Lightstone Group. The company owns and manages moderately price extended-stay hotels under five brand names: Crossland (34 hotels), Extended Stay America (363 hotels), Homestead Studio Suites (132 hotels), Extended Stay Deluxe (109 hotels) and Studio PLUS (46 hotels). The typical guest travels for training, temporary business assignments or relocation. Many are employed in fields prone to extended-stay travel, including technology, telecommunications and consulting. HVM targets large corporate customers with multi-location extended-stay needs and has customized its rooms for this purpose with full kitchens, Internet connections and work/study areas. It offers daily, weekly and monthly rates with discounts for extended stays. HVM hotels all include kitchen, living and dining areas; laundry facilities; and pet accommodations; certain locations offer pools, fitness rooms and individual DVD players. The company's properties are typically located near business centers, airports and entertainment areas. The company recently launched its Lowest Internet Price Guarantee; the program offers customers who find a lower, publicly available average hotel rate than that of a HVM hotel price matching plus an additional 10% discount.

FINANCIALS:

Sales and profits are in thousands of dollars—add 000 to get the full amount. 2009 Note: Financial information for 2009 was not available for all companies at press time.

2009 Sales: $	2009 Profits: $	**U.S. Stock Ticker: Private**
2008 Sales: $	2008 Profits: $	**Int'l Ticker:** Int'l Exchange:
2007 Sales: $101,000	2007 Profits: $	Employees:
2006 Sales: $	2006 Profits: $	Fiscal Year Ends: 12/31
2005 Sales: $	2005 Profits: $	Parent Company: LIGHTSTONE GROUP (THE)

SALARIES/BENEFITS:

Pension Plan:	ESOP Stock Plan:	Profit Sharing:	Top Exec. Salary: $	Bonus: $
Savings Plan: Y	Stock Purch. Plan:		Second Exec. Salary: $	Bonus: $

OTHER THOUGHTS:

Apparent Women Officers or Directors:
Hot Spot for Advancement for Women/Minorities:

LOCATIONS: ("Y" = Yes)

West:	Southwest:	Midwest:	Southeast:	Northeast:	International:
Y	Y	Y	Y	Y	Y

HYATT HOTELS CORPORATION

www.hyatt.com

Industry Group Code: 721110 **Ranks within this company's industry group:** Sales: 6 Profits:

Properties:		Financial Services:		Construction/Development:		Investments:		Specialty Services:		Brokerage:	
Apartments:		Mortgages:		Commercial Construction:		REIT:		Property Management:	Y	Commercial Sales:	
Malls/Shopping:		Title Insurance:		Residential Construction:				Online Services:		Residential Sales:	
Offices:		Property Insurance:		Land Development:				Software/IT:		Specialty:	
Hotels/Motels:	Y			Support Services:				Consulting:			
Industrial/Warehouses:				Design/Engineering:							
Other:	Y										

TYPES OF BUSINESS:

Hotel Ownership & Management
Timeshares
Golf Courses
Gaming
Retirement Communities
Motels & Inns
Hotel Franchising

BRANDS/DIVISIONS/AFFILIATES:

Hyatt Regency
Grand Hyatt
Hyatt Resorts
Hyatt Summerfield Suites
Andaz
Hyatt Vacation Club
Hyatt Gold Passport

CONTACTS:

Note: Officers with more than one job title may be intentionally listed here more than once.

Mark S. Hoplamazian, CEO
Mark S. Hoplamazian, Pres.
Harmit J. Singh, CFO
John Wallis, Head-Mktg. & Brand Strategy
Robert W. K. Webb, Chief Human Resources Officer
H. Charles Floyd, COO-North America Oper.
Stephen G. Haggerty, Head-Dev.
Katie Meyer, VP-Corp. Comm.
Atish Shah, Sr. VP-Investor Rel.
Steve Sokal, Sr. VP-Global Asset Mgmt.
Stephen G. Haggerty, Head-Real Estate
Thomas J. Pritzker, Chmn.
Rakesh Sarna, COO-Int'l Oper.

Phone: 312-750-1234 **Fax:** 312-750-8550
Toll-Free:
Address: 71 S. Wacker Dr., 12th Fl., Chicago, IL 60606 US

GROWTH PLANS/SPECIAL FEATURES:

Hyatt Hotels Corporation (Hyatt) owns and operates full-service luxury hotels. With its subsidiaries, Hyatt has approximately 424 resorts and hotels across 45 countries. Its best known brand, Hyatt Regency, caters mainly to corporate travel clients. Grand Hyatt hotels cater to leisure and business travelers and include accommodations for banquets and conferences. Hyatt Resorts often feature professional, PGA golf courses; adventure travel opportunities, such as scuba diving, biking, hot air balloon trips or horseback riding; Hyatt Pure spas; and activities for kids and families. Hyatt Summerfield Suites, an all-suites hotel concept designed to feel more like home, offers 32-inch HDTVs, a full kitchen and complementary shopping service for its outdoor BBQ-pits. Recently introduced Hyatt Place hotels feature high-tech amenities such as 42-inch HDTVs in every room, free Wi-Fi Internet access and a 24-hour, touch-screen room service ordering system. Park Hyatt hotels are smaller, full-service luxury hotels featuring world class art and restaurants in a few of the world's most visited cities. Andaz, the firm's newest brand, is a brand of boutique-style hotels that feature restaurants and bars aimed at local clientele as well as single travelers. Hyatt Vacation Club offers vacation ownership and vacation rental opportunities, offering members timeshare or points-based resort vacation opportunities. Hyatt hotel services include Hyatt Gold Passport, a frequent-traveler rewards program; and some properties feature casinos. Hyatt's newest locations include Curacao golf Resort, Spa and Marina; Hyatt Place in San Antonio; Hyatt Place in Madison, Wisconsin; Hyatt Miami at the Blue; Andaz San Diego; Andaz Manhattan; Hyatt Regency Clearwater in Florida; Hyatt Regency Oubaai in South Africa; Grand Hyatt Shenzen in China; Hyatt Place Long Island; and the Grand Hyatt Macau. In 2009, Hyatt launched its initial public stock offering.

Employees of Hyatt receive complementary hotel rooms; medical, dental, vision and prescription drug coverage; tuition assistance; and life insurance.

FINANCIALS:

Sales and profits are in thousands of dollars—add 000 to get the full amount. 2009 Note: Financial information for 2009 was not available for all companies at press time.

2009 Sales: $3,332,000	2009 Profits: $-43,000	**U.S. Stock Ticker: H**
2008 Sales: $3,900,000	2008 Profits: $	**Int'l Ticker:** Int'l Exchange:
2007 Sales: $3,750,000	2007 Profits: $	Employees: 125,000
2006 Sales: $3,500,000	2006 Profits: $	Fiscal Year Ends: 1/31
2005 Sales: $7,266,000	2005 Profits: $	Parent Company:

SALARIES/BENEFITS:

Pension Plan:	ESOP Stock Plan:	Profit Sharing:	Top Exec. Salary: $979,167	Bonus: $983,000
Savings Plan: Y	Stock Purch. Plan:		Second Exec. Salary: $581,000	Bonus: $370,000

OTHER THOUGHTS:

Apparent Women Officers or Directors: 2
Hot Spot for Advancement for Women/Minorities: Y

LOCATIONS: ("Y" = Yes)

West:	Southwest:	Midwest:	Southeast:	Northeast:	International:
Y	Y	Y	Y	Y	Y

HYPO REAL ESTATE HOLDING AG (HYPO BANK)

www.hyporealestate.com

Industry Group Code: 5311 **Ranks within this company's industry group:** Sales: 28 Profits: 13

Properties:		Financial Services:		Construction/Development:		Investments:		Specialty Services:		Brokerage:	
Apartments:		Mortgages:	Y	Commercial Construction:		REIT:		Property Management:		Commercial Sales:	
Malls/Shopping:		Title Insurance:		Residential Construction:				Online Services:		Residential Sales:	
Offices:		Property Insurance:		Land Development:				Software/IT:		Specialty:	
Hotels/Motels:				Support Services:				Consulting:			
Industrial/Warehouses:				Design/Engineering:							
Other:											

TYPES OF BUSINESS:

Commercial Real Estate Financing
Mortgages
Asset Management

BRANDS/DIVISIONS/AFFILIATES:

Deutsche Pfandbriefbank AG
DEPFA Bank plc
Flint Nominees Ltd.
Hypo Real Estate Capital Corp.
Hypo Real Estate Capital Japan Corporation
Hypo Real Estate Transactions S.A.S.
Hypo Real Estate Capital India Corp. Private Ltd.
Hypo Pfandbrief Bank International S.A.

CONTACTS:

Note: Officers with more than one job title may be intentionally listed here more than once.

Manuela Better, Interim CEO
Frank Krings, COO
Alexander Freiherr von Uslar-Gleichen, CFO
Kai Wilhelm Franzmeyer, Treas.
Bernhard Scholz, Head-Real Estate Finance
Bernd Thiemann, Chmn.

Phone: 49-89-2880-0	**Fax:** 49-89-2880-10319
Toll-Free:	
Address: Freisinger St. 5, Unterschleissheim, D-85716 Germany	

GROWTH PLANS/SPECIAL FEATURES:

Hypo Real Estate Holding AG (Hypo Bank) is a financial holding company with interests in real estate and related areas such as financing, consulting, brokering and other services. It does not have any direct banking operations. The firm's businesses include credit and financial service institutions, Deutsche Pfandbriefbank AG (Munich) and DEPFA Bank Plc (Dublin). Deutsche Pfandbriefbank AG, headquartered in Munich, Germany, was formed by the 2009 merger of Hypo Real Estate Bank and DEPFA Deutsche Pfandbriefbank AG. Subsidiaries of Deutsche Pfandbriefbank include Flint Nominees Ltd. in London; Hypo Real Estate Capital Corp. in New York; Hypo Real Estate Capital Japan Corporation, based in Tokyo; Hypo Real Estate Transactions S.A.S., with headquarters in Paris; Mumbai-based Hypo Real Estate Capital India Corp. Private Ltd.; and Hypo Real Estate Capital Singapore Corp. Private Ltd. DEPFA Bank plc, headquartered in Dublin, is the parent of Hypo Pfandbrief Bank International S.A. of Luxembourg; DEPFA ACS Bank in Dublin; and Hypo Public Finance Bank Dublin. Both Deutsche Pfandbriefbank AG and DEPFA bank plc are currently restructuring following the firm's June 2009 takeover by the German Financial Markets Stabilization Fund, known as SoFFin. As part of the restructuring plan, the banks will become specialist institutions focused on real estate and public finance and will take on a more regional approach, concentrating its activities primarily in Germany and Europe. Also in 2009, the group moved its headquarters to Unterschliessheim from Munich.

FINANCIALS:

Sales and profits are in thousands of dollars—add 000 to get the full amount. 2009 Note: Financial information for 2009 was not available for all companies at press time.

2009 Sales: $	2009 Profits: $	**U.S. Stock Ticker:**
2008 Sales: $309,400	2008 Profits: $594,100	**Int'l Ticker: HRXG.DE** Int'l Exchange: Frankfurt-Euronext
2007 Sales: $376,000	2007 Profits: $722,100	Employees: 2,000
2006 Sales: $300,200	2006 Profits: $856,400	Fiscal Year Ends: 12/31
2005 Sales: $270,200	2005 Profits: $600,400	Parent Company:

SALARIES/BENEFITS:

Pension Plan:	ESOP Stock Plan:	Profit Sharing:	Top Exec. Salary: $	Bonus: $
Savings Plan:	Stock Purch. Plan:		Second Exec. Salary: $	Bonus: $

OTHER THOUGHTS:

Apparent Women Officers or Directors: 1
Hot Spot for Advancement for Women/Minorities:

LOCATIONS: ("Y" = Yes)

West:	Southwest:	Midwest:	Southeast:	Northeast:	International:
				Y	Y

HYSAN DEVELOPMENT CO LTD

www.hysan.com.hk

Industry Group Code: 5311 **Ranks within this company's industry group:** Sales: 32 Profits: 16

Properties:		Financial Services:		Construction/Development:		Investments:		Specialty Services:		Brokerage:	
Apartments:	Y	Mortgages:		Commercial Construction:		REIT:		Property Management:	Y	Commercial Sales:	
Malls/Shopping:	Y	Title Insurance:		Residential Construction:				Online Services:		Residential Sales:	
Offices:	Y	Property Insurance:		Land Development:	Y			Software/IT:		Specialty:	
Hotels/Motels:				Support Services:				Consulting:			
Industrial/Warehouses:				Design/Engineering:							
Other:	Y										

TYPES OF BUSINESS:

Real Estate Development, Management & Investment
Apartments
Shopping Centers
Office Buildings
Car Parks

BRANDS/DIVISIONS/AFFILIATES:

AIA Plaza
Lee Gardens (The)
Leighton Centre
Sunning Plaza
Lee Theatre Plaza
Bamboo Grove
Causeway Bay
Lee Gardens Two

CONTACTS: *Note: Officers with more than one job title may be intentionally listed here more than once.*

Gerry Lui Fai Yim, CEO
Cissy Ching Sze Chan, Dir.-Mktg. & Retail Portfolio
Roger Shu Yan Hao, Head-IT
Wendy Wen Yee Yung, Corp. Sec./Exec. Dir.
Mark Tung, Head-Corp. Comm.
Roger Shu Yan Hao, Controller
Lai Kiu Chan, Dir.-Design & Project Affairs
Jimmy Yiu Cho Mak, Gen. Mgr.-Property Svcs.
David Akers-Jones, Chmn.

Phone: 852-2895-5777	**Fax:** 852-2577-5153
Toll-Free:	
Address: 33 Hysan Ave., 49th Fl., The Lee Gardens, Hong Kong, China	

GROWTH PLANS/SPECIAL FEATURES:

Hysan Development Co., Ltd. is a Hong Kong property development and investment firm that derives revenues by leasing space to commercial and residential tenants. Its investment portfolio totals approximately 4 million square feet of space, located primarily in the Causeway Bay district of Hong Kong. In addition, Hysan owns and manages about 1,200 carparks. The firm's commercial properties encompass office and retail space Most of the firm's commercial properties combine office and retail within a single building, these holdings include: AIA Plaza (25 floors); The Lee Gardens (53 floors); Lee Gardens Two (34 floors); Leighton Centre (28 floors); One Hysan Avenue (26 floors); Sunning Plaza (30 floors); and 111 Leighton Road (24 floors). The firm also owns Lee Theatre Plaza, a shopping and dining complex. Hysan's residential holdings encompass the 345-unit residential complex Bamboo Grove, which includes a club house and sports facilities; and the 59-unit Sunning Court. The firm's development investments consist of a 24.7% interest in The Grand Gateway, a mixed-use commercial, dining, office and residential complex in Shanghai. Additionally, the company provides property management services, based on its proprietary model, Service-Scan, and through its Satisfaction Management System, aims to monitor tenant satisfaction and respond accordingly to keep occupancy rates high.

FINANCIALS: **Sales and profits are in thousands of dollars—add 000 to get the full amount. 2009 Note: Financial information for 2009 was not available for all companies at press time.**

2009 Sales: $216,400	2009 Profits: $349,850	**U.S. Stock Ticker: HYSNY**
2008 Sales: $212,900	2008 Profits: $207,200	**Int'l Ticker: 0014** Int'l Exchange: Hong Kong-HKEX
2007 Sales: $177,800	2007 Profits: $513,400	Employees: 488
2006 Sales: $164,900	2006 Profits: $402,800	Fiscal Year Ends: 12/31
2005 Sales: $162,500	2005 Profits: $535,700	Parent Company:

SALARIES/BENEFITS:

Pension Plan:	ESOP Stock Plan:	Profit Sharing:	Top Exec. Salary: $	Bonus: $
Savings Plan:	Stock Purch. Plan:		Second Exec. Salary: $	Bonus: $

OTHER THOUGHTS:

Apparent Women Officers or Directors: 3
Hot Spot for Advancement for Women/Minorities: Y

LOCATIONS: ("Y" = Yes)

West:	Southwest:	Midwest:	Southeast:	Northeast:	International:
					Y

HYUNDAI ELEVATOR CO LTD

www.hyundaielevator.co.kr

Industry Group Code: 333 **Ranks within this company's industry group:** Sales: Profits:

Properties:		Financial Services:		Construction/Development:		Investments:		Specialty Services:		Brokerage:	
Apartments:		Mortgages:		Commercial Construction:		REIT:		Property Management:		Commercial Sales:	
Malls/Shopping:		Title Insurance:		Residential Construction:				Online Services:		Residential Sales:	
Offices:		Property Insurance:		Land Development:				Software/IT:		Specialty:	
Hotels/Motels:				Support Services:	Y			Consulting:			
Industrial/Warehouses:				Design/Engineering:	Y						
Other:											

TYPES OF BUSINESS:

Elevator Manufacture & Design
Escalator Manufacture & Design
Moving Walk Manufacture & Design
Material Handling System Manufacture & Design
Platform Screen Door Manufacture & Design
Auto Parking System Manufacture & Design

BRANDS/DIVISIONS/AFFILIATES:

Hyundai Corporation
TIME & SPACE Elevators
PASSENGER Elevators
LUXEN Elevators
yzer Elevators
Millenium Escalators
Modular Escalators
H-Series Escalators

CONTACTS:

Note: Officers with more than one job title may be intentionally listed here more than once.

Jin Cheol Song, CEO
Jin Cheol Song, Pres.
Hong Hwan Ahn, VP
Gi Ryong Suhk, Managing Dir.
Hyun Jeong-eun, Chmn.

Phone: 82-2-3670-0665 **Fax:** 82-2-3672-8763
Toll-Free:
Address: San 136-1, Ami-ri Boobal-eup, Ichon-si, Gyeonggi-do, 467-734 Korea

GROWTH PLANS/SPECIAL FEATURES:

Hyundai Elevator Co., Ltd., an affiliate of the Hyundai Business Group, is a designer and manufacturer of vertical and horizontal transportation systems, including elevators, escalators, moving walkways, material handling systems, platform screen doors and auto parking systems. The company provides installation and service for the majority of its products. Hyundai Elevator manufactures passenger, observation, hospital bed, automobile, freight and marine elevators, and modernizes existing outdated elevators. Passenger elevators, sold under the TIME & SPACE, PASSENGER, LUXEN and yzer brands, comprise high-speed traction elevators for heavy traffic high-rise commercial buildings and medium-speed traction elevators for residential or mid-rise commercial buildings. Observation elevators, with a glass wall and decorative casing visible from the building's exterior, are designed to provide an aesthetic architectural detail to hotels, shopping centers, office buildings, banks, hospitals and observation towers. Hyundai Elevator's hospital bed elevators are designed to accommodate wheelchairs and hospital beds. The firm's automobile elevators transport automobiles from one floor to another in parking garages. Its freight elevators include designs for lightweight cargoes as well as forklifts and heavier loads. Hyundai Elevator's marine elevators feature safety switches, emergency stop devices, alarms for rolling or pitching, fireproof landing doors and fire, carbon dioxide and halon alarms to warn against entering the engine room area in the eventuality of a fire or gas leak. The firm sells escalators under such brands as Millennium, which feature microprocessor controls and an ergonomic design; Modular, designed for heavy-duty use; and H-Series, designed for installation in subway stations, sports complexes, conference halls and airports. Its moving walkways include horizontal, 12-degree inclined and combination designs. Material handling systems include stacker cranes, automated guided vehicles and robotic transfer vehicles. Hyundai Elevator's platform screen doors, designed to separate subway and light rail transit platforms from railways, include hermetic, semi-hermetic and handrail options.

FINANCIALS:

Sales and profits are in thousands of dollars—add 000 to get the full amount. 2009 Note: Financial information for 2009 was not available for all companies at press time.

2009 Sales: $ | 2009 Profits: $
2008 Sales: $ | 2008 Profits: $
2007 Sales: $ | 2007 Profits: $
2006 Sales: $ | 2006 Profits: $
2005 Sales: $ | 2005 Profits: $

U.S. Stock Ticker:
Int'l Ticker: 017800 Int'l Exchange: Seoul-KRX
Employees:
Fiscal Year Ends:
Parent Company:

SALARIES/BENEFITS:

Pension Plan: ESOP Stock Plan: Profit Sharing: Top Exec. Salary: $ Bonus: $
Savings Plan: Stock Purch. Plan: Second Exec. Salary: $ Bonus: $

OTHER THOUGHTS:

Apparent Women Officers or Directors: 1
Hot Spot for Advancement for Women/Minorities:

LOCATIONS: ("Y" = Yes)

West:	Southwest:	Midwest:	Southeast:	Northeast:	International:
Y					Y

HYUNDAI ENGINEERING & CONSTRUCTION COMPANY LTD

www.hdec.co.kr

Industry Group Code: 237 **Ranks within this company's industry group:** Sales: 19 Profits: 12

Properties:		Financial Services:		Construction/Development:		Investments:		Specialty Services:		Brokerage:	
Apartments:		Mortgages:		Commercial Construction:	Y	REIT:		Property Management:		Commercial Sales:	
Malls/Shopping:		Title Insurance:		Residential Construction:	Y			Online Services:		Residential Sales:	
Offices:		Property Insurance:		Land Development:	Y			Software/IT:		Specialty:	
Hotels/Motels:				Support Services:				Consulting:			
Industrial/Warehouses:				Design/Engineering:							
Other:											

TYPES OF BUSINESS:

Construction, Heavy & Civil Engineering
Power Plant Construction
Highway & Bridge Construction
Residential Construction
Commercial Construction

BRANDS/DIVISIONS/AFFILIATES:

Hillstate
Hyundai Engineering Co., Ltd.
Hyperion

GROWTH PLANS/SPECIAL FEATURES:

Hyundai Engineering & Construction Company Ltd. (also known as HDEC) is an international construction company based in South Korea. HDEC has expertise in a variety of structures, such as civil works, highways and bridges, housing, shipyards, dams, power plants (including nuclear power), airports, stadiums, hotels and retail complexes. The firm has offices in the Pacific Rim, the Middle East, Africa, the U.K. and the U.S. HDEC is organized into nine divisions: civil & environment division; division of building works; plant division; power and energy division; investment & business development division; domestic business division; overseas business division; and management & corporate business division. Subsidiaries of the company include Hyundai Engineering Co., Ltd.; Hillstate, a construction company; and Hyperion, an upscale apartment builder. In October 2009, HDEC sold its stake in SeoulBeltway Corp.

CONTACTS: *Note: Officers with more than one job title may be intentionally listed here more than once.*

Joong-Kyum Kim, CEO
Won-Bok Kim, Co-COO
Joong-Kyum Kim, Pres.
Won-Bok Kim, Head-Power & Energy
Jong-Ho Kim, Co-COO/Head-Plant
Seung Ryeol Lee, VP
Seung Gyu Ahn, VP
Lee Ji-Song, Chmn.

Phone: 82-2-746-1114	**Fax:** 82-2-743-8963
Toll-Free:	
Address: 140-2, Kye-dong, Chongro-ku, Seoul, Korea	

FINANCIALS: **Sales and profits are in thousands of dollars—add 000 to get the full amount. 2009 Note: Financial information for 2009 was not available for all companies at press time.**

2009 Sales: $9,309,980	2009 Profits: $408,040	**U.S. Stock Ticker:**
2008 Sales: $5,782,184	2008 Profits: $296,997	**Int'l Ticker: 000720** Int'l Exchange: Seoul-KRX
2007 Sales: $4,492,324	2007 Profits: $220,584	Employees:
2006 Sales: $5,410,300	2006 Profits: $	Fiscal Year Ends:
2005 Sales: $4,152,000	2005 Profits: $	Parent Company:

SALARIES/BENEFITS:

Pension Plan:	ESOP Stock Plan:	Profit Sharing:	Top Exec. Salary: $	Bonus: $
Savings Plan:	Stock Purch. Plan:		Second Exec. Salary: $	Bonus: $

OTHER THOUGHTS:

Apparent Women Officers or Directors:
Hot Spot for Advancement for Women/Minorities:

LOCATIONS: ("Y" = Yes)

West:	Southwest:	Midwest:	Southeast:	Northeast:	International:
				Y	Y

ICAHN ENTERPRISES LP

www.icahnenterprises.com

Industry Group Code: 5311 **Ranks within this company's industry group:** Sales: 3 Profits: 35

Properties:		Financial Services:		Construction/Development:		Investments:		Specialty Services:		Brokerage:	
Apartments:	Y	Mortgages:	Y	Commercial Construction:		REIT:		Property Management:	Y	Commercial Sales:	
Malls/Shopping:	Y	Title Insurance:		Residential Construction:	Y			Online Services:		Residential Sales:	
Offices:	Y	Property Insurance:	Y	Land Development:	Y			Software/IT:		Specialty:	
Hotels/Motels:	Y			Support Services:				Consulting:			
Industrial/Warehouses:	Y			Design/Engineering:							
Other:	Y										

TYPES OF BUSINESS:

Real Estate Operations
Property Leasing, Retail & Corporate
Casinos, Hotels & Resorts
Residential Development
Home Furnishings
Automotive Parts & Components
Debt & Equity Investments
Railcar Manufacturing & Servicing

BRANDS/DIVISIONS/AFFILIATES:

American Real Estate Partners
WestPoint International, Inc.
PSC Metals, Inc.
Federal-Mogul Corporation
New Seabury Resort
American Railcar Industries, Inc.
Viskase Companies, Inc.

CONTACTS:

Note: Officers with more than one job title may be intentionally listed here more than once.

Keith A. Meister, CEO
Daniel A. Ninivaggi, Pres.
Dominick Ragone, CFO
John A. Piazza, Pres./CEO-WPI
Carl C. Icahn, Chmn.

Phone: 212-702-4300 **Fax:** 212-750-5841
Toll-Free: 800-255-2737
Address: 767 Fifth Ave., 47th Fl., New York, NY 10153 US

GROWTH PLANS/SPECIAL FEATURES:

Icahn Enterprises L.P., formerly American Real Estate Partners, is a holding company with businesses in several areas including real estate, investment management, metals, home fashion and automotive. In real estate, the company leases retail, office and industrial properties to corporations, and it constructs and sells residential property, including single-family homes, multiple-family complexes and residential lots. It owns and operates several resort properties near some of its residential development sites, namely, the New Seabury Resort in Massachusetts and several golf courses, athletic facilities and clubhouses in Vero Beach, Florida. Icahn's investment segment focuses on real estate development companies and mezzanine loans. The firm's metal division is operated through its subsidiary, PSC Metals, Inc., and is principally engaged in collecting, processing and selling ferrous and non-ferrous metals. Icahn conducts its home fashion operations through WestPoint International, Inc., or WPI, a manufacturer and distributor of home fashion consumer products. In the automotive sector, through subsidiary Federal-Mogul, the firm is a global supplier of vehicle technologies and products related to fuel economy, alternative energies, environment and safety systems, with customers primarily including original equipment manufacturers (OEMs) in the automotive, light commercial, heavy duty, agricultural, aerospace, marine, rail and off-road vehicle markets. In January 2010, Icahn completed its acquisition of a 54% stake in American Railcar Industries, Inc., a freight car manufacturing and servicing company. Also in January 2010, the firm acquired a 71% share of Viskase Companies, Inc., a provider of casings for hot dogs, sausages, lunch meats and other processed meat and poultry products. In February 2010, the company acquired a 7 million-square-foot building, currently under development, along with 25 acres of adjacent land, for approximately $150 million; the property was purchased from Fontainebleau Las Vegas, LLC.

FINANCIALS:

Sales and profits are in thousands of dollars—add 000 to get the full amount. 2009 Note: Financial information for 2009 was not available for all companies at press time.

2009 Sales: $7,865,000	2009 Profits: $1,195,000
2008 Sales: $5,027,000	2008 Profits: $-2,688,000
2007 Sales: $2,491,000	2007 Profits: $564,000
2006 Sales: $3,006,000	2006 Profits: $1,107,726
2005 Sales: $1,524,705	2005 Profits: $81,888

U.S. Stock Ticker: IEP
Int'l Ticker: Int'l Exchange:
Employees:
Fiscal Year Ends: 12/31
Parent Company:

SALARIES/BENEFITS:

Pension Plan: Y	ESOP Stock Plan:	Profit Sharing:	Top Exec. Salary: $1,229,743	Bonus: $972,603
Savings Plan: Y	Stock Purch. Plan:		Second Exec. Salary: $400,000	Bonus: $

OTHER THOUGHTS:

Apparent Women Officers or Directors:
Hot Spot for Advancement for Women/Minorities:

LOCATIONS: ("Y" = Yes)

West:	Southwest:	Midwest:	Southeast:	Northeast:	International:
Y	Y	Y	Y	Y	

IMPAC MORTGAGE HOLDINGS INC

www.impaccompanies.com

Industry Group Code: 531110 **Ranks within this company's industry group:** Sales: 2 Profits: 16

Properties:		Financial Services:		Construction/Development:		Investments:		Specialty Services:		Brokerage:	
Apartments:		Mortgages:	Y	Commercial Construction:		REIT:	Y	Property Management:		Commercial Sales:	
Malls/Shopping:		Title Insurance:		Residential Construction:				Online Services:		Residential Sales:	
Offices:		Property Insurance:		Land Development:				Software/IT:		Specialty:	
Hotels/Motels:				Support Services:				Consulting:			
Industrial/Warehouses:				Design/Engineering:							
Other:											

TYPES OF BUSINESS:

Residential Mortgages
Real Estate Investment Trust

BRANDS/DIVISIONS/AFFILIATES:

IMH Assets Corp.
Impac Funding Corporation
Impac Secured Assets Corp.
Impac Warehouse Lending Group Inc.
Impac Commercial Capital Corporation

CONTACTS: *Note: Officers with more than one job title may be intentionally listed here more than once.*

Joseph R. Tomkinson, CEO
William S. Ashmore, Pres.
Todd R. Taylor, CFO/Sr. VP
Sheralee Urbano, VP-Human Resources
Ronald M. Morrison, General Counsel/Exec. VP/Sec.
Joseph R. Tomkinson, Chmn.

Phone: 949-475-3600	**Fax:**
Toll-Free: 800-597-4101	
Address: 19500 Jamboree Rd., Irvine, CA 92612 US	

GROWTH PLANS/SPECIAL FEATURES:

Impac Mortgage Holdings, Inc. (IMH) is a mortgage real estate investment trust. The company is a nationwide acquirer, originator, seller and investor of non-conforming Alt-A residential mortgages, and to a lesser extent, small-balance, commercial mortgages and multi-family. The company's focus is long-term investment operations conducted by IMH and IMH Assets Corp. (IMH Assets). The long-term investment operations primarily invests in, and holds, adjustable rate and, to a lesser extent, fixed rate Alt-A mortgages and commercial mortgages that were acquired and originated by the, newly discontinued, mortgage and commercial operations. Alt-A mortgages are primarily first lien mortgages made to borrowers whose credit is generally within typical Fannie Mae and Freddie Mac guidelines, but have loan characteristics that make them non-conforming under those guidelines. The long-term investment operations also invested in, and holds, commercial mortgages that were primarily adjustable rate mortgages with initial fixed interest rate periods of two, three, five, seven and 10 years that subsequently converted to adjustable rate mortgages, or hybrid ARMs. The firm laid off roughly 90% of its work force in 2008 following the subprime mortgage crisis.

FINANCIALS: **Sales and profits are in thousands of dollars—add 000 to get the full amount. 2009 Note: Financial information for 2009 was not available for all companies at press time.**

2009 Sales: $1,780,923	2009 Profits: $10,837	**U.S. Stock Ticker: IMH**
2008 Sales: $1,476,972	2008 Profits: $-44,723	**Int'l Ticker:** Int'l Exchange:
2007 Sales: $1,224,821	2007 Profits: $-2,047,090	Employees: 426
2006 Sales: $1,134,002	2006 Profits: $-75,273	Fiscal Year Ends: 12/31
2005 Sales: $1,472,884	2005 Profits: $270,258	Parent Company:

SALARIES/BENEFITS:

Pension Plan:	ESOP Stock Plan:	Profit Sharing:	Top Exec. Salary: $600,000	Bonus: $
Savings Plan:	Stock Purch. Plan:		Second Exec. Salary: $500,001	Bonus: $

OTHER THOUGHTS:

Apparent Women Officers or Directors:
Hot Spot for Advancement for Women/Minorities:

LOCATIONS: ("Y" = Yes)

West:	Southwest:	Midwest:	Southeast:	Northeast:	International:
Y	Y	Y	Y	Y	

IMPREGILO SPA

www.impregilo.it

Industry Group Code: 237 **Ranks within this company's industry group:** Sales: 23 Profits: 15

Properties:		Financial Services:		Construction/Development:		Investments:		Specialty Services:		Brokerage:	
Apartments:		Mortgages:		Commercial Construction:	Y	REIT:		Property Management:		Commercial Sales:	
Malls/Shopping:		Title Insurance:		Residential Construction:				Online Services:		Residential Sales:	
Offices:		Property Insurance:		Land Development:				Software/IT:		Specialty:	
Hotels/Motels:				Support Services:				Consulting:			
Industrial/Warehouses:				Design/Engineering:	Y						
Other:											

TYPES OF BUSINESS:

Heavy Construction
Civil Engineering
Environmental Engineering
Infrastructure Management
Airport Operations

BRANDS/DIVISIONS/AFFILIATES:

Fisia Italimpianti
Fisia Babcock
IGLI SpA

CONTACTS:

Note: Officers with more than one job title may be intentionally listed here more than once.

Alberto Rubegni, CEO
Massimo Ponzellini, Chmn.

Phone: 39-02-244-22111	**Fax:** 39-02-244-22293
Toll-Free:	
Address: Viale Italia 1, Sesto San Giovanni, Milan, 20099 Italy	

GROWTH PLANS/SPECIAL FEATURES:

Impregilo S.p.A., 29%-owned by IGLI S.p.A., is a leading Italian civil engineering and construction company with over a century of experience and operations in approximately 30 countries, including the U.S. The Impregilo group is divided into three primary business segments: infrastructures, engineering and plant construction and concessions. The infrastructures unit is responsible for public-sector projects such as dams, hydroelectric plants, roads, bridges, airports, underground works and high-capacity rail projects. The engineering and plant construction segment supplies technical assistance for desalinization, water treatment, solid waste power plant facilities and remediation of contaminated areas on land and sea. It operates through Fisia Italimpianti and Fisia Babcock (Germany) and furnishes a laboratory and research center that provides backup for the segment's operations. The concessions unit manages motorways, airports, water distribution and treatment and renewable energy power production facilities. Impregilo group has had construction projects in Iceland (Karahnjukar), the Dominican Republic (Guaigui), Venezuela (Tocoma) and Ecuador (Mazar). It is currently working on the Gotthard Base Tunnel, a railway tunnel in Switzerland, expected to be completed in 2015, and the Strait of Messina Bridge project, a suspension bridge between Sicily and Southern mainland Italy, expected to be completed in 2016.

FINANCIALS:

Sales and profits are in thousands of dollars—add 000 to get the full amount. 2009 Note: Financial information for 2009 was not available for all companies at press time.

2009 Sales: $3,503,760	2009 Profits: $104,740	**U.S. Stock Ticker: IPG**
2008 Sales: $3,991,960	2008 Profits: $226,220	**Int'l Ticker: IPG** Int'l Exchange: Milan-BI
2007 Sales: $3,770,300	2007 Profits: $60,700	Employees:
2006 Sales: $3,734,700	2006 Profits: $210,800	Fiscal Year Ends: 12/31
2005 Sales: $3,114,199	2005 Profits: $-456,544	Parent Company:

SALARIES/BENEFITS:

Pension Plan:	ESOP Stock Plan:	Profit Sharing:	Top Exec. Salary: $	Bonus: $
Savings Plan:	Stock Purch. Plan:		Second Exec. Salary: $	Bonus: $

OTHER THOUGHTS:

Apparent Women Officers or Directors: 1
Hot Spot for Advancement for Women/Minorities:

LOCATIONS: ("Y" = Yes)

West:	Southwest:	Midwest:	Southeast:	Northeast:	International:
					Y

INDIAN HOTEL COMPANY LIMITED (THE)

www.tajhotels.com

Industry Group Code: 721110 **Ranks within this company's industry group:** Sales: Profits:

Properties:		Financial Services:		Construction/Development:		Investments:		Specialty Services:		Brokerage:	
Apartments:		Mortgages:		Commercial Construction:		REIT:		Property Management:	Y	Commercial Sales:	
Malls/Shopping:		Title Insurance:		Residential Construction:				Online Services:		Residential Sales:	
Offices:		Property Insurance:		Land Development:				Software/IT:		Specialty:	
Hotels/Motels:	Y			Support Services:				Consulting:			
Industrial/Warehouses:				Design/Engineering:							
Other:											

TYPES OF BUSINESS:

Hotels
Spas
Apartments
Private Jet Rental
Air Catering
Travel Agency

BRANDS/DIVISIONS/AFFILIATES:

Indian Hotels Company Ltd. (The)
Tata Group
Taj Luxury Residences
TajAir Ltd.
Taj Sats Air Catering Ltd.
IndiTravel Private Limited

CONTACTS: *Note: Officers with more than one job title may be intentionally listed here more than once.*

Raymond N. Bickson, CEO/Managing Dir.
Rajiv Gujral, COO/Sr. VP-Mergers, Acquisitions & Dev.
Anil P. Goel, Exec. Dir.-Finance
Ajoy K. Misra, Sr. VP-Sales & Mktg.
H. N. Shrinivas, Sr. VP-Human Resources
Prakash V. Shukla, CIO
Prakash V. Shukla, Sr. VP-Tech.
Sanker Parameswaran, VP-Legal/Corp. Sec.
Abhijit Mukerji, Exec. Dir.-Hotel Oper.
Sumit Guha, VP-Bus. Dev. & Projects
Sarita Hegde, Dir.-Public Rel.
Veer Vijay Singh, COO-Upper Upscale Hotels
Prabhat Pani, CEO-Roots Corp. Ltd.
Jyoti Narang, COO-Luxury Div.
Ratan N. Tata, Chmn.

Phone: 91-22-6665-1000	**Fax:** 91-22-2284-6680
Toll-Free:	
Address: Oxford House, 15/17 N.F. Rd, Apollo Bunder, Mumbai, 400 001 India	

GROWTH PLANS/SPECIAL FEATURES:

The Indian Hotels Company Limited (IHCL), which, together with its subsidiaries, does business as Taj Hotels, Resorts and Palaces (Taj), is one of the world's premier operators of luxury hotels. Part of Indian conglomerate Tata Group, Taj owns more than 60 hotels in 45 locations across India and 15 additional hotels in Sri Lanka, Bhutan, Malaysia, Australia, Africa, the Middle East, the U.S. and the U.K. IHCL operates hotels in the value, mid-market, premium and luxury segments. The firm's hotel brands include Taj, a chain of luxury full-service resorts, hotels and palaces include historic properties, modern business-oriented hotels, beach resorts and safari lodges; Taj Exotica, a resort and spa brand; Taj Safaris, ecotourism lodges in the Indian jungle; The Gateway Hotel, a mid to upscale full-service hotel and resort brand; and Ginger, a line of economy hotels. Taj offers a variety of services through Jiva Spas including yoga, meditation, Indian healing ceremonies and other treatments. Besides hotels, IHCL offers two eight-seat Falcon 2000 private luxury jets through subsidiary TajAir Ltd., and catering services for over 26 domestic and international airlines through Taj Sats Air Catering Ltd. Subsidiary Taj Luxury Residences offers apartments in three locations, staffed with personal butlers, a round-the-clock concierge and 24-hour-a-day babysitting service. Finally, IndiTravel Private Limited offers travel services from ticketing to car rentals and passport assistance. Significant developments in recent years have included the signing of a management contracts at Palm Island, Jumeirah in Dubai; the Saraya Islands in Ras Al Khaimah; Aldar Group in Abu Dhabi; Langkawi in Malaysia; and Thimpu in Bhutan. In March 2010, Taj Cape Town, a luxury hotel in Cape Town, South Africa and a joint venture between Indian Hotels Company Limited and Euro Cape, opened for business.

FINANCIALS: **Sales and profits are in thousands of dollars—add 000 to get the full amount. 2009 Note: Financial information for 2009 was not available for all companies at press time.**

2009 Sales: $	2009 Profits: $	**U.S. Stock Ticker: Subsidiary**
2008 Sales: $	2008 Profits: $	**Int'l Ticker:** Int'l Exchange:
2007 Sales: $	2007 Profits: $	Employees:
2006 Sales: $	2006 Profits: $	Fiscal Year Ends: 3/31
2005 Sales: $	2005 Profits: $	Parent Company: TATA GROUP

SALARIES/BENEFITS:

Pension Plan:	ESOP Stock Plan:	Profit Sharing:	Top Exec. Salary: $	Bonus: $
Savings Plan:	Stock Purch. Plan:		Second Exec. Salary: $	Bonus: $

OTHER THOUGHTS:

Apparent Women Officers or Directors: 1
Hot Spot for Advancement for Women/Minorities: Y

LOCATIONS: ("Y" = Yes)

West:	Southwest:	Midwest:	Southeast:	Northeast:	International:
Y				Y	Y

INDUSTRIAL DEVELOPMENTS INTERNATIONAL INC www.idi.com

Industry Group Code: 5311 **Ranks within this company's industry group:** Sales: Profits:

Properties:		Financial Services:		Construction/Development:		Investments:		Specialty Services:		Brokerage:	
Apartments:		Mortgages:		Commercial Construction:	Y	REIT:		Property Management:	Y	Commercial Sales:	
Malls/Shopping:		Title Insurance:		Residential Construction:				Online Services:		Residential Sales:	
Offices:		Property Insurance:		Land Development:	Y			Software/IT:		Specialty:	
Hotels/Motels:				Support Services:				Consulting:			
Industrial/Warehouses:	Y			Design/Engineering:							
Other:											

TYPES OF BUSINESS:

Real Estate Development
Industrial Business Parks
Warehouses
Facility Management & Leasing
Construction Management Services

BRANDS/DIVISIONS/AFFILIATES:

IDI Investment Management

CONTACTS:

Note: Officers with more than one job title may be intentionally listed here more than once.

Tim Gunter, CEO
David Birdwell, COO/Exec. VP
Tim Gunter, Pres.
Linda Booker, CFO/Sr. VP
Rita Skaggs, VP-Mktg.
Debbie Kvietkus, Dir.-Human Resources
Matt O'Sullivan, Chief Dev. Officer/Exec. VP
Rita Skaggs, VP-Comm.
Greg Ryan, Sr. VP-Investments/Dir.-Acquisitions
J. Bryan Blasingame, Jr., Sr. VP-Investments/Dir.-Dispositions
Brian Mee, Sr. VP-Strategic Dev. Svcs.
Paul Philips, Sr. VP-Investment Mgmt.

Phone: 404-479-4000	**Fax:** 404-479-4162
Toll-Free:	
Address: 1100 Peachtree St., Ste. 1100, Atlanta, GA 30309 US	

GROWTH PLANS/SPECIAL FEATURES:

Industrial Developments International, Inc. (IDI), founded in 1989, is a national, privately held, full-service industrial real estate developer that provides development, investment management, and property management and leasing services to tenants with distribution, warehouse and light manufacturing needs. Since its inception, the firm has acquired and developed over 134 million square feet of industrial space in 63 business parks in the U.S., Canada and Mexico. The company manages a portfolio of about 56 million square feet. IDI operates through eight development offices in Georgia, Illinois, Ohio, Texas, Florida, California, Tennessee and Pennsylvania. The company divides its operations among three business groups: the development group, the investment management group and the property management group. The firm's development group includes its build-to-suit services group, which offers comprehensive development services for single properties and multiple-market rollouts. Its project management services include site selection, due diligence, LEED/sustainable design consulting, permitting/incentive coordination, construction management and project financing. The investment management group is a leading buyer, seller, operating partner and investment advisor focusing on industrial real estate assets. This group includes IDI's Acquisitions division, which actively seeks to purchase warehouse and distribution facilities in the U.S. and Canada; and its Dispositions division, which directly markets and sells buildings under IDI development, as well as jointly owned buildings. The property management group provides property management, leasing, building service engineer programs and tenant-improvement construction management services to IDI and third parties, as well as leasing services for third-party owners of IDI-managed properties. In January 2009, the firm launched IDI Investment Management, a fee-based management service. In February 2009, IDI acquired 125 acres in Liberty County, Georgia; and two Class-A industrial buildings in Orlando, Florida.

IDI offers its employees medical, dental and vision coverage; life insurance; short- and long-term disability insurance; flexible spending accounts; and a 401(k) plan.

FINANCIALS:

Sales and profits are in thousands of dollars—add 000 to get the full amount. 2009 Note: Financial information for 2009 was not available for all companies at press time.

2009 Sales: $	2009 Profits: $	**U.S. Stock Ticker: Private**
2008 Sales: $	2008 Profits: $	**Int'l Ticker:** Int'l Exchange:
2007 Sales: $262,700	2007 Profits: $	Employees:
2006 Sales: $	2006 Profits: $	Fiscal Year Ends: 12/31
2005 Sales: $	2005 Profits: $	Parent Company:

SALARIES/BENEFITS:

Pension Plan:	ESOP Stock Plan:	Profit Sharing:	Top Exec. Salary: $	Bonus: $
Savings Plan: Y	Stock Purch. Plan:		Second Exec. Salary: $	Bonus: $

OTHER THOUGHTS:

Apparent Women Officers or Directors: 3
Hot Spot for Advancement for Women/Minorities: Y

LOCATIONS: ("Y" = Yes)

West:	Southwest:	Midwest:	Southeast:	Northeast:	International:
Y	Y	Y	Y	Y	

INLAND AMERICAN REAL ESTATE TRUST INC www.inland-american.com

Industry Group Code: 531110 **Ranks within this company's industry group:** Sales: Profits:

Properties:		Financial Services:		Construction/Development:		Investments:		Specialty Services:		Brokerage:	
Apartments:	Y	Mortgages:		Commercial Construction:		REIT:	Y	Property Management:		Commercial Sales:	
Malls/Shopping:	Y	Title Insurance:		Residential Construction:				Online Services:		Residential Sales:	
Offices:	Y	Property Insurance:		Land Development:				Software/IT:		Specialty:	
Hotels/Motels:	Y			Support Services:				Consulting:			
Industrial/Warehouses:	Y			Design/Engineering:							
Other:											

TYPES OF BUSINESS:

Real Estate Investment Trust

BRANDS/DIVISIONS/AFFILIATES:

Inland Real Estate Group of Companies Inc (The)
Inland American Winston Hotels Inc
Inland American Orchard Hotels Inc
Inland American Urban Hotels Inc
Inland American Lodging Corporation
Inland American Retail Management LLC
Inland American Industrial Management LLC
Inland American Office Management LLC

CONTACTS:

Note: Officers with more than one job title may be intentionally listed here more than once.

Brenda G. Gujral, Pres.
Lori J. Foust, Principal Financial Officer/Treas.
Roberta S. Matlin, VP-Admin.
Scott W. Wilton, Corp. Sec.
Jack Potts, Principal Acct. Officer
G. Joseph Cosenza, Pres., Inland Real Estate Acquisitions, Inc.
Daniel L. Goodwin, CEO/Chmn.-The Inland Real Estate Group, Inc.
Robert D. Parks, Chmn.

Phone: 630-218-8000 **Fax:** 630-218-4957
Toll-Free: 800-826-8228
Address: 2901 Butterfield Rd., Oak Brook, IL 60523 US

GROWTH PLANS/SPECIAL FEATURES:

Inland American Real Estate Trust, Inc. is a Real Estate Investment Trust (REIT) and a member of the Inland Real Estate Group of Companies. The firm operates in five segments, divided by property types. Inland American Retail Management Llc, segment consists of 944 properties totaling approximately 42 million square feet. The Inland American Lodging Corporation segment consists of the operations of three subsidiaries, namely Inland American Winston Hotels, Inc., Inland American Orchard Hotels, Inc., and Inland American Urban Hotels, Inc. Between them, these subsidiaries own 99 hotel properties primarily operating under the Marriot and Hilton brand names, containing an approximately 15,125 rooms. The Inland American Industrial Management LLC segment owns approximately 64 properties totaling approximately 15.4 million square feet of industrial space. The Inland American Office Management LLC segment includes approximately 36 properties totaling approximately 8.4 million square feet. The firm's Inland American Apartment Management LLC segment consists of approximately 19 multi-family residential properties containing 9,481 units, as well as 11 properties currently in development. Inland American's properties are located throughout the U.S., and it generally aims to acquire multiple properties grouped around major metropolitan markets. The company typically seeks properties with existing net leases, requiring tenants to cover various operating expenses such as real estate taxes, insurance and general maintenance costs. Inland American also engages in sale-leaseback transactions, in which the firm purchases a property, and then leases it back to the seller. The company's two largest customers are SunTrust Banks, Inc., and AT&T, Inc. In 2009, the company announced $154 million in new acquisitions. The new properties consist of two shopping centers totaling 397,268 square feet and two multifamily properties.

Employees of the company are offered medical and dental insurance; a flexible savings plan for health and dependent care needs; a 401(k) plan; life and AD&D insurance; and both short and long-term disability insurance.

FINANCIALS:

Sales and profits are in thousands of dollars—add 000 to get the full amount. 2009 Note: Financial information for 2009 was not available for all companies at press time.

2009 Sales: $ 2009 Profits: $
2008 Sales: $ 2008 Profits: $
2007 Sales: $ 2007 Profits: $
2006 Sales: $ 2006 Profits: $
2005 Sales: $ 2005 Profits: $

U.S. Stock Ticker: Subsidiary
Int'l Ticker: Int'l Exchange:
Employees:
Fiscal Year Ends: 12/31
Parent Company: INLAND REAL ESTATE GROUP OF COMPANIES INC (THE)

SALARIES/BENEFITS:

Pension Plan: ESOP Stock Plan: Profit Sharing: Top Exec. Salary: $ Bonus: $
Savings Plan: Y Stock Purch. Plan: Second Exec. Salary: $ Bonus: $

OTHER THOUGHTS:

Apparent Women Officers or Directors: 2
Hot Spot for Advancement for Women/Minorities:

LOCATIONS: ("Y" = Yes)

West:	Southwest:	Midwest:	Southeast:	Northeast:	International:
	Y	Y		Y	

INLAND REAL ESTATE CORPORATION

www.inlandrealestate.com

Industry Group Code: 531120 **Ranks within this company's industry group:** Sales: 57 Profits: 44

Properties:		Financial Services:		Construction/Development:		Investments:		Specialty Services:		Brokerage:	
Apartments:	Y	Mortgages:		Commercial Construction:		REIT:	Y	Property Management:	Y	Commercial Sales:	
Malls/Shopping:	Y	Title Insurance:		Residential Construction:				Online Services:		Residential Sales:	
Offices:		Property Insurance:		Land Development:				Software/IT:		Specialty:	
Hotels/Motels:				Support Services:				Consulting:			
Industrial/Warehouses:				Design/Engineering:							
Other:											

TYPES OF BUSINESS:

Real Estate Investment Trust
Property Management
Retail Properties

BRANDS/DIVISIONS/AFFILIATES:

Inland Group of Companies Inc (The)

CONTACTS:

Note: Officers with more than one job title may be intentionally listed here more than once.

Mark E. Zalatoris, CEO
Mark E. Zalatoris, Pres.
Brett A. Brown, CFO/Sr. VP
Beth Sprecher Brooks, General Counsel/Sr. VP/Corp. Sec.
Dawn Benchelt, Dir.-Investor Rel.
Brett A. Brown, Treas.
William W. Anderson, VP-Transactions
D. Scott Carr, Pres., Property Mgmt.
Theresa B. Strino, Mgr.-Investor Svcs.
Thomas P. D'Arcy, Chmn.

Phone: 708-218-8000	**Fax:**
Toll-Free: 888-331-4732	
Address: 2901 Butterfield Rd., Oak Brook, IL 60523 US	

GROWTH PLANS/SPECIAL FEATURES:

Inland Real Estate Corporation (IRC) is a self-administered real estate investment trust (REIT) owned by the Inland Real Estate Group of Companies, Inc. The firm acquires, owns, operates and develops open-air neighborhood, community and lifestyle shopping centers and single-tenant retail properties located primarily in the Midwestern U.S. Most of IRC's properties are located within a 400-mile radius of its suburban Chicago headquarters and consist of grocery anchored, discount anchored, fashion anchored and convenience retail centers. The firm will also purchase freestanding properties leased by single credit tenants, located anywhere in the country. IRC acquires both single assets and entire portfolios. Its emphasis remains on well-tenanted, well-located properties, from 75,000 to 300,000 square feet. IRC owns approximately 144 retail properties comprised of 62 neighborhood retail centers, 27 power centers, 19 community centers, one lifestyle center and 32 single-user retail properties, with more than 14 million square feet of total real estate and approximately $1.8 billion in assets. Prominent tenants of the company include Cub Foods, a subsidiary of SUPERVALU, Inc.; Dominick's Finer Foods, a subsidiary of Safeway; Bank of America; Bally's Total Fitness; Carmax; Walt Disney World; Food 4 Less; Eckerd Drug Store; Michael's; and PetSmart. Recently, through a joint venture, the company acquired a share in four office buildings purchased from Bank of America, located in Pennsylvania, Nevada, Maryland and New Mexico. The total price of the acquisition was $152.6 million, with IRC contributing approximately $60.8 million.

Employees of the company are offered medical and dental insurance; a flexible savings plan for health and dependent care needs; a 401(k) plan; life and AD&D insurance; and both short and long-term disability insurance.

FINANCIALS:

Sales and profits are in thousands of dollars—add 000 to get the full amount. 2009 Note: Financial information for 2009 was not available for all companies at press time.

2009 Sales: $170,844	2009 Profits: $8,629
2008 Sales: $188,844	2008 Profits: $30,425
2007 Sales: $184,664	2007 Profits: $42,095
2006 Sales: $175,856	2006 Profits: $45,184
2005 Sales: $181,173	2005 Profits: $47,255

U.S. Stock Ticker: IRC
Int'l Ticker: Int'l Exchange:
Employees: 103
Fiscal Year Ends: 12/31
Parent Company: INLAND REAL ESTATE GROUP OF COMPANIES INC (THE)

SALARIES/BENEFITS:

Pension Plan:	ESOP Stock Plan:	Profit Sharing:	Top Exec. Salary: $450,000	Bonus: $70,000
Savings Plan: Y	Stock Purch. Plan:		Second Exec. Salary: $300,000	Bonus: $22,500

OTHER THOUGHTS:

Apparent Women Officers or Directors: 2
Hot Spot for Advancement for Women/Minorities:

LOCATIONS: ("Y" = Yes)

West:	Southwest:	Midwest:	Southeast:	Northeast:	International:
	Y	Y	Y		

INNKEEPERS USA TRUST

www.innkeepersusa.com

Industry Group Code: 531120 **Ranks within this company's industry group:** Sales: Profits:

Properties:		Financial Services:		Construction/Development:		Investments:		Specialty Services:		Brokerage:	
Apartments:		Mortgages:		Commercial Construction:		REIT:	Y	Property Management:		Commercial Sales:	
Malls/Shopping:		Title Insurance:		Residential Construction:				Online Services:		Residential Sales:	
Offices:		Property Insurance:		Land Development:				Software/IT:		Specialty:	
Hotels/Motels:	Y			Support Services:				Consulting:			
Industrial/Warehouses:				Design/Engineering:							
Other:											

TYPES OF BUSINESS:

Real Estate Investment Trust
Hotels
Hotel Development

BRANDS/DIVISIONS/AFFILIATES:

Island Hospitality Management

CONTACTS: *Note: Officers with more than one job title may be intentionally listed here more than once.*

Tim Walker, CEO
Tim Walker, Pres.
Dennis Craven, CFO
Mark A. Murphy, General Counsel/Sec.
Richard F. Fenton, VP-Financial Planning & Analysis
Linda K. Price, VP/Controller
Bob Martin, VP-Construction & Renovation
Jeffrey H. Fisher, Chmn.

Phone: 561-835-1800	**Fax:** 561-835-0457
Toll-Free:	
Address: 340 Royal Poinciana Way, Ste. 306, Palm Beach, FL 33480 US	

GROWTH PLANS/SPECIAL FEATURES:

Innkeepers USA Trust, a subsidiary of Apollo Investment Corp., is a real estate investment trust (REIT) that specializes in the ownership of multi-brand, upscale, extended-stay hotels in the U.S. The firm seeks to acquire hotel properties in markets with high barriers to entry and with strong underlying demand growth. Innkeepers USA owns interests in 73 hotels with an aggregate of 10,000 rooms/suites in 19 states and Washington, D.C. 72 of these hotels are managed by Island Hospitality Management. The firm's hotels operate under the following brands: Residence Inn, TownePlace Suites and Courtyard by Marriott; Sheraton; Double Tree; Embassy Suites; Hyatt Summerfield Suites; Westin; Best Western; Bulfinch Hotel; Hampton Inn; and Hilton. In addition to its acquisitions of existing hotels in the upscale and extended-stay market, Innkeepers also acquires under-performing mid-priced and full service hotels that have the potential for strategic repositioning or re-flagging to a premium franchise brand in the upscale segment. Hotels in deteriorated physical condition that could benefit from renovation and/or hotels in attractive locations are acquired and repackaged under a major brand.

FINANCIALS: **Sales and profits are in thousands of dollars—add 000 to get the full amount. 2009 Note: Financial information for 2009 was not available for all companies at press time.**

2009 Sales: $	2009 Profits: $	**U.S. Stock Ticker: Private**
2008 Sales: $	2008 Profits: $	**Int'l Ticker:** Int'l Exchange:
2007 Sales: $	2007 Profits: $	Employees:
2006 Sales: $286,713	2006 Profits: $30,487	Fiscal Year Ends: 12/31
2005 Sales: $247,181	2005 Profits: $22,659	Parent Company:

SALARIES/BENEFITS:

Pension Plan:	ESOP Stock Plan:	Profit Sharing:	Top Exec. Salary: $	Bonus: $
Savings Plan:	Stock Purch. Plan:		Second Exec. Salary: $	Bonus: $

OTHER THOUGHTS:

Apparent Women Officers or Directors: 1
Hot Spot for Advancement for Women/Minorities:

LOCATIONS: ("Y" = Yes)

West:	Southwest:	Midwest:	Southeast:	Northeast:	International:
Y	Y	Y	Y	Y	

INSITUFORM TECHNOLOGIES

www.insituform.com

Industry Group Code: 2389 **Ranks within this company's industry group:** Sales: 3 Profits: 3

Properties:		Financial Services:		Construction/Development:		Investments:		Specialty Services:		Brokerage:	
Apartments:		Mortgages:		Commercial Construction:		REIT:		Property Management:		Commercial Sales:	
Malls/Shopping:		Title Insurance:		Residential Construction:				Online Services:		Residential Sales:	
Offices:		Property Insurance:		Land Development:				Software/IT:		Specialty:	
Hotels/Motels:				Support Services:	Y			Consulting:			
Industrial/Warehouses:				Design/Engineering:	Y						
Other:											

TYPES OF BUSINESS:

Construction, Heavy & Civil Engineering
Sewer & Pipe Rehabilitation Services

BRANDS/DIVISIONS/AFFILIATES:

Insituform CIPP Process
Insituform Blue
United Pipeline Systems
Corrpro Companies, Inc.
Bayou Companies (The)
Insitu Envirotech (S.E. Asia) Pte Ltd.

CONTACTS:

Note: Officers with more than one job title may be intentionally listed here more than once.

J. Joseph Burgess, CEO
J. Joseph Burgess, Pres.
David A. Martin, CFO/VP
Holly Sharp, VP-Human Resources
David F. Morris, Chief Admin. Officer
David F. Morris, General Counsel/Corp. Sec./Sr. VP
Kenneth Young, Treas./VP
Holly Sharp, VP-Environmental, Health & Safety
Charles Voltz, Sr. VP-North American Rehabilitation
Dorwin Hawn, Sr. VP-Energy & Mining
Daniel Cowan, VP-Asia Pacific
Alfred L. Woods, Chmn.
Alex Buehler, VP-Europe

Phone: 636-530-8000	**Fax:** 636-519-8010
Toll-Free: 800-234-2992	
Address: 17988 Edison Ave., Chesterfield, MO 63005 US	

GROWTH PLANS/SPECIAL FEATURES:

Insituform Technologies is provider of proprietary technologies and pipeline rehabilitation services to the sewer, water, energy and mining infrastructure markets. Most of Insituform's installation operations are project-oriented contracts for municipal entities, concerning the maintenance of municipal sewers, commercial pipes and water mains. The company and its subsidiaries operate principally in the U.S., Canada, the Netherlands, the U.K., France, Switzerland, Chile, Spain, Poland, Mexico, Belgium, Romania and India, with sales in the U.S. representing approximately 60.8% of revenues. The firm's operations comprise the five following operating segments: North American Sewer Rehabilitation, European Sewer Rehabilitation, Asia-Pacific Sewer Rehabilitation, Water Rehabilitation and Energy and Mining. Sewer rehabilitation services include the firm's proprietary Insituform Cured-In-Place Pipe (CIPP) process, a trenchless technology allowing pipeline to be repaired without digging and major service disruptions. Insituform's CIPP process involves saturating a synthetic fiber tube with a thermosetting resin, installing the tube into a host pipe and then hardening the resin, forming a new rigid pipe-within-a-pipe. While Insituform uses a variety of trenchless technologies for sewer rehabilitation, the Insituform CIPP process contributes roughly 75% of overall company revenues. Water rehabilitation activities are focused on pipelines carrying drinking water and include the firm's Insituform Blue brand of potable water pipe restoration services. The company's subsidiaries include United Pipeline Systems, a provider of high-density polyethylene (HDPE) lining systems used for the protection of internal pipelines; Corrpro Companies, Inc., a provider of corrosion protection and pipeline maintenance services in North America; and The Bayou Companies, a provider of pipeline services to energy and infrastructure firms, primarily in the Gulf of Mexico and North America. In January 2010, the firm acquired its former Singaporean licensee, Insitu Envirotech (S.E. Asia) Pte Ltd., for $1.3 million.

Employees are offered retirement plans; a 401(k) plan; disability coverage; and life insurance.

FINANCIALS:

Sales and profits are in thousands of dollars—add 000 to get the full amount. 2009 Note: Financial information for 2009 was not available for all companies at press time.

2009 Sales: $726,866	2009 Profits: $26,171	**U.S. Stock Ticker: INSU**
2008 Sales: $536,664	2008 Profits: $21,640	**Int'l Ticker:** Int'l Exchange:
2007 Sales: $495,570	2007 Profits: $2,543	Employees: 3,000
2006 Sales: $527,419	2006 Profits: $24,678	Fiscal Year Ends: 12/31
2005 Sales: $595,282	2005 Profits: $13,160	Parent Company:

SALARIES/BENEFITS:

Pension Plan: Y	ESOP Stock Plan:	Profit Sharing:	Top Exec. Salary: $358,013	Bonus: $500,000
Savings Plan: Y	Stock Purch. Plan:		Second Exec. Salary: $325,000	Bonus: $269,481

OTHER THOUGHTS:

Apparent Women Officers or Directors: 3
Hot Spot for Advancement for Women/Minorities: Y

LOCATIONS: ("Y" = Yes)

West:	Southwest:	Midwest:	Southeast:	Northeast:	International:
Y	Y	Y	Y	Y	Y

INTEGRATED ELECTRICAL SERVICES

www.ies-co.com

Industry Group Code: 238210 **Ranks within this company's industry group:** Sales: 2 Profits: 2

Properties:		Financial Services:		Construction/Development:		Investments:		Specialty Services:		Brokerage:	
Apartments:		Mortgages:		Commercial Construction:		REIT:		Property Management:		Commercial Sales:	
Malls/Shopping:		Title Insurance:		Residential Construction:				Online Services:		Residential Sales:	
Offices:		Property Insurance:		Land Development:				Software/IT:		Specialty:	
Hotels/Motels:				Support Services:	Y			Consulting:			
Industrial/Warehouses:				Design/Engineering:	Y						
Other:											

TYPES OF BUSINESS:

Electric Contractors
Electrical & Communications Installation & Maintenance
Residential Building & Remodeling
Commercial & Industrial Renovations

BRANDS/DIVISIONS/AFFILIATES:

IES Commercial
IES Industrial
IES Residential

CONTACTS: *Note: Officers with more than one job title may be intentionally listed here more than once.*

Michael J. Caliel, CEO
Michael J. Caliel, Pres.
Terryy L. Freeman, CFO/Sr. VP
Edjuan D. Bailey, VP-Mktg.
Robert B. Callahan, Sr. VP-Human Resources
Bill Fiedler, General Counsel/Sr. VP/Corp. Sec.
Harvey Hammock, VP-Safety & Productivity
Michael J. Caliel, Acting Head-IES Commercial & Industrial
Richard Nix, VP-IES Residential
Michael J. Hall, Chmn.

Phone: 713-860-1500	**Fax:** 713-222-1214
Toll-Free: 877-437-6285	
Address: 1800 W. Loop S., Ste. 500, Houston, TX 77027 US	

GROWTH PLANS/SPECIAL FEATURES:

Integrated Electrical Services (IES) is a provider of electrical contracting services in the U.S., with 89 locations in the continental 48 states. The firm's offerings include: design of the electrical distribution systems within a building; procurement and installation of wiring; connection to power sources, end-use equipment and fixtures; and long-term contract maintenance. IES works in the commercial, industrial and residential markets and its customer base encompasses general contractors; property managers and developers; corporations; government agencies and municipalities; and homeowners. The types of projects the firm engages in include high-rise residential and office buildings; power plants; manufacturing facilities; municipal infrastructure; health care facilities; and residential developments. To complement its electrical contracting services, IES provides low voltage services, utility services and maintenance services. The company's low voltage services include design and installation of external cables for corporations, universities, data centers and switching stations for data communications companies as well as the installation of fire and security alarm systems. Its utility services consist of overhead and underground installation and maintenance of electrical and other utilities transmission and distribution networks; installation and splicing of high-voltage transmission and distribution lines; substation construction; and substation and right-of-way maintenance. Maintenance is a general service provided by IES. Commercial work generated 63% of the firm's revenue during 2009, industrial work generated 13% and residential work generated 24%.

FINANCIALS: **Sales and profits are in thousands of dollars—add 000 to get the full amount. 2009 Note: Financial information for 2009 was not available for all companies at press time.**

2009 Sales: $665,997	2009 Profits: $-11,820	**U.S. Stock Ticker: IESC**
2008 Sales: $818,287	2008 Profits: $ 187	**Int'l Ticker:** Int'l Exchange:
2007 Sales: $890,351	2007 Profits: $-4,412	Employees: 3,504
2006 Sales: $933,800	2006 Profits: $- 400	Fiscal Year Ends: 9/30
2005 Sales: $856,600	2005 Profits: $-129,600	Parent Company:

SALARIES/BENEFITS:

Pension Plan:	ESOP Stock Plan:	Profit Sharing:	Top Exec. Salary: $599,250	Bonus: $
Savings Plan: Y	Stock Purch. Plan:		Second Exec. Salary: $387,500	Bonus: $

OTHER THOUGHTS:

Apparent Women Officers or Directors:
Hot Spot for Advancement for Women/Minorities:

LOCATIONS: ("Y" = Yes)

West:	Southwest:	Midwest:	Southeast:	Northeast:	International:
Y	Y	Y	Y	Y	

INTERCONTINENTAL HOTELS GROUP PLC

www.ihgplc.com

Industry Group Code: 721110 **Ranks within this company's industry group:** Sales: 9 Profits: 4

Properties:		Financial Services:		Construction/Development:		Investments:		Specialty Services:		Brokerage:	
Apartments:		Mortgages:		Commercial Construction:		REIT:		Property Management:	Y	Commercial Sales:	
Malls/Shopping:		Title Insurance:		Residential Construction:				Online Services:		Residential Sales:	
Offices:		Property Insurance:		Land Development:				Software/IT:		Specialty:	
Hotels/Motels:	Y			Support Services:				Consulting:			
Industrial/Warehouses:				Design/Engineering:							
Other:											

TYPES OF BUSINESS:

Hotel & Motel Development & Management
Hotels

BRANDS/DIVISIONS/AFFILIATES:

InterContinental Hotels and Resorts
Crowne Plaza Hotels and Resorts
Hotel Indigo
Staybridge Suites
Holiday Inn
Holiday Inn Express
Candlewood Suites
Priority Club Rewards

CONTACTS: *Note: Officers with more than one job title may be intentionally listed here more than once.*

Andrew Cosslett, CEO
Richard Solomons, CFO/Head-Commercial Dev.
Tom Seddon, Chief Mktg. Officer/Exec. VP
Tracy Robbins, Exec. VP-Global Human Resources
Tom Conophy, CIO/Exec. VP
George Turner, General Counsel/Exec. VP/Corp. Sec.
Kate Gibson, VP-Strategy, EMEA
James R. Abrahamson, Pres., Americas
John Bamsey, COO-Middle East & Africa
Allan McEwan, Sr. VP-Finance & Dev., EMEA
William Morris, Managing Dir.-U.K. & Ireland
David Webster, Chmn.
Kirk Kinsell, Pres., EMEA

Phone: 44-1895-512-000	**Fax:** 44-1753-410-101
Toll-Free:	
Address: Broadwater Park, Denham, UB9 5HR UK	

GROWTH PLANS/SPECIAL FEATURES:

InterContinental Hotels Group plc (IHG) is an international hotel firm. The company has seven hotel brands: Holiday Inn, Holiday Inn Express, Hotel Indigo, Crowne Plaza, InterContinental, Staybridge Suites and Candlewood Suites. IHG operates in approximately 4,438 hotels (646,679 rooms) in over 100 countries and territories. IHG accommodates over 130 million stays per year. Mid-scale, full-service Holiday Inn is most prevalent in the U.S., the U.K. and China. Holiday Inn Express is a value-priced, limited-service brand primarily operated by franchisees. Hotel Indigo is a boutique hotel brand located in urban, mid-town and suburban areas that are in close proximity to restaurants, businesses and entertainment venues throughout the U.S. Crowne Plaza and InterContinental cater to business and leisure travelers in nearly 60 countries. Staybridge Suites and Candlewood Suites provide upscale and extended-stay options. IHG offers Priority Club Rewards, which provides benefits like free stays and frequent flyer miles. In 2009, IHG opened several new hotels in countries including the U.S., the U.K., South Africa, Canada, France, El Salvador, Costa Rica, Vietnam, the Dominican Republic, Thailand and Argentina. Also in 2009, the firm disposed of the InterContinental Sao Paulo for $22 million. In April 2009, the firm announced plans to open 31 hotels (7,600 rooms) in India over the coming years under the InterContinental, Holiday Inn and Crowne Plaza brands. In early 2010, IHG opened new hotels throughout the U.S. and in Denmark and United Arab Emirates.

The firm typically offers employees benefits including life, disability, medical and dental insurance; paid time off; employee discounts; a 401(k); incentive programs; and educational assistance.

FINANCIALS: **Sales and profits are in thousands of dollars—add 000 to get the full amount. 2009 Note: Financial information for 2009 was not available for all companies at press time.**

2009 Sales: $2,364,810	2009 Profits: $327,510	**U.S. Stock Ticker: IHG**
2008 Sales: $1,854,000	2008 Profits: $302,000	**Int'l Ticker: IHG** Int'l Exchange: London-LSE
2007 Sales: $1,771,000	2007 Profits: $444,000	Employees:
2006 Sales: $1,548,400	2006 Profits: $797,900	Fiscal Year Ends: 12/31
2005 Sales: $1,373,100	2005 Profits: $977,100	Parent Company:

SALARIES/BENEFITS:

Pension Plan: Y	ESOP Stock Plan:	Profit Sharing:	Top Exec. Salary: $	Bonus: $
Savings Plan: Y	Stock Purch. Plan:		Second Exec. Salary: $	Bonus: $

OTHER THOUGHTS:

Apparent Women Officers or Directors: 5
Hot Spot for Advancement for Women/Minorities: Y

LOCATIONS: ("Y" = Yes)

West:	Southwest:	Midwest:	Southeast:	Northeast:	International:
Y	Y	Y	Y	Y	Y

INTERSTATE HOTELS AND RESORTS INC

www.ihrco.com

Industry Group Code: 721110 **Ranks within this company's industry group:** Sales: 16 Profits: 24

Properties:		Financial Services:		Construction/Development:		Investments:		Specialty Services:		Brokerage:	
Apartments:		Mortgages:		Commercial Construction:	Y	REIT:		Property Management:	Y	Commercial Sales:	
Malls/Shopping:		Title Insurance:		Residential Construction:				Online Services:		Residential Sales:	
Offices:		Property Insurance:		Land Development:				Software/IT:		Specialty:	
Hotels/Motels:	Y			Support Services:	Y			Consulting:			
Industrial/Warehouses:				Design/Engineering:	Y						
Other:											

TYPES OF BUSINESS:

Hotel Management
Corporate Hotel Management
Engineering & Design Consulting
Construction Management
Procurement Services

BRANDS/DIVISIONS/AFFILIATES:

Hotel Acquisition Company LLC
Thayer Hotel Investors
Shanghai Jin Jiang International Hotels
Continental Design & Supply Company
Crowne Plaza Milwaukee Airport
TownePlace Suites Bethlehem-Easton
Hilton Garden Inn Baton Rouge Airport

CONTACTS: *Note: Officers with more than one job title may be intentionally listed here more than once.*

Thomas F. Hewitt, CEO
Bruce Riggins, CFO
George J. Brennan, Exec. VP-Mktg. & Sales
Christopher L. Bennett, General Counsel/Exec. VP
Samuel E. Knighton, Pres., Hotel Oper.
C.A. Anderson, Exec. VP-Dev. & Acquisitions
Joseph A. Klam, Exec. VP-Finance
Leslie Ng, Chief Investment Officer
Thomas J. Bardenett, Exec. VP-Oper., Crossroads
Evan A. Studer, Exec. VP-Oper., Sunstone Hotel Properties
John N. Elston Jr., Exec. VP-Sales & Mktg., Sunstone Hotel Properties
Thomas F. Hewitt, Chmn.

Phone: 703-387-3100 **Fax:** 703-543-0633
Toll-Free:
Address: 4501 N. Fairfax Dr., Arlington, VA 22203 US

GROWTH PLANS/SPECIAL FEATURES:

Interstate Hotels & Resorts, Inc. is one of the world's largest independent hotel management companies. The company is a subsidiary of Hotel Acquisition Company LLC, a joint venture between subsidiaries of Thayer Hotel Investors V-A LP, a private equity fund, and Shanghai Jin Jiang International Hotels. The firm divides its operations into three primary categories: hotel management services, hotel development services and design and construction services. Interstate's hotel management services consist of finance and accounting services, including accounting, internal audit and risk management; sales and marketing services; food and beverage services, including concept development and staff training; business intelligence services; and international platform management. Interstate manages luxury, full-service, select-service and extended-stay hospitality properties, consisting of 225 properties in 36 states, Washington, D.C., Belgium, Canada, Ireland, England, Russia, Mexico and India. The company's development services comprise hotel and resort investment, business development, financing, acquisitions, franchising, owner relations and hotel operations solutions. Finally, its design and construction services, provided through subsidiary Continental Design & Supply Company, consist of supply and equipment procurement, design management, project and construction management and engineering consulting services. The company has 13 future hotels and resorts under development. The company's brand portfolio includes Best Western; Comfort Inn; Courtyard by Marriott; Crowne Plaza; Days Inn; Doubletree; Embassy Suites; Fairfield Inn by Marriott; Hampton Inn; Hilton; Holiday Inn; Homewood Suites; Hyatt Place; Marriott; Radisson; Renaissance; Residence Inn by Marriott; Sheraton; Super 8; Travelodge; and Westin. During 2009, the firm agreed to manage its first hotels in Costa Rica, India and the U.K.; opened the Crowne Plaza Milwaukee Airport in Wisconsin and the TownePlace Suites Bethlehem/Easton in Pennsylvania; and sold the Hilton Garden Inn Baton Rouge Airport for $10.6 million. In March 2010, the company was acquired by joint venture Hotel Acquisition Company.

FINANCIALS: **Sales and profits are in thousands of dollars—add 000 to get the full amount. 2009 Note: Financial information for 2009 was not available for all companies at press time.**

2009 Sales: $	2009 Profits: $	**U.S. Stock Ticker: Joint Venture**
2008 Sales: $779,453	2008 Profits: $-18,023	**Int'l Ticker:** Int'l Exchange:
2007 Sales: $800,131	2007 Profits: $22,828	Employees: 19,000
2006 Sales: $975,165	2006 Profits: $29,779	Fiscal Year Ends: 12/31
2005 Sales: $995,411	2005 Profits: $12,877	Parent Company:

SALARIES/BENEFITS:

Pension Plan:	ESOP Stock Plan:	Profit Sharing:	Top Exec. Salary: $500,000	Bonus: $125,000
Savings Plan:	Stock Purch. Plan:		Second Exec. Salary: $374,071	Bonus: $93,518

OTHER THOUGHTS:

Apparent Women Officers or Directors:
Hot Spot for Advancement for Women/Minorities: Y

LOCATIONS: ("Y" = Yes)

West:	Southwest:	Midwest:	Southeast:	Northeast:	International:
Y	Y	Y	Y	Y	Y

INTOWN SUITES MANAGEMENT INC

www.intownsuites.com

Industry Group Code: 721110 **Ranks within this company's industry group:** Sales: Profits:

Properties:		Financial Services:	Construction/Development:	Investments:	Specialty Services:		Brokerage:
Apartments:		Mortgages:	Commercial Construction:	REIT:	Property Management:	Y	Commercial Sales:
Malls/Shopping:		Title Insurance:	Residential Construction:		Online Services:		Residential Sales:
Offices:		Property Insurance:	Land Development:		Software/IT:		Specialty:
Hotels/Motels:	Y		Support Services:		Consulting:		
Industrial/Warehouses:			Design/Engineering:				
Other:							

TYPES OF BUSINESS:

Hotels
Extended-Stay Hotels

BRANDS/DIVISIONS/AFFILIATES:

Westmont Hospitality Group

CONTACTS:

Note: Officers with more than one job title may be intentionally listed here more than once.

Scott Griffith, CEO
Dennis Cassel, CFO
Stephen Bell, Dir.-IT

Phone: 770-799-5000	**Fax:** 770-437-8190
Toll-Free: 800-553-9338	
Address: 2727 Paces Ferry Rd., Ste. 2-1200, Atlanta, GA 30339 US	

GROWTH PLANS/SPECIAL FEATURES:

Intown Suites Management, Inc. is a private corporation that develops, owns and operates budget extended-stay properties. The company does not offer reservations for less than seven days and prefers long-term commitments or apartment leases. A seven-day stay at Intown Suites is generally cheaper than renting a nightly room at a traditional hotel for a few days. Most facilities are located in predominately retail-oriented locations near shops, restaurants and movie theaters, with proximity to major metropolitan areas, spanning 130 locations in 21 states. Intown's properties typically feature 121 studio suites with full amenities, including complete kitchens, high-speed Internet, a dining area, cable TV, a full size bath, voicemail service, laundry facilities, pool areas and weekly housekeeping. Intown Suites was one of the first hotel chains in the U.S. to offer free high-speed Internet access in all of its hotel rooms. The company also offers specialized services for corporate customers. Intown is currently focused on accelerating the growth of its operations, and it will convert all newly acquired properties to the Intown Suites brand. Certain locations are also undergoing renovation and development, which in some cases significantly increasing the number of rooms. Westmont Hospitality Group operates InTown Suites' properties. In 2009, the company spent $250,000 to purchase an Exinda device for each of its locations, to prioritize essential office internet traffic and block peer-to-peer internet traffic. In addition, the firm is integrating its voice and data traffic on integrated T-1 lines at each of its properties. The telecommunications company Qwest will provide the T-1 services for InTown Suites.

FINANCIALS:

Sales and profits are in thousands of dollars—add 000 to get the full amount. 2009 Note: Financial information for 2009 was not available for all companies at press time.

2009 Sales: $	2009 Profits: $	**U.S. Stock Ticker: Private**
2008 Sales: $	2008 Profits: $	**Int'l Ticker:** Int'l Exchange:
2007 Sales: $	2007 Profits: $	Employees:
2006 Sales: $	2006 Profits: $	Fiscal Year Ends: 12/31
2005 Sales: $	2005 Profits: $	Parent Company:

SALARIES/BENEFITS:

Pension Plan:	ESOP Stock Plan:	Profit Sharing:	Top Exec. Salary: $	Bonus: $
Savings Plan:	Stock Purch. Plan:		Second Exec. Salary: $	Bonus: $

OTHER THOUGHTS:

Apparent Women Officers or Directors:
Hot Spot for Advancement for Women/Minorities:

LOCATIONS: ("Y" = Yes)

West:	Southwest:	Midwest:	Southeast:	Northeast:	International:
Y	Y	Y	Y	Y	

INVESTORS REAL ESTATE TRUST

www.iret.com

Industry Group Code: 531110 **Ranks within this company's industry group:** Sales: 16 Profits: 14

Properties:		Financial Services:		Construction/Development:		Investments:		Specialty Services:		Brokerage:	
Apartments:	Y	Mortgages:		Commercial Construction:	Y	REIT:	Y	Property Management:		Commercial Sales:	
Malls/Shopping:	Y	Title Insurance:		Residential Construction:	Y			Online Services:		Residential Sales:	
Offices:	Y	Property Insurance:		Land Development:				Software/IT:		Specialty:	
Hotels/Motels:				Support Services:				Consulting:			
Industrial/Warehouses:	Y			Design/Engineering:							
Other:	Y										

TYPES OF BUSINESS:

Real Estate Investment Trust
Apartment Communities
Retail, Office & Industrial Properties
Medical Properties

BRANDS/DIVISIONS/AFFILIATES:

IRET Properties

CONTACTS:

Note: Officers with more than one job title may be intentionally listed here more than once.

Timothy P. Mihalick, CEO
Thomas A. Wentz, Jr., COO/Sr. VP
Timothy P. Mihalick, Pres.
Diane K. Bryantt, CFO/Sr. VP
Thomas A. Wentz, Sr., CIO/Sr. VP
Michael Bosh, General Counsel/Sr. VP
Karin M. Wentz, Sr. VP/Corp. Sec./Associate General Counsel
Charles A. Greenberg, Sr. VP-Asset Management Group
Jeffrey L. Miller, Chmn.

Phone: 701-837-4738 **Fax:** 701-838-7785
Toll-Free:
Address: 3015 16th St. SW, Ste. 100, Minot, ND 58701 US

GROWTH PLANS/SPECIAL FEATURES:

Investors Real Estate Trust is a self-advised real estate investment trust (REIT) involved in the ownership and operation of multi-family residential, commercial offices, medical, industrial and retail properties. The firm conducts its business operations through its operating partnership, IRET Properties. The company's portfolio consists of both residential and commercial properties. By category, the portfolio contains approximately 77 multi-family residential properties, with a total of 9,669 apartment units; 67 office properties containing 5 million square feet of leasable space; 54 medical properties, including senior housing properties, for a total of approximately 2.6 million square feet of leasable space; 19 industrial properties, with a total of 3 million square feet of leasable space; and 33 retail properties, containing approximately 1.4 million square feet of leasable space. These property types represent the company's five business segments. Investors Real Estate Trust outsources the day-to-day management of some of its properties to other companies; however, the firm has announced plans to transfer management of many of its commercial and multi-family residential properties away from third-parties. In 2010, approximately 56% of the properties in the industrial segment, 78% of the properties in the medical segment, 47% of the properties in the office segment and 92% of the properties in the retail segment were internally managed by employees of the company, while multi-family residential properties were still generally managed by third-parties. The trust's main area of concentration is in the upper Midwest, primarily Minnesota and North Dakota. The firm also owns properties in Texas, Colorado, Kansas, Nebraska, South Dakota, Wyoming, Montana, Idaho, Missouri, Iowa, Wisconsin and Michigan. During 2009, the company acquired seven multi-family residential properties, two office properties, two medical properties, one industrial property and a plot of unimproved land, for purchase prices totaling approximately $33.8 million.

FINANCIALS:

Sales and profits are in thousands of dollars—add 000 to get the full amount. 2009 Note: Financial information for 2009 was not available for all companies at press time.

2009 Sales: $240,005	2009 Profits: $8,526	**U.S. Stock Ticker: IRETS**
2008 Sales: $221,170	2008 Profits: $12,088	**Int'l Ticker:** Int'l Exchange:
2007 Sales: $197,817	2007 Profits: $14,110	Employees: 81
2006 Sales: $170,448	2006 Profits: $11,567	Fiscal Year Ends: 4/30
2005 Sales: $152,937	2005 Profits: $15,076	Parent Company:

SALARIES/BENEFITS:

Pension Plan: Y	ESOP Stock Plan:	Profit Sharing:	Top Exec. Salary: $345,244	Bonus: $41,892
Savings Plan: Y	Stock Purch. Plan:		Second Exec. Salary: $287,500	Bonus: $34,910

OTHER THOUGHTS:

Apparent Women Officers or Directors: 2
Hot Spot for Advancement for Women/Minorities: Y

LOCATIONS: ("Y" = Yes)

West:	Southwest:	Midwest:	Southeast:	Northeast:	International:
Y	Y	Y			

INVESTORS TITLE COMPANY

www.invtitle.com

Industry Group Code: 524127 **Ranks within this company's industry group:** Sales: 5 Profits: 1

Properties:		Financial Services:		Construction/Development:		Investments:		Specialty Services:		Brokerage:	
Apartments:		Mortgages:		Commercial Construction:		REIT:		Property Management:		Commercial Sales:	
Malls/Shopping:		Title Insurance:	Y	Residential Construction:				Online Services:		Residential Sales:	
Offices:		Property Insurance:		Land Development:				Software/IT:		Specialty:	
Hotels/Motels:				Support Services:				Consulting:			
Industrial/Warehouses:				Design/Engineering:							
Other:											

TYPES OF BUSINESS:

Title Insurance
Tax-Deferred Exchange Services
Reinsurance

BRANDS/DIVISIONS/AFFILIATES:

Investors Title Insurance Company (ITIC)
Northeast Investors Title Insurance (NE-ITIC)
Investors Title Exchange Corporation (ITEC)
Investors Title Accommodation Corporation (ITAC)
Investors Capital Management Company

CONTACTS:

Note: Officers with more than one job title may be intentionally listed here more than once.

J. Allen Fine, CEO
James A. Fine, Jr., Pres.
W. Morris Fine, Exec. VP/Sec.
James A. Fine, Jr., Treas.
W. Morris Fine, Pres./COO-Investors Title Insurance Company
J. Allen Fine, Chmn.

Phone: 919-968-2200	**Fax:** 919-968-2235
Toll-Free: 800-326-4842	
Address: 121 N. Columbia St., Chapel Hill, NC 27514 US	

GROWTH PLANS/SPECIAL FEATURES:

Investors Title Company is a holding company that, through its subsidiaries, issues and underwrites title insurance policies. Through its subsidiaries, Investors Title Insurance Company (ITIC) and National Investors Title Insurance (N-ITIC), the company underwrites land title insurance for owners and mortgages as a primary insurer and as a reinsurer for other title insurance companies. ITIC markets title insurance through issuing agents and branch offices in 23 states. N-ITIC writes title insurance as a primary insurer and as a reinsurer in the state of New York and is also licensed to write title insurance in 19 additional states and Washington, D.C. Investors Title also provides tax-deferred real property exchange services through subsidiaries, Investors Title Exchange Corporation (ITEC) and Investors Title Accommodation Corporation (ITAC). ITEC acts as an intermediary in tax-deferred exchanges of property held for productive use in a business or for investments. The subsidiary's income is primarily derived from fees for handling exchange transactions. ITAC serves as an exchange accommodation titleholder, offering services for accomplishing reverse exchanges when a taxpayer must acquire replacement property before selling the relinquished property. Through another wholly-owned subsidiary, Investors Capital Management Company, the firm offers investment management and trust services to individuals, companies, banks and trusts. The company owns two office buildings and property in Chapel Hill, North Carolina, which serve as its corporate headquarters and houses offices for subsidiaries. ITIC maintains leased office space in 28 locations throughout North Carolina, South Carolina, Michigan and Nebraska. N-ITIC leases office space in one location in New York.

Employees are offered medical, dental and vision insurance; disability coverage; life and AD&D insurance; flexible spending accounts; an employee assistance program; and a 401(k) plan.

FINANCIALS:

Sales and profits are in thousands of dollars—add 000 to get the full amount. 2009 Note: Financial information for 2009 was not available for all companies at press time.

2009 Sales: $71,308	2009 Profits: $4,829	**U.S. Stock Ticker: ITIC**
2008 Sales: $71,123	2008 Profits: $-1,183	**Int'l Ticker:** Int'l Exchange:
2007 Sales: $84,942	2007 Profits: $8,402	Employees: 216
2006 Sales: $86,662	2006 Profits: $13,185	Fiscal Year Ends: 12/31
2005 Sales: $87,864	2005 Profits: $13,293	Parent Company:

SALARIES/BENEFITS:

Pension Plan:	ESOP Stock Plan:	Profit Sharing:	Top Exec. Salary: $303,360	Bonus: $90,000
Savings Plan: Y	Stock Purch. Plan:		Second Exec. Salary: $255,560	Bonus: $130,000

OTHER THOUGHTS:

Apparent Women Officers or Directors: 2
Hot Spot for Advancement for Women/Minorities:

LOCATIONS: ("Y" = Yes)

West:	Southwest:	Midwest:	Southeast:	Northeast:	International:
		Y		Y	

ISTAR FINANCIAL INC

www.istarfinancial.com

Industry Group Code: 531120 **Ranks within this company's industry group:** Sales: 11 Profits: 59

Properties:		Financial Services:		Construction/Development:		Investments:		Specialty Services:		Brokerage:	
Apartments:		Mortgages:	Y	Commercial Construction:		REIT:	Y	Property Management:		Commercial Sales:	
Malls/Shopping:	Y	Title Insurance:		Residential Construction:				Online Services:		Residential Sales:	
Offices:	Y	Property Insurance:		Land Development:				Software/IT:		Specialty:	
Hotels/Motels:	Y			Support Services:				Consulting:			
Industrial/Warehouses:	Y			Design/Engineering:							
Other:											

TYPES OF BUSINESS:

Financial Services
Real Estate Investment Trust
Mortgages & Loans
Asset Services
Corporate Finance
Corporate Leasing

BRANDS/DIVISIONS/AFFILIATES:

iStar Europe Ltd
AutoStar

CONTACTS:

Note: Officers with more than one job title may be intentionally listed here more than once.

Jay Sugarman, CEO
Jay Nydick, Pres.
Andrew G. Backman, Sr. VP-Mktg.
Nina B. Matis, Chief Legal Officer
Andrew G. Backman, Sr. VP-Investor Rel.
David M. DiStaso, Chief Acct. Officer
Nina B. Matis, Chief Investment Officer
Chase S. Curtis, Jr., Exec. VP-Credit
Michelle M. MacKay, Exec. VP-Investments
Barbara Rubin, Pres., iStar Asset Svcs.
Jay Sugarman, Chmn.

Phone: 212-930-9400	**Fax:** 212-930-9494
Toll-Free:	
Address: 1114 Ave. of the Americas, 39th Fl., New York, NY 10036 US	

GROWTH PLANS/SPECIAL FEATURES:

iStar Financial, Inc. is a finance company focused on the commercial real estate industry and is taxed as a real estate investment trust (REIT). The firm provides custom-tailored financing to high-end private and corporate owners of real estate. iStar's primary lines of business are lending and corporate tenant leasing. The lending business is primarily comprised of senior and mezzanine real estate loans that typically range in size from $20 million to $150 million and have maturities generally ranging from three to 10 years. The corporate tenant leasing business operates by purchase or leasebacks and by acquiring facilities subject to existing long-term net leases such as mission-critical headquarters or distribution facilities and general-purpose real estate with residual values that represent a discount to current market values and replacement costs. The company is focused on expanding its market-leading platforms; adding key personnel; building strategic relationships; and working to deliver comprehensive capital result to the marketplace. iStar generally seeks corporate customers that are established companies with a stable core and businesses or market leadership in growing industries. Approximately 44% of iStar's assets are in First mortgages/senior debt; corporate tenant leases make up 25%; Fremont First mortgages make up 15%; mezzanine/subordinated debt makes up 6%, and other investments make up the final 10%. The company's properties are broken into the following categories: Apartment/Residential, 27%; Land, 15%; Office, 13%; Industrial, 9%; Retail, 8%; Entertainment/Leisure, 7%; Hotel, 6%; Mixed Use, 6%; Corporate (Real Estate), 5%; Corporate (Non Real Estate), 1%; and Other, 3%. Approximately 4% of the firm's portfolio is outside the U.S.

iStar provides employees benefits including health, life and disability insurance plans; a 401(k) plan; and paid time off.

FINANCIALS:

Sales and profits are in thousands of dollars—add 000 to get the full amount. 2009 Note: Financial information for 2009 was not available for all companies at press time.

2009 Sales: $893,284	2009 Profits: $-769,847	**U.S. Stock Ticker: SFI**
2008 Sales: $1,354,254	2008 Profits: $-181,767	**Int'l Ticker:** Int'l Exchange:
2007 Sales: $1,404,459	2007 Profits: $236,602	Employees: 247
2006 Sales: $933,752	2006 Profits: $374,827	Fiscal Year Ends: 12/31
2005 Sales: $781,929	2005 Profits: $287,913	Parent Company:

SALARIES/BENEFITS:

Pension Plan:	ESOP Stock Plan:	Profit Sharing:	Top Exec. Salary: $1,000,000	Bonus: $
Savings Plan: Y	Stock Purch. Plan:		Second Exec. Salary: $483,333	Bonus: $2,750,000

OTHER THOUGHTS:

Apparent Women Officers or Directors: 5
Hot Spot for Advancement for Women/Minorities: Y

LOCATIONS: ("Y" = Yes)

West:	Southwest:	Midwest:	Southeast:	Northeast:	International:
Y	Y	Y	Y	Y	

JACOBS ENGINEERING GROUP INC

www.jacobs.com

Industry Group Code: 237 **Ranks within this company's industry group:** Sales: 12 Profits: 9

Properties:		Financial Services:		Construction/Development:		Investments:		Specialty Services:		Brokerage:	
Apartments:		Mortgages:		Commercial Construction:	Y	REIT:		Property Management:	Y	Commercial Sales:	
Malls/Shopping:		Title Insurance:		Residential Construction:				Online Services:		Residential Sales:	
Offices:		Property Insurance:		Land Development:				Software/IT:		Specialty:	
Hotels/Motels:				Support Services:				Consulting:	Y		
Industrial/Warehouses:				Design/Engineering:	Y						
Other:											

TYPES OF BUSINESS:

Engineering & Design Services
Facility Management
Construction & Field Services
Technical Consulting Services
Environmental Services

BRANDS/DIVISIONS/AFFILIATES:

TYBRIN Corporation
Jordan, Jones and Goulding, Inc.
OCP SA
Jacobs Engineering SA
Jacobs Technology, Inc.

CONTACTS: *Note: Officers with more than one job title may be intentionally listed here more than once.*

Craig Martin, CEO
Craig Martin, Pres.
Andrew F. Kremer, Sr. VP-Global Sales
Patricia H. Summers, Sr. VP-Human Resources
Cora Carmody, Sr. VP-IT
John W. Prosser Jr., Exec. VP-Admin.
William C. Markley III, General Counsel/Sec./Sr. VP
Thomas R. Hammond, Exec. VP-Oper.
John McLachlan, Sr. VP-Strategy
John W. Prosser Jr., Exec. VP-Finance/Treas.
John Machlan, Sr. VP-Acquisitions
George A. Kunberger, Exec. VP-Oper.
Rogers F. Starr, Pres., Jacobs Technology, Inc.
Nazim Thawerbhoy, Sr. VP/Controller
Noel G. Watson, Chmn.

Phone: 626-578-3500	**Fax:** 626-568-7144
Toll-Free:	
Address: 1111 S. Arroyo Pkwy., Pasadena, CA 91109-7084 US	

GROWTH PLANS/SPECIAL FEATURES:

Jacobs Engineering Group, Inc. offers technical, professional, and construction services to industrial, commercial and governmental clients throughout North America, Europe, Asia, South America, India, the U.K. and Australia. The company's global network includes more than 160 offices in over 20 countries. The company provides project services, which include engineering, design and architecture; process, scientific, and systems consulting services; operations and maintenance services; and construction services, which include direct-hire construction and management services. Services are offered to selected industry groups such as oil and gas exploration, production, and refining; programs for various federal governments; pharmaceuticals and biotechnology; chemicals and polymers; buildings, which includes projects in the fields of health care and education as well as civic, governmental, and other buildings; infrastructure; technology and manufacturing; and pulp and paper, among others. Jacobs also provides pricing studies, project feasibility reports and automation and control system analysis for U.S. government agencies involved in defense and aerospace programs. In addition, the company is one of the leading providers of environmental engineering and consulting services in the U.S. and abroad, including hazardous and nuclear waste management and site cleanup and closure, providing support in such areas as underground storage tank removal, contaminated soil and water remediation, and long-term groundwater monitoring. Jacobs also designs, builds, installs, operates and maintains various types of soil and groundwater cleanup systems. In December 2009, the firm acquired TYBRIN Corporation. In January 2010, Jacobs purchased Jordan, Jones and Goulding, Inc., which specializes in water and wastewater services. In March 2010, the company formed Jacobs Engineering SA, a joint venture with OCP SA, to provide industrial services in Morocco.

Jacobs offers its employees health and disability benefits; life and AD&D insurance; an employee tock purchase plan; tuition reimbursement; retirement benefits and more.

FINANCIALS: **Sales and profits are in thousands of dollars—add 000 to get the full amount. 2009 Note: Financial information for 2009 was not available for all companies at press time.**

2009 Sales: $11,467,376	2009 Profits: $399,854	**U.S. Stock Ticker: JEC**
2008 Sales: $11,252,159	2008 Profits: $420,742	**Int'l Ticker:** Int'l Exchange:
2007 Sales: $8,473,970	2007 Profits: $287,130	Employees: 38,900
2006 Sales: $7,421,270	2006 Profits: $196,883	Fiscal Year Ends: 9/30
2005 Sales: $5,635,001	2005 Profits: $131,608	Parent Company:

SALARIES/BENEFITS:

Pension Plan:	ESOP Stock Plan:	Profit Sharing:	Top Exec. Salary: $1,150,000	Bonus: $978,254
Savings Plan: Y	Stock Purch. Plan: Y		Second Exec. Salary: $850,000	Bonus: $723,058

OTHER THOUGHTS:

Apparent Women Officers or Directors: 3
Hot Spot for Advancement for Women/Minorities: Y

LOCATIONS: ("Y" = Yes)

West:	Southwest:	Midwest:	Southeast:	Northeast:	International:
Y	Y	Y	Y	Y	Y

JAMESON INN INC

www.jamesoninns.com

Industry Group Code: 721110 **Ranks within this company's industry group:** Sales: Profits:

Properties:		Financial Services:		Construction/Development:		Investments:		Specialty Services:		Brokerage:	
Apartments:		Mortgages:		Commercial Construction:		REIT:		Property Management:	Y	Commercial Sales:	
Malls/Shopping:		Title Insurance:		Residential Construction:				Online Services:		Residential Sales:	
Offices:		Property Insurance:		Land Development:				Software/IT:		Specialty:	
Hotels/Motels:	Y			Support Services:				Consulting:			
Industrial/Warehouses:				Design/Engineering:							
Other:											

TYPES OF BUSINESS:

Hotels

BRANDS/DIVISIONS/AFFILIATES:

JER Partners
Longhouse Hospitality
Park Management Group
J.E. Robert Companies
Signature Inn

CONTACTS:

Note: Officers with more than one job title may be intentionally listed here more than once.

Craig Kitchin, Pres.
Craig Kitchin, CFO

Phone: 404-350-9990	**Fax:** 404-601-6106
Toll-Free: 800-526-3766	
Address: 4770 S. Atlanta Rd., Smyrna, GA 30080 US	

GROWTH PLANS/SPECIAL FEATURES:

Jameson Inn, Inc., a subsidiary of the private equity firm JER Partners, operates hotels in 13 states in the southeastern and Midwestern U.S. Jameson is a part of JER Partners' Longhouse Hospitality. JER Partners is the private equity investment arm of the J.E. Robert Companies. Jameson owns more than 160 hotels under the Jameson Inn, Crestwood Suites, Sun Suites, Lodge America and Signature Inn brands. The firm's hotels are managed by Park Management Group. All hotels owned by the firm typically offer amenities such as swimming pools, fitness centers, executive workstations, free cable, free USA Today, voicemail, refrigerators, microwaves and daily breakfast. In order to attract more business travelers, Jameson Inn offers workstations equipped with data ports, meeting spaces and fax and photocopy machines. Executive meeting rooms at Jameson Inn are approximately 300 square feet, with a capacity of 12 people, while the Signature Inn meeting rooms range from 300-900 square feet, with a capacity of 12-80 people.

The company offers its employees health, dental, vision, life and short- and long-term disability insurance; a 401(k) plan; paid holidays and time off; and discounts at company hotels.

FINANCIALS:

Sales and profits are in thousands of dollars—add 000 to get the full amount. 2009 Note: Financial information for 2009 was not available for all companies at press time.

2009 Sales: $
2008 Sales: $
2007 Sales: $
2006 Sales: $
2005 Sales: $91,370

2009 Profits: $
2008 Profits: $
2007 Profits: $
2006 Profits: $
2005 Profits: $605,078

U.S. Stock Ticker: Subsidiary
Int'l Ticker: Int'l Exchange:
Employees:
Fiscal Year Ends: 12/31
Parent Company: JER PARTNERS

SALARIES/BENEFITS:

Pension Plan: ESOP Stock Plan: Profit Sharing: Top Exec. Salary: $ Bonus: $
Savings Plan: Y Stock Purch. Plan: Second Exec. Salary: $ Bonus: $

OTHER THOUGHTS:

Apparent Women Officers or Directors:
Hot Spot for Advancement for Women/Minorities:

LOCATIONS: ("Y" = Yes)

West:	Southwest:	Midwest:	Southeast:	Northeast:	International:
		Y	Y	Y	

JANUS HOTELS AND RESORTS INC

www.janushotels.com

Industry Group Code: 721110 **Ranks within this company's industry group:** Sales: Profits:

Properties:		Financial Services:		Construction/Development:		Investments:		Specialty Services:		Brokerage:	
Apartments:		Mortgages:		Commercial Construction:		REIT:		Property Management:	Y	Commercial Sales:	
Malls/Shopping:		Title Insurance:		Residential Construction:				Online Services:		Residential Sales:	
Offices:		Property Insurance:		Land Development:				Software/IT:		Specialty:	
Hotels/Motels:	Y			Support Services:				Consulting:	Y		
Industrial/Warehouses:				Design/Engineering:							
Other:											

TYPES OF BUSINESS:

Hotel Management
Management, Financial & Legal Consulting
Food & Beverage Services
Staffing Services

BRANDS/DIVISIONS/AFFILIATES:

CONTACTS:

Note: Officers with more than one job title may be intentionally listed here more than once.

Louis Beck, CEO
Michael Nanosky, Pres.
Rick Tonges, CFO
Greg Cappel, VP-Mktg. & Sales
Mary Ellen Steck, Dir.-Human Resources
Joe Jeffery, Head-IT
Eric Glazer, Corp. Attorney
Deborah Chamberlin, VP-Oper.
Burton Bongard, Dir.-Dev.
Joe Jeffery, Head-Web Tech.
Barb Soete, Co-Controller
Scott Wielkiewicz, Co-Controller/Mgr.-Tax
Jennifer Wagner, Co-Controller/VP/Mgr.-Tax
Magda Khalil, Dir.-Corp. Acct.
Theresa Giordano, Mgr.-Corp. Revenue
Louis Beck, Chmn.
Rick Ziegelmeyer, VP-Purchasing & Renovations

Phone: 561-997-2325	**Fax:** 561-997-5331
Toll-Free:	
Address: 2300 Corporate Blvd. NW, Ste. 232, Boca Raton, FL 33431-8596 US	

GROWTH PLANS/SPECIAL FEATURES:

Janus Hotels and Resorts, Inc. is one of the largest independently-owned full-service hotel management companies. It owns or manages over 30 hotels with approximately 8,000 guest rooms, concentrated in Florida. Its locations sit under the signposts of nationally recognized brands, including Days Inn, Holiday Inn, Radisson, Howard Johnson and Best Western. Janus operates each hotel according to a business plan specifically tailored to the characteristics of the hotel and its market, employing centralized management, accounting and purchasing systems to reduce cost and increase operating margins. The firm focuses primarily on continuing sales and marketing to increase revenue. Janus also provides food and beverage services, including lounges, coffee shops and locally and nationally branded restaurants. The company offers support services in the areas of administration, legal issues, brand relationships, maintenance of property, staffing, cash controls, liquor license issues, financial review and management, property development and customer service strategies. The firm also provides receivership services that involve quickly securing the asset; providing management services designed to stabilize the property; and services aimed at restoring staff and customer confidence in addition to its general offerings.

FINANCIALS:

Sales and profits are in thousands of dollars—add 000 to get the full amount. 2009 Note: Financial information for 2009 was not available for all companies at press time.

2009 Sales: $	2009 Profits: $	**U.S. Stock Ticker: Private**
2008 Sales: $	2008 Profits: $	**Int'l Ticker:** Int'l Exchange:
2007 Sales: $	2007 Profits: $	Employees:
2006 Sales: $	2006 Profits: $	Fiscal Year Ends: 12/31
2005 Sales: $	2005 Profits: $	Parent Company:

SALARIES/BENEFITS:

Pension Plan:	ESOP Stock Plan:	Profit Sharing:	Top Exec. Salary: $	Bonus: $
Savings Plan:	Stock Purch. Plan:		Second Exec. Salary: $	Bonus: $

OTHER THOUGHTS:

Apparent Women Officers or Directors: 10
Hot Spot for Advancement for Women/Minorities: Y

LOCATIONS: ("Y" = Yes)

West:	Southwest:	Midwest:	Southeast:	Northeast:	International:
	Y	Y	Y	Y	

JEWETT CAMERON TRADING CO LTD

www.jewettcameron.com

Industry Group Code: 444130 **Ranks within this company's industry group:** Sales: 4 Profits: 2

Properties:		Financial Services:		Construction/Development:		Investments:		Specialty Services:		Brokerage:	
Apartments:		Mortgages:		Commercial Construction:		REIT:		Property Management:		Commercial Sales:	
Malls/Shopping:		Title Insurance:		Residential Construction:				Online Services:		Residential Sales:	
Offices:		Property Insurance:		Land Development:				Software/IT:		Specialty:	
Hotels/Motels:				Support Services:	Y			Consulting:			
Industrial/Warehouses:				Design/Engineering:							
Other:											

TYPES OF BUSINESS:

Building Materials & Hardware-Distribution
Lumber & Specialty Wood Products
Industrial Tools-Import & Distribution
Agricultural Seeds-Processing & Sales
Specialty Metal Products

BRANDS/DIVISIONS/AFFILIATES:

Jewett-Cameron Lumber Company
Greenwood Products, Inc.
Jewett-Cameron Seed Company
MSI-PRO Company
Lucky Dog
Weatherguard
Perimeter Patrol
Spring Gardener

CONTACTS: *Note: Officers with more than one job title may be intentionally listed here more than once.*

Donald M. Boone, CEO
Donald M. Boone, Pres.
Murray G. Smith, CFO
Michael C. Nasser, Corp. Sec.
Thomas Rice, Pres., Greenwood Products

Phone: 503-647-0110	**Fax:** 503-647-2272
Toll-Free: 800-547-5877	
Address: 32275 NW Hillcrest St., North Plains, OR 97133 US	

GROWTH PLANS/SPECIAL FEATURES:

Jewett-Cameron Trading Company is the holding company for Jewett-Cameron Lumber Company (JCLC), which markets wood and specialty metal products out of facilities located in North Plains, Oregon. The firm is broken into four segments: industrial wood products; lawn, garden, pet and other; seed processing and sales; and industrial tools and clamps. JCLC offers warehouse distribution and direct sales of building materials to home improvement centers. JCLC concentrates a portion of its sales efforts on the home improvement industry. Wood products include fencing and landscape timbers, while metal products include dog kennels, a proprietary gate support system, perimeter fencing and greenhouses. JCLC markets its products under the Lucky Dog, AKC Pro Breeder, Weatherguard and Spring Gardener, Adjust-A-Gate and Perimeter Patrol brands. The firm has a number of other wholly-owned subsidiaries. Greenwood Products, Inc. processes and distributes industrial wood and other specialty building products, including treated plywood that is sold primarily to boat manufacturers and the transportation industry. Jewett-Cameron Seed Company is involved in cleaning, processing, packaging, distributing and certifying grass seed and other agricultural seed products. MSI-PRO Company is an importer and distributor of pneumatic air tools, saw blades and clamps, which are primarily sold to contractor supply, industrial supply and retail wood and specialty tool stores. This subsidiary markets its products under the MSI-PRO, Avenger and Promax brands.

FINANCIALS: **Sales and profits are in thousands of dollars—add 000 to get the full amount. 2009 Note: Financial information for 2009 was not available for all companies at press time.**

2009 Sales: $42,130	2009 Profits: $1,582	**U.S. Stock Ticker: JCTCF**
2008 Sales: $64,321	2008 Profits: $2,610	**Int'l Ticker:** Int'l Exchange:
2007 Sales: $69,038	2007 Profits: $2,295	Employees: 47
2006 Sales: $76,096	2006 Profits: $2,339	Fiscal Year Ends: 8/31
2005 Sales: $74,617	2005 Profits: $ 931	Parent Company:

SALARIES/BENEFITS:

Pension Plan:	ESOP Stock Plan:	Profit Sharing:	Top Exec. Salary: $177,000	Bonus: $92,950
Savings Plan:	Stock Purch. Plan:		Second Exec. Salary: $84,000	Bonus: $

OTHER THOUGHTS:

Apparent Women Officers or Directors:
Hot Spot for Advancement for Women/Minorities:

LOCATIONS: ("Y" = Yes)

West:	Southwest:	Midwest:	Southeast:	Northeast:	International:
Y					

JOHN LAING PLC

www.john-laing.com

Industry Group Code: 5311 **Ranks within this company's industry group:** Sales: Profits:

Properties:		Financial Services:		Construction/Development:		Investments:		Specialty Services:		Brokerage:	
Apartments:		Mortgages:		Commercial Construction:	Y	REIT:		Property Management:		Commercial Sales:	
Malls/Shopping:		Title Insurance:		Residential Construction:				Online Services:		Residential Sales:	
Offices:		Property Insurance:		Land Development:				Software/IT:		Specialty:	
Hotels/Motels:				Support Services:	Y			Consulting:			
Industrial/Warehouses:				Design/Engineering:							
Other:											

TYPES OF BUSINESS:

Investor & Developer, Infrastructure Projects
Public Infrastructure Management
Rail Operations
Facilities Management
Private Finance Initiative Investor

BRANDS/DIVISIONS/AFFILIATES:

Henderson Group plc
Henderson Private Equity

CONTACTS:

Note: Officers with more than one job title may be intentionally listed here more than once.

Adrian Ewer, CEO
Dylan Jones, Dir.-IT
Roger Miller, Sec.
Chris Waples, Dir.-Oper.
Derek Potts, Managing Dir.-Bus. Dev.
Jo Young, Mgr.-Group Comm.
Lynn Macgregor, Dir.-Finance
David Marshall, Dir.-Corp. Projects
Jane Webb, Controller
Phil Nolan, Chmn.

Phone: 44-20-7901-3200 **Fax:** 44-20-7901-3520
Toll-Free:
Address: Allington House, 150 Victoria St., London, SW1E 5LB UK

GROWTH PLANS/SPECIAL FEATURES:

John Laing plc, owned by Henderson Private Equity, the private equity branch of Henderson Group plc, operates as a long-term investor, developer and operator of privately financed, public sector infrastructure such as roads, railways, hospitals, schools and other major projects in the U.K. and overseas. The firm's clients include local and education authorities, health trusts, the U.K. Ministry of Defense (MoD) and various police departments. The company operates in 11 business segments: police and criminal justice; defense; education; further education; healthcare; rail infrastructure; housing and community regeneration; local authority estates and regeneration; roads and bridges; street lighting and highway maintenance; and waste, renewable energy and utilities. In the criminal justice and police segment, John Laing serves the Department for Constitutional Affairs across all of its procurement methods, including private finance initiative (PFI), public-private partnership (PPP) and private developer schemes (PDS). In its defense segment, the company has been involved in three major MoD projects, including the Joint Services Command and Staff College in Shrivenham and the MoD Main Building in Whitehall, both of which won awards. John Laing's education portfolio includes over 60 projects, which it delivers through either PFI, PPP or as property development deals. In healthcare, the company is a leading provider for the Local Improvement Finance Trust (LIFT), a major government initiative designed to stimulate investment in local primary and social care facilities, for which it established joint-venture Primary Plus with the Bank of Scotland, providing financing and project management expertise. John Laing is involved in the development of over 30 police facilities, including stations and firearm training facilities. The company provides facilities management services to 36 sites through subsidiary John Laing Integrated Services.

FINANCIALS:

Sales and profits are in thousands of dollars—add 000 to get the full amount. 2009 Note: Financial information for 2009 was not available for all companies at press time.

2009 Sales: $	2009 Profits: $	**U.S. Stock Ticker: Private**
2008 Sales: $	2008 Profits: $	**Int'l Ticker:** Int'l Exchange:
2007 Sales: $	2007 Profits: $	Employees:
2006 Sales: $	2006 Profits: $	Fiscal Year Ends: 12/31
2005 Sales: $758,043	2005 Profits: $21,300	Parent Company: HENDERSON GROUP PLC

SALARIES/BENEFITS:

Pension Plan:	ESOP Stock Plan:	Profit Sharing:	Top Exec. Salary: $	Bonus: $
Savings Plan:	Stock Purch. Plan:		Second Exec. Salary: $	Bonus: $

OTHER THOUGHTS:

Apparent Women Officers or Directors: 3
Hot Spot for Advancement for Women/Minorities: Y

LOCATIONS: ("Y" = Yes)

West:	Southwest:	Midwest:	Southeast:	Northeast:	International:
					Y

JOHN Q HAMMONS HOTELS LLC

www.jqhhotels.com

Industry Group Code: 721110 **Ranks within this company's industry group:** Sales: Profits:

Properties:		Financial Services:		Construction/Development:		Investments:		Specialty Services:		Brokerage:	
Apartments:		Mortgages:		Commercial Construction:		REIT:		Property Management:		Commercial Sales:	
Malls/Shopping:		Title Insurance:		Residential Construction:				Online Services:		Residential Sales:	
Offices:		Property Insurance:		Land Development:				Software/IT:		Specialty:	
Hotels/Motels:	Y			Support Services:				Consulting:			
Industrial/Warehouses:				Design/Engineering:							
Other:											

TYPES OF BUSINESS:

Hotels

BRANDS/DIVISIONS/AFFILIATES:

Chateau on the Lake
World Golf Village Renaissance Resort
John Q. Hammons Hotels Management LLC
Renaissance
Marriott
Hilton
Radisson
Residence Inn by Marriott

CONTACTS: *Note: Officers with more than one job title may be intentionally listed here more than once.*

John Q. Hammons, CEO
Kent Foster, VP-Human Resources
Matt Bortniker, VP-IT
John Fulton, VP-Design
Christopher Smith, Sr. VP-Admin.
Justin Harris, General Counsel
Joe Morrissey, Sr. VP-Oper.
L. Scott Tarwater, Exec. VP-Bus. Dev.
Steve Minton, Sr. VP-Architecture
Kent Larson, VP-Capital Planning & Asset Protection
Bill Mead, Regional VP
Bob Fugazi, Regional VP
John Q. Hammons, Chmn.
John Fulton, VP-Purchasing

Phone: 417-864-4300 **Fax:**
Toll-Free: 800-641-4026
Address: 300 John Q. Hammons Pkwy., Ste. 900, Springfield, MO 65806 US

GROWTH PLANS/SPECIAL FEATURES:

John Q. Hammons Hotels LLC is a leading company that owns, manages and develops low-cost upscale hotels in main traffic areas. The company owns and operates more than 74 hotels in 25 states. These properties operate primarily under the Embassy Suites, Renaissance, Marriott, Hilton, Sheraton, Radisson, Residence Inn by Marriott, Homewood Suites by Hilton, Hampton Inn & Suites, Holiday Inn and Courtyard by Marriott trade names and are marketed to a range of customers, including frequent business travelers; groups and conventions; and leisure travelers. John Q. Hammons Hotels Management LLC manages all of the firm's hotels, which are generally located near a state capitol, university, airport, corporate headquarters or other major facility. Most of the hotels contain a multi-storied atrium, extensive meeting space and large rooms or suites. In addition, the firm owns two resorts: Chateau on the Lake, located in Branson, Missouri, and the World Golf Village Renaissance Resort in St. Augustine, Florida. In 2009, the company opened two new hotels: Courtyard by Marriott in La Vista, Nebraska; and Embassy Suites-Loveland Hotel, Spa & Conference Center in Loveland, Colorado.

FINANCIALS: **Sales and profits are in thousands of dollars—add 000 to get the full amount. 2009 Note: Financial information for 2009 was not available for all companies at press time.**

2009 Sales: $	2009 Profits: $	**U.S. Stock Ticker: Private**
2008 Sales: $	2008 Profits: $	**Int'l Ticker:** Int'l Exchange:
2007 Sales: $	2007 Profits: $	Employees:
2006 Sales: $	2006 Profits: $	Fiscal Year Ends: 12/31
2005 Sales: $	2005 Profits: $	Parent Company:

SALARIES/BENEFITS:

Pension Plan:	ESOP Stock Plan:	Profit Sharing:	Top Exec. Salary: $	Bonus: $
Savings Plan: Y	Stock Purch. Plan:		Second Exec. Salary: $	Bonus: $

OTHER THOUGHTS:

Apparent Women Officers or Directors:
Hot Spot for Advancement for Women/Minorities:

LOCATIONS: ("Y" = Yes)

West:	Southwest:	Midwest:	Southeast:	Northeast:	International:
Y	Y	Y	Y	Y	

JOHNSON CONTROLS INC

www.johnsoncontrols.com

Industry Group Code: 3363 **Ranks within this company's industry group:** Sales: 1 Profits: 1

Properties:		Financial Services:		Construction/Development:		Investments:		Specialty Services:		Brokerage:	
Apartments:		Mortgages:		Commercial Construction:		REIT:		Property Management:	Y	Commercial Sales:	
Malls/Shopping:		Title Insurance:		Residential Construction:				Online Services:		Residential Sales:	
Offices:		Property Insurance:		Land Development:				Software/IT:		Specialty:	
Hotels/Motels:				Support Services:	Y			Consulting:			
Industrial/Warehouses:				Design/Engineering:							
Other:											

TYPES OF BUSINESS:

Automobile Parts & Controls
Automotive Batteries
Facilities Management
Automotive Interior Components
Energy Management Services
Building Security, Lighting & HVAC Systems

BRANDS/DIVISIONS/AFFILIATES:

National Energy Services
Johnson Controls-Saft Advanced Power Solutions
Automotive Experience
Optima
Varta
Metasys Sustainability Manager
Heliar
LTH

CONTACTS: *Note: Officers with more than one job title may be intentionally listed here more than once.*

Stephen A. Roell, CEO
Keith Wandell, COO
Stephen A. Roell, Pres.
R. Bruce McDonald, CFO/Exec. VP
Susan F. Davis, Exec. VP-Human Resources
Colin Boyd, CIO/VP-IT
Jerome D. Okarma, General Counsel/VP/Sec.
Jacqueline F. Strayer, VP-Corp. Comm.
Glen Ponczak, Exec. Dir.-Investor Rel.
Frank A. Voltolina, Corp. Treas./VP
C. David Meyers, VP/Pres., Building Efficiency
Jeffrey G. Augustin, VP-Finance, Building Efficiency
Alex A. Molinaroli, VP/Pres., Power Solutions
Charles A. Harvey, VP-Public Affairs & Diversity
Stephen A. Roell, Chmn.
Jeffrey S. Edwards, VP-Automotive Experience, Japan & APAC

Phone: 414-524-1200	**Fax:** 414-524-2070
Toll-Free: 800-524-6220	
Address: 5757 N. Green Bay Ave., Milwaukee, WI 53209 US	

GROWTH PLANS/SPECIAL FEATURES:

Johnson Controls, Inc. is a leader in automotive interiors/batteries, building efficiency and facility management. The firm's Automotive Experience segment, which accounts for roughly 42% of the company's sales, designs and manufactures concept cars; complete seat systems; seating components; electronics; instrument panels; overhead, door and cargo management systems; cockpits; and interior trim for manufacturers of cars and light trucks. The division operates approximately 175 wholly- and majority-owned manufacturing/assembly plants in 32 countries. Johnson Control's Power Solutions division (14% of sales) manufactures and replaces automotive batteries, focusing on innovations for hybrid electric vehicles. Its battery brands include Optima, Varta, Heliar (in South America), and LTH (in Mexico). The segment produces roughly 110 million lead-acid batteries annually in approximately 55 wholly- and majority-owned manufacturing/assembly facilities in 21 countries. The Building Efficiency division (44% of sales) operates in 59 countries, supplying systems designed for heating; ventilation; air conditioning; lighting; security; and fire management. The U.S. Department of Defense utilizes Johnson Controls for the Pentagon's energy management and environmental control systems. Global WorkPlace Solutions, part of Building Efficiency, provides companies with a real-estate based approach to shareholder value. The Building Efficiency division also does facility management, using its patented Metasys Building Management System. It handles school districts, hospitals, factories, airports and government facilities. Johnson Controls has a joint venture with Saft SA, a battery company, called Johnson Controls-Saft Advanced Power Solutions. In January 2010, the firm opened two new laboratories in Pennsylvania for the testing of commercial air-conditioning equipment. In February 2010, the company and IBM agreed to jointly develop a program to reduce energy and water consumption in buildings. In March 2010, Johnson Controls acquired lighting services firm National Energy Services.

The firm offers employees benefits including health care coverage, tuition reimbursement and a 401(k) plan.

FINANCIALS: **Sales and profits are in thousands of dollars—add 000 to get the full amount. 2009 Note: Financial information for 2009 was not available for all companies at press time.**

2009 Sales: $28,497,000	2009 Profits: $-338,000	**U.S. Stock Ticker: JCI**
2008 Sales: $38,062,000	2008 Profits: $979,000	**Int'l Ticker:** Int'l Exchange:
2007 Sales: $34,624,000	2007 Profits: $1,252,000	Employees: 130,000
2006 Sales: $32,235,000	2006 Profits: $1,028,000	Fiscal Year Ends: 9/30
2005 Sales: $27,479,400	2005 Profits: $909,400	Parent Company:

SALARIES/BENEFITS:

Pension Plan:	ESOP Stock Plan:	Profit Sharing:	Top Exec. Salary: $1,371,500	Bonus: $1,097,000
Savings Plan: Y	Stock Purch. Plan:		Second Exec. Salary: $817,000	Bonus: $470,000

OTHER THOUGHTS:

Apparent Women Officers or Directors: 4
Hot Spot for Advancement for Women/Minorities: Y

LOCATIONS: ("Y" = Yes)

West:	Southwest:	Midwest:	Southeast:	Northeast:	International:
Y	Y	Y	Y	Y	Y

JOIE DE VIVRE HOSPITALITY

www.jdvhotels.com

Industry Group Code: 721110 **Ranks within this company's industry group:** Sales: Profits:

Properties:		Financial Services:		Construction/Development:		Investments:		Specialty Services:		Brokerage:	
Apartments:	Y	Mortgages:		Commercial Construction:		REIT:		Property Management:	Y	Commercial Sales:	
Malls/Shopping:		Title Insurance:		Residential Construction:				Online Services:		Residential Sales:	
Offices:		Property Insurance:		Land Development:				Software/IT:		Specialty:	
Hotels/Motels:	Y			Support Services:				Consulting:	Y		
Industrial/Warehouses:				Design/Engineering:							
Other:	Y										

TYPES OF BUSINESS:

Hotels
Day Spas
Restaurants
Hospitality Consulting
Condominium Management

BRANDS/DIVISIONS/AFFILIATES:

Hotel Rex
Phoenix Hotel
Hotel Tomo
Kabuki Springs & Spa
Spa Vitale
Millennium Restaurant
Hotel Erwin Venice Beach
Gaige House

CONTACTS: *Note: Officers with more than one job title may be intentionally listed here more than once.*

Chip Conley, CEO
Ingrid Summerfield, Pres.
Michael J. Wisner, CFO
Peter Gamez, Sr. VP-Sales & Bus. Dev.
Jane Howard, Chief People Officer
Michael Stano, VP-Tech.
Anne Conley, VP-Admin.
Karlene Holloman, Sr. VP-Oper.
Christian Strobel, Chief Dev. Officer
Kristina Hjelsand, Sr. Mgr.-Public Rel.
Linda Palermo, Chief Revenue Officer
Morgan Plant, VP-Food & Beverage
Eric Paul, VP-Northern California
Rick Patten, VP-Southern California

Phone: 415-835-0300	**Fax:** 415-835-0317
Toll-Free: 800-738-7477	
Address: 530 Bush St., Ste 501, San Francisco, CA 94108 US	

GROWTH PLANS/SPECIAL FEATURES:

Joie de Vivre Hospitality (JdV) operates primarily through subsidiary Joie de Vivre Hotels, one of California's largest independent boutique hotel operators. The company has locations throughout California, including almost 40 boutique hotels featuring a combined 20 restaurants and bars and approximately 4,500 guest rooms. JdV's boutique hotels each target a niche audience by embodying a particular lifestyle or theme, such as arts and literature, featured at the Hotel Rex; rock and roll, at the Phoenix Hotel; or Japanese pop-culture, at Hotel Tomo. It also owns and operates the Kabuki Springs & Spa in San Francisco; Spa Vitale at Hotel Vitale; Spa Elia, a day spa at the Hotel Los Gatos in Silicon Valley; and a spa located in the Ventana Inn near Big Sur. JdV's restaurants and bars are usually attached to its hotels, such as Bambuddha Lounge in the Phoenix Hotel and Cafe Andree in Hotel Rex; however, it also has free-standing restaurants such as Millennium Restaurant in Union Square, San Francisco. The firm offers approximately 150,000 combined square feet of business meeting space, with some locations able to accommodate groups of up to 1,000 people. JdV also manages an upscale residential community, Soma Grand Condos, in downtown San Francisco. The company's web site features the Yvette the Hotel Matchmaker service, which matches guests to particular hotels based on personality. In addition to managing its hotels, spas and restaurants, JdV provides hospitality consulting services, including general concept development and creative brainstorming for new projects. In February 2009, JdV acquired the 23-room Gaige House in Sonoma County. In July 2009, the firm opened its new Hotel Erwin Venice Beach location, a 119-room beachfront property. In September 2009, the company added the 168-room Avatar Hotel to its line-up, featuring a number of amenities aimed at tech-savvy business travelers visiting the Silicon Valley area.

FINANCIALS: **Sales and profits are in thousands of dollars—add 000 to get the full amount. 2009 Note: Financial information for 2009 was not available for all companies at press time.**

2009 Sales: $	2009 Profits: $	**U.S. Stock Ticker: Private**
2008 Sales: $	2008 Profits: $	**Int'l Ticker:** Int'l Exchange:
2007 Sales: $	2007 Profits: $	Employees:
2006 Sales: $	2006 Profits: $	Fiscal Year Ends: 12/31
2005 Sales: $	2005 Profits: $	Parent Company:

SALARIES/BENEFITS:

Pension Plan:	ESOP Stock Plan:	Profit Sharing:	Top Exec. Salary: $	Bonus: $
Savings Plan:	Stock Purch. Plan:		Second Exec. Salary: $	Bonus: $

OTHER THOUGHTS:

Apparent Women Officers or Directors: 6
Hot Spot for Advancement for Women/Minorities: Y

LOCATIONS: ("Y" = Yes)

West:	Southwest:	Midwest:	Southeast:	Northeast:	International:
Y					

JONES LANG LASALLE INC

www.joneslanglasalle.com

Industry Group Code: 5311 **Ranks within this company's industry group:** Sales: 11 Profits: 18

Properties:		Financial Services:		Construction/Development:		Investments:		Specialty Services:		Brokerage:	
Apartments:		Mortgages:		Commercial Construction:		REIT:		Property Management:	Y	Commercial Sales:	Y
Malls/Shopping:		Title Insurance:		Residential Construction:				Online Services:		Residential Sales:	
Offices:		Property Insurance:		Land Development:				Software/IT:		Specialty:	
Hotels/Motels:				Support Services:				Consulting:	Y		
Industrial/Warehouses:				Design/Engineering:							
Other:											

TYPES OF BUSINESS:

Real Estate Rental, Leasing & Management
Investment Management
Project Management
Consulting Services
Real Estate Investment Banking
Properties Brokerage

BRANDS/DIVISIONS/AFFILIATES:

LaSalle Investment Management, Inc.
LaSalle Investment Management (Canada), Inc.
LaSalle Investment Management Asia Pte Ltd.
LaSalle Investment Management B.V.

CONTACTS:

Note: Officers with more than one job title may be intentionally listed here more than once.

Colin Dyer, CEO
Lauralee E. Martin, COO
Colin Dyer, Pres.
Lauralee E. Martin, CFO
Charles Doyle, Chief Mktg. Officer
Nazneen Razi, Chief Human Resources Officer
David Johnson, CIO
Mark Ohringer, General Counsel/Corp. Sec.
Joe Romenesko, Global Treas.
Jeff Jacobson, CEO-LaSalle Investment Mgmt.
Peter C. Roberts, CEO-Americas
Christian Ulbrich, CEO-EMEA
James Jasionowski, Global Dir.-Tax
Sheila A. Penrose, Chmn.
Alastair Hughes, CEO-Asia Pacific

Phone: 312-782-5800 **Fax:** 312-782-4339
Toll-Free:
Address: 200 E. Randolph Dr., Chicago, IL 60601 US

GROWTH PLANS/SPECIAL FEATURES:

Jones Lang LaSalle, Inc. (JLL) is a real estate money management firm that provides integrated real estate and investment management expertise on a local, regional and global level to owner, occupier and investor clients. The firm is active in the area of property and corporate facility management services, with a portfolio encompassing roughly 1.6 billion square feet worldwide. JLL offers its real estate services across three geographically-aligned business segments: the Americas; Europe, the Middle East and Africa; and Asia Pacific. The company's range of real estate service areas includes agency leasing; property management; project and development management; valuations; brokerage of properties; capital markets; real estate investment banking and merchant banking; corporate finance; hotel advisory; space acquisition and disposition; facilities management; strategic consulting; energy management and sustainability; value recovery and receivership services; and money management. These services are offered to for-profit and not-for-profit firms, as well as to governmental entities and public-private partnerships, across a wide variety of property categories including offices, hotels, industrial, retail, multi-family residential, hospitals, data centers, sporting facilities, cultural institutions and transportation centers. A fourth business segment encompasses the operations of subsidiary LaSalle Investment Management, a leading diversified real estate investment management firm with approximately $40 billion in assets under management globally. JLL has operations in more than 750 locations in 60 countries worldwide, including 180 corporate offices. Following a flurry of acquisition activity in recent years, the company focused instead during 2009 on overall balance sheet maintenance, and announced plans to limit acquisitions substantially during 2010 as well.

Jones Lang LaSalle offers employee benefits including medical, dental and vision coverage; health savings accounts and flexible spending accounts; discounted gym memberships; life and disability insurance; a 401(k) plan; a discount stock purchase plan; an education assistance program; adoption assistance; and an employee assistance program.

FINANCIALS:

Sales and profits are in thousands of dollars—add 000 to get the full amount. 2009 Note: Financial information for 2009 was not available for all companies at press time.

2009 Sales: $2,480,736	2009 Profits: $-3,595	**U.S. Stock Ticker: JLL**
2008 Sales: $2,697,586	2008 Profits: $84,883	**Int'l Ticker:** Int'l Exchange:
2007 Sales: $2,652,075	2007 Profits: $257,832	Employees: 36,600
2006 Sales: $2,013,578	2006 Profits: $176,401	Fiscal Year Ends: 12/31
2005 Sales: $1,390,610	2005 Profits: $103,672	Parent Company:

SALARIES/BENEFITS:

Pension Plan:	ESOP Stock Plan:	Profit Sharing:	Top Exec. Salary: $750,000	Bonus: $1,162,500
Savings Plan: Y	Stock Purch. Plan: Y		Second Exec. Salary: $425,000	Bonus: $880,000

OTHER THOUGHTS:

Apparent Women Officers or Directors: 4
Hot Spot for Advancement for Women/Minorities: Y

LOCATIONS: ("Y" = Yes)

West:	Southwest:	Midwest:	Southeast:	Northeast:	International:
Y	Y	Y	Y	Y	Y

KB HOME

www.kbhome.com

Industry Group Code: 2361 **Ranks within this company's industry group:** Sales: 9 Profits: 14

Properties:		Financial Services:		Construction/Development:		Investments:		Specialty Services:		Brokerage:	
Apartments:		Mortgages:	Y	Commercial Construction:	Y	REIT:		Property Management:		Commercial Sales:	
Malls/Shopping:		Title Insurance:		Residential Construction:	Y			Online Services:		Residential Sales:	
Offices:		Property Insurance:		Land Development:				Software/IT:		Specialty:	
Hotels/Motels:				Support Services:				Consulting:			
Industrial/Warehouses:				Design/Engineering:							
Other:											

TYPES OF BUSINESS:

Residential Construction Services
Mortgage Services
Home Construction

BRANDS/DIVISIONS/AFFILIATES:

KB Home Mortgage Company
KBnxt
KB Home Studios
My Home. My Earth

CONTACTS: *Note: Officers with more than one job title may be intentionally listed here more than once.*

Jeffrey T. Mezger, CEO
Jeffrey T. Mezger, Pres.
William R. Hollinger, Principal Financial Officer
Wendy Marlett, Sr. VP-Sales & Mktg.
Thomas Norton, Sr. VP-Human Resources
Wendy C. Shiba, General Counsel/Exec. VP/Sec.
Wendy Marlett, Sr. VP-Comm.
William R. Hollinger, Chief Acct. Officer/Sr. VP
Cory F. Cohen, Sr. VP-Tax
Kelly Masuda, Sr. VP/Treas.
Glen Barnard, Sr. VP-KBnxt Group
Stephen F. Bollenbach, Chmn.

Phone: 310-231-4000	**Fax:** 310-231-4222
Toll-Free: 888-524-6637	
Address: 10990 Wilshire Blvd., Los Angeles, CA 90024 US	

GROWTH PLANS/SPECIAL FEATURES:

KB Home is one of the largest homebuilders in the U.S., with operations in 10 states. The firm's major markets are Arizona, California, Colorado, Florida, Nevada, South Carolina, North Carolina, Maryland, Virginia and Texas. KB builds innovatively designed homes catering to first-time and first-move-up homebuyers, generally in medium-sized developments close to major metropolitan areas, as well as to luxury home buyers. Through its KBnxt business model, KB Home seeks to keep construction costs and base prices as low as possible while promoting customer choice. Potential buyers may visit one of the firm's large KB Home Studios locations to select options for their home. KB Home's houses sell for an average price of approximately $207,100. KB Home also provides mortgage-banking, title and insurance services through KB Home Mortgage, LLC, a joint venture between the company and CWB Venture Management Corporation, a subsidiary of Bank of America, N.A. The firm's environmental initiative, My Home. My Earth, embodies the firm's commitment to become a leading environmentally friendly national company. The company currently installs exclusively ENERYSTAR appliances in all of its new homes in 2009, committed to build all new communities to ENERGY STAR guidelines, meaning that they must be more efficient and use less energy than typical houses. In December 2009, firm launched a new web site designed for mobile phones, which features price information, floor plans, directions and photographs of the homes.

FINANCIALS: **Sales and profits are in thousands of dollars—add 000 to get the full amount. 2009 Note: Financial information for 2009 was not available for all companies at press time.**

2009 Sales: $1,824,850	2009 Profits: $-101,784	**U.S. Stock Ticker: KBH**
2008 Sales: $3,033,936	2008 Profits: $-976,131	**Int'l Ticker:** Int'l Exchange:
2007 Sales: $6,416,526	2007 Profits: $-929,414	Employees: 1,400
2006 Sales: $9,359,843	2006 Profits: $482,351	Fiscal Year Ends: 11/30
2005 Sales: $8,154,681	2005 Profits: $823,712	Parent Company:

SALARIES/BENEFITS:

Pension Plan:	ESOP Stock Plan:	Profit Sharing:	Top Exec. Salary: $1,000,000	Bonus: $2,750,000
Savings Plan: Y	Stock Purch. Plan:		Second Exec. Salary: $457,000	Bonus: $411,300

OTHER THOUGHTS:

Apparent Women Officers or Directors: 3
Hot Spot for Advancement for Women/Minorities: Y

LOCATIONS: ("Y" = Yes)

West:	Southwest:	Midwest:	Southeast:	Northeast:	International:
Y	Y	Y	Y	Y	

KERZNER INTERNATIONAL LIMITED

www.kerzner.com

Industry Group Code: 721120 **Ranks within this company's industry group:** Sales: Profits:

Properties:		Financial Services:		Construction/Development:		Investments:		Specialty Services:		Brokerage:	
Apartments:		Mortgages:		Commercial Construction:		REIT:		Property Management:		Commercial Sales:	
Malls/Shopping:		Title Insurance:		Residential Construction:				Online Services:		Residential Sales:	
Offices:		Property Insurance:		Land Development:				Software/IT:		Specialty:	
Hotels/Motels:	Y			Support Services:				Consulting:			
Industrial/Warehouses:				Design/Engineering:							
Other:	Y										

TYPES OF BUSINESS:

Casino Hotels
Luxury Resort Hotels
Resort Development

BRANDS/DIVISIONS/AFFILIATES:

Atlantis
Atlantis, The Palm Dubai
Cove Atlantis (The)
One&Only
Mazagan Beach Resort

CONTACTS:

Note: Officers with more than one job title may be intentionally listed here more than once.

Solomon Kerzner, CEO
Paul O'Neil, COO
Robert F. Cotter, Pres.
Bruce Himelstein, Chief Mktg. Officer/Exec. VP
Megan Marchesini, Contact-Media
Solomon Kerzner, Chmn.

Phone: 242-363-6000	**Fax:** 954-809-2337
Toll-Free:	
Address: Atlantis, Coral Towers, Executive Offices, Paradise Island, C5 Bahamas	

GROWTH PLANS/SPECIAL FEATURES:

Kerzner International Holdings, Ltd., is a resort and gaming company that develops, operates and manages premier resorts, casinos and luxury hotels. The company's flagship property is the Atlantis Paradise Island in the Bahamas. The 2,900-room ocean themed resort features three interconnected hotel towers built around 100 acres of pools and marine environments, home to over 50,000 marine animals. Additionally, the resort features the world's largest open-air aquarium. The firm also operates Atlantis The Palm, Dubai, a 1,500-room ocean themed resort located on the manmade island of Palm Jumeirah; The Cove Atlantis; and six One&Only Resorts, exclusive luxury resorts, located in the Bahamas, Mexico, Mauritius, South Africa, the Maldives and Dubai. The company's newest resort is Mazagan Beach Resort, a 500-room casino resort in Morocco, which opened in October 2009. Kerzner International manages or owns interests in nine beach resorts. A seventh One&Only resort, under development in Dubai, is expected to open in October 2010.

FINANCIALS:

Sales and profits are in thousands of dollars—add 000 to get the full amount. 2009 Note: Financial information for 2009 was not available for all companies at press time.

2009 Sales: $	2009 Profits: $	**U.S. Stock Ticker: Private**
2008 Sales: $	2008 Profits: $	**Int'l Ticker:** Int'l Exchange:
2007 Sales: $	2007 Profits: $	Employees:
2006 Sales: $	2006 Profits: $	Fiscal Year Ends: 12/31
2005 Sales: $721,524	2005 Profits: $50,648	Parent Company:

SALARIES/BENEFITS:

Pension Plan:	ESOP Stock Plan:	Profit Sharing:	Top Exec. Salary: $	Bonus: $
Savings Plan:	Stock Purch. Plan:		Second Exec. Salary: $	Bonus: $

OTHER THOUGHTS:

Apparent Women Officers or Directors: 1
Hot Spot for Advancement for Women/Minorities: Y

LOCATIONS: ("Y" = Yes)

West:	Southwest:	Midwest:	Southeast:	Northeast:	International:
				Y	Y

KILROY REALTY CORPORATION

www.kilroyrealty.com

Industry Group Code: 531120 **Ranks within this company's industry group:** Sales: 48 Profits: 35

Properties:		Financial Services:		Construction/Development:		Investments:		Specialty Services:		Brokerage:	
Apartments:		Mortgages:		Commercial Construction:		REIT:	Y	Property Management:	Y	Commercial Sales:	
Malls/Shopping:		Title Insurance:		Residential Construction:				Online Services:		Residential Sales:	
Offices:	Y	Property Insurance:		Land Development:				Software/IT:		Specialty:	
Hotels/Motels:				Support Services:	Y			Consulting:			
Industrial/Warehouses:	Y			Design/Engineering:							
Other:											

TYPES OF BUSINESS:

Real Estate Investment Trust
Office & Industrial Properties
Property Management
Financial Services
Leasing
Construction Management

BRANDS/DIVISIONS/AFFILIATES:

Kilroy Realty, L.P.
Kilroy Realty Finance Partnership
Kilroy Realty Finance, Inc.
Kilroy Services, LLC
Kilroy Realty TRS, Inc.
Kilroy RB LLC
Kilroy RB II LLC

CONTACTS: *Note: Officers with more than one job title may be intentionally listed here more than once.*

John B. Kilroy, Jr., CEO
Jeffrey C. Hawken, COO/Exec. VP
John B. Kilroy, Jr., Pres.
Tyler H. Rose, CFO/Exec. VP
Tyler H. Rose, Sec.
Chris Corpuz, Exec. VP-Acquisitions & Strategic Initiatives
Heidi Roth, Controller/Sr. VP
John T. Fucci, Sr. VP-Asset Mgmt.
Steven R. Scott, Sr. VP-San Diego
Justin W. Smart, Sr. VP-Dev.
John B. Kilroy, Sr., Chmn.

Phone: 310-481-8400	**Fax:** 310-481-6501
Toll-Free:	
Address: 12200 W. Olympic Blvd., Ste. 200, Los Angeles, CA 90064 US	

GROWTH PLANS/SPECIAL FEATURES:

Kilroy Realty Corporation (KRC) is a REIT (Real Estate Investment Trust) that owns, operates, develops and acquires Class A office and industrial real estate in suburban markets, primarily in southern California. Its portfolio of operating properties comprises 93 office buildings and 41 industrial buildings, aggregating approximately 8.7 million and 3.7 million rentable square feet, respectively. The office properties were 80.6% leased to 286 tenants and the industrial properties were 88.2% leased to 58 tenants. The company has one development property in the lease-up phase encompasses 51,000 rentable square feet of new medical office space located in San Diego. The firm's tenants can be broken down into the following industry categories: Professional and business services, which generated 32.8% of the firm's rental revenue; education and health services, 21.1%; manufacturing, 18.3%; finance, insurance and real estate, 12.3%; information technology, 11.1%; wholesale and retail trade, 2%; construction, 1.4%; government, 0.5%; leisure and hospitality, 0.4%; and transportation, warehousing and public utilities, 0.1%. Its largest tenants include Intuit, Inc. (leasing a total of approximately 536,800 square feet); AMN Healthcare, Inc.; DIRECTV, Inc.; Scripps Health; CareFusion Corporation; Hewlett-Packard Company, Comcast Corporation; Northrup Grumman Corporation; and The Boeing Company. KRC owns all of its properties through subsidiary Kilroy Realty, L.P. (KRLP), which in turn owns Kilroy Realty Finance Partnership, L.P. KRLP's wholly-owned subsidiary Kilroy Services, LLC conducts substantially all of the firm's development activities. Other KRLP wholly-owned subsidiaries include Kilroy Realty Finance, Inc.; Kilroy Realty TRS, Inc.; Kilroy RB LLC; and Kilroy RB II LL.

FINANCIALS: **Sales and profits are in thousands of dollars—add 000 to get the full amount. 2009 Note: Financial information for 2009 was not available for all companies at press time.**

2009 Sales: $247,071	2009 Profits: $38,015	**U.S. Stock Ticker: KRC**
2008 Sales: $256,066	2008 Profits: $46,911	**Int'l Ticker:** Int'l Exchange:
2007 Sales: $227,811	2007 Profits: $123,317	Employees: 132
2006 Sales: $241,541	2006 Profits: $81,864	Fiscal Year Ends: 12/31
2005 Sales: $226,111	2005 Profits: $33,819	Parent Company:

SALARIES/BENEFITS:

Pension Plan:	ESOP Stock Plan:	Profit Sharing:	Top Exec. Salary: $1,050,000	Bonus: $2,500,000
Savings Plan:	Stock Purch. Plan:		Second Exec. Salary: $525,000	Bonus: $1,441,280

OTHER THOUGHTS:

Apparent Women Officers or Directors: 1
Hot Spot for Advancement for Women/Minorities:

LOCATIONS: ("Y" = Yes)

West:	Southwest:	Midwest:	Southeast:	Northeast:	International:
Y					

KIMCO REALTY CORP

www.kimcorealty.com

Industry Group Code: 531120 **Ranks within this company's industry group:** Sales: 23 Profits: 12

Properties:		Financial Services:		Construction/Development:		Investments:		Specialty Services:		Brokerage:	
Apartments:		Mortgages:		Commercial Construction:	Y	REIT:	Y	Property Management:	Y	Commercial Sales:	
Malls/Shopping:	Y	Title Insurance:		Residential Construction:				Online Services:		Residential Sales:	
Offices:	Y	Property Insurance:		Land Development:	Y			Software/IT:		Specialty:	
Hotels/Motels:				Support Services:				Consulting:	Y		
Industrial/Warehouses:				Design/Engineering:							
Other:											

TYPES OF BUSINESS:

Real Estate Investment Trust
Commercial Development
Property Services
Leasing
Consulting Services
Shopping Centers
Regional Malls
Property Management

BRANDS/DIVISIONS/AFFILIATES:

Kimco Exchange Place

CONTACTS:

Note: Officers with more than one job title may be intentionally listed here more than once.

David B. Henry, CEO
Michael V. Pappagallo, COO
David B. Henry, Pres.
Michael V. Pappagallo, CFO
Barbara Pooley, Investor Rel. Contact/Sr. VP
Chris Freeman, VP-Property Mgmt.
Milton Cooper, Chmn.

Phone: 516-869-9000 **Fax:** 516-869-9001
Toll-Free: 800-285-4626
Address: 3333 New Hyde Park Rd., Ste. 100, New Hyde Park, NY 11042 US

GROWTH PLANS/SPECIAL FEATURES:

Kimco Realty Corp. is a U.S. is a real estate investment trust (REIT) that owns and operates shopping centers. The firm owns interest in approximately 1,915 properties, including shopping centers, retail store leases, development projects and undeveloped land. These properties are located in 45 states, Puerto Rico, Canada, Mexico, Brazil, Peru and Chile. Kimco's shopping centers are anchored by a department store, supermarket or drug store tenant offering day-to-day necessities. Kimco's Property Services division provides property management services relating to the management, operation, supervision and maintenance of properties. Subsidiary Kimco Exchange Place handles 1031 tax deferred transactions. The Leasing Department assists potential renters in finding the best locations for their business ventures. The firm focuses on acquiring properties that have opportunities for redevelopment and renovation, as well as other value increasing characteristics. Generally, the company can close a transaction in 45 to 60 days. Kimco also offers retail store owners and developers preferred equity debt. In November 2009, the company acquired the remaining 85% interest in PL Retail LLC, which consists of 21 shopping centers that the company manages. In April 2010, the firm established a joint venture with the Canada Pension Plan Investment Board to acquire shopping centers in well established neighborhoods in the U.S. The company will own a 55% interest in the venture.

Employees are offered medical and dental insurance; disability coverage; life insurance; healthcare and dependent care reimbursement accounts; a 401(k) savings plan; and tuition assistance.

FINANCIALS:

Sales and profits are in thousands of dollars—add 000 to get the full amount. 2009 Note: Financial information for 2009 was not available for all companies at press time.

2009 Sales: $786,887	2009 Profits: $-3,942	**U.S. Stock Ticker: KIM**
2008 Sales: $758,704	2008 Profits: $249,902	**Int'l Ticker:** Int'l Exchange:
2007 Sales: $674,534	2007 Profits: $442,830	Employees:
2006 Sales: $580,551	2006 Profits: $428,259	Fiscal Year Ends: 12/31
2005 Sales: $501,569	2005 Profits: $363,628	Parent Company:

SALARIES/BENEFITS:

Pension Plan:	ESOP Stock Plan:	Profit Sharing:	Top Exec. Salary: $673,077	Bonus: $500,000
Savings Plan: Y	Stock Purch. Plan:		Second Exec. Salary: $661,538	Bonus: $400,000

OTHER THOUGHTS:

Apparent Women Officers or Directors: 1
Hot Spot for Advancement for Women/Minorities:

LOCATIONS: ("Y" = Yes)

West:	Southwest:	Midwest:	Southeast:	Northeast:	International:
Y	Y	Y	Y	Y	Y

KIMPTON HOTEL & RESTAURANT GROUP LLC

www.kimptonhotels.com

Industry Group Code: 721110 **Ranks within this company's industry group:** Sales: Profits:

Properties:		Financial Services:		Construction/Development:		Investments:		Specialty Services:		Brokerage:	
Apartments:		Mortgages:		Commercial Construction:	Y	REIT:		Property Management:	Y	Commercial Sales:	
Malls/Shopping:		Title Insurance:		Residential Construction:				Online Services:		Residential Sales:	
Offices:		Property Insurance:		Land Development:				Software/IT:		Specialty:	
Hotels/Motels:	Y			Support Services:				Consulting:			
Industrial/Warehouses:				Design/Engineering:							
Other:	Y										

TYPES OF BUSINESS:

Hotels
Restaurants
Hotel Management Services

BRANDS/DIVISIONS/AFFILIATES:

Hotel Vintage Plaza
Monticello Inn
Hotel Vintage Park
Hotel Burnham
Cafe Pescatore
Sazerac
Silverleaf Tavern
Mind. Body. Spa.

CONTACTS:

Note: Officers with more than one job title may be intentionally listed here more than once.

Michael Depatie, CEO
Niki Leondakis, COO
Ben Rowe, CFO/Exec. VP
Steve Pinetti, Sr. VP-Mktg. & Sales
Greg Smith, Sr. VP-Human Resources
Joe Long, CIO/Exec. VP-Dev.
Judy Miles, General Counsel/Exec. VP
David Sussman, Sr. VP-Hotel Dev. & Design
Vanessa Bortnick, Sr. Dir.-Comm.
Ken Reynolds, Sr. VP-Construction
Christine Lawson, VP-Hotel Sales
Mike DeFrino, Sr. VP-Hotel Oper.
John Inserra, Sr. VP-Restaurant Oper.

Phone: 415-397-5572	**Fax:** 415-296-8031
Toll-Free: 800-546-7866	
Address: 222 Kearny St., Ste. 200, San Francisco, CA 94108 US	

GROWTH PLANS/SPECIAL FEATURES:

Kimpton Hotel and Restaurant Group, LLC, based in San Francisco, owns 42 lifestyle boutique hotels in the U.S. and Canada. Its holdings consist of 8,270 rooms, in addition to 45 restaurants and bars beside or within its hotels. The firm specializes in renovating old buildings to transform them into unique, themed hotels and small, European-style restaurants. Its themed hotels include Hotel Vintage Plaza in Portland, OR, which has an Italian romance theme; Monticello Inn in San Francisco, reminiscent of Thomas Jefferson's famous estate; Hotel Vintage Park in Seattle, highlighting local Washington wines; and Hotel Burnham in Chicago, which actively expresses its place in Chicago's history. Some notable restaurants run by Kimpton include San Francisco bistros Cafe Pescatore, Scala's Bistro and Puccini & Pinetti; as well as Sazerac in Seattle; Atwood Cafe in Chicago; Cobalt in New Orleans; Ginger Grove in Miami; Firefly in Washington, D.C.; Ruby Room in Boston; Silverleaf Tavern in New York City; and Zin in Vancouver. Special services offered by its hotels include Mind. Body. Spa. Program, which offers in-room massage, yoga, Pilates and meditation; pet packages, which include pet-friendly amenities and services; and Hosted Evening Wine Hour. In addition to owning and running its own hotels, the company is engaged in comprehensive management services for other companies, offering everything from financial management to facilities renovation. The company's newest hotel is in Philadelphia, where Kimpton is renovating the historic Architects Building to create Hotel Palomar. The firm opened seven new locations recently, with three more scheduled to open in 2010.

Employees of the firm are offered medical, dental and vision and 100% for basic life insurance; long and short-term disability; pet care program; paid vacation time; tuition reimbursement and employee discounts.

FINANCIALS:

Sales and profits are in thousands of dollars—add 000 to get the full amount. 2009 Note: Financial information for 2009 was not available for all companies at press time.

2009 Sales: $	2009 Profits: $	**U.S. Stock Ticker: Private**
2008 Sales: $	2008 Profits: $	**Int'l Ticker:** Int'l Exchange:
2007 Sales: $	2007 Profits: $	Employees:
2006 Sales: $	2006 Profits: $	Fiscal Year Ends: 12/31
2005 Sales: $	2005 Profits: $	Parent Company:

SALARIES/BENEFITS:

Pension Plan:	ESOP Stock Plan:	Profit Sharing:	Top Exec. Salary: $	Bonus: $
Savings Plan:	Stock Purch. Plan:		Second Exec. Salary: $	Bonus: $

OTHER THOUGHTS:

Apparent Women Officers or Directors: 8
Hot Spot for Advancement for Women/Minorities: Y

LOCATIONS: ("Y" = Yes)

West:	Southwest:	Midwest:	Southeast:	Northeast:	International:
Y	Y	Y	Y	Y	Y

KUMHO INDUSTRIAL CO LTD

www.kumhoenc.com

Industry Group Code: 237 **Ranks within this company's industry group:** Sales: 17 Profits: 27

Properties:		Financial Services:		Construction/Development:		Investments:		Specialty Services:		Brokerage:	
Apartments:		Mortgages:		Commercial Construction:	Y	REIT:		Property Management:		Commercial Sales:	
Malls/Shopping:		Title Insurance:		Residential Construction:	Y			Online Services:		Residential Sales:	
Offices:		Property Insurance:		Land Development:	Y			Software/IT:		Specialty:	
Hotels/Motels:				Support Services:				Consulting:			
Industrial/Warehouses:				Design/Engineering:	Y						
Other:											

TYPES OF BUSINESS:

Engineering & Construction
Research & Development
Sewage Treatment

BRANDS/DIVISIONS/AFFILIATES:

Kumho E&C
[?]ullim
Kumho Asiana Group
ECOS
KIDEA

CONTACTS:

Note: Officers with more than one job title may be intentionally listed here more than once.

Yon-Goo Lee, CEO
Wang-Hyun Moon, Mgr.-Investor Rel. Team
Seong-San Kim, CEO-Buslines

Phone: 02-6303-0114	**Fax:**
Toll-Free:	
Address: 1095-4 SongWol Dong, NaJu City, Jeollanam-Do, Seoul, 100-061 Korea	

GROWTH PLANS/SPECIAL FEATURES:

Kumho Industrial Co. Ltd., doing business as Kumho Engineering & Construction (Kumho E&C), offers a wide range of building services. It has worked on general architectural construction projects, building commercial centers, warehouses, leisure facilities and even whole cities. Kumho E&C's civil engineering projects have run the gamut from airports, railroads and highways to tunnels and bridges. The firm has built over 600,000 new homes, including state-of-the-art apartment complexes and high-rise residential buildings. Kumho E&C's plant engineering projects have included constructing petrochemical plants; installing factory automation equipment; building environmental facilities such as incinerators and water and sewage treatment plants; and energy-related facilities, including gasoline tanks, LNG (liquefied natural gas) pipelines and power plants. The firm operates a research and development institute near its office dedicated to finding environmentally friendly building materials; stronger and faster building techniques; and new architectural designs maximizing heating and cooling systems, water-proofing and structural integrity. The firm's Electrode Contract Oxydation System (ECOS) is a solution that facilitates the decomposition of sewage and is used in the removal of pollutants. Another sewage treatment is the KIDEA process, which was developed jointly by the company and the Korea Institute of Science & Technology, and removes 70% to 80% of nutrient salt from sewage. Kumho E&C is part of the Kumho Asiana Group.

FINANCIALS:

Sales and profits are in thousands of dollars—add 000 to get the full amount. 2009 Note: Financial information for 2009 was not available for all companies at press time.

2009 Sales: $2,096,050	2009 Profits: $-2,137,490	**U.S. Stock Ticker:**
2008 Sales: $6,072,700	2008 Profits: $27,600	**Int'l Ticker: 002990** Int'l Exchange: Seoul-KRX
2007 Sales: $5,339,000	2007 Profits: $135,000	Employees:
2006 Sales: $6,207,400	2006 Profits: $56,900	Fiscal Year Ends:
2005 Sales: $	2005 Profits: $	Parent Company:

SALARIES/BENEFITS:

Pension Plan:	ESOP Stock Plan:	Profit Sharing:	Top Exec. Salary: $	Bonus: $
Savings Plan:	Stock Purch. Plan:		Second Exec. Salary: $	Bonus: $

OTHER THOUGHTS:

Apparent Women Officers or Directors:
Hot Spot for Advancement for Women/Minorities:

LOCATIONS: ("Y" = Yes)

West:	Southwest:	Midwest:	Southeast:	Northeast:	International:
					Y

LANDAMERICA FINANCIAL GROUP INC

www.landam.com

Industry Group Code: 524127 **Ranks within this company's industry group:** Sales: 3 Profits: 5

Properties:		Financial Services:		Construction/Development:		Investments:		Specialty Services:		Brokerage:	
Apartments:		Mortgages:		Commercial Construction:		REIT:		Property Management:		Commercial Sales:	
Malls/Shopping:		Title Insurance:	Y	Residential Construction:				Online Services:		Residential Sales:	
Offices:		Property Insurance:		Land Development:				Software/IT:		Specialty:	
Hotels/Motels:				Support Services:				Consulting:			
Industrial/Warehouses:				Design/Engineering:							
Other:											

TYPES OF BUSINESS:

Real Estate Services
Title Services
Transaction Management Services
Loan Servicing

BRANDS/DIVISIONS/AFFILIATES:

LandAmerica Title Insurance Company of Mexico
Capital Title Group Inc.
Aaron & Wright, Inc.
Lawyers Title Insurance Corporation
Commonwealth Land Title Insurance Company
LandAmerica NJ Title Insurance Company
United Capital Title Insurance Company
Fidelity National Financial Inc.

CONTACTS:

Note: Officers with more than one job title may be intentionally listed here more than once.

G. William Evans, CFO/Exec. VP
Richard P. Gonzalez, CIO/Exec. VP
Ross W. Dorneman, Chief Admin. Officer/Exec. VP
Michelle H. Gluck, Chief Legal Officer/Exec. VP
Christine Vlahcevic, Corp. Controller/Sr. VP
Melissa A. Hill, Pres., Residential Svcs.
Jonathan Mitchell, Chief Restructuring Officer
Thomas Snead, Jr., Chmn.

Phone:	**Fax:**
Toll-Free: 800-446-7086	
Address: 5600 Cox Rd., Glen Allen, VA 23060 US	

GROWTH PLANS/SPECIAL FEATURES:

LandAmerica Financial Group, Inc. is a holding company that provides, through more than 25 subsidiaries, real estate transaction services to agent, residential, commercial and lender customers. The company divides its operations into four segments: commercial services, residential services, lender services and agency services. Commercial services include assessment, construction disbursement, Tenant In Common (TIC), risk mitigation, valuation and ancillary services. The residential services segment, operating through Title Insurance Company of America, offers home warranty, online residential title, property inspection, relocation, title and closing services. Lender services include credit services, loan servicing, flood services, mortgage origination and refinancing, tax servicing and default services. Agency services include executive, support, transaction and technology services, as well as the AgentXtra program, a suite of products designed to assist customers with business solutions, customer service and growth opportunities. The firm conducts business in the U.S., Mexico, Canada, the Caribbean, Latin America, Europe and Asia. In May 2008, the firm announced the opening of the LandAmerica Title Insurance Company of Mexico, S.A. with headquarters in San Miguel De Allende and a satellite office in North Baja. In August 2008, LandAmerica acquired Aaron & Wright, Inc. a commercial real estate valuation company based in Houston, Texas. In November 2008, LandAmerica and LandAmerica 1031 Exchange Services, Inc. filed for Chapter 11 bankruptcy protection. In December 2008, the company sold subsidiary Lawyers Title Insurance Corporation and its subsidiaries; Commonwealth Land Title Insurance Company and its subsidiaries, including LandAmerica NJ Title Insurance Company; and United Capital Title Insurance Company to Fidelity National Financial, Inc. for a combined $298 million.

LandAmerica offers its employees medical, dental, vision and prescription drug coverage; flexible spending accounts; accident insurance; employee development resources; employee discounts; a stock ownership plan; and a 401(k) plan.

FINANCIALS:

Sales and profits are in thousands of dollars—add 000 to get the full amount. 2009 Note: Financial information for 2009 was not available for all companies at press time.

2009 Sales: $	2009 Profits: $	**U.S. Stock Ticker: LFGRQ**
2008 Sales: $2,876,000	2008 Profits: $-719,700	**Int'l Ticker:** Int'l Exchange:
2007 Sales: $3,705,800	2007 Profits: $-54,100	Employees:
2006 Sales: $4,015,900	2006 Profits: $98,800	Fiscal Year Ends: 12/31
2005 Sales: $3,959,600	2005 Profits: $165,600	Parent Company:

SALARIES/BENEFITS:

Pension Plan:	ESOP Stock Plan: Y	Profit Sharing:	Top Exec. Salary: $	Bonus: $
Savings Plan: Y	Stock Purch. Plan:		Second Exec. Salary: $	Bonus: $

OTHER THOUGHTS:

Apparent Women Officers or Directors: 3
Hot Spot for Advancement for Women/Minorities: Y

LOCATIONS: ("Y" = Yes)

West:	Southwest:	Midwest:	Southeast:	Northeast:	International:
Y	Y	Y	Y	Y	

LAS VEGAS SANDS CORP (THE VENETIAN) www.lasvegassands.com

Industry Group Code: 721120 **Ranks within this company's industry group:** Sales: 3 Profits: 4

Properties:		Financial Services:		Construction/Development:		Investments:		Specialty Services:		Brokerage:	
Apartments:		Mortgages:		Commercial Construction:		REIT:		Property Management:		Commercial Sales:	
Malls/Shopping:	Y	Title Insurance:		Residential Construction:				Online Services:		Residential Sales:	
Offices:		Property Insurance:		Land Development:				Software/IT:		Specialty:	
Hotels/Motels:	Y			Support Services:				Consulting:			
Industrial/Warehouses:				Design/Engineering:							
Other:	Y										

TYPES OF BUSINESS:

Hotel Casinos
Convention & Conference Centers
Shopping Center Development
Casino Property Development

BRANDS/DIVISIONS/AFFILIATES:

Venetian Resort Hotel Casino (The)
Sands Expo and Convention Center (The)
Congress Center (The)
Sands Macao Casino (The)
Palazzo Resort Hotel Casino (The)
Venetian Macao Resort Hotel (The)
Marina Bay Sands
Cotai Strip

CONTACTS: *Note: Officers with more than one job title may be intentionally listed here more than once.*

Sheldon G. Adelson, CEO
Michael A. Leven, COO
Michael A. Leven, Pres.
Kenneth J. Kay, CFO/Sr. VP
Ron Reese, Contact-Media
Daniel Briggs, Contact-Investment Community
Robert G. Goldstein, COO/Pres., The Venetian Las Vegas
Nigel Roberts, Pres., Marina Bay Sands
Leonard DeAngelo, Sr. VP-Asia Oper., Marina Bay Sands
Sheldon G. Adelson, Chmn.
Steven C. Jacobs, CEO-Sands China Ltd.

Phone: 702-414-1000	**Fax:** 702-414-4884
Toll-Free:	
Address: 3355 Las Vegas Blvd. S., Rm. 1A, Las Vegas, NV 89109 US	

GROWTH PLANS/SPECIAL FEATURES:

Las Vegas Sands Corp. (The Venetian) (LVSC) is an international hotel, resort and casino firm. Its flagship property is The Venetian Resort Hotel Casino, which is connected the firm's The Palazzo Resort Hotel Casino. Together, The Venetian and The Palazzo offer 225,000 square feet (sq. ft.) of gaming space with 240 table games and 3,020 slot machines; 6,080 hotel suites; and 840,000 square feet of dining, retail and entertainment space, including The Shoppes at The Palazzo. LVSC also runs the 1.2 million square foot convention and trade show facility, The Sands Expo and Convention Center, and supplemental event and conference center The Congress Center that connects to The Venetian. These properties feature 1.2 million square feet of meeting, exhibition and convention space; 1 million sq. ft. of retail and dining space; and the 15,000 seat Venetian Arena. The company's largest development projects, $12 billion Cotai Strip, is a collection of hotel properties, casinos and entertainment venues in Macao, China is expected open in 2011. The firm runs The Sands Macao and The Venetian Macao Resort Hotel, the anchor property on the Cotai Strip. One of the company's newest properties is the Sands Casino Resort Bethlehem, Philadelphia featuring 3,000 slot machines and various entertainment options. Construction on the tower of the Sands Casino Resort Bethlehem is to be completed, by May 2011. The newest international hotel and casino, Marina Sands opened on April 27 2010, in Singapore, Malaysia. In April 28 2010, the company announced the sale of retail outlets and apartments for $$12 billion to recoup construction costs on its Macau properties.

FINANCIALS: **Sales and profits are in thousands of dollars—add 000 to get the full amount. 2009 Note: Financial information for 2009 was not available for all companies at press time.**

2009 Sales: $4,929,444	2009 Profits: $-354,479	**U.S. Stock Ticker: LVS**
2008 Sales: $4,735,126	2008 Profits: $-163,558	**Int'l Ticker:** Int'l Exchange:
2007 Sales: $3,104,422	2007 Profits: $116,688	Employees: 27,000
2006 Sales: $2,340,178	2006 Profits: $442,003	Fiscal Year Ends: 12/31
2005 Sales: $1,824,225	2005 Profits: $283,686	Parent Company:

SALARIES/BENEFITS:

Pension Plan:	ESOP Stock Plan:	Profit Sharing:	Top Exec. Salary: $1,561,539	Bonus: $
Savings Plan: Y	Stock Purch. Plan:		Second Exec. Salary: $1,000,000	Bonus: $

OTHER THOUGHTS:

Apparent Women Officers or Directors:
Hot Spot for Advancement for Women/Minorities:

LOCATIONS: ("Y" = Yes)

West:	Southwest:	Midwest:	Southeast:	Northeast:	International:
Y				Y	Y

LASALLE HOTEL PROPERTIES

www.lasallehotels.com

Industry Group Code: 531120 **Ranks within this company's industry group:** Sales: 26 Profits: 42

Properties:		Financial Services:		Construction/Development:		Investments:		Specialty Services:		Brokerage:	
Apartments:		Mortgages:		Commercial Construction:		REIT:	Y	Property Management:		Commercial Sales:	
Malls/Shopping:		Title Insurance:		Residential Construction:				Online Services:		Residential Sales:	
Offices:		Property Insurance:		Land Development:				Software/IT:		Specialty:	
Hotels/Motels:	Y			Support Services:				Consulting:			
Industrial/Warehouses:				Design/Engineering:							
Other:											

TYPES OF BUSINESS:

Real Estate Investment Trust
Luxury Hotels
Property Investment

BRANDS/DIVISIONS/AFFILIATES:

LaSalle Hotel Operating Partnership
Chicago 540 LLC
Westin Copley Place
House of Blues Hotel
Sofitel Washington, DC Lafayette Square
San Diego Paradise Point Resort
Chicago Marriott Downtown
Modern Magic Hotel LLC

CONTACTS:

Note: Officers with more than one job title may be intentionally listed here more than once.

Michael D. Barnello, CEO
Alfred L. Young, COO
Michael D. Barnello, Pres.
Hans S. Weger, CFO
Hans S. Weger, Corp. Sec.
Hans S. Weger, Treas./Exec. VP
Stuart L. Scott, Chmn.

Phone: 301-941-1500 **Fax:** 301-941-1553
Toll-Free:
Address: 3 Bethesda Metro Ctr., Ste. 1200, Bethesda, MD 20814 US

GROWTH PLANS/SPECIAL FEATURES:

LaSalle Hotel Properties is a self-managed and self-administered real estate investment trust (REIT) that owns and invests in luxury hotels. The firm primarily works with hotels located in convention, resort or major urban business markets. The company currently owns interests in 31 upscale and luxury full-service hotels with approximately 8,500 rooms/suites located in 11 states and Washington, D.C. The firm is comprised of hotel investors, asset managers and financial experts, rather than hotel operators. LaSalle's hotels are operated and managed by unrelated hotel operating companies. LaSalle maintains strategic relationships with internationally recognized hotel operating companies such as Westin Hotels and Resorts; Sheraton Hotels and Resorts Worldwide, Inc.; Hilton Hotels Corporation; Hyatt Hotels Corporation; Dolce Hotels and Resorts; and others. The firm seeks to improve revenue growth through renovations, redevelopment and/or expansions; brand or franchise conversion; acquisitions of appropriate full-service hotels in the U.S. and abroad; and selective development of hotel properties in favorable upscale markets. Properties include the Le Montrose Suite Hotel, Indianapolis Marriott Downtown; Hilton San Diego Gaslamp Quarter; Westin Copley Place; Westin Michigan Avenue; and Hotel Solamar. The company maintains a 95% controlling interest in joint venture, Modern Magic Hotel LLC. In February 2010, LaSalle's joint venture with LaSalle Investment Management was mutually dissolved. In March 2010, the company acquired the Sofitel Washington, DC Lafayette Square for $95 million.

FINANCIALS:

Sales and profits are in thousands of dollars—add 000 to get the full amount. 2009 Note: Financial information for 2009 was not available for all companies at press time.

2009 Sales: $606,999	2009 Profits: $7,618	**U.S. Stock Ticker: LHO**
2008 Sales: $683,377	2008 Profits: $33,127	**Int'l Ticker:** Int'l Exchange:
2007 Sales: $661,710	2007 Profits: $89,755	Employees: 26
2006 Sales: $593,831	2006 Profits: $99,060	Fiscal Year Ends: 12/31
2005 Sales: $363,863	2005 Profits: $35,396	Parent Company:

SALARIES/BENEFITS:

Pension Plan:	ESOP Stock Plan:	Profit Sharing:	Top Exec. Salary: $529,936	Bonus: $529,936
Savings Plan:	Stock Purch. Plan:		Second Exec. Salary: $425,000	Bonus: $

OTHER THOUGHTS:

Apparent Women Officers or Directors: 1
Hot Spot for Advancement for Women/Minorities:

LOCATIONS: ("Y" = Yes)

West:	Southwest:	Midwest:	Southeast:	Northeast:	International:
Y	Y	Y		Y	

LAYNE CHRISTENSEN COMPANY

www.laynechristensen.com

Industry Group Code: 237 **Ranks within this company's industry group:** Sales: 31 Profits: 26

Properties:		Financial Services:		Construction/Development:		Investments:		Specialty Services:		Brokerage:	
Apartments:		Mortgages:		Commercial Construction:		REIT:		Property Management:		Commercial Sales:	
Malls/Shopping:		Title Insurance:		Residential Construction:				Online Services:		Residential Sales:	
Offices:		Property Insurance:		Land Development:				Software/IT:		Specialty:	
Hotels/Motels:				Support Services:	Y			Consulting:	Y		
Industrial/Warehouses:				Design/Engineering:	Y						
Other:											

TYPES OF BUSINESS:

Construction & Civil Engineering Services
Water Treatment Plant Development
Drilling Services
Oil & Gas Field Services
Unconventional Natural Gas Production

BRANDS/DIVISIONS/AFFILIATES:

CONTACTS:

Note: Officers with more than one job title may be intentionally listed here more than once.

Andrew B. Schmitt, CEO
Andrew B. Schmitt, Pres.
Steven F. Crooke, General Counsel/VP/Sec.
Jerry W. Fanska, VP-Finance/Treas.
Gregory F. Aluce, Sr. VP/Pres., Water Resources Div.
Eric Despain, Sr. VP/Pres., Mineral Exploration
Phil Winner, Pres., Layne Energy
Jeffrey J. Reynolds, Exec. VP/Pres., Water Infrastructure Div.
David A. B. Brown, Chmn.

Phone: 913-677-6800	**Fax:** 913-362-0133
Toll-Free:	
Address: 1900 Shawnee Mission Pkwy., Mission Woods, KS 66205 US	

GROWTH PLANS/SPECIAL FEATURES:

Layne Christensen Co. provides drilling and construction services and related products in two principal markets: water infrastructure and mineral exploration. In addition, the company is a producer of unconventional natural gas for the energy market. The firm operates in four segments: Water Infrastructure, Mineral Exploration, Energy Services and Other. Through the Water Infrastructure division, Layne Christensen provides water systems services, such as test hole drilling, well construction, well development and testing, pump selection, equipment installation and pipeline construction; well and pump rehabilitation services; water and wastewater treatment and plant construction services; sewer rehabilitation; and environmental assessment drilling. The Mineral Exploration division conducts aboveground and underground drilling activities for the global mineral exploration industry. The Energy Services segment provides the exploration for, and acquisition, development, and production of, unconventional natural gas. The other segment includes two small specialty energy service companies and any other specialty operations not included in the other divisions. The firm operates throughout North America, as well as Africa, Australia, Europe, Brazil and, through its affiliates, in South America. Layne Christensen's customers include municipalities, investor-owned water utilities, industrial companies, global mining companies, consulting engineering firms, heavy civil construction contractors, oil and gas companies and agribusiness.

FINANCIALS:

Sales and profits are in thousands of dollars—add 000 to get the full amount. 2009 Note: Financial information for 2009 was not available for all companies at press time.

2009 Sales: $1,008,063	2009 Profits: $26,534	**U.S. Stock Ticker: LAYN**
2008 Sales: $868,274	2008 Profits: $37,256	**Int'l Ticker:** Int'l Exchange:
2007 Sales: $722,768	2007 Profits: $26,252	Employees: 3,600
2006 Sales: $463,015	2006 Profits: $14,681	Fiscal Year Ends: 1/31
2005 Sales: $343,462	2005 Profits: $9,754	Parent Company:

SALARIES/BENEFITS:

Pension Plan:	ESOP Stock Plan:	Profit Sharing:	Top Exec. Salary: $618,462	Bonus: $562,437
Savings Plan:	Stock Purch. Plan:		Second Exec. Salary: $363,231	Bonus: $248,334

OTHER THOUGHTS:

Apparent Women Officers or Directors:
Hot Spot for Advancement for Women/Minorities:

LOCATIONS: ("Y" = Yes)

West:	Southwest:	Midwest:	Southeast:	Northeast:	International:
Y	Y	Y	Y	Y	Y

LB FOSTER COMPANY

www.lbfoster.com

Industry Group Code: 4233 **Ranks within this company's industry group:** Sales: 3 Profits: 3

Properties:		Financial Services:		Construction/Development:		Investments:		Specialty Services:		Brokerage:	
Apartments:		Mortgages:		Commercial Construction:	Y	REIT:		Property Management:		Commercial Sales:	
Malls/Shopping:		Title Insurance:		Residential Construction:				Online Services:		Residential Sales:	
Offices:		Property Insurance:		Land Development:				Software/IT:		Specialty:	
Hotels/Motels:				Support Services:	Y			Consulting:			
Industrial/Warehouses:				Design/Engineering:	Y						
Other:											

TYPES OF BUSINESS:

Engineered Building Materials
Railroad Materials

BRANDS/DIVISIONS/AFFILIATES:

LB Pipe & Coupling Products LLC
LB Pipe & Coupling Products LLC

CONTACTS:

Note: Officers with more than one job title may be intentionally listed here more than once.

Stan L. Hasselbusch, CEO
Stan L. Hasselbusch, Pres.
David J. Russo, CFO/Sr. VP/Treas.
Gregory W. Lippard, VP-Sales, Rail Prod.
Brian H. Kelly, VP-Human Resources
John F. Kasel, Sr. VP-Mfg.
David L. Voltz, General Counsel/VP/Corp. Sec.
John F. Kasel, Sr. VP-Oper.
David R. Sauder, VP-Global Bus. Dev.
Linda K. Patterson, Controller
Samuel K. Fisher, Sr. VP-Rail Prod.
Donald L. Foster, Sr. VP-Construction Prod.
Kevin R. Haugh, Pres., CXT, Inc.
Merry L. Brumbaugh, VP-Tubular Prod.
Lee B. Foster, II, Chmn.

Phone: 412-928-3417	**Fax:** 412-928-7891
Toll-Free:	
Address: 415 Holiday Dr., Pittsburgh, PA 15220 US	

GROWTH PLANS/SPECIAL FEATURES:

L.B. Foster Company, founded in 1902, manufactures, fabricates and distributes products and services for the rail, construction, energy and utility industries. The company operates in three business segments: rail products, construction products and tubular products. The rail products segment, serving the railroad industry, provides a full line of new and used rail, trackwork, and related accessories to the railroad, mining and industrial markets. L.B. Foster also designs and produces insulated rail joints, power rail, concrete railroad ties, track fasteners, coverboards and special accessories for mass transit and other rail systems worldwide. The construction products division manufactures and sells steel sheet piling, H-bearing piling and pipe piling, as well as providing rental sheet piling for foundation requirements. In addition, Foster supplies fabricated structural steel, bridge decking, bridge railing, expansion joints and other products for highway construction and repair. Foster's tubular products segment supplies pipe coatings for natural gas pipelines and utilities. The firm also produces threaded pipe products for industrial water well and irrigation markets and sells micropiles for construction foundation repair and slope stabilization. The company maintains 17 sales offices, as well as 16 warehouses and plants located throughout the U.S. Rail products account for approximately 47% of the L.B. Foster's revenues; construction products account for 48%; and tubular products account for 5%. In May 2009, the firm and L.B. Industries, Inc., formed joint venture L.B. Pipe & Coupling Products, LLC to manufacture, market and sell various products for the energy, utility and construction industries. L.B Foster owns 45% of the venture. In November 2009, the firm, Jim Legg and Lally Pipe & Tube formed couplings manufacturing joint venture L.B. Pipe & Coupling Products, LLC.

Foster offers its employees benefits which include life, AD&D, disability, medical, dental and vision insurance; flexible spending accounts; profit sharing; and an employee assistance plan.

FINANCIALS:

Sales and profits are in thousands of dollars—add 000 to get the full amount. 2009 Note: Financial information for 2009 was not available for all companies at press time.

2009 Sales: $381,962	2009 Profits: $15,727	**U.S. Stock Ticker: FSTR**
2008 Sales: $512,592	2008 Profits: $27,746	**Int'l Ticker:** Int'l Exchange:
2007 Sales: $508,981	2007 Profits: $110,724	Employees: 593
2006 Sales: $389,788	2006 Profits: $10,715	Fiscal Year Ends: 12/31
2005 Sales: $	2005 Profits: $	Parent Company:

SALARIES/BENEFITS:

Pension Plan:	ESOP Stock Plan:	Profit Sharing: Y	Top Exec. Salary: $438,000	Bonus: $218,194
Savings Plan: Y	Stock Purch. Plan:		Second Exec. Salary: $248,333	Bonus: $96,820

OTHER THOUGHTS:

Apparent Women Officers or Directors: 4
Hot Spot for Advancement for Women/Minorities: Y

LOCATIONS: ("Y" = Yes)

West:	Southwest:	Midwest:	Southeast:	Northeast:	International:
Y	Y	Y	Y	Y	

LBA REALTY LLC

www.lbarealty.com

Industry Group Code: 5311 **Ranks within this company's industry group:** Sales: Profits:

Properties:		Financial Services:		Construction/Development:		Investments:		Specialty Services:		Brokerage:	
Apartments:		Mortgages:		Commercial Construction:	Y	REIT:		Property Management:	Y	Commercial Sales:	
Malls/Shopping:		Title Insurance:		Residential Construction:				Online Services:		Residential Sales:	
Offices:	Y	Property Insurance:		Land Development:				Software/IT:		Specialty:	
Hotels/Motels:				Support Services:				Consulting:			
Industrial/Warehouses:	Y			Design/Engineering:							
Other:	Y										

TYPES OF BUSINESS:

Real Estate Operations & Development
Real Estate Management

BRANDS/DIVISIONS/AFFILIATES:

CONTACTS:

Note: Officers with more than one job title may be intentionally listed here more than once.

Mike Memoly, CFO
Claudine Gamboa, Dir.-Human Resources & Employment
Paul Thometz, Dir.-Design & Construction
Phil Belling, Principal-Oper. & Corp. Svcs.
Phil Belling, Principal-Strategy & Acquisitions
Tom Rutherford, Sr. VP-Finance
Brad Neglia, Sr. VP-Leasing
Tom Motherway, Sr. VP-Dispositions
Melanie Colbert, Sr. VP-Property Mgmt. Svcs.
Alice Wilson, VP-Corp. Svcs.

Phone: 949-833-0400	**Fax:**
Toll-Free:	
Address: 17901 Von Karman Ave, Ste. 950, Irvine, CA 92614 US	

GROWTH PLANS/SPECIAL FEATURES:

LBA Realty LLC is a leading real estate investment and management company based in California, with operations primary in the western half of the U.S. The firm has multiple properties throughout Arizona, Nevada, California, Colorado, Oregon, Texas, Utah and Washington. The company's portfolio consists of large, mixed-use properties, single and multi-tenant office buildings and industrial properties such as warehouse, distribution, light manufacturing & business park facilities. The firm has three primary acquisition targets: office and industrial properties including warehouses, multi-tenant business parks, and R&D facilities; corporate-owned facilities including industrial, office and R&D; and development opportunities such as office in select markets, industrial and R&D. LBA has acquired approximately $4 billion in real estate assets since 1995. The company's major tenants include AT&T; Colorado State Bank; Comcast; DeVry; Isuzu Motors; Liberty Mutual; Microsoft; United Healthcare; QWEST; Sun Microsystems; State Farm; Sony; Starbucks; State of California; Time Warner; Fed Ex; Jackson National Life; University of Phoenix; Verizon; and Noble Energy.

Employees of the firm are offered medical, dental and vision coverage; a 401(k) plan; life insurance; gym membership discounts; college 529 plan; a long term care program; and a flexible spending account program.

FINANCIALS:

Sales and profits are in thousands of dollars—add 000 to get the full amount. 2009 Note: Financial information for 2009 was not available for all companies at press time.

2009 Sales: $	2009 Profits: $	**U.S. Stock Ticker: Private**
2008 Sales: $	2008 Profits: $	**Int'l Ticker:** Int'l Exchange:
2007 Sales: $	2007 Profits: $	Employees:
2006 Sales: $	2006 Profits: $	Fiscal Year Ends: 12/31
2005 Sales: $	2005 Profits: $	Parent Company:

SALARIES/BENEFITS:

Pension Plan:	ESOP Stock Plan:	Profit Sharing:	Top Exec. Salary: $	Bonus: $
Savings Plan: Y	Stock Purch. Plan:		Second Exec. Salary: $	Bonus: $

OTHER THOUGHTS:

Apparent Women Officers or Directors: 3
Hot Spot for Advancement for Women/Minorities: Y

LOCATIONS: ("Y" = Yes)

West:	Southwest:	Midwest:	Southeast:	Northeast:	International:
Y	Y				

LENDER PROCESSING SERVICES INC

www.lpsvcs.com

Industry Group Code: 511210 **Ranks within this company's industry group:** Sales: 1 Profits: 1

Properties:		Financial Services:		Construction/Development:		Investments:		Specialty Services:		Brokerage:	
Apartments:		Mortgages:	Y	Commercial Construction:		REIT:		Property Management:		Commercial Sales:	
Malls/Shopping:		Title Insurance:		Residential Construction:				Online Services:		Residential Sales:	
Offices:		Property Insurance:		Land Development:				Software/IT:		Specialty:	
Hotels/Motels:				Support Services:				Consulting:			
Industrial/Warehouses:				Design/Engineering:							
Other:											

TYPES OF BUSINESS:

Mortgage Processing & Management Systems
Settlement Services
Data & Technology Solutions
Loan Facilitation Services

BRANDS/DIVISIONS/AFFILIATES:

Fidelity National Information Services, Inc.
LPS Real Estate Group
McDash Analytics
Verification Bureau

CONTACTS: *Note: Officers with more than one job title may be intentionally listed here more than once.*

Jeffrey S. Carbiener, CEO
Daniel T. Scheuble, Co-COO/Exec. VP
Jeffrey S. Carbiener, Pres.
Michelle Kersch, Sr. VP-Mktg.
Joseph M. Nackashi, CIO/Exec. VP
Todd C. Johnson, General Counsel/Exec. VP/Sec.
Parag Bhansali, Exec. VP-Corp. Dev.
Michelle Kersch, Sr. VP-Corp. Comm.
Eric D. Swenson, Co-COO/Exec. VP
Pete Maselli, Sr. VP-Strategy & Bus. Dev.
Lee A. Kennedy, Chmn.

Phone: 904-854-5100	**Fax:** 904-854-4124
Toll-Free: 800-991-1274	
Address: 601 Riverside Ave., Jacksonville, FL 32204 US	

GROWTH PLANS/SPECIAL FEATURES:

Lender Processing Services, Inc. is a provider of integrated technology and outsourced services to the mortgage lending industry. The company, formerly a subsidiary of Fidelity National Information Services, Inc. (FIS), provides mortgage processing services, settlement services, default solutions and integrated data, servicing and technology solutions through two operating segments: Technology, Data and Analytics; and Loan Transaction Services. The Technology, Data and Analytics segment provides mortgage processing and workflow management services to mortgage lenders and other lending institutions, along with related support and services. This segment constitutes approximately 30% of Lender Processing Services' consolidated revenue. The Loan Transaction Services segment consists primarily of the firm's loan facilitation services, including settlement services, property appraisals and other real estate-related services; and its default management services, provided to national lenders and loan servicers. This segment accounts for approximately 70% of revenue. The firm serves more than 1,000 financial institutions, including many of the top 50 U.S. banks, as well as other financial groups, mortgage lenders, mortgage loan service providers and real estate service providers. In July 2008, Lender Processing Services completed its spinoff from FIS. Also in July 2008, the firm acquired McDash Analytics, which provides access to one of the largest loan-level mortgage asset databases for benchmarking and analysis purposes. In August 2009, the company rebranded its real estate group division, formerly Cyberhomes and FNRES MLS, as LPS Real Estate Group. Also in August 2009, Lender Processing Services acquired Verification Bureau, a developer of fraud prevention and web-based verification solutions.

FINANCIALS: **Sales and profits are in thousands of dollars—add 000 to get the full amount. 2009 Note: Financial information for 2009 was not available for all companies at press time.**

2009 Sales: $2,370,548	2009 Profits: $275,729	**U.S. Stock Ticker: LPS**
2008 Sales: $1,837,590	2008 Profits: $230,888	**Int'l Ticker:** Int'l Exchange:
2007 Sales: $1,638,622	2007 Profits: $256,805	Employees: 8,900
2006 Sales: $	2006 Profits: $	Fiscal Year Ends: 12/31
2005 Sales: $	2005 Profits: $	Parent Company:

SALARIES/BENEFITS:

Pension Plan:	ESOP Stock Plan:	Profit Sharing:	Top Exec. Salary: $660,833	Bonus: $85,000
Savings Plan:	Stock Purch. Plan:		Second Exec. Salary: $516,823	Bonus: $54,000

OTHER THOUGHTS:

Apparent Women Officers or Directors: 1
Hot Spot for Advancement for Women/Minorities:

LOCATIONS: ("Y" = Yes)

West:	Southwest:	Midwest:	Southeast:	Northeast:	International:
Y	Y	Y	Y	Y	

LENDINGTREE LLC

www.lendingtree.com

Industry Group Code: 522310E **Ranks within this company's industry group:** Sales: Profits:

Properties:		Financial Services:		Construction/Development:		Investments:		Specialty Services:		Brokerage:	
Apartments:		Mortgages:		Commercial Construction:		REIT:		Property Management:		Commercial Sales:	
Malls/Shopping:		Title Insurance:		Residential Construction:				Online Services:	Y	Residential Sales:	
Offices:		Property Insurance:		Land Development:				Software/IT:		Specialty:	
Hotels/Motels:				Support Services:				Consulting:			
Industrial/Warehouses:				Design/Engineering:							
Other:											

TYPES OF BUSINESS:

Consumer Loans & Mortgages Internet Portal
Online Financial Information & Tools
Online Realty Services
Settlement Services
Online Homeowner Resources

BRANDS/DIVISIONS/AFFILIATES:

Tree.com, Inc
LendingTree Loans
GetSmart.com
ARM Central
LendingTree.com

CONTACTS:

Note: Officers with more than one job title may be intentionally listed here more than once.

Douglas Lebda, CEO
Matthew Packey, CFO/Sr. VP
Mark W. Fowler, Sr. VP-Sales
Claudette Hampton, Sr. VP-Human Resources
Don Norton, VP-Tech.
Mark W. Fowler, Sr. VP-Oper.
Don Norton, VP-Dev.
Mona Marimow, Contact-Press
David Norris, Pres., Lending Tree Loans
Greg Hanson, Sr. VP/Gen. Mgr.-Tree.com & Real Estate.com
Mona Marimow, Sr. VP-Mktg., LendingTree.com & Tree.com
Douglas Lebda, Chmn.

Phone: 704-541-5351	**Fax:** 704-541-1824
Toll-Free: 800-555-8733	
Address: 11115 Rushmore Dr., Charlotte, NC 28277 US	

GROWTH PLANS/SPECIAL FEATURES:

LendingTree, LLC., a subsidiary of Tree.com, Inc., is an online lending and realty services exchange. The company operates LendingTree.com a leading online lending exchange that brings consumers together with a network of lenders competing for their business. LendingTree.com provides consumers with resources to purchase and refinance home loans, home equity loans, lines of credit, auto loans, personal loans and credit cards. The firm also offers these services over the phone at 800-555-TREE. Customers begin by completing the firm's online loan request, which requires information concerning desired loan(s) and personal financial information. The customer's data and credit scores are then automatically compared to the underwriting criteria of participating lenders. The Home Loan Center, Inc., a licensed mortgage lender in every state also known as LendingTree Loans, originates, processes and funds consumer mortgage loans. Instead of using the LendingTree network of lenders, qualifying consumers may be matched with a single loan officer who will provide up to four loan offers based on rates and terms given to LendingTree Loans from its wholesale mortgage banks and investors. LendingTree also connects customers with realtors, who offer services concerning the buying and selling of homes through RealEstate.com and 1-800-REALESTATE. Other LendingTree websites and resources include getsmart.com, a web site that offers access to a range of loan services, including loan refinancing, mortgage loans, home equity loans, debt consolidation and credit reports; JustThrive.com, a personal finance management website; and ARM Central, a resource for homeowners facing an adjustable rate mortgage reset.

FINANCIALS:

Sales and profits are in thousands of dollars—add 000 to get the full amount. 2009 Note: Financial information for 2009 was not available for all companies at press time.

2009 Sales: $	2009 Profits: $	**U.S. Stock Ticker: Subsidiary**
2008 Sales: $	2008 Profits: $	**Int'l Ticker:** Int'l Exchange:
2007 Sales: $356,200	2007 Profits: $-42,700	Employees:
2006 Sales: $485,700	2006 Profits: $42,300	Fiscal Year Ends: 12/31
2005 Sales: $425,300	2005 Profits: $6,400	Parent Company: IAC/INTERACTIVECORP

SALARIES/BENEFITS:

Pension Plan:	ESOP Stock Plan:	Profit Sharing:	Top Exec. Salary: $	Bonus: $178,900
Savings Plan:	Stock Purch. Plan:		Second Exec. Salary: $	Bonus: $

OTHER THOUGHTS:

Apparent Women Officers or Directors: 2
Hot Spot for Advancement for Women/Minorities:

LOCATIONS: ("Y" = Yes)

West:	Southwest:	Midwest:	Southeast:	Northeast:	International:
Y				Y	

Note: Financial information, benefits and other data can change quickly and may vary from those stated here.

LENNAR CORPORATION

www.lennar.com

Industry Group Code: 2361 **Ranks within this company's industry group:** Sales: 5 Profits: 15

Properties:		Financial Services:		Construction/Development:		Investments:		Specialty Services:		Brokerage:	
Apartments:		Mortgages:	Y	Commercial Construction:	Y	REIT:		Property Management:		Commercial Sales:	
Malls/Shopping:		Title Insurance:	Y	Residential Construction:	Y			Online Services:		Residential Sales:	
Offices:		Property Insurance:		Land Development:				Software/IT:		Specialty:	
Hotels/Motels:				Support Services:				Consulting:			
Industrial/Warehouses:				Design/Engineering:							
Other:											

TYPES OF BUSINESS:

Home Building
Mortgages
Title Insurance & Services

BRANDS/DIVISIONS/AFFILIATES:

Universal American Mortgage LLC
Eagle Home Mortgage
Railto Investments
Starwood Land Ventures LLC

CONTACTS:

Note: Officers with more than one job title may be intentionally listed here more than once.

Stuart A. Miller, CEO
Jonathan M. Jaffe, COO/VP
Stuart A. Miller, Pres.
Bruce E. Gross, CFO/VP
John R. Nygard, III, CIO
Mark Sustana, General Counsel/Corp. Sec.
Kay L. Howard, Dir.-Comm.
Diane J. Bessette, Treas./VP
Rick Beckwitt, Exec. VP
Marshall Ames, VP
David Collins, Controller
David J. Kaiserman, Pres., Lennar Ventures
Stuart A. Miller, Chmn.

Phone: 305-559-4000 **Fax:** 305-228-8383
Toll-Free: 800-741-4663
Address: 700 NW 107th Ave., Ste 400, Miami, FL 33172 US

GROWTH PLANS/SPECIAL FEATURES:

Lennar Corporation is a U.S. homebuilder and provider of financial services operating in 16 states. The firm sells single-family attached and detached homes and, to a lesser extent, multi-level residential buildings primarily under the Lennar brand name, in communities targeted to first-time, move-up and active adult homebuyers. The company also purchases, develops and sells residential land. Lennar divides its homebuilding operations into four segments: Homebuilding East, Homebuilding Central, Homebuilding West and Homebuilding Houston. Lennar's homes have an average sale price of about $243,000. Lennar generally supervises and controls the development of land and the design and building of its residential communities with a relatively small labor force, hiring subcontractors for site improvements and virtually all of the work involved in the construction of homes. Through its financial services subsidiaries, Universal American Mortgage Company and Eagle Home Mortgage, the firm also provides mortgage financing, title insurance and closing services for both buyers of its homes and third parties. Lennar primarily provides a full spectrum of primarily originate conforming conventional, FHA-insured, VA-guaranteed residential mortgage loan products. Lennar's subsidiaries provide loans to about 87% of its homebuyers who obtain mortgage financing in areas where it offers services. The Railto Investments segment provides advisory services, ongoing asset management services and acquisition and monetization services related to distressed loans and securities portfolios. In February 2010, Lennar acquired two loan portfolios consisting of approximately $3 billion in real estate loans. Also in February 2010, the company announced an agreement with Starwood Land Ventures LLC to acquire or option more than 2,700 homesites in Florida.

Employees are offered medical, dental and vision insurance; home and auto insurance; mortgage and title benefits; short- and long-term disability coverage; life insurance; and health and dependent care spending accounts.

FINANCIALS:

Sales and profits are in thousands of dollars—add 000 to get the full amount. 2009 Note: Financial information for 2009 was not available for all companies at press time.

2009 Sales: $3,119,387
2008 Sales: $4,575,417
2007 Sales: $10,186,781
2006 Sales: $16,266,662
2005 Sales: $13,866,971

2009 Profits: $-417,147
2008 Profits: $-1,109,085
2007 Profits: $-1,941,081
2006 Profits: $593,869
2005 Profits: $1,355,155

U.S. Stock Ticker: LEN
Int'l Ticker: Int'l Exchange:
Employees: 4,704
Fiscal Year Ends: 11/30
Parent Company:

SALARIES/BENEFITS:

Pension Plan: ESOP Stock Plan: Profit Sharing: Top Exec. Salary: $1,000,000 Bonus: $
Savings Plan: Y Stock Purch. Plan: Second Exec. Salary: $800,000 Bonus: $

OTHER THOUGHTS:

Apparent Women Officers or Directors: 4
Hot Spot for Advancement for Women/Minorities: Y

LOCATIONS: ("Y" = Yes)

West:	Southwest:	Midwest:	Southeast:	Northeast:	International:
Y	Y	Y	Y	Y	

LEXINGTON REALTY TRUST

www.lxp.com

Industry Group Code: 531120 **Ranks within this company's industry group:** Sales: 41 Profits: 53

Properties:		Financial Services:		Construction/Development:		Investments:		Specialty Services:		Brokerage:	
Apartments:		Mortgages:		Commercial Construction:		REIT:	Y	Property Management:		Commercial Sales:	
Malls/Shopping:	Y	Title Insurance:		Residential Construction:				Online Services:		Residential Sales:	
Offices:	Y	Property Insurance:		Land Development:				Software/IT:		Specialty:	
Hotels/Motels:				Support Services:				Consulting:			
Industrial/Warehouses:	Y			Design/Engineering:							
Other:											

TYPES OF BUSINESS:

Real Estate Investment Trust
Investment & Asset Management
Property Management & Leasing
Office & Industrial Properties
Retail Properties
Construction Financing

BRANDS/DIVISIONS/AFFILIATES:

Lex-Win Concord LLC
Lepercq Corporate Income Fund L.P.
Lepercq Corporate Income Fund II L.P.
Net 3 Acquisition L.P.

CONTACTS:

Note: Officers with more than one job title may be intentionally listed here more than once.

T. Wilson Eglin, CEO
T. Wilson Eglin, COO
T. Wilson Eglin, Pres.
Patrick Carroll, CFO/Exec. VP/Treas.
Joseph Bonventre, General Counsel/Exec. VP
Paul R. Wood, Chief Acct. Officer/VP/Corp. Sec.
Richard J. Rouse, Chief Investment Officer/Vice Chmn.
Natasha Roberts, Exec. VP/Dir.-Real Estate
Lara Sweeney Johnson, Exec. VP-Strategic Transactions
Brendan P. Mullinix, Exec. VP-Capital Markets
E. Robert Roskind, Chmn.

Phone: 212-692-7200	**Fax:** 212-594-6600
Toll-Free:	
Address: 1 Penn Plz., Ste. 4015, New York, NY 10119-4015 US	

GROWTH PLANS/SPECIAL FEATURES:

Lexington Realty Trust (formerly Lexington Corporate Properties Trust) is a self-managed and self-administered real estate investment trust (REIT) that primarily acquires, owns and manages a portfolio of net leased office, industrial and retail properties. Lexington also acquires and holds investments in loan assets and debt securities related to real estate, primarily acquired through a 50% interest in Lex-Win Concord LLC. Substantially all of the company's properties are subject to triple-net or similar leases, in which the tenant bears all or substantially all of the costs and cost increases for real estate taxes, utilities, insurance and ordinary repairs. Lexington has ownership interests in 210 properties in 40 states and the Netherlands, for a total of approximately 38.3 million square feet. The company has diversified its portfolio by geographical location, tenant industry segment, lease term expiration and property type in an effort to insulate itself from regional recession, industry specific downturns and price fluctuations by property type. Lexington is structured as an umbrella partnership REIT, with a portion of its business conducted through its three operating subsidiaries: Lepercq Corporate Income Fund L.P.; Lepercq Corporate Income Fund II L.P.; and Net 3 Acquisition L.P. During 2009, the firm sold 15 properties to third parties for a combined total of $108.5 million, as well as executing the transfer of two other properties to lenders and the disposal of a property through bankruptcy. Also during 2009, Lexington acquired a property in Greenville, South Carolina for approximately $10.5 million; the company also acquired a parcel of land in Long Beach, California for roughly $2.5 million.

Lexington offers its employees a tuition assistance program; a 529 college savings plan; a 401(k) plan; an employee stock purchase plan; flexible spending accounts; and medical, dental, life and disability insurance.

FINANCIALS:

Sales and profits are in thousands of dollars—add 000 to get the full amount. 2009 Note: Financial information for 2009 was not available for all companies at press time.

2009 Sales: $376,621	2009 Profits: $-211,272	**U.S. Stock Ticker: LXP**
2008 Sales: $418,149	2008 Profits: $-3,468	**Int'l Ticker:** Int'l Exchange:
2007 Sales: $401,176	2007 Profits: $91,929	Employees: 59
2006 Sales: $185,963	2006 Profits: $7,753	Fiscal Year Ends: 12/31
2005 Sales: $162,383	2005 Profits: $32,695	Parent Company:

SALARIES/BENEFITS:

Pension Plan:	ESOP Stock Plan:	Profit Sharing:	Top Exec. Salary: $550,000	Bonus: $275,000
Savings Plan: Y	Stock Purch. Plan: Y		Second Exec. Salary: $475,000	Bonus: $195,000

OTHER THOUGHTS:

Apparent Women Officers or Directors: 2
Hot Spot for Advancement for Women/Minorities:

LOCATIONS: ("Y" = Yes)

West:	Southwest:	Midwest:	Southeast:	Northeast:	International:
Y	Y	Y	Y	Y	Y

LIBERTY PROPERTY TRUST

www.libertyproperty.com

Industry Group Code: 531120 **Ranks within this company's industry group:** Sales: 24 Profits: 16

Properties:		Financial Services:		Construction/Development:		Investments:		Specialty Services:		Brokerage:	
Apartments:		Mortgages:		Commercial Construction:		REIT:	Y	Property Management:	Y	Commercial Sales:	
Malls/Shopping:		Title Insurance:		Residential Construction:				Online Services:		Residential Sales:	
Offices:	Y	Property Insurance:		Land Development:				Software/IT:		Specialty:	
Hotels/Motels:				Support Services:				Consulting:			
Industrial/Warehouses:	Y			Design/Engineering:							
Other:											

TYPES OF BUSINESS:

Real Estate Investment Trust
Industrial & Office Properties
Property Management
Property Development

BRANDS/DIVISIONS/AFFILIATES:

Liberty Property, LP

CONTACTS:

Note: Officers with more than one job title may be intentionally listed here more than once.

William P. Hankowsky, CEO
Robert E. Fenza, COO/Exec. VP
William P. Hankowsky, Pres.
George J. Alburger, Jr., CFO/Exec. VP
Caren Hosansky, Sr. VP-Human Resources
Steven E. Messaros, CIO
James J. Bowes, General Counsel/Sec.
James V. Maneri, Sr. VP-Bus. Dev. & National Leasing
Mary Beth Morrissey, Sr. VP-Finance & Acct.
Donna Wagner, Sr. VP-Acquisitions
Michael T. Hagan, Chief Investment Officer/Sr. VP
Jim Lutz, Sr. VP-Dev.
Anne E. Sheppard, Sr. VP/Real Estate Counsel
William P. Hankowsky, Chmn.

Phone: 610-648-1700	**Fax:** 610-644-4129
Toll-Free:	
Address: 500 Chesterfield Pkwy., Malvern, PA 19355 US	

GROWTH PLANS/SPECIAL FEATURES:

Liberty Property Trust, headquartered in Pennsylvania, is a self-administered and self-managed real estate investment trust (REIT). The company provides leasing, property management, development, acquisition and other tenant-related services for its properties. Nearly all of the firm's assets and operations are owned and conducted through its subsidiary, Liberty Property, LP, a Pennsylvania limited partnership. Liberty's portfolio consists of 349 industrial and nearly 300 office properties, encompassing 64.4 million square feet, in 12 states and the U.K. Through joint ventures, the firm owns interest in an additional 96 (47 industrial and 49 office) properties, totaling 13.8 million square feet. Industrial properties include warehouse, distribution, service, assembly, light manufacturing and research and development facilities. Office properties include single- and multi-story office buildings located principally in suburban mixed-use developments or office parks. The firm provides property management services to over 2,000 companies in over 65 million square feet; leasing representatives with knowledge of the particular local market; and architects and space planners that aid in the design and use of tenants' leased space. Liberty also owns three properties under development and 1,355 acres of developable land, substantially all of which is zoned for commercial use.

Liberty offers its employees medical, dental and vision insurance; short- and long-term disability; paid time off; a 401(k) savings plan with a company match; a health care spending account; a dependent care spending account; a work-life balance support program; wellness programs; an employee stock purchase plan with a 15% discount; an employee referral program; educational assistance that includes both tuition reimbursement and professional certification support; employee discounts; commuter assistance; life insurance; and dependent, supplemental and AD&D insurance.

FINANCIALS:

Sales and profits are in thousands of dollars—add 000 to get the full amount. 2009 Note: Financial information for 2009 was not available for all companies at press time.

2009 Sales: $744,257	2009 Profits: $78,992	**U.S. Stock Ticker: LRY**
2008 Sales: $731,352	2008 Profits: $180,106	**Int'l Ticker:** Int'l Exchange:
2007 Sales: $669,144	2007 Profits: $190,310	Employees: 469
2006 Sales: $607,562	2006 Profits: $266,574	Fiscal Year Ends: 12/31
2005 Sales: $588,176	2005 Profits: $249,351	Parent Company:

SALARIES/BENEFITS:

Pension Plan:	ESOP Stock Plan:	Profit Sharing:	Top Exec. Salary: $525,000	Bonus: $239,715
Savings Plan: Y	Stock Purch. Plan: Y		Second Exec. Salary: $400,000	Bonus: $ 500

OTHER THOUGHTS:

Apparent Women Officers or Directors: 7
Hot Spot for Advancement for Women/Minorities: Y

LOCATIONS: ("Y" = Yes)

West:	Southwest:	Midwest:	Southeast:	Northeast:	International:
	Y	Y	Y	Y	Y

LIGHTSTONE GROUP LLC (THE)

www.lightstonegroup.com

Industry Group Code: 531110 **Ranks within this company's industry group:** Sales: Profits:

Properties:		Financial Services:		Construction/Development:		Investments:		Specialty Services:		Brokerage:	
Apartments:		Mortgages:		Commercial Construction:		REIT:	Y	Property Management:	Y	Commercial Sales:	
Malls/Shopping:	Y	Title Insurance:		Residential Construction:				Online Services:		Residential Sales:	
Offices:	Y	Property Insurance:		Land Development:				Software/IT:		Specialty:	
Hotels/Motels:	Y			Support Services:				Consulting:			
Industrial/Warehouses:				Design/Engineering:							
Other:											

TYPES OF BUSINESS:

Real Estate Company
Outlet Retail Properties
Office Building Properties
Lodging Facilities Properties
Real Estate Investment Trust

BRANDS/DIVISIONS/AFFILIATES:

Prime Retail
Extended Stay Hotels
Prime Outlets
Prime Group Realty Trust
Beacon Management
Park Avenue Funding

CONTACTS:

Note: Officers with more than one job title may be intentionally listed here more than once.

Peyton (Chip) Owen, Jr., COO/Exec. VP
Peyton (Chip) Owen, Jr., Pres.
Michael M. Schurer, CFO
Joseph E. Teichman, General Counsel/Exec. VP
Akiva Elazary, VP-Acquisitions
Pamela Meadows, Sr. VP-Human Resources, Prime Retail, Inc.
Robert Brvenik, Pres., Prime Retail
Bruno de Vinck, Sr. VP-Special Projects
Stephen Hamrick, CEO/Pres., Lightstone Securities, LLC
David Lichtenstein, Chmn.

Phone: 212-616-9969	**Fax:**
Toll-Free:	
Address: 505 Park Ave., 5th fl., New York, NY 10022 US	

GROWTH PLANS/SPECIAL FEATURES:

Lightstone Group LLC is one of the largest privately-owned real estate companies in the U.S. It currently boasts a portfolio of diversified properties in 46 U.S. states, Canada and Puerto Rico; its holdings are in excess of 22,000 residential units, 680 hotels and approximately 24 million square feet of office, industrial and retail space. Through its subsidiary Prime Retail, The Lightstone Group is also one of the largest owners of retail space in the country, with approximately 8 million square feet of retail outlets space and an additional 8 million square feet of full-price retail mall space. Operating under the Prime Outlets brand, the company has outlet locations in 15 states and Puerto Rico. Subsidiary Beacon Management, one of the foremost players in the multi-family residential housing sector, with corporate offices in the Northeast, Southeast and Midwest regions of the U.S.; and Park Avenue Funding, a real estate lending company. The firm's subsidiary Prime Group Realty Trust, is a real estate investment trust, which owns, manages, leases, develops and redevelops office and industrial properties, principally in the metropolitan Chicago area. Extended Stay Hotels, a subsidiary of the firm, operates approximately 76,000 rooms located in 44 states and Canada. The company currently operates under five brands in the extended-stay segment: Extended Stay Deluxe, Extended Stay America, Homestead Studio Suites, StudioPlus, and Crossland. In June 2009, Extended Stay Hotels filed for bankruptcy protection.

FINANCIALS:

Sales and profits are in thousands of dollars—add 000 to get the full amount. 2009 Note: Financial information for 2009 was not available for all companies at press time.

2009 Sales: $	2009 Profits: $	**U.S. Stock Ticker: Private**
2008 Sales: $	2008 Profits: $	**Int'l Ticker:** Int'l Exchange:
2007 Sales: $	2007 Profits: $	Employees:
2006 Sales: $	2006 Profits: $	Fiscal Year Ends: 12/31
2005 Sales: $	2005 Profits: $	Parent Company:

SALARIES/BENEFITS:

Pension Plan:	ESOP Stock Plan:	Profit Sharing:	Top Exec. Salary: $	Bonus: $
Savings Plan:	Stock Purch. Plan:		Second Exec. Salary: $	Bonus: $

OTHER THOUGHTS:

Apparent Women Officers or Directors: 3
Hot Spot for Advancement for Women/Minorities: Y

LOCATIONS: ("Y" = Yes)

West:	Southwest:	Midwest:	Southeast:	Northeast:	International:
Y	Y	Y	Y	Y	

LILLIBRIDGE HEALTHCARE REAL ESTATE TRUST

www.lillibridge.com

Industry Group Code: 531120 **Ranks within this company's industry group:** Sales: Profits:

Properties:		Financial Services:		Construction/Development:		Investments:		Specialty Services:		Brokerage:	
Apartments:		Mortgages:		Commercial Construction:		REIT:	Y	Property Management:	Y	Commercial Sales:	
Malls/Shopping:		Title Insurance:		Residential Construction:				Online Services:		Residential Sales:	
Offices:		Property Insurance:		Land Development:				Software/IT:		Specialty:	
Hotels/Motels:				Support Services:				Consulting:	Y		
Industrial/Warehouses:				Design/Engineering:							
Other:	Y										

TYPES OF BUSINESS:

Real Estate Investment Trust
Property Management
Health Care Properties
Consulting Services

BRANDS/DIVISIONS/AFFILIATES:

CONTACTS:

Note: Officers with more than one job title may be intentionally listed here more than once.

Todd Lillibridge, CEO
Joe Kurzydym, CFO
Carla M. Lyons, VP-Mktg./Bus. Dev.
Mary Fitzpatrick, Dir.-Human Resources
Michael Lincoln, Exec. VP-Bus. Dev.
Carla M. Lyons, Contact-Media
Jack Dudick, Sr. VP-Finance
Kevin Geraghty, Exec. VP-Asset Property Mgmt.
Margie McHugh, Sr. VP-Lillibridge Advisors
Chuck Fendrich, Sr. VP-Property Mgmt.
Thomas A. Czerniak, Sr. VP-Acquisitions
Todd Lillibridge, Chmn.

Phone: 312-408-1370 **Fax:** 312-408-1415
Toll-Free: 877-545-5430
Address: 200 W. Madison St., 32 Fl., Chicago, IL 60606 US

GROWTH PLANS/SPECIAL FEATURES:

Lillibridge Healthcare Real Estate Trust is a leading national health care real estate investment trust (REIT) that focuses on nonprofit hospitals and other healthcare facilities. The company acquires, develops and manages its properties. The firm's operations, including owned and managed property, encompasses 95 medical office facilities, totaling 5.7 million square feet across 37 local healthcare markets and across 16 states. The business serves over 6,000 physicians and hospital tenants nationwide. Lillibridge's acquisition branch purchases a client's medical office buildings. After a purchase, the development branch of the company plans the campus, physician recruitment and other operations associated with the new facility or its renovation. Lillibridge also manages the property for clients and handles compliance issues that consistently come up in the health care field when new federal and state laws are passed. The firm has developed a compliance risk-assessment checklist and paperwork that aids clients in evaluating and learning about compliance issues. Lillibridge consulting services help clients inventory strategic and non-strategic real estate assets, improve performance through operations assessment, determine the impact of a monetization on the financial position of the hospital and create an ambulatory network or leasing strategy. Recently, the firm broke ground on five properties: a new medical office building adjacent to Florida Hospital Kissimmee in Kissimmee, Florida; and two medical office buildings for two new hospitals in Waco, Texas. The company also recently completed a second medical office building adjacent to St. Peter's Hospital in Helena, Montana. In March 2009, Lillibridge acquired a 13-building portfolio, totaling 255,000 square feet, from Decatur Memorial Hospital in Decatur, Illinois.

FINANCIALS:

Sales and profits are in thousands of dollars—add 000 to get the full amount. 2009 Note: Financial information for 2009 was not available for all companies at press time.

2009 Sales: $ | 2009 Profits: $
2008 Sales: $ | 2008 Profits: $
2007 Sales: $ | 2007 Profits: $
2006 Sales: $ | 2006 Profits: $
2005 Sales: $ | 2005 Profits: $

U.S. Stock Ticker: Private
Int'l Ticker: Int'l Exchange:
Employees:
Fiscal Year Ends: 12/31
Parent Company:

SALARIES/BENEFITS:

Pension Plan: | ESOP Stock Plan: | Profit Sharing: | Top Exec. Salary: $ | Bonus: $
Savings Plan: Y | Stock Purch. Plan: | Second Exec. Salary: $ | Bonus: $

OTHER THOUGHTS:

Apparent Women Officers or Directors: 3
Hot Spot for Advancement for Women/Minorities: Y

LOCATIONS: ("Y" = Yes)

West:	Southwest:	Midwest:	Southeast:	Northeast:	International:
	Y	Y			

LINK REAL ESTATE INVESTMENT TRUST (THE) www.thelinkreit.com

Industry Group Code: 531120 **Ranks within this company's industry group:** Sales: 32 Profits: 2

Properties:		Financial Services:		Construction/Development:		Investments:		Specialty Services:		Brokerage:	
Apartments:		Mortgages:		Commercial Construction:		REIT:	Y	Property Management:		Commercial Sales:	
Malls/Shopping:	Y	Title Insurance:		Residential Construction:				Online Services:		Residential Sales:	
Offices:		Property Insurance:		Land Development:				Software/IT:		Specialty:	
Hotels/Motels:				Support Services:				Consulting:			
Industrial/Warehouses:				Design/Engineering:							
Other:	Y										

TYPES OF BUSINESS:

Real Estate Investment Trust
Asset Enhancement

BRANDS/DIVISIONS/AFFILIATES:

CONTACTS:
Note: Officers with more than one job title may be intentionally listed here more than once.

Ian David Murray Robins, CEO
Ross O'Toole, COO
George Kwok Lung Hongchoy, CFO
KT Poon, Dir.-Strategy
KT Poon, Dir.-Corp. Comm.
Nicholas Robert Sallnow-Smith, Chmn.

Phone: 852-2175-1800	**Fax:** 852-2175-1900
Toll-Free:	
Address: 100 How Ming St., One Landmark East, Hong Kong, China	

GROWTH PLANS/SPECIAL FEATURES:

The Link Real Estate Investment Trust is one of Hong Kong's largest real estate investment trusts (REIT). The company's portfolio consists of 180 retail and car park facilities, with 11 million square feet of retail space and 80,000 individual car spaces. The firm's facilities encompass a variety of tenants, including well known retail and restaurant brands. The Link's strategy is to invest in properties in Hong Kong that are primarily for car park and retail usage and to increase their value by enhancing physical structure, customer service, and developing promotional activities. Current asset enhancement projects include introducing more popular restaurants at Hau Tak Shopping Centre; remodeling vacant floors into shopping areas for the Tsz Wan Shan Shopping Centre; aligning the walkway with retail outlets and adding a coffee shop at Lung Cheung Mall; and converting a market to a retail area and therefore adding more shopping space to the Ming Tak Shopping Centre.

Employees are offered retirement savings; health coverage; and life insurance.

FINANCIALS:
Sales and profits are in thousands of dollars—add 000 to get the full amount. 2009 Note: Financial information for 2009 was not available for all companies at press time.

2009 Sales: $580,040	2009 Profits: $80,120	**U.S. Stock Ticker:**
2008 Sales: $545,900	2008 Profits: $668,100	**Int'l Ticker: 0823** Int'l Exchange: Hong Kong-HKE
2007 Sales: $514,000	2007 Profits: $566,000	Employees: 473
2006 Sales: $528,100	2006 Profits: $811,600	Fiscal Year Ends: 3/31
2005 Sales: $	2005 Profits: $	Parent Company:

SALARIES/BENEFITS:

Pension Plan:	ESOP Stock Plan:	Profit Sharing:	Top Exec. Salary: $	Bonus: $
Savings Plan: Y	Stock Purch. Plan:		Second Exec. Salary: $	Bonus: $

OTHER THOUGHTS:

Apparent Women Officers or Directors: 1
Hot Spot for Advancement for Women/Minorities:

LOCATIONS: ("Y" = Yes)

West:	Southwest:	Midwest:	Southeast:	Northeast:	International:
					Y

LODGIAN INC

www.lodgian.com

Industry Group Code: 721110 **Ranks within this company's industry group:** Sales: 27 Profits: 23

Properties:		Financial Services:		Construction/Development:		Investments:		Specialty Services:		Brokerage:	
Apartments:		Mortgages:		Commercial Construction:		REIT:		Property Management:	Y	Commercial Sales:	
Malls/Shopping:		Title Insurance:		Residential Construction:				Online Services:		Residential Sales:	
Offices:		Property Insurance:		Land Development:				Software/IT:		Specialty:	
Hotels/Motels:	Y			Support Services:				Consulting:			
Industrial/Warehouses:				Design/Engineering:							
Other:											

TYPES OF BUSINESS:

Hotels

BRANDS/DIVISIONS/AFFILIATES:

InterContinental Hotels Group plc
Marriott International Inc
Hilton Group plc
Wyndham Worldwide
Crowne Plaza
Holiday Inn
Courtyard by Marriott
Residence Inn by Marriott

CONTACTS: *Note: Officers with more than one job title may be intentionally listed here more than once.*

Daniel E. Ellis, CEO
Daniel E. Ellis, Pres.
James A. MacLennan, CFO/Exec. VP
Carol L. Mayne, VP-Human Resources
Johnny A. Green, VP-IT
Daniel E. Ellis, General Counsel/Corp. Sec.
Joseph F. Kelly, VP-Oper.
Susan King, VP-Franchise Comm.
Deborah N. (Debi) Ethridge, VP-Investor Rel.
Deborah N. (Debi) Ethridge, VP-Finance
Barbra Beaulieu, VP-Internal Audit & Controls
Kevin B. Richards, VP-Asset Mgmt.
Donna B. Cohen, Controller/VP
Stewart J. Brown, Chmn.

Phone: 404-364-9400	**Fax:** 404-364-0088
Toll-Free:	
Address: 3445 Peachtree Rd. NE, Ste. 700, Atlanta, GA 30326 US	

GROWTH PLANS/SPECIAL FEATURES:

Lodgian, Inc. is an independent owner and operator of 27 hotels containing 5,230 rooms located in 18 states. One of the firm's hotels is operated in a joint venture in which a subsidiary serves as the general partner and has a 51% voting interest. Of the firm's 27 hotels, 13 are InterContinental Hotels Group brands (Crowne Plaza and Holiday Inn), eight are Marriott brands (Marriott, Courtyard by Marriott, SpringHill Suites by Marriott and Residence Inn by Marriott), two Hilton, and four are associated with other franchisors such as Starwood, Wyndham and Carlson. The company's hotels are primarily full-service properties that offer food and beverage services; meeting and banquet facilities; and compete in the midscale and upscale market segments of the lodging industry. Lodgian operates hotel brands in the Upper Upscale; Upscale; Midscale with Food & Beverage; and Midscale without Food & Beverage segments. Transient revenues, derived from guests staying only for brief periods of time without a long-term contract, generate roughly 43% of the firm's room revenues, while demand from corporate clients generate for 28%. Groups account for 22% and contract revenues (such as contracts with airlines for crew rooms) generate 7%. In January 2010, the company agreed to be acquired by an affiliate of global investment company, Lone Star Funds for $270 million.

Employees are offered medical, dental and vision insurance; disability coverage; life insurance; a 401(k) plan; educational assistance; and discounts on hotel stays.

FINANCIALS: **Sales and profits are in thousands of dollars—add 000 to get the full amount. 2009 Note: Financial information for 2009 was not available for all companies at press time.**

2009 Sales: $188,544	2009 Profits: $-53,902	**U.S. Stock Ticker: LGN**
2008 Sales: $228,194	2008 Profits: $-11,984	**Int'l Ticker:** Int'l Exchange:
2007 Sales: $229,875	2007 Profits: $-8,446	Employees: 2,362
2006 Sales: $227,635	2006 Profits: $-15,176	Fiscal Year Ends: 12/31
2005 Sales: $222,762	2005 Profits: $12,301	Parent Company:

SALARIES/BENEFITS:

Pension Plan:	ESOP Stock Plan:	Profit Sharing:	Top Exec. Salary: $413,732	Bonus: $
Savings Plan: Y	Stock Purch. Plan:		Second Exec. Salary: $357,815	Bonus: $35,000

OTHER THOUGHTS:

Apparent Women Officers or Directors: 5
Hot Spot for Advancement for Women/Minorities: Y

LOCATIONS: ("Y" = Yes)

West:	Southwest:	Midwest:	Southeast:	Northeast:	International:
Y	Y	Y	Y	Y	

LOEWS HOTELS HOLDING CORPORATION

www.loewshotels.com

Industry Group Code: 721110 **Ranks within this company's industry group:** Sales: Profits:

Properties:		Financial Services:		Construction/Development:		Investments:		Specialty Services:		Brokerage:	
Apartments:		Mortgages:		Commercial Construction:		REIT:		Property Management:	Y	Commercial Sales:	
Malls/Shopping:		Title Insurance:		Residential Construction:				Online Services:		Residential Sales:	
Offices:		Property Insurance:		Land Development:				Software/IT:		Specialty:	
Hotels/Motels:	Y			Support Services:				Consulting:			
Industrial/Warehouses:				Design/Engineering:							
Other:											

TYPES OF BUSINESS:

Hotels, Luxury
Hotel Management Services

BRANDS/DIVISIONS/AFFILIATES:

Loews Corporation
Loews Miami Beach Hotel
Loews Philadelphia Hotel
Loews Royal Pacific Resort at Universal Orlando
Loews Portofino Bay Hotel at Universal Orlando
Loews Lake Las Vegas Resort
Don CeSar Beach Resort & Spa
Loews Le Concorde

CONTACTS:

Note: Officers with more than one job title may be intentionally listed here more than once.

Jonathan M. Tisch, CEO
Jack Adler, COO
Jack Adler, Pres.
Michael Dominguez, VP-Global Sales
Emily K. Goldfischer, VP-Public Rel.
Jonathan M. Tisch, Chmn.
Anthony Del Gaudio, VP-Global Dist.

Phone: 212-521-2000	**Fax:** 212-521-2525
Toll-Free:	
Address: 667 Madison Ave., New York, NY 10021 US	

GROWTH PLANS/SPECIAL FEATURES:

Loews Hotels Holding Corporation, a subsidiary of the Loews Corporation, currently has a portfolio of 18 owned and/or operated luxury hotels and resorts, with a combined 8,073 rooms. In all, the company owns six hotels; has a land lease on three hotels; and operates the remaining nine hotels under management contracts. Located in 16 cities throughout the U.S. and Canada, the firm's properties include the 790-room Loews Miami Beach Hotel in Florida; the 585-room Loews Philadelphia Hotel; the 493-room Loews Lake Las Vegas Resort; the 405-room Loews Le Concorde in Quebec City; and the 140-room Loews Hotel Vogue in Montreal. Loews Hotels operates three joint venture hotels with Universal Studios in Orlando, Florida: Loews Royal Pacific Resort at Universal Orlando, its largest hotel with 1,000 rooms; the 750-room Loews Portofino Bay Hotel at Universal Orlando; and the 650-room Hard Rock Hotel at Universal Orlando. Additionally, a subsidiary of the firm owns 20% of the Don CeSar Beach Resort in St. Pete Beach, Florida, which the firm manages. Loews Hotels' business amenities include high-speed Internet access; a power breakfast with notable business leaders; notarization services; private dining rooms; boardrooms; and concierge services. The YouFirst Loyalty Program rewards guests based on number of stays and offers free Internet access, late checkout, guaranteed rooms and upgrades for guests who visit at least twice a year. Loews Hotels offers facilities for weddings, meetings and special events; and special programs and services designed for people traveling with pets, children and teenagers.

FINANCIALS:

Sales and profits are in thousands of dollars—add 000 to get the full amount. 2009 Note: Financial information for 2009 was not available for all companies at press time.

2009 Sales: $	2009 Profits: $	**U.S. Stock Ticker: Subsidiary**
2008 Sales: $	2008 Profits: $	**Int'l Ticker:** Int'l Exchange:
2007 Sales: $	2007 Profits: $	Employees:
2006 Sales: $	2006 Profits: $	Fiscal Year Ends: 12/31
2005 Sales: $350,500	2005 Profits: $	Parent Company: LOEWS CORPORATION

SALARIES/BENEFITS:

Pension Plan: Y	ESOP Stock Plan:	Profit Sharing:	Top Exec. Salary: $	Bonus: $
Savings Plan: Y	Stock Purch. Plan:		Second Exec. Salary: $	Bonus: $

OTHER THOUGHTS:

Apparent Women Officers or Directors: 1
Hot Spot for Advancement for Women/Minorities:

LOCATIONS: ("Y" = Yes)

West:	Southwest:	Midwest:	Southeast:	Northeast:	International:
Y	Y		Y	Y	Y

LOUIS BERGER GROUP INC (THE)

www.louisberger.com

Industry Group Code: 237 **Ranks within this company's industry group:** Sales: Profits:

Properties:		Financial Services:		Construction/Development:		Investments:		Specialty Services:		Brokerage:	
Apartments:		Mortgages:		Commercial Construction:		REIT:		Property Management:		Commercial Sales:	
Malls/Shopping:		Title Insurance:		Residential Construction:				Online Services:		Residential Sales:	
Offices:		Property Insurance:		Land Development:				Software/IT:		Specialty:	
Hotels/Motels:				Support Services:				Consulting:			
Industrial/Warehouses:				Design/Engineering:	Y						
Other:											

TYPES OF BUSINESS:

Architectural & Engineering Services
Civil Engineering
Environmental Engineering
Transportation Infrastructure
Project Management
Consulting Services
Hydrologic Engineering
Seismic & Geotechnical Services

BRANDS/DIVISIONS/AFFILIATES:

Louis Berger SAS
Ammann & Whitney Consulting Engineers Inc
Berger/ABAM Engineers Inc
Berger Devine Yaeger Inc
Klohn Crippen Berger Ltd
Berger, Lehman Associates PC
CHELBI Engineering Consultants Inc
RBA Group Inc (The)

CONTACTS: *Note: Officers with more than one job title may be intentionally listed here more than once.*

Nicolas J. (Nick) Masucci, CEO
James G. Bach, COO
Larry D. Walker, Pres.
Luke McKinnon, CFO
Terry Williams, Dir.-Human Resources
Larry Pesesky, Sr. VP-Environmental Sciences
Connie Crawford, Sr. VP-U.S. Eng. Svcs.
D. James Stamatis, VP-U.S. Oper.
Holly Fisher, Corp. Comm. Mgr.
Dennis Conklin, VP-Transportation Eng.
Thomas Lewis, Sr. VP-Environmental Eng.
John Hotopp, Sr. VP-Cultural Resource Group
Robert J. Nardi, Sr. VP-Facilities Planning
Derish M. Wolff, Chmn.

Phone: 973-407-1000	**Fax:** 973-267-6468
Toll-Free:	
Address: 412 Mt. Kemble Ave., Morristown, NJ 07960-6654 US	

GROWTH PLANS/SPECIAL FEATURES:

The Louis Berger Group, Inc. (Berger) is an infrastructure engineering, environmental science and economic development company with more than 140 offices throughout the U.S. and in more than 60 countries worldwide. Berger offers services in civil, structural, mechanical, electrical and environmental engineering; program management; planning; environmental sciences; cultural resources; information science; finance; economics; and construction management. The group operates through a number of subsidiary companies. Louis Berger SAS, based in Paris, France, provides design and supervision services for transportation and privately financed infrastructure projects, water supply and urban sanitation systems. It also offers management and human resource development services. Berger Avart, Inc. offers architectural and engineering services within Florida. Ammann & Whitney Consulting Engineers, Inc. provides structural, civil, architectural, mechanical, electrical engineering and construction inspection services for projects including bridges, highways, airports, transit stations, schools and government and military installations. Berger/ABAM Engineers, Inc. offers planning, environmental science, civil and structural engineering, project management and construction support consulting services. Klohn Crippen Berger Ltd. designs hydroelectric power plants, dams, tunnels and pumped storage schemes; serves mining clients internationally; and provides seismic and geotechnical services throughout Canada. Berger, Lehman Associates, P.C. is one of the largest engineering, economic and environmental planning organizations in the U.S., serving state, municipal and local agencies as well as corporate and industrial clients. CHELBI Engineering Consultants, Inc. provides project support services in China. The RBA Group, Inc. offers its clients engineering, planning and architectural services. In November 2009, the firm was selected as project management for Nigeria's Lekki Port. The first phase of construction expected to be completed in 2013.

Employees are offered medical and dental coverage; life and travel insurance; a new employee hiring referral award; tuition reimbursement; flexible spending accounts; a cafeteria plan; and registration fee payment for professional licenses.

FINANCIALS: **Sales and profits are in thousands of dollars—add 000 to get the full amount. 2009 Note: Financial information for 2009 was not available for all companies at press time.**

2009 Sales: $	2009 Profits: $	**U.S. Stock Ticker: Private**
2008 Sales: $	2008 Profits: $	**Int'l Ticker:** Int'l Exchange:
2007 Sales: $	2007 Profits: $	Employees:
2006 Sales: $	2006 Profits: $	Fiscal Year Ends: 6/30
2005 Sales: $	2005 Profits: $	Parent Company:

SALARIES/BENEFITS:

Pension Plan:	ESOP Stock Plan:	Profit Sharing:	Top Exec. Salary: $	Bonus: $
Savings Plan: Y	Stock Purch. Plan:		Second Exec. Salary: $	Bonus: $

OTHER THOUGHTS:

Apparent Women Officers or Directors: 2
Hot Spot for Advancement for Women/Minorities: Y

LOCATIONS: ("Y" = Yes)

West:	Southwest:	Midwest:	Southeast:	Northeast:	International:
Y	Y	Y	Y	Y	Y

LOWE'S COMPANIES INC

www.lowes.com

Industry Group Code: 444110 **Ranks within this company's industry group:** Sales: 2 Profits: 2

Properties:		Financial Services:		Construction/Development:		Investments:		Specialty Services:		Brokerage:	
Apartments:		Mortgages:		Commercial Construction:		REIT:		Property Management:		Commercial Sales:	
Malls/Shopping:	Y	Title Insurance:		Residential Construction:				Online Services:		Residential Sales:	
Offices:		Property Insurance:		Land Development:				Software/IT:		Specialty:	
Hotels/Motels:				Support Services:	Y			Consulting:			
Industrial/Warehouses:				Design/Engineering:							
Other:											

TYPES OF BUSINESS:

Home Centers, Retail
Home Improvement Products
Home Installation Services
Special Order Sales

BRANDS/DIVISIONS/AFFILIATES:

Premier Living
Kobalt
Portfolio
Harbor Breeze
Reliabilt
Utilitech
Top Choice Lumber
Lowes.com

CONTACTS: *Note: Officers with more than one job title may be intentionally listed here more than once.*

Robert A. Niblock, CEO
Larry D. Stone, COO
Larry D. Stone, Pres.
Robert F. Hull, Jr., CFO/Exec. VP
Robert J. Gfeller, Jr., Sr. VP-Mktg. & Advertising
Maureen K. Ausura, Sr. VP-Human Resources
Scott C. Butterfield, Sr. VP-Research & Strategic Planning
Steven M. Stone, CIO/Sr. VP
Charles W. Canter, Jr., Exec. VP-Merch.
Gary E. Wyatt, Sr. VP-Eng., Real Estate & Construction
Gaither M. Keener, Jr., General Counsel/Sr. VP/Corp. Sec.
Michael K. Brown, Exec. VP-Store Oper.
Gregory M. Bridgeford, Exec. VP-Bus. Dev.
N. Brian Peace, Sr. VP-Corp. Affairs
Matthew V. Hollifield, Chief Acct. Officer/Sr. VP
Theresa A. Anderson, Sr. VP/Gen. Merch. Mgr.-Home Decor
Patricia M. Price, Sr. VP/Gen. Merch. Mgr.-Outdoor Living
Marshall A. Croom, Sr. VP-Merch. & Store Support
Clinton T. Davis, Sr. VP/Gen. Merch. Mgr.-Hardlines
Robert A. Niblock, Chmn.
Joseph M. Mabry, Jr., Exec. VP-Logistics & Distribution

Phone: 704-758-1000	**Fax:** 336-6584766
Toll-Free: 800-445-6937	
Address: 1000 Lowe's Blvd., Mooresville, NC 28117 US	

GROWTH PLANS/SPECIAL FEATURES:

Lowe's Companies, Inc., is one of the largest home improvement retailers in the world. The company owns over 1,675 superstores in 50 states and Canada, each carrying approximately 40,000 products. Hundreds of thousands of items are also available through the firm's special order system. Lowe's stores chiefly serve do-it-yourself homeowners and commercial business customers, including contractors, landscapers, electricians, painters and plumbers. Each Lowe's store carries a wide selection of national brand name merchandise such as KitchenAid, Samsung, Whirlpool, Pella, Werner, Kohler, DeWalt, JohnDeere, Troy-Bilt, Jenn-Air and Bosch; and exclusive brand names such as Premier Living, Kobalt, Portfolio, Harbor Breeze, Reliabilt, Utilitech and Top Choice Lumber. The company's web site, Lowes.com, facilitates customers researching, comparing and buying Lowe's products and services. Lowe's recently completed the remerchandising of 116 of its earlier format stores to make them more closely resemble its most current store prototypes. The remerchandising efforts focused on moving entire departments, improving adjacencies, replacing or refurbishing the selling centers, adding interior signage and installing self check-out in each of the remerchandised stores. During 2008, the company opened 115 new stores, five of which are in Canada. For 2009-2014, Lowe's plans to open approximately 35 to 40 new stores yearly.

Lowe's offers its employees benefits such as life, disability, accident, auto, home, health, dental and vision insurance; merchandise discounts; a stock purchase plan; a 401(k); and flexible spending accounts.

FINANCIALS: **Sales and profits are in thousands of dollars—add 000 to get the full amount. 2009 Note: Financial information for 2009 was not available for all companies at press time.**

2009 Sales: $48,230,000	2009 Profits: $2,195,000	**U.S. Stock Ticker: LOW**
2008 Sales: $48,283,000	2008 Profits: $2,809,000	**Int'l Ticker:** Int'l Exchange:
2007 Sales: $46,927,000	2007 Profits: $3,105,000	Employees: 229,000
2006 Sales: $43,243,000	2006 Profits: $2,765,000	Fiscal Year Ends: 1/31
2005 Sales: $36,464,000	2005 Profits: $2,167,000	Parent Company:

SALARIES/BENEFITS:

Pension Plan:	ESOP Stock Plan:	Profit Sharing:	Top Exec. Salary: $1,100,000	Bonus: $1,500,763
Savings Plan: Y	Stock Purch. Plan: Y		Second Exec. Salary: $840,000	Bonus: $765,131

OTHER THOUGHTS:

Apparent Women Officers or Directors: 5
Hot Spot for Advancement for Women/Minorities: Y

LOCATIONS: ("Y" = Yes)

West:	Southwest:	Midwest:	Southeast:	Northeast:	International:
Y	Y	Y	Y	Y	Y

LQ MANAGEMENT LLC

www.lq.com

Industry Group Code: 721110 **Ranks within this company's industry group:** Sales: Profits:

Properties:		Financial Services:		Construction/Development:		Investments:		Specialty Services:		Brokerage:	
Apartments:		Mortgages:		Commercial Construction:		REIT:	Y	Property Management:	Y	Commercial Sales:	
Malls/Shopping:		Title Insurance:		Residential Construction:				Online Services:	Y	Residential Sales:	
Offices:		Property Insurance:		Land Development:				Software/IT:		Specialty:	
Hotels/Motels:	Y			Support Services:				Consulting:			
Industrial/Warehouses:				Design/Engineering:							
Other:											

TYPES OF BUSINESS:

Hotels, Motels & Suites
Hotel Management
Franchising
REIT

BRANDS/DIVISIONS/AFFILIATES:

La Quinta Properties
La Quinta Inns
La Quinta Inns and Suites
Budgetel
Baymont Inns and Suites
Woodfield Suites
Blackstone Group LP (The)

CONTACTS: *Note: Officers with more than one job title may be intentionally listed here more than once.*

Wayne B. Goldberg, CEO
Angelo J. Lombardi, COO/Exec. VP
Wayne Goldberg, Pres.
Temple H. Weiss, CFO/Exec. VP
Julie M. Cary, Chief Mktg. Officer/Exec. VP
Jeffrey M. Schagren, Exec. VP-Human Resources
Vivek Shaiva, CIO/Exec. VP
Mark M. Chloupek, General Counsel/Exec. VP
Rajiv K. Trivedi, Chief Dev. Officer
Teresa Ferguson, Dir.-Comm. & Public Rel.
Murry J. Cathlina, Exec. VP-Design & Construction
Feliz P. Jarvis, Exec. VP-Sales
Rajiv K. Trivedi, Exec. VP-Franchise

Phone: 214-492-6600 **Fax:** 214-492-6616
Toll-Free:
Address: 909 Hidden Ridge, Ste. 600, Irving, TX 75038 US

GROWTH PLANS/SPECIAL FEATURES:

LQ Management LLC, a subsidiary of the Blackstone Group, is the operator of the La Quinta motels and suites properties. La Quinta is a leading limited-service lodging brand that provides comfortable guest rooms in convenient locations at affordable prices. The firm is one of the largest owners and operators of limited-service hotels in the U.S. It boasts more than 750 hotels and 65,000 rooms in 45 states under the brands La Quinta Inns; La Quinta Inns and Suites; Baymont Inns and Suites; Woodfield Suites; and Budgetel. The firm also licenses its brand name to franchisees for royalty and other fees. The company markets its services to both leisure guests and business travelers. All of the firm's hotels are owned through La Quinta Properties, a real estate investment trust (REIT). A typical La Quinta Inn features approximately 130 guest rooms with amenities including movies-on-demand; interactive video games; free high-speed Internet; complimentary continental breakfast; a swimming pool; fax services; and 24-hour front desk message services. La Quinta Inn and Suites properties also feature deluxe two-room suites with microwaves and refrigerators, as well as fitness centers, courtyards and expanded food offerings.

Employees of the firm are offered medical, dental and vision coverage; life insurance; long term disability; an employee assistance program; flexible spending accounts; a 401(k) plan; tuition reimbursement; internal referral bonus program; direct deposit and room rate discounts.

FINANCIALS: **Sales and profits are in thousands of dollars—add 000 to get the full amount. 2009 Note: Financial information for 2009 was not available for all companies at press time.**

2009 Sales: $	2009 Profits: $	**U.S. Stock Ticker: Private**
2008 Sales: $	2008 Profits: $	**Int'l Ticker:** Int'l Exchange:
2007 Sales: $	2007 Profits: $	Employees:
2006 Sales: $	2006 Profits: $	Fiscal Year Ends: 12/31
2005 Sales: $	2005 Profits: $	Parent Company: BLACKSTONE GROUP LP (THE)

SALARIES/BENEFITS:

Pension Plan:	ESOP Stock Plan:	Profit Sharing:	Top Exec. Salary: $	Bonus: $
Savings Plan: Y	Stock Purch. Plan:		Second Exec. Salary: $	Bonus: $

OTHER THOUGHTS:

Apparent Women Officers or Directors: 2
Hot Spot for Advancement for Women/Minorities: Y

LOCATIONS: ("Y" = Yes)

West:	Southwest:	Midwest:	Southeast:	Northeast:	International:
Y	Y	Y	Y	Y	Y

M/I HOMES INC

www.mihomes.com

Industry Group Code: 2361 **Ranks within this company's industry group:** Sales: 15 Profits: 7

Properties:		Financial Services:		Construction/Development:		Investments:		Specialty Services:		Brokerage:	
Apartments:		Mortgages:	Y	Commercial Construction:		REIT:		Property Management:		Commercial Sales:	
Malls/Shopping:		Title Insurance:	Y	Residential Construction:	Y			Online Services:		Residential Sales:	Y
Offices:		Property Insurance:		Land Development:	Y			Software/IT:		Specialty:	
Hotels/Motels:				Support Services:				Consulting:			
Industrial/Warehouses:				Design/Engineering:	Y						
Other:											

TYPES OF BUSINESS:

Construction, Residential
Real Estate Development
Mortgage Services
Title Services

BRANDS/DIVISIONS/AFFILIATES:

Showcase Homes
M/I Financial
TransOhio Residential Title Agency
M/I Title Agency
Washington/Metro Residential Title Agency
Confidence Builder Program
Personal Construction Supervisor

CONTACTS:

Note: Officers with more than one job title may be intentionally listed here more than once.

Robert H. Schottenstein, CEO
Robert H. Schottenstein, Pres.
Phillip G. Creek, CFO/Exec. VP
J. Thomas Mason, General Counsel/Exec. Sec./Sr. VP
Ann Marier Hunker, Investor Rel.
Phillip G. Creek, Treas.
Robert H. Schottenstein, Chmn.

Phone: 614-418-8000 **Fax:** 614-418-8080
Toll-Free: 888-644-4111
Address: 3 Easton Oval, Ste. 500, Columbus, OH 43219 US

GROWTH PLANS/SPECIAL FEATURES:

M/I Homes, Inc. is a leading builder of single-family homes sold to first-time homebuyers, move-up buyers, empty nesters and luxury buyers under the M/I Homes and Showcase Homes trade names. The company delivered 2,409 homes in 2009, with an average sales price of $231,000. M/I sells its homes in Columbus and Cincinnati, Ohio; Tampa and Orlando, Florida; Charlotte and Raleigh, North Carolina; Indianapolis, Indiana; Chicago, Illinois and the Virginia and Maryland suburbs of Washington, D.C. M/I operates in four segments: Midwest homebuilding, Florida homebuilding, Mid-Atlantic homebuilding and financial services. The firm's homebuilding operations comprise over 98% of its revenues. The homebuilding operations generated 99% of its own revenue from the sale of complete homes, with the remaining amount generated from the sale of land and lots. M/I's financial services operations generate revenue from originating and selling mortgages; collecting fees for title insurance; and closing services. Subsidiary M/I Financial provides financing services in its housing markets, while title services are provided through subsidiaries TransOhio Residential Title Agency, M/I Title Agency and majority-owned Washington/Metro Residential Title Agency. The company offers roughly 400 floor plans and spent $1.8 million in 2009 on research and development of its homes. The firm's Confidence Builder Program includes a pre-construction conference between the client and a Personal Construction Supervisor. The supervisors manage the development and construction process, for which M/I utilizes independent subcontractors. In March 2010, the company entered the housing market in Houston, Texas.

Employees are offered medical, dental and vision insurance; life insurance; disability coverage; medical and childcare reimbursement programs; an employee assistance program; a 401(k) plan; an employee stock purchase plan; and a home purchase plan.

FINANCIALS:

Sales and profits are in thousands of dollars—add 000 to get the full amount. 2009 Note: Financial information for 2009 was not available for all companies at press time.

2009 Sales: $569,949	2009 Profits: $-62,109
2008 Sales: $607,659	2008 Profits: $-250,323
2007 Sales: $1,016,460	2007 Profits: $-135,439
2006 Sales: $1,274,145	2006 Profits: $38,875
2005 Sales: $1,312,504	2005 Profits: $100,785

U.S. Stock Ticker: MHO
Int'l Ticker: Int'l Exchange:
Employees: 535
Fiscal Year Ends: 12/31
Parent Company:

SALARIES/BENEFITS:

Pension Plan:	ESOP Stock Plan:	Profit Sharing:	Top Exec. Salary: $750,000	Bonus: $356,501
Savings Plan: Y	Stock Purch. Plan: Y		Second Exec. Salary: $500,000	Bonus: $169,763

OTHER THOUGHTS:

Apparent Women Officers or Directors: 2
Hot Spot for Advancement for Women/Minorities:

LOCATIONS: ("Y" = Yes)

West:	Southwest:	Midwest:	Southeast:	Northeast:	International:
	Y	Y	Y	Y	

MACERICH COMPANY (THE)

www.macerich.com

Industry Group Code: 531120 **Ranks within this company's industry group:** Sales: 21 Profits: 15

Properties:		Financial Services:		Construction/Development:		Investments:		Specialty Services:		Brokerage:	
Apartments:		Mortgages:		Commercial Construction:		REIT:	Y	Property Management:	Y	Commercial Sales:	
Malls/Shopping:	Y	Title Insurance:		Residential Construction:				Online Services:		Residential Sales:	
Offices:		Property Insurance:		Land Development:	Y			Software/IT:		Specialty:	
Hotels/Motels:				Support Services:				Consulting:			
Industrial/Warehouses:				Design/Engineering:							
Other:											

TYPES OF BUSINESS:

Real Estate Investment Trust
Regional Shopping Centers
Community Shopping Centers
Property Management
Property Redevelopment

BRANDS/DIVISIONS/AFFILIATES:

Macerich Partnership, L.P.
Macerich Property Management Company, LLC
Westcor Partners, LLC
Macerich Management Company
Scottsdale Fashion Square

CONTACTS:

Note: Officers with more than one job title may be intentionally listed here more than once.

Arthur M. Coppola, CEO
Tony Grossi, COO/Sr. VP
Edward C. Coppola, Pres.
Thomas E. O'Hern, CFO/Sr. Exec. VP/Treas.
Tracey Gotsis, Exec. VP-Mktg. & Dev.
Genene Kruger, Sr. VP-Human Resources
J.P. Jones, CIO
Richard A. Bayer, Chief Legal Officer/Sr. Exec. VP/Sec.
John M. Genovese, Exec. VP-Dev.
Scott Kingsmore, Sr. VP-Finance
Dana K. Anderson, Vice Chmn.
Diana M. Laing, CFO-Thomas Properties Group, Inc.
Randy Brant, Exec. VP-Real Estate
Michael J. Busenhart, Sr. VP-Acquisitions
Arthur M. Coppola, Chmn.

Phone: 310-394-6000	**Fax:** 310-395-2791
Toll-Free:	
Address: 401 Wilshire Blvd., Ste. 700, Santa Monica, CA 90401 US	

GROWTH PLANS/SPECIAL FEATURES:

The Macerich Company is a real estate investment trust (REIT) involved in the acquisition, ownership, redevelopment, management and leasing of regional and community shopping centers located throughout the U.S. The firm is the sole general partner and has an 89% ownership interest in the Macerich Partnership, L.P. (MP), which owns or maintains ownership interests in 72 regional shopping centers and 14 community shopping centers, totaling approximately 74 million square feet of leasable area. Other subsidiaries include Macerich Property Management Company; Westcor Partners; and Macerich Management Company. Macerich's largest markets include California and Arizona, both with 20 or more shopping centers. Other properties are located in Colorado, Connecticut, Iowa, Illinois, Indiana, Kentucky, Maryland, Montana, New Jersey, New York, Oregon, South Dakota, Texas, Utah, Virginia and Washington. Macerich's integrated operations include in-house accounting, finance, legal, marketing, property management and redevelopment expertise. Macerich's regional shopping centers are generally enclosed; offer a variety of small and mid-size stores anchored by several department stores or other large retailers; and range in size from approximately 315,000 to over two million square feet, with an average of 955,000 square feet. The firm's community shopping centers, which are generally smaller open-air centers designed to attract local and neighborhood customers with anchors such as supermarkets and drug stores, average 276,000 square feet. Some key tenants in the company's properties include The Gap, Inc.; Limited Brands, Inc.; Foot Locker, Inc.; Forever 21, Inc.; AT&T Mobility, LLC; Abercrombie & Fitch Co.; Luxottica Group; American Eagle Outfitters, Inc.; and Signet Group PLC. Anchors in the firm's regional malls include Macy's, Sears, J.C. Penney, Dillard's, Nordstrom and Target. In the fall of 2009, Macerich completed a new expansion to its Scottsdale Fashion Square property in Scottsdale, Arizona; the expansion adds approximately 20 new retail outlets, including a Microsoft retail store and Barney's New York.

FINANCIALS:

Sales and profits are in thousands of dollars—add 000 to get the full amount. 2009 Note: Financial information for 2009 was not available for all companies at press time.

2009 Sales: $805,654	2009 Profits: $139,250	**U.S. Stock Ticker: MAC**
2008 Sales: $880,871	2008 Profits: $195,015	**Int'l Ticker:** Int'l Exchange:
2007 Sales: $800,842	2007 Profits: $106,062	Employees: 2,749
2006 Sales: $749,619	2006 Profits: $244,549	Fiscal Year Ends: 12/31
2005 Sales: $711,824	2005 Profits: $71,686	Parent Company:

SALARIES/BENEFITS:

Pension Plan:	ESOP Stock Plan:	Profit Sharing: Y	Top Exec. Salary: $950,000	Bonus: $3,800,000
Savings Plan: Y	Stock Purch. Plan: Y		Second Exec. Salary: $800,000	Bonus: $3,200,000

OTHER THOUGHTS:

Apparent Women Officers or Directors: 5
Hot Spot for Advancement for Women/Minorities: Y

LOCATIONS: ("Y" = Yes)

West:	Southwest:	Midwest:	Southeast:	Northeast:	International:
Y	Y	Y	Y	Y	

MACK-CALI REALTY CORP

www.mack-cali.com

Industry Group Code: 531120 **Ranks within this company's industry group:** Sales: 25 Profits: 34

Properties:		Financial Services:		Construction/Development:		Investments:		Specialty Services:		Brokerage:	
Apartments:		Mortgages:		Commercial Construction:		REIT:	Y	Property Management:	Y	Commercial Sales:	
Malls/Shopping:		Title Insurance:		Residential Construction:				Online Services:		Residential Sales:	
Offices:	Y	Property Insurance:		Land Development:				Software/IT:		Specialty:	
Hotels/Motels:				Support Services:				Consulting:			
Industrial/Warehouses:	Y			Design/Engineering:							
Other:											

TYPES OF BUSINESS:

Real Estate Investment Trust
Office & Industrial Properties
Property Management

BRANDS/DIVISIONS/AFFILIATES:

Gale Real Estate Services Company

CONTACTS:

Note: Officers with more than one job title may be intentionally listed here more than once.

Mitchell E. Hersh, CEO
Mitchell E. Hersh, Pres.
Barry Lefkowitz, CFO/Exec. VP
Ilene Jablonski, Sr. Dir.-Mktg.
Janice H. Torchinsky, VP-Human Resources
Nicholas Mitarotonda, Jr., VP-Info. Systems
Roger W. Thomas, General Counsel/Exec. VP/Corp. Sec.
John J. Crandall, Sr. VP-Dev.
Ilene Jablonski, Sr. Dir.-Public Rel.
Anthony Krug, Sr. VP-Finance
Giovanni M. DeBari, VP/Corp. Controller
William Fitzpatrick, VP/Treas.
John Adderly, VP-Leasing
James A. Bell, VP-Property Mgmt.
William L. Mack, Chmn.

Phone: 732-590-1000	**Fax:** 732-205-8237
Toll-Free:	
Address: 343 Thornall St., Edison, NJ 08837-2206 US	

GROWTH PLANS/SPECIAL FEATURES:

Mack-Cali Realty Corporation is a fully integrated, self-administered and self-managed real estate investment trust (REIT) that owns and operates a portfolio made up predominantly of Class A office and office/flex properties, located primarily in suburban markets in the Northeast U.S. The trust performs substantially all commercial real estate leasing, management, acquisition, development and construction services on an in-house basis. The company owns or has interests in 288 properties, totaling approximately 33.1 million square feet of Class A office, office/flex properties, warehouse/industrial and stand alone retail space that is leased to approximately 2,100 tenants. Mack-Cali's portfolio is approximately 88.8% leased. Many of the firm's properties have adjacent company-controlled developable land. Its major tenants include New Cingular Wireless PCS, LLC; Morgan Stanley & Co., Inc.; Citigroup Global Markets, Inc.; Keystone Mercy Health Plan; Toys 'R' Us-NJ, Inc.; IBM Corporation; Virgin Mobile USA L.P; Allstate Insurance Company; and Prentice-Hall, Inc. Through joint ventures, the company has interests in an additional 20 buildings, primarily office properties, totaling about 2.2 million square feet, and a 350-room hotel. Subsidiary, Gale Real Estate Services, offers development and leasing services, as well as real estate equity investment, asset management, property management and construction.

FINANCIALS:

Sales and profits are in thousands of dollars—add 000 to get the full amount. 2009 Note: Financial information for 2009 was not available for all companies at press time.

2009 Sales: $733,256	2009 Profits: $52,568	**U.S. Stock Ticker: CLI**
2008 Sales: $723,802	2008 Profits: $51,726	**Int'l Ticker:** Int'l Exchange:
2007 Sales: $808,350	2007 Profits: $108,466	Employees: 422
2006 Sales: $732,012	2006 Profits: $142,666	Fiscal Year Ends: 12/31
2005 Sales: $591,991	2005 Profits: $93,488	Parent Company:

SALARIES/BENEFITS:

Pension Plan:	ESOP Stock Plan:	Profit Sharing:	Top Exec. Salary: $1,050,000	Bonus: $1,000,000
Savings Plan:	Stock Purch. Plan:		Second Exec. Salary: $420,000	Bonus: $505,000

OTHER THOUGHTS:

Apparent Women Officers or Directors: 3
Hot Spot for Advancement for Women/Minorities: Y

LOCATIONS: ("Y" = Yes)

West:	Southwest:	Midwest:	Southeast:	Northeast:	International:
				Y	

MAGUIRE PROPERTIES INC

www.maguireproperties.com

Industry Group Code: 5311 **Ranks within this company's industry group:** Sales: 26 Profits: 32

Properties:		Financial Services:		Construction/Development:		Investments:		Specialty Services:		Brokerage:	
Apartments:		Mortgages:		Commercial Construction:		REIT:	Y	Property Management:	Y	Commercial Sales:	Y
Malls/Shopping:		Title Insurance:		Residential Construction:				Online Services:		Residential Sales:	
Offices:	Y	Property Insurance:		Land Development:				Software/IT:		Specialty:	
Hotels/Motels:	Y			Support Services:	Y			Consulting:			
Industrial/Warehouses:				Design/Engineering:	Y						
Other:											

TYPES OF BUSINESS:

Real Estate Investment, Development & Management
Office Properties
Property Management
Asset Management
Urban Planning

BRANDS/DIVISIONS/AFFILIATES:

Maguire Properties LP
Maguire Properties TRS Holdings Inc
Maguire Properties TRS Holdings II Inc
Maguire Properties Services Inc
Maguire Macquarie Office LLC

CONTACTS:

Note: Officers with more than one job title may be intentionally listed here more than once.

Nelson C. Rising, CEO
Nelson C. Rising, Pres.
Shant Koumrigian, CFO/Exec. VP
Peggy Moretti, Chief Admin. Officer
Jonathan L. Abrams, General Counsel/Sr. VP/Corp. Sec.
Christopher C. Rising, Sr. VP-Strategic Initiatives
Peggy Moretti, Exec. VP-Public Rel.
Peggy Moretti, Exec. VP-Investor Rel.
Mark T. Lamma,
Peter K. Johnston, Sr. VP-Leasing
Robert P. Goodwin, Sr. VP-Construction & Dev.
Travis F. Addison, Sr. VP-Asset Mgmt.
Robert J. White, Exec. VP
Paul M. Watson, Chmn.

Phone: 213-626-3300 **Fax:** 213-687-4758
Toll-Free:
Address: 355 S. Grand Ave., Ste. 3300, Los Angeles, CA 90071 US

GROWTH PLANS/SPECIAL FEATURES:

Maguire Properties, Inc. is a self-administered and self-managed real estate investment trust (REIT). The firm owns and operates high-quality office properties in the Los Angeles central business district. The company is primarily focused on owning, managing, leasing, acquiring and developing properties in Southern California. Maguire Properties operates through its controlling 87.8% interest in Maguire Properties, L.P., and subsidiaries such as Maguire Properties TRS Holdings, Inc.; Maguire Properties TRS Holdings II, Inc.; and Maguire Properties Services, Inc. It currently has properties in the greater Los Angeles area, Orange County and San Diego; and owns one in Denver, Colorado. Maguire operates through two segments: office properties and hotel. The firm's portfolio totals approximately 14.1 million square feet, consisting of 31 office and retail buildings; a 350-room hotel with 266,000 square feet; off-site parking garages; and on-site structured and surface parking. Office properties are typically leased to high credit tenants for terms ranging from 5-10 years. The firm also holds a 20% interest in Maguire Macquarie Office LLC, a joint venture with Macquarie Office Trust, and is responsible for day-to-day operations of the properties, including asset management, property management, leasing, construction management, acquisitions, dispositions and financing. Maguire also contributes planning solutions to urban planning issues as well as planning approvals for large-scale projects. In 2009, the firm sold three properties in Orange County and one in Irvine, California. In December 2009, the company sold the Santa Monica-based Lantana Media Entertainment Campus to an affiliate of Lionstone Group and sold one of the offices on the campus to NARAS Properties, Inc. In March 2010, Maguire sold Orange County property Griffin Towers to a joint venture between Angelo Gordon & Co. and Lincoln Property Company.

FINANCIALS:

Sales and profits are in thousands of dollars—add 000 to get the full amount. 2009 Note: Financial information for 2009 was not available for all companies at press time.

2009 Sales: $476,748	2009 Profits: $-869,727	**U.S. Stock Ticker: MPG**
2008 Sales: $492,015	2008 Profits: $-323,338	**Int'l Ticker:** Int'l Exchange:
2007 Sales: $462,542	2007 Profits: $19,359	Employees: 166
2006 Sales: $431,402	2006 Profits: $70,326	Fiscal Year Ends: 12/31
2005 Sales: $473,173	2005 Profits: $-23,818	Parent Company:

SALARIES/BENEFITS:

Pension Plan:	ESOP Stock Plan:	Profit Sharing:	Top Exec. Salary: $593,750	Bonus: $1,187,500
Savings Plan:	Stock Purch. Plan:		Second Exec. Salary: $375,000	Bonus: $562,500

OTHER THOUGHTS:

Apparent Women Officers or Directors: 2
Hot Spot for Advancement for Women/Minorities:

LOCATIONS: ("Y" = Yes)

West:	Southwest:	Midwest:	Southeast:	Northeast:	International:
Y					

MANDARIN ORIENTAL INTERNATIONAL LTD www.mandarinoriental.com

Industry Group Code: 721110 **Ranks within this company's industry group:** Sales: 20 Profits: 10

Properties:		Financial Services:		Construction/Development:		Investments:		Specialty Services:		Brokerage:	
Apartments:		Mortgages:		Commercial Construction:	Y	REIT:		Property Management:	Y	Commercial Sales:	
Malls/Shopping:		Title Insurance:		Residential Construction:				Online Services:		Residential Sales:	
Offices:		Property Insurance:		Land Development:				Software/IT:		Specialty:	
Hotels/Motels:	Y			Support Services:				Consulting:			
Industrial/Warehouses:				Design/Engineering:							
Other:	Y										

TYPES OF BUSINESS:

Hotels, Luxury
Condominiums

BRANDS/DIVISIONS/AFFILIATES:

Mandarin Oriental Holding Company Limited
Mandarin Oriental
Residences at Mandarin Oriental
Spa at Mandarin Oriental

CONTACTS:

Note: Officers with more than one job title may be intentionally listed here more than once.

Edouard Ettedgui, CEO
Stuart Dickie, CFO
Michael Hobson, Dir.-Sales & Mktg.
Terry L. Stinson, Dir.-Dev.
Jill Kluge, Group Dir.-Brand Comm.
Liam Lambert, Dir.-Oper., EMEA
Andrew Hirst, Dir.-Oper., Asia
Richard Baker, Exec. VP-US Northern Region
Jorge Gonzalez, Exec. VP-U.S. Southern Region
Simon L. Keswick, Chmn.
Terry L. Stinson, Pres., The Americas

Phone: 852-2895-9288	**Fax:** 852-2837-3500
Toll-Free:	
Address: 281 Gloucester Rd., 7th Fl., Hong Kong, China	

GROWTH PLANS/SPECIAL FEATURES:

Mandarin Oriental International, Ltd. (MOI) is an international hotel investment and management group. MOI operates in two business segments, hotel ownership and hotel management, and four geographical regions: Hong Kong and Macau; Other Asia; Europe; and the Americas. The hotel ownership segment generates approximately 96% of its revenue. The Hong Kong/Macau region generates about 37% of the firm's revenue; Other Asia, 23%; Europe 27%; and the Americas, 13%. The company operates or is in the process of developing 41 luxury and first class hotels with over 10,000 rooms and a presence in 26 countries worldwide. MOI has 17 hotel properties in Asia, 13 in the Americas and 11 in Europe, the Middle East and North Africa. These include the original flagship properties of the Mandarin Oriental in Hong Kong and the Oriental in Bangkok, as well as locations such as Singapore, Jakarta, Kuala Lumpur, Macau, Manila, London, Geneva, Tokyo, Munich, Prague and Bermuda. The company has U.S. hotels in New York City, San Francisco, Boston, Miami and Washington, D.C. In addition to hotel rooms, the Mandarin Oriental New York also offers the Residences at Mandarin Oriental, 65 luxury condominiums located above the hotel. Another 12 of the firm's properties also feature the Residences at Mandarin Oriental condominiums. The Spa at Mandarin Oriental can also be found in many of the firm's hotels worldwide, including in London, Miami, Boston and New York City. Each spa is unique and offers specialized treatments to clients. Properties currently under development include the Mandarin Oriental Hotels in Macau, Marrakech, Abu Dhabi, Atlanta, Beijing, Costa Rica, Grand Cayman, Guangzhou, Maldives, Marbella, Milan, Moscow, Paris, St. Kitts, Taipei and Turks and Caicos. In June 2009, the firm's wholly-owned subsidiary, Mandarin Oriental Holding Company Limited sold its 50% interest in hotel Mandarin Oriental, Macau to Sociedad de Turismo e Diversoes de Macau S.A.

FINANCIALS:

Sales and profits are in thousands of dollars—add 000 to get the full amount. 2009 Note: Financial information for 2009 was not available for all companies at press time.

2009 Sales: $438,000	2009 Profits: $83,300	**U.S. Stock Ticker:**
2008 Sales: $530,000	2008 Profits: $66,200	**Int'l Ticker: M04** Int'l Exchange: Singapore-SIN
2007 Sales: $529,500	2007 Profits: $107,400	Employees:
2006 Sales: $404,600	2006 Profits: $80,200	Fiscal Year Ends: 12/31
2005 Sales: $399,200	2005 Profits: $74,200	Parent Company:

SALARIES/BENEFITS:

Pension Plan:	ESOP Stock Plan:	Profit Sharing:	Top Exec. Salary: $	Bonus: $
Savings Plan:	Stock Purch. Plan:		Second Exec. Salary: $	Bonus: $

OTHER THOUGHTS:

Apparent Women Officers or Directors: 1
Hot Spot for Advancement for Women/Minorities:

LOCATIONS: ("Y" = Yes)

West:	Southwest:	Midwest:	Southeast:	Northeast:	International:
Y			Y	Y	Y

MANOR CARE INC

www.hcr-manorcare.com

Industry Group Code: 623110 **Ranks within this company's industry group:** Sales: 1 Profits:

Properties:		Financial Services:		Construction/Development:		Investments:		Specialty Services:		Brokerage:	
Apartments:		Mortgages:		Commercial Construction:		REIT:		Property Management:		Commercial Sales:	
Malls/Shopping:		Title Insurance:		Residential Construction:				Online Services:		Residential Sales:	
Offices:		Property Insurance:		Land Development:				Software/IT:		Specialty:	
Hotels/Motels:				Support Services:				Consulting:			
Industrial/Warehouses:				Design/Engineering:							
Other:	Y										

TYPES OF BUSINESS:

Long-Term Health Care/Nursing Homes
Home Health Care
Short-Term Care Facilities
Assisted Living Facilities
Rehabilitation Clinics

BRANDS/DIVISIONS/AFFILIATES:

HCR Manor Care
Heartland
ManorCare Health Services
Arden Courts
Carlyle Group (The)

CONTACTS:

Note: Officers with more than one job title may be intentionally listed here more than once.

Paul A. Ormond, CEO
Stephen L. Guillard, COO/Exec. VP
Paul A. Ormond, Pres.
Steven M. Cavanaugh, CFO
Chris Ullman, Dir.-Global Comm.
Paul A. Ormond, Chmn.

Phone: 419-252-5500	**Fax:** 419-252-6404
Toll-Free:	
Address: 333 N. Summit St., Toledo, OH 43604-2617 US	

GROWTH PLANS/SPECIAL FEATURES:

Manor Care, Inc., doing business as HCR Manor Care, provides a range of health care services, including skilled nursing care, assisted living, post-acute medical care, hospice care, home health care and rehabilitation therapy. Manor Care operates over 500 properties in 32 states, with facilities operating primarily under the Heartland, ManorCare Health Services and Arden Courts names. Manor Care's long-term care services consist of skilled nursing centers, assisted living services, post-acute medical and rehabilitation care and Alzheimer's care. The skilled nursing centers use interdisciplinary teams of experienced medical professionals, including registered nurses, licensed practical nurses and certified nursing assistants, to provide services prescribed by physicians. Other services include the design of Quality of Life programs to give the highest practicable level of functional independence to patients, provide physical, speech, respiratory and occupational therapy and provide quality nutrition services, social services, activities and housekeeping and laundry services. Manor Care's assisted living services provide personal care services and assistance with general activities of daily living such as dressing, bathing, meal preparation and medication management. In recent years, the firm was acquired by private equity firm The Carlyle Group for roughly $6.3 billion.

FINANCIALS:

Sales and profits are in thousands of dollars—add 000 to get the full amount. 2009 Note: Financial information for 2009 was not available for all companies at press time.

2009 Sales: $	2009 Profits: $	**U.S. Stock Ticker: Private**
2008 Sales: $3,850,000	2008 Profits: $	**Int'l Ticker:** Int'l Exchange:
2007 Sales: $3,800,000	2007 Profits: $	Employees: 60,000
2006 Sales: $3,613,185	2006 Profits: $169,560	Fiscal Year Ends: 12/31
2005 Sales: $3,417,290	2005 Profits: $160,955	Parent Company: CARLYLE GROUP (THE)

SALARIES/BENEFITS:

Pension Plan:	ESOP Stock Plan:	Profit Sharing:	Top Exec. Salary: $	Bonus: $
Savings Plan:	Stock Purch. Plan:		Second Exec. Salary: $	Bonus: $

OTHER THOUGHTS:

Apparent Women Officers or Directors:
Hot Spot for Advancement for Women/Minorities:

LOCATIONS: ("Y" = Yes)

West:	Southwest:	Midwest:	Southeast:	Northeast:	International:
Y	Y	Y	Y	Y	

MARCUS CORPORATION (THE)

www.marcuscorp.com

Industry Group Code: 721110 **Ranks within this company's industry group:** Sales: 22 Profits: 14

Properties:		Financial Services:		Construction/Development:		Investments:		Specialty Services:		Brokerage:	
Apartments:		Mortgages:		Commercial Construction:		REIT:		Property Management:	Y	Commercial Sales:	
Malls/Shopping:		Title Insurance:		Residential Construction:				Online Services:		Residential Sales:	
Offices:		Property Insurance:		Land Development:				Software/IT:		Specialty:	
Hotels/Motels:	Y			Support Services:				Consulting:			
Industrial/Warehouses:				Design/Engineering:							
Other:	Y										

TYPES OF BUSINESS:

Hotels & Motels
Movie & IMAX Theaters
Hotels/Resorts

BRANDS/DIVISIONS/AFFILIATES:

Marcus Theatres
Funset Boulevard
Marcus Majestic of Brookfield (The)
UltraScreen
AT&T Palladium
Marcus Hotels and Resorts
Skirvin Hilton
Marcus Midtown Cinema

CONTACTS:

Note: Officers with more than one job title may be intentionally listed here more than once.

Gregory S. Marcus, CEO
Gregory S. Marcus, Pres.
Douglas A. Neis, CFO
Karen Y. Spindler, Dir.-Corp. Human Resources
Jane Durment, CIO
Thomas F. Kissinger, General Counsel/Corp. Sec./VP
Douglas A. Neis, Treas.
Bruce J. Olson, Sr. VP/Pres., Marcus Theatres Corp.
William J. Otto, Pres., Marcus Hotels & Resorts
Stephen H. Marcus, Chmn.

Phone: 414-905-1100	**Fax:** 414-905-2879
Toll-Free:	
Address: 100 E. Wisconsin Ave., Ste. 1900, Milwaukee, WI 53202-4125 US	

GROWTH PLANS/SPECIAL FEATURES:

The Marcus Corporation is an owner and operator of movie theatres, hotels and resorts. The firm operates in two segments: Theatres and Hotels/Resorts. Through its Marcus Theatres subsidiary, the company owns 53 movie theatres in Wisconsin, Ohio, Illinois, Minnesota, North Dakota, Nebraska and Iowa, with 663 screens. The company also manages one six-screen movie theater in Wisconsin owned by a third party. Marcus also operates a family entertainment center, called Funset Boulevard, which is adjacent to one of its theatres in Appleton, Wisconsin. The company's 52 owned facilities include 32 megaplex theatres (12 or more screens), 19 multiplex theatres (two to 11 screens) and one single-screen theatre. The Marcus Majestic in Brookfield, Washington, features two 72-feet-wide UltraScreens and a multi-use auditorium called the AT&T Palladium with an attached kitchen, which offers a full menu. Through subsidiary Marcus Hotels and Resorts, Marcus owns and operates eight hotels and resorts and manages 12 hotels, resorts and other properties for third parties. Marcus' owned hotels and resorts include the Pfister Hotel, the InterContinental Milwaukee and The Hilton Milwaukee City Center in Milwaukee, Wisconsin; the Hilton Madison at Monona Terrace in Madison, Wisconsin; The Grand Geneva Resort & Spa in Lake Geneva, Wisconsin; the Hotel Phillips in Kansas City, Missouri; the Four Points by Sheraton Chicago Downtown/Magnificent Mile in Chicago, Illinois; and the Skirvin Hilton in Oklahoma City, Oklahoma. Marcus Theatres and Marcus Hotels and Resorts account for about 58% and 42% of Marcus' total revenue, respectively. In March 2009, the company announced plans to install 13 RealD digital 3D systems in at Marcus Theatres in the Midwest. In November 2009, Marcus Theatres opened the Marcus Midtown Cinema, a five-story entertainment destination in Omaha, Nebraska. In March 2010, the firm announced plans to install an additional 19 RealD digital 3D systems in its theaters.

FINANCIALS:

Sales and profits are in thousands of dollars—add 000 to get the full amount. 2009 Note: Financial information for 2009 was not available for all companies at press time.

2009 Sales: $383,496	2009 Profits: $17,200	**U.S. Stock Ticker: MCS**
2008 Sales: $371,075	2008 Profits: $20,486	**Int'l Ticker:** Int'l Exchange:
2007 Sales: $327,631	2007 Profits: $33,297	Employees: 6,300
2006 Sales: $289,244	2006 Profits: $28,271	Fiscal Year Ends: 5/31
2005 Sales: $272,707	2005 Profits: $99,221	Parent Company:

SALARIES/BENEFITS:

Pension Plan:	ESOP Stock Plan:	Profit Sharing:	Top Exec. Salary: $520,288	Bonus: $164,468
Savings Plan: Y	Stock Purch. Plan:		Second Exec. Salary: $464,037	Bonus: $127,914

OTHER THOUGHTS:

Apparent Women Officers or Directors: 3
Hot Spot for Advancement for Women/Minorities: Y

LOCATIONS: ("Y" = Yes)

West:	Southwest:	Midwest:	Southeast:	Northeast:	International:
Y	Y	Y			

MARRIOTT INTERNATIONAL INC

www.marriott.com

Industry Group Code: 721110 **Ranks within this company's industry group:** Sales: 1 Profits: 2

Properties:		Financial Services:		Construction/Development:		Investments:		Specialty Services:		Brokerage:	
Apartments:	Y	Mortgages:		Commercial Construction:	Y	REIT:		Property Management:	Y	Commercial Sales:	
Malls/Shopping:		Title Insurance:		Residential Construction:				Online Services:		Residential Sales:	
Offices:		Property Insurance:		Land Development:				Software/IT:		Specialty:	
Hotels/Motels:	Y			Support Services:				Consulting:			
Industrial/Warehouses:				Design/Engineering:	Y						
Other:	Y										

TYPES OF BUSINESS:

Hotels & Resorts
Hotels and Lodging
Timeshares
Extended Stay Lodging
Resorts
Corporate Apartments
Timeshares

BRANDS/DIVISIONS/AFFILIATES:

Marriott Hotels and Resorts
Ritz-Carlton (The)
Bulgari Hotel and Resort
Renaissance Hotels, Resorts and ClubSport
Courtyard Residence Inn
Fairfield Inn
ExecuStay
TownePlace Suites

CONTACTS: *Note: Officers with more than one job title may be intentionally listed here more than once.*

J. W. Marriott, Jr., CEO
Arne M. Sorenson, COO
Arne M. Sorenson, Pres.
Carl T. Berquist, CFO/Exec. VP
David A. Rodriguez, Exec. VP-Global Human Resources
Carl Wilson, CIO/Exec. VP
Edward A. Ryan, General Counsel/Exec. VP
Kathleen Matthews, Exec. VP-Global Comm. & Public Affairs
Laura E. Paugh, Sr. VP-Investor Rel.
William J. Shaw, Vice Chmn.
Robert J. McCarthy, Pres., North American Lodging Oper.
Simon F. Cooper, Pres./COO-Rtiz-Carlton Hotel Co. LLC
J. W. Marriott, Jr., Chmn.
Edwin D. Fuller, Pres./Managing Dir.-Marriott Lodging Int'l

Phone: 301-380-3000 **Fax:** 301-380-3967
Toll-Free: 800-721-7033
Address: 10400 Fernwood Rd., Bethesda, MD 20817 US

GROWTH PLANS/SPECIAL FEATURES:

Marriott International, Inc. operates 3,420 hotels and related lodging facilities in the U.S. and 65 other countries and territories. Though primarily known for the firm's various hotel brands, Marriot also has operations in time shares. The company operates through five segments: North American Full-Service; North American Limited-Service; International; Luxury; and Timeshare. Marriott develops, operates and franchises hotels under 14 brand names, including Marriott Hotels and Resorts; JW Marriott Hotels and Resorts; the Ritz-Carlton, featuring luxury hotels and resorts; Bulgari Hotel and Resort; Renaissance Hotels, Resorts and ClubSport; Courtyard; Residence Inn, the firm's extended-stay brand; Fairfield Inn; SpringHill Suites; and TownePlace Suites. The firm also provides furnished corporate housing units in 43 major markets through its ExecuStay brand, as well as operating 20 upscale serviced apartments through Marriott Executive Apartments. The company also develops, markets and operates timeshare, fractional ownership and residential properties under four separate brand names in over 50 locations. The resorts are usually adjacent to the firm's hotels, bearing the brand names Marriott Vacation Club International, Horizons by Marriott Vacation Club International, Ritz-Carlton Club and Grand Residences by Marriott. Additionally, Marriott manages approximately 42 golf resorts worldwide. The company also operates 13 systemwide hotel reservation centers: 8 in the U.S. and Canada, and five in other countries and territories. In 2009, the company announced the launch of the Autograph Collection, a new brand within the company's global portfolio that will be comprised of upper-upscale and luxury independent hotels located worldwide. The company expects to add at least 25 existing hotels to this portfolio throughout 2010.

Employees are offered medical, dental and disability insurance; a 401(k) plan; tuition reimbursement; discounts on hotel rooms, food and beverages; and work/family programs and services. Marriot was named one of the 100 Best Companies to Work For and one of the Best Companies for Hourly Workers by Working Mother Magazine.

FINANCIALS: **Sales and profits are in thousands of dollars—add 000 to get the full amount. 2009 Note: Financial information for 2009 was not available for all companies at press time.**

2009 Sales: $10,908,000	2009 Profits: $-346,000	**U.S. Stock Ticker: MAR**
2008 Sales: $12,879,000	2008 Profits: $359,000	**Int'l Ticker:** Int'l Exchange:
2007 Sales: $12,990,000	2007 Profits: $696,000	Employees: 137,000
2006 Sales: $11,995,000	2006 Profits: $608,000	Fiscal Year Ends: 12/31
2005 Sales: $11,129,000	2005 Profits: $669,000	Parent Company:

SALARIES/BENEFITS:

Pension Plan:	ESOP Stock Plan:	Profit Sharing:	Top Exec. Salary: $1,182,692	Bonus: $
Savings Plan: Y	Stock Purch. Plan:		Second Exec. Salary: $1,000,000	Bonus: $

OTHER THOUGHTS:

Apparent Women Officers or Directors: 9
Hot Spot for Advancement for Women/Minorities: Y

LOCATIONS: ("Y" = Yes)

West:	Southwest:	Midwest:	Southeast:	Northeast:	International:
Y	Y	Y	Y	Y	Y

MATRIX SERVICE COMPANY

www.matrixservice.com

Industry Group Code: 237 **Ranks within this company's industry group:** Sales: 32 Profits: 28

Properties:		Financial Services:		Construction/Development:		Investments:		Specialty Services:		Brokerage:	
Apartments:		Mortgages:		Commercial Construction:		REIT:		Property Management:		Commercial Sales:	
Malls/Shopping:		Title Insurance:		Residential Construction:				Online Services:		Residential Sales:	
Offices:		Property Insurance:		Land Development:				Software/IT:		Specialty:	
Hotels/Motels:				Support Services:	Y			Consulting:			
Industrial/Warehouses:				Design/Engineering:							
Other:											

TYPES OF BUSINESS:

Heavy Construction & Civil Engineering
Plant Maintenance Services
Storage Tank Services
Petrochemical Industry Services

BRANDS/DIVISIONS/AFFILIATES:

Matrix Service Industrial Contractors, Inc.
Matrix Service, Inc.
S.M. Electric Company, Inc.

CONTACTS:

Note: Officers with more than one job title may be intentionally listed here more than once.

Michael J. Bradley, CEO
Joseph F. Montalbano, COO/VP
Michael J. Bradley, Pres.
Thomas E. Long, CFO/VP
Nancy E. Austin, VP-Human Resources
Lansing G. Smith, VP-Eng. & Fabrication
Robert A. Long, VP-Gulf Coast Oper.
Kevin S. Cavanah, VP-Financial Reporting
Kevin S. Cavanah, VP-Acct.
James P. Ryan, Pres., Matrix Service, Inc.
Matthew J. Petrizzo, Pres., Matrix Service Industrial Contractors, Inc.
Bradley J. Rinehart, VP-Midwestern Oper.
Michael J. Hall, Chmn.
Lansing G. Smith, VP-Procurement

Phone: 866-367-6879	**Fax:** 918-838-8810
Toll-Free:	
Address: 5100 E. Skelly Dr., Ste. 700, Tulsa, OK 74135 US	

GROWTH PLANS/SPECIAL FEATURES:

Matrix Service Company and its subsidiaries provide construction, repair and maintenance services, primarily to the liquefied natural gas, petroleum, petrochemical, power generation, power delivery, terminal, pipeline, utility, chemical, transportation, pulp and paper, food and beverage, heavy industrial and industrial gas industries throughout the U.S. and Canada. The company operates in two segments: construction services and repair and maintenance services. Construction services include turnkey projects; renovations, upgrades and expansions for large and small projects, electrical and instrumentation; mechanical, piping and equipment installations; tank engineering, design, fabrication and erection; and steel, steel plate, vessel and pipe fabrication. The company's repair and maintenance services include plant maintenance, turnaround services, outages, industrial cleaning, hydroblasting and substation and above ground storage tank repair and maintenance. Matrix's major customers are Plains All American Pipeline, British Petroleum and Chevron. Subsidiaries of the company include Matrix Service, Inc. and Matrix Service Industrial Contractors, Inc. In February 2009, Matrix Service Industrial Contractors, Inc. acquired S.M. Electric Company, Inc., a private electrical contracting firm.

Employees are offered medical, dental and vision insurance; disability coverage; retirement savings plans; flexible spending accounts; pre-paid legal services; and an employee assistance program.

FINANCIALS:

Sales and profits are in thousands of dollars—add 000 to get the full amount. 2009 Note: Financial information for 2009 was not available for all companies at press time.

2009 Sales: $689,720	2009 Profits: $30,589	**U.S. Stock Ticker: MTRX**
2008 Sales: $731,301	2008 Profits: $21,414	**Int'l Ticker:** Int'l Exchange:
2007 Sales: $639,846	2007 Profits: $19,171	Employees: 2,818
2006 Sales: $493,927	2006 Profits: $7,653	Fiscal Year Ends: 5/31
2005 Sales: $439,138	2005 Profits: $-38,830	Parent Company:

SALARIES/BENEFITS:

Pension Plan:	ESOP Stock Plan:	Profit Sharing:	Top Exec. Salary: $670,000	Bonus: $335,000
Savings Plan: Y	Stock Purch. Plan:		Second Exec. Salary: $350,000	Bonus: $175,000

OTHER THOUGHTS:

Apparent Women Officers or Directors: 1
Hot Spot for Advancement for Women/Minorities:

LOCATIONS: ("Y" = Yes)

West:	Southwest:	Midwest:	Southeast:	Northeast:	International:
Y	Y	Y		Y	Y

MAX PROPERTY GROUP PLC

www.maxpropertygroup.com

Industry Group Code: 5311 **Ranks within this company's industry group:** Sales: Profits:

Properties:		Financial Services:		Construction/Development:		Investments:		Specialty Services:		Brokerage:	
Apartments:		Mortgages:		Commercial Construction:		REIT:		Property Management:	Y	Commercial Sales:	
Malls/Shopping:		Title Insurance:		Residential Construction:				Online Services:		Residential Sales:	
Offices:	Y	Property Insurance:		Land Development:				Software/IT:		Specialty:	
Hotels/Motels:				Support Services:				Consulting:			
Industrial/Warehouses:				Design/Engineering:							
Other:											

TYPES OF BUSINESS:

Real Estate Investment

BRANDS/DIVISIONS/AFFILIATES:

Solent Business Park
Overbridge Square
New Bond House
Concorde Business Park
Brooklands Business Campus
Workplace Systems Rooksley
Silbury Court
Centric MK

CONTACTS: *Note: Officers with more than one job title may be intentionally listed here more than once.*

Aubrey Adams, Chmn.

Phone: 534-814814	**Fax:** 534-814815
Toll-Free:	
Address: 26 New St., St. Helier, Jersey JE2 3RA Channel Islands	

GROWTH PLANS/SPECIAL FEATURES:

Max Property Group plc is a firm engaged in the acquisition and operation of commercial properties in the U.K. The firm, which completed an IPO in May 2009, controls a total of 83 properties comprising over 7.1 million square feet (sq. ft.) of leasable space and housing approximately 800 tenants. The company's portfolio includes over 1,250 lettable units with an average lettable unit size of 5,700 sq. ft. Max Property Group's commercial ventures include the Solent Business Park (71,000 sq. ft.) in Fareham, U.K.; the Overbridge Square in (66,000 sq. ft.) Newbury, U.K.; New Bond House (47,000 sq. ft.) in Bristol, U.K.; Aldrin Place (24,000 sq. ft.) in Farnborough, U.K.; Concorde Business Park (124,000 sq. ft.) and Westpoint(104,000 sq. ft.) in Manchester, U.K.; Brooklands Business Campus (116,000 sq. ft.) in Horsham, U.K.; and Workplace Systems Rooksley (27,000 sq. ft.), Centric MK (107,000 sq. ft.) and Silbury Court (77,000 sq. ft.) in Milton Keynes, U.K. In October 2009, the firm completed the acquisition of an industrial portfolio of properties and sold its Crawley, U.K. holdings. In December 2009, the firm sold its Farnborough property for roughly $25.2 million. In January 2010, Max Properties acquired a portfolio of office properties for approximately $59.4 million.

FINANCIALS: **Sales and profits are in thousands of dollars—add 000 to get the full amount. 2009 Note: Financial information for 2009 was not available for all companies at press time.**

2009 Sales: $	2009 Profits: $	**U.S. Stock Ticker:**
2008 Sales: $	2008 Profits: $	**Int'l Ticker: MAX** Int'l Exchange: London-LSE
2007 Sales: $	2007 Profits: $	Employees:
2006 Sales: $	2006 Profits: $	Fiscal Year Ends:
2005 Sales: $	2005 Profits: $	Parent Company:

SALARIES/BENEFITS:

Pension Plan:	ESOP Stock Plan:	Profit Sharing:	Top Exec. Salary: $	Bonus: $
Savings Plan:	Stock Purch. Plan:		Second Exec. Salary: $	Bonus: $

OTHER THOUGHTS:

Apparent Women Officers or Directors:
Hot Spot for Advancement for Women/Minorities:

LOCATIONS: ("Y" = Yes)

West:	Southwest:	Midwest:	Southeast:	Northeast:	International:
					Y

MCDERMOTT INTERNATIONAL INC

www.mcdermott.com

Industry Group Code: 541330 **Ranks within this company's industry group:** Sales: 2 Profits: 1

Properties:		Financial Services:		Construction/Development:		Investments:		Specialty Services:		Brokerage:	
Apartments:		Mortgages:		Commercial Construction:	Y	REIT:		Property Management:		Commercial Sales:	
Malls/Shopping:		Title Insurance:		Residential Construction:				Online Services:		Residential Sales:	
Offices:		Property Insurance:		Land Development:				Software/IT:		Specialty:	
Hotels/Motels:				Support Services:	Y			Consulting:			
Industrial/Warehouses:				Design/Engineering:	Y						
Other:											

TYPES OF BUSINESS:

Engineering Services
Power Generation Services
Nuclear Fuel Assemblies
Government Services
Marine Construction
Procurement Services
Project Management
Consulting

BRANDS/DIVISIONS/AFFILIATES:

J. Ray McDermott, S.A.
BWX Technologies, Inc.
Babcock & Wilcox Company (The)

CONTACTS:

Note: Officers with more than one job title may be intentionally listed here more than once.

John A. Fees, CEO
Stephen M. Johnson, COO
Stephen M. Johnson, Pres.
Michael S. Taff, CFO/Sr. VP
Preston Johnson, Jr., Sr. VP-Human Resources
John C. Knowles, CIO/VP
John T. Nesser, III, Chief Admin. & Legal Officer/Exec. VP
Liane K. Hinrichs, General Counsel/VP/Corp. Sec.
John D. Krueger, VP-Corp. Dev. & Strategic Planning
John E. Roueche, III, VP-Corp. Comm.
John E. Roueche, III, VP-Investor Rel.
Dennis S. Baldwin, Chief Acct. Officer/VP
James C. Lewis, Treas./VP
Thomas A. Henzler, Corp. Compliance Officer
Robert A. Deason, CEO/Pres., J. Ray McDermott, S.A.
Brandon C. Bethards, CEO/Pres., The Babcock & Wilson Company
Bruce W. Wilkinson, Chmn.

Phone: 281-870-5901	**Fax:**
Toll-Free:	
Address: 777 N. Eldridge Pkwy., Houston, TX 77079 US	

GROWTH PLANS/SPECIAL FEATURES:

McDermott International, Inc. is a leading energy services company that operates three main business segments: offshore oil and gas construction services; government operations; and power generation systems. The offshore construction services are provided through subsidiary J. Ray McDermott, S.A. and its subsidiaries. This segment designs, engineers, fabricates and installs offshore drilling and production facilities, as well as installs marine pipelines and subsea production systems. It operates in most major offshore oil and gas producing regions throughout the world, including Mexico, the Gulf of Mexico, the Middle East, the Caspian Sea, India and Asia Pacific. Presently, this segment also operates fabrication facilities located in Indonesia on Batam Island, in Dubai, U.A.E., Altamira, Mexico and near Morgan City, Louisiana. These facilities construct a full range of offshore structures, from conventional jacket-type fixed platforms to intermediate water and deepwater platform configurations. The government operations segment, with services performed by subsidiary BWX Technologies, Inc. and its subsidiaries, supplies nuclear components to the U.S. government, as well as processing uranium; offering environmental site restoration services; and managing and operating U.S. government-owned facilities, primarily within the nuclear weapons complex of the U.S. Department of Energy. Facilities served by the segment include the Y-12 National Security Complex, the Pantex Plant and Los Alamos National Laboratory. Currently, it is assisting in the development of a high-density, low-enriched uranium fuel required for high-enriched uranium test reactor conversions. The power generation systems segment, run by the Babcock & Wilcox Company (B&W) and its subsidiaries, provides a variety of services, equipment and systems to generate steam and electric power at energy facilities worldwide. In June 2009, B&W was awarded a contract from the PacifiCorp's Naughton power plant near Kemmerer, Wyoming to engineer, procure and construct two wet flue gas desulfurization systems, which should be operational in 2010.

FINANCIALS:

Sales and profits are in thousands of dollars—add 000 to get the full amount. 2009 Note: Financial information for 2009 was not available for all companies at press time.

2009 Sales: $6,193,077	2009 Profits: $387,056	**U.S. Stock Ticker: MDR**
2008 Sales: $6,572,423	2008 Profits: $429,302	**Int'l Ticker:** Int'l Exchange:
2007 Sales: $5,631,610	2007 Profits: $607,828	Employees: 29,000
2006 Sales: $4,120,141	2006 Profits: $330,515	Fiscal Year Ends: 12/31
2005 Sales: $1,856,311	2005 Profits: $205,687	Parent Company:

SALARIES/BENEFITS:

Pension Plan: Y	ESOP Stock Plan:	Profit Sharing:	Top Exec. Salary: $592,500	Bonus: $841,026
Savings Plan: Y	Stock Purch. Plan:		Second Exec. Salary: $562,500	Bonus: $519,298

OTHER THOUGHTS:

Apparent Women Officers or Directors: 2
Hot Spot for Advancement for Women/Minorities: Y

LOCATIONS: ("Y" = Yes)

West:	Southwest:	Midwest:	Southeast:	Northeast:	International:
Y	Y	Y	Y	Y	Y

MDC HOLDINGS INC

www.richmondamerican.com

Industry Group Code: 2361 **Ranks within this company's industry group:** Sales: 14 Profits: 10

Properties:		Financial Services:		Construction/Development:		Investments:		Specialty Services:		Brokerage:	
Apartments:		Mortgages:	Y	Commercial Construction:		REIT:		Property Management:		Commercial Sales:	
Malls/Shopping:		Title Insurance:	Y	Residential Construction:	Y			Online Services:		Residential Sales:	Y
Offices:		Property Insurance:	Y	Land Development:	Y			Software/IT:		Specialty:	
Hotels/Motels:				Support Services:				Consulting:			
Industrial/Warehouses:				Design/Engineering:	Y						
Other:											

TYPES OF BUSINESS:

Residential Construction
Land Development
Mortgages
Title Services
Insurance

BRANDS/DIVISIONS/AFFILIATES:

Richmond American Homes
HomeAmerican Mortgage Corporation
American Home Insurance Agency
American Home Title and Escrow Company
Allegiant Insurance Company Inc
StarAmerican Insurance Ltd

CONTACTS: *Note: Officers with more than one job title may be intentionally listed here more than once.*

Larry A. Mizel, CEO
David D. Mandarich, COO
David D. Mandarich, Pres.
Christopher M. Anderson, CFO/Sr. VP
Zane DeHerrera, VP-Mktg.
Michael Touff, General Counsel/Sr. VP
Bob Martin, VP-Bus. Dev.
Zane DeHerrera, VP-Corp. Comm.
Bob Martin, VP-Finance
Joseph H. Fretz, Corp. Sec.
Larry A. Mizel, Chmn.

Phone: 303-773-2727 **Fax:**
Toll-Free: 888-402-4663
Address: 4350 S. Monaco St., Ste. 500, Denver, CO 80237 US

GROWTH PLANS/SPECIAL FEATURES:

M.D.C. Holdings, Inc. is a holding company engaged in homebuilding and financial services. The company's homebuilding segment, which operates through subsidiary Richmond American Homes, builds and sells single-family homes through the following geographic segments: West (California, Nevada and Arizona); Mountain (Colorado and Utah); East (Maryland, Pennsylvania, Delaware, New Jersey and Virginia); and other homebuilding (Florida, and Illinois). The company is in the process of exiting the Illinois market. Other operations of the homebuilding segment include land acquisition and development, home construction purchasing, sales and marketing and customer service. M.D.C. also acquires entitled land for development into finished lots. The base price for its homes generally ranges from $160,000 to $450,000. M.D.C. maintains a variety of home styles in each of its markets, targeting generally first-time and first-time move-up homebuyers, and building a limited number of homes for the second-time move-up and luxury homebuyers. The firm's financial services segment consists principally of the operations of HomeAmerican Mortgage Corporation, which originates mortgage loans primarily for its homebuyers; American Home Title and Escrow Company, which provides title agency services to M.D.C. and its homebuyers in Maryland, Florida, Nevada, Colorado and Virginia; and American Home Insurance Agency, which offers third-party insurance products to its homebuyers. The segment also includes risk retention firm Allegiant Insurance Company, Inc. and reinsurer StarAmerican Insurance Ltd.

M.D.C. offers its employees medical, dental, vision, life, AD&D and disability insurance; education reimbursement; a 401(k); home purchase discounts; paid time off; floating and paid holidays; and flexible spending accounts.

FINANCIALS: **Sales and profits are in thousands of dollars—add 000 to get the full amount. 2009 Note: Financial information for 2009 was not available for all companies at press time.**

2009 Sales: $898,303	2009 Profits: $24,679
2008 Sales: $1,458,108	2008 Profits: $-380,545
2007 Sales: $2,885,659	2007 Profits: $-636,940
2006 Sales: $4,793,569	2006 Profits: $214,253
2005 Sales: $4,892,589	2005 Profits: $505,723

U.S. Stock Ticker: MDC
Int'l Ticker: Int'l Exchange:
Employees: 1,089
Fiscal Year Ends: 12/31
Parent Company:

SALARIES/BENEFITS:

Pension Plan: ESOP Stock Plan: Profit Sharing: Top Exec. Salary: $1,000,000 Bonus: $2,500,000
Savings Plan: Y Stock Purch. Plan: Second Exec. Salary: $830,000 Bonus: $2,500,000

OTHER THOUGHTS:

Apparent Women Officers or Directors:
Hot Spot for Advancement for Women/Minorities: Y

LOCATIONS: ("Y" = Yes)

West:	Southwest:	Midwest:	Southeast:	Northeast:	International:
Y	Y		Y	Y	

MEADOW VALLEY CORPORATION

www.meadowvalley.com

Industry Group Code: 237 **Ranks within this company's industry group:** Sales: Profits:

Properties:		Financial Services:		Construction/Development:		Investments:		Specialty Services:		Brokerage:	
Apartments:		Mortgages:		Commercial Construction:	Y	REIT:		Property Management:		Commercial Sales:	
Malls/Shopping:		Title Insurance:		Residential Construction:				Online Services:		Residential Sales:	
Offices:		Property Insurance:		Land Development:				Software/IT:		Specialty:	
Hotels/Motels:				Support Services:	Y			Consulting:			
Industrial/Warehouses:				Design/Engineering:	Y						
Other:											

TYPES OF BUSINESS:

Heavy Construction & Civil Engineering
Construction Materials-Concrete, Sand & Gravel
Design Services
Mining
Ready-Mix Concrete
Technical Services

BRANDS/DIVISIONS/AFFILIATES:

Meadow Valley Contractors, Inc.
Ready Mix, Inc.
Insight Equity Holdings LLC

CONTACTS:

Note: Officers with more than one job title may be intentionally listed here more than once.

Bradley E. Larson, CEO
David D. Doty, CFO
Lance Faber, Dir.-Info. Svcs.
Kenneth D. Nelson, Chief Admin. Officer
Grant E. Larson, Assistant VP-Admin. & Strategic Planning
Nicole R. Smith, Controller
Norm Watkins, Dir.-Safety/Compliance Officer
Mark Krumm, VP-Arizona

Phone: 602-437-5400 **Fax:** 602-437-1681
Toll-Free:
Address: 4602 E. Thomas Rd., Phoenix, AZ 85018 US

GROWTH PLANS/SPECIAL FEATURES:

Meadow Valley Corp., operates as Meadow Valley Contractors Inc., is engaged in the construction industry. Based in Phoenix, Arizona, the firm is a provider of construction services and a supplier of construction materials. The construction services segment (CSS) specializes in structural concrete construction of highway bridges and overpasses and the paving of highways and airport runways. The construction materials segment (CMS) provides ready-mix concrete, sand and gravel products to both itself and other contractors. The company operates throughout Nevada, Arizona and Utah, with principal operations in the Las Vegas, Nevada and Phoenix, Arizona metropolitan areas. The firm operates for both public and private infrastructure projects, including the construction of bridges and overpasses, channels, roadways, highways and airport runways. The company owns 53% of Ready Mix, Inc., which manufactures and distributes ready mix concrete, crushed landscaping rock and other miscellaneous rock and sand products. Meadow Valley owns or leases most of the equipment used in its business, including cranes, backhoes, graders, loaders, trucks, trailers, pavers, rollers, construction materials processing plants, batch plants and related equipment. The raw materials necessary for most operations are obtained from multiple sources. CMS does have one full-time mining operation in Nephi, Utah. In February 2009, Dallas-based private equity firm Insight Equity Holdings LLC acquired the company for approximately $61 million.

FINANCIALS:

Sales and profits are in thousands of dollars—add 000 to get the full amount. 2009 Note: Financial information for 2009 was not available for all companies at press time.

2009 Sales: $	2009 Profits: $	**U.S. Stock Ticker: Private**
2008 Sales: $	2008 Profits: $	**Int'l Ticker:** Int'l Exchange:
2007 Sales: $205,919	2007 Profits: $4,061	Employees:
2006 Sales: $195,522	2006 Profits: $4,166	Fiscal Year Ends: 12/31
2005 Sales: $183,872	2005 Profits: $4,203	Parent Company: INSIGHT EQUITY HOLDING LLC

SALARIES/BENEFITS:

Pension Plan:	ESOP Stock Plan:	Profit Sharing:	Top Exec. Salary: $	Bonus: $363,785
Savings Plan:	Stock Purch. Plan:		Second Exec. Salary: $	Bonus: $

OTHER THOUGHTS:

Apparent Women Officers or Directors: 1
Hot Spot for Advancement for Women/Minorities:

LOCATIONS: ("Y" = Yes)

West:	Southwest:	Midwest:	Southeast:	Northeast:	International:
Y	Y				

MERITAGE HOMES CORP

www.meritagehomes.com

Industry Group Code: 2361 **Ranks within this company's industry group:** Sales: 13 Profits: 8

Properties:		Financial Services:		Construction/Development:		Investments:		Specialty Services:		Brokerage:	
Apartments:		Mortgages:		Commercial Construction:		REIT:		Property Management:		Commercial Sales:	
Malls/Shopping:		Title Insurance:		Residential Construction:	Y			Online Services:		Residential Sales:	
Offices:		Property Insurance:		Land Development:				Software/IT:		Specialty:	
Hotels/Motels:				Support Services:				Consulting:			
Industrial/Warehouses:				Design/Engineering:	Y						
Other:											

TYPES OF BUSINESS:

Residential Construction
Home Design Services
Home Building Services

BRANDS/DIVISIONS/AFFILIATES:

Legacy Homes
Meritage Homes
Monterey Homes
Province
Simply Smart Series

CONTACTS:

Note: Officers with more than one job title may be intentionally listed here more than once.

Steven J. Hilton, CEO
Steven M. Davis, COO/Exec. VP
Larry W. Seay, CFO/Exec. VP
Jane Hays, VP-Corp. Mktg.
C. Timothy White, General Counsel/Exec. VP/Sec.
Jane Hays, VP-Corp. Comm.
Brent Anderson, VP-Investor Rel.
Hilla Sferruzza, Chief Acct. Officer/Controller/VP
Steven J. Hilton, Chmn.

Phone: 480-515-8100 **Fax:** 480-998-9162
Toll-Free: 877-275-6374
Address: 17851 N. 85th St., Ste. 300, Scottsdale, AZ 85255 US

GROWTH PLANS/SPECIAL FEATURES:

Meritage Home Corp. is a designer and builder of single-family attached and detached homes in the southern and western U.S. It offers a variety of homes that are designed to appeal to a wide range of homebuyers, including first-time, move-up, luxury and active adult buyers. The company has operations in three regions: west, central and east, which comprise 12 metropolitan areas in six states. These three regions are the firm's principal operating segments. The firm also holds a minority interest in three joint ventures with other development companies and real estate investors. Meritage's homebuilding and marketing activities are conducted under the name of Meritage Homes in each of its markets, except for certain communities in Arizona, where it operates under the name of Monterey Homes; and in Texas, where it operates in certain communities as Legacy Homes and Monterey Homes. The company sells homes in 173 communities, with base prices ranging from roughly $99,900 to $971,990. Doing business primarily on an individual basis with contractors and suppliers, Meritage Home usually completes its homes within two to four months of construction. Main strategies of the company include purchasing land subject to complete entitlement; developing smaller parcels that can be completed within a three-year period; and managing housing inventory by pre-selling and obtaining substantial customer deposits on homes prior to beginning construction. The company is also focused on offering more affordable houses in order to target first time homebuyers. In October 2009, Meritage Home acquired Arizona-based active adult community Province. In January 2010, the firm introduced Simply Smart Series, homes that include a low monthly payment and are marketed toward renters and first-time buyers; and Your Home. Your Way. 99 Days Guaranteed, a program which guarantees that the firm will build a new home for a customer within 99 days of signing the sales contract.

FINANCIALS:

Sales and profits are in thousands of dollars—add 000 to get the full amount. 2009 Note: Financial information for 2009 was not available for all companies at press time.

2009 Sales: $970,313	2009 Profits: $-66,456	**U.S. Stock Ticker: MTH**
2008 Sales: $1,523,068	2008 Profits: $-291,935	**Int'l Ticker:** Int'l Exchange:
2007 Sales: $2,343,594	2007 Profits: $-288,851	Employees: 700
2006 Sales: $3,461,320	2006 Profits: $225,354	Fiscal Year Ends: 12/31
2005 Sales: $3,001,102	2005 Profits: $255,665	Parent Company:

SALARIES/BENEFITS:

Pension Plan:	ESOP Stock Plan:	Profit Sharing:	Top Exec. Salary: $800,000	Bonus: $
Savings Plan: Y	Stock Purch. Plan:		Second Exec. Salary: $525,000	Bonus: $250,000

OTHER THOUGHTS:

Apparent Women Officers or Directors: 2
Hot Spot for Advancement for Women/Minorities:

LOCATIONS: ("Y" = Yes)

West:	Southwest:	Midwest:	Southeast:	Northeast:	International:
Y	Y		Y		

MERITUS HOTELS & RESORTS INC

www.meritus-hotels.com

Industry Group Code: 721110 **Ranks within this company's industry group:** Sales: Profits:

Properties:		Financial Services:		Construction/Development:		Investments:		Specialty Services:		Brokerage:	
Apartments:		Mortgages:		Commercial Construction:		REIT:		Property Management:		Commercial Sales:	
Malls/Shopping:		Title Insurance:		Residential Construction:				Online Services:		Residential Sales:	
Offices:		Property Insurance:		Land Development:				Software/IT:		Specialty:	
Hotels/Motels:	Y			Support Services:				Consulting:			
Industrial/Warehouses:				Design/Engineering:							
Other:											

TYPES OF BUSINESS:

Hotels & Resorts

BRANDS/DIVISIONS/AFFILIATES:

Overseas Union Enterprise Ltd
Mandarin Orchard Singapore
Meritus Mandarin Haikou
Meritus Pelangi Beach Resort & Spa, Langkawi
Meritus Shantou China
Shanghai JC Mandarin
Marina Mandarin Singapore

CONTACTS:

Note: Officers with more than one job title may be intentionally listed here more than once.

Frank Kuhn, Pres.
Kelvin Seah, VP-Mktg. & Sales
Lim Ee Jin, Assistant VP-Comm.
Lim Ee Jin, Assistant VP-Investor Rel.
Lau Ler Ling, Assistant Mgr.-Mktg. Comm.
Low Shi Ping, Assistant Mgr.-Mktg. Comm.
Linda Su, Assistant Mgr.-Mktg. Comm.
Joyce Yeung, Assistant Mgr.-Mktg. Comm.
Chitty Jiang, Mgr.-Mktg. Comm., Meritus Shantou China

Phone: 65-6235-7788	**Fax:** 65-6235 6688
Toll-Free:	
Address: 333 Orchard Rd., 37th Fl., Main Tower, Singapore, 238867 Singapore	

GROWTH PLANS/SPECIAL FEATURES:

Meritus Hotels & Resorts is a hotel management firm based in Singapore. The firm is a subsidiary of Overseas Union Enterprise Limited, a Singapore-based hospitality services, property investment and investment holding firm. Meritus operates six hotels and resorts: Mandarin Orchard Singapore; Meritus Mandarin Haikou; Meritus Pelangi Beach Resort & Spa, Langkawi (Meritus Pelangi); Meritus Shantou China; Shanghai JC Mandarin; and Marina Mandarin Singapore. Mandarin Orchard Singapore is the company's flagship 1,051-room resort; it features a swimming pool, tennis court, fitness center, wireless Internet, two restaurants, eight meeting suites, 34 suites, two Presidential suites and several banquet halls. Meritus Mandarin Haikou is a 318-room hotel with three restaurants, one lounge, a ballroom with a capacity of 1,000, two swimming pools and two outdoor tennis courts. Meritus Pelangi is a 31-acre spa in Malaysia that features 331 rooms, several restaurants, 12 meeting rooms, water sports, snorkeling, jungle trekking, swimming pools and spas. Meritus Shantou China is a 21-storey, 318-room hotel with five bars/restaurants, three recreational facilities and several meeting rooms. Shanghai JC Mandarin features 515 rooms, a pastry shop, five restaurants/lounges, a beauty salon, a swimming pool and a tennis court. Marina Mandarin Singapore is a Marina Bay waterfront hotel with 575 rooms, 19 suites, one Presidential suite, a spa, a 24-hour fitness center and several restaurants/lounges. In July 2009, the firm launched www.Meritus-Hotels.com, a new Japanese web site.

FINANCIALS:

Sales and profits are in thousands of dollars—add 000 to get the full amount. 2009 Note: Financial information for 2009 was not available for all companies at press time.

2009 Sales: $	2009 Profits: $	**U.S. Stock Ticker: Subsidiary**
2008 Sales: $	2008 Profits: $	**Int'l Ticker:** Int'l Exchange:
2007 Sales: $	2007 Profits: $	Employees:
2006 Sales: $	2006 Profits: $	Fiscal Year Ends:
2005 Sales: $	2005 Profits: $	Parent Company: OVERSEAS UNION ENTERPRISE LTD

SALARIES/BENEFITS:

Pension Plan:	ESOP Stock Plan:	Profit Sharing:	Top Exec. Salary: $	Bonus: $
Savings Plan:	Stock Purch. Plan:		Second Exec. Salary: $	Bonus: $

OTHER THOUGHTS:

Apparent Women Officers or Directors: 5
Hot Spot for Advancement for Women/Minorities: Y

LOCATIONS: ("Y" = Yes)

West:	Southwest:	Midwest:	Southeast:	Northeast:	International:
				Y	Y

MFA FINANCIAL INC

www.mfa-reit.com

Industry Group Code: 525990 **Ranks within this company's industry group:** Sales: 1 Profits: 1

Properties:		Financial Services:		Construction/Development:		Investments:		Specialty Services:		Brokerage:	
Apartments:	Y	Mortgages:	Y	Commercial Construction:		REIT:	Y	Property Management:		Commercial Sales:	
Malls/Shopping:		Title Insurance:		Residential Construction:				Online Services:		Residential Sales:	
Offices:		Property Insurance:		Land Development:				Software/IT:		Specialty:	
Hotels/Motels:				Support Services:				Consulting:			
Industrial/Warehouses:				Design/Engineering:							
Other:											

TYPES OF BUSINESS:

Mortgage-Backed Securities
Mortgage REIT
Apartment Properties

BRANDS/DIVISIONS/AFFILIATES:

CONTACTS: *Note: Officers with more than one job title may be intentionally listed here more than once.*

Stewart Zimmerman, CEO
William S. Gorin, Pres.
William S. Gorin, CFO
Timothy W. Korth II, General Counsel/Corp. Sec.
Timothy W. Korth II, Sr. VP-Bus. Dev.
Teresa D. Covello, Chief Acct. Officer/Treas./Sr. VP
Ronald A. Freydberg, Chief Investment Officer/Exec. VP
Kathleen A. Hanrahan, Sr. VP-Acct.
Craig L. Knutson, Exec. VP-RMBS Bus.
Stewart Zimmerman, Chmn.

Phone: 212-207-6400	**Fax:** 212-207-6420
Toll-Free: 800-892-7547	
Address: 350 Park Ave., 21st Fl., New York, NY 10022 US	

GROWTH PLANS/SPECIAL FEATURES:

MFA Financial, Inc., formerly, MFA Mortgage Investments, Inc., is a mortgage real estate investment trust (REIT), primarily engaged in the business of investing, on a leveraged basis, in residential agency and non-agency adjustable-rate mortgage-backed securities (ARM-MBS), which are secured by pools of residential mortgages. The company's operating policies require that at least 50% of its investment portfolio consist of ARM-MBS that are either issued or guaranteed by an agency of the U.S. government or a federally chartered corporation (Agency MBS), or rated in one of the two highest rating categories by at least one nationally recognized rating agency. The remaining 50% may be comprised of investments in other types of MBS and residential mortgage loans; other mortgage and real estate-related debt and equity; other yield instruments; and other types of assets approved by the board of directors. MFA has $9.627 billion in assets, of which $8.758 billion, or 91%, represent its MBS portfolio. Of these MBS assets, 87.5% are Agency MBS, and approximately 12.5% are non-agency MBS. MFA also has an indirect investment in a multi-family apartment property. Approximately 99.1% of the MBS in the firm's portfolio consists of ARM-MBS, with the remaining 0.9% representing fixed-rate MBS. Utilizing repurchase agreements, the firm finances the acquisition of these assets by pledging its MBS as collateral to secure loans with lenders. At the maturity of a repurchase agreement, MFA is required to repurchase its collateral at a higher price, corresponding to the interest expense, or renew its agreement at the then prevailing market interest rate. To reduce its lender-related risk, the company generally maintains repurchase agreements with at least four separate lenders with a maximum loan from any lender of no more than three times its stockholders' equity.

FINANCIALS: **Sales and profits are in thousands of dollars—add 000 to get the full amount. 2009 Note: Financial information for 2009 was not available for all companies at press time.**

2009 Sales: $504,464	2009 Profits: $268,189	**U.S. Stock Ticker: MFA**
2008 Sales: $519,788	2008 Profits: $45,797	**Int'l Ticker:** Int'l Exchange:
2007 Sales: $380,328	2007 Profits: $30,210	Employees: 25
2006 Sales: $216,871	2006 Profits: $8,758	Fiscal Year Ends: 12/31
2005 Sales: $235,798	2005 Profits: $6,708	Parent Company:

SALARIES/BENEFITS:

Pension Plan:	ESOP Stock Plan:	Profit Sharing:	Top Exec. Salary: $	Bonus: $
Savings Plan:	Stock Purch. Plan:		Second Exec. Salary: $	Bonus: $

OTHER THOUGHTS:

Apparent Women Officers or Directors: 2
Hot Spot for Advancement for Women/Minorities:

LOCATIONS: ("Y" = Yes)

West:	Southwest:	Midwest:	Southeast:	Northeast:	International:
				Y	

MGM MIRAGE

www.mgmmirage.com

Industry Group Code: 721120 **Ranks within this company's industry group:** Sales: 2 Profits: 7

Properties:		Financial Services:		Construction/Development:		Investments:		Specialty Services:		Brokerage:	
Apartments:		Mortgages:		Commercial Construction:		REIT:		Property Management:	Y	Commercial Sales:	
Malls/Shopping:		Title Insurance:		Residential Construction:				Online Services:		Residential Sales:	
Offices:		Property Insurance:		Land Development:				Software/IT:		Specialty:	
Hotels/Motels:	Y			Support Services:				Consulting:			
Industrial/Warehouses:				Design/Engineering:							
Other:	Y										

TYPES OF BUSINESS:

Casino Hotels & Resorts
Casino & Resort Management

BRANDS/DIVISIONS/AFFILIATES:

Bellagio
MGM Grand Las Vegas
Mandalay Bay
Mirage (The)
Luxor
Excalibur
CityCenter
MGM Mirage Hospitality

CONTACTS:

Note: Officers with more than one job title may be intentionally listed here more than once.

James J. Murren, CEO
Daniel J. D'Arrigo, CFO/Exec. VP
Bill Hornbuckle, Chief Mktg. Officer
Robert H. Baldwin, Chief Design & Construction Officer
Aldo Manzini, Chief Admin. Officer/Exec. VP
John M. McManus, Acting General Counsel/Sec./Sr. VP
Alan M. Feldman, Sr. VP-Public Affairs
Robert C. Selwood, Chief Acct. Officer/Exec. VP
Shawn T. Sani, Treas.
Ricky Edward, Controller/Sr. VP
Robert H. Baldwin, Pres./CEO-CityCenter
James J. Murren, Chmn.

Phone: 702-693-7120	**Fax:** 702-693-8626
Toll-Free:	
Address: 3600 Las Vegas Blvd. S., Las Vegas, NV 89109 US	

GROWTH PLANS/SPECIAL FEATURES:

MGM Mirage (MGM) and its subsidiaries operate 15 casino resorts in Nevada, Mississippi and Michigan, as well as five 50%-owned casino resorts in Nevada, Macau, New Jersey and Illinois. Its Las Vegas Strip casino resorts include Bellagio, CityCenter (50% owned), MGM Grand Las Vegas, Mandalay Bay, The Mirage, Luxor, New York-New York, Excalibur, Monte Carlo and Circus Circus Las Vegas. Combined, they feature 40,122 guestrooms, more than 1.2 million square feet of gaming space, 18,060 slot machines and 986 gaming tables. CityCenter, which MGM manages for a fee, consists of several casinos, resorts and hotels, including Aria, Mandarin Oriental Las Vegas and some rooms for rent at Vdara. Its other Nevada properties, including Circus Circus Reno, Silver Legacy (50% owned), Gold Strike and Railroad Pass, offer 4,008 guestrooms, 207,000 square feet of gaming space, 3,421 slot machines and 112 gaming tables. Finally, its other operations include MGM Grand Detroit, Beau Rivage and Gold Strike, all wholly-owned; and MGM Grand Macau, Borgata and Grand Victoria, all 50%-owned. These facilities offer 6,635 guestrooms, 630,000 square feet of gaming space, 13,485 slot machines and 887 gaming tables. MGM's casinos often feature hotel, dining, entertainment, retail and other amenities. Subsidiary MGM Mirage Hospitality manages casino and non-casino resorts internationally. Over half of MGM's revenue is generated by non-gaming activities. In March 2009, the firm sold Treasure Island Hotel & Casino to Ruffin Acquisition LLC. In March 2010, MGM agreed to sell its 50% stake in Borgata Hotel Casino and Spa. In April 2001, the firm announced a proposal to rebrand itself as MGM Resorts International.

MGM offers its employees health plans, a college savings plan, a 401(k) plan, an employee assistance program, life and disability insurance, adoption assistance, flexible spending accounts, healthy living programs and Children's Choice Learning Centers for employees' children.

FINANCIALS:

Sales and profits are in thousands of dollars—add 000 to get the full amount. 2009 Note: Financial information for 2009 was not available for all companies at press time.

2009 Sales: $5,978,589	2009 Profits: $-1,291,682	**U.S. Stock Ticker: MGM**
2008 Sales: $7,208,767	2008 Profits: $-855,286	**Int'l Ticker:** Int'l Exchange:
2007 Sales: $7,691,637	2007 Profits: $1,584,419	Employees: 62,000
2006 Sales: $7,175,956	2006 Profits: $648,264	Fiscal Year Ends: 12/31
2005 Sales: $6,128,843	2005 Profits: $443,256	Parent Company:

SALARIES/BENEFITS:

Pension Plan:	ESOP Stock Plan:	Profit Sharing:	Top Exec. Salary: $2,000,000	Bonus: $
Savings Plan: Y	Stock Purch. Plan:		Second Exec. Salary: $1,500,000	Bonus: $

OTHER THOUGHTS:

Apparent Women Officers or Directors: 2
Hot Spot for Advancement for Women/Minorities: Y

LOCATIONS: ("Y" = Yes)

West:	Southwest:	Midwest:	Southeast:	Northeast:	International:
Y		Y	Y	Y	Y

MID-AMERICA APARTMENT COMMUNITIES INC

www.maac.net

Industry Group Code: 531110 **Ranks within this company's industry group:** Sales: 11 Profits: 10

Properties:		Financial Services:		Construction/Development:		Investments:		Specialty Services:		Brokerage:	
Apartments:	Y	Mortgages:		Commercial Construction:		REIT:	Y	Property Management:	Y	Commercial Sales:	
Malls/Shopping:		Title Insurance:		Residential Construction:	Y			Online Services:		Residential Sales:	
Offices:		Property Insurance:		Land Development:				Software/IT:		Specialty:	
Hotels/Motels:				Support Services:				Consulting:			
Industrial/Warehouses:				Design/Engineering:							
Other:											

TYPES OF BUSINESS:

Real Estate Investment Trust
Apartment Communities

BRANDS/DIVISIONS/AFFILIATES:

Mid-America Apartments LP
MAC II of Delaware Inc
Mid-America Multifamily Fund I LLC
Mid-America Multifamily Fund II LLC

CONTACTS:

Note: Officers with more than one job title may be intentionally listed here more than once.

H. Eric Bolton, Jr., CEO
Albert M. Campbell, III, CFO/Exec. VP
Melintha Ogle, VP/Dir.-Mktg.
Cynthia Y. Thompson, Sr. VP/Dir.-Human Resources
Shelton Barron, VP/Dir.-MIS
Leslie Wolfgang, Corp. Sec./Sr. VP/Dir.-External Reporting
Thomas L. Grimes, Jr., Exec. VP/Dir.-Property Mgmt. Oper.
Ginny Doane, Sr. VP/Dir.-Dev. & Training
Rick Barton, Controller/Sr. VP
James Maclin, Sr. VP/Dir.-Corp. Support
Kevin P. Perkins, Sr. VP/Dir.-Physical Assets
James Andrew Taylor, Exec. VP/Dir.-Asset Mgmt.
Doug Clark, VP/Dir.-Risk Mgmt.
H. Eric Bolton, Jr., Chmn.

Phone: 901-682-6600	**Fax:** 901-682-6667
Toll-Free:	
Address: 6584 Poplar Ave., Memphis, TN 38138 US	

GROWTH PLANS/SPECIAL FEATURES:

Mid-America Apartment Communities, Inc. (MAAC) is a self-administered and self-managed real estate investment trust (REIT) that acquires, owns and operates apartment communities in the south-east and south-central U.S. The firm manages approximately 42,684 apartment homes in 144 communities, conducting business primarily through its subsidiary and sole general partner, Mid-America Apartments, LP. MAAC also maintains an REIT subsidiary, MAC II of Delaware, Inc. The company also has a 33.33% share in Mid-America Multifamily Fund I LLC and Mid-America Multifamily Fund II, LLC, which own three properties combined consisting of 920 apartment units. The firm's current investment focus involves acquiring relatively new properties (7-15 years old) within its present geographic area with the potential for above-average growth. MAAC also provides on-site property management, through which the firm handles matters concerning rent, occupancy limits and regulations. MAAC maintains an 18 month management training program for property managers, and a large majority of its property managers are Certified Apartment Managers, a designation established by the National Apartment Association. MAAC also maintains each property's physical condition through regular landscaping and exterior improvements. During 2009, the company wholly acquired five properties, with a total of 1,844 apartments, located in Texas, Arizona, Georgia and Florida. Through its interest in Fund I, MAAC acquired a one-third share in one property with 294 units located in Georgia. In 2009, the firm also disposed of three properties (840 units) in Tennessee, Mississippi and North Carolina.

MAAC offers its employees life, disability, medical and dental insurance; a 401(k); a stock ownership plan; bonuses; apartment discounts; scholarships; and an employee assistance program. In addition, as employees stay with the firm over time, benefits packages are enhanced with higher bonuses, higher company contribution to retirement savings plans, decreased healthcare costs and additional vacation and leave time.

FINANCIALS:

Sales and profits are in thousands of dollars—add 000 to get the full amount. 2009 Note: Financial information for 2009 was not available for all companies at press time.

2009 Sales: $378,544	2009 Profits: $37,211	**U.S. Stock Ticker: MAA**
2008 Sales: $370,011	2008 Profits: $30,249	**Int'l Ticker:** Int'l Exchange:
2007 Sales: $347,444	2007 Profits: $39,946	Employees: 1,282
2006 Sales: $318,370	2006 Profits: $20,945	Fiscal Year Ends: 12/31
2005 Sales: $293,786	2005 Profits: $19,744	Parent Company:

SALARIES/BENEFITS:

Pension Plan:	ESOP Stock Plan: Y	Profit Sharing:	Top Exec. Salary: $407,753	Bonus: $816,006
Savings Plan: Y	Stock Purch. Plan: Y		Second Exec. Salary: $265,907	Bonus: $532,314

OTHER THOUGHTS:

Apparent Women Officers or Directors: 10
Hot Spot for Advancement for Women/Minorities: Y

LOCATIONS: ("Y" = Yes)

West:	Southwest:	Midwest:	Southeast:	Northeast:	International:
	Y	Y	Y	Y	

MILLENNIUM & COPTHORNE HOTELS PLC

www.mill-cop.com

Industry Group Code: 721110 **Ranks within this company's industry group:** Sales: 12 Profits: 7

Properties:		Financial Services:		Construction/Development:		Investments:		Specialty Services:		Brokerage:	
Apartments:	Y	Mortgages:		Commercial Construction:		REIT:	Y	Property Management:	Y	Commercial Sales:	
Malls/Shopping:		Title Insurance:		Residential Construction:				Online Services:		Residential Sales:	
Offices:		Property Insurance:		Land Development:				Software/IT:		Specialty:	
Hotels/Motels:	Y			Support Services:				Consulting:			
Industrial/Warehouses:				Design/Engineering:							
Other:	Y										

TYPES OF BUSINESS:

Hotels, Luxury
Restaurants
Property Management
Apartments
Conference & Event Centers
Casino
Theaters
Fitness & Spa Facilities

BRANDS/DIVISIONS/AFFILIATES:

Millennium Hotels and Resorts
Copthorne Hotels

CONTACTS:

Note: Officers with more than one job title may be intentionally listed here more than once.

Richard Hartman, CEO
Adrian Bushnell, Corp. Sec.
Wong Hong Ren, Executive Dir.
Kwek Leng Beng, Chmn.
John Arnett, Head-North America

Phone: 44-0207-872-2444 **Fax:** 44-0207-872-2460
Toll-Free: 866-866-8086
Address: Scarsdale Place, Kensington, London, W8 5SR UK

GROWTH PLANS/SPECIAL FEATURES:

Millennium and Copthorne Hotels plc (MCH) is a global hotel company that owns, manages and/or operates over approximately 104 hotels in 17 countries worldwide, primarily located in Europe. The company's 25 European locations, branded under the Millennium Hotels and Resorts, Millennium and Copthorne labels, can be found in major business centers in the U.K. (including Birmingham, Cardiff, Glasgow, London, Manchester and Newcastle) as well as France and Germany. MCH's European locations include standard rooms, club accommodation and suites, as well as a club lounge, fully equipped business center and in-room business facilities. Meetings and events facilities operated by the firm include the Millennium Conference Centre in London; the Ballroom at Millennium Hotel London Mayfair; the Millennium Conference Centre at Effingham Park; and the Millennium Hotel and Resort Stuttgart with the SI-Entertainment-Centre, which features two full-scale musical theaters, 17 conference and banquet rooms, a six-screen movie theater, casino and 19 restaurants. Many hotel locations also offer health-club and fitness-spa facilities as well as restaurants, such as the Brian Turner Mayfair and Mju restaurants. In addition to MCH's European locations, the company has 15 hotels in the U.S., 30 in New Zealand, six in Singapore, six in the United Arab Emirates, five locations in China, two in Hong Kong, two in Malaysia and locations in Indonesia, the Philippines, South Korea, Taiwan, Thailand and Kuwait. During 2009, the group began management of three new hotels, one hotel under management in Orlando was closed, and the company's management contract for the Millenium Oyoun Hotel, Sharm el Sheikh in Egypt expired. Also during 2009, the company signed fifteen additional management contracts for hotels scheduled to open between 2010 and 2013, in the U.K., U.A.E, Iraq, Saudi Arabia, Yemen and Taiwan. In November 2009 MCH launched its Studio M brand, a new line of hotels with an emphasis on technology.

FINANCIALS:

Sales and profits are in thousands of dollars—add 000 to get the full amount. 2009 Note: Financial information for 2009 was not available for all companies at press time.

2009 Sales: $1,005,580	2009 Profits: $107,790
2008 Sales: $1,158,530	2008 Profits: $116,860
2007 Sales: $1,325,800	2007 Profits: $295,800
2006 Sales: $1,279,700	2006 Profits: $198,200
2005 Sales: $1,042,100	2005 Profits: $122,200

U.S. Stock Ticker:
Int'l Ticker: MLC Int'l Exchange: London-LSE
Employees: 12,778
Fiscal Year Ends: 12/31
Parent Company:

SALARIES/BENEFITS:

Pension Plan:	ESOP Stock Plan:	Profit Sharing:	Top Exec. Salary: $	Bonus: $
Savings Plan:	Stock Purch. Plan:		Second Exec. Salary: $	Bonus: $

OTHER THOUGHTS:

Apparent Women Officers or Directors:
Hot Spot for Advancement for Women/Minorities:

LOCATIONS: ("Y" = Yes)

West:	Southwest:	Midwest:	Southeast:	Northeast:	International:
Y	Y	Y	Y	Y	Y

MISSION WEST PROPERTIES

www.missionwest.com

Industry Group Code: 531120 **Ranks within this company's industry group:** Sales: 60 Profits: 48

Properties:		Financial Services:		Construction/Development:		Investments:		Specialty Services:		Brokerage:	
Apartments:		Mortgages:		Commercial Construction:		REIT:	Y	Property Management:	Y	Commercial Sales:	
Malls/Shopping:		Title Insurance:		Residential Construction:				Online Services:		Residential Sales:	
Offices:	Y	Property Insurance:		Land Development:	Y			Software/IT:		Specialty:	
Hotels/Motels:				Support Services:				Consulting:			
Industrial/Warehouses:				Design/Engineering:							
Other:	Y										

TYPES OF BUSINESS:

Real Estate Investment Trust
Research & Development Properties
Real Estate Rental, Leasing & Management
Commercial Land Development

BRANDS/DIVISIONS/AFFILIATES:

Berg Group (The)

CONTACTS:

Note: Officers with more than one job title may be intentionally listed here more than once.

Carl E. Berg, CEO
Raymond V. Marino, COO
Raymond V. Marino, Pres.
Raymond V. Marino, Corp. Sec.
Wayne N. Pham, VP-Finance/Controller
Carl E. Berg, Chmn.

Phone: 408-725-0700	**Fax:** 408-725-1626
Toll-Free:	
Address: 10050 Bandley Dr., Cupertino, CA 95014 US	

GROWTH PLANS/SPECIAL FEATURES:

Mission West Properties, Inc. is a self-managed, self-administered real estate investment trust (REIT). The firm acquires, markets, leases and manages commercial research and development properties, primarily located in the Silicon Valley portion of the San Francisco Bay area. Much of the company's business is undertaken through four general partnerships with the Berg Group, whose properties Mission West purchased at the inception of its operations. The Berg Group maintains architectural and construction personnel and therefore is responsible for the land acquisition, development and construction activities for the research and development properties that the firm is interested in. The properties, designed both for research and development and office use, in some cases include space for light manufacturing operations and logistics installations, such as loading docks. The company currently owns and manages 111 properties, totaling approximately 8 million square feet. Mission West focuses on single-tenant properties, which it leases primarily through triple net leases, in which the lessee agrees to pay real estate taxes, building insurance and many of the maintenance costs associated with the properties. The firm has approximately 71 combined tenants leasing its properties. Some of Mission West's biggest tenants include Microsoft Corporation; Apple, Inc.; JDS Uniphase Corporation; Tyco Electronics Corporation; and Fujitsu.

FINANCIALS:

Sales and profits are in thousands of dollars—add 000 to get the full amount. 2009 Note: Financial information for 2009 was not available for all companies at press time.

2009 Sales: $105,008	2009 Profits: $8,391	**U.S. Stock Ticker: MSW**
2008 Sales: $99,704	2008 Profits: $10,134	**Int'l Ticker:** Int'l Exchange:
2007 Sales: $151,583	2007 Profits: $18,888	Employees: 6
2006 Sales: $120,852	2006 Profits: $14,630	Fiscal Year Ends: 12/31
2005 Sales: $115,814	2005 Profits: $10,027	Parent Company:

SALARIES/BENEFITS:

Pension Plan:	ESOP Stock Plan:	Profit Sharing:	Top Exec. Salary: $250,000	Bonus: $
Savings Plan: Y	Stock Purch. Plan:		Second Exec. Salary: $138,000	Bonus: $

OTHER THOUGHTS:

Apparent Women Officers or Directors:
Hot Spot for Advancement for Women/Minorities:

LOCATIONS: ("Y" = Yes)

West:	Southwest:	Midwest:	Southeast:	Northeast:	International:
Y					

MODTECH HOLDINGS INC

www.modtech.com

Industry Group Code: 321991 **Ranks within this company's industry group:** Sales: Profits:

Properties:		Financial Services:		Construction/Development:		Investments:		Specialty Services:		Brokerage:	
Apartments:		Mortgages:		Commercial Construction:	Y	REIT:		Property Management:		Commercial Sales:	
Malls/Shopping:		Title Insurance:		Residential Construction:				Online Services:		Residential Sales:	
Offices:		Property Insurance:		Land Development:				Software/IT:		Specialty:	
Hotels/Motels:				Support Services:				Consulting:			
Industrial/Warehouses:				Design/Engineering:	Y						
Other:											

TYPES OF BUSINESS:

Modular Construction
Modular Design Services
Modular Educational Facilities

BRANDS/DIVISIONS/AFFILIATES:

CONTACTS:

Note: Officers with more than one job title may be intentionally listed here more than once.

Dennis L. Shogren, CEO
Dennis L. Shogren, Pres.
Kenneth Cragun, CFO
Karen Andreasen, Sr. VP-Human Resources
Karen Andreasen, Sr. VP-IT
Karen Andreasen, Sr. VP-Admin.
Karen Andreasen, Sr. VP-Legal
Ronald Savona, Sr. VP-Oper.
Karen Andreasen, Sr. VP-Comm.
Charles C. McGettigan, Chmn.

Phone: 951-943-4014	**Fax:** 951-443-3642
Toll-Free: 888-929-0998	
Address: 2830 Barrett Ave., Perris, CA 92571 US	

GROWTH PLANS/SPECIAL FEATURES:

Modtech Holdings, Inc. designs, manufactures, markets and installs modular, relocatable buildings for educational, residential, commercial, industrial, healthcare and government applications. The company has three manufacturing facilities with approximately 1.2 million square feet of space on 132 acres. Modtech aims to increase quality and strength of units, as well as achieve savings in construction time and overall costs through off-site building. Its service area includes California, Nevada, Arizona, Texas and Florida, though most of its business is done in California. The company provides pre-manufactured student facilities for schools with overcrowded classrooms. These facilities are made up of not only standard classrooms but also libraries, gymnasiums, computer labs and bathrooms, and range from two units of 960 square feet to campuses consisting of over 50,000 square feet. Additionally, the company is a designer, manufacturer and wholesaler of commercial and light industrial modular buildings. Modtech designs and builds modular buildings to customer specifications for a wide array of uses, including corporate and professional office space; governmental, educational, recreational and religious facilities; and construction site offices. The company maintains an online gift store on its web site that offers shirts, gifts, hats and outerwear bearing the Motech name.

FINANCIALS:

Sales and profits are in thousands of dollars—add 000 to get the full amount. 2009 Note: Financial information for 2009 was not available for all companies at press time.

2009 Sales: $	2009 Profits: $	**U.S. Stock Ticker: MODT**
2008 Sales: $	2008 Profits: $	**Int'l Ticker:** Int'l Exchange:
2007 Sales: $87,323	2007 Profits: $-56,908	Employees:
2006 Sales: $156,033	2006 Profits: $-54,691	Fiscal Year Ends: 12/31
2005 Sales: $230,324	2005 Profits: $-21,104	Parent Company:

SALARIES/BENEFITS:

Pension Plan:	ESOP Stock Plan:	Profit Sharing:	Top Exec. Salary: $	Bonus: $
Savings Plan: Y	Stock Purch. Plan:		Second Exec. Salary: $	Bonus: $

OTHER THOUGHTS:

Apparent Women Officers or Directors: 1
Hot Spot for Advancement for Women/Minorities:

LOCATIONS: ("Y" = Yes)

West:	Southwest:	Midwest:	Southeast:	Northeast:	International:
Y					

MORGANS HOTEL GROUP CO

www.morganshotelgroup.com

Industry Group Code: 721110 **Ranks within this company's industry group:** Sales: 23 Profits: 26

Properties:		Financial Services:		Construction/Development:		Investments:		Specialty Services:		Brokerage:	
Apartments:		Mortgages:		Commercial Construction:		REIT:		Property Management:	Y	Commercial Sales:	
Malls/Shopping:		Title Insurance:		Residential Construction:				Online Services:		Residential Sales:	
Offices:		Property Insurance:		Land Development:				Software/IT:		Specialty:	
Hotels/Motels:	Y			Support Services:				Consulting:			
Industrial/Warehouses:				Design/Engineering:							
Other:	Y										

TYPES OF BUSINESS:

Boutique Luxury Hotels & Resorts
Boutique Hotels
Property Management

BRANDS/DIVISIONS/AFFILIATES:

Morgans
Royalton
Hudson
Delano South Beach
Mondrian Los Angeles
Clift
Modrian Scottsdale
Ames

CONTACTS:

Note: Officers with more than one job title may be intentionally listed here more than once.

Fred J. Kleisner, CEO
Marc Gordon, Pres.
Richard Szymanksi, CFO
M. Thomas Buoy, Sr. VP-Customer Mktg. & Revenue Mgmt.
David Smail, General Counsel/Exec. VP
David Weidlich, Exec. VP-Oper.
James Zito, VP-Interactive Mktg.
Kim Walker, Dir.-Creative Svcs.
David Freiberger, VP-Brand Integrity
David T. Hamamoto, Chmn.

Phone: 212-277-4100	**Fax:** 212-277-4260
Toll-Free:	
Address: 475 10th Ave., New York, NY 10018 US	

GROWTH PLANS/SPECIAL FEATURES:

Morgans Hotel Group Co. (MHG) operates, owns, develops and redevelops luxury hotels. The firm, which is known for its establishment of the boutique hotel sector, primarily maintains hotels in gateway cities and select resort markets in the U.S. and Europe that feature avant-garde modern design. MHG owns/partially owns and operates 12 hotel properties in New York, Miami, Los Angeles, San Francisco, London and Las Vegas. The firm's fully-owned and managed hotels include the Morgans, Royalton, Hudson, Delano South Beach, Mondrian Los Angeles and Clift. The company also manages and owns a 50% interest in two hotels (St. Martins Lane and Sanderson) in London; a 50% interest in Mondrian South Beach in Miami; a 7% interest in the Shore Club in Miami; a 35% interest in Ames in Boston; and a 12.8% interest in the Hard Rock Hotel and Casino in Las Vegas. Significant media attention has been devoted to MHG's hotels, which it attributes to the public spaces, modern design, celebrity guests and high-profile events for which its hotels are known. Designers of MHG's hotels have included Phillippe Starck, Benjamin Noriega-Ortiz, Andree Putman and David Chipperfield. The lobby of the company's Royalton in midtown Manhattan spans a full city block and includes a series of iconic spaces. Delano South Beach features a simple white Art Deco design and the Water Salon and Orchard, comprised of a landscaped orchard and 100-foot long pool. The Sanderson, located on London's Soho district, features wall-less guest rooms in which the dressing room and bathroom are encased in a glass box wrapped in layered sheer curtains. Ames, which features 114 rooms, was opened in November 2009. MHG has a hotel under development in the SoHo neighborhood of New York that is expected to open in late 2010. Another of the firm's hotels, Mondrian Scottsdale, is in foreclosure.

FINANCIALS:

Sales and profits are in thousands of dollars—add 000 to get the full amount. 2009 Note: Financial information for 2009 was not available for all companies at press time.

2009 Sales: $232,645	2009 Profits: $-99,724	**U.S. Stock Ticker: MHGC**
2008 Sales: $314,467	2008 Profits: $-55,349	**Int'l Ticker:** Int'l Exchange:
2007 Sales: $322,985	2007 Profits: $-14,796	Employees: 4,500
2006 Sales: $281,883	2006 Profits: $-13,925	Fiscal Year Ends: 12/31
2005 Sales: $263,683	2005 Profits: $-30,216	Parent Company:

SALARIES/BENEFITS:

Pension Plan:	ESOP Stock Plan:	Profit Sharing:	Top Exec. Salary: $936,000	Bonus: $374,400
Savings Plan:	Stock Purch. Plan:		Second Exec. Salary: $709,800	Bonus: $709,800

OTHER THOUGHTS:

Apparent Women Officers or Directors: 1
Hot Spot for Advancement for Women/Minorities:

LOCATIONS: ("Y" = Yes)

West:	Southwest:	Midwest:	Southeast:	Northeast:	International:
Y			Y	Y	Y

MOVE INC

www.move.com

Industry Group Code: 519130 **Ranks within this company's industry group:** Sales: 1 Profits: 2

Properties:		Financial Services:		Construction/Development:		Investments:		Specialty Services:		Brokerage:	
Apartments:		Mortgages:		Commercial Construction:		REIT:		Property Management:		Commercial Sales:	
Malls/Shopping:		Title Insurance:		Residential Construction:				Online Services:	Y	Residential Sales:	
Offices:		Property Insurance:		Land Development:				Software/IT:	Y	Specialty:	
Hotels/Motels:				Support Services:				Consulting:			
Industrial/Warehouses:				Design/Engineering:							
Other:											

TYPES OF BUSINESS:

Online Portal-Real Estate Data
Real Estate Software
Real Estate Publishing
Real Estate Advertising

BRANDS/DIVISIONS/AFFILIATES:

Realtor.com
Move.com
Top Producer 7i
Moving.com
Move New Homes
Move Rentals

CONTACTS:

Note: Officers with more than one job title may be intentionally listed here more than once.

Steven Berkowitz, CEO
Rob Krolik, CFO
David Story, CTO
Scott Boeker, Chief Product Officer
James S. Caulfield, General Counsel/Exec. VP/Sec.
Errol Samuelson, Chief Revenue Officer
Joe F. Hanauer, Chmn.

Phone: 805-557-2300	**Fax:**
Toll-Free:	
Address: 30700 Russell Ranch Rd., Westlake Village, CA 91362 US	

GROWTH PLANS/SPECIAL FEATURES:

Move, Inc. and its subsidiaries operate a leading network of web sites for real estate search, finance, moving and home enthusiasts and provide a resource for consumers seeking information and connections needed before, during and after a move. Its flagship consumer websites are Move.com and Realtor.com. Move operates under two business segments: real estate services and consumer media, which represent approximately 90% and 10% of revenue, respectively. The company's real estate services segment, comprised of the Realtor.com, Top Producer and Move New Homes and Rentals businesses, provides marketing services that allow real estate professionals connect with the consumer audience it has attracted to its web sites. Realtor.com offers consumers a suite of services, tools and content for all aspects of the residential real estate transaction. Move's primary Top Producer product, 7i, is a web-based customer relationship management (CRM) software. The Move new homes channel of Move.com is the official new homes listing site of the National Association of Home Builders; it aggregates and displays new home listings nationwide at no charge to consumers. The Move rentals segment of Move.com aggregates and displays rental listings at no charge to consumers. The company's consumer media business segment provides advertisers such as mortgage companies, home improvement retailers, moving service providers and other consumer product and service companies with products and services designed to help them target consumers during the move cycle. These products and services include advertising products and lead generation tools including display; text-link and rich media advertising positions; directory products; price quote tools and content sponsorships on Move.com and other related web sites as well as lead generation products for professional moving, truck rental and self-storage businesses on the Move.com web site.

The firm offers its employees medical and dental coverage; disability and life insurance; and a 401(k) Plan.

FINANCIALS:

Sales and profits are in thousands of dollars—add 000 to get the full amount. 2009 Note: Financial information for 2009 was not available for all companies at press time.

2009 Sales: $212,009	2009 Profits: $-6,946	**U.S. Stock Ticker: MOVE**
2008 Sales: $242,069	2008 Profits: $-29,190	**Int'l Ticker:** Int'l Exchange:
2007 Sales: $248,919	2007 Profits: $- 316	Employees: 951
2006 Sales: $280,112	2006 Profits: $22,105	Fiscal Year Ends: 12/31
2005 Sales: $240,911	2005 Profits: $ 545	Parent Company:

SALARIES/BENEFITS:

Pension Plan:	ESOP Stock Plan:	Profit Sharing:	Top Exec. Salary: $500,000	Bonus: $356,000
Savings Plan: Y	Stock Purch. Plan:		Second Exec. Salary: $450,000	Bonus: $346,000

OTHER THOUGHTS:

Apparent Women Officers or Directors: 2
Hot Spot for Advancement for Women/Minorities: Y

LOCATIONS: ("Y" = Yes)

West:	Southwest:	Midwest:	Southeast:	Northeast:	International:
Y	Y	Y		Y	Y

MRV ENGENHARIA E PARTICIPACOES SA

www.mrv.com.br

Industry Group Code: 5311 **Ranks within this company's industry group:** Sales: 25 Profits: 17

Properties:		Financial Services:		Construction/Development:		Investments:		Specialty Services:		Brokerage:	
Apartments:		Mortgages:		Commercial Construction:		REIT:		Property Management:		Commercial Sales:	
Malls/Shopping:		Title Insurance:		Residential Construction:	Y			Online Services:		Residential Sales:	
Offices:		Property Insurance:		Land Development:	Y			Software/IT:		Specialty:	
Hotels/Motels:				Support Services:				Consulting:			
Industrial/Warehouses:				Design/Engineering:							
Other:											

TYPES OF BUSINESS:

Real Estate Development

BRANDS/DIVISIONS/AFFILIATES:

Parque
Spazio
Village
Minha Casa, Minha Vida

CONTACTS:

Note: Officers with more than one job title may be intentionally listed here more than once.

Rubens M.T. de Souza, CEO
Homero Aguiar Paiva, Chief Prod. Officer
Junia M. de Sousa Lima Galvao, Co-Chief Admin. Officer
Hudson G. de Andrade, Chief Real Estate Dev. Officer
Leonardo G.Correa, Exec. VP-Investor Rel.
Monica Simao, Dir.-Finance
Eduardo P. Barreto, Chief Commercial Officer
Jose A.T. Simao, Co-Chief Admin. Officer
Rubens M.T. de Souza, Chmn.

Phone: 55-31-3348-7150 **Fax:** 55-31-3348-7155
Toll-Free:
Address: 2720 Raja Gabaglia Ave., Estoril Belo Horizonte, MG 30494-170 Brazil

GROWTH PLANS/SPECIAL FEATURES:

MRV Engenharia e Participacoes S.A. is a Brazilian developer and builder of low-income residential real estate. The firm offers three products directed to low-income customers: the Parque line, featuring units with between 430.56 and 592 square feet of usable area and a maximum sale price of approximately $55,310; the Spazio line, which offers units with between 452 and 753.47 square feet of usable area and prices ranging between $38,728 and $77,455; and the Village line, featuring units with between 753.47 and 1,291.67 square feet of usable area and prices ranging from $55,325 to $165,975. Both the Parque and Spazio units are vertically designed condominiums with a maximum of five floors; the village line of condominiums feature a horizontal layout. MRV Engenharia operates in 75 cities located in the Federal District and the following 14 states: Sao Paulo, Rio de Janeiro, Minas Gerais, Rio Grande do Norte, Goias, Espirito Santo, Parana, Santa Catarina, Rio Grande do Sul, Bahia, Ceara, Mato Grosso, Mato Grosso do Sul and Pernambuco. Approximately 84% of the firm's customers pay for their condominiums using CEF-associative credit financing; 10% utilize bank financing; 5% pay cash; and 1% use direct financing from MRV Engenharia. The company is a member of Minha Casa, Minha Vida (My Home, My Life), a program funded by the Brazilian government to promote homeownership in the country. The program, which was launched in April 2009, aims to build 1 million new houses for families earning up to 10 times Brazil's minimum wage.

FINANCIALS:

Sales and profits are in thousands of dollars—add 000 to get the full amount. 2009 Note: Financial information for 2009 was not available for all companies at press time.

2009 Sales: $940,540	2009 Profits: $198,320	**U.S. Stock Ticker:**
2008 Sales: $634,050	2008 Profits: $131,870	**Int'l Ticker: MRVE3** Int'l Exchange: Sao Paulo-SAO
2007 Sales: $228,110	2007 Profits: $12,730	Employees:
2006 Sales: $	2006 Profits: $	Fiscal Year Ends: 12/31
2005 Sales: $	2005 Profits: $	Parent Company:

SALARIES/BENEFITS:

Pension Plan:	ESOP Stock Plan:	Profit Sharing:	Top Exec. Salary: $	Bonus: $
Savings Plan:	Stock Purch. Plan:		Second Exec. Salary: $	Bonus: $

OTHER THOUGHTS:

Apparent Women Officers or Directors: 1
Hot Spot for Advancement for Women/Minorities:

LOCATIONS: ("Y" = Yes)

West:	Southwest:	Midwest:	Southeast:	Northeast:	International:
					Y

MUNICIPAL MORTGAGE & EQUITY

www.munimae.com

Industry Group Code: 522310 **Ranks within this company's industry group:** Sales: Profits:

Properties:		Financial Services:		Construction/Development:		Investments:		Specialty Services:		Brokerage:	
Apartments:		Mortgages:	Y	Commercial Construction:		REIT:		Property Management:		Commercial Sales:	
Malls/Shopping:		Title Insurance:		Residential Construction:				Online Services:		Residential Sales:	
Offices:		Property Insurance:		Land Development:				Software/IT:		Specialty:	
Hotels/Motels:				Support Services:				Consulting:			
Industrial/Warehouses:				Design/Engineering:							
Other:											

TYPES OF BUSINESS:

Mortgages
Real Estate Services

BRANDS/DIVISIONS/AFFILIATES:

MuniMae
MMA Financial, Inc.
MMA Realty Capital
SLF Management, LLC
MMA Renewable Ventures

CONTACTS:

Note: Officers with more than one job title may be intentionally listed here more than once.

Michael L. Falcone, CEO
Charles M. Pinckney, COO
Michael L. Falcone, Pres.
David Kay, CFO
Stephen A. Goldberg, General Counsel
Gary A. Mentesana, Exec. VP/Chief Capital Officer
Earl W. Cole, Exec. VP-Corp. Credit & Portfolio Mgmt.
Mark K. Joseph, Chmn.

Phone: 443-263-2900	**Fax:** 410-727-5387
Toll-Free:	
Address: 621 E. Pratt St., Ste. 300, Baltimore, MD 21202 US	

GROWTH PLANS/SPECIAL FEATURES:

Municipal Mortgage and Equity (MuniMae) is a real estate finance company and a leading provider of debt and equity financing to real estate developers of both multi-family and commercial properties. The firm's multi-family housing segment primary focus is tax except bonds. The company also offers investment advisory services to its investor clients. MuniMae's portfolio consists of multifamily debt, equity and other real estate investments, and its assets under management exceed $18 billion, including investments in 2,800 multifamily properties in 49 states, Washington, D.C., Puerto Rico and the U.S. Virgin Islands. The company acts through its principal operating subsidiaries: MMA Financial, Inc., offers debt and equity lending and investment solutions for multifamily housing, senior and student housing, as well as construction loans, permanent financing, forward commitments and low-income tax credit equity. MMA Realty Capital provides various debt financing programs and equity investment management programs to the office, hotel, retail, medical and industrial properties markets. MMA Realty Capital offers permanent debt, construction loans, mezzanine investments and B-Notes, CMBS and private equity and investment advisory services. In April 2009, the subsidiary, MMA Renewable Ventures, LLC, sold its renewable energy business excluding its Solar Funds I and II for $19.7 million to Fotowatio Renewable Ventures, Inc. In May 2009, the firm sold its Agency lending operation to Oak Grove Commercial Mortgage LLC. In July 2009, the company completed the first closing of its low income tax credit business held by its subsidiaries, MMA Equity and MMA Financial TC Corp, to JEN Partners, LLC, for an expected $30 million after final closing.

FINANCIALS:

Sales and profits are in thousands of dollars—add 000 to get the full amount. 2009 Note: Financial information for 2009 was not available for all companies at press time.

2009 Sales: $	2009 Profits: $	**U.S. Stock Ticker: MMAB.PK**
2008 Sales: $	2008 Profits: $	**Int'l Ticker:** Int'l Exchange:
2007 Sales: $	2007 Profits: $	Employees:
2006 Sales: $	2006 Profits: $	Fiscal Year Ends: 12/31
2005 Sales: $306,554	2005 Profits: $85,791	Parent Company:

SALARIES/BENEFITS:

Pension Plan:	ESOP Stock Plan:	Profit Sharing:	Top Exec. Salary: $423,077	Bonus: $600,000
Savings Plan: Y	Stock Purch. Plan:		Second Exec. Salary: $313,573	Bonus: $525,000

OTHER THOUGHTS:

Apparent Women Officers or Directors:
Hot Spot for Advancement for Women/Minorities:

LOCATIONS: ("Y" = Yes)

West:	Southwest:	Midwest:	Southeast:	Northeast:	International:
Y	Y	Y	Y	Y	

MWH GLOBAL INC

www.mw.com

Industry Group Code: 237 **Ranks within this company's industry group:** Sales: Profits:

Properties:		Financial Services:		Construction/Development:		Investments:		Specialty Services:		Brokerage:	
Apartments:		Mortgages:		Commercial Construction:		REIT:		Property Management:		Commercial Sales:	
Malls/Shopping:		Title Insurance:		Residential Construction:				Online Services:		Residential Sales:	
Offices:		Property Insurance:		Land Development:				Software/IT:		Specialty:	
Hotels/Motels:				Support Services:				Consulting:			
Industrial/Warehouses:				Design/Engineering:	Y						
Other:											

TYPES OF BUSINESS:

Engineering & Construction Services
Environmental Engineering
Water & Waste Treatment Analysis
Facilities Development
Infrastructure Asset Management
Consulting
Government Relations & Lobbying
Software & IT Services

BRANDS/DIVISIONS/AFFILIATES:

KnowledgeNet
MWH Laboratories
Asset Group (The)
Montgomery Group (The)
MWH Constructors
MWH Automation & Information Solutions
MWH Smart Systems
MWH Applied Research

CONTACTS:

Note: Officers with more than one job title may be intentionally listed here more than once.

Robert B. Uhler, CEO
Alan J. Krause, COO
Alan J. Krause, Pres.
David Barnes, CFO
Gary Carlson, Chief Human Resources Officer
Micki Nelson, Chief IT Officer
Don Ungemah, Chief Legal Officer/Chief Risk Officer
Dan McConville, Pres., MWH Americas, Inc.
Joseph D. Adams, Jr., Pres., MWH Constructors, Inc.
Paul F. Boulos, Pres., MWH Soft, Inc. & Middle East
Bruce K. Howard, Pres., MWH Bus. Solutions
Robert B. Uhler, Chmn.
Marshall Davert, Pres., APAC

Phone: 303-533-1900 **Fax:** 303-533-1901
Toll-Free:
Address: 370 Interlocken Crescent, Ste. 200, Broomfield, CO 80021 US

GROWTH PLANS/SPECIAL FEATURES:

MWH Global, Inc. is one of the world's leading providers of consulting, engineering, construction and management services to the water, natural resources and infrastructure industries. Through roughly 123 global offices, MWH specializes in proprietary software and process automation packages in the areas of environmental engineering, power generation, facilities development, laboratory services, construction, asset management, financial services, IT consulting and government relations. One of these packages, KnowledgeNet, links the firm's worldwide employee base, allowing instant collaboration on projects and the elimination of redundancies in its system. MWH conducts its operations through several independent divisions: environmental engineering, power solutions, facilities, program management, laboratory services, asset management, financial consulting, construction, information technology, applied research and government relations. Some of its affiliates include MWH Laboratories, providing water and wastewater analysis services; mCapitol Management, which offers government relations, marketing and business development services; and MWH Soft is the creator of H2ONET, an integrated water distribution analysis software package. In August 2009, MWH and Parsons Brinckerhoff opened a joint office in Australia and MWH Soft agreed to merge with water resource management software firm Wallingford Software. In February 2010, the firm entered into a partnership with HTP, a German-based provider of engineering services for the waste sector, to provide the U.K. with a service for developing efficient waste facilities. Also in February 2010, the company introduced mCO2, a new reporting program that calculates carbon emissions.

FINANCIALS:

Sales and profits are in thousands of dollars—add 000 to get the full amount. 2009 Note: Financial information for 2009 was not available for all companies at press time.

2009 Sales: $	2009 Profits: $	**U.S. Stock Ticker: Private**
2008 Sales: $	2008 Profits: $	**Int'l Ticker:** Int'l Exchange:
2007 Sales: $	2007 Profits: $	Employees:
2006 Sales: $	2006 Profits: $	Fiscal Year Ends: 9/30
2005 Sales: $	2005 Profits: $	Parent Company:

SALARIES/BENEFITS:

Pension Plan:	ESOP Stock Plan:	Profit Sharing:	Top Exec. Salary: $	Bonus: $
Savings Plan:	Stock Purch. Plan:		Second Exec. Salary: $	Bonus: $

OTHER THOUGHTS:

Apparent Women Officers or Directors: 2
Hot Spot for Advancement for Women/Minorities: Y

LOCATIONS: ("Y" = Yes)

West:	Southwest:	Midwest:	Southeast:	Northeast:	International:
Y	Y	Y	Y	Y	Y

NAI GLOBAL INC

www.naiglobal.com

Industry Group Code: 531210 **Ranks within this company's industry group:** Sales: Profits:

Properties:		Financial Services:		Construction/Development:		Investments:		Specialty Services:		Brokerage:	
Apartments:		Mortgages:		Commercial Construction:		REIT:		Property Management:	Y	Commercial Sales:	Y
Malls/Shopping:		Title Insurance:		Residential Construction:				Online Services:	Y	Residential Sales:	
Offices:		Property Insurance:		Land Development:				Software/IT:	Y	Specialty:	
Hotels/Motels:				Support Services:				Consulting:	Y		
Industrial/Warehouses:				Design/Engineering:							
Other:											

TYPES OF BUSINESS:

Brokerage Services
Consulting & Advisory Services
Property Management
Online Transaction Services
IT Services
Real Estate Software

BRANDS/DIVISIONS/AFFILIATES:

REALTrac Online

CONTACTS:

Note: Officers with more than one job title may be intentionally listed here more than once.

Jeffrey Finn, CEO
Ed Finn, COO
Jeffrey Finn, Pres.
Mark Klionsky, Sr. VP-Mktg.
Shawn Stumbaugh, Sr. VP-Info. Svcs.
Shawn Stumbaugh, CTO/Exec. VP-Info. Systems
Ed Finn, Corp. Counsel/Exec. VP
Bobbi Jean Formosa, Exec. VP-Oper.
Peter Setaro, Dir.-Public Rel.
Marjy Smith, Sr. VP-Finance
David Blanchard, Exec. VP-Member Svcs.
Ted Parcel, Exec. VP-Corp. Svcs.
Patricia Faulkner, Sr. VP-Client Dev.
Gerald S. Monash, Exec. VP-Investment Svcs.
Gerald Finn, Chmn.
David Perry, VP-EMEA

Phone: 609-945-4000 **Fax:** 609-945-4001
Toll-Free:
Address: 4 Independence Way, Ste. 400, Princeton, NJ 08540 US

GROWTH PLANS/SPECIAL FEATURES:

NAI Global, Inc., formerly New America International, is an international commercial real estate network with more than 325 offices in 55 countries worldwide. The company manages over 200 million square feet of commercial space, with services provided local, regional, national and international businesses. The company offers leasing and brokerage agencies; disposition services; financial and investment strategies; leasing; property management; tenant representation; valuation and advice; and practice groups. Some of NAI's value-added operations include auction services, build-to-suit development services, commercial real estate due diligence, cost segregation, facilities management, lease audits, relocation studies, tax appeals and title insurance services. NAI also runs several specialty segments focusing on government, life sciences, location advisory, logistics, capital markets, investment sales, NAFTA advisory, process industries, supply chain solutions, and the office, industrial, retail, multifamily, hotel and land markets. The company also publishes market analysis reports and newsletters, including international and industry-specific reports, city-specific reports, country-specific reports and regional reports (the biggest being the NAI Asia Pacific Regional Overview). NAI runs REALTrac Online, an active platform for management of all company client transactions, with a leaning towards project coordination and transaction cycles. The company offers software for portfolio management, lease administration, online property marketing, financial analysis and demographics mapping. In April 2010, the firm launched a new unit, the Global Forms Project Management Unit, to help facilitate clients with design and building transaction services.

FINANCIALS:

Sales and profits are in thousands of dollars—add 000 to get the full amount. 2009 Note: Financial information for 2009 was not available for all companies at press time.

2009 Sales: $ | 2009 Profits: $
2008 Sales: $ | 2008 Profits: $
2007 Sales: $ | 2007 Profits: $
2006 Sales: $ | 2006 Profits: $
2005 Sales: $ | 2005 Profits: $

U.S. Stock Ticker: Private
Int'l Ticker: Int'l Exchange:
Employees:
Fiscal Year Ends: 6/30
Parent Company:

SALARIES/BENEFITS:

Pension Plan: ESOP Stock Plan: Profit Sharing: Top Exec. Salary: $ Bonus: $
Savings Plan: Stock Purch. Plan: Second Exec. Salary: $ Bonus: $

OTHER THOUGHTS:

Apparent Women Officers or Directors: 3
Hot Spot for Advancement for Women/Minorities: Y

LOCATIONS: ("Y" = Yes)

West:	Southwest:	Midwest:	Southeast:	Northeast:	International:
Y	Y	Y	Y	Y	Y

NATIONAL HEALTH INVESTORS

www.nhinvestors.com

Industry Group Code: 531120 **Ranks within this company's industry group:** Sales: 63 Profits: 32

Properties:		Financial Services:		Construction/Development:		Investments:		Specialty Services:		Brokerage:	
Apartments:		Mortgages:		Commercial Construction:		REIT:	Y	Property Management:		Commercial Sales:	
Malls/Shopping:		Title Insurance:		Residential Construction:				Online Services:		Residential Sales:	
Offices:		Property Insurance:		Land Development:				Software/IT:		Specialty:	
Hotels/Motels:				Support Services:				Consulting:			
Industrial/Warehouses:				Design/Engineering:							
Other:	Y										

TYPES OF BUSINESS:

Real Estate Investment Trust
Health Care Facilities
Long-Term Care Facilities
Retirement Centers
Mortgages

BRANDS/DIVISIONS/AFFILIATES:

National HealthCare Corporation
Sun Healthcare

CONTACTS:

Note: Officers with more than one job title may be intentionally listed here more than once.

W. Andrew Adams, CEO
J. Justin Hutchens, COO
J. Justin Hutchens, Pres.
Roger R. Hopkins, Chief Acct. Officer
W. Andrew Adams, Chmn.

Phone: 615-890-9100	**Fax:** 615-225-3030
Toll-Free:	
Address: 222 Robert Rose Dr., Murfreesboro, TN 37129 US	

GROWTH PLANS/SPECIAL FEATURES:

National Health Investors, Inc. (NHI) is a self-managed, self-administered real estate investment trust (REIT). The firm invests in healthcare properties including long-term care facilities, acute care hospitals, medical office buildings, retirement centers and assisted living facilities. NHI's portfolio includes real estate and mortgage investments in 114 health care facilities located in 20 states. These facilities consist of approximately 84 long-term care facilities, 21 assisted living facilities, four medical office buildings, four independent living centers and one acute care hospital. Of these facilities, 41 are leased to National HealthCare Corporation (NHC). All of NHI's long-term care facilities provide some combination of skilled and intermediate nursing and rehabilitative care, including speech, physical and occupational therapy. The firm's medical office buildings are specifically configured office buildings whose tenants are primarily physicians and other medical practitioners. Each of NHI's medical office buildings is leased to one lessee, who then leases out individual office space. Its assisted living facilities are either free-standing or attached to long-term care or retirement facilities and provide basic room and board functions for the elderly. NHI's independent living centers offer specially designed residential units for the active and ambulatory elderly and provide various ancillary services for their residents including restaurants, activity rooms and social areas. Three of the centers are leased to NHC and one is leased to Sun Healthcare. The company's acute care hospital offers a wide range of inpatient and outpatient services. In mid-2009, NHI acquired four skilled nursing facilities in Texas from Legend Healthcare, LLC for $56.5 million. In February 2010, the firm acquired six skilled nursing facilities in Florida from Care Foundation of America, Inc. for roughly $67 million.

FINANCIALS:

Sales and profits are in thousands of dollars—add 000 to get the full amount. 2009 Note: Financial information for 2009 was not available for all companies at press time.

2009 Sales: $64,221	2009 Profits: $64,229	**U.S. Stock Ticker: NHI**
2008 Sales: $58,005	2008 Profits: $57,510	**Int'l Ticker:** Int'l Exchange:
2007 Sales: $57,506	2007 Profits: $96,435	Employees:
2006 Sales: $60,770	2006 Profits: $69,228	Fiscal Year Ends: 12/31
2005 Sales: $62,231	2005 Profits: $54,408	Parent Company:

SALARIES/BENEFITS:

Pension Plan:	ESOP Stock Plan:	Profit Sharing:	Top Exec. Salary: $299,615	Bonus: $436,667
Savings Plan:	Stock Purch. Plan:		Second Exec. Salary: $218,269	Bonus: $75,000

OTHER THOUGHTS:

Apparent Women Officers or Directors:
Hot Spot for Advancement for Women/Minorities:

LOCATIONS: ("Y" = Yes)

West:	Southwest:	Midwest:	Southeast:	Northeast:	International:
Y	Y	Y	Y	Y	

NATIONAL HOME CENTERS INC

www.nhci.com

Industry Group Code: 444110 **Ranks within this company's industry group:** Sales: Profits:

Properties:		Financial Services:		Construction/Development:		Investments:		Specialty Services:		Brokerage:	
Apartments:		Mortgages:		Commercial Construction:		REIT:		Property Management:		Commercial Sales:	
Malls/Shopping:	Y	Title Insurance:		Residential Construction:				Online Services:		Residential Sales:	
Offices:		Property Insurance:		Land Development:				Software/IT:		Specialty:	
Hotels/Motels:				Support Services:	Y			Consulting:			
Industrial/Warehouses:				Design/Engineering:							
Other:											

TYPES OF BUSINESS:

Building Supply, Retail
Home Improvement Products
Construction Materials Manufacturing
Appliances

BRANDS/DIVISIONS/AFFILIATES:

Maumelle Appliance

CONTACTS:

Note: Officers with more than one job title may be intentionally listed here more than once.

Dwain A. Newman, CEO
Danny R. Funderburg, COO
Danny R. Funderburg, Pres.
Brent A. Hanby, CFO/Exec. VP
Jeff Newman, Sr. VP-Mktg.
Dennis Detar, CIO/VP
John Collins, VP-Merch.
Glenda Newman, VP-Admin.
C. Belle Reed, Corp. Sec.
Joe Frame, Sr. VP-Oper.
John Collins, VP-Store Dev.
Beth Epperson, Mgr.-Advertising & Web Site Admin.
C. Belle Reed, Controller
Robert H. Storment, VP-Acct.
Vickie Judy, VP-Acct.
John Walters, Merch. Mgr.-Imports, Hardware, Tools & Electrical
Dwain A. Newman, Chmn.
Jeff Newman, Sr. VP-Purchasing

Phone: 479-756-1700 **Fax:** 479-927-5797
Toll-Free:
Address: 1106 N. Old Missouri Rd., Hwy. 265 N., Springdale, AR 72764 US

GROWTH PLANS/SPECIAL FEATURES:

National Home Centers, Inc. began operations in the building supply business in 1972, serving primarily professional contractors. The company began implementing a dual-customer strategy in 1983, serving both professional contractors and retail consumers. Currently, National Home Centers operates eight retail locations and two flooring superstores in Arkansas. All of the firm's locations operate within four Arkansas markets, including Little Rock, northwest Arkansas, Russellville and Fort Smith. The company's stores offer a large selection of lumber, building materials, hardware and tools, electrical and plumbing supplies, paint, lighting, home decor, pre-hung doors, windows, appliances, cabinets, garden supplies and seasonal items. In addition, National Home Centers offers, through its fabrication facilities, custom services such as custom door shops, custom molding shops, custom countertop shops and custom granite shops. For over 20 years, National Home Centers has offered professional contractors a travel incentive program in which customers earn, through their purchases, credit toward trips arranged each year. The program, which has been highly successful in helping increase its share of the professional contractor business, affords an opportunity to present product seminars during each trip.

The company offers its employees two weeks paid vacation, health and dental insurance, a 401(k) plan and an employee discount.

FINANCIALS:

Sales and profits are in thousands of dollars—add 000 to get the full amount. 2009 Note: Financial information for 2009 was not available for all companies at press time.

2009 Sales: $	2009 Profits: $	**U.S. Stock Ticker: Private**
2008 Sales: $	2008 Profits: $	**Int'l Ticker:** Int'l Exchange:
2007 Sales: $	2007 Profits: $	Employees:
2006 Sales: $	2006 Profits: $	Fiscal Year Ends: 1/31
2005 Sales: $	2005 Profits: $	Parent Company:

SALARIES/BENEFITS:

Pension Plan:	ESOP Stock Plan:	Profit Sharing:	Top Exec. Salary: $	Bonus: $
Savings Plan: Y	Stock Purch. Plan:		Second Exec. Salary: $	Bonus: $

OTHER THOUGHTS:

Apparent Women Officers or Directors: 4
Hot Spot for Advancement for Women/Minorities: Y

LOCATIONS: ("Y" = Yes)

West:	Southwest:	Midwest:	Southeast:	Northeast:	International:
			Y		

NATIONWIDE HEALTH PROPERTIES

www.nhp-reit.com

Industry Group Code: 531120 **Ranks within this company's industry group:** Sales: 42 Profits: 11

Properties:		Financial Services:		Construction/Development:		Investments:		Specialty Services:		Brokerage:	
Apartments:		Mortgages:	Y	Commercial Construction:		REIT:	Y	Property Management:	Y	Commercial Sales:	
Malls/Shopping:		Title Insurance:		Residential Construction:				Online Services:		Residential Sales:	
Offices:	Y	Property Insurance:		Land Development:				Software/IT:		Specialty:	
Hotels/Motels:				Support Services:				Consulting:			
Industrial/Warehouses:				Design/Engineering:							
Other:	Y										

TYPES OF BUSINESS:

Real Estate Investment Trust
Health Care Facilities
Nursing & Assisted Living Facilities
Retirement Communities
Mortgage Loans

BRANDS/DIVISIONS/AFFILIATES:

Assisted Living Concepts, Inc.
Brookdale Senior Living Inc
Emeritus Corp
Extendicare Inc
HEALTHSOUTH Corp
Kindred Healthcare Inc
Pacific Medical Buildings LLC

CONTACTS: *Note: Officers with more than one job title may be intentionally listed here more than once.*

Douglas M. Pasquale, CEO
Abdo H. Khoury, CFO
Derrick D. Pete, VP-Corp. Dev.
Ron Hubbard, VP-Investor Rel. & Capital Markets
Danion Fielding, VP-Finance
Donald D. Bradley, Chief Investment Officer/Exec. VP
Abdo H. Khoury, Exec. VP/Portfolio Officer
David M. Boitano, Sr. Investment Officer-West/Sr. VP
Robert Noonan, Sr. Investment Officer-Northeast/VP
Douglas M. Pasquale, Chmn.

Phone: 949-718-4400 **Fax:** 919-759-6876
Toll-Free:
Address: 610 Newport Center Dr., Ste. 1150, Newport Beach, CA 92660 US

GROWTH PLANS/SPECIAL FEATURES:

Nationwide Health Properties, Inc. (NHP) is a real estate investment trust (REIT) that invests primarily in healthcare-related senior housing, long-term care properties and medical office buildings. NHP's operates through two segments: triple net leases and multi-tenant leases. In the triple net leases segment, the firm invests in healthcare-related properties, which it leases to unaffiliated tenants under leases that transfer the obligation for all facility operating costs, including maintenance, repairs, taxes and insurance, to the tenant. In the multi-tenant leases segment, NHP invests in medical office buildings that have several tenants under separate leases per building, thus requiring active management. NHP has investments in 576 healthcare facilities located in 43 states, comprised of 251 assisted and independent living facilities; 167 skilled nursing facilities; 10 continuing care retirement communities; seven specialty hospitals; 19 triple-net medical office buildings, one of which is operated by a joint venture; and 60 multi-tenant medical office buildings, 15 of which are operated by consolidated joint ventures. The firm also has indirect ownership of 36 facilities through unconsolidated joint ventures. Additionally, NHP provides mortgage loans to tenants secured by 16 skilled nursing facilities; nine assisted and independent living facilities; one medical office building; and one land parcel. NHP's directly owned properties are operated by approximately 83 tenants, including Assisted Living Concepts, Inc., operating four facilities; Brookdale Senior Living, Inc., operating 96 facilities; Emeritus Corporation, operating six facilities; Extendicare, Inc., operating one facility; HEALTHSOUTH Corporation, operating two facilities; Kindred Healthcare, Inc., operating one facility; and Sun Healthcare Group, Inc., operating four facilities. Leases account for 93% of NHP's revenues; mortgage loans and other activities account for the remaining 7%. In February 2010, the company acquired two medical office buildings in California from Pacific Medical Buildings LLC (Pac Med); in March, NHP acquired five additional medical buildings from Pac Med.

FINANCIALS: **Sales and profits are in thousands of dollars—add 000 to get the full amount. 2009 Note: Financial information for 2009 was not available for all companies at press time.**

2009 Sales: $390,512
2008 Sales: $368,319
2007 Sales: $306,269
2006 Sales: $222,910
2005 Sales: $179,662

2009 Profits: $148,390
2008 Profits: $268,138
2007 Profits: $224,458
2006 Profits: $185,577
2005 Profits: $69,941

U.S. Stock Ticker: NHP
Int'l Ticker: Int'l Exchange:
Employees: 36
Fiscal Year Ends: 12/31
Parent Company:

SALARIES/BENEFITS:

Pension Plan: ESOP Stock Plan: Profit Sharing: Top Exec. Salary: $562,500 Bonus: $1,153,750
Savings Plan: Stock Purch. Plan: Second Exec. Salary: $330,000 Bonus: $500,000

OTHER THOUGHTS:

Apparent Women Officers or Directors:
Hot Spot for Advancement for Women/Minorities:

LOCATIONS: ("Y" = Yes)

West:	Southwest:	Midwest:	Southeast:	Northeast:	International:
Y	Y	Y	Y	Y	

NCI BUILDING SYSTEMS INC

www.ncilp.com

Industry Group Code: 332311 **Ranks within this company's industry group:** Sales: 1 Profits: 1

Properties:		Financial Services:		Construction/Development:		Investments:		Specialty Services:		Brokerage:	
Apartments:		Mortgages:		Commercial Construction:		REIT:		Property Management:		Commercial Sales:	
Malls/Shopping:		Title Insurance:		Residential Construction:				Online Services:		Residential Sales:	
Offices:		Property Insurance:		Land Development:				Software/IT:		Specialty:	
Hotels/Motels:				Support Services:	Y			Consulting:			
Industrial/Warehouses:				Design/Engineering:	Y						
Other:											

TYPES OF BUSINESS:

Prefabricated Metal Buildings
Metal Building Components
Engineered Building Systems

BRANDS/DIVISIONS/AFFILIATES:

Metallic Buildings
Metallic de Mexico
Mid-West Steel Buildings
All American Systems
Metal Building Components, Inc.
American Building Components
Doublecote
Robertson-Ceco Corporation

CONTACTS:

Note: Officers with more than one job title may be intentionally listed here more than once.

Norman C. Chambers, CEO
Mark W. Dobbins, COO/Exec. VP
Norman C. Chambers, Pres.
Mark E. Johnson, CFO
Eric J. Brown, CIO/Exec. VP
Todd R. Moore, General Counsel/Sec./Exec. VP
Mark T. Golladay, VP-Corp. Dev.
Mark E. Johnson, Treas./Exec. VP
C. Wayne Dickinson, Pres., Metal Components Div.
Bradley D. Robeson, Pres., NCI Buildings
John Kuzdal, Pres., Metal Coil Coating Div.
Norman C. Chambers, Chmn.

Phone: 281-897-7788 **Fax:** 281-477-9674
Toll-Free: 888-624-8677
Address: 10943 N. Sam Houston Pkwy. W., Houston, TX 77064 US

GROWTH PLANS/SPECIAL FEATURES:

NCI Building Systems, Inc. is one of North America's largest manufacturers of metal products for the construction and building industry. Comprised of a family of companies and 32 manufacturing facilities located throughout the U.S. states and Mexico, the company is a viable national presence, offering a diversified product line. The firm operates in three business segments: metal components; engineered building systems; and metal coil coating services. The metal component segment produces metal roof and wall systems, metal partitions, metal trim, doors and other related accessories. These products are used in new construction and repair applications for industrial, commercial, institutional, agricultural and rural use. Some of this segment's brand names are Metal Building Components (MBCI); American Building Components; Insulated Panel Systems (IPS); NCI Metal Depots; and DBCI. The engineered building systems segment encompasses the manufacturing of structural framing, complemented by engineering and drafting services, and includes the manufacturing of main house frames. It also offers value-added engineering and drafting services, which are typically not part of metal building component or metal coil coating products or services. This segment's brand names include A & S Building Systems; All American Systems; Ceco Building Systems; Garco Building Systems; Heritage Building Systems; Mesco Building Solutions; Metallic Building Company; and Star Building Systems. The metal coil coating business, operating as Metal Coaters and Metal-Prep, is engaged in the cleaning, treating and painting of continuous steel coils before the steel is fabricated for use by construction and industrial users.

Employees are offered medical, dental and vision benefits; a 401(k) plan; life and AD&D insurance; dependent life insurance; short- and long-term disability coverage; an employee assistance program; and credit union membership.

FINANCIALS:

Sales and profits are in thousands of dollars—add 000 to get the full amount. 2009 Note: Financial information for 2009 was not available for all companies at press time.

2009 Sales: $967,923	2009 Profits: $-746,964
2008 Sales: $1,764,159	2008 Profits: $78,881
2007 Sales: $1,625,068	2007 Profits: $63,729
2006 Sales: $1,571,183	2006 Profits: $73,796
2005 Sales: $1,130,066	2005 Profits: $55,951

U.S. Stock Ticker: NCS
Int'l Ticker: Int'l Exchange:
Employees: 3,673
Fiscal Year Ends: 10/31
Parent Company:

SALARIES/BENEFITS:

Pension Plan:	ESOP Stock Plan:	Profit Sharing:	Top Exec. Salary: $750,000	Bonus: $
Savings Plan: Y	Stock Purch. Plan:		Second Exec. Salary: $332,000	Bonus: $

OTHER THOUGHTS:

Apparent Women Officers or Directors: 1
Hot Spot for Advancement for Women/Minorities:

LOCATIONS: ("Y" = Yes)

West:	Southwest:	Midwest:	Southeast:	Northeast:	International:
Y	Y	Y	Y	Y	Y

NEW PLAN EXCEL REALTY TRUST INC

http://www.centroprop.com/NewPlanBondholders.aspx

Industry Group Code: 531120 **Ranks within this company's industry group:** Sales: Profits:

Properties:		Financial Services:		Construction/Development:		Investments:		Specialty Services:		Brokerage:	
Apartments:		Mortgages:		Commercial Construction:	Y	REIT:	Y	Property Management:	Y	Commercial Sales:	
Malls/Shopping:	Y	Title Insurance:		Residential Construction:				Online Services:		Residential Sales:	
Offices:		Property Insurance:		Land Development:	Y			Software/IT:		Specialty:	
Hotels/Motels:				Support Services:	Y			Consulting:			
Industrial/Warehouses:				Design/Engineering:							
Other:											

TYPES OF BUSINESS:

Real Estate Investment Trust
Community Shopping Centers

BRANDS/DIVISIONS/AFFILIATES:

CONTACTS:

Note: Officers with more than one job title may be intentionally listed here more than once.

Michael Carroll, CEO
John Braddon, CFO/Exec. VP
Steven Siegel, General Counsel/Exec. VP/Corp. Sec.
Dean Bernstein, Exec. VP-Acquisitions & Dispositions
Leonard Brumberg, Exec. VP-Portfolio Mgmt.
Steve Splain, Exec. VP
Michael Moss, Exec. VP
William Newman, Chmn.

Phone: 212-869-3000	**Fax:**
Toll-Free:	
Address: 420 Lexington Ave., New York, NY 10170 US	

GROWTH PLANS/SPECIAL FEATURES:

Centro Np LLC, formerly New Plan Excel Realty Trust, Inc. (NP) is a U.S. shopping center Real Estate Investment Trust (REIT). The firm is a subsidiary of Centro Properties Group. The company engages in the ownership, management and development of community and neighborhood shopping centers, with approximately 467 properties in 38 states with 68.3 million square feet of gross leasable area. The company's portfolio includes 289 wholly-owned properties; one property owned by a consolidated joint venture; and 177 properties held through unconsolidated joint ventures. The firm has a mix of convenience shopping and general merchandise properties, with both grocery and non-grocery anchors. The company also holds stakes in several joint ventures that invest in and develop retail real estate. In regards to new development, the firm has a policy of having a lease executed with an anchor tenant prior to making an investment. The firm's model for growth is both internal and external, focusing on aggressive management to maintain high occupancy rates and recognized anchor tenants, as well as on selective acquisitions of income-producing shopping centers or of centers that the firm can add value to through redevelopment or management. The gross leasable area of the firm's portfolio is over 90% leased and major tenants such as Hobby Lobby, Kroger, Wal-Mart, Sears, Publix Super Markets, Ahold USA, Safeway, and Walgreens serve as its anchor stores.

FINANCIALS:

Sales and profits are in thousands of dollars—add 000 to get the full amount. 2009 Note: Financial information for 2009 was not available for all companies at press time.

2009 Sales: $	2009 Profits: $	**U.S. Stock Ticker: Subsidiary**
2008 Sales: $	2008 Profits: $	**Int'l Ticker:** Int'l Exchange:
2007 Sales: $	2007 Profits: $	Employees:
2006 Sales: $456,975	2006 Profits: $135,217	Fiscal Year Ends: 12/31
2005 Sales: $473,293	2005 Profits: $306,324	Parent Company: CENTRO PROPERTIES GROUP

SALARIES/BENEFITS:

Pension Plan:	ESOP Stock Plan:	Profit Sharing:	Top Exec. Salary: $1,166,769	Bonus: $1,866,438
Savings Plan:	Stock Purch. Plan:		Second Exec. Salary: $404,423	Bonus: $605,001

OTHER THOUGHTS:

Apparent Women Officers or Directors: 2
Hot Spot for Advancement for Women/Minorities:

LOCATIONS: ("Y" = Yes)

West:	Southwest:	Midwest:	Southeast:	Northeast:	International:
Y	Y	Y	Y	Y	Y

NEW WORLD DEVELOPMENT COMPANY LIMITED www.nwd.com.hk

Industry Group Code: 5311 **Ranks within this company's industry group:** Sales: 6 Profits: 5

Properties:		Financial Services:		Construction/Development:		Investments:		Specialty Services:		Brokerage:	
Apartments:	Y	Mortgages:		Commercial Construction:	Y	REIT:		Property Management:	Y	Commercial Sales:	
Malls/Shopping:	Y	Title Insurance:		Residential Construction:	Y			Online Services:		Residential Sales:	
Offices:	Y	Property Insurance:	Y	Land Development:	Y			Software/IT:		Specialty:	
Hotels/Motels:	Y			Support Services:	Y			Consulting:			
Industrial/Warehouses:	Y			Design/Engineering:	Y						
Other:	Y										

TYPES OF BUSINESS:

Real Estate Holdings & Development

BRANDS/DIVISIONS/AFFILIATES:

New World China Land Limited
Hong Kong Property
Mainland China Property
Hotel Investment
New World Insurance
Hip Hing Construction
Taifook Securities
New World China Enterprises Projects Limited

CONTACTS:

Note: Officers with more than one job title may be intentionally listed here more than once.

Henry Cheng Kar-Shun, Managing Dir.
Adrian Cheng Chi-Kong, Exec. Dir.
Stewart Leung Chi-Kin, Exec. Dir.
David Liang Chong-Hou, Exec. Dir.
David Sin Wai-Kin, Exec. Dir.
Cheng Yu-Tung, Chmn.

Phone: 852-2523-1056 **Fax:** 852-2810-4673
Toll-Free:
Address: 18 Queen's Rd. Central, New World Tower, 30th Fl., Hong Kong, China

GROWTH PLANS/SPECIAL FEATURES:

New World Development Company Limited is a Hong Kong-based real estate investment holding firm operating in three primary segments: Property; Infrastructure and Service; and Department Store. The Property segment operates in three divisions: Hong Kong Property, Mainland China Property and Hotel Investment. Its Hong Kong property includes 46 projects totaling over 28.8 million square feet. Mainland China property is managed by subsidiary New World China Land Limited and encompasses properties in 21 metropolitan areas totaling approximately 28 million square feet of developable floor area. The hotel division has investments in 20 operational hotels throughout Hong Kong, Mainland China and Southeast Asia. The Infrastructure and Service segment is involved in infrastructure investments and facility management. It is focused on investments in energy, roads, water and ports projects, with a portfolio encompassing 384 miles of toll roads; a number of power plants; a coal trading company; wastewater treatment facilities; and container terminals with an annual capacity of 7.1 million twenty-foot equivalent units (TEUs). Its main facility management operations include the management of the Hong Kong Convention & Exhibition Centre and the ATL Logistics Centre; contracting activities, performed mostly through subsidiaries Hip Hing Construction and NWS Engineering; and financial services, offered through subsidiaries Taifook Securities and New World Insurance. The Department Store segment includes the activities of subsidiary New World Department Store China Limited, which operates 34 department stores totaling over 3 million square feet, located in 17 cities in Mainland China. The firm, through wholly-owned subsidiary New World Strategic Investment Limited, also invests in growing private companies that are within one to three years of an initial public stock listing in a variety of industries. New World China Enterprises Projects Limited, another subsidiary, provides project management services to several of the company's businesses.

FINANCIALS:

Sales and profits are in thousands of dollars—add 000 to get the full amount. 2009 Note: Financial information for 2009 was not available for all companies at press time.

2009 Sales: $3,144,740	2009 Profits: $268,360	**U.S. Stock Ticker:**
2008 Sales: $3,788,350	2008 Profits: $1,248,270	**Int'l Ticker: 0017** Int'l Exchange: Hong Kong-HKE
2007 Sales: $3,004,340	2007 Profits: $556,480	Employees:
2006 Sales: $	2006 Profits: $	Fiscal Year Ends: 6/30
2005 Sales: $	2005 Profits: $	Parent Company:

SALARIES/BENEFITS:

Pension Plan:	ESOP Stock Plan:	Profit Sharing:	Top Exec. Salary: $	Bonus: $
Savings Plan:	Stock Purch. Plan:		Second Exec. Salary: $	Bonus: $

OTHER THOUGHTS:

Apparent Women Officers or Directors: 1
Hot Spot for Advancement for Women/Minorities:

LOCATIONS: ("Y" = Yes)

West:	Southwest:	Midwest:	Southeast:	Northeast:	International:
					Y

NEWCASTLE INVESTMENT CORP

www.newcastleinv.com

Industry Group Code: 531120 **Ranks within this company's industry group:** Sales: 37 Profits: 63

Properties:		Financial Services:		Construction/Development:		Investments:		Specialty Services:		Brokerage:	
Apartments:		Mortgages:	Y	Commercial Construction:		REIT:	Y	Property Management:	Y	Commercial Sales:	
Malls/Shopping:		Title Insurance:		Residential Construction:				Online Services:		Residential Sales:	
Offices:		Property Insurance:		Land Development:				Software/IT:		Specialty:	
Hotels/Motels:				Support Services:				Consulting:			
Industrial/Warehouses:				Design/Engineering:							
Other:											

TYPES OF BUSINESS:

Real Estate Investment Trust
Real Estate Securities
Real Estate Loan Investments
Loans & Mortgages
Property Management

BRANDS/DIVISIONS/AFFILIATES:

Fortress Investment Group LLC
Nationstar Mortgage LLC

CONTACTS:

Note: Officers with more than one job title may be intentionally listed here more than once.

Kenneth M. Riis, CEO
Jonathan Ashley, COO
Kenneth M. Riis, Pres.
Brian C. Sigman, CFO
Randal A. Nardone, Corp. Sec.
Lily Donohue, Dir.-Investor Rel.
Phillip J. Evanski, Chief Investment Officer
Wesley R. Edens, Chmn.

Phone: 212-798-6100	**Fax:** 212-798-6133
Toll-Free:	
Address: 1345 Ave. of the Americas, New York, NY 10105 US	

GROWTH PLANS/SPECIAL FEATURES:

Newcastle Investment Corp. is a REIT (Real Estate Investment Trust) and finance company that invests in real estate securities and other real estate-related assets. An affiliate of Fortress Investment Group LLC provides day-to-day management of the firm's operations. Fortress owns approximately 10% of Newcastle. The company has a $5.6 billion investment portfolio, consisting of $3.5 billion in commercial assets, $1.2 billion in residential assets, and $0.9 in corporate assets. Its activities cover four major categories: Real Estate Securities, which represent 52.1% of Newcastle's assets; Real Estate Related Loans, 16.3%; Residential Mortgage Loans, 10.9%; and Operating Real Estate, 0.3%. Additionally, 8.9% of its assets consist of restricted and unrestricted cash and other miscellaneous net assets. The firm's Real Estate Securities activities consist of diversified, credit-sensitive real estate securities, including commercial mortgage-backed securities, asset backed securities, REIT debt and Federal National Mortgage Association (Fannie Mae) and Federal Home Loan Mortgage Corporation (Freddie Mac) securities. Its Real Estate Related Loans activities consist of acquired and company-originated loans made to well-capitalized real estate owners, including B-notes, mezzanine loans, corporate bank loans and real estate loans. Newcastle's Residential Mortgage Loans activities consist of acquiring residential loans, manufactured housing loans and subprime mortgage loans. The Operating Real Estate activities consist of acquiring and managing direct and indirect interests in the operating real estate sector.

FINANCIALS:

Sales and profits are in thousands of dollars—add 000 to get the full amount. 2009 Note: Financial information for 2009 was not available for all companies at press time.

2009 Sales: $361,866	2009 Profits: $-209,904	**U.S. Stock Ticker: NCT**
2008 Sales: $468,867	2008 Profits: $-2,985,352	**Int'l Ticker:** Int'l Exchange:
2007 Sales: $680,535	2007 Profits: $-65,457	Employees:
2006 Sales: $529,818	2006 Profits: $127,923	Fiscal Year Ends: 12/31
2005 Sales: $378,213	2005 Profits: $116,955	Parent Company:

SALARIES/BENEFITS:

Pension Plan:	ESOP Stock Plan:	Profit Sharing:	Top Exec. Salary: $	Bonus: $
Savings Plan:	Stock Purch. Plan:		Second Exec. Salary: $	Bonus: $

OTHER THOUGHTS:

Apparent Women Officers or Directors: 1
Hot Spot for Advancement for Women/Minorities:

LOCATIONS: ("Y" = Yes)

West:	Southwest:	Midwest:	Southeast:	Northeast:	International:
				Y	Y

NEWHALL LAND & FARMING

www.valencia.com

Industry Group Code: 5311 **Ranks within this company's industry group:** Sales: Profits:

Properties:		Financial Services:		Construction/Development:		Investments:		Specialty Services:		Brokerage:	
Apartments:	Y	Mortgages:		Commercial Construction:	Y	REIT:		Property Management:	Y	Commercial Sales:	Y
Malls/Shopping:	Y	Title Insurance:		Residential Construction:	Y			Online Services:		Residential Sales:	Y
Offices:	Y	Property Insurance:		Land Development:	Y			Software/IT:		Specialty:	Y
Hotels/Motels:				Support Services:				Consulting:			
Industrial/Warehouses:	Y			Design/Engineering:							
Other:	Y										

TYPES OF BUSINESS:

Real Estate Investment & Development
Master-Planned Communities
Commercial Property Management
Agricultural Land Management
Residential Development
Land Sales

BRANDS/DIVISIONS/AFFILIATES:

LandSource Communities Development LLC
Newhall Land Development LLC
West Hills
RiverVillage
Valencia
Newhall Ranch
West Creek

CONTACTS: *Note: Officers with more than one job title may be intentionally listed here more than once.*

Gregory H. McWilliams, Pres.
Donald L. Kimball, CFO/Sr. VP
Gary M. Cusumano, Chmn.

Phone: 661-255-4000	**Fax:** 661-255-3960
Toll-Free: 888-897-6815	
Address: 23823 Valencia Blvd., Valencia, CA 91355 US	

GROWTH PLANS/SPECIAL FEATURES:

The Newhall Land and Farming Company, a subsidiary of Newhall Land Development LLC (formerly LandSource Communities Development LLC), develops new towns and master-planned, mixed-use communities. Newhall owns 15,000 acres in California from the original 48,000 acres acquired by Henry Mayo Newhall in 1882. The land, initially used for ranching, agriculture and oil production, today includes the towns of Valencia, 30 miles north of downtown Los Angeles, and Newhall Ranch, which is being planned to include 20,000 homes on 12,000 acres adjacent to Valencia. The company expects to break ground on Newhall Ranch in 2010. Since 1965, Newhall has been developing the town of Valencia on a portion of the company's landholdings, which now provides over 60,000 jobs. Valencia is notable for its environmentally sensitive planning, with natural amenities such as an extensive network of pedestrian walkways, 10 square miles acres of open space, long range water planning and 30 miles of the free-flowing Santa Clara River. Valencia is comprised of villages West Creek, West Hills and RiverVillage. Within its communities, Newhall sells residential lots to merchant builders, operates a portfolio of commercial properties, provides building-ready sites for sale to industrial and commercial developers and users and owns a public water utility, the Valencia Water Company. In August 2009, the firm and its parent emerged from Chapter 11 bankruptcy; LandSource emerged as Newhall Land Development.

FINANCIALS: **Sales and profits are in thousands of dollars—add 000 to get the full amount. 2009 Note: Financial information for 2009 was not available for all companies at press time.**

2009 Sales: $	2009 Profits: $	**U.S. Stock Ticker: Subsidiary**
2008 Sales: $	2008 Profits: $	**Int'l Ticker:** Int'l Exchange:
2007 Sales: $	2007 Profits: $	Employees:
2006 Sales: $	2006 Profits: $	Fiscal Year Ends: 12/31
2005 Sales: $	2005 Profits: $	Parent Company: NEWHALL LAND DEVELOMENT LLC

SALARIES/BENEFITS:

Pension Plan:	ESOP Stock Plan:	Profit Sharing:	Top Exec. Salary: $	Bonus: $
Savings Plan: Y	Stock Purch. Plan:		Second Exec. Salary: $	Bonus: $

OTHER THOUGHTS:

Apparent Women Officers or Directors:
Hot Spot for Advancement for Women/Minorities:

LOCATIONS: ("Y" = Yes)

West:	Southwest:	Midwest:	Southeast:	Northeast:	International:
Y					

NH HOTELES SA

www.nh-hotels.com

Industry Group Code: 721110 **Ranks within this company's industry group:** Sales: 7 Profits: 12

Properties:		Financial Services:		Construction/Development:		Investments:		Specialty Services:		Brokerage:	
Apartments:		Mortgages:		Commercial Construction:	Y	REIT:		Property Management:	Y	Commercial Sales:	
Malls/Shopping:		Title Insurance:		Residential Construction:	Y			Online Services:		Residential Sales:	
Offices:		Property Insurance:		Land Development:	Y			Software/IT:		Specialty:	
Hotels/Motels:	Y			Support Services:				Consulting:			
Industrial/Warehouses:				Design/Engineering:							
Other:	Y										

TYPES OF BUSINESS:

Hotels
Golf Courses
Restaurants

BRANDS/DIVISIONS/AFFILIATES:

Sotogrande SA
Aymerich Golf Management
Grand Jolly Srl
Compagnia Italiana dei Jolly Hotels SpA

CONTACTS: *Note: Officers with more than one job title may be intentionally listed here more than once.*

Gabriele Burgio, CEO
Francisco Zinser, COO
Gabriele Burgio, Pres.
Roberto Chollet, CFO
Andreas Westerburg, Dir.-Sales
Juan Mora, Dir.-Human Resources
Francisco Souto, Dir.-IT
Luis Ortega, Dir.-Eng., Environment & Maintenance
Domingo Benet, Dir.-Admin. & Finance
Leopoldo Gonzalez, General Counsel
Paolo Gobbetti, Dir.-European Resort Oper.
Ignacio Aranguren, Chief Strategy Officer
Victor Bermejo, Corp. Controller
Juan Mora, Dir.-Corp. Responsibility & Institutional Rel.
Ignacio Diaz, Dir.-Auditing
Santiago Lopez, Dir.-Buildings & Real Estate
Inigo Onieva, Dir.-Mktg.
Gabriele Burgio, Chmn.
Francisco Medina, Dir.-Mexico & Caribbean Area
Pedro Martinez, Dir.-Purchasing

Phone: 34-91-451-97-18	**Fax:** 34-91-451-97-64
Toll-Free: 800-232-9860	
Address: Santa Engracia 120, Edifico Central, Madrid, 28003 Spain	

GROWTH PLANS/SPECIAL FEATURES:

NH Hoteles S.A., based in Spain, is a hotel operator with 398 hotels with 60,000 rooms in 24 countries across Europe, the Americas and Africa, ranging from budget hotels to four-star resorts. In Europe, NH has hotels in Spain, Andorra, Germany, Italy, Luxembourg, Switzerland, the Netherlands, Belgium, Austria, the U.K., France, Portugal, Poland, the Czech Republic, Romania and Hungary. In the Americas, the firm has hotels in Mexico, the U.S., Argentina, Cuba, Chile, Uruguay and the Dominican Republic. In South Africa, the company has two hotels, one in Plettenberg Bay and the other in Cape Town. Subsidiary Sotogrande S.A. operates a residential property development site in Spain, and controls a 55% interest in Aymerich Golf Management, a golf course management and development company with approximately 40 active courses in Spain and Portugal. Also, through majority-owned subsidiary Grand Jolly S.r.l., the firm maintains an interest in Compagnia Italiana dei Jolly Hotels S.p.A., which operates approximately 45 hotels in Europe and one in the U.S., the Jolly Hotel Madison Towers in New York, New York. In October 2009, the firm completed its acquisition of Grupo Hesperia, a hotel management company, adding 51 hotels to its portfolio. In February 2010, the firm sold three of its Hilton-branded properties in Mexico for $57 million. In April 2010, NH Hoteles agreed to sell the Jolly St. Ermin's Hotel in London to investors Angelo, Gordon & Co.; Amerimar Enterprises; and Gracemark Invesments.

FINANCIALS: **Sales and profits are in thousands of dollars—add 000 to get the full amount. 2009 Note: Financial information for 2009 was not available for all companies at press time.**

2009 Sales: $1,615,110	2009 Profits: $-129,530	**U.S. Stock Ticker: NHHEY.PK**
2008 Sales: $1,997,070	2008 Profits: $34,930	**Int'l Ticker: NHH** Int'l Exchange: Madrid-MCE
2007 Sales: $1,962,270	2007 Profits: $100,870	Employees:
2006 Sales: $1,630,100	2006 Profits: $91,800	Fiscal Year Ends: 12/31
2005 Sales: $1,461,200	2005 Profits: $91,500	Parent Company:

SALARIES/BENEFITS:

Pension Plan:	ESOP Stock Plan:	Profit Sharing:	Top Exec. Salary: $	Bonus: $
Savings Plan:	Stock Purch. Plan:		Second Exec. Salary: $	Bonus: $

OTHER THOUGHTS:

Apparent Women Officers or Directors: 2
Hot Spot for Advancement for Women/Minorities:

LOCATIONS: ("Y" = Yes)

West:	Southwest:	Midwest:	Southeast:	Northeast:	International:
	Y		Y	Y	Y

NRT INCORPORATED

www.nrtllc.com

Industry Group Code: 531210 **Ranks within this company's industry group:** Sales: Profits:

Properties:		Financial Services:		Construction/Development:		Investments:		Specialty Services:		Brokerage:	
Apartments:		Mortgages:	Y	Commercial Construction:		REIT:		Property Management:		Commercial Sales:	Y
Malls/Shopping:		Title Insurance:		Residential Construction:				Online Services:		Residential Sales:	Y
Offices:		Property Insurance:		Land Development:				Software/IT:		Specialty:	
Hotels/Motels:				Support Services:				Consulting:			
Industrial/Warehouses:				Design/Engineering:							
Other:											

TYPES OF BUSINESS:

Real Estate Brokerage
Mortgage Lending
Real Estate Services

BRANDS/DIVISIONS/AFFILIATES:

Realogy Corporation
Coldwell Banker Real Estate Corp
ERA
Sotheby's International Realty
Corcoran Group (The)
Coldwell Banker Commercial NRT
ERA Mortgage
Home Sellers Inc

CONTACTS: *Note: Officers with more than one job title may be intentionally listed here more than once.*

Bruce G. Zipf, CEO
Judy Reeves, COO/Exec. VP
Bruce G. Zipf, Pres.
Kevin Greene, CFO/Sr. VP
Dan Barnett, Sr. VP-Mktg.
Lauren De Simon Johnson, Sr. VP-Human Resources
Ken Hoffert, General Counsel/Sr. VP
Mike Goad, Sr. VP-Oper.
Peter J. Sobeck, Sr. VP-Bus. Dev.
Jeff Culbertson, Exec. VP-Southwest & Sacramento Region
Budge Huskey, Exec. VP-Southeast Region
Greg Macres, Exec. VP-Western Region
Monty D. Smith, Sr. VP-Strategic Initiatives
Robert M. Becker, Chmn.

Phone: 973-407-5296	**Fax:** 973-407-7999
Toll-Free:	
Address: 1 Campus Dr., Parsippany, NJ 07054 US	

GROWTH PLANS/SPECIAL FEATURES:

NRT LLC, a subsidiary of Realogy Corporation, is a leading residential real estate brokerage company. The company, through subsidiaries Coldwell Banker, ERA, Sotheby's International Realty and The Corcoran Group has operations in more than 35 of the largest markets in the U.S., with about 760 offices in its extended family. Coldwell Banker operates through a handful of various divisions, which offer commercial and residential real estate brokerage services and mortgage lending. Coldwell Banker Commercial NRT is the firm's commercial real estate brokerage division, with operation in 21 states. Additionally, Coldwell Banker Commercial affiliates operate throughout North America, South America, Europe, Africa, Asia and Australia. ERA is a worldwide franchised real estate brokerage that also provides mortgage lending through its subsidiary ERA Mortgage. Sotheby's International Realty, acquired from Sotheby Holding Corporation, the owners of Sotheby Auction House, specializes in luxury commercial and residential real estate worldwide. The Corcoran Group operates in New York City, the Hamptons and Palm Beach. NRT's growth strategy involves an aggressive attitude towards expansion focusing on companies that have established themselves locally. Acquired companies are then affiliated with one of NRT's brands and allowed to continue a relatively independent management, simply building upon pre-established success and local identity. . In May 2009, Sotheby's acquired Teton Village Realty of Jackson Hole, Wyoming. Coldwell Banker has recently acquired several companies throughout 2009 and 2010, sequentially including Home Sellers, Inc. of Portland, Maine in March 2009; Drake Realtors Inc. of Dupage County, Illinois in July 2009; Tourtelot Brothers, Inc. of St. Petersburg, Florida in August; Blue Realty GMAC of New Jersey in October 2009; Coldwell Banker Wikle Properties of Palm Harbor, Florida in November 2009; and Fine Homes Connecticut/USA of Westport, Connecticut in April 2010.

FINANCIALS: **Sales and profits are in thousands of dollars—add 000 to get the full amount. 2009 Note: Financial information for 2009 was not available for all companies at press time.**

2009 Sales: $	2009 Profits: $	**U.S. Stock Ticker: Subsidiary**
2008 Sales: $	2008 Profits: $	**Int'l Ticker:** Int'l Exchange:
2007 Sales: $	2007 Profits: $	Employees:
2006 Sales: $	2006 Profits: $	Fiscal Year Ends: 12/31
2005 Sales: $	2005 Profits: $	Parent Company: REALOGY CORPORATION

SALARIES/BENEFITS:

Pension Plan:	ESOP Stock Plan:	Profit Sharing:	Top Exec. Salary: $	Bonus: $
Savings Plan:	Stock Purch. Plan:		Second Exec. Salary: $	Bonus: $

OTHER THOUGHTS:

Apparent Women Officers or Directors: 4
Hot Spot for Advancement for Women/Minorities: Y

LOCATIONS: ("Y" = Yes)

West:	Southwest:	Midwest:	Southeast:	Northeast:	International:
Y	Y	Y	Y	Y	Y

NVR INC

www.nvrinc.com

Industry Group Code: 2361 **Ranks within this company's industry group:** Sales: 6 Profits: 2

Properties:		Financial Services:		Construction/Development:		Investments:		Specialty Services:		Brokerage:	
Apartments:		Mortgages:	Y	Commercial Construction:		REIT:		Property Management:		Commercial Sales:	
Malls/Shopping:		Title Insurance:	Y	Residential Construction:	Y			Online Services:		Residential Sales:	Y
Offices:		Property Insurance:		Land Development:				Software/IT:		Specialty:	
Hotels/Motels:				Support Services:				Consulting:			
Industrial/Warehouses:				Design/Engineering:							
Other:											

TYPES OF BUSINESS:

Residential Construction
Mortgages
Townhouse Construction
Condominium Construction

BRANDS/DIVISIONS/AFFILIATES:

Ryan Homes
NVHomes
Fox Ridge Homes
NVR Mortgage Finance Inc
Rymarc Homes

CONTACTS: *Note: Officers with more than one job title may be intentionally listed here more than once.*

Paul Saville, CEO
Dennis Seremet, CFO
Robert Henley, Controller
William Inman, Pres., NVR Mortgage Finance, Inc.
Dwight C. Schar, Chmn.

Phone: 703-956-4000	**Fax:** 703-956-4750
Toll-Free:	
Address: 11700 Plz. America Dr., Ste. 500, Reston, VA 20190 US	

GROWTH PLANS/SPECIAL FEATURES:

NVR, Inc. is primarily engaged in the construction and sale of single-family detached homes, townhomes and condominium buildings. Additionally, NVR offers mortgage banking services through its subsidiary NVR Mortgage Finance, Inc. (NVRM). The company operates in 14 states, with concentration in the Washington, D.C. and Baltimore, Maryland metropolitan areas, which accounted for 48% of revenues. NVR's homebuilding operations include the sale and construction of single-family detached homes, townhomes and condominium buildings under four brand names: Ryan Homes, NVHomes, Fox Ridge Homes and Rymarc Homes. The Ryan, Fox Ridge and Rymarc products are moderately priced and marketed primarily to first-time homeowners and first-time move-up buyers. Ryan Homes are currently sold in 25 metropolitan areas, including Maryland, Virginia, West Virginia, Pennsylvania, New York, Indiana, Florida, North Carolina, South Carolina, Ohio, New Jersey, Delaware and Kentucky. NVHomes are marketed primarily to move-up and upscale buyers and is sold in the Washington, D.C., Baltimore, Philadelphia and the Maryland Eastern Shore metropolitan areas. The Fox Ridge product is sold in the Nashville, Tennessee, metropolitan area and Rymarc homes are sold in Columbia, South Carolina. The average price of a unit sold is roughly $296,000. NVR also provides mortgage-related services through its mortgage banking operations, which include subsidiaries that broker title insurance and perform title searches. NVRM originates mortgage loans for NVR's homebuilding customers, making it dependent on the homebuilding operations. NVRM sells all mortgage loans it closes to investors in the secondary markets on a servicing released basis; it is an approved seller/servicer for FHLMC, VA, FNMA, GNMA and FHA mortgage loans.

Employees are offered benefits including life, AD&D, medical and dental insurance; home purchase, mortgage and settlement services discounts; paid holidays; an employee assistance program; and dependent scholarship awards.

FINANCIALS: **Sales and profits are in thousands of dollars—add 000 to get the full amount. 2009 Note: Financial information for 2009 was not available for all companies at press time.**

2009 Sales: $2,683,467	2009 Profits: $192,180	**U.S. Stock Ticker: NVR**
2008 Sales: $3,638,702	2008 Profits: $100,892	**Int'l Ticker:** Int'l Exchange:
2007 Sales: $5,048,187	2007 Profits: $333,955	Employees: 2,688
2006 Sales: $6,036,236	2006 Profits: $587,412	Fiscal Year Ends: 12/31
2005 Sales: $5,177,743	2005 Profits: $697,559	Parent Company:

SALARIES/BENEFITS:

Pension Plan:	ESOP Stock Plan: Y	Profit Sharing: Y	Top Exec. Salary: $800,000	Bonus: $400,000
Savings Plan: Y	Stock Purch. Plan:		Second Exec. Salary: $475,000	Bonus: $237,500

OTHER THOUGHTS:

Apparent Women Officers or Directors:
Hot Spot for Advancement for Women/Minorities:

LOCATIONS: ("Y" = Yes)

West:	Southwest:	Midwest:	Southeast:	Northeast:	International:
		Y	Y	Y	

OAKWOOD WORLDWIDE

www.oakwood.com

Industry Group Code: 721110 **Ranks within this company's industry group:** Sales: Profits:

Properties:		Financial Services:		Construction/Development:		Investments:		Specialty Services:		Brokerage:	
Apartments:		Mortgages:		Commercial Construction:		REIT:		Property Management:		Commercial Sales:	
Malls/Shopping:		Title Insurance:		Residential Construction:				Online Services:		Residential Sales:	
Offices:		Property Insurance:		Land Development:				Software/IT:		Specialty:	
Hotels/Motels:	Y			Support Services:				Consulting:			
Industrial/Warehouses:				Design/Engineering:							
Other:											

TYPES OF BUSINESS:

Rental Housing
Temporary Housing
Corporate Apartments

BRANDS/DIVISIONS/AFFILIATES:

Oakwood Corporate Housing
Oakwood Premier
Oakwood Residence
Oakwood Apartment

CONTACTS:

Note: Officers with more than one job title may be intentionally listed here more than once.

Howard Ruby, CEO
Ric Villarreal, Pres.
Bill Foltz, CFO/Sr. VP
Chris Ahearn, Sr. VP-Worldwide Sales & Mktg.
Bill Maxwell, Sr. VP-Human Resources
Marina Lubinsky, CIO/Sr. VP
Gavan James, Sr. VP/Gen. Mgr.-Oakwood Corp. Housing
Howard Ruby, Chmn.
P.G. Mathew, Managing Dir.-Oakwood Asia Pacific

Phone: 310-478-1021 **Fax:** 310-444-2210
Toll-Free: 877-902-0832
Address: 2222 Corinth Ave., Los Angeles, CA 90064 US

GROWTH PLANS/SPECIAL FEATURES:

Oakwood Worldwide offers temporary housing, corporate housing and multifamily property management. The firm provides approximately 15,000 furnished and unfurnished accommodations in roughly 4,000 locations throughout the U.S., the U.K., and the Asia Pacific region through its Oakwood Corporate Housing, Oakwood Premier, Oakwood Residence and Oakwood Apartment brands. Each apartment is equipped with fine furnishings, housewares, telephone service and cable television service. Oakwood services for temporary housing include weekly housekeeping, an on-call concierge and maintenance services. These services are available in most areas nationwide on a day-by-day pay schedule, and are often used by production crews for the footage of television shows or movies. The company also manages traditional long-term apartment residences through its 40 apartment communities in the U.S., with both furnished and unfurnished apartments. Oakwood has apartments of all styles, residing in differing natural environments, and will custom fit its models to its clients. During 2009, Oakwood expanded its international presence with the acquisitions and openings of properties in Mumbai, India; London, U.K.; Pune, India; Bangkok, Thailand; Hangzhou, China; and Manila, Philippines.

Oakwood offers its employees medical, dental, vision, prescription, life and AD&D insurance; short- and long-term disability; a 401(k) plan; access to a credit union; career development through Oakwood University; educational reimbursement; an employee assistance program; corporate discounts; bonus opportunities; annual company functions; flexible spending accounts; and referral bonuses.

FINANCIALS:

Sales and profits are in thousands of dollars—add 000 to get the full amount. 2009 Note: Financial information for 2009 was not available for all companies at press time.

2009 Sales: $	2009 Profits: $	**U.S. Stock Ticker: Private**
2008 Sales: $	2008 Profits: $	**Int'l Ticker:** Int'l Exchange:
2007 Sales: $	2007 Profits: $	Employees:
2006 Sales: $	2006 Profits: $	Fiscal Year Ends:
2005 Sales: $	2005 Profits: $	Parent Company:

SALARIES/BENEFITS:

Pension Plan:	ESOP Stock Plan:	Profit Sharing:	Top Exec. Salary: $	Bonus: $
Savings Plan: Y	Stock Purch. Plan:		Second Exec. Salary: $	Bonus: $

OTHER THOUGHTS:

Apparent Women Officers or Directors: 1
Hot Spot for Advancement for Women/Minorities:

LOCATIONS: ("Y" = Yes)

West:	Southwest:	Midwest:	Southeast:	Northeast:	International:
Y	Y	Y	Y	Y	Y

OBEROI GROUP (EIH LTD)

www.oberoihotels.com

Industry Group Code: 721110 **Ranks within this company's industry group:** Sales: 24 Profits: 11

Properties:		Financial Services:		Construction/Development:		Investments:		Specialty Services:		Brokerage:	
Apartments:		Mortgages:		Commercial Construction:		REIT:		Property Management:	Y	Commercial Sales:	
Malls/Shopping:		Title Insurance:		Residential Construction:				Online Services:		Residential Sales:	
Offices:		Property Insurance:		Land Development:				Software/IT:		Specialty:	
Hotels/Motels:	Y			Support Services:				Consulting:			
Industrial/Warehouses:				Design/Engineering:							
Other:											

TYPES OF BUSINESS:

Luxury Hotels
Commercial Hotels
Cruise Ships
Travel Agency
Charter Aircraft
Tour Services
Inflight Catering
Car Rental

BRANDS/DIVISIONS/AFFILIATES:

EIH Limited
Trident Hotels
Oberoi Hotels and Resorts
Mercury Travels
Clarke's Hotel
Maidens Hotel

CONTACTS: *Note: Officers with more than one job title may be intentionally listed here more than once.*

P.R.S. Oberoi, CEO
Mark Allvey, VP-Sales & Mktg., EMEA
Justin Purves, Dir.-Sales, Leisure, Europe
P.R.S. Oberoi, Chmn.
Samantha Steckbeck, VP-Leisure Sales, The Americas

Phone: 91-11-2389-0505	**Fax:** 91-11-2389-0582
Toll-Free: 800-562-3764	
Address: 7 Sham Nath Marg, Delhi, 110 054 India	

GROWTH PLANS/SPECIAL FEATURES:

The Oberoi Group, also known as EIH, Ltd., owns or manages 28 Oberoi and Trident brand luxury hotels and three small cruiser ships in five countries. Additionally, the group operates airport restaurants, travel and tour services, in-flight catering, car rentals, project management and corporate air charters. The firm has locations across the Asia-Pacific region: 11 hotels in India; two hotels in Indonesia; two hotels and two Nile river boats in Egypt; one hotel in Mauritius; and one hotel in Saudi Arabia. The company also operates two heritage hotels, the Maidens Hotel and the Clarke's Hotel, which are located in historic colonial areas. The firm offers a member program called Connections, which rewards points for staying at the hotels. These points can be redeemed for a variety of things, including additional stay at the Group's hotels. Many of the hotels feature spas, which can also be used by non-guests. Additionally, the firm operates its own travel agency through subsidiary Mercury Travels. Mercury has 15 offices in India and marketing locations in New York and Frankfurt. Although Mercury primarily works to book corporate travel and leisure travelers staying at an Oberoi location, it does offer limited services for other travelers. The Oberoi Aviation segment of the group offers two aircraft for charter: a Hawker 850 XP and a King Air C-90A. The planes can be booked with as little as 72 hours notice and fly between locations within India along with a limited international service. The flagship Oberoi hotel and the adjoining Trident in Mumbai were attacked by terrorists in November 2008, with significant damage and some lives lost. The Trident was reopened in late 2008, and the Oberoi Mumbai reopened in April 2009 after extensive renovations.

Oberoi Group maintains The Oberoi Centre of Learning and Development (OCLD), which offers a specialized two year course in hospitality management.

FINANCIALS: **Sales and profits are in thousands of dollars—add 000 to get the full amount. 2009 Note: Financial information for 2009 was not available for all companies at press time.**

2009 Sales: $	2009 Profits: $	**U.S. Stock Ticker:**
2008 Sales: $270,000	2008 Profits: $47,000	**Int'l Ticker: 500840** Int'l Exchange: Bombay-BSE
2007 Sales: $	2007 Profits: $	Employees: 9,175
2006 Sales: $	2006 Profits: $	Fiscal Year Ends: 3/31
2005 Sales: $	2005 Profits: $	Parent Company:

SALARIES/BENEFITS:

Pension Plan:	ESOP Stock Plan:	Profit Sharing:	Top Exec. Salary: $	Bonus: $
Savings Plan:	Stock Purch. Plan:		Second Exec. Salary: $	Bonus: $

OTHER THOUGHTS:

Apparent Women Officers or Directors:
Hot Spot for Advancement for Women/Minorities:

LOCATIONS: ("Y" = Yes)

West:	Southwest:	Midwest:	Southeast:	Northeast:	International:
					Y

ODEBRECHT SA

www.odebrecht.com.br

Industry Group Code: 237 **Ranks within this company's industry group:** Sales: Profits:

Properties:		Financial Services:		Construction/Development:		Investments:		Specialty Services:		Brokerage:	
Apartments:		Mortgages:		Commercial Construction:	Y	REIT:		Property Management:		Commercial Sales:	
Malls/Shopping:		Title Insurance:		Residential Construction:				Online Services:		Residential Sales:	
Offices:		Property Insurance:		Land Development:	Y			Software/IT:		Specialty:	
Hotels/Motels:				Support Services:				Consulting:			
Industrial/Warehouses:				Design/Engineering:							
Other:											

TYPES OF BUSINESS:

Engineering & Construction
Environmental Engineering
Real Estate Development
Insurance and Warranties Services
Ethanol and Sugar

BRANDS/DIVISIONS/AFFILIATES:

Construtora Norbeto Odebrecht SA
Odebrecht Oleo e Gas Ldta
Foz do Brazil SA
Odebrecht Realizacoes Imobiliarias SA
Braskem SA
ETH Bioenergia SA
Odebrecht Investimentos em Infraestrutura
Odeprev Odebrecht Previdencia

CONTACTS: *Note: Officers with more than one job title may be intentionally listed here more than once.*

Jose de Freitas Mascarenhas, Opportunities Dev. & Representation
Emilio Odebrecht, Chmn.

Phone: 55-71-2105-1111 **Fax:** 55-71-2105-1112
Toll-Free:
Address: Av. Luis Viana, 2841 Parelela Edificio Odebrecht, Salvador, 41730-900 Brazil

GROWTH PLANS/SPECIAL FEATURES:

Odebrecht SA is a Brazilian company with operations in several diversified sectors. These include engineering and construction; oil and gas; real estate development; ethanol and sugar; chemicals and petrochemical; environmental engineering; and support services. The company conducts its operations via its many subsidiaries. Construtora Norbeto Odebrecht SA is the company's engineering and construction sector subsidiary that focuses on such projects as highways, thermal electric plants, railroads, airports, steel mills, offshore operation rigs and buildings. Subsidiary, Odebrecht Oleo e Gas Ldta, operates the company's oil and gas sector, which focuses on field exploration, production and services. Subsidiary, Odebrecht Realizacoes Imobiliarias SA conducts the company's real estate development activities that include residential, corporate, commercial, tourism and mixed use developments. Subsidiary, ETH Bioenergia SA operates the ethanol and sugar sector, and includes sugarcane cultivation, harvesting, ethanol production and energy cogeneration. Subsidiary, Braskem operates the chemical and petrochemical sector, which focuses primarily on thermoplastic resins. Foz do Brazil SA, is the subsidiary that operates the environmental engineering sector, which provides waste and industrial effluent treatment, sanitation services and urban solid waste disposal. Additionally, the company also offers support services in the areas of infrastructure investment, insurance, warranties and pension funds. Subsidiary, Odebrecht Investimentos em Infraestrutura provides infrastructure investments in energy, transportation and logistics. Subsidiary, Odebrecht Administradora e Corretora de Seguros Ltda provides insurance and warranties services that focus on protecting assets and managing risks. Lastly, the company offers pension fund services through its subsidiary Odeprev Odebrecht Previdencia.

FINANCIALS: **Sales and profits are in thousands of dollars—add 000 to get the full amount. 2009 Note: Financial information for 2009 was not available for all companies at press time.**

2009 Sales: $	2009 Profits: $	**U.S. Stock Ticker: Private**
2008 Sales: $	2008 Profits: $	**Int'l Ticker:** Int'l Exchange:
2007 Sales: $	2007 Profits: $	Employees:
2006 Sales: $	2006 Profits: $	Fiscal Year Ends:
2005 Sales: $	2005 Profits: $	Parent Company:

SALARIES/BENEFITS:

Pension Plan:	ESOP Stock Plan:	Profit Sharing:	Top Exec. Salary: $	Bonus: $
Savings Plan:	Stock Purch. Plan:		Second Exec. Salary: $	Bonus: $

OTHER THOUGHTS:

Apparent Women Officers or Directors:
Hot Spot for Advancement for Women/Minorities:

LOCATIONS: ("Y" = Yes)

West:	Southwest:	Midwest:	Southeast:	Northeast:	International:
					Y

OMEGA HEALTHCARE INVESTORS

www.omegahealthcare.com

Industry Group Code: 531120 **Ranks within this company's industry group:** Sales: 56 Profits: 27

Properties:		Financial Services:		Construction/Development:		Investments:		Specialty Services:		Brokerage:	
Apartments:		Mortgages:	Y	Commercial Construction:		REIT:	Y	Property Management:	Y	Commercial Sales:	
Malls/Shopping:		Title Insurance:		Residential Construction:				Online Services:		Residential Sales:	
Offices:		Property Insurance:		Land Development:				Software/IT:		Specialty:	
Hotels/Motels:				Support Services:				Consulting:			
Industrial/Warehouses:				Design/Engineering:							
Other:	Y										

TYPES OF BUSINESS:

Real Estate Investment Trust
Health Care Facilities
Long-Term Care Facilities
Lease & Mortgage Financing

BRANDS/DIVISIONS/AFFILIATES:

CONTACTS:

Note: Officers with more than one job title may be intentionally listed here more than once.

C. Taylor Pickett, CEO
Daniel J. Booth, COO
Robert O. Stephenson, CFO
R. Lee Crabill, Jr., Sr. VP-Oper.
Michael D. Ritz, Chief Acct. Officer
Bernard J. Korman, Chmn.

Phone: 410-427-1700	**Fax:** 410-427-8800
Toll-Free: 866-996-6342	
Address: 200 International Cir., Ste. 3500, Hunt Valley, MD 21030 US	

GROWTH PLANS/SPECIAL FEATURES:

Omega Healthcare Investors, Inc. is a self-administered Real Estate Investment Trust (REIT) investing in healthcare facilities, particularly long-term care facilities located in the U.S. The firm provides lease or mortgage financing to qualified operators of skilled nursing facilities and, to a lesser extent, assisted living facilities, independent living facilities and rehabilitation and acute care facilities. Omega's portfolio of investments is comprised of 293 healthcare facilities (approximately 34,312 licensed beds) located in 31 states and operated by 35 third-party operators. The portfolio includes 265 skilled nursing facilities; seven assisted living facilities; and five specialty facilities. In addition, the firm maintains fixed rate mortgages on 14 long-term healthcare facilities, as well as two skilled nursing facilities owned and operated by Omega and one skilled nursing facility as held-for-sale. The company has sought to maintain a diversified investment portfolio in terms of geography and operators, and generally focuses on established, creditworthy, middle-market healthcare operators. Factors considered by Omega in evaluating potential investments include the quality and experience of management; the facility's historical and forecasted cash flow; the construction quality, condition and design of the facility; the geographic area of the facility; the occupancy and demand for similar healthcare facilities in the same or nearby communities; and the payer mix of private, Medicare and Medicaid patients. One of Omega's fundamental investment strategies is to obtain contractual rent escalations under long-term, non-cancelable, triple-net leases and fixed-rate mortgage loans, and to obtain substantial liquidity deposits. Approximately 61% of Omega's properties are managed by the following six companies: Sun Healthcare Group; CommuniCare Health Services; Advocat, Inc.; Guardian LTC Management, Inc.; Formation Capital Corporation; and Signature Holding II LLC. During 2009, the company added approximately 37 properties to its portfolio. In April 2010, Omega agreed to acquire 63 long-term care facilities CapitalSource, Inc.

FINANCIALS:

Sales and profits are in thousands of dollars—add 000 to get the full amount. 2009 Note: Financial information for 2009 was not available for all companies at press time.

2009 Sales: $197,438	2009 Profits: $82,111	**U.S. Stock Ticker: OHI**
2008 Sales: $193,762	2008 Profits: $78,137	**Int'l Ticker:** Int'l Exchange:
2007 Sales: $159,558	2007 Profits: $69,374	Employees: 19
2006 Sales: $135,513	2006 Profits: $55,697	Fiscal Year Ends: 12/31
2005 Sales: $109,535	2005 Profits: $25,355	Parent Company:

SALARIES/BENEFITS:

Pension Plan:	ESOP Stock Plan:	Profit Sharing:	Top Exec. Salary: $558,000	Bonus: $558,000
Savings Plan: Y	Stock Purch. Plan:		Second Exec. Salary: $344,000	Bonus: $172,000

OTHER THOUGHTS:

Apparent Women Officers or Directors:
Hot Spot for Advancement for Women/Minorities:

LOCATIONS: ("Y" = Yes)

West:	Southwest:	Midwest:	Southeast:	Northeast:	International:
Y	Y	Y	Y	Y	

ORIENT OVERSEAS (INTERNATIONAL) LTD

www.ooilgroup.com

Industry Group Code: 4885 **Ranks within this company's industry group:** Sales: 1 Profits: 1

Properties:		Financial Services:		Construction/Development:		Investments:		Specialty Services:		Brokerage:	
Apartments:		Mortgages:		Commercial Construction:		REIT:		Property Management:		Commercial Sales:	
Malls/Shopping:		Title Insurance:		Residential Construction:				Online Services:		Residential Sales:	
Offices:	Y	Property Insurance:		Land Development:	Y			Software/IT:		Specialty:	
Hotels/Motels:				Support Services:				Consulting:			
Industrial/Warehouses:	Y			Design/Engineering:							
Other:	Y										

TYPES OF BUSINESS:

Freight Logistics
Deep Sea Shipping
Port & Terminal Operations
Logistics Software & Services
Real Estate Development & Investment
Office Buildings
Residential Property Development

BRANDS/DIVISIONS/AFFILIATES:

Orient Overseas Container Line, Ltd.
OOCL China Domestic, Ltd.
CargoSmart, Ltd.
OOCL Logistics, Ltd.
Kaohsiung Terminal
Long Beach Container Terminal

CONTACTS: *Note: Officers with more than one job title may be intentionally listed here more than once.*

Chee Chen Tung, CEO
Chee Chen Tung, Pres.
Kenneth Gilbert Cambie, CFO
Paul Devine, Sr. VP-Sales
Lammy Chee Fun Lee, Corp. Sec.
Stanley Shen, Dir.-Investor Rel.
Alan Lieh Sing Tung, Managing Dir.-Orient Overseas Dev. Ltd.
Philip Yiu Wah Chow, CEO-Orient Overseas Container Line, Ltd.
Stephen Ng, Dir.-Transpacific Trade
Chee Chen Tung, Chmn.
Erxin Yao, Pres., OOCL USA
Henry Wong, Dir.-Corp. Logistics Dept.

Phone: 852-2833-3167 **Fax:** 852-2531-8221
Toll-Free:
Address: Harbour Center, 25 Harbour Rd., 33rd Fl., Wanchai, Hong Kong, China

GROWTH PLANS/SPECIAL FEATURES:

Orient Overseas (International) Ltd. (OOIL) is engaged in international container transport and logistics services, port and terminal operation, and property development. It has more than 230 offices in 58 countries. OOIL's primary subsidiary, Orient Overseas Container Line (OOCL), is an integrated international logistics company offering intermodal transport services worldwide. OOCL has a fleet of 86 ships. It is one of the leading international carriers serving China, through sub-subsidiary OOCL China Domestic, Ltd., which provides a full range of logistics and transportation services throughout the country. OOCL subsidiary CargoSmart, Ltd., uses information and e-commerce to manage the entire cargo process, while its OOCL Logistics, Ltd. subsidiary provides logistics services. OOIL's ports and terminal business operates two private terminals (meaning they are open only to the company and alliance partners): the Kaosiung Terminal in Hong Kong, China and the Long Beach Container Terminal in California. The firm's property development and investment division, The company has a grand alliance with Hapag-Lloyd, MISC Berhad and Nippon Yusen Kaisha, in which they share the same routes for cargos. In addition, the company has strategic alliances with St. Lawrence Co-ordinated Services members; Hapag-Lloyd; Tokyo Senpaku Kaisha Ltd.; and COSCO Container Lines Co., Ltd. In 2009, the firm re-established some of its routes, which includes a direct Vietnam call at Cay Mep; the Montreal Express 1, in Canada; the MEX (Middle East Express); and suspended the ABX service between Asia and Black Sea/East Mediterranean. In 2010, the firm announced sold Orient Overseas Developments Ltd. (OODL) to CapitaLand China (RE) Holdings Co., Ltd. OODL has an 80% interest in Beijing Oriental Plaza, one of Beijing's most prestigious commercial and office developments, and owns Wall Street Plaza in New York City. In addition to these long-term property investments, this division is engaged in residential property development in Shanghai and Hangzhou in China.

FINANCIALS: **Sales and profits are in thousands of dollars—add 000 to get the full amount. 2009 Note: Financial information for 2009 was not available for all companies at press time.**

2009 Sales: $4,350,200	2009 Profits: $-402,300	**U.S. Stock Ticker:**
2008 Sales: $6,545,140	2008 Profits: $275,529	**Int'l Ticker: 0316** Int'l Exchange: Hong Kong-HKEX
2007 Sales: $5,651,030	2007 Profits: $2,548,402	Employees:
2006 Sales: $4,609,751	2006 Profits: $580,603	Fiscal Year Ends: 12/31
2005 Sales: $4,696,241	2005 Profits: $651,291	Parent Company:

SALARIES/BENEFITS:

Pension Plan: Y	ESOP Stock Plan:	Profit Sharing:	Top Exec. Salary: $	Bonus: $
Savings Plan:	Stock Purch. Plan:		Second Exec. Salary: $	Bonus: $

OTHER THOUGHTS:

Apparent Women Officers or Directors: 1
Hot Spot for Advancement for Women/Minorities:

LOCATIONS: ("Y" = Yes)

West:	Southwest:	Midwest:	Southeast:	Northeast:	International:
Y			Y	Y	Y

ORIENT-EXPRESS HOTELS LTD

www.orient-express.com

Industry Group Code: 721110 **Ranks within this company's industry group:** Sales: 21 Profits: 25

Properties:		Financial Services:		Construction/Development:		Investments:		Specialty Services:		Brokerage:	
Apartments:		Mortgages:		Commercial Construction:	Y	REIT:		Property Management:	Y	Commercial Sales:	
Malls/Shopping:		Title Insurance:		Residential Construction:				Online Services:		Residential Sales:	
Offices:		Property Insurance:		Land Development:	Y			Software/IT:		Specialty:	
Hotels/Motels:	Y			Support Services:				Consulting:			
Industrial/Warehouses:				Design/Engineering:							
Other:	Y										

TYPES OF BUSINESS:

Hotels, Luxury
Tourist Railroads
Cruise Lines
Safari Tours

BRANDS/DIVISIONS/AFFILIATES:

Le Manoir aux Quat'Saisons
Grand Hotel Europe
Copacabana Palace
Le Residence d'Angkor
Eastern & Oriental Express Railway
Royal Scotsman Railway
The Inn at Perry Cabin
21 Club

CONTACTS:

Note: Officers with more than one job title may be intentionally listed here more than once.

Paul M. White, CEO
Filip Boyen, COO/VP
Paul M. White, Pres.
Martin O'Grady, CFO/VP
David C. Williams, VP-Sales & Mktg.
Roger V. Collins, VP-Tech. Svcs. & Design
Edwin S. Hetherington, General Counsel/Sec./VP
Nicholas R. Varian, Chief Dev. Officer/VP
Pippa Isbell, VP-Corp. Comm.
Phillip Gesue, VP-Real Estate
James B. Hurlock, Chmn.
Maurizio Saccani, VP-Italy

Phone: 441-295-2244	**Fax:** 441-292-8666
Toll-Free:	
Address: 22 Victoria St., Hamilton, HM 12 Bermuda	

GROWTH PLANS/SPECIAL FEATURES:

Orient-Express Hotels, Ltd. (OEH) manages and owns complete or partial interests in a portfolio of 50 properties in 24 countries. Its properties include 41 deluxe hotels (with 3,595 individual guestrooms and multi-room suites); one stand-alone restaurant; six tourist trains; and two river or canal cruise businesses. Avoiding chain branding, the company relies on a business model that emphasizes maintaining distinctive properties of cultural, historic or recreational interest in order to provide luxury travel experiences. During 2009, the hotels and restaurants segment generated approximately 87% of revenues, while tourist trains and cruises together accounted for 13%. In 2009, approximately 40% of OEH customers came from North America, 40% from Europe, and 20% from elsewhere in the world; approximately 70% of its customers were leisure travelers. The daily room rate for its hotels averaged $407 in 2009. OEH's properties include hotels such as Le Manoir aux Quat'Saisons, a 16th Century manor house in England; Grand Hotel Europe, which occupies an entire city block in St. Petersburg, Russia; The Inn at Perry Cabin, a country inn in St. Michaels, Maryland dating back to 1812; Copacabana Palace in Rio de Janeiro, Brazil, complete with a casino and a 500-seat theater; three safari camps in Botswana, featuring wildlife viewing from open vehicles or boats; and Le Residence d'Angkor, located in Siem Reap, Cambodia, near the famous Temples of Angkor. The firm's trains include the Venice Simplon-Orient-Express, refurbished in 1920s and '30s decor, traveling between Venice and London; the Royal Scotsman, which visits clan castles, historic battlegrounds and famous Scotch whiskey distilleries in Scotland; and the Eastern & Oriental Express, which travels weekly between Singapore, Kuala Lumpur and Bangkok. The company also owns the historic 21 Club restaurant in New York City; which originated as a Prohibition-era speakeasy. In January 2010, the company acquired two historic hotels in Taormina, Sicily for approximately $117 million.

FINANCIALS:

Sales and profits are in thousands of dollars—add 000 to get the full amount. 2009 Note: Financial information for 2009 was not available for all companies at press time.

2009 Sales: $456,956	2009 Profits: $-68,797	**U.S. Stock Ticker: OEH**
2008 Sales: $502,838	2008 Profits: $-26,551	**Int'l Ticker:** Int'l Exchange:
2007 Sales: $528,956	2007 Profits: $33,642	Employees: 7,100
2006 Sales: $479,364	2006 Profits: $39,767	Fiscal Year Ends: 12/31
2005 Sales: $421,090	2005 Profits: $41,539	Parent Company:

SALARIES/BENEFITS:

Pension Plan:	ESOP Stock Plan:	Profit Sharing:	Top Exec. Salary: $	Bonus: $
Savings Plan:	Stock Purch. Plan:		Second Exec. Salary: $	Bonus: $

OTHER THOUGHTS:

Apparent Women Officers or Directors: 2
Hot Spot for Advancement for Women/Minorities: Y

LOCATIONS: ("Y" = Yes)

West:	Southwest:	Midwest:	Southeast:	Northeast:	International:
				Y	Y

ORIGEN FINANCIAL INC

www.origenfinancial.com

Industry Group Code: 522291 **Ranks within this company's industry group:** Sales: Profits: 1

Properties:		Financial Services:		Construction/Development:		Investments:		Specialty Services:		Brokerage:	
Apartments:		Mortgages:		Commercial Construction:		REIT:	Y	Property Management:		Commercial Sales:	
Malls/Shopping:		Title Insurance:		Residential Construction:				Online Services:		Residential Sales:	
Offices:		Property Insurance:		Land Development:				Software/IT:		Specialty:	
Hotels/Motels:				Support Services:				Consulting:			
Industrial/Warehouses:				Design/Engineering:							
Other:											

TYPES OF BUSINESS:

REIT
Managing Manufactured Home Loans

BRANDS/DIVISIONS/AFFILIATES:

Origen Financial L.L.C.

GROWTH PLANS/SPECIAL FEATURES:

Origen Financial, Inc. is an internally-managed and internally-advised real estate investment trust (REIT) specializing in the manufactured housing business. The company manages a portfolio of approximately $1 billion made up of manufactured housing loans and asset backed securities. Although the company no long engages in its former businesses of originating and servicing loans, it remains focused on the management of its residual interests in its securitized loan portfolios. The firm's operations are carried out by its wholly-owned subsidiary, Origen Financial L.L.C.

CONTACTS: *Note: Officers with more than one job title may be intentionally listed here more than once.*

Ronald A. Klein, CEO
J. Peter Scherer, COO
J. Peter Scherer, Pres.
W. Anderson Geater, Jr., CFO
Laura Campbell, Sr. VP-Human Resources
Paul J. Galaspie, CIO/Sr. VP
W. Anderson Geater, Jr., Sec.
Gina Sheahan, Controller
Mark Landschulz, Exec. VP-Portfolio Mgmt.
Paul A. Halpern, Chmn.

Phone: 248-746-7000	**Fax:** 248-746-7094
Toll-Free:	
Address: 27777 Franklin Rd., Ste. 1700, Southfield, MI 48034 US	

FINANCIALS: **Sales and profits are in thousands of dollars—add 000 to get the full amount. 2009 Note: Financial information for 2009 was not available for all companies at press time.**

2009 Sales: $12,200	2009 Profits: $-8,567	**U.S. Stock Ticker: ORGN**
2008 Sales: $	2008 Profits: $-35,364	**Int'l Ticker:** Int'l Exchange:
2007 Sales: $26,400	2007 Profits: $-31,767	Employees:
2006 Sales: $92,082	2006 Profits: $6,971	Fiscal Year Ends: 12/31
2005 Sales: $74,000	2005 Profits: $-2,700	Parent Company:

SALARIES/BENEFITS:

Pension Plan:	ESOP Stock Plan:	Profit Sharing:	Top Exec. Salary: $531,058	Bonus: $250,000
Savings Plan:	Stock Purch. Plan:		Second Exec. Salary: $280,096	Bonus: $150,000

OTHER THOUGHTS:

Apparent Women Officers or Directors: 2
Hot Spot for Advancement for Women/Minorities: Y

LOCATIONS: ("Y" = Yes)

West:	Southwest:	Midwest:	Southeast:	Northeast:	International:
		Y			

ORION MARINE GROUP INC

www.orionmarinegroup.com

Industry Group Code: 2389 **Ranks within this company's industry group:** Sales: 4 Profits: 4

Properties:		Financial Services:		Construction/Development:		Investments:		Specialty Services:		Brokerage:	
Apartments:		Mortgages:		Commercial Construction:		REIT:		Property Management:		Commercial Sales:	
Malls/Shopping:		Title Insurance:		Residential Construction:				Online Services:		Residential Sales:	
Offices:		Property Insurance:		Land Development:				Software/IT:		Specialty:	
Hotels/Motels:				Support Services:	Y			Consulting:			
Industrial/Warehouses:				Design/Engineering:	Y						
Other:											

TYPES OF BUSINESS:

Marine Construction & Specialty Services
Dredging Services

BRANDS/DIVISIONS/AFFILIATES:

TW LaQuay Dredging LLC

CONTACTS:

Note: Officers with more than one job title may be intentionally listed here more than once.

J. Michael Pearson, CEO
J. Michael Pearson, Pres.
Mark R. Stauffer, CFO/Exec. VP
Pete Buchler, General Counsel/VP/Corp. Sec.
Elliott J. Kennedy, Exec. VP-Gulf Coast
James L. Rose, Exec. VP-Atlantic Seaboard & Caribbean
Richard L. Daerr, Jr., Chmn.

Phone: 713-852-6500	**Fax:** 713-852-6530
Toll-Free:	
Address: 12000 Aerospace, Ste. 300, Houston, TX 77034 US	

GROWTH PLANS/SPECIAL FEATURES:

Orion Marine Group, Inc. is a marine specialty contractor that serves the heavy civil marine infrastructure industry. The firm offers an array of marine construction services on, over and under the water along the Atlantic Seaboard, the Gulf Coast and in the Caribbean Basin. The company's customers, for which Orion Marine acts as a single-source turnkey solution, include private commercial and industrial enterprises; and federal, state and municipal governments. The firm offers three types of services: marine construction, dredging and specialty services. Its marine construction services include construction of marine transportation facilities, bridges, causeways, marine pipelines and marine environmental structures. Marine transportation facility construction projects include public port facilities; private and special-use Navy terminals; cruise ship port facilities; and recreational use marinas and docks. The firm's bridge and causeway projects include the construction, repair and maintenance of bridges and causeways; and the development of fendering systems in marine environments. Its marine pipeline service projects generally include the installation and removal of underwater buried pipeline transmission lines; installation of pipeline intakes and outfalls for industrial facilities; construction of pipeline outfalls for wastewater and industrial discharges; river crossing and directional drilling; creation of hot taps and tie-ins; and inspection, maintenance and repair services. Orion Marine's dredging services involve removing mud and silt from the channel floor by means of pipeline systems and a mechanical backhoe, crane/bucket or cutter suction dredge. The company's specialty services include demolition; surveying; diving; salvage; towing; and underwater inspection, excavation and repair. In January 2010, the firm acquired specialty dredging services firm T.W. LaQuay Dredging, LLC for $60 million. In February 2010, Orion Marine agreed to establish a new base to serve the Pacific Northwest and West Coast.

The firm offers employees medical, dental vision, life, AD&D and disability insurance; an employee assistance plan; and a 401(k).

FINANCIALS:

Sales and profits are in thousands of dollars—add 000 to get the full amount. 2009 Note: Financial information for 2009 was not available for all companies at press time.

2009 Sales: $293,494	2009 Profits: $20,030	**U.S. Stock Ticker: ORN**
2008 Sales: $261,802	2008 Profits: $14,475	**Int'l Ticker:** Int'l Exchange:
2007 Sales: $210,360	2007 Profits: $16,617	Employees: 1,040
2006 Sales: $	2006 Profits: $	Fiscal Year Ends: 12/31
2005 Sales: $	2005 Profits: $	Parent Company:

SALARIES/BENEFITS:

Pension Plan:	ESOP Stock Plan:	Profit Sharing:	Top Exec. Salary: $423,385	Bonus: $621,857
Savings Plan: Y	Stock Purch. Plan:		Second Exec. Salary: $269,520	Bonus: $302,606

OTHER THOUGHTS:

Apparent Women Officers or Directors:
Hot Spot for Advancement for Women/Minorities:

LOCATIONS: ("Y" = Yes)

West:	Southwest:	Midwest:	Southeast:	Northeast:	International:
	Y		Y	Y	

ORLEANS HOMEBUILDERS

www.orleanshomes.com

Industry Group Code: 2361 **Ranks within this company's industry group:** Sales: 16 Profits: 6

Properties:		Financial Services:		Construction/Development:		Investments:		Specialty Services:		Brokerage:	
Apartments:		Mortgages:		Commercial Construction:		REIT:		Property Management:		Commercial Sales:	
Malls/Shopping:		Title Insurance:		Residential Construction:	Y			Online Services:		Residential Sales:	Y
Offices:		Property Insurance:		Land Development:	Y			Software/IT:		Specialty:	
Hotels/Motels:				Support Services:				Consulting:			
Industrial/Warehouses:				Design/Engineering:							
Other:											

TYPES OF BUSINESS:

Residential Construction
Residential Community Development
Townhouses & Condominiums
Residential Brokerage

BRANDS/DIVISIONS/AFFILIATES:

CONTACTS:

Note: Officers with more than one job title may be intentionally listed here more than once.

Jeffrey P. Orleans, CEO
Michael T. Vesey, COO
Michael T. Vesey, Pres.
Garry P. Herdler, CFO/Exec. VP
Benjamin D. Goldman, Vice Chmn.
C. Dean Amann, II, Exec. VP-Northern & Midwestern Regions
Thomas R. Vesey, Exec. VP-Southern Region
Kyle J. Upper, Exec. VP-Florida Region & Land
Jeffrey P. Orleans, Chmn.

Phone: 215-245-7500	**Fax:**
Toll-Free:	
Address: 1 Greenwood Square, 3333 St. Rd., Ste. 101, Bensalem, PA 19020 US	

GROWTH PLANS/SPECIAL FEATURES:

Orleans Homebuilders, Inc. and its subsidiaries primarily develop, build and market upper-price range single-family homes, townhouses and condominiums. The company sells homes in eight states and owns or controls approximately 7,299 building lots. The firm divides its business into four regions. The first of these is the Northern region, which includes Southeastern Pennsylvania; Central and Southern New Jersey and Orange County New York markets. Second is the firm's Southern region, which includes the Richmond and Tidewater, Virginia and Charlotte, Raleigh and Greensboro, North Carolina markets (some adjacent South Carolina counties are also served). The company's third region is Florida, which includes the Orlando, Palm Coast and Palm Bay markets. The Midwestern region consists entirely of operations in the Chicago area. In March 2010, the company filed for Chapter 11 bankruptcy protection. In April 2010, the firm sells most of its assets to rival NVR for $170 million.

FINANCIALS:

Sales and profits are in thousands of dollars—add 000 to get the full amount. 2009 Note: Financial information for 2009 was not available for all companies at press time.

2009 Sales: $	2009 Profits: $	**U.S. Stock Ticker: OHBIQ**
2008 Sales: $583,282	2008 Profits: $-143,413	**Int'l Ticker:** Int'l Exchange:
2007 Sales: $682,534	2007 Profits: $-66,850	Employees: 544
2006 Sales: $987,193	2006 Profits: $63,041	Fiscal Year Ends: 6/30
2005 Sales: $919,230	2005 Profits: $55,584	Parent Company:

SALARIES/BENEFITS:

Pension Plan:	ESOP Stock Plan:	Profit Sharing:	Top Exec. Salary: $	Bonus: $
Savings Plan: Y	Stock Purch. Plan:		Second Exec. Salary: $	Bonus: $

OTHER THOUGHTS:

Apparent Women Officers or Directors:
Hot Spot for Advancement for Women/Minorities:

LOCATIONS: ("Y" = Yes)

West:	Southwest:	Midwest:	Southeast:	Northeast:	International:
		Y	Y	Y	

PACIFIC COAST BUILDING PRODUCTS

www.paccoast.com

Industry Group Code: 444130 **Ranks within this company's industry group:** Sales: Profits:

Properties:		Financial Services:		Construction/Development:		Investments:		Specialty Services:		Brokerage:	
Apartments:		Mortgages:		Commercial Construction:		REIT:		Property Management:		Commercial Sales:	
Malls/Shopping:		Title Insurance:		Residential Construction:				Online Services:		Residential Sales:	
Offices:		Property Insurance:		Land Development:				Software/IT:		Specialty:	
Hotels/Motels:				Support Services:	Y			Consulting:			
Industrial/Warehouses:				Design/Engineering:							
Other:											

TYPES OF BUSINESS:

Building Materials-Manufacturing & Distribution
Contracting Services
Transportation Services
Charter Aviation Services

BRANDS/DIVISIONS/AFFILIATES:

Basalite Concrete Products LLC
Epic Plastics, Inc.
Pabco Building Products LLC
Pacific Coast Supply LLC
Transportation Services, Inc.
Pacific Coast Jet Charter, Inc.
Alcal Arcade Contracting, Inc.
Pacific Coast Companies, Inc.

CONTACTS: *Note: Officers with more than one job title may be intentionally listed here more than once.*

Darren Morris, CFO
Elaine Keane, Dir.-Mktg.
Heather Miller, VP-Human Resources
Megan Vincent, Dir.-Community Rel.

Phone: 916-631-6500	**Fax:**
Toll-Free:	
Address: 10600 White Rock Rd., Bldg. B, Ste. 100, Rancho Cordova, CA 95670-6032 US	

GROWTH PLANS/SPECIAL FEATURES:

Pacific Coast Building Products, Inc. is a manufacturer and distributor of building materials for residential, commercial and industrial construction on the west coast. The firm operates through its family of companies: Basalite Concrete Products, LLC; Pabco Building Products, LLC; Pacific Coast Building Services, Inc; Pacific Coast Supply, LLC; Transportation Services, Inc; Pacific Coast Jet Charter, Inc.; Pacific Coast Companies, Inc.; and PCBP Properties, Inc. The companies under the Basalite Concrete Products division include Blocklite and Epic Plastics, Inc. The companies under Pabco Building Products division include Gladding McBean; H.C. Muddox; Interstate Brick; Pabco Gypsum; and Pabco Roofing Products. Divisions under the Pacific Coast Building Services include Alcal/Arcade Contracting, Inc.; and Pacific Coast Contracting Specialties, Inc. The divisions under Pacific Coast Supply include Anderson Lumber; Anderson Truss; Diamond Pacific; Pacific Supply and P.C. Wholesale. The transportation division operates through Material Transport, which moves products and raw materials to and from the company's subsidiaries; and Pacific Coast Jet Charter, Inc., which operates a King Air 350 turboprop that is available for charter to destinations throughout the U.S., Canada and Mexico. The Pacific Coast Companies, Inc. team is in charge of much of the administrative work that corresponds to the family of companies. Finally, the firm's subsidiary, PCBP Properties, Inc. invests and manages a number of properties in the western U.S.

FINANCIALS: **Sales and profits are in thousands of dollars—add 000 to get the full amount. 2009 Note: Financial information for 2009 was not available for all companies at press time.**

2009 Sales: $	2009 Profits: $	**U.S. Stock Ticker: Private**
2008 Sales: $	2008 Profits: $	**Int'l Ticker:** Int'l Exchange:
2007 Sales: $	2007 Profits: $	Employees:
2006 Sales: $	2006 Profits: $	Fiscal Year Ends: 3/31
2005 Sales: $1,077,000	2005 Profits: $	Parent Company:

SALARIES/BENEFITS:

Pension Plan:	ESOP Stock Plan:	Profit Sharing:	Top Exec. Salary: $	Bonus: $
Savings Plan: Y	Stock Purch. Plan:		Second Exec. Salary: $	Bonus: $

OTHER THOUGHTS:

Apparent Women Officers or Directors: 3
Hot Spot for Advancement for Women/Minorities: Y

LOCATIONS: ("Y" = Yes)

West:	Southwest:	Midwest:	Southeast:	Northeast:	International:
Y					Y

PALM HARBOR HOMES INC

www.palmharbor.com

Industry Group Code: 321991 **Ranks within this company's industry group:** Sales: 2 Profits: 3

Properties:		Financial Services:		Construction/Development:		Investments:		Specialty Services:		Brokerage:	
Apartments:		Mortgages:	Y	Commercial Construction:		REIT:		Property Management:		Commercial Sales:	
Malls/Shopping:		Title Insurance:		Residential Construction:	Y			Online Services:		Residential Sales:	Y
Offices:		Property Insurance:	Y	Land Development:				Software/IT:		Specialty:	
Hotels/Motels:				Support Services:				Consulting:			
Industrial/Warehouses:				Design/Engineering:							
Other:											

TYPES OF BUSINESS:

Manufactured & Modular Housing
Mortgages
Property & Casualty Insurance

BRANDS/DIVISIONS/AFFILIATES:

Standard Casualty Company
CountryPlace Mortgage, Ltd.
SmartPlus Construction
Masterpiece
Discovery Custom Homes
Windsor Homes
Nationwide Custom Homes, Inc.

CONTACTS:

Note: Officers with more than one job title may be intentionally listed here more than once.

Larry Keener, CEO
Larry Keener, Pres.
Kelly Tacke, CFO/Exec. VP
Kelly Tacke, Corp. Sec.
Larry Keener, Chmn.

Phone: 972-991-2422	**Fax:** 972-991-5949
Toll-Free: 800-456-8744	
Address: 15303 Dallas Pkwy., Ste. 800, Addison, TX 75001 US	

GROWTH PLANS/SPECIAL FEATURES:

Palm Harbor Homes, Inc. is a U.S. manufacturer and marketer of factory-built and modular homes. The firm markets nationwide through vertically integrated operations encompassing manufactured housing; modular housing; retailing; chattel; and mortgage bank financing and insurance. The company operates nine manufacturing facilities in seven states that sell homes through 86 company-owned retail superstores and approximately 150 independent retail dealers and builders. Subsidiary CountryPlace Mortgage, Ltd. offers chattel and non-conforming land and home mortgages to purchasers of manufactured homes sold by Palm Harbor. In addition, the firm offers property and casualty insurance through subsidiary Standard Casualty Company. Palm Harbor's products include single- and multi-section manufactured homes sold under brand names including Palm Harbor, Masterpiece, Keystone, CountryPlace, River Bend and Windsor Homes. The average retail sales price of the company's manufactured homes is approximately $73,000. The firm also helps customers find an appropriate lot or look for a pre-owned home. Palm Harbor's building system, SmartPlus Construction, uses a process called EnerGmiser, an energy management system that includes added insulation and other efficiency-increasing products. Modular homes are manufactured through subsidiary Nationwide Custom Homes, Inc., principally under the brand name Discovery Custom Homes. Modular offerings include single-story ranch homes, split-levels and two- and three-story homes with an average retail sales price of $175,000.

The company offers its employees benefits including medical, dental and vision coverage; disability protection; life insurance; a home purchase plan; a down payment assistance plan; tuition reimbursement; a scholarship program; an employee assistance program; a 401(k) plan; and a stock purchase plan.

FINANCIALS:

Sales and profits are in thousands of dollars—add 000 to get the full amount. 2009 Note: Financial information for 2009 was not available for all companies at press time.

2009 Sales: $409,274	2009 Profits: $-26,304	**U.S. Stock Ticker: PHHM**
2008 Sales: $555,096	2008 Profits: $-124,262	**Int'l Ticker:** Int'l Exchange:
2007 Sales: $661,247	2007 Profits: $-11,565	Employees:
2006 Sales: $710,635	2006 Profits: $11,114	Fiscal Year Ends: 3/31
2005 Sales: $610,538	2005 Profits: $-3,823	Parent Company:

SALARIES/BENEFITS:

Pension Plan:	ESOP Stock Plan:	Profit Sharing:	Top Exec. Salary: $300,000	Bonus: $265,000
Savings Plan: Y	Stock Purch. Plan: Y		Second Exec. Salary: $170,000	Bonus: $225,000

OTHER THOUGHTS:

Apparent Women Officers or Directors: 1
Hot Spot for Advancement for Women/Minorities:

LOCATIONS: ("Y" = Yes)

West:	Southwest:	Midwest:	Southeast:	Northeast:	International:
Y	Y	Y	Y	Y	

PARKWAY PROPERTIES INC

www.pky.com

Industry Group Code: 531120 **Ranks within this company's industry group:** Sales: 47 Profits: 50

Properties:		Financial Services:		Construction/Development:		Investments:		Specialty Services:		Brokerage:	
Apartments:		Mortgages:		Commercial Construction:		REIT:	Y	Property Management:	Y	Commercial Sales:	
Malls/Shopping:		Title Insurance:		Residential Construction:				Online Services:		Residential Sales:	
Offices:	Y	Property Insurance:		Land Development:				Software/IT:		Specialty:	
Hotels/Motels:				Support Services:				Consulting:			
Industrial/Warehouses:				Design/Engineering:							
Other:											

TYPES OF BUSINESS:

Real Estate Investment Trust
Office Buildings
Property Management

BRANDS/DIVISIONS/AFFILIATES:

Parkway Realty Services
One Park Ten

CONTACTS:

Note: Officers with more than one job title may be intentionally listed here more than once.

Steven G. Rogers, CEO
William R. Flatt, COO/Exec. VP
Steven G. Rogers, Pres.
Mandy M. Pope, Interim CFO/Exec. VP
Warren Speed, Sr. VP-Human Resources
W. Randy Lominick, III, VP-IT
Jack R. Sullenberger, Sr. VP-Tech. Svcs.
Sarah P. Clark, Sr. VP-Strategy
Sarah P. Clark, Sr. VP-Investor Rel.
Roy H. Butts, Sr. VP/Treas.
James M. Ingram, Chief Investment Officer/Exec. VP
O. Darryl Waltman, VP/Assistant Controller
R. Bradley Antici, VP-Investments
G. Mitch Mattingly, Exec. VP/Senior Asset Mgr.
Leland R. Speed, Chmn.

Phone: 601-948-4091	**Fax:** 601-949-4077
Toll-Free: 800-748-1667	
Address: 188 E. Capitol St., 1 Jackson Pl., Ste. 1000, Jackson, MS 39201 US	

GROWTH PLANS/SPECIAL FEATURES:

Parkway Properties, Inc. is a self-administered real estate investment trust (REIT) specializing in the operation, acquisition, ownership and leasing of office properties, with a focus on Chicago and the southeastern and southwestern U.S. Parkway owns or has interest in 65 office properties located in 11 states, totaling approximately 13.4 million square feet. Parkway leases its office properties to customers in the banking, insurance, professional services, legal, accounting, consulting, energy, financial services and telecommunications industries. The company provides investment, administrative, management and maintenance services internally. Through wholly-owned subsidiary Parkway Realty Services LLC, the company manages and/or leases 5.2 million square feet of rentable space for third-party owners, joint venture interests and fund properties.

Parkway is currently attempting to transform itself into an operator-owner rather than an owner-operator in order to leverage its core strength of operating office properties. The company's strategy for achieving this focuses on forming joint ventures; managing its balance sheet; providing public stockholders with higher returns; and recycling assets. Recently, Parkway sold four of its office properties: One Park Ten in Texas, for $15.7 million; Town Point Center in Virginia, for $12.75 million; and Lynnwood Plaza in Virginia, for $7.8 million. In January 2010, Parkway Realty Services expanded its presence in Jacksonville, Florida.

Parkway offers its employees stock grants; health, vision, life and disability insurance; a 401(k) plan; an employee advocate program; wellness programs and health club benefits; mentoring programs; and monthly company-wide lunches.

FINANCIALS:

Sales and profits are in thousands of dollars—add 000 to get the full amount. 2009 Note: Financial information for 2009 was not available for all companies at press time.

2009 Sales: $268,215	2009 Profits: $-11,603	**U.S. Stock Ticker: PKY**
2008 Sales: $265,411	2008 Profits: $9,274	**Int'l Ticker:** Int'l Exchange:
2007 Sales: $234,909	2007 Profits: $19,692	Employees:
2006 Sales: $203,218	2006 Profits: $25,682	Fiscal Year Ends: 12/31
2005 Sales: $191,483	2005 Profits: $20,807	Parent Company:

SALARIES/BENEFITS:

Pension Plan:	ESOP Stock Plan:	Profit Sharing:	Top Exec. Salary: $544,405	Bonus: $163,322
Savings Plan: Y	Stock Purch. Plan:		Second Exec. Salary: $295,000	Bonus: $73,750

OTHER THOUGHTS:

Apparent Women Officers or Directors: 6
Hot Spot for Advancement for Women/Minorities: Y

LOCATIONS: ("Y" = Yes)

West:	Southwest:	Midwest:	Southeast:	Northeast:	International:
	Y	Y	Y	Y	

PARSONS BRINCKERHOFF INC

www.pbworld.com

Industry Group Code: 237 **Ranks within this company's industry group:** Sales: 27 Profits: 22

Properties:		Financial Services:		Construction/Development:		Investments:		Specialty Services:		Brokerage:	
Apartments:		Mortgages:		Commercial Construction:	Y	REIT:		Property Management:		Commercial Sales:	
Malls/Shopping:		Title Insurance:		Residential Construction:				Online Services:		Residential Sales:	
Offices:		Property Insurance:		Land Development:				Software/IT:		Specialty:	
Hotels/Motels:				Support Services:				Consulting:	Y		
Industrial/Warehouses:				Design/Engineering:	Y						
Other:											

TYPES OF BUSINESS:

Engineering Services
Planning, Design & Construction
Civic Construction Projects
Commercial Construction
Transportation Consulting
Program Management Services
Telecommunications & Environmental Projects

BRANDS/DIVISIONS/AFFILIATES:

Balfour Beatty PLC
PB Research Library

CONTACTS:

Note: Officers with more than one job title may be intentionally listed here more than once.

George J. Pierson, CEO
Richard A. Schrader, CFO/Exec. VP
John J. Ryan, Exec. VP/Dir.-Human Resources
Lisa M. Palumbo, General Counsel
Hugh Inglis, Sr. VP-Alltech
Gay Knipper, Dir.-National Program Mgmt., PB Americas
Paul Skoutelas, Market Leader-Transit, PB Americas
Keith J. Hawksworth, Chmn.

Phone: 212-465-5000	**Fax:** 212-465-5096
Toll-Free:	
Address: 1 Penn Plz., New York, NY 10119 US	

GROWTH PLANS/SPECIAL FEATURES:

Parsons Brinckerhoff, Inc. provides engineering, consulting, and management services to local governments and the transportation, energy, and commercial market sectors. The company also offers construction services, program and project management, and facilities management. Parsons Brinckerhoff has taken on projects for clients such as Bangkok Mass Transit System Corporation and the City of Austin, Texas; and its signature works include the design of New York City's first subway and the reconfiguration of the Fort Washington Way interstate connector in Cincinnati. The company also worked with the Delhi Metro Rail Corporation to build a mass transit system designed as an urban transport system to move over 3 million passengers a day. Other relevant projects have included a gas fired power station in Kuwait; a web site and communications plan for lower Manhattan, known as lowermanhatten.info; and designing and engineering the Greater Cairo Metro system. Potential clients can view the company's work through the PB Research Library, a body that showcases and publishes the details of important projects. The firm is organized into three divisions: Americas, International and Facilities. The company is employee-owned with 150 offices worldwide. In October 2009, the firm was acquired by U.K.-based construction company Balfour Beatty PLC for $626 million.

FINANCIALS:

Sales and profits are in thousands of dollars—add 000 to get the full amount. 2009 Note: Financial information for 2009 was not available for all companies at press time.

2009 Sales: $	2009 Profits: $	**U.S. Stock Ticker: Private**
2008 Sales: $2,343,117	2008 Profits: $73,882	**Int'l Ticker:** Int'l Exchange:
2007 Sales: $1,853,741	2007 Profits: $62,117	Employees: 13,010
2006 Sales: $1,689,964	2006 Profits: $46,386	Fiscal Year Ends: 10/31
2005 Sales: $1,447,756	2005 Profits: $27,160	Parent Company: BALFOUR BEATTY PLC

SALARIES/BENEFITS:

Pension Plan:	ESOP Stock Plan:	Profit Sharing:	Top Exec. Salary: $	Bonus: $
Savings Plan:	Stock Purch. Plan:		Second Exec. Salary: $	Bonus: $

OTHER THOUGHTS:

Apparent Women Officers or Directors: 2
Hot Spot for Advancement for Women/Minorities: Y

LOCATIONS: ("Y" = Yes)

West:	Southwest:	Midwest:	Southeast:	Northeast:	International:
Y	Y	Y	Y	Y	Y

PCL CONSTRUCTION GROUP INC

www.pcl.com

Industry Group Code: 237 **Ranks within this company's industry group:** Sales: Profits:

Properties:		Financial Services:		Construction/Development:		Investments:		Specialty Services:		Brokerage:	
Apartments:		Mortgages:		Commercial Construction:	Y	REIT:		Property Management:		Commercial Sales:	
Malls/Shopping:		Title Insurance:		Residential Construction:				Online Services:		Residential Sales:	
Offices:		Property Insurance:		Land Development:				Software/IT:		Specialty:	
Hotels/Motels:				Support Services:				Consulting:			
Industrial/Warehouses:				Design/Engineering:	Y						
Other:											

TYPES OF BUSINESS:

Construction
Financial and Accounting Reporting
Development, Support and Project Management
Engineering Services

BRANDS/DIVISIONS/AFFILIATES:

Melloy Industrial Services
Monad Industrial Constructors
PCL Civil Constructors
PCL Industrial Services
PCL Intracon Power
Teton Industrial Construction

CONTACTS: *Note: Officers with more than one job title may be intentionally listed here more than once.*

Ross Grieve, CEO
Peter Beaupre, COO/Pres., PCL Construction Enterprises, Inc.
Ross Grieve, Pres.
Gordon Maron, CFO
Gordon Panas, Exec. VP-Admin.
Doug Stollery, Legal Counsel
Joe Watson, Dir.-Corp. Bus. Dev., Canadian Oper.
Gordon Panas, Exec. VP-Finance
Brad Nelson, COO/Pres., Canadian Buildings
Peter Stalenhoef, COO/Pres., Heavy Industrial
Al Troppmann, Pres., U.S. Buildings
Paul Douglas, CEO/Pres., PCL Constructors Inc.
Joseph D. Thompson, Chmn.

Phone: 780-733-5000 **Fax:** 780-733-5075
Toll-Free:
Address: 5410 99 St., Edmonton, AB T6E 3P4 Canada

GROWTH PLANS/SPECIAL FEATURES:

PCL Construction Group, Inc., founded in 1906, is an employee-owned group of construction companies in 27 locations throughout Canada, the U.S. and the Bahamas, with operations in the buildings, infrastructure and heavy industrial sectors. The firm focuses on three main areas of construction: buildings, infrastructure and heavy industrial. The buildings segment, conducts projects throughout North America and is able to work on an array of projects including commercial; institutional; educational; residential; adaptive reuse, which entails upgrading and converting an existing facility; cultural consideration, including on-site and on-the-job employment and training opportunities; green building; high-tech projects, for meeting cleanliness protocols in the medical, bio-tech and research working environments; and historical preservation, including repair, exterior masonry, renovations combining typical construction methods with scenic construction technology. The infrastructure segment undertakes various civil structure projects including bridges, overpasses, tunnels, interchanges, water treatment facilities, interchanges and light rail transportation projects. The heavy industrial division offers construction assistance to the petrochemical; oil and gas; pulp and paper; mining; and power and generation industries. PCL's building operations include larger projects, such as airports, sports facilities and office towers, and smaller projects, such as renovations, restorations and repairs. Subsidiaries include Melloy Industrial Services; Monad Industrial Constructors; PCL Civil Constructors; PCL Industrial Services; PCL Intracon Power; and Teton Industrial Construction.

Employees of the firm are offered medical, vision and dental insurance; flexible spending accounts; a prescription drug plan; a 401(k); a profit sharing bonus; and an employee assistance programs. Additionally, in 2009, the firm ranked among the top 100 companies to work for according to Fortune Magazine.

FINANCIALS: **Sales and profits are in thousands of dollars—add 000 to get the full amount. 2009 Note: Financial information for 2009 was not available for all companies at press time.**

2009 Sales: $ | 2009 Profits: $
2008 Sales: $ | 2008 Profits: $
2007 Sales: $ | 2007 Profits: $
2006 Sales: $ | 2006 Profits: $
2005 Sales: $3,120,000 | 2005 Profits: $

U.S. Stock Ticker: Private
Int'l Ticker: Int'l Exchange:
Employees: 9,989
Fiscal Year Ends:
Parent Company:

SALARIES/BENEFITS:

Pension Plan: ESOP Stock Plan: Profit Sharing: Top Exec. Salary: $ Bonus: $
Savings Plan: Y Stock Purch. Plan: Second Exec. Salary: $ Bonus: $

OTHER THOUGHTS:

Apparent Women Officers or Directors:
Hot Spot for Advancement for Women/Minorities:

LOCATIONS: ("Y" = Yes)

West:	Southwest:	Midwest:	Southeast:	Northeast:	International:
Y	Y	Y	Y		Y

PDG REALTY SA EMPREENDIMENTOS E PARTICIPACOES

www.pdgrealty.com.br

Industry Group Code: 5311 **Ranks within this company's industry group:** Sales: Profits:

Properties:		Financial Services:		Construction/Development:		Investments:		Specialty Services:		Brokerage:	
Apartments:		Mortgages:		Commercial Construction:		REIT:		Property Management:		Commercial Sales:	
Malls/Shopping:		Title Insurance:		Residential Construction:				Online Services:		Residential Sales:	
Offices:		Property Insurance:		Land Development:	Y			Software/IT:		Specialty:	
Hotels/Motels:				Support Services:				Consulting:			
Industrial/Warehouses:				Design/Engineering:							
Other:											

TYPES OF BUSINESS:

Real Estate Investments

BRANDS/DIVISIONS/AFFILIATES:

TGLT
REP Desenvolvimento Imobiliario S.A.
Goldfarb Incorporacoes e Construcoes S.A

CONTACTS:

Note: Officers with more than one job title may be intentionally listed here more than once.

Jose Antonio Grabowsky, CEO
Marcus Vinicius Medeiros Cardoso de Sa, COO
Michel Wurman, CFO
Caue Castello Veiga Innocencio Cardoso, Legal Affairs Officer
Carneio da Cunha, Exec. Dir.-Oper.
Carneiro da Cunha, Exec. Dir.-Real Estate Dev.
Michel Wurman, Investor Rel. Officer
Gilberto Sayao da Silva, Chmn.

Phone: 55-21-3504-3800	**Fax:** 55-21-35043849
Toll-Free:	
Address: 501 Praia de Botafogo, Botafogo, RJ 22290-140 Brazil	

GROWTH PLANS/SPECIAL FEATURES:

PDG Realty SA Empreemdimentos e Participacoes is a Brazilian firm that operates in the real estate industry. The company operates in five segments of the real estate industry: the development of residential projects targeted at income classes ranging from the low middle-income class to the high-income class; the development of residential lots; investments in commercial developments for the generation of rental income; the purchase of commercial and residential units for subsequent resale; and the offering of rendering services as a real estate brokerage and consulting firm. PDG Realty develops real estate projects through investments in its portfolio companies and is involved in co-development real estate projects with several other Brazilian real estate developers. Its portfolio firms include wholly-owned Goldfarb Incorporacoes e Construcoes S.A., which develops residential housing for middle and low middle-income classes in the states of Rio de Janeiro and Sao Paulo; commercial developer REP Real Estate Partners Desenvolvimento Imobiliario S.A. (36.9% owned); wholly-owned CHL, which develops commercial real estate and housing for middle, high-middle, and high-income classes in the state of Rio de Janeiro; residential real estate seller Brasil Brokers (5.47% owned); residential developer Cipasa (15.92% owned). Sao Paulo general real estate developer Lindencorp (15.92% owned); and Argentinian residential building developer TGLT (30% owned).

FINANCIALS:

Sales and profits are in thousands of dollars—add 000 to get the full amount. 2009 Note: Financial information for 2009 was not available for all companies at press time.

2009 Sales: $	2009 Profits: $	**U.S. Stock Ticker:**
2008 Sales: $	2008 Profits: $	**Int'l Ticker: PDGR3** Int'l Exchange: Sao Paulo-SAO
2007 Sales: $	2007 Profits: $	Employees:
2006 Sales: $	2006 Profits: $	Fiscal Year Ends: 12/31
2005 Sales: $	2005 Profits: $	Parent Company:

SALARIES/BENEFITS:

Pension Plan:	ESOP Stock Plan:	Profit Sharing:	Top Exec. Salary: $	Bonus: $
Savings Plan:	Stock Purch. Plan:		Second Exec. Salary: $	Bonus: $

OTHER THOUGHTS:

Apparent Women Officers or Directors:
Hot Spot for Advancement for Women/Minorities:

LOCATIONS: ("Y" = Yes)

West:	Southwest:	Midwest:	Southeast:	Northeast:	International:
					Y

PENNSYLVANIA REIT

www.preit.com

Industry Group Code: 531120 **Ranks within this company's industry group:** Sales: 38 Profits: 55

Properties:		Financial Services:		Construction/Development:		Investments:		Specialty Services:		Brokerage:	
Apartments:		Mortgages:		Commercial Construction:	Y	REIT:	Y	Property Management:	Y	Commercial Sales:	
Malls/Shopping:	Y	Title Insurance:		Residential Construction:				Online Services:		Residential Sales:	
Offices:		Property Insurance:		Land Development:	Y			Software/IT:		Specialty:	
Hotels/Motels:				Support Services:				Consulting:			
Industrial/Warehouses:				Design/Engineering:							
Other:											

TYPES OF BUSINESS:

Real Estate Investment Trust
Retail Properties
Industrial Properties
Multi-Family Residential Properties
Property Development & Redevelopment

BRANDS/DIVISIONS/AFFILIATES:

PREIT Associates LP
PREIT Services LLC
PREIT RUBIN Inc

CONTACTS:

Note: Officers with more than one job title may be intentionally listed here more than once.

Ronald Rubin, CEO
Edward A. Glickman, COO
Edward A. Glickman, Pres.
Robert F. McCadden, CFO/Exec. VP
Judith Trias, VP-Retail Mktg.
Judith E. Baker, Sr. VP-Human Resources
Bruce Goldman, General Counsel/Exec. VP/Sec.
Douglas S. Grayson, Exec. VP-Dev.
Nurit Yaron, VP-Investor Rel.
Jonathan Bell, Chief Acct. Officer/Sr. VP
Jeffrey A. Linn, Exec. VP-Acquisitions
Timothy R. Rubin, Exec. VP-Leasing
Joseph F. Coradino, Pres., PREIT Services LLC & PREIT-RUBIN, Inc.
Andrew M. Ioannou, Sr. VP-Capital Markets/Treas.
Ronald Rubin, Chmn.

Phone: 215-875-0700 **Fax:** 215-546-7311
Toll-Free: 866-875-0700
Address: 200 S. Broad St., Philadelphia, PA 19102 US

GROWTH PLANS/SPECIAL FEATURES:

Pennsylvania REIT (PREIT) is a fully integrated, self-administered and self-managed real estate investment trust (REIT), whose primary investment focus is on retail shopping malls, strip centers and power centers. It acquires, develops, redevelops and operates properties in the Eastern U.S. The company offers a full complement of real estate capabilities including leasing, acquisition, development, construction, management, property management and marketing. The firm's portfolio currently consists of 54 retail properties in 13 states, of which 38 are shopping malls; 13 are strip and power centers; and three are under development. Overall, PREIT controls approximately 34.6 million square feet of rentable property. Prominent tenants of the firm include Gap, Inc.; Foot Locker; J.C. Penney Company, Inc.; Sears; and Limited Brands, Inc. PREIT holds its interests in its portfolio of properties through its operating partnership PREIT Associates, LP, in which the company is the sole general partner, with a 95% controlling interest. The company provides management, leasing and real estate development services through two of its subsidiaries, PREIT Services, LLC and PREIT-RUBIN, Inc. PREIT Services generally develops and manages properties which the firm intends to consolidate for financial reporting purposes. PREIT-RUBIN generally develops and manages properties which the firm does not consolidate for financial reporting purposes, including properties in which the firm owns interests through partnerships with third parties and properties that are owned by third parties in which the firm does not own an interest.

PREIT employees receive benefits including a 401(k) plan; an employee share purchase plan; flexible spending accounts; corporate flex time hours; tuition reimbursement; disability, life and AD&D insurance; and an employee assistance program.

FINANCIALS:

Sales and profits are in thousands of dollars—add 000 to get the full amount. 2009 Note: Financial information for 2009 was not available for all companies at press time.

2009 Sales: $463,088
2008 Sales: $467,993
2007 Sales: $460,590
2006 Sales: $459,308
2005 Sales: $428,875

2009 Profits: $-90,091
2008 Profits: $-16,355
2007 Profits: $23,120
2006 Profits: $28,021
2005 Profits: $57,629

U.S. Stock Ticker: PEI
Int'l Ticker: Int'l Exchange:
Employees: 712
Fiscal Year Ends: 12/31
Parent Company:

SALARIES/BENEFITS:

Pension Plan:
Savings Plan: Y
ESOP Stock Plan:
Stock Purch. Plan: Y
Profit Sharing:
Top Exec. Salary: $562,648 Bonus: $321,960
Second Exec. Salary: $503,880 Bonus: $249,141

OTHER THOUGHTS:

Apparent Women Officers or Directors: 8
Hot Spot for Advancement for Women/Minorities: Y

LOCATIONS: ("Y" = Yes)

West:	Southwest:	Midwest:	Southeast:	Northeast:	International:
		Y	Y	Y	

PLUM CREEK TIMBER CO INC

www.plumcreek.com

Industry Group Code: 444130 **Ranks within this company's industry group:** Sales: 2 Profits: 1

Properties:		Financial Services:		Construction/Development:		Investments:		Specialty Services:		Brokerage:	
Apartments:		Mortgages:		Commercial Construction:		REIT:	Y	Property Management:		Commercial Sales:	
Malls/Shopping:		Title Insurance:		Residential Construction:				Online Services:		Residential Sales:	
Offices:		Property Insurance:		Land Development:	Y			Software/IT:		Specialty:	Y
Hotels/Motels:				Support Services:				Consulting:			
Industrial/Warehouses:				Design/Engineering:							
Other:	Y										

TYPES OF BUSINESS:

Forestry & Logging
Real Estate Investment Trust
Land Management & Development
Manufactured Timber Products
Specialty Brokerage
Land Investments
Mineral Rights

BRANDS/DIVISIONS/AFFILIATES:

CONTACTS:

Note: Officers with more than one job title may be intentionally listed here more than once.

Rick R. Holley, CEO
Thomas M. Lindquist, COO/Exec. VP
Rick R. Holley, Pres.
David W. Lambert, CFO/Sr. VP
Barbara L. Crowe, VP-Human Resources
Joan K. Fitzmaurice, VP-IT
Thomas G. Ray, VP-Northwest Resources & Mfg.
James A. Kraft, General Counsel/Sr. VP/Corp. Sec.
Larry D. Neilson, Sr. VP-Bus. Dev.
Joan K. Fitzmaurice, VP-Corp. Comm. & Audit
John Hobbs, VP-Investor Rel.
David A. Brown, Chief Acct. Officer/VP
James A. Kilberg, Sr. VP-Real Estate
Thomas M. Reed, VP-Southern Resources
Dan Tucker, VP-Tax
John F. Morgan, Chmn.

Phone: 206-467-3600	**Fax:** 206-467-3795
Toll-Free: 800-858-5347	
Address: 999 3rd Ave., Ste. 4300, Seattle, WA 98104-4096 US	

GROWTH PLANS/SPECIAL FEATURES:

Plum Creek Timber Co., Inc. is a real estate investment trust (REIT) that owns, harvests and redevelops timberland. The company is one of the largest private timberland owners in the U.S., with approximately seven million acres in 19 states. Plum Creek's timber assets are well diversified by both geography and by species mix and age distribution. The firm harvests trees and then markets the lumber to the paper and forest products industry and replants and fertilizes the harvested lands. Plum Creek is operated in four divisions: two regional timberland management divisions; a real estate segment; a manufactured products division; and an Other Businesses segment. The Northern Resources segment covers timberlands in Maine, Michigan, Montana, New Hampshire, Oregon, Vermont, Washington, West Virginia and Wisconsin; while the Southern Resources segment covers Alabama, Arkansas, Florida, Georgia, Louisiana, Mississippi, Oklahoma, Texas and the Carolinas. Plum Creek operates six nurseries to provide seedlings for reforestation projects. The real estate division handles the sale and management of higher value lands, sales of non-strategic timberlands and development of certain properties. The manufacturing segment includes two lumber mills, two plywood plants, two medium density fiberboard facilities and two lumber remanufacturing facilities. These operations, located near the firm's Montana timberlands, turn logs into saleable items, including veneer logs, plywood, planks and other materials, which are distributed through a nationwide network of field inventory points. The company's other businesses segment focuses on opportunities related to mineral extraction, natural gas, and communication and transportation rights of way on company lands.

Employees are offered health care coverage; health and dependent daycare funds; savings and retirement benefits; and life and disability protection.

FINANCIALS:

Sales and profits are in thousands of dollars—add 000 to get the full amount. 2009 Note: Financial information for 2009 was not available for all companies at press time.

2009 Sales: $1,294,000	2009 Profits: $236,000	**U.S. Stock Ticker: PCL**
2008 Sales: $1,614,000	2008 Profits: $233,000	**Int'l Ticker:** Int'l Exchange:
2007 Sales: $1,675,000	2007 Profits: $282,000	Employees: 1,252
2006 Sales: $1,627,000	2006 Profits: $317,000	Fiscal Year Ends: 12/31
2005 Sales: $1,576,000	2005 Profits: $354,000	Parent Company:

SALARIES/BENEFITS:

Pension Plan:	ESOP Stock Plan:	Profit Sharing: Y	Top Exec. Salary: $830,000	Bonus: $828,340
Savings Plan: Y	Stock Purch. Plan:		Second Exec. Salary: $500,000	Bonus: $408,500

OTHER THOUGHTS:

Apparent Women Officers or Directors: 3
Hot Spot for Advancement for Women/Minorities: Y

LOCATIONS: ("Y" = Yes)

West:	Southwest:	Midwest:	Southeast:	Northeast:	International:
Y	Y	Y	Y	Y	

PMI GROUP INC (THE)

www.pmigroup.com

Industry Group Code: 524126 **Ranks within this company's industry group:** Sales: 2 Profits: 2

Properties:		Financial Services:		Construction/Development:		Investments:		Specialty Services:		Brokerage:	
Apartments:		Mortgages:	Y	Commercial Construction:		REIT:		Property Management:		Commercial Sales:	
Malls/Shopping:		Title Insurance:		Residential Construction:				Online Services:		Residential Sales:	
Offices:		Property Insurance:		Land Development:				Software/IT:		Specialty:	
Hotels/Motels:				Support Services:				Consulting:			
Industrial/Warehouses:				Design/Engineering:							
Other:											

TYPES OF BUSINESS:

Insurance-Financial Guaranty
Mortgage Insurance & Reinsurance
Structured Finance Insurance

BRANDS/DIVISIONS/AFFILIATES:

PMI Mortgage Insurance Co.
PMI Europe
PMI Canada
CMG Mortgage Insurance Company
FCIG Group

CONTACTS:
Note: Officers with more than one job title may be intentionally listed here more than once.

L. Stephen Smith, CEO
Donald P. Lofe, Jr., CFO/Exec. VP
Charles F. Broom, Sr. VP-Human Resources & Organizational Dev.
Donald P. Lofe, Jr., Chief Admin. Officer
Andrew D. Cameron, General Counsel/Exec. VP/Sec.
David Berson, Chief Strategist & Economist/Sr. VP
Tom Taggart, VP-Public Rel.
Bill Horning, VP-Investor Rel.
Thomas H. Jeter, Chief Acct. Officer/Corp. Controller/Sr. VP
Ray D. Chang, Corp. Treas./Sr. VP
Lloyd A. Porter, Chief Enterprise Risk Officer/Exec. VP
Joanne M. Berkowitz, Chief Insurance Oper. Officer/Exec. VP
David H. Katkov, Chief Bus. Officer/Exec. VP
L. Stephen Smith, Chmn.

Phone: 925-658-7878 **Fax:** 925-658-6931
Toll-Free: 800-280-4764
Address: 3003 Oak Rd., Walnut Creek, CA 94597 US

GROWTH PLANS/SPECIAL FEATURES:

The PMI Group, Inc. provides financial products for residential mortgages, public finance obligations and asset-backed securities. Products include mortgage insurance and reinsurance; structured finance solutions; and financial guaranty. The company operates in four segments: U.S. mortgage insurance operations; international operations; financial guaranty; and corporate and other. The U.S. mortgage insurance operations segment, through PMI Mortgage Insurance Co., offers mortgage insurance and structured financial products to meet the capital and credit risk mitigation needs of its customers the U.S. market. CMG Mortgage Insurance Company, a 50%-owned joint venture, provides mortgage insurance exclusively to credit unions. The international segment consists of PMI Europe and PMI Canada. PMI Europe has since ceased operations to conserve capital, and the firm is in the process of closing PMI Canada. The financial guaranty segment includes the company's investment in RAM Holdings Ltd. and FGIC Corporation, whose subsidiary Financial Guaranty Insurance Company provides financial guaranty insurance for public finance and structured finance obligations. Both RAM Holdings Ltd. and FGIC Corporation have both ceased operations. The corporate and other segment consists of corporate debt and expenses of the company. It also focuses on contract underwriting operations and equity in earnings or losses from investments in certain limited partnerships. In October 2008, the company sold its Australian operations (PMI Australia) to QBE Insurance Group Limited for $920 million. In December of the same year, the firm sold its Asia operations (PMI Asia) to QBE Lenders' Mortgage Insurance Limited for $51.6 million.

Employees are offered medical, dental and vision insurance; life insurance; disability coverage; an employee assistance program; domestic partner benefits; a pension plan; a 401(k) plan; an employee stock purchase plan; flexible spending accounts; a first-time homebuyer program; onsite yoga classes; adoption reimbursement; and tuition reimbursement.

FINANCIALS:
Sales and profits are in thousands of dollars—add 000 to get the full amount. 2009 Note: Financial information for 2009 was not available for all companies at press time.

2009 Sales: $923,909 — 2009 Profits: $-659,326
2008 Sales: $907,787 — 2008 Profits: $-928,508
2007 Sales: $923,185 — 2007 Profits: $-915,326
2006 Sales: $868,344 — 2006 Profits: $419,651
2005 Sales: $1,019,898 — 2005 Profits: $409,169

U.S. Stock Ticker: PMI
Int'l Ticker: Int'l Exchange:
Employees: 600
Fiscal Year Ends: 12/31
Parent Company:

SALARIES/BENEFITS:

Pension Plan: Y | ESOP Stock Plan: | Profit Sharing: | Top Exec. Salary: $830,000 | Bonus: $
Savings Plan: Y | Stock Purch. Plan: Y | | Second Exec. Salary: $481,990 | Bonus: $

OTHER THOUGHTS:

Apparent Women Officers or Directors: 5
Hot Spot for Advancement for Women/Minorities: Y

LOCATIONS: ("Y" = Yes)

West:	Southwest:	Midwest:	Southeast:	Northeast:	International:
Y	Y	Y	Y	Y	Y

POST PROPERTIES INC

www.postproperties.com

Industry Group Code: 531110 **Ranks within this company's industry group:** Sales: 14 Profits: 15

Properties:		Financial Services:		Construction/Development:		Investments:		Specialty Services:		Brokerage:	
Apartments:	Y	Mortgages:		Commercial Construction:		REIT:	Y	Property Management:	Y	Commercial Sales:	
Malls/Shopping:		Title Insurance:		Residential Construction:				Online Services:		Residential Sales:	
Offices:		Property Insurance:		Land Development:	Y			Software/IT:		Specialty:	
Hotels/Motels:				Support Services:	Y			Consulting:			
Industrial/Warehouses:				Design/Engineering:	Y						
Other:											

TYPES OF BUSINESS:

Real Estate Investment Trust
Apartment Communities
Landscaping & Design Services
Apartment Management & Development
Corporate Apartments
Condominiums
Retail Space
Preferred Homes

BRANDS/DIVISIONS/AFFILIATES:

Post Apartment Management
Post Investment Group
Post Corporate Services
Post Construction and Property Services
Post Ridge
Post Forest

CONTACTS: *Note: Officers with more than one job title may be intentionally listed here more than once.*

David P. Stockert, CEO
David P. Stockert, Pres.
Christopher J. Papa, CFO/Exec. VP
Terri Sherrod, Dir.-Mktg. & Branding
Linda J. Ricklef, Sr. VP-Human Resources
Bill NeSmith, VP-IT Oper.
Sherry W. Cohen, Corp. Sec./Exec. VP
Steve Sadler, VP-Strategic Bus. Svcs.
Arthur J. Quirk, Chief Acct. Officer/Sr. VP
Charles A. Konas, Exec. VP-Construction & Property Svcs.
Kathleen M. Mason, VP-Taxation
Glen P. Smith, VP-Legal Affairs
S. Jamie Teabo, Exec. VP-Post Apartment Mgmt.
Robert C. Goddard, III, Chmn.

Phone: 404-846-5000	**Fax:** 404-846-6282
Toll-Free:	
Address: 4401 Northside Pkwy, Ste. 800, Atlanta, GA 30327 US	

GROWTH PLANS/SPECIAL FEATURES:

Post Properties, Inc. is a self-administered and self-managed equity real estate investment trust (REIT). The firm owns, develops and manages upscale multifamily apartment communities in Atlanta, Georgia; Dallas, Texas; and the greater Washington, D.C., and Tampa, Florida metropolitan areas. The company owns approximately 19,863 apartment units in 55 apartment communities, including 1,747 units in five communities held in unconsolidated entities and 1,428 units in four communities currently under construction or in lease-up. Post is also in the process of developing and selling 277 luxury for-sale condominium homes in two communities, including 129 units in one community held in an unconsolidated entity; and is completing the sell out of units in one condominium community. The firm's major operating divisions include Post Apartment Management; Post Investment Group; Post Corporate Services; and Post Construction and Property Services. Post Apartment Management is responsible for the day-to-day operations of all Post communities and also conducts short-term corporate apartment leasing activities. Post Investment Group handles the company's acquisition, development, rehabilitation, disposition, condominium sales and asset management operations. Post Corporate Services provides all compliance, information systems, human resources, accounting, management reporting, legal, security, personnel recruiting, training/development, risk management and insurance services for Post. The Post Construction and Property Services division oversees all construction and physical asset maintenance activities at each Post community. In July 2009, Post Properties sold its Post Ridge apartment community (434 units) in Atlanta, Georgia, to an affiliate of Centennial Holding Company, LLC for approximately $44.8 million; and sold its Post Forest apartment community (364 units) in Fairfax, Virginia, to an affiliate of Pantzer Properties, Inc. for roughly $57.5 million.

Employees are offered benefits including life, disability, auto, homeowners, medical, dental and vision insurance; educational assistance; a 401(k); a stock purchase program; an employee assistance program; a group legal plan; and credit union membership.

FINANCIALS: **Sales and profits are in thousands of dollars—add 000 to get the full amount. 2009 Note: Financial information for 2009 was not available for all companies at press time.**

2009 Sales: $276,323	2009 Profits: $-11,489	**U.S. Stock Ticker: PPS**
2008 Sales: $281,940	2008 Profits: $-8,370	**Int'l Ticker:** Int'l Exchange:
2007 Sales: $277,324	2007 Profits: $182,949	Employees: 590
2006 Sales: $262,324	2006 Profits: $101,469	Fiscal Year Ends: 12/31
2005 Sales: $272,271	2005 Profits: $141,948	Parent Company:

SALARIES/BENEFITS:

Pension Plan:	ESOP Stock Plan:	Profit Sharing:	Top Exec. Salary: $420,000	Bonus: $
Savings Plan: Y	Stock Purch. Plan: Y		Second Exec. Salary: $352,000	Bonus: $158,400

OTHER THOUGHTS:

Apparent Women Officers or Directors: 8
Hot Spot for Advancement for Women/Minorities: Y

LOCATIONS: ("Y" = Yes)

West:	Southwest:	Midwest:	Southeast:	Northeast:	International:
	Y		Y	Y	

PRIME GROUP REALTY TRUST

www.pgrt.com

Industry Group Code: 531120 **Ranks within this company's industry group:** Sales: 62 Profits: 57

Properties:		Financial Services:		Construction/Development:		Investments:		Specialty Services:		Brokerage:	
Apartments:		Mortgages:		Commercial Construction:		REIT:	Y	Property Management:	Y	Commercial Sales:	
Malls/Shopping:		Title Insurance:		Residential Construction:				Online Services:		Residential Sales:	
Offices:	Y	Property Insurance:		Land Development:	Y			Software/IT:		Specialty:	
Hotels/Motels:				Support Services:				Consulting:			
Industrial/Warehouses:	Y			Design/Engineering:							
Other:											

TYPES OF BUSINESS:

Real Estate Investment Trust
Office & Industrial Properties
Land Development
Property Management

BRANDS/DIVISIONS/AFFILIATES:

Lightstone Group LLC
Prime Group Realty Services, Inc.

GROWTH PLANS/SPECIAL FEATURES:

Prime Group Realty Trust (PGRT), a subsidiary of The Lightstone Group, LLC, is a real estate investment trust (REIT) that owns and operates 8 office properties in metropolitan Chicago, which contain an aggregate of nearly 3.3 million square feet. It also owns and operates one industrial property in the Chicago metropolitan area and shares interest in an office property joint venture consisting of 101,000 square feet. PGRT provides its own property management, leasing, marketing, acquisition, development, redevelopment and finance services. In addition, the company is the managing and leasing agent for the 1.5 million square foot Citadel Center office building located at 131 South Dearborn Street in Chicago, Illinois. Subsidiary Prime Group Realty Services Inc. offers property management services to third parties. The REIT also owns a joint venture interest in an office complex in Phoenix, Arizona.

CONTACTS: *Note: Officers with more than one job title may be intentionally listed here more than once.*

Jeffrey A. Patterson, CEO
Jeffrey A. Patterson, Pres.
James F. Hoffman, General Counsel/Sr. VP/Corp. Sec.
Steven R. Baron, Exec. VP- Office Leasing
Paul G. Del Vecchio, Exec. VP-Capital Markets
Victoria A. Cory, Sr VP-Loan Admin., Real Estate Tax & Due Diligence
George R. Whittemore, Trustee
David Lichtenstein, Chmn.

Phone: 312-917-1300 **Fax:** 312-917-1310
Toll-Free:
Address: 330 N. Wabash Ave. Ste. 2800, Chicago, IL 60611 US

FINANCIALS: **Sales and profits are in thousands of dollars—add 000 to get the full amount. 2009 Note: Financial information for 2009 was not available for all companies at press time.**

2009 Sales: $
2008 Sales: $64,840
2007 Sales: $73,174
2006 Sales: $
2005 Sales: $

2009 Profits: $
2008 Profits: $-73,336
2007 Profits: $-59,018
2006 Profits: $
2005 Profits: $

U.S. Stock Ticker: Subsidiary
Int'l Ticker: Int'l Exchange:
Employees:
Fiscal Year Ends: 12/31
Parent Company: LIGHTSTONE GROUP LLC (THE)

SALARIES/BENEFITS:

Pension Plan: ESOP Stock Plan: Profit Sharing: Top Exec. Salary: $ Bonus: $
Savings Plan: Stock Purch. Plan: Second Exec. Salary: $ Bonus: $

OTHER THOUGHTS:

Apparent Women Officers or Directors: 1
Hot Spot for Advancement for Women/Minorities:

LOCATIONS: ("Y" = Yes)

West:	Southwest:	Midwest:	Southeast:	Northeast:	International:
		Y			

PRIME RETAIL INC

www.primeretail.com

Industry Group Code: 531120 **Ranks within this company's industry group:** Sales: Profits:

Properties:		Financial Services:		Construction/Development:		Investments:		Specialty Services:		Brokerage:	
Apartments:		Mortgages:		Commercial Construction:		REIT:	Y	Property Management:	Y	Commercial Sales:	
Malls/Shopping:	Y	Title Insurance:		Residential Construction:				Online Services:		Residential Sales:	
Offices:		Property Insurance:		Land Development:				Software/IT:		Specialty:	
Hotels/Motels:				Support Services:				Consulting:			
Industrial/Warehouses:				Design/Engineering:							
Other:											

TYPES OF BUSINESS:

Real Estate Investment Trust
Shopping & Outlet Centers
Property Management

BRANDS/DIVISIONS/AFFILIATES:

Lightstone Group LLC
Prime Retail, LP
Prime Outlets
Prime Tourism

CONTACTS:

Note: Officers with more than one job title may be intentionally listed here more than once.

Nicholas G. King, COO
Robert A. Brvenik, Pres.
William G. Ellis, CFO
Karen Fluharty, Sr. VP-Mktg.
Pamela Meadows, Sr. VP-Human Resources
Kelvin Antill, General Counsel/Exec. VP
Bruce Zalaznick, Exec. VP-Real Estate
Lisa H. Kessler, Sr. VP-Leasing Outlet Shopping Centers
Salem LaHood, Sr. VP-Design & Construction
W. Paul Reed, Sr. VP-Construction

Phone: 410-234-0782	**Fax:**
Toll-Free:	
Address: 217 E. Redwood St., 20 fl., Baltimore, MD 21202 US	

GROWTH PLANS/SPECIAL FEATURES:

Prime Retail, Inc., a subsidiary of Lightstone Group LLC, owns and operates outlet mall and commercial real estate properties. The company is organized as an REIT (Real Estate Investment Trust). The company is divided into three divisions Prime Retail, Prime Outlet and Prime Tourism. The Prime Retail division operates shopping centers across the U.S. The firm's Prime Outlet is mainly discount-type shopping centers that enable value-oriented shoppers to purchase designer and brand name products directly from manufacturers at discounts. The Prime Tourism division provides services such as, itinerary planning assistance, group reservations, meet and greet services and travel packages. Prime's portfolio consists of 21 properties in 15 states and Puerto Rico, totaling more than 8 million square feet of retail outlets space and 8 million square feet of mall space. Most of these properties are located outside metropolitan areas, and ten of them are standard indoor shopping malls. These outlet centers feature a diversified mix of nationally recognized manufacturers of brand-name merchandise, including 3,000 stores and 450 designer and brand names. Companies currently utilizing Prime Retail's properties include American Eagle Outfitters; Avon; Banana Republic; Barneys New York; Bath & Body Works; Brooks Brothers; Calvin Klein; Disney; DKNY Jeans; Eddie Bauer; Gap; Giorgio Armani; Gucci; GUESS; Lee Wrangler; Saks Fifth Avenue OFF 5th; and Victoria's Secret Outlet. As a fully integrated real estate firm, the company provides accounting, finance, leasing, marketing and management services to its properties. Prime conducts substantially all of its business through operating subsidiary Prime Retail, LP. The company's business strategy includes seeking a tenant mix that represents the biggest and best draws in the outlet industry; operating under the Prime Outlets brand name and using on-site management teams to develop individualized marketing programs; and managing and leasing its properties with in-house personnel, reducing its reliance on third-party service providers and thereby lowering operating expenses.

FINANCIALS:

Sales and profits are in thousands of dollars—add 000 to get the full amount. 2009 Note: Financial information for 2009 was not available for all companies at press time.

2009 Sales: $	2009 Profits: $	**U.S. Stock Ticker: Subsidiary**
2008 Sales: $	2008 Profits: $	**Int'l Ticker:** Int'l Exchange:
2007 Sales: $	2007 Profits: $	Employees:
2006 Sales: $	2006 Profits: $	Fiscal Year Ends: 12/31
2005 Sales: $	2005 Profits: $	Parent Company: LIGHTSTONE GROUP LLC (THE)

SALARIES/BENEFITS:

Pension Plan:	ESOP Stock Plan:	Profit Sharing:	Top Exec. Salary: $	Bonus: $
Savings Plan:	Stock Purch. Plan:		Second Exec. Salary: $	Bonus: $

OTHER THOUGHTS:

Apparent Women Officers or Directors: 3
Hot Spot for Advancement for Women/Minorities: Y

LOCATIONS: ("Y" = Yes)

West:	Southwest:	Midwest:	Southeast:	Northeast:	International:
Y	Y	Y	Y	Y	

PROLOGIS

www.prologis.com

Industry Group Code: 531120 **Ranks within this company's industry group:** Sales: 1 Profits: 60

Properties:		Financial Services:		Construction/Development:		Investments:		Specialty Services:		Brokerage:	
Apartments:		Mortgages:		Commercial Construction:		REIT:	Y	Property Management:	Y	Commercial Sales:	
Malls/Shopping:		Title Insurance:		Residential Construction:				Online Services:		Residential Sales:	
Offices:		Property Insurance:		Land Development:	Y			Software/IT:	Y	Specialty:	
Hotels/Motels:				Support Services:	Y			Consulting:	Y		
Industrial/Warehouses:	Y			Design/Engineering:	Y						
Other:											

TYPES OF BUSINESS:

Real Estate Operations
REIT
Property Management
Property Development

BRANDS/DIVISIONS/AFFILIATES:

ProLogis Parc Narashino III

CONTACTS:

Note: Officers with more than one job title may be intentionally listed here more than once.

Walter C. Rakowich, CEO
Ted R. Antenucci, Pres./CIO
William E. Sullivan, CFO
John Morland, Managing Dir.-Global Human Resources
Edward S. Nekritz, General Counsel/Corp. Sec./Head-Global Risk
Charles E. Sullivan, Head-Global Oper.
Mo Sheahan, Public Rel.
Robbin Lee, Contact-Shareholder
Larry H. Harmsen, Pres., US & Canada
John R. Rizzo, Chief Sustainability Officer
Gary E. Anderson, Head-Global Investment Mgmt.
Mike Yamada, Pres., Japan
Stephen L. Feinberg, Chmn.
Philip Dunne, Pres., Europe

Phone: 303-567-5000	**Fax:** 303-567-5605
Toll-Free: 800-566-2706	
Address: 4545 Airport Way, Denver, CO 80239 US	

GROWTH PLANS/SPECIAL FEATURES:

ProLogis, formerly ProLogis Trust, is a real estate investment trust (REIT), based in Colorado, with more than 2,600 facilities owned, managed and under development in 136 markets throughout Europe, Asia, and North America. Most of the real estate properties managed, operated and in development by the company are generic bulk industrial complexes. The company is a leading global provider of industrial distribution facilities, with more than 475 million square feet of industrial space under management, which is leased to more than 4,500 clients, including manufacturers, retailers, transportation companies, third-party logistics providers and other companies with large-scale distribution needs. The firm manages its business through two operating segments: direct owned and investment management. The direct-owned segment includes the long-term ownership of industrial and retail properties, as well as industrial properties currently under development, land available for development and land subject to ground leases. The investment management segment represents the investment management of unconsolidated property funds and certain joint ventures, as well as the properties they own. In August 2009, ProLogis entered a portfolio development alliance with Japan Logistics Fund, Inc. and Mitsui & Co. In September 2009, the company formed a Global Renewable Energy Group to manage installations, provide development management services for and expand its portfolio of renewable energy projects. In March 2010, the firm completed the contribution of ProLogis Parc Narashino III to its alliance with Japan Logistics Fund and Mitsui & Co.

FINANCIALS:

Sales and profits are in thousands of dollars—add 000 to get the full amount. 2009 Note: Financial information for 2009 was not available for all companies at press time.

2009 Sales: $1,223,082	2009 Profits: $23,929	**U.S. Stock Ticker: PLD**
2008 Sales: $5,565,983	2008 Profits: $-449,966	**Int'l Ticker:** Int'l Exchange:
2007 Sales: $6,106,471	2007 Profits: $1,057,872	Employees: 1,135
2006 Sales: $2,446,392	2006 Profits: $874,367	Fiscal Year Ends: 12/31
2005 Sales: $1,817,207	2005 Profits: $396,163	Parent Company:

SALARIES/BENEFITS:

Pension Plan:	ESOP Stock Plan:	Profit Sharing:	Top Exec. Salary: $987,870	Bonus: $1,600,000
Savings Plan: Y	Stock Purch. Plan: Y		Second Exec. Salary: $630,000	Bonus: $696,000

OTHER THOUGHTS:

Apparent Women Officers or Directors: 4
Hot Spot for Advancement for Women/Minorities: Y

LOCATIONS: ("Y" = Yes)

West:	Southwest:	Midwest:	Southeast:	Northeast:	International:
Y	Y	Y	Y	Y	Y

PRUDENTIAL REAL ESTATE AFFILIATES INC

www.prudential.com

Industry Group Code: 531210 **Ranks within this company's industry group:** Sales: Profits:

Properties:		Financial Services:		Construction/Development:		Investments:		Specialty Services:		Brokerage:	
Apartments:		Mortgages:		Commercial Construction:		REIT:		Property Management:		Commercial Sales:	
Malls/Shopping:		Title Insurance:		Residential Construction:				Online Services:	Y	Residential Sales:	Y
Offices:		Property Insurance:		Land Development:				Software/IT:		Specialty:	
Hotels/Motels:				Support Services:				Consulting:			
Industrial/Warehouses:				Design/Engineering:							
Other:											

TYPES OF BUSINESS:

Real Estate Brokerage
Residential Sales
Online Databases & Information

BRANDS/DIVISIONS/AFFILIATES:

Prudential Financial
Prudential Lovejoy Realty, Inc.
Prudential Carruthers Realtors
Prudential Douglas Elliman
Prudential Vista
Triple S Realty
Prudential California Realty

CONTACTS:

Note: Officers with more than one job title may be intentionally listed here more than once.

Laurie Keenan, Pres.
Jack Frost, Sr. VP-Eastern Region Sales & Service
Patti Ray, Sr. VP-Western Region Sales & Service

Phone: 949-794-7900	**Fax:** 949-794-7035
Toll-Free:	
Address: 3333 Michelson Dr., Ste. 1000, Irvine, CA 92612 US	

GROWTH PLANS/SPECIAL FEATURES:

Prudential Real Estate Affiliates, Inc. (PREA), a subsidiary of Prudential Financial, is a collection of independently owned and operated franchises engaged in the brokerage of residential real estate throughout every state in the U.S., nine Canadian provinces and Mexico under the Prudential flag. The operations of this group of companies, consisting of more than 2,100 brokerages with more than 48,000 sales associates, are facilitated by an online database. Additionally, 800 affiliated independent commercial brokers make use of the PREA network. The firm's web site offers a search engine for homebuyers that features a home search, a neighborhood search, a brokerage office search and an e-mail registry that updates customers according to their profiles. Homebuyers can also access online guides for buying a home, selling a home and moving. The company also offers an online center for brokers. To its franchisees, PREA offers the well-known and respectable brand name and the symbolic rock of Prudential, as well as educational assistance, advance technology, a referral and relocation program and extensive networking between franchises and Prudential. Through other divisions and affiliates, the firm offers commercial real estate brokerage services, as well as all the financial services involved in buying a home.

FINANCIALS:

Sales and profits are in thousands of dollars—add 000 to get the full amount. 2009 Note: Financial information for 2009 was not available for all companies at press time.

2009 Sales: $	2009 Profits: $	**U.S. Stock Ticker: Subsidiary**
2008 Sales: $	2008 Profits: $	**Int'l Ticker:** Int'l Exchange:
2007 Sales: $	2007 Profits: $	Employees:
2006 Sales: $	2006 Profits: $	Fiscal Year Ends: 12/31
2005 Sales: $	2005 Profits: $	Parent Company: PRUDENTIAL FINANCIAL INC

SALARIES/BENEFITS:

Pension Plan:	ESOP Stock Plan:	Profit Sharing:	Top Exec. Salary: $	Bonus: $
Savings Plan:	Stock Purch. Plan:		Second Exec. Salary: $	Bonus: $

OTHER THOUGHTS:

Apparent Women Officers or Directors: 2
Hot Spot for Advancement for Women/Minorities:

LOCATIONS: ("Y" = Yes)

West:	Southwest:	Midwest:	Southeast:	Northeast:	International:
Y	Y	Y	Y	Y	Y

PS BUSINESS PARKS INC

www.psbusinessparks.com

Industry Group Code: 531120 **Ranks within this company's industry group:** Sales: 46 Profits: 30

Properties:		Financial Services:		Construction/Development:		Investments:		Specialty Services:		Brokerage:	
Apartments:		Mortgages:		Commercial Construction:		REIT:	Y	Property Management:	Y	Commercial Sales:	
Malls/Shopping:		Title Insurance:		Residential Construction:				Online Services:		Residential Sales:	
Offices:	Y	Property Insurance:		Land Development:				Software/IT:		Specialty:	
Hotels/Motels:				Support Services:				Consulting:			
Industrial/Warehouses:	Y			Design/Engineering:							
Other:											

TYPES OF BUSINESS:

Real Estate Investment Trust
Industrial Properties
Office Properties
Retail Properties
Business Parks
Property Management

BRANDS/DIVISIONS/AFFILIATES:

PS Business Parks LP
Public Storage Inc
Shady Grove Executive Center

CONTACTS:

Note: Officers with more than one job title may be intentionally listed here more than once.

Joseph D. Russell, Jr., CEO
John W. Petersen, COO/Exec. VP
Joseph D. Russell, Jr., Pres.
Edward Stokx, CFO/Exec. VP
Trenton Groves, Controller/VP
Viola I. Sanchez, VP-Southeast
Robin Mather, VP-Southern California
Maria Hawthorne, Sr. VP-East Coast
Coby Holley, VP-Pacific Northwest
Ronald L. Havner, Jr., Chmn.

Phone: 818-244-8080	**Fax:** 818-242-0566
Toll-Free:	
Address: 701 Western Ave., Glendale, CA 91201-2397 US	

GROWTH PLANS/SPECIAL FEATURES:

PS Business Parks, Inc. (PSB) is a self-advised and self-managed Real Estate Investment Trust (REIT). It acquires, owns, operates and develops commercial properties, primarily multi-tenant flex, office and industrial space. The company does business primarily through an operating partnership, PS Business Parks LP, in which PSB holds a 77% share, with the remainder being held by Public Storage, Inc. As the sole general partner of PS Business Parks LP, PSB maintains complete responsibility and discretion in managing and controlling the operating partnership. The firm's portfolio includes more than 150 properties totaling approximately 19.8 million square feet of commercial space located in eight states: Arizona, California, Florida, Maryland, Oregon, Texas, Virginia and Washington. Approximately 12.2 million square feet of the firm's owned property is classified as flex space. Flex space includes buildings that are configured with a combination of office, assembly, showroom, laboratory, light manufacturing and warehouse space, suitable to a variety of business needs. Approximately 3.9 million square feet of the firm's owned property is classified as industrial space, also suitable for a variety of uses. The remaining 3.4 million square feet consists of low-rise office space. The company also manages approximately 1.4 million rentable square feet on behalf of Public Storage and its affiliated entities. PSB targets properties in select sub-markets located in high-growth areas across the U.S. with above average education and personal income levels, access to critical infrastructure and with universities and major transportation arteries in close proximity. In March 2010, the firm acquired a 350,000 square foot office park in Maryland (Shady Grove Executive Center) for roughly $60 million.

PS Business Parks offers its employees benefits including a 401(k) plan; life and disability insurance; paid vacation; and comprehensive medical and dental coverage.

FINANCIALS:

Sales and profits are in thousands of dollars—add 000 to get the full amount. 2009 Note: Financial information for 2009 was not available for all companies at press time.

2009 Sales: $271,655	2009 Profits: $77,178	**U.S. Stock Ticker: PSB**
2008 Sales: $281,843	2008 Profits: $70,044	**Int'l Ticker:** Int'l Exchange:
2007 Sales: $269,298	2007 Profits: $68,666	Employees: 138
2006 Sales: $242,839	2006 Profits: $64,580	Fiscal Year Ends: 12/31
2005 Sales: $220,183	2005 Profits: $75,294	Parent Company:

SALARIES/BENEFITS:

Pension Plan:	ESOP Stock Plan:	Profit Sharing:	Top Exec. Salary: $425,790	Bonus: $340,550
Savings Plan: Y	Stock Purch. Plan:		Second Exec. Salary: $300,790	Bonus: $223,050

OTHER THOUGHTS:

Apparent Women Officers or Directors: 5
Hot Spot for Advancement for Women/Minorities: Y

LOCATIONS: ("Y" = Yes)

West:	Southwest:	Midwest:	Southeast:	Northeast:	International:
Y	Y		Y	Y	

PUBLIC STORAGE INC

www.publicstorage.com

Industry Group Code: 531120 **Ranks within this company's industry group:** Sales: 9 Profits: 1

Properties:		Financial Services:		Construction/Development:		Investments:		Specialty Services:		Brokerage:	
Apartments:		Mortgages:		Commercial Construction:		REIT:	Y	Property Management:		Commercial Sales:	
Malls/Shopping:		Title Insurance:		Residential Construction:				Online Services:	Y	Residential Sales:	
Offices:		Property Insurance:	Y	Land Development:				Software/IT:		Specialty:	
Hotels/Motels:				Support Services:				Consulting:			
Industrial/Warehouses:	Y			Design/Engineering:							
Other:	Y										

TYPES OF BUSINESS:

Real Estate Investment Trust
Self-Storage Facilities
Commercial Properties
Online Storage Reservations
Transportation Equipment

BRANDS/DIVISIONS/AFFILIATES:

PS Business Parks, Inc.
Shurgard Europe
PS Partners, Ltd.

CONTACTS: *Note: Officers with more than one job title may be intentionally listed here more than once.*

Ronald L. Havner, Jr., CEO
Mark C. Good, COO/Sr. VP
Ronald L. Havner, Jr., Pres./Vice Chmn.
John Reyes, CFO/Sr. VP
Candace N. Krol, Sr. VP-Human Resources
Steven M. Glick, Chief Legal Officer/Sr. VP
John M. Sambucho, Exec. VP-Oper., US Self-Storage
Obren P. Gerich, Pres., PS Insurance
David F. Doll, Pres., Real Estate Group
Stephanie G. Heim, Corp. Counsel/VP/Sec.
Joseph D. Russell Jr., Pres./CEO-PS Business Parks, Inc.
B. Wayne Hughes, Chmn.
StevenDe Tollenaere, CEO-Shurgard Europe

Phone: 818-244-8080	**Fax:** 818-244-9530
Toll-Free: 800-688-8057	
Address: 701 Western Ave., Glendale, CA 91201 US	

GROWTH PLANS/SPECIAL FEATURES:

Public Storage, Inc. is a fully integrated, self-administered and self-managed equity real estate investment trust (REIT) that acquires, develops, owns and operates self-storage facilities primarily used for month-to-month personal and business use. It is one of the largest owners and operators of self-storage space in the U.S. The company operates in three segments: Domestic Self-Storage, Europe Self-Storage and Commercial. The Domestic Self-Storage segment consists of the firm's direct and indirect equity interests in 2,010 self-storage facilities, containing approximately 127 million square feet of net rentable space, in 38 states under the Public Storage brand name. The self-storage facilities consist of three to seven buildings containing 350-750 storages spaces, most of which have 25-400 square feet and an interior height of eight to 12 feet. The Europe Self-Storage segment comprises the firm's 49% interest in Shurgard Europe, which owns 179 storage facilities in seven countries in Europe, with 10 million square feet of net rentable space. This segment also manages one facility in the U.K. that is wholly owned by Public Storage. Finally, the Commercial segment includes the company's direct and indirect equity interests in 21 million net rentable square feet of commercial space in 11 states, partially held through its 41% interest in PS Business Parks, Inc., a publicly traded REIT. In April 2010, Public Storage agreed to acquire 30 self-storage facilities in the Los Angeles, California and Chicago, Illinois areas for $189 million.

Employees are offered medical, dental and vision insurance; prescription drug coverage; short and long-term disability coverage; life insurance; medical and dependent care spending plans; an employee assistance program; employee discounts; and a 401(k) plan.

FINANCIALS: **Sales and profits are in thousands of dollars—add 000 to get the full amount. 2009 Note: Financial information for 2009 was not available for all companies at press time.**

2009 Sales: $1,627,702	2009 Profits: $834,621	**U.S. Stock Ticker: PSA**
2008 Sales: $1,723,593	2008 Profits: $935,176	**Int'l Ticker:** Int'l Exchange:
2007 Sales: $1,787,202	2007 Profits: $457,535	Employees: 4,900
2006 Sales: $1,379,066	2006 Profits: $314,026	Fiscal Year Ends: 12/31
2005 Sales: $1,059,838	2005 Profits: $456,393	Parent Company:

SALARIES/BENEFITS:

Pension Plan:	ESOP Stock Plan:	Profit Sharing:	Top Exec. Salary: $1,000,000	Bonus: $800,000
Savings Plan: Y	Stock Purch. Plan:		Second Exec. Salary: $600,000	Bonus: $700,000

OTHER THOUGHTS:

Apparent Women Officers or Directors: 2
Hot Spot for Advancement for Women/Minorities:

LOCATIONS: ("Y" = Yes)

West:	Southwest:	Midwest:	Southeast:	Northeast:	International:
Y	Y	Y	Y	Y	

PULTEGROUP INC

www.pulte.com

Industry Group Code: 2361 **Ranks within this company's industry group:** Sales: 4 Profits: 18

Properties:		Financial Services:		Construction/Development:		Investments:		Specialty Services:		Brokerage:	
Apartments:		Mortgages:	Y	Commercial Construction:		REIT:		Property Management:		Commercial Sales:	
Malls/Shopping:		Title Insurance:		Residential Construction:	Y			Online Services:		Residential Sales:	
Offices:		Property Insurance:		Land Development:	Y			Software/IT:		Specialty:	
Hotels/Motels:				Support Services:				Consulting:			
Industrial/Warehouses:				Design/Engineering:							
Other:											

TYPES OF BUSINESS:

Residential Construction
Financial Services
Mortgages
Land Development
Adult Communities

BRANDS/DIVISIONS/AFFILIATES:

Pulte Diversified Companies Inc
Del Webb Corp
Pulte Home Corp
Pulte International Corp
Pulte Mortgage LLC
DiVosta Homes
Centex Corp

CONTACTS:

Note: Officers with more than one job title may be intentionally listed here more than once.

Richard J. Dugas, Jr., CEO
Steven C. Petruska, COO/Exec. VP
Richard J. Dugas, Jr., Pres.
Roger A. Cregg, CFO/Exec. VP
Deborah W. Meyer, Chief Mktg. Officer/Sr. VP
James R. Ellinghausen, Exec. VP-Human Resources
Jerry R. Batt, CIO/VP
Janice M. Jones, VP-Merch.
Steven M. Cook, General Counsel/Sr. VP/Sec.
Anthony C. Koblinski, VP-Homebuilder Oper.
James P. Zeumer, VP-Corp. Comm.
James P. Zeumer, VP-Investor Rel.
Timothy M. Stewart, VP-Finance
Peter J. Keane, Sr. VP-Project Mgmt. Office
Bruce E. Robinson, Treas./VP
Michael J. Schweninger, Controller/VP
Richard J. Dugas, Jr., Chmn.

Phone: 248-647-2750 **Fax:** 248-433-4598
Toll-Free: 866-785-8325
Address: 100 Bloomfield Hills Pkwy., Ste. 300, Bloomfield Hills, MI 48304 US

GROWTH PLANS/SPECIAL FEATURES:

PulteGroup, Inc. is a holding company with subsidiaries in the homebuilding and financial services industries. These subsidiaries include Pulte Diversified Companies, Inc.; Del Webb Corp.; Pulte Home Corp.; Pulte International Corp.; Fox & Jacobs; DiVosta; and Pulte Mortgage LLC. The firm's business operation consists of two units: homebuilding and financial services. Pulte's core homebuilding business is engaged in the acquisition and development of land, primarily for residential purposes, within the U.S. and Puerto Rico. It facilitates the construction of housing on such land targeted for first-time, first and second move-up and active adult home buyers. Pulte builds a wide variety of homes including detached units, townhouses, condominium apartments and duplexes, with varying prices, models, options and lot sizes. Pulte's homebuilding business operates in 69 markets spanning 29 states, offering homes in 882 communities, with the average unit selling price of $258,000. Pulte's Homebuilding segments consist of the Atlantic Coast, including Connecticut, Delaware, Georgia, Maryland, Massachusetts, New Jersey, New York, North Carolina, Pennsylvania, Rhode Island, South Carolina, Tennessee and Virginia; the Gulf Coast, including Florida and Texas; the Midwest, including Colorado, Illinois, Indiana, Michigan, Minnesota and Ohio; the Southwest, including Arizona, Nevada and New Mexico; and the California segment, including California and Reno, Nevada. The firm's strategy is based on extensive market research that reveals well-defined buying profiles, job demographics and lifestyle choices. Pulte's financial services segment consists principally of mortgage operations conducted through Pulte Mortgage and its subsidiaries. Through its Del Webb brand, the company builds active adult communities. In August 2009, the company completed the acquisition of Centex Corporation for $1.3 billion.

Employees are offered medical, dental and vision insurance; a 401(k) plan; life and AD&D insurance; business travel accident insurance; short- and long-term disability; a tuition reimbursement plan; an employee assistance program; and time off for volunteering.

FINANCIALS:

Sales and profits are in thousands of dollars—add 000 to get the full amount. 2009 Note: Financial information for 2009 was not available for all companies at press time.

2009 Sales: $3,966,589	2009 Profits: $-1,182,567	**U.S. Stock Ticker: PHM**
2008 Sales: $6,112,038	2008 Profits: $-1,473,113	**Int'l Ticker:** Int'l Exchange:
2007 Sales: $9,121,730	2007 Profits: $-2,255,755	Employees: 5,700
2006 Sales: $14,075,248	2006 Profits: $687,471	Fiscal Year Ends: 12/31
2005 Sales: $14,528,236	2005 Profits: $1,491,913	Parent Company:

SALARIES/BENEFITS:

Pension Plan:	ESOP Stock Plan:	Profit Sharing:	Top Exec. Salary: $1,000,000	Bonus: $1,799,933
Savings Plan: Y	Stock Purch. Plan:		Second Exec. Salary: $775,010	Bonus: $1,195,670

OTHER THOUGHTS:

Apparent Women Officers or Directors: 4
Hot Spot for Advancement for Women/Minorities: Y

LOCATIONS: ("Y" = Yes)

West:	Southwest:	Midwest:	Southeast:	Northeast:	International:
Y	Y	Y	Y	Y	

QMH UK LTD

www.qmh-hotels.com

Industry Group Code: 721110 **Ranks within this company's industry group:** Sales: Profits:

Properties:		Financial Services:		Construction/Development:		Investments:		Specialty Services:		Brokerage:	
Apartments:		Mortgages:		Commercial Construction:		REIT:		Property Management:		Commercial Sales:	
Malls/Shopping:		Title Insurance:		Residential Construction:				Online Services:		Residential Sales:	
Offices:		Property Insurance:		Land Development:				Software/IT:		Specialty:	
Hotels/Motels:	Y			Support Services:				Consulting:			
Industrial/Warehouses:				Design/Engineering:							
Other:	Y										

TYPES OF BUSINESS:

Hotels
Fitness Clubs
Event Planning Services

BRANDS/DIVISIONS/AFFILIATES:

Holiday Inn
Crowne Plaza
Best Western
Club Moativation
Queens Moat Houses plc

GROWTH PLANS/SPECIAL FEATURES:

QMH UK Ltd., formerly Queens Moat Houses plc, owns and operates hotels throughout the U.K. In total, it has 18 hotels: 12 Holiday Inns, three Crowne Plaza hotels and three Best Western hotels. QMH also runs 15 Club Moativation health and fitness clubs. The clubs are located on hotel property but make memberships available to anyone, not just hotel guests. All of QMH's hotels offer conference suites that can accommodate groups ranging from 40-800 delegates, as well as providing wireless Internet, a dedicated meeting host and extra rooms for smaller meetings. QMH hotels are all three- or four-star standard. Almost all of the firm's hotels have been awarded Civil Marriage Licenses, allowing couples to utilize the hotel as a dedicated venue for both wedding ceremonies and receptions. Individual hotels offer wedding planning services including table plans, flower arrangements, photographers, catering and entertainment booking. They also provide discounted room rates for wedding guests. The private company is owned by a group of investors that includes Goldman Sachs; Regina Investments Sarl.; and Whitehall 2001 Funds, a real estate private equity fund sponsored and managed by Goldman Sachs affiliates.

CONTACTS: *Note: Officers with more than one job title may be intentionally listed here more than once.*

Richard Moore, Managing Dir.

Phone: 44-1708-730-522	**Fax:** 44-1708-762-691
Toll-Free:	
Address: Queens Ct., 9-17 Eastern Rd., Romford, Essex RM1 3NG UK	

FINANCIALS: **Sales and profits are in thousands of dollars—add 000 to get the full amount. 2009 Note: Financial information for 2009 was not available for all companies at press time.**

2009 Sales: $	2009 Profits: $	**U.S. Stock Ticker: Private**
2008 Sales: $	2008 Profits: $	**Int'l Ticker:** Int'l Exchange:
2007 Sales: $	2007 Profits: $	Employees:
2006 Sales: $	2006 Profits: $	Fiscal Year Ends: 12/31
2005 Sales: $	2005 Profits: $	Parent Company:

SALARIES/BENEFITS:

Pension Plan:	ESOP Stock Plan:	Profit Sharing:	Top Exec. Salary: $	Bonus: $
Savings Plan:	Stock Purch. Plan:		Second Exec. Salary: $	Bonus: $

OTHER THOUGHTS:

Apparent Women Officers or Directors: 1
Hot Spot for Advancement for Women/Minorities:

LOCATIONS: ("Y" = Yes)

West:	Southwest:	Midwest:	Southeast:	Northeast:	International:
					Y

RADIAN GROUP INC

www.radian.biz

Industry Group Code: 524126 **Ranks within this company's industry group:** Sales: 1 Profits: 1

Properties:		Financial Services:		Construction/Development:		Investments:		Specialty Services:		Brokerage:	
Apartments:		Mortgages:	Y	Commercial Construction:		REIT:		Property Management:		Commercial Sales:	
Malls/Shopping:		Title Insurance:		Residential Construction:				Online Services:	Y	Residential Sales:	
Offices:		Property Insurance:		Land Development:				Software/IT:		Specialty:	
Hotels/Motels:				Support Services:				Consulting:			
Industrial/Warehouses:				Design/Engineering:							
Other:											

TYPES OF BUSINESS:

Insurance-Financial Guaranty
Mortgage Insurance & Services
Insurance-Related Services
Financial Services
Consumer Asset Services

BRANDS/DIVISIONS/AFFILIATES:

Radian Guaranty, Inc.
Radian Insurance, Inc.
Amerin Guaranty Corp.
Radian Asset Assurance
RAAL
Sherman Financial Services Group LLC
C-BASS

CONTACTS:

Note: Officers with more than one job title may be intentionally listed here more than once.

S. A. Ibrahim, CEO
C. Robert Quint, CFO/Exec. VP
Lawrence DelGatto, CIO/Exec. VP
Rick Altman, Chief Admin. Officer/Exec. VP
Ted Hoffman, General Counsel/Corp. Sec.
Terri Williams-Perry, Investor Rel.
Cathy Jackson, Controller/Sr. VP
Teresa Bryce, Pres., Radian Guaranty, Inc.
David J. Beidler, Pres., Radian Asset Assurance, Inc.
Paul F. Bognanno, Chmn.-Radian Guaranty Inc.
H. Scott Theobald, Exec. VP/Chief Risk Officer-Radian Guaranty, Inc.
Herbert Wender, Chmn.

Phone: 215-231-1000	**Fax:**
Toll-Free: 800-523-1988	
Address: 1601 Market St., Philadelphia, PA 19103 US	

GROWTH PLANS/SPECIAL FEATURES:

Radian Group, Inc. is a global credit enhancement company focused on domestic residential mortgage insurance. The firm operates in three segments: mortgage insurance, financial guaranty and financial services. The mortgage insurance segment provides credit protection for mortgage lenders and other financial services companies on residential mortgage assets, primarily through traditional mortgage insurance. The company provides these products and services through wholly-owned subsidiaries Radian Guaranty, Inc.; Radian Insurance, Inc.; and Amerin Guaranty Corp. The financial guaranty segment insures and reinsures municipal bonds, structured finance transactions and other credit-based risks, and provides synthetic credit protection on various asset classes through credit default swaps. Major industries served by this segment include telecommunications, financial solutions, insurance, retail and utilities. This segment operates primarily through Radian Asset Assurance, a wholly-owned subsidiary of Radian Guaranty, and Radian Asset Assurance's subsidiary RAAL, located in the U.K. The financial services segment consists mainly of the company's 28.7% ownership stake in Sherman Financial Services Group LLC, a consumer asset and servicing firm specializing in credit card and bankruptcy-plan consumer assets. This segment also includes the firm's 46% interest in Credit-Based Asset Servicing and Securitization LLC (C-BASS), a mortgage investment company whose operations are in run-off. In late 2008, Radian announced a temporary discontinuation of writing any new financial guaranty business, including accepting new financial guaranty reinsurance.

The company offers its employees medical, dental and vision insurance; a 401(k) plan; an employee stock purchase plan; life insurance; a pension plan; short- and long-term disability insurance; tuition reimbursement; and an employee assistance program.

FINANCIALS:

Sales and profits are in thousands of dollars—add 000 to get the full amount. 2009 Note: Financial information for 2009 was not available for all companies at press time.

2009 Sales: $1,313,378	2009 Profits: $-147,879	**U.S. Stock Ticker: RDN**
2008 Sales: $1,808,036	2008 Profits: $-410,579	**Int'l Ticker:** Int'l Exchange:
2007 Sales: $201,051	2007 Profits: $-1,290,299	Employees: 803
2006 Sales: $1,327,946	2006 Profits: $582,172	Fiscal Year Ends: 12/31
2005 Sales: $1,298,151	2005 Profits: $522,854	Parent Company:

SALARIES/BENEFITS:

Pension Plan: Y	ESOP Stock Plan:	Profit Sharing:	Top Exec. Salary: $800,000	Bonus: $
Savings Plan: Y	Stock Purch. Plan: Y		Second Exec. Salary: $383,846	Bonus: $

OTHER THOUGHTS:

Apparent Women Officers or Directors: 3
Hot Spot for Advancement for Women/Minorities: Y

LOCATIONS: ("Y" = Yes)

West:	Southwest:	Midwest:	Southeast:	Northeast:	International:
Y	Y	Y	Y	Y	Y

RAILWORKS CORP

www.railworks.com

Industry Group Code: 237 **Ranks within this company's industry group:** Sales: Profits:

Properties:		Financial Services:		Construction/Development:		Investments:		Specialty Services:		Brokerage:	
Apartments:		Mortgages:		Commercial Construction:	Y	REIT:		Property Management:		Commercial Sales:	
Malls/Shopping:		Title Insurance:		Residential Construction:				Online Services:		Residential Sales:	
Offices:		Property Insurance:		Land Development:				Software/IT:		Specialty:	
Hotels/Motels:				Support Services:	Y			Consulting:			
Industrial/Warehouses:				Design/Engineering:	Y						
Other:											

TYPES OF BUSINESS:

Railroad Construction & Maintenance
Rail Technologies
Electrical & Mechanical Installations
Communications Technologies

BRANDS/DIVISIONS/AFFILIATES:

Railworks Transit, Inc.
Railworks Track Systems, Inc.
RailWorks Track Systems-Texas, Inc.
HSQ Technology
L.K. Comstock & Company, Inc.
PNR Railworks, Inc.
PNR Leasing, Ltd.
Railworks Track Services, Inc.

CONTACTS: *Note: Officers with more than one job title may be intentionally listed here more than once.*

Jeffrey M. Levy, CEO
Jeffrey M. Levy, Pres.
Veronica Lubatkin, CFO/Exec. VP
Harry Z. Glantz, VP-Human Resources
Steven G. Milewicz, General Counsel/Sec./Exec. VP
James R. Hansen, VP-Bus. Dev.
Gene Cellini, Sr. VP-Tax
John August, Exec. VP
Michael Holt, Pres., RailWorks Transit Inc.
Ben D'Alessandro, Pres., RailWorks Transit, Inc.
Scott Brace, Exec. VP-RailWorks Track Systems Inc.
Jamey Craig, Pres., PNR RailWorks Inc.

Phone: 212-502-7900	**Fax:** 212-502-1865
Toll-Free:	
Address: 5 Penn Plz., New York, NY 10001 US	

GROWTH PLANS/SPECIAL FEATURES:

RailWorks Corporation and its network of affiliated companies provide track and transit systems construction and maintenance services for the rail and rail-transit industries in the U.S. and Canada. The firm is owned by Wind Point Partners, a private equity investment firm. The company's business serves a range of railroads, public transit authorities and commuter railroads, as well as private industries. The firm divides its operations into two business units: transit systems and tracks. In total, RailWorks has twelve subsidiaries: HSQ Technology; L.K. Comstock & Company, Inc.; L.K. Comstock National Transit, Inc.; PNR RailWorks, Inc.; PNR Leasing, Ltd.; PNR Coyle Inc.; RailWorks Signals & Communications, Inc.; RailWorks Systems, Inc.; RailWorks Track Services, Inc.; RailWorks Track Systems, Inc.; RailWorks Track Systems-Texas, Inc.; and RailWorks Transit, Inc. The transit systems segment handles automatic train controls and systems; traction power systems, including overhead catenary; transit facilities, including general and mechanical contracting; communication systems, including systems that incorporate fiber/Sonet, radio/microwave, cellular and WiFi technology; Supervisory Control and Data Acquisition System (SCADA) and system integration; and rain construction, maintenance and rehabilitation. In addition to these services, the transit systems unit provides design support, construction engineering and installation, testing, start-up and maintenance services for heavy rail, light rail and automated people mover facilities. The track segment designs, builds, manages and supplies railways and railway construction, maintenance and rehabilitation projects. This business involves, in addition to rail and tie installation techniques, the development of signals and crossings, production involving steel and tie gangs, maintenance-of-way services, communication systems, scheduled maintenance work and emergency repairs, which include derailment response.

RailWorks offers its employees medical and dental insurance and a 401(k) plan.

FINANCIALS: **Sales and profits are in thousands of dollars—add 000 to get the full amount. 2009 Note: Financial information for 2009 was not available for all companies at press time.**

2009 Sales: $	2009 Profits: $	**U.S. Stock Ticker: Private**
2008 Sales: $	2008 Profits: $	**Int'l Ticker:** Int'l Exchange:
2007 Sales: $	2007 Profits: $	Employees:
2006 Sales: $	2006 Profits: $	Fiscal Year Ends: 12/31
2005 Sales: $350,000	2005 Profits: $	Parent Company:

SALARIES/BENEFITS:

Pension Plan:	ESOP Stock Plan:	Profit Sharing:	Top Exec. Salary: $	Bonus: $
Savings Plan: Y	Stock Purch. Plan:		Second Exec. Salary: $	Bonus: $

OTHER THOUGHTS:

Apparent Women Officers or Directors: 2
Hot Spot for Advancement for Women/Minorities:

LOCATIONS: ("Y" = Yes)

West:	Southwest:	Midwest:	Southeast:	Northeast:	International:
Y	Y	Y	Y	Y	Y

RAMADA WORLDWIDE INC

www.ramada.com

Industry Group Code: 721110 **Ranks within this company's industry group:** Sales: Profits:

Properties:		Financial Services:		Construction/Development:		Investments:		Specialty Services:		Brokerage:	
Apartments:		Mortgages:		Commercial Construction:		REIT:		Property Management:		Commercial Sales:	
Malls/Shopping:		Title Insurance:		Residential Construction:				Online Services:		Residential Sales:	
Offices:		Property Insurance:		Land Development:				Software/IT:		Specialty:	
Hotels/Motels:	Y			Support Services:				Consulting:			
Industrial/Warehouses:				Design/Engineering:							
Other:											

TYPES OF BUSINESS:

Hotels & Motels

BRANDS/DIVISIONS/AFFILIATES:

Wyndham Worldwide
Ramada Inn
Ramada Plaza Hotel
Ramada Limited
Ramada Hotel & Suites
Ramada Resort
Ramada Hotel & Resorts
Ramada Encore

CONTACTS:

Note: Officers with more than one job title may be intentionally listed here more than once.

Keith J. Pierce, Pres.
Mark F. Young, Sr. VP-Brand
Stephen P. Holmes, CEO-Wyndham Worldwide

Phone: 973-428-9700	**Fax:** 605-229-8938
Toll-Free: 800-272-6232	
Address: 1 Sylvan Way, Parsippany, NJ 07054 US	

GROWTH PLANS/SPECIAL FEATURES:

Ramada Worldwide, Inc., a subsidiary of Wyndham Worldwide, is a leading franchisor of hotel and motel properties. The company owns approximately 900 Ramada Limited, Ramada Inn and Ramada Plaza Hotel properties throughout the U.S. and in 45 other countries, and offers discounts for seniors, groups, government employees and AAA and AARP members. The franchise also participates in the Wyndham Rewards program, in which guests can earn rewards points, gift cards or resort vacations by staying in participating hotels. The company's core brand, Ramada, offers room service, bell service, on-site restaurants and cocktail lounges, and full-service meeting facilities. Ramada Limited and Ramada Encore properties offer less expensive rates and limited amenities. Ramada Plaza Hotel properties offer on-site restaurants, lounges and banquet rooms, concierge services and fitness centers. Ramada Resort properties, franchised both domestically and internationally, are designed for leisure travelers on extended stays and offer playgrounds, pools, spas, fitness centers, dining room services and car rental facilities. The franchise's resort properties, principally located outside the U.S. and Canada, include Ramada Hotel & Resorts, which feature oversized rooms, pools, saunas, golf and tennis facilities, restaurants and lounges; and Ramada Hotel & Suites, offering luxury suites, restaurants and meeting and banquet facilities. Recently, Ramada has formed and expanded agreements for the development of hotels in Kuwait, Jordan, Moldova, Thailand, China and India. In September 2009, the company opened its first hotel in Russia, Ramada Yekaterinburg. In February 2010, the franchise opened the Ramada Plaza Waikiki in Hawaii.

Wyndham Worldwide and its subsidiaries offer employees a choice of medical, dental and vision plans, flexible spending accounts, adoption reimbursement, business travel accident insurance, an educational assistance program and a 401(k) plan.

FINANCIALS:

Sales and profits are in thousands of dollars—add 000 to get the full amount. 2009 Note: Financial information for 2009 was not available for all companies at press time.

2009 Sales: $	2009 Profits: $	**U.S. Stock Ticker: Subsidiary**
2008 Sales: $	2008 Profits: $	**Int'l Ticker:** Int'l Exchange:
2007 Sales: $	2007 Profits: $	Employees:
2006 Sales: $	2006 Profits: $	Fiscal Year Ends: 12/31
2005 Sales: $	2005 Profits: $	Parent Company: WYNDHAM WORLDWIDE

SALARIES/BENEFITS:

Pension Plan:	ESOP Stock Plan:	Profit Sharing:	Top Exec. Salary: $	Bonus: $
Savings Plan: Y	Stock Purch. Plan:		Second Exec. Salary: $	Bonus: $

OTHER THOUGHTS:

Apparent Women Officers or Directors:
Hot Spot for Advancement for Women/Minorities:

LOCATIONS: ("Y" = Yes)

West:	Southwest:	Midwest:	Southeast:	Northeast:	International:
Y	Y	Y	Y	Y	Y

RE/MAX INTERNATIONAL INC

www.remax.com

Industry Group Code: 531210 **Ranks within this company's industry group:** Sales: Profits:

Properties:		Financial Services:		Construction/Development:		Investments:		Specialty Services:		Brokerage:	
Apartments:		Mortgages:		Commercial Construction:		REIT:		Property Management:		Commercial Sales:	Y
Malls/Shopping:		Title Insurance:		Residential Construction:				Online Services:	Y	Residential Sales:	Y
Offices:		Property Insurance:		Land Development:				Software/IT:		Specialty:	Y
Hotels/Motels:				Support Services:				Consulting:			
Industrial/Warehouses:				Design/Engineering:							
Other:											

TYPES OF BUSINESS:

Real Estate Brokerage
Moving & Relocation Services
Online Database

BRANDS/DIVISIONS/AFFILIATES:

RE/MAX Collection
RE/MAX Commercial Services
E-Loan
CCIMnet

CONTACTS:

Note: Officers with more than one job title may be intentionally listed here more than once.

Margaret Kelly, CEO
Bruce Benham, COO
Vinnie Tracey, Pres.
David M.K. Metzger, CFO
Mike Reagan, Sr. VP-Brand Mktg.
Pat Lawrence, Sr. VP-Human Resources
Kristi Graning, Sr. VP-IT
Geoff Lewis, Chief Legal Officer/Sr. VP
John DuPont, Sr. VP-Global Brand Mgmt. & Strategic Planning
Kristi Graning, Sr. VP-eBusiness
Mike Ryan, Sr. VP-Media & Training
Kelly Hickey, Controller
Joe Reynolds, Exec. VP-Affiliated Companies
Jack Kreider, Exec. VP-Regional Svcs.
Peter Gilmour, Sr. VP-Int'l Franchise Sales & Brokerage
Pam Newman, VP-Event Mgmt.
Dave Liniger, Chmn.
William E. Soteroff, Sr. VP-Int'l Dev.

Phone: 303-770-5531	**Fax:** 303-796-3599
Toll-Free:	
Address: 5075 S. Syracuse St., Denver, CO 80237-2712 US	

GROWTH PLANS/SPECIAL FEATURES:

RE/MAX International, Inc. is a real estate brokerage company. Its focus is to aid clients in buying, selling, financing and moving into properties. The firm's network is divided into over 70 regions. These regions can vary in size from a metropolitan area to an entire country. Residential sales make up the majority of the firm's revenue, but it also operates a commercial brokerage division. The firm has a franchised network of approximately 100,000 sales associates operating in more than 65 countries, including Canada, Australia, the U.K. and Mexico, as well as countries in Central and South America, the Caribbean Islands, Europe, the Middle East and southern Africa. The company's commercial properties division gives customers access to the CCIMnet database of commercial properties, which allows clients to find commercial office space, as well as industrial locations, shopping centers, retail-commercial, multi-family, vacant land, hospitality and farm/ranch properties. RE/MAX's commercial associates aid clients in the selling, buying or leasing of their property interests. Through a partnership with E-Loan, the Lending Center on RE/MAX's web site provides customers with access to mortgage information, while realtor.com allows customers to quickly search through its property listings. The RE/MAX Collection program focuses on exclusive properties. Many of the agents that work within this program are Certified Luxury Home Marketing Specialists. All RE/MAX Collection sales associates have additional training concerning the luxury real estate market. RE/MAX uses a hot air balloon as its corporate logo, and it owns it owns the world's largest balloon fleet with 80 balloons.

FINANCIALS:

Sales and profits are in thousands of dollars—add 000 to get the full amount. 2009 Note: Financial information for 2009 was not available for all companies at press time.

2009 Sales: $	2009 Profits: $	**U.S. Stock Ticker: Private**
2008 Sales: $	2008 Profits: $	**Int'l Ticker:** Int'l Exchange:
2007 Sales: $	2007 Profits: $	Employees:
2006 Sales: $	2006 Profits: $	Fiscal Year Ends: 12/31
2005 Sales: $	2005 Profits: $	Parent Company:

SALARIES/BENEFITS:

Pension Plan:	ESOP Stock Plan:	Profit Sharing:	Top Exec. Salary: $	Bonus: $
Savings Plan:	Stock Purch. Plan:		Second Exec. Salary: $	Bonus: $

OTHER THOUGHTS:

Apparent Women Officers or Directors: 10
Hot Spot for Advancement for Women/Minorities: Y

LOCATIONS: ("Y" = Yes)

West:	Southwest:	Midwest:	Southeast:	Northeast:	International:
Y	Y	Y	Y	Y	Y

REALOGY CORPORATION

www.realogy.com

Industry Group Code: 5311 **Ranks within this company's industry group:** Sales: 4 Profits: 34

Properties:		Financial Services:		Construction/Development:		Investments:		Specialty Services:		Brokerage:	
Apartments:		Mortgages:	Y	Commercial Construction:		REIT:		Property Management:		Commercial Sales:	Y
Malls/Shopping:		Title Insurance:	Y	Residential Construction:				Online Services:		Residential Sales:	Y
Offices:		Property Insurance:		Land Development:				Software/IT:		Specialty:	
Hotels/Motels:				Support Services:				Consulting:			
Industrial/Warehouses:				Design/Engineering:							
Other:											

TYPES OF BUSINESS:

Real Estate Services
Real Estate Brokerages
Settlement Services
Property Financing Services

BRANDS/DIVISIONS/AFFILIATES:

Apollo Management LP
NRT LLC
Realogy Franchise Group
Better Homes and Gardens Real Estate
Century 21 Real Estate Corp
Coldwell Banker Real Estate LLC
ERA
Sotheby's International Realty

CONTACTS: *Note: Officers with more than one job title may be intentionally listed here more than once.*

Richard A. Smith, CEO
Richard A. Smith, Pres.
Anthony E. Hull, CFO/Exec. VP
Dave Weaving, Chief Admin. Officer/Exec. VP
Marilyn Wasser, General Counsel/Corp. Sec./Exec. VP
Mark Panus, Sr. VP-Corp. Comm.
Alicia Swift, Contact-Investor Rel.
Dea Benson, Chief Acct. Officer/Sr. VP/Controller
Kevin J. Kelleher, CEO/Pres., Cartus Corp.
Alexander E. Perriello III, CEO/Pres., Realogy Franchise Group
Bruce Zipf, CEO/Pres., NRT LLC
Don Casey, CEO/Pres., Title Resource Group LLC

Phone: 973-407-2000	**Fax:**
Toll-Free:	
Address: 1 Campus Dr., Parsippany, NJ 07054 US	

GROWTH PLANS/SPECIAL FEATURES:

Realogy Corporation, a subsidiary of Apollo Management, is an integrated provider of real estate and relocation services throughout the U.S., as well as internationally. More specifically, the firm offers a variety of services including real estate franchising, brokerage, relocation and title services. Through the Realogy Franchise Group, the firm operates six brands in the real estate industry: Better Homes and Gardens Real Estate; Century 21 Real Estate LLC; Coldwell Banker; Coldwell Banker Commercial; ERA; and Sotheby's International Realty. Better Homes and Gardens Real Estate is building a new international residential real estate franchise company. Century 21 Real Estate is a residential real estate brokerage franchise with locations in 64 countries around the world. Coldwell Banker is a real estate brokerage franchisor. Coldwell Banker Commercial is a brokerage firm that concentrates on the sale of commercial properties. ERA is a residential brokerage franchisor with locations in 50 countries. Sotheby's International Realty is a real estate franchise that focuses on luxury properties around the world. Additional Realogy business units include NRT LLC, a leading owner and operator of residential real estate brokerages in over 35 major metropolitan markets of the U.S.; Cartus Corporation, a leading global relocation service provider; and Title Resource Group LLC, a provider of title and settlement services with approximately 385 offices throughout the U.S. Recently, Realogy made a minority equity investment in Century 21 China Real Estate, the master franchisor for its Century 21 brand in China. In April 2009, the firm's subsidiary Better Homes and Gardens Real Estate expanded to 15 States. In March 2010, company's subsidiary Sotheby's International Realty Affiliates announced the signing of an exclusive 25-year licensing agreement with Countrywide to use the Sotheby's name.

Employees of the firm are offered medical, dental and vision coverage; flexible spending accounts for dependent care and health care.

FINANCIALS: **Sales and profits are in thousands of dollars—add 000 to get the full amount. 2009 Note: Financial information for 2009 was not available for all companies at press time.**

2009 Sales: $3,932,000	2009 Profits: $-262,000	**U.S. Stock Ticker: Private**
2008 Sales: $4,725,000	2008 Profits: $-1,912,000	**Int'l Ticker:** Int'l Exchange:
2007 Sales: $	2007 Profits: $	Employees:
2006 Sales: $	2006 Profits: $	Fiscal Year Ends: 12/31
2005 Sales: $	2005 Profits: $	Parent Company: APOLLO MANAGEMENT LP

SALARIES/BENEFITS:

Pension Plan:	ESOP Stock Plan:	Profit Sharing:	Top Exec. Salary: $1,000,000	Bonus: $
Savings Plan: Y	Stock Purch. Plan:		Second Exec. Salary: $525,000	Bonus: $262,500

OTHER THOUGHTS:

Apparent Women Officers or Directors: 4
Hot Spot for Advancement for Women/Minorities: Y

LOCATIONS: ("Y" = Yes)

West:	Southwest:	Midwest:	Southeast:	Northeast:	International:
Y	Y	Y	Y	Y	Y

REALTY INCOME CORP

www.realtyincome.com

Industry Group Code: 531120 **Ranks within this company's industry group:** Sales: 43 Profits: 20

Properties:		Financial Services:		Construction/Development:		Investments:		Specialty Services:		Brokerage:	
Apartments:		Mortgages:		Commercial Construction:	Y	REIT:	Y	Property Management:	Y	Commercial Sales:	
Malls/Shopping:	Y	Title Insurance:		Residential Construction:				Online Services:		Residential Sales:	
Offices:	Y	Property Insurance:		Land Development:				Software/IT:		Specialty:	
Hotels/Motels:				Support Services:				Consulting:			
Industrial/Warehouses:				Design/Engineering:							
Other:											

TYPES OF BUSINESS:

Real Estate Investment Trust
Retail Property
Property Management

BRANDS/DIVISIONS/AFFILIATES:

Crest Net Lease Inc

CONTACTS:

Note: Officers with more than one job title may be intentionally listed here more than once.

Thomas A. Lewis, CEO
Gary M. Malino, COO
Gary M. Malino, Pres.
Paul M. Meurer, CFO/Exec. VP/Treas.
Robert J. Israel, Sr. VP-Research
Michael R. Pfeiffer, General Counsel/Exec. VP/Corp. Sec.
Tere H. Miller, VP-Corp. Comm.
Tere H. Miller, VP-Investor Rel.
Gregory J. Fahey, Controller/VP
Richard G. Collins, Exec. VP-Portfolio Mgmt.
Laura S. King, Sr. VP/Assistant General Counsel/Assistant Sec.
Donald R. Cameron, Chmn.

Phone: 760-741-2111	**Fax:** 760-741-2235
Toll-Free:	
Address: 600 La Terraza Blvd., Escondido, CA 92025 US	

GROWTH PLANS/SPECIAL FEATURES:

Realty Income Corporation (RIC) is a real estate investment trust (REIT). The firm's primary objective is to generate stable monthly cash distributions based on its portfolio of retail properties leased to regional and national chains. The company's portfolio management focus includes contractual rent increases on existing leases; rent increases at the termination of existing leases, when market conditions permit; the re-leasing of vacant properties; and the selective sale of other properties. Of the 2,339 retail properties owned by the company, 2,328 (approximately 99.5%) are single-tenant retail locations; the remaining 11 are multi-tenant, distribution and office properties. RIC leases its properties under long-term, net-lease agreements (usually 15-20 years) that generally require the tenant to pay for maintenance, minimum monthly rents and property operating expenses such as taxes and insurance. The company's acquisition strategy includes a focus on freestanding, commercially-zoned, single-tenant properties, in important retail locations, that can be purchased with the simultaneous execution or assumption of long-term, net-lease agreements, offering both current income and the potential for rent increases. The firm's properties are located in 49 states, are leased to 118 different retail chains in 30 separate industries and have an average of 8,200 square feet of leasable retail space. Additionally, the company's wholly-owned taxable REIT subsidiary, Crest Net Lease, Inc., owns three properties with a total investment value of $3.8 million, which are currently classified as held for sale. Crest Net Lease primarily engages in the buying and selling of properties, mainly to individual investors involved in tax-deferred exchanges. During 2009, RIC invested a total of $57.9 million in 16 new retail properties located in five states and containing over 278,000 square feet of leasable space.

FINANCIALS:

Sales and profits are in thousands of dollars—add 000 to get the full amount. 2009 Note: Financial information for 2009 was not available for all companies at press time.

2009 Sales: $327,581	2009 Profits: $131,127	**U.S. Stock Ticker: O**
2008 Sales: $327,773	2008 Profits: $131,841	**Int'l Ticker:** Int'l Exchange:
2007 Sales: $291,483	2007 Profits: $140,409	Employees: 72
2006 Sales: $237,416	2006 Profits: $110,781	Fiscal Year Ends: 12/31
2005 Sales: $195,453	2005 Profits: $99,119	Parent Company:

SALARIES/BENEFITS:

Pension Plan:	ESOP Stock Plan:	Profit Sharing:	Top Exec. Salary: $350,000	Bonus: $1,015,000
Savings Plan: Y	Stock Purch. Plan:		Second Exec. Salary: $325,000	Bonus: $480,000

OTHER THOUGHTS:

Apparent Women Officers or Directors: 4
Hot Spot for Advancement for Women/Minorities: Y

LOCATIONS: ("Y" = Yes)

West:	Southwest:	Midwest:	Southeast:	Northeast:	International:
Y	Y	Y	Y	Y	

RED LION HOTELS CORPORATION

www.rdln.com

Industry Group Code: 721110 **Ranks within this company's industry group:** Sales: 28 Profits: 22

Properties:		Financial Services:		Construction/Development:		Investments:		Specialty Services:		Brokerage:	
Apartments:		Mortgages:		Commercial Construction:		REIT:		Property Management:		Commercial Sales:	
Malls/Shopping:		Title Insurance:		Residential Construction:				Online Services:	Y	Residential Sales:	
Offices:		Property Insurance:		Land Development:				Software/IT:		Specialty:	
Hotels/Motels:	Y			Support Services:				Consulting:			
Industrial/Warehouses:				Design/Engineering:							
Other:											

TYPES OF BUSINESS:

Hotels
Event Ticketing Services
Property Management Services
Entertainment Productions
Guest Loyalty Programs

BRANDS/DIVISIONS/AFFILIATES:

Red Lion Hotels
WestCoast Hotel Partners
Red Lion R&R Club
TicketsWest
WestCoast Entertainment
Red Lion Hotel Anaheim

CONTACTS:

Note: Officers with more than one job title may be intentionally listed here more than once.

Jon E. Eliasson, Interim CEO
Jon E. Eliasson, Interim Pres.
Anthony F. Dombrowik, CFO/Sr. VP
Harry Sladich, Exec. VP-Sales & Mktg.
Krisann Hatch, VP-Human Resources
David Barbieri, CIO/VP
Thomas L. McKeirnan, General Counsel/Sec./Sr. VP
George Schweitzer, Sr. VP/COO-Hotel Oper.
Richard P. Carlson, VP-Lodging Dev.
Mark D. Mahoney, VP/Managing Dir.-Spokane
Jack G. Lucas, VP/Pres., Tickets West
Jason W. Thielbahr, VP-Revenue Mgmt.
Donald K. Barbieri, Chmn.
Barry A. Hughes, Sr. VP-Dist. & Mktg.

Phone: 509-459-6100 **Fax:** 509-325-7324
Toll-Free: 800-733-5466
Address: 201 W. North River Dr., Ste. 100, Spokane, WA 99201 US

GROWTH PLANS/SPECIAL FEATURES:

Red Lion Hotels Corporation is engaged in the ownership, operation and franchising of midscale, full, select and limited service hotels in the western U.S. under the Red Lion Hotels brand. The firm currently holds interests in approximately 45 hotels across eight states and one Canadian province, offering 8,671 rooms in total. Red Lion operates in three segments: hotels, franchise and entertainment. The hotels segment consists of the operations of its 32 company-operated hotels, of which 19 are wholly-owned and 13 are leased. This segment accounts for about 90% of total revenue. The franchise segment licenses the firm's 13 franchised hotels. WestCoast Hotel Partners, part of this segment, operates a hotel in Ketchikan, Alaska. The franchise segment accounts for approximately 1% of revenue. To support its hotels, Red Lion provides services in marketing, sales, advertising, guest loyalty programs, revenue management, reservation systems, quality assurance and brand standards. Its guest loyalty program is the Red Lion R&R Club, a point system used by guests to redeem complimentary hotel stays, air miles, car rentals and other entertainment and merchandising incentives. Finally, the entertainment segment, operating through TicketsWest and WestCoast Entertainment, offers ticketing services, ticketing inventory management systems, call center services, promotion services and outlet/electronic channel distribution for event locations. TicketsWest offers tickets for live music, sporting events, family events (such as circuses, expos and fairs) and theater events. The company has also developed an electronic ticketing platform that integrates with its electronic hotel distribution system. In May 2009, Red Lion opened the Red Lion Hotel Anaheim adjacent to Disneyland in Anaheim, California.

Employees are offered medical, dental and vision insurance; a flexible spending plan; access to a nurse hotline; life insurance; a 401(k) plan; a stock purchase plan; an associate travel program; employee discounts; and an employee assistance program.

FINANCIALS:

Sales and profits are in thousands of dollars—add 000 to get the full amount. 2009 Note: Financial information for 2009 was not available for all companies at press time.

2009 Sales: $165,388	2009 Profits: $-6,647	**U.S. Stock Ticker: RLH**
2008 Sales: $187,570	2008 Profits: $-1,704	**Int'l Ticker:** Int'l Exchange:
2007 Sales: $186,893	2007 Profits: $6,050	Employees: 2,479
2006 Sales: $170,368	2006 Profits: $- 575	Fiscal Year Ends: 12/31
2005 Sales: $163,053	2005 Profits: $4,495	Parent Company:

SALARIES/BENEFITS:

Pension Plan:	ESOP Stock Plan:	Profit Sharing:	Top Exec. Salary: $357,363	Bonus: $
Savings Plan: Y	Stock Purch. Plan: Y		Second Exec. Salary: $208,461	Bonus: $

OTHER THOUGHTS:

Apparent Women Officers or Directors: 1
Hot Spot for Advancement for Women/Minorities: Y

LOCATIONS: ("Y" = Yes)

West:	Southwest:	Midwest:	Southeast:	Northeast:	International:
Y					Y

REGENCY CENTERS CORP

www.regencycenters.com

Industry Group Code: 531120 **Ranks within this company's industry group:** Sales: 36 Profits: 18

Properties:		Financial Services:		Construction/Development:		Investments:		Specialty Services:		Brokerage:	
Apartments:		Mortgages:		Commercial Construction:		REIT:	Y	Property Management:	Y	Commercial Sales:	
Malls/Shopping:	Y	Title Insurance:		Residential Construction:				Online Services:		Residential Sales:	
Offices:		Property Insurance:		Land Development:				Software/IT:		Specialty:	
Hotels/Motels:				Support Services:				Consulting:			
Industrial/Warehouses:				Design/Engineering:							
Other:											

TYPES OF BUSINESS:

Real Estate Investment Trust
Shopping Centers
Property Management

BRANDS/DIVISIONS/AFFILIATES:

Regency Centers, L.P.
Providence Commons
Premier Customer Initiative

CONTACTS:
Note: Officers with more than one job title may be intentionally listed here more than once.

Martin Stein, Jr., CEO
Brian Smith, COO
Brian Smith, Pres.
Bruce Johnson, CFO/Exec. VP
Patrick Krejs, Sr. VP-Oper.
Bonnie Hayflick, Contact-Media
Jim Thompson, Managing Dir.-East
Mac Chandler, Managing Dir.-West
John Delatour, Managing Dir.-Central
Martin Stein, Jr., Chmn.

Phone: 904-598-7000	**Fax:** 904-634-3428
Toll-Free: 800-950-6333	
Address: 1 Independent Dr., Ste. 114, Jacksonville, FL 32202-5019 US	

GROWTH PLANS/SPECIAL FEATURES:

Regency Centers Corporation (REG) is a real estate investment trust (REIT) engaged in the ownership, operation and development of grocery-anchored and community shopping centers located in areas with above-average household incomes and population densities. The firm's operations are conducted primarily through its majority-owned operating partnership, Regency Centers, L.P., of which it owns 99%. REG owns and manages 217 shopping centers in 23 states, representing 23 million square feet of rentable space, and owns partial interests in 184 shopping centers in 25 states. REG leases space in its shopping centers to grocers, specialty side-shop retailers, restaurants and major retail anchors. The company's largest grocery tenants include Kroger, with 55 stores; Publix, with 55 stores; Safeway, with 61 stores; and Super Valu, with 31 stores. REG has developed a formal partnering process called the Premier Customer Initiative, where the company builds a base of specialty tenants that represent the best operators in their respective merchandising categories. Such connections help stabilize a shopping center's occupancy, reduce re-leasing downtime and tenant turnover and yield higher sustainable rent. The firm also holds a self-funding business model that utilizes center recycling as a key component. In March 2010, the company acquired Providence Commons, a 91,301 square-foot retail center in Charlotte, North Carolina.

Employees are offered medical, dental, vision, life and disability insurance; a 401(k) plan; profit sharing; stock grant awards; wellness programs; and educational assistance.

FINANCIALS:
Sales and profits are in thousands of dollars—add 000 to get the full amount. 2009 Note: Financial information for 2009 was not available for all companies at press time.

2009 Sales: $489,232	2009 Profits: $-36,704	**U.S. Stock Ticker: REG**
2008 Sales: $495,895	2008 Profits: $136,188	**Int'l Ticker:** Int'l Exchange:
2007 Sales: $436,006	2007 Profits: $203,651	Employees: 380
2006 Sales: $404,034	2006 Profits: $218,511	Fiscal Year Ends: 12/31
2005 Sales: $383,623	2005 Profits: $162,647	Parent Company:

SALARIES/BENEFITS:

Pension Plan:	ESOP Stock Plan:	Profit Sharing: Y	Top Exec. Salary: $660,000	Bonus: $300,000
Savings Plan: Y	Stock Purch. Plan:		Second Exec. Salary: $450,000	Bonus: $175,000

OTHER THOUGHTS:

Apparent Women Officers or Directors: 2
Hot Spot for Advancement for Women/Minorities: Y

LOCATIONS: ("Y" = Yes)

West:	Southwest:	Midwest:	Southeast:	Northeast:	International:
Y	Y	Y	Y	Y	

REIS INC

www.reis.com

Industry Group Code: 511210J **Ranks within this company's industry group:** Sales: 1 Profits: 1

Properties:		Financial Services:		Construction/Development:		Investments:		Specialty Services:		Brokerage:	
Apartments:		Mortgages:		Commercial Construction:		REIT:		Property Management:	Y	Commercial Sales:	
Malls/Shopping:		Title Insurance:		Residential Construction:				Online Services:		Residential Sales:	
Offices:		Property Insurance:		Land Development:				Software/IT:	Y	Specialty:	
Hotels/Motels:				Support Services:				Consulting:			
Industrial/Warehouses:				Design/Engineering:							
Other:											

TYPES OF BUSINESS:

Real Estate Information & Analytics

BRANDS/DIVISIONS/AFFILIATES:

Reis Services
Reis SE
Reis Value Alert

CONTACTS:

Note: Officers with more than one job title may be intentionally listed here more than once.

Lloyd Lynford, CEO
Lloyd Lynford, Pres.
Mark P. Cantaluppi, CFO/VP
Jonathan Garfield, Exec. VP
William Sander, COO-Reis Services LLC
Jeffrey H. Lynford, Chmn.

Phone: 212-921-1122	**Fax:** 212-421-7442
Toll-Free: 800-366-7347	
Address: 530 5th Ave., New York, NY 10036 US	

GROWTH PLANS/SPECIAL FEATURES:

Reis, Inc. is a provider of commercial real estate market information and analytical tools. The company offers these services through its subsidiary, Reis Services. Reis Services maintains a proprietary database that contains detailed information on commercial properties in metropolitan markets and neighborhoods. This database offers information on retail, apartment, office and industrial properties. It currently lists information on 140 retail, 169 apartment, 44 industrial and 132 office metropolitan markets throughout the U.S. The database is utilized by real estate investors, lenders and other professionals that wish to make informed selling, buying and financing decisions. The firm's data is also used by debt and equity investors to assess, quantify and manage the risks of default and loss associated with individual mortgages, properties, portfolios and real estate backed securities. Reis Services' flagship product, Reis SE, provides web-based access to commercial real estate information and analytical tools designed to facilitate debt/equity transactions and ongoing evaluations. Reis SE offers trend and forecast analysis at metropolitan and neighborhood levels; and also provides detailed building-specific information such as vacancy rates, rents, property sales, lease terms, new construction listings and property valuation estimates. The product is designed to meet the needs of banks, developers/builders, property owners, non-bank lenders and equity investors. Reis currently serves roughly 670 companies, most of which have multiple users entitled to access Reis SE. In early 2009, the firm introduced Reis Value Alert, a program that identifies potentially troubled assets; it is especially useful for property and portfolio analysis during recapitalizations and bank consolidations. In February 2010, Reis sold a 235-acre residential development project in Claverack, New York, for roughly $2.75 million. The land included 46 lots and two model homes.

FINANCIALS:

Sales and profits are in thousands of dollars—add 000 to get the full amount. 2009 Note: Financial information for 2009 was not available for all companies at press time.

2009 Sales: $30,951	2009 Profits: $1,004	**U.S. Stock Ticker: REIS**
2008 Sales: $47,621	2008 Profits: $-7,480	**Int'l Ticker:** Int'l Exchange:
2007 Sales: $36,367	2007 Profits: $-1,290	Employees: 122
2006 Sales: $	2006 Profits: $	Fiscal Year Ends: 12/31
2005 Sales: $	2005 Profits: $	Parent Company:

SALARIES/BENEFITS:

Pension Plan:	ESOP Stock Plan:	Profit Sharing:	Top Exec. Salary: $841,875	Bonus: $427,000
Savings Plan:	Stock Purch. Plan:		Second Exec. Salary: $645,000	Bonus: $191,250

OTHER THOUGHTS:

Apparent Women Officers or Directors:
Hot Spot for Advancement for Women/Minorities:

LOCATIONS: ("Y" = Yes)

West:	Southwest:	Midwest:	Southeast:	Northeast:	International:
				Y	

RELATED GROUP (THE)

www.relatedgroup.com

Industry Group Code: 5311 **Ranks within this company's industry group:** Sales: Profits:

Properties:		Financial Services:		Construction/Development:		Investments:		Specialty Services:		Brokerage:	
Apartments:	Y	Mortgages:	Y	Commercial Construction:	Y	REIT:		Property Management:	Y	Commercial Sales:	
Malls/Shopping:	Y	Title Insurance:		Residential Construction:	Y			Online Services:		Residential Sales:	
Offices:	Y	Property Insurance:		Land Development:	Y			Software/IT:		Specialty:	
Hotels/Motels:				Support Services:	Y			Consulting:			
Industrial/Warehouses:				Design/Engineering:							
Other:	Y										

TYPES OF BUSINESS:

Condominium Construction & Management
Multi-Family Residence Development
Mixed-Use Urban Environments
Financing Services
Property Management
Construction

BRANDS/DIVISIONS/AFFILIATES:

CityPlace
Related Asset Advisors
Related Financial
Related Cervera Realty Services
TRG Management
Fortune Construction Company
Related International

CONTACTS: *Note: Officers with more than one job title may be intentionally listed here more than once.*

Jorge M. Perez, CEO
Matthew J. Allen, COO/Exec. VP
Jeffery Hoyos, Chief Admin. Officer/Sr. VP
Douglas K. Bischoff, General Counsel/Sr. VP
James M. Werbelow, Sr. VP-Construction
Barbara Salk, Sr. VP
Carlos Rosso, VP
Larry Lennon, Pres., TRG Mgmt.
Jorge M. Perez, Chmn.

Phone: 305-460-9900	**Fax:** 305-460-9911
Toll-Free:	
Address: 315 S. Biscayne Blvd., Miami, FL 33131 US	

GROWTH PLANS/SPECIAL FEATURES:

The Related Group is a multi-family real estate development firm and one of the nation's leading builders of luxury condominiums. Over the past 30 years, it has built and managed over 55,000 residential units throughout its home state of Florida. The Related Group's buildings have signature characteristics, such as very artistic, often decadent designs that are often located in unknown or under-developed neighborhoods, although it has set up some run-of-the-mill country club villas and other smaller scale projects as well. Some of the company's buildings are rental properties. Also in Related Group's portfolio are so-called urban mixed-use environments, which are planned neighborhoods that integrate housing, shopping and entertainment. The company's flagship community, considered to have changed the cityscape forever, is CityPlace in West Palm Beach, Florida. Other major Florida projects include Trump Towers, Trump Hollywood and St. Regis Resort & Residences. The Group operates various subsidiaries to supplement its chief real estate business, including Related Financial, which offers financing services; Related Cervera Realty Services and TRG Management, which cover sales and property management; Realty Asset Advisors, which offers property management, sales, construction management, leasing and loan workout services; Fortune Construction, which serves as the firm's own private contractor; and Related International, which was created to drive the companies $1 billion urbanization project in Mexico. In February 2009, the company completed construction of CityPlace South Tower, a residential condominium building in West Palm Beach, Florida.

The firm offers its employees medical, dental and vision benefits; disability and life insurance; tuition reimbursement; and employee discounts.

FINANCIALS: **Sales and profits are in thousands of dollars—add 000 to get the full amount. 2009 Note: Financial information for 2009 was not available for all companies at press time.**

2009 Sales: $	2009 Profits: $	**U.S. Stock Ticker: Private**
2008 Sales: $	2008 Profits: $	**Int'l Ticker:** Int'l Exchange:
2007 Sales: $	2007 Profits: $	Employees:
2006 Sales: $1,400,000	2006 Profits: $	Fiscal Year Ends: 12/31
2005 Sales: $	2005 Profits: $	Parent Company:

SALARIES/BENEFITS:

Pension Plan:	ESOP Stock Plan:	Profit Sharing:	Top Exec. Salary: $	Bonus: $
Savings Plan: Y	Stock Purch. Plan:		Second Exec. Salary: $	Bonus: $

OTHER THOUGHTS:

Apparent Women Officers or Directors: 3
Hot Spot for Advancement for Women/Minorities: Y

LOCATIONS: ("Y" = Yes)

West:	Southwest:	Midwest:	Southeast:	Northeast:	International:
Y			Y		

RESORTQUEST INTERNATIONAL INC

www.resortquest.com

Industry Group Code: 721110 **Ranks within this company's industry group:** Sales: Profits:

Properties:		Financial Services:		Construction/Development:		Investments:		Specialty Services:		Brokerage:	
Apartments:		Mortgages:		Commercial Construction:		REIT:		Property Management:	Y	Commercial Sales:	
Malls/Shopping:		Title Insurance:		Residential Construction:				Online Services:	Y	Residential Sales:	
Offices:		Property Insurance:		Land Development:				Software/IT:	Y	Specialty:	Y
Hotels/Motels:	Y			Support Services:				Consulting:			
Industrial/Warehouses:				Design/Engineering:							
Other:	Y										

TYPES OF BUSINESS:

Vacation Homes & Condominiums
Property Management Services
Real Estate Sales
Real Estate Software

BRANDS/DIVISIONS/AFFILIATES:

Leucadia National Corp

CONTACTS:

Note: Officers with more than one job title may be intentionally listed here more than once.

Park Brady, CEO
Park Brady, Pres.
Eileen Erstad, CFO
Cheryl Spezia, VP-Mktg.

Phone: 850-837-4774	**Fax:** 850-873-5390
Toll-Free: 800-862-4853	
Address: 546 Mary Esther Cut-Off NW, Ste. 3, Fort Walton Beach, FL 32548 US	

GROWTH PLANS/SPECIAL FEATURES:

ResortQuest International, Inc., a subsidiary of Leucadia National Corp., provides vacation condominium and home rental property management services. The company markets and provides management services in premier destination resort locations in the U.S. and Canada. In conjunction with Partner Affiliates in North America and Europe, ResortQuest provides management services to approximately 100,000 vacation rental properties. ResortQuest conducts its business through two divisions: vacation rentals and real estate sales. Vacation rental properties are generally second homes or investment properties owned by individuals who assign ResortQuest the responsibility of managing, marketing and renting their properties. Vacation properties include hotels, lodges, condominiums, town homes, cottages, villas and vacation homes. Properties are located across the country and internationally, including Aspen, Colorado; Venice, Italy; Maui, Hawaii; and Sarasota, Florida. The company offers real estate brokerage services throughout its U.S. resort locations. This division provides customers with a choice from over 400 realtors, through whom customers can list a home as a ResortQuest property or buy a vacation home.

The company offers its employees benefits that include medical, dental and vision insurance; and a 401(k) plan.

FINANCIALS:

Sales and profits are in thousands of dollars—add 000 to get the full amount. 2009 Note: Financial information for 2009 was not available for all companies at press time.

2009 Sales: $	2009 Profits: $	**U.S. Stock Ticker: Subsidiary**
2008 Sales: $	2008 Profits: $	**Int'l Ticker:** Int'l Exchange:
2007 Sales: $168,300	2007 Profits: $	Employees:
2006 Sales: $	2006 Profits: $	Fiscal Year Ends: 12/31
2005 Sales: $	2005 Profits: $	Parent Company: LEUCADIA NATIONAL CORP

SALARIES/BENEFITS:

Pension Plan:	ESOP Stock Plan:	Profit Sharing:	Top Exec. Salary: $	Bonus: $
Savings Plan: Y	Stock Purch. Plan:		Second Exec. Salary: $	Bonus: $

OTHER THOUGHTS:

Apparent Women Officers or Directors: 2
Hot Spot for Advancement for Women/Minorities: Y

LOCATIONS: ("Y" = Yes)

West:	Southwest:	Midwest:	Southeast:	Northeast:	International:
Y	Y		Y	Y	Y

REZIDOR HOTEL GROUP AB

www.rezidors.com

Industry Group Code: 721110 **Ranks within this company's industry group:** Sales: Profits:

Properties:		Financial Services:		Construction/Development:		Investments:		Specialty Services:		Brokerage:	
Apartments:		Mortgages:		Commercial Construction:		REIT:		Property Management:		Commercial Sales:	
Malls/Shopping:		Title Insurance:		Residential Construction:				Online Services:		Residential Sales:	
Offices:		Property Insurance:		Land Development:				Software/IT:		Specialty:	
Hotels/Motels:	Y			Support Services:				Consulting:			
Industrial/Warehouses:				Design/Engineering:							
Other:											

TYPES OF BUSINESS:

Hotel Management

BRANDS/DIVISIONS/AFFILIATES:

Carlson Hotels Worldwide
Hotel Missoni
Regent
Radisson
Park Inn
Country Inn

CONTACTS:

Note: Officers with more than one job title may be intentionally listed here more than once.

Kurt Ritter, CEO
Jacques Dubois, COO/Sr. VP
Kurt Ritter, Pres.
Knut Kleiven, CFO/Deputy Pres.
Olivier Jacquin, Sr. VP-Mktg. & Sales
Beath-Jeanette Lunde, Sr. VP-People Dev.
Eugene P.E. Staal, VP-Tech. Dev.
Marianne Ruhngard, General Counsel/Sr. VP/Sec.
Puneet Chhatwal, Chief Dev. Officer/Sr. VP
Urban Jansson, Chmn.
Olivier Jacquin, Sr. VP-Dist.

Phone: 32-2-702-9200 **Fax:** 32-2-702-9300
Toll-Free:
Address: Ave. du Bourget 44, Brussels, B-1130 Belgium

GROWTH PLANS/SPECIAL FEATURES:

Rezidor Hotel Group AB, formerly Rezidor SAS Hospitality, is a hospitality management company that franchises, leases and manages hotel properties. The company currently has about 390 hotels in operation, with 83,000 operational and developmental rooms. The company's brands include Hotel Missoni, Radisson Blu, Park Inn, Regent and Country Inn; the latter three are operated under a franchise agreement with Carlson Hotels Worldwide. Rezidor's network has grown to its current size, from just 29 hotels 10 years ago, primarily through the Carlson franchise agreement. Radisson Blu is a first-class full-service hotel brand that currently operates almost 240 hotels in Europe, the Middle East and Africa, and is a leading luxury brand in the European Union. Park Inn is an up and coming mid-market hotel brand primarily located across Europe, the Middle East and Africa. Country Inn is an international mid-tier lodging chain. Regent is an international brand that offers luxury and high-quality service in its hotels and resorts; the firm operates three Regent hotels in Germany, Croatia and France, with more in development in Croatia and the United Arab Emirates; three in Asia, with five more under construction; and one in the Caribbean, with one more slated to open soon. Hotel Missoni is the newest member of the Rezidor family, born of the recently signed worldwide licensing agreement with the global fashion brand of the same name. The brand is currently in development in South Africa, Brazil, Oman and Kuwait, with its first opening in Scotland. Rezidor's hotels are primarily located in Western Europe, with additional locations in Scandinavia, Eastern Europe, Russia, Turkey, Malta, Azerbaijan, Kazakhstan, Uzbekistan, Iran, the Arabian Peninsula, Egypt, South Africa and China, among others. The firm actively continues to enlarge its network, with recent additions in France, Iceland, Nigeria, Saudi Arabia, and Switzerland. The firm opened the Radisson Royal Hotel, Moscow in May 2010.

FINANCIALS:

Sales and profits are in thousands of dollars—add 000 to get the full amount. 2009 Note: Financial information for 2009 was not available for all companies at press time.

2009 Sales: $	2009 Profits: $	**U.S. Stock Ticker:**
2008 Sales: $	2008 Profits: $	**Int'l Ticker: REZT** Int'l Exchange: Stockholm-SS
2007 Sales: $	2007 Profits: $	Employees:
2006 Sales: $	2006 Profits: $	Fiscal Year Ends: 12/31
2005 Sales: $	2005 Profits: $	Parent Company:

SALARIES/BENEFITS:

Pension Plan:	ESOP Stock Plan:	Profit Sharing:	Top Exec. Salary: $	Bonus: $
Savings Plan:	Stock Purch. Plan:		Second Exec. Salary: $	Bonus: $

OTHER THOUGHTS:

Apparent Women Officers or Directors: 3
Hot Spot for Advancement for Women/Minorities: Y

LOCATIONS: ("Y" = Yes)

West:	Southwest:	Midwest:	Southeast:	Northeast:	International:
					Y

Note: Financial information, benefits and other data can change quickly and may vary from those stated here.

RIO PROPERTIES INC www.harrahs.com/casinos/rio/hotel-casino/property-home.shtml

Industry Group Code: 721120 **Ranks within this company's industry group:** Sales: Profits:

Properties:		Financial Services:		Construction/Development:		Investments:		Specialty Services:		Brokerage:	
Apartments:		Mortgages:		Commercial Construction:		REIT:		Property Management:	Y	Commercial Sales:	
Malls/Shopping:		Title Insurance:		Residential Construction:				Online Services:		Residential Sales:	
Offices:		Property Insurance:		Land Development:				Software/IT:		Specialty:	
Hotels/Motels:	Y			Support Services:				Consulting:			
Industrial/Warehouses:				Design/Engineering:							
Other:	Y										

TYPES OF BUSINESS:

Hotels & Casinos
Wine Shop
Golf Course

BRANDS/DIVISIONS/AFFILIATES:

Harrah's Entertainment Inc
Rio All-Suite Hotel and Casino
Rio Spa & Salon
Masquerade Village Shops
Rio Secco Golf Club
Carnivale Masquerade Show In The Sky
Lucy Strike Lanes
Wine Cellar & Tasting Room

CONTACTS: *Note: Officers with more than one job title may be intentionally listed here more than once.*

Madeleine Weekly, Dir.-Mktg.
Stephen Thayer, VP-Hotel Oper.
Marilyn G. Winn, Gen. Mgr./Sr. VP

Phone: 702-777-7777	**Fax:** 702-777-7781
Toll-Free: 888-746-7153	
Address: 3700 W. Flamingo Rd., Las Vegas, NV 89103 US	

GROWTH PLANS/SPECIAL FEATURES:

Rio Properties, Inc., a subsidiary of Harrah's Entertainment, Inc., operates the Rio All-Suite Hotel and Casino in Las Vegas, Nevada. Harrah's Entertainment is a diversified U.S. casino company that operates over 28 establishments under the brand names Harrah's, Caesars, Showboat, Horseshoe, Bally's, Casino Windsor, Flamingo, Imperial Palace and Harveys. The Rio All-Suite Hotel and Casino features over 600 square feet of space for every room as part of its all-suite concept. The suites are equipped with such amenities as a separate dressing area, a couch, a 32-inch TV, a table with chairs, a hairdryer, a refrigerator, an iron, an ironing board and a safe. Rio's hotel additionally features 100,000 square feet of gaming space; such restaurants as Antonio's Italian Ristorante, Café Martorano, Gaylord Indian Restaurant and Carnival World Buffet; the Rio Spa & Salon; the Masquerade Village Shops, with over 60,000 square feet of shops; access to nearby Rio Secco Golf Club; the Carnivale Masquerade Show In The Sky, a free carnival-themed show with suspended floats; and Lucky Strike Lanes bowling alley. Gaming amenities include slot machines, video poker machines, Keno Lounge, a full-service Race & Sports Book and more than 80 table games, including blackjack, craps, baccarat, roulette, Let It Ride, Caribbean Stud Poker and Mini-Baccarat. Rio's Wine Cellar & Tasting Room, a wine bar and retail shop, showcases approximately 50,000 bottles valued at more than $10 million. The company actively markets its services and facilities to both local residents and Las Vegas visitors. Rio believes that its all-suite concept, diverse high-quality dining, easy access and ample parking provide an attractive alternative to the Las Vegas Strip, which is 15 minutes away.

FINANCIALS: **Sales and profits are in thousands of dollars—add 000 to get the full amount. 2009 Note: Financial information for 2009 was not available for all companies at press time.**

2009 Sales: $	2009 Profits: $	**U.S. Stock Ticker: Subsidiary**
2008 Sales: $	2008 Profits: $	**Int'l Ticker:** Int'l Exchange:
2007 Sales: $134,700	2007 Profits: $	Employees:
2006 Sales: $	2006 Profits: $	Fiscal Year Ends: 12/31
2005 Sales: $	2005 Profits: $	Parent Company: HARRAH'S ENTERTAINMENT INC

SALARIES/BENEFITS:

Pension Plan:	ESOP Stock Plan:	Profit Sharing:	Top Exec. Salary: $	Bonus: $
Savings Plan:	Stock Purch. Plan:		Second Exec. Salary: $	Bonus: $

OTHER THOUGHTS:

Apparent Women Officers or Directors: 2
Hot Spot for Advancement for Women/Minorities: Y

LOCATIONS: ("Y" = Yes)

West:	Southwest:	Midwest:	Southeast:	Northeast:	International:
Y					

RITZ-CARLTON HOTEL COMPANY LLC (THE) www.ritzcarlton.com

Industry Group Code: 721110 **Ranks within this company's industry group:** Sales: Profits:

Properties:		Financial Services:		Construction/Development:		Investments:		Specialty Services:		Brokerage:	
Apartments:		Mortgages:		Commercial Construction:		REIT:		Property Management:	Y	Commercial Sales:	
Malls/Shopping:		Title Insurance:		Residential Construction:				Online Services:		Residential Sales:	
Offices:		Property Insurance:		Land Development:				Software/IT:		Specialty:	
Hotels/Motels:	Y			Support Services:				Consulting:			
Industrial/Warehouses:				Design/Engineering:							
Other:	Y										

TYPES OF BUSINESS:

Hotels, Luxury
Condominiums
Golf Courses
Spas
Time Share Units

BRANDS/DIVISIONS/AFFILIATES:

Marriott International Inc
Ritz-Carlton Club
Taj Boston
Six Senses
La Prairie
ESPA

CONTACTS:

Note: Officers with more than one job title may be intentionally listed here more than once.

Simon F. Cooper, COO
Simon F. Cooper, Pres.
Peter Cole, CFO
Vivian A. Deuschl, Corp. VP-Public Rel.
Daniel Ford, Regional Dir.-Public Rel., Asia Pacific
Vivienne Gan, Regional Dir.-Public Rel., Middle East
Marion Schumacher, Regional Dir.-Public Rel., Europe
Jacqueline V. Ader-Grob, Mgr.-Public Rel., Ritz-Carlton Destination Club
Herve Humler, Pres., Int'l

Phone: 301-547-4700 **Fax:** 301-547-4723
Toll-Free:
Address: 4445 Willard Ave., Ste. 800, Chevy Chase, MD 20815 US

GROWTH PLANS/SPECIAL FEATURES:

The Ritz-Carlton Hotel Co., LLC, a subsidiary of Marriott International, Inc., is one of the world's best-known luxury hotel chains, operating 73 hotels in 24 countries. The firm also maintains 12 international sales offices in various locations including Chicago, New York, Los Angeles, Dubai, Shanghai, Tokyo and London. In an attempt to cater to an upscale clientele base, full-service luxury spas are offered at most of the company's resorts, and plans have been made for additional spas at new or existing hotel locations. Some spas at Ritz-Carlton hotels operate under the brand names Six Senses, La Prairie and ESPA. Ritz-Carlton also markets its 15 luxury golf courses (many designed by leading names in the golf world such as Greg Norman and Jack Nicklaus) and fitness facilities to both local residents and visitors. The Ritz-Carlton Club is the firm's time-share ownership unit, offering a flexible alternative to a second home. This concept features luxury condominiums located at Ritz-Carlton's hotels and resorts worldwide, with features such as marble foyers, walk-in closets, daily housekeeping services, 24-hour room service and access to fitness facilities and spa services. Membership is currently available in locations such as Aspen, St. Thomas, Bachelor Gulch and Jupiter, Florida. The firm plans to expand hotel operations to such locations as Toronto, Canada and Rose Island, Bahamas. In 2009, the firm opened several new hotels: Ritz-Carlton, Dove Mountain, Arizona; The Ritz-Carlton, Charlotte, North Carolina; Phulay Bay, a Ritz-Carlton Reserve, Krabi South Thailand; The Ritz-Carlton, and Los Angeles, California.

Employees of the firm are offered benefits that include medical, dental and vision coverage; domestic partner benefits; leave of absence and bereavement leave; a 401(k) plan; a credit union; an employee stock purchase plan; an employee assistance program; educational assistance program; career development programs; uniforms; and employee discounts on hotel rooms, food and retail items.

FINANCIALS:

Sales and profits are in thousands of dollars—add 000 to get the full amount. 2009 Note: Financial information for 2009 was not available for all companies at press time.

2009 Sales: $	2009 Profits: $
2008 Sales: $	2008 Profits: $
2007 Sales: $1,576,000	2007 Profits: $72,000
2006 Sales: $1,423,000	2006 Profits: $
2005 Sales: $	2005 Profits: $

U.S. Stock Ticker: Subsidiary
Int'l Ticker: Int'l Exchange:
Employees: 38,000
Fiscal Year Ends: 12/31
Parent Company: MARRIOTT INTERNATIONAL INC

SALARIES/BENEFITS:

Pension Plan:	ESOP Stock Plan:	Profit Sharing:	Top Exec. Salary: $	Bonus: $
Savings Plan: Y	Stock Purch. Plan: Y		Second Exec. Salary: $	Bonus: $

OTHER THOUGHTS:

Apparent Women Officers or Directors: 4
Hot Spot for Advancement for Women/Minorities: Y

LOCATIONS: ("Y" = Yes)

West:	Southwest:	Midwest:	Southeast:	Northeast:	International:
Y	Y	Y	Y	Y	Y

RIVIERA HOLDINGS CORP

www.rivierahotel.com

Industry Group Code: 721120 **Ranks within this company's industry group:** Sales: 8 Profits: 2

Properties:		Financial Services:		Construction/Development:		Investments:		Specialty Services:		Brokerage:	
Apartments:		Mortgages:		Commercial Construction:		REIT:		Property Management:	Y	Commercial Sales:	
Malls/Shopping:		Title Insurance:		Residential Construction:				Online Services:	Y	Residential Sales:	
Offices:		Property Insurance:		Land Development:				Software/IT:		Specialty:	
Hotels/Motels:	Y			Support Services:				Consulting:			
Industrial/Warehouses:				Design/Engineering:							
Other:	Y										

TYPES OF BUSINESS:

Casino Hotel
Casino Management

BRANDS/DIVISIONS/AFFILIATES:

Riviera Hotel and Casino
Black Hawk Casino
Riviera Operating Corporation
An Evening at La Cage
Crazy Girls
Riviera Black Hawk Player's Club

CONTACTS:

Note: Officers with more than one job title may be intentionally listed here more than once.

Robert A. Vannucci, COO
Phillip B. Simons, CFO
Tullio J. Marchionne, General Counsel/Sec.
Phillip B. Simons, Treas.
Phillip B. Simons, VP-Finance, Riviera Operating Corp.
Tullio J. Marchionne, Exec. VP-Riviera Operating Corp.

Phone: 702-734-5110	**Fax:** 702-794-9442
Toll-Free: 800-634-3420	
Address: 2901 Las Vegas Blvd. S., Las Vegas, NV 89109 US	

GROWTH PLANS/SPECIAL FEATURES:

Riviera Holdings Corp., through wholly-owned subsidiary Riviera Operating Corporation (ROC), owns and operates the Riviera Hotel and Casino. The Riviera is located on Las Vegas Boulevard (The Strip) in Las Vegas. The Riviera opened in 1955 and has a reputation for delivering high-quality, traditional Las Vegas-style gaming, entertainment and other amenities. The casino has approximately 100,000 square feet of gaming space with approximately 900 slot machines and 40 gaming tables, including blackjack, craps, poker and roulette. The hotel has 2,075 guest rooms, including 177 suites, in five towers. It has approximately 160,000 square feet of convention, meeting and banquet space. The Riviera offers live entertainment shows, such as An Evening at La Cage, a female impersonation show; and Crazy Girls, an adult revue. Subsidiary Riviera Black Hawk, Inc. owns and operates the Riviera Black Hawk Casino, a limited-stakes casino, in Black Hawk, Colorado. The Black Hawk, located about 40 miles west of Denver, is one of the largest full-service casinos in Colorado, with approximately 750 slot machines and nine live game tables. The firm offers the Riviera Black Hawk Player's Club, rewarding frequent players and collecting data about Club members which the company uses to customize promotions to attract repeat visitors. The company's web site allows travelers to book rooms, buy souvenirs, check Player's Club point balances and make other reservations before a trip.

FINANCIALS:

Sales and profits are in thousands of dollars—add 000 to get the full amount. 2009 Note: Financial information for 2009 was not available for all companies at press time.

2009 Sales: $	2009 Profits: $	**U.S. Stock Ticker: RVHL**
2008 Sales: $169,760	2008 Profits: $-11,862	**Int'l Ticker:** Int'l Exchange:
2007 Sales: $205,495	2007 Profits: $-18,258	Employees: 1,137
2006 Sales: $200,944	2006 Profits: $- 335	Fiscal Year Ends: 12/31
2005 Sales: $202,227	2005 Profits: $-3,999	Parent Company:

SALARIES/BENEFITS:

Pension Plan:	ESOP Stock Plan: Y	Profit Sharing:	Top Exec. Salary: $	Bonus: $
Savings Plan: Y	Stock Purch. Plan:		Second Exec. Salary: $	Bonus: $

OTHER THOUGHTS:

Apparent Women Officers or Directors:
Hot Spot for Advancement for Women/Minorities:

LOCATIONS: ("Y" = Yes)

West:	Southwest:	Midwest:	Southeast:	Northeast:	International:
Y					

ROSEWOOD HOTELS & RESORTS LLC

www.rosewoodhotels.com

Industry Group Code: 721110 **Ranks within this company's industry group:** Sales: Profits:

Properties:		Financial Services:		Construction/Development:		Investments:		Specialty Services:		Brokerage:	
Apartments:		Mortgages:		Commercial Construction:		REIT:		Property Management:		Commercial Sales:	
Malls/Shopping:		Title Insurance:		Residential Construction:				Online Services:		Residential Sales:	
Offices:		Property Insurance:		Land Development:				Software/IT:		Specialty:	
Hotels/Motels:	Y			Support Services:				Consulting:			
Industrial/Warehouses:				Design/Engineering:							
Other:											

TYPES OF BUSINESS:

Hotel & Resort Management
Spas
Private Residences

BRANDS/DIVISIONS/AFFILIATES:

Rosewood Dubai
Rosewood San Miguel de Allende in Mexico
Rosewood Costa Carmel
Rosewood Inn of the Anasazi
San Ysidro Ranch, A Rosewood Resort

CONTACTS:

Note: Officers with more than one job title may be intentionally listed here more than once.

John M. Scott, CEO
Robert Boulogne, COO
John M. Scott, Pres.
Ralph Aruzza, VP-Sales
Sheri Line, Corp. Dir.-Human Resources
Fred Crespo, VP-IT
George Fong, Sr. VP-Architecture & Design
Susan Aldridge, General Counsel/Sr. VP-Legal
Michael A. Gibb, VP-Oper.
Alex Alt, VP-Dev. & Strategy
Kersten Rettig, Dir.-Public Rel.
Ernest Glidden, Sr. VP-Finance
Katherine Blaisdell, VP-Construction Dev.
Elias Assaly, VP-Oper. Dev.
Gert Kopera, VP-Food & Beverage
Marcie Lieberman, Sr. Dir.-Oper., Rooms
Stephen H. Sands, Chmn.
Peter Finamore, Managing Dir.-Al Faisaliah Rosewood Hotel
James A. Brackensick, Sr. VP-Purchasing

Phone: 214-880-4200	**Fax:**
Toll-Free: 888-767-3966	
Address: 500 Crescent Court, Ste. 300, Dallas, TX 75201 US	

GROWTH PLANS/SPECIAL FEATURES:

Rosewood Hotels & Resorts, LLC operates ultra-luxury boutique hotels and resorts worldwide. It has 10 hotels and eight resorts, with over 2,000 rooms, villas and suites, in the U.S., Canada, Mexico, the Caribbean, Saudi Arabia and Japan. It also has various locations under construction, including Rosewood Dubai, in the U.A.E. (scheduled to open by 2011), Rosewood San Miguel de Allende in Mexico (late 2010) and Rosewood Costa Carmel in Costa Rica (2012). Besides constructing its own facilities, Rosewood has acquired existing properties and management contracts, including the Rosewood Inn of the Anasazi in Santa Fe, New Mexico and the San Ysidro Ranch, A Rosewood Resort, located in Santa Barbara, California. Its facilities are generally small, featuring less than 200 accommodations ranging from 350-square-foot rooms to 3,200-square-foot suites. The company uses architecture and decor to attempt to capture the unique history, geography and culture of each hotel or resort location. Services offered at Rosewood facilities can include tennis courts, a courtesy car with 5-mile radius, unpack and packing services, babysitting services, twice-daily housekeeping with nightly turndown service, pools and fitness centers, as well as shops and various dining facilities. Some locations also offer business centers stocked with computers, printers, faxes and copiers. Eight locations also offer spa services, such as exercise training and facilities, facials, aromabaths, hydrotherapy, massages, manicures and pedicures. In addition, three hotels and resorts also feature private residences, which offer owners the same services and amenities as resort guests. The private residences often come fully furnished and feature floor plan inclusions such as full kitchens, fireplaces, private pools and terraces. In 2009, the company has opened its newest resort, Rosewood Sand Hill, in Menlo Park, California.

FINANCIALS:

Sales and profits are in thousands of dollars—add 000 to get the full amount. 2009 Note: Financial information for 2009 was not available for all companies at press time.

2009 Sales: $	2009 Profits: $	**U.S. Stock Ticker: Private**
2008 Sales: $	2008 Profits: $	**Int'l Ticker:** Int'l Exchange:
2007 Sales: $	2007 Profits: $	Employees:
2006 Sales: $	2006 Profits: $	Fiscal Year Ends:
2005 Sales: $	2005 Profits: $	Parent Company:

SALARIES/BENEFITS:

Pension Plan:	ESOP Stock Plan:	Profit Sharing:	Top Exec. Salary: $	Bonus: $
Savings Plan:	Stock Purch. Plan:		Second Exec. Salary: $	Bonus: $

OTHER THOUGHTS:

Apparent Women Officers or Directors: 5
Hot Spot for Advancement for Women/Minorities: Y

LOCATIONS: ("Y" = Yes)

West:	Southwest:	Midwest:	Southeast:	Northeast:	International:
Y	Y	Y	Y	Y	Y

ROSSI RESIDENCIAL SA

www.rossiresidencial.com.br

Industry Group Code: 5311 **Ranks within this company's industry group:** Sales: 23 Profits: 20

Properties:		Financial Services:		Construction/Development:		Investments:		Specialty Services:		Brokerage:	
Apartments:		Mortgages:		Commercial Construction:	Y	REIT:		Property Management:		Commercial Sales:	
Malls/Shopping:		Title Insurance:		Residential Construction:	Y			Online Services:		Residential Sales:	
Offices:		Property Insurance:		Land Development:	Y			Software/IT:		Specialty:	
Hotels/Motels:				Support Services:				Consulting:			
Industrial/Warehouses:				Design/Engineering:							
Other:											

TYPES OF BUSINESS:

Real Estate Development

BRANDS/DIVISIONS/AFFILIATES:

CONTACTS:

Note: Officers with more than one job title may be intentionally listed here more than once.

Heitor Cantergiani, CEO
Cassio Elias Audi, CFO
Leonardo Nogueira Diniz, Sales Officer
Renato Gamba Rocha Diniz, Mgr.-Eng.
Cassio Elias Audi, Investor Rel. Officer
Edmundo Rossi Cuppoloni, Vice-Chmn.
Renato Gamba Rocha Diniz, Economic Segment Officer
Joao Rossi Cuppoloni, Chmn.

Phone: 55-11-3759-7516	**Fax:** 55-11-3759-8547
Toll-Free:	
Address: 5200 Major Sylvio de Magalhaes Padilha Ave. 3rd Fl, Sao Paulo, 05693-000 Brazil	

GROWTH PLANS/SPECIAL FEATURES:

Rossi Residencial SA is a Brazilian holding company involved in real estate and construction. The firm is part of construction, engineering and development conglomerate Grupo Rossi. Rossi Residencial is primarily involved in the construction, development, sale and commercialization of residential and commercial real estate properties. The firm operates in 61 cities located in 14 Brazilian states and the Federal District. Its most important state is Sao Paulo, which accounts for approximately 42% of the company's business. Rossi Residencial has 12 offices located in the cities of Sao Paulo, Rio de Janeiro, Porto Alegre, Curitiba, Vitoria, Salvador, Campinas, Recife, Natal, Fortaleza, Belo Horizonte and Goiania. Approximately 25% of the company's income is derived from residential real estate valued at over $276,625; 22% is derived from economic housing ($88,520-$94,052); 21% from houses valued between $193,638 and $276,624; 17% from houses valued between $110,650 and $193,638; 8% from residential housing worth up to $193,637; and 7% is derived from commercial real estate.

FINANCIALS:

Sales and profits are in thousands of dollars—add 000 to get the full amount. 2009 Note: Financial information for 2009 was not available for all companies at press time.

2009 Sales: $897,550	2009 Profits: $124,500	**U.S. Stock Ticker:**
2008 Sales: $703,920	2008 Profits: $67,700	**Int'l Ticker: RSID3** Int'l Exchange: Sao Paulo-SAO
2007 Sales: $431,510	2007 Profits: $41,960	Employees:
2006 Sales: $	2006 Profits: $	Fiscal Year Ends: 12/31
2005 Sales: $	2005 Profits: $	Parent Company:

SALARIES/BENEFITS:

Pension Plan:	ESOP Stock Plan: Y	Profit Sharing:	Top Exec. Salary: $	Bonus: $
Savings Plan:	Stock Purch. Plan:		Second Exec. Salary: $	Bonus: $

OTHER THOUGHTS:

Apparent Women Officers or Directors:
Hot Spot for Advancement for Women/Minorities:

LOCATIONS: ("Y" = Yes)

West:	Southwest:	Midwest:	Southeast:	Northeast:	International:
					Y

ROYAL GROUP INC

www.royalgrouptech.com

Industry Group Code: 326199 **Ranks within this company's industry group:** Sales: Profits:

Properties:		Financial Services:		Construction/Development:		Investments:		Specialty Services:		Brokerage:	
Apartments:		Mortgages:		Commercial Construction:		REIT:		Property Management:		Commercial Sales:	
Malls/Shopping:		Title Insurance:		Residential Construction:				Online Services:		Residential Sales:	
Offices:		Property Insurance:		Land Development:				Software/IT:		Specialty:	
Hotels/Motels:				Support Services:	Y			Consulting:			
Industrial/Warehouses:				Design/Engineering:							
Other:											

TYPES OF BUSINESS:

Building Materials

BRANDS/DIVISIONS/AFFILIATES:

Georgia Gulf Corporation
Royal Group Technologies Limited

CONTACTS:

Note: Officers with more than one job title may be intentionally listed here more than once.

Paul D. Carrico, CEO
Gregory Thompson, CFO
Mark O. Badger, VP-Mktg.
Mark O. Badger, VP-Corp. Comm.

Phone: 905-850-9700	**Fax:** 905-850-9184
Toll-Free:	
Address: 91 Royal Gate Blvd., Woodbridge, ON L4H 1X9 Canada	

GROWTH PLANS/SPECIAL FEATURES:

Royal Group, Inc., formerly Royal Group Technologies Limited, manufactures and sells PVC and vinyl construction, improvement and building products. The firm is a subsidiary of Georgia Gulf Corporation, a North American manufacturer and international marketer of commodity chemicals, polymers and durable, custom and other vinyl-based building and home improvement products. Royal Group Inc. operates primarily in Canada and the U.S., and also has international operations in Mexico, Asia, Europe and South America. The majority of Royal's sales come from the U.S. The firm operates through five divisions: Royal Building Products; Royal Mouldings Limited; Royal Outdoor Products; Royal Pipe Systems; and Royal Window and Door Profiles. Royal Building Products offers soffit, shutters, premium vinyl siding, mounts, vents, vinyl/aluminum columns and accessories. Royal Mouldings Limited manufacturers decorative polymer and cellular vinyl molding extrusion components and systems. Royal Outdoor Products produces products such as railings, decking systems, columns and fencing. Royal Pipe Systems products include pipes for municipal potable water, sewer systems and storm drains; plumbing pipes; ducts, conduit and other pipes and fittings for electrical construction; and fittings for backwater valves, inspection chambers and controlled settlement joints. Royal Window and Door Profiles utilizes polymer fenestration technologies to produce patio door systems, custom window profiles and window systems.

FINANCIALS:

Sales and profits are in thousands of dollars—add 000 to get the full amount. 2009 Note: Financial information for 2009 was not available for all companies at press time.

2009 Sales: $	2009 Profits: $	**U.S. Stock Ticker: Subsidiary**
2008 Sales: $	2008 Profits: $	**Int'l Ticker:** Int'l Exchange:
2007 Sales: $1,271,600	2007 Profits: $	Employees:
2006 Sales: $	2006 Profits: $	Fiscal Year Ends: 12/31
2005 Sales: $1,458,700	2005 Profits: $-232,600	Parent Company: GEORGIA GULF CORPORATION

SALARIES/BENEFITS:

Pension Plan:	ESOP Stock Plan:	Profit Sharing:	Top Exec. Salary: $	Bonus: $
Savings Plan:	Stock Purch. Plan:		Second Exec. Salary: $	Bonus: $

OTHER THOUGHTS:

Apparent Women Officers or Directors:
Hot Spot for Advancement for Women/Minorities:

LOCATIONS: ("Y" = Yes)

West:	Southwest:	Midwest:	Southeast:	Northeast:	International:
Y	Y	Y	Y	Y	Y

RXR REALTY

www.rxrrealty.com

Industry Group Code: 531120 **Ranks within this company's industry group:** Sales: Profits:

Properties:		Financial Services:		Construction/Development:		Investments:		Specialty Services:		Brokerage:	
Apartments:		Mortgages:		Commercial Construction:		REIT:	Y	Property Management:		Commercial Sales:	
Malls/Shopping:		Title Insurance:		Residential Construction:				Online Services:		Residential Sales:	
Offices:	Y	Property Insurance:		Land Development:				Software/IT:		Specialty:	
Hotels/Motels:				Support Services:				Consulting:			
Industrial/Warehouses:	Y			Design/Engineering:							
Other:											

TYPES OF BUSINESS:

Real Estate Investment Trust
Office & Industrial Properties
Commercial Construction & Development
Property Management

BRANDS/DIVISIONS/AFFILIATES:

Reckson Associates Realty Corp.
SL Green Realty Corporation
RexCorp Realty

CONTACTS:

Note: Officers with more than one job title may be intentionally listed here more than once.

Scott Rechler, CEO
Richard Conniff, COO
Michael Maturo, Pres.
Michael Maturo, CFO
Carol Allen, Sr. VP-Mktg.
Ylisa Kunze, VP-Human Resources
Jason Barnett, General Counsel
Walt Smith, VP-Oper.
Glenn Wasserman, Exec. VP-Strategic Planning, Capital & Markets
Tom Carey, Controller/Exec. VP
Richard Conniff, Fund Mgr.
Todd Rechler, Pres., RXR Construction & Dev.
David Frank, Exec. VP/Legal Counsel
Mitchell C. Hochberg, Managing Dir.-Residential & Hospitality
Scott Rechler, Chmn.

Phone: 516-506-6000	**Fax:** 516-506-6800
Toll-Free:	
Address: 625 RXR Plz., Uniondale, NY 11556 US	

GROWTH PLANS/SPECIAL FEATURES:

RXR Realty, formerly RexCorp Realty, is a self-administered and self-managed real estate investment trust (REIT) that acquires, owns, develops, constructs, manages and leases office and industrial properties in the New York Tri-State area. The former members of Reckson Associates Realty Corp's management formed the company in recent years after the completion of the original company's acquisition by and merger with SL Green Realty Corp. RXR Realty's primary investment funds include the Tri-State Prime Property Joint Venture, which offers 15 office properties located in Long Island and New Jersey; and Core Plus Value Enhanced Strategy, which includes the Opportunity Fund I, Opportunity Fund II and Value Enhanced Portfolio. The Core Plus portfolios include 48 developed properties in New Jersey, Long Island, Westchester and Connecticut and several active development projects. In total, RXR Realty owns approximately $2.8 billion in class-A properties consisting of a combined 11 million square feet, making the company one of the Tri-State area's leading real estate companies. RXR Realty offers its tenants cross-leasing opportunities to provide enhanced flexibility and the convenience of being able to work with a single owner/manager over multiple spaces. A few of the firm's current tenants include AT&T; Bank of America; Citibank N.A., Del Laboratories, Inc.; Hewlett Packard Company; Merrill Lynch Pierce Fenner; Starbucks Corporation; and Xerox Corporation.

FINANCIALS:

Sales and profits are in thousands of dollars—add 000 to get the full amount. 2009 Note: Financial information for 2009 was not available for all companies at press time.

2009 Sales: $	2009 Profits: $	**U.S. Stock Ticker: Private**
2008 Sales: $	2008 Profits: $	**Int'l Ticker:** Int'l Exchange:
2007 Sales: $	2007 Profits: $	Employees:
2006 Sales: $	2006 Profits: $	Fiscal Year Ends: 12/31
2005 Sales: $546,148	2005 Profits: $197,641	Parent Company:

SALARIES/BENEFITS:

Pension Plan:	ESOP Stock Plan:	Profit Sharing:	Top Exec. Salary: $	Bonus: $
Savings Plan:	Stock Purch. Plan:		Second Exec. Salary: $	Bonus: $

OTHER THOUGHTS:

Apparent Women Officers or Directors: 3
Hot Spot for Advancement for Women/Minorities: Y

LOCATIONS: ("Y" = Yes)

West:	Southwest:	Midwest:	Southeast:	Northeast:	International:
				Y	

RYLAND GROUP INC (THE)

www.ryland.com

Industry Group Code: 2361 **Ranks within this company's industry group:** Sales: 10 Profits: 11

Properties:		Financial Services:		Construction/Development:		Investments:		Specialty Services:		Brokerage:	
Apartments:		Mortgages:	Y	Commercial Construction:		REIT:		Property Management:		Commercial Sales:	
Malls/Shopping:		Title Insurance:	Y	Residential Construction:	Y			Online Services:		Residential Sales:	Y
Offices:		Property Insurance:	Y	Land Development:				Software/IT:		Specialty:	
Hotels/Motels:				Support Services:				Consulting:			
Industrial/Warehouses:				Design/Engineering:	Y						
Other:											

TYPES OF BUSINESS:

Home Building
Mortgages
Title Services
Insurance Brokerage
Escrow Services
Home Brokerage
Homeowners' Warranties

BRANDS/DIVISIONS/AFFILIATES:

Ryland Mortgage Co
Cornerstone Title Co
RH Insurance Company
LPS Holdings Corporation
Columbia National Risk Retention Group Inc

CONTACTS: *Note: Officers with more than one job title may be intentionally listed here more than once.*

Larry T. Nicholson, CEO
Larry T. Nicholson, Pres.
Gordon A. Milne, CFO/Exec. VP
Eric E. Elder, Sr. VP-Mktg.
Robert J. Cunnion, III, Sr. VP-Human Resources
Craig McSpadden, CIO/VP
Timothy J. Geckle, General Counsel/Sr. VP/Corp. Sec.
Eric E. Elder, Sr. VP-Corp. Comm.
Drew P. Mackintosh, VP-Investor Rel.
David L. Fristoe, Chief Acct. Officer/Controller/Sr. VP
Charles W. Jenkins, VP-Sales Training
Peter G. Skelly, Pres., North & West Regions
Keith E. Bass, Pres., South Region
Daniel G. Schreiner, Pres., Ryland Mortgage Company
William L. Jews, Chmn.
Steven M. Dwyer, VP-Purchasing

Phone: 818-223-7500 **Fax:** 818-223-7667
Toll-Free:
Address: 24025 Park Sorrento, Ste. 400, Calabasas, CA 91302 US

GROWTH PLANS/SPECIAL FEATURES:

The Ryland Group, Inc. is one of the largest homebuilding and mortgage finance companies in the U.S. The company has built over 285,000 homes and financed more than 235,000 mortgages since its founding in 1967. The firm's operations span all aspects of the home-buying process from design, construction and sale to mortgage origination, title insurance, escrow and insurance services. The company focuses on marketing single-family homes to entry-level and move-up buyers, as well as to adults seeking retirement housing. Its homes are available in approximately 28 markets in 15 states across the country, which are divided into four broad geographic operating units: including North, Southeast, Texas and West. Moreover, its product line is tailored to local styles and preferences found in each geographic market. The company's prices range from $100,000 to over $450,000, with the average price of a Ryland home closed being roughly $240,000. Although homebuilding represents about 97% of the firm's annual revenue, it is also involved in financial services. Ryland's financial services segment is comprised of Ryland Mortgage Company (RMC); RH Insurance Company; Cornerstone Title Company, which does business as Ryland Title Company; LPS Holdings Corporation and its subsidiaries; and Columbia National Risk Retention Group, Inc. (Columbia). Mortgage financing and related services are provided by RMC and LPS Holdings. RH Insurance Company provides insurance brokerage services to the firm's homebuyers. Cornerstone provides title services and acts as a title insurance agent. Columbia directly insures liability risks, specifically homeowners' warranty coverage, arising in connection with the homebuilding business of the company.

Ryland offers its employees a benefits program including life, AD&D, disability, medical, vision and dental insurance; a 401(k) plan; a stock purchase plan; tuition reimbursement; a mortgage discount program; and paid vacations and holidays.

FINANCIALS: **Sales and profits are in thousands of dollars—add 000 to get the full amount. 2009 Note: Financial information for 2009 was not available for all companies at press time.**

2009 Sales: $1,284,000
2008 Sales: $1,976,000
2007 Sales: $3,052,000
2006 Sales: $4,780,000
2005 Sales: $4,817,566

2009 Profits: $-162,000
2008 Profits: $-397,000
2007 Profits: $-333,526
2006 Profits: $359,942
2005 Profits: $447,052

U.S. Stock Ticker: RYL
Int'l Ticker: Int'l Exchange:
Employees: 1,019
Fiscal Year Ends: 12/31
Parent Company:

SALARIES/BENEFITS:

Pension Plan: ESOP Stock Plan: Profit Sharing: Top Exec. Salary: $868,269 Bonus: $1,500,000
Savings Plan: Y Stock Purch. Plan: Y Second Exec. Salary: $726,923 Bonus: $400,000

OTHER THOUGHTS:

Apparent Women Officers or Directors: 2
Hot Spot for Advancement for Women/Minorities: Y

LOCATIONS: ("Y" = Yes)

West:	Southwest:	Midwest:	Southeast:	Northeast:	International:
Y	Y	Y	Y	Y	

SAHA PATHANA INTER-HOLDING PCL

www.spi.co.th

Industry Group Code: 5311 **Ranks within this company's industry group:** Sales: 35 Profits: 25

Properties:		Financial Services:		Construction/Development:		Investments:		Specialty Services:		Brokerage:	
Apartments:		Mortgages:		Commercial Construction:	Y	REIT:		Property Management:		Commercial Sales:	
Malls/Shopping:		Title Insurance:		Residential Construction:				Online Services:		Residential Sales:	
Offices:	Y	Property Insurance:		Land Development:	Y			Software/IT:		Specialty:	
Hotels/Motels:				Support Services:				Consulting:			
Industrial/Warehouses:	Y			Design/Engineering:							
Other:											

TYPES OF BUSINESS:

Industrial Real Estate Holdings

BRANDS/DIVISIONS/AFFILIATES:

Brahma Park
Health Park

CONTACTS:

Note: Officers with more than one job title may be intentionally listed here more than once.

Boonsithi Chokwatana, Chmn.-Exec. Board
Santi Vilatsakdanont, Pres.
Somchai Puntaprukesa, Mgr.-Finance
Sauwanee Numbenjapol, Mgr.-Human Resources
Anant Soonpan, Mgr.-R&D
Sontaya Tabkhan, Mgr.-Eng. Dept.
Tasanee Intapura, Mgr.-Project Admin.
Vichai Aramrueng, Mgr.-Legal
Nisa Chindasombatcharoen, Mgr.-Acct.
Tanong Srichit, Exec. VP
Pimsiri Kuansuwan, Mgr.-Bus. Promotion
Pirom Thongging, Mgr.-Internal Audit
Tinakorn Bunnag, Mgr.-Land Dev.
Chokchai Aksoranan, Chmn.

Phone: 66-2-293-0030 **Fax:** 66-2-293-0040
Toll-Free:
Address: 757/10 Soi Pradoo 1, Sathupradit Rd., Bangkok, 10120 Thailand

GROWTH PLANS/SPECIAL FEATURES:

Saha Pathana Inter-Holding Public Company Limited is a Thailand-based real estate holding and development company investing primarily in industrial parks. The company is currently invested in three industrial parks in Sriracha, Kabinburi and Lamphun. The Sriracha park features a 186 megawatt (MW) power plant; a centralized water treatment plant with a daily capacity of 423,776 cubic feet; a private air field; a trade exhibition center; a 30 million cubic foot water reservoir; and a park. The park located in Kabinburi contains two 50 megavolt ampere (MVA) electrical substations; a centralized waste water treatment plant with a daily capacity of 565,035 cubic feet; a private air field; a 35.3 million cubic foot water reservoir; and an industrial incinerator with a 220 pound per hour capacity. The Lamphun park features two 50 megavolt ampere (MVA) electrical substations; a centralized water treatment plant with a daily capacity of 300,175 cubic feet; a private water supply of 127,133 cubic feet per day; a private air field; a 17.6 million cubic foot water reservoir; a golf driving range; a meeting room; and Brahma Park and Health Park. The company, to a lesser extent, is invested in consumer products, distribution, manufacturing, service and investment firms.

FINANCIALS:

Sales and profits are in thousands of dollars—add 000 to get the full amount. 2009 Note: Financial information for 2009 was not available for all companies at press time.

2009 Sales: $93,250	2009 Profits: $31,050	**U.S. Stock Ticker:**
2008 Sales: $86,500	2008 Profits: $28,000	**Int'l Ticker: SPI** Int'l Exchange: Bangkok-BAK
2007 Sales: $73,700	2007 Profits: $17,800	Employees:
2006 Sales: $78,900	2006 Profits: $21,600	Fiscal Year Ends:
2005 Sales: $	2005 Profits: $	Parent Company:

SALARIES/BENEFITS:

Pension Plan:	ESOP Stock Plan:	Profit Sharing:	Top Exec. Salary: $	Bonus: $
Savings Plan:	Stock Purch. Plan:		Second Exec. Salary: $	Bonus: $

OTHER THOUGHTS:

Apparent Women Officers or Directors: 5
Hot Spot for Advancement for Women/Minorities: Y

LOCATIONS: ("Y" = Yes)

West:	Southwest:	Midwest:	Southeast:	Northeast:	International:
					Y

SAMWHAN CORPORATION

www.samwhan.co.kr/sw/english

Industry Group Code: 23 **Ranks within this company's industry group:** Sales: Profits:

Properties:		Financial Services:		Construction/Development:		Investments:		Specialty Services:		Brokerage:	
Apartments:		Mortgages:		Commercial Construction:	Y	REIT:		Property Management:		Commercial Sales:	
Malls/Shopping:		Title Insurance:		Residential Construction:	Y			Online Services:		Residential Sales:	
Offices:		Property Insurance:		Land Development:				Software/IT:		Specialty:	
Hotels/Motels:				Support Services:				Consulting:			
Industrial/Warehouses:				Design/Engineering:							
Other:											

TYPES OF BUSINESS:

Construction
General Importing & Exporting
Precast Concrete

BRANDS/DIVISIONS/AFFILIATES:

Samwhan Camus Co
Samwhan Machinery Co Ltd
Sinmin Mutual Savings Bank
Whoihyun Co Ltd
Woosung Development Co Ltd

CONTACTS:

Note: Officers with more than one job title may be intentionally listed here more than once.

Sang Guk Park, Co-CEO/VP
Jong Huh, Pres./Co-CEO
Sang Tae Choi, Head/Dir.-Construction Bus.
Youn-Kwon Choi, Chmn.

Phone: 82-2-740-2114	**Fax:** 82-2-742-1849
Toll-Free:	
Address: 98-20 Wooni-dong, Jongno-Gu, Seoul, 110-742 Korea	

GROWTH PLANS/SPECIAL FEATURES:

Samwhan Corporation, established in 1946, is a Korean construction company. It has experience building housing units; commercial buildings; offices; ports and airports; industrial plants; fabrication facilities; power distribution and transmission systems; pipelines and pumping systems; and highways and bridges. More specifically, its projects have included intelligent buildings; resorts and recreational complexes; hospital and medical healthcare facilities; retail complexes, department stores and shopping malls; remodeling and rehabilitation; real estate development; thermal, nuclear and hydraulic power plants; municipal solid waste treatment plants; natural gas pipelines; oil refineries; subways and underground works; dams; and land reclamation. Samwhan offers engineering and consulting services, including feasibility studies; basic and detailed design; and construction management and supervisory services. The firm is also engaged in a general import and export business; and the production and supply of precast concrete. The company has branches in Afghanistan, California, Vietnam, Bangladesh, Japan, Saudi Arabia, Turkey, Russia, Algeria, Libya and the Republic of Yemen. Besides these locations, Samwhan has completed major projects in Afghanistan, Jordan, Papua New Guinea, Guam, Malaysia, Indonesia, Laos and Singapore. It was one of the first Korean contractors to work in Mongolia, and has worked on numerous U.S. military bases in Korea. Samwhan's affiliates include Samwhan Camus Co., which focuses on pre-cast concrete production and construction; Samwhan Machinery Co., Ltd., a manufacturer of materials for metal structures; Sinmin Mutual Savings Bank, a banking and financing company; Whoihyun Co., Ltd., a real estate leasing service; and Woosung Development Co., Ltd., a company involved with land development.

FINANCIALS:

Sales and profits are in thousands of dollars—add 000 to get the full amount. 2009 Note: Financial information for 2009 was not available for all companies at press time.

2009 Sales: $	2009 Profits: $	**U.S. Stock Ticker:**
2008 Sales: $	2008 Profits: $	**Int'l Ticker: 000360** Int'l Exchange: Seoul-KRX
2007 Sales: $	2007 Profits: $	Employees:
2006 Sales: $	2006 Profits: $	Fiscal Year Ends:
2005 Sales: $	2005 Profits: $	Parent Company:

SALARIES/BENEFITS:

Pension Plan:	ESOP Stock Plan:	Profit Sharing:	Top Exec. Salary: $	Bonus: $
Savings Plan:	Stock Purch. Plan:		Second Exec. Salary: $	Bonus: $

OTHER THOUGHTS:

Apparent Women Officers or Directors:
Hot Spot for Advancement for Women/Minorities:

LOCATIONS: ("Y" = Yes)

West:	Southwest:	Midwest:	Southeast:	Northeast:	International:
Y					Y

SANDS REGENT

www.sandsregency.com

Industry Group Code: 721120 **Ranks within this company's industry group:** Sales: Profits:

Properties:		Financial Services:		Construction/Development:		Investments:		Specialty Services:		Brokerage:	
Apartments:		Mortgages:		Commercial Construction:		REIT:		Property Management:		Commercial Sales:	
Malls/Shopping:		Title Insurance:		Residential Construction:				Online Services:		Residential Sales:	
Offices:		Property Insurance:		Land Development:				Software/IT:		Specialty:	
Hotels/Motels:	Y			Support Services:				Consulting:			
Industrial/Warehouses:				Design/Engineering:							
Other:	Y										

TYPES OF BUSINESS:

Casino Hotel
Convention Center

BRANDS/DIVISIONS/AFFILIATES:

Herbst Gaming Inc
Sands Regency Casino & Hotel
Terrible's Gold Ranch Casino & RV Resort
Terrible's Rail City Casino

CONTACTS:

Note: Officers with more than one job title may be intentionally listed here more than once.

Troy D. Herbst, CEO
David Ross, COO-Gaming
Ferenc Szony, Pres.
Mary E. Higgins, CFO
Sean T. Higgins, General Counsel
Edward J. Herbst, Exec. VP
Timothy P. Herbst, Chmn./Exec. VP

Phone: 702-889-7695	**Fax:** 702-889-7691
Toll-Free:	
Address: 3440 W. Russel Rd., Reno, NV 89118 US	

GROWTH PLANS/SPECIAL FEATURES:

Sands Regent owns and operates casinos and related tourist amenities in Nevada within the Terrible Herbst family of properties. The company portfolio consists of 12 casinos in Northern and Southern Nevada and three casinos in Missouri and Iowa. The company's marquee operation, the Sands Regency Casino and Hotel in downtown Reno, features some 850 hotel rooms and 29,000 square feet of gaming space. While the company derives most of its revenue from its 17 gaming tables, 539 slot machines and sportsbook, it also operates a comedy club, cocktail lounges, a video arcade and a music lounge. Other services include beauty and gift shops; restaurants and fast-food eateries; and a 12,000-square-foot convention and meeting center that accommodates 1,000 people. Some notable properties include: Terrible's Gold Ranch Casino & RV Resort in Verdi, Nevada, 12 miles west of Reno, is the first casino gaming attraction that travelers encounter on Interstate 80 when entering Nevada from California, and the last when leaving. Its facilities include an 8,300-square-foot casino with 235 slot machines, two restaurants, two bars, a California lottery station, an ARCO gas station and a convenience store, as well as a 47-space RV park. Terrible's Rail City Casino in Sparks, Nevada has approximately 16,600 square feet of gaming space and features more than 650 slots, six table games, keno and a sportsbook. It also has a family-style restaurant and a sports bar, with a convenient off-highway location. In addition, the company operations include Terrible Herbst gas stations and convenience stores. Lastly, the firm's operations include installation and operation of slot machines in chain store and street account locations and as of December 31, 2009, it owned approximately 6,200 slot machines in chain stores throughout the state of Nevada. Herbst Gaming, Inc. owns the firm. In March 2009, Herbst Gaming, Inc. has filed for reorganization of its company under Chapter 11 bankruptcy protection.

FINANCIALS:

Sales and profits are in thousands of dollars—add 000 to get the full amount. 2009 Note: Financial information for 2009 was not available for all companies at press time.

2009 Sales: $	2009 Profits: $	**U.S. Stock Ticker: Subsidiary**
2008 Sales: $	2008 Profits: $	**Int'l Ticker:** Int'l Exchange:
2007 Sales: $	2007 Profits: $	Employees:
2006 Sales: $92,574	2006 Profits: $2,431	Fiscal Year Ends: 6/30
2005 Sales: $81,132	2005 Profits: $3,831	Parent Company: HERBST GAMING INC

SALARIES/BENEFITS:

Pension Plan:	ESOP Stock Plan:	Profit Sharing:	Top Exec. Salary: $992,822	Bonus: $
Savings Plan: Y	Stock Purch. Plan:		Second Exec. Salary: $567,211	Bonus: $

OTHER THOUGHTS:

Apparent Women Officers or Directors:
Hot Spot for Advancement for Women/Minorities:

LOCATIONS: ("Y" = Yes)

West:	Southwest:	Midwest:	Southeast:	Northeast:	International:
Y		Y			

SAWYER REALTY HOLDINGS LLC

www.sawyerapts.com

Industry Group Code: 531110 **Ranks within this company's industry group:** Sales: Profits:

Properties:		Financial Services:		Construction/Development:		Investments:		Specialty Services:		Brokerage:	
Apartments:	Y	Mortgages:		Commercial Construction:	Y	REIT:		Property Management:	Y	Commercial Sales:	
Malls/Shopping:		Title Insurance:		Residential Construction:	Y			Online Services:		Residential Sales:	
Offices:		Property Insurance:		Land Development:	Y			Software/IT:		Specialty:	
Hotels/Motels:				Support Services:				Consulting:			
Industrial/Warehouses:				Design/Engineering:							
Other:	Y										

TYPES OF BUSINESS:

Real Estate Investment Trust
Apartment Communities
Property Management

BRANDS/DIVISIONS/AFFILIATES:

Forewinds Hospitality, LLC

CONTACTS:

Note: Officers with more than one job title may be intentionally listed here more than once.

David M. Rosenberg, CEO
Gregg Clickstein, COO
Gregg Clickstein, Pres.
Gary J. Gianino, CFO
Tom Rucker, VP-Real Estate Oper., Sawyer Property Mgmt.
Gary J. Gianino, COO-Sawyer Property Mgmt. Companies, LLC

Phone: 301-479-1600	**Fax:** 301-479-1700
Toll-Free:	
Address: 9658 Baltimore Ave., Ste 300, College Park, MD 20740 US	

GROWTH PLANS/SPECIAL FEATURES:

Sawyer Realty Holdings, LLC is a privately held real estate investment and management firm that acquires, maintains and operates undervalued multifamily properties. The company works to add value to its acquisitions through teams of mostly autonomous property specialists across the east coast and throughout the Midwest, and offices in Massachusetts, Maryland and Georgia. Sawyer's multifamily portfolio consists of approximately 39,814 apartment units located inside 137 apartment communities, primarily in Florida and the Southeast, up the East coast into Baltimore, Washington D.C. and New England. Sawyer utilizes real estate as an investment mechanism to enrich all of its stakeholders, including its employees, lenders, suppliers, investors, officers, and principals. In addition to Sawyer's multi-family focus, the company invests in ground up development projects for multifamily, hotel, and commercial projects, which includes the purchase or joint venture of permitted or raw land and acquisition of existing properties for significant redevelopment. Sawyer has also invested in numerous golf course assets through its wholly-owned subsidiary, Forewinds Hospitality, LLC.

Employees of the firm are offered medical, dental, vision and prescription drug plan; flexible spending account for health care and dependent care; long-term and short-term disability; employee assistance program; accidental death, dismemberment and basic life insurance; and a discount program.

FINANCIALS:

Sales and profits are in thousands of dollars—add 000 to get the full amount. 2009 Note: Financial information for 2009 was not available for all companies at press time.

2009 Sales: $	2009 Profits: $	**U.S. Stock Ticker: Private**
2008 Sales: $	2008 Profits: $	**Int'l Ticker:** Int'l Exchange:
2007 Sales: $	2007 Profits: $	Employees:
2006 Sales: $	2006 Profits: $	Fiscal Year Ends: 12/31
2005 Sales: $131,697	2005 Profits: $5,192	Parent Company:

SALARIES/BENEFITS:

Pension Plan:	ESOP Stock Plan:	Profit Sharing:	Top Exec. Salary: $	Bonus: $
Savings Plan: Y	Stock Purch. Plan:		Second Exec. Salary: $	Bonus: $

OTHER THOUGHTS:

Apparent Women Officers or Directors:
Hot Spot for Advancement for Women/Minorities:

LOCATIONS: ("Y" = Yes)

West:	Southwest:	Midwest:	Southeast:	Northeast:	International:
				Y	

SCANDIC HOTELS AB

www.scandichotels.com

Industry Group Code: 721110 **Ranks within this company's industry group:** Sales: 13 Profits: 6

Properties:		Financial Services:		Construction/Development:		Investments:		Specialty Services:		Brokerage:	
Apartments:		Mortgages:		Commercial Construction:		REIT:		Property Management:		Commercial Sales:	
Malls/Shopping:		Title Insurance:		Residential Construction:				Online Services:		Residential Sales:	
Offices:		Property Insurance:		Land Development:				Software/IT:		Specialty:	
Hotels/Motels:	Y			Support Services:				Consulting:			
Industrial/Warehouses:				Design/Engineering:							
Other:											

TYPES OF BUSINESS:

Hotels

BRANDS/DIVISIONS/AFFILIATES:

Hotel Rivoli
Hotel Linnea
Hotel Salpaus

CONTACTS:

Note: Officers with more than one job title may be intentionally listed here more than once.

Frank Fiskers, CEO
Frank Fiskers, Pres.
Gunilla Rudebjer, CFO
Roger Olofsson, Sr. VP-Human Resources
Thomas Engelhart, Sr. VP-Commercial Oper.
Jessica Agert, Mgr.-Media Rel.
Gunilla Rudebjer, Sr. VP-Finance
Martin Creydt, Sr. VP-Hotel Oper.
Ulrika Kjellstrom Attar, Mgr.-Brand Experience
Vagn Sørensen, Chmn.

Phone: 46-85-17-350-00	**Fax:** 46-85-17-350-11
Toll-Free:	
Address: Halsingegatan 40, Stockholm, SE-102 33 Sweden	

GROWTH PLANS/SPECIAL FEATURES:

Scandic Hotels AB, which is owned by private equity firm EQT Partners AB, is one of Scandinavia's largest hotel operators. The firm has approximately 151 hotels located in 10 countries: Sweden, Norway, Finland, Denmark, Estonia, Germany, Belgium, Poland, the Netherlands and Lithuania. Every year, Scandic Hotels serve over 8 million guests. Scandic Hotels has a long history of being environmentally conscious, and all of its Swedish hotels carry the Swan eco-label, a certification earned for effort and results toward sustainable practices. Scandic also has partnerships with numerous hotel, travel and entertainment companies to provide more options to its customers. In an effort to simplify services for customers, Scandic Hotels' pricing plan offers two price levels: early and flex. Early means a reduced price reservation without the option to cancel or change, while flex is a higher, flexible reservation price. The company hopes expand and operate a total of 200 hotels within the next few years. In February 2010, Scandic Hotels and The Lunde Group agreed to open a new hotel in Lindesnes, Norway. In March 2010, the firm agreed to acquire the Finland-based Hotel Rivoli, Hotel Linnea, Hotel Salpaus and a hotel under construction from Next Hotels Finland Oy.

FINANCIALS:

Sales and profits are in thousands of dollars—add 000 to get the full amount. 2009 Note: Financial information for 2009 was not available for all companies at press time.

2009 Sales: $	2009 Profits: $	**U.S. Stock Ticker: Private**
2008 Sales: $982,670	2008 Profits: $143,930	**Int'l Ticker:** Int'l Exchange:
2007 Sales: $	2007 Profits: $	Employees:
2006 Sales: $	2006 Profits: $	Fiscal Year Ends: 12/31
2005 Sales: $	2005 Profits: $	Parent Company: EQT PARTNERS AB

SALARIES/BENEFITS:

Pension Plan:	ESOP Stock Plan:	Profit Sharing:	Top Exec. Salary: $	Bonus: $
Savings Plan:	Stock Purch. Plan:		Second Exec. Salary: $	Bonus: $

OTHER THOUGHTS:

Apparent Women Officers or Directors: 2
Hot Spot for Advancement for Women/Minorities: Y

LOCATIONS: ("Y" = Yes)

West:	Southwest:	Midwest:	Southeast:	Northeast:	International:
					Y

SCHUFF INTERNATIONAL INC

www.schuff.com

Industry Group Code: 2389 **Ranks within this company's industry group:** Sales: 2 Profits: 2

Properties:		Financial Services:		Construction/Development:		Investments:		Specialty Services:		Brokerage:	
Apartments:		Mortgages:		Commercial Construction:	Y	REIT:		Property Management:		Commercial Sales:	
Malls/Shopping:		Title Insurance:		Residential Construction:				Online Services:		Residential Sales:	
Offices:		Property Insurance:		Land Development:				Software/IT:	Y	Specialty:	
Hotels/Motels:				Support Services:	Y			Consulting:	Y		
Industrial/Warehouses:				Design/Engineering:	Y						
Other:											

TYPES OF BUSINESS:

Construction Services
Structural Steel Fabrication & Erection
Project Management Services
Design & Engineering Consulting Services
Subcontract Management

BRANDS/DIVISIONS/AFFILIATES:

Schuff Steel Company
Schuff Steel-Midwest Inc
Schuff Steel-Atlantic Inc
Quincy Joist Company
Schuff Steel Management Company-Southwest, Inc.
Schuff Steel-Gulf Coast Inc
Aitken, Inc.

CONTACTS: *Note: Officers with more than one job title may be intentionally listed here more than once.*

Scott A. Schuff, CEO
Scott A. Schuff, Pres.
Michael R. Hill, CFO/VP
Ryan S. Schuff, Pres./CEO-Schuff Steel Company
Robert N. Waldrep, VP
David A. Schuff, Chmn.

Phone: 602-252-7787	**Fax:** 602-452-4465
Toll-Free: 800-435-8528	
Address: 420 S. 19th Ave., Phoenix, AZ 85009 US	

GROWTH PLANS/SPECIAL FEATURES:

Schuff International, Inc. is a fully integrated steel fabrication and erection company primarily serving the commercial, industrial, public works, healthcare, gaming and hospitality, mixed-use, retail and transportation markets. The firm fabricates and erects structural steel for construction projects such as arenas and stadiums, bridges, casinos and hotels, convention centers, hospitals, power plants, office buildings, parking structures, retail centers, warehouses and distribution facilities. Schuff divides its services into six categories: Design-Assist/Design-Build; Preconstruction Design and Budgeting; Steel Management; Fabrication; Erection; and Building Information Modeling (BIM) Services. Design-Assist and Design-Build services utilize BIM systems and a proprietary management system, SSIMS (Schuff Steel Integrated Management System), to provide real-time reporting, 3-D model information and cost-effective design. The Steel Management division provides steel subcontract management services. The Fabrication division operates ten structural steel fabrication plants, with an annual fabrication capacity of over 300,000 tons. Products include joists and joist girders. Schuff's projects are concentrated in Arizona, Nevada, Colorado, Florida and California. It offers services primarily to developers, general contractors and engineering firms, including Hunt Construction; Fluor Corp.; and Perini Building Company. Representative projects include the Orlando Events Center in Florida, home of the Orlando Magic; the Maricopa County Court Tower, a 16-story justice center in Phoenix, Arizona; Silver Cross Replacement Hospital, a 500,000-square-foot facility in Illinois; and the Sands Casino Resort in Pennsylvania. The company operates through its subsidiaries, which include Schuff Steel Company; Schuff Steel-Midwest; Schuff Steel-Atlantic, Inc.; Quincy Joist Company; Aitken, Inc.; Schuff Steel-Gulf Coast, Inc.; and Schuff Steel Management Company-Southwest, Inc. In December 2009, Schuff Steel Company acquired a steel fabrication plant in Stockton, California.

Employees are offered medical, dental, vision and prescription drug insurance; a 401(k) plan; short-and long-term disability coverage; life and AD&D insurance; an employee assistance program; and tuition reimbursement.

FINANCIALS: **Sales and profits are in thousands of dollars—add 000 to get the full amount. 2009 Note: Financial information for 2009 was not available for all companies at press time.**

2009 Sales: $420,871	2009 Profits: $18,951	**U.S. Stock Ticker: SHFK**
2008 Sales: $681,629	2008 Profits: $56,315	**Int'l Ticker:** Int'l Exchange:
2007 Sales: $736,194	2007 Profits: $59,874	Employees:
2006 Sales: $	2006 Profits: $	Fiscal Year Ends: 12/31
2005 Sales: $	2005 Profits: $	Parent Company:

SALARIES/BENEFITS:

Pension Plan:	ESOP Stock Plan:	Profit Sharing:	Top Exec. Salary: $	Bonus: $
Savings Plan: Y	Stock Purch. Plan:		Second Exec. Salary: $	Bonus: $

OTHER THOUGHTS:

Apparent Women Officers or Directors:
Hot Spot for Advancement for Women/Minorities:

LOCATIONS: ("Y" = Yes)

West:	Southwest:	Midwest:	Southeast:	Northeast:	International:
Y	Y	Y	Y		

SEKISUI HOUSE LTD

www.sekisuihouse.co.jp

Industry Group Code: 2361 **Ranks within this company's industry group:** Sales: 1 Profits: 1

Properties:		Financial Services:		Construction/Development:		Investments:		Specialty Services:		Brokerage:	
Apartments:	Y	Mortgages:		Commercial Construction:	Y	REIT:		Property Management:		Commercial Sales:	
Malls/Shopping:		Title Insurance:		Residential Construction:	Y			Online Services:		Residential Sales:	Y
Offices:	Y	Property Insurance:		Land Development:	Y			Software/IT:		Specialty:	
Hotels/Motels:				Support Services:				Consulting:			
Industrial/Warehouses:	Y			Design/Engineering:	Y						
Other:											

TYPES OF BUSINESS:

Residential Construction
Real Estate Sales
Real Estate Leasing
Urban Construction
Garden Design

BRANDS/DIVISIONS/AFFILIATES:

CONTACTS:

Note: Officers with more than one job title may be intentionally listed here more than once.

Isami Wada, CEO
Toshinori Abe, COO
Toshinori Abe, Pres.
Takashi Uchida, Managing Exec. Officer/Dir.-Finance & Acct.
Naoki Ishii, Exec. Officer
Shiro Inagaki, Sr. Managing Officer
Sumio Wada, Sr. Managing Officer
Kotaro Asano, Exec. Officer
Isami Wada, Chmn.

Phone: 81-66-440-3111 **Fax:** 81-66-440-3369
Toll-Free:
Address: 1-88 Oyodonaka, 1-Chome, Osaka, 531-0076 Japan

GROWTH PLANS/SPECIAL FEATURES:

Sekisui House, Ltd., based in Japan, and its subsidiaries engage primarily in the contract design, construction and leasing of pre-fabricated houses. Sekisui House's corporate philosophy is Love of Humanity. It attempts to fulfill this philosophy by reducing consumption and providing high-quality homes that last for generations, as well as creating new residential designs that will provide a greater value to society. These residences are built-to-order and include both single- and multi-family houses, condominiums, dormitories and resort accommodations. The company is also involved in comprehensive urban development projects, including the construction of office buildings; school buildings; clinics; factories; and other buildings constructed with steel- and wood-frame and in ferro-concrete. Sekisui House manufactures and sells construction materials; purchases and sells materials for reforestation, landscaping and other civil engineering and construction works; and undertakes research, planning, design, execution, supervision, engineering, management and consulting business related to regional development, urban development, land preparation and environmental improvement. The firm designs, executes, contracts and supervises civil engineering works; carpentering; earthwork; roofing works; piping; painting; waterproofing; interior finishing; furnishing; electrical work; telecommunication works; installation works of machinery and tools; steel structure and reinforcing works; waterworks; and fire fighting equipment works. In real estate, the company buys and sells properties; operating a management consultant business; and acts as a broker for the purchase and sale of properties. Sekisui House also engages in the cultivation, purchase and sale of plants and the design, construction and cultivation of gardens. The company has a total of 92 subsidiaries and affiliate companies. In February 2010, Sekisui House, and Spring Investment Co., Ltd. agreed to jointly acquire asset management firm Joint Capital Partners Co., Ltd. from Joint Corporation.

FINANCIALS:

Sales and profits are in thousands of dollars—add 000 to get the full amount. 2009 Note: Financial information for 2009 was not available for all companies at press time.

2009 Sales: $16,083,100	2009 Profits: $122,320	**U.S. Stock Ticker: SKHSY**
2008 Sales: $15,978,100	2008 Profits: $603,500	**Int'l Ticker: 1928** Int'l Exchange: Tokyo-TSE
2007 Sales: $15,961,800	2007 Profits: $626,600	Employees:
2006 Sales: $15,018,600	2006 Profits: $430,300	Fiscal Year Ends: 1/31
2005 Sales: $12,592,200	2005 Profits: $360,770	Parent Company:

SALARIES/BENEFITS:

Pension Plan:	ESOP Stock Plan:	Profit Sharing:	Top Exec. Salary: $	Bonus: $
Savings Plan:	Stock Purch. Plan:		Second Exec. Salary: $	Bonus: $

OTHER THOUGHTS:

Apparent Women Officers or Directors:
Hot Spot for Advancement for Women/Minorities:

LOCATIONS: ("Y" = Yes)

West:	Southwest:	Midwest:	Southeast:	Northeast:	International:
					Y

SEMBCORP INDUSTRIES LTD

www.sembcorp.com.sg

Industry Group Code: 237 **Ranks within this company's industry group:** Sales: 16 Profits: 7

Properties:		Financial Services:		Construction/Development:		Investments:		Specialty Services:		Brokerage:	
Apartments:		Mortgages:		Commercial Construction:	Y	REIT:		Property Management:		Commercial Sales:	
Malls/Shopping:		Title Insurance:		Residential Construction:				Online Services:		Residential Sales:	
Offices:		Property Insurance:		Land Development:				Software/IT:		Specialty:	
Hotels/Motels:				Support Services:				Consulting:			
Industrial/Warehouses:				Design/Engineering:							
Other:											

TYPES OF BUSINESS:

Heavy Construction
Marine Construction & Shipbuilding
Utilities Services
Environmental Engineering & Waste Management
Industrial Parks
Internet Service Provider
Floating Oil Production Platforms
Pipelines

BRANDS/DIVISIONS/AFFILIATES:

SembCorp Marine
SembCorp Environment
SembCorp Utilities
SembCorp Gas
SembCorp Cogen
Singapore Mint
Singapore Precision Industries
SembCorp Design and Production

CONTACTS:

Note: Officers with more than one job title may be intentionally listed here more than once.

Tang Kin Fei, CEO
Tang Kin Fei, Pres.
Lim Joke Mui, CFO
Tan Cheng Guan, Exec. VP-Group Bus. & Strategic Dev.
Francis Joseph Gomez, Exec. VP-Energy
Paul Gavens, Exec. VP-Sembcorp Utilities (U.K.)
Wong Weng Sun, Pres./CEO-SembCorp Marine
Goh Swee Ooi, COO-SembCorp Environment

Phone: 65-6723-3113	**Fax:** 65-6822-3254
Toll-Free:	
Address: 30 Hill St., #05-04, Singapore, 179360 Singapore	

GROWTH PLANS/SPECIAL FEATURES:

Sembcorp Industries, Ltd. is one of Singapore's leading utilities and marine groups. The firm's primary businesses include Sembcorp Utilities; Sembcorp Marine; Sembcorp Environment; and Sembcorp Industrial Parks. Sembcorp Utilities provides integrated utilities, energy and water solutions to the chemical and petrochemical industry in Singapore, the U.K. and China. In addition, the firm operates power a desalination plants in Vietnam and the United Arab Emirates (U.A.E.). The firm offers a variety of industrial utilities services including water supply and wastewater treatment; power generation; process stream production and distribution; chemical feedstock; and asset protection. The utility segment's operation has a generation capacity of 3,300 megawatts. Sembcorp Marine has one of the largest ship repair, shipbuilding and ship conversion operations in East Asia. The company offers a full range of marine and offshore engineering solutions including container ships, chemical tankers, production platforms; and converts Floating Production, Storage and Offloading units (FPSO) for the oil and gas industry. Sembcorp Environment provides treatment methods and waste-to-resource technologies to 1.2 million households, 47,000 industrial and commercial customers and government agencies, plus 9,000 healthcare establishments in Singapore, India and Australia. The Sembcorp Industrial Parks segment owns, develops, markets and manages multinational industrial parks predominately located in China, Indonesia and Vietnam. Sembcorp Industries operates numerous subsidiaries including Sembcorp Gas; Sembcorp Cogen; Sembcorp Power; Singapore Mint; SembCorp Design and Production; and Singapore Precision Industries.

SembCorp offers employees health benefits; loan/interest subsidy; a stock ownership plan; a bonus program; and a job development program.

FINANCIALS:

Sales and profits are in thousands of dollars—add 000 to get the full amount. 2009 Note: Financial information for 2009 was not available for all companies at press time.

2009 Sales: $6,870,650	2009 Profits: $490,010	**U.S. Stock Ticker: SCRPF**
2008 Sales: $6,548,910	2008 Profits: $482,170	**Int'l Ticker: U96** Int'l Exchange: Singapore-SIN
2007 Sales: $5,990,000	2007 Profits: $370,000	Employees:
2006 Sales: $4,880,000	2006 Profits: $670,000	Fiscal Year Ends: 12/31
2005 Sales: $4,604,000	2005 Profits: $258,000	Parent Company:

SALARIES/BENEFITS:

Pension Plan:	ESOP Stock Plan: Y	Profit Sharing:	Top Exec. Salary: $	Bonus: $1,165,529
Savings Plan:	Stock Purch. Plan:		Second Exec. Salary: $	Bonus: $

OTHER THOUGHTS:

Apparent Women Officers or Directors: 1
Hot Spot for Advancement for Women/Minorities:

LOCATIONS: ("Y" = Yes)

West:	Southwest:	Midwest:	Southeast:	Northeast:	International:
					Y

SENIOR HOUSING PROPERTIES

www.snhreit.com

Industry Group Code: 531120 **Ranks within this company's industry group:** Sales: 53 Profits: 25

Properties:		Financial Services:		Construction/Development:		Investments:		Specialty Services:		Brokerage:	
Apartments:	Y	Mortgages:		Commercial Construction:		REIT:	Y	Property Management:		Commercial Sales:	
Malls/Shopping:		Title Insurance:		Residential Construction:				Online Services:		Residential Sales:	
Offices:	Y	Property Insurance:		Land Development:				Software/IT:		Specialty:	
Hotels/Motels:				Support Services:				Consulting:			
Industrial/Warehouses:				Design/Engineering:							
Other:	Y										

TYPES OF BUSINESS:

Real Estate Investment Trust
Senior Housing Properties

BRANDS/DIVISIONS/AFFILIATES:

Reit Management and Research LLC

CONTACTS:

Note: Officers with more than one job title may be intentionally listed here more than once.

David J. Hegarty, COO
David J. Hegarty, Pres.
Richard A. Doyle, CFO
Jennifer B. Clark, Corp. Sec.
Richard A. Doyle, Treas.
William J. Sheehan, Dir.-Internal Audit & Compliance

Phone: 617-796-8350	**Fax:** 617-796-8349
Toll-Free:	
Address: 400 Centre St., Newton, MA 02458-2076 US	

GROWTH PLANS/SPECIAL FEATURES:

Senior Housing Properties (SHP) is a real estate investment trust (REIT) that invests in properties such as apartments for aged residents, assisted living facilities and nursing homes. SHP owns 298 properties in 35 states and Washington, D.C. The firm's portfolio includes 232 senior living properties, with 26,937 units; 56 medical office, clinic and biotech laboratory buildings, totaling 2.9 million square feet; and 10 wellness centers, with approximately 812,000 square feet of space. The company is managed by Reit Management & Research LLC (RMR), a real estate management company that oversees a large portfolio of publicly owned real estate in the U.S., Puerto Rico and Canada. SHP has no direct employees and day-to-day company activities are conducted by RMR and SHP's managing trustees and officers. All SHP properties are triple net leased, meaning that each tenant pays rent and is also responsible for such expenses as taxes, insurance and maintenance costs. SHP has adapted its business strategy to focus on high-quality properties in which revenues are received entirely from residents' private resources and not from the government. Currently, approximately 90% of the firm's annual rent revenues come from properties where 80% or more of operating revenues are derived from residents who pay from private resources rather than from Medicare or Medicaid.
The firm's properties include senior apartments, in which residents care for themselves; independent living properties, which include services such as meals and maid service; assisted living properties, typically offering private units with 24-hour availability of various types of assistance to residents; nursing homes, which generally provide extensive nursing and healthcare services; rehabilitation hospitals, which provide services such as physical therapy, occupational therapy and speech language pathology; and wellness centers, which offer features such as gymnasiums, strength and cardiovascular equipment areas, tennis and racquet sports facilities, pools and spas.

FINANCIALS:

Sales and profits are in thousands of dollars—add 000 to get the full amount. 2009 Note: Financial information for 2009 was not available for all companies at press time.

2009 Sales: $297,780	2009 Profits: $109,715	**U.S. Stock Ticker: SNH**
2008 Sales: $235,537	2008 Profits: $106,511	**Int'l Ticker:** Int'l Exchange:
2007 Sales: $188,022	2007 Profits: $85,303	Employees: 600
2006 Sales: $179,806	2006 Profits: $66,101	Fiscal Year Ends: 12/31
2005 Sales: $163,187	2005 Profits: $63,912	Parent Company:

SALARIES/BENEFITS:

Pension Plan:	ESOP Stock Plan:	Profit Sharing:	Top Exec. Salary: $	Bonus: $
Savings Plan:	Stock Purch. Plan:		Second Exec. Salary: $	Bonus: $

OTHER THOUGHTS:

Apparent Women Officers or Directors: 1
Hot Spot for Advancement for Women/Minorities:

LOCATIONS: ("Y" = Yes)

West:	Southwest:	Midwest:	Southeast:	Northeast:	International:
Y	Y	Y	Y	Y	Y

SERVICEMASTER COMPANY (THE)

www.servicemaster.com

Industry Group Code: 561720 **Ranks within this company's industry group:** Sales: 1 Profits: 1

Properties:		Financial Services:		Construction/Development:		Investments:		Specialty Services:		Brokerage:	
Apartments:		Mortgages:		Commercial Construction:		REIT:		Property Management:		Commercial Sales:	
Malls/Shopping:		Title Insurance:		Residential Construction:				Online Services:		Residential Sales:	
Offices:		Property Insurance:		Land Development:				Software/IT:		Specialty:	
Hotels/Motels:				Support Services:	Y			Consulting:			
Industrial/Warehouses:				Design/Engineering:							
Other:											

TYPES OF BUSINESS:

Lawn Care Services
Landscaping Services
Termite & Pest Control
Home Warranty
Disaster Restoration & Cleaning
Furniture Repair
Home Inspection

BRANDS/DIVISIONS/AFFILIATES:

TrueGreen LawnCare
TrueGreen LandCare
Terminix
American Home Shield
AmeriSpec
Furniture Medic
ServiceMaster Clean
Merry Maids

CONTACTS: *Note: Officers with more than one job title may be intentionally listed here more than once.*

J. Patrick Spainhour, CEO
Steven J. Martin, CFO/Sr. VP
Jim Kunihiro, Sr. VP-Mktg.
Jed Norden, Sr. VP-Human Resources
Dan J. Marks, CIO
Greer McMullen, General Counsel/Sr. VP
Jim Kunihiro, Sr. VP-Corp. Strategy
Pete Tosches, VP-Corp. Comm.
Mark Peterson, Corp. Treas./Sr. VP
David Martin, Corp. Controller/Sr. VP
Laura Hendricks, Pres., Merry Maids
Rick Ascolese, Pres., TruGreen LandCare
Thomas G. Brackett, CEO/Pres., Terminix
George W. Tamke, Chmn.

Phone: 901-597-1400	**Fax:**
Toll-Free: 888-937-3783	
Address: 860 Ridge Lake Blvd., Memphis, TN 38120 US	

GROWTH PLANS/SPECIAL FEATURES:

The ServiceMaster Company provides various cleaning and maintenance services to residential and commercial customers through a network of approximately 5,500 company-owned or franchised locations. ServiceMaster is divided into nine principal segments: TruGreen; Terminix; TruGreen LandCare; American Home Shield (AHS); ServiceMaster Clean; Merry Maids; Furniture Medic; and AmeriSpec. TruGreen provides lawn care services including lawn care; tree and shrub care; nuisance pest control; and landscaping care. Terminix provides termite and pest control services in 45 U.S. states and 14 countries worldwide. TruGreen LandCare provides landscaping services through more than 100 locations throughout the U.S. Services include landscape maintenance; golf course management; design and installation; irrigation services; snow and ice management; tree care; sports turf management; and fertilization and weed control. AHS provides home warranty contracts for systems and appliances, administering contracts throughout the U.S. ServiceMaster Clean offers residential cleaning, commercial cleaning and disaster restoration services through 4,500 franchises around the world. Merry Maids offers house cleaning services worldwide through more than 600 global locations. Furniture Medic offers residential and commercial furniture repair and restoration services. Residential services include wood color matching, watermark removal, furniture structural repair and stabilization, refinishing and polishing and cabinet refacing. Commercial services offers wood and furniture repair and restoration services for commercial properties. This segment specializes in lobby and greeting areas repairs, conference rooms, executive suites and restaurants. There are approximately 300 franchised Furniture Medic locations in the U.S., Canada and Europe. Finally, AmeriSpec offers home inspection services through 288 franchised locations in the U.S. and Canada.

FINANCIALS: **Sales and profits are in thousands of dollars—add 000 to get the full amount. 2009 Note: Financial information for 2009 was not available for all companies at press time.**

2009 Sales: $3,240,079	2009 Profits: $13,495	**U.S. Stock Ticker: Private**
2008 Sales: $3,311,432	2008 Profits: $-126,399	**Int'l Ticker:** Int'l Exchange:
2007 Sales: $3,356,748	2007 Profits: $-42,419	Employees: 27,000
2006 Sales: $3,322,703	2006 Profits: $169,699	Fiscal Year Ends: 12/31
2005 Sales: $3,239,478	2005 Profits: $198,925	Parent Company: CLAYTON DUBILIER & RICE INC

SALARIES/BENEFITS:

Pension Plan:	ESOP Stock Plan:	Profit Sharing:	Top Exec. Salary: $	Bonus: $
Savings Plan:	Stock Purch. Plan:		Second Exec. Salary: $	Bonus: $

OTHER THOUGHTS:

Apparent Women Officers or Directors: 1
Hot Spot for Advancement for Women/Minorities:

LOCATIONS: ("Y" = Yes)

West:	Southwest:	Midwest:	Southeast:	Northeast:	International:
Y	Y	Y	Y	Y	Y

SHANGRI-LA ASIA LTD

www.shangri-la.com

Industry Group Code: 721110 **Ranks within this company's industry group:** Sales: 11 Profits: 5

Properties:		Financial Services:		Construction/Development:		Investments:		Specialty Services:		Brokerage:	
Apartments:		Mortgages:		Commercial Construction:		REIT:		Property Management:	Y	Commercial Sales:	
Malls/Shopping:		Title Insurance:		Residential Construction:				Online Services:		Residential Sales:	
Offices:		Property Insurance:		Land Development:				Software/IT:		Specialty:	
Hotels/Motels:	Y			Support Services:				Consulting:			
Industrial/Warehouses:				Design/Engineering:							
Other:	Y										

TYPES OF BUSINESS:

Hotels, Luxury
Property Management
Health Spas
Golf Courses

BRANDS/DIVISIONS/AFFILIATES:

Shangri-La
Rasa
Summer Palace
Shang Palace
Traders
Chi, The Spa at the Shangri-La
Shangri-La Hotel (Malaysia) Berhad
Shangri-La Hotel Public Company Limited

CONTACTS:

Note: Officers with more than one job title may be intentionally listed here more than once.

Rao Madhu, CEO/Managing Dir.
Greg Dogan, COO
S. S. Mohan Ram, Group Financial Controller
Kent Zhu, Group Dir.-Sales & Mktg.
June Ng, Group Dir.-Human Resources
Anand Rao, CIO
Harold Lee, Group Dir.-Eng.
Ching Leun Teo, Corp. Sec.
Vincent Leung, VP-Finance
Ben Lui, Group Dir.-Projects
Jean Michel Offe, Group Dir.-Food & Beverage
Brenden Inns, VP-Brand Comm.
Caroline Cheah, Group Dir.-Rooms
Edward Kuok Khoon Loong, Chmn.
Bernhard Haechler, VP/Gen. Mgr.-Shangri La Hotel Dubai

Phone: 852-2599-3000 **Fax:** 852-2599-3131
Toll-Free:
Address: 20F Tower 1, Enterprise Square 5, 38 Wang Chiu Rd., Hong Kong, China

GROWTH PLANS/SPECIAL FEATURES:

Shangri-La Asia, Ltd. is an investment holding company that owns and manages hotels and resorts, primarily under the Shangri-La, Rasa, Summer Palace, Shang Palace and Traders brands. Its portfolio consists of 65 luxury resorts and hotels located in Australia, China, Hong Kong, the Fiji Islands, India, Indonesia, Malaysia, the Republic of Maldives, Myanmar, Oman, the Philippines, Singapore, Taiwan, Thailand, the United Arab Emirates and Canada. Shangri-La owns and manages 47 hotels (consisting of roughly 24,000 rooms); manages 17 hotels owned by third parties (5,881 rooms); and owns one additional hotel managed by a third party. In addition, the firm's 18 Chi Spa locations, inspired by the Shangri-La legend and located at Shangri-La hotels in 11 countries, feature a variety of treatments and therapies derived from Chinese, Thai and other Asian traditions. Subsidiaries Shangri-La Hotel (Malaysia) Berhad and Shangri-La Hotel Public Company Limited are engaged in the operation of hotels, resorts, golf courses and related facilities in Malaysia and Thailand, respectively. Shangri-La Asia has whole or partial interests in approximately 20 projects currently in development, including new hotels in China, Singapore, Mongolia, Malaysia, India, Qatar, Turkey, the U.K., France, Austria, Canada and Russia. In February 2009, Shangri-La began offering free Internet to all hotel guests, with access available in guestrooms, function areas and on-site restaurants and lounges. In March 2009, the company opened two new hotels: the Shangri-La Hotel, Tokyo and Shangri-La's Boracay Resort and Spa, in the Philippines. Later in 2009, three additional new hotels were opened: Shangri-La Maldives, in the Republic of Maldives, and Shangri-La Wenzhou and Shangri-La Ningbo, both in China. In early 2010, the firm opened its new Shangri-La Guilin property in China.

FINANCIALS:

Sales and profits are in thousands of dollars—add 000 to get the full amount. 2009 Note: Financial information for 2009 was not available for all companies at press time.

2009 Sales: $1,230,000	2009 Profits: $255,500	**U.S. Stock Ticker: SHALF**
2008 Sales: $1,353,300	2008 Profits: $165,900	**Int'l Ticker: 0069** Int'l Exchange: Hong Kong-HKEX
2007 Sales: $1,219,200	2007 Profits: $340,900	Employees:
2006 Sales: $1,002,900	2006 Profits: $202,200	Fiscal Year Ends: 12/31
2005 Sales: $842,000	2005 Profits: $	Parent Company:

SALARIES/BENEFITS:

Pension Plan:	ESOP Stock Plan:	Profit Sharing:	Top Exec. Salary: $	Bonus: $
Savings Plan:	Stock Purch. Plan:		Second Exec. Salary: $	Bonus: $

OTHER THOUGHTS:

Apparent Women Officers or Directors: 6
Hot Spot for Advancement for Women/Minorities: Y

LOCATIONS: ("Y" = Yes)

West:	Southwest:	Midwest:	Southeast:	Northeast:	International:
Y				Y	Y

SHAW GROUP INC (THE)

www.shawgrp.com

Industry Group Code: 237 **Ranks within this company's industry group:** Sales: 14 Profits: 18

Properties:		Financial Services:		Construction/Development:		Investments:		Specialty Services:		Brokerage:	
Apartments:		Mortgages:		Commercial Construction:		REIT:		Property Management:		Commercial Sales:	
Malls/Shopping:		Title Insurance:		Residential Construction:				Online Services:		Residential Sales:	
Offices:		Property Insurance:		Land Development:				Software/IT:		Specialty:	
Hotels/Motels:				Support Services:				Consulting:			
Industrial/Warehouses:				Design/Engineering:	Y						
Other:											

TYPES OF BUSINESS:

Pipe Manufacturing
Construction & Engineering
Consulting Services
Environmental Services
Facilities Management
Power Plant Construction
Nuclear Power Plant Construction

BRANDS/DIVISIONS/AFFILIATES:

Westinghouse

CONTACTS:

Note: Officers with more than one job title may be intentionally listed here more than once.

James M. Bernhard, Jr., CEO
Gary P. Graphia, COO/Exec. VP
James M. Bernhard, Jr., Pres.
Brian K. Ferraioli, CFO/Exec. VP
Gentry Brann, Dir.-Mktg.
David L. Chapman, Sr., Pres., Fabrication & Mfg. Group
John Donofrio, General Counsel/Exec. VP/Corp. Sec.
Lee Elder, Sr. VP-Bus. Dev., Power Group
Gentry Brann, Dir.-Corp. Comm.
Michael J. Kershaw, Chief Acct. Officer/Sr. VP
Frederick W. Buckman, Pres., Power Group
Louis J. Pucher, Pres., Energy & Chemicals Group
George P. Bevan, Pres., Environmental & Infrastructure Group
Ron Barnes, Pres., Fossil, Renewables & Nuclear Div.
James M. Bernhard, Jr., Chmn.
Ronald W. Oakley, Managing Dir.-Europe

Phone: 225-932-2500	**Fax:** 225-987-3328
Toll-Free:	
Address: 4171 Essen Ln., Baton Rouge, LA 70809 US	

GROWTH PLANS/SPECIAL FEATURES:

The Shaw Group, Inc. is a construction and engineering contractor firm. It is involved in engineering; technology; construction; fabrication; and environmental and industrial services. The company operates in six segments: fossil, renewables & nuclear (FR&N); energy & chemicals (E&C); environmental & infrastructure (E&I); maintenance; fabrication & manufacturing (F&M); investment in Westinghouse; and corporate. The FR&N segment provides a range of project-related services, primarily to the global fossil and nuclear power generation industries. The E&C division's offerings include design, engineering, construction, procurement, technology and consulting services, primarily to the oil and gas, refinery, petrochemical and chemical industries. The E&I segment designs and executes remediation solutions involving contaminants in soil, air and water. It also provides project/facilities management for non-environmental construction, watershed restoration, emergency response services, program management and solutions to support and enhance domestic and global land, water and air transportation systems. The maintenance segment performs routine and outage/turnaround maintenance, engineering, construction, recovery and specialty services. The maintenance sector' services include fossil/nuclear maintenance and turbine generator repair. The F&M segment supplies fabricated piping systems. Shaw's Investment in Westinghouse division includes its 20% equity interest in Westinghouse, which offers advanced licensing, nuclear plant designs, engineering services, equipment, fuel and other products and services to the international nuclear electric power industry. The corporate segment includes the corporate management and expenses associated with managing the firm. The company's customer base includes multinational oil companies and industrial corporations; regulated utilities; independent and merchant power producers; government agencies; and other equipment manufacturers. In March 2009, Shaw opened a new office in United Arab Emirates.

FINANCIALS:

Sales and profits are in thousands of dollars—add 000 to get the full amount. 2009 Note: Financial information for 2009 was not available for all companies at press time.

2009 Sales: $7,279,690	2009 Profits: $14,995	**U.S. Stock Ticker: SGR**
2008 Sales: $6,998,011	2008 Profits: $140,717	**Int'l Ticker:** Int'l Exchange:
2007 Sales: $5,723,712	2007 Profits: $-19,000	Employees: 28,000
2006 Sales: $4,775,649	2006 Profits: $50,226	Fiscal Year Ends: 8/31
2005 Sales: $3,267,702	2005 Profits: $15,671	Parent Company:

SALARIES/BENEFITS:

Pension Plan:	ESOP Stock Plan:	Profit Sharing:	Top Exec. Salary: $1,767,617	Bonus: $2,376,000
Savings Plan: Y	Stock Purch. Plan:		Second Exec. Salary: $759,449	Bonus: $996,050

OTHER THOUGHTS:

Apparent Women Officers or Directors:
Hot Spot for Advancement for Women/Minorities:

LOCATIONS: ("Y" = Yes)

West:	Southwest:	Midwest:	Southeast:	Northeast:	International:
Y	Y	Y	Y	Y	Y

SHIMAO PROPERTY HOLDINGS LTD

www.shimaoproperty.com/en

Industry Group Code: 5311 **Ranks within this company's industry group:** Sales: 16 Profits: 12

Properties:		Financial Services:		Construction/Development:		Investments:		Specialty Services:		Brokerage:	
Apartments:	Y	Mortgages:		Commercial Construction:		REIT:		Property Management:		Commercial Sales:	
Malls/Shopping:	Y	Title Insurance:		Residential Construction:				Online Services:		Residential Sales:	
Offices:	Y	Property Insurance:		Land Development:	Y			Software/IT:		Specialty:	
Hotels/Motels:	Y			Support Services:				Consulting:			
Industrial/Warehouses:				Design/Engineering:							
Other:	Y										

TYPES OF BUSINESS:

Real Estate Holdings & Development

BRANDS/DIVISIONS/AFFILIATES:

Shimao Group
Shanghai Shimao Riviera Garden
Shanghai Shimao International Plaza
Shanghai Le Meridien Sheshan hotel
Wuhan Shimao Splendid River
Shanghai Shimao Real Estate Co., Ltd
Shanghai Shimao International Plaza Co., Ltd
Shimao Manor Real Estate Co., Ltd

CONTACTS:

Note: Officers with more than one job title may be intentionally listed here more than once.

Wai Man Hui, CFO
Sai Tan Hui, Exec. Dir.-Mktg. & Sales.
Sai Tan Hui, Exec. Dir./Vice Chmn.
Chi Shing Tung, Exec. Dir.
Wing Mau Hui, Chmn.

Phone: 852-2511-9968	**Fax:** 852-2511-0278
Toll-Free:	
Address: 1 Harbour Rd., Units 4307-12, 43rd Fl., Hong Kong, China	

GROWTH PLANS/SPECIAL FEATURES:

Shimao Property Holdings Limited, along with its subsidiaries, is engaged in investment holding and develops residential, hotel, office and commercial properties in large cities in China. The company currently has over 30 projects under development in over 20 cities. The firm utilizes its Riviera Model, which combines landscape, waterside, gardening and architectural design. Some of its properties include Shanghai Shimao Riviera Garden; Shanghai Shimao International Plaza; the Shanghai Le Meridien Sheshan hotel; Beijing Shimao Olive Garden; Fuzhou Shimao Bund Garden; Wuhan Shimao Splendid River; Nanjing Shimao Rivera New City; The Genesis; and Shanghai Hyatt On The Bund. Subsidiaries of the company that are involved in property development include Shanghai Shimao Real Estate Co., Ltd.; Shanghai Shimao International Plaza Co., Ltd.; and Shanghai Shimao Manor Real Estate Co., Ltd. Subsidiary Shanghai Shimao Jianse Co., Ltd, is focused on investment holding operations. In October 2009, Shimao Property and Shanghai Shimao Co., Ltd jointly acquired nearly 323,000 square feet of coastal property in Xiamen, Fujian, for roughly \$103.88 million. Also in October 2009, the firm acquired two properties in the province of Zhejiang totaling nearly 861,113 square feet for roughly \$52.74 million. In November 2009, the company acquired a 4.95 million square foot property in a residential area in Shenyang City for roughly \$103.88 million. In March 2010, Shimao Property opened a new urban complex in Shaanxi Province.

FINANCIALS:

Sales and profits are in thousands of dollars—add 000 to get the full amount. 2009 Note: Financial information for 2009 was not available for all companies at press time.

2009 Sales: \$2,490,950	2009 Profits: \$513,510	**U.S. Stock Ticker:**
2008 Sales: \$1,356,270	2008 Profits: \$598,280	**Int'l Ticker: 0813** Int'l Exchange: Hong Kong-HKE
2007 Sales: \$1,010,840	2007 Profits: \$333,190	Employees:
2006 Sales: \$365,600	2006 Profits: \$132,760	Fiscal Year Ends:
2005 Sales: \$	2005 Profits: \$	Parent Company:

SALARIES/BENEFITS:

Pension Plan:	ESOP Stock Plan:	Profit Sharing:	Top Exec. Salary: \$	Bonus: \$
Savings Plan:	Stock Purch. Plan:		Second Exec. Salary: \$	Bonus: \$

OTHER THOUGHTS:

Apparent Women Officers or Directors:
Hot Spot for Advancement for Women/Minorities:

LOCATIONS: ("Y" = Yes)

West:	Southwest:	Midwest:	Southeast:	Northeast:	International:
					Y

SHUN TAK HOLDINGS LIMITED

www.shuntakgroup.com

Industry Group Code: 721110 **Ranks within this company's industry group:** Sales: 19 Profits: 15

Properties:		Financial Services:		Construction/Development:		Investments:		Specialty Services:		Brokerage:	
Apartments:		Mortgages:		Commercial Construction:	Y	REIT:		Property Management:	Y	Commercial Sales:	
Malls/Shopping:		Title Insurance:		Residential Construction:	Y			Online Services:		Residential Sales:	
Offices:		Property Insurance:		Land Development:				Software/IT:		Specialty:	
Hotels/Motels:	Y			Support Services:				Consulting:			
Industrial/Warehouses:				Design/Engineering:							
Other:											

TYPES OF BUSINESS:

Investment Holding Company
High-Speed Ferry Services
Real Estate Investment
Hotel Management
Casino Management

BRANDS/DIVISIONS/AFFILIATES:

Far East Hydrofoil Co. Ltd.
Shun Tak-China Travel Ship Management Limited
TuboJET
Belcher's (The)
Sociedade de Turismo e Diversoes de Macau, S.A.
Shun Tak Business Centre
Shun Tak Hospitality Services Limited
Liberte

CONTACTS: *Note: Officers with more than one job title may be intentionally listed here more than once.*

Pansy Ho, Managing Dir.
Daisy Ho, CFO/Deputy Managing Dir.
Pansy Ho, Exec. Dir.-Strategic Dev.
Maisy Ho, Exec. Dir.-Planning & Oper., Property Mgmt. Div.
David Shum, Exec. Dir.
Michael Ng, Exec. Dir.
Ambrose So, Exec. Dir.
Stanley Ho, Chmn.

Phone: 852-2859-3111	**Fax:** 852-2857-7181
Toll-Free:	
Address: Penthouse, 39 Fl. West Tower, 200 Connaught Rd., Hong Kong, China	

GROWTH PLANS/SPECIAL FEATURES:

Shun Tak Holdings Limited is a publicly traded Hong Kong-based conglomerate with core businesses in the transportation, property, investments and hospitality sectors. The transportation segment is operated through the joint venture, Shun Tak-China Travel Ship Management Limited, which is known under the brand name, TurboJET. The company's shares ownership of TurboJET with China Travel International Investment Hong Kong Limited. The segment also includes subsidiary Far East Hydrofoil Co. Ltd., which offers 24-hour-a-day passenger ferry service between Hong Kong and Macau. The company operates bus services in Macau and the Guangdong province through joint venture, Shun Tak & CITS Coach (Macao) Limited. Shun Tak's property division develops and invests in property in Hong Kong and Macau. Its major interests in residential and commercial properties include Nova City, one of the largest luxury property developments in Macau; The Belcher's, a complex of six residential towers on a retail podium that covers 2.9 million square feet; Liberte, a complex of seven residential towers on a retail podium that covers 1.9 million square feet; and Shun Tak Business Centre, an office and retail property that covers 521,467 square feet. The group's investments segment has interests in the Sociedade de Turismo e Diversoes de Macau, S.A. (SDTM), which owns the Macau Tower Convention & Entertainment Centre. Shun Tak's hospitality segment, operated by Shun Tak Hospitality Services Limited, is engaged in hotel and casino management, with a 50% interest in Mandarin Oriental; a 34.9% interest in the Westin Resort Macau; and a 70% interest in the Hong Kong SkyCity Marriott Hotel. In December 2009, the firm announced the opening of One Central Macau, a mixed-use, waterfront development featuring luxury apartment, hotel and retail facilities, developed jointly with HongKong Land Limited.

FINANCIALS: **Sales and profits are in thousands of dollars—add 000 to get the full amount. 2009 Note: Financial information for 2009 was not available for all companies at press time.**

2009 Sales: $429,370	2009 Profits: $370,060	**U.S. Stock Ticker:**
2008 Sales: $561,240	2008 Profits: $14,860	**Int'l Ticker: 0242** Int'l Exchange: Hong Kong-HKEX
2007 Sales: $431,400	2007 Profits: $131,800	Employees: 2,880
2006 Sales: $360,400	2006 Profits: $86,300	Fiscal Year Ends: 12/31
2005 Sales: $343,400	2005 Profits: $47,400	Parent Company:

SALARIES/BENEFITS:

Pension Plan:	ESOP Stock Plan:	Profit Sharing:	Top Exec. Salary: $	Bonus: $
Savings Plan:	Stock Purch. Plan:		Second Exec. Salary: $	Bonus: $

OTHER THOUGHTS:

Apparent Women Officers or Directors: 4
Hot Spot for Advancement for Women/Minorities: Y

LOCATIONS: ("Y" = Yes)

West:	Southwest:	Midwest:	Southeast:	Northeast:	International:
					Y

SIEMENS BUILDING TECHNOLOGIES

www.buildingtechnologies.siemens.com

Industry Group Code: 541310 **Ranks within this company's industry group:** Sales: Profits:

Properties:		Financial Services:		Construction/Development:		Investments:		Specialty Services:		Brokerage:	
Apartments:		Mortgages:		Commercial Construction:		REIT:		Property Management:		Commercial Sales:	
Malls/Shopping:		Title Insurance:		Residential Construction:				Online Services:		Residential Sales:	
Offices:		Property Insurance:		Land Development:				Software/IT:		Specialty:	
Hotels/Motels:				Support Services:	Y			Consulting:			
Industrial/Warehouses:				Design/Engineering:							
Other:											

TYPES OF BUSINESS:

Residential & Commercial HVAC Systems

BRANDS/DIVISIONS/AFFILIATES:

Siemens AG

CONTACTS:

Note: Officers with more than one job title may be intentionally listed here more than once.

Johannes Milde, CEO
Heribert Stumpf, CFO
Matthias Rebellius, Head-Fire Safety & Security Prod.
Frank Pedersen, Head-Security Solutions
Andreas Schierenbeck, Head-Building Automation
Stephan Bauer, Head-Control Prod. & Systems
Paulo Ricardo Stark, Head-Low Voltage Dist.

Phone: 41-41-724-2424	**Fax:** 41-41-724-35-22
Toll-Free:	
Address: Gubelstrasse 22, Zug, CH-6301 Switzerland	

GROWTH PLANS/SPECIAL FEATURES:

Siemens Building Technologies (SBT) provides products, services and solutions for public, industrial, commercial and residential buildings. Based in Switzerland, SBT is a division of Siemens AG's Industry Sector segment, along with five other divisions: OSRAM, Drive Technologies, Industry Automation, Industry Solutions and Mobility. The division's building specialties include services related to comfort, automation, safety, security and operations. SBT also offers energy solutions aimed at improving buildings' energy costs, reliability and performance while minimizing their impact on the environment. The division operates through five business units: security solutions; building automation; control products and systems; fire safety and security products; and low voltage distribution. Its security solutions unit offers intruder detection, video surveillance and building access control products. The building automation unit offers computerized, distributed control systems that monitor and control a building's mechanical and lighting systems. SBT's control products and systems unit offers includes heating and ventilation controls. The fire safety and security products unit offers fire detectors, protection alarm systems and non-water based fire extinguishers. The low voltage distribution unit, which until recently was part of the Industry Automation division, offers electrical installation equipment for buildings, including low-voltage switchgear, sockets and circuit breakers. SBT operates through approximately 110 branches across the U.S., and maintains operations in 46 other countries on five continents.

FINANCIALS:

Sales and profits are in thousands of dollars—add 000 to get the full amount. 2009 Note: Financial information for 2009 was not available for all companies at press time.

2009 Sales: $	2009 Profits: $	**U.S. Stock Ticker: Subsidiary**
2008 Sales: $	2008 Profits: $	**Int'l Ticker:** Int'l Exchange:
2007 Sales: $	2007 Profits: $	Employees:
2006 Sales: $	2006 Profits: $	Fiscal Year Ends: 9/30
2005 Sales: $	2005 Profits: $	Parent Company: SIEMENS AG

SALARIES/BENEFITS:

Pension Plan:	ESOP Stock Plan:	Profit Sharing:	Top Exec. Salary: $	Bonus: $
Savings Plan:	Stock Purch. Plan:		Second Exec. Salary: $	Bonus: $

OTHER THOUGHTS:

Apparent Women Officers or Directors:
Hot Spot for Advancement for Women/Minorities:

LOCATIONS: ("Y" = Yes)

West:	Southwest:	Midwest:	Southeast:	Northeast:	International:
Y	Y	Y	Y	Y	Y

SIMON PROPERTY GROUP INC

www.simon.com

Industry Group Code: 531120 **Ranks within this company's industry group:** Sales: 3 Profits: 5

Properties:		Financial Services:		Construction/Development:		Investments:		Specialty Services:		Brokerage:	
Apartments:		Mortgages:		Commercial Construction:	Y	REIT:	Y	Property Management:	Y	Commercial Sales:	
Malls/Shopping:	Y	Title Insurance:		Residential Construction:				Online Services:		Residential Sales:	
Offices:	Y	Property Insurance:		Land Development:				Software/IT:		Specialty:	
Hotels/Motels:				Support Services:				Consulting:	Y		
Industrial/Warehouses:				Design/Engineering:							
Other:											

TYPES OF BUSINESS:

Real Estate Investment Trust
Malls, Shopping & Outlet Centers
Office & Mixed-Use Properties
Real Estate Development
Real Estate Consulting
Marketing Services
Property Management

BRANDS/DIVISIONS/AFFILIATES:

Simon Property Group, L.P.
Chelsea Japan Co., Ltd
Chelsea Premium Outlets
Premium Outlets de Mexico
Shinsegae Chelsea Co., Ltd

CONTACTS: *Note: Officers with more than one job title may be intentionally listed here more than once.*

David Simon, CEO
Richard S. Sokolov, COO
Richard S. Sokolov, Pres.
Stephen E. Sterrett, CFO/Exec. VP
James M. Barkley, General Counsel/Corp. Sec.
Michael E. McCarty, Exec. VP-Dev. Oper.
Steve Broadwater, Chief Acct. Officer/Sr. VP
Gregg M. Goodman, Pres., The Mills
John R. Klein, Pres., Premium Outlet Centers
John Rulli, Exec. VP/Pres., Simon Mgmt. Group
Andrew Juster, Exec.. VP/Treas.
David Simon, Chmn.
Hans C. Mautner, Pres., Int'l Division, Simon Global Limited

Phone: 317-636-1600	**Fax:** 317-685-7222
Toll-Free:	
Address: 225 W. Washington St., Indianapolis, IN 46204 US	

GROWTH PLANS/SPECIAL FEATURES:

Simon Property Group, Inc. (SPG) is a self-managed real estate investment trust (REIT). It is engaged in owning, managing and developing retail real estate, primarily regional malls, outlet centers and community/lifestyle centers. The company owns all of its real estate properties through Simon Property Group, L.P., a majority-owned subsidiary. The company owns or holds an interest in 321 properties in 41 states. SPG maintains interests in 51 shopping centers in Europe and one in China. The firm's Chelsea Premium Outlets brand, operated through three joint ventures, maintains eight outlet locations in Japan (Chelsea Japan Co., Ltd.); one in Korea (Shinsegae Chelsea Co., Ltd.); and one in Mexico (Premium Outlets de Mexico). SPG's strategy includes aggressively marketing available space and renewing existing leases at higher rents, pursuing acquisitions, developing new properties in major metropolitan areas and expanding and renovating existing properties. Through Simon Brand Ventures, the company develops national, regional and local marketing and media plans for clients. In Aril 2009, the company opened a new outlet location in Camarillo, California. In July 2009, Chelsea Japan Co., Ltd. opened a new outlet in Japan. In December 2009, SPG agreed to acquire Prime Outlets Acquisition Company for roughly $2.325 billion. In February 2010, the firm agreed to sell all of the interests in Simon Ivanhoe S.a.r.l, which owns seven shopping centers located in France and Poland.

Simon offers its employees benefits including sick pay, supplemental voluntary programs, flexible spending accounts, educational assistance and a 401(k) plan.

FINANCIALS: **Sales and profits are in thousands of dollars—add 000 to get the full amount. 2009 Note: Financial information for 2009 was not available for all companies at press time.**

2009 Sales: $3,775,216	2009 Profits: $	**U.S. Stock Ticker: SPG**
2008 Sales: $3,783,155	2008 Profits: $463,636	**Int'l Ticker:** Int'l Exchange:
2007 Sales: $3,650,799	2007 Profits: $491,239	Employees: 5,300
2006 Sales: $3,332,154	2006 Profits: $563,840	Fiscal Year Ends: 12/31
2005 Sales: $3,166,853	2005 Profits: $475,749	Parent Company:

SALARIES/BENEFITS:

Pension Plan:	ESOP Stock Plan:	Profit Sharing:	Top Exec. Salary: $1,038,462	Bonus: $3,000,000
Savings Plan: Y	Stock Purch. Plan:		Second Exec. Salary: $812,077	Bonus: $1,000,000

OTHER THOUGHTS:

Apparent Women Officers or Directors: 3
Hot Spot for Advancement for Women/Minorities: Y

LOCATIONS: ("Y" = Yes)

West:	Southwest:	Midwest:	Southeast:	Northeast:	International:
Y	Y	Y	Y	Y	Y

SINO LAND COMPANY LIMITED

www.sino.com

Industry Group Code: 5311 **Ranks within this company's industry group:** Sales: 22 Profits: 7

Properties:		Financial Services:		Construction/Development:		Investments:		Specialty Services:		Brokerage:	
Apartments:	Y	Mortgages:		Commercial Construction:	Y	REIT:		Property Management:	Y	Commercial Sales:	
Malls/Shopping:	Y	Title Insurance:		Residential Construction:	Y			Online Services:		Residential Sales:	Y
Offices:	Y	Property Insurance:		Land Development:	Y			Software/IT:		Specialty:	
Hotels/Motels:	Y			Support Services:	Y			Consulting:			
Industrial/Warehouses:	Y			Design/Engineering:	Y						
Other:	Y										

TYPES OF BUSINESS:

Real Estate Holdings & Development
Commercial & Residential Construction
Property Management Services

BRANDS/DIVISIONS/AFFILIATES:

Sino Hotels (Holdings) Limited
Sino Estates Management Limited
Sino Parking Services Limited
Sino Security Services Limited
Best Results Cleaning Services Limited

CONTACTS:

Note: Officers with more than one job title may be intentionally listed here more than once.

Thomas Tang Wing Yung, CFO
Ringo Chan Wing Kwong, Exec. VP-Treasury
Sunny Yeung Kwong, Exec. Dir.-Sino Property Svcs.
Yu Wai Wai, Exec. Dir.-Dev. Div.
Daryl Ng Win Kong, Exec. Dir.
Robert Ng Chee Siong, Chmn.

Phone: 852-2721-8388 **Fax:** 852-2723-5901
Toll-Free:
Address: 11th-12th Fl., Tsim Sha Tsui Centre, Salisbury Rd., Hong Kong, China

GROWTH PLANS/SPECIAL FEATURES:

Sino Land Company Limited is a Hong Kong-based real estate firm whose core business involves the development of property for both sale and investment purposes. The company holds a property portfolio totaling approximately 43.2 million square feet, consisting of five primary property types: residential, accounting for 66.1% of the firm's portfolio; commercial, accounting for 23.1%; industrial, accounting for 4.9%; car parks, accounting for 3.4%; and hotels, also accounting for 2.5% of the portfolio. Commercial and industrial properties, as well as hotels and car parks, are typically held by the firm as long-term investments to generate recurrent income, while Sino Land generally acquires residential properties with the intention of developing them for resale. The firm aims to acquire residential properties in popular urban areas, with convenient access to various forms of transportation, such as subways and rail lines. Of the company's total holdings, approximately 30.7 million square feet consist of properties currently under development; approximately 10.9 million square feet represent properties held either as investments or for the firm's own use; and approximately 1.6 million square feet are completed properties held for sale. Subsidiary Sino Hotels (Holdings) Limited operates four upscale hotels in Hong Kong, as well as a yacht and country club; and manages a hotel in Singapore. In addition to its real estate investment operations, the company is also involved in building construction; property management, offered through subsidiary Sino Estates Management Limited; car park operations and management, offered through subsidiary Sino Parking Services Limited; security services, provided by Sino Security Services Limited; cleaning services, provided by subsidiary Best Results Cleaning Services Limited; and real estate agency services.

FINANCIALS:

Sales and profits are in thousands of dollars—add 000 to get the full amount. 2009 Note: Financial information for 2009 was not available for all companies at press time.

2009 Sales: $1,248,460	2009 Profits: $480,520	**U.S. Stock Ticker:**
2008 Sales: $812,600	2008 Profits: $1,003,700	**Int'l Ticker: 0083** Int'l Exchange: Hong Kong-HKE
2007 Sales: $979,200	2007 Profits: $814,700	Employees:
2006 Sales: $1,082,700	2006 Profits: $782,300	Fiscal Year Ends: 6/30
2005 Sales: $	2005 Profits: $	Parent Company:

SALARIES/BENEFITS:

Pension Plan:	ESOP Stock Plan:	Profit Sharing:	Top Exec. Salary: $	Bonus: $
Savings Plan:	Stock Purch. Plan:		Second Exec. Salary: $	Bonus: $

OTHER THOUGHTS:

Apparent Women Officers or Directors:
Hot Spot for Advancement for Women/Minorities:

LOCATIONS: ("Y" = Yes)

West:	Southwest:	Midwest:	Southeast:	Northeast:	International:
					Y

SKIDMORE OWINGS & MERRILL LLP

www.som.com

Industry Group Code: 541330 **Ranks within this company's industry group:** Sales: Profits:

Properties:		Financial Services:		Construction/Development:		Investments:		Specialty Services:		Brokerage:	
Apartments:		Mortgages:		Commercial Construction:		REIT:		Property Management:		Commercial Sales:	
Malls/Shopping:		Title Insurance:		Residential Construction:				Online Services:		Residential Sales:	
Offices:		Property Insurance:		Land Development:				Software/IT:		Specialty:	
Hotels/Motels:				Support Services:				Consulting:	Y		
Industrial/Warehouses:				Design/Engineering:	Y						
Other:											

TYPES OF BUSINESS:

Architectural & Engineering Services
Urban Design Services
Transportation Planning
Seismic Analysis & Consulting
Environmental Engineering

BRANDS/DIVISIONS/AFFILIATES:

Mechanical and Electrical Engineering Group
MEP Engineering
SOM Interiors

CONTACTS:

Note: Officers with more than one job title may be intentionally listed here more than once.

Jeffrey J. McCarthy, Managing Partner-Chicago
Carl Galioto, Partner-Tech.
Gene Schnair, Managing Partner-West Coast
Gary P. Haney, Design Partner
William F. Baker, Partner-Civil & Structural Eng.

Phone: 312-554-9090	**Fax:** 312-360-4545
Toll-Free: 866-269-2688	
Address: 224 S. Michigan Ave., Ste. 1000, Chicago, IL 60604 US	

GROWTH PLANS/SPECIAL FEATURES:

Skidmore, Owings & Merrill, LLP (SOM) is one of the world's leading architecture, urban design, engineering and interior architecture firms. Its services span architectural design and engineering of individual buildings to the master planning and design of entire communities. The firm's projects include corporate offices, banking and financial institutions, government buildings, public and private institutions, health care facilities, religious buildings, airports, recreational and sports facilities, university buildings and residential developments. SOM's graphics group provides branding, corporate identity and graphic design services, with expansive projects for clients including the Bay Area Discovery Museum and Dublin Airport. The SOM Interiors group provides interior design solutions for corporate facilities, educational facilities, retail spaces, performing arts spaces, hotels and residential complexes among others. SOM's Mechanical and Electrical Engineering Group (MEP Engineering) provides design engineering services for new and existing buildings, such as developing solar heating and cooling for new and existing buildings; modeling energy consumption patterns; forecasting probable operating costs; and developing energy recovery systems. Additionally, the firm offers structural and civil engineering services; sustainable design services; and urban design and planning services. Signature projects include 7 World Trade Center, the Willis Tower (formerly known as the Sears Tower) and the John Hancock Tower. One of the firm's latest projects is 73-story residential Infinity Tower in Dubai, which features a twisting helix shape that gradually rotates 90 degrees while maintaining a consistent structural and architectural floor plate throughout its height.

FINANCIALS:

Sales and profits are in thousands of dollars—add 000 to get the full amount. 2009 Note: Financial information for 2009 was not available for all companies at press time.

2009 Sales: $	2009 Profits: $	**U.S. Stock Ticker: Private**
2008 Sales: $	2008 Profits: $	**Int'l Ticker:** Int'l Exchange:
2007 Sales: $228,000	2007 Profits: $	Employees:
2006 Sales: $228,000	2006 Profits: $	Fiscal Year Ends: 9/30
2005 Sales: $225,000	2005 Profits: $	Parent Company:

SALARIES/BENEFITS:

Pension Plan:	ESOP Stock Plan:	Profit Sharing:	Top Exec. Salary: $	Bonus: $
Savings Plan:	Stock Purch. Plan:		Second Exec. Salary: $	Bonus: $

OTHER THOUGHTS:

Apparent Women Officers or Directors: 2
Hot Spot for Advancement for Women/Minorities:

LOCATIONS: ("Y" = Yes)

West:	Southwest:	Midwest:	Southeast:	Northeast:	International:
Y		Y		Y	Y

SKYLINE CORPORATION

www.skylinecorp.com

Industry Group Code: 332311 **Ranks within this company's industry group:** Sales: 2 Profits: 2

Properties:		Financial Services:		Construction/Development:		Investments:		Specialty Services:		Brokerage:	
Apartments:		Mortgages:		Commercial Construction:		REIT:		Property Management:		Commercial Sales:	
Malls/Shopping:		Title Insurance:		Residential Construction:	Y			Online Services:		Residential Sales:	
Offices:		Property Insurance:		Land Development:				Software/IT:		Specialty:	
Hotels/Motels:				Support Services:	Y			Consulting:			
Industrial/Warehouses:				Design/Engineering:	Y						
Other:											

TYPES OF BUSINESS:

Manufactured Housing
Recreational Vehicles
Prefabricated Metal Buildings & Components

BRANDS/DIVISIONS/AFFILIATES:

Nomad
Shyline Homes
Aljo
Weekender
Hillcrest Homes
Rampage
Trailrider
Wagoneer

CONTACTS:

Note: Officers with more than one job title may be intentionally listed here more than once.

Thomas G. Deranek, CEO
Jon S. Pilarski, CFO
Terrence M. Decio, VP-Mktg. & Sales
Charles W. Chambliss, VP-Prod. Dev.
Charles W. Chambliss, VP-Eng.
Martin R. Fransted, Sec.
Christopher R. Leader, VP-Oper.
Jon S. Pilarski, VP-Finance/Treas.
Bruce G. Page, VP-Oper.
Martin R. Fransted, Corp. Controller
Thomas G. Deranek, Chmn.

Phone: 574-294-6521	**Fax:** 574-293-7574
Toll-Free: 800-348-7469	
Address: 2520 By-Pass Rd., P.O. Box 743, Elkhart, IN 46515 US	

GROWTH PLANS/SPECIAL FEATURES:

Skyline Corporation, along with its consolidated subsidiaries, designs, produces and distributes manufactured housing, including single-section, multi-section and modular homes and towable RVs, including travel trailers, fifth wheels and park models. The firm sold 2,712 manufactured homes in 2009. The company also sold 2,832 recreational vehicles in 2009, which are sold under a number of trademarks for travel trailers, fifth wheels and park models. Skyline has 14 manufacturing facilities in 10 states; of which 11 produce housing and 3 produce RVs. The firm's manufactured homes are distributed by approximately 240 independent dealers at 400 locations throughout the U.S., and its RVs are distributed by approximately 130 independent dealers at 150 locations throughout the U.S. The company sells a variety of RVs: Aljo; Aljo Ultra-Lite; Layton; Layton Ultra-Lite; Mountain View; Nomad; Nomad Ultra-Lite; Texan; Wagoneer; Weekender; Freestyle; Trail Rider; and Rampage. The RV market is made up primarily of vacationing middle-income families, retired couples traveling around the country and sports enthusiasts pursuing four-season hobbies. Housing options include Skyline Homes, Hillcrest Homes and Skyline Park Models. Skyline Homes and Hillcrest Homes by Skyline can range from a one bedroom, 400 square foot home to a 5 bedroom, 2,700 square foot multi-sectional modular home, nearly indistinguishable from conventionally built homes, which can be assembled on commercial lots. The Skyline Park Models are meant for temporary use and are commonly used in resort or vacation locations.

FINANCIALS:

Sales and profits are in thousands of dollars—add 000 to get the full amount. 2009 Note: Financial information for 2009 was not available for all companies at press time.

2009 Sales: $166,676	2009 Profits: $-15,434	**U.S. Stock Ticker: SKY**
2008 Sales: $301,765	2008 Profits: $-5,556	**Int'l Ticker:** Int'l Exchange:
2007 Sales: $365,473	2007 Profits: $2,593	Employees: 1,300
2006 Sales: $508,543	2006 Profits: $14,292	Fiscal Year Ends: 5/31
2005 Sales: $454,324	2005 Profits: $5,452	Parent Company:

SALARIES/BENEFITS:

Pension Plan:	ESOP Stock Plan:	Profit Sharing:	Top Exec. Salary: $300,000	Bonus: $
Savings Plan:	Stock Purch. Plan:		Second Exec. Salary: $290,000	Bonus: $

OTHER THOUGHTS:

Apparent Women Officers or Directors:
Hot Spot for Advancement for Women/Minorities:

LOCATIONS: ("Y" = Yes)

West:	Southwest:	Midwest:	Southeast:	Northeast:	International:
Y	Y	Y	Y	Y	

SL GREEN REALTY CORP

www.slgreen.com

Industry Group Code: 531120 **Ranks within this company's industry group:** Sales: 18 Profits: 8

Properties:		Financial Services:		Construction/Development:		Investments:		Specialty Services:		Brokerage:	
Apartments:	Y	Mortgages:		Commercial Construction:	Y	REIT:	Y	Property Management:	Y	Commercial Sales:	
Malls/Shopping:	Y	Title Insurance:		Residential Construction:				Online Services:		Residential Sales:	
Offices:	Y	Property Insurance:		Land Development:				Software/IT:		Specialty:	
Hotels/Motels:				Support Services:				Consulting:			
Industrial/Warehouses:				Design/Engineering:							
Other:											

TYPES OF BUSINESS:

Real Estate Investment Trust
Commercial Properties
Property Management

BRANDS/DIVISIONS/AFFILIATES:

CONTACTS:

Note: Officers with more than one job title may be intentionally listed here more than once.

Marc Holliday, CEO
Gregory F. Hughes, COO
Andrew W. Mathias, Pres.
Gregory F. Hughes, CFO
Andrew S. Levine, Chief Legal Officer
Andrew W. Mathias, Chief Investment Officer
Steven M. Durels, Exec. VP/Dir.-Leasing
Edward V. Piccinich, Exec. VP-Property Mgmt. & Construction
Neil H. Kessner, Exec. VP-Legal Counsel
Stephen L. Green, Chmn.

Phone: 212-594-2700	**Fax:** 212-216-1785
Toll-Free:	
Address: 420 Lexington Ave., New York, NY 10170 US	

GROWTH PLANS/SPECIAL FEATURES:

SL Green Realty Corp. is a self-managed REIT (Real Estate Investment Trust). The firm specializes in property management, acquisitions, financing, development, construction and leasing. The company's portfolio consists of 29 properties in Manhattan, totaling 23.2 million square feet; and 31 properties in the New York Metro area, including Long Island, Brooklyn, Queens, Westchester County, Connecticut and New Jersey, totaling 6.8 million square feet. SL Green's interests in these properties consist of fee ownership of 52 properties, including condominium units; leasehold ownership in six properties; and operating sublease ownership in two properties. Under operating sublease agreements, SL Green is responsible for collecting rent from subtenants and payment of all expenses relating to the property. In addition to commercial properties, SL Green also holds interests in eight retail properties with approximately 374,812 square feet; three development properties with 399,800 square feet; and two land interests. The company also manages three office properties owned by third-parties and affiliated companies with 1 million square feet. In April 2009, the firm completed a $40 million redevelopment construction project on three of its properties.

FINANCIALS:

Sales and profits are in thousands of dollars—add 000 to get the full amount. 2009 Note: Financial information for 2009 was not available for all companies at press time.

2009 Sales: $1,010,659	2009 Profits: $37,669	**U.S. Stock Ticker: SLG**
2008 Sales: $1,079,422	2008 Profits: $360,935	**Int'l Ticker:** Int'l Exchange:
2007 Sales: $974,830	2007 Profits: $626,355	Employees: 961
2006 Sales: $469,854	2006 Profits: $220,719	Fiscal Year Ends: 12/31
2005 Sales: $368,684	2005 Profits: $157,419	Parent Company:

SALARIES/BENEFITS:

Pension Plan:	ESOP Stock Plan:	Profit Sharing:	Top Exec. Salary: $824,446	Bonus: $4,750,000
Savings Plan: Y	Stock Purch. Plan:		Second Exec. Salary: $600,000	Bonus: $2,659,000

OTHER THOUGHTS:

Apparent Women Officers or Directors:
Hot Spot for Advancement for Women/Minorities:

LOCATIONS: ("Y" = Yes)

West:	Southwest:	Midwest:	Southeast:	Northeast:	International:
				Y	

SOCIETE DES BAINS DE MER ET DU CERCLE en.montecarloresort.com

Industry Group Code: 721120 **Ranks within this company's industry group:** Sales: Profits:

Properties:		Financial Services:		Construction/Development:		Investments:		Specialty Services:		Brokerage:	
Apartments:		Mortgages:		Commercial Construction:	Y	REIT:		Property Management:	Y	Commercial Sales:	
Malls/Shopping:	Y	Title Insurance:		Residential Construction:				Online Services:		Residential Sales:	
Offices:		Property Insurance:		Land Development:	Y			Software/IT:		Specialty:	
Hotels/Motels:	Y			Support Services:				Consulting:			
Industrial/Warehouses:				Design/Engineering:							
Other:	Y										

TYPES OF BUSINESS:

Hotels
Casinos
Restaurants
Resorts

BRANDS/DIVISIONS/AFFILIATES:

Monte-Carlo SBM
Hotel Hermitage
Hotel de Paris
Monte-Carlo Beach Hotel
Monte-Carlo Bay Hotel & Resort
Les Thermes Marins de Monte-Carlo
Casinos de Monte Carlo
Le Louis XV-Alain Ducasse

CONTACTS: *Note: Officers with more than one job title may be intentionally listed here more than once.*

Bernard Lambert, Managing Dir.
Jean-Luc Biamonti, Chmn.

Phone: 377-98-06-20-00	**Fax:** 377-98-06-58-00
Toll-Free:	
Address: Place du Casino, Monaco, 98000 Monaco	

GROWTH PLANS/SPECIAL FEATURES:

Societe Anonyme des Bains de Mer et du Cercle des Etrangers a Monaco (SBM) is a hotel and resort company that manages luxury properties in the Principality of Monaco, located next to France on the Mediterranean coast. It generally refers to all its properties as a single resort: Monte-Carlo SBM. The firm owns and manages four hotels: Hotel Hermitage, with 280 rooms and suites; Hotel de Paris, 182 rooms and suites; Monte-Carlo Beach Hotel, 40 rooms; and Monte-Carlo Bay Hotel & Resort, 334 rooms. Each hotel features luxury accommodations. The Hotel Hermitage and Hotel de Paris directly link to the firm's Les Thermes Marins de Monte-Carlo, one of the most prestigious spas in Europe; the Beach Hotel features an Olympic-sized seawater swimming pool; and the newer, high-tech Bay Hotel & Resort, located on 10 acres of land, features a sand-bottomed lagoon and the Cinq Mondes spa. SBM's five casinos include the legendary Casino de Monte-Carlo, Cafe de Paris Casino, Sun Casino, Bay Casino and Summer Casino. The casinos, some of which require guests to follow a strict dress code, feature a wide variety of European and American table games, as well as slot machines. Monte-Carlo SBM also offers 33 bars and restaurants, including Le Louis XV-Alain Ducasse, the oldest restaurant in Monaco; 26 conference rooms; an 18-hole golf course; 23 tennis courts; retail outlets; cocktail rooms for up to 1,000 people; an opera company; a live performance arena with regular entertainment; and multiple night clubs. The firm also hosts the annual Grand Prix de Monaco, a Formula One auto race. SBM intertwines all its segments in order to create package deals for its guests. In December 2009, the company announced that Mangas Gaming, its 50% owned subsidiary, acquired 60% stake in Everest Gaming from GigaMedia.

FINANCIALS: **Sales and profits are in thousands of dollars—add 000 to get the full amount. 2009 Note: Financial information for 2009 was not available for all companies at press time.**

2009 Sales: $	2009 Profits: $	**U.S. Stock Ticker: Subsidiary**
2008 Sales: $	2008 Profits: $	**Int'l Ticker:** Int'l Exchange:
2007 Sales: $	2007 Profits: $	Employees:
2006 Sales: $	2006 Profits: $	Fiscal Year Ends: 3/31
2005 Sales: $	2005 Profits: $	Parent Company: MONTE CARLO RESORTS

SALARIES/BENEFITS:

Pension Plan:	ESOP Stock Plan:	Profit Sharing:	Top Exec. Salary: $	Bonus: $
Savings Plan:	Stock Purch. Plan:		Second Exec. Salary: $	Bonus: $

OTHER THOUGHTS:

Apparent Women Officers or Directors:
Hot Spot for Advancement for Women/Minorities:

LOCATIONS: ("Y" = Yes)

West:	Southwest:	Midwest:	Southeast:	Northeast:	International:
					Y

SOL MELIA SA

www.solmelia.com

Industry Group Code: 721110 **Ranks within this company's industry group:** Sales: 10 Profits: 9

Properties:		Financial Services:		Construction/Development:		Investments:		Specialty Services:		Brokerage:	
Apartments:		Mortgages:		Commercial Construction:	Y	REIT:		Property Management:	Y	Commercial Sales:	
Malls/Shopping:		Title Insurance:		Residential Construction:				Online Services:		Residential Sales:	
Offices:		Property Insurance:		Land Development:	Y			Software/IT:		Specialty:	
Hotels/Motels:	Y			Support Services:				Consulting:			
Industrial/Warehouses:				Design/Engineering:							
Other:											

TYPES OF BUSINESS:

Hotel & Resort Management
Real Estate Development

BRANDS/DIVISIONS/AFFILIATES:

Melia Hotels
TRYP Hotels
Sol Hotels
Paradisus Resorts
Hard Rock Hotels
ME
Gran Melia

CONTACTS:

Note: Officers with more than one job title may be intentionally listed here more than once.

Gabriel Juan Escarrer Jaume, Co-CEO
Luis Del Olmo Pinero, Exec. VP-Mktg.
Fernando De Cevallos Aguaron, Exec. VP-Human Resources
Jose Maria Lafuente Lopez, Sec.
Onofre Servera Andreu, Exec. VP-Finance
Sebastian Escarrer Jaume, Vice-Chmn./Exec. Dir.
Andre Gerandeau, Exec. VP-Hotels
Mark Maurice Hoddinott, Exec. VP-Hospitality Bus. Solutions Unit
Luis Miguel Martin Ortiz, Exec. VP-Real Estate
Gabriel Escarrer Julia, Chmn.

Phone: 34-97-122-4554	**Fax:** 34-97-122-44-98
Toll-Free: 888-956-3542	
Address: Gremio Toneleros 24, Palma de Mallorca, 07009 Spain	

GROWTH PLANS/SPECIAL FEATURES:

Sol Melia S.A. is a leading Spanish hotel chain in the city and resort markets, the third-largest hotel chain in Europe, and the twelfth-largest hotel chain in the world. It engages in the management and operation of hotels and resorts under management or franchise agreements. Sol Melia boasts more than 300 city and resort hotels in 30 countries on four continents. The company has locations throughout Europe, the Americas, the Mediterranean, the Middle East and Asia-Pacific. Its brand names include Melia Hotels, TRYP Hotels, Sol Hotels, Paradisus Resorts, Gran Melia, ME, Innside and Sol Melia Vacation Club. Melia hotels are usually in the four-to five-star range, offering luxury accommodations and amenities. The TRYP brand of hotels is designed to appeal to upscale business travelers by providing the latest in technology services and conference facilities within the setting of a scenic resort. The Sol brand is designed for family vacations, while Paradisus Resorts cater to destination-driven resort vacations. The ME brand of luxury hotels, located in select urban and resort destinations, integrates contemporary cuisine, design, and music. Innside is an upscale German hotel chain featuring modern, minimalist architecture and the latest in communications technology for business travelers. Gran Melia advertises a luxurious red carpet atmosphere and Sol Melia is a chain of membership resorts offering family villas and condominiums with the option to upgrade or exchange units. The firm, through its subsidiaries, is also engaged in real estate activities, primarily the development of new hotels. In recent years, the company has formed alliances with U.S.-based travel and tourism companies such as Cendant Corporation and lastminute.com to allow access to new markets. Sol Melia operates through 30 sales offices in 19 countries. During 2009, the company sold two of its Spanish hotels, Melia Madrid Princesa and Tryp Alondras.

FINANCIALS:

Sales and profits are in thousands of dollars—add 000 to get the full amount. 2009 Note: Financial information for 2009 was not available for all companies at press time.

2009 Sales: $1,532,400	2009 Profits: $50,830	**U.S. Stock Ticker:**
2008 Sales: $1,657,000	2008 Profits: $66,330	**Int'l Ticker: SOL** Int'l Exchange: Madrid-MCE
2007 Sales: $1,749,890	2007 Profits: $209,750	Employees:
2006 Sales: $1,847,800	2006 Profits: $200,300	Fiscal Year Ends: 12/31
2005 Sales: $1,713,000	2005 Profits: $132,400	Parent Company:

SALARIES/BENEFITS:

Pension Plan:	ESOP Stock Plan:	Profit Sharing:	Top Exec. Salary: $	Bonus: $
Savings Plan:	Stock Purch. Plan:		Second Exec. Salary: $	Bonus: $

OTHER THOUGHTS:

Apparent Women Officers or Directors: 1
Hot Spot for Advancement for Women/Minorities:

LOCATIONS: ("Y" = Yes)

West:	Southwest:	Midwest:	Southeast:	Northeast:	International:
					Y

SONESTA INTERNATIONAL HOTELS CORP

www.sonesta.com

Industry Group Code: 721110 **Ranks within this company's industry group:** Sales: 29 Profits: 19

Properties:		Financial Services:		Construction/Development:		Investments:		Specialty Services:		Brokerage:	
Apartments:		Mortgages:		Commercial Construction:		REIT:		Property Management:	Y	Commercial Sales:	
Malls/Shopping:		Title Insurance:		Residential Construction:				Online Services:		Residential Sales:	
Offices:		Property Insurance:		Land Development:				Software/IT:		Specialty:	
Hotels/Motels:	Y			Support Services:				Consulting:			
Industrial/Warehouses:				Design/Engineering:							
Other:											

TYPES OF BUSINESS:

Hotels
River Cruise Ships
Hotels
Resorts

BRANDS/DIVISIONS/AFFILIATES:

Sonesta Art Collection
Just Us Kids
Sonesta Mikado Hotel
Sonesta Sole
Sonesta Dahabeya

CONTACTS: *Note: Officers with more than one job title may be intentionally listed here more than once.*

Stephanie Sonnabend, CEO
Stephanie Sonnabend, Pres.
Carol Beggs, VP-Tech.
Philip M. Silberstein, Exec. VP-Dev.
Boy Van Riel, Treas./VP
Kathy Rowe, Sr. VP
Jacqueline Sonnabend, Exec. VP
Peter J. Sonnabend, Exec. Chmn.
Felix Madera, VP-Int'l

Phone: 617-421-5400	**Fax:** 617-421-5402
Toll-Free: 800-766-3378	
Address: 116 Huntington Ave., Boston, MA 02116 US	

GROWTH PLANS/SPECIAL FEATURES:

Sonesta International Hotels Corp., doing business as Sonesta Collection, specializes in providing upscale accommodation. There are currently 26 Sonesta hotels and resorts, including six Nile cruise ships. The properties are located in Boston, Miami, New Orleans, Orlando, St. Maarten, Brazil, Peru and Egypt. The company has also entered into management agreements to operate new hotels being created in Jaco, Costa Rica; Miami, Florida; and San Carlos, Mexico. In addition, the firm has franchise agreements for two hotels in St. Maarten, two in Brazil, three in Chile, one in Colombia and seven in Peru. Locations feature the Sonesta Art Collection. This group of art consists of more than 7,000 contemporary paintings, sculptures, original prints and tapestries by world-renowned artists, which are placed in public places and guestrooms inside its hotels. Some of the company's resorts also offer Just Us Kids, a complimentary supervised children's program for ages 5-13. Family packages, children's menus, baby-sitting and discounts on a second room add to the appeal for families. Sonesta's strategy is to consolidate assets and position the company for opportunities to expand with more hotels and resorts. The firm intends for its growth to be continuous, but at a pace that will preserve the character that distinguishes each Sonesta property. In December 2009, the firm announced the Sonesta Hotel Orlando Downtown, the first property in its new U.S. franchise program. The announcement is the result of a franchise agreement between Sonesta Franchise Corporation, a subsidiary of the company, and RSLLC Orlando Downtown Hotel, LLC. In January 2010, the company announced plans to add six new hotels by mid-2010, which will total an additional 1,011 rooms worldwide.

Employees are offered health and dental insurance; life insurance short-and long-term disability coverage; Sonesta Hotel discounts; educational assistance; and credit union membership.

FINANCIALS: **Sales and profits are in thousands of dollars—add 000 to get the full amount. 2009 Note: Financial information for 2009 was not available for all companies at press time.**

2009 Sales: $64,800	2009 Profits: $25,300	**U.S. Stock Ticker: SNSTA**
2008 Sales: $80,517	2008 Profits: $4,080	**Int'l Ticker:** Int'l Exchange:
2007 Sales: $86,685	2007 Profits: $1,337	Employees: 723
2006 Sales: $98,832	2006 Profits: $-3,523	Fiscal Year Ends: 12/31
2005 Sales: $102,668	2005 Profits: $4,668	Parent Company:

SALARIES/BENEFITS:

Pension Plan:	ESOP Stock Plan:	Profit Sharing:	Top Exec. Salary: $414,557	Bonus: $5,541
Savings Plan: Y	Stock Purch. Plan:		Second Exec. Salary: $400,000	Bonus: $

OTHER THOUGHTS:

Apparent Women Officers or Directors: 5
Hot Spot for Advancement for Women/Minorities: Y

LOCATIONS: ("Y" = Yes)

West:	Southwest:	Midwest:	Southeast:	Northeast:	International:
	Y		Y	Y	Y

SOUTHERN ENERGY HOMES INC

www.sehomes.com

Industry Group Code: 321991 **Ranks within this company's industry group:** Sales: Profits:

Properties:		Financial Services:		Construction/Development:		Investments:		Specialty Services:		Brokerage:	
Apartments:		Mortgages:	Y	Commercial Construction:		REIT:		Property Management:		Commercial Sales:	
Malls/Shopping:		Title Insurance:		Residential Construction:	Y			Online Services:		Residential Sales:	
Offices:		Property Insurance:		Land Development:				Software/IT:		Specialty:	
Hotels/Motels:				Support Services:				Consulting:			
Industrial/Warehouses:				Design/Engineering:							
Other:											

TYPES OF BUSINESS:

Manufactured Housing
Home Financing

BRANDS/DIVISIONS/AFFILIATES:

Southern Homes
Southern Energy
Southern Energy of Texas
Southern Estates
Giles Industries, Inc.
Cavalier Homes
Southern Energy Homes Renew Center

CONTACTS:

Note: Officers with more than one job title may be intentionally listed here more than once.

Keith Holdbrooks, CEO
Keith Holdbrooks, Pres.
James Stariha, CFO
Dan Batchelor, General Counsel/Exec. VP/Corp. Sec.
James Stariha, Treas.
Doug Southern, Contact-SEhomes Renew Center
Wendell L. Batchelor, Chmn.

Phone: 256-747-8589	**Fax:** 256-747-7586
Toll-Free: 866-896-2737	
Address: 144 Corporate Way, Addison, AL 35540 US	

GROWTH PLANS/SPECIAL FEATURES:

Southern Energy Homes, Inc. (SE Homes), a subsidiary of Clayton Homes Inc., builds and sells pre-manufactured homes and operates five home manufacturing facilities: four in Alabama and one in Texas. The company offers 200 different floor plans for clients to choose from, ranging from under 1,000 to over 2,500 square foot. SE Homes custom-designs and manufactures homes intended for primary residences in 20 states, primarily in the Southeastern and Southwest U.S., and sold through 300 independent dealers. The company builds homes in sections at one of its production facilities and then employs independent trucking companies to transport the sections to dealer locations. The firm's homes are marketed under four brand names: Energy Homes, Southern Estates, Southern Homes, Giles Industries and Southern Energy of Texas. Additionally, SE Homes sells pre-owned homes through its Southern Energy Homes Renew Center division. In September 2009, the firm acquired manufactured home company Cavalier Homes for nearly $50 million.

FINANCIALS:

Sales and profits are in thousands of dollars—add 000 to get the full amount. 2009 Note: Financial information for 2009 was not available for all companies at press time.

2009 Sales: $	2009 Profits: $	**U.S. Stock Ticker: Subsidiary**
2008 Sales: $	2008 Profits: $	**Int'l Ticker:** Int'l Exchange:
2007 Sales: $	2007 Profits: $	Employees:
2006 Sales: $	2006 Profits: $	Fiscal Year Ends: 12/31
2005 Sales: $202,752	2005 Profits: $8,979	Parent Company: CLAYTON HOMES INC

SALARIES/BENEFITS:

Pension Plan:	ESOP Stock Plan:	Profit Sharing:	Top Exec. Salary: $	Bonus: $
Savings Plan:	Stock Purch. Plan:		Second Exec. Salary: $	Bonus: $

OTHER THOUGHTS:

Apparent Women Officers or Directors:
Hot Spot for Advancement for Women/Minorities:

LOCATIONS: ("Y" = Yes)

West:	Southwest:	Midwest:	Southeast:	Northeast:	International:
	Y	Y	Y	Y	

SOVRAN SELF STORAGE INC

www.unclebobs.com

Industry Group Code: 531120 **Ranks within this company's industry group:** Sales: 55 Profits: 38

Properties:		Financial Services:		Construction/Development:		Investments:		Specialty Services:		Brokerage:	
Apartments:		Mortgages:		Commercial Construction:		REIT:	Y	Property Management:	Y	Commercial Sales:	
Malls/Shopping:		Title Insurance:		Residential Construction:				Online Services:		Residential Sales:	
Offices:		Property Insurance:		Land Development:				Software/IT:		Specialty:	
Hotels/Motels:				Support Services:				Consulting:			
Industrial/Warehouses:				Design/Engineering:							
Other:	Y										

TYPES OF BUSINESS:

Real Estate Investment Trust
Self-Storage Properties
Truck Rental
Moving & Storage Products
Property Management

BRANDS/DIVISIONS/AFFILIATES:

Uncle Bob's Self Storage
Dri-guard
Uncle Bob's Rental Trucks
AllBoxes.com

CONTACTS: *Note: Officers with more than one job title may be intentionally listed here more than once.*

Robert J. Attea, CEO
Kenneth F. Myszka, COO
Kenneth F. Myszka, Pres.
David L. Rogers, CFO/Sec.
Edward Killeen, Exec. VP-Sales
Jennifer Kozub, Dir.-Human Resources
Jeffrey O'Donnell, Dir.-IT
Sandra Herberger, VP-Admin.
Sandra Herberger, VP-Legal Compliance
Edward Killeen, Exec. VP-Oper.
Diane Piegza, VP-Corp. Comm.
Andrew Gregoire, VP-Finance
Paul Powell, Exec. VP-Real Estate
John Rogers, VP-Special Oper.
Robert Myszka, VP-Joint Ventures
Jeffrey Myszka, Regional VP
Robert J. Attea, Chmn.

Phone: 716-633-1850	**Fax:** 716-633-3397
Toll-Free: 800-242-1715	
Address: 6467 Main St., Williamsville, NY 14221 US	

GROWTH PLANS/SPECIAL FEATURES:

Sovran Self Storage, Inc. is a self-administered and self-managed REIT (Real Estate Investment Trust) that acquires, owns and manages self-storage properties. It owns and manages 381 self-storage facilities (including 52 properties that are managed on behalf of two joint ventures) comprising 24.7 million square feet, making it one of the largest self-storage companies in the U.S. Sovran operates its stores under the trade name Uncle Bob's Self Storage, serving over 170,000 customers in 24 states. The states with the largest number of Uncle Bob's stores include Texas, with 90 stores; Florida, 57; New York, 28; Georgia, 27; Ohio, 23; Alabama, 22; Virginia, 19; North Carolina, 14; Louisiana, 14; Massachusetts, 12; and Mississippi, 12. Stores range in size from 21,000-187,000 rentable square feet, with an average size of 65,000 rentable square feet. Sovran's stores typically offer various value-added products and services including the following. Dri-guard, its state-of-the art centrally controlled dehumidification system, is available either singly or paired with the firm's climate controlled storage system. Dri-guard is used by the Smithsonian, Boeing, Volvo and the U.S. Military, including for the storage of Air Force One and Two. Uncle Bob's Rental Trucks offers moving trucks with 750 cubic feet of storage space on a two-way, local basis only. The firm also sells locks, boxes, tarps and other ancillary items used by its customers, offering these products both at its stores and through its affiliate web site, AllBoxes.com.

Corporate employees are offered health insurance; a 401(k) plan; life insurance; long-term disability; vacation time; personal time; and paid holidays and sick leave. Full-time employees receive a 401(k) plan; life and health insurance; vacation time; and paid holidays and sick leave. Part-time employees receive a 401(k) plan, life insurance and vacations.

FINANCIALS: **Sales and profits are in thousands of dollars—add 000 to get the full amount. 2009 Note: Financial information for 2009 was not available for all companies at press time.**

2009 Sales: $195,011	2009 Profits: $19,916	**U.S. Stock Ticker: SSS**
2008 Sales: $200,193	2008 Profits: $37,399	**Int'l Ticker:** Int'l Exchange:
2007 Sales: $190,013	2007 Profits: $37,958	Employees: 1,051
2006 Sales: $165,369	2006 Profits: $36,610	Fiscal Year Ends: 12/31
2005 Sales: $138,305	2005 Profits: $34,790	Parent Company:

SALARIES/BENEFITS:

Pension Plan:	ESOP Stock Plan:	Profit Sharing:	Top Exec. Salary: $419,000	Bonus: $
Savings Plan: Y	Stock Purch. Plan:		Second Exec. Salary: $408,000	Bonus: $

OTHER THOUGHTS:

Apparent Women Officers or Directors: 6
Hot Spot for Advancement for Women/Minorities: Y

LOCATIONS: ("Y" = Yes)

West:	Southwest:	Midwest:	Southeast:	Northeast:	International:
	Y	Y	Y	Y	

ST JOE COMPANY (THE)

www.joe.com

Industry Group Code: 5311 **Ranks within this company's industry group:** Sales: 29 Profits: 28

Properties:		Financial Services:		Construction/Development:		Investments:		Specialty Services:		Brokerage:	
Apartments:		Mortgages:		Commercial Construction:		REIT:		Property Management:		Commercial Sales:	
Malls/Shopping:		Title Insurance:		Residential Construction:				Online Services:		Residential Sales:	
Offices:	Y	Property Insurance:		Land Development:	Y			Software/IT:		Specialty:	
Hotels/Motels:				Support Services:				Consulting:			
Industrial/Warehouses:	Y			Design/Engineering:							
Other:	Y										

TYPES OF BUSINESS:

Real Estate Development, Investment & Operations
Residential Communities
Commercial Real Estate Development
Retail, Office & Industrial Properties
Forestry Operations

BRANDS/DIVISIONS/AFFILIATES:

WaterColor
WaterSound Beach
WasterSound West Beach
WaterSound
SummerCamp Beach
RiverCamps
WindMark Beach
SouthWood

CONTACTS:

Note: Officers with more than one job title may be intentionally listed here more than once.

William Britton Greene, CEO
William Britton Greene, Pres.
William S. McCalmont, CFO/Exec. VP
Hugh Durden, Chmn.

Phone: 904-301-4200	**Fax:** 904-301-4201
Toll-Free: 866-417-7133	
Address: 245 Riverside Ave., Ste. 500, Jacksonville, FL 32202 US	

GROWTH PLANS/SPECIAL FEATURES:

The St. Joe Company, founded in 1936, is a real estate development company with ownership of approximately 580,000 acres primarily in Northwest Florida, approximately 405,000 acres of which are within 15 miles of the Gulf of Mexico coast. St. Joe is engaged in town and resort development; commercial and industrial development; and rural land sales, with significant interests in timber. St. Joe operates through four segments: residential real estate; commercial real estate; rural land sales; and forestry. The residential segment develops large-scale, mixed-use resort, seasonal and primary residential communities including large tracts of land in Northwest Florida and significant Gulf of Mexico beach frontage and waterfront properties. Prominent properties within this category include WaterColor, WaterSound Beach, WaterSound West Beach, WaterSound, RiverCamps, WindMark Beach, SummerCamp Beach, SouthWood and RiverTown. St. Joe's commercial real estate segment develops and sells real estate for commercial purposes primarily in Northwest Florida. Often times the firm either manages the conceptual design, planning and permitting process for each of its new communities and developments; or enters into plans to either partner with or sell land to third party developers or investors. The rural land sales segment markets undeveloped timberland for rural residential and recreational uses in Northwest Florida. St. Joe's forestry segment manages and harvests its timber holdings. The firm has been undergoing massive restructuring in 2008-2009 to better deal with the economic downturn. It cut the employee count by 200, shut down its homebuilding operations and outsourced the management of its hotels, marinas and golf courses. In October 2009, the company entered into a strategic agreement with Southwest Airlines to help the company ease into a new international airport in Northwest Florida. St. Joe's owns several tracts of land around the new airport and will share in any immediate losses or profits that Southwest experiences.

FINANCIALS:

Sales and profits are in thousands of dollars—add 000 to get the full amount. 2009 Note: Financial information for 2009 was not available for all companies at press time.

2009 Sales: $138,257	2009 Profits: $-130,019	**U.S. Stock Ticker: JOE**
2008 Sales: $258,158	2008 Profits: $-35,883	**Int'l Ticker:** Int'l Exchange:
2007 Sales: $371,551	2007 Profits: $39,207	Employees: 143
2006 Sales: $525,024	2006 Profits: $51,020	Fiscal Year Ends: 12/31
2005 Sales: $717,677	2005 Profits: $126,600	Parent Company:

SALARIES/BENEFITS:

Pension Plan: Y	ESOP Stock Plan:	Profit Sharing:	Top Exec. Salary: $726,923	Bonus: $750,000
Savings Plan: Y	Stock Purch. Plan: Y		Second Exec. Salary: $407,789	Bonus: $325,000

OTHER THOUGHTS:

Apparent Women Officers or Directors: 2
Hot Spot for Advancement for Women/Minorities: Y

LOCATIONS: ("Y" = Yes)

West:	Southwest:	Midwest:	Southeast:	Northeast:	International:
			Y		

STANDARD PACIFIC CORP

www.standardpacifichomes.com

Industry Group Code: 2361 **Ranks within this company's industry group:** Sales: 12 Profits: 17

Properties:		Financial Services:		Construction/Development:		Investments:		Specialty Services:		Brokerage:	
Apartments:		Mortgages:	Y	Commercial Construction:		REIT:		Property Management:		Commercial Sales:	
Malls/Shopping:		Title Insurance:	Y	Residential Construction:	Y			Online Services:		Residential Sales:	
Offices:		Property Insurance:		Land Development:	Y			Software/IT:		Specialty:	
Hotels/Motels:				Support Services:				Consulting:			
Industrial/Warehouses:				Design/Engineering:							
Other:											

TYPES OF BUSINESS:

Residential Construction
Mortgage Financing
Title Services

BRANDS/DIVISIONS/AFFILIATES:

SPH Title
SPH Home Mortgage
Universal Land Title of South Florida
Standard Pacific Mortgage, Inc.

CONTACTS:

Note: Officers with more than one job title may be intentionally listed here more than once.

Kenneth L. Cambell III, CEO
Scott D. Stowell, COO
Kenneth L. Campbell III, Pres.
John M. Stephens, CFO/Sr. VP
John P. Babel, General Counsel/Sr. VP/Corp. Sec.
Todd J. Palmaer, Pres., California Region
Kathleen R. Wade, Pres., Southwest & Southeast Regions
Ronald R. Foell, Chmn.

Phone: 949-789-1600	**Fax:** 949-789-1609
Toll-Free:	
Address: 26 Technology Dr., Irvine, CA 92618 US	

GROWTH PLANS/SPECIAL FEATURES:

Standard Pacific Homes (SPH) is a builder of single-family detached and attached homes. The firm maintains operations in major metropolitan areas in California, Florida, Arizona, Texas, North Carolina, South Carolina, Colorado and Nevada, with California home deliveries accounting for 41% of total deliveries in 2009. Single-family detached dwellings accounted for 74% of deliveries. The company offers a wide variety of products and prices for its homes, which can range in price from $100,000 to $1,000,000 and typically range from 1,500 to 3,500 square feet. The firm currently constructs homes through seven operating divisions, with 198 projects under development, of which 122 are actively selling. SPH typically purchases unimproved or improved land zoned for residential use and employs independent architectural, design, engineering and other third-party consulting firms to assist in project planning and design. SPH supervisory employees are responsible for coordinating and directing subcontractors. The firm also enters into land development and homebuilding joint ventures as a means of accessing lot positions, expanding market opportunities and establishing strategic alliances. In addition to homebuilding operations, SPH provides mortgage financing and title services through subsidiaries and joint ventures such as Standard Pacific Mortgage, Inc.; SPH Home Mortgage; Universal Land Title of South Florida; and SPH Title.

Employees are offered medical, dental, vision, and life insurance; a home purchase discount program; a home mortgage/loan discount program; a college savings plan; work/life programs; paid maternity and military leave; tuition reimbursement programs; health care reimbursement accounts; a dependent care reimbursement program; 401(k) employer contributions; local vendor/supplier discounts; concierge services; and free financial planning/investment advice.

FINANCIALS:

Sales and profits are in thousands of dollars—add 000 to get the full amount. 2009 Note: Financial information for 2009 was not available for all companies at press time.

2009 Sales: $1,179,542	2009 Profits: $-13,786	**U.S. Stock Ticker: SPF**
2008 Sales: $1,549,203	2008 Profits: $-1,233,615	**Int'l Ticker:** Int'l Exchange:
2007 Sales: $2,905,510	2007 Profits: $-737,380	Employees: 800
2006 Sales: $3,765,336	2006 Profits: $123,693	Fiscal Year Ends: 12/31
2005 Sales: $3,893,019	2005 Profits: $440,984	Parent Company:

SALARIES/BENEFITS:

Pension Plan:	ESOP Stock Plan:	Profit Sharing:	Top Exec. Salary: $750,000	Bonus: $432,000
Savings Plan: Y	Stock Purch. Plan:		Second Exec. Salary: $703,833	Bonus: $615,000

OTHER THOUGHTS:

Apparent Women Officers or Directors: 1
Hot Spot for Advancement for Women/Minorities:

LOCATIONS: ("Y" = Yes)

West:	Southwest:	Midwest:	Southeast:	Northeast:	International:
Y	Y		Y	Y	

STARWOOD CAPITAL GROUP GLOBAL LLC www.starwoodcapital.com

Industry Group Code: 721110 **Ranks within this company's industry group:** Sales: Profits:

Properties:		Financial Services:		Construction/Development:		Investments:		Specialty Services:		Brokerage:	
Apartments:	Y	Mortgages:		Commercial Construction:		REIT:	Y	Property Management:		Commercial Sales:	
Malls/Shopping:	Y	Title Insurance:		Residential Construction:				Online Services:		Residential Sales:	
Offices:	Y	Property Insurance:		Land Development:				Software/IT:		Specialty:	
Hotels/Motels:	Y			Support Services:				Consulting:			
Industrial/Warehouses:				Design/Engineering:							
Other:	Y										

TYPES OF BUSINESS:

Real Estate Investments
Energy Investments
Commercial and Residential Development
Industrial Properties
Recreational Properties
Retail Properties
Office Buildings
Golf Courses

BRANDS/DIVISIONS/AFFILIATES:

Starwood Energy Group Global LLC
Starwood Property Trust Inc
Starwood Hotels & Resorts Worldwide Inc
Baccarat Hotels & Resorts
Hotel Crillon
Concorde Hotels & Resorts
Four Points by Sheraton
1Hotel & Resorts

CONTACTS: *Note: Officers with more than one job title may be intentionally listed here more than once.*

Barry S. Sternlicht, CEO
Daniel Yih, COO/Exec. VP
Jerry C. Silvey, CFO/Exec. VP
Ellis F. Rinaldi, Co-General Counsel/Exec. VP
Heather S. Goldman, Sr. VP-Investor Rel.
Jeffrey G. Dishner, Sr. Managing Dir.
Madison F. Grose, Co-General Counsel/Sr. Managing Dir.
Karl Frey, Managing Dir.
Christopher D. Graham, Managing Dir.-Acquisitions
Barry S. Sternlicht, Chmn.
Gregory Stuppler, Managing Dir. Starwood Capital Japan Oper.

Phone: 203-422-7700	**Fax:** 203-422-7784
Toll-Free:	
Address: 591 W. Putnam Ave., Greenwich, CT 06830 US	

GROWTH PLANS/SPECIAL FEATURES:

Starwood Capital Group Global, LLC is a private equity real estate investment firm. The company specializes in real estate-related investments on behalf of select private and institutional investor partners. It has invested in a wide range of property types, including multifamily, office, retail, hotel, industrial, residential and commercial land, mixed-use and golf. Through its Starwood Hotels & Resorts Worldwide, Inc., the company owns brands such as Sheraton, W Hotels, The St. Regis, Le Meridien, The Luxury Collection and Four Points by Sheraton; and develops, launches, oversees and manages the following brands: Baccarat Hotels and Resorts, Hotel Crillon and eco-focused brand 1Hotel and Resorts in the luxury segment; Concorde Hotels and Resorts in the business segment; Campanile, Kyriad and Premiere Classe in the budget segment; and B.R. Guest in the Restaurant segment. The company has also partnered with a variety of firms to complete such projects as building or acquiring more than 14 million square feet of retail assets, building a $500 million portfolio of senior housing assets and buying a large group of office buildings on the west coast of the U.S. Customers include public and private retirement programs; university endowments; foundations; and international and high net worth investor. Subsidiary Starwood Energy Group Global, LLC is involved in the investment of energy infrastructure. The firm's newest subsidiary Starwood Property Trust, Inc., a real estate investment trust (REIT), provides financing and managing commercial mortgage loans and other commercial real estate-related debt investments. In October 2009, the company partnered with TPG Capital, Perry Capital and WLR LeFrak and acquired real estate assets and construction loans owned by Corus Bank, NA. In January 2010, the company's Starwood Energy Group Global laid plans to construct and finance a 20-megawatt (MW) solar power generator project in Ontario, Canada.

FINANCIALS:

Sales and profits are in thousands of dollars—add 000 to get the full amount. 2009 Note: Financial information for 2009 was not available for all companies at press time.

2009 Sales: $	2009 Profits: $	**U.S. Stock Ticker: Private**
2008 Sales: $	2008 Profits: $	**Int'l Ticker:** Int'l Exchange:
2007 Sales: $	2007 Profits: $	Employees:
2006 Sales: $	2006 Profits: $	Fiscal Year Ends:
2005 Sales: $	2005 Profits: $	Parent Company:

SALARIES/BENEFITS:

Pension Plan:	ESOP Stock Plan:	Profit Sharing:	Top Exec. Salary: $	Bonus: $
Savings Plan:	Stock Purch. Plan:		Second Exec. Salary: $	Bonus: $

OTHER THOUGHTS:

Apparent Women Officers or Directors: 2
Hot Spot for Advancement for Women/Minorities: Y

LOCATIONS: ("Y" = Yes)

West:	Southwest:	Midwest:	Southeast:	Northeast:	International:
Y			Y	Y	Y

STARWOOD HOTELS & RESORTS WORLDWIDE INC

www.starwoodhotels.com

Industry Group Code: 721110 **Ranks within this company's industry group:** Sales: 4 Profits: 3

Properties:		Financial Services:		Construction/Development:		Investments:		Specialty Services:		Brokerage:	
Apartments:		Mortgages:		Commercial Construction:		REIT:		Property Management:	Y	Commercial Sales:	
Malls/Shopping:		Title Insurance:		Residential Construction:				Online Services:		Residential Sales:	
Offices:		Property Insurance:		Land Development:				Software/IT:		Specialty:	
Hotels/Motels:	Y			Support Services:				Consulting:			
Industrial/Warehouses:				Design/Engineering:							
Other:											

TYPES OF BUSINESS:

Hotels & Resorts
Financial Services
Hotel Management & Franchising
Spa Services
Online Auction Web Site
Preferred Guest Club

BRANDS/DIVISIONS/AFFILIATES:

Sheraton
W
Four Points
Westin
Le Meridien
St. Regis
Luxury Collection
Aloft

CONTACTS: *Note: Officers with more than one job title may be intentionally listed here more than once.*

Frits van Paasschen, CEO
Frits van Paasschen, Pres.
Vasant M. Prabhu, CFO
Christie Hicks, Sr. VP-Global Sales
Jeffrey M. Cava, Chief Human Resources Officer/Exec. VP
Phil McAveety, Exec. VP/Chief Brand Officer
Kenneth S. Siegel, Chief Admin. Officer
Kenneth S. Siegel, General Counsel
Simon Turner, Pres., Global Dev.
Alan Schnaid, Controller/Sr. VP
Roeland Vos, Pres., EMEA
Denise M. Coll, Pres., North America
Phil McAveety, Exec. VP/Chief Brand Officer
Matthew E. Avril, Pres., Hotel Group
Bruce W. Duncan, Chmn.
Osvaldo V. Librizzi, Pres., Latin America

Phone: 914-640-8100 **Fax:** 914-640-8310
Toll-Free:
Address: 1111 Westchester Ave., White Plains, NY 10604 US

GROWTH PLANS/SPECIAL FEATURES:

Starwood Hotels & Resorts Worldwide, Inc. manages the global operation of hotels and resorts, primarily in the luxury and upscale segments of the industry. It owns, leases, manages or franchises approximately 979 hotels containing about 292,000 rooms in roughly 100 countries. The company's hotel brand names include St. Regis, The Luxury Collection, W, Westin, Sheraton, Four Points, Le Meridien, Aloft and Element. The firm's earnings are derived mainly from its hotel and leisure operations; the receipt of franchise fees; and the development, ownership and operation of vacation ownership resorts. Additionally, Starwood provides financing to customers who purchase interests in resorts. The firm's frequent guest loyalty program, Starwood Preferred Guest, is unique in the hotel industry for its lack of capacity controls and blackout dates. Starwood's property portfolio includes the St. Regis in New York, New York; The Phoenician in Scottsdale, Arizona; the Hotel Gritti Palace in Venice, Italy; and the St. Regis in Beijing, China. In 2009, Starwood opened over 40 new hotels in locations such as Georgia (W); Maryland (Aloft and Element); New York (Four Points by Sheraton); Colorado (Element); Abu Dhabi (Aloft); Mumbai (Westin); and Florida (Westin). In July 2009, the firm sold its W San Francisco to Keck Seng Investments (Hong Kong) Limited for $90 million. In January 2010, the company sold Bliss, a spa and related product firm, to Steiner Leisure Limited for $100 million. In early 2010, Starwood opened new Westin hotels in Vancouver, Canada and Austin, Texas.

The company offers its employees life, disability, medical, dental and vision insurance; a 401(k) plan; an employee stock purchase plan; an employee assistance program; and domestic partner benefits.

FINANCIALS: **Sales and profits are in thousands of dollars—add 000 to get the full amount. 2009 Note: Financial information for 2009 was not available for all companies at press time.**

2009 Sales: $4,712,000	2009 Profits: $73,000	**U.S. Stock Ticker: HOT**
2008 Sales: $5,754,000	2008 Profits: $329,000	**Int'l Ticker:** Int'l Exchange:
2007 Sales: $5,999,000	2007 Profits: $542,000	Employees: 145,000
2006 Sales: $5,979,000	2006 Profits: $1,043,000	Fiscal Year Ends: 12/31
2005 Sales: $5,977,000	2005 Profits: $422,000	Parent Company:

SALARIES/BENEFITS:

Pension Plan:	ESOP Stock Plan:	Profit Sharing:	Top Exec. Salary: $1,000,000	Bonus: $1,875,000
Savings Plan: Y	Stock Purch. Plan:		Second Exec. Salary: $640,658	Bonus: $563,812

OTHER THOUGHTS:

Apparent Women Officers or Directors: 8
Hot Spot for Advancement for Women/Minorities: Y

LOCATIONS: ("Y" = Yes)

West:	Southwest:	Midwest:	Southeast:	Northeast:	International:
Y	Y	Y	Y	Y	Y

STATION CASINOS INC

www.stationcasinos.com

Industry Group Code: 721120 **Ranks within this company's industry group:** Sales: Profits:

Properties:		Financial Services:		Construction/Development:		Investments:		Specialty Services:		Brokerage:	
Apartments:		Mortgages:		Commercial Construction:		REIT:		Property Management:	Y	Commercial Sales:	
Malls/Shopping:		Title Insurance:		Residential Construction:				Online Services:		Residential Sales:	
Offices:		Property Insurance:		Land Development:				Software/IT:		Specialty:	
Hotels/Motels:	Y			Support Services:				Consulting:			
Industrial/Warehouses:				Design/Engineering:							
Other:	Y										

TYPES OF BUSINESS:

Casino Hotel
Casino Management
Restaurants
Movie Theaters & Entertainment Venues

BRANDS/DIVISIONS/AFFILIATES:

Palace Station Hotel & Casino
Texas Station Gambling Hall & Hotel
Boulder Station Hotel & Casino
Santa Fe Station Hotel & Casino
Barley's Casino & Brewing Company
Sunset Station Hotel & Casino
Fiesta Rancho Casino Hotel
Thunder Valley Casino

CONTACTS:

Note: Officers with more than one job title may be intentionally listed here more than once.

Frank J. Fertitta, III, CEO
Kevin L. Kelley, COO/Exec. VP
Frank J. Fertitta, III, Pres.
Richard J. Haskins, General Counsel/Exec. VP
Scott M. Nielson, Chief Dev. Officer/Exec. VP
Lori Nelson, Dir.-Corp. Comm.
Thomas M. Friel, Chief Acct. Officer/Treas./Exec. VP
Lorenzo J. Fertitta, Vice Chmn.
Frank J. Fertitta III, Chmn.

Phone: 702-495-3000	**Fax:**
Toll-Free: 800-634-3101	
Address: 1505 S. Pavilion Ctr. Dr., Las Vegas, NV 89135 US	

GROWTH PLANS/SPECIAL FEATURES:

Station Casinos, Inc. is a gaming and entertainment company concentrated in the Las Vegas area, mainly targeting locals and repeat customers. Its properties include nine major casino and hotel properties and eight smaller casino properties, featuring a total of 4,048 hotel rooms, 2,676 slot machines, 100 gaming tables, 54 restaurants, 112 movie screens and 288 bowling lanes. Other offerings include live entertainment venues, retail outlets, sports betting and convention banquet space. Station's owned and operated casinos include, in Las Vegas, Palace Station Hotel & Casino; Boulder Station Hotel & Casino; Santa Fe Station Hotel & Casino; Red Rock Casino Resort Spa; Wild Wild West Gambling Hall & Hotel; Wildfire Rancho; Texas Station Gambling Hall & Hotel and Fiesta Rancho Casino Hotel. Finally, in Henderson, Nevada, it owns Sunset Station Hotel & Casino; Fiesta Henderson Casino Hotel; Wildfire Boulder; Lake Mead Casino; and Gold Rush Casino. The firm owns 50% of five properties in Henderson: Green Valley Ranch Station Casino; Barley's Casino & Brewing Company; The Greens; Aliante Station Hotel & Casino; and Wildfire Casino & Lanes. It also manages the Thunder Valley Casino in Sacramento, California for the United Auburn Indian Community. Fertitta Colony Partners LLC, comprising two partners, Fertitta Partners LLC and FCP Holding, Inc., privately owns the firm. In July 2009, the firm filed for Chapter 11 bankruptcy protection, also announcing that its casinos will continue to operate during the bankruptcy and go through a re-organization. In March 2010, the firm filed a separate reorganization proposal to make an $85.6 million investment to retain stakes in the Red Rock Casino Spa, Palace Station, Boulder Station and Sunset Station. In April 2010, as part of the bankruptcy proceedings, a company was created to hold Station Casino's former assets, including (nine casinos plus five joint ventures). The company will then sign long-term lease agreements with the new company and continuing operating the casinos.

FINANCIALS:

Sales and profits are in thousands of dollars—add 000 to get the full amount. 2009 Note: Financial information for 2009 was not available for all companies at press time.

2009 Sales: $	2009 Profits: $	**U.S. Stock Ticker: Private**
2008 Sales: $	2008 Profits: $	**Int'l Ticker:** Int'l Exchange:
2007 Sales: $1,446,995	2007 Profits: $-375,610	Employees:
2006 Sales: $1,339,024	2006 Profits: $110,212	Fiscal Year Ends: 12/31
2005 Sales: $1,108,833	2005 Profits: $161,886	Parent Company: FERTITTA COLONY PARTNERS LLC

SALARIES/BENEFITS:

Pension Plan:	ESOP Stock Plan:	Profit Sharing:	Top Exec. Salary: $	Bonus: $
Savings Plan: Y	Stock Purch. Plan:		Second Exec. Salary: $	Bonus: $

OTHER THOUGHTS:

Apparent Women Officers or Directors: 1
Hot Spot for Advancement for Women/Minorities:

LOCATIONS: ("Y" = Yes)

West:	Southwest:	Midwest:	Southeast:	Northeast:	International:
Y	Y				

STERLING CONSTRUCTION COMPANY www.sterlingconstructionco.com

Industry Group Code: 237 **Ranks within this company's industry group:** Sales: 33 Profits: 29

Properties:		Financial Services:		Construction/Development:		Investments:		Specialty Services:		Brokerage:	
Apartments:		Mortgages:		Commercial Construction:	Y	REIT:		Property Management:		Commercial Sales:	
Malls/Shopping:		Title Insurance:		Residential Construction:				Online Services:		Residential Sales:	
Offices:		Property Insurance:		Land Development:				Software/IT:		Specialty:	
Hotels/Motels:				Support Services:	Y			Consulting:			
Industrial/Warehouses:				Design/Engineering:	Y						
Other:											

TYPES OF BUSINESS:

Heavy Construction & Reconstruction, Civil
Transportation & Water Infrastructure
Municipal Construction

BRANDS/DIVISIONS/AFFILIATES:

Texas Sterling Construction LP
Road and Highway Builders LLC
Ralph L Wadsworth Construction Co LLC

CONTACTS: *Note: Officers with more than one job title may be intentionally listed here more than once.*

Patrick T. Manning, CEO
Joseph P. Harper, Sr., COO
Joseph P. Harper, Sr., Pres.
James H. Allen, Jr., CFO/Sr. VP
Roger M. Barzun, General Counsel/Sr. VP
Brian Manning, VP-Bus. Dev.
Joseph P. Harper, Sr., Treas.
Patrick T. Manning, Chmn.

Phone: 281-821-9091	**Fax:** 281-821-2995
Toll-Free:	
Address: 20810 Fernbush Ln., Houston, TX 77073 US	

GROWTH PLANS/SPECIAL FEATURES:

Sterling Construction Company is a civil construction company that builds and reconstructs water infrastructure and transportation in Nevada and Texas. It operates in the Texas markets of Houston, San Antonio, Dallas/Fort Worth and Austin; and provides services in Utah and Nevada. The firm operates entirely through three subsidiaries: Texas Sterling Construction, LP; Road and Highway Builders, LLC (Nevada); and Ralph L. Wadsworth Construction Company, LLC (Utah). Sterling Construction's activities include concrete and asphalt paving; concrete slip forming; concrete crushing; concrete batch plant operations; installation of large-diameter water and wastewater distribution systems; bridge construction; and the building of light rail infrastructure. The company provides general contracting services to both public sector and municipal clients, while utilizing its own employees and equipment for activities including excavating, paving, pipe installation and concrete placement. The firm normally purchases its own materials, using subcontractors only for ancillary services. Sterling Construction's largest customer is the Nevada Department of Transportation, which accounts for approximately 23.6% of the company's revenues; the Texas Department of Transportation, its second largest customer, represents 20.9% of Sterling Construction's total revenues. The firm's other major customer, North Texas Tollroad Authority, accounts for roughly 13.4% of revenues. In December 2009, the company acquired 80% stake in Ralph L. Wadsworth Construction Company, LLC.

FINANCIALS: **Sales and profits are in thousands of dollars—add 000 to get the full amount. 2009 Note: Financial information for 2009 was not available for all companies at press time.**

2009 Sales: $390,847	2009 Profits: $23,704	**U.S. Stock Ticker: STRL**
2008 Sales: $415,074	2008 Profits: $18,066	**Int'l Ticker:** Int'l Exchange:
2007 Sales: $306,220	2007 Profits: $14,444	Employees: 1,100
2006 Sales: $249,348	2006 Profits: $13,320	Fiscal Year Ends: 12/31
2005 Sales: $219,439	2005 Profits: $11,100	Parent Company:

SALARIES/BENEFITS:

Pension Plan:	ESOP Stock Plan:	Profit Sharing:	Top Exec. Salary: $365,000	Bonus: $325,000
Savings Plan:	Stock Purch. Plan:		Second Exec. Salary: $365,000	Bonus: $325,000

OTHER THOUGHTS:

Apparent Women Officers or Directors: 1
Hot Spot for Advancement for Women/Minorities:

LOCATIONS: ("Y" = Yes)

West:	Southwest:	Midwest:	Southeast:	Northeast:	International:
Y	Y				

STEWART INFORMATION SERVICES CORP

www.stewart.com

Industry Group Code: 524127 **Ranks within this company's industry group:** Sales: 4 Profits: 4

Properties:		Financial Services:		Construction/Development:		Investments:		Specialty Services:		Brokerage:	
Apartments:		Mortgages:		Commercial Construction:		REIT:		Property Management:		Commercial Sales:	
Malls/Shopping:		Title Insurance:	Y	Residential Construction:				Online Services:		Residential Sales:	
Offices:		Property Insurance:		Land Development:				Software/IT:		Specialty:	
Hotels/Motels:				Support Services:				Consulting:			
Industrial/Warehouses:				Design/Engineering:							
Other:											

TYPES OF BUSINESS:

Title Insurance
Real Estate Information Services & Software

BRANDS/DIVISIONS/AFFILIATES:

Stewart Title Guaranty Co.
Stewart Title Insurance Co.
Landata Technologies, Inc.
Stewart REI Data, Inc.
LANSCAN
Brief Convey Software
Gulf Coast Title

CONTACTS:

Note: Officers with more than one job title may be intentionally listed here more than once.

Malcom S. Morris, Co-CEO
Stewart Morris, Jr., Pres./Co-CEO
Allen Berryman, CFO/Exec. VP
Murshid Khan, CIO
E. Ashley Smith, Chief Legal Officer/Exec. VP
Ted Jones, Dir.-Investor Rel.
Joseph Berryman, Treas./Sec.
Matthew Morris, Sr. Exec. VP
Rand Zimmerman, Pres., Region Prod. Centers
Pat L. Vaden, Pres., PropertyInfo Corp. & Real Estate Info.
Bob Oakland, Pres., Western State Direct Oper.
Malcom S. Morris, Chmn.

Phone: 713-625-4100	**Fax:** 713-625-4129
Toll-Free:	
Address: 1990 Post Oak Blvd., Ste. 100, Houston, TX 77056 US	

GROWTH PLANS/SPECIAL FEATURES:

Stewart Information Services Corp. is a real estate information, title insurance and transaction management company. The firm provides title insurance and related information services to the real estate and mortgage industries through more than 9,500 policy-issuing offices and agencies in the U.S. and international markets. Stewart also provides post-closing lender services, automated county clerk land records, property ownership mapping, geographic information systems, property information reports, document preparation, background checks and expertise in tax-deferred exchanges. The company operates in two main segments: title insurance-related services, which includes the functions of searching, examining, closing and insuring the condition of the title to real property; and real estate information (REI), which primarily provides electronic delivery of data, products and services related to real estate. The firm's international division delivers products and services protecting and promoting private land ownership worldwide, through its subsidiaries, business partners and its own offices, in more than 70 countries. Its primary international operations are in Canada, the U.K., Mexico, Central America and Australia. Subsidiary Stewart REI Data, Inc. offers information solutions to title agents, lenders, brokers and real estate agents; federal, state and local governments; and other markets with similar needs. Subsidiary Landata Technologies, Inc. offers automation for government recording and registration via the LANSCAN courthouse automation system. In September 2008, the company's subsidiary Gulf Coast Title changed its name to Stewart Title Co. In November 2008, Stewart Title Guaranty, Co. acquired Brief Convey Software, a conveyance program used to process residential real estate transactions. In December 2008, this subsidiary also created the Agency Services Group to streamline interactions with independent title agencies.

The firm offers its employees medical, dental and vision insurance; life insurance; short- and long-term disability insurance; flexible spending accounts; a 401(k) plan; a stock purchase plan; a college savings plan; and an educational assistance program.

FINANCIALS:

Sales and profits are in thousands of dollars—add 000 to get the full amount. 2009 Note: Financial information for 2009 was not available for all companies at press time.

2009 Sales: $1,707,300	2009 Profits: $-50,975	**U.S. Stock Ticker: STC**
2008 Sales: $1,555,294	2008 Profits: $-247,455	**Int'l Ticker:** Int'l Exchange:
2007 Sales: $2,106,691	2007 Profits: $-40,220	Employees: 6,100
2006 Sales: $2,471,481	2006 Profits: $43,252	Fiscal Year Ends: 12/31
2005 Sales: $2,430,627	2005 Profits: $88,765	Parent Company:

SALARIES/BENEFITS:

Pension Plan:	ESOP Stock Plan:	Profit Sharing:	Top Exec. Salary: $300,000	Bonus: $
Savings Plan: Y	Stock Purch. Plan: Y		Second Exec. Salary: $225,000	Bonus: $

OTHER THOUGHTS:

Apparent Women Officers or Directors: 3
Hot Spot for Advancement for Women/Minorities: Y

LOCATIONS: ("Y" = Yes)

West:	Southwest:	Midwest:	Southeast:	Northeast:	International:
Y	Y	Y	Y	Y	Y

STOCK BUILDING SUPPLY INC

www.stockbuildingsupply.com

Industry Group Code: 444130 **Ranks within this company's industry group:** Sales: Profits:

Properties:		Financial Services:		Construction/Development:		Investments:		Specialty Services:		Brokerage:	
Apartments:		Mortgages:		Commercial Construction:		REIT:		Property Management:		Commercial Sales:	
Malls/Shopping:		Title Insurance:		Residential Construction:				Online Services:		Residential Sales:	
Offices:		Property Insurance:		Land Development:				Software/IT:		Specialty:	
Hotels/Motels:				Support Services:	Y			Consulting:			
Industrial/Warehouses:				Design/Engineering:							
Other:											

TYPES OF BUSINESS:

Building Materials/Hardware Stores
Design & Installation Services

BRANDS/DIVISIONS/AFFILIATES:

Wolseley plc
Smoot Lumber Co.
Portrait
Kitchen Factor (The)
Wolseley plc
Gores Group (The)

CONTACTS:

Note: Officers with more than one job title may be intentionally listed here more than once.

Joseph Appelmann, CEO
Steve Short, COO
Joseph Appelmann, Pres.
Jim Major, CFO
Tim Krall, Market Mgr.-Eastern Pennsylvania
Timothy Meyer, Chmn.

Phone: 919-431-1000	**Fax:** 919-431-1700
Toll-Free:	
Address: 8020 Arco Corporate Dr., Raleigh, NC 27617 US	

GROWTH PLANS/SPECIAL FEATURES:

Stock Building Supply, Inc. (SBS) is a supplier of building materials to professional homebuilders and contractors in the U.S. The firm is a joint venture between The Gores Group and Wolseley plc. The company is currently focused on operations in the following states and Washington, D.C.: New Mexico, North Carolina, South Carolina, Georgia, Texas, Pennsylvania, Utah, Idaho and California. Its brands include Portrait millwork products, Smoot Lumber, The Kitchen Factor, and PROSELECT professional materials. It supplies building materials (dimensional lumber, plywood, sheetrock, windows, doors, siding and shingles), components (roof trusses, floor trusses, laminated beams and wall panels), brand-name tools (Dewalt, Milwaukee, Freud, Paslode, Porter Cable, Senco, Stabila and Stanley), interior products (carpet, tile, wall coverings and flooring) and custom and pre-fab millworks (doors, windows, stairs, molding, rail, wainscoting and trim). The firm also provides design services such as stair design, custom millwork, laminated beams, trusses, kitchen cabinets, decks and fences. SBS additionally offers installation services. SBS has several stock house plans on file. In addition, the firm offers financial services including credit accounts, construction loans, insurance and permanent financing. In June 2009, the firm announced plans to close 94 locations, representing nearly half of its 201 retail outlets. In July 2009, the company emerged from Chapter 11 bankruptcy. As a result of its Chapter 11 reorganization, SBS is now 51% owned by the Gores Group; its former parent company, Wolseley plc, controls the remaining 49%. In November 2009, the firm announced plans to consolidate its three Pennsylvania facilities into one factory. Also in November 2009, SBS sold its Connecticut, Wisconsin and Central New York operations to US LBM, a new company formed by a partnership between BlackEagle Partners, LLC, and Building Industry Partners, LLC.

The company offers its employees life, disability, medical, dental and vision insurance; a 401(k) plan; an employee stock purchase plan; and tuition reimbursement.

FINANCIALS:

Sales and profits are in thousands of dollars—add 000 to get the full amount. 2009 Note: Financial information for 2009 was not available for all companies at press time.

2009 Sales: $	2009 Profits: $	**U.S. Stock Ticker: Joint Venture**
2008 Sales: $	2008 Profits: $	**Int'l Ticker:** Int'l Exchange:
2007 Sales: $4,600,000	2007 Profits: $	Employees:
2006 Sales: $3,300,000	2006 Profits: $	Fiscal Year Ends: 7/31
2005 Sales: $3,953,100	2005 Profits: $	Parent Company:

SALARIES/BENEFITS:

Pension Plan:	ESOP Stock Plan:	Profit Sharing:	Top Exec. Salary: $	Bonus: $
Savings Plan: Y	Stock Purch. Plan: Y		Second Exec. Salary: $	Bonus: $

OTHER THOUGHTS:

Apparent Women Officers or Directors:
Hot Spot for Advancement for Women/Minorities:

LOCATIONS: ("Y" = Yes)

West:	Southwest:	Midwest:	Southeast:	Northeast:	International:
Y	Y	Y	Y	Y	

STRATEGIC HOTELS AND RESORTS INC

www.strategichotels.com

Industry Group Code: 721110 **Ranks within this company's industry group:** Sales: 15 Profits: 27

Properties:		Financial Services:		Construction/Development:		Investments:		Specialty Services:		Brokerage:	
Apartments:		Mortgages:		Commercial Construction:		REIT:	Y	Property Management:	Y	Commercial Sales:	
Malls/Shopping:		Title Insurance:		Residential Construction:				Online Services:		Residential Sales:	
Offices:		Property Insurance:		Land Development:				Software/IT:		Specialty:	
Hotels/Motels:	Y			Support Services:				Consulting:			
Industrial/Warehouses:				Design/Engineering:							
Other:											

TYPES OF BUSINESS:

Real Estate Investment Trust
Hotels

BRANDS/DIVISIONS/AFFILIATES:

Westin
InterContinental
Fairmont
Four Seasons
Hyatt
Loews
Marriott
Ritz-Carlton

CONTACTS:

Note: Officers with more than one job title may be intentionally listed here more than once.

Laurence S. Geller, CEO
Laurence S. Geller, Pres.
Diane M. Morefield, CFO/Exec. VP
Paula C. Maggio, General Counsel/Corp. Sec./Sr. VP
Stephen Briggs, Chief Acct. Officer/Sr. VP
Richard J. Moreau, Exec. VP-Asset Mgmt.
William Prezant, Chmn.

Phone: 312-658-5000	**Fax:**
Toll-Free:	
Address: 200 W. Madison St., Ste. 1700, Chicago, IL 60606 US	

GROWTH PLANS/SPECIAL FEATURES:

Strategic Hotels & Resorts, Inc. (SHR) is a real estate investment trust (REIT). The firm owns and manages upper upscale and luxury hotels in North America and Europe through its direct and indirect subsidiaries, including SH Funding. The company owns or leases 14 hotels, comprising 7,245 rooms; owns a 51% interest in affiliates that own two hotels that are asset-managed by SHR; and owns a 45% interest in a joint venture that owns one hotel (for which SHR also acts as asset manager). The company also owns a 31% interest in and acts as asset manager for a joint venture with two third parties that is developing the Four Seasons Residence Club Punta Mita, a luxury vacation home product on property adjacent to its Four Seasons Punta Mita Resort hotel in Mexico. The firm does not operate any of its hotels directly; instead, it employs internationally known hotel management companies to operate them under management contracts or operating leases. The company's existing hotels are operated under the Fairmont, Four Seasons, Hyatt, InterContinental, Loews, Marriott, Ritz-Carlton and Westin brands. The Hotel del Coronado is operated by specialty management company, SHC KSL Partners, LP, in which SHR owns 45% interest. SHR manages properties in Arizona, California, Illinois, Florida and Washington, D.C., as well as worldwide in Mexico, Germany, France, the U.K. and the Czech Republic. In October 2009, the firm sold its 240-room Four Seasons Mexico City property to a Meridia Capital affiliate for approximately $54.0 million. In December 2009, SHR sold its 116-room Renaissance Paris Hotel Le Parc Trocadero property to an investment group led by a Westmont Hospitality affiliate for roughly $51.5 million.

FINANCIALS:

Sales and profits are in thousands of dollars—add 000 to get the full amount. 2009 Note: Financial information for 2009 was not available for all companies at press time.

2009 Sales: $723,799	2009 Profits: $-243,945	**U.S. Stock Ticker: BEE**
2008 Sales: $928,389	2008 Profits: $-317,291	**Int'l Ticker:** Int'l Exchange:
2007 Sales: $967,552	2007 Profits: $69,158	Employees: 43
2006 Sales: $680,944	2006 Profits: $120,129	Fiscal Year Ends: 12/31
2005 Sales: $389,531	2005 Profits: $30,260	Parent Company:

SALARIES/BENEFITS:

Pension Plan:	ESOP Stock Plan:	Profit Sharing:	Top Exec. Salary: $750,000	Bonus: $615,000
Savings Plan:	Stock Purch. Plan:		Second Exec. Salary: $420,000	Bonus: $358,300

OTHER THOUGHTS:

Apparent Women Officers or Directors: 2
Hot Spot for Advancement for Women/Minorities:

LOCATIONS: ("Y" = Yes)

West:	Southwest:	Midwest:	Southeast:	Northeast:	International:
Y	Y	Y	Y	Y	Y

STRATOSPHERE CORPORATION

www.stratospherehotel.com

Industry Group Code: 721120 **Ranks within this company's industry group:** Sales: Profits:

Properties:		Financial Services:	Construction/Development:	Investments:	Specialty Services:	Brokerage:
Apartments:		Mortgages:	Commercial Construction:	REIT:	Property Management:	Commercial Sales:
Malls/Shopping:	Y	Title Insurance:	Residential Construction:		Online Services:	Residential Sales:
Offices:		Property Insurance:	Land Development:		Software/IT:	Specialty:
Hotels/Motels:	Y		Support Services:		Consulting:	
Industrial/Warehouses:			Design/Engineering:			
Other:	Y					

TYPES OF BUSINESS:

Casino Hotel
Retail Outlets
Restaurants
Nightclubs
Spa
Thrill Rides

BRANDS/DIVISIONS/AFFILIATES:

Stratosphere Casino Hotel & Tower
Top of the World Restaurant & Lounge

CONTACTS:

Note: Officers with more than one job title may be intentionally listed here more than once.

Frank Riolo, CEO
Arthur Keith, Pres.

Phone: 702-380-7777	**Fax:**
Toll-Free: 800-998-6937	
Address: 2000 S. Las Vegas Blvd., Las Vegas, NV 89104 US	

GROWTH PLANS/SPECIAL FEATURES:

Stratosphere Corporation operates the Stratosphere Casino Hotel and Tower property at the north end of the Las Vegas Strip. The Stratosphere Tower is centerpiece of the Stratosphere property. At 1,149-feet, the Stratosphere Tower is the tallest freestanding observation tower in the U.S. The tower features a revolving restaurant, observation decks and a roller coaster that wraps around the tower. Visitors are brought to the top of the tower by double-decker elevators traveling at speeds of 1,800 feet per minute or three floors a second. The company also owns the adjacent hotel, with 2,427 guest rooms (including 133 suites), services ranging from car rentals to dry cleaning through its guest services and business needs such as faxing and next-day delivery through its business services. Stratosphere's casino has 80,000 square feet of casino space with over 50 table games, 1,500 slot and video poker machines, keno, poker room, and a race and space book. The hotel also features a 650-seat Broadway showroom and a retail center with shops, fast-food outlets and thrill rides on top of the Stratosphere Tower. Stratosphere dining facilities include the Top of the World Restaurant and Lounge, sitting 833 feet above the Strip, as well as other themed restaurants, nightclubs and coffee shops. Recently, American Real Estate Partners, L.P. sold Stratosphere Corporation to Whitehall Street Real Estate Fund for $1.3 billion. The purchase also included 17 acres of undeveloped land adjacent to the hotel.

FINANCIALS:

Sales and profits are in thousands of dollars—add 000 to get the full amount. 2009 Note: Financial information for 2009 was not available for all companies at press time.

2009 Sales: $
2008 Sales: $
2007 Sales: $182,900
2006 Sales: $
2005 Sales: $

2009 Profits: $
2008 Profits: $
2007 Profits: $
2006 Profits: $
2005 Profits: $

U.S. Stock Ticker: Private
Int'l Ticker: Int'l Exchange:
Employees:
Fiscal Year Ends: 12/31
Parent Company: WHITEHALL STREET REAL ESTATE FUND

SALARIES/BENEFITS:

Pension Plan:	ESOP Stock Plan:	Profit Sharing:	Top Exec. Salary: $	Bonus: $
Savings Plan:	Stock Purch. Plan:		Second Exec. Salary: $	Bonus: $

OTHER THOUGHTS:

Apparent Women Officers or Directors: 1
Hot Spot for Advancement for Women/Minorities: Y

LOCATIONS: ("Y" = Yes)

West:	Southwest:	Midwest:	Southeast:	Northeast:	International:
Y					

STV GROUP INC

www.stvinc.com

Industry Group Code: 541330 **Ranks within this company's industry group:** Sales: 9 Profits:

Properties:		Financial Services:		Construction/Development:		Investments:		Specialty Services:		Brokerage:	
Apartments:		Mortgages:		Commercial Construction:	Y	REIT:		Property Management:		Commercial Sales:	
Malls/Shopping:		Title Insurance:		Residential Construction:				Online Services:		Residential Sales:	
Offices:		Property Insurance:		Land Development:	Y			Software/IT:		Specialty:	
Hotels/Motels:				Support Services:	Y			Consulting:			
Industrial/Warehouses:				Design/Engineering:	Y						
Other:											

TYPES OF BUSINESS:

Architectural & Engineering Services
Construction Management
Infrastructure Design
Defense Systems Engineering
Industrial Process Engineering

BRANDS/DIVISIONS/AFFILIATES:

STV Security Solutions
STV Architects
STV Construction
STV Canada Consulting Inc

CONTACTS:

Note: Officers with more than one job title may be intentionally listed here more than once.

Dominick M. Servedio, CEO
Milo E. Riverso, Pres.
Peter W. Knipe, CFO
Linda Rosenberg, Sr. VP-Mktg. & Comm.
Patrick M. Austin, Dir.-Human Resources
Ronald Wiseman, CIO
James R. Vilbert, Sr. VP-Oper. Buildings & Facilities Div.
Debra B. Trace, Mgr.-Corp. Comm. STV Group
Maher Z. Labib, Exec. VP/COO-Buildings & Facilities Div.
William F. Matts, Exec. VP/COO-Transportation & Infrastructure
John A. Agro Jr., Sr. VP/Deputy Dir.-Transportation & Infrastructure
Jill Bonamusa, Mgr.-Corp. Comm., STV Inc.
Dominick M. Servedio, Chmn.

Phone: 610-385-8200 **Fax:** 610-385-8500
Toll-Free:
Address: 205 W. Welsh Dr., Douglassville, PA 19518 US

GROWTH PLANS/SPECIAL FEATURES:

STV Group, Inc. is an architectural, engineering, planning, environmental and construction management firm. The firm specializes in constructing airports, highways, bridges, ports, railroad systems and schools, almost all of which are in the U.S. It operates through three divisions: Construction Management; Buildings/Facilities; and Transportation/Infrastructure. STV Construction Management undertakes design and building contracts in nearly every field of industry; the firm's personnel oversees construction programs through administrative, inspection and surveillance. The Buildings/Facilities division works directly with architects, to address the safety, practicality, cost and efficiency of its buildings. STV's Transportation and Infrastructure sector focuses on the management, planning and design of transportation systems and facilities. Specialties of the firm include aviation/transportation architecture, defense systems, and sustainable design. The company's subsidiary, STV Security Solutions Group, Inc., offers security, as well as risk, crisis and emergency management to its clients. Some of the STV Group's representative projects include the MetroLink in St. Louis, Missouri; the Villanova University Center for Engineering Education and Research; Sprint PCS Environmental Site Assessments in seven states; the Metra Inner Circumferential Rail Study in Chicago, Illinois; Shea Stadium in Queens, New York; and engineering and technical services for the U.S. Naval Air Warfare Center in Patuxent River, Maryland. In May 2009, the firm launched STV Canada Consulting Inc., adding an office in Toronto, Canada.

Employees are offered health and life insurance; short- and long-term disability benefits; employee assistance program; paid time off; and a credit union membership.

FINANCIALS:

Sales and profits are in thousands of dollars—add 000 to get the full amount. 2009 Note: Financial information for 2009 was not available for all companies at press time.

2009 Sales: $	2009 Profits: $	**U.S. Stock Ticker: Private**
2008 Sales: $250,000	2008 Profits: $	**Int'l Ticker:** Int'l Exchange:
2007 Sales: $205,000	2007 Profits: $	Employees:
2006 Sales: $	2006 Profits: $	Fiscal Year Ends: 9/30
2005 Sales: $	2005 Profits: $	Parent Company:

SALARIES/BENEFITS:

Pension Plan:	ESOP Stock Plan: Y	Profit Sharing:	Top Exec. Salary: $	Bonus: $
Savings Plan: Y	Stock Purch. Plan:		Second Exec. Salary: $	Bonus: $

OTHER THOUGHTS:

Apparent Women Officers or Directors: 4
Hot Spot for Advancement for Women/Minorities: Y

LOCATIONS: ("Y" = Yes)

West:	Southwest:	Midwest:	Southeast:	Northeast:	International:
Y	Y	Y	Y	Y	Y

SUN COMMUNITIES INC

www.suncommunities.com

Industry Group Code: 531120 **Ranks within this company's industry group:** Sales: 49 Profits: 56

Properties:		Financial Services:		Construction/Development:		Investments:		Specialty Services:		Brokerage:	
Apartments:		Mortgages:		Commercial Construction:		REIT:	Y	Property Management:	Y	Commercial Sales:	
Malls/Shopping:		Title Insurance:		Residential Construction:				Online Services:		Residential Sales:	Y
Offices:		Property Insurance:		Land Development:	Y			Software/IT:		Specialty:	
Hotels/Motels:				Support Services:				Consulting:			
Industrial/Warehouses:				Design/Engineering:							
Other:	Y										

TYPES OF BUSINESS:

Real Estate Investment Trust
Manufactured Housing Communities
Recreational Vehicle Communities
Manufactured Home Sales
Property Management

BRANDS/DIVISIONS/AFFILIATES:

Sun Home Services, Inc.

CONTACTS:

Note: Officers with more than one job title may be intentionally listed here more than once.

Gary A. Shiffman, CEO
John B. McLaren, COO/Exec. VP
Gary A. Shiffman, Pres.
Karen J. Dearing, CFO/Exec. VP
Karen J. Dearing, Sec.
Karen J. Dearing, Treas.
Jonathan M. Colman, Exec. VP
Gary A. Shiffman, Chmn.

Phone: 248-208-2500	**Fax:** 248-932-3072
Toll-Free:	
Address: 27777 Franklin Rd., Ste. 200, Southfield, MI 48034 US	

GROWTH PLANS/SPECIAL FEATURES:

Sun Communities, Inc. is a self-administered and self-managed Real Estate Investment Trust (REIT) that owns, operates and develops manufactured housing communities concentrated in the midwestern, southern and southeastern U.S. Sun, together with its affiliates and predecessors, has been in the business of acquiring, operating and expanding manufactured housing communities since 1975. The company owns and operates a portfolio of 136 properties in 18 states, including 124 manufactured housing communities; four recreational vehicle (RV) communities; and eight multi-use properties containing both manufactured housing and RV sites. The properties contain a total of 47,572 developed sites, including approximately 42,294 developed manufactured home sites, 3,176 permanent RV sites, 2,102 seasonal recreational vehicle sites and an additional 6,000 manufactured home sites suitable for development. The firm leases individual sites and utility access to customers for the placement of manufactured homes and RVs. Communities may contain improvements similar to other garden-style residential developments, including centralized entrances, paved streets, curbs and gutters and parkways; and often provide of amenities such as a clubhouse, a swimming pool, shuffleboard courts, tennis courts and laundry facilities. Subsidiary Sun Home Services, Inc. markets, sells and leases new and pre-owned manufactured homes for placement in the properties. The firm expands primarily through the acquisition of manufactured housing and RV communities. In its acquisitions, Sun focuses on communities with a minimum of 200 home sites, located near large metropolitan areas; land/lease communities, rather than rental homes; RV communities with more than 50% annual leases; public utilities access; and the potential to expand. Headquartered in Southfield, Michigan, the company also maintains management offices in Texas, Ohio, Indiana and Florida.

Employees of Sun receive medical and prescription coverage; dental and vision plans; life, AD&D and identity theft insurance; a 401(k) plan; an employee assistance program; tuition reimbursement; and health and dependent care reimbursement accounts.

FINANCIALS:

Sales and profits are in thousands of dollars—add 000 to get the full amount. 2009 Note: Financial information for 2009 was not available for all companies at press time.

2009 Sales: $256,609	2009 Profits: $-6,302	**U.S. Stock Ticker: SUI**
2008 Sales: $254,291	2008 Profits: $-34,448	**Int'l Ticker:** Int'l Exchange:
2007 Sales: $235,075	2007 Profits: $-16,643	Employees: 664
2006 Sales: $227,778	2006 Profits: $-24,968	Fiscal Year Ends: 12/31
2005 Sales: $211,964	2005 Profits: $-5,452	Parent Company:

SALARIES/BENEFITS:

Pension Plan:	ESOP Stock Plan:	Profit Sharing:	Top Exec. Salary: $598,150	Bonus: $239,260
Savings Plan: Y	Stock Purch. Plan:		Second Exec. Salary: $345,000	Bonus: $86,250

OTHER THOUGHTS:

Apparent Women Officers or Directors: 2
Hot Spot for Advancement for Women/Minorities:

LOCATIONS: ("Y" = Yes)

West:	Southwest:	Midwest:	Southeast:	Northeast:	International:
Y	Y	Y	Y	Y	

SUN HUNG KAI PROPERTIES

www.shkp.com.hk

Industry Group Code: 5311 **Ranks within this company's industry group:** Sales: 9 Profits: 1

Properties:		Financial Services:		Construction/Development:		Investments:		Specialty Services:		Brokerage:	
Apartments:	Y	Mortgages:	Y	Commercial Construction:	Y	REIT:		Property Management:	Y	Commercial Sales:	
Malls/Shopping:	Y	Title Insurance:		Residential Construction:	Y			Online Services:		Residential Sales:	
Offices:	Y	Property Insurance:		Land Development:	Y			Software/IT:	Y	Specialty:	
Hotels/Motels:	Y			Support Services:	Y			Consulting:			
Industrial/Warehouses:	Y			Design/Engineering:	Y						
Other:	Y										

TYPES OF BUSINESS:

Real Estate Operations & Development
Land Development
Engineering Services
Hotels & Shopping Malls
Insurance & Financial Services
Logistics & Transportation
Ocean Port Terminals
Infrastructure

BRANDS/DIVISIONS/AFFILIATES:

Royal Garden
Royal Park Hotel
Royal Plaza Hotel
River Trade Terminal Company Limited
Hoi Kong Container Services Company Limited
Sun Hung Kai Logistics Limited

CONTACTS: *Note: Officers with more than one job title may be intentionally listed here more than once.*

Thomas Kwok Ping-kwong, Co-Managing Dir./Vice Chmn.
Raymonf Kwok Ping-luen, Co-Managing Dir./Vice Chmn.
Patrick Chan Kwok-wai, CFO
Chan Kai-ming, Exec. Dir.-Architecture & Eng.
Sandy Yung Sheung-tat, Company Sec.
Kwong Chun, Exec. Dir.
Mike Wong Chik-wing, Exec. Dir.
Thomas Chan Kui-yuen, Exec. Dir.
Kwong Siu-hing, Chmn.

Phone: 852-2827-8111 **Fax:** 852-2827-2862
Toll-Free:
Address: Sun Hung Kai Ctr., 30 Harbour Rd., 45th Fl., Hong Kong, China

GROWTH PLANS/SPECIAL FEATURES:

Sun Hung Kai Properties (SHKP) is one of the largest property developers in Hong Kong. The company's core areas of business include construction, land acquisition and property management; non-core businesses include hotels, insurance and financial services; it also has investments in transportation, infrastructure, logistics, telecommunications and information technology. SHKP's land bank is one of the largest private landholders in Hong Kong, with 26.1 million square feet of completed investment property; over 25 million square feet of agricultural land, much of which is in the process of land use conversion for future residential development; and 18 million square feet of space currently under development. The firm's mainland China land bank has approximately 85 million square feet under development and 3.3 million square feet of completed investment properties, with a strategic focus on acquisitions in major cities such as Beijing, Shanghai, Guangzhou and Nanjing. SHKP also owns approximately 50 shopping malls in Hong Kong and two in mainland China. The firm owns three luxury hotels in Hong Kong: the Royal Garden, the Royal Park Hotel and the Royal Plaza Hotel. It also manages five other Hong Kong hotels, with one additional hotel currently under construction. The company's financial division provides mortgages and related services in support of SHKP's property development activities. SHKP is also active in a number of additional business areas, including bus operations, toll roads, port operations, department stores, broadband telecommunications infrastructure development and IT venture capital investments. In addition, SHKP is involved in air transportation and logistics, with subsidiaries focused on international air cargo consolidation and freight forwarding; airport services such as storage, X-ray scanning, loading and unloading, collection and delivery, palletization and containerization; and aviation services such as aircraft parking, marshalling, towing, fuelling, potable water supply and other turn-around operations. In February 2010, the firm purchased a new residential site in Hong Kong for $432 million.

FINANCIALS: **Sales and profits are in thousands of dollars—add 000 to get the full amount. 2009 Note: Financial information for 2009 was not available for all companies at press time.**

2009 Sales: $4,411,600	2009 Profits: $1,334,540	**U.S. Stock Ticker: SUHJY**
2008 Sales: $3,154,710	2008 Profits: $2,956,560	**Int'l Ticker: 0016** Int'l Exchange: Hong Kong-HKEX
2007 Sales: $4,029,200	2007 Profits: $2,759,400	Employees: 31,500
2006 Sales: $3,327,700	2006 Profits: $2,580,500	Fiscal Year Ends: 5/31
2005 Sales: $2,982,900	2005 Profits: $2,327,000	Parent Company:

SALARIES/BENEFITS:

Pension Plan:	ESOP Stock Plan:	Profit Sharing:	Top Exec. Salary: $	Bonus: $
Savings Plan:	Stock Purch. Plan:		Second Exec. Salary: $	Bonus: $

OTHER THOUGHTS:

Apparent Women Officers or Directors: 2
Hot Spot for Advancement for Women/Minorities:

LOCATIONS: ("Y" = Yes)

West:	Southwest:	Midwest:	Southeast:	Northeast:	International:
					Y

SUNBURST HOSPITALITY CORPORATION

www.snbhotels.com

Industry Group Code: 721110 **Ranks within this company's industry group:** Sales: Profits:

Properties:		Financial Services:		Construction/Development:		Investments:		Specialty Services:		Brokerage:	
Apartments:		Mortgages:		Commercial Construction:		REIT:		Property Management:	Y	Commercial Sales:	
Malls/Shopping:		Title Insurance:		Residential Construction:				Online Services:		Residential Sales:	
Offices:		Property Insurance:		Land Development:				Software/IT:		Specialty:	
Hotels/Motels:	Y			Support Services:				Consulting:			
Industrial/Warehouses:	Y			Design/Engineering:							
Other:	Y										

TYPES OF BUSINESS:

Hotels
Hotel Management

BRANDS/DIVISIONS/AFFILIATES:

Comfort Inns & Suites
Holiday Inn Express
Crowne Plaza
Quality Inn
Glenwood Golf Club
Sleep Inn
Clarion Collection Hotel
Best Western

CONTACTS: *Note: Officers with more than one job title may be intentionally listed here more than once.*

Kevin Hanley, CEO
Kevin Hanley, Pres.
Joe Smith, CFO/VP
Julie Thompson, VP-Mktg. & Sales
Mark Elbaum, VP-Info. Systems
Pam Williams, Chief Admin. Officer
Pam Williams, General Counsel/Exec. VP
Tom Murphy, VP-Oper.
Chris Milke, VP-Acquisitions & Dev.
Joe Smith, Treas.
Randy Hartig, VP-Construction
Leon Vainikos, Regional General Counsel/VP
Ned Heiss, VP-Oper.

Phone: 301-592-3800	**Fax:** 301-592-3830
Toll-Free:	
Address: 10770 Columbia Pike, Ste. 200, Silver Spring, MD 20901-4448 US	

GROWTH PLANS/SPECIAL FEATURES:

Sunburst Hospitality Corp. owns, acquires and manages hotels, a championship golf course and townhomes, with operations in 17 states. The company additionally develops residential real estate, with current projects in Virginia and Arkansas. Sunburst owns and operates 31 hotels under such brand names as Comfort Inns and Suites; Holiday Inn Express; Crowne Plaza; Quality Inn; Clarion; Sleep Inn; Best Western; and AmeriHost. The company actively seeks to expand its hotel business through the acquisition of 100-300 room hotels. The firm's Glenwood Golf Club in Glenwood, Arkansas features a full service pro shop, a snack bar and a driving range, and is rated four and a half out of five stars by Golf Digest. Recently, Sunburst acquired a 110-room beachfront hotel in Ocean City, Maryland that it plans to renovate; and completed an $18 million redevelopment of its Arlington, Virginia hotel, which now operates as a high-end, extended stay Clarion Collection Hotel under the Arlington Residence Court brand. In January 2010, the firm announced the sale of its Vista on Courthouse apartments to Equity Residential.

FINANCIALS: **Sales and profits are in thousands of dollars—add 000 to get the full amount. 2009 Note: Financial information for 2009 was not available for all companies at press time.**

2009 Sales: $	2009 Profits: $	**U.S. Stock Ticker: Private**
2008 Sales: $	2008 Profits: $	**Int'l Ticker:** Int'l Exchange:
2007 Sales: $84,600	2007 Profits: $	Employees:
2006 Sales: $	2006 Profits: $	Fiscal Year Ends: 12/31
2005 Sales: $	2005 Profits: $	Parent Company:

SALARIES/BENEFITS:

Pension Plan:	ESOP Stock Plan:	Profit Sharing:	Top Exec. Salary: $	Bonus: $
Savings Plan:	Stock Purch. Plan:		Second Exec. Salary: $	Bonus: $

OTHER THOUGHTS:

Apparent Women Officers or Directors: 2
Hot Spot for Advancement for Women/Minorities: Y

LOCATIONS: ("Y" = Yes)

West:	Southwest:	Midwest:	Southeast:	Northeast:	International:
Y	Y	Y	Y	Y	

SUNRISE SENIOR LIVING

www.sunriseseniorliving.com

Industry Group Code: 623110 **Ranks within this company's industry group:** Sales: 4 Profits: 6

Properties:		Financial Services:		Construction/Development:		Investments:		Specialty Services:		Brokerage:	
Apartments:		Mortgages:		Commercial Construction:		REIT:		Property Management:	Y	Commercial Sales:	
Malls/Shopping:		Title Insurance:		Residential Construction:				Online Services:		Residential Sales:	
Offices:		Property Insurance:		Land Development:				Software/IT:		Specialty:	
Hotels/Motels:				Support Services:				Consulting:			
Industrial/Warehouses:				Design/Engineering:							
Other:	Y										

TYPES OF BUSINESS:

Long-Term Health Care
Assisted Living Centers
Independent Living Centers
Nursing Homes

BRANDS/DIVISIONS/AFFILIATES:

Sunrise Assisted Living

CONTACTS:

Note: Officers with more than one job title may be intentionally listed here more than once.

Mark S. Ordan, CEO
Julie A. Pangelinan, CFO
Jeffery M. Jasnoff, Sr. VP-Human Resources
Meghan Lublin, Sr. Dir.-Corp. Comm.
Meghan Lublin, Sr. Dir.-Investor Comm.
Julie A. Pangelinan, Treas.
Teresa M. Klaassen, Chief Cultural Officer
Greg Neeb, Chief Investment Officer
Paul J. Klaassen, Chmn.

Phone: 703-273-7500 **Fax:** 703-744-1601
Toll-Free: 888-434-4648
Address: 7902 Westpark Dr., McLean, VA 22102 US

GROWTH PLANS/SPECIAL FEATURES:

Sunrise Senior Living is an international provider of senior living services. The firm operates approximately 335 senior living communities in the U.S., 27 in the U.K., seven in Germany and 15 in Canada, with a resident capacity of approximately 40,400. These 384 communities include 201 that Sunrise owns in unconsolidated ventures; 135 that are owned by third parties; 27 operated under leases; 20 that the company wholly owns; and one consolidated as a variable interest entity. Sunrise Senior Living offers services tailored to the unique needs of each of its residents, typically in apartment-like assisted living environments. Upon move-in, Sunrise assists the resident in developing an individualized service plan, including selection of resident accommodations and the appropriate level of care. Services provided range from basic care, consisting of assistance with activities of daily living; to reminiscence care, which consists of programs and services to help cognitively impaired residents, including residents with Alzheimer's disease. The firm targets sites for development located in major metropolitan areas and their surrounding suburban communities, considering factors such as population, age demographics and estimated level of market demand. In 2009, the firm opened a total of 23 facilities with a combined occupant capacity of 2,100. In November 2009, Sunrise sold 21 of its wholly owned assisted living communities to BLC Acquisitions, Inc., an affiliate of Brookdale Senior Living Inc., for roughly $204 million.

Sunrise offers employees health, dental, vision, disability and life insurance; flexible spending accounts; a scholarship program; tuition assistance; a meal discount program; and a 401(k).

FINANCIALS:

Sales and profits are in thousands of dollars—add 000 to get the full amount. 2009 Note: Financial information for 2009 was not available for all companies at press time.

2009 Sales: $1,464,144	2009 Profits: $-133,915
2008 Sales: $1,570,974	2008 Profits: $-439,179
2007 Sales: $1,482,020	2007 Profits: $-70,275
2006 Sales: $1,628,605	2006 Profits: $15,284
2005 Sales: $1,509,438	2005 Profits: $87,089

U.S. Stock Ticker: SRZ
Int'l Ticker: Int'l Exchange:
Employees: 37,600
Fiscal Year Ends: 12/31
Parent Company:

SALARIES/BENEFITS:

Pension Plan:	ESOP Stock Plan:	Profit Sharing:	Top Exec. Salary: $652,500	Bonus: $1,775,000
Savings Plan: Y	Stock Purch. Plan: Y		Second Exec. Salary: $401,538	Bonus: $710,000

OTHER THOUGHTS:

Apparent Women Officers or Directors: 4
Hot Spot for Advancement for Women/Minorities: Y

LOCATIONS: ("Y" = Yes)

West:	Southwest:	Midwest:	Southeast:	Northeast:	International:
Y	Y	Y	Y	Y	Y

SUNSTONE HOTEL INVESTORS INC

www.sunstonehotels.com

Industry Group Code: 531120 **Ranks within this company's industry group:** Sales: 20 Profits: 28

Properties:		Financial Services:		Construction/Development:		Investments:		Specialty Services:		Brokerage:	
Apartments:		Mortgages:		Commercial Construction:		REIT:	Y	Property Management:		Commercial Sales:	
Malls/Shopping:		Title Insurance:		Residential Construction:				Online Services:	Y	Residential Sales:	
Offices:		Property Insurance:		Land Development:				Software/IT:		Specialty:	
Hotels/Motels:	Y			Support Services:				Consulting:			
Industrial/Warehouses:				Design/Engineering:							
Other:											

TYPES OF BUSINESS:

Real Estate Investment Trust
Hotel Ownership
Online Purchasing Systems

BRANDS/DIVISIONS/AFFILIATES:

Sunstone Hotel TRS Lessee Inc
Sunstone Hotel Properties Inc
Interstate Hotels and Resorts Inc
Strategic Hotels and Resorts Inc
BuyEfficient LLC

CONTACTS: *Note: Officers with more than one job title may be intentionally listed here more than once.*

Arthur L. Buser, CEO
Marc A. Hoffman, COO/Exec. VP
Arthur L. Buser, Pres.
Kenneth E. Cruse, CFO/Exec. VP
David Sloan, VP-Legal
Bryan Giglia, Sr. VP-Finance
Oliver Kolpin, VP-Tax
Denise Hertle, VP-Corp. Acct.
Michael Harvey, VP-Asset Mgmt.
W. Guy Lindsey, Sr. VP-Design & Construction
Robert A. Alter, Exec. Chmn.

Phone: 949-369-4000	**Fax:** 949-369-4110
Toll-Free:	
Address: 903 Calle Amanecer, Ste. 100, San Clemente, CA 92673 US	

GROWTH PLANS/SPECIAL FEATURES:

Sunstone Hotel Investors, Inc., a REIT (Real Estate Investment Trust), acquires, owns, asset manages and renovates primarily luxury, upper upscale and upscale full service hotels. Sunstone owns 29 hotels with a total of 10,966 rooms, located in 13 U.S. states and Washington, D.C. The firm's portfolio includes 27 upscale or upper upscale hotels, one luxury hotel and one mid-scale hotel. Sunstone also owns a 38% equity interest in the 460-room Doubletree Guest Suites Hotel Times Square in New York. Third-party managers operate the company's hotels through agreements with wholly-owned subsidiary Sunstone Hotel TRS Lessee, Inc. Approximately 15 hotels are operated by Sunstone Hotel Properties Inc., a division of Interstate Hotels and Resorts, Inc. Other hotels are managed as follows: subsidiaries of either Marriott International, Inc. or Marriot Services, Inc. operate 11 of the firm's hotels; and Hyatt Corporation, Fairmont Hotels & Resorts and Hilton Hotels Corp. operate one hotel each. Sunstone specializes in acquiring under-performing properties and developing them into profitable upscale and luxury properties. The firm prefers to acquire major brand properties situated in one of the top 25 U.S. markets, with upscale potential and a location with high barriers to entry. Besides its normal operations, the firm has a joint venture, BuyEfficient, LLC, an electronic purchasing management platform that helps to simplify procurement and accounting activities.

FINANCIALS: **Sales and profits are in thousands of dollars—add 000 to get the full amount. 2009 Note: Financial information for 2009 was not available for all companies at press time.**

2009 Sales: $717,823	2009 Profits: $-269,608	**U.S. Stock Ticker: SHO**
2008 Sales: $881,494	2008 Profits: $71,238	**Int'l Ticker:** Int'l Exchange:
2007 Sales: $866,494	2007 Profits: $123,876	Employees: 30
2006 Sales: $771,219	2006 Profits: $53,237	Fiscal Year Ends: 12/31
2005 Sales: $541,747	2005 Profits: $30,205	Parent Company:

SALARIES/BENEFITS:

Pension Plan:	ESOP Stock Plan:	Profit Sharing:	Top Exec. Salary: $650,769	Bonus: $359,423
Savings Plan:	Stock Purch. Plan:		Second Exec. Salary: $317,354	Bonus: $44,760

OTHER THOUGHTS:

Apparent Women Officers or Directors: 2
Hot Spot for Advancement for Women/Minorities:

LOCATIONS: ("Y" = Yes)

West:	Southwest:	Midwest:	Southeast:	Northeast:	International:
Y	Y	Y	Y	Y	

SUPER 8 MOTELS INC

www.super8.com

Industry Group Code: 721110 **Ranks within this company's industry group:** Sales: Profits:

Properties:		Financial Services:		Construction/Development:		Investments:		Specialty Services:		Brokerage:	
Apartments:		Mortgages:		Commercial Construction:		REIT:		Property Management:		Commercial Sales:	
Malls/Shopping:		Title Insurance:		Residential Construction:				Online Services:	Y	Residential Sales:	
Offices:		Property Insurance:		Land Development:				Software/IT:		Specialty:	
Hotels/Motels:	Y			Support Services:				Consulting:			
Industrial/Warehouses:				Design/Engineering:							
Other:											

TYPES OF BUSINESS:

Hotel Franchising
Economy Motels
Online Reservations & Services

BRANDS/DIVISIONS/AFFILIATES:

Wyndham Worldwide
TripRewards
Guaranteed Best Rate
TripFinder

CONTACTS:

Note: Officers with more than one job title may be intentionally listed here more than once.

John Valletta, Pres.
Heny Gabay, VP-Mktg.
Jim Darby, VP-Oper.

Phone: 973-428-9700 **Fax:** 973-496-7307
Toll-Free: 800-800-8000
Address: 1 Sylvan Way, Parsippany, NJ 07054 US

GROWTH PLANS/SPECIAL FEATURES:

Super 8 Motels, Inc., a subsidiary of Wyndham Worldwide, is one of the world's largest franchised economy lodging chains, with a total of nearly 2,000 motels. The firm offers lodging for the budget traveler, with many rooms below $50 per night. Super 8 motels, which are found in every domestic state besides Hawaii and in every Canadian province, contain an average of 61 single rooms, totaling over 124,000 rooms. The company offers numerous promotions, such as guaranteed best rates, group and corporate rates and AAA and AARP discounts. Super 8 also offers TripFinder packages, which allow guests to construct their custom vacation package including hotel reservation, flight and rental car, as well as hotel package deals organized by the company around Super 8 properties. In addition, the firm is a member of Wyndham Rewards, one of the largest hotel reward programs in the world based on the 6,000 participating hotels. The program allows customers to earn points toward hotel stays, as well as airline miles, gifts, meals and other incentives. Super 8's web site offers customers a wide array of integrated travel resources, including flight tracking, driving directions, street maps, airport maps, destination guides and weather information, in addition to online reservations, location information and special promotional programs. A search feature can automatically find the Super 8 motel and room with the best available rate for a given date in the travel area. The company offers several in-room products and services, including in-room coffee makers, bath amenities and expanded breakfast choices.

FINANCIALS:

Sales and profits are in thousands of dollars—add 000 to get the full amount. 2009 Note: Financial information for 2009 was not available for all companies at press time.

2009 Sales: $ — 2009 Profits: $
2008 Sales: $ — 2008 Profits: $
2007 Sales: $1,335,800 — 2007 Profits: $
2006 Sales: $ — 2006 Profits: $
2005 Sales: $ — 2005 Profits: $

U.S. Stock Ticker: Subsidiary
Int'l Ticker: Int'l Exchange:
Employees:
Fiscal Year Ends: 12/31
Parent Company: WYNDHAM WORLDWIDE

SALARIES/BENEFITS:

Pension Plan: ESOP Stock Plan: Profit Sharing: Top Exec. Salary: $ Bonus: $
Savings Plan: Stock Purch. Plan: Second Exec. Salary: $ Bonus: $

OTHER THOUGHTS:

Apparent Women Officers or Directors:
Hot Spot for Advancement for Women/Minorities:

LOCATIONS: ("Y" = Yes)

West:	Southwest:	Midwest:	Southeast:	Northeast:	International:
Y	Y	Y	Y	Y	Y

SUPERTEL HOSPITALITY INC

www.supertelinc.com

Industry Group Code: 531120 **Ranks within this company's industry group:** Sales: 61 Profits: 51

Properties:		Financial Services:		Construction/Development:		Investments:		Specialty Services:		Brokerage:	
Apartments:		Mortgages:		Commercial Construction:		REIT:	Y	Property Management:		Commercial Sales:	
Malls/Shopping:		Title Insurance:		Residential Construction:				Online Services:		Residential Sales:	
Offices:		Property Insurance:		Land Development:				Software/IT:		Specialty:	
Hotels/Motels:	Y			Support Services:				Consulting:			
Industrial/Warehouses:				Design/Engineering:							
Other:											

TYPES OF BUSINESS:

Real Estate Investment Trust
Hotels & Motels

BRANDS/DIVISIONS/AFFILIATES:

Supertel Hospitality REIT Trust
E&P REIT Trust
Supertel Limited Partnership
E&P Financing Limited Partnership
Supertel Hospitality Management, Inc.
TRS Leasing, Inc.
Royco Hotels, Inc.
HLC Hotels, Inc

CONTACTS: *Note: Officers with more than one job title may be intentionally listed here more than once.*

Kelly A. Walters, CEO
Stephen C. Gilbert, COO
Kelly A. Walters, Pres.
Corrine L. Scarpello, CFO
Donavon A. Heimes, Sec.
Donavon A. Heimes, Treas./Sr. VP
William C. Latham, Chmn.

Phone: 402-371-2520	**Fax:** 402-371-4229
Toll-Free:	
Address: 309 N. 5th St., Norfolk, NE 68701 US	

GROWTH PLANS/SPECIAL FEATURES:

Supertel Hospitality, Inc. (SHI) is a self-administered REIT (Real Estate Investment Trust) primarily engaged in acquiring and owning hotels. Its portfolio includes 115 limited-service hotels in 24 states under the following franchise brands: Super 8; Comfort Inn/Comfort Suites; Days Inn; Hampton Inn; Holiday Inn Express; Ramada, Ltd.; Tara Inn; Baymont Inn; Key West Inns; Savannah Suites; Masters Inn; Supertel Inn; Guest House Inn/Guesthouse Inn and Suites; and Sleep Inn. Standard guestroom amenities include high-speed wireless Internet, free local calls, cable TV, including movie channels, and iron and ironing board. Select Supertel properties also have complimentary continental breakfast, pools, suites, conference centers and meeting facilities. Through its two wholly-owned subsidiaries, Supertel Hospitality REIT Trust and E&P REIT Trust, the firm owns a 99% interest in Supertel Limited Partnership and 100% of E&P Financing Limited Partnership. Together, these four firms, along with other subsidiaries and partnerships, own the firm's properties. Those other subsidiaries and partnerships include Supertel Hospitality Management, Inc.; SPPR-South Bend LLC; SPPR-Hotels LLC; SPPR-BMI LLC; and Solomon's Beacon Inn Limited Partnership. To enter into management agreements with independent contractors, in compliance with the REIT Modernization Act of 1999, Supertel created TRS Leasing, Inc. and its subsidiaries TRS Subsidiary LLC; SPPR TRS Subsidiary LLC; and SPPR-BMI TRS Subsidiary LLC. All SHI hotels are leased to TRS Leasing and are managed by Royco Hotels, Inc. and HLC Hotels, Inc. TRS also holds the firm's furniture, fixtures and equipment.

FINANCIALS: **Sales and profits are in thousands of dollars—add 000 to get the full amount. 2009 Note: Financial information for 2009 was not available for all companies at press time.**

2009 Sales: $88,970	2009 Profits: $-27,395	**U.S. Stock Ticker: SPPR**
2008 Sales: $99,256	2008 Profits: $6,656	**Int'l Ticker:** Int'l Exchange:
2007 Sales: $90,084	2007 Profits: $4,078	Employees: 1,557
2006 Sales: $77,134	2006 Profits: $3,721	Fiscal Year Ends: 12/31
2005 Sales: $60,537	2005 Profits: $2,778	Parent Company:

SALARIES/BENEFITS:

Pension Plan:	ESOP Stock Plan:	Profit Sharing:	Top Exec. Salary: $270,000	Bonus: $
Savings Plan:	Stock Purch. Plan:		Second Exec. Salary: $184,807	Bonus: $

OTHER THOUGHTS:

Apparent Women Officers or Directors:
Hot Spot for Advancement for Women/Minorities:

LOCATIONS: ("Y" = Yes)

West:	Southwest:	Midwest:	Southeast:	Northeast:	International:
Y		Y	Y	Y	

SWIRE PACIFIC LTD

www.swirepacific.com

Industry Group Code: 483111 **Ranks within this company's industry group:** Sales: 1 Profits: 1

Properties:		Financial Services:		Construction/Development:		Investments:		Specialty Services:		Brokerage:	
Apartments:	Y	Mortgages:		Commercial Construction:		REIT:		Property Management:		Commercial Sales:	
Malls/Shopping:	Y	Title Insurance:		Residential Construction:				Online Services:		Residential Sales:	
Offices:	Y	Property Insurance:		Land Development:				Software/IT:		Specialty:	
Hotels/Motels:	Y			Support Services:				Consulting:			
Industrial/Warehouses:				Design/Engineering:							
Other:											

TYPES OF BUSINESS:

Deep Sea Shipping
Airlines and Air Freight
International & Regional Airlines
Apparel Retail
Real Estate, Hotels, Commercial Properties
Aircraft Maintenance
Airline Catering Service
Beverage Manufacturing & Distribution

BRANDS/DIVISIONS/AFFILIATES:

Swire Group (The)
Swire Properties, Ltd.
Cathay Pacific Airways, Ltd.
Swire Beverages, Ltd.
Swire Resources, Ltd.
Swire Pacific Offshore Holdings
HUD Group (The)
Hong Kong Dragon Airlines (Dragonair)

CONTACTS:

Note: Officers with more than one job title may be intentionally listed here more than once.

Christopher Dale Pratt, Managing Dir.
Peter Alan Kilgour, Exec. Dir.-Group Finance
Yat Hung David Fu, Corp. Sec.
Antony Nigel Tyler, CEO-Cathay Pacific Airways, Ltd.
Geoffrey Leslie Cundle, Exec. Dir.-Beverages Div.
John Bruce Rae-Smith, Exec. Dir.-Swire Pacific Offshore
Christopher D. Pratt, Chmn.

Phone: 852-2840-8098 **Fax:** 852-2526-9365
Toll-Free:
Address: 2 Pacific Place, 88 Queensway, 35th Fl., Hong Kong, China

GROWTH PLANS/SPECIAL FEATURES:

Swire Pacific Ltd., is part of the Swire Group and one of Hong Kong's leading listed companies. It operates several core businesses, organized into five divisions: property; aviation; beverages; marine services; and trading and industrial. Swire Properties, Ltd., a property developer based in Hong Kong, has invested in roughly 17.8 million square feet of real estate. Swire Properties, Inc., its U.S. subsidiary, develops and trades properties in Florida, specifically downtown Miami, including office space, retail space and hotels. The company's aviation holdings include international passenger and freight airline Cathay Pacific Airways, Ltd., with nearly 120 worldwide destinations; an all-cargo carrier, AHK Air Hong Kong Ltd.; Cathay Pacific subsidiary, Hong Kong Dragon Airlines (Dragonair), with more than 30 Asian destinations and cargo operations in Asia, Europe, the U.S. and the Middle East; Hong Kong Air Cargo Terminals, with a handling capacity of 3.5 million tons annually; and a leading Asian aeronautical engineering company, Hong Kong Aircraft Engineering Company, a provider of base and line maintenance at Hong Kong International Airport. Swire Beverages, Ltd. owns the franchise to manufacture and distribute Coca-Cola products in Hong Kong, Taiwan, 11 U.S. states and seven provinces in China, representing a total franchise population of over 420 million. Swire Beverages is one of The Coca-Cola Company's major international bottlers and works with Coca-Cola on brand development and marketing. The firm's marine services holdings include Swire Pacific Offshore Holdings Ltd., one of the largest offshore energy support fleets in the world, with over 70 vessels; the HUD Group, which provides ship repair, towage and salvage, mechanical and electrical engineering and steelwork services; and Swire Pacific Ship Management Ltd., a provider of fleet personnel services. Trading and industrial subsidiary Swire Resources acts as the holding company for various retail and wholesale interests in sports and active footwear and apparel, operating more than 200 retail locations in China.

FINANCIALS:

Sales and profits are in thousands of dollars—add 000 to get the full amount. 2009 Note: Financial information for 2009 was not available for all companies at press time.

2009 Sales: $3,209,370 — 2009 Profits: $2,565,380
2008 Sales: $3,183,030 — 2008 Profits: $215,210
2007 Sales: $2,780,860 — 2007 Profits: $2,589,000
2006 Sales: $2,445,120 — 2006 Profits: $1,115,150
2005 Sales: $2,440,520 — 2005 Profits: $1,054,460

U.S. Stock Ticker: SWRAY
Int'l Ticker: 0019 Int'l Exchange: Hong Kong-HKEX
Employees:
Fiscal Year Ends: 12/31
Parent Company:

SALARIES/BENEFITS:

Pension Plan: ESOP Stock Plan: Profit Sharing: Top Exec. Salary: $ Bonus: $
Savings Plan: Stock Purch. Plan: Second Exec. Salary: $ Bonus: $

OTHER THOUGHTS:

Apparent Women Officers or Directors: 2
Hot Spot for Advancement for Women/Minorities: Y

LOCATIONS: ("Y" = Yes)

West:	Southwest:	Midwest:	Southeast:	Northeast:	International:
Y	Y	Y		Y	Y

TANGER FACTORY OUTLET CENTERS

www.tangeroutlet.com

Industry Group Code: 531120 **Ranks within this company's industry group:** Sales: 51 Profits: 45

Properties:		Financial Services:		Construction/Development:		Investments:		Specialty Services:		Brokerage:	
Apartments:		Mortgages:		Commercial Construction:		REIT:	Y	Property Management:	Y	Commercial Sales:	
Malls/Shopping:	Y	Title Insurance:		Residential Construction:				Online Services:		Residential Sales:	
Offices:		Property Insurance:		Land Development:				Software/IT:		Specialty:	
Hotels/Motels:				Support Services:				Consulting:			
Industrial/Warehouses:				Design/Engineering:							
Other:											

TYPES OF BUSINESS:

Factory Outlet Shopping Centers
Real Estate Investment Trust
Property Management

BRANDS/DIVISIONS/AFFILIATES:

Tanger Outlet Centers
Relax, It's Guaranteed
TangerClub

CONTACTS:

Note: Officers with more than one job title may be intentionally listed here more than once.

Steven B. Tanger, CEO
Steven B. Tanger, Pres.
Frank C. Marchisello, Jr., CFO/Exec. VP
Carrie A. Warren, Sr. VP-Mktg.
Mary Anne Williams, VP-Human Resources
Ricky L. Farrar, VP-Info. Systems
Patti Ross, Dir.-Admin.
Frank C. Marchisello, Jr., Corp. Sec.
Betty Coleman, Sr. VP-Oper.
Virgina R. Summerell, VP-Finance/Treas.
Lisa J. Morrison, Sr. VP-Leasing
James F. Williams, Sr. VP/Controller
Kevin M. Dillon, Sr. VP-Construction & Site Selection
Jack Africk, Interim Chmn.

Phone: 336-292-3010 **Fax:** 336-852-2096
Toll-Free:
Address: 3200 Northline Ave., Ste. 360, Greensboro, NC 27408 US

GROWTH PLANS/SPECIAL FEATURES:

Tanger Factory Outlet Centers, Inc. (Tanger) is a self-administered and self-managed real estate investment trust (REIT). Through operating subsidiary Tanger Properties Limited Partnership, the company develops, acquires, owns, operates and manages factory outlet shopping centers under the brand name Tanger Outlet Center. The firm owns 33 centers in 22 states with a total gross leasable area of approximately 10.2 million square feet of retail space containing over 2,200 stores. Through unconsolidated joint ventures, Tanger also operates and owns interest in two outlet centers with approximately 950,000 square feet. Tanger Outlet Centers typically incorporate a mix of leading designer and brand name manufacturers, allowing customers to buy discounted products directly from the manufacturer. In addition, frequent shoppers are eligible for TangerClub membership, entitling them to various seasonal discounts, special coupons and fee waivers. The firm also has a money-back, low-price guarantee program called 'Relax, It's Guaranteed,' which gives customers a cash refund equal to the difference in price. The roughly 330 brand names sold at Tanger Outlet Centers include Liz Claiborne, GAP, Old Navy, Polo Ralph Lauren, Adidas, Nike, Tommy Hilfiger, Nautica, Maurice's and Reebok. In December 2009, the firm began construction on a new 317,000 square foot, 80-store outlet location in Mebane, North Carolina.

FINANCIALS:

Sales and profits are in thousands of dollars—add 000 to get the full amount. 2009 Note: Financial information for 2009 was not available for all companies at press time.

2009 Sales: $271,685	2009 Profits: $58,019	**U.S. Stock Ticker: SKT**
2008 Sales: $245,391	2008 Profits: $25,786	**Int'l Ticker:** Int'l Exchange:
2007 Sales: $228,765	2007 Profits: $26,458	Employees: 407
2006 Sales: $210,962	2006 Profits: $37,309	Fiscal Year Ends: 12/31
2005 Sales: $197,949	2005 Profits: $5,089	Parent Company:

SALARIES/BENEFITS:

Pension Plan:	ESOP Stock Plan:	Profit Sharing:	Top Exec. Salary: $538,900	Bonus: $931,250
Savings Plan:	Stock Purch. Plan:		Second Exec. Salary: $438,020	Bonus: $652,650

OTHER THOUGHTS:

Apparent Women Officers or Directors: 7
Hot Spot for Advancement for Women/Minorities: Y

LOCATIONS: ("Y" = Yes)

West:	Southwest:	Midwest:	Southeast:	Northeast:	International:
Y	Y	Y	Y	Y	

TARRAGON CORPORATION

www.tarragoncorp.com

Industry Group Code: 5311 **Ranks within this company's industry group:** Sales: Profits:

Properties:		Financial Services:		Construction/Development:		Investments:		Specialty Services:		Brokerage:	
Apartments:	Y	Mortgages:		Commercial Construction:		REIT:		Property Management:	Y	Commercial Sales:	
Malls/Shopping:		Title Insurance:		Residential Construction:	Y			Online Services:		Residential Sales:	
Offices:	Y	Property Insurance:		Land Development:	Y			Software/IT:		Specialty:	
Hotels/Motels:				Support Services:				Consulting:			
Industrial/Warehouses:				Design/Engineering:							
Other:											

TYPES OF BUSINESS:

Real Estate Operations
Apartment Communities
Property Management
Real Estate Development
Office & Retail Properties
Condominium Conversions
Planned Communities

BRANDS/DIVISIONS/AFFILIATES:

GROWTH PLANS/SPECIAL FEATURES:

Tarragon Corporation develops, owns and manages real estate. It operates the Real Estate Development Division, run by wholly-owned subsidiary Tarragon Development, Inc.; and the Investment Division, run by wholly-owned subsidiary Tarragon Management, Inc. The Development Division concentrates on five areas: Developing low- and mid-rise rental apartment communities; high- and mid-rise condominiums designed for luxury and urban living; townhomes, traditional and new developments and low-rise condominiums ranging in price from $219,000 to $500,000 or more; and converting apartment communities into condominiums. The Investment Division focuses on property management, mainly for third parties; opportunistic acquisitions through joint ventures; property sales; and complementary financial services. In early 2009, Tarragon Corporation filed for Chapter 11 bankruptcy protection. The firm plans to emerge from Chapter 11 in June 2010.

CONTACTS:

Note: Officers with more than one job title may be intentionally listed here more than once.

William S. Friedman, CEO
Robert P. Rothenberg, COO
Robert P. Rothenberg, Pres.
Erin D. Pickens, CFO/Exec. VP
Kathryn Mansfield, General Counsel/Sec./Exec. VP
Todd C. Minor, Treas./Exec. VP
Michael C. Johnson, Exec. VP-Tarragon Mgmt.
William J. Rosato, Pres., Tarragon Dev. Corp.
Charles Rubenstein, Chief Real Estate Counsel/Exec. VP
William S. Friedman, Chmn.

Phone: 212-949-5000 **Fax:** 212-949-8001
Toll-Free:
Address: 423 W. 55th St., 12th Fl., New York, NY 10019 US

FINANCIALS:

Sales and profits are in thousands of dollars—add 000 to get the full amount. 2009 Note: Financial information for 2009 was not available for all companies at press time.

2009 Sales: $	2009 Profits: $	**U.S. Stock Ticker: TARR**
2008 Sales: $	2008 Profits: $	**Int'l Ticker:** Int'l Exchange:
2007 Sales: $358,911	2007 Profits: $-388,441	Employees:
2006 Sales: $444,274	2006 Profits: $11,153	Fiscal Year Ends: 12/31
2005 Sales: $504,722	2005 Profits: $88,498	Parent Company:

SALARIES/BENEFITS:

Pension Plan:	ESOP Stock Plan:	Profit Sharing:	Top Exec. Salary: $	Bonus: $
Savings Plan:	Stock Purch. Plan:		Second Exec. Salary: $	Bonus: $

OTHER THOUGHTS:

Apparent Women Officers or Directors: 3
Hot Spot for Advancement for Women/Minorities: Y

LOCATIONS: ("Y" = Yes)

West:	Southwest:	Midwest:	Southeast:	Northeast:	International:
	Y		Y	Y	

TAUBMAN CENTERS INC

www.taubman.com

Industry Group Code: 531120 **Ranks within this company's industry group:** Sales: 27 Profits: 54

Properties:		Financial Services:		Construction/Development:		Investments:		Specialty Services:		Brokerage:	
Apartments:		Mortgages:		Commercial Construction:		REIT:	Y	Property Management:	Y	Commercial Sales:	
Malls/Shopping:	Y	Title Insurance:		Residential Construction:				Online Services:		Residential Sales:	
Offices:		Property Insurance:		Land Development:				Software/IT:		Specialty:	
Hotels/Motels:				Support Services:				Consulting:			
Industrial/Warehouses:				Design/Engineering:							
Other:											

TYPES OF BUSINESS:

Real Estate Investment Trust
Malls & Shopping Centers
Property Management

BRANDS/DIVISIONS/AFFILIATES:

Taubman Realty Group Ltd. Partnership (The)
Taubman Company LLC (The)
Taubman Asia

CONTACTS: *Note: Officers with more than one job title may be intentionally listed here more than once.*

Robert S. Taubman, CEO
William S. Taubman, COO
Robert S. Taubman, Pres.
Lisa A. Payne, CFO
Glenda Cole, VP-Mktg. & Sponsorship
Robert R. Reese, Chief Admin. Officer/Sr. VP
Chris B. Heaphy, General Counsel/Sr. VP/Corp. Sec.
Steven J. Kieras, Sr. VP-Dev.
Karen MacDonald, Dir.-Comm.
Barbara Baker, VP-Investor Rel.
Esther R. Blum, Chief Acct. Officer/Sr. VP/Controller
Denise Anton, Sr. VP-Center Oper.
Steven E. Eder, Treas./Sr. VP
David T. Weinert, Sr. VP-Leasing
Robert S. Taubman, Chmn.
Morgan Parker, Pres., Taubman Asia

Phone: 248-258-6800 **Fax:** 248-258-7596
Toll-Free:
Address: 200 E. Long Lake Rd., Ste. 300, Bloomfield Hills, MI 48304 US

GROWTH PLANS/SPECIAL FEATURES:

Taubman Centers, Inc. is a real estate investment trust (REIT) that owns, develops, acquires and operates regional luxury shopping centers. Headquartered in Michigan with offices in the San Francisco Bay area, Virginia and New York, the company's portfolio includes 23 urban and suburban shopping centers in ten states, 18 of which are super-regional shopping centers. Taubman Centers owns a majority interest in The Taubman Realty Group Ltd. Partnership, through which all operations are conducted. The Taubman Realty Group Ltd. Partnership also owns certain regional retail shopping center development projects and majority interest in The Taubman Company LLC, which manages the shopping centers and provides other services to the operating partnership. 90% of the firm's revenue comes from national retail chains such as Forever 21, Limited Brands and The Gap. Taubman Asia is the platform for Taubman's expansion into the Asia-Pacific region; it is headquartered in Hong Kong and is engaged in projects that leverage the company's retail planning, design and operational capabilities. In 2009, Taubman's malls averaged sales per square foot of store space of $498, an amount that is significantly higher than most other mall operators.

The company offers its employees medical, dental, vision, prescription drug and domestic partner benefits; life and AD&D insurance; short- and long-term disability; flexible spending accounts; an employee assistance program; and pet insurance.

FINANCIALS: **Sales and profits are in thousands of dollars—add 000 to get the full amount. 2009 Note: Financial information for 2009 was not available for all companies at press time.**

2009 Sales: $666,104	2009 Profits: $-79,161	**U.S. Stock Ticker: TCO**
2008 Sales: $671,498	2008 Profits: $-8,052	**Int'l Ticker:** Int'l Exchange:
2007 Sales: $626,822	2007 Profits: $116,236	Employees: 590
2006 Sales: $579,284	2006 Profits: $45,117	Fiscal Year Ends: 12/31
2005 Sales: $479,405	2005 Profits: $71,735	Parent Company:

SALARIES/BENEFITS:

Pension Plan: Y	ESOP Stock Plan:	Profit Sharing:	Top Exec. Salary: $825,000	Bonus: $
Savings Plan: Y	Stock Purch. Plan:		Second Exec. Salary: $677,625	Bonus: $

OTHER THOUGHTS:

Apparent Women Officers or Directors: 3
Hot Spot for Advancement for Women/Minorities: Y

LOCATIONS: ("Y" = Yes)

West:	Southwest:	Midwest:	Southeast:	Northeast:	International:
Y	Y	Y	Y	Y	Y

TDINDUSTRIES

www.tdindustries.com

Industry Group Code: 237 **Ranks within this company's industry group:** Sales: Profits:

Properties:		Financial Services:		Construction/Development:		Investments:		Specialty Services:		Brokerage:	
Apartments:		Mortgages:		Commercial Construction:	Y	REIT:		Property Management:		Commercial Sales:	
Malls/Shopping:		Title Insurance:		Residential Construction:	Y			Online Services:		Residential Sales:	
Offices:	Y	Property Insurance:		Land Development:	Y			Software/IT:		Specialty:	
Hotels/Motels:	Y			Support Services:	Y			Consulting:			
Industrial/Warehouses:	Y			Design/Engineering:	Y						
Other:											

TYPES OF BUSINESS:

Construction
Facilities Services
HVAC

BRANDS/DIVISIONS/AFFILIATES:

Camden Development Inc
Clark Construction Group
Fairfield Development
Gables Residential
Hanover Company (The)
Trammell Crow Residential
ServiceLink Wireless Technology
Building Protection Systems Inc

CONTACTS:

Note: Officers with more than one job title may be intentionally listed here more than once.

Harold MacDowell, CEO
Mike Fitzpatrick, CFO
Maureen Underwood, Sr. VP-People Dept.
Jim Bivins, VP-IT
Jason Cinek, VP-Tech.
L. Steve Canter, Sr. VP-Eng.
L. Steve Canter, Sr. VP-Mfg.
Rod Johannsen, Pres., North Texas Construction
Graham T. Moore, Pres., Houston
Bob Richards, Pres., Central Texas
Ed Reeve, Exec. VP-Major Projects
John B. Lowe Jr, Chmn.

Phone: 972-888-9500	**Fax:** 972-888-9507
Toll-Free:	
Address: 13850 Diplomat Dr., Dallas, TX 75234-8849 US	

GROWTH PLANS/SPECIAL FEATURES:

TDIndustries is a leading facilities service and specialty construction company. The Dallas, Texas-based firm offers construction, installation and operations services for commercial, industrial and institutional buildings in these following industries: education, food service, government, healthcare, historic properties, hotels, multifamily, sports and assembly, pharmaceutical, semiconductor manufacturing and telecom. The company offers its services in these key areas: heating ventilation, air conditioning, electrical, mechanical, millwright, steel fabrication, life safety, facilities management, plumbing, process and high purity piping, life cycle planning, building automation refrigeration and specialty fabrication and installation. The firm provides services in the energy and environment sector, which includes energy audits and energy efficiency modeling of buildings; and the design and construction of LEED (Leadership in Energy and Environmental Design) buildings. Lastly, the company constructs intelligent buildings, which monitors security, controls heating, and air conditioning throughout the property. The firm has construction partnerships with Camden Development, Inc., Clark Construction Group, Fairfield Development, Gables Residential, The Hanover Company and Trammell Crow Residential. Prominent clients include Dallas Cowboys Stadium, the Texas Governor's Mansion and Tyson Foods. In 2009, the company launched the ServiceLink Wireless Technology, which ensures accuracy in reporting of time and billing. In January 2010, TDIndustries signed an exclusive distribution contract with Building Protection Systems, Inc. (BPSI), to provide and distribute the CBRN (Chemical, Biological, Radiological, Nuclear) detection system for Texas and Arizona.

Employees of the firm are offered an employee stock option program. TDIndustries is 100%-owned by its over 900 employees and retirees with no one employee controlling more than 3% of the company's stock. TDIndustries was ranked 37 on FORTUNE magazine's 100 Best Companies to Work For List. The firm has consistently earned placement on the prestigious list since its inception and as a result holds Fortune's All Star distinction, an honor only held by 13 companies.

FINANCIALS:

Sales and profits are in thousands of dollars—add 000 to get the full amount. 2009 Note: Financial information for 2009 was not available for all companies at press time.

2009 Sales: $	2009 Profits: $	**U.S. Stock Ticker: Private**
2008 Sales: $	2008 Profits: $	**Int'l Ticker:** Int'l Exchange:
2007 Sales: $	2007 Profits: $	Employees: 1,713
2006 Sales: $	2006 Profits: $	Fiscal Year Ends: 12/31
2005 Sales: $	2005 Profits: $	Parent Company:

SALARIES/BENEFITS:

Pension Plan:	ESOP Stock Plan: Y	Profit Sharing:	Top Exec. Salary: $	Bonus: $
Savings Plan:	Stock Purch. Plan:		Second Exec. Salary: $	Bonus: $

OTHER THOUGHTS:

Apparent Women Officers or Directors: 1
Hot Spot for Advancement for Women/Minorities:

LOCATIONS: ("Y" = Yes)

West:	Southwest:	Midwest:	Southeast:	Northeast:	International:
	Y				

TECHNICAL OLYMPIC USA INC

www.tousa.com

Industry Group Code: 2361 **Ranks within this company's industry group:** Sales: Profits:

Properties:		Financial Services:		Construction/Development:		Investments:		Specialty Services:		Brokerage:	
Apartments:		Mortgages:	Y	Commercial Construction:		REIT:		Property Management:		Commercial Sales:	
Malls/Shopping:		Title Insurance:	Y	Residential Construction:	Y			Online Services:		Residential Sales:	
Offices:		Property Insurance:	Y	Land Development:				Software/IT:		Specialty:	
Hotels/Motels:				Support Services:				Consulting:			
Industrial/Warehouses:				Design/Engineering:							
Other:											

TYPES OF BUSINESS:

Residential Construction
Closing & Settlement Services
Mortgages
Title & Homeowner's Insurance

BRANDS/DIVISIONS/AFFILIATES:

TOUSA Homes Inc
Engle Homes
Newmark Homes
Fedrick, Harris Estate Homes
Trophy Homes
Universal Land Title Inc
Preferred Home Mortgage Company

CONTACTS:

Note: Officers with more than one job title may be intentionally listed here more than once.
Tommy L. McAden, CFO/Exec. VP
George Yeonas, Exec. VP/COO-Homebuilding Oper.
Angie Valdes, Chief Acct. Officer
Peter J. Strawser, Pres., Preferred Home Mortgage Company

Phone: 954-364-4000 **Fax:** 954-364-4010
Toll-Free:
Address: 4000 Hollywood Blvd., Ste. 500 N., Hollywood, FL 33021 US

GROWTH PLANS/SPECIAL FEATURES:

Technical Olympic USA, Inc. (TOUSA) designs, builds and markets detached single-family residences, town homes and condominiums. It builds homes through subsidiary TOUSA Homes, Inc., operating in five states: Texas, Virginia, Colorado, Tennessee and Arizona. TOUSA markets its homes to a diverse group of homebuyers, including first-time, move-up and active-adult homebuyers; buyers who are relocating to a new city or state; and those buying a second or vacation home. Houses are marketed under the brand names Engle Homes in Texas, Colorado, Arizona and Virginia; Newmark Homes and Fedrick, Harris Estate Homes (a division of Newmark Homes) in Texas and Tennessee; and Trophy Homes in Texas. The company also offers complementary financial services, providing mortgage financing, closing and settlement services and offers title, homeowners' and other insurance products. These services are marketed through subsidiaries Preferred Home Mortgage Company and Universal Land Title, Inc. TOUSA selects its target markets based on population growth; projected job and income growth; regional economic conditions; availability of management with local expertise; single-family home permit activity and price; housing inventory and secondary home sales activity, among other criteria. The firm and many of its non-financial services subsidiaries are currently in Chapter 11 bankruptcy. The company is in the process of reorganization with the intent to emerge from Chapter 11. In early 2010, TOUSA sold 5,449 undeveloped lots and 36 model homes to Starwood Land Ventures, LLC for roughly $81 million. The property sold represented the vast majority of the firm's Florida operations.

FINANCIALS:

Sales and profits are in thousands of dollars—add 000 to get the full amount. 2009 Note: Financial information for 2009 was not available for all companies at press time.

2009 Sales: $	2009 Profits: $	**U.S. Stock Ticker: TOUSQ**
2008 Sales: $	2008 Profits: $	**Int'l Ticker:** Int'l Exchange:
2007 Sales: $2,195,300	2007 Profits: $-1,347,200	Employees:
2006 Sales: $2,441,300	2006 Profits: $-201,200	Fiscal Year Ends: 12/31
2005 Sales: $2,461,500	2005 Profits: $218,300	Parent Company:

SALARIES/BENEFITS:

Pension Plan:	ESOP Stock Plan:	Profit Sharing:	Top Exec. Salary: $	Bonus: $
Savings Plan:	Stock Purch. Plan:		Second Exec. Salary: $	Bonus: $

OTHER THOUGHTS:

Apparent Women Officers or Directors: 3
Hot Spot for Advancement for Women/Minorities: Y

LOCATIONS: ("Y" = Yes)

West:	Southwest:	Midwest:	Southeast:	Northeast:	International:
Y	Y		Y	Y	

THARALDSON ENTERPRISES INC

www.tharaldson.com

Industry Group Code: 721110 **Ranks within this company's industry group:** Sales: Profits:

Properties:		Financial Services:		Construction/Development:		Investments:		Specialty Services:		Brokerage:	
Apartments:		Mortgages:		Commercial Construction:		REIT:		Property Management:	Y	Commercial Sales:	
Malls/Shopping:		Title Insurance:		Residential Construction:				Online Services:		Residential Sales:	
Offices:		Property Insurance:		Land Development:				Software/IT:		Specialty:	
Hotels/Motels:	Y			Support Services:				Consulting:			
Industrial/Warehouses:				Design/Engineering:							
Other:											

TYPES OF BUSINESS:

Hotels
Construction Services
Communications Services
Property Management

BRANDS/DIVISIONS/AFFILIATES:

Tharaldson Property Management, Inc.
Tharaldson Development Company, Inc.
Tharaldson Communications
Tharaldson Lodging Co.
Room In The Inn Program
Courtyard
Residence Inn
Fairfield Inn

CONTACTS:

Note: Officers with more than one job title may be intentionally listed here more than once.

Richard Larson, Pres.
Douglas Dobmeier, Sr. VP-Oper.
Annette Croves, Controller
Charles A. Krumwiede, VP-Oper. & Property Support

Phone: 701-235-1060	**Fax:** 701-235-0948
Toll-Free:	
Address: 1202 Westrac Dr., Fargo, ND 58103-2344 US	

GROWTH PLANS/SPECIAL FEATURES:

Tharaldson Enterprises, Inc. builds and operates select-service and extended-service hotels across the U.S. The firm's Tharaldson Property Management, Inc. subsidiary is a leading independent hotel property-management company in the U.S., operating 222 hotels in 30 states. Tharaldson Communications, Inc. provides nationwide telecommunications services to the hospitality industry. Tharaldson Development Company, Inc., one of the largest developers of new hotels in the U.S., has more than 20 hotel projects currently in development. Tharaldson Enterprises operates properties under brand names including Courtyard, Residence Inn, Fairfield Inn, Springhill Suites and TownePlace Suites by Marriott; Homewood Suites and Hampton Inn by Hilton; Country Inn and Suites; Holiday Inn Express; and Comfort Inn and Suites. Tharaldson properties offer many amenities including cable television; indoor and outdoor pools; complimentary breakfast; free local phone calls; and 24-hour coffee service. In addition, children under 18 stay free. The firm also provides its Room In The Inn Program, which offers free rooms to guests visiting friends or family members in a hospital, nursing home or treatment facility during the Christmas and Thanksgiving seasons. In March 2010, the firm's Courtyard by Marriott brand redesigned its lobbies to a more open floor plan, offering the latest technology, healthy food and beverage options. The new redesigned lobby is based on consumer research and is designed to get consumers into the lobby.

Employees of the firm are offered tuition reimbursement, lodging discounts, a flexible spending account and medical, dental and life insurance. The company is 100% employee owned through its employee stock ownership program.

FINANCIALS:

Sales and profits are in thousands of dollars—add 000 to get the full amount. 2009 Note: Financial information for 2009 was not available for all companies at press time.

2009 Sales: $	2009 Profits: $	**U.S. Stock Ticker: Private**
2008 Sales: $	2008 Profits: $	**Int'l Ticker:** Int'l Exchange:
2007 Sales: $312,700	2007 Profits: $	Employees:
2006 Sales: $	2006 Profits: $	Fiscal Year Ends: 12/31
2005 Sales: $	2005 Profits: $	Parent Company:

SALARIES/BENEFITS:

Pension Plan:	ESOP Stock Plan: Y	Profit Sharing:	Top Exec. Salary: $	Bonus: $
Savings Plan: Y	Stock Purch. Plan:		Second Exec. Salary: $	Bonus: $

OTHER THOUGHTS:

Apparent Women Officers or Directors: 1
Hot Spot for Advancement for Women/Minorities: Y

LOCATIONS: ("Y" = Yes)

West:	Southwest:	Midwest:	Southeast:	Northeast:	International:
Y	Y	Y	Y	Y	

TOLL BROTHERS INC

www.tollbrothers.com

Industry Group Code: 2361 **Ranks within this company's industry group:** Sales: 8 Profits: 9

Properties:		Financial Services:		Construction/Development:		Investments:		Specialty Services:		Brokerage:	
Apartments:		Mortgages:	Y	Commercial Construction:		REIT:		Property Management:	Y	Commercial Sales:	
Malls/Shopping:		Title Insurance:		Residential Construction:	Y			Online Services:		Residential Sales:	Y
Offices:		Property Insurance:		Land Development:	Y			Software/IT:		Specialty:	
Hotels/Motels:				Support Services:	Y			Consulting:			
Industrial/Warehouses:				Design/Engineering:	Y						
Other:	Y										

TYPES OF BUSINESS:

Home Building
Mortgages & Insurance
Property Management
Landscaping
Country Club Communities
Golf Courses
Security Monitoring
Lumber Distribution

BRANDS/DIVISIONS/AFFILIATES:

CONTACTS:

Note: Officers with more than one job title may be intentionally listed here more than once.

Robert I. Toll, CEO
Zvi Barzilay, COO
Zvi Barzilay, Pres.
Joel H. Rassman, CFO/Exec. VP
Joel H. Rassman, Treas.
Douglas C. Yearley, Jr., Exec. VP
Robert I. Toll, Chmn.

Phone: 215-938-8000 **Fax:** 215-938-8010
Toll-Free: 800-289-8655
Address: 250 Gibralter Rd., Horsham, PA 19044 US

GROWTH PLANS/SPECIAL FEATURES:

Toll Brothers, Inc. designs, builds, markets and arranges financing for single-family detached and attached homes in luxury residential communities. The firm is also involved, both directly and through joint ventures, in building or converting existing rental apartment buildings into high-, mid- and low-rise luxury homes. Toll Brothers markets its services to move-up, empty-nester, active-adult, age-qualified and second-home buyers through its operations in 20 U.S. states. The company operates in major suburban and urban residential areas including the Philadelphia, Pennsylvania metropolitan area; the Eastern Shore of Maryland and Delaware; central and northern New Jersey; Washington, D.C.; Boston, Massachusetts; Westchester County, New York; Palm Springs, California; the San Francisco Bay area; Phoenix, Arizona; Las Vegas and Reno, Nevada; and Chicago, Illinois, among others. Toll Brothers emphasizes high-quality construction and customer satisfaction. The average base sales price of the company's homes is about $626,300 for detached homes and approximately $508,700 for attached homes. However, its typical home buyer often adds customized options and lot premiums, and prices can range to over $1.9 million. Toll Brothers operates its own land development, architectural, engineering, mortgage, title, landscaping, lumber distribution, house component assembly and manufacturing operations. In addition, the company owns and operates golf courses in conjunction with several of its master planned communities (of which it has 24). Over the past five years, the firm has delivered over 32,189 homes in 604 communities, including approximately 2,965 homes in 318 communities delivered in 2009. In June 2009, Toll Brothers began operating in Houston, Texas. Between late 2009 and early 2010, the company purchased or took control of roughly 3,000 housing sites throughout its various operating areas.

Toll Brothers offers its employees discounts on company-built homes; educational reimbursement; a 401(k) plan; a discount stock purchase plan; short and long term disability insurance; and medical and dental coverage.

FINANCIALS:

Sales and profits are in thousands of dollars—add 000 to get the full amount. 2009 Note: Financial information for 2009 was not available for all companies at press time.

2009 Sales: $1,755,310	2009 Profits: $-755,825	**U.S. Stock Ticker: TOL**
2008 Sales: $3,148,166	2008 Profits: $-297,810	**Int'l Ticker:** Int'l Exchange:
2007 Sales: $4,635,093	2007 Profits: $35,651	Employees: 2,066
2006 Sales: $6,123,453	2006 Profits: $687,213	Fiscal Year Ends: 10/31
2005 Sales: $5,793,425	2005 Profits: $806,110	Parent Company:

SALARIES/BENEFITS:

Pension Plan:	ESOP Stock Plan:	Profit Sharing:	Top Exec. Salary: $1,170,000	Bonus: $1,344,000
Savings Plan: Y	Stock Purch. Plan: Y		Second Exec. Salary: $1,000,000	Bonus: $1,672,000

OTHER THOUGHTS:

Apparent Women Officers or Directors: 1
Hot Spot for Advancement for Women/Minorities:

LOCATIONS: ("Y" = Yes)

West:	Southwest:	Midwest:	Southeast:	Northeast:	International:
Y	Y	Y	Y	Y	

TRACO

www.traco.com

Industry Group Code: 326199 **Ranks within this company's industry group:** Sales: Profits:

Properties:	Financial Services:	Construction/Development:		Investments:	Specialty Services:	Brokerage:
Apartments:	Mortgages:	Commercial Construction:		REIT:	Property Management:	Commercial Sales:
Malls/Shopping:	Title Insurance:	Residential Construction:			Online Services:	Residential Sales:
Offices:	Property Insurance:	Land Development:			Software/IT:	Specialty:
Hotels/Motels:		Support Services:	Y		Consulting:	
Industrial/Warehouses:		Design/Engineering:				
Other:						

TYPES OF BUSINESS:

Windows & Doors-Manufacturing

BRANDS/DIVISIONS/AFFILIATES:

NRG
Nexgen
Biscayne Windows and Doors
Valu
NX-3000
Three Rivers Aluminum Company

CONTACTS:

Note: Officers with more than one job title may be intentionally listed here more than once.

Robert P. Randall, CEO
Robert P. Randall, Pres.
Fran Stephen, CFO
Brett Randall, VP-Commercial Sales
Chris Randall, VP-Mfg.
Denise Abraham, Mgr.-Mktg. Comm.

Phone: 724-776-7000	**Fax:** 724-776-7014
Toll-Free: 800-837-7001	
Address: 71 Progress Ave., Cranberry Township, PA 16066 US	

GROWTH PLANS/SPECIAL FEATURES:

TRACO, formerly Three Rivers Aluminum Company, is a designer and manufacturer of custom-made windows and doors primarily for the commercial and residential real estate markets. The firm fashions impact resistant and energy efficient windows and doors, as well as entranceways, skylights sunrooms and curtain walls for buildings in the educational, healthcare, multi-family, office, hotel and government sectors. TRACO's areas of expertise include glass tempering, paint finishing, anodizing, glass insulating and aluminum extruding. The company provides products for new construction projects, as well as historical landmarks. TRACO has serviced notable buildings and structures such as the Empire State Building, the Statue of Liberty, the Waldorf Astoria and the Flat Iron Building in New York, the National Theatre in Washington D.C. and the College of William and Mary in Williamsburg, Virginia. Customers consist primarily of homeowners, general contractors, architects and developers. Commercial product lines include NRG, for aluminum window and door items; Nexgen, for glass and frame insulation; Biscayne Windows and Doors, for aluminum products designed for coastal environments; and Valu products for low-mid rise building applications. The firm sells its products through dealers and distributors nationwide. Recently, TRACO sold its residential vinyl replacement division to Echo Windows LLC. In early 2009, the company introduced the NX-3000 line of architectural windows with casement solutions designed to provide improved thermal insulation.

FINANCIALS:

Sales and profits are in thousands of dollars—add 000 to get the full amount. 2009 Note: Financial information for 2009 was not available for all companies at press time.

2009 Sales: $	2009 Profits: $	**U.S. Stock Ticker: Private**
2008 Sales: $	2008 Profits: $	**Int'l Ticker:** Int'l Exchange:
2007 Sales: $	2007 Profits: $	Employees:
2006 Sales: $	2006 Profits: $	Fiscal Year Ends: 12/31
2005 Sales: $	2005 Profits: $	Parent Company:

SALARIES/BENEFITS:

Pension Plan:	ESOP Stock Plan:	Profit Sharing:	Top Exec. Salary: $	Bonus: $
Savings Plan:	Stock Purch. Plan:		Second Exec. Salary: $	Bonus: $

OTHER THOUGHTS:

Apparent Women Officers or Directors: 2
Hot Spot for Advancement for Women/Minorities:

LOCATIONS: ("Y" = Yes)

West:	Southwest:	Midwest:	Southeast:	Northeast:	International:
				Y	

TRAMMELL CROW COMPANY

www.trammellcrow.com

Industry Group Code: 5311 **Ranks within this company's industry group:** Sales: Profits:

Properties:		Financial Services:		Construction/Development:		Investments:		Specialty Services:		Brokerage:	
Apartments:		Mortgages:		Commercial Construction:		REIT:		Property Management:	Y	Commercial Sales:	Y
Malls/Shopping:		Title Insurance:		Residential Construction:				Online Services:		Residential Sales:	
Offices:		Property Insurance:		Land Development:				Software/IT:		Specialty:	Y
Hotels/Motels:				Support Services:	Y			Consulting:	Y		
Industrial/Warehouses:				Design/Engineering:	Y						
Other:											

TYPES OF BUSINESS:

Real Estate Development & Investment Services
Building Management
Brokerage Services
Project Management Services
Development Services
Property & Facility Management

BRANDS/DIVISIONS/AFFILIATES:

Partners Health Trust
CB Richard Ellis

CONTACTS:

Note: Officers with more than one job title may be intentionally listed here more than once.

Robert E. Sulentic, CEO
Chris Kirk, COO
Chris Kirk, General Counsel
John Stirek, Pres., Western Oper.
Chris Roth, Pres., Northeast Oper.
Robert E. Sulentic, Chmn.

Phone: 214-863-4104 **Fax:** 214-863-3138
Toll-Free:
Address: 2001 Ross Ave., Ste. 3400, Dallas, TX 75201 US

GROWTH PLANS/SPECIAL FEATURES:

Trammell Crow Company, a subsidiary of CB Richard Ellis, is one of the largest diversified commercial real estate service companies in the world, providing real estate services primarily in North America. The company has offices throughout the U.S., as well as one in Toronto, Canada. Trammel Crow serves the office, industrial, retail, healthcare, student housing, on-airport distribution and multi-family residential markets by delivering project management and development to both user and investor clients. As the manager of development projects, the firm offers services including the evaluation of project feasibility, budgeting and scheduling; site identification, due diligence and acquisition; cash flow analysis; the procurement of approvals and permits, including zoning and other entitlements; project finance advisory services; coordination of project design and engineering; construction bidding and management; tenant finish coordination; and project close-out and tenant move coordination. The company currently has approximately $4.7 billion in development projects in process. Trammell Crow's outsourcing is done on a contractual basis, aiming at long-term and full-service agreements with its clients. In December 2009, the company's joint venture, Partners Health Trust (owned with a public pension fund advised by Kennedy Associates) acquired Duke Medicine Plaza, an 85,000 square foot building located on the campus of Duke Raleigh Hospital.

Employee benefits include: medical, dental and vision insurance; educational assistance; life insurance; and long-term disability coverage.

FINANCIALS:

Sales and profits are in thousands of dollars—add 000 to get the full amount. 2009 Note: Financial information for 2009 was not available for all companies at press time.

2009 Sales: $	2009 Profits: $	**U.S. Stock Ticker: Subsidiary**
2008 Sales: $	2008 Profits: $	**Int'l Ticker:** Int'l Exchange:
2007 Sales: $	2007 Profits: $	Employees:
2006 Sales: $	2006 Profits: $	Fiscal Year Ends: 12/31
2005 Sales: $895,950	2005 Profits: $59,407	Parent Company: CB RICHARD ELLIS GROUP INC (CBRE)

SALARIES/BENEFITS:

Pension Plan:	ESOP Stock Plan:	Profit Sharing:	Top Exec. Salary: $	Bonus: $
Savings Plan: Y	Stock Purch. Plan:		Second Exec. Salary: $	Bonus: $

OTHER THOUGHTS:

Apparent Women Officers or Directors:
Hot Spot for Advancement for Women/Minorities:

LOCATIONS: ("Y" = Yes)

West:	Southwest:	Midwest:	Southeast:	Northeast:	International:
Y	Y	Y	Y	Y	Y

TRANSCONTINENTAL REALTY

www.transconrealty-invest.com

Industry Group Code: 531120 **Ranks within this company's industry group:** Sales: 59 Profits: 43

Properties:		Financial Services:		Construction/Development:		Investments:		Specialty Services:		Brokerage:	
Apartments:	Y	Mortgages:		Commercial Construction:		REIT:		Property Management:	Y	Commercial Sales:	
Malls/Shopping:	Y	Title Insurance:		Residential Construction:				Online Services:		Residential Sales:	
Offices:	Y	Property Insurance:		Land Development:				Software/IT:		Specialty:	
Hotels/Motels:				Support Services:				Consulting:			
Industrial/Warehouses:	Y			Design/Engineering:							
Other:											

TYPES OF BUSINESS:

Real Estate Investment Trust
Warehouses
Apartments
Office Properties
Retail Properties

BRANDS/DIVISIONS/AFFILIATES:

American Realty Investment
Prime Asset Management
Income Opportunity Realty Investors Inc
Keller Springs Technical Center

CONTACTS:

Note: Officers with more than one job title may be intentionally listed here more than once.

Daniel J. Moos, CEO
Daniel J. Moos, Pres.
Gene S. Bertcher, CFO/Exec. VP
Louis J. Corna, General Counsel/Corp. Sec./Exec. VP-Tax
Daeho Kim, Treas.
Alfred Crozier, Exec. VP-Residential Construction
Henry A. Butler, Chmn.

Phone: 469-522-4200 **Fax:** 469-522-4299
Toll-Free: 800-400-6407
Address: 1 Hickory Centre, 1800 Valley View Ln., Ste. 300, Dallas, TX 75234 US

GROWTH PLANS/SPECIAL FEATURES:

Transcontinental Realty Investors, Inc. (TCI) is an externally advised real estate investment company. The firm specializes in the acquisition, development and ownership of income-producing residential and commercial real estate properties. TCI also acquires land for future development in in-fill or high-growth suburban markets. The company owns approximately 57 residential apartment communities totaling roughly 11,354 units. With regard to commercial property, the firm owns 19 office buildings, three retail centers, and six industrial properties totaling nearly 5.1 million square feet. In addition, TCI owns 6,813 acres of undeveloped and partially developed land. The company produces revenue by managing previously undervalued or underperforming office buildings, apartments, retail centers and warehouses. Day-to-day management of TCI's business is contracted to Prime Asset Management, whose employees serve as company officers. Subsidiaries of American Realty Investment own approximately 82.8% of the company's stock. In July 2009, TCI acquired roughly 60.4% interest in Income Opportunity Realty Investors, Inc. (IORI) from Syntek West, Inc.; the firm now owns approximately 85.3% of IORI. Also in July 2009, the firm sold a 101,500 square foot commercial facility located in San Antonio, Texas, and a 30,000 square foot commercial facility located in Atlanta, Georgia, for $4 million. In October 2009, the company sold a 40,666 square foot facility located in Farmers Branch, Texas, for $3.2 million; and the Parkway Centre retail shopping center, a 28,374 square foot facility located in Dallas, Texas, for $4 million. In November 2009, TCI acquired 27.192 acres of McKinney Ranch land located in McKinney, Texas, and Keller Springs Technical Center, an 80,000 square foot commercial building located in Carrollton, Texas. In December 2009, the firm sold the Bridges on Kinsey Apartments, a 232-unit complex located in Tyler, Texas, for $20.5 million.

FINANCIALS:

Sales and profits are in thousands of dollars—add 000 to get the full amount. 2009 Note: Financial information for 2009 was not available for all companies at press time.

2009 Sales: $151,647	2009 Profits: $-79,573	**U.S. Stock Ticker: TCI**
2008 Sales: $138,337	2008 Profits: $32,209	**Int'l Ticker:** Int'l Exchange:
2007 Sales: $123,704	2007 Profits: $11,111	Employees:
2006 Sales: $100,591	2006 Profits: $3,506	Fiscal Year Ends: 12/31
2005 Sales: $81,630	2005 Profits: $9,069	Parent Company:

SALARIES/BENEFITS:

Pension Plan:	ESOP Stock Plan:	Profit Sharing:	Top Exec. Salary: $	Bonus: $
Savings Plan:	Stock Purch. Plan:		Second Exec. Salary: $	Bonus: $

OTHER THOUGHTS:

Apparent Women Officers or Directors: 1
Hot Spot for Advancement for Women/Minorities:

LOCATIONS: ("Y" = Yes)

West:	Southwest:	Midwest:	Southeast:	Northeast:	International:
Y	Y	Y	Y	Y	Y

TRANSWESTERN COMMERCIAL SERVICES

www.transwestern.net

Industry Group Code: 5311 **Ranks within this company's industry group:** Sales: Profits:

Properties:		Financial Services:		Construction/Development:		Investments:		Specialty Services:		Brokerage:	
Apartments:		Mortgages:	Y	Commercial Construction:	Y	REIT:		Property Management:	Y	Commercial Sales:	Y
Malls/Shopping:		Title Insurance:		Residential Construction:	Y			Online Services:		Residential Sales:	
Offices:		Property Insurance:		Land Development:				Software/IT:		Specialty:	
Hotels/Motels:				Support Services:				Consulting:	Y		
Industrial/Warehouses:				Design/Engineering:							
Other:											

TYPES OF BUSINESS:

Real Estate Operations
Property Management
Advisory Services
Development & Research Services
Tenant Representation
Investment & Finance Services

BRANDS/DIVISIONS/AFFILIATES:

Delta Associates
Investment Services Group

CONTACTS:

Note: Officers with more than one job title may be intentionally listed here more than once.

Larry P. Heard, CEO
Mark Doran, COO
Larry P. Heard, Pres.
Steve Harding, CFO
Kim Chapman, National Dir.-Mktg.
Colleen Dolan, Sr. VP-Human Resources
Chris Saah, CIO
Tom McNearney, Exec. Managing Dir.-Dev. & Investment
Kim Chapman, National Dir.-Comm.
Steve Pumper, Exec. Managing Dir.-Investment Svcs.
Robert Duncan, Chmn.

Phone: 713-270-7700	**Fax:** 713-270-6285
Toll-Free:	
Address: 1900 W. Loop S., Ste. 1300, Houston, TX 77027 US	

GROWTH PLANS/SPECIAL FEATURES:

Transwestern Commercial Services is one of the largest privately held full-service real estate firms in the U.S. The company operates in 25 cities across the U.S. and oversees the leasing and management of more than 900 properties. The firm offers a range of services including agency leasing; development; property and facility management; investment services; tenant advisory; and research. Transwestern's agency leasing services utilize local market knowledge to provide customized marketing plans for each asset being considered by its clients. The development offerings include site analysis and acquisition, construction management and project marketing. Property and facility management services aim at maximizing property values through tenant relations programs, strategic planning, building enhancement and accurate accounting. The company offers its investment services through its Investment Services Group which provides clients with the firm's experience with real estate capital markets and investment banking to improve the financial performance of their assets. The firm's tenant advisory services include strategic planning, needs analysis, market research/analysis, disposition services, document management/negotiation, lease administration and project management. Transwestern's research services, provided by wholly-owned subsidiary Delta Associates, include national economic updates and regional market reports designed for the commercial real estate industry.

The company offers its employees health, dental and vision insurance; a 401(k) plan; flexible spending accounts; life and AD&D insurance; long-term disability insurance; and an employee assistance program.

FINANCIALS:

Sales and profits are in thousands of dollars—add 000 to get the full amount. 2009 Note: Financial information for 2009 was not available for all companies at press time.

2009 Sales: $	2009 Profits: $	**U.S. Stock Ticker: Private**
2008 Sales: $	2008 Profits: $	**Int'l Ticker:** Int'l Exchange:
2007 Sales: $70,600	2007 Profits: $	Employees:
2006 Sales: $	2006 Profits: $	Fiscal Year Ends: 12/31
2005 Sales: $	2005 Profits: $	Parent Company:

SALARIES/BENEFITS:

Pension Plan:	ESOP Stock Plan:	Profit Sharing:	Top Exec. Salary: $	Bonus: $
Savings Plan: Y	Stock Purch. Plan:		Second Exec. Salary: $	Bonus: $

OTHER THOUGHTS:

Apparent Women Officers or Directors: 2
Hot Spot for Advancement for Women/Minorities: Y

LOCATIONS: ("Y" = Yes)

West:	Southwest:	Midwest:	Southeast:	Northeast:	International:
Y	Y	Y	Y	Y	

TRANSWESTERN INVESTMENT CO LLC

www.transinvestco.com

Industry Group Code: 531110 **Ranks within this company's industry group:** Sales: Profits:

Properties:		Financial Services:		Construction/Development:		Investments:		Specialty Services:		Brokerage:	
Apartments:	Y	Mortgages:		Commercial Construction:		REIT:	Y	Property Management:		Commercial Sales:	
Malls/Shopping:		Title Insurance:		Residential Construction:				Online Services:		Residential Sales:	
Offices:	Y	Property Insurance:		Land Development:				Software/IT:		Specialty:	
Hotels/Motels:				Support Services:				Consulting:			
Industrial/Warehouses:	Y			Design/Engineering:							
Other:											

TYPES OF BUSINESS:

Real Estate Investment Trust
Industrial/Flex Properties
Multi-Family Residential Properties
Retail Properties
Mezzanine Loans

BRANDS/DIVISIONS/AFFILIATES:

Transwestern Commercial Services, LLC
Aslan Realty Partners III, LP
Transwestern Mezzanine Realty Partners II, LP
Transwestern Securities Management
Transwestern Realty Finance Partners

CONTACTS:

Note: Officers with more than one job title may be intentionally listed here more than once.

Stephen R. Quazzo, CEO/Managing Principal
James A. Fox, CFO
Jeffrey L. Johnson, CIO/Managing Dir.
John W. Collins, Controller
Adam J. Falk, Managing Dir.-Mezzanine & Equity Investments
Bradley S. Beile, Dir.-Capital Markets & Portfolio Mgmt.
Dirk Degenaars, Dir.-Retail Investments
Timothy E. McChesney, Managing Dir.-Ownership Representation
Robert D.Duncan, Chmn.

Phone: 312-499-1900	**Fax:** 312-499-1901
Toll-Free:	
Address: 150 N. Wacker Dr., Ste. 800, Chicago, IL 60606 US	

GROWTH PLANS/SPECIAL FEATURES:

Transwestern Investment Co., LLC is a Chicago-based real estate principal investment firm specializing in commercial real estate. Since its founding in 1996, the company has invested in more than 455 properties totaling $10.8 billion throughout the U.S. through its nine sponsored investment funds. In addition to 57 office properties, the company's portfolio includes 10 retail properties totaling in excess of 19 million square feet. Transwestern's other current investments include 10 multi-family complexes totaling 3,300 units and 90 mezzanine loan investments. Currently, the firm is seeking U.S. equity investment opportunities for Aslan Realty Partners III, L.L.C., a fully discretionary equity fund that targets office, industrial, and retail investments nationwide. Transwestern also pursues U.S. mezzanine-debt investment opportunities for Transwestern Mezzanine Realty Partners II, L.P., a fully discretionary fund; and multifamily investments through Transwestern Multifamily Partners, L.L.C. The company is affiliated with one of the largest privately-held real estate operating companies in the country, Transwestern Commercial Services, L.L.C., which specializes in development, tenant advisory, brokerage, leasing, and research for office, industrial, healthcare, retail and multifamily properties. Other subsidiaries include Transwestern Securities Management, which offers public real estate securities and Transwestern Realty Finance Partners, which manages high yield and senior mortgage investment activities. Recently the firm acquired Galaxy Office Park in Concord, California, totaling 173,000 square feet in office space and acquired a 24,000 occupied Bed Bath & Beyond building in Vienna, Virginia. In 2010, the firm was awarded with 2010 Energy Star Sustained Excellence Award from the U.S. Environmental Protection Agency (EPA). This award is to recognize leadership and commitment in operating buildings efficiently by reducing waste and its carbon footprint. The firm was previously recognized in 2004 and 2005 as an Energy Star Partner of the Year and is the first third party commercial real estate provider to achieve both awards.

FINANCIALS:

Sales and profits are in thousands of dollars—add 000 to get the full amount. 2009 Note: Financial information for 2009 was not available for all companies at press time.

2009 Sales: $	2009 Profits: $	**U.S. Stock Ticker: Private**
2008 Sales: $	2008 Profits: $	**Int'l Ticker:** Int'l Exchange:
2007 Sales: $	2007 Profits: $	Employees:
2006 Sales: $	2006 Profits: $	Fiscal Year Ends: 12/31
2005 Sales: $	2005 Profits: $	Parent Company:

SALARIES/BENEFITS:

Pension Plan:	ESOP Stock Plan:	Profit Sharing:	Top Exec. Salary: $	Bonus: $
Savings Plan:	Stock Purch. Plan:		Second Exec. Salary: $	Bonus: $

OTHER THOUGHTS:

Apparent Women Officers or Directors:
Hot Spot for Advancement for Women/Minorities:

LOCATIONS: ("Y" = Yes)

West:	Southwest:	Midwest:	Southeast:	Northeast:	International:
Y	Y	Y	Y	Y	

TREVI-FINANZIARIA INDUSTRIALE SPA (TREVI GROUP)

www.trevifin.com

Industry Group Code: 541330 **Ranks within this company's industry group:** Sales: 7 Profits: 4

Properties:		Financial Services:		Construction/Development:		Investments:		Specialty Services:		Brokerage:	
Apartments:		Mortgages:		Commercial Construction:	Y	REIT:		Property Management:		Commercial Sales:	
Malls/Shopping:		Title Insurance:		Residential Construction:				Online Services:		Residential Sales:	
Offices:		Property Insurance:		Land Development:				Software/IT:		Specialty:	
Hotels/Motels:				Support Services:	Y			Consulting:			
Industrial/Warehouses:				Design/Engineering:	Y						
Other:											

TYPES OF BUSINESS:

Engineering & Construction Services
Underground Construction Services
Foundation & Drilling Machinery & Services
Wind Farms

BRANDS/DIVISIONS/AFFILIATES:

Trevi Group
TREVI S.p.A.
SOILMEC S.p.A.
DRILLMEC S.p.A.
Trevi Energy S.p.A.
Galante SA
Arabian Soil Contractors Ltd
Watson, Inc.

CONTACTS: *Note: Officers with more than one job title may be intentionally listed here more than once.*

Gianluigi Trevisani, Managing Dir./VP
Daniele Forti, CFO
Stefano Trevisani, Managing Dir.
Cesare Trevisani, Managing Dir.
Davide Trevisani, Chmn.

Phone: 39-05-473-19111	**Fax:** 39-05-473-19313
Toll-Free:	
Address: 201 via Larga, Cesena, 47023 Italy	

GROWTH PLANS/SPECIAL FEATURES:

Trevi-Finanziaria Industriale (Trevi Group) is a global leader in foundation engineering and drilling and provides project management services supporting related projects around the world. It has branches in as over 30 countries. The group operates through four main subsidiaries: Trevi, Petreven, Soilmec and Drillmec. Trevi provides construction services for underground engineering projects, such as special foundations for bridges, railways, dams, industrial systems and tunnels. Petreven is the company's segment in charge of oil drilling. Soilmec manufactures plants and rigs used for foundation engineering. Drillmec specializes in drilling projects and manufactures hydraulic rigs for oil, geothermal and water drilling. The company, through its subsidiaries, also has operations in well drilling for water research, as well as having completed numerous automated car park projects. Trevi Group's strong worldwide presence is illustrated by such past projects as the foundation works for the Third Mainland Bridge of Lagos in Nigeria; the Alicura in Argentina; the Port of Bandar Abbas in Iran; and the Khao dam in Thailand. The company also owns and operates Trevi Energy S.p.A., which is engaged in the design, development and engineering of offshore wind farms. In 2009, the company acquired Galante S.A. in Colombia; Arabian Soil Contractors Ltd. in Saudi Arabia; and Watson, Inc. in the U.S.

FINANCIALS: **Sales and profits are in thousands of dollars—add 000 to get the full amount. 2009 Note: Financial information for 2009 was not available for all companies at press time.**

2009 Sales: $1,366,660	2009 Profits: $111,680	**U.S. Stock Ticker:**
2008 Sales: $1,443,130	2008 Profits: $100,830	**Int'l Ticker: TFI** Int'l Exchange: Milan-BI
2007 Sales: $1,323,600	2007 Profits: $87,600	Employees:
2006 Sales: $1,019,100	2006 Profits: $42,000	Fiscal Year Ends: 12/31
2005 Sales: $676,728	2005 Profits: $18,623	Parent Company:

SALARIES/BENEFITS:

Pension Plan:	ESOP Stock Plan:	Profit Sharing:	Top Exec. Salary: $	Bonus: $
Savings Plan:	Stock Purch. Plan:		Second Exec. Salary: $	Bonus: $

OTHER THOUGHTS:

Apparent Women Officers or Directors:
Hot Spot for Advancement for Women/Minorities:

LOCATIONS: ("Y" = Yes)

West:	Southwest:	Midwest:	Southeast:	Northeast:	International:
Y	Y		Y	Y	Y

TRINITY LTD

www.trinity.com.au

Industry Group Code: 523920 **Ranks within this company's industry group:** Sales: Profits:

Properties:		Financial Services:		Construction/Development:		Investments:		Specialty Services:		Brokerage:	
Apartments:	Y	Mortgages:		Commercial Construction:		REIT:		Property Management:	Y	Commercial Sales:	
Malls/Shopping:	Y	Title Insurance:		Residential Construction:				Online Services:		Residential Sales:	
Offices:	Y	Property Insurance:		Land Development:				Software/IT:		Specialty:	
Hotels/Motels:				Support Services:				Consulting:			
Industrial/Warehouses:	Y			Design/Engineering:							
Other:											

TYPES OF BUSINESS:

Investment Fund Management
Property Management

BRANDS/DIVISIONS/AFFILIATES:

Trinity Funds Management
Trinity Property Trust
Trinity Enhanced Return Fund
Trinity Development Trust
Trinity Land Trust
Trinity Opportunistic Property

CONTACTS: *Note: Officers with more than one job title may be intentionally listed here more than once.*

Craig Bellamy, CEO
Lisa Myers, Legal Counsel/Corp. Sec.
David Asplin, Gen. Mgr.-Institutional Funds Mgmt.
Chris Morton, Joint Managing Dir.
Steve Leigh, Joint Managing Dir.
Brett Heading, Chmn.

Phone: 61-7-3002-4200 **Fax:** 61-7-3002-4201
Toll-Free:
Address: 88 Creek St. Mezzanine Level, The Tower, Brisbane, QLD 4000 Australia

GROWTH PLANS/SPECIAL FEATURES:

Trinity Limited is a publicly traded Australian property fund management firm. Its core businesses are funds management and direct property investment. Its funds management business, operated by Trinity Funds Management (TFM), manages a portfolio of trusts and funds including Trinity Property Trust (TPT), a direct property fund; Trinity Enhanced Return Fund (TERF), an unlisted, wholesale direct property fund; Trinity Development Trust (TDT) which makes equity investments in commercial, retail, industrial and residential (non-land) developments; the Trinity Land Trust (TLT), an unlisted, residential land development trust, investing in residential subdivision and master-planned Australian communities; and Trinity Opportunistic Property (TOP), which invests in a variety of commercial, industrial and residential properties. The company's direct portfolio, the Trinity Stapled Trust (TST) includes retail, commercial and industrial properties. Trinity also provides property services to its investment properties under management by TFM including day-to-day property management; occupant maximization and tenant retention programs; leasing; strategic asset management; capital transactions; and property due diligence. In April 2010, Trinity sold its 38.5% interest in TERF for $5.87 million to its subsidiary, TPT, and an unaffiliated institutional investor. TPT now owns a 75% interest in TERF and the institutional investor holds the remaining 25%.

FINANCIALS: **Sales and profits are in thousands of dollars—add 000 to get the full amount. 2009 Note: Financial information for 2009 was not available for all companies at press time.**

2009 Sales: $	2009 Profits: $	**U.S. Stock Ticker:**
2008 Sales: $	2008 Profits: $	**Int'l Ticker: TCQ** Int'l Exchange: Sydney-ASX
2007 Sales: $	2007 Profits: $	Employees:
2006 Sales: $	2006 Profits: $	Fiscal Year Ends:
2005 Sales: $	2005 Profits: $	Parent Company:

SALARIES/BENEFITS:

Pension Plan:	ESOP Stock Plan:	Profit Sharing:	Top Exec. Salary: $	Bonus: $
Savings Plan:	Stock Purch. Plan:		Second Exec. Salary: $	Bonus: $

OTHER THOUGHTS:

Apparent Women Officers or Directors:
Hot Spot for Advancement for Women/Minorities:

LOCATIONS: ("Y" = Yes)

West:	Southwest:	Midwest:	Southeast:	Northeast:	International:
					Y

TRIPLE FIVE GROUP

www.triplefive.com

Industry Group Code: 5311 **Ranks within this company's industry group:** Sales: Profits:

Properties:		Financial Services:		Construction/Development:		Investments:		Specialty Services:		Brokerage:	
Apartments:	Y	Mortgages:	Y	Commercial Construction:	Y	REIT:		Property Management:	Y	Commercial Sales:	
Malls/Shopping:	Y	Title Insurance:		Residential Construction:				Online Services:		Residential Sales:	
Offices:	Y	Property Insurance:		Land Development:	Y			Software/IT:		Specialty:	
Hotels/Motels:	Y			Support Services:				Consulting:			
Industrial/Warehouses:				Design/Engineering:							
Other:	Y										

TYPES OF BUSINESS:

Shopping Malls
Hotels
Office Buildings
Mixed-Use Developments
Entertainment Venues & Amusement Parks
Banking
Venture Capital
Oil & Gas Exploration

BRANDS/DIVISIONS/AFFILIATES:

Mall of America
West Edmonton Mall
First Nuclear Corporation
People's Trust
T5 Equity Partners LLC
Celonex Pharmaceuticals
Wayne Engineering

CONTACTS:

Note: Officers with more than one job title may be intentionally listed here more than once.

Don Ghermezian, Pres.
Stacey Claffey, Contact-Media
Nader Ghermezian, Chmn.

Phone: 702-430-5800	**Fax:** 702-430-5810
Toll-Free:	
Address: 9440 W. Sahara, Ste. 240, Las Vegas, NV 89117 US	

GROWTH PLANS/SPECIAL FEATURES:

Triple Five Group is a multi-segmented corporation engaged in real estate; resource development and mining; venture capital; hotels; banking; private equity; engineering; industrial manufacturing; and retail operations. Together with its extended group of affiliates, the firm owns major shopping centers and other commercial real estate. It also focuses on planning and development; tourism projects; residential planned communities; and technology. Its real estate division is one of the most diverse real estate developers in the U.S., with activities that include suburban city establishment, urban entertainment venues, amusement parks, commercial real estate and industrial real estate. The firm also has projects in Japan, England, Taiwan and the Middle East, as well as Ontario, British Columbia and Alberta in Canada. Subsidiary People's Trust operates throughout Canada and provides investment and lending services, estate and trust asset management and mortgage servicing. Subsidiary T5 Equity Partners LLC provides venture and equity capital investments. The company's Venture Capital group and other investment arms provide funds for development in the wireless, Internet and high technology industries; and through subsidiary First Nuclear Corporation, also active in resource development and exploration within the oil, gas and metallurgical industries and is involved in production, business management and technical aspects of these industries. Subsidiaries of the firm include Maverick Engineering, Inc.; Wayne Engineering; Celonex Pharmaceuticals, Celonex Life Science and DiamondGear. Triple Five's most well-known projects include the West Edmonton Mall in Canada and the Mall of America in Bloomington, Minnesota, respectively the first- and second-largest mixed-use tourism, retail and entertainment complexes in the world. The company has also developed five-star hotel complexes, high-rise office buildings and apartments. Triple Five, which owns a controlling interest in the Mall of America, plans to enlarge this property to over 9 million square feet, making it the largest single real estate complex in the world.

FINANCIALS:

Sales and profits are in thousands of dollars—add 000 to get the full amount. 2009 Note: Financial information for 2009 was not available for all companies at press time.

2009 Sales: $	2009 Profits: $	**U.S. Stock Ticker: Private**
2008 Sales: $	2008 Profits: $	**Int'l Ticker:** Int'l Exchange:
2007 Sales: $	2007 Profits: $	Employees:
2006 Sales: $	2006 Profits: $	Fiscal Year Ends: 7/31
2005 Sales: $	2005 Profits: $	Parent Company:

SALARIES/BENEFITS:

Pension Plan:	ESOP Stock Plan:	Profit Sharing:	Top Exec. Salary: $	Bonus: $
Savings Plan:	Stock Purch. Plan:		Second Exec. Salary: $	Bonus: $

OTHER THOUGHTS:

Apparent Women Officers or Directors: 1
Hot Spot for Advancement for Women/Minorities:

LOCATIONS: ("Y" = Yes)

West:	Southwest:	Midwest:	Southeast:	Northeast:	International:
Y	Y	Y	Y	Y	Y

TRT HOLDINGS

www.omnihotels.com

Industry Group Code: 721110 **Ranks within this company's industry group:** Sales: Profits:

Properties:		Financial Services:		Construction/Development:		Investments:		Specialty Services:		Brokerage:	
Apartments:		Mortgages:		Commercial Construction:		REIT:		Property Management:	Y	Commercial Sales:	
Malls/Shopping:		Title Insurance:		Residential Construction:				Online Services:	Y	Residential Sales:	
Offices:		Property Insurance:		Land Development:				Software/IT:		Specialty:	
Hotels/Motels:	Y			Support Services:				Consulting:			
Industrial/Warehouses:				Design/Engineering:							
Other:	Y										

TYPES OF BUSINESS:

Hotels
Gymnasiums
Oil & Gas Exploration

BRANDS/DIVISIONS/AFFILIATES:

Omni Hotels
Executive Service Plan
Select Guest
Omni Express
Omni Kids
Select Guest Gold
Gold's Gym International
Tana Exploration Company

CONTACTS: *Note: Officers with more than one job title may be intentionally listed here more than once.*

James D. Caldwell, CEO
Mike Deitemeyer, Pres.
Mike Garcia, CFO
Tom Santora, Chief Mktg. Officer/Sr. VP-Sales
Joy Rothschild, Sr. VP-Human Resources
Michael G. Smith, General Counsel/Sr. VP
Jeff Smith, Sr. VP-Oper.
Mike Garcia, Sr. VP-Dev. & Acquisitions
Paul Dietzler, Exec. VP-Asset Mgmt.
Jeff Smith, Sr. VP-Loyalty Svcs.
Stephen Rosenstock, Sr. VP-Food & Beverage/Brand Standards
Robert B. Rowling, Chmn.

Phone: 972-730-6664	**Fax:** 972-871-5665
Toll-Free: 800-843-6664	
Address: 420 Decker Dr., Ste. 200, Irving, TX 75062-3952 US	

GROWTH PLANS/SPECIAL FEATURES:

TRT Holdings owns and franchises the Omni Hotel chain. Omni Hotels offer luxury and first-class accommodations at 47 locations across North America, totaling more than 14,000 rooms. The company owns or manages 43 of the properties and franchises four. A typical Omni Hotel has 350-500 rooms, and it offers amenities such as marble bathrooms, voicemail, modem connections, high-speed Internet access, gourmet dining, fitness centers; 24-hour and online room service; valet ordering, baggage retrieval and housekeeping, among other services. The firm's specialty programs operate at all locations and include the Executive Service Plan, designed to aid corporate travelers; and the Select Guest and Select Guest Gold customer loyalty programs, whereby members are rewarded on business and other types of stays, including most government, leisure and group discounts. Omni Express is a direct hotline for meeting planners and Omni Kids caters to the needs of younger guests. The hotel chain caters primarily to corporate business and upscale leisure travelers. The Omni is part of The Global Hotel Alliance (GHA), which consists of 12 prominent hotel brands in more than 47 countries. Additionally, TRT owns Gold's Gym International, a franchiser of more than 550 fitness centers in 25 countries. Apart from these operations, the company holds stakes in businesses involved in oil and gas exploration (the Tana Exploration Company), as well as retail chains in Mexico and other real estate investments. In January 2009, the Omni Fort Worth Hotel opens. In February 2009, the Dallas City Council named the company as the operator of the new Dallas Convention Center Hotel. In February 2010, the firm launched a new brand of upscale hotels called Mokara Hotel and Spa.

Employees receive tuition reimbursement; relocation allowances; a flexible spending account; short term and long-term disability; discounted associate room rates; and medical, dental, life and disability insurance.

FINANCIALS: **Sales and profits are in thousands of dollars—add 000 to get the full amount. 2009 Note: Financial information for 2009 was not available for all companies at press time.**

2009 Sales: $	2009 Profits: $	**U.S. Stock Ticker: Private**
2008 Sales: $	2008 Profits: $	**Int'l Ticker:** Int'l Exchange:
2007 Sales: $404,000	2007 Profits: $	Employees:
2006 Sales: $	2006 Profits: $	Fiscal Year Ends: 12/31
2005 Sales: $	2005 Profits: $	Parent Company:

SALARIES/BENEFITS:

Pension Plan:	ESOP Stock Plan:	Profit Sharing:	Top Exec. Salary: $	Bonus: $
Savings Plan: Y	Stock Purch. Plan:		Second Exec. Salary: $	Bonus: $

OTHER THOUGHTS:

Apparent Women Officers or Directors: 1
Hot Spot for Advancement for Women/Minorities: Y

LOCATIONS: ("Y" = Yes)

West:	Southwest:	Midwest:	Southeast:	Northeast:	International:
Y	Y	Y	Y	Y	Y

TRUE HOME VALUE INC

www.thv.com

Industry Group Code: 444130 **Ranks within this company's industry group:** Sales: Profits:

Properties:		Financial Services:		Construction/Development:		Investments:		Specialty Services:		Brokerage:	
Apartments:		Mortgages:		Commercial Construction:		REIT:		Property Management:		Commercial Sales:	
Malls/Shopping:		Title Insurance:		Residential Construction:	Y			Online Services:		Residential Sales:	
Offices:		Property Insurance:		Land Development:				Software/IT:		Specialty:	
Hotels/Motels:				Support Services:	Y			Consulting:			
Industrial/Warehouses:				Design/Engineering:	Y						
Other:											

TYPES OF BUSINESS:

Building Materials
Door & Window Assemblies
Retail & Installation
Roofing & Siding Materials
Coatings

BRANDS/DIVISIONS/AFFILIATES:

Thermal Line Windows, Inc.
Leingang Home Center
Primax Home Center
Rolox Home Center
Thomas Home Center
ThermoView Industries, Inc.
THV, Inc.

CONTACTS: *Note: Officers with more than one job title may be intentionally listed here more than once.*

Phone: 502-968-2020	**Fax:** 502-968-7798
Toll-Free: 800-669-2020	
Address: 5611 Fern Valley Rd., Louisville, KY 40228 US	

GROWTH PLANS/SPECIAL FEATURES:

True Home Value, Inc., or THV, (formerly ThermoView Industries, Inc.) is one of the largest full-service national home improvement companies in the U.S. It designs, manufactures, sells and installs custom vinyl replacement for residential and retail commercial customers. These customers reside primarily in the Midwestern U.S. The company sells and installs thermal replacement windows, doors, textured coatings, vinyl siding, patio decks, patio enclosures, cabinet refacings, bathroom and kitchen remodeling products and residential roofing. THV operates in 16 states under the retail trade names Primax Home Center; Leingang Home Center; Thomas Home Center; and Rolox Home Center. The firm's primary business is in the replacement window market. THV has a single manufacturing subsidiary, Thermal Line Windows, Inc. in Mandan, ND, which produces one of its three lines of replacement windows; the other two lines are manufactured in Toledo, Ohio and Saltsburg, Pennsylvania by unaffiliated third parties. Its windows use high-technology glass that allows sunlight in while keeping damaging ultraviolet rays out. THV offers a 50-year non-prorated glass and window warranty as well as a 25% fuel savings pledge in writing on all its window products. The firm offers custom-made insulated steel doors with a wood grain finish in 36 different styles and 150 color combinations, as well as six variations of sliding glass doors. The company's primary goal is to become a national leader in the home improvement and replacement window industry by building a network of sales and installation subsidiaries.

FINANCIALS: **Sales and profits are in thousands of dollars—add 000 to get the full amount. 2009 Note: Financial information for 2009 was not available for all companies at press time.**

2009 Sales: $	2009 Profits: $	**U.S. Stock Ticker: Private**
2008 Sales: $	2008 Profits: $	**Int'l Ticker:** Int'l Exchange:
2007 Sales: $	2007 Profits: $	Employees:
2006 Sales: $	2006 Profits: $	Fiscal Year Ends: 12/31
2005 Sales: $	2005 Profits: $	Parent Company:

SALARIES/BENEFITS:

Pension Plan:	ESOP Stock Plan:	Profit Sharing:	Top Exec. Salary: $	Bonus: $
Savings Plan:	Stock Purch. Plan:		Second Exec. Salary: $	Bonus: $

OTHER THOUGHTS:

Apparent Women Officers or Directors:
Hot Spot for Advancement for Women/Minorities:

LOCATIONS: ("Y" = Yes)

West:	Southwest:	Midwest:	Southeast:	Northeast:	International:
	Y	Y	Y	Y	

TRUMP ENTERTAINMENT RESORTS INC

www.trumpcasinos.com

Industry Group Code: 721120 **Ranks within this company's industry group:** Sales: 7 Profits: 6

Properties:		Financial Services:		Construction/Development:		Investments:		Specialty Services:		Brokerage:	
Apartments:		Mortgages:		Commercial Construction:		REIT:		Property Management:		Commercial Sales:	
Malls/Shopping:		Title Insurance:		Residential Construction:				Online Services:		Residential Sales:	
Offices:		Property Insurance:		Land Development:				Software/IT:		Specialty:	
Hotels/Motels:	Y			Support Services:				Consulting:			
Industrial/Warehouses:				Design/Engineering:							
Other:	Y										

TYPES OF BUSINESS:

Casino Hotels
Casino Management

BRANDS/DIVISIONS/AFFILIATES:

Trump Taj Mahal Casino Resort
Trump Plaza Hotel & Casino
Trump Marina Hotel Casino
Xanadu Theater
Il Mulino New York
Trattoria Il Mulino (The)

CONTACTS:

Note: Officers with more than one job title may be intentionally listed here more than once.

Mark Juliano, CEO
John P. Burke, CFO
Craig D. Keyser, Exec. VP-Human Resources
Robert M. Pickus, Chief Admin. Officer
Robert M. Pickus, General Counsel/Sec.
Tom Hickey, Dir.-Corp. Comm.
John P. Burke, Corp. Treas./Exec. VP
Richard M. Santoro, Exec. VP-Asset Protection & Risk Mgmt.
Joseph A. Fusco, Exec VP-Gov't Affairs
Donald J. Trump, Chmn.

Phone: 609-449-5866 **Fax:** 609-449-6586
Toll-Free: 800-777-1177
Address: 15 S. Pennsylvania Ave., Atlantic City, NJ 08401 US

GROWTH PLANS/SPECIAL FEATURES:

Trump Entertainment Resorts, Inc. (TER) operates three casino properties, all in Atlantic City: Trump Taj Mahal Casino Resort; Trump Plaza Hotel and Casino; and Trump Marina Hotel and Casino. Trump Taj Mahal is located on 39.4 acres of land features the new, 782-room Chairman Tower, which includes 66 suites and 8 penthouse suites. The Taj Mahal also houses 1,228 hotel rooms, which include 243 suites and 7 penthouse suites; 16 dining locations; five cocktail lounges; and 143,000 square feet of ballroom, meeting room and pre-function area space. It features 162,000 square feet of gaming space with approximately 204 gaming tables, 2,996 slot machines and 12,500 square feet dedicated to Asian gaming favorites; and the Xanadu Theater, a 20,000 square foot entertainment complex with seating capacity for 1,200. Trump Plaza, sitting on 10.9 acres, features 906 hotel rooms and 87,000 square feet of casino space for 1,808 slot machines and 71 gaming tables. Additional amenities include 18,000 square feet of conference space, a 750-seat cabaret theater, 11 dining locations and two cocktail lounges. Trump Marina, covering 14 acres, offers a 27-story hotel with 728 guest rooms and 79,000 square feet of gaming space for 1,815 slot machines, 71 gaming tables 30,500 square feet of convention, ballroom and meeting space. In February 2009, the firm filed for bankruptcy protection while facing declining revenues.

Employees of TER receive an employee assistance program; health benefits; tuition reimbursement; a 401(k) plan; a free employee cafeteria; and a credit union.

FINANCIALS:

Sales and profits are in thousands of dollars—add 000 to get the full amount. 2009 Note: Financial information for 2009 was not available for all companies at press time.

2009 Sales: $792,149	2009 Profits: $-533,938	**U.S. Stock Ticker: TRMP**
2008 Sales: $908,008	2008 Profits: $-232,203	**Int'l Ticker:** Int'l Exchange:
2007 Sales: $988,235	2007 Profits: $-188,681	Employees: 5,500
2006 Sales: $1,007,775	2006 Profits: $-18,507	Fiscal Year Ends: 12/31
2005 Sales: $992,221	2005 Profits: $251,856	Parent Company:

SALARIES/BENEFITS:

Pension Plan:	ESOP Stock Plan:	Profit Sharing:	Top Exec. Salary: $	Bonus: $
Savings Plan: Y	Stock Purch. Plan:		Second Exec. Salary: $	Bonus: $

OTHER THOUGHTS:

Apparent Women Officers or Directors:
Hot Spot for Advancement for Women/Minorities:

LOCATIONS: ("Y" = Yes)

West:	Southwest:	Midwest:	Southeast:	Northeast:	International:
				Y	

TRUMP ORGANIZATION (THE)

www.trump.com

Industry Group Code: 5311 **Ranks within this company's industry group:** Sales: Profits:

Properties:		Financial Services:		Construction/Development:		Investments:		Specialty Services:		Brokerage:	
Apartments:	Y	Mortgages:		Commercial Construction:	Y	REIT:		Property Management:	Y	Commercial Sales:	Y
Malls/Shopping:	Y	Title Insurance:		Residential Construction:	Y			Online Services:		Residential Sales:	Y
Offices:	Y	Property Insurance:		Land Development:	Y			Software/IT:		Specialty:	
Hotels/Motels:	Y			Support Services:				Consulting:			
Industrial/Warehouses:				Design/Engineering:							
Other:	Y										

TYPES OF BUSINESS:

Real Estate Investment, Development & Operations
Property Management
Residential & Commercial Brokerage
Hotel, Casino & Resort Management
Golf Courses

BRANDS/DIVISIONS/AFFILIATES:

Miss Teen USA
Trump Sales and Leasing
Trump International Hotel & Tower
Trump Golf
Trump Productions LLC
Miss Universe
Miss USA
Trump Super Premium Vodka

CONTACTS:

Note: Officers with more than one job title may be intentionally listed here more than once.

Matthew F. Calamari, COO/Exec. VP
Donald J. Trump, Pres.
Allen Weisselberg, CFO/Exec. VP
Donald Trump, Jr., Exec. VP-Dev. & Acquisitions
Ivanka Trump, Exec. VP-Dev. & Acquisitions
Eric Trump, Exec. VP-Dev. & Acquisitions
Cathy Hoffman Glosser, Exec. VP-Global Licensing
Donald J. Trump, Chmn.

Phone: 212-832-2000	**Fax:** 212-935-0141
Toll-Free:	
Address: 725 5th Ave., New York, NY 10022 US	

GROWTH PLANS/SPECIAL FEATURES:

The Trump Organization is a global firm active in luxury real estate development, sales and marketing, as well as entertainment and brand licensing activities. The company's portfolio includes residential, commercial, hotel and golf properties, with over 70 projects current and in development. The Trump real estate portfolio includes a number of well-known buildings, such as the 68-story Trump Tower in Manhattan and the Taj Mahal casino in Atlantic City, New Jersey. Trump Sales and Leasing is the firm's residential brokerage division, which purchases, sells or leases luxury real estate. The luxury Trump International Hotel & Tower, itself a redevelopment of Gulf and Western's landmark Manhattan office building, is a mixed-use residential and hotel property re-designated as One Central Park West. Additional Trump International Hotel & Tower locations recently opened in Chicago, Illinois, and Waikiki, Hawaii, with development begun on sites in Toronto, Canada; Dubai, United Arab Emirates; Punta Pacifica, Panama; New Orleans, Louisiana; and Fort Lauderdale, Florida. Trump Golf is the developer and operator of 12 premium golf clubs in New York, New Jersey, Washington, D.C., California, Florida, Scotland, Puerto Rico and the Caribbean. In addition, The Trump Organization owns the rights to 50% of the Miss USA, Miss Teen USA and Miss Universe beauty pageants, while subsidiary Trump Productions LLC oversees television programming such as The Apprentice on NBC. The company also has several licensing ventures, such as a partnership with Drinks Americas for the production and marketing of Trump Super Premium Vodka. In early 2009, subsidiary Trump Entertainment Resorts filed for Chapter 11 bankruptcy protection. In December 2009, The Trump Organization acquired two new golf courses in New York and New Jersey. In April 2010, the firm and Serta introduced the Trump Home Luxury mattress series.

FINANCIALS:

Sales and profits are in thousands of dollars—add 000 to get the full amount. 2009 Note: Financial information for 2009 was not available for all companies at press time.

2009 Sales: $	2009 Profits: $	**U.S. Stock Ticker: Private**
2008 Sales: $	2008 Profits: $	**Int'l Ticker:** Int'l Exchange:
2007 Sales: $10,700,000	2007 Profits: $	Employees: 22,000
2006 Sales: $	2006 Profits: $	Fiscal Year Ends: 12/31
2005 Sales: $	2005 Profits: $	Parent Company:

SALARIES/BENEFITS:

Pension Plan:	ESOP Stock Plan:	Profit Sharing:	Top Exec. Salary: $	Bonus: $
Savings Plan:	Stock Purch. Plan:		Second Exec. Salary: $	Bonus: $

OTHER THOUGHTS:

Apparent Women Officers or Directors: 2
Hot Spot for Advancement for Women/Minorities: Y

LOCATIONS: ("Y" = Yes)

West:	Southwest:	Midwest:	Southeast:	Northeast:	International:
Y		Y	Y	Y	Y

TUTOR PERINI CORPORATION

www.tutorperini.com

Industry Group Code: 237 **Ranks within this company's industry group:** Sales: 20 Profits: 31

Properties:		Financial Services:		Construction/Development:		Investments:		Specialty Services:		Brokerage:	
Apartments:		Mortgages:		Commercial Construction:	Y	REIT:		Property Management:		Commercial Sales:	
Malls/Shopping:		Title Insurance:		Residential Construction:	Y			Online Services:		Residential Sales:	
Offices:		Property Insurance:		Land Development:				Software/IT:		Specialty:	
Hotels/Motels:				Support Services:	Y			Consulting:	Y		
Industrial/Warehouses:				Design/Engineering:	Y						
Other:											

TYPES OF BUSINESS:

Construction Services
Hospitality & Casino Construction
Construction Management Services
Civic & Infrastructure Construction
Design Services

BRANDS/DIVISIONS/AFFILIATES:

Perini Building Company
James A. Cummings, Inc.
Rudolph and Sletten, Inc.
Perini Civil Construction
Cherry Hill Construction, Inc.
Tutor-Saliba Corporation
Keating Building Corporation
Perini Corporation

CONTACTS:

Note: Officers with more than one job title may be intentionally listed here more than once.

Ronald N. Tutor, CEO
Robert Band, COO
Robert Band, Pres.
Kenneth R. Burk, CFO/Exec. VP
William B. Sparks, Corp. Sec./Clerk/Exec. VP
William B. Sparks, Treas./Exec. VP
Robert Band, Pres./CEO-Mgmt. Svcs.
Mark Caspers, Exec. VP/CEO-Building Group
James A. Frost, Exec. VP/CEO-Civil Group
Craig W. Shaw, Pres./CEO-Perini Building Company Inc.
Ronald N. Tutor, Chmn.

Phone: 818-362-8391	**Fax:** 818-367-5379
Toll-Free:	
Address: 15901 Olden St., Sylmar, CA 91342 US	

GROWTH PLANS/SPECIAL FEATURES:

Tutor Perini Corporation (formerly Perini Corporation) and its subsidiaries provide general contracting, construction management and design-build services worldwide. It operates in three segments: building, civil and management services. The building segment is comprised of Perini Building Company; James A. Cummings, Inc.; Rudolph and Sletten, Inc.; Keating Building Company; Desert Plumbing & Heating Company, Inc.; and Powerco Electric Corporation. This segment focuses on large, complex projects in the hospitality and gaming, transportation, healthcare, municipal offices, sports and entertainment, education, correctional facilities, biotech, pharmaceutical, industrial and high-tech markets. The civil segment is comprised of Tutor Perini Civil Construction, Tutor-Saliba Corporation and Cherry Hill Construction, Inc. The segment focuses on public works construction, including the new construction, repair, replacement and reconstruction of public infrastructure such as highways, bridges, mass transit systems and wastewater treatment facilities. The company's customers primarily award contracts through the public competitive bid, in which price is the major determining factor; or through a request for proposals, where contracts are awarded based on a combination of technical capability and price. The management services segment, comprised of Perini Management Services, Inc. and Black Construction's operation in Guam, provides diversified construction, design-build and maintenance services to the U.S. military and government agencies, as well as surety companies and multi-national corporations domestically and overseas. In January 2009, the firm acquired Keating Building Corporation, a private construction management and designing and building company. In May 2009, the company changed its name to Tutor Perini Corporation. In October 2009, the firm relocated its headquarters to Los Angeles. In December 2009, subsidiary Perini Building Company completed CityCenter, the largest private development in the U.S. to date.

Employees are offered medical and dental insurance; a 401(k) plan; medical and dependent care spending accounts; life and accident insurance; disability coverage; educational assistance; and an employee assistance program.

FINANCIALS:

Sales and profits are in thousands of dollars—add 000 to get the full amount. 2009 Note: Financial information for 2009 was not available for all companies at press time.

2009 Sales: $5,151,966	2009 Profits: $137,061	**U.S. Stock Ticker: TPC**
2008 Sales: $5,660,286	2008 Profits: $-75,140	**Int'l Ticker:** Int'l Exchange:
2007 Sales: $4,628,358	2007 Profits: $97,114	Employees: 5,449
2006 Sales: $3,042,839	2006 Profits: $41,536	Fiscal Year Ends: 12/31
2005 Sales: $1,733,477	2005 Profits: $4,049	Parent Company:

SALARIES/BENEFITS:

Pension Plan:	ESOP Stock Plan:	Profit Sharing:	Top Exec. Salary: $576,000	Bonus: $576,000
Savings Plan: Y	Stock Purch. Plan:		Second Exec. Salary: $540,400	Bonus: $517,400

OTHER THOUGHTS:

Apparent Women Officers or Directors: 1
Hot Spot for Advancement for Women/Minorities:

LOCATIONS: ("Y" = Yes)

West:	Southwest:	Midwest:	Southeast:	Northeast:	International:
Y			Y	Y	Y

UDR INC

www.udrt.com

Industry Group Code: 531110 **Ranks within this company's industry group:** Sales: 5 Profits: 1

Properties:		Financial Services:		Construction/Development:		Investments:		Specialty Services:		Brokerage:	
Apartments:	Y	Mortgages:		Commercial Construction:		REIT:	Y	Property Management:	Y	Commercial Sales:	
Malls/Shopping:		Title Insurance:		Residential Construction:	Y			Online Services:		Residential Sales:	
Offices:		Property Insurance:		Land Development:	Y			Software/IT:		Specialty:	
Hotels/Motels:				Support Services:				Consulting:			
Industrial/Warehouses:				Design/Engineering:							
Other:	Y										

TYPES OF BUSINESS:

Real Estate Investment Trust
Apartment Communities

BRANDS/DIVISIONS/AFFILIATES:

Heritage Communities LP
United Dominion Realty LP
RE3
Vitruvian Park

CONTACTS:

Note: Officers with more than one job title may be intentionally listed here more than once.

Thomas W. Toomey, CEO
Thomas W. Toomey, Pres.
David L. Messenger, CFO/Sr. VP
Steven H. Taraborelli, VP/Dir.-Mktg. & Sales
Katie Miles-Ley, Sr. VP-Human Resources
Warren L. Troupe, General Counsel/Sr. Exec. VP/Corp. Sec.
Jerry A. Davis, Sr. VP-Property Oper.
Thomas A. Spangler, Sr. VP-Bus. Dev.
H. Andrew Cantor, VP-Investor Rel.
William T. O'Shields, Treas./VP
Matthew T. Akin, Sr. VP-Acquisitions & Dispositions
Richard A. Giannotti, Exec. VP-Redevelopment
W. Mark Wallis, Sr. Exec. VP
S. Douglas Walker, Sr. VP-Transactions
James D. Klingbeil, Chmn.

Phone: 720-283-6120 **Fax:** 720-283-2451
Toll-Free:
Address: 1745 Shea Center Dr., Ste. 200, Highlands Ranch, CO 80129 US

GROWTH PLANS/SPECIAL FEATURES:

UDR, Inc., formerly United Dominion Realty Trust, Inc., is a self-administered real estate investment trust (REIT) that owns, acquires, renovates, develops and manages multifamily apartment communities nationwide. UDR's property portfolio includes 165 communities located in 23 markets in 10 U.S. states and Washington, D.C. The firm currently owns 45,913 completed apartment homes and maintains an ownership interest in 3,992 apartment units through joint ventures. United's subsidiaries include two operating partnerships: Heritage Communities L.P. and United Dominion Realty L.P. Another subsidiary, RE3, provides development, land entitlement and short-term hold investment services. UDR's upgrade and rehabilitation programs enable it to raise rents and attract residents with higher levels of disposable income who are more likely to accept the transfer of expenses, such as water and sewer costs, from the landlord to the resident. It focuses on the middle-market segment of the apartment market, generally renters-by-necessity, including young professionals, blue-collar families, single-parent households, singles, immigrants and families renting while waiting to purchase a home. The company believes this renting-by-necessity population provides the highest profit potential in terms of rent growth, stability of occupancy and investment opportunities. In the future, UDR will continue to emphasize aggressive lease management, improved expense control, increased resident retention efforts and the realignment of employee incentive plans tied to its bottom line performance. In 2009, the company continued development on four projects in Raleigh, North Carolina; Dallas, Texas; Addison, Texas; and Woodbridge, Virginia. In August 2009, the company formed a $450 million joint venture with the Kuwait Finance House to develop multifamily properties. In February 2010, the firm opened the first phase of its Vitruvian Park multifamily development in Addison, Texas.

UDR offers its employees benefits which include medical, dental and vision coverage; a 401(k) plan; a stock purchase plan; life and disability insurance; educational assistance; and apartment discounts.

FINANCIALS:

Sales and profits are in thousands of dollars—add 000 to get the full amount. 2009 Note: Financial information for 2009 was not available for all companies at press time.

2009 Sales: $602,899	2009 Profits: $-95,858
2008 Sales: $563,408	2008 Profits: $688,708
2007 Sales: $501,618	2007 Profits: $198,958
2006 Sales: $467,511	2006 Profits: $128,605
2005 Sales: $427,702	2005 Profits: $155,166

U.S. Stock Ticker: UDR
Int'l Ticker: Int'l Exchange:
Employees: 1,363
Fiscal Year Ends: 12/31
Parent Company:

SALARIES/BENEFITS:

Pension Plan: ESOP Stock Plan: Profit Sharing: Top Exec. Salary: $500,000 Bonus: $1,336,000
Savings Plan: Y Stock Purch. Plan: Second Exec. Salary: $450,000 Bonus: $850,000

OTHER THOUGHTS:

Apparent Women Officers or Directors: 9
Hot Spot for Advancement for Women/Minorities: Y

LOCATIONS: ("Y" = Yes)

West:	Southwest:	Midwest:	Southeast:	Northeast:	International:
Y	Y		Y	Y	

UNIBAIL-RODAMCO

www.unibail.com

Industry Group Code: 531120 **Ranks within this company's industry group:** Sales: 8 Profits: 61

Properties:		Financial Services:		Construction/Development:		Investments:		Specialty Services:		Brokerage:	
Apartments:		Mortgages:		Commercial Construction:		REIT:		Property Management:		Commercial Sales:	
Malls/Shopping:	Y	Title Insurance:		Residential Construction:				Online Services:		Residential Sales:	
Offices:	Y	Property Insurance:		Land Development:				Software/IT:		Specialty:	
Hotels/Motels:				Support Services:				Consulting:			
Industrial/Warehouses:				Design/Engineering:							
Other:	Y										

TYPES OF BUSINESS:

Commercial Property Investment Company
Office Buildings
Shopping Center Real Estate
Convention Center Real Estate

BRANDS/DIVISIONS/AFFILIATES:

Rodamco Europe NV
Unibail Holdings SA
La Maquinista
Habaneras

CONTACTS: *Note: Officers with more than one job title may be intentionally listed here more than once.*

Guillaume Poitrinal, CEO
Michel Dessolain, COO
Peter van Rossum, CFO
Catherine Pourre, Chief Resources Officer
Jaap L. Tonckens, General Counsel
Bertrand Julien-Laferrier, Chief Dev. Officer
Guillaume Poitrinal, Chmn.

Phone: 33-1-53-43-74-37 **Fax:**
Toll-Free:
Address: 7 Place du Chancelier Adenauer, Paris, Cedex 16, CS 31622-75722 France

GROWTH PLANS/SPECIAL FEATURES:

Unibail-Rodamco, formed by the July 2007 merger of Rodamco Europe NV and Unibail Holdings SA, is a Paris-based commercial property investment company that spans across 12 European countries. It operates within three business sectors: offices; shopping centers; and exhibition and convention complexes. The firm's office portfolio is comprised of office buildings, mainly located in the Paris central business district and its western outskirts. This segment has a portfolio of 16 office buildings and is focused on large buildings of over 10,000 square meters, which have been refurbished and equipped with advanced technical installations. Unibail's portfolio of 95 shopping centers is almost exclusively made up of very large shopping centers. This portfolio includes 12 regional centers, which are made up of four multi-region regional centers. The exhibition and convention centers segment is divided into two companies, VIPARIS and Comexposium, which are jointly owned by the company and the Paris Chamber of Commerce and Industry. This segment consists of 10 venues, are located in Paris and its western outskirts, and spread over 360,000 square meters. In February 2010, the company agreed to sell five Dutch shopping centers to Wereldhave for $312 million. Also in February 2010, the company entered into an agreement with Simon Property Group and Ivanhoe Cambridge to acquire the Simon Ivanhoe portfolio in Europe for $949 million. The Simon Ivanhoe portfolio consists of seven shopping centers in Poland and France.

FINANCIALS: **Sales and profits are in thousands of dollars—add 000 to get the full amount. 2009 Note: Financial information for 2009 was not available for all companies at press time.**

2009 Sales: $1,942,350 | 2009 Profits: $-1,958,090
2008 Sales: $1,893,300 | 2008 Profits: $-1,484,300
2007 Sales: $1,180,900 | 2007 Profits: $1,256,600
2006 Sales: $869,000 | 2006 Profits: $2,845,900
2005 Sales: $785,700 | 2005 Profits: $2,188,800

U.S. Stock Ticker:
Int'l Ticker: UL Int'l Exchange: Paris-Euronext
Employees: 1,717
Fiscal Year Ends:
Parent Company:

SALARIES/BENEFITS:

Pension Plan: | ESOP Stock Plan: | Profit Sharing: | Top Exec. Salary: $ | Bonus: $
Savings Plan: | Stock Purch. Plan: | | Second Exec. Salary: $ | Bonus: $

OTHER THOUGHTS:

Apparent Women Officers or Directors: 2
Hot Spot for Advancement for Women/Minorities:

LOCATIONS: ("Y" = Yes)

West:	Southwest:	Midwest:	Southeast:	Northeast:	International:
					Y

UNITECH LIMITED

www.unitechgroup.com

Industry Group Code: 5311 **Ranks within this company's industry group:** Sales: 21 Profits: 15

Properties:		Financial Services:		Construction/Development:		Investments:		Specialty Services:		Brokerage:	
Apartments:	Y	Mortgages:		Commercial Construction:	Y	REIT:		Property Management:		Commercial Sales:	
Malls/Shopping:		Title Insurance:		Residential Construction:	Y			Online Services:		Residential Sales:	
Offices:		Property Insurance:		Land Development:				Software/IT:		Specialty:	
Hotels/Motels:				Support Services:				Consulting:			
Industrial/Warehouses:				Design/Engineering:							
Other:											

TYPES OF BUSINESS:

Real Estate Development
Construction and Civil Engineering Services
Telecommunications

BRANDS/DIVISIONS/AFFILIATES:

CONTACTS:

Note: Officers with more than one job title may be intentionally listed here more than once.

Sanjay Chandra, Managing Dir.
Manoj Popli, CFO
Deepak Jain, Sec./Compliance Officer
Ajay Chandra, Joint Managing Dir./Executive Dir.
Ramesh Chandra, Chmn.

Phone: 91-11-4166-4040	**Fax:** 91-11-2685-7338
Toll-Free:	
Address: 6, Community Centre, New Delhi, 110 017 India	

GROWTH PLANS/SPECIAL FEATURES:

Unitech Limited is an India-based real estate development and construction firm. The company's operations are organized into five categories: Residential, Commercial, Retail & Leisure, Construction and Wireless. The residential category includes housing units in such areas as Bangalore, Mumbai, Gurgaon, Mohali, Noida, Lucknow, and Kolkata. The commercial category includes office complexes and business parks in Kolkata, Gurgaon and Noida. The retail & leisure category includes an amusement park, hotel and shopping centers in Noida, as well as shopping malls in Gurgaon. The construction category is focused on various industrial and residential construction projects, including highways, transmission lines and overseas turnkey projects. Completed projects in the construction category include exhaust chimneys at power plants in various parts of India, steel and cement plant construction projects, a 305-room hotel in New Delhi, a multi-purpose indoor stadium in Madras and a residential apartment complex in Gurgaon, as well as various highway construction and expansion projects. The wireless segment operates through Uninor Cellular Services, a joint venture with Norweigeian mobile communications group Telenor. The firm owns 32.75% interest in the venture. Uninor Cellular Services currently offers mobile telephony services in Uttaranchal, Bihar, Orissa, Tamil Nadu, Karnataka, Kerala and Andhra Pradesh, India. Unitech maintains business offices in Gurgaon, Agra, Bangalore, Chennai, Hyderabad, Kochi, Lucknow and Mumbai.

FINANCIALS:

Sales and profits are in thousands of dollars—add 000 to get the full amount. 2009 Note: Financial information for 2009 was not available for all companies at press time.

2009 Sales: $747,730	2009 Profits: $269,820	**U.S. Stock Ticker:**
2008 Sales: $844,600	2008 Profits: $327,730	**Int'l Ticker: 507878** Int'l Exchange: Bombay-BSE
2007 Sales: $668,580	2007 Profits: $257,740	Employees: 967
2006 Sales: $185,770	2006 Profits: $16,690	Fiscal Year Ends: 3/31
2005 Sales: $	2005 Profits: $	Parent Company:

SALARIES/BENEFITS:

Pension Plan:	ESOP Stock Plan:	Profit Sharing:	Top Exec. Salary: $	Bonus: $
Savings Plan:	Stock Purch. Plan:		Second Exec. Salary: $	Bonus: $

OTHER THOUGHTS:

Apparent Women Officers or Directors:
Hot Spot for Advancement for Women/Minorities:

LOCATIONS: ("Y" = Yes)

West:	Southwest:	Midwest:	Southeast:	Northeast:	International:
					Y

URS CORPORATION

www.urscorp.com

Industry Group Code: 541330 **Ranks within this company's industry group:** Sales: 1 Profits: 2

Properties:		Financial Services:		Construction/Development:		Investments:		Specialty Services:		Brokerage:	
Apartments:		Mortgages:		Commercial Construction:		REIT:		Property Management:		Commercial Sales:	
Malls/Shopping:		Title Insurance:		Residential Construction:				Online Services:		Residential Sales:	
Offices:		Property Insurance:		Land Development:				Software/IT:		Specialty:	
Hotels/Motels:				Support Services:	Y			Consulting:			
Industrial/Warehouses:				Design/Engineering:	Y						
Other:											

TYPES OF BUSINESS:

Engineering Design Services
Systems Engineering & Technical Assistance
Operations & Maintenance Services
Construction

BRANDS/DIVISIONS/AFFILIATES:

EG&G Division
URS Division
Washington Division

CONTACTS:

Note: Officers with more than one job title may be intentionally listed here more than once.

Martin M. Koffel, CEO
Martin M. Koffel, Pres.
H. Thomas Hicks, CFO/VP-Finance
Joseph Masters, General Counsel/Sec.
Thomas W. Bishop, VP-Strategy/Sr. VP-Construction Svcs.
Susan B. Kilgannon, VP-Comm.
Reed N. Brimhall, Chief Acct. Officer/Controller/VP
Thomas H. Zarges, Pres., Washington Div.
Gary V. Jandegian, VP/Pres., URS Div.
Randall A. Wotring, VP/Pres., EG&G Div.
Martin M. Koffel, Chmn.

Phone: 415-774-2700	**Fax:** 415-398-1905
Toll-Free:	
Address: 600 Montgomery St., Fl. 26, San Francisco, CA 94111 US	

GROWTH PLANS/SPECIAL FEATURES:

URS Corp. is a worldwide engineering design services firm and a U.S. federal government contractor for systems engineering, technical assistance, operations and maintenance services. The company focuses primarily on providing fee-based professional and technical services in the engineering and construction services and defense markets. The firm operates in three divisions: URS, EG&G and the Washington division. The URS division provides professional planning and design; program management; construction management; and operations and maintenance services to various government agencies and departments in the U.S. and internationally, as well as to private industry clients. The EG&G division provides planning; systems engineering and technical assistance; operations and maintenance; and program management services to various U.S. governmental agencies, including the Departments of Defense and Homeland Security. The Washington division builds transportation infrastructure, including airports, mass transit systems and tolls roads. The unit also performs intricate tasks such as nuclear waste disposal, mining, engineering and facility management. The company has a network of offices and job sites across the U.S. and in more than 30 foreign countries in the Americas, Europe, the Middle East and Asia-Pacific. The federal government accounted for 35% of the company's revenues in 2008, while industrial and commercial, power and infrastructure projects accounted for 29%, 19% and 17%, respectively. In June 2009, the company sold its stake in the German mining and power joint venture MIBRAG.

URS offers its employees medical, vision and dental insurance; a 401(k) plan; an employee stock purchase plan; short- and long-term insurance; life and AD&D insurance; an employee assistance program; flexible spending accounts; and tuition reimbursement.

FINANCIALS:

Sales and profits are in thousands of dollars—add 000 to get the full amount. 2009 Note: Financial information for 2009 was not available for all companies at press time.

2009 Sales: $9,249,100	2009 Profits: $269,100	**U.S. Stock Ticker: URS**
2008 Sales: $10,086,289	2008 Profits: $219,791	**Int'l Ticker:** Int'l Exchange:
2007 Sales: $5,383,007	2007 Profits: $132,243	Employees: 45,000
2006 Sales: $4,222,869	2006 Profits: $113,012	Fiscal Year Ends: 12/31
2005 Sales: $3,890,282	2005 Profits: $82,475	Parent Company:

SALARIES/BENEFITS:

Pension Plan: Y	ESOP Stock Plan:	Profit Sharing:	Top Exec. Salary: $1,019,232	Bonus: $2,500,003
Savings Plan: Y	Stock Purch. Plan: Y		Second Exec. Salary: $713,462	Bonus: $1,047,122

OTHER THOUGHTS:

Apparent Women Officers or Directors: 2
Hot Spot for Advancement for Women/Minorities: Y

LOCATIONS: ("Y" = Yes)

West:	Southwest:	Midwest:	Southeast:	Northeast:	International:
Y	Y	Y	Y	Y	Y

VENTAS INC

www.ventasreit.com

Industry Group Code: 531120 **Ranks within this company's industry group:** Sales: 19 Profits: 14

Properties:		Financial Services:		Construction/Development:		Investments:		Specialty Services:		Brokerage:	
Apartments:		Mortgages:		Commercial Construction:		REIT:	Y	Property Management:		Commercial Sales:	
Malls/Shopping:		Title Insurance:		Residential Construction:				Online Services:		Residential Sales:	
Offices:		Property Insurance:		Land Development:				Software/IT:		Specialty:	
Hotels/Motels:				Support Services:				Consulting:			
Industrial/Warehouses:				Design/Engineering:							
Other:	Y										

TYPES OF BUSINESS:

Real Estate Investment Trust
Hospitals
Senior Housing Properties
Medical Office Buildings
Skilled Nursing Facilities

BRANDS/DIVISIONS/AFFILIATES:

Ventas Realty LP
Ventas SSL Inc
PSLT OP LP

CONTACTS: *Note: Officers with more than one job title may be intentionally listed here more than once.*

Debra A. Cafaro, CEO
Debra A. Cafaro, Pres.
Richard A. Schweinhart, CFO/Exec. VP
Julie M. Dreixler, Sr. VP-Human Resources
T. Richard Riney, Chief Admin. Officer/Exec. VP
T. Richard Riney, General Counsel/Corp. Sec.
David J. Smith, VP-Investor Rel.
Robert J. Brehl, Chief Acct. Officer/Controller
Raymond Lewis, Exec. VP/Chief Investment Officer
Timothy A. Doman, Sr. VP-Asset Mgmt.
Brian K. Wood, Sr. VP-Tax
Kristen M. Benson, VP/Senior Securities Counsel
Debra A. Cafaro, Chmn.

Phone: 312-660-3800 **Fax:** 312-660-3850
Toll-Free:
Address: 111 S. Wacker Dr., Ste. 4800, Chicago, IL 60606 US

GROWTH PLANS/SPECIAL FEATURES:

Ventas, Inc. is a health care real estate investment trust (REIT) with a geographically diverse portfolio of health care facilities. This portfolio consists of 40 hospitals, 187 skilled nursing facilities, 34 medical office buildings and 244 senior housing facilities in 43 states and two Canadian provinces. The company is the sole owner of 439 of these assets, and holds a majority interest in all remaining 66 properties. The firm conducts substantially all of its business through three wholly-owned subsidiaries: Ventas Realty, LP, PSLT OP, L.P., and Ventas SSL, Inc. The company leases its facilities to health care operating companies under triple-net or absolute-net leases. Kindred Healthcare, Inc. and its subsidiaries lease Ventas' nursing facilities and some of its hospitals; Brookdale Living Communities, Inc., and Sunrise Senior Living, Inc. are the company's other major customers. The firm's business strategy includes three primary objectives: diversifying its portfolio of properties; maintaining a strong balance sheet and liquidity; and increasing its earnings. In early 2009, Ventas sold four senior housing properties to Benchmark Assisted Living affiliates for $58.7 million; and sold Samaritan, an acute care hospital in Lexington, Kentucky, to affiliates of the University of Kentucky for $35 million. In April 2009, the company dissolved operating partnership ElderTrust Operating, LP. In July 2009, the firm sold six skilled nursing facilities to Kindred Healthcare, Inc. for roughly $58 million. In December 2009, Ventas acquired three medical office buildings for $62.5 million.

FINANCIALS: **Sales and profits are in thousands of dollars—add 000 to get the full amount. 2009 Note: Financial information for 2009 was not available for all companies at press time.**

2009 Sales: $936,094 | 2009 Profits: $266,495
2008 Sales: $923,698 | 2008 Profits: $222,603
2007 Sales: $746,697 | 2007 Profits: $273,681
2006 Sales: $397,951 | 2006 Profits: $131,430
2005 Sales: $355,939 | 2005 Profits: $130,583

U.S. Stock Ticker: VTR
Int'l Ticker: Int'l Exchange:
Employees: 61
Fiscal Year Ends: 12/31
Parent Company:

SALARIES/BENEFITS:

Pension Plan: ESOP Stock Plan: Profit Sharing: Top Exec. Salary: $652,000 Bonus: $2,013,865
Savings Plan: Stock Purch. Plan: Second Exec. Salary: $407,000 Bonus: $854,700

OTHER THOUGHTS:

Apparent Women Officers or Directors: 3
Hot Spot for Advancement for Women/Minorities: Y

LOCATIONS: ("Y" = Yes)

West:	Southwest:	Midwest:	Southeast:	Northeast:	International:
Y	Y	Y	Y	Y	

VINCI

www.vinci.com

Industry Group Code: 237 **Ranks within this company's industry group:** Sales: 2 Profits: 2

Properties:		Financial Services:		Construction/Development:		Investments:		Specialty Services:		Brokerage:	
Apartments:		Mortgages:		Commercial Construction:	Y	REIT:		Property Management:	Y	Commercial Sales:	
Malls/Shopping:		Title Insurance:		Residential Construction:				Online Services:		Residential Sales:	
Offices:		Property Insurance:		Land Development:	Y			Software/IT:	Y	Specialty:	
Hotels/Motels:				Support Services:	Y			Consulting:			
Industrial/Warehouses:				Design/Engineering:	Y						
Other:											

TYPES OF BUSINESS:

Heavy Construction
Infrastructure Management
Information & Energy Technologies
Commercial Construction
Engineering Services
Highway Construction
Airport Management & Support Services
Power Transmission Services

BRANDS/DIVISIONS/AFFILIATES:

VINCI Concessions
VINCI Energies
Eurovia
VINCI Construction
Taylor Woodrow Construction
Autoroutes Du Sud De La France (ASF)
Haymills Property Solutions

CONTACTS: *Note: Officers with more than one job title may be intentionally listed here more than once.*

Xavier Huillard, CEO
Christian Labeyrie, CFO/Exec. VP
Franck Mougin, Dir.-Human Resources & Sustainable Dev.
Patrick Richard, Dir.-Legal Affairs
Jean-Luc Pommier, VP-Bus. Dev.
Pierre Duprat, Dir.-Corp. Comm.
Jean-Yves le Brouster, CEO-VINCI Energies
Xavier Huillard, CEO-VINCI Concessions
Louis-Roch Burgard, COO-VINCI Concessions
Jacques Tavernier, CEO-Eurovia
Yves-Thibault de Silguy, Chmn.
John Stanion, Chmn.-VINCI PLC (UK)

Phone: 33-1-47-16-3500 **Fax:** 33-1-47-51-9102
Toll-Free:
Address: 1 Cours Ferdinand-de-Lesseps, Rueil-Malmaison, 92851 France

GROWTH PLANS/SPECIAL FEATURES:

VINCI, one of the largest companies operating in construction and related services worldwide, consists of four major divisions: VINCI Concessions, VINCI Energies, Eurovia and VINCI Construction. VINCI Concessions is engaged in the design, turnkey construction, financing and operation of facilities, as well as outsourced infrastructure management. Its comprehensive approach is applied to major public facilities such as the Stade de France stadium near Paris, as well as to the operation of various motorways, car parks and airports. The overall Concessions business line accounts for approximately 15% of company revenues. VINCI Energies is a leading European producer of information and energy technologies for infrastructure, industry, the service sector and telecommunications. It operates through several brands in Europe, including Actemium, offering energy services to industry; Axians, offering voice-data-image communication services; Citeos, specializing in urban lighting; Graniou, supporting telecommunications infrastructure; Omexom, specializing in high-voltage power; and Opteor, offering industrial and services maintenance. The Energies business line accounts for approximately 15% of company revenues. Eurovia is a leading European company in the road industry and in recycled materials, operating in roadworks, materials production, environment-related activities and services. It accounts for approximately 25% of company revenues. VINCI Construction, representing roughly 45% of overall company revenues, is an industry leader in building, civil engineering, hydraulics and facilities management. The division is composed of three main components: Mainland France; Local Markets outside mainland France; and Worldwide activities, including major structures, specialized civil engineering and dredging. VINCI is engaged in a design-build project for a causeway between Qatar and Bahrain, which will be among the world's longest bridges. In September 2008, the company acquired the Taylor Woodrow Construction Unit from U.K.-based Taylor Wimpey PLC for approximately $122 million. In August 2009, VINCI Construction acquired U.K. property and construction firm Haymills Property Solutions.

FINANCIALS: **Sales and profits are in thousands of dollars—add 000 to get the full amount. 2009 Note: Financial information for 2009 was not available for all companies at press time.**

2009 Sales: $44,101,500	2009 Profits: $2,168,390	**U.S. Stock Ticker:**
2008 Sales: $42,717,900	2008 Profits: $2,003,070	**Int'l Ticker: DG** Int'l Exchange: Paris-Euronext
2007 Sales: $33,820,000	2007 Profits: $1,680,000	Employees:
2006 Sales: $35,200,919	2006 Profits: $	Fiscal Year Ends: 12/31
2005 Sales: $31,785,190	2005 Profits: $1,053,100	Parent Company:

SALARIES/BENEFITS:

Pension Plan:	ESOP Stock Plan:	Profit Sharing:	Top Exec. Salary: $	Bonus: $
Savings Plan:	Stock Purch. Plan:		Second Exec. Salary: $	Bonus: $

OTHER THOUGHTS:

Apparent Women Officers or Directors:
Hot Spot for Advancement for Women/Minorities:

LOCATIONS: ("Y" = Yes)

West:	Southwest:	Midwest:	Southeast:	Northeast:	International:
Y	Y	Y	Y	Y	Y

VORNADO REALTY TRUST

www.vno.com

Industry Group Code: 531120 **Ranks within this company's industry group:** Sales: 7 Profits: 7

Properties:		Financial Services:		Construction/Development:		Investments:		Specialty Services:		Brokerage:	
Apartments:		Mortgages:		Commercial Construction:		REIT:	Y	Property Management:		Commercial Sales:	
Malls/Shopping:	Y	Title Insurance:		Residential Construction:				Online Services:		Residential Sales:	
Offices:	Y	Property Insurance:		Land Development:				Software/IT:		Specialty:	
Hotels/Motels:	Y			Support Services:				Consulting:			
Industrial/Warehouses:	Y			Design/Engineering:							
Other:	Y										

TYPES OF BUSINESS:

Real Estate Investment Trust
Office Properties
Retail Properties
Toys
Merchandise

BRANDS/DIVISIONS/AFFILIATES:

Merchandise Mart
Toys-R-Us Inc
Alexander's
Hotel Pennsylvania
Vornado Retail Portfolio

CONTACTS:

Note: Officers with more than one job title may be intentionally listed here more than once.

Michael D. Fascitelli, CEO
Michael D. Fascitelli, Pres.
Joseph Macnow, CFO
Joseph Macnow, Exec. VP-Admin.
Joseph Macnow, Exec. VP-Finance
David R. Greenbaum, Pres., New York Office Div.
Sandeep Mathrani, Exec. VP-Retail Real Estate Div.
Michelle Felman, Exec. VP-Acquisitions
Wendy Silverstein, Exec. VP-Capital Markets
Steven Roth, Chmn.

Phone: 212-894-7000	**Fax:** 201-587-0600
Toll-Free:	
Address: 888 7th Ave., New York, NY 10019 US	

GROWTH PLANS/SPECIAL FEATURES:

Vornado Realty Trust, which conducts its business through Vornado Realty L.P., is a fully integrated real estate investment trust (REIT). It is one of the largest property owners in New York City, primarily in Manhattan. The firm has four different platforms: office, retail, merchandise mart and toys. The office portfolio is made up of 109 wholly- or partially-owned office properties (36.2 million square feet) in the New York City metropolitan area; Washington, D.C.; northern Virginia; and San Francisco. The Vornado Retail Portfolio controls and/or manages 164 properties (22.1 million square feet) in 21 states, Puerto Rico and Washington, D.C. The Merchandise Mart division includes eight properties in five states and Washington, D.C., with 8.9 million square feet of showroom and office space. The toys division holds a 32.7% interest in Toys-R-Us, Inc., which owns and/or operates approximately 1,567 stores worldwide. Vornado's additional properties include the Hotel Pennsylvania in Manhattan, containing 1 million square feet with 1,700 rooms and 400,000 square feet of retail and office space; and a 32.4% interest in Alexander's, which owns seven properties in the greater New York metropolitan area. In 2009, Vornado sold 15 retail properties in separate transactions. In September 2009, the firm sold its 1999 K Street office property in the business district of Washington, D.C.

FINANCIALS:

Sales and profits are in thousands of dollars—add 000 to get the full amount. 2009 Note: Financial information for 2009 was not available for all companies at press time.

2009 Sales: $2,742,578	2009 Profits: $128,450	**U.S. Stock Ticker: VNO**
2008 Sales: $2,692,686	2008 Profits: $411,445	**Int'l Ticker:** Int'l Exchange:
2007 Sales: $2,405,243	2007 Profits: $607,833	Employees: 4,597
2006 Sales: $1,909,100	2006 Profits: $560,140	Fiscal Year Ends: 12/31
2005 Sales: $2,519,861	2005 Profits: $539,604	Parent Company:

SALARIES/BENEFITS:

Pension Plan:	ESOP Stock Plan:	Profit Sharing:	Top Exec. Salary: $1,000,000	Bonus: $750,000
Savings Plan:	Stock Purch. Plan:		Second Exec. Salary: $1,000,000	Bonus: $750,000

OTHER THOUGHTS:

Apparent Women Officers or Directors: 2
Hot Spot for Advancement for Women/Minorities: Y

LOCATIONS: ("Y" = Yes)

West:	Southwest:	Midwest:	Southeast:	Northeast:	International:
Y	Y	Y	Y	Y	Y

WASHINGTON REAL ESTATE INVESTMENT TRUST www.writ.com

Industry Group Code: 531110 **Ranks within this company's industry group:** Sales: 15 Profits: 11

Properties:		Financial Services:		Construction/Development:		Investments:		Specialty Services:		Brokerage:	
Apartments:	Y	Mortgages:		Commercial Construction:		REIT:	Y	Property Management:		Commercial Sales:	
Malls/Shopping:	Y	Title Insurance:		Residential Construction:				Online Services:		Residential Sales:	
Offices:	Y	Property Insurance:		Land Development:				Software/IT:		Specialty:	
Hotels/Motels:				Support Services:				Consulting:			
Industrial/Warehouses:	Y			Design/Engineering:							
Other:											

TYPES OF BUSINESS:

Real Estate Investment Trust
Office Buildings
Industrial Properties
Retail Properties
Apartments
Medical Office Buildings

BRANDS/DIVISIONS/AFFILIATES:

CONTACTS:

Note: Officers with more than one job title may be intentionally listed here more than once.

George F. McKenzie, CEO
George F. McKenzie, Pres.
William T. Camp, CFO/Exec. VP
Laura M. Franklin, Exec. VP-Admin.
Thomas C. Morey, General Counsel/Sr. VP
Laura M. Franklin, Exec. VP-Acct.
Michael Paukstitus, Sr. VP-Real Estate
Thomas L. Regnell, Sr. VP-Acquisitions
David A. DiNardo, Managing Dir.-Leasing
James B. Cederdahl, Managing Dir.-Property Mgmt.
Edmund B. Cronin, Jr., Chmn.

Phone: 301-984-9400	**Fax:** 301-984-9610
Toll-Free: 800-565-9748	
Address: 6110 Executive Blvd., Ste. 800, Rockville, MD 20852 US	

GROWTH PLANS/SPECIAL FEATURES:

Washington Real Estate Investment Trust (WRIT) is a self-administered, self-managed, equity real estate investment trust (REIT) that owns and develops income-producing real properties in the greater Washington, D.C./Baltimore region. Its portfolio contains general purpose office buildings, medical office buildings, industrial/flex properties, multifamily buildings and retail centers. WRIT owns 90 properties consisting of 27 general purpose office properties; 20 industrial/flex properties and land held for development; 14 retail centers; 18 medical office properties; and 11 multifamily properties. Its principal objective is to invest in high quality properties in prime locations, then proactively manage, lease and develop ongoing capital improvement programs to improve their economic performance. The company's geographic focus is based on two principles: real estate is a local business and is more effectively selected and managed by owners located and with expertise in the region; and geographic markets deserving of focus must be among the nation's best with a strong primary industry and diversified enough to withstand downturns in their primary industry. In May 2009, WRIT sold Avondale Apartments, a multifamily property, for $7 million. In July 2009, the company sold Tech 100 Industrial Park, an industrial property, for $4.2 million. Also in July 2009, WRIT sold Brandywine Center, an office property, for $3.3 million. In August 2009, the firm acquired Lansdowne Medical Office Building for $19.9 million. In November 2009, the company sold Crossroads Distribution Center, another industrial property, for $1.6 million.

The company offers its employees medical, dental and vision insurance; a 401(k) plan; tuition reimbursement; short- and long-term disability; flexible spending accounts; an annual incentive bonus program; an employee assistance program; and an in-house fitness center.

FINANCIALS:

Sales and profits are in thousands of dollars—add 000 to get the full amount. 2009 Note: Financial information for 2009 was not available for all companies at press time.

2009 Sales: $306,929	2009 Profits: $40,948	**U.S. Stock Ticker: WRE**
2008 Sales: $278,691	2008 Profits: $27,082	**Int'l Ticker:** Int'l Exchange:
2007 Sales: $248,899	2007 Profits: $57,451	Employees: 301
2006 Sales: $205,940	2006 Profits: $38,661	Fiscal Year Ends: 12/31
2005 Sales: $180,255	2005 Profits: $77,638	Parent Company:

SALARIES/BENEFITS:

Pension Plan:	ESOP Stock Plan:	Profit Sharing:	Top Exec. Salary: $405,521	Bonus: $466,735
Savings Plan: Y	Stock Purch. Plan:		Second Exec. Salary: $320,925	Bonus: $284,729

OTHER THOUGHTS:

Apparent Women Officers or Directors: 2
Hot Spot for Advancement for Women/Minorities: Y

LOCATIONS: ("Y" = Yes)

West:	Southwest:	Midwest:	Southeast:	Northeast:	International:
				Y	

WATSON LAND COMPANY

www.watsonlandcompany.com

Industry Group Code: 5311 **Ranks within this company's industry group:** Sales: Profits:

Properties:		Financial Services:		Construction/Development:		Investments:		Specialty Services:		Brokerage:	
Apartments:		Mortgages:		Commercial Construction:	Y	REIT:		Property Management:	Y	Commercial Sales:	
Malls/Shopping:		Title Insurance:		Residential Construction:				Online Services:		Residential Sales:	
Offices:	Y	Property Insurance:		Land Development:	Y			Software/IT:		Specialty:	
Hotels/Motels:				Support Services:	Y			Consulting:			
Industrial/Warehouses:	Y			Design/Engineering:	Y						
Other:											

TYPES OF BUSINESS:

Office & Industrial Properties
Land Development
Commercial Construction
Property Management
Building Maintenance & Operations

BRANDS/DIVISIONS/AFFILIATES:

Heritage Customer Service Program
Legacy Building Series

CONTACTS:

Note: Officers with more than one job title may be intentionally listed here more than once.

Bruce A. Choate, CEO
Bruce A. Choate, Pres.
Roger von Ting, CFO
Lance P. Ryan, VP-Mktg. & Leasing
Bradley D. Frazier, General Counsel/Corp. Sec.
Kirk R. Johnson, Exec. VP-Real Estate Oper.
Craig B. Halverson, VP-Acquisitions
Pilar M. Hoyos, VP-Public Affairs
Jeffrey R. Jennison, VP-Real Estate Asset Mgmt.
Thomas W. Huston, VP-Leasing & Real Estate Asset Mgmt.
Christopher L. Trujillo, VP-Construction
Robert W. Huston, Chmn.

Phone: 310-952-6400 **Fax:** 310-522-8788
Toll-Free:
Address: 22010 S. Wilmington Ave., Ste. 400, Carson, CA 90745 US

GROWTH PLANS/SPECIAL FEATURES:

Watson Land Company is a private REIT (Real Estate Investment Trust) that develops, owns and manages industrial properties in Southern California including the Los Angeles area. It is one of the largest developers of industrial centers in Los Angeles County, having planned more than 1,000 acres of industrial and commercial property in addition to owning and managing approximately 14 million square feet of industrial, office and technology buildings and business centers. Watson specializes in building master-planned facilities for warehousing, distribution, assembly and manufacturing. It also builds office buildings and multi-tenant business centers that serve as corporate headquarters; administrative and general offices; and computer operations, data processing, technology and service-related centers. Watson's Heritage Customer Service Program offers clients a unique lease structure through which Watson assumes and manages the maintenance and operating functions typically performed by the customer. The Heritage program is tailored to the client and can include roofing, yard, lighting, painting and HVAC maintenance repair and replacement services. Watson's Legacy Building Series consists of build-to-suit industrial buildings and corporate headquarters for clients such as Mercedes-Benz, Kmart, NEC Logistics, TRW, McDonnell Douglas and Honda. Watson has also completed the incorporation of several master-planned business centers into a General Purpose Zone Site as part of Foreign Trade Zone (FTZ) 202, sponsored by the Port of Los Angeles. FTZ status is intended to provide approved customers enhanced cost savings and operating benefits to maximize efficiency. In addition, the company has land holdings available for development in the Inland Empire region of California. Other notable customers have included Boeing; BP West Coast Products; DHL; Hansen's; Hitachi Transport; Target Logistics; The Pasha Group; Union Pacific Railroad; the United States Postal Service; and Whirlpool.

FINANCIALS:

Sales and profits are in thousands of dollars—add 000 to get the full amount. 2009 Note: Financial information for 2009 was not available for all companies at press time.

2009 Sales: $	2009 Profits: $	**U.S. Stock Ticker: Private**
2008 Sales: $	2008 Profits: $	**Int'l Ticker:** Int'l Exchange:
2007 Sales: $	2007 Profits: $	Employees:
2006 Sales: $	2006 Profits: $	Fiscal Year Ends: 12/31
2005 Sales: $	2005 Profits: $	Parent Company:

SALARIES/BENEFITS:

Pension Plan:	ESOP Stock Plan:	Profit Sharing:	Top Exec. Salary: $	Bonus: $
Savings Plan:	Stock Purch. Plan:		Second Exec. Salary: $	Bonus: $

OTHER THOUGHTS:

Apparent Women Officers or Directors:
Hot Spot for Advancement for Women/Minorities:

LOCATIONS: ("Y" = Yes)

West:	Southwest:	Midwest:	Southeast:	Northeast:	International:
Y					

WCI COMMUNITIES INC

www.wcicommunities.com

Industry Group Code: 2361 **Ranks within this company's industry group:** Sales: 17 Profits: 12

Properties:		Financial Services:		Construction/Development:		Investments:		Specialty Services:		Brokerage:	
Apartments:	Y	Mortgages:	Y	Commercial Construction:	Y	REIT:		Property Management:	Y	Commercial Sales:	
Malls/Shopping:		Title Insurance:	Y	Residential Construction:	Y			Online Services:		Residential Sales:	Y
Offices:		Property Insurance:		Land Development:	Y			Software/IT:		Specialty:	
Hotels/Motels:				Support Services:	Y			Consulting:			
Industrial/Warehouses:				Design/Engineering:	Y						
Other:	Y										

TYPES OF BUSINESS:

Homebuilding
Country Club Management
Title Insurance
Design & Engineering Services
Residential Brokerage
Land Development
Mortgages

BRANDS/DIVISIONS/AFFILIATES:

Prudential Florida WCI Realty
WCI Amenities
Florida Title & Guarantee

CONTACTS:

Note: Officers with more than one job title may be intentionally listed here more than once.

David L. Fry, CEO
David L. Fry, Pres.
Russel Devendorf, CFO/Sr. VP
Diana Walker, Sr. VP-Human Resources
Diana Walker, CIO
Vivien N. Hastings, General Counsel/Sr. VP
Douglas L. Schwartz, Sr. VP-Asset Mgmt.

Phone: 239-498-8200 **Fax:** 239-498-8338
Toll-Free: 800-924-4005
Address: 24301 Walden Ctr. Dr., Ste. 300, Bonita Springs, FL 34134 US

GROWTH PLANS/SPECIAL FEATURES:

WCI Communities, Inc. is a designer, builder and seller of traditional and luxury high-rise homes, which are typically part of master planned communities. WCI has locations in Florida, Connecticut New Jersey and New York. The company's community and mid-rise and high-rise tower (known as Sky Homes) locations contain homes ranging in price from around $100,000 to over $10 million. WCI owns approximately 13,000 acres of land, some if which it sells to other builders. WCI communities offer a wide array of world-class amenities including hotel services, boating, river clubs, marinas, championship golf courses, tennis complexes, fine dining, concierge services, nature trails, spas and fitness studios. The company's Prudential Florida WCI Realty division operates its mortgage and title business; Florida Title & Guarantee underwrites its policies on behalf of large national title insurers. The firm's amenities division, WCI Amenities, operates many of the clubhouses, golf courses, restaurants and marinas within WCI communities. After filing for Chapter 11 bankruptcy protection in 2008, the firm emerged from bankruptcy in September 2009 as a private company. In December 2009, the company sold its Oceanside property located in Pompano Beach Florida for $38.5 million. In February 2010, WCI Communities sold 102 homesites at its Four Corners community in East Fishkill, New York to Toll Brothers, Inc. for $8.9 million.

Employees are offered medical and dental insurance; a vision reimbursement plan; life insurance; flexible spending accounts; a pre-paid legal plan; tuition assistance; adoption assistance; an employee assistance plan; and a home purchase discount.

FINANCIALS:

Sales and profits are in thousands of dollars—add 000 to get the full amount. 2009 Note: Financial information for 2009 was not available for all companies at press time.

2009 Sales: $	2009 Profits: $	**U.S. Stock Ticker: Private**
2008 Sales: $556,077	2008 Profits: $-936,796	**Int'l Ticker:** Int'l Exchange:
2007 Sales: $936,376	2007 Profits: $-578,531	Employees: 1,450
2006 Sales: $2,044,585	2006 Profits: $9,014	Fiscal Year Ends: 12/31
2005 Sales: $2,593,648	2005 Profits: $186,150	Parent Company:

SALARIES/BENEFITS:

Pension Plan:	ESOP Stock Plan:	Profit Sharing:	Top Exec. Salary: $	Bonus: $
Savings Plan: Y	Stock Purch. Plan:		Second Exec. Salary: $	Bonus: $

OTHER THOUGHTS:

Apparent Women Officers or Directors: 3
Hot Spot for Advancement for Women/Minorities: Y

LOCATIONS: ("Y" = Yes)

West:	Southwest:	Midwest:	Southeast:	Northeast:	International:
			Y	Y	

WEINGARTEN REALTY INVESTORS

www.weingarten.com

Industry Group Code: 531120 **Ranks within this company's industry group:** Sales: 29 Profits: 17

Properties:		Financial Services:		Construction/Development:		Investments:		Specialty Services:		Brokerage:	
Apartments:		Mortgages:		Commercial Construction:	Y	REIT:	Y	Property Management:	Y	Commercial Sales:	
Malls/Shopping:	Y	Title Insurance:		Residential Construction:				Online Services:		Residential Sales:	
Offices:	Y	Property Insurance:		Land Development:	Y			Software/IT:		Specialty:	
Hotels/Motels:				Support Services:				Consulting:			
Industrial/Warehouses:	Y			Design/Engineering:							
Other:											

TYPES OF BUSINESS:

Real Estate Investment Trust
Industrial & Office Properties
Shopping Centers
Commercial Construction
Property Management

BRANDS/DIVISIONS/AFFILIATES:

CONTACTS:

Note: Officers with more than one job title may be intentionally listed here more than once.

Andrew M. Alexander, CEO
Andrew M. Alexander, Pres.
Stephen C. Richter, CFO/Exec. VP
Michael Townsell, VP-Human Resources
Lee Pearson, CIO/VP
Jeffrey A. Tucker, General Counsel/Sr. VP
Robert Smith, Sr. VP-New Dev.
Kristin Gandy, Dir.-Investor Rel.
Joe D. Shafer, Chief Acct. Officer/Sr. VP
Patricia A. Bender, Exec. VP-Leasing
Johnny L. Hendrix, Exec. VP-Asset Mgmt.
Gary Greenberg, Sr. VP-Capital Markets
M. Candace DuFour, Sr. VP-Acquisitions/Corp. Sec.
Stanford Alexander, Chmn.

Phone: 713-886-6000	**Fax:** 713-886-6049
Toll-Free:	
Address: 2600 Citadel Plz. Dr., Ste. 125, Houston, TX 77008 US	

GROWTH PLANS/SPECIAL FEATURES:

Weingarten Realty Investors, a Real Estate Investment Trust (REIT), primarily owns and develops neighborhood and community shopping centers, as well as industrial properties. It owns or operates under long-term leases, directly and through interests in joint ventures or partnerships, a total of 376 income-producing properties and 13 properties in various stages of construction and development. The firm's portfolio, totaling roughly 70 million square feet, includes 307 neighborhood and community shopping centers, accounting for 89.4% of Weingarten's revenues; 76 industrial properties, representing 9.3%; and three other properties, representing 1.3% of revenues. 88 of Weingarten's properties are located in the Houston metropolitan area and 66 are located in other parts of Texas; in all, its properties are divided between 23 states, including retail properties in 22 states and industrial properties in six states. The company's operating strategy consists of intensive hands-on management with a focus on long-term ownership. When acquiring properties, it attempts to accumulate enough to establish a regional office, enabling the company to obtain in-depth knowledge of the market from a leasing perspective and to have easy access to the property and tenants from a management standpoint. Weingarten's criteria for retail acquisition includes an anchored community, neighborhood or power shopping center; 100,000 to 400,000 square feet; multiple tenants, including an existing anchor store or accommodations for one; properties that can be leased-up, re-merchandised or renovated; a trade area with a minimum population of 50,000; and a location at a major intersection of two thoroughfares. The firm's criterion for industrial acquisition includes bulk warehouses, office/warehouse or service center/flex buildings; and good location within first- and second-tier markets. During 2009, the company sold 12 retail properties, five industrial properties and 11 retail buildings at seven operating properties.

Weingarten offers its employees benefits including medical, dental, life and disability insurance; a 401(k); and education reimbursement.

FINANCIALS:

Sales and profits are in thousands of dollars—add 000 to get the full amount. 2009 Note: Financial information for 2009 was not available for all companies at press time.

2009 Sales: $572,108	2009 Profits: $175,276	**U.S. Stock Ticker: WRI**
2008 Sales: $592,748	2008 Profits: $154,595	**Int'l Ticker:** Int'l Exchange:
2007 Sales: $561,200	2007 Profits: $240,338	Employees:
2006 Sales: $523,424	2006 Profits: $305,010	Fiscal Year Ends: 12/31
2005 Sales: $487,856	2005 Profits: $219,653	Parent Company:

SALARIES/BENEFITS:

Pension Plan: Y	ESOP Stock Plan:	Profit Sharing:	Top Exec. Salary: $700,000	Bonus: $525,000
Savings Plan: Y	Stock Purch. Plan:		Second Exec. Salary: $675,000	Bonus: $354,400

OTHER THOUGHTS:

Apparent Women Officers or Directors: 5
Hot Spot for Advancement for Women/Minorities: Y

LOCATIONS: ("Y" = Yes)

West:	Southwest:	Midwest:	Southeast:	Northeast:	International:
Y	Y		Y	Y	

WELLS REAL ESTATE FUNDS INC

www.wellsref.com

Industry Group Code: 531120 **Ranks within this company's industry group:** Sales: Profits:

Properties:		Financial Services:		Construction/Development:		Investments:		Specialty Services:		Brokerage:	
Apartments:		Mortgages:		Commercial Construction:	Y	REIT:	Y	Property Management:	Y	Commercial Sales:	
Malls/Shopping:		Title Insurance:		Residential Construction:				Online Services:		Residential Sales:	
Offices:	Y	Property Insurance:		Land Development:				Software/IT:		Specialty:	
Hotels/Motels:				Support Services:				Consulting:			
Industrial/Warehouses:	Y			Design/Engineering:							
Other:											

TYPES OF BUSINESS:

Real Estate Investment Trust
Office & Industrial Properties
Property Management
Construction Management

BRANDS/DIVISIONS/AFFILIATES:

Wells REIT II
Wells S&P REIT Index Mutual Fund
Wells Money Market Fund
Wells Limited Partnership Program
Wells Timberland
Wells Capital

CONTACTS: *Note: Officers with more than one job title may be intentionally listed here more than once.*

Leo F. Wells, III, Pres.
Robert Bowers, CFO
Michael Dobbs, Chief Mktg. Officer
Rebecca Padgett, Chief People Officer
Thomas Brittelle, CIO
Steve Franklin, VP-New Bus. Dev.
Kevin Race, Chief-Financial Strategy
Jess Jarratt, Pres., Wells Timberland Mgmt. Organization
Don Henry, Chief Real Estate Officer
Doug Williams, Prod. Chief Financial Officer
Doug Buce, Chief Learning Officer

Phone: 770-449-7800	**Fax:** 770-243-8199
Toll-Free: 800-448-1010	
Address: 6200 The Corners Pkwy, Norcross, GA 30092-3365 US	

GROWTH PLANS/SPECIAL FEATURES:

Wells Real Estate Funds, Inc. is a national real estate investment management firm that purchases corporate and industrial property. It leases its holdings on a long-term basis to tenants with a net worth of at least $100 million. The company offers three chief investment products: the Wells REIT II, a private real estate investment trust that owns over 115 office buildings; the Wells S&P REIT Index Mutual Fund, a REIT tracking fund based on the S&P REIT Composite Index; and the Wells Money Market Fund, offering a portfolio with minimal credit risk. In total, Wells manages more than $12 billion in assets for over 250,000 investors nationwide. The firm generally maintains a conservative investment strategy that focuses on acquiring and managing high-quality properties. Part of its strategy is leasing only to credit-worthy tenants; securing leases with major clients before acquiring a property; and using net leases in which the tenant pays all cost of taxes, insurance and maintenance. The firm maintains a diversified portfolio consisting of various geographic regions, tenants, industries and staggered lease terms. Complementing the investment business, property acquisitions and leasing, Wells also oversees property management, construction, and tenant relations. Wells Limited Partnerships is a wholly-owned subsidiary of the company, for the purpose of acquiring, developing, owning, operating, leasing, and managing income-producing commercial properties for investment purposes. Wells Capital manages investment assets for its clients. Wells Timberland is the firm's nature resource division, which maintains and distributes timber. Wells Timberland also may lease timberland to others for recreational and extraction purposes. The timberland properties are located in Georgia and Alabama.

FINANCIALS: **Sales and profits are in thousands of dollars—add 000 to get the full amount. 2009 Note: Financial information for 2009 was not available for all companies at press time.**

2009 Sales: $	2009 Profits: $	**U.S. Stock Ticker: Private**
2008 Sales: $	2008 Profits: $	**Int'l Ticker:** Int'l Exchange:
2007 Sales: $	2007 Profits: $	Employees:
2006 Sales: $	2006 Profits: $	Fiscal Year Ends: 12/31
2005 Sales: $	2005 Profits: $	Parent Company:

SALARIES/BENEFITS:

Pension Plan:	ESOP Stock Plan:	Profit Sharing:	Top Exec. Salary: $	Bonus: $
Savings Plan:	Stock Purch. Plan:		Second Exec. Salary: $	Bonus: $

OTHER THOUGHTS:

Apparent Women Officers or Directors: 1
Hot Spot for Advancement for Women/Minorities:

LOCATIONS: ("Y" = Yes)

West:	Southwest:	Midwest:	Southeast:	Northeast:	International:
Y	Y	Y	Y	Y	

WESTFIELD GROUP (THE)

www.westfield.com

Industry Group Code: 531120 **Ranks within this company's industry group:** Sales: 5 Profits: 62

Properties:		Financial Services:		Construction/Development:		Investments:		Specialty Services:		Brokerage:	
Apartments:		Mortgages:		Commercial Construction:	Y	REIT:		Property Management:	Y	Commercial Sales:	
Malls/Shopping:	Y	Title Insurance:		Residential Construction:				Online Services:		Residential Sales:	
Offices:		Property Insurance:		Land Development:	Y			Software/IT:		Specialty:	
Hotels/Motels:				Support Services:	Y			Consulting:			
Industrial/Warehouses:				Design/Engineering:	Y						
Other:											

TYPES OF BUSINESS:

Real Estate Operations
Shopping Centers
Design & Construction
Asset Management
Property Management
Leasing
Marketing

BRANDS/DIVISIONS/AFFILIATES:

Westfield Shoppingtowns
Westfield America Trust
Westfield Holdings
Westfield Trust
Statford City Development

CONTACTS: *Note: Officers with more than one job title may be intentionally listed here more than once.*

Steven M. Lowy, Co-Managing Dir.
Peter Allen, CFO
Gary Williams, Dir.-Mktg. & New Revenue
Ian Cornell, Dir.-Human Resources, Australia
Gerhard Karba, CIO
Simon Tuxen, General Counsel/Corp. Sec.
Greg Miles, Dir.-Dev, Australia
Mark Ryan, Dir.-Corp. Affairs
Mark Bloom, Deputy CFO
Peter S. Lowy, Co-Managing Dir./Managing Dit.-US
Eamonn Cunningham, Chief Risk Officer
John Widdup, COO-US
Catharine C. Dickey, Exec. VP-Corp. Comm., US
Frank P. Lowy, Chmn.
Michael Gutman, Managing Dir.-U.K. & Europe

Phone: 61-02-9358-7000 **Fax:** 61-02-9358-7079
Toll-Free:
Address: 100 William St., Westfield Towers, Sydney, NSW 2011 Australia

GROWTH PLANS/SPECIAL FEATURES:

The Westfield Group is an internally managed retail property group based in Sydney, Australia with other offices throughout Australia, New Zealand, the U.K. and the U.S. The company is currently one of the largest retail property groups in the world by equity market capitalization as well as a leading entity on the Australian Stock Exchange. It has investment interests in 119 shopping centers in four countries. The firm divides its services into the following three categories: property investments; property and project management; and development. The property investments segment is responsible for all income from shopping centers and other completed developments and revaluations of existing centers. The firm's property and project management activities derive their income from fees paid by third parties for property and asset management services. The development segment includes development, redevelopment and revaluation projects. Additionally, the company offers marketing space and services in its shopping centers. During 2009, the group completed four major projects in Riccarton, New Zealand; Santa Anita, California; Culver City, California; and Roseville, California. The group is currently developing Westfield Stratford City in East London, adjacent to the site of the 2012 Olympic Games and scheduled to open in 2011.

FINANCIALS: **Sales and profits are in thousands of dollars—add 000 to get the full amount. 2009 Note: Financial information for 2009 was not available for all companies at press time.**

2009 Sales: $3,834,110 | 2009 Profits: $-424,810
2008 Sales: $3,167,100 | 2008 Profits: $-1,581,600
2007 Sales: $3,019,800 | 2007 Profits: $2,474,800
2006 Sales: $2,739,000 | 2006 Profits: $4,019,800
2005 Sales: $5,052,600 | 2005 Profits: $546,000

U.S. Stock Ticker:
Int'l Ticker: WDC Int'l Exchange: Sydney-ASX
Employees:
Fiscal Year Ends: 6/30
Parent Company:

SALARIES/BENEFITS:

Pension Plan: ESOP Stock Plan: Profit Sharing: Top Exec. Salary: $ Bonus: $
Savings Plan: Stock Purch. Plan: Second Exec. Salary: $ Bonus: $

OTHER THOUGHTS:

Apparent Women Officers or Directors: 7
Hot Spot for Advancement for Women/Minorities: Y

LOCATIONS: ("Y" = Yes)

West:	Southwest:	Midwest:	Southeast:	Northeast:	International:
Y		Y	Y	Y	Y

WHARF (HOLDINGS) LIMITED, THE

www.wharfholdings.com

Industry Group Code: 5311 **Ranks within this company's industry group:** Sales: Profits:

Properties:		Financial Services:		Construction/Development:		Investments:		Specialty Services:		Brokerage:	
Apartments:	Y	Mortgages:		Commercial Construction:	Y	REIT:		Property Management:		Commercial Sales:	
Malls/Shopping:	Y	Title Insurance:		Residential Construction:	Y			Online Services:		Residential Sales:	
Offices:	Y	Property Insurance:		Land Development:	Y			Software/IT:		Specialty:	
Hotels/Motels:	Y			Support Services:				Consulting:			
Industrial/Warehouses:				Design/Engineering:							
Other:	Y										

TYPES OF BUSINESS:

Real Estate Holdings & Development

BRANDS/DIVISIONS/AFFILIATES:

Modern Terminals Limited
i-Cable Communications Limited
Harbour Centre Development Limited
Marco Polo Hongkong Hotel

CONTACTS: *Note: Officers with more than one job title may be intentionally listed here more than once.*

Paul Yiu Cheung Tsui, CFO/Exec. Dir.
T Y Ng, Exec. Dir.
Stephen Tin Hoi Ng, Deputy Chmn./Managing Dir.
Doreen Yuk Fong Lee, Exec. Dir.
Peter Kwong Ching Woo, Chmn.

Phone: 852-2118-8118 **Fax:** 852-2118-8018
Toll-Free:
Address: 16th Fl., Ocean Centre, Canton Rd., Hong Kong, China

GROWTH PLANS/SPECIAL FEATURES:

The Wharf (Holding) Limited is a Hong Kong-based real estate investment holding firm. The company's two core properties, both located in Hong Kong, are Harbour City and Times Square. Harbour City, located in the commercial center of Tsim Sha Tsui, is Wharf Holding's flagship property, typically generating 60% of the company's annual rental income. With roughly 700 shops, the center encompasses approximately 8.4 million total square feet of commercial space consisting of offices, retail stores, serviced apartments, clubs, hotels and parking facilities. The Times Square property, located in the Causeway Bay commercial district of northern Hong Kong, encompasses approximately 900,000 square feet of retail space and over 1 million square feet of office space. Other Hong Kong properties include Plaza Hollywood, a retail center totaling over 562,000 square feet, as well as a number of upscale residential properties. In addition to its Hong Kong investments, Wharf Holding has been expanding its activities in Mainland China in recent years, having acquired a land bank there totaling approximately 95 million square feet, primarily in or near metropolitan areas such as Beijing, Shanghai, Chongqing, Wuhan, Dalian, Chengdu, Suzhou, Wuxi, Hangzhou, Nanjing and Changzhou. The firm currently operates three investment properties in Beijing, Shanghai and Chongqing under its Times Square brand. The company also holds a 67.6% share in Modern Terminals Limited, a provider of container terminal services in the South China region since 1969. Modern Terminals is currently engaged in developing new container terminal locations in the Pearl River Delta and Yangtze River Delta areas, in addition to other projects along the coast of China. Additional subsidiaries include i-Cable Communications Limited, a telecommunications firm; and Harbour Centre Development Limited, a property developer and owner of the Marco Polo Hongkong Hotel in Hong Kong.

FINANCIALS: **Sales and profits are in thousands of dollars—add 000 to get the full amount. 2009 Note: Financial information for 2009 was not available for all companies at press time.**

2009 Sales: $	2009 Profits: $	**U.S. Stock Ticker: Subsidiary**
2008 Sales: $	2008 Profits: $	**Int'l Ticker:** Int'l Exchange:
2007 Sales: $	2007 Profits: $	Employees:
2006 Sales: $	2006 Profits: $	Fiscal Year Ends:
2005 Sales: $	2005 Profits: $	Parent Company: WHEELOCK AND COMPANY LIMITED

SALARIES/BENEFITS:

Pension Plan:	ESOP Stock Plan:	Profit Sharing:	Top Exec. Salary: $	Bonus: $
Savings Plan:	Stock Purch. Plan:		Second Exec. Salary: $	Bonus: $

OTHER THOUGHTS:

Apparent Women Officers or Directors: 1
Hot Spot for Advancement for Women/Minorities:

LOCATIONS: ("Y" = Yes)

West:	Southwest:	Midwest:	Southeast:	Northeast:	International:
					Y

WHEELOCK AND COMPANY LIMITED

http://www.wheelockcompany.com/index_main.htm

Industry Group Code: 5311 **Ranks within this company's industry group:** Sales: 10 Profits: 6

Properties:		Financial Services:		Construction/Development:		Investments:		Specialty Services:		Brokerage:	
Apartments:	Y	Mortgages:		Commercial Construction:		REIT:		Property Management:		Commercial Sales:	
Malls/Shopping:	Y	Title Insurance:		Residential Construction:				Online Services:		Residential Sales:	
Offices:	Y	Property Insurance:		Land Development:	Y			Software/IT:		Specialty:	
Hotels/Motels:	Y			Support Services:				Consulting:			
Industrial/Warehouses:				Design/Engineering:							
Other:	Y										

TYPES OF BUSINESS:

Real Estate Holdings & Development

BRANDS/DIVISIONS/AFFILIATES:

Wharf (Holdings) Limited (The)
Wheelock Properties Limited
Modern Terminals
COL
Hong Kong Cable Television
Harbour City
Gateway Apartments
Plaza Hollywood

CONTACTS:

Note: Officers with more than one job title may be intentionally listed here more than once.

Paul Y. C. Tsui, Exec. Dir.
Paul Y. C. Tsui, CFO
Wilson W. S. Chan, Corp. Sec.
Peter K.C. Woo, Chmn.

Phone: 852-2118-2118 **Fax:** 852-2118-2018
Toll-Free:
Address: Wheelock House 20 Pedder St., 23rd Fl., Hong Kong, China

GROWTH PLANS/SPECIAL FEATURES:

Wheelock and Company Limited (Wheelock & Co), founded in 1857, is an investment holding company based in Hong Kong, with services offered in China and Singapore. The firm operates through two main subsidiaries: The Wharf (Holdings) Limited and Wheelock Properties Limited. The Wharf (Holdings) Limited, with consolidated assets $22 billion, focuses on property and infrastructure in Hong Kong and China. Its core properties include Harbour City, Times Square in Hong Kong and more than two-thirds of Modern Terminals, a shipping terminal operator in southern China. In addition, Wharf has interests in cable television, Internet access and telecommunications providers in Hong Kong. Some of Wharf's group of companies includes COL, an IT service provider; Gateway Apartments, in Harbour City in Hong Kong; Hong Kong Cable Television, a cable provider; Marco Polo Hotels; i-CABLE Communications, a telecommunications company; and Plaza Hollywood, one of the largest shopping malls in Hong Kong. These properties account for half of the subsidiary's total assets. Wharf also has 95 million square feet of investment properties and developable land in China. It is currently developing container terminals in the Pearl River Delta and the Yangtze River Delta and other projects along China's coast. Wheelock & Co has a 50% interest in Wharf Holdings. Wheelock Properties Limited's primary business is property with a land bank of 1.2 million square feet in Hong Kong. It aims to increase its development opportunities in China, having already acquired two sites in the Guangdong province. Wheelock Properties currently holds approximately 3.88 million square feet in China. It has offices in Singapore and Hong Kong. Wheelock & Co has a 74% controlling interest in this subsidiary. In April 2010, the firm announced plans to take Wheelock Properties private for $889 million.

FINANCIALS:

Sales and profits are in thousands of dollars—add 000 to get the full amount. 2009 Note: Financial information for 2009 was not available for all companies at press time.

2009 Sales: $2,441,730	2009 Profits: $1,240,510
2008 Sales: $2,913,850	2008 Profits: $1,219,710
2007 Sales: $2,311,550	2007 Profits: $1,345,510
2006 Sales: $	2006 Profits: $
2005 Sales: $	2005 Profits: $

U.S. Stock Ticker:
Int'l Ticker: 0020 Int'l Exchange: Hong Kong-HKE
Employees: 13,400
Fiscal Year Ends: 12/31
Parent Company:

SALARIES/BENEFITS:

Pension Plan:	ESOP Stock Plan:	Profit Sharing:	Top Exec. Salary: $	Bonus: $
Savings Plan:	Stock Purch. Plan:		Second Exec. Salary: $	Bonus: $

OTHER THOUGHTS:

Apparent Women Officers or Directors:
Hot Spot for Advancement for Women/Minorities:

LOCATIONS: ("Y" = Yes)

West:	Southwest:	Midwest:	Southeast:	Northeast:	International:
					Y

WILLIAM LYON HOMES

www.lyonhomes.com

Industry Group Code: 2361 **Ranks within this company's industry group:** Sales: 18 Profits: 4

Properties:		Financial Services:		Construction/Development:		Investments:		Specialty Services:		Brokerage:	
Apartments:		Mortgages:	Y	Commercial Construction:		REIT:		Property Management:		Commercial Sales:	
Malls/Shopping:		Title Insurance:	Y	Residential Construction:	Y			Online Services:		Residential Sales:	Y
Offices:		Property Insurance:		Land Development:	Y			Software/IT:		Specialty:	
Hotels/Motels:				Support Services:				Consulting:			
Industrial/Warehouses:				Design/Engineering:	Y						
Other:											

TYPES OF BUSINESS:

Residential Construction
Land Development
Home Sales
Home Financing
Home Design
Title Reinsurance

BRANDS/DIVISIONS/AFFILIATES:

William Lyon Financial Services
Duxford Escrow
Duxford Title Reinsurace Company
William Lyon Mortgage

CONTACTS:

Note: Officers with more than one job title may be intentionally listed here more than once.

William Lyon, Sr., CEO
William H. Lyon, Jr., COO
William H. Lyon, Jr., Pres.
Colin T. Severn, CFO/VP
Maureen L. Singer, VP-Human Resources
Colin T. Severn, Corp. Sec.
Richard S. Robinson, Sr. VP-Finance
Cynthia E. Hardgrave, VP-Tax & Internal Audit
Mary J. Connelly, Sr. VP/Pres., Nevada Div.
W. Thomas Hickox, Sr. VP/Pres., Arizona Div.
William Lyon, Sr., Chmn.

Phone: 949-833-3600	**Fax:** 949-476-2178
Toll-Free:	
Address: 4490 Von Karman Ave., Newport Beach, CA 92660 US	

GROWTH PLANS/SPECIAL FEATURES:

William Lyon Homes, Inc. and its subsidiaries design, construct and sell single-family detached and attached homes in California, Arizona and Nevada. The company has four homebuilding operations, which are geographically divided into Southern California, Northern California, Arizona and Nevada and include both wholly-owned projects and projects being developed in unconsolidated joint ventures. The majority of the firm's home closings occur in California. William Lyon markets its homes through 60 sales locations; its homes range in price from $76,000 to $1,725,000. The company offers a wide range of homes, primarily emphasizing sales to the entry-level and move-up homebuyer markets. Since its founding in 1956 as a company that provided homes for military families, William Lyon and its joint ventures have sold over 100,000 homes. Subsidiaries William Lyon Financial Services, Duxford Escrow and Duxford Title Reinsurance Company provide home financing loans, title reinsurance and financial assistance to William Lyon customers. In the near future, the company expects to temporarily suspend all development, sales and marketing activities at 10 of its actively-selling projects which are in the early stages of development.

FINANCIALS:

Sales and profits are in thousands of dollars—add 000 to get the full amount. 2009 Note: Financial information for 2009 was not available for all companies at press time.

2009 Sales: $309,243	2009 Profits: $-20,525	**U.S. Stock Ticker: Private**
2008 Sales: $526,078	2008 Profits: $-111,638	**Int'l Ticker:** Int'l Exchange:
2007 Sales: $1,105,357	2007 Profits: $-349,408	Employees:
2006 Sales: $	2006 Profits: $	Fiscal Year Ends: 12/31
2005 Sales: $1,856,383	2005 Profits: $190,631	Parent Company:

SALARIES/BENEFITS:

Pension Plan:	ESOP Stock Plan:	Profit Sharing:	Top Exec. Salary: $	Bonus: $
Savings Plan:	Stock Purch. Plan:		Second Exec. Salary: $	Bonus: $

OTHER THOUGHTS:

Apparent Women Officers or Directors: 3
Hot Spot for Advancement for Women/Minorities: Y

LOCATIONS: ("Y" = Yes)

West:	Southwest:	Midwest:	Southeast:	Northeast:	International:
Y	Y				

WOLSELEY PLC

www.wolseley.com

Industry Group Code: 4233 **Ranks within this company's industry group:** Sales: 1 Profits: 2

Properties:		Financial Services:		Construction/Development:		Investments:		Specialty Services:		Brokerage:	
Apartments:		Mortgages:		Commercial Construction:		REIT:		Property Management:		Commercial Sales:	
Malls/Shopping:		Title Insurance:		Residential Construction:				Online Services:		Residential Sales:	
Offices:		Property Insurance:		Land Development:				Software/IT:		Specialty:	
Hotels/Motels:				Support Services:	Y			Consulting:			
Industrial/Warehouses:				Design/Engineering:							
Other:											

TYPES OF BUSINESS:

Building Materials Wholesale Distribution
Plumbing & Heating Products Distribution

BRANDS/DIVISIONS/AFFILIATES:

Ferguson Enterprises Inc
Wolseley Canada

CONTACTS:

Note: Officers with more than one job title may be intentionally listed here more than once.

Ian K. Meakins, CEO
John Martin, CFO
Richard Shoylekov, General Counsel/Group Company Sec.
John W. Whybrow, Chmn.
Frank W. Roach, CEO-North America

Phone: 44-118-929-8700 **Fax:** 44-118-929-8701
Toll-Free:
Address: Parkview 1220, Arlington Business Park, Theale, RG7 4GA UK

GROWTH PLANS/SPECIAL FEATURES:

Wolseley plc is one of the world's largest distributors of residential construction materials, including plumbing, building and heating equipment. It operates 4,400 branches in 25 countries across Europe and North America, dividing its business into two geographic divisions: North America, which includes both a plumbing and heating distribution and a building materials distribution segment; and Europe. The North American plumbing and heating distribution segment supplies plumbing and heating products such as industrial pipes, valves and fittings to markets in North America. It consists of the businesses of U.S. subsidiary Ferguson Enterprises, Inc., with 1,228 locations in the U.S., Puerto Rico and Mexico; and Wolseley Canada, which has 255 branches. Ferguson and Wolseley have integrated their operations, but maintain separate brands. Wolseley's U.S. building materials distribution segment is one of the largest wholesalers and retailers of lumber and building materials to professional contractors in the U.S. This segment supplies lumber and building materials, including value-added pre-assembled components such as roof and floor trusses and wall panels and floor systems, doors, windows and staircases, to house builders and professional contractors. The Europe division, with almost 3,000 branches, is one of the largest specialty distributors of building materials, electrical supplies and plumbing and heating products to the professional contractor and specialist installer markets in Europe. It is divided into four geographic areas: U.K. and Ireland; Central and Eastern Europe; the Nordic region; and France. In May 2009, the firm entered into a joint venture of stock building supply agreement with The Gores Group, LLC, with Wolseley retaining 49% interest. In January 2010, the company announced the sale of Wolseley Ireland Holdings Limited to WBHM Limited, a private investor-backed company, for $35.1 million.

FINANCIALS:

Sales and profits are in thousands of dollars—add 000 to get the full amount. 2009 Note: Financial information for 2009 was not available for all companies at press time.

2009 Sales: $23,382,600	2009 Profits: $-189,930	**U.S. Stock Ticker:**
2008 Sales: $24,071,500	2008 Profits: $437,820	**Int'l Ticker: WOS** Int'l Exchange: London-LSE
2007 Sales: $23,594,400	2007 Profits: $1,095,280	Employees: 51,000
2006 Sales: $26,384,800	2006 Profits: $950,400	Fiscal Year Ends: 7/31
2005 Sales: $19,786,500	2005 Profits: $810,600	Parent Company:

SALARIES/BENEFITS:

Pension Plan:	ESOP Stock Plan:	Profit Sharing:	Top Exec. Salary: $	Bonus: $
Savings Plan:	Stock Purch. Plan:		Second Exec. Salary: $	Bonus: $

OTHER THOUGHTS:

Apparent Women Officers or Directors:
Hot Spot for Advancement for Women/Minorities:

LOCATIONS: ("Y" = Yes)

West:	Southwest:	Midwest:	Southeast:	Northeast:	International:
Y	Y	Y	Y	Y	Y

WORLDMARK BY WYNDHAM INC

www.worldmarktheclub.com

Industry Group Code: 561599 **Ranks within this company's industry group:** Sales: Profits:

Properties:		Financial Services:		Construction/Development:		Investments:		Specialty Services:		Brokerage:	
Apartments:		Mortgages:		Commercial Construction:		REIT:		Property Management:	Y	Commercial Sales:	
Malls/Shopping:		Title Insurance:		Residential Construction:				Online Services:		Residential Sales:	
Offices:		Property Insurance:		Land Development:				Software/IT:		Specialty:	
Hotels/Motels:	Y			Support Services:				Consulting:			
Industrial/Warehouses:				Design/Engineering:							
Other:	Y										

TYPES OF BUSINESS:

Timeshare Resorts
Property Management

BRANDS/DIVISIONS/AFFILIATES:

Wyndham Worldwide
Wyndham Vacation Ownership
WorldMark, The Club
Resort Condominiums International

CONTACTS:

Note: Officers with more than one job title may be intentionally listed here more than once.

Dave Akins, VP-Resort Oper.
Franz S. Hanning, Pres./CEO-Wyndham Vacation Ownership
Gary Byrd, Chief Customer Officer
Dave Herrick, Sr. VP
Peggy Fry, VP-WorldMark Owner Svcs.

Phone: 425-498-2500 **Fax:** 425-498-3050
Toll-Free:
Address: 9805 Willows Rd., Redmond, WA 98052 US

GROWTH PLANS/SPECIAL FEATURES:

WorldMark by Wyndham, Inc. (formerly Trendwest Resorts, Inc.), a wholly-owned subsidiary of Wyndham Worldwide, develops and markets the vacation ownership program WorldMark, The Club. It is one of the three brands operated by Wyndham Vacation Ownership, another subsidiary of Wyndham Worldwide. Unlike traditional timeshare owners, who have access to a specific time at a specific place, WorldMark, The Club member-owners purchase credits, which are renewed annually, to spend them like currency to reserve vacations in WorldMark resorts, giving member-owners flexibility about vacation dates and locations. The firm operates more than 50 WorldMark resorts, concentrated in the U.S., but including one resort in Fiji, four in Hawaii, two in Mexico and four in British Columbia, Canada. Approximately 80% of the resorts are designed to be a short drive away from major metropolitan areas, and the remaining resorts are in exotic locations, such as those in Hawaii and Fiji. Resorts are often located near golf courses, beaches, sightseeing locations, hiking trails, romantic getaways, shopping centers, skiing slopes or family-friendly entertainment. A typical resort room includes a stocked kitchen; laundry facilities; television and video player; stereo; fireplace; private deck with access to swimming pools; indoor and outdoor spas; exercise rooms; arcade games; and sports facilities. WorldMark, The Club has over 250,000 member-owners. The firm also operates a vacation exchange partnership with Resort Condominiums International (RCI), one of the largest vacation ownership companies in the world. This partnership grants WorldMark, The Club member-owners access to thousands of resorts worldwide, for an exchange fee.

Employees of Wyndham Vacation Ownership receive medical, dental and vision plans; long- and short-term disability benefits; an educational assistance plan; adoption assistance; domestic partner benefits; paid time off; an employee assistance program; and discounts on various products and services, including hotels.

FINANCIALS:

Sales and profits are in thousands of dollars—add 000 to get the full amount. 2009 Note: Financial information for 2009 was not available for all companies at press time.

2009 Sales: $	2009 Profits: $	**U.S. Stock Ticker: Subsidiary**
2008 Sales: $	2008 Profits: $	**Int'l Ticker:** Int'l Exchange:
2007 Sales: $	2007 Profits: $	Employees:
2006 Sales: $	2006 Profits: $	Fiscal Year Ends: 12/31
2005 Sales: $	2005 Profits: $	Parent Company: WYNDHAM WORLDWIDE

SALARIES/BENEFITS:

Pension Plan:	ESOP Stock Plan:	Profit Sharing:	Top Exec. Salary: $	Bonus: $
Savings Plan: Y	Stock Purch. Plan:		Second Exec. Salary: $	Bonus: $

OTHER THOUGHTS:

Apparent Women Officers or Directors:
Hot Spot for Advancement for Women/Minorities:

LOCATIONS: ("Y" = Yes)

West:	Southwest:	Midwest:	Southeast:	Northeast:	International:
Y	Y	Y	Y		Y

WP CAREY & CO LLC

www.wpcarey.com

Industry Group Code: 5311 **Ranks within this company's industry group:** Sales: 30 Profits: 19

Properties:		Financial Services:		Construction/Development:		Investments:		Specialty Services:		Brokerage:	
Apartments:		Mortgages:		Commercial Construction:		REIT:	Y	Property Management:	Y	Commercial Sales:	Y
Malls/Shopping:		Title Insurance:		Residential Construction:				Online Services:		Residential Sales:	
Offices:	Y	Property Insurance:		Land Development:				Software/IT:		Specialty:	
Hotels/Motels:				Support Services:				Consulting:			
Industrial/Warehouses:	Y			Design/Engineering:							
Other:											

TYPES OF BUSINESS:

Real Estate Operations
Commercial Properties
Property Management & Leasing
Real Estate Financing
Commercial Construction
Commercial Brokerage

BRANDS/DIVISIONS/AFFILIATES:

Corporate Property Associates 14 Inc
Corporate Property Associates 15 Inc
Corporate Property Associates 16-Global Inc
Corporate Property Associates 17-Global Inc

CONTACTS: *Note: Officers with more than one job title may be intentionally listed here more than once.*

Gordon F. DuGan, CEO
Thomas E. Zacharias, COO
Gordon F. DuGan, Pres.
Mark J. DeCesaris, Interim CFO
Mark J. DeCesaris, Chief Admin. Officer
Douglas E. Barzelay, General Counsel
Susan C. Hyde, Dir.-Investor Rel./Corp. Sec.
Thomas Ridings, Chief Acct. Officer
John D. Miller, Chief Investment Officer
Thomas E. Zacharias, Pres., CPA 16-Global, Inc./Dir.-Asset Mgmt.
Jan F. Karst, Pres., CPA 17-Global, Inc.
Gino Sabatini, Pres., CPA 14-Global, Inc.
William P. Carey, Chmn.
Greg Butchart, Head-Int'l Asset Mgmt. Group

Phone: 212-492-1100 **Fax:** 212-492-8922
Toll-Free: 800-972-2739
Address: 50 Rockefeller Plz., New York, NY 10020 US

GROWTH PLANS/SPECIAL FEATURES:

W.P. Carey & Co., LLC is a real estate advisory and investment company that invests primarily in commercial properties that are each triple-net leased to single corporate tenants, domestically and internationally. Founded in 1973, the company is one of the world's largest publicly traded limited liability companies; it has nearly $10 billion in assets, owning approximately 880 commercial and industrial facilities in 15 countries, mainly in Europe and the U.S. The company operates in two segments: investment management, which generates approximately 66% of the firm's revenue; and real estate ownership, 53%. The investment management segment, operating mainly through various subsidiaries, consists primarily of advising REITs (Real Estate Investment Trusts) that it sponsors, including Corporate Property Associates 14 Incorporated (CPA 14, Inc.), CPA 15, Inc., CPA 16-Global, Inc. and CPA 17-Global, Inc., which it collectively refers to as the CPA REITs. The firm provides various services to the CPA REITs, including day-to-day management, transaction related services and asset management. The real estate ownership segment typically acquires a property and leases it back to the tenant company (referred to as sale-leaseback) on a triple-net long-term basis, meaning the tenant company bears the responsibility for maintaining the premises, insuring the building and paying real estate taxes, among other operating costs. As a result, the tenant company preserves operational control of the property and benefits from the immediate access to capital, which can be used to improve its balance sheet, fund future growth or reduce debt. Most of the firm's real estate acquisitions in recent years have been done on behalf of the CPA REITs. In December 2009, CPA 17–Global acquired the North American headquarters of Mori Seiki Co. Ltd. for $33 million; the corporate headquarters of US Oncology, Inc. for $45 million; and 13 retail facilities from Eroski Sociedad Cooperativa, a Spanish supermarket operator, for $51 million.

FINANCIALS: **Sales and profits are in thousands of dollars—add 000 to get the full amount. 2009 Note: Financial information for 2009 was not available for all companies at press time.**

2009 Sales: $235,876	2009 Profits: $69,023	**U.S. Stock Ticker: WPC**
2008 Sales: $238,624	2008 Profits: $78,047	**Int'l Ticker:** Int'l Exchange:
2007 Sales: $257,956	2007 Profits: $79,252	Employees:
2006 Sales: $267,487	2006 Profits: $86,303	Fiscal Year Ends: 12/31
2005 Sales: $163,240	2005 Profits: $48,604	Parent Company:

SALARIES/BENEFITS:

Pension Plan:	ESOP Stock Plan:	Profit Sharing: Y	Top Exec. Salary: $600,000	Bonus: $896,000
Savings Plan: Y	Stock Purch. Plan:		Second Exec. Salary: $350,000	Bonus: $760,000

OTHER THOUGHTS:

Apparent Women Officers or Directors: 2
Hot Spot for Advancement for Women/Minorities: Y

LOCATIONS: ("Y" = Yes)

West:	Southwest:	Midwest:	Southeast:	Northeast:	International:
Y	Y			Y	Y

WS ATKINS PLC

www.atkinsglobal.com

Industry Group Code: 541330 **Ranks within this company's industry group:** Sales: 6 Profits: 3

Properties:		Financial Services:		Construction/Development:		Investments:		Specialty Services:		Brokerage:	
Apartments:		Mortgages:		Commercial Construction:		REIT:		Property Management:		Commercial Sales:	
Malls/Shopping:		Title Insurance:		Residential Construction:				Online Services:		Residential Sales:	
Offices:		Property Insurance:		Land Development:				Software/IT:		Specialty:	
Hotels/Motels:				Support Services:	Y			Consulting:	Y		
Industrial/Warehouses:				Design/Engineering:	Y						
Other:											

TYPES OF BUSINESS:

Engineering Services-Building Design
Infrastructure & Transportation Engineering
Consulting
Technology Support Services

BRANDS/DIVISIONS/AFFILIATES:

Faithful & Gould

CONTACTS:

Note: Officers with more than one job title may be intentionally listed here more than once.

Keith Clarke, CEO
Heath Drewett, Dir.-Finance
Alun Griffiths, Dir.-Human Resources
Paul Dollin, Managing Dir.-Eng. & Design
Sara Lipscombe, Dir.-Comm
Richard Barrett, Managing Dir.-Europe
Richard Hall, Managing Dir.-Faithful & Gould
Neil Thomas, Managing Dir.-Highways & Transportation
Samson Sin, Managing Dir.-Atkins China
Allan Cook, Chmn.
Tim Askew, Managing Dir.-Middle East & India

Phone: 44-372-726-140 **Fax:** 44-372-740-055
Toll-Free:
Address: Woodcote Grove, Ashley Rd., Epsom, Surrey KT18 5BW UK

GROWTH PLANS/SPECIAL FEATURES:

WS Atkins plc, an engineering consultancy company, plans, designs and enables delivery of complex infrastructure and buildings, primarily in the U.K. It has five primary business segments: Design and Engineering Solutions; Highways and Transportation; Rail; Middle East, China and Europe; Management and Project Services; and Asset Management. The Design and Engineering Solutions segment operates in the following areas: water, nuclear, defense, environment, oil/gas, urban development, buildings, communications, aerospace, education and other. The Highways and Transportation segment is involved in designing new roads; developing intelligent transport systems; transport planning; road improvements; integrated road network management; and road maintenance management. The Rail segment offers electrification, civil and signaling engineering services, as well as strategic planning, systems integration, asset management and safety specialist services. The Middle East, China and Europe segment offers engineering, design and project management services for infrastructure including transportation and buildings. Project and cost management consultancy subsidiary Faithful & Gould, Inc. operates in both the Middle East and China and Management and Project Services segments. The Management and Project Services segment mainly offers IT and management consultancy, as well as cost, project and program management services. Lastly, the Asset Management segment manages property for private and public sector clients. Atkins has over 200 offices in 27 countries and ongoing projects in more than 80.

FINANCIALS:

Sales and profits are in thousands of dollars—add 000 to get the full amount. 2009 Note: Financial information for 2009 was not available for all companies at press time.

2009 Sales: $2,287,330	2009 Profits: $129,500	**U.S. Stock Ticker:**
2008 Sales: $2,076,210	2008 Profits: $148,360	**Int'l Ticker: ATK** Int'l Exchange: London-LSE
2007 Sales: $1,840,040	2007 Profits: $-85,010	Employees: 17,026
2006 Sales: $2,150,000	2006 Profits: $113,800	Fiscal Year Ends: 3/31
2005 Sales: $1,910,000	2005 Profits: $77,800	Parent Company:

SALARIES/BENEFITS:

Pension Plan:	ESOP Stock Plan:	Profit Sharing:	Top Exec. Salary: $	Bonus: $345,327
Savings Plan:	Stock Purch. Plan:		Second Exec. Salary: $	Bonus: $

OTHER THOUGHTS:

Apparent Women Officers or Directors: 3
Hot Spot for Advancement for Women/Minorities: Y

LOCATIONS: ("Y" = Yes)

West:	Southwest:	Midwest:	Southeast:	Northeast:	International:
Y	Y	Y	Y	Y	Y

WYNDHAM VACATION OWNERSHIP

www.fairfieldresorts.com

Industry Group Code: 561599 **Ranks within this company's industry group:** Sales: Profits:

Properties:		Financial Services:		Construction/Development:		Investments:		Specialty Services:		Brokerage:	
Apartments:		Mortgages:		Commercial Construction:		REIT:		Property Management:		Commercial Sales:	
Malls/Shopping:		Title Insurance:		Residential Construction:				Online Services:		Residential Sales:	
Offices:		Property Insurance:		Land Development:				Software/IT:		Specialty:	Y
Hotels/Motels:	Y			Support Services:				Consulting:			
Industrial/Warehouses:				Design/Engineering:							
Other:	Y										

TYPES OF BUSINESS:

Resorts
Timeshare Resorts
Property Management

BRANDS/DIVISIONS/AFFILIATES:

Wyndham Worldwide
Wyndham Vacation Resorts
Fairfield Resorts Inc.

CONTACTS: *Note: Officers with more than one job title may be intentionally listed here more than once.*

Franz S. Hanning, CEO
Franz S. Hanning, Pres.
Mike Hug, CFO
Geoff Richards, Exec. VP-Global Sales & Mktg. Oper.
Adam Schwartz, Sr. VP-Corp. Rel.
Mike Hug, Exec. VP-Finance

Phone: 407-370-5200 **Fax:** 407-370-5143
Toll-Free: 800-251-8736
Address: 8427 SouthPark Cir., Ste. 500, Orlando, FL 32819 US

GROWTH PLANS/SPECIAL FEATURES:

Wyndham Vacation Ownership (WVO), a subsidiary of Wyndham Worldwide Corp., is one of the world's leading time share companies. The firm markets point-based vacation ownership through the brands Wyndham Vacation Resorts and Trendwest. WVO primarily operates through Wyndham Vacation Resorts (WVR), formerly Fairfield Resorts, Inc. Through WVR, it markets, sells and finances vacation ownership interests and develops vacation ownership resorts. Additionally, WVR provides property management services to property owners' associations. The firm maintains over 150 resort properties as well as over 20,000 individual vacation ownership units across the U.S., Canada, Mexico, the Caribbean and the South Pacific. Domestic locations can be found in every region of the U.S., including Texas, California, Florida and Massachusetts. WVR's units are fully furnished, and many include washers/dryers, whirlpool spas, fireplaces and VCRs. The company offers travel discounts and other member specials to all vacation ownership members.

The company offers employees a variety of benefits including medical and life insurance; short- and long-term disability; a 401(k); an employee stock purchase program; adoption assistance; educational assistance; and discounts.

FINANCIALS: **Sales and profits are in thousands of dollars—add 000 to get the full amount. 2009 Note: Financial information for 2009 was not available for all companies at press time.**

2009 Sales: $ | 2009 Profits: $
2008 Sales: $ | 2008 Profits: $
2007 Sales: $ | 2007 Profits: $
2006 Sales: $ | 2006 Profits: $
2005 Sales: $ | 2005 Profits: $

U.S. Stock Ticker: Subsidiary
Int'l Ticker: Int'l Exchange:
Employees:
Fiscal Year Ends: 12/31
Parent Company: WYNDHAM WORLDWIDE

SALARIES/BENEFITS:

Pension Plan: | ESOP Stock Plan: | Profit Sharing: | Top Exec. Salary: $ | Bonus: $
Savings Plan: Y | Stock Purch. Plan: Y | | Second Exec. Salary: $ | Bonus: $

OTHER THOUGHTS:

Apparent Women Officers or Directors:
Hot Spot for Advancement for Women/Minorities:

LOCATIONS: ("Y" = Yes)

West:	Southwest:	Midwest:	Southeast:	Northeast:	International:
Y	Y	Y	Y	Y	Y

WYNDHAM WORLDWIDE

www.wyndhamworldwide.com

Industry Group Code: 721110 **Ranks within this company's industry group:** Sales: 5 Profits: 28

Properties:		Financial Services:		Construction/Development:		Investments:		Specialty Services:		Brokerage:	
Apartments:		Mortgages:		Commercial Construction:		REIT:		Property Management:	Y	Commercial Sales:	
Malls/Shopping:		Title Insurance:		Residential Construction:				Online Services:		Residential Sales:	
Offices:		Property Insurance:		Land Development:				Software/IT:		Specialty:	
Hotels/Motels:	Y			Support Services:				Consulting:			
Industrial/Warehouses:				Design/Engineering:							
Other:	Y										

TYPES OF BUSINESS:

Hotels, Motels & Resorts
Property Management
Hotel Development
Vacation Property Exchange and Rental
Timeshare Resorts
Franchising
Vacation Ownership

BRANDS/DIVISIONS/AFFILIATES:

Wyndham Hotels
Wingate Inns
Ramada
Days Inn
Super 8
Howard Johnson
AmeriHost
Trendwest

CONTACTS: *Note: Officers with more than one job title may be intentionally listed here more than once.*

Stephen P. Holmes, CEO
Virginia M. Wilson, CFO/Exec. VP
Betsy O'Rourke, Sr. VP-Mktg.
Mary R. Falvey, Exec. VP/Chief Human Resources Officer
Scott G. McLester, General Counsel/Exec. VP
Betsy O'Rourke, Sr. VP-Comm.
Nicola Rossi, Sr. VP/Chief Acct. Officer
Franz S. Hanning, Pres./CEO-Wyndham Vacation Ownership
Steven A. Rudnitsky, Pres./CEO-Wyndham Hotel Group
Geoff Ballotti, Pres./CEO-Group RCI
Tom Anderson, Exec. VP/Chief Real Estate Dev. Officer
Stephen P. Holmes, Chmn.

Phone: 973-428-9700 **Fax:**
Toll-Free:
Address: 7 Sylvan Way, Parsippany, NJ 07054 US

GROWTH PLANS/SPECIAL FEATURES:

Wyndham Worldwide (WW) is a hospitality company offering individual consumers and business customers an array of hospitality products and services, as well as various accommodation alternatives and price ranges through its portfolio of world-renowned brands. The company encompasses over 7,100 hotels representing almost 597,700 rooms on six continents and another 950 hotels representing 108,100 rooms in development. Wyndham Hotel Group offers the TripRewards loyalty program. Group RCI, the firm's vacation exchange business, offers its 3.8 million members access for specified periods to over 4,000 vacation properties in 100 countries around the world. WW also offers Wyndham Vacation Ownership, which includes marketing and sales of vacation ownership interests, consumer financing in conjunction with the purchase of vacation ownership interests, property management services to property owners' associations and development and acquisition of vacation ownership resorts. Wyndham Vacation has over 155 vacation ownership resorts in U.S., Canada, Mexico, the Caribbean and the South Pacific that represent over 820,000 owners of vacation ownership interests. WW's extensive portfolio of brands includes Wyndham Hotels and Resorts; Ramada; Days Inn; Super 8; Wyndham Rewards; Wingate by Wyndham; Microtel; RCI; The Registry Collection; Endless Vacation Rentals; Landal GreenParks; Cottages4You; Novasol; Wyndham Vacation Resorts; and WorldMark by Wyndham. The firm also holds 30% interest in CHI Limited; this joint venture provides management services to luxury and upscale hotels in Europe, the Middle East and Africa. In March 2010, WW announced that its Registry Collection program welcomed 24 new resort destinations, increasing its total number of properties to 175.

Employees are offers medical, dental and vision insurance; flexible spending accounts; long-term disability; business travel accident insurance; life and personal accident insurance; supplemental life insurance; a 401(k) plan; an educational assistance program; an employee assistance program; adoption reimbursement; flexible work arrangements; and travel discounts.

FINANCIALS: **Sales and profits are in thousands of dollars—add 000 to get the full amount. 2009 Note: Financial information for 2009 was not available for all companies at press time.**

2009 Sales: $3,750,000	2009 Profits: $293,000	**U.S. Stock Ticker: WYN**
2008 Sales: $4,281,000	2008 Profits: $-1,074,000	**Int'l Ticker:** Int'l Exchange:
2007 Sales: $4,360,000	2007 Profits: $403,000	Employees: 24,600
2006 Sales: $3,842,000	2006 Profits: $287,000	Fiscal Year Ends: 12/31
2005 Sales: $3,471,000	2005 Profits: $431,000	Parent Company:

SALARIES/BENEFITS:

Pension Plan:	ESOP Stock Plan:	Profit Sharing:	Top Exec. Salary: $1,076,355	Bonus: $
Savings Plan: Y	Stock Purch. Plan:		Second Exec. Salary: $599,470	Bonus: $2,462,000

OTHER THOUGHTS:

Apparent Women Officers or Directors: 4
Hot Spot for Advancement for Women/Minorities: Y

LOCATIONS: ("Y" = Yes)

West:	Southwest:	Midwest:	Southeast:	Northeast:	International:
Y	Y	Y	Y	Y	Y

WYNN RESORTS LIMITED

www.wynnresorts.com

Industry Group Code: 721120 **Ranks within this company's industry group:** Sales: 4 Profits: 1

Properties:		Financial Services:		Construction/Development:		Investments:		Specialty Services:		Brokerage:	
Apartments:		Mortgages:		Commercial Construction:		REIT:		Property Management:		Commercial Sales:	
Malls/Shopping:		Title Insurance:		Residential Construction:				Online Services:		Residential Sales:	
Offices:		Property Insurance:		Land Development:				Software/IT:		Specialty:	
Hotels/Motels:	Y			Support Services:				Consulting:			
Industrial/Warehouses:				Design/Engineering:							
Other:	Y										

TYPES OF BUSINESS:

Hotel Casinos

BRANDS/DIVISIONS/AFFILIATES:

Wynn Las Vegas, LLC
Wynn Resorts (Macau), S.A.
Encore Suites at Wynn Las Vegas
Encore Suites at Wynn Macau

CONTACTS:

Note: Officers with more than one job title may be intentionally listed here more than once.

Stephen A. Wynn, CEO
Marc D. Schorr, COO
Matt Maddox, CFO
Linda Chen, Pres., Wynn Int'l Mktg., Ltd.
John Strzemp, Chief Admin. Officer/Exec. VP
Kim Sinatra, General Counsel/Sec./Sr. VP
Matt Maddox, Treas.
Andrew Pascal, Pres., Wynn Las Vegas, LLC
Maurice Wooden, COO-Wynn Las Vegas, LLC
Scott Peterson, Sr. VP/CFO-Wynn Las Vegas, LLC
Stephen A. Wynn, Chmn.
Ian M. Coughlan, Pres., Wynn Resorts (Macau), S.A.

Phone: 702-770-7555	**Fax:**
Toll-Free:	
Address: 3131 Las Vegas Blvd. S., Las Vegas, NV 89109 US	

GROWTH PLANS/SPECIAL FEATURES:

Wynn Resorts Limited is a developer, owner and operator of destination casino resorts. It owns and operates two destination casino resorts: The Wynn Las Vegas on the Strip in Las Vegas, Nevada, which includes Encore at Wynn Las Vegas, and the Wynn Macau in the Macau Special Administrative Region of China. Wynn Las Vegas offers 2,716 rooms and suites. The 111,000-square-foot casino features 130 table games, a baccarat salon, private VIP gaming rooms, a poker room, 1,920 slot machines, and a race and sports book. The resort's 22 food and beverage outlets feature six fine dining restaurants. Other amenities include two nightclubs; a spa and salon; a Ferrari and Maserati automobile dealership; wedding chapels; an 18-hole golf course; 223,000 square feet of meeting space; and a 74,000 square foot retail promenade featuring boutiques from Alexander McQueen, Cartier, Chanel, and Louis Vuitton. Wynn Las Vegas also has a showroom which features "Le Rêve," a water-based theatrical production. The Encore at Wynn Las Vegas features 2,034 suites, a 76,000 square feet casino with 90 table games, a baccarat salon, 790 slot machines and a sports book. It also features 12 food and beverage outlets; a night club; a spa and salon; meeting space; and upscale retail outlets, as well as The Encore Theater. The Wynn Macau features 600 hotel rooms and suites; 390 table games, 1,200 slot machines and a poker room; six restaurants; a spa and salon; lounges; meeting facilities; and 48,000 square feet of retail space. In April 2010, the company's newest boutique hotel, the Encore, began operations next door to the Wynn Macau.

Employees are offered medical, dental, vision and life insurance; disability insurance; short- and long-term disability; an employee assistance program; educational assistance; classes to assist employees taking the U.S. Citizenship test; and a 401(k) plan.

FINANCIALS:

Sales and profits are in thousands of dollars—add 000 to get the full amount. 2009 Note: Financial information for 2009 was not available for all companies at press time.

2009 Sales: $3,045,611	2009 Profits: $20,654	**U.S. Stock Ticker: WYNN**
2008 Sales: $2,987,324	2008 Profits: $210,479	**Int'l Ticker:** Int'l Exchange:
2007 Sales: $2,687,519	2007 Profits: $196,336	Employees: 18,900
2006 Sales: $1,432,257	2006 Profits: $628,728	Fiscal Year Ends: 12/31
2005 Sales: $721,981	2005 Profits: $-90,836	Parent Company:

SALARIES/BENEFITS:

Pension Plan:	ESOP Stock Plan:	Profit Sharing:	Top Exec. Salary: $2,953,125	Bonus: $4,062,500
Savings Plan: Y	Stock Purch. Plan:		Second Exec. Salary: $1,817,308	Bonus: $2,000,000

OTHER THOUGHTS:

Apparent Women Officers or Directors: 3
Hot Spot for Advancement for Women/Minorities: Y

LOCATIONS: ("Y" = Yes)

West:	Southwest:	Midwest:	Southeast:	Northeast:	International:
Y					Y

XANTERRA PARKS AND RESORTS

www.xanterra.com

Industry Group Code: 721110 **Ranks within this company's industry group:** Sales: Profits:

Properties:		Financial Services:		Construction/Development:		Investments:		Specialty Services:		Brokerage:	
Apartments:		Mortgages:		Commercial Construction:		REIT:		Property Management:		Commercial Sales:	
Malls/Shopping:		Title Insurance:		Residential Construction:				Online Services:		Residential Sales:	
Offices:		Property Insurance:		Land Development:				Software/IT:		Specialty:	
Hotels/Motels:	Y			Support Services:				Consulting:			
Industrial/Warehouses:				Design/Engineering:							
Other:											

TYPES OF BUSINESS:

Hotel & Restaurant Management
Conference Center Management

BRANDS/DIVISIONS/AFFILIATES:

Anshutz Company (The)
Xanterra South Rim LLC

CONTACTS:

Note: Officers with more than one job title may be intentionally listed here more than once.

Andrew N. Todd, CEO
Andrew N. Todd, Pres.
Michael F. Welch, CFO/VP-Finance
Dave M. Hartvigsen, VP-Mktg. & Sales
Kate A. Longenecker, VP-Human Resources
John W. Wimmer, CIO
Richard Rabinoff, Dir.-Hospitality Tech.
Susan J. Jessup, Dir.-Retail Merch.
Kirk H. Anderson, General Counsel/VP
Susan Jessup, Dir.-Oper.
Shane J. Harvey, Dir.-Bus. Dev. & Legal Affairs
Lonnie S. Clark, Controller
Stephen W. Tedder, VP-National Parks
Hans Desai, VP-State Parks & Resorts
Chris R. Lane, VP-Environmental Affairs
Bill J. Bub, VP-Retail
Rebecca L. Ritter, Dir.-Purchasing

Phone: 303-600-3400	**Fax:** 303-600-3600
Toll-Free:	
Address: 6312 South Fiddlers Green Cir., Ste. 600N, Greenwood Village, CO 80111 US	

GROWTH PLANS/SPECIAL FEATURES:

Xanterra Parks and Resorts is a parks concessions management company operating in national parks and state parks across the U.S. The company operates hotels, including the world-famous Old Faithful Inn in Yellowstone National Park and the El Tovar in Grand Canyon National Park; 68 restaurants; and gift shops in some of the U.S.'s most popular parks, including Yellowstone, Bryce Canyon, Zion, Crater Lake, Death Valley, Rocky Mountain and Petrified Forest National Parks. Additionally, the company operates conference facilities, premium golf courses, tennis courts and spa amenities. Outside of its national park operations, Xanterra offers services at Mount Rushmore National Memorial and eight Ohio state parks. Other operations of the firm include resorts in Napa Valley and Death Valley, California, and the Grand Canyon Railway in Williams, Arizona via affiliate Xanterra South Rim, L.L.C. The firm is owned by The Anschutz Company.

The firm offers a number of seasonal employment opportunities for both U.S. citizens and foreign nationals.

FINANCIALS:

Sales and profits are in thousands of dollars—add 000 to get the full amount. 2009 Note: Financial information for 2009 was not available for all companies at press time.

2009 Sales: $	2009 Profits: $	**U.S. Stock Ticker: Subsidiary**
2008 Sales: $	2008 Profits: $	**Int'l Ticker:** Int'l Exchange:
2007 Sales: $	2007 Profits: $	Employees:
2006 Sales: $	2006 Profits: $	Fiscal Year Ends:
2005 Sales: $	2005 Profits: $	Parent Company: ANSCHUTZ COMPANY (THE)

SALARIES/BENEFITS:

Pension Plan:	ESOP Stock Plan:	Profit Sharing:	Top Exec. Salary: $	Bonus: $
Savings Plan:	Stock Purch. Plan:		Second Exec. Salary: $	Bonus: $

OTHER THOUGHTS:

Apparent Women Officers or Directors: 6
Hot Spot for Advancement for Women/Minorities: Y

LOCATIONS: ("Y" = Yes)

West:	Southwest:	Midwest:	Southeast:	Northeast:	International:
Y	Y	Y			

YIT CORPORATION

www.yitgroup.com

Industry Group Code: 23 **Ranks within this company's industry group:** Sales: 2 Profits: 2

Properties:		Financial Services:		Construction/Development:		Investments:		Specialty Services:		Brokerage:	
Apartments:		Mortgages:		Commercial Construction:	Y	REIT:		Property Management:		Commercial Sales:	
Malls/Shopping:		Title Insurance:		Residential Construction:	Y			Online Services:		Residential Sales:	
Offices:		Property Insurance:		Land Development:				Software/IT:		Specialty:	
Hotels/Motels:				Support Services:	Y			Consulting:			
Industrial/Warehouses:				Design/Engineering:	Y						
Other:											

TYPES OF BUSINESS:

Development of Living Environments
Building Systems
Construction Services
Industrial Services
Network Services

BRANDS/DIVISIONS/AFFILIATES:

YIT Construction Ltd
YIT Industrial and Network Services Ltd
YIT Building Systems Ltd

CONTACTS:

Note: Officers with more than one job title may be intentionally listed here more than once.

Juhani Pitkakoski, CEO
Juhani Pitkakoski, Pres.
Sakari Ahdekivi, CFO
Antero Saarilahti, Sr. VP-Human Resources
Antero Saarilahti, Sr. VP-Admin.
Antero Saarilahti, Corp. Sec.
Sakari Toikkanen, Sr. VP-Bus. Dev.
Petra Thoren, Sr. VP-Investor Rel.
Pekka Frantti, Pres., YIT Industrial & Network Svcs. Ltd.
Tero Kiviniemi, Pres., YIT Construction Svcs.
Arne Malonaes, Head-Building & Industrial Svcs.
Henrik Ehrnrooth, Chmn.
Kari Kauniskangas, Head-Int'l Construction Svcs.

Phone: 358-20-433-111 **Fax:** 358-20-433-370
Toll-Free:
Address: PO Box 36, Panuntie 11, Helsinki, 00621 Finland

GROWTH PLANS/SPECIAL FEATURES:

YIT Corporation is a Helsinki-based company whose mission is to build, develop and maintain a good living environment for people. The company, which operates as a group of companies, offers technical infrastructure investment and upkeep services for the property, construction, industry and telecommunications sectors. In all sectors of operations, YIT Group's services cover the entire lifecycle of its projects. The firm's main market areas are the Nordic countries, Central Europe, the Baltic countries and Russia. The YIT Group's operations are divided into three business segments: Building and Industrial Systems, which accounted for 61% of 2009 revenues; Construction Services Finland, which accounted for 29%; and International Construction Services, accounting for 10%. Building and Industrial Systems offers technical building systems, infrastructure upgrading, building maintenance, industrial piping, tanks and pulp towers, access-control systems, industrial maintenance, and energy-efficiency services. The Construction Services segments are primarily focused on the construction of residential, commercial and industrial properties, as well as the provision of civil engineering, water and environmental services. YIT's strategy for building an international presence is to bolster its construction services in the Baltic countries and Russia, building system services in the Nordic and Baltic countries as well as industrial and data network services in its entire market area. In November 2009, the firm sold a Finnish shopping center to Fennia Mutual Insurance Company for about $33.7 million. In February 2010, YIT sold a Finnish office building to IVG Institutional Funds GmbH for approximately $10.6 million.

FINANCIALS:

Sales and profits are in thousands of dollars—add 000 to get the full amount. 2009 Note: Financial information for 2009 was not available for all companies at press time.

2009 Sales: $4,608,410	2009 Profits: $89,110	**U.S. Stock Ticker:**
2008 Sales: $5,245,600	2008 Profits: $176,800	**Int'l Ticker: YTY1V** Int'l Exchange: Helsinki
2007 Sales: $4,931,900	2007 Profits: $299,100	Employees: 25,784
2006 Sales: $4,373,400	2006 Profits: $227,400	Fiscal Year Ends:
2005 Sales: $4,781,700	2005 Profits: $245,700	Parent Company:

SALARIES/BENEFITS:

Pension Plan:	ESOP Stock Plan:	Profit Sharing:	Top Exec. Salary: $	Bonus: $
Savings Plan:	Stock Purch. Plan:		Second Exec. Salary: $	Bonus: $

OTHER THOUGHTS:

Apparent Women Officers or Directors:
Hot Spot for Advancement for Women/Minorities:

LOCATIONS: ("Y" = Yes)

West:	Southwest:	Midwest:	Southeast:	Northeast:	International:
					Y

ZIPREALTY INC

www.ziprealty.com

Industry Group Code: 531210 **Ranks within this company's industry group:** Sales: 4 Profits: 1

Properties:		Financial Services:		Construction/Development:		Investments:		Specialty Services:		Brokerage:	
Apartments:		Mortgages:		Commercial Construction:		REIT:		Property Management:		Commercial Sales:	
Malls/Shopping:		Title Insurance:		Residential Construction:				Online Services:	Y	Residential Sales:	Y
Offices:		Property Insurance:		Land Development:				Software/IT:		Specialty:	
Hotels/Motels:				Support Services:				Consulting:			
Industrial/Warehouses:				Design/Engineering:							
Other:											

TYPES OF BUSINESS:

Real Estate Brokerage

BRANDS/DIVISIONS/AFFILIATES:

ZipNotify
ZipAgents
Zip Agent Platform

CONTACTS:

Note: Officers with more than one job title may be intentionally listed here more than once.

Patrick Lashinsky, CEO
Patrick Lashinsky, Pres.
Charles C. Baker, CFO/Exec. VP
Robert Yakominich, Sr. VP-Sales
Joan Burke, VP-Human Resources
Joe Trifoglio, CIO/VP
Genevieve Combes, Sr. VP-Tech.
Samantha Harnett, General Counsel/VP/Corp. Sec.
William C. Sinclair, Exec. VP-Oper.
William C. Sinclair, Exec. VP-Bus. Dev.
Genevieve Combes, Sr. VP-Oper. Strategy
Leslie Tyler, VP-Mktg.
Donald F. Wood, Chmn.

Phone: 510-735-2600 **Fax:** 510-735-2850
Toll-Free: 800-225-5947
Address: 2000 Powell St., Ste. 300, Emeryville, CA 94608 US

GROWTH PLANS/SPECIAL FEATURES:

ZipRealty, Inc. is a full-service residential real estate brokerage firm that utilizes the Internet, proprietary technology, local agents and efficient business processes to provide home buyers and sellers with the appropriate tools for the home-buying process. The company employs a client-centric approach, a sophisticated web site and a proprietary business management technology platform. The firm operates in 35 markets and employs over 3,000 sales agents, known as ZipAgents. ZipRealty's web site provides users with direct access to comprehensive local Multiple Listing Services, home listings data, asking prices, home layouts and other features. The company also provides further information such as neighborhood attributes, school district information, comparable home sales data, maps and driving directions. The firm attracts users to its web site through a number of marketing channels, including online advertising, word-of-mouth and traditional media advertisements. The proprietary ZipAgent Platform, or ZAP, automatically matches registered users with local agents who market and provide the company's comprehensive real estate brokerage services, including showing properties to buyers and listing and marketing properties on behalf of its sellers, as well as negotiating, advisory, transaction processing and closing services. The company's website features ZipNotify, a tool that sends an automatic email notification once a property with a set of predetermined qualities comes onto the market. The firm has roughly 26.1 million active registered users and has closed over 100,000 real estate transactions with an aggregate transaction value of about $29 billion.

FINANCIALS:

Sales and profits are in thousands of dollars—add 000 to get the full amount. 2009 Note: Financial information for 2009 was not available for all companies at press time.

2009 Sales: $123,130	2009 Profits: $-12,892
2008 Sales: $107,450	2008 Profits: $-13,342
2007 Sales: $103,862	2007 Profits: $-14,884
2006 Sales: $95,387	2006 Profits: $-20,594
2005 Sales: $93,405	2005 Profits: $20,467

U.S. Stock Ticker: ZIPR
Int'l Ticker: Int'l Exchange:
Employees: 3,346
Fiscal Year Ends: 12/31
Parent Company:

SALARIES/BENEFITS:

Pension Plan: ESOP Stock Plan: Profit Sharing: Top Exec. Salary: $379,167 Bonus: $122,345
Savings Plan: Stock Purch. Plan: Second Exec. Salary: $300,000 Bonus: $61,200

OTHER THOUGHTS:

Apparent Women Officers or Directors: 5
Hot Spot for Advancement for Women/Minorities: Y

LOCATIONS: ("Y" = Yes)

West:	Southwest:	Midwest:	Southeast:	Northeast:	International:
Y	Y	Y	Y	Y	

ADDITIONAL INDEXES

Contents:

INDEX OF FIRMS NOTED AS HOT SPOTS FOR ADVANCEMENT FOR WOMEN & MINORITIES

INTERCONTINENTAL HOTELS GROUP PLC
INTERSTATE HOTELS AND RESORTS INC
INVESTORS REAL ESTATE TRUST
ISTAR FINANCIAL INC
JACOBS ENGINEERING GROUP INC
JANUS HOTELS AND RESORTS INC
JOHN LAING PLC
JOHNSON CONTROLS INC
JOIE DE VIVRE HOSPITALITY
JONES LANG LASALLE INC
KB HOME
KERZNER INTERNATIONAL LIMITED
KIMPTON HOTEL & RESTAURANT GROUP LLC
LANDAMERICA FINANCIAL GROUP INC
LB FOSTER COMPANY
LBA REALTY LLC
LENNAR CORPORATION
LIBERTY PROPERTY TRUST
LIGHTSTONE GROUP LLC (THE)
LILLIBRIDGE HEALTHCARE REAL ESTATE TRUST
LODGIAN INC
LOUIS BERGER GROUP INC (THE)
LOWE'S COMPANIES INC
LQ MANAGEMENT LLC
MACERICH COMPANY (THE)
MACK-CALI REALTY CORP
MARCUS CORPORATION (THE)
MARRIOTT INTERNATIONAL INC
MCDERMOTT INTERNATIONAL INC
MDC HOLDINGS INC
MERITUS HOTELS & RESORTS INC
MGM MIRAGE
MID-AMERICA APARTMENT COMMUNITIES INC
MOVE INC
MWH GLOBAL INC
NAI GLOBAL INC
NATIONAL HOME CENTERS INC
NRT INCORPORATED
ORIENT-EXPRESS HOTELS LTD
ORIGEN FINANCIAL INC
PACIFIC COAST BUILDING PRODUCTS
PARKWAY PROPERTIES INC
PARSONS BRINCKERHOFF INC
PENNSYLVANIA REIT
PLUM CREEK TIMBER CO INC
PMI GROUP INC (THE)
POST PROPERTIES INC
PRIME RETAIL INC
PROLOGIS
PS BUSINESS PARKS INC
PULTEGROUP INC
RADIAN GROUP INC
RE/MAX INTERNATIONAL INC
REALOGY CORPORATION
REALTY INCOME CORP
RED LION HOTELS CORPORATION
REGENCY CENTERS CORP
RELATED GROUP (THE)
RESORTQUEST INTERNATIONAL INC
REZIDOR HOTEL GROUP AB
RIO PROPERTIES INC
RITZ-CARLTON HOTEL COMPANY LLC (THE)
ROSEWOOD HOTELS & RESORTS LLC
RXR REALTY
RYLAND GROUP INC (THE)
SAHA PATHANA INTER-HOLDING PCL
SCANDIC HOTELS AB
SHANGRI-LA ASIA LTD
SHUN TAK HOLDINGS LIMITED
SIMON PROPERTY GROUP INC
SONESTA INTERNATIONAL HOTELS CORP
SOVRAN SELF STORAGE INC
ST JOE COMPANY (THE)
STARWOOD CAPITAL GROUP GLOBAL LLC
STARWOOD HOTELS & RESORTS WORLDWIDE INC
STEWART INFORMATION SERVICES CORP
STRATOSPHERE CORPORATION
STV GROUP INC
SUNBURST HOSPITALITY CORPORATION
SUNRISE SENIOR LIVING
SWIRE PACIFIC LTD
TANGER FACTORY OUTLET CENTERS
TARRAGON CORPORATION
TAUBMAN CENTERS INC
TECHNICAL OLYMPIC USA INC
THARALDSON ENTERPRISES INC
TRANSWESTERN COMMERCIAL SERVICES
TRT HOLDINGS
TRUMP ORGANIZATION (THE)
UDR INC
URS CORPORATION
VENTAS INC
VORNADO REALTY TRUST
WASHINGTON REAL ESTATE INVESTMENT TRUST
WCI COMMUNITIES INC
WEINGARTEN REALTY INVESTORS
WESTFIELD GROUP (THE)
WILLIAM LYON HOMES
WP CAREY & CO LLC
WS ATKINS PLC
WYNDHAM WORLDWIDE
WYNN RESORTS LIMITED
XANTERRA PARKS AND RESORTS
ZIPREALTY INC

INDEX OF SUBSIDIARIES, BRAND NAMES AND AFFILIATIONS

Brand or subsidiary, followed by the name of the related corporation

INDEX OF SUBSIDIARIES, BRAND NAMES AND AFFILIATIONS, CONT.

INDEX OF SUBSIDIARIES, BRAND NAMES AND AFFILIATIONS, CONT.

INDEX OF SUBSIDIARIES, BRAND NAMES AND AFFILIATIONS, CONT.

INDEX OF SUBSIDIARIES, BRAND NAMES AND AFFILIATIONS, CONT.

INDEX OF SUBSIDIARIES, BRAND NAMES AND AFFILIATIONS, CONT.

INDEX OF SUBSIDIARIES, BRAND NAMES AND AFFILIATIONS, CONT.

INDEX OF SUBSIDIARIES, BRAND NAMES AND AFFILIATIONS, CONT.

INDEX OF SUBSIDIARIES, BRAND NAMES AND AFFILIATIONS, CONT.

INDEX OF SUBSIDIARIES, BRAND NAMES AND AFFILIATIONS, CONT.

INDEX OF SUBSIDIARIES, BRAND NAMES AND AFFILIATIONS, CONT.

INDEX OF SUBSIDIARIES, BRAND NAMES AND AFFILIATIONS, CONT.

INDEX OF SUBSIDIARIES, BRAND NAMES AND AFFILIATIONS, CONT.

INDEX OF SUBSIDIARIES, BRAND NAMES AND AFFILIATIONS, CONT.

INDEX OF SUBSIDIARIES, BRAND NAMES AND AFFILIATIONS, CONT.

INDEX OF SUBSIDIARIES, BRAND NAMES AND AFFILIATIONS, CONT.

INDEX OF SUBSIDIARIES, BRAND NAMES AND AFFILIATIONS, CONT.

INDEX OF SUBSIDIARIES, BRAND NAMES AND AFFILIATIONS, CONT.

INDEX OF SUBSIDIARIES, BRAND NAMES AND AFFILIATIONS, CONT.

INDEX OF SUBSIDIARIES, BRAND NAMES AND AFFILIATIONS, CONT.

INDEX OF SUBSIDIARIES, BRAND NAMES AND AFFILIATIONS, CONT.

INDEX OF SUBSIDIARIES, BRAND NAMES AND AFFILIATIONS, CONT.

INDEX OF SUBSIDIARIES, BRAND NAMES AND AFFILIATIONS, CONT.

INDEX OF SUBSIDIARIES, BRAND NAMES AND AFFILIATIONS, CONT.

INDEX OF SUBSIDIARIES, BRAND NAMES AND AFFILIATIONS, CONT.

INDEX OF SUBSIDIARIES, BRAND NAMES AND AFFILIATIONS, CONT.

INDEX OF SUBSIDIARIES, BRAND NAMES AND AFFILIATIONS, CONT.

INDEX OF SUBSIDIARIES, BRAND NAMES AND AFFILIATIONS, CONT.